Dictionary of American Classical Composers

Second Edition

Books by Neil Butterworth

English for Business and Professional Examinations

400 Aural Training Exercises

Haydn, His Life and Times

A Music Quiz Book

Dvořák, His Life and Times

The Music of Aaron Copland

Ralph Vaughan Williams : A Guide to Research

Neglected Music

The American Symphony

The Music of Samuel Barber (in preparation)

Film Music: An International Catalog (in preparation)

DICTIONARY OF AMERICAN CLASSICAL COMPOSERS

Second Edition

NEIL BUTTERWORTH

ROUTLEDGE
NEW YORK AND LONDON

Published in 2005 by
Routledge
270 Madison Aveune
New York, NY 10016
www.routledge-ny.com

Published in Great Britain by
Routledge
2 Park Square
Milton Park, Abingdon
Oxon, OX14 4RN U.K.
www.routledge.co.uk

Routledge is an imprint of the Taylor & Francis Group.

Printed in the United States of America on acid-free paper.

10 9 8 7 6 5 4 3 2 1

Cataloging-in-Publication Data
Butterworth, Neil, 1934–
    Dictionary of American classical composers / Neil Butterworth. — 2nd ed.
       p. cm.
    Includes bibliographical references (p. 513) and index.
    ISBN 0-415-93848-1 (hb : alk. paper)
    1. Music—United States—Bio-bibliography—Dictionaries. 2. Composers—United States—Biography
    —Dictionaries. I. Title.

ML106.U3B87 2004
780'.92'273--dc22

                                                                    2004021382

Contents

Introduction
to the First Edition

The principal aim of this book is to be informative and readable. Critical opinions where expressed represent either the consensus of writers and musicians with regard to composers of the past or personal assessment.

Although it is difficult to describe a composer's style in objective terms, where possible I have given some indication of the musical language used—e.g., serial, neo-classical, neo-romantic—even if these terms tend to be generalizations.

Inevitably, many composers both past and present have been excluded. Each university music faculty has its own gathering of musicians who compose, and new stars are rising every year. In subsequent editions of this book further names will be added; my apologies go to any who feel they should be included but are not. The criterion for inclusion is hard to establish, but all composers listed have their music performed widely beyond their own immediate circle.

Where composers from other countries have emigrated to the United States, I have usually included them if they have become naturalized citizens. In these cases, to give a complete survey of their work, music written abroad has also been mentioned. Those composers who enjoyed prolonged residence in America but were not naturalized do not appear. I have omitted Stravinsky, partly as he is so well documented elsewhere and partly because the majority of his major works were composed in Europe.

Not included are composers of light music and jazz and song-writers unless they have produced works in other media. Thus George Gershwin and Ethelbert Nevin are represented, Harold Arlen and Irving Berlin are not. One exception is Stephen Foster, whose songs exerted such an influence during the nineteenth century that it was felt his historical significance warranted his inclusion.

Where possible biographies have been submitted to the composers themselves for correction, and I am deeply grateful for their help especially in providing information impossible to obtain from any other source.

Because music by American composers is not as widely known or performed in Europe, and Britain in particular, as it deserves to be, I hope this dictionary may bring to the notice of musicians on the east side of the Atlantic a new repertory of works worthy to stand beside the long tradition of European music.

Neil Butterworth
Edinburgh 1983

Introduction
to the Second Edition

In this revised edition of the *Dictionary of American Composer*, my criteria remain the same. Every entry has undergone close scrutiny and rewriting with an updating of the list of works.

John Cage, Aaron Copland, Walter Piston, William Schuman, Roger Sessions, and Virgil Thomson were some of those who assisted me in compiling the first edition. I am again greatly indebted to many distinguished composers who took time to correct their entries and provide a wealth of additional material for this new publication.

I am deeply grateful to my daughter Alexa, and Sam Albertson who explored the internet on my behalf to seek out remote information.

Neil Butterworth
Greenlaw, Scotland 2003

Photo Acknowledgments

Thanks to the many composers and their families for providing photographs for use in this work, and for checking their entries for accuracy. In addition, the following archivists, librarians, and collections were helpful in providing photographs and information used in this work: Denise Anderson, University of Iowa Libraries; Katie Behrman, Carnegie Mellon University Libraries; John Bewley, Music Library, State University of New York, Buffalo; Richard Boursy and Suzanne Eggleston Lovejoy, Gilmore Music Library, Yale University; Lisa Breede, Media Lab, MIT; Brendan Carroll, the Erich Wolfgang Korngold Society Archive; Dongshin Chang, New York University Archives; The Chicago Historical Society; Columbia Electronic Music Center; David Peter Coppen, Sibley Music Library, Eastman School of Music; Michael N. Crotty, Duke University Library; Kay DeCicco-Carey, Harvard University Archives; Suzanne Finck, University of Cincinnati Archives; Heather Ford, Dept. of Music, University of California, Davis; Kristin M. Giacoletto, J. Willard Marriott Library, University of Utah; Anna Gordon, Diehn Fine and Performing Arts Center, Old Dominion University; Jane Gottlieb, The Juilliard School; William Gottlieb; Kathy Haines, University of Pittsburgh Library; Irene Haupt; Kathryn Hodson, University of Iowa Libraries; Tom Hyry, Yale University Libraries, Manuscripts and Archives; Frances Kern and Anne Skilton, University of North Carolina at Chapel Hill Library; Karen Klinkenberg, University of Minnesota Archives; Kathy Lafferty, Kenneth Spencer Research Library, University of Kansas; Kevin B. Leonard, Northwestern University Library; Morgen MacIntosh, DePaul University Library; Carolyn Marr, Museum of History & Industry (Seattle, Washington) Library; The Morrison Foundation for Musical Research, Inc.; Gordon Mumma; Ann Stevens-Naftel, Editio Helios Publications; The New York Public Library, Music Division; Jon Newsom and his staff, Library of Congress, Music Division; Vincent J. Novara, Michelle Smith Performing Arts Library, University of Maryland; Kristen J. Nyitray, Frank Melville, Jr. Memorial Library, Stony Brook University; Jean Parker, Oakland University, Dept. of Music, Theatre and Dance; Lucy Patrick and Burt Altman, Florida State University Libraries; Sandra Peck, The Archives & Museum of Tuskegee University; Anne Prichard, University of Arkansas Libraries; Kevin Proffitt, American Jewish Archives; Rathaus Archives, Queens College; Claire Robbins, Nordoff-Robbins Center for Music Therapy; Dean M. Rogers, Vassar College Library; David Saladino: Elizabeth Scaaf and Nick Homenda, Peabody Institute of John Hopkins University Library; Bernard Schermetzler, University of Wisconsin-Madison Archives; Joanne M. Seitter, Curtis Institute of Music; Kathleen Shimeta; Christopher Slavik, Chicago Symphony Orchestra; Dave Stein, Kurt Weill Foundation; Howard Stokar; Rosina Tammany, Eastern Michigan University Archives; F. Anthony Thurman, American Guild of Organists; Sydney C. Van Nort, Cohen Library, City University of New York; Cassandra M. Volpe, American Music Research Center, University of Colorado at Boulder; and Nancy Young, Smith College Archives.

A

ACHRON, JOSEPH

b. Lozdzeje, Lithuania, 13 May 1886
d. Hollywood, California, 29 April 1943

At a very early age, Achron was a violin prodigy. He studied in Warsaw and at the St. Petersburg Conservatory (1898-1904) where he was a pupil of Leopold Auer; he was also a member of Anatoly Liadov's composition class. In 1913, he joined the teaching staff of Kharkhov Conservatory. After a year in Palestine, he went to America in 1925, where he became an American citizen in 1928, settling first in New York, moving in 1934 to Hollywood.

Most of Achron's important works are for violin and reveal the strong influence of Hebrew music. His best-known composition, *Hebrew Melody* for violin and orchestra, was published in 1911. He composed three violin concertos (1927, 1936, 1939), the third dedicated to Jascha Heifetz, and *Konzertaten-Kapelle* (1929), also for violin and orchestra. For orchestra he wrote *Hazan* (with cello solo) (1914); *The Fiddler's Soul* (1920); *Belshazzar* (1924); *Elegy for Strings* (1927); *Golem Suite* for small orchestra, performed at the I.S.C.M. Festival in Venice in 1932; *Little Dance Fantasy* (1933); and a Piano Concerto (1941).

His chamber music includes a String Sextet; *Chromatic String Quartet* (1907); two sonatas for violin and piano (1914, 1918); *Elegy* for string quartet (1927); Sinfonietta for string quartet (1935); Sextet for woodwind and trumpet (1938) and *Children's Suite* for piano, clarinet, and string quartet (1938). He also composed several pieces for piano solo: *Symphonic Variation* (1915); *Sonata on a Jewish Theme* (1915); *Traum* (1923); *Begrüssung* (*Welcome*) (1923); and *Seven Statuettes* (1930). His major choral works are *Epitaph* (*In memory of Scriabine*) (1916); *Salome's Dance* for chorus, piano, and percussion (1925): and an *Evening Service for the Sabbath* for baritone, chorus, and orchestra (1932). The ballet *Spring Night* was written in 1935 for a film.

His brother Isador (1892–1948) settled in the United States in 1922, where he pursued a career as pianist, teacher, and composer. He was also the accompanist to Jascha Heifetz (1922–33).

ADAMS, JOHN (COOLIDGE)

b. Worcester, Massachusetts, 15 February 1947

Adams began learning the clarinet with his father, playing in local bands and later earning a living as a freelance orchestral musician. As a student at Harvard University (B.A. 1969; M.A. 1971) he was a pupil of Leon Kirchner. In addition he studied conducting at Dartmouth College (summer 1965), a skill he has developed with his own music. Adams was Composer-in-Residence at the Marlboro Festival (1970) and with the San Francisco Symphony Orchestra (1982–85). From 1972 to 1982 he taught at the San Francisco Conservatory, where he also directed the New Music Ensemble. He acted as creative advisor to the St. Paul (Minnesota) Chamber Orchestra (1986–90).

Adams came to minimalism after its basic features had been established by Steve Reich and Philip Glass. Compared to them, he has been less single-minded than the former and less ritualistic than the latter. Since 1990 he has become the most performed living American composer, with his orchestral works appearing in concerts throughout the world. The electrifying driving rhythms and colorful textures present audiences with a new musical language that is of immediate appeal.

Adams earliest extant work, the experimental *Piano Quintet*, written in 1970, contains aleatoric elements. In addition to a tape composition, *Onyx*, he used

John Adams with Morton Feldman,
January 10, 1987.
*Courtesy Music Library, State
University of New York, Buffalo, Morton
Feldman Papers, Box 15, no. 43.*

electronics in *Groundings* with three solo voices and instruments (1975), which was influenced by the ensemble pieces of Reich. Two piano pieces of 1977, *China Gates* and *Phrygian Gates*, epitomize the typical minimalist relentless pulse and repetitions.

His first orchestral work, *Christian Zeal and Activity* (the central part of a triptych *American Standard*), dating from 1973, drastically slows down the hymn tune *Onward Christian Soldiers* to provide a gradually changing harmonic sound base. *Shaker Loops* for string septet (1978, arranged for string orchestra in 1983) abandons the single pulse to provide a greater variety of tempi for the seven "loops" given to each instrument. Adams describes "shaking" as "the fast, tightly rhythmical motion of the bow across the strings." *Common Tones in Simple Time* (1979, rev. 1986) for orchestra is dedicated to the composer's teacher Leon Kirchner.

Harmonium (1980) immediately brought Adams's name to wide popular attention. Scored for choir and large orchestra, it sets three poems, *Negative Love* by John Donne and *Because I Could Not Stop For Death* and *Wild Nights* by Emily Dickinson. In the following year he composed *Grand Pianola Music* for two sopranos, two pianos, and chamber orchestra. Other orchestral pieces include *Harmonielehre* (1984–85); *The Chairman Dances* (1985), described as a foxtrot, a byproduct of the opera *Nixon in China*; the frenetic *Short Ride in a Fast Machine* (1986); a fanfare, *Tromba Lontana* (1986); *Fearful Symmetries* (1988); *Eros Piano* for piano and orchestra (1989); and *El Dorado* (1991).

With the Chamber Symphony (1992) and the Violin Concerto (1993), Adams adopted a more dissonant harmonic language with a greater degree of freedom from the insistent pulse of minimalism. *Lollapalooza*, named after an American term for something large and outrageous, is a lively jazzy novelty composed in 1995 to celebrate the 40th birthday of the conductor Sir Simon Rattle.

Recent orchestral pieces are *Gnarly Buttons* (1996); *Slonimsky's Earbox* (1997); *Century Rolls* (Piano Concerto no. 1), written for Emanuel Ax (1997); *Naïve and Sentimental Music* (1999); *Guide to Strange Places* (2001); and *My Father Knew Charles Ives*, premiered by the San Francisco Symphony Orchestra in April 2003. Adams' most recent orchestral work, *The Dharma at Big Sur* for the Los Angeles Symphony Orchestra, opened the 2003–2004 season in October 2003.

To date, all of Adams' operas have taken as their subjects recent historical and political events. *Nixon in China* concerns the visit in 1972 of the American president to Mao Tse-Tung. With a libretto written mostly in couplets by Alice Goodman and production by Peter Sellars, it is a historical account, not a satire. The premiere production by the Houston Grand Opera on 22 October 1987, received with great acclaim, was repeated at the Brooklyn Academy of Music (December 1987), John F. Kennedy Center, Washington, D.C. (March 1988), Netherlands Opera (June 1988), and the Edinburgh International Festival (August 1988). Adams's second opera, *The Death of Klinghoffer*, again with a libretto by Alice Goodman, was first staged in Brussels on 19 March 1991. The plot is based on a real event, the hijacking of the liner *Achille Lauro* (1985) by Arab terrorists, who murdered an elderly disabled Jewish man.

I Was Looking at the Ceiling and Then I Saw the Sky is described as a song play. Depicting an earthquake in Los Angeles, it was performed in Berkeley, California on 11 May 1995. Currently Adams is writing an opera, *Doctor Atomic*, based on the life of the nuclear scientist Robert Oppenheimer at Los Alamos. It will be presented by the San Francisco Opera in the 2005/2006 season.

Adams has composed two ballets, *Available Light* (1983) and *Hallelujah Junction* (Copenhagen, 2001); and two film scores, *Matter at Heart* (1982) and *An American Tapestry* (1999).

The nativity oratorio *El Niño* was given a virtual staging with film projection at its premiere in Paris on 15 December 2000. Adams had long held a deep love for Handel's *Messiah*: "I wanted to write a *Messiah*." The text in Spanish, Latin, and English draws on a multitude of sources from the Bible to the present day. It is scored for soprano, mezzo-soprano, baritone, a trio of countertenors, chorus, children's chorus, and orchestra.

Adams's most recent choral work, *The Transmigration of Souls* for four solo voices, choruses, and orchestra, was composed to commemorate the 9/11 disaster in New York. The music is enhanced by familiar sounds of the city on tape, performed against a litany of the victims' names. The premiere was given on 19 September 2002 by the New York Philharmonic Orchestra under Lorin Maazel. It was awarded the Pulitzer Prize in 2003 and performed in the summer of that year at the Promenade Concerts in London.

Among his vocal works are *The Wound Dresser*, a setting of Walt Whitman for baritone and orchestra (1989), and a group of songs for voice and electronics dating from 1993: *Bump, Cerulean, Disappointment Lake, Hoodoo Zephyr,* and *Tourist Song.* Adams has composed a handful of instrumental pieces, including *Light Over Water* for brass and synthesizer (1983); *John's Book of Alleged Dances* for string quartet and foot-controller sampler (1994); *Road Movies* for violin and piano (1995); and *Scratchboard* for ensemble (1996).

ADLER, SAMUEL (HANS)
b. Mannheim, Germany, 4 March 1928

As a child, Adler began violin studies before emigrating with his family to the United States in January 1939, where he studied composition privately with Herbert Fromm (1941–46). At Boston University (1946–48) he was a pupil of Hugo Norden and Karl Geiringer. Later at Harvard University (1948–50) he studied with Walter Piston and Randall Thompson. He was also a composition pupil of Aaron Copland and Paul Hindemith, and

at Tanglewood (1949, 1950) he received conducting lessons from Serge Koussevitzky.

During his army service in Germany, Adler organized the 7th Army Symphony Orchestra; he was to devote much time to conducting throughout his career. From 1953 to 1966 he was musical director of the Temple Emanu-El in Dallas, Texas. In 1957 he became professor of composition at North Texas State University, Denton. From 1966 until his retirement in 1995, he was professor of composition at the Eastman School of Music, Rochester, New York, serving as chairman of the composition department from 1974 to 1994. Subsequently he has taught at the Juilliard School in New York.

Adler has composed six symphonies: no. 1 (Dallas, 1953); no. 2 (Dallas, 1958); no. 3, *Diptych* (1960, rev. 1980-81); no. 4, *Geometrics* (1967); no. 5, *We Are the Echoes* for mezzo-soprano and orchestra (1975); and no. 6 (1985). His early orchestral compositions include *American Comedy* Overture (1946); a symphonic poem *Kinnereth* (1947): and a Concerto for flute, bassoon, and strings (1949-50), all now withdrawn. Among his surviving pieces from his early works are: *Song and Dance* for violin and orchestra (1953); Concertino no. 1 (1954); Toccata (1954); *Overture: Summer Stock* (1955); *The Feast of Lights* (1955); *Jubilee* (1958); *Rhapsody* for violin and orchestra (1961); *Four Early American Folk Songs* for strings (1962); *Elegy* for strings (1962); and *Requiescat in Pace* (1963) in memory of John F. Kennedy.

Later orchestral works are *City by the Lake*, a portrait of Rochester (1968); Sinfonietta (1970); Concerto for Orchestra (1971); Concertino no. 2 for strings (1976), premiered in 1977 by the St. Louis Symphony Orchestra; *A Little Bit* for strings (1976); a ballet, *The Waking*, composed for the Louisville Orchestra in 1978; *Joi, Amor, Cortezia* for chamber orchestra (1982); an overture, *In Just Spring* (1984); *The Fixed Desire of the Human Heart* (1988); *Beyond the Land* (1988); *Shadow Dances* (1990); *To Celebrate a Miracle* (1991); *Celebration*, for the centenary of the Cincinnati Symphony Orchestra (1993); Concertino no. 3 for strings (1993); *Art Creates Artists* (1996); *Lux Perpetua* for organ and orchestra (1997); and *Show an Affirming Flame* (2001), composed for the New York Philharmonic Orchestra in memory of the destruction of the World Trade Center. Adler has composed several concertos for solo instruments and orchestra: organ (1970); flute (1977); two for piano (1983, 1996); a saxophone quartet (1985); wind quintet (1991); guitar (1994); cello (1995); viola (1999); horn (2001); and *Beyond the Pale* for clarinet and strings (2002).

Adler's important choral works are principally settings of religious texts: a cantata, *Vision of Isaiah* (1962); *B'shaaray Tefilah: Sabbath Service* (1963); an oratorio, *The Binding* (1967); a cantata, *From Out of Bondage* (1968); a cantata, *A Falling of Saints* for tenor, baritone, chorus, and orchestra, completed in 1977; *It is to God I Shall Sing* for chorus and organ (1977); an oratorio, *Chosen Life* (1989); a cantata, *Ever Since Babylon* for soloists, chorus, and orchestra (1991); and two pieces for unaccompanied voices, *Psalm Trilogy* (1997) and *My Beloved is Mine* (1998). Secular choral items include a cantata, *A Whole Bunch of Fun* (1969); *Serenade on Texts by Blake* for chorus and winds (1971); *The Flames of Freedom* for chorus and piano (1982); an oratorio, *Choose Life* for mezzo-soprano, tenor, chorus, and orchestra (1986); *High Flight* for chorus and chamber orchestra (1986); *'Round the Globe* for treble voices and piano (1986); a cantata, *Stars in the Dust* for soloists, chorus, and orchestra (1988); a cantata, *Any Human to Another* for chorus, piano, and orchestra (1989); *A Prolific Source of Sorrow* for chorus and flute (1994); and two pieces for chorus and band, *Family Portraits* (1995) and *Rogues and Lovers* (1995).

Adler's eight string quartets represent the nucleus of his chamber works. They date respectively from 1945, 1950, 1955 (rev. 1964), 1963, 1969, 1975, 1981, and 1987. The Fourth and Fifth make use of certain aleatoric effects, and the Sixth, subtitled *A Whitman Sampler*, includes a part for mezzo-soprano. He has also composed four violin sonatas (1948, 1956, 1965, 1989); Horn Sonata (1948); two piano trios (1964, 1979); Sonata for unaccompanied cello (1966); *Music for 11* (1964); *L'olam Vaed* for cello and piano (1976); *Dialogues* for euphonium and marimba (1977); *Aeolus, God of the Winds* for clarinet and piano trio (1978-79); Sonata for solo flute (1981); *Gottschalkiana* for brass quintet (1982); Viola Sonata (1984); Guitar Sonata (1984); Oboe Sonata (1985); *Double Portrait* for violin and piano (1985); *Acrostics* for flute, oboe, clarinet, violin, cello, and harpsichord (1986); *Herinnering* for string quartet (1987) and *Pasiphae* for piano and percussion (1987).

More recent instrumental music includes a Clarinet Sonata (1989); *Five Etudes* for violin (1989); *Triolet* for flute, viola, and harp (1989); *Close Encounters* for violin and cello (1989); *Sounding* for alto saxophone and piano (1989); *Ports of Call* for two violins and guitar (1992); *Into the Radiant Boundaries of Light* for viola and guitar (1993); *Clarion Calls* for trumpet and organ (1995); *Diary of a Journey: Four Snapshots* for flute, bassoon, and cello (1995); *Be Not Afraid, the Isle is Full of Noises* for brass quintet (1999); *Pensive Soliloquy* for saxophone and piano (1997); and a Piano Quintet (2000).

Adler has written many pieces for wind ensemble and concert band: *Southwestern Sketches* (1961); *Festive Prelude* (1965); Concerto for winds, brass, and percussion (1968); *A Little Night and Day Music* (1976); *An American Duo* (1981); *Merrymakers* (1982); *Double Vision* (1987); *Ultralight* (1990); *We Live* (1995); *Serenata Concertante* (1996); *Dawn to Glory* (1998): and *American Airs and Dances* (1998). For brass ensemble there are *Concert Piece* (1946); *Praeludium* (1947); Divertimento (1948); *Five Vignettes* for trombone choir (1967); *Histrionics* for brass and percussion (1966); *Brass Fragments* for 25-piece brass choir (1971); *Trumpet Triptych* for seven trumpets (1979); *Brahmsiana* for eight horns (1997); and *Scherzo Schmerzo* for brass and percussion (2000).

In 1970, Adler began a series of pieces entitled *Canto*, mostly for solo instruments: *I*, trumpet (1970); *II*, trombone (1971); *III*, violin (1976); *IV*, saxophone (1974); *V*, for soprano; flute, cello, and three percussion players (1974); *VI*, double bass (1973); *VII*, tuba (1975); *VIII*, piano (1974); *IX*, five timpani and six rototoms (1978); *X*, cello (1979); *XI*, horn (1984); *XII*, bassoon (1989); *XIII*, piccolo (1994); *XIV A Kletzmer Fantasy* for clarinet (1996); and *XV*, English horn (1997).

Among his piano works are *Sonata Breve* (1963); Sonatina (1979); *The Sense of Touch* (1983); *Composers' Portraits* (2002); and *Duo Sonata* for two pianos (1983). A Sonata for harpsichord dates from 1982.

Adler has published eight song-cycles, the last of which, *Musique, Poetrie, Art, Nature and Love*, for medium voice, flute, and piano, was composed in 1979. Recent vocal music includes: *Snow Tracks* for high voice and wind ensemble (1981); *Reconciliation* for soprano, flute, clarinet, violin, cello, and piano (1992); *Time in Tempest Everywhere* (W. H. Auden) for soprano, oboe, piano, and chamber orchestra (1994); and *The Challenge of Music* for soprano, tenor, and orchestra (2003).

A one-act opera, *The Outcast of Poker Flat* (1959), based on a story by Bret Harte set in a gold-rush town, was produced at the Eastman School on 25 April 1968. The American Guild of Organists commissioned a second opera, *The Wrestler*, in one act with libretto by Judah Stampfer and based on Jacob's reconciliation with his brother Esau. It was first staged on 22 June 1972 in Dallas, Texas. In 1973 he completed a music drama, *The Lodge of Shadows*, for baritone solo, dancers, and orchestra. His reconstruction of the first American opera, *The Disappointment*, received its premiere in 1976 at the Library of Congress, Washington, D.C.

Adler is the author of three textbooks: *Anthology for the Teaching of Choral Conducting* (1971, rev. 1985); *Sight-Singing: Pitch, Interval and Rhythm* (1979, rev. 1997); and *The Study of Orchestration*, 3 volumes with workbooks (1982, 1989, 2002), widely used in universities throughout the United States.

AITKEN, HUGH

b. New York, New York, 7 September 1924

Aitken studied the clarinet before undertaking a chemistry major for two years at New York University (1941–43). Following service in the U.S. Army Air Corps during World War II (1943–46), he enrolled at the Juilliard School (1946–50), where he was a composition pupil of Bernard Wagenaar, Vincent Persichetti, and Robert Ward. Aitken taught there (1960–70) before being appointed professor of music at William Paterson College, Wayne, New Jersey (1970–96).

As several of the titles of his works suggest, Aitken has been strongly influenced by music of the past. For the stage he has written two operas, *Fables* (after La Fontaine) (1975) and the three-act *Felipe* (after Cervantes) (1981); and four dance scores (1949–63), including *The Moirai* (1961) for José Limón. Among his works for full orchestra are a Piano Concerto (1953); three violin concertos (1984, 1988, 1992); *Happy Birthday* (1988); *Songdance* (1992); *Harmonic Rhythms* for strings (1997); a Symphony (1998); and *Songs and Caprices* (2001). For smaller ensembles he has composed a Chamber Concerto for piano, winds, brass, and string quintet (1947, rev. 1957); *Short Suite* for strings (1954); four *Partitas*: *I* (1957), *II* (1959), *III* (1964), and *IV* (1964); *Partita for strings* (1960); *Partita* for string quartet and orchestra (1964); *Rameau Remembered* for flute and chamber orchestra (1980); and *In Praise of Ockeghem* for strings (1981). Aitken also has contributed valuable items to the band repertory including *Suite in Six* (1961); *Four Quiet Pieces* (1962); *Partita* (1967); *Variations on a Toccata* (1968); and *Songdance* (1992).

Aitken's major choral composition is *The Revelation of St John the Divine* for soloists, chorus, and orchestra (1953–1990). There are also two settings of the Mass (1950, 1964) and a sequence of 10 secular cantatas (1958–94) for solo voices and instrumental ensemble. *Thirteen Ways of Looking at a Blackbird* (Wallace Stevens) for baritone and chamber ensemble dates from 1996.

An extensive catalog of instrumental works includes *Short Suite* for wind quintet and piano (1948); String Trio (1951); *Short Fantasy* for violin and piano (1954, rev. 1980); *Partita for Six* (1956); Quintet for oboe and strings (1957); *Eight Studies* for wind quintet (1958); Quartet for clarinet and strings (1959); Serenade for oboe and string trio (1965); *Tromba* for trumpet and string quartet (1976); and Trio for flute, clarinet, and cello (1984). Recent chamber works include *Duo* for cello and piano (1989) written for Yo-Yo Ma; *Two Tales from Grimm* for narrator and chamber ensemble (1991); and *Laura Goes to India* (1998) for the Emerson Quartet.

In addition, Aitken has produced a number of pieces for unaccompanied instruments: *Partita* (violin) (1958); *Trombone Music* (1961); *Suite for Bass* (1961); *Montages* (bassoon) (1962); *Trumpet!* (1974); *Oboe Music* (1975); *For the Violin* (1978); *For the Cello* (1980); *Flute Music* (1981); and *Music for the Horn* (1985).

ALBERT, STEPHEN (JOEL)

b. New York, New York, 6 February 1941
d. Truro, Massachusetts, 27 December 1992

At school, Albert learned to play the piano, horn, and trombone. He studied composition with Elie Siegmeister (1956–58) and with Darius Milhaud at Aspen (1956). At the Eastman School of Music, Rochester, N.Y., he was a pupil of Bernard Rogers (1959–60). Later he took composition lessons in Stockholm with Karl-Birger Blomdahl (1960) and with George Rochberg at the University of Pennsylvania (1963). He graduated from the Philadelphia Musical Academy in 1962. Albert taught at the Philadelphia Musical Academy (1968–70), Stanford University (1970–71), Smith College, Northampton, Massachusetts (1974–76), Boston University (1981–84), and the Juilliard School (1986–92). He was the recipient of numerous awards, including two Guggenheim Fellowships (1967–68, 1978–79) and two Rome Prizes (1985–86). From 1985 to 1988 he was composer-in-residence with the Seattle Symphony Orchestra. He died in an automobile accident.

For orchestra, Albert composed *Bacchae Prologue* (1967); *Leaves From the Golden Notebook* (1970); *Voices Within* (1975); Symphony no. 1: *RiverRun* (1983-84), which won the Pulitzer Prize in 1985; a Violin Concerto subtitled *In Concordium* (1986, rev. 1988); *Anthem and Processionals* (1988); a Cello Concerto (1990) for Yo Yo Ma; *Tapioca Pudding* (1991); and Symphony no. 2 (1992) performed in New York in 1994.

Albert wrote extensively for the voice including *Supernatural Songs* (W. B. Yeats), for soprano and orchestra (1964); *Winter Songs* for tenor and orchestra (1965); *Wedding Songs* for soprano and piano (1965); *Bacchae Canticles* (Euripides) for narrator, chorus, and orchestra (1968); *Wolf Time* (Icelandic tenth-century texts) for soprano, amplified instruments, and orchestra (1968-69); *To Wake the Dead* (Joyce: *Finnegans Wake*) for soprano and ensemble (1978); *Into Eclipse* (Ted Hughes's adaptation of Seneca's *Oedipus*) for tenor and 13 instruments (1981); *TreeStone* (Joyce: *Finnegans Wake*) for soprano, tenor, and 12 instruments (1983-84); *Flower of the Mountain* (Joyce: *Ulysses*) for soprano and orchestra (1985); *Distant Hills* for soprano, tenor, and 11 instruments (1989); *Sun's Heat* for tenor and 11 instruments (1989); *Rilke Song* for soprano, flute, clarinet, violin, cello, and piano (1991); and *Ecce Puer* for soprano, oboe, horn, and piano (1992).

Among Albert's instrumental pieces are Two Toccatas for piano (1958-59); *Illuminations* for two pianos, harp, and percussion (1962); *Imitations* (after Bartók) for string quartet (1963); *Canons* for string quartet (1964); *Cathedral Music–Concerto for Four Quartets* for two amplified flutes, two amplified cellos, brass, and percussion (1971–72); *Tribute* for violin and piano (1980); and *Music From the Stone Harp* for seven players (1979–80).

ALBRIGHT, WILLIAM
b. Gary, Indiana, 20 October 1944
d. Ann Arbor, Michigan, 17 September 1998

At the Juilliard Preparatory School (1959–62), Albright was a pupil of Hugh Aitken (composition) and Rosetta Goodkind (piano). At the University of Michigan (1963–70), he studied with Ross Lee Finney and Leslie Bassett and received organ lessons from Marilyn Mason. In 1969 he spent a year at the Paris Conservatory with Olivier Messiaen and studied privately with Max Deutsch. A Guggenheim Fellowship in 1976 again took him to Paris. At Tanglewood he was a pupil of George Rochberg.

From 1970 until his death Albright taught composition at the University of Michigan, where he became associate director of the Electronic Music Studio. In 1979 he was composer-in-residence at the American Academy in Rome. In addition to his reputation as a composer, Albright was noted throughout the United States and Europe as an organist and pianist, especially with regard to new music. He also specialized in the performance of classic ragtime and early jazz for piano.

For large orchestra Albright wrote *Alliance*, a symphonic suite in three movements, completed in 1970 and first performed by the Buffalo Philharmonic Orchestra. Other orchestral pieces include *Night Procession* (1972); *Gothic Suite* for organ, strings, and percussion (1973); *Backhand* for organ and orchestra (1981); *Chasm*, a symphonic fragment (1988); and Concerto for harpsichord and strings (1991).

Many of Albright's compositions are for various instrumental ensembles: *Foils* for winds (1963–64); *Frescoes* for wind quintet (1964); *Two Pieces* for nine instruments (1965–66); *Caroms* for seven instruments (1966); *Danse Macabre* for violin, cello, flute, clarinet, and piano (1971); *Marginal Worlds* for small orchestra (1972); *Take That* for percussion (1972);

Stipendium peccati for three players (1973); *Introduction, Passacaglia and Rondo Capriciosso* for solo tackpiano and winds (1974); *Doo-dah* for three alto saxophones (1975); and *Seven Deadly Sins* for flute, clarinet, string quartet, piano, and optional narrator (1974).

Later chamber music includes *Peace Pipe* for two bassoons (1976); *Saints Preserve Us* for solo clarinet (1976); *Heater* for alto saxophone band (1977); *Shadows* for guitar (1977); *The Enigma Syncopations* for flute, double bass, percussion, and organ (1982); Sonata for alto saxophone and piano (1984); *Sphaera* for ensemble and 4-track tape (1985); Clarinet Quintet (1987); *Abiding Passions* for wind quintet (1988); *The Great Amen* for flute and piano (1992); *Pit Band* for alto saxophone, bass clarinet, and piano (1993); *Fantasy Etudes* for saxophone quartet (1993–94); and *Rustles of Spring* for flute, saxophone, and piano trio (1994).

For his own instrument, the organ, Albright wrote *Chorale Partita in an Old Style* (1963); *Juba* (1965); *Pneuma* (1966); three *Organ Books* (1967, 1971, 1978), his most widely known works; *De Spiritum* (1980–81); *That Sinking Feeling* (1982); *In Memoriam* (1983); *Carillon-Bombarde* (1985); *Chasm* (with optional tape) (1985); *Whistler Nocturnes* (1989); *Flights of Fancy* (1992); *Chorale Prelude for Advent* (1997); and *Cod Piece* (1998). To expand the organ repertory he composed *Stipendium Peccati* for organ, piano, and percussion (1973); *Dream and Dance* for organ and percussion (1974); *Jericho Battle Music* for trumpet and organ (1976); *Halo* for organ and metal instruments (1978); *King of Instruments* for narrator and orchestra (1978); *Romance* for horn and organ (1981); *1732: In Memoriam Johannes Albrecht* for narrator and organ (1984) and Symphony for organ and tape (1986).

His piano pieces include *Pianoagogo* (1965–66); *Grand Sonata in Rag* (1968); *The Dream Rags* (1970); *Five Chromatic Dances* (1976); *New Leaves* (1991); and *Four Dance Tributes* (1987–96).

Albright composed three multimedia works: *Tic* for soloist, two jazz-rock improvisation ensembles, film, and tape (1967); *Beulahland Rag* for narrator, jazz quartet, improvisation ensemble, tape, film, and slides (1967–68); and *Cross of Gold* for actors, chorus, and instruments (1974). His single opera, *The Magic City* (1978), was performed in 1982.

Albright's choral compositions include *An Alleluia Super-round* (1973); Mass in D (1974); *The Chichester Mass* (1974); *Pax in Terra* for alto, tenor, and chorus (1981); *David's Psalms* for soloists and chorus (1982); *Six New Hymns* (1974–83); *A Song of David* (Christopher Smart) for two choruses and organ (1983); *Take Up the Song* for soprano, chorus, and piano (1986); *Deum de Deo* for chorus and organ (1989); *Dona Nobis*

Pacem for chorus and piano (1992); and *Missa Brevis* for soprano and organ (1996).

ALEXANDER, JOSEF
b. Boston, Massachusetts, 15 May 1907
d. New York, New York, 28 February 1992

Alexander studied the piano at the New England Conservatory (1922–25) and undertook a piano career in 1934 before entering Harvard University, where he was a pupil of Walter Piston and Edward Burlingame Hill (1935–38). He spent the following year in Paris where he was taught by Nadia Boulanger. At the Berkshire Center he studied composition with Aaron Copland and conducting with Serge Koussevitzky. From 1943 until 1977 he taught at Brooklyn College of the City University of New York.

In his compositions Alexander steered a middle course between conventional tonality and dissonant modernism, often using colorful and exotic scoring. Alexander's orchestral music includes four symphonies: no. 1 (*Clockwork*) for strings (1947); no. 2 (1954); no. 3 (1961); and no. 4 (1968); Piano Concerto in C minor (1936); a symphonic poem, *The Ancient Mariner* (1938); *Doina* (1940); *A New England Overture* (1943); *Williamsburg Suite* (1943); *Dithyrambe* (1947); *Epitaphs* (1947); *Andante and Allegro* for strings (1952); *Duo Concertante* for trombone, percussion, and strings (1959); *Quiet Music* for strings (1965); Concertino for trumpet and strings (1959); and *Trinity* for brass and percussion (1976).

Among his numerous vocal works are *Dialogues Spirituels* for men's chorus and orchestra (1945); *Songs of Eve* for soprano and four instruments (1957); *Canticle of the Night* (Tagore) for mezzo-soprano and orchestra (1959); *Gitanjali* (Tagore) for soprano, harpsichord, and percussion (1973); *Aspects of Love* for soprano and ensemble (1974); *Symphonic Odes* for men's chorus and orchestra (1975); *Salute to the Whole World* (Whitman) for narrator and orchestra (1976); and *Adventures of Alice* (Lewis Carroll) for female voices and piano (1976).

Alexander was also a prolific composer of chamber music, including: String Quartet (1940); Piano Quintet (1942); Piano Trio (1944); Wind Quintet (1949); Piano Quartet (1952); Violin Sonata (1953); Cello Sonata (1953); Flute Sonata (1954); Clarinet Sonata (1957); Trombone Sonata (1959); *Three Pieces for Six* (1965); Brass Trio (1971); Horn Sonata (1979); *Hexagon* for wind quintet and piano (1980); *Of Masks and Mirrors* for soprano saxophone, cello, piano, and percussion (1981); *Five Fables* for oboe, bassoon, and piano (1981); and sonatas for viola and trombone.

Among over 100 piano solos are two sonatas (1936, 1943); *10 Bagatelles* (1967); *Twelve Signs of the Zodiac* (1974); and *Nine Etudes* (1979).

AMRAM, DAVID
b. Philadelphia, Pennsylvania, 17 November 1930

Amram studied piano from the age of seven and soon developed an enthusiasm for jazz, which he still plays. At age sixteen he began to study the horn seriously and became an expert player. On 1948 he entered Oberlin (Ohio) Conservatory, moving the following year to George Washington University. There he played as a professional in the National Symphony Orchestra. While serving in the U.S. Army in Germany from 1952 to 1954, he was a member of the 7th Army Symphony Orchestra. After this he spent a year in Paris where he played in various jazz groups including the Lionel Hampton Band.

On his return to America in 1955 Amram became a pupil of Vittorio Giannini at the Manhattan School of Music. From 1956 to 1967 he was musical director for Joseph Papp's New York Shakespeare Festival, composing over 30 scores for various productions. He was awarded a Pulitzer Prize in 1959 for the incidental music to Archibald McLeish's play *JB*. In 1966 he was appointed the first Composer-in-Residence at the New York Philharmonic Orchestra. Amram has appeared as guest conductor with many of the leading orchestras throughout the world. In 1971 he became Director of Youth and Family Concerts for the Brooklyn Academy of Music. He has also toured with his own jazz and folklore group.

David Amram conducting.
Photo: Sedar Pakay, courtesy the composer.

Amram is equally at home in the theater, the synagogue, the symphony orchestra, and the jazz band, and his numerous compositions reflect his very wide interest in all aspects of music. His musical language is relatively conservative and tonal. The first of his two operas, *The Final Ingredient* (libretto: Arnold Weinstein), portrays a Passover Eve service in a concentration camp. It was commissioned by ABC Televison and first performed in 1965. The choice of *Twelfth Night* for a second opera came from his close association with the productions of Shakespeare plays on stage. It was performed on 1 August 1968 at the Lake George Opera Festival at Hunter College, New York.

In addition to his theatrical work, Amram has provided music for a number of television productions, including *The Taming of the Shrew* starring Ingrid Bergman. He also composed the scores for several significant films: *Echo of an Era* (1957); *The Young Savages* (1960); *Splendor in the Grass* (1961); *The Manchurian Candidate* (1962); *The Subject Was Roses* (1968); *The Arrangement* (1969); *This Song for Jake* (1982); *The Beat Generation* (1987); and *Boys of Winter* (2001). In 1967 he collaborated with Allen Ginsberg and Jack Kerouac on Robert Frank's cult beat film *Pull My Daisy*.

The *King Lear Variations*, performed in 1967 by the New York Philharmonic Orchestra, was Amram's first important work for orchestra. It was followed by the Triple Concerto for woodwind, brass, jazz quartet, and orchestra, performed in New York in January 1971 by the American Symphony Orchestra; *Elegy* for violin and orchestra (1971); and a Horn Concerto that was premiered in 1971 by Mason Jones and the Philadelphia Orchestra. A Bassoon Concerto, completed in 1972, was performed in Washington umder Antal Dorati. Three later orchestral pieces are a Violin Concerto, premiered by the Chicago Symphony Orchestra in 1976; *The Trail of Beauty* for mezzo-soprano, oboe, and orchestra (1977), settings of American Indian writings commissioned for the Bicentennial by the Philadelphia Orchestra; and *En memoria de Chano Pozo* (1977).

Among Amram's other orchestral works are *Ode to Lord Buckley* for alto saxophone and orchestra (1980); *Honor Song for Sitting Bull* for cello and orchestra (1983); *Across the Wide Missouri: A Musical Tribute to Harry S. Truman* (1984); *Fox Hunt* (1984); *Travels* for trumpet and orchestra (1985); *American Dance Suite* (1986); *A Little Rebellion: A Portrait of Thomas Jefferson* for narrator and orchestra (1995); *Kokopelli– A Symphony* (1996); and *Giants of the Night* (1997); and a flute concerto for James Galway. Amram has composed a large quantity of instrumental music that has achieved wide success. Many of these compositions have been recorded, including the *Shakespeare Concerto* for viola, two horns, and strings (1959); a Sonata for violin and piano (1960); a Piano Sonata (1960); and *Dirge and Variations* for piano trio (1962). Other important chamber works are a Trio for alto saxophone, bassoon, and horn (1958); *Overture and Allegro* for solo flute (1959); *Discussions* for flute, cello, piano, and percussion (1960); String Quartet (1961); *Three Songs for Marlboro* for cello and horn (1962); *The Wind and the Rain* for viola and piano (1963); a Sonata for solo violin (1964); *Fanfare and Procession* for brass quintet (1966); Woodwind Quintet (1968); *Zohar* for solo flute (1974); *Native American Portraits* for violin, piano, and percussion (1976); and *Landscapes* for percussion quartet (1980).

In 1961 Amram set the *Jewish Sacred Service for the Sabbath Eve "Shir L'Erev Shabbat"* for tenor, choir, and organ. Other works for chorus include *Two Anthems* (1961); *May the Word of the Lord* (1962); *Thou Shalt Love the Lord Thy God* (1962); and two cantatas for soloists, chorus, and orchestra: *A Year in Our Land* (1964) and *Let us Remember* (1965), to words by Langston Hughes, which premiered in San Francisco. *Missa Manhattan* for narrator, chorus, and orchestra dates from 2000.

Amram has written an autobiography, *Vibrations: The Adventures and Musical Times of David Amram*, published in 1968, and *Offbeat: Collaborating with Kerouac, 1956–69* (2002).

ANDERSON, LEROY
b. Cambridge, Massachusetts, 29 June 1908
d. Woodbury, Connecticut, 18 May 1975

Born of Swedish ancestry, Anderson studied at the New England Conservatory, Boston, from the age of eleven. At Harvard he was a pupil of Walter Spalding and Walter Piston, graduating in 1929, earning a master's degree a year later. In 1929, he was appointed organist and choirmaster at the East Congregational Church in Milton, Massachusetts. He taught at Radcliffe College (1930–32) and directed the Harvard Band from 1931 to 1935. From 1936 to 1950 Anderson was pianist and arranger for the Boston Pops Orchestra for whom he wrote most of his short, brilliantly conceived light orchestral works, of which *Sleigh Ride* (1948) has reached almost legendary status. The first of these novelty pieces, *Jazz Legato* and *Jazz Pizzicato*, both for strings, date from 1938. For the same forces he wrote *Fiddle Faddle* (1947) and *Plink, Plank, Plunk* (1951). In 1950, Anderson signed a recording contract with Decca Records, and a year later won his first Gold Record, for one million sales, for his recording of *Blue Tango."*

Full orchestra pieces include *The Syncopated Clock* (1945), used as the theme for *The Late Show* on televi-

Leroy Anderson.
Courtesy Eleanor Anderson.

sion; *Promenade* (1945); *Chicken Reel* (1946); *Irish Suite* (1947); *The Typewriter* (1950); *The Waltzing Cat* (1950); *Belle of the Ball* (1951); *China Dog* (1951); *Blue Tango* (1951); *Horse and Buggy* (1951); *Bugler's Holiday* (1954); *Sandpaper Ballet* (1954); and *Clarinet Candy* (1962). He also wrote a Piano Concerto (1953). Except for a Broadway musical, *Goldilocks* (1958), and a ballet, *Lady in Waiting* (1959), Anderson did not attempt to compose works on a larger scale.

Anderson was elected posthumously to the Songwriters Hall of Fame in 1988, and in 1995 Harvard University opened its Anderson Band Center, named in his honor.

ANTES, JOHN

b. Fredericktownship, Pennsylvania, 24 March 1740

d. Bristol, England, 17 December 1811

Antes was born in the Moravian community of Fredericktownship. As a young man he took an active part in music as a performer and composer and maker of stringed instruments. A violin he made, dated 1759, is preserved in the Moravian Historical Society Museum in Nazareth, Pennsylvania. At the age of 25 he left America as a missionary. At first he went to England and then to Europe where he met Haydn. Ordained a minister, from 1769 to December 1781 he was in Egypt where he was tortured by the Bey, who attempted to extort money from him.

In 1782 he returned to Europe, living first in Neuwied, Germany, before settling in the Moravian community in Fulnick, England.

Antes took a particular interest in writing church music, and his hymn tune *Monkland* (Let us with a gladsome mind) is still widely sung. He composed many anthems, of which notable examples are *Loveliest Immanuel*; *Go, Congregations, Go* for soprano and strings; and *Sure He Has Been Born* for chorus and strings.

In 1790, John Bland published in London a set of Trios, op. 3, for two violins and cello, that Antes had composed in Egypt in 1779 for the Swedish ambassador to the Porte. They show the strong influence of Haydn but rate as important instrumental works by an American-born composer of the eighteenth century. A set of six string quartets also written in 1779 has been lost.

In 1806 Antes published a pamphlet outlining improvements he had made to violin bows, keyboard hammers, and the tuning of violins. He also invented a device for automatically turning the pages of music. In 1809, Antes moved to Bristol where he set up as a watchmaker.

His lengthy memoirs, written shortly before his death, are entitled *Lebenslauf des Bruders John Antes* (publ. 1815); strangely, they make no reference to his activities as a musician.

ANTHEIL, GEORGE

b. Trenton, New Jersey, 8 July 1900

d. New York, New York, 12 February 1959

Antheil was born of Polish parents. He studied piano in Philadelphia (1916–19) with Constantine von Sternberg, a pupil of Liszt, and composition in New York (1919–21) with Ernest Bloch. After a short stay at the Curtis Institute in Philadelphia, he went to Europe as a concert pianist and spent the 1920s and 1930s there, dividing his time mostly between Berlin and Paris. He also made two excursions into North Africa, where he acquired a considerable interest in Arab music.

From the age of 12, Antheil took a great liking to modern music, and his first significant compositions were influenced by jazz. His wildly avant-garde works written between 1922 and 1927 earned him a wide notoriety. (His musical autobiography, published in 1945, is aptly titled *Bad Boy of Music*.) The first of the iconoclastic pieces was *Zingareska* (1921) (later called Symphony no. 1.), which he had begun while a pupil of Bloch. It was given its premiere by the Berlin Philharmonic Orchestra in 1922. Also making use of jazz is the *Jazz Symphony* for chamber orchestra (1925), based on the finale of *Zingareska*, and Symphony in F (1927) originally called no. 1. There followed a String Quintet and a group of violently dissonant piano pieces—

Sonata Sauvage (1922), *Airplane Sonata* (1922), and *Mechanisms* (c. 1923)—which frequently caused riots when they were performed. He moved from Berlin to Paris in 1923, where he wrote his First String Quartet in 1924. In 1926 a *Piano Concerto* proved a failure at its premiere, also in Paris.

On 19 June 1926 the first performance in Paris of Antheil's "succès de scandale," *Ballet Mécanique*, was given. The score had been written three years earlier to accompany an abstract film by Fernand Léger concerning time and space. After a performance on 10 April 1927 in Carnegie Hall, it went down in history as the peak of modernity from this "enfant terrible." Aaron Copland and Colin McPhee were among the pianists involved in the New York premiere. The piece is scored for a group of normal musical instruments and a collection of noise-producing machines: anvils, airplane engine, electric bells, two octaves of motor horns, pieces of tin and steel, player piano, and up to ten pianos. Not surprisingly, the result is principally an exercise in rhythm and noise. Subsequent performances of *Ballet Mécanique* in London, Paris, and New York served to confirm the composer's reputation as a violent musical rebel. Years later Antheil found this a considerable handicap, because musicians on both sides of the Atlantic refused to accept his more orthodox works.

In 1929, Antheil was appointed assistant musical director of the Berlin State Theater,, and in the same year composed incidental music for a production of Sophocles' *Oedipus*. In the following year he began a Second Symphony, completed in 1938 and revised in 1943, and a full-length opera, *Transatlantic*, which was performed with great success at the Frankfurt-am-Main State Theater on 25 May 1930. It is a satire on American life involving a hero named Hector, who is eventually elected President of the United States, and a heroine of doubtful character named Helen. In the light of recent political history, the work might warrant a revival. Fittingly, Antheil made use of 1920 jazz idioms to suit the nature of the plot.

Two Guggenheim Fellowships in 1932 and 1933 enabled Antheil to compose a second opera, *Helen Retires*, first heard at the Juilliard School in New York in 1934, shortly after the composer's return to America. The musical language is a mixture of Puccini and Richard Strauss, again laced with jazz. Towards the end of his life Antheil composed five more operas: *The Rascal* (1948); *Volpone* in three acts, performed in Los Angeles on 9 January 1953; and three one-act operas— *The Brothers* (1954); *The Wish*, the latter commissioned by the Louisville Orchestra in 1955; and *Venus in Africa*, produced in Denver in 1957.

Antheil composed four dance scores. In 1929 he made use of a text by W. B. Yeats for a ballet entitled *Fighting the Waves*, produced at the Abbey Theatre in Dublin. The other ballets were *Flight* (1930) for puppets; *Dreams* (1935); and *Capital of the World.* The scenario for this last work is based on a Hemingway bullfight story set in Madrid. It was performed in 1953. Several other ballet scores are believed to have been lost.

For orchestra, Antheil composed six symphonies. The Third (*American*) was written between 1936 and 1939 and performed by Hans Kindler and the National Orchestra of Washington, D.C. The Fourth, completed in 1942, was first performed two years later by Leopold Stokowski and the NBC Symphony Orchestra. By this time in his career, Antheil's modernisms had mellowed into a more compromising language. The influences in the Fourth Symphony seem to be Shostakovich and American folk music. Major events of the Second World War, especially the battles of El Alamein and Stalingrad, served as the stimulus for the patriotic character of the music.

In *Bad Boy of Music*, Antheil wrote that his Fifth Symphony, subtitled *Tragic* and composed 1945–46, was a requiem for those who died in World War II, including his younger brother Henry. Later a quite different work, also called the Fifth Symphony (but subtitled *Joyous*), appeared (1947–48). Taking the same basic precepts of his Symphony no. 4., Antheil used American themes as the material. It was first performed in Philadelphia under Eugene Ormandy on 31 December 1948. Symphony no. 6., subtitled *After Descartes*, completed in 1949, received its premiere by the San Francisco Symphony Orchestra conducted by Pierre Monteux. Among Antheil's other orchestral compositions are Piano Concerto no. 2. (1927); *Archipelago* (1933); *Nocturne* (1943); Violin Concerto (1947); *Serenade for Strings* (1948); *Over the Plains* (1948); a concert overture, *McKonkey's Ferry*, his most widely performed work (1948); and *Tom Sawyer, A Mark Twain Overture* (1950).

Antheil's output of chamber music includes three string quartets (1924, 1928, 1948); four violin sonatas (1923, 1924, 1924, 1948); a Trumpet Sonata (1951); and six piano sonatas. The fourth of these, written in 1948, reveals the final refuge of a rebel in conformity, with quotations from Beethoven's *Appassionata*. In his last works, Antheil avoided all pretensions of being a modern composer, seekng eventual solace in the music of previous centuries. His Fifth Piano Sonata (1950) is entirely Lisztian in concept.

In 1939 Antheil settled in Hollywood, where he devoted his time to writing film music for Paramount Pictures and contributing articles on a wide range of subjects, especially international affairs, to *Esquire* magazine. To supplement his income, he wrote a syndicated lonely-hearts column and published anonymously a book, *The Shape of War to Come*. He had made his debut as an author in 1926 with a detective novel. *Death in the Dark*, published by Faber. The manuscript was edited by a distinguished literary trio: Ezra Pound, T. S. Eliot, and Franz Werfel. In Paris, he had befriended Pound, who championed the young composer. In turn Antheil helped Pound in composing two operas. One of Antheil's more bizarre activities was the invention, in co-operation with the film star Hedy Lemarr, of a radio-guided torpedo. Although the device was rejected by the U.S. Navy, it was the predecessor of satellite communications today.

Among Antheil's numerous film scores are *Harlem Picture* (1934); *The Scoundrel* (1935); *Millions in the Air* (1935); *Once in a Blue Moon* (1935); *The Plainsman* (1936); *The Buccaneer* (1937); *Make Way For Tomorrow* (1937); *Union Pacific* (1938); *Angels Over Broadway* (1940); *Orchids for Charlie* (1941); *The Plainsman and the Lady* (1946); *Specter of the Rose* (1946); *Repeat Performance* (1946); *That Brennan Girl* (1946); *Ballerina* (1947); *Knock on Any Door* (1948); *We Were Strangers* (1949); *Tokyo Joe* (1949); *The Fighting Kentuckian* (1949); *House by the River* (1950); *In a Lonely Place* (1950); *Sirocco* (1951); *The Sniper* (1952); *Actors and Sin* (1952); *The Juggler* (1953); *Not as a Stranger* (1955); *Dementia* (1955); *Hunters of the Deep* (1956); *The Young Don't Cry* (1957); *The Pride and the Passion* (1957); and *Woman Without a Shadow* (1957). Antheil's two choral works are *Fragments from Shelley* for chorus and piano (1951) and *Cabezza de Vacca*, first performed posthumously on CBS television in 1962. As a teacher, Antheil numbered Henry Brant, Benjamin Lees, and Tom Scott among his pupils.

ANTONIOU, THEODORE
b. Athens, Greece, 10 February 1935

Antoniou studied violin and theory at the National Conservatory, Athens (1947–58), where Manolis Kalomoiris was his composition teacher. At the Hellenic Conservatory, Athens (1958–61), Yannis A. Papaioannou was his teacher. At the Hochschule für Musik in Munich (1961–65), he was a pupil of Adolph Mennerich (conducting) and Gunter Bialas (composition). Also in Munich he worked at the Siemens Studio for Electronic Music with Josef Riedl (1964–65). At Darmstadt (1963, 1966) he received instruction from Luciano Berio, Pierre Boulez, György Ligeti, and Karlheinz Stockhausen.

Antoniou taught at the National Conservatory in Athens (1956–61) and was the founder of the Heinrich Schütz Society and director of the Hellenic Group of Contemporary Composers. In 1969 he joined the music faculty at Stanford University, moving the following year to the University of Utah. From 1970 he taught

at the Philadelphia College of Performing Arts and in 1978 was a visiting professor at the University of Pennsylvania. Antoniou was appointed professor of composition at Boston University in 1979 and was Assistant Director of Contemporary Activities at the Berkshire Music Center, Tanglewood (1974–85) where he also taught and conducted. In addition to directing various ensembles in Philadelphia, he has conducted extensively in Europe and the United States, most notably for the Politis Composition Prize and with Alea II at Stanford University and Alea III in residence at Boston University. Antoniou has received several awards, including grants from the Guggenheim Foundation and the National Endowment for the Arts and commissions from the Koussevitzky and Fromm Foundations.

In many of his works he has combined conventional techniques with electronic means. For orchestra he has written an *Overture* (1961); *Antithesis* (1962); *Micrographies* (1964); *Kinesis ABCD* for strings (1966); *OP Overture* (with tape) (1966); *Events II* (1969); *Events III* (with tape and slides) (1969); *Threnos* for wind orchestra (1972); *Fluxus I* (1974–75); and *Circle of Accusation* (1975). Works for solo instruments and orchestra include Triple Concerto for violin, clarinet, and trumpet (1959); Concertino for piano, strings, and percussion (1962); *Jeux* for cello and strings (1963); Concertino for piano, winds, and strings (1963); a Violin Concerto (1965); *Events I* for violin, piano, and orchestra (1967–68); *Katharsis* for flute, orchestra, tape, and projections (1968); *Flexus II* for piano and chamber orchestra (1975); and *Double Concerto* for percussion (1977).

Later orchestral pieces are *The GBYSO Music* (1982); *Skolion* (1986); *Paean* (1989); *Celebration* (1994); *Moto Perpetuo* (1995); and *Kommos B* (1996). Other works for solo instruments and orchestra include Concerto for tambura and chamber orchestra (1988); *Concerto/Fantasia* for violin and chamber orchestra (1989); *North/South* for piano and chamber orchestra (1990); Concerto for strings and optional percussion (1992); *Chania* for piano and strings (1992); Concerto for violin and strings (1995); Concerto for marimba, harp, and orchestra (1995); *Zon B* for small orchestra and tape (1996); Guitar Concerto (1997); Piano Concerto (1998), with a version for two pianos (1999); *Celebration VII* for strings (2000); Concerto for double bass (2000); *Concerto per Cinque* (2001); *Concerto Piccolo* for alto saxophone (2001); Horn Concerto (2002): and Symphony no. 1 (2002–03).

Among Antoniou's choral compositions are *Greek Folk Songs* for a cappella voices (1961); *Kontakion* for soloists, chorus, and strings (1965); *Ten School Songs* (1965–66); *Nenikikamen* (*We are Victorious*), a cantata for narrator, mezzo-soprano, baritone, chorus, and orchestra (1971); *Verleih und Frieden* for three choruses

(1971–72); *Die Weisse Rose*, a cantata for boys' chorus, choir, narrators, baritone, and orchestra (1974–75) and a cantata, *Circle of Thanatos and Genesis* (1977–78).

His vocal music includes *Eight Musical Pictures* for voice and piano (1953); *Melos*, a cantata for medium voice and orchestra (1962); *Epilogue* (after the *Odyssey* of Homer) for mezzo-soprano, narrator, oboe, horn, piano, percussion, and double bass (1963); *Climate of Absence* for medium voice and orchestra (1968); *Parodies* for voice and piano (1970); and *Moirologhia for Jani Christou* for medium voice and piano (1970), written in memory of the Greek composer who died in an automobile accident in that year.

Later choral works are *Die Revolution de Toten: Antiliturgy*, a cantata for soloists, chorus, and orchestra (1981); a cantata, *Prometheus* (Aeschylus) (1983); *Oraseis Opsonde* for chorus, flute, brass, and percussion (1988); *Eros I* for chorus and orchestra (1990); *Agape* for chorus, flute, brass, and percussion (1990); *Celebration III* for chorus and orchestra (1995); *Music of the Myth* for chorus, cello, double bass, and percussion (1996); and *Cantata Concertante* for mezzo-soprano, chorus, violin, piano, and orchestra (1998).

Other vocal music include *Epigrams* for soprano and chamber orchestra (1981); *11 Aphighisis* (Kavafis) for medium voice and piano (1983; orchestrated 1984); *Kriti: Oneiro Mega* for soprano, tenor, narrator, and chamber orchestra (1984); *Eros II* for mezzo-soprano, flute, brass, and percussion (1990); *Westwinds* (1991); *Ode* (1992) for soprano and orchestra; and *Kie Rodo Mesa Mou Poly* (*And Plentiful Rose in Me*) for soprano, baritone, projectors, and orchestra (1998).

For the stage Antoniou has composed two ballets, *Bacchae* (1980) and *The Imaginary Cosmos* (1984); and two operas, *Bacchae* (1991–92), produced in Athens in 1995, and *Oedipus at Colonus*, also premiered in Athens in May 1998. In addition to incidental music for the theater and television, he has composed a number of multimedia works for dramatic presentation. These include *Noh Musik* for four musician/actors (1965); *Clytemnestra* for actress, dancers, orchestra, and tape (1967); *Cassandra* for dancers, actors, orchestra, tape, lights, and projections (1969); *Protest I* for actors and tape (1970); *Protest II* for voice, actors, tape, lights, and ensemble (1971); *Afrosyngentrossipetrama* for mixed media (1972); *Chorochronos I* for narrator, baritone, four percussion, four trombones, tape, film, slides, and lights (1973); *Chronochronos II* for narrator and orchestra (1973); *Chronochronos III* for medium voice, piano (or percussion), and tape (1975); *Periander*, a mixed-media opera (1977–79); and *A Comedy* for four voices, actors, and orchestra (2002).

Antoniou's output of instrumental works is considerable. Important among these are two string quartets (1960, 1998); Sonatina for violin and piano (1958);

Suite for eight players (1960); Trio for flute, viola, and cello (1961); *Dialogues* for flute and guitar (1962); *Quartetto Giocoso* for oboe and piano trio (1965); *Six Likes* for solo tuba (1967); *Lyrics* for violin and piano (1967); *Katharsis* for flute, ensemble, tape, and lights (1968); *Synthesis* for oboe, hammond organ, percussion, double bass, and four synthesizers (1971); *Cheironomiai* (*Gestures*) for eight performers (1971); *Four Likes* for solo violin (1972); *Three Likes* for solo clarinet (1973); *Stichomythia I* for flute and guitar (1976); *Two Likes* for solo double bass (1976); *Stichomythia II* for guitar (1977); *Parastasis* for solo percussion and tape (1977); *Parastasis II* for solo percussion, optional dancer, and ensemble (1978) and *The Do Quintet* for brass (1978).

Later instrumental pieces include *Aphierosis* (*Dedication*) for flute, clarinet, violin, cello, and piano (1984); Octet (1986); *Ertnos* for nine players (1987); *Commos* for cello and piano (1989); *Dexiotechnika Idiomela* for nine performers (1989); Suite for brass and optional organ and percussion (1993); Brass Quintet (1995); *Zen* for eight players (1996); *Celebration V for Jacques Cousteau* for violin and piano (1996); *Decem Inventions* for wind quintet (1996); *Eros II* for clarinet, violin, and piano (1997); *Trio Concertante* for two violins and piano (1998); *Trio SLS* for bassoon, cello, and piano (1999); *Double Reed and Strings* for oboe and string trio (1999); *Saxquar* for saxophone quartet (1999–2000); Piano Trio (2000); Trio for clarinet, violin, and piano (2001); and *Celebration IX* for chamber ensemble (2002).

APPLEBAUM, EDWARD (EVEREST)
b. Los Angeles, California, 28 September 1937

Applebaum studied at the University of California, Los Angeles with Lukas Foss and Henri Lazarof where he was awarded a Ph.D. in composition in 1966. He also received composition lessons from Ingvar Lidholm in Stockholm.

In 1969 he was Composer-in-Residence with the Oakland Symphony Orchestra. From 1971 to 1985 he was professor of composition at the University of California, Santa Barbara, becoming Composer-in-Residence with the Santa Barbara Symphony Orchestra (1985–87). After teaching at the Music Academy of the West in Santa Barbara (1988–89), he was appointed professor of composition, Florida State University, Tallahassee. He spent the years 1991–1994 as professor of music at the Edith Cowan University, Perth, Western Australia. Later he taught at the Shepherd School of Music at Rice University.

Applebaum was a child prodigy, a gifted pianist at the age of eight, soon becoming deeply interested in jazz. The first work he acknowledges is the *Piano Sonata* of 1965, dedicated to his teacher Henri Lazarof.

For orchestra he has composed five symphonies: no. 1 (1970); no. 2 (1983); no. 3 (1989); no. 4 (1995); no. 5 (1997). Other orchestral works include: Variations (1966); a Concerto for viola and chamber orchestra (1967); *The Princess in the Garden* for strings (1985); a *Piano Concerto: Dreams and Voyage* (1986); a Guitar Concerto; *Night Waltz* (1987); and *Waltz in 2* for narrator and orchestra (1988).

Applebaum's chamber works include a String Trio (1966); *Montages* for clarinet, cello, and piano (1968); *Shantih* for cello and piano (1969); *Foci* for viola and piano (1971); a Piano Trio (1972); *The Face in the Cameo* for clarinet and piano (1973); *To Remember, a Trio* for clarinet, cello, and piano (1976); Piano Sonata no. 2. (1980); *Prelude* for string quartet (1984); and *Whispers of Yesterday* for wind quintet (1988).

Among his vocal compositions is the unusual *When Dreams Do Show Thee Me, a* triple concerto for clarinet, cello, and piano with chamber orchestra and nine voices (1972); *The Garden* for soprano, chamber ensemble, and tape (1979); *And with and to* for men's chorus (1984); and an oratorio, *Song of the Sparrows* for soloists, narrator, chorus, and orchestra (1988). A chamber opera, *The Frieze of Life*, was completed in 1974.

Applebaum is currently working on a book, *Psychotherapy in the Arts*.

AREL, BULENT
b. Constantinople, Turkey, 23 April 1919
d. Stony Brook, New York, 24 November 1990

Arel studied at the Ankara State Conservatory (1940–47) with Ferhunde Erkin (piano), Necil Kâzim Akses (composition), Ernst Praetorius (conducting), and Edward Zuckmayer (twentieth-century music). From 1947 to 1959 he lectured in harmony, counterpoint, and orchestration at the Ankara Teachers College and the Ankara State Conservatory; from 1951 to 1959 he served as engineer and director of the Western Music Program, Radio Ankara. On a Rockefeller research grant, Arel worked at the Columbia-Princeton Electronic Music Center (1959–63) and also taught electronic music at Yale (1961–62, 1965–71) and at Columbia University (1970–71). He became an American citizen in 1973. From 1971 to 1989 he was professor of music and director of the Electronic Music Studios at the State University of New York at Stony Brook.

Arel's early music is neoclassical in style, but after 1957 he adopted 12-tone techniques and worked extensively in the electronic music medium.

Bulent Arel.
Courtesy Communications Department, Stony Brook University.

For orchestra he wrote *Six Bagatelles* for strings (1958) and *Short Piece* commissioned by the New Haven Symphony Orchestra in 1967. He also composed a Piano Concerto (1946); two symphonies (1951, 1952); *Suite intime* (1949); and *Masques* for wind and strings (1949). His chamber works include *Music for Strings and Tape* (1958, rev. 1962); *Music for Unaccompanied Viola* (or violin) (1962); *For Violin and Piano* (1966); *Interrupted Preludes* for organ (1967); and *Fantasy and Dance* for five viols and tape (1974), commissioned by the New York Consort of Viols.

Arel's electronic music includes *Short Study* (1960); *Fragment* (1960); *Electronic Music No. 1* (1960); *Stereo Electronic Music I* (1960), commissioned by the Columbia-Princeton Electronic Music Center and the Martha Baird Rockefeller Foundation; *Impressions of Wall Street* (1961); *Music for a Sacred Service* (1961); *The Scapegoat* (incidental music for a play by John F. Matthews based on Kafka's *The Trial*) (1961); *Capriccio for T.V.* (1969), commissioned by National Educational Television; *Stereo Electronic Music No. 2* (1970), commissioned for the 10th anniversary of the Columbia-Princeton Electronic Music Center; *Mimiana I* (1968), *II* (1969), and *III* (1973), dance scores with choreography by Mimi Garrard; and *Out of Into* (1972) for an animated film by Irving Kreisberg.

Dominick Argento, 1961.
Courtesy University of Minnesota Archives.

ARGENTO, DOMINICK

b. York, Pennsylvania, 27 October 1927

The son of Italian immigrants, Argento studied at the Peabody Conservatory, Baltimore from 1947 to 1951 and again from 1953 to 1954, where he was a pupil of Hugo Weisgall, Nicolas Nabokov, and Henry Cowell. He also attended the Cherubini Conservatory in Florence (1951–52), where he studied with Luigi Dallapiccola.

At the Eastman School of Music, Rochester, New York, he received composition lessons from Bernard Rogers, Howard Hanson, and Alan Hovhaness (1955–57), earning his Ph.D. in 1957. From 1952 to 1955, he taught theory at Hampton Institute, Virginia. From 1958–1997, he was a faculty member at the University of Minnesota, Minneapolis, being appointed Regents Professor in 1980. He has been awarded a Guggenheim Fellowship (1957) and two Fulbright Fellowships (1951, 1964).

Argento's greatest successes have been in the theater. His first opera, *Sicilian Limes* (now withdrawn), was staged at the Peabody Conservatory in 1954. An opera buffa, *The Boor*, based on a play by Chekhov, was produced at the Eastman School on 6 May 1957. It was followed by *Colonel Jonathan the Saint* (1953–60), a comedy set shortly after the Civil War, performed at Loretto Heights College, Denver on 31 December 1971. His fourth opera, *Christopher Sly*, based on the Introduction to Shakespeare's *The Taming of the Shrew*, was first performed at the University of Minnesota on 31 May 1963. The one-act *The Masque of Angels* was staged by the Minnesota Center Opera Company on 9 January 1964. The English Elizabethan theatre provided the source for *The Shoemakers' Holiday*, a ballad opera derived from Thomas Dekker's play. It was premiered by the Minnesota Theatre Company on 1 June 1967.

Postcard From Morocco, Argento's seventh opera, was commissioned by the Minnesota Center Opera Company and performed in Minneapolis on 14 October 1971. In 1976, for a commission from the University of Minnesota, Argento composed an opera to mark the Bicentennial. As its subject, he took the final days in the life of Edgar Allan Poe. Entitled *The Voyage of Edgar Allan Poe*, it was first staged by the Minnesota Opera Company on 24 April 1976 and later performed in Sweden.

For a commission from the National Endowment for the Arts, Argento wrote a ninth opera, *A Water Bird Talk*, a monodrama for baritone and chamber orchestra, based on Chekhov's "On the Harmfulness of Tobacco," which was premiered in Brooklyn on 19 May 1977. In 1978 the New York City Opera commissioned *Miss Havisham's Fire* for Beverly Sills. It was produced in New York on 22 March 1979. This was followed by a one-act monodrama, *Miss Havisham's Wedding Night*, performed by Rita Shane with the Minnesota Opera on 1 May 1981. Minnesota Opera also first staged *Casanova's Homecoming* on 12 April 1985. *The Aspern Papers*, based on Henry James's novella, was premiered by Dallas Opera on 19 November 1988. Argento's most recent opera, *The Dream of Valentino*, was premiered at the John F. Kennedy Center by Washington Opera on 15 January 1994.

Also for the stage are two ballets: *The Resurrection of Don Juan*, composed in 1956 and produced in Karlsruhe, Germany in 1959, and *Royal Invitation* or *Homage to the Queen of Tonga* (1964).

Vocal music forms an important part of Argento's other compositions. He has written *Songs About Spring* (e.e. cummings) for soprano and chamber orchestra (1956); *Six Elizabethan Songs* for high voice and baroque ensemble (1962); *Letters From Composers*, a song cycle for tenor and guitar (1968); *To Be Sung on the Water* for high voice, clarinet, bass clarinet, and piano (1973); and *From the Diary of Virginia Woolf* for voice and piano (1979), commissioned by Janet Baker, which received the Pulitzer Prize. The song cycle *The Andree Expedition* (1982) for baritone and piano draws texts from the diaries of three Swedish explorers. *Casa Guidi*, settings of texts from letters from Elizabeth Barrett Browning to her sister for mezzo-soprano and orchestra, was premiered by Frederica von Stade on 28 September 1983. His most recent vocal work is *A Few Words About Chekhov* for mezzo-soprano, baritone, and chamber ensemble (2001).

Argento's choral works include *Let All the World in Every Corner Sing* for chorus, brass quintet, harp, and organ (1960); *The Revelations of St. John the Divine*, a rhapsody for tenor, men's voices, brass, and percussion (1966); *Tria Carmina Paschalia* for female voices, harp, and guitar (1970); *A Nation of Cowslips*, a song cycle for chorus (1973); *Jonah and the Whale* for soloists, chorus, and orchestra (1973); and *Peter Quince at the Clavier* (Wallace Stevens) for chorus and piano concertante (1979).

In 1982, Argento composed *I Hate and I Love*, a song cycle for mixed chorus and percussion. An extended setting of the *Te Deum* for chorus and orchestra was performed in March 1987 by the Buffalo Philharmonic Orchestra and Buffalo Schola Cantorum conducted by Thomas Swan. *A Toccata of Galuppi* (1989) sets Browning's poem for chamber choir, harpsichord, and string quartet.

Recent music for unaccompanied chorus includes *Easter Day* (1988); *Everyone Sang* (1991); *Spirituals and Swedish Chorales* (1994); *To God* (*In Memoriam M.B. 1994*); and *Walden Pond* (1996) for SATB chorus, three cellos, and harp, based on extracts from the writings of Henry Davis Thoreau.

For orchestra Argento has written a Divertimento for piano and strings (1955); *From the Album of Allegra Harper . . . 1867*, a suite of dances from the opera *Colonel Jonathan the Saint* (1961); *Variations for Orchestra* (*The Mask of Night*) with solo soprano (1965); *Bravo Mozart!*, a concerto for oboe, violin, and horn with chamber orchestra (1969); *A Ring of Time*, subtitled *Preludes and Pageants*, for orchestra and bells, performed by the Minnesota Orchestra in October 1972 to celebrate its 70th anniversary; and *In Praise of Music*, composed for the same orchestra in 1977. Other orchestral works derived from operas include *Fire Variations* (1982), based on a theme from *Miss Havisham's Fire*; *Le Tombeau d'Edgar Poe* (1985), a suite from *The Voyage of Edgar Allan Poe*; and *Valentino Dances* (1994), adapted from *The Dream of Valentino*.

Recent works for orchestra are *Valse Triste* for harp and strings, written in 1996 to celebrate the 60th birthday of the conductor David Zinman, and *Reverie: Reflections on a Hymn Tune*, performed in 1997 by the Minnesota Orchestra. *Bremen Town Musicians* for chamber orchestra dates from 1999.

ASHLEY, ROBERT (REYNOLDS)
b. Ann Arbor, Michigan, 28 March 1930

Ashley graduated from the University of Michigan in 1952 and the Manhattan School of Music in 1954. He returned to the University of Michigan in 1957 to undertake postgraduate studies in psychoacoustics, and in 1958, with Gordon Mumma, he established the Cooperative Studio for Electronic Music, the first independent electronic music studio in the United States. With Mumma and Roger Reynolds, he was a founder of the ONCE Festival, an annual festival of contemporary music (1961–69), and he founded and directed the ONCE Group (1965–69), a music theater ensemble that toured extensively in the United States. Ashley was director of the Center for Contemporary Music at Mills College, Oakland, California from 1969 to 1981.

Ashley's major works have been in the area of electronic music theater, initially experimental in character. *In memoriam . . . Kit Carson* (1964), described as an opera, was realized by the composer from schematic outlines (score) for 16 speaking voices and domestic sound producers (radio, television, phonographs). *She Was a Visitor* for speaking voice and chorus (1967) consists of vocal amplification of micro-components of the title phrase in rhythmic repetition. Other music theater creations include *The Wolfman* for amplified voice and "The Wolfman Tape" (1964); *Four Ways*, *Frogs*, and *Purposeful Lady Slow Afternoon*, performed in Ann Arbor in 1968; *That Morning Thing*, an opera for five voices, eight dancers, chorus, and tape (Ann Arbor, 1968); *Music With Roots in the Aether*, a series

Gordon Mumma and Robert Ashley, at Ashley's section of the Coopertive Studio for Electronic Music. Ann Arbor, MI, circa 1960. *Courtesy Gordon Mumma.*

of videotapes illustrating the work and ideas of nine radical composers, produced on television in Paris in 1976; *Title Withdrawn*, also televised in Paris in 1976; *Perfect Lives* (*Private Parts*), an opera in seven episodes (1977–81) broadcast on PBS in 1981; *The Lessons*, seen on television in New York in 1981; *Tap Dancing in the Sand* (1982); and *Atalanta* (*Acts of God*), an opera in three episodes based on Max Ernst, premiered in Paris in 1982 and produced in New York in 1986. A concert version is titled *Songs from Atalanta*.

Later theater pieces are *Atalanta Strategy*, a television opera (New York, 1984); an opera, e*L/Aficianado* (1987); a tetralogy, *Now Eleanor's Idea* (1984–93); *Yellow Man With Heart With Wings* for voice and tape (1990); *Love is a Good Example* for voice (1994); *When Famous Last Words Fail You* for voice and orchestra (1994); *Yes, But is It Edible?* for voice (1994); *Dust*, produced in Yokohama in 1998; and a radio opera *Your Money My Life Goodbye* (1999). Ashley's creations often have original and exotic titles: *The Fourth of July* for tape (1960); *Something* for clarinet, piano, and tape (1961); *Detroit Divided* for tape (1962); *Complete With Heat* (1962); *Trios* (*White on White*) for various instruments (1963); *in memoriam . . . Esteban Gomez* (*Quartet*) for any instruments (1963); *Untitled Mixes* for tape (1965); and *Factory Preset* for tape (1993).

Ashley has composed a number of pieces termed "electronic music theater": *Heat* (1961); *Public Opinion Descends Upon the Demonstartors* (1961); *Boxing* (Detroit, 1963); *Combination Wedding and Funeral* (1964); *Interludes for the Space Theater* (Cleveland, 1964); *Kitty Hawk* (*An Antigravity Piece*) (1964); *The Wolfgang Motorcity Revue* (1964); *The Lecture Series* (with Mary Ashley) (New York: 1965); *Morton Feldman Says* (1965); *Orange Dessert* (1965); *Unmasked Interchange* (1965); *Night Train* (1966); *The Trial of Anne Opie Wehrer and Unknown Accomplices for Crimes Against Humanity* (1968); *Fancy Free or It's There* (1970); *Over the Telephone* (1975); and *What She Thinks* (1976). Other works include *Illusion Models* for hypothetical computer (1970); *String Quartet Describing the Motions of Large Real Bodies* (1972); *In Sara, Mencken, Christ and Beethoven There Were Men and Women* (1973); and *Exposure in Little Light* (1974).

Ashley's instrumental music includes a Piano Sonata (1959, rev. 1979) with the extended title *Christopher Columbus Crosses to the New World in the Nina, the Pinta and the Santa Maria Using Only Dead Reckoning and an Crude Astyrolabe*; a Quartet for any string or wind instruments (1961); *Fives* for two pianos, two percussion, and string quartet (1962); *Details* for two pianos (1962); and *The Entrance* for electric organ

(1965). Ashley's oeuvre also includes scores for films by George Manupelli: *The Image in Time* (1957), *The Bottleman* (1960), *The House* (1961), *Jenny and the Poet* (1964), *My May* (1965), *Overdrive* (1968), and *Portraits, Self-portraits and Still-lifes* (1969); four feature-length experimental comedies of the "Dr, Chicago" series (1968–70); and music for films by Philip Makenna: *Battery Davis* (1970), *Shoot the Whale* (1972), and *Home on the Range* (1974). Later he wrote music for several dance companies: *Ideas for the Church* (1978; Douglas Dunn); *The Park* and *The Backyard* (1978; Steve Paxton); *Son of Gone Fishin'* (1983; Trisha Brown); and *Problems in the Flying Saucer* (1988; Merce Cunningham).

Music without electronics include *Odalisque* for voice, chorus, and 24 instruments (1973); *Superior Seven* for flute, chorus, and instruments (1988); *Outcome Inevitable* for chamber orchestra (1991); *Van Cao's Meditation* for piano (1991); and *Tract* for voice and string trio or keyboards (1992).

ASIA, DANIEL
b. Seattle, Washington, 27 June 1953

As a student at Hampshire College, Amherst, Massachusetts, Asia was a pupil of Randall McClellan before he moved on to Smith College, Northampton, Massachusetts, where he studied with Stephen Albert and Ronald Perera. He obtained his M.M. at Yale University in 1977, where he studied with Jacob Druckman, Arthur Weisberg, and Krzysztof Penderecki. At Tanglewood (1979), Asia received lessons from Gunther Schuller. On a Fulbright Fellowship in 1980 he spent a year at the Hochschule für Musik, Berlin, as a pupil of Isang Yun. In New York in 1977, he founded the Musical Elements ensemble to perform new music. Asia taught at Oberlin (Ohio) College Conservatory of Music (1980–86) and City University, London (1986–88). He joined the faculty of the University of Arizona, Tucson, in 1988, becoming professor and head of the Composition Department in 1997. In 1991 he served as Composer-in-Residence with the Phoenix Symphony Orchestra.

Asia's early compositions are dense in texture with complex rhythmic features. He has gradually evolved a music of simpler textures, color, and rhythmic material, utilizing more developed and sophisticated formal designs. At the center of his compositional career are four symphonies. Symphony no. 1 was commissioned jointly by the Seattle Symphony Orchestra and the American Composers Orchestra and performed in Seattle in 1990. It is based on five movements of the *Scherzo Sonata* for piano (1987). Similarly, Symphony no. 2 (1989–90) is derived from an earlier work, *Celebration* (1988). It bears a double title: *Celebration Symphony: Khagiga, In Memoriam Leonard Bernstein*. Symphony no. 3 incorporates a work, *At the Far Edge*, written for the Seattle Youth Orchestra in 1991, into the score. It was premiered in Phoenix in May 1992. Symphony no. 4, also a Phoenix Symphony Orchestra commission, was completed in 1994.

Asia's other orchestral works are *Black Light*, an American Composers Orchestra commission (1990); *At the Far Edge* (1991); *Gateways* (1993); a Piano Concerto for Andre-Michel Schub, (1994, rev. 1995–96); a Cello Concerto for Carter Bray (1997); *Then Something Happened*, written for the Tucson Symphony Orchestra (1999); *Once Again* (2000), a Knoxville Symphony Orchestra commission; and *Bear Down Arizona* (2002).

Asia's instrumental music includes *On the Surface* for chamber ensemble (1974-75); *Dream Sequence No. 1.* for amplified trombone (1976); *No. 2.* for flute (1977); two string quartets (1976–77, 1985); *Sand I* for flute, horn, and double bass (1977); *Line Images* for four winds (1978); *Rivalries* for ensemble (1980-81); *Music* for trumpet and organ (1983); Piano Quartet (1989); *Five Images* for flute and bassoon (1994); *Embers* for flute and guitar (1995); *The Alex Set* for solo oboe (1995); Piano Trio (1996); *Guitar Set I* for solo guitar (1998); Wind Quintet (1998); *Songs of Trascendence* for guitar (1999); *A Lament* for cello and piano (2000); Violin Sonata (2000); Cello Suite (2002); and Brass Quintet, commissioned in 2002 by the American Brass Quintet. For piano solo he has written two *Piano Sets* (1976, 1977); *Scherzo Sonata* (1978); *Why? Jacob* (1983); and *Piano Variations* (1996).

Among Asia's vocal and choral music are two pieces for mezzo-soprano and chamber orchestra, *Sand II* (1978) and *Ossabaw Island Dream* (1982); *Pine Songs I* for voice and piano (1983–85); *V'shamru* for baritone and chamber ensemble (1985); *Psalm 30* for baritone, violin, and piano (1986); *Songs From the Page of Swords* for bass-baritone, oboe, and chamber ensemble (1986); *Celebration* for baritone, chorus, brass quintet, and organ (1988); *Sacred Songs* for soprano, flute, guitar, and cello (1989); *Breath in a Ram's Horn* for high voice and piano (1995); *My Father's Name Was* for soprano, piano, and bass (1995); three pieces for chorus: *Purer Than Purest Pure, Summer is Over, Out of More* (1996); *An e. e. cummings Songbook* for high voice and piano (1997–98); and *Pine Songs II* for tenor and piano (2002).

With his colleague Kip Haaheim, Asia produced a cycle of electro-acoustic music, *Sacred and Profane* (1999–2000), in both stereo and surround-sound formats.

Larry Austin.
Photo: Don Lee, Banff Center for the Arts.

AUSTIN, LARRY (DON)
b. Duncan, Oklahoma, 12 September 1930

Austin studied with Violet Archer at North Texas State University, Denton (1948–52), and from 1955 to 1958 at the University of California, Berkeley, where he was a pupil of Andrew Imbrie and Seymour Shifrin. Earlier, at Mills College, Oakland, California, he received lessons from Darius Milhaud (summer 1955).

In 1958, Austin joined the music faculty at the University of California, Davis, becoming a professor in 1970. There he founded the New Music Ensemble in 1963 and spent the following year in Rome. In 1966 he was editor and co-founder of the avant-garde music magazine *Source* In 1972, Austin was appointed chairman of the Department of Music at the University of Southern Florida in Tampa. From 1973 to 1978 he was director of the System Complex for the Studio and Performing Arts, College of Fine Arts in Tampa. In 1978 he accepted the position of director of music at North Texas State University, where he taught computer music and composition. He retired in 1996.

With Gunther Schuller, Austin was a pioneer among the exclusive group of musicians known in the jazz world as "Third Stream." Later he made extensive use of electronic sounds and computer techniques in his compositions. His early works emphasize wind instruments: a Wind Quartet (1948); Wind Quintet (1949); Brass Quintet (1949); Concertino for flute, trumpet, and strings (1952); and Fanfare for nine brass (1958). Austin's "Third Stream" creations include *Homecoming*, a cantata for soprano and jazz quartet (1959); *Fantasy on a Theme of Berg* for jazz band (1960); and his best-known composition, *Improvisations for Jazz Soloists and Orchestra* (1961), performed by the New York Philharmonic Orchestra under Leonard Bernstein in January 1964.

Apart from these pieces, Austin has composed little for orchestra, the exceptions being *Prosidy* (1953) and *Open Style* for orchestra with piano solo (1965), performed in Buffalo in September 1968, which also incorporates improvisation techniques. Other instrumental compositions of this period include a String Quartet (1955); *Broken Consort* for seven instruments (1962); *Collage* for a variety of instruments (1963); *Continuum* for two to seven instruments (1964); *Quartet in Open Style* (1964); *Catharsis* (1965); and *Current* for clarinet and piano (1967).

For concert band he has composed *Fanfare and Procession* (1953); *Music Galore* (1958); *Suite for Massed Bands* (1961); and *In Memoriam J. F. Kennedy* (1964). Austin has provided music for three plays: *Elektra* (Giradoux) (1963); *Richard II* (Shakespeare) (1963); and *Amphitryon 38* (Giradoux) (1967).

Since 1965 many of Austin's compositions use electronic tape as a major element: *The Maze*, a theater piece in open style for three percussionists, tape, machines, and projections (1965); *Roma Due*, sound and movements for improvisation ensemble, dancers, and tape (1965; rev. 1997); *Duet Amphitryon* for tape (1967); *Cyclotron Stew* for cyclotron with tape montage (1967); *Changes* for trombone and tape (1968); *Transmission One*, an audio-visual electronic composition for color television (1969); and *Agape*, a celebration for priests, musicians, actors, and poets (1970).

From 1966 to 1971 Austin composed a number of "portraits" for specific performers. These include *Bass* for double bass, tape, and film for Bertram Turetzky (1966); *Accidents* for prepared piano, magnetic tape, mirrors, actors, and projections for David Tudor (1967); *Brass* for the American Brass Quintet (1967); *The Musicians* for children, tape, and lights for the composer's own children (1968); *Plastic Surgery with Prelude and Postlude* for Robert Lloyd (1969–71); and *Walter* for viola, viola d'amore, tape, and film for Walter Trampler (1970–71). For solo keyboard he has composed several pieces of which the Piano Variations (1960), *Piano Set in Open Style* (1964), *Tango Violets* (1984), and *Violets Invention* (1988) are the most frequently performed. In addition he has written *Sonata Concertante* for piano and tape (1983–84).

In the 1970s Austin wrote three four-channel electronic-music compositions—*Quartet Three* (1971), *Quartet Four* (1971), and *Primal Hybrid* (1972)—and a series of eleven pieces combining tape with instruments and voices: *No. 1, Events/Complex* for symphonic wind ensemble (1972); *No. 2* for chorus (1972); *Nos 3 – 7* for flute, clarinet, and piano trio (1973); *No. 8* for viola (1973); *No. 9* for percussion (1974); *No. 10* for trombone (1976); and *No. 11* for double bass (1977). *Tableaux Vivants*, a sonograph for any combination of voices and instruments (1973), composed in collaboration with the graphic artist Charles Ringness, was performed in Tampa, Florida in November 1973.

Austin has taken a considerable interest in the last few years in an incomplete score by Charles Ives, the *Universe Symphony*. In addition to a performing version for large orchestra on which he worked from 1974 to 1994, he has also used the material for his own compositions, including *Fantasy No. 1* for double brass quintet, narrator, and tape (1975); *Fantasy No. 2* for clarinet, viola, keyboards, percussion, and tape (1976); *Phantasmagoria*, a fantasy for narrator, orchestra, tape, and synthesizer (1977); and *Life Pulse* for 20 percussion (1984).

Later works include *Beachcombers* for four musicians and tape, a dance piece for Merce Cunningham (1983); *Canadian Coastlines* for eight variable musicians and tape (1984); *Life Pulse Prelude* for piccolo, piano, and orchestra (1984); *Sinfonia Concertante: A Mozartean Episode* for chamber orchestra and tape (1986); *Concertante Cibernetica*, interactions for performer and synclavier (1987); *Euphoria 2344*, an intermezzo in five scenes for vocal quartet and tape (1988); *Transmission 2: The Great Excursion* for chorus, computer music ensemble, and recorded dialogue (1989–90); *La Barbara: The Name/The Sounds/The Music* for voice and computer (1991); *Accidents 2*, sound projections for piano and computer music (1992); and *Variations...beyond Pierrot*, sound-play for soprano, flute, clarinet, violin, cello, piano, hypermedia system, and computer music on tape (1993–95).

Among Austin's most recent compositions are *BluesAx* for saxophone and computer music on tape (1995); *Shin-Edo: CityscapeSet* for computer on tape (1994–96); *Singing! the music of my own time*, a sound-portrait of the singer Thomas Buckner for voice and octophonic computer music (1996–99); *Djuro's Tree* for computer (1997); *Tarogato* for tarogato and octophone computer (1998); *Willam(re)Mix(ed)* for computer based on John Cage's *Williams Mix* (1997-2000); and *Ottoplo!* for four inter-episodes of real and virtual string quartet (1998–2000).

With T. Clark, Austin is the author of a book, *Learning to Compose: Modes, Materials and Models of Musical Invention* (1989).

Jacob Avshalomov.
Photo by Doris Avshalomov.

AVSHALOMOV, JACOB (DAVID)

b. Tsingtao, China, 28 March 1919

Avshalomov was born of an American mother and a Russian father, the composer Aaron Avshalomov (1894–1965); he received his first musical training in China from his father. Jacob and his mother went to the United States in 1937 and he became a naturalized citizen in 1944. In Los Angeles, he was taught privately by Ernst Toch. The following year he became a student at Reed College, Portland, Oregon, moving in 1941 to the Eastman School of Music, Rochester, New York, where he was a pupil of Bernard Rogers. War service (1943–44) briefly interrupted his musical career.

Avshalomov joined the music faculty of Columbia University in 1947, becoming an assistant professor in 1954. In that year he was appointed conductor of the Portland Junior Symphony Orchestra, a post he held until 1994. The orchestra, renamed the Portland Youth Philharmonic in 1978, was the first youth orchestra in America. He has been the recipient of several awards, including a Ditson Fellowship in 1946 and a Guggenheim Fellowship in 1951.

Avshalomov's orchestral works include three Symphonies: no. 1, *The Oregon* (1959-61), composed for the Oregon Centennial in 1962; no. 2, *Glorious the*

Assembled Fires for choir and orchestra (1985); and no. 3, *Symphony of Songs* (1993), composed for the 70th anniversary of the Portland Youth Philharmonic. Among his other orchestral pieces are *The Taking of T'ung Kuan* (1943, rev. 1953); *Slow Dance* (1945); Sinfonietta (1946), which won a Naumburg Recording Prize; *Evocations* for clarinet and chamber orchestra (1947, rev. 1952), first performed in New York in 1953 under the direction of Leopold Stokowski; *The Plywood Age*, a suite (1955); *Phases of the Great Land*, commissioned in 1959 for the Anchorage (Alaska) Symphony Orchestra; *Raptures* (1975); *Open Sesame!* (1985); *Up at Timberline* for winds and brasses (1986), and *Season's Greetings* (1995-96) for orchestra.

Avshalomov is a noted conductor who gave the United States premiere of Michael Tippett's oratorio *A Child of Our Time* at Columbia University in 1952. Other works performed in America for the first time under his direction include Bruckner's Mass in D and Handel's *The Triumph of Time and Truth*.

Avshalomov's choral works include *Prophecy* for cantor, chorus, and organ (1948); *How Long, O Lord*, a cantata (1948–49); *Tom O'Bedlam*, sung by the Robert Shaw Chorale at Carnegie Hall, New York in 1953 and winner of the New York Critics' Circle Award; and *Proverbs of Hell* for men's chorus (1954). Also for chorus are a setting of *Psalm 100: Make a Joyful Noise Unto the Lord* for chorus and winds (1956); *Inscriptions at the City of Brass* for female narrator, large chorus, and orchestra (1956); *City Upon the Hill* (William Blake) for narrator, chorus, orchestra, and the Liberty Bell (1965); and *Praises from the Corners of the Earth* for chorus and organ or orchestra (1964).

Avshalomov also has written pieces for chorus with instrumental accompaniment: *Now Welcome Somer* with flute (1957); *I Saw a Stranger Yestere'en* with violin (1968); *The Most Triumphant Bird* with viola and piano (1985); *Songs from the Goliards* with cello (1992); and *Songs in Season* with piano and double bass (1993). In 2000 he set words by Ruth Pittes as *When Summer Shines* for unaccompanied chorus. In 1973, to celebrate the 50th anniversary of the Portland Youth Philharmonic, he composed a setting of James Thurber's *The Thirteen Clocks* for two narrators and orchestra.

Instrumental music includes a *Sonatine* for viola and piano (1943); *Evocations* for clarinet (or viola) and piano (1947); *Two Bagatelles* for clarinet and piano; *Disconsolate Music* for flute and piano; and *Quodlibet Montagna* for brass sextet (1975).

Avshalomov is the author of *Music is Where You Make It* (vol.1. 1959; vol.2. 1979); *The Concerts Reviewed: 65 Years of the Portland Youth Philharmonic* (1991); and *Avshalomov's Winding Way: Composer Out of China* (2002).

AYRES, FREDERIC
(REAL NAME FREDERIC AYRES JOHNSON)

b. Binghampton, New York, 17 March 1876
d. Colorado Springs, Colorado, 23 November 1926

Ayres trained as an engineer at Cornell University, Ithaca, New York, and undertook a career in designing electric motors. Later he received composition lessons from Edgar Stillman Kelley (1897-1901) and Arthur Foote (1899) before moving to Colorado Springs for health reasons, where he taught composition and theory privately until his death.

Ayres was best known for his songs, including the cycle *The Seeonee Wolves* (Kipling) (1918) and other settings of Kipling and Shakespeare. His single orchestral work, an overture *From the Plains* composed in 1914, enjoyed a brief success. Most of his other compositions are instrumental: Piano Trio (1914); Violin Sonata no. 1 in B minor (1914); String Quartet (1916); Piano Trio no. 2. in D minor (1925); Violin Sonata no. 2; Cello Sonata; and String Quartet no. 2 (*The West Wind*).

B

BABBITT, MILTON (BYRON)
b. Philadelphia, Pennsylvania, 19 May 1916

As a child, Babbitt moved from Philadelphia to Jackson, Mississippi, where he learned to play the violin and clarinet. Following his father's example, he entered the University of Pennsylvania in 1931 to study mathematics but transferred to New York University changing his major to music where his teachers included Marion Bauer and Philip James. After graduating in 1935, he received private lessons from Roger Sessions, joining him on the music faculty at Princeton University in 1938. During the 1930s, he worked in Tin Pan Alley for Harms Music arranging popular songs; he also wrote a musical, *Fabulous Voyager*, in 1946.

In 1942, Babbitt received his M.F.A. and taught mathematics at Princeton (1942–45). He returned to the music faculty there in 1948, succeeding Sessions as William Shubael Conant Professor in 1966, retiring in 1984. From 1973 he also taught at the Juilliard School, Tanglewood, Salzburg Seminar in American Studies, New England Conservatory, and Darmstadt. He received a Guggenheim Fellowship (1960–61) and a Special Pulitzer Citation in 1982, and is a member of the editorial board of *Perspectives of New Music*.

In his early music, Babbitt was much influenced by Stravinsky, Varèse, Schoenberg, and Berg. He has applied total serialism and, as a trained mathematician, has added a discipline of note values to the standard 12-tone system derived from Schoenberg and Webern. In *Composition for Twelve Instruments* (1948), for example, Babbitt used, in addition to the 12-tone system, 12 different intervals of time between the successive instrumental entries. The entire method of composing has been rigorously systematized. Just as abstract painters have eschewed picturesque names for their works, Babbitt adopted abstract titles for his pieces: *Composi-*

tion for Four Instruments (1948); *Composition for Viola and Piano* (1950); and *Concerto for Four Woodwind Instruments* (1953, renamed Woodwind Quintet). His early works include *Music for the Mass I* (1940); *Music for the Mass II* (1942); and a film score, *Into the Good Ground* (1949), all now withdrawn.

For orchestra Babbitt has written *Relata I* (1965); *Relata II* (1968), composed for the 125th anniversary of the New York Philharmonic Orchestra; *Concerti* for small orchestra and tape (1976); *Ars Combinatoria* (1980), commissioned for Indiana University; two piano concertos (1985, 1998); and *Transfigured Notes* for string orchestra (1986). In addition to a String Quartet (1948), now withdrawn, his instrumental music includes five further string quartets (1954, 1969–70, 1970, 1982, 1993); a String Trio (1951); Woodwind Octet (1953); *All Set* for jazz ensemble (1957); *Sextets* for violin and piano (1966); *Arie Da Capo* for flute, clarinet, and piano trio (1973–74); *My Ends Are My Beginnings* for solo clarinet (1978); *Paraphrases* for ten instruments (1979); *Dual* for cello and piano (1981); *Melismata* for solo violin (1982); and *Groupwise* for five players (1983).

Since his official retirement, Babbitt has produced a considerable amount of chamber music, often with curious, whimsical titles: *Four Play* for clarinet, violin, cello, and piano (1984); *Composition: Sheer Pluck* for guitar (1984); *Whirled Series* for saxophone and piano (1987); *The Crowded Air* for 11 instruments (1988); *Consortini* for five instruments (1989); *Play It Again, Sam* for solo viola (1989); *Soli e Duettini* for two guitars (1989); *None But the Lonely Flute* for solo flute (1991); *Septet But Equal* for three clarinets, string trio, and piano (1992); *Counterparts* for brass quintet (1992); and *Around the Horn* for horn (1993). With undiminished energy, he has continued these instrumental works into the 21st century, with *Fanfare for All* for

Milton Babbitt with Samuel Rhodes, December 1990. Publicity photo for Samuel Rhodes's faculty recital, Jan. 24, 1991, which featured *Play it Again Sam* by Babbitt (composed for Rhodes in 1989), #9236-11.
Photo: David Archer, courtesy The Juilliard School.

brass quintet (1993); *Triad* for clarinet, viola, and piano (1994); *Arrivals and Departures* for two violins (1994); *Accompanied Recitative* for soprano saxophone and piano (1994); *Bicenquinquagenamy Fanfare* for brass quintet (1995); Quartet for piano and string trio (1995); Quintet for clarinet and strings (1996); *When Shall We Three Meet Again?* for flute, clarinet, and vibraphone (1996); *Concertino Piccolino* for vibraphone (1999); *Little Goes a Long Way* for violin and piano (2001); and *Swan Song no. 1* for six instruments (2002–03).

For piano Babbitt has written *Three Compositions* (1947); *Duet* (1956); *Semi-Simple Variations* (1956); *Partitions* (1957); *Post-Partitions* (1966); *Tableaux* (1972); *Minute Waltz* (1977); *Playing for Time* (1977); *My Compliments to Roger* (1978); *About Time* (1982); *Canonical Form* (1983); *It Takes Twelve to Tango* (1984); *Lagnaippe* (1985); *Emblems (Ars Emblematical)* (1989); *Preludes, Interludes, Postlude* (1991); *Tutte le Corde* (1994); *The Old Order Changeth* (1998); *Allegro Penseroso* (1999); and *A Gloss on "Round Midnight"* (2001). For piano four-hands are *Don* (1981) and *Envoi* (1990). His single work for organ is *Manifold Music* (1995).

Babbitt was one of the founders of the Columbia-Princeton Electronic Music Center in 1959. He has made effective use of electronic tape in *Composition* for synthesizer and four-track tape (1961); *Ensembles* for synthesizer (1961-64); the widely performed *Philomel* for soprano and tape (1964); *Correspondences* for string orchestra and tape (1967); *Occasional Variations* for synthesizer (1969); *Phonemena* for soprano and tape (1974); *Reflections* for piano and tape (1974–75); and *Images* for saxophone and tape (1979).

Vocal works include *Three Theatrical Songs* for voice and piano (1946); *The Widow's Lament in Springtime* (William Carlos Williams) for soprano and piano (1950); *Du* (A. Shramm), a cycle to German texts performed at the I.S.C.M. Festival in Oslo in 1953; *Two Sonnets of Gerard Manley Hopkins* for baritone, clarinet, viola, and cello (1955); *Composition* for tenor and six instruments (1960); *Sounds and Words* for soprano and piano (1960); *Vision and Prayer* to words of Dylan Thomas for soprano and electronic tape (1961); *Phonemena* for soprano and piano (1969–70); *A Solo Requiem* for soprano and two pianos (1976–77); *The Head of the Bed* (John Hollander) for soprano, flute, clarinet, violin, and cello (1982); *Four Cavalier Settings* for tenor and guitar (1991); *Mehr "Du'* for soprano, viola, and piano (1991); *Quatrains* for soprano and two clarinets (1993); *No Longer Very Clear* for soprano and four instruments (1994); *Pantun* (John Hollander) for mezzo-soprano and piano (2001); *From the Psaltery* for soprano and strings (2002); and *From "Italian Eclogues'* for soprano and piano (2002). Babbitt's choral music includes *Four Canons* (after Schoenberg) for female choir (1968); *An Elizabethan Sextette* for six-part female chorus (1977); and *More Phonemena* for twelve voices (1978).

BACON, ERNST
b. Chicago, Illinois, 26 May 1898
d. Orinda, California, 16 March 1990

Bacon was a piano pupil of Alexander Raab in Chicago from 1916 to 1921. He attended Northwestern

University, Evanston, Illinois (1915–1918), the University of Chicago (1919–20), and the University of California (1935). In 1924 he studied piano with Franz Schmidt and theory with Karl Weigl in Vienna. In the following year, he embarked on a career as a concert pianist in Europe and America. Later he became assistant conductor to Eugene Goossens at the Rochester (New York) Opera Company and teacher of piano at the Eastman School of Music in Rochester in 1925. From 1928 to 1930 he taught at the San Francisco Conservatory, during which time he briefly took composition lessons from Ernest Bloch in the city.

In 1936 Bacon was appointed Supervisor of Federal (WPA) Music in San Francisco, where he also conducted various orchestras. In the following year he was acting professor of Music at Hamilton College, Clifton, New York. From 1938 to 1945 he was Dean of the School of Music at Converse College, Spartanburg, South Carolina. In 1945 he became Dean of the School of Music and later Composer-in-Residence at Syracuse University, New York, retiring in 1963. In that year he taught at the Center for Advanced Studies at Wesleyan University, Middletown, Connecticut. Bacon was awarded a Pulitzer Prize in 1932 for his Symphony no. 1, three Guggenheim Fellowships, and a National Academy of Arts and Letters Award. In 1935 he founded the Carmel (California) Bach Festival and (later) the New Spartanburg Festival, South Carolina.

The literature and folk music of America exerted a deep effect upon Bacon's own compositions. He published various collections of choral and solo songs based on folk sources. For orchestra he wrote four symphonies: no. 1 in D with piano solo (1932); no. 2 (1937); no. 3, *Great River*, to poems of Paul Hogan for narrator (1956); and no. 4 (1962–63). Other orchestral works include *Symphonic Fantasy and Fugue* (1926); *Symphonic Fugue* (1932); and *Bearwalla* (1936), both for piano and strings; *Country Roads Unpaved* (1936); a suite, *Ford's Theater* (1939–43), describing events which led up to the assassination of Abraham Lincoln; a second suite, *From These States* (1951); *Fables* for narrator and orchestra (1953); and *The Enchanting Island* (depicting characters from Shakespeare's *The Tempest*), commissioned in 1954 by the Louisville Orchestra. Later orchestral pieces include a *Concerto Grosso* (1957); *Elegy* for oboe and strings (1957); *Erie Waters* (1961); two piano concertos, no. 1, *Riolama* (1962) and no. 2 (1982); an overture, *Over the Waves* (1976); and *Remembering Ansel Adams* for clarinet and orchestra (1985).

Bacon's works for the stage include the children's opera, *A Drumlin Legend*, staged in New York in 1949; a folk opera, *A Tree on the Plains* (1940, rev. 1962), commissioned by the League of Composers and first produced in May 1942 in Spartanburg, South Carolina;

Ernst Bacon.
Photo by Art Bacon; courtesy of the Ernst Bacon Society, www.ernstbacon.org.

a musical comedy, *Take Your Choice* (San Francisco; 1936); and a musical, *Dr. Franklin* (1976). With John Edmunds he wrote two ballets: *Arrival on Ararat* (*Jehovah and the Ark*) (1968–70) and *The Parliament of Fowls* (1975).

Bacon's choral music includes two short oratorios, *On Ecclesiastes* (1936) and *By Blue Ontario* (Whitman) (1958); a cantata, *The Lord Star* (1950); *Requiem: The Last Invocation* for bass, chorus, and orchestra (1968–71); an oratorio, *Usania* (1977); and an oratorio for children's chorus, narrator, and piano, *The Animals' Christmas* (1982). There are also two song cycles for female voices and piano, *From Emily's Diary* (1944) and *Nature* (1971). In addition Bacon composed over one hundred choral songs for amateur choirs. His solo songs number over 250 to texts by Walt Whitman, Emily Dickinson, A. E. Housman, Blake, Herrick, Stevenson, Sandburg, E. B. Browning, Goethe, Lenau, and others. His most inclusive volumes are *Ten Songs* to German texts (1928); *Songs of Parting* (Whitman) (1930); *Songs of Eternity* (Dickinson) (1932); *Black and White Songs* (1932); *Twilight Songs* (1932); *Midnight Special* (1932); *My River* (1932); *Six Songs* (1942); *Five Poems* to German texts (1943); *Among Unpaved Roads* (1944); *Quiet Airs* (1952); and *Fifty Songs* (1974).

Bacon's chamber works include a Cello Sonata (1946); two quintets, one with piano (1946), the other with double bass (1951); *Peterborough Suite* for viola and piano (1961–82); *A Life Suite* for cello and piano (1966–81); *Tumbleweeds* for violin and piano (1979); Piano Trio (1979); Violin Sonata (1982); and Viola Sonata (1987). For organ he wrote a *Trumpet Tune and Intrada* and an untitled cycle (1976). There are also many pieces for piano solo.

Bacon was the author of seven books: *Words on Music* (1960); *Notes on the Piano* (1963); *100 Fables and Apologues*; *The Honor of Music*; *Irreverent Quillets*; *Imaginary Dialogues*; and *Advice to Patrons*.

BALLANTINE, EDWARD

b. Oberlin, Ohio, 6 August 1886
d. Oak Bluffs, Massachusetts, 2 July 1971

Ballantine studied with Walter Spalding and Frederick Converse at Harvard University (1904–07), and was a piano pupil of Artur Schnabel and Rudolf Ganz in Berlin (1907–09). He was appointed an instructor at Harvard in 1912, becoming an assistant professor in 1926 and associate professor in 1932; he retired in 1947.

For orchestra Ballantine wrote *Prelude to the Delectable Forest* (1914); *The Eve of St Agnes* (1917); *By a Lake in Russia* (1922); *From the Garden of Hellas* (1923); *Overture to the Piper*; and a tone poem, *The Awakening of the Woods*. His choral works include *Song for the Future* and *Lake Werna's Water*. In his lifetime Ballantine was widely known for the witty *Variations on Mary Had a Little Lamb* for piano, composed in 1924 in various musical styles. It was followed in 1943 by a second set parodying 20th century composers. He also composed a Violin Sonata.

BARAB, SEYMOUR

b. Chicago, Illinois, 9 January 1921

In addition to his work as a composer, Barab is widely known as a cellist and viol da gamba player. He was a pupil of Gregor Piatigorsky and Edmund Kurtz, and played in many leading orchestras, including the Indianapolis Symphony, Cleveland Orchestra, CBS Symphony, and San Francisco Symphony, and was a member of the Galimir String Quartet. Among his composition teachers were Vincent Persichetti, Edgard Varèse, and Lou Harrison. He has taught at Rutgers, the State University of New Jersey; Black Mountain College; and the New England Conservatory, Boston.

Barab has made a major contribution to American opera with over 42 works in this medium to his credit. For these he has been dubbed "the present day Rossini" by his fellow composer Miriam Gideon. *A Piece of*

String (based on Maupassant) is in three acts (Colorado, 1965). Five of them are cast in two acts: *Phillip Marshall* (1967); *Sleeping Beauty* (2000); *License to Marry*, a zarzuela (2001); an operetta, *A Perfect Plan* (2002); and *Gods of Mischief* (2003). The others are in one act and include (in alphabetical order): *American Punchlines*; *At Last I Have Found You* (1984); *The Betrothal of Becky Brown*; *Chanticleer* (based on Chaucer) (1954); *Everything Must Be Perfect* (1986); *Fortune's Favorites, A Game of Chance* (1960); *The Husband, the Wife, the Lover*; *I Can't Stand Wagner* (1985); *Jewish Humor From Oy to Vey*; *Let's Not Talk About Lenny Anymore*; *Little Stories in Tomorrow's Paper* (1966); *The Maledroit Door* (1963); *Mating Habits of the Radical Chic*; *A Matter of Time* (1959); *Not a Spanish Kiss* (1981); *Out the Window* (1985); *Passion in the Principal's Office* (1987); *The Perfect Wife* (after Pergolesi); *La Pizza con Funghi* (*The Mushroom Pie*; 1988); *Predators* (1987); *Public Defender*; *The Rajah's Ruby* (1954); *Reba*; *The Ruined Maid* (1982); and *Say Cheese*.

Barab has also written operas for children and family audiences, including *Androcles and the Lion*; *Cinderella*; *Fair Means or Foul* (1983); *How Far to Bethlehem?* (1963); *Little Red Riding Hood* (1962); *The Maker of Illusions* (1985); *Pied Piper of Hamelin* (1998); *Sleeping Beauty*; *Snow White and the Seven Dwarfs* (1988); *The Toy Shop* (1978); and *Who Am I?* (1966). For children to perform Barab has composed three one-act operas: *No Laughing Matter*; *The Pink Siamese*; and *A Very Special Gift*. Another work for the stage, *Tales of Rhyme and Reason*, for narrator, dancers, and orchestra, dates from 1967.

His major choral work, *Cosmos Cantata*, is a setting of a text by Kurt Vonnegut for soprano, tenor, baritone, and chamber orchestra. Other vocal works include *Tennyson Songs*, six songs for soprano, harp, and strings; *Moments Macabres* for voice, flute, oboe, clarinet, string quartet, and double bass (1976); *Bawd Ballads* for voice and string trio; *A Child's Garden of Verse* for voice and chamber orchestra; and *Songs of Perfect Propriety* to poems of Dorothy Parker.

For orchestra, Barab has composed a *Concerto Grosso* for strings; *Suite on Armenian Themes* for strings; *Dances* for oboe and strings; concertos for alto saxophone and winds, cello, and orchestra "in classical mode"; and concertinos for alto saxophone and strings, saxophone quartet and strings, and violin. Among his instrumental works are four string quartets; seven piano trios; three saxophone quartets; a Wind Quintet; Flute Quintet; Piano Sextet; *Little Suite* and Sonatina for three flutes; Trio for flute, viola, and harp; and numerous duos and suites for various instrumental groupings.

BARBER, SAMUEL
b. West Chester, Pennsylvania, 9 March 1910
d. New York, New York, 23 January 1981

Barber began piano lessons at the age of six and composed his first piece of music, a song, a year later. At the age of ten he began an opera, *The Rose Tree*, to a libretto by the family cook. His aunt was the singer Louise Homer (1871–1947), whose husband, Sidney (1864–1953), was a composer noted for his many songs. She performed some of her nephew's songs in recitals as early as 1927. While still in high school, Barber studied at the newly founded Curtis Institute of Music in Philadelphia where he received composition lessons from Rosario Scalero and piano instruction from Isabella Vengerova, a former pupil of Theodor Leschetizky. He was also a student of singing and later earned the distinction of making a commercial recording of his own setting of Matthew Arnold's poem, *Dover Beach*, singing the solo part himself.

It was at the Curtis Institute in 1928 that he first met Gian-Carlo Menotti, a fellow student of composition. In that year he was awarded the Bearns Prize of $1,000 for a Violin Sonata, which has remained unpublished. This enabled him to travel to Europe, first to France and then through Switzerland to the Italian Alps. There he stayed with his teacher Scalero; he later traveled to Venice where he met George Antheil. He spent each summer from 1929 to 1931 at Cadegliano on Lake Lugano with Menotti and his family. In 1931 Barber was appointed piano instructor at the Curtis Institute, a post he retained for two years, resigning in 1933 to devote himself to composition. A second Bearns Prize in 1933 allowed him to visit Vienna, where he studied conducting and singing.

On his return to the United States, Barber lived for a time in New York where he attempted to earn a living as a singer. At a second application, he won the Prix de Rome in 1935. During his stay in Italy he composed the First Symphony and the *James Joyce Songs*. In March 1937 he returned to the United States.

In 1939, after a visit to London, Barber settled in Switzerland where he began to compose the Violin Concerto. At the outbreak if the Second World War he left Europe for the United States where he taught at the Curtis Institute from 1939 to 1942. He subsequently joined the U. S. Army, and was later assigned to the Army Air Force. In 1943 he bought a house named "Capricorn," near Mount Kisco, New York, where he lived until shortly before his death, sharing it with Menotti. Barber was a fine pianist and occasionally performed in public as an accompanist, usually giving recitals of his own songs and lieder with the soprano Leontyne Price. Less frequently he appeared as a conductor.

Orchestral Works

The first of his published works, Serenade for string quartet or string orchestra, op. 1 (1929) was first performed in its original form for string quartet at the Curtis Institute in 1930. The string orchestra arrangement dates from 1942. It was followed by the *Overture: The School for Scandal*, op. 5 (1931), which received its premiere in Philadelphia in August 1933, and *Music for a Scene from Shelley*, op. 7 (1933), inspired by a passage from *Prometheus Unbound*.

Symphony no. 1, op. 9 (1936, rev. 1942) was first performed in Rome by the Augusteo Orchestra under Bernardino Molinari on 13 December 1936. The American premiere took place in Cleveland under Rodzinski in January 1937, and he introduced it at the Salzburg Festival in July 1937. It was the first work by an American composer to be heard there. The revised version, with an altered scherzo section, was performed in February 1944 by Bruno Walter and the New York Philharmonic Symphony Orchestra, which recorded it. Cast in a single movement, it is described by the composer as "a synthetic treatment of the four-movement classical symphony."

Samuel Barber, 1944.
Photo: Carl Van Vechten, from the Collections of the Library of Congress.

The *Adagio for Strings*, arranged from the slow movement of the String Quartet, op. 11, was performed by Arturo Toscanini and the NBC Symphony Orchestra on 5 November 1938. It has subsequently become one of the most widely known works by an American composer. In the same concert, Toscanini conducted the *First Essay for Orchestra*, op. 12.

The Violin Concerto, op. 14, begun in Switzerland in 1939 and completed in the United States the following year, was performed by Albert Spalding and the Philadelphia Orchestra under Eugene Ormandy on 7 February 1941. The quiet, sad lyricism of the first two movements and the virtuosity of the finale were not to the taste of those who had commissioned the work, but it has become the most frequently played concerto for the instrument written by an American.

The *Second Essay for Orchestra*, op. 17, is an impressive exercise in orchestral writing and has been used by American orchestras on tour as a brilliant display piece. It received its premiere under Bruno Walter with the New York Philharmonic Symphony Orchestra on 16 April 1942.

Symphony no. 2, op. 19 was commissioned by the U. S. Army Air Force to whom it is dedicated. It was first performed in Boston by Koussevitzky on 3 March 1944 and revised in 1947. Lack of further performances persuaded the composer to withdraw the work, issuing a revised version of the slow movement in 1964, published separately as *Night Flight*, op. 19a. The complete Symphony no. 2 was restored to the catalog in 1984 and recorded several times.

Capricorn Concerto, op. 21, named after Barber's home, is a concerto grosso in appropriately neo-Baroque style, scored for flute, oboe, trumpet, and strings; it dates from 1944. The Concerto for Cello and Orchestra, op. 22 (1945) is a more assertive work than the Violin Concerto, but contains much lyrical writing for the soloist. It was performed by Raya Garbousova with the Boston Symphony Orchestra, conducted by Koussevitzky, on 5 April 1946. Barber's next orchestral work, *Toccata Festiva*, op. 36 for organ and large orchestra, was composed for the new Aeolian-Skinner organ presented to the Curtis Institute in 1960. The soloist in the premiere with the Philadelphia Orchestra was Paul Callaway. *Die Natali*, op. 37, commissioned to celebrate the 75th anniversary of the Boston Symphony Orchestra in 1960, is a sequence of choral preludes based on familiar Christmas carols.

The Piano Concerto, op. 38 was commissioned by Barber's publisher, G. Schirmer, Inc., for the centenary of the company in 1961. It was completed in 1962 and performed in September of that year with John Browning as soloist with the Boston Symphony Orchestra under Erich Leinsdorf in Philharmonic Hall, New York City. It won the Pulitzer Prize in 1963 and has been performed in locations throughout the world, including the Soviet Union in 1965. Cast in the mold of the great concertos of the nineteenth century, it provides the soloist with a virtuosic role in the outer movements; but there is much expressive, lyrical music in the central *Canzona*. Instead of the customary commissioning fee, the publisher presented the composer with a swimming pool for his home.

Fadograph on a Yestern Scene (based on *Finnegans Wake*), op. 44 shows a continued interest in the writings of James Joyce. It was performed by the Pittsburgh Symphony Orchestra on 11 September 1971. In October 1978 Zubin Mehta conducted the premiere of *Third Essay for Orchestra*, op. 47. The same conductor also commissioned an Oboe Concerto, op.48 from the composer, but only a slow movement entitled *Canzonetta* was completed in short score. At the end of his life, Barber was considering the composition of a Second Piano Concerto.

Stage Works

Vanessa, op. 32., the first of Barber's two grand operas, was performed at the Metropolitan Opera House, New York on 15 January 1958. It was produced by Menotti, who had also written the libretto. In the same year it was awarded the Pulitzer Prize and was presented at the Salzburg Festival. A romantic opera in the old tradition, it possesses a plot that might have suited Richard Strauss. Vanessa has waited many years for the return of her lover, Anatol. When his son, also named Anatol, arrives at her home, she falls in love with him. Anatol Jr. seduces Erika, Vanessasa's niece, but leaves with Vanessa, whom he marries. It is now Erika's turn to wait for a husband. Much acclaimed by the critics, it is a work of great dramatic tension, with lyrical tenderness and a wealth of expressive melody.

Antony and Cleopatra, op. 40 was commissioned for the opening of the new Metropolitan Opera House at Lincoln Center, New York City on 16 September 1966. In spite of a lavish production and the importance of the occasion, it received a less favorable response from the critics than had *Vanessa*. Leontyne Price as Cleopatra was highly praised for her performance, but the inadequate production was withdrawn after the initial performances. Barber revised the score in 1974 and a new production was mounted by Menotti at the Juilliard School Opera Center on 6 February 1975 with much success.

Hand of Bridge, op. 35 for four soloists and small orchestra is a brief chamber opera lasting only nine minutes. Composed in 1959 for the Festival of the Two Worlds in Spoleto, Italy, it explores the thoughts and personalities of two couples as they play bridge.

Barber composed two ballet scores. For Martha

Graham, the Ditson Fund of Columbia University commissioned *The Serpent Heart*, op. 23, performed by her company in New York City in May 1946 and later revised and retitled *Cave of the Heart*. From this ballet the composer drew an orchestral suite, *Medea*. In 1952, Ballet Society commissioned *Souvenirs*, op. 28 originally written as a set of duets for piano. The separate movements (Waltz, Schottische, Pas-de-Deux, Two-Step and Hesitation Tango, and Galop) recall with nostalgia the Palm Court Orchestra of the early 1900s.

Choral Music

Barber's first pieces for chorus were *The Virgin Martyrs*, op. 8, no. 1, for women's voices to words by Helen Waddell, translated from the Latin of Sigbert of Benbloux, and *Let Down the Bars, O Death*, op. 8, no. 2, a setting of a poem by Emily Dickinson for mixed voices. These date from 1935 and 1936, respectively.

A Stopwatch and an Ordnance Map, op. 15 for men's voices and kettledrums, with optional brass, was performed at the Curtis Institute on 23 April 1940 under the composer's direction. The poem by Stephen Spender upon which it is based was inspired by the Spanish Civil War and is a lament for one of the fallen. *Reincarnations*, op. 16 for unaccompanied chorus are settings of three poems by James Stephens—"Mary Hynes," "Anthony O'Daly," and "The Coolin'"—all composed between 1938 and 1940.

Not until 1954 did Barber compose a work for choir and orchestra. *The Prayers of Kierkegaard*, op. 30 for soprano, mixed chorus, and orchestra was first performed in Boston on 3 December 1954 under Charles Munch. In 1970 Barber wrote two short pieces for chorus, *Twelfth Night* and *To Be Sung on the Water*, op. 42. *The Lovers*, op. 43 for baritone, chorus, and orchestra to poems by Pablo Neruda was premiered in Philadelphia on 22 November 1971, conducted by Eugene Ormandy.

Vocal Works

The songs of Samuel Barber occupy an important place in his compositions. There are some 60 unpublished early songs by Barber. Among his earliest publications are *Three Songs*, op. 2: comprising "The Daisies" (James Stephens), "With Rue My Heart is Laden" (A. E. Housman), and "Bessie Bobtail" (James Stephens), written between 1927 and 1934. *Dover Beach*, op. 3 (1931), a setting of Matthew Arnold's poem for voice and string quartet, brought Barber's name before the American public and, later in Europe, where Poulenc was greatly impressed. *Three Songs from James Joyce's "Chamber Music'*, op. 10: "Rain Has Fallen," "Sleep Now," and "I Hear an Army" (1936) are among the composer's most frequently heard vocal music.

Four Songs, op. 13, comprising "The Nun Takes the Veil" (Gerard Manley Hopkins), "The Secrets of the Old" (W. B. Yeats), "Sure on This Shining Night" (James Agee), and "Nocturne" (Frederic Prokosch), date from 1938. *Two Songs*, op. 18—"The Queen's Face on the Summery Coin" (Robert Horan) and "Monks and Raisins" (Jose Garcia Villa)—were completed in 1943. *Nuvoletta*, op. 25 for voice and piano (1947) again sets words by James Joyce. On 21 January 1952, Pierre Bernac and Francis Poulenc gave the first performance at Dumbarton Oaks, Washington, D.C., of the song cycle *Mélodies Passagères*, op. 27, five settings of poems by Rainer Maria Rilke. These songs, composed in France in 1950, are dedicated to Poulenc.

Ten Hermit Songs, op. 29, to anonymous Irish poems of the eighth to thirteenth centuries, marked the first collaboration between the composer and the soprano Leontyne Price who performed the cycle at the Library of Congress, Washington, D.C, in October 1953. For the same singer he wrote the song cycle *Despite and Still*, op. 41 (1969). For Dietrich Fischer-Dieskau, Barber composed *Three Songs*, op. 45: "How I Have Fed and Eaten Up the Rose" (Gottfried Keller, translated by James Joyce), "A Green Lowland of Pianos" (Jerzy Harasymowicz), and "O Boundless, Boundless Evening" (George Heym). They were performed in Alice Tully Hall in New York on 30 April 1974 with Charles Wadsworth at the piano.

Barber wrote two extended works for voice and orchestra. *Knoxville: Summer 1915*, op. 24, commissioned in 1947 by Eleanor Steber, is based on a prose fragment from James Agee's Pulitzer Prize-winning autobiographical novel *A Death in the Family*. It is one of the few scores by him to have a distinctly American national flavor and homespun nostalgia. *Andromache's Farewell*, op. 39 is a dramatic scene for soprano and orchestra, based on an extract from *The Trojan Women* by Euripides. It was commissioned by the New York Philharmonic Orchestra for the opening of the Lincoln Center in New York City and first performed on 4 April 1963.

Instrumental Music

The Sonata *for cello and piano*, op. 6 (1932) was one of the works that led Barber to be awarded the Prix de Rome. Dedicated to his teacher Rosario Scalero, it is a valuable addition to the limited repertory of the cello. It was first performed in Rome by Orlando Cole and the composer in 1932.

Although the *Adagio for Strings* is frequently heard, the String Quartet in B minor, op. 11 from which it comes is sadly neglected. Written during a stay in St. Wolfgang near Salzburg in 1936, it received its premiere in Rome by the Pro Arte Quartet in December

1936. The delightful *Four Excursions*, op. 20 for piano was performed in New York in 1945 with Vladimir Horowitz as soloist. The title implies excursions into different styles described by the composer as "contrast pieces using classical forms, in an American setting." Horowitz also gave the premiere of Barber's Piano Sonata, op. 26 in Havana on 9 December 1949; it was commissioned to celebrate the 25th anniversary of the American League of Composers. *Summer Music*, op. 31. for wind quintet was commissioned by the Chamber Music Society of Detroit and first performed there on 20 March 1956.

Other instrumental pieces include *Nocturne: Homage to John Field*, op. 33 (1958) and *Ballade*, op. 46 (1977), both for piano; *Variations on "Wondrous Love"*, op. 34 for organ (1959); and *Mutations from Bach's "Christ du Lammas Gott"* for brass and timpani (1968).

BARLOW, SAMUEL L(ATHAM MITCHELL)

b. New York, New York, 1 June 1892
d. Wyndmoor, Pennsylvania, 19 September 1982

Barlow studied at Harvard University (B.A. 1914) and later with Isador Philipp in Paris and Respighi in Rome (1923). He taught music in settlement schools in New York City and took an active part in international relations and liberal political movements, including the American Committees for Spanish Freedom.

For the stage, Barlow composed a ballet, *Ballo Sardo* (1928), and three operas: *Mon Ami Pierrot*, based on the life of Lully, commissioned by Sacha Guitry in 1934 and performed at the Opera Comique in Paris; *Amanda*, composed in 1936; and *Eugenie*.

Barlow's orchestral music includes *Vocalise* (1926); a symphonic poem *Alba* (1927); *Circus Overture* (1930); *Biedermeier Waltzes* (1935); *Babar*, a concerto for magic lantern and orchestra (1936); music for Giraudoux's *Amphitryon 38* (1937); *Leda* (1939); *Sousa ad Parnassum* (1939); and *Overture: Mardi Gras*. He was himself the soloist in the premiere in Rochester, New York, of his Piano Concerto, composed in 1931. His major instrumental works are *Ballad and Scherzo* for string quartet (1933); *Conversations with Tchekhov* for piano trio (1940); and *Three Songs from the Chinese* for tenor and seven instruments (1924).

Barlow published a autobiography, *The Astonished Muse* (1961).

BARLOW, WAYNE (BREWSTER)

b. Elyria, Ohio, 6 September 1912
d. Rochester, New York, 17 December 1996

Barlow was a graduate of the Eastman School of Music, Rochester, New York (B.M. 1934; M.M. 1935; Ph.D. 1937) where he studied with Bernard Rogers, Howard Hanson, and Edward Royce. He was also briefly a pupil of Arnold Schoenberg at the University of Southern California (1935). At the University of Toronto (1963–64), he studied electronic music with R. Murray Schafer. In 1937 he joined the music faculty at the Eastman School, becoming chairman of the Composition Department and director of the Electronic Music Studio in 1968. He retired in 1978.

Barlow's best-known composition is a short rhapsody for oboe and strings, *The Winter's Passed*. Written in 1938, it makes use of two Appalachian folk songs from the Carolinas, "A Poor Wayfaring Stranger" and "Black is the Color of My True Love's Hair," in a lyrical modal setting with an appealing, naïve simplicity. His other works for solo instruments are *Lyrical Piece* for clarinet and strings (1943); *Images* for harp and orchestra (1961); a Concerto for saxophone and band (1970);

Handbill for a lecture by Samuel Barlow, 1949.
From the Collections of the Library of Congress.

and *Divertissement* for flute and chamber orchestra (1980). Among his other orchestral compositions are a *Prelude: De Profundis* (1934); a ballet suite, *False Faces* (1935); Sinfonietta no. 1 in C (1936); two ballets, *Three Moods for Dancing* (1940) and *The Black Madonna* (1941); *Nocturne* for 18 instruments (1946); *Rondo Overture* (1947); Sinfonietta no. 2 in C (1950); *Lento and Allegro* (1955); *Night Song* (1957); *Rota* for chamber orchestra (1959); *Sinfonia da Camera* (1962); *Vistas* (1963); and *Overture: Hampton Beech* (1971). For concert band he wrote *Frontiers* (1982).

Barlow's important choral works are the cantata *Zion in Exile* for soloists, chorus, and orchestra (1937); *The Twenty Third Psalm* for chorus and orchestra (1944); Mass in G for chorus and orchestra (1953); *Missa Sancti Thomae* for chorus and organ (1959); *We All Believe in One God* for chorus, brass quartet, and organ (1965); a cantata, *Wait for the Promise of the Father* for tenor, baritone, chorus, and small orchestra (1968); a secular cantata, *Voices of Faith* for reader, soprano, chorus, and orchestra (1976); and *The Seven Seals* for soloists, chorus, and orchestra (1991). For soprano and orchestra he wrote *Songs from the Silence of Amor* (1939) and *Poems for Music* (1958).

Barlow's instrumental music includes a Piano Sonata (1948); *Prelude, Air and Variations* for bassoon, piano, and string quartet (1949); a Piano Quintet (1951); *Triptych* for string quartet (1953); *Intrada, Fugue and Postlude* for brass (1959); Trio for oboe, viola, and piano (1964); *Dynamisms* for two pianos (1967); *Elegy* for viola and piano (1967); *Dialogues* for harp and tape (1969); *Vocalise and Canon* for tuba and piano (1976); *Intermezzo* for viola and harp (1980); *Hymn and Voluntaries for the Church Year* (four books) for organ (1963–81); and *Sonatine for Four* for flute, clarinet, cello, and harp (1984).

Barlow's association with the Electronic Music Studio at the Eastman School led to three compositions for prerecorded tape: *Study in Electronic Sound* (1965); *Moonflight* (1970); and *Soundprints in Concrete* (1975). Other pieces combining tape with instruments and voices are *Duo* for harp and tape (1969); *Soundscapes* for tape and orchestra (1972); *Voices of Darkness* for reader, piano, percussion, and tape (1974); and *Out of the Cradle Endlessly Rocking* for tenor, chorus, clarinet, viola, piano, and tape (1978).

In 1953 Barlow published a book on music appreciation, *Foundations of Music.*

BARTH, HANS

b. Leipzig, Germany, 25 June 1897
d. Jacksonville, Florida, 8 December 1956

At the age of six, Barth came to the United States, but later returned to Germany to study at the Leipzig Conservatoire with Carl Reinecke. He made his debut as a pianist at the age of twelve in New York City. He became director of the Yonkers Institute of Musical Art and taught at the Mannes School in New York (1948–50).

Today he is remembered mainly for his experiments in microtones. He composed several works using quarter-tones, including two sonatas (1929, 1932), a Concerto (1928), a Quintet (1930); and *Ten Etudes* for piano and orchestra (1943), using a specially constructed piano. A Suite for strings and timpani (1930) also employs microtones. Barth lectured throughout the United States on his system and on music in general. His book, *Technic* (1935), discusses these theories of microtonality. He also toured extensively as a concert pianist.

In normal tonal music he composed a Piano Concerto (1925, rev. 1928); *Pantomime Symphony* (1937); *Symphony: Prince of Peace* (1940); and an operetta, *Miragia* (1928).

BASSETT, LESLIE RAYMOND

b. Hanford, California, 22 January 1923

Bassett attended Fresno State College, California (1940–47). His college studies were interrupted by war service in France and Germany, where he served as a trombonist and arranger in various orchestras and bands. He undertook graduate work at the University of Michigan, Ann Arbor (1947–49, 1953–56), where he was a pupil of Ross Lee Finney. On a Fulbright Fellowship (1950–51), Bassett studied composition in Paris privately with Nadia Boulanger and at the Ecole Normale de Musique with Arthur Honegger. In 1960 he worked with Roberto Gerhard and spent several months in 1964 with Mario Davidovsky studying electronic music. Except for a time in Rome as a fellow of the American Academy of Arts and Letters(1961–63), Bassett taught at the University of Michigan from 1952, becoming Chairman of the Composition Department in 1977 and retiring in 1992. Bassett has received many awards including a grant from the National Institute of Arts and Letters (1964), a National Council on the Arts and Humanities Fellowship (1966–67), and two Guggenheim Fellowships (1973–74, 1980–81). He was a founding member of the University of Michigan Electronic Music Studio.

In addition to a Symphony in B (1949), now withdrawn, his orchestral works are a Symphony (1955-56); *Five Movements* (1961); *Variations* (1963), which received the Pulitzer Prize in 1966; *Colloquy* (1969); *Forces* (1972); *Echoes From an Invisible World* (1974–75), commissioned by the Philadelphia Orchestra for the Bicentennial; and a Concerto for two pianos (1976).

Leslie Raymond Bassett.
Photo: Richard Singleton, courtesy the composer.

Recent additions include a Concerto for Orchestra (1981); *Concerto Lirico* for trombone (1983); *From a Source Evolving* (1985); *Thoughts That Sing, Breathe and Burn* (1995); and a Concerto for alto saxophone (1999). For band he has written *Designs, Images and Textures* (1964), commissioned by the Ithaca (New York) High School Band; *Sounds, Shapes and Symbols* (1977); *Concerto Grosso* for brass quintet, winds, and percussion (1982); *Colors and Contours* (1984); *Lullaby for Kirsten* (1985); *Fantasy* for clarinet and winds (1986); and *Wood and Reed Transformed* for bassoon and wind ensemble (1998).

Among Bassett's many choral compositions are *Cantata: For City, Nation, World* for tenor, chorus, children's choir, four trombones, and organ (1959); *Moonrise* for female voices and 10 instruments (1960); *Eclogue, Encomium and Evocation* for female voices, piano, harp, and percussion (1962); *Notes in the Silence* for chorus and piano (1966); *Moon Canticle* for chorus, cello, and amplified speaker (1969); *Collect* for chorus and tape (1969); *Celebration: In Praise of Earth* for chorus, amplified speaker, and orchestra (1970); two pieces for choir and piano, *Of Wind and Earth* (1973) and *A Ring of Emeralds* (1979); and four anthems for choir and organ: *Lord Who Hast Formed Me* (1981), *Sing to the Lord* (1981), *Almighty Eternal* (1990), and *Maker of Our Being* (1993).

Bassett's extensive chamber music includes four string quartets (1951, 1957, 1962, 1978); a Horn Sonata (1952); a Brass Trio (1953); Trio for clarinet, viola, and piano (1953); String Quintet (1954); Trombone Sonata (1954); Viola Sonata (1956); *Five Pieces* for string quartet (1957); Suite for unaccompanied trombone (1957); *Easter Triptych* for tenor and brass ensemble (1958); Wind Quintet (1958); Violin Sonata (1959); *Cello Duets* (1959); Piano Quintet (1962); *Music* for cello and piano (1966); *Nonet* (1967); *Music* for alto saxophone and piano (1968); Piano Sextet (1971); *Sounds Remembered* for violin and piano (1972); *Music* for four horns (1974); *Wind Music* for sextet (1975); Sextet (1979); *Five Temperaments* for guitar (1979); Trio for violin, clarinet, and piano (1980); and *A Masque of Bells* for carillon and optional dancers (1980). More recent instrumental pieces include *Concerto da Camera* for flute, clarinet, trumpet, violin, cello, piano, and percussion (1981); *Duo Concertante* for alto saxophone and piano (1984); *Dialogues* for oboe and piano (1987); Brass Quintet (1988); *Duo Inventions* for two cellos (1988); *Illuminations* for flute and piano (1989); *Metamorphoses*, eight pieces for solo bassoon (1990); *Arias* for clarinet and piano (1992); *Narratives* for guitar quartet (1993); *Song and Dance* for tuba and piano (1996); *Trio-Inventions* for three cellos (1996); *Three Graces* for three flutes (2000); and *Song of Aulos* for solo oboe (2000).

For solo piano Bassett has written *Six Pieces* (1951); *Mobile* (1961); *Elaborations* (1966); *Seven Preludes* (1984) and *Configurations* (1987). Important vocal works include *Four Songs* (1953); *To Music* (1962); *The Jade Garden* (1973); *Time and Beyond* for baritone, clarinet, cello, and piano (1973); *Love Songs* (1975); *Pierrot Songs* (Andre Giraud) for soprano, flute, clarinet, violin, cello, and piano (1988); and *Two Stephens Songs* for baritone and piano (1996–98).

BAUER, MARION EUGENIE
b. Walla Walla, Washington, 15 August 1887
d. South Hadley, Massachusetts, 9 August 1955

Marion Bauer was born of French parents. She received her musical education from Walter Henry Rothwell and Henry Holden Huss in New York City. Later she went to Paris where she was a pupil of Raoul Pugno, the French pianist (1905–07), and Nadia Boulanger (1923). She also studied in Berlin in 1910. In 1926 Bauer was appointed an associate professor at New York University, and in 1940 she became an associate professor at the Juilliard School of Music. For a number of years she was the New York editor and critic for the *Musical Leader*.

Bauer's French training is clearly evident in much of her music, which adopts impressionistic character-

Marion Bauer.
Courtesy The Juilliard School.

istics similar to those found in the works of Charles Griffes. Her most important orchestral pieces include three tone-poems, *Up the Ocklawaha* (1913), *Indian Pipes* (1927), and *Sun Splendor* (1936); *American Youth Concerto* for piano and orchestra (1943); and a Symphony (1947–50). Among her compositions for chamber orchestra are *Lament on African Themes* (1928); *Symphonic Suite* for strings (1940); and *Prelude and Fugue* (1948) for flute and strings.

For chorus Bauer wrote *The Thinker* (1938) for a cappella voices and *China* (1943–44) for choir and orchestra. The influence of Ravel is strong in *Orientale* for soprano and orchestra (1914, orch. 1934) and in *Four Songs* for voice and string quartet (1935). Her instrumental music includes a Violin Sonata (1921); *From New Hampshire Woods* for piano (1923); a String Quartet (1927); *Fantasia Quasi una Sonata* for violin and piano (1932); *Duo* for oboe and clarinet (1932); *Dance Sonata* for piano (1932); a Sonata for viola (or clarinet) (1935); a neo-classical Concertino for oboe, clarinet, and string quartet (1939–43); and two trios for flute, cello, and piano (1941, 1951).

Marion Bauer was the author of a comprehensive book, *Twentieth Century Music* which, although published in 1933, contains much perspicacious comment that remains valid today. Her other books are *How*

Music Grew (with Ethel R. Peyser; 1925); *Music Through the Ages* (1932); *Musical Questions and Quizzes* (1941); and *How Opera Grew* (with Ethel R. Peyser; 1955). With Aaron Copland, Howard Hanson, Quincy Porter, and Otto Luening, Bauer was one of the founders of the American Music Center in New York in 1940.

BAZELON, IRWIN ALLEN
b. Evanston, Illinois, 4 June, 1922
d. New York, New York, 2 August 1995

After graduating from DePaul University, Chicago in 1945, Bazelon spent two years at Mills College, Oakland, California, where he was a pupil of Darius Milhaud. At the University of California, Berkeley, he studied advanced analysis with Ernest Bloch.

Bazelon's important orchestral works include ten symphonies: no. 1 (1960); no. 2, *Testament of a Big City* (1961); no. 3 for brass, percussion, piano, and string sextet (1962); no. 4 (1964–65); no. 5 (1966); no. 6 (1969); no. 7, *Ballet for orchestra* (1980); no. 8 for strings (1986); no. 8 -1/2 (1988); and no. 9 *Sunday Silence* (1990), named after a racehorse. A Tenth Symphony for narrator, chorus, and orchestra (1992-95) remained incomplete. Other orchestral pieces include a *Suite for Strings*; a *Concert Overture* (1951-52); *Adagio and Fugue* for strings (1952); *Overture: The Taming of the Shrew* (1959); *Symphonie Concertante* for clarinet, trumpet, marimba, and orchestra (1963); *Excursion* (1965); *Dramatic Fanfare* (1970); *Chamber Concerto "Churchill Downs"* (1970), which shows the influence of jazz; *Dramatic Movement* (1974); *A Quiet Piece for a Violent Time* (1975); *De-tonations* for brass quintet and orchestra (1975-76); *Spirits in the Night* (1976); *Tides* for clarinet and small orchestra (1980); *Memories of a Winter Childhood* (1981); *Spires* for trumpet and small orchestra (1981); *Jubilee Overture* (1982) for the Boston Pops Orchestra; *Fusions* for chamber orchestra (1983); a Piano Concerto (1983); and *Motivations* for trumpet and orchestra (1986). Bazelon's later orchestral music includes *Fourscore + 2* for four solo percussionists and orchestra (1987); *Midnight Music* for symphonic wind band (1990); *Prelude to Hart Crane's The Bridge* for strings (1991); *Entre Nous* for cello and small orchestra (1992); and *Fire and Smoke* for timpani and wind band (1993).

Among his chamber compositions are three string quartets (1946, 1947, 1995); *Five Pieces* for cello and piano (1950); *Five Piano Pieces* (1952); *Chamber Concerto* for flute, clarinet, trumpet, tuba, violin, piano, and percussion (1956); a Brass Quintet (1963); *Duo* for viola and piano (1963, rev. 1969–70); *Early American Suite* for wind quintet and harpsichord (1965); *Propulsions* for percussion ensemble (1974); a *Woodwind*

31

Quintet (1975); *Concatenations* for viola and percussion quartet (1976); *Double Crossings* for trumpet and percussion (1977); *Sound Dreams* for chamber ensemble (1977); *Cross-Currents* for brass quintet and percussion (1978); *Imprints on Ivory and Strings* for piano (1978); *Three Men on a Dis-Course* for clarinet, cello, and percussion (1979); *Partnership* for five timpani and marimba (1980); *Triple Play* for two trombones and percussion (1981); *Sound Play* for six players (1982); *Repercussions* for two pianos (1982); *For Tuba With Strings Attached* for tuba and string quartet (1982); *Quintessentials* for flute, clarinet, and marimba (1983); *Fairy Tale* for viola and chamber ensemble (1989); *Alliances* for cello and piano (1989); and *Bazz Ma Tazz* for large brass ensemble and percussion (1993).

Among Bazelon's vocal compositions are three pieces for soprano and orchestra, *Phenomena* (1972), *Junctures* (1979), and *Legends and Love Letters* (1988), and a song cycle for soprano and piano, *Four... Parts of a World* (1991). Bazelon provided incidental music for *The Taming of the Shrew* (1958) and *The Merry Wives of Windsor* (1959) for the Shakespeare Festival Theatre, Stratford, Connecticut and, for NBC Television, *What Makes Sammy Run* (1959) and *Wilma* (1977). In addition he composed scores for three documentary films: *Rice* (1962), *Survival* (1967), and *The Glory of These Times* (1970). He was also the author of a book, *Knowing the Score: Notes on Film Music* (1975).

BEACH, AMY MARCY CHENEY (MRS. H. H. A.)

b. Henniker, New Hampshire, 5 September 1867
d. New York, New York, 27 December 1944

As a child Amy Marcy Cheney was musically precocious, learning to play the piano at four and composing her own music before she was eight. In her teens she established a reputation as a concert pianist, making her debut at the age of 16 with a performance of Moscheles's Piano Concerto in G minor with the Boston Symphony Orchestra.

After her marriage in 1885 to a Boston surgeon, she gave up using her maiden name and was thereafter known as Mrs. H. H. A. Beach. From 1911, a year after her husband's death, she spent three years in Europe where her Piano Concerto in C# minor (1900), Piano Quintet in F# minor (1909), and *Gaelic Symphony* were performed. The *Gaelic*, which had been played in 1896 by the Boston Symphony Orchestra, was among the first important symphonies to be written by an American. She returned to the United States in 1914, settling in New York.

At one time her songs, which number over 125, enjoyed considerable popularity. After years of neglect they are being rediscovered, as are her numerous piano solos. Her choral works were also frequently performed during her lifetime. These include Mass in E flat (1892); *Festival Jubilate* (Chicago, 1893); *Te Deum in F minor* for men's chorus and organ (1922); *Canticle of the Sun* (1928); *Communion Responses* for soloists, chorus, and organ (1928); and *Christ in the Universe* (1931). In 1932 she wrote a one-act opera, *Cabildo*, performed in Athens, Georgia, in 1947.

Beach's instrumental compositions, besides the Piano Quintet, include *Romance* for violin and piano (1893); Violin Sonata in A minor (1896); *Theme and Variations* for flute and string quartet (1916); *Pastorale* for flute, cello, and piano (1921); a string quartet in one movement (1929); Piano Trio in A minor (1938); *Pastorale* for wind quintet (1942); and numerous piano solos.

BEACH, JOHN PARSONS

b. Gloversville, New York, 11 October 1877
d. Pasadena, California, 6 November 1953

After graduating from the New England Conservatory in Boston, where his teachers included George Chadwick and Charles Loeffler, Beach taught at the Northwestern Conservatory in Minneapolis (1904–10) and at the University of Minnesota. Later he went to Europe to study piano in Paris with Harold Bauer and composition with Malipiero in Venice. On his return he settled in Pasadena, devoting himself to composition.

For orchestra Beach wrote a suite, *The Asolani* (1922), and *New Orleans Alley* (1926). He composed several works for the stage including a dramatic prelude, *Pippa's Holiday* for soprano and orchestra (1916), based on Browning's poem "Pippa Passes." He also wrote a short opera, *Jornida and Jornidel*, and two ballets, *Phantom Satyr* (1923) and *Mardi Gras* (1925). His instrumental pieces include *Naïve Landscapes* for wind trio and piano (1917); *Poem* for string quartet (1920); and *Concert* for six instruments (1929). Beach's best-known work, *Angelo's Letter* for tenor and 17 instruments, dates from 1926.

BECKER, JOHN J(OSEPH)

b. Henderson, Kentucky, 22 January 1886
d. Wilmette, Illinois, 21 January 1961

Becker was educated at the Cincinatti Conservatory (1902–05) and the Wisconsin Conservatory where he obtained a doctorate. His teachers there included Carl Busch. In 1917 he became director of music at the University of Notre Dame, St. Louis, Missouri, and was

John Becker with student choir members.
Courtesy Paul University Archives, Chicago, Illinois.

conductor of several choirs and orchestras in St. Paul, Minnesota. From 1929 to 1935 he was chairman of the Fine Arts Department at the College of St. Thomas in St. Paul and then served as director of the Federal Music Project for Minnesota State (1935–41). He was a professor at Barat College of the Sacred Heart, Lake Forest, Illinois (1943–57) and also taught at the Chicago Musical College.

Throughout his life Becker was a champion of modern music in the Midwest, and took part in the promotion of new works. His own music, underestimated in his lifetime, has not received the attention it deserves since his death. His admiration for sixteenth century contrapuntalists is evident in his compositions, although the harmonic language is modern.

Becker's most significant works are a set of pieces entitled *Stageworks* in various dramatic media. No. 1, *Dance Figure* for solo voice and large orchestra (1932), is based on a poem by Ezra Pound. No. 2, *Abongo*, a ballet also composed in 1932, is scored for 29 percussion instruments. No. 3, *A Marriage with Space* for solo and choral recitation, solo and group of dancers, and orchestra, dating from 1934, was arranged in 1940 as his Symphony no. 4, entitled *Dramatic Episodes.* No. 4, *The Life of Man* (1937) is a ballet based on a play by Leonid Andreiev. *Stagework no. 5* incorporates three separate pieces: (*a*) is incidental music to a play by Alfred Kreymborg, *Rain Down Death* (1939), for choir and orchestra, later rescored for orchestra alone

as Suite no. 1 (1940); (*b*) is music for another Kreymborg play, *When the Willow Nods*, for speaker and chamber orchestra (1940), revised as Suite no. 2 for orchestra; and (*c*) is an opera, *Privilege and Privation* (1938), staged in Amsterdam in 1982. *Stagework 6* is another opera, *Deirdre of the Sorrows*, based on the play by J. M. Synge, begun in 1945 but left unfinished.

Other operas are *The City of Shagpur* (1926–27); *Faust*, a monodrama for tenor and piano (1951) produced on television in 1985; and *The Queen of Cornwall*, based on Thomas Hardy, dating from 1956, also unfinished. He wrote three other ballets: *The Season of Pan* (1910); *Nostalgic Songs of Earth* (1938); and *Vigilante* (1938). Becker provided incidental music for *Trap Doors* (A. Kreymborg) (1945, unfinished); *Antigone* (Sophocles) (1940–41); and *Madeleine et Judas* (R. Bruckbecker) (1958). He composed four film scores: *Salome* (1931); *Julius Caesar* (1949); *The Tiger of Eschanapur, Part 2* (1958); and *The Song of the Scaffold* (1959).

Becker wrote seven symphonies, the first of them in 1912. The second, *Fantasia Tragica* (1920), was performed at the I.S.C.M. Festival in Frankfurt in 1927, but the third symphony, *Sinfonia Breve*, his best-known work, composed in 1929, did not receive its premiere until 1958 under the direction of Leonard Bernstein. Symphony no. 4, *Dramatic Episodes* was adapted in 1940 from *A Marriage With Space.* Symphony no. 5, *Homage to Mozart* was completed in 1942, and Symphony no. 6 for speaker, chorus, and orchestra dates from 1943. Symphony no. 7, subtitled *Sermon on the Mount* (1954), is scored for female voices, speaking chorus, and orchestra. Becker's other orchestral works include *Concertino Pastorale: A Forest Rhapsodie* for two flutes and orchestra (1933); a Horn Concerto (1933); *Prelude to Shakespeare* (1935); Viola Concerto (1937); *The Snow Goose: A Legend for the Second World War* (1944); and Violin Concerto (1948). His *Concerto Arabesque* for piano and orchestra (1930) was at one time comparatively widely performed in the United States. A second piano concerto, subtitled *Satirico*, dates from 1938.

Becker's important choral work is *Out of the Cradle Endlessly Rocking*, a setting of Whitman's poem for soprano, tenor, speaker, chorus, and orchestra (1929). He also wrote much unaccompanied choral music, including *Missa Symphonica* for male voices (1933); and *Mass in Honor of the Sacred Heart* (1943); *Moments from the Passion* (1945); and *The Seven Last Words* (1947), all three pieces for either women's or men's voices. These works epitomize his amalgamation of sixteenth-century polyphony with twentieth-century harmonic language. *Moments From the Liturgical Year* for speaker, speaking chorus, vocal soloists, and choir was written in 1948.

Among Becker's instrumental music is a series of works for various chamber ensembles entitled *Soundpieces*: *no. 1*, a piano concerto (1935); *no. 2*, *Homage to Haydn* for strings (1935); *no. 3* for violin and piano (1936); *no. 4*, a string quartet (1937); *no. 5*, a piano sonata (1938); *no. 6* for flute and clarinet (1941); *no. 7* for two pianos (1949); and *no. 8* for string quartet (1959). He also composed a *Romance* for brass sextet; *Sonate American* for violin and piano (1925); and *Fantasia Tragica* for organ.

BEESON, JACK HAMILTON

b. Muncie, Indiana, 15 July 1921

Beeson received certificates from the University of Toronto (1938) and two degrees from Eastman School of Music, Rochester, New York (1939–44), where his teachers included Burrill Phillips, Howard Hanson, and Bernard Rogers. He also received lessons from Béla Bartók in New York (1944–45). In 1944 he joined the Columbia University Opera Workshop and shortly thereafter began teaching at Columbia University, where he was appointed MacDowell Professor of Music in 1967. He retired in 1988. He also lectured at the Juilliard School, New York (1961–63). Beeson won a Prix de Rome Fellowship in 1948, a Fulbright Fellowship in 1949, and a Guggenheim Fellowship in 1958. In 1968 he gained the Marc Blitzstein Award for the Musical

Theater from the American Academy of Arts and Letters, of which he became a member in 1976.

It is with his operas that Beeson has made his greatest impression. As an actor he has performed in one of them himself. The first opera, *Jonah*, based on a play by Paul Goodman, was completed in 1950. His initial success came with a production of the opera *Hello Out There* (1953) in New York in 1954. Adapted from the play by William Saroyan, it is scored for three singers and 13 instruments. Its sustained lyricism has something in common with the music of Douglas Moore and Leonard Bernstein. A third opera, *The Sweet Bye and Bye* (libretto: Kenward Elmslie; 1956), was performed at the Juilliard School in New York City in 1957. The story concerns the activities of a woman evangelist. The three-act *Lizzie Borden* (1964), based on the 1892 Boston murders, was staged by the New York City Opera on 25 March 1965. The text is again by Kenward Elmslie.

In 1969 Beeson wrote for the National Educational Television Theater a two-act chamber opera *My Heart's in the Highlands*, based on a play by William Saroyan. In 1975 he completed *Captain Jinks and the Horse Marines*, based on a play by Clyde Fitch. It was commissioned by the National Endowment for the Arts and produced by the Kansas City Lyric Opera. Beeson's next opera, *Dr. Heidegger's Fountain of Youth*, based on a story by Nathaniel Hawthorne, was commissioned by the National Arts Club and first performed in New York in November 1978. In collaboration with Sheldon Harnick, the librettist for his previous two operas, he composed an operatic adaptation of Rostand's *Cyrano de Bergerac* (1980–91). His next opera, *Sorry, Wrong Number*, dates from 1996. In the same year he composed an "operina," *Practice in the Art of Elocution* for soprano and piano, to his own libretto.

In addition to his operas, Beeson has composed three important orchestral works: Symphony *in A* (1959); *Transformations* (1959); and *Hymns and Dances from The Sweet Bye and Bye* (1965). Beeson's instrumental music includes two published *Piano Sonatas*; *Interlude* for violin and piano (1945; rev. 1951); Sonata for viola and piano (1953); and *The Hoosier Balks* and *The Hawksley Blues* for ten instruments (1967).

Among his choral works are: *A Round for Christmas* (1942; rev. 1951); *Three Psalms* (1951); *Three Settings from the Bay Psalm Book* (1951); *Knots: Jack and Jill for Grownups* (R. D. Laing; 1979); *Magicke Pieces* (1991); and *Epitaphs* (1993). There are many smaller choral pieces for mixed voices including *Summer Rounds and Canons* (2002) in addition to numerous rounds for various voices.

His solo vocal music includes *Three Love Songs* (W. B. Yeats) for contralto and piano (1944; rev. 1959); *Three Songs* (William Blake) for soprano and piano

(1945; rev. 1951); *Five Songs* Francis Quarles) for soprano and piano (1946; rev. 1950; rev. 1959); *Two Songs* (John Betjamin) for baritone and piano (1952); *Six Lyrics* for high voice and piano (1952); *A Creole Mystery* for mezzo-soprano and string quartet (1971); *The Day's No Rounder Than Its Angles Aqre*, for the same forces, premiered in New York in 1972); and *From a Watchtower*, five songs for baritone and piano (1976). Recent vocal works include *Two Millay Songs* for mezzo-soprano (1992); *The Daring Young Man on the Flying Trapeze* for countertenor and ensemble (1999); *Orphelia Sings, a Mad Scene with Ditties* for mezzo-soprano and instruments (2000); *The Equilibrists*, an elegiac cycle for soprano, tenor, and chamber ensemble (2001); and *A Rupert Brooke Cycle* (2002) for bass and piano.

BELCHER, SUPPLY
b. Stoughton (now Sharon), Massachusetts, 29 March (9 April new style) 1752
d. Farmington, Maine, 9 June 1836

After operating a tavern in Stoughton, Belcher settled in Farmington, Maine, where he taught in the local schools and became a much-respected citizen. His use of fugal counterpoint and a certain Handelian turn of melody in his compositions earned him the nickname "The Handel of Maine."

A collection of his hymns, psalms, and other religious music entitled *The Harmony of Maine* was published in Boston in 1794. Contained within it are Belcher's surviving hymn tunes: *Cumberland, Plenitude, Omega,* and *York.* His anthems include *While Shepherds Watched Their Flocks By Night*; *An Anthem of Praise (Psalm 100)*; *An Anthem of Easter*; *Blow Ye the Trumpet (Jubilate)*; *Welcome to Spring*; and *Deep North Spirituals* (1794).

BENNETT, ROBERT RUSSELL
b. Kansas City, Missouri, 15 June 1894
d. New York, New York, 18 August 1981

As a child, Bennett was taught the piano by his mother, and he learned to play several other instruments as well. As his father was an orchestral musician, the boy came into contact with other players. When barely in his teens he often deputized in local bands, usually on violin or trombone. At the age of 15, Bennett began harmony lessons with Carl Busch in Kansas City. He later became an arranger and copyist in New York, a career interrupted by a year in the First World War. Thus began his long association with Broadway musicals. He was awarded Guggenheim Fellowships which enabled

him to study in Paris with Nadia Boulanger (1926–30). During his stay in Europe he visited London, Berlin, and Vienna. In spite of the prevailing influences, especially in Paris, Bennett remained essentially American, as the titles of most of his pieces indicate.

Except for the *Charleston Rhapsody* for orchestra composed in America in 1926 (rev. 1933), most of his early serious compositions date from his years in Europe. His *First* Symphony was completed in 1926. The *Abraham Lincoln Symphony* (1927) and *Sights and Sounds* (1929) won awards in the Victor Symphony Contest in 1929. Also composed in these years were *Paysage* for orchestra (1927) and *March* for two pianos and orchestra (1930). His knowledge of popular music inspired the *Concerto Grosso* for dance band and orchestra (1932). A third and somewhat light-hearted *Symphony in D for the Dodgers* was composed in 1941. In the following year the Philadelphia Orchestra performed his *Eight Etudes*, composed in 1938, Symphony no. 4, *The Four Freedoms* (1941), inspired by paintings by Norman Rockwell, was given its premiere in 1943 by the NBC Symphony Orchestra. Symphony no. 5, subtitled *Commemoration Symphony: Stephen Collins Foster*, completed in 1959, is scored for soprano, tenor, chorus, and orchestra. He composed two further symphonies, no. 6 (1946) and no. 7 (1963).

Louis Kaufmann was the soloist in the premiere of his Violin Concerto in A, in New York in 1941. Bennett also composed a Concerto for viola, harp, and orchestra (1940) revised in 1959 for harp, cello, and orchestra; *Antique Suite* for clarinet and orchestra (1941); Piano Concerto (1947); Double Concerto for violin and piano (1958); *Nocturne and Appassionata* for piano and orchestra (1941); *Concert Variations on a Crooner's Theme* for violin (1949); and Harmonica Concerto (1971). His other orchestral works of note include *Hollywood (Introduction and Scherzo*; 1936); *Symphonic Story of Jerome Kern* (1946); *Overture to an Imaginary Drama* (1946); *Kansas City Album: 7 Songs for Orchestra* (1949); *Overture to the Mississippi* (1950); *Rose Variations* (1955); *Concerto Grosso* for wind quintet and orchestra (1957); *Ohio River Suite* (1959); and *The Fun and Faith of William Billings, American* (with chorus), composed for Antal Dorati and the National Symphony Orchestra of Washington to mark the Bicentennial in 1976.

Bennett's considerable experience in the theater assisted him in writing for the stage. He composed a five-act operetta, *Endymion* (1927); two one-act operas, *An Hour of Delusion* (1927) and *The Enchanted Kiss* (1944); and a full-length opera, *Crystal* (1972). His major work is the three-act opera *Maria Malibran* (1935) to a libretto by the critic Robert A. Simon. The story concerns the two-year stay in the United States of the famous singer. He also wrote a pantomime ballet, *Columbine* (1916) and a musical play, *Hold Your Horses* (1933).

Bennett's chamber music includes a Violin Sonata (1927); an *Organ* Sonata *in G* (1929); a *Sonatina* for flute, cello, and harp (1936); *Water Music* for string quartet (1937); A *Song Sonata* for violin and piano (1947); Clarinet Quartet (1941); String Quartet (1956); and *Arabesque* for brass quintet (1978). In addition he composed a number of short instrumental pieces, often using jazz and dance idioms. The best known of these is *Hexapoda*, five studies in "Jitteroptera" for violin and piano (1940), a favorite with Kaufmann and Heifetz. Among his last works are four *Carol Cantatas* (1976), composed for the First Presbyterian Church, Orlando, Florida; and *Easter Story* for chorus and orchestra (1978).

By far the greatest part of Bennett's talent and time was devoted to orchestrating Broadway shows both for the stage and the screen. He orchestrated over 230 scores for musicals, and his skill often turned a routine work into a masterpiece. Some of these near legendary productions are *Rose-Marie* (Rudolf Friml, 1924); *Sunny* (Jerome Kern, 1925); *Showboat* (Kern, 1927); *The Cat and the Fiddle* (Kern, 1931); *Music in the Air* (Kern, 1932); *Face the Music* (Irving Berlin, 1932); *Roberta* (Kern, 1933); *Louisiana Purchase* (Berlin, 1939); *Panama Hattie* (Cole Porter, 1940); *Oklahoma !* (Richard Rodgers, 1948); *The Gay Divorcee* (Porter, 1944); *Annie Get Your Gun* (Berlin, 1946); *South Pacific* (Rodgers, 1948); *Kiss Me Kate* (Porter, 1948); *The King and I* (Rodgers, 1951); *My Fair Lady* (Frederick Loewe, 1956); *The Sound of Music* (Rodgers, 1959); and *Camelot* (Loewe, 1960).

Bennett's successful music for feature films include *Fugitives for a Night* (1937); *Annabel Takes a Tour* (1937); *Carlot* (1938); *Career* (1939); *Twelve Crowded Hours* (1939); *Pacific Liner* (1939); *Fifth Avenue Girl* (1939); and a documentary, *Willow Run* (1942). He won an Academy Award for the scoring and background music for *Oklahoma!* (1955). He also contributed scores for television, notably *He is Risen* (Emmy Award, 1962); *The Coming of Christ*; and *The War in Korea* (1965). Also for television he scored Richard Rodgers' music for *Victory at Sea* (1953).

Bennett made a valuable contribution to the more permanent repertory of concert bands with such pieces as *Tone Poems* (1939); *Suite of Old American Dances* (1949); *Symphonic Songs* (1957); *West Virginia Epic* (1960); *Overture to Ty, Tris and Willie* (1961); *Kentucky* (1961); *Twain and the River* (1968); and *Zimmer's American Greeting* (1974).

He was the author of a book on orchestration, *Instrumentally Speaking*, published in 1974, and *Autobiography* (1980).

BENSON, WARREN F(RANK)

b. *Detroit, Michigan, 26 January 1924*

Benson began his musical career as a percussion player at the age of 14 and was a teacher at 19, becoming timpanist in the Detroit Symphony Orchestra in 1946. He graduated from the University of Michigan, Ann Arbor, in 1949. On two Fulbright Fellowship he taught at Anatolia College, Thessalonika, Greece (1950–52) before becoming director of the band and orchestra at Mars Hill College, North Carolina (1952–53). In 1953 he was appointed professor of music and Composer-in-Residence at Ithaca College, Ithaca, New York. From 1967 to retirement in 1994 he was professor of composition at the Eastman School of Music, Rochester, New York. He was awarded a Guggenheim Fellowship in 1981.

Many of Benson's compositions reflect a concern with the concert band; works for winds and percussion predominate. Works for band include *Transylvanian Fanfare Concert March* (1953); *Concertino* for alto saxophone (1953); *Night Song* (1958); *Juniperus* (1959); *Remembrance* (1962–63); *The Leaves Are Falling* (1963–64); *Symphony for Drums and Wind Orchestra* (1964); *Star-edge* for alto saxophone and winds (1965); *Helix* for tuba and winds (1966); *The Solitary Dancer* for wind ensemble (1966); *The Mask of Night* (1968); *The Passing Bell* (1974); *Ginger Marmalade* (1978); Symphony no. 2. *Lost Songs* (1982); *Other Rivers* (1984); *Wings* (1984); *Dawn's Early Light* (1987); *Meditation on I am For Peace* (1990); *Adagietto* (1991); *Danzon – memory* (1991); *Dux Variations* (1992); *Divertissement* (1993); *Daughter of the Stars* (*A Reminiscence on Shenandoah*) (1998); *Still Dancing* (2001); *Scherzo Robusto and Aria Serena* (2002); and *Vilandoe* (2003).

For orchestra he has written *A Delphic Serenade* (1953); *Vignettes* for small orchestra (1961); *Theme and Excursions* for strings (1963); *Chants and Graces* for piccolo, harp, percussion, and strings (1964); *Bailando*, a ballet score (1965); a Horn Concerto (1971); *The Man With the Blue Guitar* (1980); *Beyond Winter: Sweet Aftershowers* for strings, written in memory of the composer Alec Wilder in 1981; and *Concertino* for flute, strings, and percussion (1983).

Benson's chamber music is extensive: *Marche-Encore* for wind quintet (1955); Quintet for oboe, soprano saxophone, and strings (1957); Trio for percussion (1957); Trio for clarinet, cello, and piano (1959); *Three Pieces* for percussion quartet (1960); *Invocation* for soprano saxophone, alto saxophone, and percussion (1960); *Streams* for seven percussionists (1961); *Recuerdo* for oboe, English horn and wind ensemble (1965); *Wind Rose* for saxophone quartet (1967); two

Warren Benson.
Photo: Louis Ouzer, courtesy the composer.

string quartets (1969, 1985); *Capriccio* for piano quartet (1971); *Serpentine Shadows* for two tubas (1973); *The Dream Net* for alto saxophone and string quartet (1976); *Largo Tah* for bass trombone and marimba (1977); *Embers* for trumpet, trombone, and percussion (1978); *Elegy* for horn and organ (1982); *Thorgard's Song* for horn and percussion (1982); *Fair Game* for clarinet, trumpet, violin, cello, piano, and percussion (1986); *The Red Lion* for vibraphone and piano (1988); *Steps* for brass quintet (1988); String Quartet no. 3; *Cat's Cradle* (1995); *Trio Tertulia* for clarinet, violin, and cello (2001); and *Meditation on E* for solo violin (2002).

Choral music includes *Something of the Sea* for chorus (1949); *Psalm 24* for female chorus and strings (1959); *Love Is* for double chorus (1967); *Songs of O* for chorus, brass quintet, and percussion (1974); *Of Rounds* for chorus and chamber ensemble (1975); *Earth, Sky, Sea, Trees, Birds* (Kenneth Rexroth) for chorus, flute, bass trombone, and percussion (1975); *Meditation, Prayer and Sweet Hallelujah* for chorus and piano (1979); *Psalm 139* for chorus and organ (1981); *A Score of Praises* for chorus (1983); *The Drums of Summer* for double chorus, large wind ensemble, and percussion (1997); and *Sing and Rejoice* for double chorus (1997).

Among his solo vocal pieces are *Shadow Wood* (Tennessee Williams) for soprano and wind ensemble (1970); *Nara* for soprano, flute, piano, and percussion (1970); *The Beaded Leaf* (A. Hecht) for bass and wind ensemble (1974); *Five Lyrics of Louise Bogan* for mezzo-soprano and flute (1977); *Songs for the End of World* for mezzo-soprano, English horn, horn, cello, and marimba (1980); *Moon Rain and Memory Jane*, a song cycle for soprano and two cellos (1982); *Hills, Woods, Brook: Three Love Songs* for voice, clarinet, trumpet, violin, cello, piano, and percussion (1982); *Dos Antifonas Lindas* for soprano, mezzo-soprano, and viola (1985); *Songs and Asides About Love* for baritone, viola, and guitar (1999); and *Love and the Lady* for mezzo-soprano and cello (1999). A dance-drama, *Odysseus*, was performed in Greece in May 1971.

Benson is the author of three books: *Creative Projects in Musicianship* (1967); *Compositional Processes and Writing Skills* (1974); and a collection of musical limericks, *And My Daddy Will Play the Drums* (1998). He is currently writing a musical primer, *Problems for the Pedagogy of Composition*, and an autobiography provisionally entitled *Memoires*.

BEREZOWSKY, NICOLAI
b. St. Petersburg, Russia, 17 May 1900
d. New York, New York, 27 August 1953

Berezowsky received his basic musical training at the Imperial Chapel in his native city of St. Petersburg (1908–16); at the age of 18 he became a violinist in the opera orchestras of Saratov and, two years later, the Bolshoi Theatre in Moscow. He was also a student of conducting at the School of Modern Art in Moscow. In 1922, he emigrated to America where for five years he was a violinist in the New York Philharmonic Orchestra. During that time he also studied at the Juilliard School with Rubin Goldmark. He was a member of the Coolidge String Quartet (1935–40). Although he remained a violinist all his life, he devoted much time to composition and was active as an orchestral conductor. In 1944 he won an award from the American Academy of Arts and Letters and in 1948 he gained a Guggenheim Fellowship.

Berezowsky's major were works were four symphonies: no. 1 (1925); no. 2 (1933); no. 3 (1936); and no. 4 (1943). His output of orchestral works was considerable and includes a Violin Concerto written for Carl Flesch (1930); *Concerto Lirico* for cello (1935), performed by Piatigorsky; a Viola Concerto (1941); a Clarinet Concerto (1941); a Harp Concerto (1945); *Hebrew Suite* (1928); *Concert Fantasy* for two pianos and orchestra (1931); *Sinfonietta* (1932); *Toccata, Variations and Finale* for string quartet and orchestra (1938); *Introduction and Waltz* (1939); *Christmas Festival Overture on a Ukranian Noel* (1943); *Soldiers on the Town* (1943); *Passacaglia* for theremin and orchestra (1947) and *Sextet Concerto* for strings (1953).

Among his instrumental works are a Piano Sonata (1926); *Theme and Fantastic Variations in A flat* for clarinet, string quartet, and piano (1926); two woodwind quintets (1928, 1937); Sextet for strings (1928); *Fantasy* for two pianos (1930); *Duo* for clarinet and viola (1931); two string quartets (1931, 1934); a Suite for brass (1939); and a Suite for wind quintet (1941).

Berezowsky composed two operas, *Prince Batrak* (1920) and *Ship South* (1941), and a one-act opera for children, *Babar the Elephant* (1953). In 1927 he completed a *Cantata* for soprano, tenor, bass, chorus, and orchestra; a second cantata, *Gilgamesh*, dates from 1946.

BERGER, ARTHUR (VICTOR)
b. *New York, New York, 15 May 1912*
d. *Cambridge, Massachusetts, 7 October 2003*

Berger was educated at City College of New York (1928–30), New York University (1930–33), and Harvard University (1934–37), where he studied with Walter Piston. From 1937 to 1939 he studied in Paris with Nadia Boulanger on a John Knowles Paine Fellowship from Harvard. On his return to the United States, he taught at Mills College, Oakland, California (1939–41), where he also received composition lessons from Milhaud. After a year at North Texas College, Denton, he taught at Brooklyn College (1942–43) and the Juilliard School. In 1953 he joined the faculty at Brandeis University, Waltham, Massachusetts, becoming Naumburg Professor in 1963 and Irving Fine Professor Emeritus in 1980, the year in which he joined the faculty at the New England Conservatory in Boston, retiring in 1999. For many years he was a music critic for the *New York Herald Tribune* and was founding editor of *Perspectives in New Music*.

The influences on Berger's early music come primarily from Copland, who encouraged him as a young composer. The strong insistence on ostinato figures was derived from the music of Stravinsky. One of Berger's most important work is *Ideas of Order* written in a neoclassical idiom in the manner of Stravinsky. It was first performed on 11 April 1953 by the New York Philharmonic Orchestra under Dimitri Mitropoulos who had commissioned it. Another major composition is *Serenade Concertante* in one movement, written in 1944 and revised in 1951. In the form of a concerto grosso, it is scored for flute, oboe, clarinet, bassoon, violin, and orchestra. It was commissioned by CBS radio for

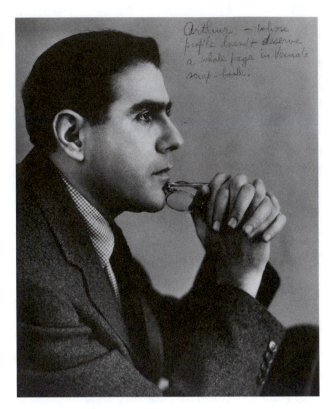

Arthur Berger, c. 1953.
Irving Fine Collection, Music Division, Library of Congress.

performance under the direction of Bernard Herrmann. His *Polyphony* was composed for the Louisville Orchestra in 1956. A *Concerto for Chamber Orchestra* was completed in 1960 and withdrawn in 1978 and revised in 1986 as *Perspectives* for chamber orchestra.. For string orchestra he has composed *Three Pieces* (1945, rev. 1982).

Berger concentrated principally upon instrumental music. Among his works in this field are the neoclassical Quartet in C major for woodwinds (1941); four duos: no. 1 for violin and piano (1948), no. 2 for violin and piano (1950), no. *3* for cello and piano (1951) and no. 4 for oboe and clarinet (1952), arranged for clarinet and piano (1957); *Chamber Music for Thirteen Players* (1956); *Movement* for chamber orchestra (1959, rev. 1969); Septet (1966); Trio for violin, guitar, and piano (1972); a Piano Trio written for the Beaux Arts Trio in 1980; Wind Quintet (1984); *Diptych: Collage I & II* for flute, clarinet, and piano trio (1990); and *Collage III* for flute, clarinet, violin, cello, percussion, and piano (1992). His String Quartet (1958) makes use of the 12-tone method similar to late Stravinsky, and was cited by the New York Music Critics' Circle in 1962.

Berger composed several major works for keyboard including *Two Episodes* (1933), which experiment with atonality; *Piano Fantasy* (1940); *Rondo* (1945); *Capriccio* (1945); *Three Bagatelles* (1946); *Intermezzo* for harpsichord (or piano) (1946); *Partita* (1947); *Five Pieces* (1968); *For Elliott Carter at 75* (1983); *Four Two-Part Inventions* (1993); and *Birthday Cards* (1980–94, 1985–96), all for piano. *Three Pieces* for two pianos (1962) makes use of prepared piano effects. For piano four-hands he has written *Perspectives III* (1982).

For the theater Berger composed a ballet *Entertainment Piece* (1940). Also dating from 1940 is his best-known vocal work, *Music for Words, Perhaps*, three songs to poems by W.B. Yeats for mezzo-soprano, flute, clarinet, and violin. Other vocal music includes *Garlands* for mezzo-soprano and piano (1945); *Boo Hoo at the Zoo: Tails of Woe* for two voices (1978); *Five Settings of European Poets* for tenor (1978–79); and *Ode of Ronsard* for soprano and piano (1987), transcribed in 2002 for flute, cello, and piano. His two choral works are a setting of *Psalm 92* (1946) and *Love, Sweet Animal* (Delmore Schwartz) (1982) for mixed voices and piano four-hands.

Berger was the author of an important book, *Aaron Copland*, published in 1953, and a collection of his own writings, *Reflections of an American Composer* (2002).

BERGSMA, WILLIAM (LAWRENCE)

b. Oakland, California, 1 April 1921
d. Seattle, Washington, 18 March 1994

Bergsma was educated at Stanford University (1938–40) and the Eastman School of Music, Rochester, New York (1940–44) where he was a pupil of Howard Hanson and Bernard Rogers. For a while he taught at the Eastman School, but later he settled in New York where he was on the faculty of the Juilliard School (1946–63). From 1963 to 1986 he was director of the School of Music at the University of Washington, Seattle. In 1946 he was awarded a Guggenheim Fellowship.

Bergsma's style is essentially chromatic and romantic. He composed scores for two ballets: *Paul Bunyan*, written in 1937, while he was still in school (rev. 1945), and *Gold and the Senor Commandante* (1940–41, rev. 1963). His first opera, *The Wife of Martin Guerre*, a tragedy in three acts, was staged at the Juilliard School in 1956. In 1976 he wrote a second opera, *The Murder of Comrade Sharik*.

Bergsma's earliest orchestral work is *Pioneer Saga*, heard at an Eastman concert in 1939. This was followed by *Dances From a New England Album of 1865* (1939, rev. 1969); *Music on a Quiet Theme* (1943); a Symphony for chamber orchestra (1943); and *The Fortunate Islands* for string orchestra, composed in 1947 while he was vacationing in the West Indies; it was revised in 1956. Other major orchestral pieces are Symphony no. 1. (1946–49); *A Carol for Twelfth* Night,

commissioned by the Louisville Orchestra in 1954; *Chameleon Variations* (1959); *In Celebration: Toccata for the Sixth Day* (1962); *Documentary One: Portrait of a City* (1963, rev. 1968); *Serenade to Await the Moon* for small orchestra (1962); and a Violin Concerto (1965). Later orchestral works include *Documentary Two: Billie's World* (1968); *Changes* (1971); Symphony no. 2. (*Voyages*) for soloists, chorus, and orchestra (1976); *Sweet Was the Song the Virgin Sung: Tristan Revisted*, variations and fantasy for viola and orchestra, commissioned by the Seattle Symphony Orchestra in 1977; and *In Campo Aperto* for oboe, two bassoons, and strings (1981).

Bergsma composed six string quartets (1942, 1944, 1953, 1970 [rev. 1974], 1982, 1991). Among his other instrumental music are a Suite for brass quartet (1940, rev. 1945); *Pastorale and Scherzo* for recorder (or flute) and two violas (1943); Concerto *for wind quintet* (1958); *Fantastic Variations on a Theme from Tristan and Isolde* for viola and piano (1961); *Illegible Canons* for clarinet and percussion (1969); *Clandestine Dialogues* for cello and piano (1976); *Blatant Hypotheses* for trombone and percussion (1977); Quintet for flute and strings (1980, rev. 1981); *The Voice of the Coelacanth* for horn, violin, and piano, commissioned by the Chamber Music Society of Lincoln Center in 1980; *4 All* for clarinet, trombone, cello, and percussion (1981); *Symmetries* for oboe, bassoon, and piano

William Bergsma.
William Schuman Photo Collection #1, neg #135.
Courtesy The Juilliard School.

(1982); *Masquerade* for wind quintet (1986); and *A Lick and a Promise* for saxophone and chimes (1988). For piano he wrote *Three Fantasies* (1943, rev. 1983); *Tangents* (1951); and *Variations* (1984).

His most important choral work, *Confrontation*, from the Book of Job, for chorus and orchestra (1963, rev. 1966), is a declamatory setting owing something to both Copland and Stravinsky, with much expressive lyrical writing. In 1968, to a commission from the American Choral Directors Association, he composed *The Sun, The Soaring Eagle, The Turquoise Prince, The God* for chorus, brass, and percussion. Other choral items include *In a Glass of Water Before Retiring* (S.V. Benet) (1945); *Black Salt, Black Provender* (Louise Bogan) (1946); *On the Beach at Night* (Whitman) (1946); *Let True Love Among Us Be* (1948); *Riddle Me This* (1957); *Praise* (George Herbert) for chorus and organ (1958); and *Wishes, Wonders, Portents, Charms* for soloists, chorus, and instruments (1974).

For solo voice he wrote *Three Songs* (e.e.cummings) (1944–45); *Bathsabe, Bathing* (George Peele) (1961); *In Space* for soprano and instruments (1975); *Four Songs* for medium voice, clarinet, bassoon, and piano (1981); and *I Told You So*, four songs for voice and percussion (1986).

BERNSTEIN, LEONARD (REAL NAME: LOUIS)
b. Lawrence, Massachusetts, 25 August 1918
d. New York, New York, 14 October 1990

Bernstein's first piano teachers were Heinrich Gebhard and Helen Coates, who later became his secretary. At Harvard University, he was a pupil of Walter Piston, A. Jillman Merritt, and Edward Burlingame Hill. In 1939 he continued his studies at the Curtis Institute in Philadelphia, where his teachers were Isabella Vengerova (piano), Fritz Reiner (conducting), and Randall Thompson (composition). At the Berkshire Music Center, Tanglewood, Massachusetts he was in Koussevitzky's conducting class, becoming his assistant in 1942. In 1951 he succeeded Koussevitzky as director of the class.

In 1943 Bernstein was appointed assistant conductor of the New York Philharmonic Symphony Orchestra. He was conductor of the New York City Center Orchestra from 1944 to 1947. His outstanding talent as a conductor was soon recognized throughout the world. Bernstein was the first American conductor to perform regularly at La Scala, Milan in 1953. In 1958, succeeding Dimitri Mitropoulos, he was appointed musical director and conductor of the New York Philharmonic Orchestra, the first American-born musician to become conductor of a major American orchestra. He held the post until 1969, when he resigned to devote more time

to composition. Bernstein was also a brilliant pianist, appearing as a soloist throughout his career. As a presenter of music programs on television he had no equal.

In his principal role as a composer, Bernstein showed a remarkable versatility in every medium and musical language. His works range from the intensely dramatic and serious orchestral works to the delightful songs of his early musicals, which reflect a complete command of popular music and jazz. His first important work is the *Jeremiah Symphony*, composed in 1942 and performed in Pittsburgh under the composer's direction. It won the New York Music Critics' Circle award in that year. The melodic inspiration in the three movements, entitled *Prophesy – Profanation – Lamentation*, is derived, in part, from Jewish liturgical music. The finale uses material from the previous movements and sets words from the Book of Lamentation in Hebrew for mezzo-soprano. Another Jewish work, *Hashkivenu*, for tenor, chorus and organ, dates from 1945.

Symphony no. 2, *The Age of Anxiety*, is based on a poem by W. H. Auden. Closely paralleling the form of the poem in six sections, the music illustrates the story of four lonely people, three men and a woman. There is an important concertante part for solo piano. At the premiere in April 1949, the composer was the pianist with the Boston Symphony Orchestra under Koussevitzky. Bernstein subsequently revised the finale to include the piano. *Serenade* for violin and string orchestra, harp, timpani, and percussion was inspired by another literary work, Plato's *Symposium*; each movement is named after a character at the banquet described in the book. Isaac Stern was the soloist in the first performance at the Venice Festival in September 1954.

Symphony no. 3 was commissioned by the Koussevitzky Foundation and dedicated to the memory of John F. Kennedy. It is subtitled *Kaddish*, after the Jewish prayer associated with the dead. It is scored for speaker, mezzo-soprano, chorus, and orchestra. The spoken text in English, written by the composer, reaches an outburst in which God is accused of breaking faith with man. Such sentiments caused a degree of disapproval from some religious sources. In 1977 Bernstein made certain revisions, cutting the text and providing hummed chorus and orchestra support to the spoken voice. The choir and a boys' chorus sing the Kaddish prayer in Hebrew. In this work Bernstein uses a motto theme he calls the "Kaddish" tune as a unifying element. The musical language is often extremely chromatic, abandoning tonality, and is based in part on two tone-rows, one a chain of fourths. Bernstein requires a large orchestra including four flutes, four clarinets, and a huge percussion section. Although commissioned originally for the 75th anniversary of the Boston Sym-

Leonard Bernstein in his apartment, c. 1946–48.
Photo: William P. Gottlieb, used with permission.

phony Orchestra in 1955, the first performance of the symphony was given in Tel Aviv on 10 December 1963 by the Israel Philharmonic Orchestra conducted by the composer.

Chichester Psalms was commissioned by the Dean of Chichester, England for the Southern Cathedrals Festival in 1965. The three sections are settings in Hebrew of parts of Psalms 108, 100, 23, 131, and 133. The accompaniment is scored for brass, two harps, percussion, and strings.

For the opening of the John F. Kennedy Center for the Performing Arts in Washington, D.C., Bernstein composed *Mass*, described as "a theater piece for singers, players, and dancers." Between the sections of the Latin text of the Roman Mass are interpolated settings of additional texts in English, written by Stephen Sondheim and the composer. Enormous and varied forces are used in the scoring. The Celebrant, a baritone, is the central figure throughout. He is assisted by a solo boy's voice, a boy's choir, a large group of solo singers, some pre-recorded, a formal chorus of 60 mixed voices, pre-recorded solo oboe, and orchestra. The orchestra is divided into two parts: a pit orchestra of strings and percussion, with two organs (one "concert," one "rock"), and a stage orchestra of brass, woodwind, electric guitars, and keyboards. The stage players provide a brass marching band, a rock band, and several varied ensembles. The instrumentalists are in costume and act as members of the cast. In addition, a group of dancers augment the movements of the solo singers and players. The original choreography was by Alvin Ailey. Some of the Latin Mass sections are reminiscent of the

choral and orchestral writing in *Chichester Psalms*, especially the preference for seven-beat measures. The musical styles cover the complete spectrum of music today in all forms: pop, rock, blues, pre-recorded tape, band music, atonality.

The premiere took place in Washington on 8 September 1971 under the musical direction of Maurice Peress. The impact of the first performance was strong, and critics were far from unanimous in their assessment. Some felt the banalities of the English words weakened the musical force; others considered that the wide range of styles could not be welded into a single successful composition. All agreed that it was a work of considerable significance, if flawed in certain respects, with sufficient fine moments for it to become established as a major creation of its time. The level of energy required and the complexity and length of the score will keep live performances limited in number, but recordings and television appearances may well make it a "classic" in its own right. This is a landmark in the attempt to create "one-music," a fusion of all current musical styles, breaking down barriers between them.

On 11 October 1977, the National Symphony Orchestra of Washington, D.C. performed three Bernstein premieres: *Overture Slava!*, the title taken from the name of the dedicatee, the cellist Mstislav Rostropovich; *Meditations from Mass* for cello and orchestra; and *Songfest*, for six solo voices and orchestra. This last work was originally commissioned to celebrate the American Bicentennial. Appropriately, *Songfest* represents a survey of American poetry, ranging from "To My Dear and Loving Husband" by Anne Bradstreet (1612–1672) to "Zizi's Lament" by Gregory Corso (1930–2001). In the setting of 13 poems, Bernstein uses the six singers in various groupings. *Songfest* is dedicated to the composer's mother.

Bernstein's last orchestral pieces are a Divertimento performed in Boston in September 1980; *A Musical Toast* in memory of André Kostelanetz, for the New York Philharmonic Orchestra in October 1980; and *Halil* for flute, strings, and percussion (1981) written in memory of a young Israeli soldier. On 23 September 1981, *Olympic Hymn* to words by Gunther Kuhnert was performed in Baden Baden. Bernstein's final orchestral composition, *Jubilee Games*, began as a two-movement work to celebrate the 50th anniversary of the Israel Philharmonic Orchestra in 1986. In the same year he added a *Benediction* for baritone and orchestra. In 1989 he made it a four-movement score with a set of variations entitled *Mixed Doubles*.

Bernstein's last choral work, *Missa Brevis* for treble voice, chorus, and percussion, was first performed in Atlanta, Georgia under the direction of Robert Shaw on April 21 1988.

Ballets

Bernstein wrote three ballets. *Fancy Free* (1944) was his first collaboration with dancer-choreographer Jerome Robbins. The scenario describes the adventures of three sailors and their girlfriends in New York for one day. After its premiere on 18 April 1944 by Ballet Theatre, it was such a success that the original season was extended. The ballet was performed 161 times in its first year. *Facsimile*, also composed for Jerome Robbins and Ballet Theatre, was produced on Broadway in October 1946. The story explores the theme of loneliness, as does *The Age of Anxiety*. A woman escapes from the city to the beach but finds no consolation in the emptiness. Bernstein's last ballet, *Dybbuk* (now entitled *Dybbuk Variations*), was also choreographed by Robbins. It was performed on 16 March 1974 by the New York City Ballet at Lincoln Center. Two suites from the score were given their premiere on 16 August 1974 by the New York Philharmonic Orchestra under the composer's direction in Auckland, New Zealond.

Musicals and Operas

Bernstein's widest success as a composer has come with his musical scores for Broadway. The first of these, *On The Town* (1944), took the plot of *Fancy Free*, but provided totally new music, even for the extended dances. It received 463 performances in its original production. The story again follows the adventures of three sailors on leave for a day in New York. The brilliant score contains a number of outstanding songs: "Come Up to My Place," "Carried Away," "Lucky to Be Me," "Some Other Time," and ensemble items much superior to and more ambitious than those usually found in Broadway musicals. A film version containing additional songs by Roger Edens, with a cast including Frank Sinatra, followed the success of the stage production. Bernstein provided songs and choruses for a production of J. M. Barrie's *Peter Pan*, which opened at the Imperial Theatre, New York on 24 April 1950.

His first opera, the satirical one-act *Trouble in Tahiti*, to his own libretto, depicts the empty lives of a suburban couple and is meant to serve as a warning to us all. It was first conducted by the composer at the Festival of Creative Arts, Brandeis University, Waltham, Massachusetts, on 12 June 1952. It has subsequently been produced many times, including on television.

Wonderful Town (1952), Bernstein's second musical, also enjoyed great acclaim on Broadway. Unfortunately, the close association of the story with New York and its immediate locale has prevented its being produced widely throughout the world, although it has been staged in England, Austria, and Germany. *Wonderful Town* is based on the stories of Ruth McKenney, which appeared in the *New Yorker* magazine in the 1930s and were subsequently published as *My Sister Eileen*. Set in Greenwich Village in the summer of 1935, it tells of the impact of New York on two sisters, Ruth and Eileen Sherwood, who come from Ohio seeking their fortune. The electric presence and performance of Rosalind Russell as Ruth ensured the success of *Wonderful Town*. Again Bernstein produced a number of memorable songs which deserve wider popularity: "Ohio," "Pass That Football," and "A Quiet Girl." In 1955 Bernstein provided incidental music for Lillian Hellman's adaptation of Jean Anouilh's play *The Lark*, from which two choruses were published separately.

Candide, a musical comedy after Voltaire's novel, was first performed in New York in December 1956 at the Martin Beck Theater. In many ways it is the most skillful of Bernstein's stage works, but its very subtlety, with frequent use of parody of operatic styles, presents a difficult challenge to the audience. The demands upon singers make *Candide* a piece that could be best performed by an opera company; the leading parts of Candide and Cunegonde are appropriate roles for opera singers with an extensive vocal technique. Every major composer of opera seems to have been invoked in this score. The "Jewel Song" is a clever parody of Gounod's *Faust* with echoes of Richard Strauss. "I am Easily Assimilated" is appropriately cast in a Stravinsky-like Latin-American idiom. Even the music of Gilbert and Sullivan is detectable in the chorus of "The Best of All Possible Worlds." A revision of *Candide*, with a new book by Hugh Wheeler replacing Lillian Hellman's original libretto, opened in March 1974 under the direction of Harold Price with greater success than the original. A more operatic version made in collaboration with the conductor John Mauceri was produced in New York in 1982 and with further changes in Glasgow in 1988.

West Side Story, Bernstein's next stage work, has had a phenomenal success unparalleled by any other American musical. More a music drama, it occupies a position closer to opera than musical comedy. Since its premiere in Washington, D.C., on 19 August 1957, it has been performed throughout the world, and the excellent film adaptation has ensured it a permanent place in the twentieth century. Many of the individual songs have already entered music history: "Tonight," "America," "Maria," "I Feel Pretty," and the composer's favorite, "Something's Coming." Only Gershwin's *Porgy and Bess* has as many established songs in a single work of this kind. The stark realism of gang warfare between the Sharks and the Jets and racial prejudice are presented with frightening brutality. There is an obvious parallel between Shakespeare's *Romeo and Juliet* and *West Side Story*, but the musical is decidedly a work of our time. As in Bernstein's previous stage presentations, the writing for vocal ensemble and the orchestration show a masterly hand.

After *West Side Story* he made several attempts at writing other musicals which he abandoned. On 24 February 1976 his last musical, *1600 Pennsylvania Avenue*, was produced at the Forrest Theatre, Philadelphia. With book and lyrics by Alan Jay Lerner, it traces the lives of ten presidents in the White House. The unsuccessful New York premiere took place at the Mark Hellinger Theater on 8 May 1976. Music from the show was salvaged to create a concert work, *A White House Cantata*, performed in London in 1997.

Sadly, Bernstein's last work for the theater, a full-length opera in which he had so much faith, was very poorly received on the opening night in Houston on 17 June 1983. *A Quiet Place*, with libretto by Stephen Wadsworth, concerns a family coping with death. Like Sam in the opera, Bernstein had lost his own wife in 1978. The deeply guilt-ridden, autobiographical character of the plot proved embarrassing to the audience. A drastic revision of the score, whereby almost the entire music of his first opera, *Trouble in Tahiti*, was incorporated into the second scene as a flashback, did little to alter critical opinion. The new version was staged at La Scala, Milan, on 19 June 1984 to greater initial acclaim, but the opera remains an oddity.

Other Works

Bernstein composed the Academy Award-winning score for Elia Kazan's film *On the Waterfront* (1954). He also took a considerable interest in jazz and in 1949 wrote *Prelude, Fugue and Riffs* for the Woody Herman Band. Although not performed by them, it was premiered on television in 1955 by Bernstein and Benny Goodman. He also wrote three song cycles: *I Hate Music,: a Cycle of Five Kids' Songs* (1943); *La Bonne Cuisine* (1947), settings of French recipes; and *Arias and Barcarolles* for four singers and piano duet (1988).

In addition to three early works—a Piano Trio (1937), a Piano Sonata (1938), and a Violin Sonata (1940)—he composed several instrumental pieces, including a Clarinet Sonata (1941–42); *Five Pieces* for brass (1948); and a sequence of piano solos: *Seven Anniversaries* (1943); *Four Anniversaries* (1948); *Five Anniversaries* (1949–51); *Touches* (1981); *Moby Diptych* (1981); *13 Anniversaries* (1988); and *For Nicky, an Ancient Friendship* (1989) for the 95th birthday of Nicolas Slonimsky.

Bernstein was a distinguished communicator in words as well as music. His first book, *The Joy of Music*, published in 1959, was partly based on programs he had presented on television. *Leonard Bernstein's Young People's Concerts* (1962) contains scripts written for these television concerts. His third book, *The Infinite Variety of Music*, also first appeared in 1962. Texts of his six talks at Harvard University, *The Unanswered Question*, were issued in 1978. A collection of essays written throughout his life were published in *Findings* in 1982.

BEVERSDORF, (SAMUEL) THOMAS
b. Yoakum, Texas, 8 August 1924
d. Bloomington, Indiana, 15 February 1981

As a child, Beversdorf was taught the trombone by his father, a band master. In 1942 he entered the University of Texas where he was a pupil of Eric DeLamarter, Kent Kennan, and Anthony Donato. After graduating in 1945, he continued his studies at the Eastman School, University of Rochester, New York with Bernard Rogers and Howard Hanson. At the Berkshire Center in 1947, he received composition lessons from Arthur Honegger and Aaron Copland. Beversdorf was a trombonist in the Rochester Philharmonic Orchestra (1945–46), Houston Symphony (1946–48), and Pittsburgh Symphony Orchestra (1948–49). After teaching at the University of Houston (1946–48) he was appointed professor of Music at the Indiana University School of Music, Bloomington in 1951, retiring in 1977.

For the stage Beversdorf composed two operas: *The Hooligan* (after Chekhov) (1964–69) and *Metamorphosis* (Kafka; 1968); a ballet, *Threnody: The Funeral of Youth* (1968); and music for a mystery play *Vision of Christ* (1971). In 1958 he composed an oratorio, *The Rock*, based on texts by T.S. Eliot.

His orchestral works include four symphonies: no. 1. (1946); no. 2. (1950); no. 3. for wind and percussion (1954, rev. for orchestra 1958); no. 4. (1958); *Essay on Mass Production* (1946); *Reflections* (1947); Suite for clarinet, cello, and strings (1947); *Mexican Portrait* (1948, rev. 1952); *Concerto Grosso* for oboe and chamber orchestra (1948); Concerto for two pianos (1951); *Ode* (1952); *New Frontiers* (1952); *Serenade* (1956); a Violin Concerto (1959); *Variations (Threnody)* (1963); *Generation With a Torch Overture* (1965); *Divertimento Concertante* (1970); *Murals, Tapestries and Icons* for symphonic band, electric bass, and electric piano (1975); and a Concerto for tuba and wind orchestra (1976).

Among his instrumental compositions are a *Horn* Sonata *"Christmas'* (1942); a Piano Sonata (1944); *Cathedral Music* for brass (1950); *Prelude and Fugue* for wind quintet (1950); two string quartets (1951, 1955); *Three Epitaphs* for brass quintet (1955); a *Tuba* Sonata (1956); *Serenade* for winds and percussion (1957); a *Trumpet* Sonata (1962); a Violin Sonata (1964-65); a Flute Sonata (1965–66); *Divertimento da Camera* for flute, oboe, double bass, and harpsichord (1968); a Cello Sonata (1967-69); a Sonata for viola and harp (1976); and *Corelliana Variations* for two flutes and cello (1980).

BILLINGS, WILLIAM
b. Boston, Massachusetts, 7 October 1746
d. Boston, Massachusetts, 26 September 1800

A tanner by trade, Billings gave up business to devote himself to music. In this way he became probably the first full-time professional musician in America; not surprisingly, he died penniless.

Billings was self-taught and acquired a strikingly personal style quite unrelated to any music he could have heard at the time. The works of his contemporaries in Europe were totally unknown to him. His contempt for old-fashioned musical theory is summed up in his famous dictum: "I don't think myself confined to any Rules for Composition laid down by any that went before me. I think it better for every composer to be his own learner. All the hard dry rules will not enable any person to form an Air without genius. Nature must inspire the thought." Billings's music is the earliest written by an American that is still frequently performed today. It established a choral tradition of church music that has continued to the present. The hymn tune *Chester* survived at least until the end of the nineteenth century, and several anthems have been revived recently with success.

Billings's first collection of pieces, *The New England Psalm Singer, or American Chorister*, was published in Boston in 1770 when he was only 24 years old. It contains psalm tunes, anthems, and "fuging pieces," simple canonical compositions. Other publications were *The Singing Master's Assistant* (1776); *Music in Miniature* (1779); *The Psalm Singer's Amusement* (1781); *The Suffolk Harmony* (1786); and *Continental Harmony* (1794).

His style is charmingly naïve with a simplicity that is particularly effective, as heard in the setting of words from the Song of Solomon, *I Am the Rose of Sharon*. The modal harmony and abrupt modulations make it strangely twentieth-century in character. *Lamentation over Boston* paraphrases Psalm 137 and describes the sorrow at the occupation of the city by British soldiers: "By the rivers of Watertown we sat down and wept,/ Yea, we wept as we remembered Boston."

In answer to criticism that his harmony was too simple, Billings composed a short but highly discordant part-song entitled *Jargon* in which every chord is dissonant. If this piece could be treated seriously, it would be considered nearly 150 years ahead of its time.

Billings was fond of writing long bombastic prefaces to his published works, and just as his music looks forward to the present, his literary style foreshadows the poetry of Walt Whitman. Here is a portion of his grandiose description of a piece of music which he calls a "Fuging Tune": "Now the solemn Bass demands their attention; next the/manly Tenor; now the lofty Counter; now the volatile/Treble. Now here, now there, now here again! O ecstatic!/Rush on, ye sons of Harmony!"

Billings as a man and musician provoked considerable hostility, and his uncompromising nature alienated even his few friends. He died in poverty and was buried in an unmarked grave on Boston Common.

BINDER, ALEXANDER WOLFE
b. New York, New York, 13 January 1895
d. New York, New York, 10 October 1966

Binder received his musical education at the New York College of Music and graduated from Columbia University in 1926. In 1918 he was appointed director of music to the Young Men's Hebrew Association and became director of the New York Free Synagogue in 1923. In 1922 he took up the post of instructor in liturgical music at the Jewish Institute of Religion in New York, becoming a professor in 1937.

Almost every one of Binder's compositions is directly influenced by Jewish sources. His orchestral works include an *Israel Suite*; an overture, *Ha Chalutsin (The Pioneers)* (1931); three *Symphonic Suites*: no. 1, subtitled *Holy Land Impressions* (1933), no. 2 (1934), and no. 3 (1937); a symphonic fantasy, *The Valley of Dry Bones* (1936); an *Overture Fantasy "Theodore Herzl,"* (1935–39); and *Three Palestine Pioneer Pictures* (1936–38). For string orchestra he wrote a *Concertino Concertante* (1938); and *Night Music*. Later works for orchestra are *Rhapsody "King David'* with piano solo (1941–42); *Poem of Freedom*; and *Lament in Memory of the Defenders of the Warsaw Ghetto*. His chamber music includes a Trio (1927); a String Quartet (1935); an Oboe Trio (1936); and *Dybbuk Suite* for clarinet, piano, and string quartet.

Among his many choral pieces are a musical narrative, *Esther, the Queen of Persia*; two choral poems, *Amos on Times Square* and *Israel Reborn*; a children's oratorio, *Judas Maccabeus*; three cantatas:*The Childhood of Samuel* (1928); *Horas Vehoday (Prayer and Dance)* for soloists, chorus, and orchestra; and *The Legend of the Ari* (1962), to a text by George Alexander Kohut, for tenor, bass-baritone, chorus, and orchestra; and an operetta, *In the Land of Promise* (1937). Binder also provided music for a number of Jewish services and composed an oratorio, *Requiem Yiskor*.

Binder was an active collector and arranger of both Israeli and Armenian folksongs, and published two books of Palestinian folksongs, collected on location in 1925. He also published a book on Biblical chant.

BINGHAM, SETH (DANIELS)
b. Bloomfield, New Jersey, 16 April 1882
d. New York, New York, 21 June 1972

Bingham studied the organ with Charles-Marie Widor and Alexandre Guilmant in Paris, where he also received composition lessons from Vincent D'Indy (1906–7). At Yale University he was a pupil of Horatio Parker; later he joined the faculty there (1908–19). He taught organ at Columbia University (1919-54) and at Union Theological College, New York (1954–65), and became renowned throughout the world as a recitalist. For 35 years he was music director of Madison Avenue Presbyterian Church, New York.

Although most of Bingham's compositions are for organ, he wrote an opera, *La Charelzenn* (1917); a number of choral pieces, including a folk cantata, *Wilderness Stone* (1933) and *Canticle of the Sun* (1942); and much church music. For orchestra he composed *Wall Street Fantasy* (1912); *Passacaglia* (1918); *Pioneer American Suite* (1919); *Suite "Memories of France'* (1920); and *The Breton Cadence* (1928). Among a hand-

Seth Bingham.
Courtesy The American Organist.

ful of instrumental pieces are a Suite for winds (1915); a String Quartet (1916); and *Tame Animal Tunes* for 18 instruments (1918).

His concert works for organ are a Concerto (1946); a Concerto for brass, snare drum, and organ (1954); and *Connecticut Suite* for organ and strings (1954). Solo organ pieces include a *Suite* (1923); *Pioneer America* (1926); *Harmonies of Florence* (1929); *Baroque Suite* (1943); *Variations Studies* (1950); and *36 Hymn and Carol Canons in Free Style* (1952).

BINKERD, GORDON WARE
b. Lynch, Nebraska, 22 May 1916
d. Urbana, Illinois, 5 September 2003

After studying the piano, Binkerd became a pupil of Gail Kubik at Wesleyan University, South Dakota (1933–37). He also received composition lessons from Bernard Rogers at the Eastman School of Music, Rochester, New York (1940–41) and Walter Piston and Irving Fine at Harvard University (1946–49). From 1949 to 1971 he was head of theory and composition at the University of Illinois before devoting himself entirely to composition. He received a Guggenheim Fellowship in 1959 and an award from the National Institute of Arts and Letters in 1964.

Binkerd's major works are four symphonies: no. 1 (1955); no. 2, commissioned by the Fromm Foundation in 1957; no. 3 (1959); and no. 4 (1963), written for the St. Louis Symphony Orchestra, later revised and retitled *Movement for Orchestra* (1972). Also for orchestra are *Four Chorale Preludes*; *Sun Singer* (1956); and *A Part of Heaven* with violin solo (1972).

Instrumental music includes two string quartets (1958, 1961); Sonatina for flute and piano (1947); Cello Sonata (1952); Trio for clarinet, violin, and cello (1955); *Three Canzonas* for brass choir (1960); Violin Sonata (1974); *Duo* for flute and oboe; *The Battle* for brass and percussion (1972); String Trio (1979); and *Noble Numbers* for wind ensemble. Among his many piano pieces are four sonatas (1955, 1981, 1982, 1983); *Entertainments* (1960); *Concert Set* (1969); and *Piano Miscellany* (1969).

Four important choral compositions are a setting of *Psalm 93: The Lord is King* for choir and chamber orchestra; *At te levavi* for unaccompanied chorus (1959); *Jesus Weeping*, to words by Henry Vaughan for double chorus, commissioned by the Ford Foundation in 1964; and *On the King's Highway*, to words by James Stephens for children's chorus and chamber orchestra. Other choral pieces include *The Recommendation* (Crashaw; 1962); *A Christmas Caroll* (Herrick; 1964); *Nocturne* for chorus and cello (William Carlos Williams; 1966); *Autumn Flowers* (Jones Very; 1966); *In a*

Gordon Binkerd.
Courtesy The Larry Kanfer Photography Gallery.

Whispering Gallery (Hardy; 1966); *To Electra*, nine choruses setting poems by Herrick (1968-73); *Choral Strands* (1976); *Sung Under the Silver Umbrella* for voices and piano (1977); *Requiem for Soldiers Lost in Ocean Transports* (Herman Melville; 1983-84); and *Dakota Day* (Tennyson) for mixed voices, flute, oboe, clarinet, and harp (1985). For male voices he composed *A Scotch Mist* (Burns) (1976) and *Houses at Dusk* (1984).

Binkerd's vocal music includes a song cycle *Shut Out That Moon* (Hardy; 1966); *The Fair Morning* (Jones Very) (1969); *Three Songs* (Herrick) for mezzo-soprano and string quartet (1970); *Portrait Interieur* (Rilke) for mezzo-soprano, violin, and cello (1972); *Four Songs for High Soprano* (1976); *Secret-Love* (Dryden) for mezzo-soprano, cello, and harp (1977); *Heart Songs* (Burns) for tenor and piano (1980); and *Secret Love* for mezzo-soprano and string quartet.

BIRD, ARTHUR HOMER

b. Cambridge, Massachusetts, 23 July 1856
d. Berlin, Germany, 22 December 1923

In 1875, Bird went to Berlin where he studied piano and organ with Eduard Rohde, August Haupt, and Albert Loschhorn. Although he later visited the United States several times, he made his home in Germany. His debut as an organist took place in Berlin in 1876. In 1883 he met Liszt in Weimar and became acquainted with most of the leading musicians in Europe at the time. For many years he acted as the Berlin music correspondent for various American journals.

Bird was the first American composer to write a ballet, *Folk Festival*, composed in 1886 and premiered in Berlin in the following year. A second ballet, *Rubezahl*, in two acts, was completed in 1888, revised in 1891, and produced in that year. His third stage work, a comic opera in three acts entitled *Daphne* or *The Pipes of Arcadia*, received its first performance in New York in December 1897.

For orchestra he composed three *Little Suites* (no. 1, 1883-84; no. 2, 1884-85; no. 3, 1890); a *Pastorale Concert Overture in D* (1884); *A Carnival Scene* (1884); *Symphony in A* (1885), first performed in 1886 in Berlin under the composer's direction; *Introduction and Fugue in D minor* for organ and orchestra (1886, rev. 1888); *Two Episodes* (1887-88); *Two Poems* (1888); and *Symphonic Suite in E-flat* (c.1908).

Among his early compositions are two pieces for string orchestra, Suite in E (1882) and a Serenade (1882), Towards the end of his short composing career he wrote two notable works for wind ensemble, the first for this medium by an American composer: Suite in D (1889), and a Serenade (1898), which was awarded the Paderewski Prize in 1901. In addition Bird composed many pieces for piano duet, piano solo, and organ, and a number of vocal items, including *Wanderlieder* (*Hiking Songs*) for men's chorus and piano (1891).

BLACKWOOD, EASLEY

b. Indianapolis, Indiana, 21 April 1933

Blackwood studied the piano at an early age. In 1948 he attended the composition classes at Tanglewood, Massachusetts, and in the following year studied there with Olivier Messiaen. His other teachers in America were Bernhard Heiden and Paul Hindemith (1950-54). For three years (1954-57) he studied in Paris with Nadia Boulanger. From 1958 to his retirement in 1997 he was on the faculty of the University of Chicago. A brilliant pianist, Blackwood has traveled widely, giving solo recitals and concerts with violinist Esther Glazer, helping to promote contemporary American music in particular.

Blackwood completed his Symphony no. 1 in Paris in December 1955; it was first performed three days before Blackwood's 25th birthday by the Boston Symphony Orchestra under Richard Burgin. Symphony no. 2 (1960) was commissioned by G. Schirmer Inc., the music publishing house, to mark the 100th anniversary of the firm's founding. It was premiered in February 1961 by the Cleveland Orchestra, directed by George Szell. Symphony no. 3 was performed by the Chicago Symphony Orchestra under Jean Martinon in 1963. *Symphonic Fantasy* for orchestra was composed in 1965 for the Indianapolis Symphony Orchestra. Symphony no. 4, commissioned to celebrate the Illinois Sesquicentennial in 1968, was first performed by the Chicago Symphony Orchestra under Georg Solti on 22 November 1978. Symphony no. 5 was completed in 1990 and Symphony no. 6 dates from 1995.

Blackwood has composed concertos for clarinet (1963); oboe and strings (1966); violin (1967); flute and strings (1968); and piano (1970). His String Quartet no. 1, written in Paris in 1957, was performed in that year at Tanglewood. String Quartet no. 2 (1959) seems to recall consciously the chamber music of Beethoven in its similar textures and scoring. A Third Quartet dates from 1998. Other instrumental works include a *Viola Sonata* (1953); a *Chamber Symphony* for 14 instruments (1955); Concertino for flute, oboe, and string trio (1959); *Fantasy* for cello and piano (1960); two violin sonatas (1960, 1973); *Pastorale and Variations* for wind quintet (1961); Sonata for flute and harpsichord (1962); *Fantasy* for flute, clarinet, and piano (1965); a Piano Trio (1967); a Clarinet Sonata (1994); and a Sonatina for piccolo clarinet (1994). For synthesizer he has composed *12 Microtonal Etudes* (1982).

Un Voyage à Cythère, a setting of Baudelaire for soprano and ten instruments, was performed in January 1967 as part of the 75th anniversary celebrations of the University of Chicago. *Four Letter Scenes* from "Gulliver's Last Voyage," for mezzo-soprano, baritone, and tape, dates from 1972.

BLITZSTEIN, MARC
b. *Philadelphia, Pennylvania, 2 March 1905*
d. *Fort-de-France, Martinique, 22 January 1964*

Blitzstein received his musical education at the University of Pennsylvania, Philadelphia (1921–23) and at the Curtis Institute in Philadelphia (1924–26), where he was a composition pupil of Rosario Scalero. He also studied piano with Alexander Siloti in New York. In 1926 he went to Europe and worked with Nadia Boulanger in Paris. Later he attended the Akademie der Kunste in Berlin where he received lessons from Arnold Schoenberg. On his return to the United States he became a solo pianist, lecturer, and playwright, in addition to devoting much time to composition. He taught for a while at the New School for Social Research in New York City. In the Second World War he served with the U. S. Army in Britain.

Marc Blitzstein with Leonard Bernstein (at piano) in Bernstein's apartment, March 1946.
From the Collections of the Library of Congress.

With Aaron Copland, Lehman Engel, and Virgil Thomson, he was a founder of the Arrow Music Press in 1937. He won several awards, including a Guggenheim Fellowship in 1940 and a National Institute of Arts and Letters Award in 1946.

Blitzstein had a particular gift for writing for the stage, and his principal works are all theater pieces. The first of these, an opera-farce in one act, *Triple Sec*, was performed in Philadelphia in 1928. There followed a one-act opera-ballet, *Parabola and Circula* (1929); a ballet *Cain* (1930); and *The Harpies*, a one-act opera commissioned by the League of Composers. It was completed in 1931 but had to wait until May 1953 for its premiere at the Manhattan School of Music in New York.

In 1937 Blitzstein wrote his best-known work, the one-act opera *The Cradle Will Rock*. It was staged in New York in June 1937 with the composer directing from the piano. The score was arranged for a small orchestra and performed in this version in New York by Leonard Bernstein in 1947, in defiance of attempts to prevent this left-wing satire from opening to the public. It was influenced by Brecht and Weill's *Threepenny Opera* with dialogue, songs, set numbers, and background music. His adaptation of *Threepenny Opera* enjoyed a six-year run after opening off-Broadway in 1954. As with all his operas, the composer wrote his own libretto so as to express his political views directly through music of "social significance." The plot concerns a wicked capitalist, Mister Mister, and his unscrupulous activities in Steeltown, U.S.A. It was revived in New York in 1960 and again in 1964.

In 1937 Blitzstein also composed a short opera for radio, *I've Got a Tune*, an allegory about a composer that is clearly autobiographical in character. His next opera, or "play in music" as he described it, *No For an Answer*, was written in 1941. The tragic story again has satirical overtones depicting corruption in New York. A ballet for Jerome Robbins, *The Guests*, was completed in 1948.

In 1949 he was commissioned by the Koussevitzky Foundation to composer an opera. He chose Lillian Hellman's play *The Little Foxes* as the basis for *Regina*. It was produced in New York in October 1949 with 56 performances, and the New York City Opera successfully revived it in April 1953. The corruption of capitalism is here confined to a family. Set in the Deep South, the opera makes use of jazz idioms.

Blitzstein wrote three other music dramas: *Goloopchik* (1943, unfinished); *Reuben, Reuben* (1953); and *Juno* (1959), derived from Sean O'Casey's play *Juno and the Paycock*. A one-act opera, *Idiot's First*, to a libretto based on a story by Bernard Malamud, was unfinished at the time of the composer's death. It was completed by Leonard Lehman and performed at Indiana University in March 1976. Two other stage projects remain unfinished: a one-act opera, *The Magic Barrel*, also based on a Malamud story; and another opera on a political subject, *Sacco and Vanzetti*, commissioned by the Ford Foundation for production at the Metropolitan Opera in New York. Only two of its three acts were completed.

Among Blitzstein's other works are several early orchestral pieces, which he later withdrew; *Jigg-Saw* (1927), a ballet suite; *Romantic Piece* (1930); a Piano Concerto (1931); *Variations* (1934); and a symphonic poem, *Freedom Morning*, composed in London and performed there in 1943. For choir and orchestra he wrote an oratorio, *The Condemned* (1930); *The Airborne* (1943–44), a ballad symphony for narrator, tenor, baritone, men's chorus, and orchestra; and a cantata, *This is the Garden* (1957).

Blitzstein provided incidental music for a number of plays: Orson Welles' production of *Julius Caesar* (1937); *Danton's Death* (Georg Buchner); *Androcles and the Lion* (G. B. Shaw; 1938); *Another Part of the Forest* (Lillian Hellman; 1946); *King Lear* (1951); A *Midsummer Night's Dream* (1958); *The Winter's Tale* (1958); and *Toys in the Attic.*. His film scores include *Hands* (1927); *Surf and Seaweed* (1931); *Chesapeake Bay Retriever* (1936); *The Spanish Earth* (with Virgil Thomson; 1937); *Valley Town* (1940); *Native Land* (1941); and *Night Shift* (1942).

Among his early instrumental music are a Piano Sonata (1927); *Percussion Music* for piano (1929); a String Quartet (1930); and a Serenade for string quartet (1932). He wrote many songs to texts by Walt Whitman, e. e. cummings, and other American writers, as well as a solo cantata, *Gods*, for mezzo-soprano, cello, and string orchestra dating from 1926.

Blitzstein died from a brain injury resulting from a brawl after an argument in a bar.

BLOCH, ERNEST
b. Geneva, Switzerland, 24 July 1880
d. Portland, Oregon, 15 July 1959

Bloch studied with Emile Jaques-Dalcroze in Geneva and received violin lessons from Louis Rey. At the age of 16 he was a pupil of Eugène Ysaÿe at the Brussels Conservatory. In 1900 he went to Frankfurt, where he studied composition with Iwan Knorr and later with Ludwig Thuille in Munich. After a visit to Paris he returned to Geneva in 1904, initially to teach, but soon he entered the family clock-making business, writing music only in his spare time. After a successful performance of his opera *Macbeth* in Paris in 1910, he returned, at the age of 30, to music. In 1911 he became a professor of composition at the Geneva Conservatory.

In 1916 he toured America as conductor to the dancer Maud Allan. He settled in New York City in the following year where he taught at the Mannes School of Music. He became a naturalized citizen in 1926. From 1920 to 1925 he was director of the Cleveland Institute of Music and from 1925 to 1930 director of the San Francisco Conservatory. A generous patron allowed Bloch to devote ten years solely to composing, and in 1930 he went to Switzerland, returning to America in 1939 shortly before the outbreak of the Second World War. From 1939 to 1952 he taught at the University of California, Berkeley. His influence as a teacher was considerable, and a list of his principal pupils appears in the Appendix.

The prime influence upon the music of Ernest Bloch were the Jewish faith and Hebrew tradition. More than half of his compositions derive their inspiration from religious belief. The production of his opera *Macbeth* at the Opera Comique in Paris in November 1910 persuaded the composer to concentrate exclusively on music. A second opera, *Jezebel*, begun in 1918, remained unfinished.

His earliest orchestral works were all performed in Geneva: a symphonic poem, *Viver et Aimer* (1900); Symphony in C # minor (1901); and a symphonic poem, *Hiver-Printemps* (1905). *Trois Poèmes Juifs* for orchestra, composed in 1913, were not heard until 1917 in Boston. *Schelomo, Hebraic Rhapsody* for cello was inspired by a large statue of Solomon, which the composer had seen in Switzerland. Bloch's best-known work, it was composed in Geneva in 1916 and first performed in New York in May 1917. There followed *In the Night*, a nocturne for orchestra (1923), and *Poems of the Sea* (1923). Concerto Grosso no. 1 for string orchestra and piano was written as a model of neo-classical form for his pupils at the Cleveland Institute of Music. Completed in 1925, it was presented at the Institute that year under the direction of the composer.

In 1927 the magazine *Musical America* offered a prize of $3,000 for an American symphonic work. The panel of judges, five conductors (Stokowski, Koussevitzky, Walter Damrosch, Frederick Stock, and Alfred Herz), selected Bloch's epic rhapsody *America* as the winning entry. It was performed simultaneously on 21 December 1928 in Philadelphia, Boston, New York, Chicago, and San Francisco. The three movements seek to portray life in America from 1620 to 1926 in musical terms. The work is dedicated "to the memory of Abraham Lincoln and Walt Whitman whose vision has upheld its inspiration." It is ironic that a resident of the United States for only ten years should have won such a competition. Although the thematic material has its origin in national songs such as "Old Folks at Home," "Hail, Columbia," "John Brown's Body," "Dixie," and even "Pop Goes the Weasel," the musical language is derived from the European Romantic tradition. In spite of the composer's sincerity toward the subject, the result is little more than a pastiche of folk songs in sophisticated dress that can be heard today only as a historical curiosity.

Bloch's next work, a symphonic poem, *Helvetia*, composed in 1928 and performed in Rome in 1933, is a tribute to the land of his birth, to which he returned in 1930. *Voice in the Wilderness* for cello and orchestra (1936) is closely related to *Schelomo* in character. It was first heard in Los Angeles in 1937. Two other works composed in Switzerland received their premieres in the United States. The symphonic poem *Evocations* (1937) was performed in San Francisco in 1938, and Szigeti was the soloist in the Violin Concerto presented in Cleveland in the same year.

On his return to America, Bloch composed *Suite Symphonique* (1944); *Concerto Symphonique* for piano and orchestra (1950); Concertino for flute, viola, and strings (1950); *In Memoriam* (1952); and *Suite Hébraique* for viola and orchestra (1953). In April 1953 the BBC in London performed *Sinfonia Breve* and the Second Concerto *Grosso* for string orchestra. Originally the two works were designed to be played as a pair, but they were subsequently separated, and the Second Concerto Grosso won the New York Music Critics' Circle Award in 1954. Bloch's last orchestral

works were Symphony for trombone and orchestra (1953–54); Symphony in E-Flat (1954–55), also first performed in London; and *Proclamation* for trumpet and orchestra (1955).

Bloch's early vocal music includes *Poèmes d'Automne* for mezzo-soprano and orchestra (1906); *Prelude and Two Psalms* (nos. 114 and 137) for soprano and orchestra (1912–14); *Israel Symphony* for two sopranos, two contraltos, bass, and orchestra (1912-16); and *Psalm 22* for baritone and orchestra (1914), performed at the I.S.C.M. Festival in Prague in 1924. His major choral work is the *Sacred Service: Avodath Hakodesh* for baritone (cantor), chorus, and orchestra. This setting of the Morning Service was completed in 1933 and first performed in Turin in January 1934.

Bloch's chamber music occupies an important place among his works. The five string quartets deserve a significant position in the twentieth century alongside those of Bartók and Shostakovich. The Quartet no. 1 in B minor was performed by the Flonzaley Quartet in New York in 1916. Quartet no. 2 (1946) won the New York Music Critics' Circle Award in 1947. It was performed in that year at the I.S.C.M. Festival in Copenhagen. Quartet no. 3 (1951), dedicated to the Griller Quartet, was premiered by them in New York in 1953 and also won the New York Music Critics' Circle Award. In 1953 he composed the Quartet no. 4. Quartet no. 5, completed in 1956, makes reference to the 12-tone method but remains tonal throughout.

Quintet no. 1 (1923) established Bloch's reputation outside the United States. At certain points within this piece he used quarter tones as modal inflections. It was performed at the I.S.C.M. Festival in Siena in 1928. A Second Quintet was composed in 1957. The two violin sonatas—no. 1 (1920), and no. 2, *Poème Mystique* in one movement (1924)—are among his finest music, although the suite *Baal Shem* (1923), also for violin and piano, is perhaps better known and more widely played. Bloch's other instrumental works include a Suite for viola and piano which won the Coolidge Prize in 1919; *Three Nocturnes* for piano trio (1924); two suites for string quartet (1925); and three suites for solo cello (1958).

Among his music for piano is a Sonata (1935); performed at the I.S.C.M. Festival in San Francisco in 1942; *Enfantines* (1923); and *Five Sketches in Sepia.*

BOATWRIGHT, HOWARD LEAKE, JR.

b. Newport News, Virginia, 16 March 1918
d. Syracuse, New York, 20 February 1999

As a child Boatwright studied violin with Israel Feldman in Norfolk, Virginia, making his solo concert debut at the age of 17. At Yale University (1945-48), Boatwright was a pupil of Paul Hindemith. He taught violin at the University of Texas, Austin (1943–45) and theory at Yale (1948–64). From 1952 to 1960 he was conductor of the Yale University Orchestra. He was also music director at St. Thomas' Church, New Haven, Connecticut (1949–64). In 1964 he was appointed Dean of the School of Music at Syracuse University. He was active as a violinist and conductor and gave many concerts in America and Europe with his wife, the soprano Helen Boatwright.

For orchestra Boatwright wrote *A Song for St. Cecilia's Day* for large string ensemble (1948); *Variations* for small orchestra (1949); *Movement* (1971); and a Symphony (1976). Among his instrumental music are two string quartets (1947, 1974); a Trio for two violins and viola (1948); *Serenade* for two strings and two winds (1952); and a Clarinet Quartet (1958), winner of the 1962 award of the Society for the Publication of American Music and his best-known work. In 1977 he completed a virtuoso cycle for solo violin entitled *Twelve Pieces*. A Clarinet Sonata dates from 1983. His last instrumental piece was an incomplete Piano Sonata (1993/95).

Boatwright composed much choral music including *The Women of Trachis* for female voices and chamber orchestra, a setting of Sophocles in a translation by Ezra Pound (1955); Mass in C for chorus and organ (1958); *The Passion According to St. Matthew* for soloists, chorus, and organ (1962); *Canticle of the Sun* (St. Francis of Assisi) for soprano, chorus, and orchestra (1963); *Music for Temple Service* for cantor, chorus, and organ (1964); *The Ship of Death* (D.H. Lawrence) for vocal quartet and string quartet (1966); *A Song for St. Cecilia's Day* for soprano, chorus, and orchestra (1981); and *Magnifical and Nunc Dimittis* for chorus and organ (1996).

For solo voice he wrote *The False Knight upon the Road* for baritone and orchestra (1961); *Lament of Mary Stuart* for soprano and continuo (1968); *Six Prayers of Kierkegaard*, a cycle for soprano and piano (1978); *Prologue, Narrative and Lament* (Whitman) for tenor and string quartet (1987); and *Five Poems of Sylvia Plath* for soprano and piano (1993).

An authority on Indian music, Boatwright was a Fulbright lecturer in India from 1956 to 1960. From this experience he wrote two valuable books: *A Handbook on Staff Notation for Indian Music* and *Indian Classical Music and the Western Listener*, both published in Bombay in 1960. He was also the author of a widely used text book, *Introduction to the Theory of Music* (1956), and editor of Charles Ives's *Essays Before a Sonata and Other Writings* (1962).

BOLCOM, WILLIAM (ELDEN)
b. Seattle, Washington, 26 May 1938:

After graduating from the University of Washington, Seattle, in 1958, where he had been a pupil of George McKay and John Verrall, Bolcom attended Mills College, Oakland, California (1958–59, 1961) where he studied with Darius Milhaud. From 1959 to 1961 on a French Government scholarship, he was at the Paris Conservatory, numbering Milhaud, Jean Rivier, and Olivier Messiaen among his teachers. From 1961 to 1964 he was a pupil of Leland Smith at Stanford University.

After teaching at the University of Washington (1965–66), he joined the music faculty at Queens College, New York (1966–68). In 1973 he began teaching at the University of Michigan, Ann Arbor, becoming associate professor in 1977, professor in 1983, and chairman of the music department from 1994. He has served as Composer-in-Residence with Yale University Drama School (1968–70), New York University (1969), Detroit Symphony Orchestra (1987-88), Ithaca College (1990–91), and New York Philharmonic Orchestra (1993).

Attendance at classes held by Pierre Boulez at Darmstadt, Germany in 1960 led Balcom to adopt interval-series techniques in his early works. With a one-act "pop" opera, *Dynamite Tonite*, performed off-Broadway in 1963, his music broadened in scope to take in American idioms with a gradual trend towards a more diatonic language.

At the core of his orchestral works are seven symphonies: no. 1, a student work composed when he was nineteen, at the suggestion of his teacher Milhaud and performed at the Aspen Festival in 1957; no. 2 (*Oracles*) written in 1964 and later withdrawn for revision; no. 3 (*Symphony for Chamber Orchestra*), commissioned in 1979 by the St. Paul's Chamber Orchestra; no. 4 (1986) in two movements, the second of which is a setting for soprano of a poem *The Rose* by Theodore Roethke; no. 5, a Philadelphia Orchestra commission (1990); no. 6, performed in Washington, D.C., in 1998; and no. 7, completed in 2002.

Bolcom's other orchestral works include several pieces for solo instruments: *Concertante* for three instruments and orchestra (1961); *Fives* for solo violin, piano, and three string orchestras (1965–66); *Concerto-Serenade* for violin and strings (1966); a Piano Concerto (1976) to mark the American Bicentennial; *Humoresk* for organ and orchestra (1979); Violin Concerto *in D* (1983); *Fantasia Concertante* for viola, cello, and orchestra, performed by the Vienna Philharmonic Orchestra at the Salzburg Festival in 1985; *Spring Concertino* for oboe and chamber orchestra (1986–87);

William Bolcom.
Photo: Bach Brothers, courtesy ICM Artists/the composer.

Clarinet Concerto, written in 1990 for Stanley Drucker; *Lyric Concerto* for flute, commissioned by James Galway (1993); and *GAEA*, a concerto for two pianists, left hands only, written for Gary Graffman and Leon Fleisher in 1995.

Also for orchestra are *Commedia* for almost eighteenth-century orchestra (1966); *Summer Divertimento* (1973); *Ragomania* (1982); *Seattle Slew*, a dance suite of three movements (1985–86); *Fanfare: Converging on a Mountain* (1989); *MC – MXC Tanglewood* (1990); *Gala Variations* (1996); *Classic Action Samba* (1997); *Three Delagado Palacios Dances* (1995); and *Fanfare for a New President* (1997).

For the band repertory he has provided *Broadside* (1981); *Liberty Enlightening the World* (1985); and *Concert Suite* for saxophone and band (1999).

Among his instrumental compositions are ten string quartets, the first seven of which (1950–61) have been withdrawn; the surviving three date from 1965, 1972, and 1988. Other chamber music includes four violin sonatas (1956, rev. 1984; 1978); *Sonata Stromba*, 1992; 1995); *Decalage* for cello and piano (1961–62); *Octet* (1962); and four *Sessions*: *no. 1* for flute, oboe, English horn, bassoon, trombone, violin, cello, and percussion (1965); *no. 2* for violin and viola (1966); *no. 3*

for E-flat clarinet, violin, cello, piano, and percussion (1967); and *no. 4* for clarinet, two violas, cello, trombone, harp, piano, percussion, and tape (1967).

There followed *Black Host* for organ, percussion, and tape (1967); *Praeludium* for organ and vibraphone (1969); *Dark Music* for timpani and cello (1969–70); *Frescoes* (*War in Heaven* and *The Caves of Orcus*) for two pianos (doubling harmonium and harpsichord) (1971); *Whisper Moon* for flute, clarinet, violin, cello, and piano (1971); *Duo Fantasy* for violin and piano (1973); two piano quartets (1976, 1996); Brass Quintet (1980); *Orpheus Serenade* for piano and strings (1984); *Five Fold Five* for wind quintet and piano (1987); Cello Sonata, composed in 1989 for Yo-Yo Ma; Trio for clarinet, violin, and piano (1994); Suite no. 1. for solo cello (1994–95); *Trez Piezas Lindas* for flute and guitar (1995); *Spring Trio* for violin, cello, and piano (1996); and Piano Quintet (2002).

Latter stage works by Bolcom include an actors' opera, *Greatshot* (1967–69) with libretto by Arnold Weinstein; *Theatre of the Absurd* for actor and chamber group (1970); a music theater piece, *Casino Paradise* (1986–90); and two operas: *McTeague*, based on a book by Frank Norris, commissioned to celebrate the 500th anniversary of the discovery of America, premiered in Chicago in 1992; and *A View From the Bridge*, based on the play by Arthur Miller, also first performed in Chicago in 1999. Currently he is writing his third opera, an adaptation of Robert Altman's film *The Wedding*, with libretto by Altman and Arnold Weinstein, scheduled for the 2004–05 season. He has also plans for an opera to be staged in 2009.

Bolcom's masterpiece is the three-hour complete setting of the 46 poems that constitute William Blake's *Songs of Innocence and Experience*. This massive project, involving nine solo voices, three choirs, children's chorus, and large orchestra, occupied the composer from 1956 to 1981. It was first performed in Stuttgart, Germany on 8 January 1984.

An important part of his career has been devoted to concerts he has given accompanying his wife the mezzo-soprano Joan Morris, whom he married in 1975. Their recitals of American songs of the 19th and 20th century have produced over 20 recorded albums. Vocal music has naturally formed a significant part of his compositional output. The song cycle *Open House* (1975) sets poems by Theodore Roethke for tenor and chamber orchestra. *Six Cabaret Songs* to texts by Arnold Weinstein (1978) has been followed by *Six New Cabaret Songs* (1983) and *Cabaret Songs, Volumes 3 & 4* (1997). Other vocal works include *Three Irish Songs* (Thomas Moore) for mezzo-soprano (or baritone) and ensemble (1978); *Three Donald Hall Songs* (1979); a cycle, *I Will Breathe a Mountain*, written in 1990 for

Marilyn Horne; *Let Evening Come*, a cycle in memory of Tatiana Troyanos (1994); *Turbulence: A Romance* for soprano, baritone, and piano (1996); *Briefly It Enters* (Jane Kenyon) a cycle for soprano and piano (1996); *The Whitman Triptych* for mezzo-soprano and orchestra (1997); *The Miracle*, nine madrigals for medium voice, wind quintet, and two pianos (1999); *The Digital Wonder Watch* for voice and piano (1999); *From the Diary of Sally Heming* (2000); and the *Naumburg Cycle* (2001).

As a pianist Bolcom played a significant part in the revival of the music of Scott Joplin in the 1960s and 1970s, writing several rags, most notably the popular *The Graceful Ghost* (1970). His other piano solos include *Romantic Pieces* (1959); *12 Etudes* (1959–66); *Fantasy Sonata* (1960–62); *Garden of Eden* (suite; 1968); *Field of Flowers* (1978); *12 New Etudes*, which won the Pulitzer Prize in 1988; *9 Bagatelles* (1996); *Bird Spirits* (1999–2000); *11.59* (2000); and *Collusions* (2000). For two pianos he has written *Interlude* (1963) and a Sonata (1993). For organ he has composed *Chorale Prelude on Abide With Me* (1970); *Hydraulis* (1971); *Mysteries* (1976); *Gospel Preludes: 4 volumes* (1979–84); and *Borborygm* (2001).

As an author Bolcom has written a book on popular piano music, *Reminiscing with Sissle and Blake* (with Robert Kimbal; 1973, reissued 1999), and edited the writings of George Rochberg, *The Aesthetics of Survival: A Composer' View of Twentieth Century Music* (1984).

Franz Bornschein.
Photo: Bachrach, courtesy Peabody Conservatory/John Hopkins University.

BORNSCHEIN, FRANZ (CARL)

b. Baltimore, Maryland, 10 February 1879
d. Baltimore, Maryland, 8 June 1948

A native of Baltimore, where he remained his entire life, Bornschein first studied violin privately with Lawrence Rosenberger and Julius Zech. He then enrolled at the Peabody Conservatory, studying violin with Joan Van Hulsteyn and theory with Phillip Kahmer and Otis Boise, graduating in 1902. Bornschein began teaching at the Peabody Prepatory School in 1905, the same year he also was made a local reporter for *Musical America*; he subsequently reviewed local musical events for the *Baltimore Sun* from 1910–13. In 1919, he joined Peabody Conservatory's faculty as a violin, conducting, and composition teacher, a position he held until his death.

Among his large output of orchestral works are two violin concertos and several symphonic poems, including *The Sea God's Daughter* (1924, rev. 1940); *Southern Nights* (1935); *Leif Ericson* (1935); *The Mission Road* (1937); *Ode to the Brave* (1944); and *The Earth Sings* (1944); a symphonic ballad, *Old Louisiana* (1920); and the orchestral suites *The Phantom Canoe* (1920) and *Cape Cod Impressions* (1935). Other shorter pieces are *Low Tide*; *Midsummer on South Mountain*; *Gremlins* (a burlesque overture); *Palestinian Lament*; *Persian Festivals* (1922); *Moon Over Taos* (1939); *Symphonic Fantasy*; and *Theirs Be the Glory*.

He was awarded many prizes for choral works, of which the most important are *The Djinns* (1913); the cantata *Onawa* (1916); *The Sea* (1923); *Vision of Sir Launfal* (1928); *The Minute Man* (1930); *The Mystic Trumpeter* (Whitman; 1931); *Tuscan Cypress* (1931); *The Word Made Flesh*; and *The Conqueror Worm*, all for chorus and orchestra.

His operetta *The Willow Pattern Plate* was produced by the Baltimore Civic Opera in 1937. Also for the stage he wrote a children's operetta, *Mother Goose's Goslings* (1918), and a two-act lyric opera, *Song of Songs* (1934). Among his instrumental pieces are a String Quartet (1900) and a Piano Quintet (1904).

BOROWSKI, FELIX

b. Burton-in-Kendal, Westmoreland, England, 10 March 1872

d. Chicago, Illinois, 6 September 1956

Borowski was the son of Polish nobleman who had settled in England. After studying in Cologne he made a name for himself in England as a composer. In 1897 he went to the United States and settled permanently in Chicago, becoming a naturalized citizen. He was equally famous as a composer, violinist, violin teacher, and critic. His first musical post was as professor of violin and composition at the Chicago Musical College from 1897 to 1915, being appointed President of the College in 1915. In 1926 he became Superintendent at the Civic Music Association in Chicago. For many years he was the music editor for several Chicago newspapers, including the *Chicago Sun*. From 1937 until his retirement in 1942 he was professor of musicology at Northwestern University in Evanston, Illinois.

Borowski's large output of orchestral works includes three symphonies (1932, 1933, 1937); *Suite Rococo* for strings (1900); *Two Pieces* for strings (1905); *Elegie Symphonique* (1916); *Peintures* (1917); *Anacreon Overture* (1917); a tone poem, *Le Printemps Passione* (1920); *Fantasy Overture: Youth* (1922); a symphonic

Felix Borowski.
Courtesy James P. Murphy Collection, Georgetown University Library.

poem, *Ecce Homo* (1924); a tone poem, *Semirimis* (1925); and *Requiem for a Child* (1944). One of his last works, *The Mirror*, was composed in 1953 to a commission from the Louisville Orchestra. For solo instruments and orchestra Borowski wrote a Piano Concerto (1913) and a *Rhapsody and Allegro de Concert* for organ and orchestra (1926). He composed one opera, *Fernando del Nonsensico* (1935), and three ballets: *Boudoir* (1918); *Pierrot in Arcady* (1920); and *A Century of the Dance* (1934).

Borowski set Hans Christian Andersen's story *The Little Match Girl* for narrator and orchestra (1945). His chamber music includes three string quartets (1897, 1928, 1944); three organ sonatas; a Violin Sonata subtitled *Russian*; a Piano Sonata; and a number of anthems and songs.

He was the author of a textbook *The Standard Concert Guide* (1932).

BOTTJE, WILL GAY

b. Grand Rapids, Michigan, 30 June 1925

Bottje studied flute and composition at the Juilliard School, New York where he was a pupil of Vittorio Giannini. On graduating in 1947 he was a freelance flutist, conductor, and teacher. In Europe (1952–53) he received composition lessons from Nadia Boulanger in Paris and Henk Badings in Holland. He earned a doctorate at the Eastman School of Music, Rochester, New York (1955), where he studied with Bernard Rogers and Howard Hanson. At the University of Utrecht (1962–63) and in Stockholm (1973) he made a study of electronic music. Bottje taught at the University of Mississippi (1955–57) and Southern Illinois University, Carbondale (1957–81), where he founded the electronic music studio in 1965. Since 1981 he has devoted himself solely to composition.

For the stage he has composed two operas—*Altgeld* to his own text, produced in Carbondale in 1968, and a comedy, *Root !* (1971)—and a musical comedy, *The Village That Voted the Earth Was Flat* (1983–85).

His orchestral works include *The Ballad Singer* (1951); Concerto for flute, trumpet, harp, and strings (1955); Concertino for piccolo and orchestra (1956; arr. for band, 1994); *Rhapsodic Variations* for viola, piano, and strings (1962); *Chiaroscuros* (1975); Tuba Concerto (1977); *Mutations* for small orchestra (1977); Concerto for oboe, bassoon, chamber orchestra, and piano (1981); *Chamber Concerto* for oboe, bassoon, and small orchestra (1981, rev. 1998); *Commentaries* for guitar and chamber orchestra (1983); *Sounds From the West Shore* (1983); Concerto for violin, oboe, and small orchestra (1984); Concerto for two flutes and orchestra (1984); *Full Circle* (1987); *Opener* (1988);

Evolutions for solo wind quintet and orchestra (1988, rev. 1999); Sinfonia for strings (1993); Concerto for horn and small orchestra (1994); *Flavors* (1995); and *Symphony on One Movement* (2000).

Bottje has contributed major works to the band repertory: *Contrasts* (1952); Symphony no. 4. (1956); *Theme and Variations* (1959); Concerto for trumpet, trombone, and band (1959); Sinfonietta (1960); Symphony no. 6. for large brass ensemble, organ, and percussion (1965); *Sinfonia Concertante* for brass quintet and band (1966); *Duo Sonatina* for two euphoniums and wind ensemble (1970); *Symphonic Allegro* for brass ensemble and percussion (1971); *Facets* for piano and band (1975); Concerto for cello and wind ensemble (1975); Concerto for band (1982); and Suite for concert band (2000).

Among his many instrumental pieces are seven string quartets (1959, 1962, 1982 [rev. 1984], 1998, 2001, 2002, 2002); Quintet for flute and strings (1954); two wind quintets (1957, 1984); three cello sonatas (1958 [rev.1994], 1989, 1989); Trumpet Sonata (1959, rev. 1994); *Diversions* for narrator, wind quintet, and piano (1962); Saxophone Quartet (1963, rev. 1994); Sextet for brass, organ, and percussion (1964); *Interplays* for horn, harpsichord, piano, and tape (1970); Concertino for English horn and string quartet (1972, rev. 1992); *Modules* for clarinet and piano (1973); *Dances, Real and Imagined* for guitar and string quartet (1976); Piano Trio (1978, rev. 1998); *Mallets* for xylophone, marimba, and vibraphone (1978); *The Country Wife* for wind quintet (1979, rev. 1996); Guitar Sonata (1980); Symphony for cello and piano (four hands) (1980, rev. 1997); Flute Sonata (1981); two sonatas for oboe and harpsichord (1981); Divertimento for flute, clarinet, violin, viola, and cello (1982); Quintet for clarinet, bassoon, horn, cello, and double bass (1983); Sonata for two cellos (1994; arr. for violin and viola, 1999); String Sextet (1996); Violin Sonata (1996); *Concertato* for piano and wind quintet (2000); Quintet for piano and strings (2001); String Trio (2001); Trio for two violins and viola (2001); Concertino for violin and string quartet (2001); String Quintet (2002); Quintet for clarinet and strings (2002–03); and Viola Sonata no. 2. (2003).

Bottje's choral works include *Credo* for double chorus (1950, rev. 1993); *What is Man?* (Walt Whitman) for narrator, chorus, two pianos, and band (1959); *Wayward Pilgrim* (Emily Dickinson) for soprano, chorus, and chamber orchestra (1961); *The Case is New* for female voices and piano (1963); *Thrush Song* for double chorus and flute (1970); *Cantata for the 53rd Sunday* for soloists and chorus (1974); *Exhortation of the Dawn* for chorus, organ, piano, and brass ensemble (1977); *Diptych* (Rilke) for double chorus and keyboard (1977, rev. 1997); *Songs From the Land Between the Rivers* for chorus and instruments (1980); *Last Minute Message for a Time Capsule* for chorus and keyboard (1990, rev. 1997); *Radiant Musings* for narrator, chorus, and keyboard (1991); and *Sunsets and Star-rise* for chorus and keyboard (2001).

For solo voice he has composed *Patterns* for alto and piano (1953); *In Praise of Music* for soprano and string quartet (1959); *Quests of Odysseus* for tenor and piano (1960, rev. 1994); *In Caverns All Alone*, seven songs for tenor, flute, bassoon, and piano (1977, rev. 1996); and *A Sentence Once Begun* (Christopher Fry) for soprano and string quartet or piano (1982).

Two theater pieces are *From the Winds and the Farthest Spaces* (L. Eiseley) for narrator, dancers, wind quintet, tape, and slides (1977), and *To Charm the Cloudy Crystal* (Eisley) for two narrators, dancer, and chamber ensemble (1983).

In the 1980s Bottje explored alternative tunings, both equal and unequal, with the assistance of a tuneable synthesizer. Among the fifty or so pieces he produced with these experiments are *Saraband and Double* and *Theme and Nine Variations* (15 tones); *Fickle* (16 tones); *Call to Prayer*, *Waltz Chain*, and *Casuals* (17 tones); *Bagatelle* (18 unequal tones); *Sonata* and *Suite* (19 tones); *Kids at Play*, *Finale*, and *Lyric Interlude* (22 tones); *March of the Ghouls* (24 random tones); *Suite* and *31 Variations* (31 tones); and *Thirteen Ways of Looking at a Rainbow* for various alternative tunings.

BOWLES, PAUL (FREDERIC)
b. New York, New York, 30 December 1910
d. Tangiers, Morocco, 18 November 1999

Bowles studied at the University of Virginia and later with Aaron Copland in New York (1930–31) and Virgil Thomson and Nadia Boulanger in Paris (1931). After 1929 he travelled extensively in Spain, South and Central America, and in North Africa, where he made his home for many years. From 1947 until his death he lived in Tangiers. In 1941 he was awarded a Guggenheim Fellowship and in 1959 he received a Rockefeller Foundation Grant to collect on tape Moroccan and Berber folk music, both for the archives of the Library of Congress and for issue on recordings. He received two grants from the National Endowment for the Arts in 1978 and 1980. He joined the staff of the *New York Herald Tribune* in 1942 as a music critic, resigning in 1945. Following the publication of his novel *The Sheltering Sky* in 1949, he devoted most of his varied talents to writing books.

Bowles's important musical works are for the stage. He wrote three operas: *Denmark Vesey* in three acts to a libretto by Charles Henri Ford (1937); *The Wind Remains*, a zarazuela based on a play by Federico Garcia

Lorca (1943); and *Yerma* (1956), also a setting of a Lorca play. His first ballet, *Yankee Clipper*, composed in 1936, was produced by Ballet Caravan in 1938. Other ballets are *The Ballroom Guide* (1937); *Pastorela* (1941); and *Colloque Sentimental*, written in 1944 and produced with sets and costumes by Salvador Dali.

Bowles provided incidental music for many major plays, including *The Glass Menagerie, Summer and Smoke, Sweet Bird of Youth*, and *The Milk Train Doesn't Stop Here Any More* (all by Tennessee Williams); *My Heart's in the Highlands* and *Love's Old Sweet Song* (William Saroyan); *Horse Eats Hat* (Eugene Labiche); *Twelfth Night* (Shakespeare); *Jacobowsky and the Colonel* (Franz Werfel); *Watch on the Rhine* (Lillian Hellman); *Cyrano de Bergerac* (Edmond Rostand); *In the Summer House* (Jane Bowles); and *Twilight Bar* (Arthur Kostler). Bowles also composed 16 film scores, including *Dreams That Money Can Buy* (1948); *The Yellow Cabman* (1950); and two documentaries, *Roots in the Earth* (1940) and *Congo* (1944).

His few orchestral works are for chamber ensemble, including a Suite (1933); *Iquitos* (1933); *Music for a Farce* (1938); *Romantic Suite* (1939); and a Concerto for two pianos, wind, and percussion (1947). He also wrote a Sonata for oboe and clarinet (1930); a Sonata for flute and piano (1932); and *Nocturne* (1935) and a Sonata (1949), both for two pianos.

Vocal music includes *Scènes d'Anabase* for voice, oboe, and piano (1932); *Cantata* for soprano, male quartet, and harmonium (1938); *Three Pastoral Songs* for tenor, piano, and strings (1944); *Blue Mountain Ballads* (Tennessee Williams) for voice and piano (1946); and *A Picnic Cantata* for four female voices, two pianos, and percussion (1954). He composed and published many songs.

In addition to *The Sheltering Sky*, which was issued in an acclaimed film version in 1990, Bowles wrote three collections of short stories—*The Delicate Prey* (1950), *The Time of Friendship* (1967), and *Things Gone and Things Still Here* (1977)—and the novels *Let It Come Down* (1952), *The Spider's House* (1955), and *Up Above the World* (1966), all praised by critics who were often unaware of his musical activities. He has also published a collection of short stories, *A Hundred Camels in the Courtyard* (1962); a book of travel essays, *Their Heads Are Green and Their Hands Are Blue* (1963); and an autobiography, *Without Stopping* (1972). His last literary works were *39 Collected Stories* (1979); *Points in Time* (1982); and *Call at Corazon* (1988). His collected writings on music, *Paul Bowles on Music*, were published in 2003.

His wife, Jane Bowles, whom he married in 1938, was also an author who wrote a fine novel, *Two Serious Ladies* (1943), and a play, *In the Summer House*, produced on Broadway, for which her husband pro-

vided incidental music. She died in Malaga, Spain in 1973.

BRAINE, ROBERT

b. Springfield, Ohio, 27 May 1896
d. New York, New York, 22 August 1940

At the age of seven Braine began to study the violin and entered the Cincinnati College of Music when only 15. After playing in the Cincinnati Symphony Orchestra, he moved to New York City in 1929 where he was appointed pianist and conductor with NBC, a post he retained until his death.

Braine composed four operas: *The Wandering Jew* (1924); *The Eternal Light* (1924); *Virginia* (1926); and *Diane* (1927). His orchestral works include *S.O.S.* (1927); *The Raven* (Poe) for baritone and orchestra (1928); a suite, *The Song of Hiawatha* (1930); a symphonic poem, *The House of Usher* (1931); *Variations on a Theme of Chopin* (1935); and *Choreographic Impressions* (1937).

His *Concerto in Jazz* for violin and orchestra received its premiere in 1930. In addition to a String Quartet in A (1921), he wrote a *Jazz Quartet* (1935); a Suite for violin and piano (1926); a *Barbaric Sonata* for piano; and over 50 songs.

Braine's death was a suicide.

BRANSCOMBE, GENA

b. Picton, Ontario, Canada, 4 November 1881
d. New York, New York, 26 July 1977

Gena Branscombe studied with Felix Borowski and Rudolf Ganz at the Chicago Musical College (1900–03) and with Engelbert Humperdinck in Berlin (1909–10). From 1903 to 1907 she taught piano at the Chicago Musical College and was director of the piano department at Whitman College, Walla Walla, Washington (1907–09). After moving to New York in 1910 she was active in women's art organizations and as a choral conductor until retirement in 1954. She wrote a number of orchestral works, including a *Festival Prelude* (1913); a symphonic suite, *Quebec* (with tenor solo; 1926), based on the music of an unfinished opera, *The Bells of Circumstance*; *Elegie* (1937); and *Rigaudon* and *Wings* (both 1946).

Branscombe's reputation rests on her choral music and over 150 songs. *Pilgrims of Destiny*, a choral drama with a libretto by the composer for soloists, chorus, and orchestra (1919) won a prize in 1928 from the National League of American Pen Women. Other important choral items are *The Dancer of Fjaard* for female voices and orchestra (1926); *The Phantom*

Gena Branscombe.
Courtesy Kathleen Shimeta.

Caravan for men's chorus and orchestra (1927); *Youth and the World* (1932) and *Coventry's Choir* (1944), both for female voices and orchestra; and *A Joyful Litany* for female chorus (1967). In 1973, at the age of 92, she composed *Introit, Prayer Responses and Amen* for the Riverside Church, New York City. As with many of her pieces she wrote both text and music.

Her song cycles *Love in a Life* (Elizabeth Barrett Browning; 1907), *A Lute of Jade* (1913), *The Sun Dial* (1913); and *Songs of the Unafraid* (1919) are still heard in concerts in the United States. Among her chamber works are a Violin Sonata (1920); *Carnival Fantasy* for flute, harp, piano, and strings (1932); two works for horn and piano, *Pacific Sketches* (1956) and *American Suite* (1959); and many pieces for piano solo and for violin and piano for children.

BRANT, HENRY DREYFUS

b. Montreal, Canada, 15 September 1913

Born of American parents, Brant studied at McGill University, Montreal (1926–29), the Institute of Musical Art, New York City (1929–34), and at the Juilliard School (1932–34), where he was a pupil of Rubin Goldmark. He also received private teaching from Wallingford Riegger (1930–31), George Antheil (1934–35), and Aaron Copland. He taught at Columbia University (1945–52) and the Juilliard School (1947–55).

From 1957 to 1980 he was a member of the music faculty of Bennington College. He received Guggenheim Fellowships in 1946 and 1956; in 1955, he was given an award from the National Institute of Arts and Letters. He has also been a member of the editorial board of the American Composers Alliance.

Although in most cases Brant's early works are comparatively orthodox in form, experiments appear in certain pieces. *Angels and Devils*, a concerto for flute and ten-piece flute orchestra (1931, rev. 1947), makes use of tone clusters in the manner of Charles Ives, with bird sounds and other novel effects and dissonant harmony. The composer was only 18 years old when he wrote the work.

The extensive catalog of Brant's orchestral pieces in the 1930s shows a prolific talent: Symphony in B-Flat *"The Thirties"* (1931); *Four Choral Preludes* (1932); *Intrada and Ricercata* (1933); *Galloping Colloquy*, a scherzo ballad (1934); and Symphony in C minor (1937). The influence of jazz and popular music is evident in the *Whoopie Overture in D* (1937); *The Marx Brothers: Three Faithful Portraits* for tin whistle, fife, piccolo, and orchestra (1938); and Concerto for clarinet and jazz orchestra (1939). These were followed by *Good Weather Overture* (1940); *Fantasy and Caprice* for violin and orchestra (1941); Concerto for alto saxophone (1941); *Dedication in Memory of a Great Man* (1945); and *Music for an Imaginary Ballet* (1947).

In 1940 Brant was hired to write scores for documentary films for the United States Government. These included *Capitol Story* (1944); *The Pale Horseman* (1944); *Journey into Medicine* (1946); *Your Community* (1956); *Endowing the Future* (1957); and *United Nations Day* (1959). In addition he composed music for the following feature films: *Valley of Tennessee* (1944); *My Father's House* (1947); *Osmosis* (1948); *The Big Break* (1951); *Ode to a Grecian Urn* (1953); *The Secret Thief* (1956); *Doctor "B'* (1957); *Early Birds* (1961); *Fire in the Cities* (1961); *Jael Levine* (1964); and *Voyage Four* (1964). He also provided arrangements for Benny Goodman and Andre Kostelanetz. In 1947 he composed a cantata, *Spanish Underground*. From the 1947 film score of *My Father's House* he produced an extended work, *The Promised Land*, a symphony for Palestine, performed by the Cincinnati Symphony Orchestra in 1948.

Brant's early chamber music includes the experimental *Variations in Oblique Harmony* (1930), to be played on any four instruments; a Sonata for two pianos (1931); Suite for flute and string quartet (1932); *Five and Two Cents Store Music* for piano and 20 instruments (1932); an Oboe Sonata (1932); *Lyric Piece* for chamber ensemble (1933); a Sonata for hardware and piano (1936); *Lyric Cycle* for soprano, three violas, and piano (1937);

Sonata for viola or cello (1937, rev. 1962); and *Prelude and Fugue* for string octet and winds (1938).

For the stage Brant wrote *Dis Chard*, a two-act burlesque (1932); a one-act opera, *Miss O'Grady* (1938); *Entente Cordiale*, a musical satire in one act (1936); and an opera, *Alisaunde* (1940). His principal successs in this medium was the ballet-play, *The Great American Goof*, to a text by William Saroyan. It was performed in New York in 1940 by Ballet Theatre. That year, Ballet Caravan produced another ballet, *City Portrait*, also in New York.

After 1950 Brant began to experiment with the spacing of instruments to produce directional sound. The exploration of sonorities has been of particular concern to him, resulting in his remarkable use of unusual instrumental combinations. *Millennium I* for eight trumpets, bells, and cymbals (1950) marks the turning point in his style. This and most of his subsequent compositions make use of spatial features now familiar throughout the works of Karlheinz Stockhausen and his followers. Brant, however, made such experiments before his European contemporaries. He followed *Millennium I* with *Origins* (1952), a percussion symphony; *Signs and Alarms* (1953) and *Rural Antiphonies* (1954),

Henry Brant.
Photo: Irene Haupt, courtesy Music Library, State University of New York, Buffalo.

both for chamber ensemble; and *Encephalograms* (1954).

Millenium II (1954) is scored for ten trumpets, ten trombones, eight horns, two tubas, and four percussion instruments with solo soprano. The performers are spaced across the platform, and up to 24 different tempi prevail simultaneously. *Climax*, also composed in 1954, employs six conductors with no co-ordination among them. Here 18 unrelated strands of music coexist. *December* for chorus and instruments, *Ceremony* for spaced choirs, and *Galaxy I and II* for chamber ensemble also date from 1954. *The Grand Universal Circus*, a spatial theater piece, and *On the Nature of Things after Lucretius* for orchestra were completed in 1956.

Atlantis, an antiphonal symphony for narrator, chorus, and band; *The Fire Garden* for voices and instruments; and *Bird with Passenger* for viola d'amore and musical boxes were all composed in 1960. The year 1961 produced *Fire in Cities* for chorus, wind instruments, and percussion; *Violin Concerto with Lights* for violin and five electric switches; and *Barricades* for tenor, soprano saxophone, and ensemble.

Voyage Four (1964), a spatial concert piece, uses 83 instrumentalists and a singer with three conductors. *Hieroglyphics I, II, and III* were composed in 1966. *Consort for True Violins* (1968) employs eight assorted violins especially constructed for the work. *Verticals Ascending* (1967) is conceived for two antiphonal instrumental groups; *Windjammer* (1969) is scored for four mobile players.

Brant continued to employ unusual combinations of voices and instruments. *Spatial Concerto* (*Questions from Genesis*; 1977) is a setting of texts by Patricia Brant for piano and orchestra divided into various groups, with eight sopranos and eight altos. *Orbits* (1979) is scored for soprano, 80 trombones, and organ. *Meteor Farm* (1982) is a multicultural work for expanded orchestra, two choruses, jazz band, gamelan ensemble, African drummers and singers, and South Indian soloists, in which each group retains its own traditional music.

Equally exotic is *Western Springs* (1983), a three-hour aquatic procession through the canals of Amsterdam employing two orchestras, two choirs, four church carillons, three brass bands, and four street organs. In similarly extravagant manner are *Bran(d)t aan de Amstel* (*Burning/Brant on the Amstel*), an environmental piece for 100 flutes, three orchestras, four hurdy-gurdys, three choirs, and four optional carillons (1984); *Desert Forests* (1985) for multiple orchestral groups; and *Northern Lights Over the Twin Cities* (1986) for two choruses, orchestra, jazz band, large wind ensemble, large percussion ensemble, five pianos, bagpipe band, and five solo singers spaced throughout a sports arena in St. Paul, Minnesota.

An expanded version of 1954's *Millennium II*, produced in 1988, makes use of a 35-piece brass orchestra, jazz combo, percussion ensemble, gospel choir, gamelan ensemble, bluegrass group, boys' choir, three pianos, organ, and ten vocal soloists. Brant's energies remained indefatigable with *Flight Over a Global Map* for 100 trumpets (1989); *Rosewood* for 75 guitars (1989); and *Prisons of the Mind*, a spatial symphony for 314 players in eight separated groups with eight conductors, performed in April 1990 by a greatly enlarged Dallas Symphony Orchestra.

The next decade Brant's enthusiasm for creation and experiment continued unabated. In August 1992, Lincoln Center, New York, was the venue for the premiere of *500: Hidden Hemisphere*, an hour-long piece for three separate concert bands and a steel drum ensemble. His project to orchestrate Charles Ives's *Concord Sonata* for piano, begun in 1958, was finally completed in 1994. In October of that same year, a seven-hour "marathon" of 22 of Brant's works were performed at the Cultuurcentrum De Oosterpoort in Groningen, Holland. The range of music stretched from *Angels and Devils* of 1931 to the premiere of *Trajectory*, an acoustic, spatial experience with abstract silent film.

Among his most recent works are *Seventy* for three concert bands (1994); *Dormant Craters* for 16 percussionists (1995); *Ploughshares and Swords* for an orchestra spaced throughout the auditorium of Carnegie Hall, New York (1996); *Festive 80* for 26 brass, 18 winds, and four percussion (1997); and *Crystal Antiphonies* for wind band and orchestra, performed in Hannover, Germany in September 2000.

BRICKEN, CARL ERNEST
b. Shelbyville, Kentucky, 28 December 1898
d. Sweet Briar, Virginia, 25 January 1971

Bricken studied with Rosario Scalero at the Mannes School of Music, New York City, and at Yale University (B.A. 1922) before going to Vienna and the Ecole Normale de Musique in Paris where he became a pupil of Alfred Cortot. From 1925 to 1928 he was a member of the faculty at the Mannes School as a piano teacher, and later taught at the Institute of Musical Art, New York. He was awarded a Pulitzer Prize in 1929 and a Guggenheim Fellowship in 1930. In 1931 he founded the department of music at the University of Chicago, becoming its chairman. In 1938 he was appointed professor of music at the University of Wisconsin. He moved to Seattle in 1944 to become musical director of the Seattle Symphony Orchestra, a post he held until 1948. From 1954 to 1963 he was Resident Professor at Sweet Briar College, Sweet Briar, Virginia. Thereafter he abandoned composition and devoted himself to painting.

Bricken's orchestral works include three symphonies; a Suite (1930); *The Prairie Years*; *Daniel Boone Legend*; and *Five Etchings*. He also provided incidental music for Euripides' *Trojan Women* and the film score for *The Making of the River*. His most important contribution was in the field of chamber music. He composed a Piano Quintet *in D minor* (1930); a String Quartet in C minor (1925); two violin sonatas; a Cello Sonata; and a number of songs.

Bricken was also the author of a book entitled *Some Analytical Approaches to Musical Criticism*.

Carl Bricken in rehearsal.
Photo: Seattle Post-Intelligencer
Collection, Museum of History &
Industry, Seattle, WA.

BRISTOW, GEORGE F(REDERICK)
b. Brooklyn, New York, 19 December 1825
d. New York, New York, 13 December 1898

Bristow was the son of as English musician, William Richard Bristow (1803–67), who had come to the United States in 1824. George studied at the Royal Academy of Music in London under Sir George Macfarren. He became a violinist and played in the New York Philharmonic Society from 1842, the year of its foundation, until 1879. From 1852 until his death he was a music teacher in New York City. He was also conductor of the New York Harmonic Society (1851–63).

Like William Henry Fry, Bristow devoted much of his energy to promoting concerts of American music and himself wrote pieces that reflect the American spirit. He composed the second American grand opera, *Rip Van Winkle*, based on the story by Washington Irving. It was produced at Niblo's Gardens in New York on 27 September 1855 where it ran for four weeks. It was revived with great success in 1870.

Bristow composed at least six symphonies. Louis Antoine Jullien, the famous French conductor, performed Bristow's *Jullien Symphony* in D minor (c. 1853), the *Arcadian Symphony*, and Symphony in F# minor in his New York season of 1855-56. Among Bristow's other orchestral works are a *Concert Overture* (1847); *Overture: Columbus* (1866); an overture to *The Winter's Tale* (1856); and *The Jibbenainosay Overture* (1889). He also composed two string quartets (1849). His choral works include two oratorios, *Praise to God* (1861) and *Daniel* (1867); four cantatas: *Eleutheria* (1849), *The Pioneer* or *Westward Ho!* (1874), *The Great Republic* (1879), and *Niagara* (1893); and a Mass in C (1885).

Bristow died before completing his second opera, *King of the Mountains*.

BRITAIN, RADIE
b. Amarillo, Texas, 17 March 1899
d. Palm Springs, California, 23 May 1994

Britain studied at Clarendon College, Texas, and at the American Conservatory in Chicago (1919–21) where she was a pupil of Henriot Levy (piano) and Von Dusen (organ). After teaching at Clarendon College (1921–23), she went to Paris where she studied with Marcel Dupré; in Munich she was a pupil of Albert Noelte for composition. She also received lessons from Godowsky (piano) and Pietro Yon (organ). On her return to the United States she taught at the Girvin Institute of Music, Chicago (1930–34) and the Chicago Conservatory (1934–39). From 1940 to 1960 she lived in Hollywood, where she taught piano and composition. She continued to compose after retirement.

For orchestra, Britain wrote *Epic Poem* (1927); *Nirvana* (1927); *Symphonic Intermezzo* (1927); *Heroic Poem* (1928), commemorating Lindburgh's flight; *Prelude to a Drama* (1928); *Overture: Pygmalion* (1930); *Rhapsodie Phantasie* for piano and orchestra (1931); *Saturnale* (1933); *Nocturne* (1934); *Light* (1935), a tribute to Edison; *Southern Symphony* (1936–37); *Drouth* (1939); *Canyon* (1939); *Ontonagon Sketches* (1939); *Prison* (1940); *Suite for Strings* (1940); *Serenada del Coronado* (1940); *Franciscan Sketches* (1941); *Fantasie* for oboe and orchestra (1941); *We Believe* (1942); *Serenata Sorrentino* for small orchestra (1946); *Cactus Rhapsody* (1950); *Chicken in the Rough* (1951); *Radiation* (1955); *Cowboy Rhapsody* (1956); *Minha Terra* (1958); *Cosmic Mist Symphony* (1962); *Les Femeux Douze* (1965); *Pyramids of Giza* (1973); *Anwar Sadat (In Memory)* (1982); *Earth of God* for strings (1984); *Sam Houston* (1984); and *Texas* (1987).

Her many choral works include *Drums of Africa* (1934); *Prayer* (1934); *Noontide* (1935); *Rain* (1937); *Immortality* (1937); *Lasso of Time* (1940); *Nisan* for female chorus, piano, and strings (1961); *Harvest Heritage* (1963); *Brothers of the Clouds* for male voices and organ (1964); and *Flute Song*.

For the stage she wrote two operas, *Carillon* (1952) and *Kuthara* (1960); two operettas, *Happyland* (1946) and *The Spider and the Butterfly* (for children) (1953); and two music dramas, *Ubiquity* (1937) and *Western Temperament* (1963). She also composed four ballets: *Wheel of Life* (1933); *Shepherd in the Distance* (1937); *The Dark Lady Within* (1962); and *Kumbu* (1963).

Among her chamber works are two string quartets (1934, 1935); *Epic Poem* for string quartet (1927); *Nocturne* for nine instruments (1934); *Chipmunks* for woodwinds, harp, and percussion (1940); Serenade for violin and piano (1944); *Barcarola* for violin and piano (1948); a Piano Sonata (1958); *Phantasy* for flute and piano (1962); *In the Beginning* for eight horns (1962); *Awake to Life* for brass quintet (1968); *Hebraic Poem* for string quartet (1976); *Ode to NASA* for brass quintet (1981); and *Soul of the Sea* for cello and piano (1984). In 1969 she commemorated the moon landing with *Translunar Cycle* for voice and piano.

She was the author of a book entitled *Composer's Corner* (1978); her autobiography *From Ridin' Herd to Writing Symphonies* was published posthumously in 1996.

BROCKWAY, HOWARD A.
b. Brooklyn, New York, 22 November 1870
d. New York, New York, 20 February 1951

After studying in Berlin (1890–93), Brockway settled in New York City as a teacher and pianist. From 1903 to 1910 he taught at the Peabody Institute in Baltimore, after which he spent the rest of his life in New York, teaching at the Institute of Musical Art and the Mannes College of Music.

For orchestra, Brockway composed a Symphony in D, performed in Berlin in 1895 and in Boston in 1907 under Karl Muck; *Cavatina* for violin and orchestra (1895); *Sylvan Suite* (Boston, 1901); and a Suite for cello and orchestra. His choral works include a cantata, *Herr Oluf* (1913), and *Des Sangers Fluch* for eight-part chorus (1902). With Loraine Wyman, he published two sets of Kentucky folk songs, *Lonesome Tunes* (1916) and *Twenty Kentucky Mountain Songs* (1920).

BROWN, EARLE
b. Lunenburg, Massachusetts, 26 December 1926
d. Rye, New York, 2 July 2002

Brown entered Northeastern University in Boston to study mathematics and engineering. Later he was a pupil of Roslyn Brogue Henning in composition and studied the Schillinger System of composition with Kenneth McKillop at the Schillinger House School of Music in Boston (1946–50). From 1950 to 1952 he taught the Schillinger System in Denver, Colorado, before moving to New York to become a member of the "Project for Music for Magnetic Tape" with John Cage and David Tudor. In 1952 he invented a form of non-metric notation that indicates spatial relationships and duration of notes but allows a degree of flexibility. From 1955 to 1960 he was a recording engineer and editor for Capitol Records, moving to Mainstream Records (1960–68).

Brown held positions as Composer-in-Residence at the Peabody Conservatory (1968–73), the Rotterdam Philharmonic Orchestra (1974), and California Institute of the Arts (1974–83). He also worked on the "Kunstler Programm" in West Germany (1970–71). In addition he was a visiting professor at the State University of New York, Buffalo (1975), University of California, Berkeley (1976), University of Southern California, Los Angeles (1978), Yale University (1980–81, 1986–87), and the American Academy in Rome (1987). From 1986 to 1989 he was President of the American Music Center in New York. He received many honors including a Guggenheim Fellowship (1965–66), the National Institute of Arts and Letters Award (1972),

Earle Brown, Spring 1978.
Courtesy Music Library, State University of New York, Buffalo.

the Brandeis University Award (1974), and an Honorary Doctorate from the Peabody Institute Conservatory of Music (1970).

Brown's early works are comparatively orthodox: *Three Pieces* for piano (1951); *Perspectives* for piano (1952); *Music for violin, cello and piano* (1952); and *Music for cello and piano* (1954). However, coming under the influence of Cage and his avant-garde circle in New York, Brown soon developed a unique approach to composition.

Brown stated that he was much influenced by the creations of Alexander Calder and Jackson Pollock and by the writings of Pollock. In his "open-form" works, Brown was affected by the aesthetic principles of the Calder mobiles, creating works whose musical content is fixed and composed but subject to many different formal configurations from performance to performance. In several pieces the conductors or soloists are able to select the order in which they perform the fragments of musical material that are given. In this category are *25 Pages* (1953); *Available Forms I* for 18 players (1961); and *Available Forms II* for 98 players (1962), requiring two conductors, which was performed under the direction of the composer and Bruno Maderna in 1962 and Leonard Bernstein in 1964. *Event: Synergy II* (1967–68) is intended for a chamber group of up to 19 performers with one or two conductors.

The "open-form" approach to composition is seen in Brown's work of the 1950s. *Folio* (1952-53) contains the first "graphic" scores, "open-form" score, and proportional notation. In addition to *25 Pages* for one to 25 pianos (1953), other "open-form" works include *Nine Rarebits* for one or two harpsichords (1965), *Modules I* and *II* (1966), and *Modules III* (1969) for orchestra. *Indices* for 12 players (1954); *Pentathis* for nine instruments (1957–58); *Hadograph I* for flute, glockenspiel, vibraphone, marimba, celeste, and piano (1959); and *Corroboree* for two or three pianos (1964). *Calder Piece* for four percussionists and mobile (1964) and the String Quartet (1965) are "closed-form" works with "mobile" inner structures. Other works from this period are *Novara* for flute, bass clarinet, trumpet, piano, and string quartet (1962) and *From Here* for 20 musicians on specified instruments and optional chorus of 16 voices (1963).

Brown's collaboration with John Cage and David Tudor led to the exploration of electronic music. In this genre he produced two *Octets* for eight magnetic tapes (1953, 1957); *Light Music* for electric light, electronic equipment, and instruments (1961); and *Times Five* for four tapes and five instruments (1963). Later works include *Syntagm III* (1970) and *Sign Sounds* (1972), both for instrumental ensemble; *New Piece: Loops* for chorus and orchestra (1971–72), performed at the Venice Biennale in 1972; *Time Spans* for large orchestra (1971–72); *Centering* for violin and ten instruments, commissioned by the London Sinfonietta in 1973; *Small Pieces* for large orchestra (1973); *Cross Section and Color Fields* for large orchestra (1975); and *Windsor Jambs* for chamber ensemble (1978–80).

Among his last compositions were *Sounder Rounds* for orchestra (1982), commissioned by the New York State Council on the Arts; *Tracer* for flute, oboe, bassoon, violin, cello, double bass, and four-track tape (1984); *Four Systems* for amplified percussion and sustaining instruments (1986); *Tracking Pierrot* for ensemble (1992); *Special Events* for cello and piano (1999); and *Octet* for eight loudspeakers (2000).

BROWN, RAYNER

b. Des Moines, Iowa, 23 February 1912
d. Los Angeles, California, 16 June 1999

After studying at the University of Southern California (1935–38) under Ingolf Dahl and Lucien Cailliet, Brown established himself as an organist in Los Angeles where he held a post at Wilshire Presbyterian Church (1944–77). From 1950 to 1977 he was professor of music at Biola University, La Mirada, California.

For orchestra he composed six symphonies (1952, 1957, 1958, 1980, 1982, 1982); eight organ concertos (1960–94); and *Variations on a Hymn* (1957). Many of his other solo concertos have wind accompaniment: Concertino for harp and brass (1964); Concertino for piano (1966); Concerto for two pianos, brass, and percussion (1972); Clarinet Concerto (1979); Flute Concerto (1980); Concerto for bass trombone (1987); and

Concerto for two organs, brass, and percussion (1987).

With orchestral accompaniment he wrote three further clarinet concertos; a Concerto Grosso for brass and percussion (1965); a Concerto for piano, strings, bassoon, and percussion (1985); a Concerto for harp and violin (1987); Concerto for soprano saxophone, strings, and piano (1988); Concerto for organ duet (1989); and Concerto for cello and English horn (1995).

Most of Brown's other compositions are for instrumental groups. These include four flute sonatas (1944, 1959, 1985, 1988); four brass quintets (1957, 1960, 1981, 1985); two wind quintets (1955, 1957); Piano Quartet (1947); String Quartet (1953); *Prelude and Scherzo* for seven flutes (1956); Trio for flute, clarinet, and viola (1957); *Five Pieces* for organ, harp, brass, and percussion (1963); *Prelude and Fugue* for brass and percussion (1963); *Fantasy and Fugue* for brass (1965); Symphony for clarinet choir (1968); *Sonata Breve* for baritone saxophone and piano (1969); Sonata for flute and organ (1970); Violin Sonata (1977); Sonata for six trombones (1980); Tuba Quartet (1980); *Music* for three clarinets (1980); Trio for trumpet, cello, and piano (1982); Sonata for violin and harp (1985); Clarinet Sonata (1986); Cello Sonata (1986); Sonata for English horn and organ (1989); and Sonata for harp and organ (1990). Among his numerous pieces for organ are 20 sonatas (1958–87) and 35 sonatinas (1945–80).

Among his choral works are two cantatas: *True Singularity* for chorus, flute, oboe, and strings (1992) and *Levania de Nuestro Senor Don Quijote* for chorus, brass, and percussion (1993).

Rayner Brown.
Courtesy Biola University, Conservatory of Music.

BRUNSWICK, MARK

b. New York, New York, 6 January 1902
d. London, England, 26 May 1971

Brunswick was educated at the Horace Mann School in Riverdale, New York and studied privately with Rubin Goldmark. He was also a pupil of Ernest Bloch and Roger Sessions, and in Paris with Nadia Boulanger. From 1925 to 1938 he lived in England. Before returning to the United States in 1938, he received lessons from Anton Webern. In 1938 he was appointed head of the department of compositon at the Greenwich House School of Music. Brunswick relinquished this post in 1942, and four years later became chairman of the music department of the City College of New York, a position he held until 1967. For many years he was a respected writer on musical subjects.

Brunswick's most frequently performed composition is a suite from his ballet *Lysistrata* (1934), scored for chorus and orchestra. His other large-scale works include a Symphony in B-Flat (1945) and a choral symphony, *Eros and Death*, written in 1937. At his death he left an unfinished opera, *The Master Builder*, based on the play by Ibsen. The *Sappho Chorus* for mixed voices (1932) reveals the influence of his particular interest in pre-Bach music.

The two early *Movements* for string quartet (1926), published in Vienna, were the first pieces to bring Brunswick's name to a wider musical public. They were performed at the 1936 I.S.C.M. Festival in Barcelona. His other chamber works include *Sonata and Fantasia* for solo viola (1932); *Seven Trios* for string quartet (1956); a String Quartet (1957); a *Septet in Seven Movements* (1957); Quartet for violin, viola, cello, and double bass (1958); and *Six Bagatelles* (1958) for piano.

BUCCI, MARC

b. New York, New York, 26 February 1924
d. Camp Verde, Arizona, 22 August 2002

Bucci studied at St. John's University, New York (1941–42) before taking private lessons in composition with Tibor Serly (1944–46). An Irving Berlin Scholarship enabled him to attend the Juilliard School of Music (1948–51), where he was a pupil of Frederick Jacobi and Vittorio Giannini. In 1949 he received instruction from Aaron Copland at Tanglewood, Massachusetts. He was the recipient of two Guggenheim Fellowships (1953, 1957), a grant from the National Institute of Arts and Letters (1959) and co-winner of the International Television Italia Prize (1966).

Bucci achieved wide acclaim for his music for the theater. His first opera, *The Boor*, based on a short story by Chekhov to a libretto by Eugene Haun, was premiered in New York City in December 1949. Two one-act operas to his own libretti, *The Dress* and *Sweet Betsy from Pike (a Horse Opera)*, were presented at the Kaufman Auditorium, New York City on 8 December 1953. These three operas are collectively called *The Triad* and were first staged together in November 1958 at the Theatre Marque, New York City. *The Hero*, a one-act opera based on Frank D. Gilroy's "Far Rockaway" with libretto by David Rogers, was presented on television on 24 September 1965 by PBS. Other operas include *Myron, It's Deep Down Here*, to his own text (1972); *Midas* (text: H. Hackaday; 1981); and a jazz opera, *The Square One*.

In addition to these operas, Bucci composed many musicals, including *Caucasian Chalk Circle* (Brecht; 1948); *The Thirteen Clocks* (James Thurber; 1953); *The Adamses* (Paula Jacobi; 1956); *Time and Again* (1958); *The Girl From Outside* (Tally Brown; 1959); *The Old Lady Shows Her Medals* (J.M. Barrie; 1960); *Cheaper by the Dozen* (1960); *Pink Party Dress* (1960); *Chain of Jade* (1960); *Johnny Mishuga* (1961); *The Best of Broadway* (1961); *Pocahontas Wore a Hat* (1961); *Our Miss Brooks* (1962); *Ask Any Girl* (1963); *Along Came Brady* (1963); *The Mouse That Roared* (1969); *Young Ben* (1976); *Second Coming* (1971–79); and *Monsterwood* (1980).

He also provided incidental music for several plays, including *Cadenza* (Holland Dills; 1947); *The Beggar's Opera* (Gay; 1950); *Elmer and Lily* (Saroyan; 1952); *Summer Afternoon* (Bucci; 1952); *The Western*, a mime play (1954); *Thistle in My Bed* (Powers; 1963); *The Sorcerer's Apprentice* (1969); and *I Wish I Were a Trumpet* (Elizabeth Berryhill; 1969).

In addition, Bucci was the author of a number of plays with and without music: *Summer Afternoon* (1952); *Days on End* (1961); *Time and Again* (with Donna Jones; 1963); *Two Angels on Duty* (Wibberly; 1967); *Fool the Eye* (with Thomas Millott; 1969); *The Fastest Curlin' Iron in the West* (with Rod Arrants; 1970); *The Diary of Adam and Eve* (Mark Twain; 1971); *The Cop and the Anthem* (O. Henry; 1972); *The Court of the Stone Children* (Cameron; 1978); and *Paul's Case* (Willa Cather; 1980). His film scores include *A Time to Play* (1967); *Seven in Darkness* (1969); *Honeymoon With a Stranger* (1969); *Echo of a Marriage* (1973); *The Chinese Caper* (1975); *Human Experiments* (1979); *Hart to Hart* (TV; 1979); and *Beyond the Gate* (1980).

Bucci's single orchestral work is a *Concerto for a Singing Instrument* with accompaniment for string orchestra, harp, and piano/celeste, intended for any instrument which covers the range of a twelfth, including the human voice. The finale, "Tug-of-War," was first performed by Anita Darian on kazoo with the New York Philharmonic Orchestra under Leonard Bernstein at Carnegie Hall on 26 March 1960. His other instrumental works include an *Introduction and Allegro* for eight woodwinds (1946) and Divertimento for violin and piano (1949).

Bucci composed two choral works: *The Wondrous Kingdom* (*Flora and Fauna*) for unaccompanied voices to poems of Blake, Emerson, and George Herbert (1962); and *The Trojan Women*, a semi-operatic score based on Edith Hamilton's translation of Euripides' work for women's chorus and chamber ensemble (1967). *Nocturne* for solo voice (or instrument) was premiered in 1962 with Carolyn Stanford and the Vienna State Opera Orchestra under Gene Farrell.

BUCK, DUDLEY
b. Hartford, Connecticut, 10 March 1839
d. West Orange, New Jersey, 6 October 1909

Like his contemporary John Knowles Paine, Buck studied at Harvard University before going to Germany. At the Leipzig Conservatory in 1858 he was a pupil of Julius Rietz, Ernst Friedrich Richter, Louis Plaidy, and Ignaz Moscheles. Later he studied in Dresden (1860) and Paris (1861). On his return to America in 1862 he held a number of posts as organist in Hartford, Chicago, Boston, and Brooklyn, and in 1875 became assistant conductor to Theodore Thomas in New York. It was at this time that he began to compose, concentrating especially upon choral music of a practical nature, often intended for amateur performance.

The score of his first important choral work, *The Culprit Fay* (1870), a setting of Drake's poem, was lost in the great fire in Chicago in 1871. Other works written in Chicago are *Festival Hymn* (1872) and *Psalm 46*, performed by the Handel and Haydn Society in 1873. *The Legend of Don Munio*, to a text by Washington Irving, was published in 1874. *Centennial Meditation of Columbus*, the setting of a specially written poem by Sidney Lanier, was performed in Philadelphia in 1876 under Theodore Thomas.

His next three choral works were to words by Longfellow: *The Nun of Nidaros* (1879); *The Golden Legend*, which won a prize of $1,000 at the Cincinnati Festival in 1880; and *King Olaf's Christmas* (1881). The performance of *The Light of Asia* in London in 1885 helped to extend Buck's reputation abroad. His last major choral work, *The Voyage of Columbus*, to words by Washington Irving, was completed in 1886. He also wrote two operas, *Deseret* (1880) and *Serapis* (1889).

Buck composed much church music, including three short cantatas—*The Story of the Cross* (1892), *The Coming of the King* (1895), and *Christ the Victor* (1896)—and a setting of the *Midnight Service for the New Year* (1880).

For orchestra he wrote a Symphony *"In Springtime,"* now lost; an overture to Scott's *Marmion* (1878); *Festival Overture on "The Star Spangled Banner'* (1891); and a *Romance* for four horns and orchestra (1891). Among his instrumental pieces are numerous works for organ including two sonatas (1866, 1877).

He was the author of two useful books for organists and choir trainers: *Illustrations in Choir Accompaniment* (1877) and *The Influence of the Organ in History* (1882).

BURLEIGH, CECIL
b. Wyoming, New York, 17 April 1885
d. Madison, Wisconsin, 28 July 1980

At the age of nine, Burleigh moved with his family to Omaha, Nebraska. As a child, he studied the violin first in Omaha and Bloomington, Illinois, then attended the Klindworth-Scharwenka Conservatory in Berlin (1903–05). On his return to the United States he studied in

Cecil Burleigh.
Courtesy University of Wisconsin-Madison Archives.

Chicago under Emil Sauret and Felix Borowski. In 1919 he was a composition pupil of Ernest Bloch in New York and received violin lessons from Leopold Auer. From 1909 to 1911 he was violin instructor at the Denver Institute of Music. His next three years were spent in a similar capacity at Morningside College, Souix City, Iowa. From 1914 to 1919 he taught the violin at the University of Montana. In 1921 he was appointed professor of violin and composition at the University of Wisconsin, Madison, a post from which he retired in 1955.

Burleigh's important compositions are three symphonies (1944), entitled *Creation, Prophesy*, and *Revelation*; three violin concertos; and two orchestral pieces, *Mountain Pictures* (1917) and *Evangeline* (1918, rev. 1930). The First Violin Concerto in E minor won a prize in Chicago in 1916; the other two were written in 1919 and 1925. He composed two violin sonatas with subtitles, *The Ascension* (1914) and *From the Life of St. Paul* (1926); *Two Essays* for string quartet (1945); and two works for piano duo, *Leaders of Men* (1943) and *From the Muses* (1945). He also wrote many piano solos and songs and numerous teaching pieces for violin and piano.

BURLEIGH, HENRY THACKER
b. Erie, Pennsylvania, 2 December 1866
d. Stamford, Connecticut, 12 September 1949

An African-American, Burleigh became a pupil of Antonín Dvořák at the New York National Conservatory in 1892, and was the first person to introduce Negro spirituals to his teacher. His career as a concert baritone lasted 52 years, and he performed widely as a piano accompanist. He is remembered today for his numerous arrangements of spirituals for solo and choral performance. Particularly popular is his version of *Deep River* (1917). Paul Robeson made recordings of them in which he was accompanied on the piano by Burleigh. In this way he brought spirituals directly into the corpus of the twentieth-century tradition.

Burleigh composed three song cycles: *Saracen Songs* (1914); *Passionale* (1915); and *Five Songs to Poems of Lawrence Hope* (1915). In addition he published two collections, *Jubilee Songs of the U.S.A.* (1916) and *Old Songs Hymnal* (1929).

Among his instrumental works are *Six Plantation Melodies* (1901) and *Southland Sketches* both for violin and piano.

C

CADMAN, CHARLES WAKEFIELD
b. Johnstown, Pennsylvania, 24 December 1881
d. Los Angeles, California, 30 December 1946

Cadman learned to play the piano as a child and began composing songs while in his teens. He studied in Pittsburgh with Emil Paur and was an organist and conductor in that city. From 1908 to 1910, he was music critic for the *Pittsburgh Dispatch*. In 1916 he settled in Los Angeles where he was director of the department of music at the University of Southern California in 1926.

His first success with a publisher came in 1905, and in the following year his best-known song, "At Dawning," was issued. As part of *Four American Indian Songs*, another song, "From the Land of Sky Blue Water," brought him increased fame. It seems that Cadman's reputation rests solely upon these two pieces, although he composed much else of greater significance.

Beginning in 1909, he made a study of the Omaha Indians and recorded their music. He lectured on the subject throughout the United States and Europe. This interest led him to use Indian melodies in his own music. His two most important operas incorporate Indian melodies. *Shanewis (The Robin Woman)*, in one act, to a libretto by Nelle Richmond Eberhart, was produced at the Metropolitan Opera in New York on 23 March 1918 and enjoyed performances elsewhere in America. *The Sunset Trail* (1920) was staged by the American Opera Company in Denver in 1922 and taken on tour. His other operas are *Daoma or The Land of Misty Water* (1912), revised as *Ramala, The Garden of Mystery* (1915); *A Witch of Salem*, produced in Chicago in December 1926; and *The Willow Tree*, a radio opera broadcast in 1932. Also for the stage, Cadman composed four operettas: *The Ghost of Lollipop Bay* (1926); *Lelawala* (1926); *The Belle of Havana* (1928); and *South in Sonora* (1932).

His best-known orchestral work, *The Thunderbird Suite* (1914), originally for piano, is based on Omaha Indian themes. Also for orchestra he composed *Prairie Sketches* (1906); *To a Vanishing Race* for strings (1913); *Oriental Rhapsody* (1917); *Hollywood Suite* (1932); *Dark Dancers of the Mardi Gras* (with piano) (1933); *American Suite* for strings (1936); *Suite on American Folk Tunes* (1937); Symphony in E minor *"Pennsylvania'* (1939); *Aurora Borealis*, with solo piano (1942); *A Mad Empress Remembers*, with solo violin (1944);and an overture, *Huckleberry Finn Goes Fishing* (1945).

Cadman composed a Piano Trio in D (1914); a Piano Sonata in A (1915); a String Quartet (1917); a Violin Sonata (1930);and a Piano Quintet in G minor (1937). He wrote several choral works, including *The Vision of Sir Launfal* for men's chorus (1909), and four cantatas: *The Father of Waters* (1928); *The Far Horizon* (1934); *Home of Joy* and *Indian Love Charm*. He was also the composer of one of earliest film scores, *Captain of the Guard*, written in 1930.

Apart from the two songs mentioned above, Cadman wrote a number of song cycles: *From Wigwam to Tepee* (1914); *The Willow Wind* (1922); *Birds of Flame* and *White Enchantment*. Like many of his 300 separate songs, these reflect the folklore of the American Indian. Cadman was a successful administrator, founding the Society for the Encouragement of American Music in 1915, which presented a festival in Los Angeles. He was also active in the establishment of the Hollywood Bowl.

CAGE, JOHN (MILTON JR.)
b. Los Angeles, California, 5 September 1912
d. New York, New York, 13 August 1992

Cage attended Pomona College, Claremont, California (1928–30) and studied privately with Richard Buhlig (1932), Henry Cowell (1933–34), Arnold Schoenberg (1935–37), and Adolph Weiss (1933). He was a composer-accompanist for modern dance, working with Bonnie Bird at the Cornish School in Seattle, Washington (1937–39), and taught at the School of Design in Chicago (1941–42). In 1943 he moved to New York City and the following year began his long association with Merce Cunningham and his dance company, of which Cage was musical director for two decades. From 1955 to 1960 he was a member of the music faculty of the New School for Social Research in New York. Cage was also a Fellow at the Center for Advanced Studies at Wesleyan University, Middletown, Connecticut (1960–61) and Composer-in-Residence at the University of Cincinnati (1966–67) and the University of Illinois, Urbana (1967–69). He was awarded a Guggenheim Fellowship in 1949 and was elected a member of the National Institute of Arts and Letters (1968).

In all his compositions, Cage was free of influences from most earlier music. He avoided every established association from European tradition and pursued innovation with remarkable single-mindedness. His earliest extant works are highly chromatic: Sonata *for clarinet solo* (1933); *Six Short Inventions* for seven instruments (1934); *Three Pieces* for flute duet (1935);and *Five Songs for Contralto* (e.e. cummings; 1938). The Sonata *for two voices* (1933) and *Composition for three voices* (1934) already explore the problems of using two octaves in each part, with no repeat of any of the 25 notes within a single part until all the notes have been expressed.

In the works composed after 1937 there is little melody, harmony, or rhythm in the accepted sense. Instead he concentrated on single tones and timbres. He sought to be "free of individual taste and memory in the order of events." Thus the only continuity arises in relation to time. To take the place of a tonal structure, he established a rhythm structure in which the phraseology of each unit of the whole is mirrored in the division of that whole into larger parts. In a 1937 lecture he stated prophetically: "I believe that the use of noise to make music will continue and increase until we reach a music produced through the aid of electrical instruments, which will make available for musical purposes any and all sounds that can be heard." Experiments in sound for their own sake had already been made in the post-Debussy era by Henry Cowell (Cage's teacher), Edgar Varèse, George Antheil, and Leo Ornstein. None of these, however, had gone as far as Cage in creating a totally new concept of musical creation with sound. For him "the composer will be faced with the entire field of sound."

It is not insignificant that his father was an inventor, and Cage himself was always moving to new fields of exploration with an urgent sense of discovery. *First Construction in Metal* (1939) is scored for six percussion players who perform on orchestral bells, thunder sheets, gongs, anvils, cowbells, automobile brake-drums, and cymbals. The rhythmical patterns are built on mathematical relations with 16 measures played 16 times, followed by a 12-measure coda. It was first performed under the composer's direction in Seattle in December 1939.

In 1938, Cage began his experiments with what he called a "prepared" piano. The sound of a grand piano is changed by the insertion of pieces of rubber, wood, and metal between the strings to produce a wide range of timbres. Although Henry Cowell had employed new techniques for playing the strings on a piano, Cage opened up still further possibilities. *Bacchanale* (1938) was Cage's first piece for prepared piano, where the composer wished to use percussive sounds without percussion instruments. It was designed to accompany a dance by Syvilla Fort. *Amores* (1943) comprises two solo movements for prepared piano, surrounding two Trios, the first for nine tom-toms and pod rattle, the second for seven woodblocks. *Perilous Night* for prepared piano was completed in 1944. *Daughters of the Lonesome Isle* (1945) and *Mysterious Adventure* (1945), both for prepared piano, are notated conventionally. They were used for dances, the first by Jean Erdman, the second by Merce Cunningham. The most significant composition for prepared piano is *Sixteen Sonatas and Four Interludes*. The piano requires elaborate preparation, which can take up to six hours. Duos for two prepared pianos include *A Book of Music* (1944) and *Three Dances* (1945).

After 1950 Cage introduced what Pierre Boulez has termed "aleatoric techniques"; Cage himself used the term "chance operations." His study of Zen Buddhism paralleled this development. From the Chinese *I Ching: Book of Changes*, he derived these chance operations. He also introduced indeterminacy into his works, with performers being given more freedom than is customary. The four volumes of *Music of Changes* for piano (1951) are the first works using chance operations.

Concerto for Prepared Piano and Orchestra, completed in 1951, before *Music of Changes*, makes use of charts based on the "Magic Square." In the first movement, the piano is totally independent of the other instruments; indeed it is set in opposition to them. In the remaining two movements, the solo part "studies" then follows the master (orchestral) chart. This work was first performed in 1952 by David Tudor, who would be closely associated with the composer for many years in the performance of his music. Half the music of the slow movement of the *Concerto* is in fact silence. The ultimate in silence is reached in *4' 33"* (1952), marked "tacet" for any instrument or combination of instruments. The piece is cast in three movements in which the performer makes no sound at all. Other works with precise timings as their titles are *59 ½ for a String Player* (1953) notated on a graph, giving details of bowing pressures, noises on the box, and varied vibrato; *26'1.1499* (1955), also for a string player; *27'10.554* (1956) for percussionist; and two pieces for prepared piano, *31'57.9864* (1954) and *34'46.776* (1954), both indicated as space equal to time.

In the 1950s, also with David Tudor, Cage began to use recording tape to create new compositions. The first important production in this manner, *Williams Mix* (1952), incorporating over six hundred recordings, is depicted on 192 pages of score on eight tracks of tape, using natural sounds of the city and country and electronic effects in one extended aural collage. Recordings had already been part of *Imaginary Landscape No. 1* (1939), which employs two variable-speed gramophones, frequency recordings, muted piano, and cymbal. *Imaginary Landscape No. 2* (*March* 1942) is for percussion quintet and an amplified coil of wire. *Imaginary Landscape No. 3* (1942) combines a percussion sextet with a formidable array of electronics and mechanical devices, including audio-frequency oscillators and amplification. *Imaginary Landscape No. 4.* (March 2; 1951) is scored for 12 radios, each with two players.

Imaginary Landscape No. 5 (1952) employs a recording on tape derived from any 42 records. The chance selection is indicated on a graph. Like so many of Cage's works, it became the basis of a dance piece. Under the title *Portrait of a Lady*, it was performed in New York in 1952 by Jean Erdman. Another tape work, *Fontana Mix* (1958), was first compiled in the Studio di Fonologia of Italian Radio in Rome. It was constructed from a score for a production of eight tracks on tape. There are ten transparent sheets of ten drawings having six differentiated curved lines and a graph with one hundred units plotted which determine all aspects of sound manipulation, tape splicing, and compilation of material. *Aria* for voice (1958) can also be performed with *Fontana Mix*.

Concerto for Piano and Orchestra (1957–58) has no score as such but each part is carefully but indeterminately written. The 63-page piano part can be played complete or in part and in any sequence; it contains 84 different kinds of sound aggregates. Of this work Cage said: "The orchestral accompaniment may involve any number of players or more or fewer instruments and a given performance may be extended or shorter in length.

Indeed I regard the work as one 'in progress' which I intend never to consider as a final state, although I find each performance definitive." The instruments are subject to many special effects: the trombone sometimes plays without the bell, the viola may be played across the knees and the pianist sometimes produces noises on the piano structure.

Other works of particular interest of the early period are *The Wonderful Widow of Eighteen Springs* (1940), the text taken from James Joyce's *Finnegans Wake*, for voice and closed piano, where the instrument is used for percussive and resonant effects, and *She Is Asleep* (1945) in two parts: the first for 12 tom-toms based on rhythmical structure, the second for soprano vocalist and prepared piano.

The seemingly simple *String Quartet in Four Parts* (1950) is carefully constructed on multiples of 22 measures. The four movements are related to the seasons of the year, beginning with *Summer in France*, where the work was started, *Fall in America* where it was completed, *Winter* (*Canon*), and *Spring* (*Quodlibet*). *Sixteen Dances* (1951) for flute, trumpet, violin, cello, piano, and percussion makes use of charts related to the Magic Square. It was written for Merce Cunningham and Company of Three. *Water Music* for piano and accessory instruments dates from 1952. *Music for Piano* (1953–55) in 84 parts is derived from imperfections in the paper on which the music was written. *Water Music* can be performed with *Atlas Eclipticalis* for orchestra (1957). The latter work, commissioned by the Montreal Festivals Society, became the dance *Aeon* for Merce Cunningham. *Cartridge Music* (1960) uses gramophone pick-ups into which various materials are inserted and stroked to produce sounds that are amplified. *Music for Toy Pianos* (1960) comprises eight sheets of transparent paper marked with points and circles referring to actions to be made on the toy pianos. It uses live electronic amplification and manipulation.

The set of *Variations* are intended for any instruments: *I* (1958), *II* (1961), *III* (1963), *IV* (1963), *V* (1965), and *VI* (1966). *HPSCHD* (1968–69) was composed in collaboration with Lejeran Hiller at the University of Illinois, Urban-Champaign. Lasting four and a half hours at its premiere on 16 May 1969 at the University, it required massive preparation. In addition to seven harpsichords, there were 52 tape recorders, 59 amplifiers and loudspeakers, and 208 computer-generated tapes. To these were added 6,400 slides and eight movie projectors with 40 films. Sound and kinetic art combined in one huge environmental experience witnessed by an audience of 18,000 people who moved about the auditorium as it took place. Here Cage "let sounds be themselves" with no attempt at producing what might be termed "art." This "happening" or multimedia activity demonstrated the composer's approach to the world of sound.

Cage's admiration for Erik Satie is acknowledged in *Cheap Imitation*, based on Satie's *Socrate*. This entirely monodic work dates initially from 1969 as a piano solo. Later Cage scored it for an orchestra of between 24 and 96 players; in this version it was to be presented at the Holland Festival in 1972 but it was withdrawn because of inadequate rehearsal time. Also dating from 1972 is a tape piece, *62 Mesostics re Merce Cunningham*, played simultaneously with a tape by David Tudor called *Untitled*.

Four books for piano, the *32 Etudes Australes*, were completed in 1975. As with *Atlas Eclipticalis*, the composer used star charts of the Southern Hemisphere to produce the notes fixed in pitch but free in interpretation. Dating from the same year is *Score (40 Drawings of Thoreau) and 23 Parts together with a Recording of the Dawn at Stony Point, New York August 6th 1974* for any instrument and/or voice (*Twelve Haiku*)).

To mark the Bicentennial, Cage composed *Renga* with *Apartment House 1776*, performed at the I.S.C.M. Festival in Boston in 1976 under Seiji Ozawa. *Renga* is the name given to a sequence of poems called "wakas." Scored for four solo voices, four instrumental soloists, four quartets, and large orchestra, the work represents a collage of music that might have been heard in 1776, with simultaneous activities against an explosive accompaniment, suggestive of events in nature, producing what the composer called "the pleasures of chaos." Cage drew on music of African-Americans, American Indians, Protestant hymns, Sephardic chant, and instrumental items of the eighteenth century.

In 1976 Cage began working intensively in collaboration with Paul Zukovsky, producing several works for solo violin: *Cheap Imitation*, *Nine Chorales*, *Freeman Etudes*, and *Eight Whiskus*. *Empty Words* (1977) is derived through chance operations from the Journal of Henry David Thoreau. Lasting eleven and a half hours in performance, the work makes a gradual metamorphosis from isolated phrases, words, syllables, and letters to music.

Cage's music generated considerable interest in Europe. In Bonn on 9 December 1977, the Cologne Radio Orchestra under Hiroshi Wakasugi gave the first performance of *Quartets I – VIII* for orchestra. In June 1978, Dutch Radio devoted a whole day to *Sounday*, a musical event especially devised by Cage. This was followed in Bologna by *Il Treno*, three variations on a theme by Tito Gotti involving prepared trains and music choruses in stations visited.

Among later compositions are two works for percussion: *Branches* (1976), and *Child of Tree* for solo performer using botanical instruments, including cactus, etc. (1975). Other pieces include *Inlets*, for three players with a conch shell using circular breathing and the sound of fire; *Lecture on the Weather* (1975); *Telephone and Birds* for three to perform (1977); *Circus On*, comprising three pages of instructions (1979);and *Forever and Sunsmell* for voice and percussion duo (1980).

On 10 June 1979, the Cologne Radio Chorus under Hubert Schernus gave the premiere of *Hymns and Variations* for 12 amplified voices. Also in 1979, Cage made *Roaratorio, an Irish Circus on Finnegans Wake* with technical assistance from John Fullemann at IRCAM in Paris for WDR, SDR, and KRO broadcasting stations. It is a radio play with music and was awarded the Carl Szucka Prize and Donaueschingen, Germany in the same year.

In 1985 Cage began a series of multimedia theater works entitled *Europeras*. *Nos. 1 and 2*, for any combination of voices, chamber orchestra, tape, and organ, was performed in Frankfurt-am-Main in 1987. *Nos. 3 and 4* for at least six voices, chamber orchestra, tape, and light operation received its premiere in London in 1990. *No. 5* for two voices, piano, phonograph, and sound and light operations was staged in Buffalo, New York, in 1991.

Cage continued composing with undiminished imagination until his death, completing an astonishing quantity of works. Among his pieces in the final year of his life are a sequence of instrumental and orchestral items titled according to the number of performers required: *Twenty-Six* (violins); *Twenty-Eight* (winds and brass); *Twenty-Nine*; *Sixty-Eight*; *Eighty*; *103*; and *108*. Instrumental works are similarly designated: *One* for violin, *Two* for trombone and piano, *Two* for violin and piano, *Four* for saxophone quartet, *One*, *Three*, *Four*, and *Six* for percussionists, etc.

Cage's writings on music have stimulated much interest and his various essays have been gathered into book-form: *Silence* (1961), *A Year From Monday* (1967), *To Describe the Process of Not Wanting to Say Anything About Marcel* (1969), *Notations* (1969), *M: Writings "67–'72* (1973), *Empty Words* (1979), *Another Song* (1981), *Mind Book* (1982, 2nd ed. 1988), *Themes and Variations* (1982), *I – IV* (1990), and *Composition in Retrospect* (1993). With Kathleen Hoover he wrote a biography of Virgil Thomson, published in 1959.

CAMPBELL-TIPTON, LOUIS
b. *Chicago, Illinois, 21 November 1877*
d. *Paris, France, 1 May 1921*

Campbell-Tipton studied in Chicago and Boston before moving to Germany where he was a pupil of Carl Reinecke at the Leipzig Conservatoire (1896–99). He taught at the Chicago Musical College (1901–04) before settling permanently in Paris.

He was best known for his piano pieces, including *Sonata Heroic* (1904); *Two Legends* (1908); *Etude en Octaves* (1912); and *Day's End* (1921). His songs were at one time widely performed, including *Four Sea Lyrics* (1907) and *The Opium Smoker* (1907). Two operas remained in manuscript.

CARPENTER, JOHN ALDEN
b. Park Ridge, Illinois, 28 February 1876
d. Chicago, Illinois, 26 April 1951

Like Charles Ives, Carpenter was a professionally trained composer who undertook a career in business. He studied with John Knowles Paine at Harvard from 1893 to 1897 and later was briefly a pupil of Elgar in Rome in 1906. From 1909 to 1936 he worked in his father's shipping supply company in Chicago, writing music only in his spare time. He then retired to devote himself to his composing. Carpenter's early compositions attempted none of the daring experiments of Ives, with the result that they were widely performed throughout the composer's lifetime. His works are among the first technically accomplished music to represent the American spirit and way of life, devoid of almost every European influence.

Carpenter's first important work is the orchestral suite *Adventures in a Perambulator*, written in 1914. It portrays the impressions experienced by a baby on an outing with his nurse. The titles of each movement describe what he met: "En voiture," "the policeman," "the hurdy-gurdy man (eventually stopped by the policeman!)," "the lake," "dogs," and "dreams." This simple music, with its naïve extrovert characteristics and vitality, contains the essence of what is now felt to be "American."

The first of Carpenter's three ballets, *The Birthday of the Infanta*, was composed in 1917 and revised in 1940. *Krazy Kat*, written in 1920 (rev. 1939), uses jazz idioms to accompany dances based on newspaper cartoon figures. Carpenter's third ballet, *Skyscrapers*, is his best-known work. Commissioned by dance impresario Serge Diaghilev, it attempts to portray the noisy elements of American cities. Completed in 1925, *Skyscrapers* is the composer's most advanced impressionistic music. A note at the head of the score states: "*Skyscrapers* is a ballet which seeks to reflects some of the many rhythmic movements and sounds of modern American life. It has no story in the usual sense, but proceeds on the simple fact that American life reduces itself to violent alternatives of work and play, each with its own peculiar and distinctive character." With choreography by Heinrich Kroller, *Skyscrapers* was first produced in 1925 in Monte Carlo by the Ballet Russe. Its American premiere took place in New York at the Metropolitan Opera on 19 February 1926. From all these works, almost every trace of nineteenth-century European influence has disappeared.

Carpenter wrote three symphonies. The First, subtitled *Sermon in Stones*, was composed in 1916, soon after *Adventures in a Perambulator*. A *Symphony in one movement*, based on a theme from the First Symphony, was completed in 1940 to mark the 50th anniversary of the Chicago Symphony Orchestra. Symphony no. 2. appeared in 1942 and was performed for the first time by Bruno Walter and the New York Philharmonic Orchestra; like most of Carpenter's music, it is witty and optimistic in mood.

Carpenter composed a Concertino for piano and orchestra (1915), which contains elements of ragtime and was premiered with Percy Grainger as soloist with the Chicago Symphony Orchestra; a Violin Concerto (1937); and *Patterns* for piano and orchestra (1932). His other orchestral works are *A Pilgrim Vision*, commissioned in 1920 to celebrate the tercentenary of the landing of the Mayflower; *Sea Drift* (1933); *Danza* (1935); *Blue Gal* for cello and orchestra (1943); a symphonic poem, *The Anxious Bugler* (1943); *The Seven Ages*, first performed by the New York Philharmonic Orchestra in 1945; and *Carmel Concerto* (1948) for piano and orchestra, which was premiered in 1949 by the New York Philharmonic Orchestra under Leopold Stokowski. In a lighter vein, he composed a number of short jazz numbers for Paul Whiteman and other band leaders; among these items are *A Little Jazz Piece* (1925) and *Oil and Vinegar* (1926).

For voice and orchestra Carpenter composed a cycle of six songs, *Gitanjali* (1913, orch. 1932), to words by Rabindranath Tagore; and *Water Colors* (1918), settings of four Chinese poems for mezzo-soprano and orchestra. *Four Negro Songs*, to words by Langston Hughes, were completed in 1927. *Songs of Faith*, for narrator, chorus, organ, and orchestra, was commissioned in 1931 (rev. 1937) for the bicentenary celebration of the birth of George Washington the following year. His last two choral works are *Song of Freedom* (1941) and *Song of David* for women's voices, cello, and orchestra (1951).

At one time in the United States, Carpenter's three major chamber works were frequently performed: Violin Sonata (1911); String Quartet (1927); and Piano Quintet (1934), commissioned by the Elizabeth Sprague Coolidge Foundation.

CARR, BENJAMIN
b. London, England, 12 September 1768
d. Philadelphia, Pennsylvania, 24 May 1831

Carr was a pupil of Samuel Arnold and Charles Wesley

in London. His first known work, the pastoral opera *Philander and Silvia* or *Love Crowned at Last*, was produced at Sadler's Wells in London on 16 October 1792.

Carr went to the United States in 1793, followed a year later by his father and brother, and settled eventually in Philadelphia. Through his considerable versatility, he gained a reputation as a composer, conductor, singer, organist, and pianist. He also founded music businesses in Baltimore, Philadelphia, and New York, publishing works by Haydn, Mozart, and Pleyel, and printing some of the earliest copies of American songs, including "The Star-Spangled Banner," "Yankee Doodle," and "Hail, Columbia." After 1797, Carr became a central figure in the musical life in Philadelphia, and, with Raynor Taylor, was a founder member of the Musical Fund Society in 1820. From 1801 until his death, Carr was organist at St. Augustine's Roman Catholic Church.

Carr's compositions include church music, ballads, instrumental pieces, and several orchestral works, of which a *Federal Overture* (1794), a medley of popular tunes, is one of the few early American pieces to be in print today. He also published six piano sonatas (1796) and *Dead March and Monody for George Washington* (with voices) (1800).

Carr's opera *The Archers* or *The Mountaineers of Switzerland*, based on Schiller's *William Tell*, was produced in New York on 18 April 1796, 33 years before Rossini's opera on the same subject. Carr also composed incidental music for *Macbeth* (New York, 1795) and a ballet, *Caledonian Frolic* (1794). The song cycle *The Lady of the Lake* was composed in 1811, only one year after the publication of Sir Walter Scott's poem.

In 1800 he edited *The Musical Journal* in two sections, one of vocal and the other of instrumental music. From 1812 to 1825 he issued *Carr's Musical Miscellany* and three music textbooks.

CARTER, ELLIOTT (COOK, JR.)
b. New York, New York, 11 December 1908

Carter received his first musical training at Horace Mann High School, New York from which he graduated in 1926. At Harvard University (1926–32) he studied with Walter Piston and Edward Burlingame Hill and briefly with Gustav Holst before going to Paris in 1932 to become a pupil of Nadia Boulanger. Back in the United States in 1936 he turned to musical journalism and serious composition. From 1937 to 1939 he was musical director of Lincoln Kirstein's Ballet Caravan. In 1940 he was appointed Chairman of the music Department at St. John's College, Annapolis, Maryland. During World War II, from 1942 to 1944 he was Music

Elliott Carter.
Courtesy Music Library, State University of New York, Buffalo.

Controller in the U.S. Office of War Information. He taught at the Peabody Conservatory, Baltimore (1946–48), Columbia University (1948–50), and Queens College, New York (1955–56), and was a professor at Yale University from 1960 to 1962. In 1962 he went to Rome, where he was Composer-in-Residence at the American Academy; in 1964, he was Composer-in-Residence in the city of West Berlin. In addition he taught at the Juilliard School, New York (1964–84).

Carter has been the recipient of Guggenheim Fellowships (1945, 1950), the Prix de Rome (1953); and the Ernst von Siemens Prize (1981). He has been on the board of directors of the League of Composers (1939–52), the International Society for Contemporary Music (1946–52); and the American Composers' Alliance (1939–52). In 1956 he was elected a Member of the Institute of Arts and Letters, and to membership of the American Academy of Arts and Sciences (1963) and the American Academy of Arts and Letters (1969), from which he received the Gold Medal for Music in 1971. In 1968 he was awarded the Premio Delle Muse by the city of Florence, Italy and was elected as an honorary member of the Akademie der Kunst in West Berlin (1972). In celebration of his 70th birthday, the City of New York presented Carter with the Handel Medallion, and the mayor of Los Angeles proclaimed 27th April 1979 "Elliott Carter Day."

Carter's earliest extant works include a ballet, *Pocahontas* (1936), performed in a revised version in New York in 1939, and incidental music to Sophocles's *Philoctetes* (1933); Plautus's *Mostellaria* (1936); and Shakespeare's *The Merchant of Venice* (1937). A Symphony, composed in 1942 was performed in Rochester, New York, but later was withdrawn and revised in 1954. Also dating from this period are *Tarantella* for men's chorus and orchestra (1936) and two pieces for a cappella voices, *To Music* (1937) and *Heart Not So Heavy As Mine* (1938). Other choral works are *The Defense of Corinth* (after Rabelais) for narrator, men's chorus, and piano duet, performed in Cambridge, Massachusetts, in March 1942; *The Harmony of Morning* (Mark Van Doren) for female chorus and small orchestra (1944); *Musicians Wrestle Everywhere* for mixed voices with optional string accompaniment (1945); and *Emblems* (1947) for men's chorus and piano to words by Allan Tate, performed by the Harvard Glee Club in 1951.

The emergence of a more personal style is heard in the extrovert ebullient *Holiday Overture*, composed in 1944 and revised in 1961. A second ballet, *The Minotaur*, was produced by Ballet Society in New York in 1947. The Louisville Orchestra commissioned *Variations for Orchestra*, composed between 1953 and 1955 and performed in April 1956. The elaborate construction of the material is typical of Carter's complex language. It is the first of his impressive orchestral works that have established him as a composer of international stature. The second of these pieces is the Double Concerto for harpsichord, piano, and two chamber ensembles. Each solo instrument has its own instrumental group with separate musical ideas and intervals. The interaction and contrasts between the two forces reflect some elements of the Concerto Grosso form. It was commissioned by the Fromm Foundation and first performed in New York in September 1961. It won the New York Music Critics' Circle Award in that year.

The Piano Concerto was composed as an 85th birthday offering to Stravinsky. It was commissioned through the Ford Foundation and written during 1964 and 1965 for Jacob Latenier, who premiered it in Boston in January 1967. Here the composer often places the soloist in opposition to the orchestra, providing a virtuoso but never purely exhibitionistic part for the piano. The Concerto for Orchestra was commissioned by the New York Philharmonic Orchestra for its 125th anniversary and first performed by them under Leonard Bernstein in February 1970. The continuous flow of this work was inspired by the poem "Vents" (Winds) by St. John Perse.

On 17 February 1977, Pierre Boulez conducted the premiere of *A Symphony for Three Orchestras* with the New York Philharmonic Orchestra. The music was suggested by Hart Crane's poem "The Bridge," a symbolic description of the Brooklyn Bridge. The opening invokes the sound of sea gulls that appear in the first lines of the poem. It is scored for large forces divided into three groups, One on the left is Orchestra I, comprising brass, timpani, and strings; Orchestra II, placed centrally, is a concertante ensemble of three clarinets, piano, percussion, and strings; Orchestra III on the right has triple woodwind (without clarinets), two horns and strings (without cellos), and untuned percussion. There are 12 brief, interlocked movements, four for each orchestra. Of the work the composer wrote: "The listener of course is not meant, on a first hearing, to identify the details of this continually shifting web of sound, but rather to hear and grasp the character of the kaleidoscope of musical themes as they are presented in varying context."

Later orchestral pieces include *Three Occasions* comprising three works originally written separately: *A Celebration of Some 100 x 150 Notes*, composed in 1986 for the Houston Symphony Orchestra, *Remembrance* (Tanglewood, 1989), and *Anniversary*, composed in 1989 for the B.B.C. Symphony Orchestra; an Oboe Concerto, commissioned in 1986 by Paul Sacher for Heinz Hollinger; a Violin Concerto performed in San Francisco in 1990; a Clarinet Concerto, premiered in Paris in 1997; and *Symphonia: Sum Flexae Pretium Spei*, like *Three Occasions*, a gathering together of three separate works: *Partita* (Chicago Symphony Orchestra, 1993); *Adagio tenebrosa* (B.B.C. Symphony Orchestra, 1996); and *Allegro scorrevole* (Cleveland Orchestra, 1996). The complete *Symphonia*, lasting 50 minutes, was first performed in 1998.

Carter's recent orchestral works are *Asko Concerto* (1999–2000), written for the Asko Ensemble and first performed in the Concertgebouw, Amsterdam in 2000; a Cello Concerto (2000) for Yo-Yo Ma; *Micomicón* (Boston 2003); and *Boston Concerto*, premiered in April 2003 by the Boston Symphony Orchestra. In the same month, the Chicago Symphony Orchestra gave the first performance of *Of Rewaking*, a setting for soprano and orchestra of words by William Carlos Williams, Daniel Barenboim conducting with Michell DeYoung as soloist. Currently he is writing *Dialogues* for piano and orchestra to be premiered by Nicolas Hodges and the London Sinfonetta in January 2004.

The Piano Sonata of 1945, Carter has said, "takes as its point of departure the sonorities of the modern piano and is thought of as being completely idiomatic for that instrument. I have in this work attempted to translate into a special virtuoso style my general musical outlook, my thoughts and feelings. I approach writing for the piano as if it were an art all its own, requiring a special musical vocabulary and a particular character unrelated to other kinds of music." It is a powerful work and a major contribution to the twentieth-century repertoire of the piano.

The Piano Sonata began a sequence of chamber works that rank in importance with the orchestral compositions. These are among the most significant works of instrumental music composed in the last sixty years. Of the Sonata In 1948 Carter composed a *Woodwind Quintet* and a *Cello Sonata*. The Cello Sonata, commissioned by Bernard Greenhouse, uses what the composer calls "metric modulation." Here the tempi of the whole work are related and regulated so that speed becomes an integral part of the structure. In 1950 there followed another composition for wind instruments, *Eight Etudes and a Fantasy* for flute, oboe, clarinet, and bassoon. Herein every technical device is explored in the *Etudes*, culminating in an extended *Fantasy* that refers back to earlier material and includes elaborate contrapuntal writing for the instruments. The impressive First String Quartet also uses "structural tempi." Composed in 1950, it is conceived on a large scale, lasting about 45 minutes. It received an award in the Liege International Concourse.

Carter's interest in unusual instrumental forces is seen in the Sonata for flute, oboe, cello, and harpsichord (1952) and *Six Pieces* for four timpani (1952, rev. 1966). This last work was written as exercises in metrical modulation and was not originally intended for public performance. *Recitative* and *Improvisations* for timpani were published in 1960, and as a result of the interest shown by percussionists, the complete work was issued in 1968.

Carter has stated that when he came to write his Second String Quartet, originally commissioned by the Stanley Quartet of the University of Michigan, he initially found great difficulty in adopting a method of approach to the work. The nine short movements are designed to give prominence in turn to each instrument. In addition, each instrument is given certain separate and distinct characteristics. The first violin is a virtuoso using intervals of minor thirds, perfect fifths, major ninths, and major elevenths. The second violin is non-virtuoso, maintaining peaceful features with major thirds and minor sixths. The viola has sustained lamenting phrases using augmented fourths and minor sevenths. The cello attempts to avoid settling to a regular metrical pattern; its intervals are fourths and major sixths. Carter has described the Second String Quartet as "a series of events in time." It was first performed at the Juilliard School by the Juilliard Quartet in March 1960 and immediately received wide critical acclaim. It won the Pulitzer Prize (the first chamber work to do so), the New York Music Critics' Circle Award, and, in 1961, a UNESCO Prize in Europe.

String Quartet no. 3 was composed in 1971 for the Juilliard Quartet. Like the Second Quartet, it was pre-miered by them at the Juilliard School in January 1973 and awarded the Pulitzer Prize in that year. In this work, the four instruments are arranged as two duos: first violin and cello, balanced by the second violin and viola. Each pair of instruments is assigned a different set of movements, and each movement of one duo is poised against one part of every movement of the other duo. The Brass Quintet, composed for the American Brass Quintet, was premiered by them on BBC radio in London on the centenary of the birth of Charles Ives, 20 October 1974. Also for the American Brass Quintet he wrote *A Fantasy About Purcell's Fantasia on One Note* (1974) as a Christmas present.

Carter's solo vocal music includes *Voyage* for voice and piano to words of Hart Crane (1942–43, orchestrated 1975, rev. 1979); *Warble for Lilac Time* (Walt Whitman) for soprano and piano (1943, rev. 1954); and *Three Poems of Robert Frost* for medium voice and piano (1943).

A song cycle, *A Mirror on Which to Dwell* (1975) to six poems by Elizabeth Bishop, was performed by Susan Davenny Wyner (wife of the composer Yehudi Wyner) and Speculum Musicae, which had commissioned it for the American Bicentennial. *Syringa*, a setting of a poem by John Ashbery for mezzo-soprano, bass, guitar, and chamber ensemble received its first performance in New York on 10 December 1978.

Still prolific in his nineties, Carter has continued to write much instrumental music for varied ensembles. These pieces include *Triple Duo* for violin, cello, flute, clarinet, piano, and percussion (1982–83); *Penthode* for five instrumental quartets, commissioned in 1984 for the London Sinfonietta; *Canon for Four* for flute, bass clarinet, violin, and cello, or four clarinets (1984); String Quartet no. 4. (1986) for the Composers' Quartet; *Enchanted Preludes* for flute and cello (1988); *Con leggerezza pensosa* for clarinet, violin, and cello (1990); Quintet for piano and winds (1991); *Trilogy: Baniolage* (harp); *Immer Nea* (oboe and harp); *Inner Song* (oboe; 1992) for Heinz and Ursula Hollinger; *Esprit Rude/ Esprit Doux II* for flute, clarinet, and marimba (1994); *Figment* for solo cello (1994); *Gra* for clarinet, composed in 1993 for the 80th birthday of Witold Lutoslawski; String Quartet no. 5. (1995); *A Six-Letter Letter* (in memory of Paul Sacher) for English horn (1996); *Shard* (1997) for guitar; *Luimen* for ensemble (1998); *Two Fragments* for string quartet (1994/1999); three pieces for solo violin: *Statement (remembering Aaron)*, *Fantasy (remembering Roger)*, and *Riconoscenza (for Goffredo Petrassi*; 1984–2000); an Oboe Quartet (2001) for Heinz Hollinger; *Scrivo in Vento* for solo flute (2001); *Hiyoku* for two clarinets (2001); *Rhapsodic Musings* for solo violin (2001); *Au Quai* for bassoon or viola (2002);and *Retracing* for solo bassoon (2002).

In recent years Carter has returned to writing for the piano with *90+* (1998) to mark the 90th birthday of Petrassi; *Two Diversions* (1999); and *Retrouvailles* (*Recollections*) (2000). His latest vocal works are *In Sleep, In Thunder* (Robert Lowell) for tenor and 14 instruments, commissioned by the London Sinfonietta (1981); *Of Challenge and Love* for soprano and piano performed at the Aldeburgh Festival, England in June 1995; and *Tempo e Tempi*, a song cycle for soprano and ensemble (1998–99), also an Aldeburgh commission.

In his ninetieth year, he embarked on his first opera, *What Next?* in one act to a libretto by Paul Griffiths, concerning the aftermath of a car crash. The premiere conducted by Daniel Barenboim took place on 16 September 1999 at the Berlin Staatsoper.

Flawed and Stubborn Sounds, a conversation with Elliott Carter by Allen Edwards, was published in 1971. *The Writings of Elliott Carter: An American Composer Looks at Modern Music* was published in 1977. *Elliott Carter: Harmony Book*, edited by Nicholas Hopkins and John Flunk, was issued in 2002.

CASTELNUOVO-TEDESCO, MARIO
b. Florence, Italy, 3 April 1895
d. Hollywood, California, 17 March 1968

Castelnuovo-Tedesco studied at the Cherubini Royal Institute in Florence (1913–18), where he was a pupil of Pizzetti. The Italian Fascist racial laws against Jews forced him to emigrate to the United States in 1939. He settled in Hollywood where he composed film scores, and from 1942 to 1959 he taught at the Los Angeles Conservatory. He became an American citizen in 1946.

The dramatic works of Shakespeare provided inspiration for many of his compositions. In addition to the operas *All's Well That Ends Well* (1955–58) and *The Merchant of Venice* (1956–58), he composed overtures for ten of the plays: *The Taming of the Shrew* (1930); *Twelfth Night* (1933); *Julius Caesar* (1934); *The Winter's Tale* (1934); *A Midsummer Night's Dream* (1940); *King John* (1941); *Antony and Cleopatra* (1947); *Coriolanus* (1947); *As You Like It* (1953);and *Much Ado About Nothing* (1953). He also set all the songs from Shakespeare's plays (1921–25).

His orchestral works include *Symphonic Variation* for violin and orchestra (1930); *Cipressi* (1940), performed by Koussevitzky and the Boston Symphony Orchestra; *Poem* for violin and orchestra (1942); *Indian Songs and Dances* (1943); *An American Rhapsody* (1943); *Five Humoresques on Foster's Themes* (1943); *Noah's Ark* for narrator and orchestra (1947); *Concerto da Camera* for oboe and strings (1950);and *The Little Siren and the Blue Fish.*

He composed three violin concertos: no. 1, *Concerto Italiano* in G minor (1926); no. 2, *The Prophets* (1933), performed by Jascha Heifetz with the New York Philharmonic Orchestra under Toscanini; and no. 3 (1939). Other concertos include two for piano: no. 1 in G (1927) and no. 2 in F (1939); the composer was the soloist in their first performances. In addition there are two concertos for harp, and a Cello Concerto in one movement (1935), performed by Piatigorsky with the New York Philharmonic Orchestra conducted by Toscanini.

Castelnuovo-Tadesco made a significant contribution to the guitar repertoire with two concertos (1939, 1959); a Concerto for two guitars (1962); *Serenade* for guitar and orchestra (1943); a Quintet for guitar and strings (1950); *Fantasia* for guitar and piano (1950); *The Well-Tempered Guitar*, a set of 24 preludes for two guitars (1962); and several solo pieces, including a Sonata (*Homage to Boccherini*; 1934); *Capriccio Diabolico* (*Homage to Paganini*; 1935);and *Plantero and I* (1960).

For violin and piano he wrote *Signorine* (1918); *Ritmi* (1920); *Capitan Fracassa* (1920); *Notturno Adriatico* (1922); *Sonata quasi una Fantasia* (1929); *The Lark* (1930); and *Ballade* (1940). His other instrumental works include three string quartets (1928, 1948, 1964); a Cello Sonata in E-Flat (1928); Piano Trio no. 1. (1928); two piano quintets (1932, 1951); Piano Trio no. 2. (1932); Concertino for harp and seven instruments (1937); Sonata for violin and viola (1945); Clarinet Sonata (1945); Sonatina for bassoon and piano (1946); Sonata for viola and cello (1950); Sonata for viola and cello (1950);and Sonata for cello and harp (1966). He composed many piano pieces, including a Sonata (1928).

Castelnuovo-Tadesco wrote seven operas: *La Mandragola* (after Machiavelli; 1920–23), produced in Venice in May 1926; *Bacco in Toscanna* (1925–26), performed in Milan in 1931; *The Princess and the Pea* (1943); *All's Well That Ends Well* (1955–58); *The Merchant of Venice* (1956–58), produced in Florence in 1961; *Saul* (1958–60);and *The Importance of Being Earnest* (1962). Also for the stage he wrote three ballets: *Aucassin et Nicolette,*a puppet show (1938); *The Birthday of the Infanta* (1942), produced in New Orleans in January 1947; and *Octaroon Ball* (1947).

Among his choral works are five oratorios: *The Book of Ruth* (1949), *Jonah* (1951), *The Book of Esther* (1962), *The Song of Songs* (1963), and *Tobias and the Angel* (1964–65). He also composed three cantatas: *Naomi and Ruth* (1947), *The Queen of Sheba* (1953), and *The Fiery Furnace* (1960); a setting of the *Jewish Sacred Service* for baritone, chorus, and organ (1943); and *The Giants of the Mountain* for chorus and orchestra.

In addition to the *Shakespeare Songs*, his solo vocal music includes a cycle on Spanish texts by the composer, *Coplas* (1915, rev. 1967); *Lauda di Nostra Donna* ((*In Praise of Our Lady*)) (Savonarola) for soprano and orchestra; *Six Scottish Songs* for soprano, tenor, harp, and strings (1939); *Three Sephardic Songs* for medium voice and chamber orchestra; and *Two Old Romances* for soprano and orchestra.

His Hollywood film scores include *Tortilla Flat* (1942); *Forgotten Treasure* (1943); *Dorian Gray* (1944); *Gaslight* (1944); *The Return of the Vampire* (1944); *Two-Man Submarine* (1944); *She's A Soldier Too* (1944); *Sergeant Mike* (1944); *Dancing in Manhattan* (1944); *The Black Parachute* (1944); *The Crime Doctor's Courage* (1945); *Mark of the Whistler* (1945); *Prison Ship* (1945); *Ten Little Indians* (1945); *I Love a Mystery* (1945); *Night Editor* (1946); *Dangerous Business* (1946); *Shadowed* (1946); *Time Out of Mind* (1947); *The Loves of Carmen* (1948); *Everybody Does It* (1949); *The Brave Bulls* (1950); *Mask of the Avenger* (1951); *The Brigand* (1952); *The Long Wait* (1954); *Mr Charmley Meets a Lady* (1956); and *The Day of the Fox* (1956).

CAZDEN, NORMAN

b. *New York, New York, 23 September 1914*
d. *Bangor, Maine, 18 August 1980*

Cazden began his public career as a pianist at age of ten, and a decade later he toured the eastern United States. He studied at the Institute of Musical Art in New York (later the Juilliard School), where he was a pupil of Arthur Newstead, Charles L. Seeger, and Leopold Mannes. He received diplomas is piano (1931, 1932) and teaching (1932). He entered the Juilliard Graduate School for study in piano under Ernest Hutcheson and in composition with Bernard Wagenaar, completing the program in 1939.

In 1934 Cazden joined the piano teaching faculty at the Juilliard School, although he chiefly taught theory, composition, and musicology. In addition, from 1926 to 1943 he was pianist with several modern dance groups. In 1938 he became a student at City College of New York where he earned a degree in Social Science in 1943. In that year he entered Harvard University where he was taught composition by Walter Piston and Aaron Copland in the musicology program, and studied psychology of music with Carroll C. Pratt. In 1948 he was awarded a doctorate in music. Cazden taught at a number of colleges and universities, including Vassar College, Poughkeepsie, New York (1947–48, 1956), Peabody Conservatory, Baltimore (1948–49), the University of Michigan, Ann Arbor (1949–50), the University of Illinois, Urbana-Champaign (1950–53), and the New School for Social Research, New York City (1956–58). He last taught at the University of Maine, Orono

Norman Cazden.
Courtesy The Juilliard School.

where he was professor of music from 1969 to 1980. Melodically his music reflects a deep interest in folk music, which he combined with strong rhythmic vitality.

For orchestra Cazden composed *Concerto for Ten Instruments* (1937); *Preamble* (1938); *On the Death of a Spanish Child* (1939); *Six Definitions* for chamber orchestra (1930-39); *Three Dances* (1940); *Stony Hollow* (1944); a Symphony (1948); *Three Ballads* (1949); *Songs From the Catskills* (1950); *Three Times a Round* (1953–57); *Woodland Valley Sketches* (1960); *Adventure* (1963); *Chamber Concerto* for clarinet and strings (1965);and a Viola Concerto (1972).

Among his instrumental works are five piano sonatas, a String Quartet (1936); Sonata for viola and clarinet (1938); Quartet for clarinet and strings (1939); a String Quintet (1941); two wind quintets (1941, 1966); Suite for violin and piano (1943); Suite for brass sextet (1951); Quintet for oboe and strings (1960); a Piano Trio (1969);and *Six Preludes and Fugues* for piano (1974. Cazden wrote a valuable series of sonatas for solo instrument and piano: horn (1941), flute (1941), recorder (and harp) (1971), bassoon (1971), cello (1971), English horn (1974), tuba (1974), viola (1974), clarinet (1974), and double bass (1974). He contributed many pieces to the repertory of educational music for piano and other instruments.

Among his stage works, Cazden composed a musical play, *Dingle Hill* (1958); music for Shakespeare's *The Merry Wives of Windsor* (1962) and *The Tempest* (1963); and numerous dance settings for the New Dance Group, the Humphrey-Weidman Company and others. These include *Hunger Dance* (1933); *etcetera* (1941); *Three Modern Dances* (1943); *The Lonely Ones* (1944); *Five Rejections and an Epilogue* (1951);and *Desert Sands* (1964).

Cazden published three books: *Musical Consonance and Dissonance* (1948), *A Book of Nonsense Songs* (1961), and *Folk Songs of the Catskills* (with Herbert Haufrecht) (1982).

CHADWICK, GEORGE WHITEFIELD
b. Lowell, Massachusetts, 13 November 1854
d. Boston, Massachusetts, 4 April 1931

Chadwick received his first piano instruction from his older brother; after leaving school he entered his father's insurance company. He went to Boston for piano lessons and played the organ in his local church. In 1876 he left business to teach for a year at Olivet College, Michigan, before going to Germany in 1877, against parental wishes, to study music. In Leipzig he attended the composition classes of Carl Reinecke and Solomon Jadassohn, a pupil of Liszt; it was here in 1879 that he composed his first important work, an overture *Rip Van Winkle*. In that year he moved to Munich where he received lessons from Rheinberger.

Chadwick returned to Boston in 1880 and set himself up as an organist and teacher of organ at the South Congregational Church. Among his first pupils were Horatio Parker and Arthur Whiting. In 1882 he joined the faculty of the New England Conservatory, becoming its director in 1897. He remained there until his death. As a greatly respected teacher, Chadwick laid the foundation of serious musical study, and his influence in this respect was widely felt through the activities of his pupils.

Chadwick's compositions, now sadly neglected, are numerous, especially in the orchestral and choral field. They show that he absorbed certain European features, especially from Dvořák, but his own personality is evident in a work such as the *Symphonic Sketches*, the single piece of his which is sometimes heard today. Its four movements—*Jubilee, Noel, Hobgoblin,* and *A Vogrom Ballad*, composed between 1895 and 1904—possess a wit and skill that should establish the work

as one of the most significant orchestral compositions by an American at the turn of the century.

Chadwick's many other orchestral works include three symphonies (no. 1 in C, 1882; no. 2 in B-flat, 1883-85; no. 3 in F, 1893-94); a waltz, *Schon Munchen* (1980); three symphonic poems: *Cleopatra* (1904), *Aphrodite* (1910–11), and *The Angel of Death* (1917); seven overtures: *Rip Van Winkle* (1879), *Thalia* (1883), *Melpemone* (1886), *The Miller's Daughter* (1886), *Adonais* (1899), *Euterpe* (1903), and *An American Overture* (1922); *Pastoral Prelude* (1890); *Serenade for Strings* (1890); *Andante* for strings (1892); Sinfonietta in D (1904); *Theme and Variations* for organ and orchestra (1908); *Suite Symphonique in E-flat* (1909); a symphonic ballad, *Tam O'Shanter* (1914–15); *Elegy in Memory of Horatio Parker* (1919); and *Anniversary Overture* (1922).

For the stage, Chadwick composed five operas. The first two, written in 1894, *The Quiet Lodging* and *Tabasco*, are both comedies, almost burlesque operettas. The lyric drama *Judith*, received a concert performance at the Worcester Festival in 1901. *The Padrone*, dating from 1912, concerns Italian immigrants in New England engaged in organized crime. It was never performed on stage. *Love's Sacrifice*, a pastoral opera, was composed in 1917. Chadwick also wrote an operetta, *The Peer and the Pauper* (1884), and incidental music for *Everywoman: Her Pilgrimage in Quest of Love* (1910).

His choral works earned Chadwick a wide reputation in his lifetime. The first of these, *The Viking's Last Voyage* for baritone, male chorus, and orchestra, was composed in 1881. In the following year he wrote *The Song of the Viking* for male voices. A choral ballad, *Lovely Rosabelle,* a setting of Sir Walter Scott's poem for chorus and orchestra was performed in 1889. For the Worcester Festival he wrote *Phoenix Expirans* (1892) and *The Lily Nymph* (1895). *Noel*, for soloists, chorus, and orchestra was heard at the Norfolk Festival in 1908. Shorter choral pieces include *Dedication Ode* (1883); *The Pilgrims* (1990); *Ecce Jam Noctis* (1897); *Land of Our Hearts* (1917);and *Fathers of the Free* (1927). Chadwick also composed five string quartets (1878, 1878, 1885, 1896, 1898); a Piano Quintet in E-Flat (1887);and over 130 songs.

Chadwick was the author of two textbooks, *Harmony: A Course of Study* (1897) and *A Key to Chadwick's Harmony* (1902).

CHANCE, JOHN BARNES
b. Beaumont, Texas, 20 November 1932
d. Lexington, Kentucky, 16 August 1972

Chance studied at the University of Texas where he was a pupil of Kent Kennan, Paul Pisk, and Clifton

Williams. He was timpanist in the Austin Symphony Orchestra before being appointed Composer-in-Residence in Greenboro, North Carolina for the Ford Foundation Young Composers Project (1960–62). From 1966 until his death in a domestic accident in 1972 he taught at the University of Kentucky, Lexington.

Chance's reputation rests on his expertise in writing for concert band: *Incantation and Dance* (1963); *Introduction and Caprice* for piano and band (1966); *Variations on a Korean Folk Song* (1967); *Blue Lake Overture* (1971); *Elegy* (1972);and his masterpiece, Symphony no. 2. (1972). For orchestra he composed Symphony no. 1. *in C* (1956); *Overture to a Fairy Tale* (1957); *Fiesta!* (1960);and *Satiric Suite* for strings (1961).

Among his choral works are *Blessed Are They That Mourn* for chorus, horns, strings, and bass drum (1961); *The Noiseless, Patient Spider* for female voices and flutes (1962); two pieces for chorus and band, *Alleluia* (1962) and *Ballad and March* (1962);and *Kyrie and Alleluia* for chorus and orchestra (1967). *Three Songs* (e.e.cummings) for soprano, flute, and piano date from 1962.

CHANLER, THEODORE (WARD)
b. Newport, Rhode Island, 29 April 1902
d. Boston, Massachusetts, 27 July 1961

Chanler began piano lessons at the age of six and was composing by his teens. He graduated from the Institute of Musical Art in New York City in 1921 and studied with Arthur Shepherd and Ernest Bloch in the U. S. After this he took a degree at Oxford University (1923–25), followed by three years in Paris as a pupil of Nadia Boulanger, returning to the United States in 1933. Chanler was equally celebrated as a composer and a critic. For many years he wrote articles for *Modern Music* and was on the staff of the *Boston Herald.* In 1955 he was appointed a teacher at the Peabody Institute in Baltimore. Two years later he took up a post at the Longy School in Cambridge, Massachusetts. He was awarded a Guggenheim Fellowship in 1944.

Most of Chanler's compositions are on a modest scale; he is best remembered as a writer of songs, many of which betray a French influence with their Fauré-like simplicity. His favorite poet, Walter De La Mare, provided the words for the two song cycles, *Epitaphs*, both written in 1937, and *Four Rhymes from "Peacock Pie."* (1940). The song cycle *The Children*, to words by Leonard Feeney, was composed in 1945.

The chorus *Her, whose faith lives for ever* is a setting of an English translation of words by the sixteenth-century French poet Bertaut. Also for choir he composed *Four Chorales for Summer* (1947). For female chorus and organ he wrote a Mass (1930).

Chanler's few extended works include a ballet, *Pas de Trois*, composed in 1942 for piano; a Violin Sonata (1925); *The Second Joyful Mystery* for two pianos (1942-43); and an opera, *The Pot of Fat*, performed in Cambridge, Massachusetts in 1955.

CHASINS, ABRAM
b. New York, New York, 17 August 1903
d. New York, New York, 21 June 1987

Chasins was born of Russian parents. He showed promise at an early age and studied piano with Ernest Hutcheson and composition with Rubin Goldmark at the Juilliard School. In 1926 he became a protégé, pupil, and assistant of Josef Hofmann at the Curtis Institute in Philadelphia. He also attended Columbia University. He won the friendship of Leopold Stokowski and Serge Rachmaninoff. In 1936, Chasins

Abram Chasins.
Courtesy The International Piano Archives.

resigned from teaching at the Curtis Institute to devote himself to performing, research, and composition. In 1940 he became music director of the *New York Times* radio station, WQXR. He retired from the concert platform in 1946 after a farewell tour as soloist with the Boston Symphony Orchestra under Koussevitzky. Chasins left WQXR in 1965 after 25 years service. From 1972 to 1977 he was musician-in-residence and director of the KUSC-FM radio station at the University of Southern California, Los Angeles.

As a composer, Chasins followed conservative lines, modelling his style on the romantic masters. Almost all his one hundred works are for piano solo, although he did write two piano concertos, two orchestral pieces—*Parade* (1930) and *Period Suite*—,songs, and a number of two-piano compositions. Piano Concerto no. 1. in F minor was premiered in January 1929 with the Philadelphia Orchestra under Ossip Gabrilowitsch, with the composer as soloist. The Second Piano Concerto in F# minor, composed three years later, is in a more experimental idiom. It was also first performed by the composer and the Philadelphia Orchestra, conducted by Stokowski in March 1933. Neither of these works satisfied the composer; he declined to release them for publication or recording and only he performed them in the United States and Europe.

Chasin's name is best known through his *Three Chinese Pieces* (1925), which were widely performed at one time and were taken up by Hofmann, Moisewitsch, Lhevinne, and other famous pianists. Chasins orchestrated them in 1929. His major piano work is a set of *Twenty-four Preludes* in all keys.

Chasins was the author of five books: *Speaking of Pianists* (1957), *The Van Cliburn Legend* (1959), *The Appreciation of Music* (1965), *Music at the Crossroads* (1972), and *Leopold Stokowski: A Profile* (1979).

CHESLOCK, LOUIS
b. London, England, 25 September 1899
d. Baltimore, Maryland, 19 July 1981

Cheslock was taken as a child to the United States in 1901, becoming an American citizen in 1913. He graduated from the Peabody Conservatory in violin in 1917 and in composition in 1921, where he had been a pupil of Franz Bornschein and Gustave Strube. He taught there from 1922, retiring as a violin instructor in 1976. For twenty-one years he was a violinist in the Baltimore Symphony Orchestra.

Cheslock composed an opera, *The Jewel Merchants*, in 1930, and a ballet for children, *Cinderella*, staged by the Peabody Ballet in 1946. For orchestra he wrote a Violin Concerto (1921); *Three Tone Poems* (*Cathedral at Sundown*, *'Neath Washington Monument*, *At the*

Railway Station; 1922); *Two Dances* (1922); *Symphonic Prelude* (1927); *Serenade for Strings* (1930); *Two Miniatures* for strings (1930); *Rhapsody* for strings and harp (1932); a Symphony in D (1932); *Theme and Variations* for horn and strings (1934); a *Horn* Concerto (1936); *Legend of Sleepy Hollow* (1936); *American Divertissement* (1941); *Rhapsody in Red and White* (1948); *Set of Six* for small orchestra (1950); *Suite* for oboe and strings (1953); and *Homage à Mendelssohn* for strings (1960).

Cheslock's choral music includes a setting of *Psalm 150* for chorus (1931); an oratorio *David* (1937); *Three Period Pieces* for chorus (1940); and an oratorio, *The Congo* based on the poem by Vachel Lindsay (1942).

Among Cheslock's instrumental works are a Violin Sonata (1917); Piano *Sonatina* (1932); *Shite Ami* (*Songs of My People*) *I* for harp and string quartet and *II* for violin, cello, and harp (1932); a String Quartet (1941); a Cello Sonatina (1943); *Concertinetto* for brass, piano, and percussion (1954); and *Bagatelle* for cello and piano (1969).

He was the author of a textbook, *Introductory Study on Violin Vibrato*, published in 1931.

CHIHARA, PAUL SEIKO
b. Seattle, Washington, 9 July 1938

After graduating from the University of Wisconsin as an English major in 1962, Chihara went to Paris to study with Nadia Boulanger. From 1963 to 1965 he attended Cornell University where he was a pupil of Robert Palmer. Later on a Fulbright Fellowship he studied with Ernst Pepping in Berlin. At Tanglewood he received composition lessons from Gunther Schuller. Until 1977 he was professor of music at the University of Southern California in Los Angeles where he founded the Twice Ensemble. From 1973 to 1986 he was Composer-in-Residence with San Francisco Ballet.

Chihara's *Four Pieces for Orchestra* won the Lili Boulanger Memorial Prize in 1963 and was premiered the following year at Carnegie Hall, New York by the National Orchestral Association. In 1965 his Viola Concerto was performed by the Baltimore Symphony Orchestra.

While studying at Tanglewood, Massachusetts with Gunther Schuller in 1966, Chihara began his *Tree Music* series of compositions. These include *Driftwood* for string quartet (1967); *Redwood* for viola and percussion (1968); *Willow, Willow* for bass flute, tuba, and percussion (1968); *Branches* for two bassoons and percussion (1968); *Logs* for doublebass and tape (1969); and *Logos XVI* for tape. They were first performed as a series in Carnegie Hall on 20 February 1970. Another "tree" piece for orchestra, *Forest Music*,

Paul Chihara.
Photo: Robert Millard, courtesy the composer.

"*Kisses Sweeter Than Wine*" (1997–2000); and *Love Music*, a Concerto for violin, clarinet, and orchestra (2000).

For the stage, Chihara has composed four ballets—*Phaedra* (1975), *Shinju* (*Lovers' Suicide*; 1975), *Mistletoe Bride* (1979), and *The Tempest* (1980)—and a musical,*The Infernal Machine*, retitled *Oedipus Rag* (1978–80).

Chihara's instrumental pieces include *Elegy* for piano trio (1974); *The Beauty of the Rose is in its Passing* for bassoon, two horns, harp, and percussion (1976); String Quartet (*Primavera*; 1977); *Sinfonia Concertante* for nine instruments (1980); *Sequoia* for string quartet and tape (1984); *Shogun Trio* for violin, clarinet, and piano (1982); String *Trio* (1984); *Forever Escher* for string quartet and saxophone quartet (1995); *Mambo Cane* (*A Dog's Mambo*) for concert wind ensemble (1996); *Minidoka* for viola, clarinet, harp, percussion, and tape (1996);and a Viola Sonata (*De Profundis*; 1998).

Among Chihara's choral pieces are *Magnificat* for six female voices (1965); *Psalm 90* (1965); *Nocturne* for 24 voices (1966); *Ave Maria – Scarborough Fair* for six male voices (1971); *Lie Lightly Gentle Earth* for chorus (1973); and *Missa Carminum* (*Folk Song Mass*) for eight voices (1975).

Since 1975 he has been active in providing scores for feature films, mainly for television. Among his one hundred titles are *Death Race 2000* (1975); *The Bad Seed* (1982); *The Legend of Far Walk Woman* (1982); *The Survivors* (1983); *Crossing Delancey* (1988); and *Passport to Terror* (1989).

CHILDS, BARNEY (SANFORD)
b. Spokane, Washington, 13 February 1926
d. Redlands, California, 11 January 2000

Childs studied English Literature at the universities of Nevada, Las Vegas (B.A. 1949), Oxford (M.A. 1955), and Stanford (Ph.D. 1959). He was self-taught in composition until his late 20s when he received lessons from Carlos Chávez (1953), Aaron Copland (1954), and Elliott Carter (1964–55). Childs taught English at the University of Arizona, Tucson (1956–65); from 1965 to 1969 he was Dean of Deep Springs College, Nevada; and from 1969 to 1971 he was a member of the music faculty of the Wisconsin College Conservatory in Milwaukee. From 1971 to 1994 he taught at the University of Redlands, California where he became professor of composition.

Childs's works after 1961 made use of a fairly considerable degree of indeterminacy, subordinated in the 1970s to musical structures concerned with balances and arrangements other than the traditional introduction-development-climax-resolution.

begun in 1966, was premiered by the Los Angeles Philharmonic Orchestra under Zubin Mehta in 1971 and was subsequently played in Japan in 1972 and at the Edinburgh Festival in 1973. Chihara's Cello Concerto, entitled *Wind Song*, was performed by Jeffery Solow in New York on 2 February 1971.

A second series of pieces entitled *Ceremonies* dates from the 1970s: *Ceremony I* for oboe, two cellos, doublebass, and percussion (1971); *Ceremony II*, subtitled *Incantations*, for flute, two amplified cellos, and percussion (1972); *Ceremony III* for flute and small orchestra (1973) for the Los Angeles Chamber Orchestra; *Ceremony IV* (1974) for the Los Angeles Philharmonic Orchestra; and *Ceremony V* (*Last of the Ceremonies*, later renamed *Symphony in Celebration*; 1973–75), commissioned by the Fromm Foundation for the Houston Symphony Orchestra.

Later orchestral pieces include a *Doublebass* Concerto, subtitled *Grass* (1972); a *Guitar* Concerto (1975); *Saxophone* Concerto (1978); Symphony no. 2 "*Birds of Sorrow*' (1979); *Aubade* for chamber orchestra (1989); Concerto for string quartet and orchestra

Child's few orchestral works include two symphonies (1954, 1956); a Concerto for English horn, strings, harp, and percussion (1955); *Music for Almost Everybody* (1964); *Music for piano and strings* (1965); *Variations on a theme of Harold Budd* for strings (1969); Concerto for clarinet and orchestra (1970); and a Concerto for timpani (1989). For concert band he wrote *Six Events for 68 players* (1965); *Supposes: imago mundi* (1971); *Concertpiece* for tuba and band (1974); *Golden Shore* (1975); *Courses of the Crimson Dawn* (1977); *September with Band* (1978); *A Continuance in Seven Parts* (1979);and *Orrery* (1980).

The contribution Childs made to instrumental music was extensive. He wrote eight string quartets (1951–69); five wind quintets (1951–69); five brass quintets (1954–75);and sonatas or similarly scaled works for violin (1956), solo clarinet (1951), solo horn (1955, 1963), solo viola (1954), bassoon (1953), solo oboe (1959), flute (1960), solo trombone (1961), and solo cello (1962, 1978). Some pieces are scored for unusual instrumental groups: *Quartet for bassoons* (1958); *Changes for three oboes* (1959); *Quartet* for flute, oboe, doublebass, and percussion (1964); *Music for doublebass and friend* (1964); *Mary's Idea* for tuba and harpsichord (1967); *The Golden Bubble* for contrabass sarrusophone and solo percussion (1967); *Operation*

Flabby Sleep for any instruments (1968); *Lanterns and Candlelight* for marimba and soprano (1975); *A Question of Summer* for tuba and harp (1976); *The Edge of the World* for bass clarinet and organ (1981); and a Horn Octet (1984).

Childs composed close to a dozen choral works, including a major setting of Whitman's poem *When lilacs last at the dooryard bloom'd* for soloists, chorus, and symphonic band (1970–71).

Other instrumental pieces include *Welcome to Whipperginny* for percussion nonet (1961); *The Bayonne Barrel and Drum Company* for improvising solo wind instruments, 13 winds, piano, and percussion (1968); *Music for two flute players* (1963); *37 Songs* for piano solo (1971); *Of Place, As Altered* for five clarinets (1972); *Trio* for clarinet, cello, and piano (1972); *Bowling Again with the Champs* for six improvisers and pre-recorded tape (1976); *Overture to "Measuring a Meridian'* for wind quintet, also saxophone, and solo percussion (1978); *Seven Quiet Studies* for percussion (1978); *Pastorale* for bass clarinet and tape (1983); *Sunshine Lunchh* (sic) *and Like Matters* for bass clarinet, baritone, percussion, and electronics (1984); *A Box of Views* for wind quintet and piano (1988); *Quite a row of them sitting there* for clarinet and piano (1992); and *Intrada, Be Someone Else* for saxophone quartet (1992).

Childs composed two theater works, *The Roachville Project* for four to ten people (1967) and *Banana Flannelboard!* for three readers and tape (1980).

CHOU WEN-CHUNG
b. Yantai, Shandong, China, 29 June 1923

Chou Wen-Chung studied in Shanghai, Kweilin, and at Chungking National University (1941–45) before coming to the United States in 1946 on a scholarship to study architecture. After a short time he turned to music and entered the New England Conservatory of Music, Boston, where he was a pupil of Nicolas Slonimsky and Carl McKinley (1946–49). In 1949 he moved to New York where he studied with Edgar Varèse; at Columbia University he studied with Otto Luening. He was also a pupil of Bohuslav Martinů in 1949. He became an American citizen in 1958.

In 1958 he was Composer-in-Residence at the University of Illinois, Urbana. After teaching at Brooklyn College (1961–62) and Hunter College, New York (1963–64) he joined the faculty of Columbia University in 1964, becoming a professor in 1972. He was Dean of the School of Music (1976–87) and the first Fritz Reiner Professor of Composition (1984–91).He has been the recipient of two Guggenheim Fellowships (1957, 1959) and many other awards. He was a

Barney Childs.
Courtesy University of the Redlands.

founder of the American Society of University Composers.

In his music Chou Wen-chung combines atonality with Chinese characteristics, as implied by many of the titles of his compositions. His principal works are *Landscapes* (1949), performed by Stokowski and the San Francisco Symphony Orchestra in 1953, *Seven Poems of the T'ang Dynasty* for tenor and chamber orchestra (1952); *All in the Spring Wind* for orchestra (1952–53); *And the Fallen Petals* (1954), commissioned by the Louisville Orchestra (1956); *In the Mode of Shang* for chamber orchestra (1956); *Two Miniatures of the T'ang Dynasty* for chamber orchestra (1957); *To a Wayfarer* for clarinet, harp, percussion, and strings (1958); *Poems of White Stone* for chorus and instrumental ensemble (1958–59); *Metaphors* for large wind orchestra (1961); *Riding the Wind* for similar forces (1964); *Beijing in the Mist* (1985);and a Cello Concerto composed in 1992 for Janos Staker.

He has also written several instrumental works, including *Suite* for harp and wind quintet (1950); *Two Chinese Folksongs* for harp (1950); *Three Folk Songs* for flute and harp (1950); *Willows Are New* for chamber ensemble (1957); *Soliloquy of a Bhiksuni* for trumpet, brass, and percussion (1958); *Cursive* for flute and piano (1963); *The Dark and the Light* for piano, percussion, and strings (1964); *Yu Ko* for nine players (1965); *Pien* for piano, winds, and percussion (1966); *Ceremonial* for three trumpets and three trombones (1968); *Yun* for winds, two pianos, and percussion (1969); *Echoes of the Gorge* for chamber ensemble (1989); *Windswept Peaks* for violin, cello, clarinet, and piano (1990); and *Clouds* for string quartet (1997).

Among his scores for documentary films are *Hong Kong* (1960); *White Paper of Red China* (1962); *A Day at the Fair* (1964); and *Red Chna's Year of the Gun* (1968).

In addition to writing numerous articles on Asian music, Chou has edited works by his teacher Varèse: *Amériques*, *Integrales*, and *Octandre*; he completed *Nocturnal*, left unfinished at the composer's death. In 1998 he rediscovered two lost Varèse scores, *Tuning Up* for orchestra and *Dance Burgess* for chamber orchestra.

CITKOWITZ, ISRAEL

b. *Skierniewice, Russia (now Poland), 6 February 1909*

d. *London, England, 4 May 1974*

As a young child, Citkowitz was taken to the United States. He studied with Aaron Copland and Roger Sessions in New York, and in Paris with Nadia Boulanger from 1927 to 1931. From 1939 to 1969 he taught at the Dalcroze Institute in New York. He moved to London in 1969.

Most of Citkowitz's works are in the field of chamber music, piano music, and songs. He composed a String Quartet (1932) and *Movements* for string quartet. His songs to poems by James Joyce, *Chamber Music* (1930), were heard at the I.S.C.M. Festival in London in 1931. His other important song cycles are to words by William Blake and Robert Frost (1934, 1936) and *Strings in the Earth and Air* (1930). Citkowitz's best-known choral works are the setting for mixed voices of Blake's *The Lamb*, composed in 1936, and *Songs of Protest* (1936).

CLAASSEN, ARTHUR

b. *Stargard, Prussia, 19 February 1859*

d. *San Francisco, California, 16 March 1920*

Claassen studied in Weimar (1875–78) with Karl Miller-Hartung, Alexander Wilhelm Gottschalg, and B. Sulze. In 1878 he became acquainted with Liszt. From 1880 to 1884, he conducted theater orchestras in Gottingen and Magdeburg. In 1884 he was appointed director of the Brooklyn Arion Choir. He settled in San Antonio, Texas, in 1910 where he founded the San Antonio Orchestra.

Claassen composed a symphonic poem, *Höhenfriedberg*, *Waltz Idyll* for string orchestra (1885); *Sanssouci* for strings (1890); and two choral pieces, *Festival Hymn* and *The Battle*.

CLAFLIN, (ALAN) AVERY

b. *Keene, New Hampshire, 21 June 1898*

d. *Greenwich, Connecticut, 9 January 1979*

Claflin studied composition with John P. Marshall, organist of the Boston Symphony Orchestra, and at Harvard University with Archibald T. Davison. Interrupting his studies there in May 1917, he went to France to drive an ambulance during World War I, and did not return permanently to the United States until June 1919. In France, Claflin became acquainted with Auric, Milhaud, and Poulenc, and received some musical guidance from Erik Satie. As the loss of a finger at Verdun ended his pianistic aspirations, Claflin turned to banking as a livelihood but, like Charles Ives, composed music regularly in the evenings and on weekends throughout his business career. In 1947 he was elected President of the French America Banking Corporation, an international bank in New York City, from which he retired in 1954.

Claflin's earliest works of significance are for the stage: a one-act opera, *The Fall of the House of Usher*

(1921), and a ballet *Hewlett*, composed in 1928 but not scored until 1943–44. He composed three other operas: *Hester Prynne* in three acts, completed in 1932 and based on Hawthorne's *The Scarlet Letter*; *La grande bretèche* in one act (1945–47); and his final work, *Uncle Tom's Cabin* in three acts, completed in 1964.

Among Claflin's orchestral pieces are *Moby Dick Suite* (1929); Symphony no. 1. *in D minor* (1936); *Concert Allegro* (1938); Symphony no. 2. (1942–44); *Larghetto and Shuffle* (1944); *Fishhouse Punch* (1947–48); *Teen Scenes* for strings (1954–55); *Four Pieces for Orchestra* (Symphony no. 3; 1955–56); *Seven Meditations for Holy Week* for chamber orchestra (1956–57); and a Piano Concerto subtitled *Concerto Giocoso* (1956–57).

Two large-scale works for chorus and organ are *Mary of Nazareth* (1949–60) and *Saul of Tarsus* (1960–61). The clever *Lament for April 15* for chorus (1955) uses as its text a portion of the Internal Revenue Service's tax code.

Claflin's chamber music includes a Piano Trio (1921); a String Quartet (*Laudate Dominum*) (1940-41); a Violin Sonata (1954); *Finale from "The Dunciad'* for soprano and string quartet (1954); *Pastoral "The Oriole'* for wind quintet (1957); and *Recitativo, Aria and Stretta* (1958) for violin, viola, horn, and cello. For keyboard he wrote *Prelude, Chaconne and Finale* (1953) and *An American Legend* (1959), both for piano, and *Three Pieces* for organ (1959).

Claflin was coauthor with Bernard Fäy of *The American Experiment* published in 1929.

CLAPP, PHILIP GREELEY
b. Boston Massachusetts, 4 August 1888
d. Iowa City, Iowa, 9 April 1954

Clapp graduated from Harvard University (B.A., 1908; M.A., 1909; Ph.D., 1911). On a Frederick Sheldon Fellowship (1909–11), he worked at the British Museum and studied conducting and composition with Max von Schillings in Stuttgart. On his return to the United States Clapp taught at Harvard until 1911, and later at Dartmouth College (1915–18). During the First World War, he served as a bandmaster with the 73rd Artillery in the American Expeditionary Forces in France. In 1919 he was appointed professor and director of music at the University of Iowa in Iowa City, a post he held until his death in 1954. He conducted the University Symphony Orchestra and Chorus and was guest conductor with the American Orchestral Society in New York and the Cincinnati Symphony Orchestra. The Bruckner Society awarded him the Bruckner Medal of Honour in 1940 and the Mahler Medal in 1942 for services to music.

Philip Clapp.
Courtesy University of Iowa Libraries, Kent Collection.

Clapp's major orchestral works are 12 symphonies: no. 1 in E (1908; Boston 1912); no. 2 in E minor (1911; Boston, 1914); no. 3 in E-Flat (1917); no. 4 in A (1919); no. 5 in D (1926); no. 6 in B, "Golden Gate" (1926); no. 7 in A (1928); no. 8 in C (1930); no. 9 in E-Flat, "The Pioneers," commissioned for the Chicago Century of Progress Exposition (1931); no. 10 in F, "Heroic Symphony" (1935); no. 11 in C (1942); and no. 12 in B-Flat, "The Rime of the Ancient Mariner" (1944).

Also for orchestra he composed three symphonic poems: *Norge* (Harvard, 1908, Boston, 1909), *A Song of Youth* (1910, rev. 1950); and *In Summer* (St. Louis, 1912); *Dramatic Poem* for trombone and orchestra (1912); *Academic Diversion on Seven Notes* for small orchestra (Chicago, 1931); *Overture to a Comedy* (1937); *Fantasia on an Old Plainchant* for cello and orchestra (1937, rev. 1939); *Prologue to a Tragedy* (1939); a Concerto *for two* pianos *in B minor* (1941); *A Hill Rhapsody* (1945); and an overture, *Open Road* (1948).

Clapp's instrumental music includes a String Quartet (1909); a Violin Sonata (1909); a Piano *Sonatina in*

E (1923); a Suite for brass sextet (1938); *A Fanfare Prelude* for brass (1940); and a *Prelude and Finale* for wind quintet (1954). He wrote two operas, *The Taming of the Shrew* (1945–48) and *The Flaming Brand* (1949–53), and a choral work, *A Chant of Darkness* (1919–24) to words by Helen Keller.

CLARKE, HENRY LELAND
b. Dover, New Hampshire, 9 March 1907
d. Seattle, Washington, 30 March 1992

Clarke graduated from Harvard University in 1928, receiving a Master's degree the following year and a doctorate in 1947. At Harvard he had been a pupil of Holst. From 1929 to 1931 he studied with Nadia Boulanger at the Ecole Normale in Paris. From 1932 to 1936 he was assistant librarian at the New York Public Library.

While teaching at Bennington College, Vermont (1936–38), he received lessons from Otto Luening. In 1938 he was appointed Chairman of the Graduate Faculty of Westminster Choir College, Princeton where he remained for four years. After teaching at the University of California, Los Angeles (1947–48, 1949–58) and at Vassar College, Poughkeepsie, New York (1948–49), he joined the music faculty of the University of Washington, Seattle in 1958, retiring as professor Emeritus in 1977.

He used scales restricted to certain notes and a form of the 12-note system he called "rotating triskadecaphony." For orchestra, Clarke composed *Lyric Sonata* for strings (1932, rev. 1960); *Monograph* (1952); *Saraband for the Golden Goose* (1957); *Points West* (1960); *Encounter* for viola and orchestra (1961); and *Variegation* (1961). He composed two operas: *The Loafer and the Loaf* in one act (1951), produced in Los Angeles in 1956; and *Lysistrata* (Aristophanes; 1969), which was staged in Marlboro, Vermont in 1984.

Among his many instrumental compositions are three string quartets (1928, 1956, 1958); *Nocturne* for viola and piano (1935); *A Game That Two Can Play* for flute and clarinet (1959); *Concatenata* (*Quodlibet*) for wind quintet (1969); *Three From Foster* for instrumental trio (1980); *Mason's Hamburg* for organ (1980); and *Salute to Justin Morgan* for flute, violin, and harpsichord (1982). *Danza de la Muerte* for oboe and piano (1937), choreographed by José Limón was followed 38 years later by *Danza de la Vida* (1975), also for oboe and piano.

Clarke wrote many choral pieces. Of note are *Gloria in the Five Official Languages of the United Nations* for chorus and orchestra, *Happy is the Man* for choir and orchestra (1935); *No Man is an Island* (Donne) for men's voices and band (1951); *Love-in-the-World* for tenor, women's voices, and piano (1953); and *Wonders Are Many* for tenor, baritone, and men's chorus (1954). Later choral works include *Patriot Primer* (1974); *Mass for All Souls* (1975); *These Are the Times That Try Men's Souls* (1976); *I Call That Mind Free* (1979); *We Believe* (1984); and *The Earth Mourns* (after Isaiah 24) (1984). He also composed many solo songs.

Clarke was the author of a book, *Sound and Unsound: Ideas on Music* (1973).

COATES, GLORIA
b. Wausau, Wisconsin, 10 October 1938

Coates began composing music at a very early age. She later studied at De Paul University of Chicago with Alexander Tcherepnin, Louisiana State University (B.Mus., M.M.), and Columbia University, where she was a pupil of Otto Luening. Later she attended the Mozarteum in Salzburg. From 1969 to 1989, Coates lived in Europe, teaching at the University of Wisconsin International Programs in Munich (1975–84). She also organized the German American Contemporary Music Series (1971–84). Since then she has divided her time between Europe and the United States. In addition she has been a visiting teacher at Harvard University; University of Wisconsin, Madison; Boston University; and the conservatories of New Delhi, Bombay, and Calcutta.

The uniquely personal style of Coates's works has few antecedents, with only Krzysztof Penderecki and Witold Lutoslawski as possible influences. Her compositional techniques are complex but the results for the listener are in essence relatively simple. Although the basic pulse of much of her music is slow, it usually contains a mass of internal activity. The ends can be seen in some respects minimal, but the means are intricate and rigidly controlled.

Coates's most significant works are fourteen symphonies. Not until Symphony no. 7 (1990–91) did she use the term "symphony," numbering the previous six retrospectively. Symphony no. 1 for string orchestra, her best-known composition, is subtitled *Music on Open Strings*. It was composed between 1973 and 1974 and first performed in August 1978 at the Warsaw Autumn Festival. Symphony no. 2, doubly subtitled *Illuminatio in Tenebris* and *Music in Abstract Lines*, was commissioned for New Music America 1989. Dedicated to the memory of the composer's father, it was first performed in New York by the Brooklyn Philharmonic Orchestra in May 1989.

Symphony Nocturne (Symphony no. 3) for string orchestra was completed in 1977 and premiered in Heidelberg, Germany, by the Uppsala Festival Strings in June 1988. Symphony no. 4, *Chiaroscuro* was com-

Gloria Coates, 1982.
*Photo: Hilde Zemann,
courtesy the composer.*

posed in 1984 and revised in 1990. Scored for full orchestra with a large percussion section including a flexatone, it was performed by the Stuttgart Philharmonic Orchestra in June 1990. In Symphony no. 5, *Three Mystical Songs* (1985–86), a double chorus vocalizes on texts by Alexandra Coates. The first performance took place in November 1990 during the American Week in Berlin.

Music in Microtones (Symphony no. 6), also subtitled *Time Frozen*, was commissioned by Theodore Antoniou, who conducted the premiere with the Alea III orchestra in November 1987 during the American Week in Boston. Symphony no. 7 was composed in 1991 to a commission from South German Radio, Stuttgart. It is dedicated to "those who brought down the (Berlin) wall in PEACE." The first performance was given by the Stuttgart Philharmonic Orchestra in January 1992. Symphony no. 8, subtitled *Indian Sounds*, was composed in 1991 and performed in Munich in February 1992. It is scored for small orchestra to which are added exotic percussion, including American Indian instruments, and chanting voices. *Symphony* no. 9 (*The Quinces Quandary*) *Homage to Van Gogh* (1992–93) was premiered in Dresden in 1995. Symphony no. 10, *Drones of Druids on Celtic Runes* (1993–94) was performed in Erding, Germany in 1995. Coates's Symphony, no. 11 (*Philemon and Baucis*) was heard in Zell on the Pram, Austria, in 1999. Symphonies no. 12 and 13, both for large orchestra, were premiered together in 2001 at the Festival of American Music in Nurmberg, Germany. Her most recent Symphony no. *14* was first performed in Munich in October 2003. Other orchestral works include *Planets* (1974); *Sinfonietta della Notte* (1974–82), premiered in Sweden in 1982; and *Transitions* for chamber orchestra (Munich, 1984).

Balancing this formidable sequence of symphonies,

Coates has composed eight string quartets (1966, 1971–72, 1975, 1977, 1988, 2000, 2001, 2001). Her other instrumental pieces includes *Sylken* for flute, oboe, and piano (1962); *Trio* for three flutes (1966); *Five Abstractions of Poems by Emily Dickinson* for woodwind quartet (1966–75); *Halley's Comet* for nine instruments (1974); *May the Morning Star Rise* for viola and organ (1974); *Spring Morning in Grobholzes' Garden* for three flutes and tape (1976); *Breaking Through* for recorder (1977); *Lunar Loops* for two guitars (1987–88); *Floating Down the Mississippi* for eight guitars (1987–88); *Lichtsplitter* for flute, harp, and viola (1988); two pieces for flute and tape, *Fiori* (1987) and *Fiori and the Princess* (1988); *Blue Monday* for guitar and two roto-toms (1988); and *Floating Down the Mississippi* for eight guitars (1988).

Later instrumental pieces are *Transfer 482* for flute, harp, viola, and two percussion (1988, 1991); *In the Mt. Tremper Zen Monastery* for two percussionists, viola, and harp or piano (1988–92); *In the Glacier* for ten flutes and harp (1992); *Königshymne* (*Royal Anthem*) for ten flutes and percussion (1992); *Blue Flowers* for ten flutes (1992); *Night Music* for tenor saxophone, piano, and gongs (1992); *Im Finstern sei des Geistes Licht und Sonne* for organ, cello, and ocarina (1993); *Turning To* for two flutes (1995); *Homage to Novalis* for flute, harp, and two cellos or cello and viola (1996); *Lyric Suite* for piano trio (1996); *Fairytale Suite* for solo flute (1997); *Ode to the Moon* for tenor saxophone, piano, cello, and percussion (1998); Sonata for solo violin (2000–01); and Piano Sonata no. 2 (2001–02).

Among Coates's choral works are *Missa Brevis* for female voices and organ (1964); *Anima della Terra* for solo voices and orchesra (1972–73); *The Elements* for chorus and orchestra (1975); *Fonte di Rimini* (*Sinfonia*

Brevis) for chorus and orchestra (1976–84), performed in Bayreuth, Germany in 1984, *The Beatitudes* for chorus and organ (1978); and *Rainbow Across the Night Sky* for women's voices, violin, viola, cello, and two percussionists (1991). For solo voice Coates has written *Voices of Women in Wartime* for soprano, piano, viola, cello, and two percussion (1972); *Seven Songs with Poems by Emily Dickinson* for voice and chamber orchestra (1962–88); *15 Songs on Poems by Emily Dickinson* for voice and piano (1965–97); *The Force for Peace in War* for soprano and chamber orchestra (1973–88); *Fragments from Leonardo's Notebooks* for solo voices and orchestra (1976-88); *Five Songs to Words of E.D.* (Emily Dickinson) for voice, piano, and percussion (1978–89); *The Swan* (Mallarmé), a dramatic scene for soprano, oboe or English horn, timpani, and two percussionists (1988); *Cette Blanche Agonie* (Mallarmé) for soprano and chamber orchestra (1988–91); *Wir tönen allein* (Celan) for soprano and chamber orchestra (1989–91); *Einsamkeit* for alto and piano (1999); *Komplementar* for soprano, mezzo-soprano, and piano (1999); *Im Ausland* for soprano and piano (2000); and *Mirage* for baritone, flute, cello, and piano (2002–03).

For the stage Coates has composed incidental music for *Thieves Carneval* (Anouilh) (1961); *Everyman* (1962); *St. Joan* (G. B. Shaw) (1964); *Hamlet* (Shakespeare) (1964–65); and an incomplete opera, *The Fall of the House of Usher* (1962–66).

COERNE, LOUIS (ADOLPHE)
b. Newark, New Jersey, 27 February 1870
d. Boston, Massachusetts, 11 September 1922

Coerne was a pupil of John Knowles Paine at Harvard University (1888–90) and later studied in Munich with Joseph Rheinberger (1890–92). He taught at Smith College, Northampton, Massachusetts (1903–04), Olivet College, Michigan (1909–10), and was head of the music Department of the University of Wisconsin from 1910 to 1915. He was professor of music at the Connecticut College for Women in New London (1915–22).

Of his huge output, Coerne is remembered today solely for the opera *Zenobia* (1902), premiered in Bremen, Germany in 1905. It was the first opera by an American composer to be produced in that country. With this work and a thesis entitled "The Evolution of the Modern Orchestra," Coerne became in 1905 the first recipient of a Ph.D. in music from Harvard University. It was published in 1908. Coerne composed four other operas: *A Woman of Marblehead, Sakuntula* (1904), *The Maiden Queen*, and *The Belle of Beaujolais*. He also wrote a ballet, *Evadne* (1892).

Coerne's orchestral music includes a Suite *in D minor* for strings (1892); a Concerto for organ, two horns, harp, and strings (1893); a symphonic poem, *Hiawatha* (1894); a Violin Concerto, a *Concert Overture* in D, and a symphonic poem, *Excalibur* (1921).

COHN, ARTHUR
b. Philadelphia, Pennsylvania, 6 November 1910
d. New York, New York, 15 February 1998

Cohn studied at the Combs Conservatory of Music, Philadelphia (1920–28) and also privately in Philadelphia with William F. Happich for composition (1929–32) and Sascha Jacobinoff for violin (1930–31). At the University of Pennsylvania (1930-31) he studied chamber music with Emil Folgmann and, at the Juilliard School in New York City (1932–34), he was a pupil of Rubin Goldmark. From 1934 to 1952 he was Curator of the Edwin A. Fleisher Music Collection at the Free Library of Philadelphia where he also served as head of the Music Department (1946–52). He was director of the University of Pennsylvania Museum Concerts (1949–56) and executive director of the Settlement Music School in Philadelphia (1952–56).

In 1956 Cohn moved to New York where he became head of the Symphonic and Foreign Music Department of Mills Music (1956–66), director of Serious Music, M.C.A. (1966–73), moving to a similar position with Carl Fischer, Inc in 1973.

Cohn's career as a conductor began in Philadelphia where he directed the Symphony Club Orchestra (1942–73), children's concerts for the Philadelphia Orchestra (1954 and 1956), and the Philadelphia Little Symphony (1952–56). From 1958 he was music director and Conductor of the Haddonfield Symphony Orchestra and was guest conductor with several other organizations.

For orchestra Cohn wrote two suites; *Five Nature Studies* (1932); *Retrospections* for strings (1933); *Four Preludes* for strings, a larger setting of String Quartet no. 1. (1937); *Symphony for Double Orchestra* (1937), later withdrawn, Suite for viola and orchestra (1937); *Four Symphonic Documents* (1939); Suite for violin and orchestra (1935–39); *Quintuple Concerto* for five ancient instruments and modern orchestra (1940); *Histrionics* for strings, a larger setting of *Quartet* no. 4. (1940); a *Flute* Concerto (1941); *Variations* for clarinet, saxophone, and strings (1945); *Kaddish* (1964); and a *Percussion* Concerto (1970).

Cohn's major instrumental works are six string quartets (1928, 1930, 1932, 1935, 1935, 1945). Other chamber compositions are a Suite *in E minor* for violin and piano (1932); *Music for Brass Instruments* (1934, rev. 1939); *Machine Music* for two pianos (1937); *Piano Preludes* (1939); *Music for Ancient Instruments* (1939);

Pot-bellied Gods (R. Abramson) for narrator and string quartet (1940); *Bet It's a Boy* for piano and strings with film slides (1941); *Hebraic Study and Declamation and Toccata*, both for bassoon solo or bassoon and piano (1944); and *Quotations in Percussion* for 103 instruments and six players, commissioned in 1958 by Arizona State University.

In addition to writing articles and reviews for various newspapers and journals, including the *American Record Guide, Modern Music, Tempo,* and *The Musical Courier*, Cohn was the author of a number of books: *Addendum to the Collector's Haydn* (1960), *The Collector's Twentieth-Century Music in the Western Hemisphere* (1961), *Twentieth-Century Music in Western Europe* (1965), *Musical Quizzical* (1968), *Recorded Classical Music: A Critical Guide to the Compositions and the Performances* (1981), and an *Encyclopedia of Chamber Music* (1990).

COLE, FRANCIS ULRIC
b. New York, New York, 9 September 1905
d. Bridgeport, Connecticut, 21 May 1992.

Cole studied with John Grunn in Los Angeles (1913–23) and Percy Goetschius in New York (1923–24). A Juilliard Fellowship (1924–27) enabled her to become a pupil of Rubin Goldmark (composition) and Josef Llevinne (piano). From 1927 to 1929 she studied with Nadia Boulanger in Paris. She taught at the Mannes School of Music, New York (1936–42), and was on the editorial staff of *Time* magazine for eight years.

As a child she made her debut as a pianist in concertos. She was the soloist in the premieres of her two piano concertos (1931, 1946) and the Divertimento for piano and strings. For orchestra she wrote *Two Sketches for strings* (1932–37); a Suite (1937); *Metropolitones*; *Purple Shadows*; *Nevada*; *Sunlight Channel*; and *Andante Sostenuto* for English horn (or cello) and chamber orchestra. Her instrumental music includes two violin sonatas (1927, 1929); a Suite for a piano trio (1931); a Piano Quintet (1936); Suite for string quartet (1936); two string quartets; and a *Fantasy Sonata* for piano (1933).

COLGRASS, MICHAEL (CHARLES)
b. 22 April, 1932: Chicago, Illinois

At the University of Illinois, Urbana (1950–54), Colgrass studied percussion and composition. At Tanglewood, Massachusetts, he was a pupil of Lukas Foss (1952, 1954); at Aspen, Colorado, he received lessons from Darius Milhaud. In New York City he studied with Wallingford Riegger (1958) and Ben Weber

Michael Colgrass.
Photo: Paul Hoeffler, courtesy the composer.

(1958–60). He was awarded two Guggenheim Fellowships (1964, 1968) and the Pulitzer Prize in 1978. Currently he lives in Toronto.

Until 1967 Colgrass was by profession a percussionist. He was the inventor of roto-toms, tom-toms without a shell. His practical work in both the orchestral field and jazz is often reflected in his compositions: *Three Brothers* for percussion (1950); *Percussion Music* for four percussionists (1953); *Chamber Music* for percussionist quintet (1954); *Invention on a Motive* for percussion quartet (1955); *Variations* for four drums and viola (1957); *Fantasy Variations* for solo percussion and percussion sextet (1960); *Divertimento* for eight drums, piano, and strings (1961); *Light Spirit* for flute, viola, guitar, and percussion (1963); *Rhapsodic Fantasy* for solo percussion and orchestra (1965); and Concerto for four percussionists and orchestra, titled *Deja vu* (1977), which won the Pulitzer Prize in the following year.

Five important works were premiered in 1976: *Concertmasters* for three solo violins and orchestra, commissioned by the Detroit Symphony Orchestra; *Wolf* for solo cello for the Young Concert Artists, Inc., of New York; *Theatre of the Universe* for soloists, chorus, and orchestra, performed in Minneapolis; *Best Wishes U.S.A.* for black and white choruses, jazz band, folk instruments, and orchestra, commissioned by the Springfield Symphony Orchestra; and *Letter From Mozart*, commissioned by the Musica Aeterna Orchestra, New York.

Other instrumental pieces include a *Wind Quintet* (1962); *Light Spirit* for flute, viola, guitar, and two guitars (1962); *Rhapsody* for clarinet, viola, and piano (1963); *Wolf* for solo cello (1976); *Night of the Racoon* for harp, flute, keyboard, and percussion (1978); *Mystery Flowers of Spring* for violin and piano (1978); *Flashbacks* for brass quintet (1979) for the Canadian Brass Quintet; *Winds of Nagual* for wind ensemble (1985); *Strangers: Irreconcilable Variations* for clarinet, viola, and piano (1986); a *String Quartet: Folklines* (1987); *Memento Trio* for flute, cello, and piano (1999); and *Chameleon* for alto saxophone (2001).

For orchestra Colgrass has composed *As Quiet As . . .*, commissioned by the Fromm Foundation in 1966, *Sea Shadow* for small orchestra (1966); *Aurus* for harp and orchestra (1973) to a Ford Foundation commission; *Chaconne* for viola and orchestra (1979); *Delta* for clarinet, viola, percussion, and orchestra (1979); *Memento* for two pianos and orchestra (1982); *Demon* for amplified piano, percussion, tape, radio, and orchestra (1984); *The Schubert Birds* (1989); *Snow Walker* for organ and orchestra (1990); *Arias* for clarinet and orchestra (1992); *Ghosts of Pangea* (2000); *Dream Dancer* for alto saxophone and orchestra (2001); and *Crossworlds* for flute, piano, and orchestra, composed in 2002 for the Boston Symphony Orchestra. Two recent works for wind band are *Arctic Dreams* (1991) and *Urban Requiem* (1995).

Colgrass's choral works include *Earth's a Baked Apple* (1968), commissioned by the Boston Symphony Orchestra; *Image of Man* for soloists, chorus, and orchestra, performed at Expo 74 in Montreal, Canada; and *Theatre of the Universe* for soloists, chorus and orchestra (1975). For the stage he has composed *Virgil's Dream* for four actor/singers and four mime/musicians, performed at the Brighton Festival, England in 1967; a ballet for Gerald Arpino, *Sea Shadow*, produced in New York in 1967 under the composer's direction; a one-act comic opera, *Nightingale Inc.* (1975); and a one-act children's musical, *Something's Gonna Happen* (1978).

Colgrass is the author of a book, *My Lessons With Kumi* (2002).

CONE, EDWARD TONER
b. Greensboro, North Carolina, 4 May 1917

Cone studied at Princeton University (1935–39, 1941–42) where he was a pupil of Roger Sessions. At Co-lumbia University (1939–41) he studied musicology with Paul Henry Lang. He studied piano with Edward Steuermann and Karl Ulrich Schnabel. In 1947 he was awarded a Guggenheim Fellowship. That same year, he joined the music faculty at Princeton University, first as an assistant professor, then in 1952 as an associate professor and in 1960 as a professor of music, a position he held until his retirement in 1985. In addition to teaching at Princeton, Cohn was appointed professor at the University of California, Berkeley, in 1972 for a year, and was named a professor-at-large at Cornell University in 1979.

For orchestra, Cone has written *Elegy* (1953); a Symphony (1953); *Nocturne and Rondo* for piano and orchestra (1955–57); a *Violin* Concerto (1959); *Music for Strings* (1965); *Variations for Orchestra* (1968); and *Cadenzas* for violin, oboe, and strings (1979).

His important chamber works are two *Violin* Sonatas (1940, 1948); *Clarinet Quintet* (1941); a String Quartet (1949); a String Sextet (1966), performed at the I.S.C.M. Festival in New York in 1973, *Duet* for clarinet and violin (1969); a String Trio (1973) that was premiered in the following year by members of the Pro Arte Quartet; and *Serenade* for flute and string trio (1975).

For chorus he has set two *Psalms* (90 and 91; 1948) and composed a cantata, *The Lotus Eaters* (1939–47). Among his vocal works are *Nightingale Songs* (1954–70), performed by Bethany Beardslee in 1973, *Four Songs from "Mythical Story'* (Seferis; 1961); and *Nine Lyrics from "In Memoriam"* (Tennyson) for baritone and piano (1978).

Cone has contributed many articles to musical journals and is the author of three books: *Musical Form and Musical Performance* (1968), *The Composer's Voice* (1974), and *Music: A View from the Delft* (with Robert P. Morgan; 1989).

CONVERSE, CHARLES CROZAT (PSEUD. KARL REDAN)
b. Warren, Massachusetts, 7 October 1832
d. Englewood, New Jersey, 18 October 1918

After studying in Leipzig from 1855 to 1859 with Hans Richter (conducting), Moritz Hauptmann (theory), and Louis Plaidy (piano), Converse returned to the United States where he practiced as a lawyer and musician, first in Erie, Pennsylvania, later in Highwood, New Jersey.

For orchestra he wrote two symphonies, ten suites, an *American Concert Overture* on "Hail, Columbia' (1869); and a *Festival Overture: In Springtime*, performed by Theodore Thomas in Brooklyn in 1868. Converse is remembered today for the hymn *What a*

Frederick Shepherd Converse.
From The Archives at the New England Conservatory of Music, Boston.

Friend We Have in Jesus and an anthem, *God For Us* (1867).

CONVERSE, FREDERICK SHEPHERD
b. *Newton, Massachusetts, 5 January 1871*
d. *Westwood, Massachusetts, 8 June 1940*

Converse graduated from Harvard University in 1893 where he had been a pupil of John Knowles Paine. After studying piano with Carl Baermann and receiving composition lessons from Chadwick in Boston, he went to Munich in 1896 where he studied with Rheinberger. On his return to America in 1899 he taught at the New England Conservatory in Boston. Converse was appointed a Teacher of Composition at Harvard in 1901 where he later became an assistant professor. For a while he devoted himself solely to composition, but returned to the New England Conservatory where he became Dean of the Faculty in 1931. He retired due to ill-health in 1938.

Converse acquired fame by becoming the first American composer to have an opera produced at the Metropolitan in New York. *The Pipe of Desire*, a one-act tragic fairy tale, was performed on 18 March 1910. A second opera, *The Sacrifice*, was staged in Boston in 1911. He composed three other operas: *Beauty and the*

Beast (Boston, 1906); *The Immigrants* (Boston, 1911); and *Sinbad the Sailor* (1913).

The first of his five symphonies (no. 1. *in D minor*) was composed in 1898 while he was a student in Munich. The other symphonies are spaced throughout his composing career: no. 2. *in C minor* (1920); no. 3. *in E minor* (1922); no. 4. *in F* (1933); and no. 5. *in F minor* (1940). Converse's best-known orchestral work, *Flivver 10 Million* (1927), was inspired by Arthur Honegger's *Pacific 231* and is a burlesque tribute to the ten millionth Ford automobile. The score bears the heading "a joyous epic inspired by the familiar legend—-the ten millionth Ford is now serving its owner."

For orchestra he also composed an overture, *Youth* (1897); *Festival March* (1899); *Festival of Pan* (1900); *Euphrosyne Overture* (1901); a tone poem, *Endymion's Narrative* (1903); *Indian Serenade* for small orchestra (1903); a symphonic poem, *The Mystic Trumpeter* (Whitman) (1904); *Jeanne d'Arc* (1906); a symphonic poem, *Ormazd* (1912); *Ave Atque Vale* (1916); a tone poem, *Song of the Sea*: *On the Beach at Night* (1923); *Puritan Passions*, based on music for a film, *The Scarecrow* (1923); *Elegiac Poem* (1925); *California Suite* (1928); *American Sketches* (1929); *Salutation March* (1935); and *Haul Away Joe*, variations for small orchestra (1939). Converse also composed *Night and Day* based on two poems by Whitman, for piano and orchestra (1901); a *Violin* Concerto (1903); *Fantasy* for piano and orchestra (1922); Concerto for piano and orchestra (1932); and *Rhapsody* for clarinet and orchestra (1938).

His most important choral works are the dramatic poem *Job* for soloists, chorus, and orchestra, performed at the Worcester Festival in 1907, and a cantata, *The Peace Pipe* (1914), to words by Longfellow. *Masque of St. Louis* was composed in 1914 for the 150th anniversary of St. Louis. A cantata, *An Answer of the Stars* was composed in the following year. A dramatic narrative for contralto and orchestra, *Hagar in the Desert*, was heard in Hamburg in 1908. Also for voice and orchestra are a setting of Keats' poem *La Belle Dame Sans Merci* (1902), and a tone poem for soprano and orchestra, *Prophesy* (1932), based on words from Isaiah. His last choral works were *Psalm: I Will Praise Thee, O Lord* for chorus (1924), and *The Flight of the Eagle* for baritone, chorus, and orchestra (1930).

Among his chamber works are Sonata for violin (1983); a *Septet* for piano, winds, and strings (1897); *Adagio* for woodwind and two harps (1897); three string quartets: no. 1. in E minor (1896, rev. 1901), no. 2. in A minor (1904), and no. 3. in E minor (1935); Sonata for cello (1912); Piano Trio *in E minor* (1931); Piano Sonata (1935); *Prelude and Intermezzo* for brass sextet (1938); and *Two Lyric Pieces* for brass quintet (1939).

COOK, WILL MARION
b. Washington, D.C., 27 January 1869
d. New York, New York, 19 July 1944

The son of a law professor at Howard University, Washington, D.C., Cook won a violin scholarship to the Oberlin Conservatory at the age of thirteen. Two years later as the result of funds collected by the Washington community, he travelled to Berlin to study with Joachim. On his return to the United States in the early 1890s, he enrolled at the National Conservatory in New York where he joined Dvořák's composition class. After graduating in 1898 he turned to the theatre composing the first black musical *Clorindy, or The Origin of the Cakewalk*, produced on Broadway in that year.

He wrote the music for a sequence of similar shows: *Jes' Like White Folk* (1899); *The Sons of Ham* (1900); *The Cannibal King* (1901); *Dahomey* (1902); *The Southerners* (1904); *Abyssinia* (1906); *Bandona Land* (1907); *The Traitor* (1913); *Darkydom* (1915); and *Swing Along* (in collaboration with W. Vodery; 1929). He also composed an unstaged opera *St. Louis 'ooman* depicting life beside the Mississippi in the 1890s. From 1900 to 1908 he was musical director to the Broadway comedy duo Bert Williams and George Walker.

Cook took an active interest in ragtime and jazz by training all-black bands. He developed a conducting career when he founded the American Syncopated Orchestra in 1919 which toured America and Europe for the next three years. One of its members was Sidney Bechet.

During the last two decades of his life, in addition to conducting he turned to teaching, numbering Duke Ellington and Harold Arlen among his pupils. His wife the soprano Abbie Mitchell sang the part of Clara in the premiere of Gershwin's *Porgy and Bess* in 1935, thereby introducing the song *Summertime* to the world. His son Mercer was the United States ambassador to Senegal in the 1960s.

COOPER, PAUL
b. Victoria, Illinois, 19 May 1926
d. Houston, Texas, 4 April 1996

Cooper studied at the University of Southern California with Ernest Kanitz, Ingolf Dahl, Halsey Stevens, and Roger Sessions. From 1953 to 1954 he was a pupil of Nadia Boulanger in Paris. He was the recipient of two Guggenheim Fellowships (1965, 1972) and a Fulbright Fellowship (1953). Cooper was professor of music at the University of Michigan (1955–67) and Composer-in-Residence at the University of Cincinnati (1968–74). From 1974 to 1996 he taught at the Shepherd School of Music, Rice University, Houston, Texas.

For orchestra Cooper wrote six symphonies: no. 1, *Concertant* (1966); no. 2, *Antiphons* for oboe and winds (1971); no. 3, *Lamentations* for strings (1971); no. 4, *Landscape* for flute, trumpet, viola, and orchestra (1973–75); no. 5, *Symphony in Two Movements* (1983); and no. 6, *In Memoriam* (1987). Other orchestral works include *Sinfonia* for strings (1952); *Overture* (1953); *Sinfonia for winds* (1958); Concerto *for orchestra* (1966); two *Violin* Concertos (1967, 1980–82); *Liturgies* for winds, brass, and percussion (1968); *A Shenandoah for Burl Ives* for flute, trumpet, viola, and orchestra (1974); *Descants* for viola and chamber orchestra (1975); *Homage* for flute, trumpet, viola, and orchestra (1976); *Cello* Concerto (1976–78); *Variants* (1978); *Flute* Concerto (1980–81); *Organ* Concerto (1982); *Saxophone* Concerto (1982); *Duo Concertante* for violin, viola, and orchestra (1985); *Jubilate* for winds and percussion (1985–86); and Double Concerto for violin and viola (1985–87).

Among his choral works are *Missa Brevis* (1954); *Chorales of the Nativity* (1954); an oratorio *Job* (1956); *Four Madrigals* (1956); *Two Anthems* (1959); *Sacred Service* (1960); *Gloria Patri* (1960); *Benedicite* (1966); *Genesis II* (1969); *Credo* (1970); *Psalm of Penitence* (1971); *Cantigas* (1972); *Eqiunox* for chorus, flute, and cello (1976); *Refrains* for double chorus and orchestra (1976); *Celebration* for soprano, chorus, and organ (1983); *Voyages* for chorus, brass, and organ (1983); and *Omnia Tempus Habent* for chorus and organ (1987).

Among his chamber music are six string quartets (no. 1, 1952, rev. 1978; no. 2, 1954, rev. 1979; no. 3, 1959; no. 4, 1964; no. 5, *Umbrae*, 1975; and no. 6, 1977); *Sonata à 3* (1955); *Canonic Variations* for wind quintet (1960); Viola Sonata (1961); *Divertimento* for two flutes (1962); Violin Sonata (1962); two cello sonatas (1962, 1965); Sonata for two flutes and piano (1962); Double bass Sonata (1964); *Concert for Two* for cello and piano (1965); *Concert for Four* for flute, oboe, harpsichord ad double bass (1965); *Concert for Five* for wind quintet (1966); *Variations* for violin and piano (1967); *Epitaphs* for alto flute, harp, and double bass (1969); *Soliloquies* for violin and piano (1970); *Chimera* for piano quartet (1972); *Variants II* for viola and piano (1972); *Antiphons* for oboe and brass (1973); and *Aegina Music* for piano trio (1973).

Later instrumental pieces include *Canons d'amour* for violin and viola (1981); *Canti* for viola and piano (1981); *Chamber Music I* for flute, two clarinets, violin, cello, and piano (1982); *Four Impromptus* for alto saxophone and piano (1983); *Tre Voci* for piano trio (1986); and *Variants IV* for alto saxophone and piano (1986).

For keyboard he composed two piano sonatas (1949, 1962–63); *Cycles* (1969), *Changes* (1973), and *Four Intermezzi* (1980), all for piano; a Concerto for harpsichord and organ (1962); *Variants* for organ (1971–72); and *Requiem* for organ and percussion (1978).

Among Cooper's vocal compositions are *Silences* for soprano and instrumental ensemble (1973); *Tomorrow's Songs* for soprano, alto flute, and piano (1974); *Coram morte* for soprano, synthesizer, and 12 instruments (1978); *Songs of Antigone* for soprano and seven instruments (1979); and *From the Sacred Heart* for mezzo-soprano (1982).

Cooper was the author of two books, *Perspectives in Music Theory* (1973; 2nd edition 1981) and *Music for Sight Singing* (1980).

COPLAND, AARON

b. Brooklyn, New York, 14 November 1900
d. North Tarrytown, New York, 2 December 1990

Copland's father, Harris Kaplan, was born in Shavel, Lithuania, in 1860, the eldest of eight children. At the age of 15, Harris emigrated from Russia; on his entry into Britain, an immigration official mistakenly wrote his name as Harris Copland, and he decided to retain this spelling. He arrived in Brooklyn in 1877. Aaron Copland's mother, Sarah Mittenthal, was born in 1862 in Vistinich, Lithuania, only a few miles from the home of her future husband. In 1869 she was taken to the United States; she and Harris Copland were married in New York City in 1885. Aaron was the youngest of their five children.

Copland's first musical influences were the music of the synagogue and the lessons in violin, piano, and singing that his older brother and sister received. He began lessons with his sister Laurine and later he studied at Leopold Wolfsohn's studio. His first attempts at composition were made in his early teens, and at the age of 16 he announced to a friend that he wished to be a composer. In September 1917 he went to Rubin Goldmark for lessons in theory and composition, and the following month he became a piano pupil of Victor Wittgenstein. After graduation from high school in 1918, he was able to spend more time on music. From 1919 to 1921 he studied the piano with Clarence Adler.

Instead of continuing on to college, Copland decided to devote himself entirely to the study of music. In June 1921 he set sail on the liner *France* with a party of American students about to enter the newly-founded Summer School of Music for Americans at the palace of Fontainebleau. On the voyage he met the French artist Marcel Duchamp who was to help him in Paris. Almost at once he had a success with the publication of a piano piece, *Scherzo Humoristique: The Cat and the Mouse*, which he had written in New York in 1920 while a pupil of Rubin Goldmark. Paris at that time was the center of the musical world, with Ravel, Stravinsky,

Satie, Roussel, Prokofiev, and "Les Six" the leading figures. At Fontainebleau he was initially a pupil of Paul Vidal, but the growing reputation of Nadia Boulanger as a teacher led the young composer to her classes. During his years in Paris (1921–24), Copland became acquainted with most of the musicians of significance; he also met the literary giants of the time: James Joyce, Ernest Hemingway, and Ezra Pound. Among the Americans who became his close friends were George Antheil and Virgil Thomson. He became the first of Boulanger's American composition pupils, and her unbounded enthusiasm was of great value to him.

The new music of Paris encouraged Copland in his own compositions. The first exposure to the works of Prokofiev, Stravinsky, Milhaud, Poulenc, and Honegger opened up a new world with which he felt totally in sympathy. His own works met with general critical acclaim, and two more pieces, the song *Old Poem* and *Passacaglia* for piano, were published in Paris in 1922. That French publishers accepted work by a young, unknown American is in itself an indication of his remarkable achievement. *Four Motets* on biblical texts for unaccompanied chorus written as exercises for Boulanger in 1921 were performed in Paris in 1924, conducted by a fellow American music student, Melville Smith. They were published in 1979.

Copland's first orchestral work, the one-act ballet *Grohg*, was inspired by his seeing the German horror film *Nosferatu*. To a scenario by his friend Harold Clurman, the ballet concerns a vampire who sucks blood from dead people. The Diaghilev Company was commissioning ballets from Stravinsky, Prokofiev, and others, so it was natural Copland should do likewise. Although he spent a considerable time on its composition, *Grohg* was never staged. From the score he extracted *Cortège Macabre* (1923), performed by the Rochester Philharmonic Orchestra under Howard Hanson in 1925, and *Dance Symphony* (1925), first heard in Philadelphia in April 1931 under Leopold Stokowski's direction. While in Europe, Copland took the opportunity to visit London, Rome, and Berlin. In Vienna during the summer of 1923, he completed a song, *As It Fell Upon a Day* for soprano, flute, and clarinet to a poem by Richard Barnfield. It was performed by Ada MacLeish, wife of the poet Archibald MacLeish, at a concert in Paris in February 1924.

In 1924 Nadia Boulanger was invited by Serge Koussevitzky and Walter Damrosch to appear as solo organist with the Boston Symphony Orchestra and the New York Symphony Orchestra. She had the foresight and generosity to ask her young American pupil to write a work for her to play. Copland began on a piece for organ and orchestra in the summer of 1924 while staying at Milford, Pennsylvania, where he was earning a living playing the piano in a hotel trio. Despite the circumstances, he was able to complete the whole score by the fall of the same year. As promised, on 11 January 1925, Boulanger played the Symphony for Organ and Orchestra with the New York Symphony Orchestra under Walter Damrosch in New York City. After the performance the conductor remarked to the audience: "If a young man at the age of twenty-three can write a symphony like that, in five years he will be ready to commit murder." A second performance in Boston in February of the same year marked the beginning of a valuable friendship between the composer and Koussevitzky. An alternative version of the Symphony (without organ) adds a saxophone, four more horns, two trumpets, piano, tam-tam, and glockenspiel to the score. This version was completed in 1929 and premiered by the Boston Symphony Orchestra under Ernest Ansermet in December 1931. In 1925 Copland was the recipient of the first Guggenheim Fellowship awarded for music.

At Koussevitzky's suggestion, the League of Composers commissioned *Music for the Theater*, performed by Koussevitzky in Boston in November 1925. The jazz elements and polyrhythms heard in the *Dance* Symphony and the Symphony for Organ are more evident in this work. It was mostly composed while Copland was working at the MacDowell Colony in Peterborough, New Hampshire. The suite in five movements has no specific literary or dramatic associations. In 1926 Copland and his friend Harold Clurman returned to Paris for six months. He renewed his friendship with Boulanger and met Roger Sessions for the first time. Dating from this time are the Piano Concerto and two pieces for violin and piano, *Ukulele Serenade* and *Nocturne*.

On 12 February 1924, George Gershwin had surprised the audience at Aeolian Hall, New York City with his *Rhapsody in Blue*. It was followed in 1925 by Gershwin's more ambitious Piano Concerto in F, the first idiomatically American concerto for the instrument. By October 1926, Copland had completed his own Piano Concerto, but although it included jazz features, it differed fundamentally from Gershwin's work. It is cast in two linked movements; the first is lyrical, not too distant from Gershwin in rhapsodic mood. The second part bursts into activity with a wild, sardonic jazzy piano solo, a kind of irreverent cadenza. The whole movement is aggressively assertive; in addition to the jazz in the piano part, Copland creates a jazz band within the orchestra itself. The piano vamps a tonic–dominant accompaniment while a soprano saxophone, piccolo, E-flat clarinet, muted trumpet, and muted trombone each have solo "breaks." The additions of a side drum with a brush and a Chinese drum complete the band. There is little of the ingratiating charm of Gershwin in Copland's Concerto, and its forceful character alienated both critics and audience. At its premiere in Boston on 28 January 1927 the composer was soloist. Philip Hale of the *Boston Herald* commented, "We found little to attract, little to admire, much to repel." Only Lawrence Gilman had a kind word for the work. He described it as having "a fullness and authenticity of life which makes it at once perturbing and richly treasurable." After the Piano Concerto, Copland turned away from jazz as a significant element in his compositions.

In April 1927, Copland again went to Europe for several months. On his return he began lecturing at the New School for Social Research in New York. With Roger Sessions he organized the Copland-Sessions Concerts of Modern Music, which were held from 1928 to 1931. Copland's next published works were the *Two Pieces for String Orchestra*. The second of these, *Rondino on the Name of Gabriel Fauré*, had been played at Fontainebleau in September 1924 in its original form for string quartet. The Piano Trio (*Vitebsk*; 1929) is a rare example of Copland's inspiration derived from Jewish music. In the first theme, quarter tones are used to imitate the melismas of the cantor in a synagogue.

As early as 1927, Copland had begun work on *Symphonic Ode*, commissioned to celebrate the 50th anniversary of the Boston Symphony Orchestra. Although the score was completed in 1929, the music was not performed until 19 February 1932 under the baton of Koussevitzky. At first the orchestra found difficulty in following the alternating time signatures, and the conductor suggested that the notation should be altered to facilitate the reading of complex rhythms. Copland made several changes of time signatures and rhythmic notation. The composer explained that the title *Symphonic Ode* "is not meant to imply any connection with a literary idea. It is not an ode to anything . . . other that the particular spirit to be found in the music itself. What that particular spirit is, is not for me to say." In 1929 Copland hoped to enter the *Symphonic Ode* in the RCA Victor Company Competition for a symphonic composition. Because it was not completed in time, he hurriedly assembled the *Dance Symphony* from the music for the ballet *Grohg*, and was awarded $5,000 when the prize was divided equally among five works. The other winning composers were Louis Gruenberg, Ernest Bloch, and Robert Russell Bennett (who had submitted two works).

The *Piano Variations* of 1930 mark a new movement toward absolute music. The rhythmic complexities and pungent harmonies are an extension of the language of the *Symphonic Ode*. In his study of Aaron Copland, Arthur Berger states that as an example of conciseness, one could scarcely find anything better than the *Piano Variations*. Although critical consensus now judges the *Variations* as a masterpiece, the spare textures and fragmentary melodic features were at first so disconcerting that the significance of the work was not apparent. It introduced a radically new ascetic style that eliminated the earlier influences of jazz; gone also are diatonic melody and harmony and the lyricism of the Piano Concerto and First Symphony. As with the *Symphonic Ode*, Copland restricts the initial material to five notes. This "row" serves for all the variations with remarkable ingenuity and craftsmanship in an uncompromising declamatory manner. The *Piano Variations* were first performed by the composer at a concert sponsored by the League of Composers in New York on 4 January 1931. In April of that year Copland went to Europe with Paul Bowles, visiting Paris, Berlin, and London, where the I.S.C.M. Festival was being held. Later he traveled to Morocco where he stayed for three months.

In 1932, Copland began work on the *Short Symphony* (Symphony no. 2) and *Statements for Orchestra*. During this time he met Carlos Chávez, an active supporter of new music and himself a composer of great originality. At Chávez's invitation Copland visited Mexico for performance of his music in Mexico City. Here he also came into contact with Mexican folk music, and its intricate rhythms much appealed to him. The *Short Symphony* was completed in 1933 and first performed in Mexico City in November 1934 under Chávez, to whom it is dedicated. Although it was scheduled for performance in the United States on several occasions, it was found too taxing for the performers. It was not heard in America until 1944, when it was broadcast by the NBC Symphony Orchestra conducted by Stokowski. As late as 1962 it was withdrawn before a scheduled concert because of insufficient time to prepare it adequately. The problems of performance led the composer to rescore the *Short Symphony* in 1937 as a Sextet for clarinet, string quartet, and piano; in this form it has been heard more frequently. Although the original music remains unchanged except for the removal of the final two chords, certain bar-lines and time signatures are altered to simplify the complicated rhythms.

The scoring of the *Short Symphony* is for a medium-sized orchestra without timpani, percussion, and trombones, but including the almost obsolete heckelphone, which doubles English horn and can be replaced by that instrument if necessary. A curious feature of the first movement is that the opening 82 measures are entirely in unison except for punctuating chords and a brief passage of two-part counterpoint near the beginning. Its nearest musical relatives are the *Piano Variations* and *Statements*, which Copland was composing at the same time. Also dating from 1934 is the ballet *Hear Ye! Hear Ye!*, composed for the choreographer Ruth Page. It was staged in Chicago at the Opera House in November 1934.

Statements for Orchestra was completed in 1935. Commissioned by the League of Composers; it was intended for performance by the Minneapolis Symphony Orchestra. At its premiere, however, only the last two movements were presented in an NBC broadcast in January 1936 with the Minneapolis Symphony Orchestra under Eugene Ormandy. Not until January 1942 was the complete work given, conducted by Dimitri Mitropoulos with the New York Philharmonic Orchestra. In a program note for the first performance, Copland wrote: "The title *Statements* was chosen to indicate a short terse orchestral movement of a well-defined character lasting about three minutes. The separate movements were given suggestive titles as an aid to the public in understanding what the composer had in mind when writing these pieces." The titles are "Militant," "Cryptic," "Dogmatic," "Subjective," "Jingo," and "Prophetic." In "Dogmatic" the composer quotes the theme of the *Piano Variations*, and "Jingo" makes use of the popular song "The Sidewalks of New York."

In the early 1930s Copland began to voice doubts regarding the role of the composer and the musical public. In an autobiographical essay he wrote, "'It seemed to me that composers were in danger of working in a vacuum. Moreover, an entirely new public for music had grown up around the radio and the phonograph. It made no sense to ignore them and to continue writing as though they did not exist. I felt it was worth the effort to see if I couldn't say what I had to say in the simplest possible terms." In 1935 he began the opera *The Second Hurricane* to a libretto by Edwin Denby for high school performance. It tells of the adventures of the principal of a school and six students who are faced by a hurricane and flood. Naturally the music is in a simple form appropriate for untrained amateur voices. The opera was produced by Orson Welles at the Playhouse Theatre, New York in April 1937. In this work Copland introduced at least one folk song and other tunes in a folk idiom.

Copland's first composition to gain worldwide popular success, *El Salón México*, was completed in 1936. The idea of writing a piece inspired by Mexican music came during his visit to that country in 1932. At the dance hall "Salón México" in Mexico City, he heard the folk music with asymmetrical rhythms and brilliant coloring that provided the initial inspiration for his own work. This lively score was first performed in Mexico City under Chávez on 25 August 1937. The recording made by Koussevitzky and the Boston Symphony Orchestra brought Copland's music to audience throughout the world and established its permanent popularity. The Columbia Broadcasting System commissioned *Music for Radio* in 1937. It was first performed on radio in New York in July of that year. CBS also organized a competition for a subtitle to the work; the winning entry was *Saga of the Prairie*. It was retitled *Prairie Journal* in 1968.

In 1937 Copland became chairman of the board of the newly founded American Composers' Alliance, organized to protect the performing rights of American composers. The executive board included Marion Bauer, Roy Harris, Goddard Lieberson, Douglas Moore, Quincy Porter, Wallingford Riegger, Elie Siegmeister, Roger Sessions, and Bernard Wagenaar.

In addition to *Grohg*, which remained unperformed, and *Hear Ye! Hear Ye!*, Copland's music was adapted for two ballets: *Olympus Americanus* (1922), based on *Passacaglia* for piano, and *Dithyrambic*, produced by Martha Graham in 1932 using the music of the *Piano Variations*. The first of his popular ballets, *Billy the Kid*, was composed for Lincoln Kirstein's Ballet Caravan and produced with choreography by Eugene Loring in Chicago in October 1938. From the score the composer produced a concert suite in seven sections, comprising about two-thirds of the entire score. Several cowboy tunes are used and assimilated into Copland's own style, including "The Old Chisholm Trail," "Git Along Little Dogies," "Goodbye Old Paint," and "Bury Me Not on the Lone Prairie."

Following the success of *The Second Hurricane*, Copland wrote *An Outdoor Overture* (1938) for the orchestra of the High School of Music and Art in New York City. At the request of Harold Clurman, Copland provided music for *Quiet City*, an experimental play by Irwin Shaw. From this he adapted the score for a short piece with the same title for English horn, trumpet, and strings. First performed in New York in January 1941, it has become one of his best-loved short works, frequently heard in concerts and recorded many times.

Ten years after the *Piano Variations*, Copland began the Piano Sonata, completed it in South America in 1941. He gave the first performance in Buenos Aires on 14 May 1942. Like the *Variations*, it is an intensely serious and personal work, and was received by the critics in New York in 1943 with only muted respect.

Copland's next large-scale composition, *Lincoln Portrait*, was commissioned by André Kostelanetz and performed by him with the Cincinnati Symphony Orchestra on 14 May 1942. An unashamedly patriotic piece, it sets the words of Lincoln for narrator and orchestra. In spite of the composer's injunction at the head of the score ("the speaker is cautioned against undue emphasis in the delivery of Lincoln's words"), it is difficult to recite such famous lines without incongruous histrionics. With Europe in the turmoil of the Second World War, the emotional sentiments of Lincoln's speech, especially such lines as "That government of the people, by the people, for the people shall not perish from the earth," had a particular relevance in 1942.

The long orchestral introduction makes reference to Stephen Foster's "Camptown Races' and the ballad "Springfield Mountain."

The considerable success of *Billy the Kid* encouraged the Ballet Russe de Monte Carlo to commission a second "cowboy" ballet. With choreography by Agnes de Mille who danced in it, *Rodeo* exactly captures the flavor of the American western. The story concerns a cowgirl who eventually captures her cowboy lover. *Rodeo* was produced at the Metropolitan Opera in New York on 16 October 1942. The *Four Dance Episodes* of the concert suite are among the composer's most frequently heard music. They were premiered by the Boston "Pops" Orchestra under Arthur Fiedler on 28 May 1943. *Danzón Cubano* was composed to celebrate the 20th anniversary of the League of Composers and first performed in the version for two pianos by the composer and Leonard Bernstein in New York in December 1942. The orchestral transcription premiered in 1946 makes the work a companion "travel souvenir" to *El Salón México*.

For the 1942–43 season of the Cincinnati Symphony Orchestra, Eugene Goossens commissioned ten American composers to write patriotic fanfares. Copland composed *Fanfare for the Common Man* for brass and percussion, first played on 14 March 1943. He later used the music to open the last movement of the Third Symphony.

The Violin Sonata (1943) differs from both the *Piano Variations* and Piano Sonata in that it adopts a simpler style with a strong relationship to folk song, although all the melodic material is original. Much of the music is in a hymn-like pastoral vein, elegiac in mood and sparse in texture. It is dedicated to the memory of Lieutenant Harry H. Dunham, who died in action in 1943. The first performance was given by Ruth Posselt and the composer at Times Hall, New York on 17 January 1944.

In 1944, to a commission from the Elizabeth Sprague Coolidge Foundation, Copland wrote the ballet *Appalachian Spring* for Martha Graham. With its original scoring for 13 instruments it was produced at the Library of Congress, Washington, D.C., on 30 October 1944. It received the New York Music Critics' Circle Award for the outstanding theatrical work of the 1944–45 season and won the Pulitzer Prize in 1945. The concert suite for full orchestra was performed by the New York Philharmonic Orchestra in October 1945 under Artur Rodzinski. The story tells of the preparations for a wedding in a Pennsylvania farming community. Although the music reflects the folk songs of Appalachia, the only quotation is the Shaker song "Simple Gifts," on which Copland writes a sequence of variations.

Also in 1944 Copland began the Third Symphony,

completed in September 1946, less than a month before its premiere on 18 October by the Boston Symphony Orchestra under Koussevitzky. The haste in finishing the score is indicated by the revision of the closing pages where two short sections were omitted in later performances. Although the composer stated that the Symphony contains no folk or popular material, the idiom of folk song and dance is present in many parts of the score. The lyrical writing in the third and fourth movements especially recalls folk song. The Third Symphony was commissioned by the Koussevitzky Music Foundation and is dedicated "to the memory of my dear friend, Natalie Koussevitzky." It received the New York Music Critics' Circle Award for the best orchestral work of the 1946–47 concert season. The Third Symphony is the longest and most impressive of Copland's orchestral works. Like so many American symphonies, the first movement acts as an introduction rather than a weighty sonata-form movement in the classical mold. The finale is the musical kernel of the piece. It opens with the *Fanfare for the Common Man*, composed in 1942. The fanfare provides the initial material for the movement, which builds to a massive conclusion.

For the Harvard University Symposium on Music Criticism in May 1947, Copland wrote *In the Beginning*, his only extended choral work. Scored for mezzo-soprano and unaccompanied chorus, it uses a text from the Book of Genesis presented in rondo form with the refrain for each of the seven days of Creation as the theme. In 1948 for Benny Goodman, Copland composed the Concerto for clarinet, string orchestra, harp, and piano. Like the Piano Concerto, it is cast in two movements, the first slow and lyrical, connected by a virtuoso cadenza to the fast, jazzy second movement. It was premiered on radio by Benny Goodman and the NBC Symphony Orchestra under Fritz Reiner on 6 November 1950. In 1951 the Concerto was used for a ballet by Jerome Robbins for the New York City Ballet entitled *Pied Piper*.

In 1949 the National Broadcasting Company commissioned Copland to write a work to commemorate the adoption of the Declaration of Human Rights by the United Nations. *Preamble for a Solemn Occasion* sets the opening text of the United Nations Charter for narrator and orchestra. The first performance took place in Carnegie Hall on 10 December 1949 with Leonard Bernstein conducting the Boston Symphony Orchestra and Laurence Olivier as narrator.

The Quartet for piano and strings (1950) marks the beginning of Copland's return to the musical language of his earliest works. It is based on an 11-note serial row and is most closely related in character to the *Piano Variations*. It was premiered by the New York Piano Quartet at the Library of Congress, Washington, D.C., on 29 October 1950, and is dedicated to Elizabeth Sprague Coolidge to celebrate the 25th anniversary of the Coolidge Foundation.

Although he wrote solo songs at various times during his long career, not until 1950 did Copland complete a major solo vocal work. *Twelve Poems of Emily Dickinson*, composed between March 1949 and March 1950, is not only his most important set of songs, but also one of the most significant song cycles by any composer of the 20th century. The composer parallels the compactness of the poems with an economy of musical resources, both in the directness of the vocal lines and in the relative simplicity of the piano part. Alice Howland and the composer gave the first performance of this work at the Columbia University Sixth Annual Festival of Contemporary Music in New York on 18 May 1950. Each song is dedicated to a fellow composer. In 1970 Copland orchestrated eight of the songs, which were premiered by Gwendolyn Killebrew at the Juilliard School on his 70th birthday.

The two sets of *Old American Songs* (1950, 1952) for voice and piano mark a distinct change from the Dickinson settings. In his popular style, these songs have idiomatic and ingenious accompaniments. The first set was performed by Peter Pears and Benjamin Britten at the Aldeburgh Festival, England on 17 June 1950. The second set was presented by William Warfield and the composer at the Castle Hill Concerts, Ipswich, Massachusetts, on 24 July 1953. Both sets were subsequently arranged for medium voice and orchestra in 1955 and 1958 respectively.

To celebrate the 30th anniversary of the League of Composers, Richard Rodgers and Oscar Hammerstein II commissioned the opera *The Tender Land* with libretto by Horace Everett. After the premiere on 1 April 1954 by the New York City Opera, Copland and Everett made certain revisions to improve the dramatic character of the plot. The revised version, in three acts instead of the original two, was produced at the Oberlin Conservatory, Ohio, on 20 May 1955. Its musical language belongs to that of the three popular ballets, and the work can be considered a truly American folk opera. Two drifters, Martin and Top, arrive at the farm of Grandpa Moss, looking for work. Laurie Moss is about to graduate from high school and longs to leave home to see the words. Martin, who has wandered from one place to another all his life, wants to settle down. Laurie and Martin plan to elope, but on the advice of Top, the two men leave secretly during the night without Laurie. The anticlimactic ending to the story weakens the drama and leaves the plot hanging inconclusively. The folk-song lyricism provides much fine music for the singers. There is a charming aria, "Laurie's Song," and two impressive set pieces, "The Promise of Living" and the choral square-dance "Stomp Your Foot Upon the Ground," which are sometimes heard in concert performance to great effect.

Canticle of Freedom for chorus and orchestra was commissioned by the Massachusetts Institute of Technology, Cambridge for the opening of the Kresge Auditorium on 8 May 1955. That same year, a joint commission from the Boston Symphony Orchestra (to celebrate its 175th anniversary) and the Koussevitzky Foundation offered Copland an opportunity to revise the *Symphonic Ode* of 1929. The revisions were intended to reduce the size of the orchestra for practical reasons, although a fairly large orchestra is still required. In addition, since some of the rhythms had caused considerable performance difficulties, an alteration of the notation of phrases, but not the rhythms themselves, was helpful in making reading a little simpler. Certain passages were also made fuller in texture, and high-lying parts for the brass were rescored lower for the instruments. A few measures were rewritten and restoration made of some others that had been cut before the first performance of the original version in 1929. The first version is now withdrawn. The new *Symphonic Ode* was performed by the Boston Symphony Orchestra under Charles Munch on 3 February 1956.

Copland's third extended keyboard work, the *Piano Fantasy*, was begun in 1955 and completed in 1957. It was commissioned by the Juilliard School for its 50th anniversary and dedicated to the memory of William Kapell, the pianist who died in an airplane crash in 1953. It was performed by William Masselos at the Juilliard School Concert Hall, New York City on 25 October 1957. Cast in a single movement of large proportions lasting half an hour, it makes use of serial techniques. Like the *Piano Variations*, the *Fantasy* is based on the first few notes presented in a similarly declamatory style. It possesses an impressive grandeur that makes it a major keyboard work by any standard.

In 1957, to a commission from the Louisville Orchestra, Copland orchestrated the *Piano Variations*. The composition of the *Piano Fantasy* no doubt renewed his interest in the *Variations*, to which it is closely related in character. The revision of the *Symphonic Ode* also drew him back to earlier music, and the potential of the *Variations* as an orchestral work led him to look at it in a new light. The *Orchestral Variations* is a remarkable successful composition in its own right, offering new opportunities to explore orchestral sonorities with powerful results. It was performed on 5 March 1958 under the direction of Robert Whitney.

The Nonet for strings (1960) was commissioned by the Dumbarton Oaks Research Library, Washington, D.C., in honor of the 50th wedding anniversary of Mr.

and Mrs. Robert W. Bliss. The score is dedicated to Nadia Boulanger. Although composed for trios of violins, violas, and cellos, it can be played by proportionally larger forces but not by a normal string orchestra. In this work, the composer returned to diatonicism, but certain serial methods are used.

In 1963 Copland completed his last ballet, *Dance Panels*, begun as early as 1959 and revised in 1962. Cast in seven sections, it has no specific scenario; the composer allowed choreographers to interpret the music in abstract terms or with a story. It was commissioned by Jerome Robbins and first produced by the Bavarian State Opera in Munich on 3 December 1963, conducted by the composer with choreography by Heinz Rosen. The concert premiere under the direction of Ingolf Dahl was given at the Ojai Festival, California on 21 May 1966.

To celebrate the opening of Philharmonic Hall (now Avery Fisher) in Lincoln Center in 1963, the New York Philharmonic Orchestra commissioned *Connotations*. In a program note for the first performance, the composer explained the intention behind the music: "I decided to compose a work that would bring to the opening exercise a contemporary note, expressing something of the tensions, aspirations, and drama inherent in the world today. The *Connotations* also represent the first orchestral work of mine in which I made use of the twelve tone principles." The 12 semitones are heard at the outset in three four-note chords. The work is structurally in the form of a Chaconne with each variations based on the opening chords. In its form and to some extent its melodic character, it resembles the *Orchestral Variations*, especially in the frequent use of the interval of a minor ninth. Like the *Variations*, it is an essay in contrasts. It is scored for a large orchestra, including six horns and a percussion section requiring five players in addition to timpani.

Music for a Great City was commissioned by the London Symphony Orchestra to celebrate its 60th anniversary in 1964. Much of the musical material was taken from the film score for *Something Wild*, composed in 1961. The "Great City" of the title is not London but New York, where the film is set. The four movements reflect different views of New York: Skyline, Night Thoughts, Subway Jam, and Towards the Bridge. The first performance was given in London under the composer on 26 May 1964.

The 125th anniversary of the New York Philharmonic in 1967 gave rise to commissions for 18 American and European composers. Copland's contribution was *Inscape*. The title is taken from the English poet Gerard Manley Hopkins. To Copland the word "inscape" suggested "a quasi-mystical illumination, a sudden perception of that deeper pattern, order, and unity which gives meaning to external forms." The work is based on two separate tone-rows, the first heard at the opening as a 12-note chord. In character, *Inscape* is closest to *Connotations* with a particular concentration upon texture and sonority. It was first performed by the New York Philharmonic Orchestra under Leonard Bernstein at the University of Michigan, Ann Arbor, on 13 September 1967.

The *Duo* for flute and piano was composed in response to a commission from a number of pupils and friends of William Kincaid (1895–1967), for many years first flute in the Philadelphia Orchestra. It was premiered by Elaine Shaffer and Hephzibah Menuhin at the Settlement Music School in Philadelphia on 3 October 1971.

In 1959 the Festival of Two Worlds in Spoleto, Italy, asked Copland for a short orchestral work. Although the *Two Mexican Pieces* were completed on time, only the second of them, *Danza de Jalisco*, was performed at the Festival in July of that year. Both pieces (the first is entitled *Paisaje Mexicano*) were heard in a concert of the Pan American Union in Washington, D.C. on 20 April 1965, conducted by the composer. Still not satisfied with them, Copland added a third movement, *Estribillo*, in 1971, making some revisions in *Danza de Jalisco*. The three pieces were reissued in 1975 under the title *Three Latin-American Sketches*.

Copland's last compositions are all instrumental works. The two *Threnodies*, the first in memory of Igor Stravinsky for flute and string trio, the second for alto flute and string trio in memory of Beatrice Cunningham, date from 1971 and 1973. The last published pieces are all for piano solo. The most substantial of them, *Night Thoughts*, was composed for the Van Cliburn International Piano Competition, held in Fort Worth, Texas in September 1973. Completed the previous year, it makes use of subtle piano sonorities by careful pedaling effects. It is subtitled *Homage to Ives*, and the forceful, often dissonant writing is a reminder of that composer.

Copland's remaining piano pieces, all reworkings of earlier sketches, are in a disarmingly simple, vein, presenting few difficulties to either listener or performer: *In Evening Air* (1966/1972); *Midsummer Nocturne* (1947/1972); *Midday Thoughts* (1947/1983); and *Proclamation* (1973/1983).

Copland contributed incidental music to several plays, including *Miracle at Verdun* (Hans Chlumberg; 1931); *The Five Kings* (for Orson Welles' composite production of five Shakespeare history plays; 1939); *From Sorcery to Science* (puppet show; 1939); *Quiet City* (Irwin Shaw; 1939); and *The World of Nick Adams* (Ernest Hemingway; 1957). His film scores include *The City* (Pare Lorenz, Henwar Rodakiewitz, and Oscar Serlin; 1939); *Of Mice and Men* (John Steinbeck; 1940); *Our Town* (Thornton Wilder; 1940; the five-movement *Music for the Movies* of 1942 is based on excerpts from the three films above); *North Star* (Lilliam Hellman; 1943); *The Cummington Story* (documentary for the U.S. Office of War Information; 1945); *The Red Pony* (John Steinbeck; 1948); *The Heiress* (based on Henry James' novel *Washington Square*; 1949; Academy Award); and *Something Wild* (1961).

Copland was the author of four significant books: *What to Listen For in Music* (1939, rev. 1957); *Our New Music* (1941), revised as *The New Music 1900–1960* (1968); *Music and Imagination* (1952); and *Copland on Music* (1963). With the co-operation of Vivian Perlis he published an autobiography in two volumes (1984, 1989).

CORIGLIANO, JOHN (PAUL), JR.
b. New York, New York, 16 February 1938

Corigliano is the son of John Corigliano, violinist and concertmaster of the New York Philharmonic Orchestra from 1943 to 1966. He graduated from Columbia University in 1959 where he had been a pupil of Otto Luening. He studied privately with Paul Creston and with Vittorio Giannini at the Manhattan School of Music (1962–63). From 1959 to 1961 he worked for WQXR radio and from 1962 to 1964 for WBAI-FM, both in New York City. He was director of Music for Theater, a composers' group which he founded in 1966. From 1967 to 1968 he taught at the College of Church Musicians. From 1971, he taught composition at the Manhattan School of Music, and in 1973 he was appointed associate professor at Lehman College, New York City. From 1991 he has taught at the Juilliard School of Music. He has also served as Composer-in-Residence with the Chicago Symphony Orchestra (1987–90).

Corigliano's first important orchestral work, *Elegy*, was written in 1965 for the San Francisco Symphony Orchestra. Other early orchestral works include *Journey* (1959); *Tournaments* (1967); *Gazebo Dances* (1974; also arranged for concert band); an Oboe Concerto (1975); and *Voyage* for strings (1976), arranged in 1983 for flute and orchestra for James Galway.

A Piano Concerto, composed in 1968, was performed in April 1978 by Hilde Somer with the San Antonio (Texas) Symphony Orchestra. Stanley Drucker and the New York Philharmonic Orchestra under Leonard Bernstein presented the premiere of Corigliano's Clarinet Concerto in 1977. His *Flute Concerto: Pied Piper Fantasy*, commissioned by James Galway, was performed at Hollywood Bowl in February 1982. The score was expanded into a full-length ballet,

The Pied Piper, performed at the Lincoln Center, New York in May 2001. Orchestral works of this period include *Promenade Overture*, a "reversal" of Haydn's *Farewell Symphony* (1981); *Three Hallucinations from "Altered States"* (1981); *Echoes of Forgotten Rites: Summer Fanfare* (1982); *Fantasia on an Ostinato* (1986); and *Capagne di Ravello*, a celebration piece for the 75th birthday of Sir Georg Solti (1987).

Symphony no. 1 for large orchestra, commissioned by the Chicago Symphony Orchestra, was composed as a response to the devastation of the AIDS epidemic in the United States. After the premiere under Daniel Barenboim in 1990, it was performed by over 60 orchestras in the following five years. A choral work based on part of the last movement, *Of Rage and Remembrance*, to words by William Hoffman, for mezzo soprano, men's chorus, chimes, timpani, eight cellos, and four double basses was completed in 1991.

Among Corigliano's more recent orchestral pieces are *Troubadours*, variations for guitar and chamber orchestra (1993); *Fanfares To Music* (later retitled *To Music*), based on Schubert's song (1994, rev. 1995); *Nocturne* (1997); *D.C. Fanfare* (1997); *Mannheim Rocket* (2000); and Symphony no. 2, premiered in November 2000 by the Boston Symphony Orchestra under Seiji Osawa. Scored for strings only, it is an expansion of his Quartet no. 1. It was awarded the Pulitzer Prize in 2001.

Corigliano's principal choral compositions are a setting of Dylan Thomas's poem *Fern Hill* for mezzo-soprano, chorus, and orchestra, performed in New York in 1960; and *What I Expected Was . . .* (Stephen Spender) for chorus, brass, and percussion, completed in 1961. A second Dylan Thomas work, *Poem in October* for tenor and eight instruments, was composed in 1970 for the Chamber Music Society of Lincoln Center. In 1976 he completed the *Dylan Thomas Trilogy* with *Poem on His Birthday* for baritone, chorus, and orchestra, commissioned by Washington Cathedral to celebrate the American Bicentennial. The complete set was revised in 1999.

For unaccompanied voices Corigliano has composed *L'Invitation au Voyage* (after Baudelaire; 1971) and two settings of poems by Richard Wilbur: *A Black November Turkey* (1972) and *Amen* (1994). For chorus and organ are *Christmas at the Cloisters* (1966) and *Psalm VIII* (1976). His solo vocal music includes *Petit Fours* for voice and piano (1958); *The Cloisters* for mezzo-soprano and orchestra to four poems by William Hoffman (1965); *First Marriage Service* (*Wedding Song*) for voice, oboe, and organ (1972); *Creations* (Genesis) for narrator and orchestra (1972, rev. 1984); *Three Irish Folk Song Settings* for voice and flute (1988); *Vocalise* for soprano, electronics, and orches-

tra (1999); *Mr Tambourine Man*, seven songs to words by Bob Dylan for voice and piano (2000); and *Irreverent Heart* for tenor and piano (2001).

Corigliano has composed a multimedia opera, *The Naked Carmen*, based on Bizet's opera, completed in 1971 and revised in 1976 for a Broadway production. A second opera, *A Figaro for Antonio*, was composed in 1985. His major stage success is the two-act opera *The Ghosts of Versailles* (1984–1991), commissioned by the New York Metropolitan Opera to mark the centenary of the house, premiered under James Levine on December 19th 1992. It proved to be one of the most successful new operas in modern times.

Corigliano has composed four film scores: *A Williamsburg Sampler* (1974); *Altered States* (1980); *Revolution* (1985); and *The Red Violin*, for which he received an Academy Award in 2000. His *Chaconne* for violin and orchestra performed by Joshua Bell in San Francisco in November 1997 was incorporated into the music for *The Red Violin*.

Among Corigliano's instrumental works are *Pastorale* for cello and piano (1958); *Four Fugues* for string quartet (1959); *Kaleidoscope* for two pianos (1959); Violin Sonata, premiered at the Spoleto Festival in 1964; *Scherzo* for oboe and percussion (1975); *Etude Fantasy* for piano (1976); *Aria* for oboe and string quartet (1985); *Phantasmagoria* (on *The Ghosts of Versailles*) for cello and piano (1993); *Amen* for double brass ensemble (1994); String Quartet, composed in 1995 for the farewell concert of the Cleveland Quartet in 1995; *Soliloquy* for clarinet and string quartet (1995); *Dodecaphonia* for violin and piano (1997); and *Chiaroscuro* for two pianos, tuned a quarter-tone apart (1997).

COWELL, HENRY DIXON
b. Menlo Park, California, 11 March 1897
d. Shady, New York, 10 December 1965

A violin prodigy, Cowell gave up playing at the age of eight for health reasons. In his early teens he experimented with dissonance at the keyboard, and had written over one hundred works before he was 17. He studied at the Institute of Applied Music in New York and at the University of California, Berkeley (1914–16) and privately with Charles Seeger. Briefly during World War I he was an army bandmaster. From 1923 to 1933 he toured Europe five times as a pianist playing his own compositions. In 1931 a Guggenheim Fellowship allowed him to study non-European music at Berlin University with Erich von Hornbostel.

In 1928, after visiting Russia, Cowell joined the music faculty at the New School for Social Research in New York, teaching there until 1936 and again from

Henry Cowell (left) with Charles Ives at Ives's home in Connecticut, c. 1952. *Courtesy Electra Yourke.*

1940 to 1965. From 1932 to 1936 he also taught at Mills College, Oakland, California. In 1941 he taught at Mills Training School in New York. He was also music consultant and senior musical editor of the Radio Division of War Information from 1943 to 1945. He was appointed to the faculty of Columbia University in 1948, retiring in 1960. He also taught at Bennington College, Vermont; Adelphi University, Garden City, New York; and the Peabody Institute in Baltimore.

In 1927 Cowell founded the magazine *New Music Quarterly*. In its 104 issues from 1927 to 1943, 180 works by American composers were published with parallel projects for orchestral music and recordings. He received many honors, including an award from the National Institute of Arts and Letters (1948), and served on the board of several organizations, including the League of Composers, New Music Society, American Composers' Alliance, and the Contemporary Music Society.

Two early compositions reveal his intense interest in original experimentation with complex rhythms. *Quartet Romantic* for two flutes, violin, and viola (1915–17) and *Quartet Euphometric* for strings (1916–19) provide each instrument with separate time values throughout. At the time they were written, both works were beyond human performing capabilities and were not published until 1974. His early works, while exploring a remarkable world of experimentation, at times show the influence of his Irish ancestry, especially in the use of dances such as reels. In several symphonies, the scherzo movement is a jig. Later in his career, after visits to the Far East, India, and Iceland, he made use of oriental instruments and exotic folk song in works whose titles indicate the country of origin.

In a public concert on 12 March 1912, the day after his 15th birthday, Cowell played his own compositions, including *The Tides of Manaunaun* in which he used "tone-clusters," groups of notes on both black and white keys, played sometimes by the fist or the forearm. Charles Ives and Leo Ornstein both used tone-clusters in their piano pieces, but Cowell seems to have discovered them unaided. Although he later received conventional composition lessons in New York from Percy Goetschius, his original approach to keyboard music remained with him.

In *Aeolian Harp* (1923), the pianist is instructed to depress the keys soundlessly with one hand while playing the open strings directly with the other hand. This form of impressionism predates by many years what is considered avant-garde in composers of today. *The Banshee* (1925) is also performed "inside" the piano, where the composer indicates 12 different methods of sounding the open strings to produce novel effects, with glissandi and other sounds hitherto unexplored. *Tiger* (1928) includes massive tone-clusters that have to be played with both forearms together. *Sinister Resonances* (1930) uses various tone qualities created by interfering with the notes played on the keyboard by one hand dampening the strings with the other, producing muted and harmonic effects. In *Synchony* for orchestra (1930), Cowell employs a piano in the score with the instruction that the five lowest strings should be played on directly by a gong stick. At the time of the latest of these experimental devices in piano writing, Stockhausen was two years old.

Another instrumental curiosity is *Ensemble* for string quartet and thundersticks, composed in 1925. In 1931 with Leon Theremin, the inventor of the electronic musical instrument bearing his name, Cowell developed a new musical instrument, the "Rhythmicon," which was capable of producing multiple cross-rhythms. For this he wrote *Rhythmicana* (1931) with orchestral accompaniment. After this period, Cowell's interest in mere innovation declined; except for the oriental influence in later works, his music became more conventional, and his Celtic ancestry and the American heritage held increasing significance.

In all Cowell composed over 1,000 pieces of music, and he remained prolific to the end of his life. The set of 20 symphonies forms the backbone of his orchestral works: no. 1 in B minor (1918); no. 2, *Anthropos* (Mankind; 1938–39); no. 3, *Gaelic* (1942–43); no. 4, *Short* (1945); no. 5 (1948–49); no. 6 (1951); no. 7 (1952); no. 8, *Choral* (1952); no. 9 (1953); no. 10 for chamber orchestra (1953); no. 11, *Seven Rituals of Music* (1953); no. 12 (1954); no. 13, *Madras* for Indian instruments (1955); no. 14 (1956); no. 15 *Thesis* (1960); no. 16, *Icelandic* (1962); no. 17, *Lancaster* (1962); no. 18 (1964); no. 19 (1964); and no. 20 (1965). Sketches for a Symphony no. 21 were completed by Lou Harrison (1965).

Cowell's other orchestral compositions, too numerous to list completely, include *Vestiges* (1924); *Sinfonietta* (1928), performed in Vienna in 1932 under the direction of Anton Webern; *Two Reels* (1932); *Four Continuations* for strings (1933); *Old American Country Set* (1937); *Shipshape Overture* (1939); *Ancient Desert Drone* (1940); *Pastorale* and *Fiddler's Delight* (1940); *United Music* (1944); *Festival Overture* for two orchestras (1946); *Ballad* for strings (1954); *Variations* (1956); *Music for Orchestra* (1957); *Ongaku* (1957); and *Persian Set* with Persian instruments (1957).

Between 1942 and 1957, Cowell composed 17 pieces with the title *Hymn and Fuging Tune*, a direct tribute to William Billings and his contemporaries. In form they resemble preludes and fugues: nos. 2, 5 and 8 are for strings, nos. 3 and 16 are for orchestra. The others are for various instrumental ensembles.

Among his works for soloist and orchestra are a Piano Concerto (1929); *Tales from the Countryside* for piano (1941), at one time his most popular composition; *Little Suite* for piano (1942); Suite for piano and strings (1943); *Concerto Brevis* for accordion (1960); Concerto for percussion and orchestra (1961); two koto concertos (1961–2, 1965); *Duo Concertante* for flute and harp (1961); and *Variations* for two violas (1960).

Cowell contributed several important pieces to the concert band repertory. These include *Suite in Five Movements* (1936); *A Curse and a Blessing* (1938); *Celtic Set* (1939); *The Exuberant Mexican* (1939); *Shoonthree* (1940); *Festive Occasion* (1942); *Animal Magic* (1945); *Fantasie* (1952); *Singing Band* (1953); and *Sleep Music*.

His extensive instrumental music includes five string quartets. The First was composed in 1927, the Second (entitled *Movement*) in 1934. The Third Quartet (*Mosaic*") (1935) makes use of an element of indeterminacy. The players choose the material from what the composer calls "compositional blocks," and the five movements may be performed in any order. The Fourth Quartet (*United*) dates from 1936. Other chamber music includes *Seven Paragraphs* for string trio (1926); Suite for violin and piano (1927); Violin Sonata (1945); *Homage to Iran* for violin and piano (1959); and a Piano Trio (1965).

Cowell's music for choir is also extensive. The principal works are *The Thistle Flower* for female voices (1928); *The Coming of Light* (1939); *American Muse* (1943); *The Road Leads to Tomorrow* (1947); *If He Pleases* for chorus, boys' choir, and orchestra (1954); *Thanksgiving Psalm from the Dead Sea Scrolls* for men's chorus and orchestra (1956); *The Commission*, a cantata for four voices and orchestra to a libretto by Colin McPhee (1954); *Edson Hymns and Fuging Tunes* for chorus and orchestra (1960); and *The Creator* for double chorus and orchestra (1963). His works for the stage are an unfinished opera, *O'Higgins of Chile* (1947), and two ballets, *The Building of Banba*, with chorus (1922) and *Atlantis* (1926).

Cowell produced three important books: *New Musical Resources*, written in 1919 but not published until 1930; *American Composers on American Music* (1937,); and *Charles Ives and His Music* (1955), written in collaboration with his wife, Sidney.

COWLES, CECIL MARION
b. San Francisco, California, 14 January 1898
d. Sewanee, Tennessee, 20 November 1966

Cowles studied at the Von Ende School in New York and at the Von Meyernich School, California. Among her teachers were Hugo Mansfeldt, Otto Bendix, Sigismund Stojowski, Carl Dies, and Wallingford Riegger. She made her debut as a pianist at the age of six. Among her compositions are a Mass (*Jesu Bambino*), *Oriental Sketches* for orchestra, and songs. Her once popular piano pieces often have exotic titles: *Song of Persia*, *Shanghai Bound*, and *Lotus Flower*.

COWLES, WALTER RUEL
b. New Haven, Connecticut, 4 September 1881
d. Tallahassee, Florida, 8 December 1959

Cowles graduated in 1906 from Yale University where he had been a pupil of Horatio Parker. After studying at the Schola Cantorum in Paris, he returned to the

Walter Cowles.
Courtesy Special Collections Department, Florida State University Libraries, Tallahassee, Florida.

United States in 1911 to take up a position as Instructor of Piano at Yale where he remained until 1919. He was professor of Theory at Florida State College for Women (1930–51). He composed a Piano Concerto, a Piano Trio, piano pieces, and songs.

CRAWFORD (SEEGER), RUTH PORTER
b. *East Liverpool, Ohio, 3 July 1901*
d. *Chevy Chase, Maryland, 18 November 1953*

Ruth Crawford taught piano at Jacksonville School of Music, Florida (1918–1921) before moving to Chicago, where she studied at the American Conservatory (1921–25). After teaching there she went to Berlin and Paris in 1930 on a Guggenheim Fellowship. After her marriage in 1932 to Charles Seeger, she devoted much of her effort helping her husband in the Resettlement Administration in Washington, D.C. It was at this time that she took a great interest on folk song and assisted John and Alan Lomax in editing the second volume of *American Folk-Songs and Ballads.* All her family have earned an international reputation in the field of folk song, especially her daughter Peggy, son Mike, and stepson Pete.

Her own compositions were at the opposite extreme to folk song, being complex and dissonant. Most of her works are scored for chamber ensembles. *Three Songs* to words by Carl Sandburg for contralto, oboe,

piano, and percussion (1932) were performed at the I.S.C.M. Festival in Amsterdam in 1933. The String Quartet of 1931 looks forward to the experiments of the 1950s with its systematic relationship between melody, rhythm, dynamics, and duration on an almost mathematical basis. It was published in 1941 by Henry Cowell.

The other important pieces among her small output of works include *Nine Preludes* for piano (1924–28); *Two Movements* for chamber ensemble (1926); Violin Sonata (1926); Suite no. 1 for five winds (1927); Suite no. 2 for piano and string quartet (1927); *Two Movements* (Sonata) for woodwind and piano (1928); *Four Diaphonic Suites* (no. 1 for two cellos; no. 2, two clarinets; no. 3, flute solo; and no. 4, oboe [or viola] and cello; 1930); Suite for small orchestra (1932); *Andante* for strings (1938); *Rissolty Rossolty* for ten wind instruments (1941); and Suite for wind quintet (1952). A Piano *Quintet* dating from 1927 is now lost. Her other vocal music comprises *Adventures of Tom Thumb* for narrator and piano (1925); *Five Songs* (Sandburg; 1929); *Three Chants* for chorus (1930); and *Two Ricercari* for voice and piano (1932).

With her husband she wrote an unpublished book on dissonant counterpoint, *Tradition and Experiment in the New Music.* In later life she published several folk song collections still in print, including *American Folksongs for Children.*

Ruth Crawford.
Courtesy The Family of Ruth Crawford Seeger.

CRESTON, PAUL

b. New York, New York, 10 October 1906
d. San Diego, California, 24 August 1985

Creston was born of Italian parents; he was christened Giuseppe Guttivergi, later changed to Guttoveggio. A childhood nickname "Cress" was later to become his surname, Creston. He was completely self-taught in composition, but was an organ pupil of Pietro Yon and a piano student of Giuseppe Randegger and Gaston Dethier. It was not until he was 26 that he decided to devote himself entirely to composition; for many years before that he wavered between music and literature as a career.

In 1938 Creston was awarded a Guggenheim Fellowship, renewed for the following year. He became a lecturer at Swarthmore College in 1958, and taught at the New York College of Music (1963–67). He was organist at St. Malachy's Church in New York City from 1934 to 1967. From 1968 to 1975 he was Composer-in-Residence and professor of music at Central Washington State College, Ellensburg, retiring with emeritus status. In 1975 he moved to San Diego, California.

Although at times Creston's music is dissonant, he followed conservative models, incorporating a vital rhythmic element into all his works. He made use of Gregorian chant as a basis of several major compositions, including the *Missa Solemnis*, Third Symphony, and *Corinthians: XIII*. The inspiration of the dance on his music is seen in his first published work, *Five Dances* for piano; the word "dance" appears no fewer than ten times in the titles of his compositions and several times as part of a prelude and dance under other titles, such as *Pastorale and Tarantella*. Creston's reputation was first established in 1940 with *Two Choric Dances*, op. 17 (1938), which has been performed by many orchestras in America and Europe.

Creston's First Symphony, op. 20, was composed in 1940 and premiered the following year. It received the New York Music Critics' Circle Award in a season that included the first performance of works by Copland, Harris, and Schuman. The other symphonies which are among his most heard works are no. 2, op. 35 (1944); no. 3, op. 48, subtitled *Three Mysteries* (1950); no. 4, op. 52 (1951); no. 5, op. 64 (1955); and no. 6 (*Organ Symphony*), op. 118 (1981).

Among his many other orchestral compositions are *Out of the Cradle*, op. 5 (1934); *Threnody*, op. 16 (1938); *Prelude and Dance*, op. 25 (1941); *A Rumour*, op. 27 (1941); *Pastorale and Dance*, op. 28 (1941); *Chant of 1942*, op. 33 (1942); *Frontiers*, op. 34 (1943); *Walt Whitman*, op. 53 (1952); *Invocation and Dance*, op. 58 (1953); *Dance Overture*, op. 62 (1954); and *Lydian Ode*, op. 67 (1956).

Toccata, op. 68 (1957) was commissioned by George Szell for the 40th anniversary of the Cleveland Orches-

Paul Creston, in rehearsal.
Courtesy Central Washington State University.

tra. Later works for orchestra include *Pre-Classical Suite*, op. 71 (1957); *Janus*, op. 77 (1959); *Corinthians XIII*, op. 82 (1963); *Choreografic Suite*, op. 86 (1965); *Pavane Variations*, op. 89 (1966), commissioned by the La Jolla Musical Arts Society; and *Chthonic Ode (Homage to Henry Moore)*, op. 90, commissioned by Sixten Ehrling and premiered by the Detroit Symphony Orchestra in 1966. Among his last orchestral pieces are *Thanatopsis*, op, 101, completed in 1971; *Suite for Strings*, op. 109 (1978); and *Sadhana* for cello and chamber orchestra, op. 117 (1981).

In addition to two violin concertos, op. 65 (1956) and op. 78 (1960), Creston composed a Marimba Concertino, op. 21 (1940), and concertos for saxophone, op. 26 (1941), piano, op. 43 (1949), two pianos, op. 50 (1951), and accordion, op. 75 (1958). Also for solo instruments and orchestra are *Partita* for flute, violin, and strings, op. 12 (1937); *Fantasy* for piano, op. 32 (1942); *Poem* for harp, op. 39 (1945); *Fantasy* for trombone, op. 42 (1947); and *Fantasy* for accordion, op. 75 (1958).

Creston contributed several significant works to the repertory of school and college bands, including *Legend*, op. 31 (1942); *Zanoni*, op. 40 (1946); *Celebration Overture*, op. 61 (1954); *Prelude and Dance*, op. 76 (1959); *Anatolia (Turkish Rhapsody)*, op. 93 (1967); *Kalevala (Fantasy on Finnish Folk-Songs)*, op. 95 (1968); and *Jubilee*, op. 102 (1971). For the Bicentennial celebrations he composed *Square Dance 76* for wind symphony orchestra, op. 105 (1975). In the same year he wrote *Liberty Song*, op. 107, also for concert band.

Creston's choral music includes a Requiem, op. 15 for male voices and organ (1938); *Missa Solemnis*, op. 44 for chorus and organ (1949); *Missa "Adoro Te,"* op. 54 for female or mixed voices and organ (1952); and *The Celestial Vision*, op. 60 for men's voices (1954). Other choral works are a Christmas oratorio, *Isaiah's Prophesy*, op. 80, for soloists, chorus, and orchestra (1962); *Missa "Cum Jubilo,"* op. 97 for a cappella chorus (1968); *The Northwest* (retitled *Hyas Illahee*), op. 98 for chorus and orchestra (1969); *Leaves of Grass* (Whitman), five songs for mixed voices and piano, op. 100 (1970); *Calamus*, op. 104 for chorus, brass, and percussion (1972); and *Prodigal*, op. 115 for mixed voices and piano (1980). For solo voice and orchestra he wrote *Dance Variations*, op. 30 (1942); *Psalm XXIII*, op. 37 (1945); *Nocturne*, op. 83 for soprano and ensemble (1964); and *The Psalmist*, op. 91 (1967).

Throughout his career, Creston showed a particular interest in providing pieces for neglected instruments, notably saxophone: Suite, op. 6 (1935); Sonata, op. 19 (1939); *Rapsodie*, op. 108 for saxophone and organ (1974); and Suite, op. 111 for saxophone quartet (1976). In addition to those mentioned above, his accordion works include *Prelude and Dance*, op. 69 (1957); Suite,

op. 96 (1968); and the *Embryo Suite*.

Other chamber music includes a String Quartet, op. 8 (1936); four suites: op. 13. for viola and piano (1937), op. 18 for violin and piano (1939), op. 56 for flute, viola, and piano (1952), and op. 66 for cello and piano (1956); Concertino for piano and wind quintet, op. 99 (1969); *Ceremonial*, op. 103 for percussion ensemble (1972); and Trio, op. 112 for piano, violin, and cello (1979). In addition to the *Poem* for harp and orchestra, Creston wrote two pieces for harp solo: *Lydian Song*, op. 55 (1952) and *Olympia*, op. 94 (1968).

His many pieces for piano solo include a Sonata, op. 9 (1936); *Six Preludes*, op. 38 (1945); *Three Narratives*, op. 79 (1962); *Metamorphoses*, op. 84 (1964); *Romanza*, op. 110 (1978); *Offertory*, op. 113 (1980); *Interlude*, op. 114 (1980); and *Rhythmicon*, ten books of progressive studies in rhythm. For organ he composed a Suite, op. 70. (1957); *Fantasia*, op. 74 (1958); and *Rapsodia Breve*, op. 81, (1963). Creston's single stage work, the ballet *A Tale About the Land*, op. 23 (1940), was later withdrawn.

Creston was the author of three books: *Principles of Rhythm*, published in 1964; *Creative Harmony* (1970); and *Rational Metrical Notation* (1979). He also contributed numerous articles to various musical periodicals, the first three on dance when he was only 17 years old.

CRIST, BAINBRIDGE
b. Lawrenceburg, Indiana, 13 February 1883
d. Barnstable, Massachusetts, 7 February 1969

Crist began piano lessons at the age of five with his mother, and later learned to play the flute. He studied law at George Washington University, Washington, D.C., and after being admitted to the bar, practiced in Boston for six years. Thereafter he abandoned law and went to Europe in 1912 to pursue music as a pupil of Claude Landi in London and Paul Juon in Berlin. He also studied voice in London, Paris, and Berlin. With the outbreak of the First World War, he returned to America, establishing himself as a singing teacher, first in Boston and later in Washington, D.C. He was again in Europe from 1923 to 1927.

It was as a composer of songs and piano pieces that Crist was best known; as the titles suggest, many of his works possess an oriental flavor: *Chinese Mother Goose Rhymes* (seven songs; 1917); *Drolleries from an Oriental Doll's House* (six songs; 1920); and the piano pieces *Egyptian Impressions* (1913), *Oriental Dances* (1923), and *Chinese Sketches* (1925). Among his many songs for voice and orchestra are *A Bag of Whistles* (1915); *The Parting* (1917); *O Come Hither !* (1918); *Colored Stars* (1921); *Remember* (1930); *Evening*

(1931); *The Way That Lovers Use* (1931); *Noontime* (1931); and *By a Silent Shore* (1932).

For the stage he composed *La Pied de la Momie* (1913), a choreographic drama performed in Bournemouth, England in 1925; a second choreographic drama, *The Sorceress* (1926); and a Javanese ballet, *Pregiwa's Marriage* (1922).

His orchestral pieces include *Intermezzo* (1921); *Abhisarika* for violin and orchestra (1921); *Chinese Dance* (1922); *Arabian Dance* (1922); *Nautch Dance* (1922); *An Old Portrait* (1924); *Dreams* (1924); *Yearning* (1924); *La Nuit Revéçue* (1933); *Vienna 1913* (1933); *Frivolité* (1934); *Romance* (1934); *Hymn to Nefertiti* (1936); *Hindu Rhapsody* (1939); *Festival Overture* (1939); and *American Epic 1620* (1943).

Crist was the author of a book, *The Art of Setting Words to Music*, published in 1944.

CRUMB, GEORGE
b. Charleston, West Virginia, 24 October 1929

Crumb was educated at the Mason College of Music, Charleston, West Virginia (1947–50), and at the University of Illinois, Urbana (1950–52). In 1954 he entered the University of Michigan where he was a composition pupil of Ross Lee Finney. In the summer of 1955 he studied with Boris Blacher, first at the Berkshire Music Center and later at the Hochschule für Musik, Berlin. On his return to the United States in 1950 he spent five years on the piano music faculty at the University of Colorado. From 1965 he taught at the University of Pennsylvania, retiring in 1997. He has been the recipient of many awards, including a Fulbright Scholarship (1954), a Rockefeller Award (1964), Koussevitzky Award (1965), Guggenheim Fellowships (1967, 1973), National Institute of Arts and Letters (1967), the Pulitzer Prize (1968), International Rostrum of Composers (UNESCO) (1971), and the Brandeis University Arts Award Medal (1979).

Crumb's early works include *Five Early Songs* (1947); a String Quartet (1954); a Sonata for solo cello (1955); and *Variazioni* for orchestra (1959). The *Five Piano Pieces* date from 1962. After these compositions, his style became more advanced in idiom, concentrating upon timbre and texture more than upon thematic development. He employs electronic amplification of instruments in certain pieces, but has not required prerecorded tape.

With notable single-mindedness he has set poems by Federico Garcia Lorca in most of his vocal works. The first of these, *Night Music I* for soprano, celeste, piano, and percussion, was composed in 1963 and revised in 1976. The following year he wrote *Four Nocturnes* (*Night Music II*) for violin and piano. *Eleven*

George Crumb.
Photo © 2003 Betsy Starobin,
courtesy Bridge Records/the composer.

Echoes of Autumn 1965 for alto flute, clarinet, violin, and piano (1966) was commissioned by Bowdoin College, Brunswick, Maine.

The four books of *Madrigals*, settings of fragmentary texts by Lorca, were composed between 1965 and 1969. The first two books, dedicated to the memory of Serge and Natalie Koussevitzky, are scored for soprano solo with vibraphone and double bass (Book I), and flute (doubling alto flute and piccolo) and percussion (Book II). The other two books followed in 1969: Book III for soprano, harp, and percussion, and Book IV for soprano, flute, double bass, harp, and percussion. The singer has to use a wide range of expressive styles, including "Sprechstimme," quarter-tones, and virtuosic coloratura. Various devices are applied to the instruments: the vibraphone plays harmonics, cymbals stroked with coins, glockenspiels played with brushes, and harp struck with metal rods, hard sticks, and wire brushes.

Echoes of Time and the River (*Four Processionals for Orchestra*), also subtitled *Echoes II*, was commissioned by the University of Chicago and first performed by the Chicago Symphony Orchestra in 1967. It was awarded the Pulitzer Prize in the following year. *Songs, Drones and Refrains of Death* for baritone, electric guitar, electric double bass, electric piano, and percussion was composed in 1968. Crumb's next work, *Night of the Four Moon* (1969), is scored for alto voice, alto flute, banjo, electric cello, and percussion. *Ancient Voices of Children*, commissioned by the Elizabeth Sprague Coolidge Foundation, settings of poems by Lorca for soprano, boy soprano, and seven instruments was composed in 1970. The music was used for a ballet with choreography by Christopher Bruce produced by Ballet Rambert in July 1975. Another work of 1970 is *Black Angels* (*Image I*), subtitled *Thirteen Images from the Dark Land*, for amplified string quartet. The composer describes it as "a voyage of the soul," portraying the struggle between God and the Devil.

Vox Balanae (*Voice of the Whale*), composed in 1971 to a commission from the New York Camarata and scored for flute, cello, and piano, uses the instruments to evoke the singing of the humpback whale. *Lux Aeterna* for soprano, bass flute (doubling soprano recorder), sitar, and two percussionists, was also composed in 1971 and is based on the traditional Latin text. In 1972 Crumb completed *Makrokosmos Volume I* for amplified piano. *Makrokosmos II* followed in 1973. *Music for a Summer Evening* (*Makrokosmos III*) for two amplified pianos and percussion was composed in 1974.

Dream Sequence (*Images II*) for violin, cello, piano, and percussion with off-stage glass harmonica dates from 1976. *Star Child*, Crumb's first work for symphony orchestra since 1967, received its premiere by the New York Philharmonic Orchestra under the direction of Pierre Boulez in May 1977. It is scored for large forces: quadruple woodwind, six horns, seven trumpets, organ, and vast percussion. The solo soprano and two children's choruses sing texts from the Requiem Mass, the Book of St. John, and the Medieval Massacre of the Innocents. The performance required four conductors.

Celestial Mechanics (*Makrokosmos IV*) for amplified piano (four hands) was completed in 1979. In the same year Crumb produced his first representational vocal work on an English text. *Apparition* (*Elegiac Songs and Vocalises*) on poems of Walt Whitman for soprano and amplified piano.

Never a prolific composer, Crumb has produced works at a rate of approximately one per year. Three pieces for piano solo—*A Little Suite for Christmas 1979*, *Gnomic Variations* (1981), and *Processional* (1983)—and his sole composition for organ, *Partial Drone* (1982), followed. *A Haunted Landscape* was premiered in 1984 by the New York Philharmonic Orchestra under Zubin Mehta. The remaining works for this decade are a setting of Poe's poem, *The Sleeper* for mezzo-soprano and piano (1984); *An Idyll for the Misbegotten* for amplified flute and three percussionists (1985); *Federico's Little Songs for Children* (Lorca)

for soprano, flute, and percussion (1986); and *Zeitgeist* for two amplified pianos. Crumb's most recent compositions include *Quest* for guitar, soprano saxophone, two percussion, harp, and double bass (1990, rev. 1994); *Easter Dawning* for carillon (1991); and *Mundus Canis: Five Humoresques* for guitar and percussion (1998).

Since retiring from teaching in the mid-1990s, Crumb has returned to sustained composition. Recent works include *Eine Kleine Mitternachtmusik* (*A Little Midnight Music*), *Ruminations on a theme by Thelonius Monk* for amplified piano (2001); *Unto the Hills* (*Songs of Sadness, Yearning and Innocence*) (*American Songbook I*), a cycle of Appalachian folk songs for singer, percussion quartet, and amplified piano (2002); *Otherworldly Sonorities* for two amplified pianos (2001); and *A Journey Beyond Time* (*Songs of Despair, Hope and Humor*; *American Songbook II*), a cycle of African-American spirituals for singer, percussion quartet, and amplified piano (2003). Currently he is working on two further *American Songbooks*.

CUSTER, ARTHUR
b. Manchester, Connecticut, 21 April 1923
d. New York City, New York, 17 September 1998

After studying engineering at the University of Hartford (1940–42), Custer turned to music and graduated from the University of Connecticut, Storrs in 1949. He continued his training at the University of Redlands, California (1949–51), where he was a pupil of Paul Pisk (M.M. 1951), and at the University of Iowa (1956–59) where he studied with Philip Bezanson (Ph.D., 1959). From 1960 to 1962, he was a pupil of Nadia Boulanger in Paris; he also received composition lessons from Hindemith.

Custer taught at Kansas Wesleyan University, Salina (1952–55) and the University of Omaha (1955–58), and from 1959 to 1962 was supervisor of music for the U.S. Air Force in Spain. From 1962 to 1965 he was assistant dean of fine arts at the University of Rhode Island; from 1965 to 1967, he served as Dean of the Philadelphia Musical Academy. In 1967 he became director of the Metropolitan Educational Center for the Arts in St. Louis. From 1970 to 1973 he was director of the Arts in Education Project for the Rhode Island State Council on the Arts. In 1973 he was appointed Composer-in-Residence to the Rhode Island State Council on the Arts; from 1975, he was a freelance composer.

In most of his compositions until the mid-1960s, Custer adopted serial techniques, but later his music used pre-recorded tape and a greater freedom of language. For orchestra he composed a *Passacaglia* (1957); *Concert Piece* (1959); Symphony no. 1, *Sinfonia de Madrid* (1961); *Five Dialogues* for cello and orchestra

(1962); a ballet, *Petrouchka '65*, commissioned by the American Festival Ballet (1965); *Rhapsodality Brass!* (*Found Objects II*; 1969); and *Doubles* for violin and small orchestra (1972, rev. 1975).

His large output of chamber music includes three string quartets: no. 1, *Colloquy* (1961); no. 2, *Concertino for Second Violin and Strings* (1964); and no. 3, *Interface I* with tape (1969). Other pieces are *Rhapsody and Allegro* for cello and piano (1957); *Three Pieces* for brass sextet (1958); Sextet for woodwinds and piano (1959); Divertimento for bassoon and piano (1961); *Cycle* for nine instruments (1963); *Two Movements* for wind quintet (1964); *Parabolas* for trombone and percussion (1967); *Permutations* for violin, clarinet, and cello (1967); Concerto for brass quintet (1968); and *Parabolas* for viola and piano (1970). Custer continued the series of pieces entitled *Found Objects* for instruments and tape: *III* for double bass (1971); *IV* for cello (1972); *V* (*A Little Sight Music*) for six players (1973); *VI* for flutes (1973); *VII* for piano (1973); and *VIII* for violin (1974).

Other instrumental pieces include *I Used to Play by Ear* for one piano, two pianists, and four selected objects (1971); *Eyepieces* for oboe and tape (1974); *Magic Dragon* for tuba and tape (1975); *Sweet Sixteen* for clarinet and piano (1976); and *Interface II* for ensemble, slide projectors, and audience (1976).

Custer's principal vocal compositions are *Three Songs of Death* for mezzo-soprano and piano (1958); *Songs of the Seasons* for soprano and small orchestra (1963); *Cartagena Songs* for bass-baritone, oboe, horn, and piano (1964); *Three Love Lyrics* for tenor, flute, viola, and harp (1965); and *Comments on This World* for contralto and string quartet (1967).

D

DAHL, INGOLF
b. Hamburg, Germany, 9 June 1912
d. Frutigen, Switzerland, 7 August 1970

Dahl was born of Swedish parents. He studied at the Music Academy in Cologne with Phillip Jarnach (1930–32). From 1932 to 1936 he was a student at Zurich University and the Zurich Conservatory, where he received conducting lessons from Volkmar Andreae. He gave piano recitals in Switzerland and was conductor of the Municipal Opera Orchestra in Zurich.

Dahl settled in the United States in 1938, taking American citizenship in 1943. From 1942 to 1945 he worked in Hollywood as an arranger and conductor. In California in 1944, he studied with Nadia Boulanger. From 1945 to his death he was professor of music at the University of Southern California, Los Angeles, and conductor of the University Symphony Orchestra (1945–60, 1968–69). He also taught at Tanglewood (1952–55) and was director of the Ojai Music Festival (1964–66).

Dahl's most important work is the symphonic legend *The Tower of St. Barbara*, commissioned in 1955 by the Louisville Orchestra. He also composed a Saxophone Concerto (1949, rev. 1953) and a *Symphonia Concertante* for two clarinets, written in 1952 for Benny Goodman. Other works for orchestra are *Aria Sinfonica* (1965) and *Variations on a Theme by C.P.E. Bach* for strings (1967). His last work, *Elegy Concerto* for violin and chamber orchestra, begun in 1963, was intended for Eunice Shapiro and is dedicated to the memory of her husband, Victor Gottlieb. Left unfinished at Dahl's death, the score was completed in September 1971 by Donal Michalsky.

Dahl concentrated particularly upon chamber music. Among his considerable number of instrumental works are *Allegro and Arioso* for wind quintet (1942);

Music for Brass Instruments (1944); *Concerto a Tre* for clarinet, violin, and cello (1946); *Duo* for cello and piano (1946); Divertimento for viola and piano (1948); Piano Quartet (1957); Piano Trio (1962); *Duettino Concertante* for flute and percussion (1966); *Variations on a French Folk Song* for flute and piano (1970); and *Sonata da Camera* for clarinet and piano (1970).

For piano solo he wrote *Sonata Seria* (1953); *Sonata Pastorale* (1959); *Reflections* (1967); and *Quodlibet on Six American Folk Songs* for two pianos, eight hands (1953), which he orchestrated in 1965. He also composed a Sinfonietta for concert band (1961).

DAMROSCH, WALTER (JOHANNES)
b. Breslau, Germany (now Wroclaw, Poland), 30 January 1862
d. New York, New York, 22 December 1950

Damrosch was the son of Leopold Damrosch (1832–1885), a distinguished orchestral conductor. As a child he studied piano and composition in Germany before being taken to America in 1871. He was appointed conductor of the New York Oratorio Society and the New York Symphony Orchestra on the death of his father. He also took his father's opera company on tour to Chicago and Boston, where he performed Wagner's *Die Walküre* and *Tannhäuser*.

It is as a pioneering conductor that Damrosch is remembered today; he took the New York Symphony Orchestra to every state, and in 1910 he became the first conductor to tour Europe with an American orchestra. Damrosch was also the first conductor to make a nationwide radio broadcast, and in 1927 he was appointed music adviser to NBC. He was responsible for introducing the music of Tchaikovsky to America. The many first performances which he conducted include

Walter Damrosch.
Courtesy The Morrison Foundation for Music Resaerch, Inc.

the piano concertos of Gershwin and Copland, Copland's First Symphony, and *Tapiola* by Sibelius, which Damrosch had commissioned. He was also responsible for the first American performance of the Third and Fourth Symphonies of Brahms and several works by Elgar.

Damrosch's own compositions, few in number, were written at the beginning and end of his career. His major works are five operas: *The Scarlet Letter* (after Hawthorne) was produced by the composer in Boston on 1 February 1896. A comic opera, *The Dove of Peace,* to a text by Wallace Irwin, received its premiere in Philadelphia on 15 November 1912. Three months later, *Cyrano de Bergerac*, based on the play by Rostand, with libretto by William J. Henderson, was performed at the Metropolitan Opera House on 27 February 1913. Damrosch's fourth opera, *The Man Without a Country,* to a text by Arthur Guiterman from the novel by Edward Everett Hal, was also staged at the Metropolitan Opera on 12 May 1937. This work marked his return to composition after a silence of almost 20 years. A fantasy in one act, *The Opera Cloak*, was first heard in New York on 4 November 1942.

Besides these operas, Damrosch's other important works are a *Manila Te Deum* for chorus and orchestra (1898); *Abraham Lincoln's Song* for baritone; chorus,

and orchestra (1935); a cantata; *The Canterbury Pilgrims*; and a setting of Robert Nathan's poem *Dunkirk;* for baritone; male chorus, and orchestra (1943). He also composed incidental music for three plays by Euripides: *Iphigenia in Aulis* (1915), *Medea* (1915), and *Electra* (1917), as well as several songs, of which *Danny Deever* (1897), to words by Kipling, became very popular.

Damrosch wrote an autobiography, *My Musical Life,* published in 1923.

DANIELPOUR, RICHARD
b. *New York, New York, 28 January 1956*

Danielpour studied at the Oberlin (Ohio) College Conservatory and the New England Conservatory, Boston where he graduated in 1980. At the Juilliard School, New York he was a pupil of Victor Persichetti and Peter Mennin (M.A., 1982, D.M.A., 1986). In addition he received piano lessons from Lorin Hollander, Theodore Lettvin, and Gabriel Chados. In 1989 he was awarded a Guggenheim Fellowship. From 1984 to 1988 he taught at the College of New Rochelle and Marymount Manhattan College (both in New York) and was guest composer at the Accademia di Santa Cecilia, Rome in 1988 and Composer-in-Residence with the Seattle Symphony Orchestra (1991–92). Currently he teaches at the Curtis Institute, Philadelphia and the Manhattan School of Music, New York. Danielpour belongs to the post-modernists who emerged towards the end of the 20th century. His music is rooted in tradition with an original voice marked by startling orchestration. He cites Copland, Shostakovich, Britten, Bartók, and Stravinsky among the composers he most admires.

Among his orchestral works are four symphonies: no. 1, *Dona Nobis Pacem* (1984–85); no. 2, *Vision* for soprano, tenor, and orchestra (Dylan Thomas) premiered in San Francisco in 1986; no. 3, *Journey Without Distance* for soprano, chorus, and orchestra (after Schumann; 1989–90); and no. 4, *Celestial Night* (1997). His other orchestral pieces include *First Light* for chamber orchestra (1988); *The Awakened Heart* (1990); two piano concertos, no. 1 *Metamorphosis* (1990), and no. 2 (1993); *Song of Remembrance* (1991); *Toward the Splendid City* (1992); a Cello Concerto written in 1994 for Yo-Yo Ma; *Concerto for Orchestra: Zoroastrian Riddles,* commissioned in 1996 to celebrate the centenary of the Pittsburgh Symphony Orchestra; *Vox Populi* (1998); *The Night Rainbow* (1999); *Violin Concerto: A Fool's Paradise* (1999); *Voices of Remembrance,* a concerto for string quartet and orchestra (2000); and a Double Concerto for violin and cello, composed in 2002 for Jaime Laredo and Sharon Robinson. For the stage Danielpour has composed two ballets, *Anima Mundi*

(1995) and *Urban Dances: Dance Suite in Five Movements* (1996).

Among his instrumental music are three string quartets, the first now withdrawn; no. 2, *Shadow Dances* (1992); and no. 3, *Psalm of Sorrow* for baritone and string quartet (1994). Other works are the Piano Quintet (1988); *Urban Dances I* (1989) and *II* for brass quintet (1993); *Feast of Fools* for bassoon and string quartet (1998); and *A Child's Reliquary* for piano trio (1999). For solo piano there are *Piano Fantasy* (1980), *Psalms* (1985), a Sonata (1986), and *The Enchanted Garden* (1992),

Danielpour's solo vocal music includes *Sonnets of Orpheus I* for soprano and ensemble (1991) and *II* for baritone and ensemble (1994), both settings of Rilke; *Songs of the Night* for tenor and piano trio (1993); *I Am Not Prey* for soprano and piano, four hands (1996); *Sweet Talk,* four songs to texts by Toni Morrison, for soprano, cello, double bass, and piano, composed in 1997 for Jessye Norman;, and *Spirits in the Well* (Toni Morrison), a song cycle for soprano, and orchestra (1998). In 1997, Danielpour was commissioned to write *Elegies.* Scored for mezzo-soprano, baritone, and orchestra, it sets sections of letters written home by the father of the singer Frederica von Stade, who was killed in Germany in April 1945, six weeks before she was born.

Besides the two symphonies with choirs, his choral music includes *Prologue and Prayer* for chorus and strings (1982, rev. 1989) and *Canticle of Peace* for baritone and mixed voices (1995). *An American Requiem* for choir and orchestra (2001) combines words by Whitman, Emerson, and other American writers with the Latin text.

DANIELS, MABEL WHEELER
b. Swampscott, Massachusetts, 27 November 1878
d. Boston, Massachusetts, 10 March 1971

Mabel Daniels graduated from Radcliffe College, Cambridge, Massachusetts in 1900 and later studied with Chadwick in Boston and with Ludwig Thuille in Munich (1903). From 1913 to 1918 she was head of music at Simmons College, Boston. In 1931 she held a MacDowell Fellowship.

She was widely known for her choral and vocal music, for which she won several prizes. *The Desolate City* for baritone, chorus, and orchestra was performed at the MacDowell Festival in Peterboro, New Hampshire in 1913. She is remembered today solely for the choral works: *In Springtime* for women's voices (1910); two pieces for women's voices; two violins, and piano, *Eastern Song* and *The Voice of My Beloved* (1911); *Flowerwagon* for women's voices and piano (1914);

Mabel Wheeler Daniels.
Courtesy Notable American Unitarians.

The Guests of Sleep (1914); *Peace With a Sword* (1917); *The Girl Scouts Marching Song* (1918); *Songs of Elfland* (1924); *A Psalm of Praise* (1924); *The Holy Star* (1928); *Exultate Deo* (1929); *O God of All Our Glorious Past* (1930); *Through the Dark the Dreamers Came* for women's or mixed voices (1930, rev. 1961); and *The Christ Child* for chorus and piano (1931). The cantata *Song of Jael* was heard at the Worcester Festival in 1940. Later choral pieces include *A Psalm of Praise* (1954) and *Piper, Play On !* (1960).

For the stage she composed four operettas: *A Copper Complication* (1900); *The Court of Hearts* (1901); *The Show Girl* (1902); and *The Legend of Marietta* (1909); and an operatic sketch, *Alice in Wonderland Continued* (1904). Her ballet *A Night in Bethlehem* dates from 1954.

At one time her two orchestral pieces—*Deep Forest,* composed in 1931 for 13 instruments (rev. for full orchestra, 1934) and *Pirates' Island* (1934)—were performed throughout the United States, but they have now disappeared from the repertory. She also composed a Suite for strings (1910); *Pastoral Ode* for flute and strings (1940); *In Memoriam* (1945); *Digressions* for strings (1947); and an Overture (1951).

Daniels wrote a Violin Sonata; *Three Observations* for woodwind (1943); *Four Observations* for four strings (1945); and many songs. She was the author of an entertaining book, *The American Girl in Munich*, published in 1905.

DAUGHERTY, MICHAEL
b. *Cedar Rapids, Iowa, 28 April 1954*

Daugherty was born into a family of musicians and at an early age was playing in jazz bands in Iowa. American popular music culture is much reflected in his compositions. He began his musical education at North Texas State University, Denton (1972–76) and the Manhattan School of Music (M.A., 1976), where he was a pupil of Charles Wuorinen. At Yale University (M.M.A., 1982; D.M.A., 1986), he studied with Jacob Druckman, Earle Brown, and Roger Reynolds. From 1982 to 1984 he received composition lessons from Gyorgy Ligeti at the Hochschule für Musik in Hamburg. He worked at IRCAM in Paris (1979–1980). Daugherty taught at the Oberlin (Ohio) College Conservatory of Music (1986–91), then joined the music faculty at the University of Michigan, Ann Arbor, where he is currently professor of composition. In addition he was Composer-in-Residence with the Detroit Symphony Orchestra (1999–2003) and the Colorado Symphony Orchestra (2001–02).

For orchestra Daugherty has written *Mxyzptlk* (1988); his most popular work *Metropolis Symphony* (1988–93); *Oh Lois!* (1989); *Lex* (1990); *Flamingo* for chamber orchestra (1991); *Dead Elvis* for bassoon and orchestra (1993); *Le Tombeau de Liberace* for piano and orchestra (1996); *Jackie's Song* for cello and orchestra (1996); *Second Symphony: MotorCity Triptych* (Detroit: 2000); and *Philadelphia Stories* (Philadelphia: 2001). His contribution to the wind band repertoire includes *Desi* (1991); *Bizarro* (1993); *Motown Metal* (1994); *Niagara Falls* (1997); *Red Café Tango* (1999); *UFO* (2000); *Rosa Parks Boulevard* (2001); and *Bells for Stokowski* (2002).

Among his instrumental works are *Piano Plus* (1985); *Blue Like an Orange* (1987); *Snap ! Blue Like an Orange* for chamber ensemble (1987), which won the Kennedy Friedheim Award; *Bounce I* (1988); *Sing, Sing, J. Edgar Hoover* for string quartet and tape (1992); *Elvis Everywhere* for three Elvis impersonators and string quartet (1993); *Paul Robeson Told Me* for string quartet and tape (1994); *Shaken, Not Stirred* for percussion ensemble (1995); and *What's That Spel?l* for chamber ensemble (1995),

Daugherty's opera *Jackie O,* based on the life of the widow of President Kennedy, was produced in New York in 1997.

DAVIDOVSKY, MARIO
b. *Medanos, Buenos Aires, Argentina, 4 March 1934*

After studying in Buenos Aires, Davidovsky went to the United States in 1958, where he became a pupil of Otto Luening and Aaron Copland. He also studied with Milton Babbitt at Tanglewood in the summer of 1958. He taught at the University of Michigan (1964), Institute di Tella, Buenos Aires (1965), Manhattan School of Music (1968–69), Yale University (1969–70), City College of New York (1968–81), and Columbia University (1981–94). From 1994 he has been director of the Columbia-Princeton Electronic Music Center.

Davidovsky has received an award from the American Academy and Institute of Arts and Letters (1965), two Guggenheim Fellowships (1960, 1971), and commissions from such bodies as the Koussevitzky Foundation (1964), the Library of Congress (1964), Fromm Foundation (1963), New York State Council on the Arts, and the National Endowment for the Arts.

For orchestra he has composed a Concertino for percussion and strings (1954); *Sinfonia sinfonica para el Payaso* (1955); *Contrastes No. 1,* for string orchestra and electronic tape (1960); *Planos* (1961); *Transientes* (1972); Divertimento for cello and orchestra (1984); Concerto for string quartet and orchestra (1990); and Concertino for violin and chamber orchestra (1996). For concert band he has written *Consorts* (1980). His instrumental music includes four string quartets (1954, 1958, 1976, 1980); Clarinet Quintet (1955); *Three Pieces* for wind quintet (1956); *Nonetto* (1956); Trio for clarinet, trumpet, and viola (1962); *Inflexions* for 14 players, commissioned by the Fromm Foundation in 1965 and performed in Chicago in 1967; *Junctures* for flute, clarinet, and violin (1966); *Music* for solo violin (1968); *Chacona* for piano trio (1971); *Pennplay* for 16 players (1978); String Trio (1982), commissioned by the Guggenheim Foundation; *Capriccio* for two pianos (1985); *Quartetto 1* for flute and string trio (1987); *Festino* for guitar, violin, cello, and double bass (1994); *Flashbacks* for flutes, clarinets, violin, cello, piano, and percussion (1995); and *Quartetto 2* for oboe and string trio (1996).

Davidovsky is an expert in the field of electronic music, and a number of his compositions make use of such resources. Generally these works are divided into two categories. The *Electronic Studies* (1961–65), of which there are three, are for tape alone. *Synchronisms* combine tape and instruments: no. 1 for flute (1963); no. 2 for flute, clarinet, violin, and cello (1964); *no. 3* for cello (1964); *no. 4* for chorus (Psalm 70; 1967); *no. 5* for percussion (1968); *no. 6* for piano (1970); *no. 7* for orchestra (1976); *no. 8* for woodwind quintet (1974); *no. 9* for solo violin (1988); and *no. 10* for guitar (1992). *No. 6* won the Pulitzer Prize in 1971.

His vocal music includes a cantata-opera, *Scenes from Shir-ha-shirim* (*Song of Songs*) for soprano, two tenors, baritone, and chamber orchestra (1975); *Romancero* for soprano, flute, clarinet, violin, and cello (1983); *Biblical Songs* for soprano and ensemble (1990); and *Shulamot's Dream* for soprano and orchestra (1993).

DAWSON, WILLIAM LEVI

b. Anniston, Alabama, 23 September 1899
d. Tuskegee, Alabama, 2 May 1990

After thorough musical training at the Tuskegee Instutute, Kansas City where he studied trombone (B.A.,1921) and the American Conservatory, Chicago (M.A., 1927), Dawson played trombone in the Chicago Civic Orchestra (1926–30). In 1931 he was appointed director of Tuskegee School of Music, remaining there until 1955. Under his direction from 1931 to 1935 the Tuskegee Choir gained a national reputation.

William Dawson.
Courtesy Tuskegee University Archives.

Dawson's *Negro Symphony*, composed in 1932 and revised in 1952, has achieved wide success throughout America. It was recorded by Stokowski, who had given its first performance with the Philadelphia Orchestra in 1934. Based on African-American spirituals, the Symphony relies upon naïve manipulation of the musical material, but the work hardly gains symphonic stature.

His other compositions include two works for orchestra, *Scherzo* (1930) and *A Negro Work Song* (1940); *Out of the Fields* for soprano and orchestra (1928); a Piano Trio in A (1925); Violin Sonata in A (1928); and several short choral pieces, including arrangements of spirituals.

DE FILIPPI, AMEDEO

b. Ariano, Italy, 20 February 1900

De Filippi was brought to the United States in 1905 and became a naturalized citizen in 1926. After attending school in New York he studied at the Juilliard School (1925–29) where he was a pupil of Rubin Goldmark. He also trained as a violinist and pianist. He worked extensively as a composer, arranger, and orchestrator for the theatre, radio, films, ballet, and recording companies. In these capacities he was associated RCA Victor (1925–29), Pathé Sound Studios (1929–30), and the Columbia Broadcasting System (1930–59).

For orchestra he wrote a Suite (1920); Concerto for flute, bassoon, horn, trumpet, and strings (1928); a Symphony (1930); *Overture: Twelfth Night* (1937); *Raftman's Dance* (1939); *Five Medieval Court Dances* (1939); *Brazilian Excursion* (1945); *Manhattan Isle Suite* (1961); *Four American Dances* (1971); *Helenic Rhapsody* (1971); and *Variations on "Peter, Peter, Pumpkin Eater"* for piano and orchestra. He also composed four pieces for string orchestra: Serenade (1930); *Provencal Airs* (1938); *Music for Recreation* (1938); and *Diversions* (1939).

Among his vocal music are several works for voice and orchestra, including *Two Sonnets* (1920); *Five Arabian Songs* (1925); *Five Norman Songs* (1929); *The Testament of Villon* (1957); and *Magnificat* (1970). De Filippi's principal choral works are a cantata, *Children of Adam* (1926); *Three Walden Portraits* (Thoreau) (1938); *Seven Psalm Settings* (1969); and *Missa Brevis* (1970).

His output of instrumental music was considerable; important among these are a String Quartet (1926); Piano Quintet (1928); Viola Sonata (1929); Suite for violin and piano (1929); *Corydon Suite* for wind trio (1964); *Duo* for violin and cello (1965); Divertimento for solo cello (1967); String Trio (1967); *Capriccio Dodecafonico* for solo violin (1968); *Variations* for violin and cello (1969); and *Quadrivium* for brass quartet (1970).

To the repertory of the piano De Filippi contributed a Sonata (1922); six sonatinas (1926); *Prelude, Passacaglia and Toccata* (1927); *Partita* (1928); *Mobiles* (1967); *Three Preludes and Fugues* (1970); and numerous teaching pieces. He also wrote many works for guitar, including *Nostalgic Waltzes* (1958), *Twelve Preludes* (1959), and *The Magic Circle* (1969).

For the stage he composed incidental music for John Drinkwater's play, *Robert E. Lee* (1925); a one-act opera, *The Green Cockatoo* (1927); and *Malvolio*, a two-act opera based on Shakespeare's *Twelfth Night* (1937). His film scores include *Trial Marriage* (1929); *Leatherneck* (1930); *The Jazz Age* (1930); *Blockade* (1938); *Housekeeper's Daughter* (1938); and *Everything on Ice* (1938).

DE KOVEN, (HENRY LOUIS) REGINALD

b. *Middletown, Connecticut, 3 April 1859 (not 1861)*

d. *Chicago, Illinois, 2 May 1920*

At the age of 13 De Koven moved with his parents to England, where in 1879 he graduated from Oxford University. Later he studied in Stuttgart and Florence and was a pupil of Léo Delibes in Paris and Franz Suppé in Vienna. On his return to America in 1882 he earned his living as a music critic with the *Chicago Evening Post* (1989–99), *Harper's Weekly* (1895–97), *New York World* (1898–1900), and *New York Herald* (1907–12). In 1902 he founded the Washington Philharmonic Society, which he conducted for three years.

It was from Delibes and other French composers that De Koven learned the art of writing comic opera. His first, *The Begum*, was composed in 1887. With *Robin Hood*, premiered in Chicago on 9 June 1890, the composer achieved considerable success. This romantic three-act opera received three thousand performances. In England it was performed in 1903 under the title *Maid Marion*.

In all De Koven wrote 21 operettas, including *Don Quixote* (1889); *The Fencing Master* (1892); *The Knickerbockers* (1893); *The Algerian* (1893); *Rob Roy* (1894); *The Tzigane* (1895); *The Mandarin* (1896); *The Highwayman* (1897); *The Paris Doll* (1897); *The Three Dragoons* (1899); *The Men in the Moon* (1899); *Papa's Wife* (1899); *Red Feathers* (1903); *Happyland* (1905); *The Student King* (1906); *The Golden Butterfly* (1907); *The Beauty Spot* (1909); *The Wedding Trip* (1911); and *Her Little Highness* (1913) He also composed two grand operas: *The Canterbury Pilgrims*, produced at the Metropolitan Opera on 8 March 1917; and *Rip Van Winkle*, performed in both Chicago and New York in 1920.

Among his other compositions are a Suite for orchestra, a Piano Sonata, many solo piano pieces, and over 400 songs.

DE LEONE, FRANCESCO BARTOLOMEO

b. *Ravenna, Ohio, 28 July 1887*

d. *Akron, Ohio, 10 December 1948*

De Leone studied at Dana's Musical Institute, Warren, Ohio (1901–03) and the Royal Conservatory, Naples (1913–10). He was also a pupil of Ernest Bloch. He made his debut as a conductor in Naples in 1910. He was conductor of the Cleveland Opera Guild (1927–29) and the Akron Symphony Orchestra (1930–31). He founded the department of music at the University of Akron and was head of the department of piano at the De Leone School of Music, Akron (1939–48).

For orchestra De Leone composed a Symphony in D minor; *Six Italian Dances; Italian Rhapsody; Gibraltar Suite; Amalfi Suite; Portage Trail Suite*; and *In Sunny Italy Suite*.

His opera, *Algada*, staged in Akron in 1924, won the David Bispham Memorial Medal. He wrote three operettas: *A Millionaire's Caprice* (Naples, 1910, in Italian), *Princess Ting-Ah-Ling*, and *Cave Man Stuff*. Among his choral works are four sacred music dramas: *Ruth, The Prodigal Son, The Golden Calf*, and *David*; an oratorio, *The Triumph of Joseph*; a music drama, *Death Ray*; and a musical fantasy, *The Spinner*.

DE LAMARTER, ERIC

b. *Lansing, Michigan, 18 February 1880*

d. *Orlando, Florida, 17 May 1953*

De Lamarter studied in Chicago and with Charles-Marie Widor and Alexandre Guilmant in Paris (1901–02). He was an organist and conductor, acting as assistant to Frederick Stock with the Chicago Symphony Orchestra (1918–24).

De Lamarter composed four symphonies—no. 1 in D (1914), no. 2 in G minor (after Whitman) (1926), no. 3 in E minor (1931), and no. 4 (1932)—and a large quantity of orchestral music, including five overtures: *The Faun* (1914), *Masquerade* (1916), *The Giddy Puritan* (1921), *Huckleberry Finn* (1948), and *Ol' Kaintuck* (1948). Also for orchestra are a Serenade (1915); *Fable of the Hapless Folk Tune* (1917); *Serenade near Taos* for strings (1930–33); *At Christmastide* (*Fantasia on Christmas Carols*) (1948); and a *Suite for Strings* (1946). For organ and orchestra he wrote two concertos, no. 1 in E (1920) and no. 2 in A (1922), and *The Weaver of Tales* (1926).

Eric De Lamarter.
Courtesy Rosenthal Archives, Chicago Symphony Orchestra.

De Lamarter composed a Violin Sonata in E-flat (1915); two string quartets (1943, 1948); *Piety Doe's Gremlins*, a ballet for wind instruments; and much incidental music for plays, including *The Betrothed* (Maeterlinck), produced in New York in 1918. For the stage he wrote two ballets, *The Black Orchid* and *The Dance of Life*, both dating from 1931.

DEL TREDICI, DAVID (WALTER)

b. Cloverdale, California, 16 March 1937

Del Tredici studied with Seymour Shifrin and Arnold Elstron at the University of California, Berkeley (1955–59), and with Roger Sessions and Earl Kim at Princeton (1959, 1963–64). He was also a piano pupil of Bernhard Abramowitsch at Berkeley (1953–59) and Robert Helps in New York (1962–64). At the Aspen (Colorado) Festival (1958) he received composition lessons from Darius Milhaud. At the age of 16, Del Tredici was pianist with the San Francesco Symphony Orchestra. He has taught at Harvard University (1966–72), the State University of New York, Buffalo (1973) and Boston University (1973–84). In 1984 he joined the music faculty of City College and Graduate School, City University of New York, where he is currently a Distinguished Professor. From 1988 to 1990 he was Composer-in-Residence with the New York Philharmonic Orchestra.

Most of Del Tredici's works have literary associations; if not the actual settings of words, they are usually based on the writings of major authors, in particular James Joyce and Lewis Carroll. His best-known early work, *Syzygy,* commissioned in 1966 by the Koussevitzky Foundation, is a setting of two poems by James Joyce for two groups of performers: soprano, horn, and tubular bells, balanced by a chamber orchestra. Other Joyce pieces are four *Songs to Texts by James Joyce* for soprano and piano (1959); *Two Songs* (1959, rev. 1978); *I Hear an Army* for voice and string quartet (1963–64); and *Night Conjure-Verse,* two songs for soprano, counter-tenor, and chamber ensemble (1965).

Del Tredici has been obsessed with the works of Lewis Carroll. Since the late 1960's, most of his large-scale compositions have been based on the *Alice* books. The first of these, *The Lobster Quadrille* for orchestra with optional soprano (1969), has been widely performed in the United States and Europe. In this piece the composer has combined basic 12-note melodies with tonal material, accentuated by the unusual instrumental forces, including a "folk group" of mandolin, banjo, accordion, marimba, and two soprano saxophones. Other works based on the *Alice* books and scored for soprano, folk group, and orchestra include *Alice Part I* (1969, rev. 1974); *Vintage Alice (Fantascene on a Madhatter's Tea-Party;* 1972); *Adventures Underground* (1973, rev. 1979); *Alice Part II* (1975); and *Annotated Alice* (1976).

An Alice Symphony, comprising two independent works, *Illustrated Alice* (incorporating *The Lobster Quadrille*) and *In Wonderland,* was performed in 1975. It was followed by *Child Alice* (1980–81), which combines four separate pieces: *In Memory of a Summer Day*, which won the Pulitzer Prize in 1980; *Happy Voices*, which was given a Friedheim Award in 1980; *Quaint Events* (1981); and *All in the Golden Afternoon* (1981). *Pot-pourri* for amplified soprano, mezzo-soprano, chorus, rock group, and orchestra was completed in 1968 and revised in 1973. Further *Alice* scores are *Adventures Underground* for amplified soprano, folk group, and orchestra (1971–77); *The Final Alice* (1976), setting a chapter from *Through the Looking Glass* for amplified soprano and orchestra (a Bicentennial commission originally written for the Chicago Symphony Orchestra but first performed by Barbara Hendricks with the New York Philharmonic Orchestra under Erich Leinsdorf in 1977); *Haddock's Eyes* for soprano and chamber ensemble (1985–86); and *Dum Dee Tweedle* for voices and orchestra (1993). The last two in the sequence were *Heavy Metal Alice* for brass quintet

David Del Tredici, 1972.
Courtesy Music Library, State University of New York, Buffalo.

(1994) and *Cabbages and Kings* for soprano, chorus, clarinet, four violins, and orchestra (1996).

A non-Alice work in a similar vein, *The Last Gospel,* a setting of words from the Gospel of St. John, scored for soprano, chorus, and rock group was completed in 1967 and revised in 1984. During the mid-to-late 1980s, Del Tredici composed three orchestral works: *March to Tonality* for the Chicago Symphony Orchestra (1983–85), *Tattoo* (1986); and *Steps* (1990).

In the later 1990s, Del Tredici has moved on from Lewis Carroll to setting American poetry in over 50 songs. His later vocal music includes *Dracula* for soprano and orchestra (New York, 1997); *The Spider and the Fly* (Mary Howarth) for soprano and orchestra (New York, 1998); *Chana's Story* for mezzo-soprano and piano (1998); *Three Baritone Songs* (1999); *Gay Life,* a song cycle for baritone and orchestra (San Francisco, 2000); *Honey Money Loves* (Colette Inez) for soprano, clarinet, bass clarinet, violin, cello, and double bass (2000); *Miz Inez Sez* (Colette Inez) a song cycle for soprano and piano (2000); *What My Lips Have Kissed* (Edna St. Vincent Millay) for voice and piano (2000); *Lament for the Death of a Bulfighter* for soprano and piano (1999–2001); and *Wondrous the Merge* for narrator/singer and string quartet (2003).

Among his instrumental music are a String Trio (1959); *Brass Symphony* for brass quintet (1992); *Cello Acrostic* for solo cello (1995); and *Grand Trio* for the Kalichstein, Laredo, Robinson Piano Trio (2002). He has written several piano pieces, including *Soliloquy* (1958); *Fantasy Pieces* (1960); *Virtuoso Alice: Grand Fantasy* (1984); *Opposites Attract* (*Portrait of Virgil Thomson*; 1996); *Ballad in Yellow* (1998); *Wildwood Etude* (1999); and *Wedding Song* (2000). He also wrote a *Scherzo* for piano duet (1960).

For a commission from the NEA and Rockefeller Foundation, Del Tredici composed a theater piece, *BROTHER,* a setting of eight songs to words by John Kelly, performed in May 2001 in New York City. His most recent composition is *Four Heartfelt Anthems* for treble voices, with solo soprano and piano in the last one (2003). Currently he is writing a work for the Da Ponte String Quartet.

DELANEY, ROBERT (MILLS)
b. Baltimore, Maryland, 24 July 1903
d. Santa Barbara, California, 21 September 1956

Delaney studied in America and Italy, returning home in 1921 when he entered the University of Southern California. He returned to Europe the following year, and in Paris he became a pupil of Nadia Boulanger and Arthur Honegger for composition and Lucien Capet for violin (1922–27). He taught at the School of Music in Concord, Massachusetts; the Santa Barbara School, California; and Northwestern University. He won a Guggenheim Fellowship in 1929 and was awarded a Pulitzer Prize in 1933 for his setting of Stephen Vincent Benet's *John Brown's Body,* a choral symphony.

For orchestra Delaney wrote *The Constant Couple Suite* (1926); a *Don Quixote Symphony* (1927); two *Symphonic Pieces* (1935, 1937); *Pastorale Movement* (1930); *Adagio* for violin and strings (1935); an overture, *Work 22* (1937); *Going to Town Suite* (1940); and a Second Symphony (1942). Delaney composed three string quartets (1930) and several choral works, including *Night,* a setting of words by William Blake for chorus, strings, and piano (1934) and *Western Star* for chorus and orchestra (1944).

DELLO JOIO, NORMAN
b. New York, New York, 24 January 1913

Born to Italian parents, Dello Joio was first taught by his father, an organist in New York City. At the age of 15 he became a pupil of his godfather, Piotro Yon, a composer and organist at St. Patrick's Cathedral, New York. At this time he organized his own dance band at school. He was an excellent baseball player and was even offered a professional contract, but chose instead to attend the Institute of Musical Art, New York (1933–38) and the Juilliard School (1939–41), where he studied composition with Bernard Wagenaar. At Yale University (1941–43) he was a pupil of Paul Hindemith, who exerted a strong influence upon his early works. From 1941 to 1943 he was musical director of the Dance Players, and this experience was of great value when he came to write for the stage. He was awarded Guggenheim Fellowships in 1944 and 1945.

In 1944, Dello Joio taught at Sarah Lawrence College, Bronxville, New York. In 1951 he was a member of the composition faculty of the Mannes College of Music, New York. In 1967 he was appointed chairman of the Contemporary Music Project of the Music Educators' National Conference. From 1972 to 1979 he was Dean of the School of the Arts, Boston University. Dello Joio has composed music in every form: opera, ballet, orchestral, choral, and instrumental. A large number of his compositions have been commissioned by leading organizations, and he has won many awards. A strong melodic gift, influenced by folk music, plainsong, and other traditional sources, permeates all his music.

He has composed four operas. *The Triumph of St. Joan* was performed at Sarah Lawrence College in May 1950. The New York City Opera staged it in April 1959.

(It has been subsequently withdrawn.) In May 1955 his one-act opera *The Ruby* was produced at Indiana University, Bloomington. The story to a text by William Mass, is set in England. His third opera, also on the subject of Joan of Arc, is entitled *The Trial at Rouen.* It was commissioned by NBC and performed on television in April 1956. The last opera, *Blood Moon,* was staged in San Francisco in 1961. Dello Joio has also written the score for a musical play, *The Tall Kentuckian* (1952).

While working with the Dance Players, he wrote two ballets for them. *Prairie,* an epic in four movements based on a poem by Carl Sandburg with choreography by Eugene Loring, was performed in Washington, D.C. in 1942. In the same year, *The Duke of Sacramento* (or *Hobo of the Hills*) was produced in New Hope, Pennsylvania. For Ballet Theater he composed *On Stage,* depicting a rehearsal and audition in a ballet company, a subject very familiar to him. It was produced in 1945 at the Metropolitan Opera House in New York.

Martha Graham commissioned *Wilderness Star,* performed in 1948 in New London, Connecticut. In that year she adapted his *Serenade* for orchestra as another ballet, *Diversion of Angels* (1948). Other ballets are *Seraphic Dialogue* (Graham; 1948) and *A Time of Snow* (Graham; 1968), with baritone solo, based on the Heloise and Abelard story. In 1956 José Limón

Norman Dello Joio (left) with Aaron Copland, c. 1946–47.
From the Collections of the Library of Congress.

produced the ballet *There is a Time* to the score of *Meditations on Ecclesiastes* for strings; the piece won the Pulitzer Prize in 1957, and deserves to take its place among twentieth-century masterpieces for string orchestra.

Dello Joio's early orchestral works are a Sinfonietta (1940); *Ballade* for strings (1941); *Magnificat* (1942); *To a Lone Sentry* (1943); and *Concert Music* (1944). *Variations, Chaconne and Finale* (1947) won the New York Music Critics' Circle Award in 1948. Originally entitled *Three Symphonic Dances,* it was widely played throughout the United States and firmly established the composer's reputation. It was followed by a Serenade (1948); *New York Profiles* (1949); *Epigraph* (1951); a symphonic suite from the opera *The Triumph of St. Joan* (1951); and *Five Images* (1953). *Antiphonal Fantasy on a Theme of Vincenzo Albrici* for organ, brass, and strings was completed in 1966.

In 1969 Dello Joio was commissioned to write a work to celebrate the 100th anniversary of the founding of the State of Arkansas. The result, *Homage to Haydn,* was performed by the Philadelphia Orchestra in May 1969. More recent orchestral works include *Choreography* for strings (1972); *Colonial Variants* (1974); *Southern Echoes* (1977); *Arietta* for strings (1978); *Ballabili* (1981); *East Hampton Sketches* for strings (1984); *Variants on a Bach Chorale* (1985); *Lyric Movement* for strings (1993); *Reflections on an Ancient Hymn* for chamber orchestra (1996); and Divertimento for chamber orchestra (1997).

Dello Joio has composed several scores for CBS documentary programs, including *Profile of a Composer* (1957); *Here is New York* (1959); *The Saintmaker's Christmas Eve* (1959); *Time of Decision* (1962); and *The Louvre* (1965), which won an Emmy Award. From one of these, *Air Power,* he extracted a symphonic suite (1956–57). He has also made a significant contribution to the concert band repertory, including: *From Every Horizon* (1952); *Variants on a Medieval Tune* (1963); *Scenes from the Louvre* (1968); *Fantasies on a Theme of Haydn* (1968); *Songs of Abelard* (1969); *Concertante* (1973); *Satiric Dances for a Comedy* (1975); *Colonial Ballads* (1975); *Caccia* (1978); and *Air and Roulade* (1984).

For solo instruments and orchestra he has written three concertinos—no. 1 for piano and chamber orchestra (1939), no. 2 for flute and strings (1940), and no. 3 for harmonica and chamber orchestra (1942)—all later withdrawn; a Concerto for two pianos (1942); *Ricercari* for piano and orchestra, performed in 1946 with the composer as soloist; a Harp Concerto (1943); *Concertato* for clarinet and orchestra (1949); *A Ballad: The Seven Living Arts* (1957) and *Fantasy and Variations* (1962), both for piano and orchestra; and *Lyric Fantasies* for viola and strings (1973).

Dello Joio has composed a great amount of impressive choral music. The first of these works is *Vigil Strange* for chorus and piano duet (1942). It was followed in the next year by a setting of Whitman's poem *The Mystic Trumpeter* for soloists, chorus, and French horn. To a commission from the Robert Shaw Chorale in 1944 he set words by Stephen Vincent Benet as *Western Star* for narrator, soloists, chorus, and orchestra. Whitman's words were also used for *Jubilant Song* for female voices and piano (1946). *A Fable*, to a poem by Vachel Lindsay, for tenor, chorus, and piano was composed in 1947. The Crane Department of Music at the State University Teachers' College at Potsdam, New York commissioned *A Psalm of David*, a setting in Latin of Psalm 50 (Psalm 51 in the Protestant Bible), *Miserere Mei Dei*. As a "cantus firmus" throughout the work, the composer uses a phrase from Josquin des Pres' setting of the same psalm. It is scored for chorus, brass, strings, and percussion and was first performed in 1951.

Song of the Open Road for unaccompanied chorus was written in 1952. The cantata *To St. Cecilia* for chorus, brass, and percussion, a setting of verses from John Dryden's "A Song for St. Cecilia's Day 1687," dates from the summer of 1958. To celebrate the 100th anniversary of the Cincinnati College of Music in 1967, Dello Joio again chose the poems of Whitman for his cantata *Proud Music of the Storm* for chorus, brass, and organ. Later choral works include *Years of the Modern* for chorus, brass, and percussion (1968), *Songs of Walt Whitman* for chorus, and orchestra (1969); three settings of the Mass: no. 1, for chorus, brass, and organ (1969), no. 2, *Mass in Honor of the Eucharist* for chorus, cantor, congregation, brass, and organ (1973), and no. 3, *Mass to the Blessed Virgin* for baritone, chorus, and organ (1975); *Evocations* for chorus and orchestra (1970); and four pieces for chorus and piano: *Of Crows and Clusters* (1971), *Come to Me, My Love* (1972), *The Poet's Song* (1973); and *The Psalmist's Meditation* (1979).

In 1978 he completed a large-scale composition, *Masque,* settings of poems by Walt Whitman for soloists, chorus, actors, dancers, and orchestra. *Songs of Remembrance* for voice and piano to words by Hall Weenock was composed in 1979. Three more recent choral works are *I Dreamed of an Invisible City* for chorus and piano (1984); *The Vigil* for chorus, brass, and percussion (1985); and *Nativity* for soloists, chorus, and orchestra (1987).

Dello Joio's early instrumental works have been withdrawn, including a Piano Trio, which won the Elizabeth Sprague Coolidge Prize in 1939; a Violin Sonata (1939); a Cello Sonata (1939); a Woodwind Quartet (1940); and a Woodwind Trio (1942). Surviving pieces are *Fantasy on a Gregorian Theme* for violin and piano (1942); Sextet for three recorders and string trio

(1943); Trio for flute, cello, and piano (1944); *Duo Concertante* for cello and piano (1945); *Variations and Capriccio* for violin and piano (1949); *Colloquys,* a suite for violin and piano (1964); Suite for flute (1971); Suite for clarinet (1972); *Three Essays* for clarinet and piano; Sonata for trumpet and piano (1978); and *Reflections on a Christmas Tune* for wind quintet (1981).

Important among his many works for piano are three sonatas (1942, 1943, 1947), the last based on the *Variations, Chaconne and Finale* for orchestra; Suite for Piano (1941); *Prelude to a Young Musician* and *Prelude to a Young Dancer* (1945–46); *Diversions* (1955); *Concert Variations* (1980); *Intervallic Etudes* and *Simple Sketches* (1997); a piece for two pianos, *Aria and Toccata* (1958); and *Songs at Springtime* for piano duet (1984). For harpsichord he has written *Salute to Scarlatti,* a suite of sonatas (1979).

DEMPSTER, STUART (ROSS)
b. Berkeley, California, 7 July 1936

In addition to his achievements as a composer, Dempster is a trombone virtuoso who has commissioned works for the instrument. He studied composition and trombone at the San Francisco State College (1955–58). He taught at San Francisco Conservatory of Music (1961–66) while playing in the Oakland Symphony Orchestra (1962–66); he also taught at the California State College, Hayward (1963–66). In 1968 he was appointed a member of the music faculty of the University of Washington, Seattle, becoming an associate professor in 1978; he left this position in the late 1990s.

As a brass player he has explored new instrumental sounds and systems of breathing. Among his works in this area are *Didjeridervish* for didjeridu (1976); *Sonic Breathing and Circular Meditations* for trombone and didjeridu (1981); *Fog Calling* for didjeridu and trombone (1981); *JDBBBDJ* for didjeridu and audience (1983); *Hornfinder* for trombone and audience (1983); *Roulette* for trombone and audience (1983); *Don't Worry, It Will Come* for garden hoses and audience (1983); and *Sound Massage Parlor* for didjeridu, garden hoses, shell, and audience (1986).

His instrumental compositions include *Five Pieces* for brass quintet (1957–59); *Prelude and Two Movements* for violin and piano (1959); Bass Trombone Sonata (1961); *Adagio and Canonic Variations* for brass quintet (1962); *Chamber Music 12* for voice and trombones (1964); *Standing Waves* for trombone and tape (1978); and *Aix en Providence* for multiple trombones (1983).

Dempster's more conventional music includes a show, *Life Begins at 40* (1976); a ballet, *Ten Grand*

Hosery (1971–72); and a choral piece, *The Road Not Taken* for voice, chorus, and orchestra (1967).

He is the author of a textbook, *The Modern Trombone: A Definition of Its Idioms* published in 1979.

DENCKE, JEREMIAH
b. Langenbielau, Silesia (now Bielawa, Poland), 2 October 1725
d. Bethlehem, Pennsylvania, 28 May 1795

In 1761 with Johann Friedrich Peter, Sr., Dencke arrived in America, where he joined the Moravian sect in Bethlehem, Pennsylvania as minister and organist. From 1772 to 1784 he was warden of the congregation. For the community he composed much church music, of which the anthems *I Speak of Things* and *I Will Make an Everlasting Covenant,* dating from 1767, are examples.

Dencke wrote three sets of sacred songs for soprano and string orchestra (1767–68) in the tradition of the *pastorales* composed by many Bohemian and Moravian musicians at this time. These were the first of their kind written in America. Among them are *My Soul Does Magnify the Lord, O Be Glad Ye Daughters of the People,* and *Go Forth in His Name.*

DENNISON, SAM
b. Geary, Oklahoma, 27 September 1926

Dennison studied with Spencer Norton and Harrison Kerr at the University of Oklahoma, Norman (1946–50) and with Halsey Stevens at the University of Southern California, Los Angeles (1951–53). He was a teacher and librarian at the Louisville Academy of Music (1955–60), a teacher of theory and composition at the Inter-American University of Puerto Rico (1960–64), and a music librarian at the Free Library of Philadelphia (1964–74). In 1975 he was appointed curator of the Edwin A. Fleisher Collection of Orchestral Music at the Free Library of Philadelphia, a position he held until retiring in 1993.

Dennison's stage works include an opera, *The Last Man on Earth,* first performed in Norman, Oklahoma in 1952; a ballet-musical, *The Descent* (1980); and incidental music for *Ruby of Secrets* (1981). He has also written a one-act opera, *Conrad Crispin's Broom* (1985).

In addition to *Lyric Piece and Rondo* for tuba and strings (1977) and the *Adagio* for horn and orchestra (1978), his instrumental pieces include *Quodlibet* for flute, oboe, and bassoon (1953); Suite for solo flute (1968); *Cirrus* for flute, oboe, and cello (1977); *Suite on Jazz Themes of the 40s and 50s* for flute, double bass, piano, and percussion (1978); and three piano sonatas (1949, 1950, 1963).

Dennison is the author of *Orchestra Librarianship* and *Scandalize My Name* (1982), a study of African-American imagery in American popular music.

DENNY, WILLIAM D.

b. Seattle, Washington, 2 July 1910
d. Berkeley, California, 2 September 1980

Denny studied at the University of California (A.B., 1931; M.A, 1933) and with Paul Dukas in Paris (1933–35). In 1939 he went to Rome for two years on a Horatio Parker Fellowship. After three years at Harvard University, he joined the faculty of the University of California, Berkeley in 1945 where he remained until 1978. His highly dissonant music features intricate, complex counterpoint.

For orchestra he composed three symphonies (1939, 1949, 1955–57); *Bacchanale* (1935); a Concertino for small orchestra (1939); Sinfonietta for strings (1940); an *Overture for Strings* (1945); *Praeludium* (1947); and incidental music for *A Horace Festival*. Among his instrumental works are three string quartets (1938, 1952, 1955); a Viola Sonata (1943–44); a *Partita* for organ (1958); and a Piano Trio (1965).

DES MARAIS, PAUL EMILE

b. Menominee, Michigan, 23 June 1920

Des Marais studied in Chicago under Leo Sowerby (1937–41) and in Cambridge, Massachusetts with Nadia Boulanger (1941–42). After the Second World War he attended Harvard University, where he was a pupil of Walter Piston (1946–53). In 1949 he was again a pupil of Boulanger in Paris. After teaching at Harvard (1953–56), he joined the faculty of the University of California, Los Angeles in 1960, becoming professor in 1971, then retiring in 1988.

His early works are neo-classical and strongly influenced by Stravinsky. These features are clearly seen in the Mass for six voices (1949) and the two piano sonatas (1947, 1952). In the mid-1950s he began to make use of serialism while maintaining a fundamentally tonal language. The first works to emerge in this new style were settings of *Psalm 121* for unaccompanied chorus (1959); *Motet* for unaccompanied voices, cellos, and double basses (1959); and *Capriccio* for two pianos, percussion, and celeste (1962).

A chamber opera using film sequences, *Epiphanies,* was completed on 1968. He has composed incidental music for several theatrical productions, including Dryden's *A Secular Masque* (1976); *A Midsummer Night's Dream* (Shakespeare; 1976); *Oedipus* (Sophocles) (1978); *St. Joan* (Shaw; 1980); *Marriage à la Mode* (Dryden; 1981); *As You Like It* (Shakespeare; 1983); and *The Man of Mode* (George Etherege; 1984). A theater piece, *Orpheus,* dating from 1987, was followed by two others, *Dances Before God* (1999) and *Cuirass* (2000).

Des Marais's instrumental music includes two piano sonatas; *Three Movements* for two pianos and percussion (1972, 1975); *Triplum* for organ and percussion (1981); *Touch* for two pianos (1984); *Baroque Isles: The Voyages Out* for two keyboard percussionists (1986); and *The French Park* for two guitars (1988).

Among his choral works are *Organum 1–5* for chorus, organ, and percussion (1972); *Brief Mass* for the same forces (1973); *Organum 6* (1980); similarly scored; *Seasons of the Mind,* five movements for chamber chorus, piano (four hands), and celeste (1980); and *Paradise* for chorus (1995). His vocal music includes *Reflections on Fauré,* a cycle for voice and piano (1972); *Late Songs* (in French) (1978–79); *Le cimetière marin* (Paul Valery) for voice, keyboards, and percussion (1971); and *Everything Moves,* three songs for high voice and piano (2001). In 2001 he provided the score for an animated film, *Family Dinner.*

Des Marais is the author of a book, *Harmony,* published in 1962.

DETT, ROBERT NATHANIEL

b. Drummondville, Quebec, Canada, 11 October 1882
d. Battle Creek, Michigan, 2 October 1943

Dett was the first black composer of serious music to receive recognition in America. He studied at Oberlin College, Ohio (1903–08); the Eastman School of Music, Rochester, New York (M.M.); Columbia University; University of Pennsylvania; American Conservatory of Music; and Harvard University, where he was a pupil of Arthur Foote. In 1924 he was awarded a doctorate from Howard University, Washington, D.C. He later received composition lessons from Nadia Boulanger in Paris (1929). He was director of Lane College (1908–11) and Lincoln Institute (1911–1913), and was director of music at the Hampton Institute, Virginia from 1913 to 1931. In 1935 he taught at Samuel Houston College in Austin, Texas, moving in 1937 to Bennett College, Greensboro, North Carolina.

Dett's important works are the cantata *The Chariot Jubilee* (1921); the oratorio *The Ordering of Moses* for soloists, chorus, and orchestra (1937); *American Sampler* for chorus and orchestra (1937); and two pieces for orchestra, *Juba Dance* (1913) and a Symphony in

Robert Nathaniel Dett.
Courtesy Hampton University Archives.

E minor. His choral arrangement of Negro spirituals earned him a well-deserved reputation.

For piano he composed many pieces, including five suites—*Magnolia* (1911), *In the Bottoms* (1913), *Enchantment* (1922), *The Cinnamon Grove* (1927), and *Tropic Winter* (1938)—as well as an unpublished Sonata. His songs usually reflect the Negro idiom.

In recognition of his work, Dett was awarded honorary doctorates from Oberlin College and Harvard University.

DEYO, FELIX

b. Poughkeepsie, New York, 21 April 1888
d. Baldwin, New York, 21 June 1959

After receiving training in piano from his mother, Mary Foster Deyo (1857–1947), Deyo attended the Brooklyn Conservatory of Music. From 1911 to 1939 he taught there before being appointed director of the Baldwin (New York) Conservatory of Music. Other members of his family were also prominent pianists, including his wife, Asta Nygren Deyo (1898–1953) and

his second cousin, Ruth Lydia Deyo (1884–1960); the latter also composed an opera, *The Diadem of Stars* (1930), set in ancient Egypt; only the prelude was performed, by Leopold Stokowski and the Philadelphia Orchestra in 1931.

For orchestra Felix Deyo composed *A Lyric Symphony* (1949); *An Ancient Symphony;* and *A Primeval Symphony*. He also wrote a violin sonata, two piano sonatas, and many piano pieces.

DIAMOND, DAVID (LEO)

b. Rochester, New York, 9 July 1915

Diamond was born of Austrian-Polish parents. He began to study music at an early age and had completed over one hundred works by the time he was 18. In 1927 he became a pupil of Andre de Ribaupierre at the Cleveland Institute. Later he studied with Bernard Rogers at the Eastman School of Music, Rochester, New York. From 1934 to 1936 he attended the Dalcroze Institute and New Music School in New York, where he was a pupil of Roger Sessions.

After spending the summer of 1937 at Fontainebleau, Diamond went to Paris in 1938 on a Guggenheim Fellowship to continue his lessons with Nadia Boulanger. He remained in Paris until the spring of 1939. He returned to Europe in 1949 and settled in Italy in 1951, living in Rome and Florence. He did not return permanently to the United States until 1965. From 1966 to 1967 he was on the faculty of the Manhattan School of Music and later taught composition and held seminars at the Juilliard School of Music.

During his student days, Diamond was a prolific composer, achieving his first success with a Sinfonietta, which won him an Elfrida Whiteman Fellowship in 1935. In 1933 he composed *Hommage à Satie* for chamber orchestra, his first orchestral work to be heard in New York. Both pieces have subsequently been withdrawn by the composer. Two symphonies (1933, 1935) and a *Chamber Symphony* (1936) have also been withdrawn. His ballet *Formal Dance* (1935) was choreographed by Martha Graham. Diamond's important compositions dating from 1935 to 1937 are *Partita* for oboe, bassoon, and piano (1935); Violin Concerto no. 1 (1936); *Psalm for Orchestra* (1936), which was granted a Juilliard Publication Award; *Variations on an Original Theme* (1937); *Aria and Hymn* for orchestra (1937); and a full-length ballet, *TOM* (1936), to a scenario by e.e. cummings.

In 1938 he wrote *Heroic Piece* for small orchestra; a Cello Concerto; and *Elegy in Memory of Maurice Ravel*, originally scored for brass, harps, and percussion but later arranged for strings and percussion. Both versions are published. Also dating from 1938 is *Music* for double string orchestra, brass, and timpani, revised in 1968. Instrumental pieces composed during this time were a Quintet for flute, string trio, and piano (1937); Piano Quartet (1938); and a Cello Sonata (1938). The Concerto for string quartet (1936, rev. 1958) was dedicated to Albert Roussel, who had introduced Diamond to Charles Munch (who later conducted Diamond's Third and Sixth Symphonies).

After 1940, Diamond adopted a more romantic style in contrast to the mildly neo-classical language of his early works. During the next ten years he completed his first two published symphonies, no. 1 (1941), and no. 2 (1942), which combine a directness akin to that of Shostakovich, with folk-song-like modality. The year 1945 produced the Third Symphony and Fourth Symphony, commissioned by the Boston Symphony Orchestra and conducted in 1948 by Leonard Bernstein. At the 1942 I.S.C.M. Festival in San Francisco he was represented by a *Concerto for Small Orchestra* (1941). Also dating from this decade are Diamond's most widely performed compositions, *Rounds* for string orchestra (1944); Violin Sonata no. 1 (1946); incidental music for Shakespeare's *Romeo and Juliet* (1947); and *Portrait for Orchestra: Timon of Athens* (1949). In addition he composed a ballet, *The Dream of Audubon* (1942); incidental music for the Margaret Webster production of Shakespeare's *The Tempest* (1944); Piano Sonata no. 1, written for Rosalyn Tureck (1947); Violin Concerto no. 2. (1947); and *The Enormous Room* (after e.e. cummings) for orchestra (1948). His first three string quartets date from the 1940s: no. 1 (1940); no. 2 (1943); and no. 3 (1946); which won the New York Music Critics' Circle Award in the following year. A Piano Concerto (1949–50) was premiered in New York under Bernstein in 1966.

During the 1950s, Diamond again expanded his musical language through increasing chromaticism. This is heard clearly in his Sixth Symphony of 1951 and the Seventh Symphony (1959). The former was premiered by Charles Munch and the Boston Symphony Orchestra, the latter by Eugene Ormandy and the Philadelphia Orchestra. In 1957 for the Portland Junior Symphony Orchestra on a Rockefeller Commission he wrote *The World of Paul Klee,* a work illustrating Klee's paintings and designed to give young performers a showpiece for their individual virtuosity. *Sinfonia Concertante* (1954–55) was first performed in Rochester, New York in 1957. His other major compositions of the 1950s include a Piano Concerto, written in 1950 but not performed until 1966 by Thomas Shumacker with the New York Philharmonic Orchestra under the composer's direction; Quintet for clarinet, two violins, and two cellos (1950); Piano Trio (1951); the important Fourth String Quartet (1951); *Sinfonia Concertante* (1954–56); *Diaphony* for brass, two pianos, timpani,

and organ (1956); and a Wind Quintet (1958). He also composed two solo sonatas, one for violin (1954), the other for cello (1956).

Diamond's considerable energy in composition continued unabated with Symphony no. 8. (1960) and *Elegies in Memory of William Faulkner and e.e. cummings* for flute, English horn, and string orchestra, performed by the Philadelphia Orchestra under Eugene Ormandy in January 1966. The *Nonet for Strings* (1964) was composed for Stravinsky's 80th birthday. His remaining string quartets date from this period: no. 5 (1960); no. 6 (1962); no. 7 (1963); no. 8 (1964); no. 9 (1966); and no. 10 (1966).

Later orchestral works include a Third Violin Concerto (1968) and Symphony no. 5, begun in 1947 before the Third Symphony but not finished until 1964. It is dedicated to Leonard Bernstein, who performed it in 1966 with the New York Philharmonic Orchestra. His Symphony no. 9. is a setting of Michelangelo Buonarroti for baritone and orchestra, conducted by Bernstein in 1985. In 1992 he began work on two further symphonies: no. 10, commissioned by Gerard Schwartz and the Seattle Symphony Orchestra; and no. 11, composed for the 150th anniversary of the New York Philharmonic Orchestra, which performed it under Kurt Masur. Other orchestral pieces are Sinfonietta (no. 2; 1989) and *Kaddish* for cello and orchestra (1989).

Diamond's important choral pieces are *Young Joseph* (Thomas Mann) for female voices and strings (1944); *Mizmor L'David*, a sacred service for the Park Avenue Synagogue in New York, for tenor solo, chorus, and orchestra, or organ (1951); *This Sacred Ground*, a setting of the Gettysburg Address (1963); *To Music*, a choral symphony to poems by John Masefield and Longfellow (1966); and *Chorale and Warning* to poems by James Agee. In 1980 he completed a setting of John Milton's *Ode on the Morning of Christ's Nativity*.

Diamond has also composed nine song cycles: *Four Ladies* (Ezra Pound; 1935, rev. 1962); *Three Epitaphs* (Sylvia Townsend Warner; 1938); *Five Songs from the Tempest* (Shakespeare; 1944); *L'âme de Debussy* (1949); *The Midnight Meditation* (Eldon Olson; 1950); *We Two* (Shakespeare sonnets; 1964); *Hebrew Melodies* (Byron) (1967); *Love and Time* (Katie Louchheim; 1969); and *The Fall* (James Agee; 1971). In addition there are over 75 miscellaneous songs, including *Vocalises* for soprano and viola (1935); *Two Elegies* (Christina Rossetti) for soprano and string quartet (1935); *The Mad Maid's Song* (Herrick) for soprano, flute, and harpsichord (or piano; 1937, rev. 1953); and *Somewhere I have never traveled* (e.e. cummings) for voice and orchestra (1938).

For the stage he has composed two operas, now withdrawn: *David* (1935) and *Twisting the Rope* (Yeats;

1940). He composed a musical comedy, *Mirandolina* (1958). An opera, *The Noblest Game*, to a libretto by Katie Louchheim and commissioned by the National Opera Institute of Washington, D.C., occupied him from 1971 to 1975.

Diamond has composed the following film scores: *A Place to Live* (1941); *Dreams That Money Can Buy* (1943); *Strange Victory* (1948); *Anna Lucasta* (1949); *Lippold's The Sun* (1965); and *Life in the Balance* (1966).

DICKINSON, CLARENCE

b. Lafayette, Indiana, 7 May 1873
d. New York, New York, 2 August 1969

Dickinson studied with Wild and Adolf Weidig at Northwestern University, Evanston, Illinois (A.M., 1909; D.M., 1917) and with Hugo Riemann in Berlin. In Paris he was a pupil of Moritz Moszkowski (piano), Alexandre Guilmant and Louis Vierne (organ), and Gabriel Pierné (composition). He settled in New York in 1909 as an organist and in 1912 was appointed professor of church music at the Union Theological Seminary, where he founded the School of Sacred Music in 1928, retiring in 1945.

Among his compositions are two operas, *The Medicine Man* (Chicago, 1895) and *Pricilla*; a symphony for organ and orchestra, *Storm King* (1920); and an Easter cantata, *The Redeemer*. He is principally remembered as the editor of American church music, especially the anthems of the Moravians.

Dickinson was the author of an influential textbook, *The Technique and Art of Organ Playing* (New York, 1922).

DICKMAN, STEPHEN (ALLAN)

b. Chicago, Illinois, 2 March 1943

Dickman studied at Bard College (1962–65) and Brandeis University (1968), where he was a pupil of Harold Shapero and Arthur Berger. In 1971 in Rome he received composition lessons from Goffredo Petrassi; he was also a pupil of Jacob Druckman and Ernst Krenek. During the 1970s he traveled widely in Asia, becoming much influenced by the music of India. From 1976 to 1981 he taught at Mills College, California, where he directed the Tape Music Center. He has since devoted his time to composing.

For the stage he has composed an opera, *Real Magic in New York* (1971); an a cappella opera, *Tibetan Dreams* (1987–90); and a musical, *The Violin Maker* (2002). His single work for chamber orchestra, *The Wheels of Ezekiel,* was completed in 1985.

Dickman has concentrated on vocal music. Among his pieces are *The Snow Man* (Wallace Stevens) for soprano and ensemble (1966); *On Mere Being* (Wallace Stevens) for soprano and ensemble (1968); *Continual Conversations with a Silent Man* (Stevens) for solo soprano (1969); *Song Cycle* for three sopranos and three violins (1975–77); *Magic Circle* for chorus and ensemble (1980); *Orchestra by the Sea* for four sopranos and orchestra (1983); *Maximus Song Cycle* for soprano and ensemble (1987); *Rabbi Nathan's Prayer* for soprano and violin (1995); *Four for Tom* for baritone and piano (1997); *The Music of Eric Zann* for baritone solo (1998); and *The Epic of Gilgamesh* for mezzo-soprano, baritone, violin, cello, flute, and percussion (2002).

Among Dickman's instrumental works are four string quartets (1967, 1978, 1978, 1978); two string trios (1965, 1970–71); *Damsel* for 16 instruments (1968); and *Influence of India* for flute, string trio, and piano (1980).

DIEMER, EMMA LOU

b. Kansas City, Missouri, 24 November 1927

Emma Lou Diemer began to compose at the age of seven. At Yale University (1946–50) she was a pupil of Richard Donovan and Paul Hindemith. On a Fulbright Fellowship (1954–55) she spent a year at the Royal Conservatory in Brussels. At Tanglewood (1954–55) she received composition lessons from Roger Sessions and Ernst Toch. She studied with Bernard Rogers and Howard Hanson at the Eastman School of Music, Rochester, New York, where she received her Ph.D. in 1960. She served as Composer-in Residence with the Arlington, Virginia schools (1959–61) and with the Santa Barbara, California Symphony Orchestra (1990–92). From 1965 to 1970 she was professor of theory and composition at the University of Maryland, then moved to the University of California, Santa Barbara, where she taught until 1991. A year later, she won a Kennedy Center Friedheim Award.

Diemer has composed three symphonies: no. 1 (1952–53); no. 2, *On American Indian Themes* (1959); and no. 3, *Symphonie Antique* (1961). Her other orchestral music includes two piano concertos (1953, 1991); a Suite (1954); Concerto for harpsichord and chamber orchestra (1959); *Pavane* for strings (1959); *Youth Overture* (1959); *Festival Overture* (1960); *Rondo Concertante* (1960); *Nineteen Sixty Two Overture* (1962); Flute Concerto (1963); *Fairfax Festival Overture* (1967); *Concert Piece* for organ and orchestra (1977); *Winter Day* (1982); Trumpet Concerto, revised as a Violin Concerto (1983); *Suite of Homages* (1985); *Serenade for Strings* (1988); Marimba Concerto (1990); *Concerto: "Alaska"* in one movement for organ and

Emma Lou Diemer.
Courtesy the composer.

chamber orchestra (1995); *Santa Barbara Overture* (1996); and *Homage to Tchaikovsky* (2000). She has also written two pieces for concert band, *Brass Menagerie* (1960) and *La Rag* (1981).

Among Diemer's numerous instrumental items are a Violin Sonata (1948); Piano Quartet (1954); *Toccata* for marimba (1955); Flute Sonata (1958); Wind Quintet (1960); Sextet for piano and wind quintet (1962); *Toccata* for flute chorus (1968); *Music* for wind quintet (1972); *Movement* for flute, oboe, and organ (1974); *Movement* for flute, oboe, clarinet, and piano (1976); *Quadralogue* for flute quartet (1978); *Solotrio* for xylophone, vibraphone, and marimba (1980); *Echospace* for guitar (1982); *Summer of '82* for cello and piano (1982); String Quartet (1987); *Catch-a-Turian* for violin and piano (1988); *Laudate* for trumpet and organ (1990); *A Quiet Lovely Piece* for clarinet and piano (1991); Sextet for flute, oboe, clarinet, violin, cello, and piano (1992); *Before Spring* for violin and piano (1997); *Homage to Paderewski* for viola and piano (1997); *Psalms* for flute and organ (1998); *Psalm 121* for organ, brass, and percussion (1998); *Psalms* for organ and percussion (1998); *Psalm 122* for bass trombone and organ (1999); Piano Trio (2001); Quartet for trumpet, horn, trombone, and piano (2002); and *Toccata* for timpani (2002).

For piano Diemer has written *Seven Etudes* (1965); *Toccata* (1979); *Encore* (1981); *Three Piano Pieces* (1992); *Fantasy* (1993); Piano Sonata no. 3 (1996–2000); *Spirituals* (2002); and *Homage to Cowell, Cage, Crumb and Czerny* for two pianos (1981). To the solo organ repertory she has contributed *Fantasie* (1958); *Ten Hymn Tune Preludes* (1964); *Fantasy on "O Sacred Head"* (1967); *Toccata and Fugue* (1969); *Celebration* (1970); *Declarations* (1973); *With Praise and Love* (1978–79); *Toccata* (1979); *Four Biblical Settings* (1993); and *Variations on "Rendez a Dieu"* (1993).

Among her choral works are *Fragments From the Mass* for female voices (1960); *Three Madrigals* (Shakespeare) for chorus and piano (1960); *Sing a Glory* for chorus, orchestra, and band (1964); *Verses from the Rubaiyat* for unaccompanied mixed voices (1967); *The Prophesy* for female chorus and piano (1968); *Anniversary Choruses* for choir and orchestra (1970); *Three Madrigals* for chorus and piano (1972); *Laughing Song* (William Blake) for chorus and piano duet (1974); *Wild Nights! Wild Nights!* (Emily Dickinson) for chorus and piano (1978); *Christmas Cantata: The Holy Child* (1988); *A Feast for Christmas* for chorus and brass quintet (1988); *Kyrie* and *Gloria* for chorus, two pianos, and percussion (1993, 1996); *O Viridissima Virga* for women's chorus, organ, and percussion (1998); *An Emily Dickinson Suite* for female voices and keyboard (2000); and Mass for chorus, two pianos, and percussion (2000).

Solo vocal music includes *Psalm CXXI* for soprano, tenor, and organ (1957); *Songs of Reminiscence* for soprano and piano (1958); *Three Mystic Songs* (Hindu poetry) for soprano, baritone, and piano (1963); *Four Chinese Love Poems* for soprano and harpsichord (1965); *Four Seasons* (Edmund Spenser) for soprano, tenor, and piano (1969); *Four Poems of Alice Meynell* for soprano and chamber orchestra (1976); *Lute Songs on Renaissance Poetry* for tenor and piano (1986); *Three Christmas Songs* for high voice and organ (1994); and *Seven Somewhat Silly Songs* for soprano and piano (1997).

For a decade Diemer experimented by combining electronic tape with instruments and voices. The results of this exploration are Trio for flute, oboe, and harpsichord (1973); Quartet for flute, viola, cello, and harpsichord (1974); *Add One no. 1,* for amplified piano (1981); *Add One nos.2–3* for synthesizer (1981); and *God is Love* for chorus (1982). For tape alone she composed *Patchworks* (1978), *Harpsichord Quartet* (1981), and *Scherzo* (1981).

DLUGOSZEWSKI, LUCIA

b. Detroit, Michigan, 16 June 1925 (alternatively, 1931 or 1934)

d. New York, New York, 11 April 2000

In 1940 Dlugoszewski began piano lessons at the Detroit Conservatory. At Wayne State University, Detroit (1946–49) she studied physics and mathematics. In New York she attended the Mannes School of Music (1950–51) and received composition lessons from Varèse. From 1960 she taught at New York University and the New School for Social Research, New York.

Her work with the Foundation for Modern Dance gave rise to many dance scores, especially for the Erick Hawkins Dance Company (she was married to dancer/choreographer Hawkins). After 1951 she explored the sound textures of percussion and invented over one hundred instruments, using various materials such as wood, glass, metal, skin, paper, and plastic. Her timbre piano, which incorporates bows and plectra in addition to the keyboard, was included in many of her compositions. The sound generated by these new instruments have features in common with oriental music.

Theater works include incidental music for two plays, *Desire* by Picasso (1952) and *Ubu Roi* by Jarry (1952); *Variations on Noguchi,* an opera of everyday sounds and voices for a film (1953); *Tiny Opera* (1953); *Women of Trachis,* based on Ezra Pound's translation of Sophocles (1960); and *The Heidi Songs,* an opera to a libretto by John Ashbery (1967–70).

Among her numerous dance scores, mostly for the Hawkins Company, are *Openings of the Eye* (1952); *Here and Now With Watchers* (1954–57); *Eight Clear Places* (1958–61); *To Everyone Out There* (1964); *Geography of Noon* (1964); *Cantilever II* (1964); *Lords of Persia* (1965); *Dazzle on a Knife's Edge* (1966); *Tight Rope* (1968); *Lords of Persia II* (1968); *Agathlon Algebra* (1968); *Black Lake* (1969); *Lords of Persia III* (1971); *Of Love . . . or is he a cry, she is his ear* (1971); *Angels of the Innermost Heaven* (1972); *Avanti* (1983); and *This Woman Duendo Amor* (1983–84). Most of these include the timbre piano and other invented percussion.

The exotic titles of many of Dlugoszewski's pieces derive from her interest in Buddhism and the novels of James Joyce. Her orchestral music includes *Orchestra Structure for the Poetry of Everyday Sounds* (1952);

Orchestral Radiant Ground (1955); *Arithmetic Points* (1955); *Flow Music for Left Ear in a Small Room* (1956); *Instants in Form and Movement,* a concerto for three timbre pianos and chamber orchestra (1957); *Four Attention Spans* (1964); *Naked Flight Nageiro* for chamber orchestra (1966); *Skylark Concert* (1969–71); *Kireji: Spring and Tender Speed* (1972); *Abyss and Caress* for trumpet and ensemble (1974–75); *Fire Fragile Flight* (1976); *Strange Tenderness of Naked Leaping* (1978); *Amor New Tiling Night* for chamber orchestra (1978); *Startle Transparent Terrible Freedom* (1981); *Wilderness Elegant Tilt,* a concerto for 11 instruments (1981–84); *Quidditar Sorrow Terrible Freedom* (1983–84); and *Duende Amor* (1983–84).

Her output of instrumental music is extensive, beginning with three piano sonatas (1949–51) and a Flute Sonata (1950). Later works include *Transparencies no. 1,* for harp (1952), *no. 2,* for flute (1952) and *no. 3,* for harp and six instruments (1956); *Naked Wabin* for five instruments and timbre piano (1956); *Flower Music* (1959) and *Hanging Bridges* (1967), both for string quartet; *Skylark Cicada* for violin and timbre piano (1964); *Balance Naked Flung* for six instruments (1966); *Naked Quintet* for brass (1967); *Leap and Fall, Quick Structures* for two trumpets, clarinet, two violins, and percussion (1968); *Space is a Diamond* for solo trumpet (1970); *Velocity Shells* for trumpet, percussion, and timbre piano (1970); *Sabi Music* for violin (1970); *Pure Flight* for string quartet (1970); *Angels of the Innermost Heaven* for brass (1971); *Tender Theatre Flight Nageire* for brass and percussion (1971–78); and *Amor Elusive Empty August* for wind quintet (1979).

Her final instrumental works include *Cicada Terrible Freedom* for flute, bass trombone, and string quintet (1980–81); *Duende Newfallen* for bass trombone and timbre piano (1982–83); and three pieces for flute, clarinet, trumpet, trombone, violin, and double bass: *Radical Otherness Concert* (1991), *Radical Suchness Concert* (1991), and *Radical Narrowness Concert* (1992).

Many of her numerous works using invented percussion instruments have curious names that recall the idiosyncratic titles of Chinese music in particular: *Silent Paper Spring and Summer Fried Songs* (1953–70); *Suchness Concert* for an orchestra of 100 percussion instruments; *Rates of Speed in Space* for ladder harp quintet (1959); *Concert of Man Rooms and Moving Space* (1960); *Beauty Music I – III* (1965); *Quick Dichotomies* for two trumpets, clarinet, and an orchestra of invented instruments (1965); *Naked Swift Music* (1968); *Kititail Beauty Music* (1968); *A Zen in Tyoko-In,* a film score (1971); and *Radical Quidditas for an Unborn Baby* for large percussion ensemble (1991).

Her single choral work is a setting of words by Frank

O'Hara, *In Memory of My Feelings* for tenor and chorus (1972). In addition to *Variations on Noguchi* (1953) and *A Zen in Ryoko-in* (1961), Dlugoszewski composed the music for a third film, *Guns for the Trees* (1961).

DODGE, CHARLES MALCOLM

b. Ames, Iowa, 5 June 1942

Dodge studied at the University of Iowa (1960–64) and at Columbia University (1964–70), where he was a pupil of Jack Beeson, Chou Wen-chung, and Otto Luening for composition and Vladimir Ussachevsky for electronic music. From 1966 to 1967 he also studied computer music programming at Princeton University. In the summer of 1964 he received lessons from Gunther Schuller and Arthur Berger at Tanglewood. He was also a pupil of Darius Milhaud at Aspen in 1961.

He taught at Columbia University (1967–68, 1970–77) and at Princeton University (1969–70). In 1977 he joined the faculty of Brooklyn College, CUNY, where he served as professor of music from 1980 to 1995, at one time directing the Center for Computer Music. In addition he was visiting professor of music at Dartmouth College (1993–94, 1995). In 1967 he became a member of the executive board of the American Composers' Alliance; he was elected chairman of the American Music Center in 1979. Dodge has received two Guggenheim Fellowships (1972, 1975) and the American Academy of Arts and Letters Award (1975).

For orchestra he has written *Threnody* for strings (1962); *Textures* (1963); *Study* (1964); *Rota* (1966); *Palindrome* for computer-synthesized tape and orchestra (1976); and *The One and the Other* for chamber orchestra (1993). His instrumental music includes *Solos and Combinations* for flute and/or clarinet and/or oboe (1964); *Composition in Five Parts* for cello and piano (1964); *Folia* for flute, bass clarinet, English horn, tuba, violin, piano, and percussion (1965); and *Distribution: Retribution* for clarinet, violin, and piano (1982).

Since the mid-1960s, Dodge has extensively used computer techniques and synthesized sound in his works: *Changes* (1967–70); *Earth's Magnetic Field* (1970); *Profile* (1984); *Song Without Words* (1986); *A Fraction for Wiley* (1987); *Allemande* (1988); *The Voice of Binky* (1989); and *Imaginary Narrative* (1989). In addition he has combined solo instruments and computer synthesis in a sequence of pieces: *Extensions* for trumpet (1973); *Viola Elegy* (1987); *Clarinet Elegy* for bass clarinet (1988); *Wedding Music* for violin (1988); and *Concert Etudes* (1994). *Speech Songs* (1972), *The Story of Our Lives* (1974), and *In Celebration* (1975) are all settings of poems by Mark Strand, realized by means of computer-synthesized voices. *Cascando* (1978) is an electronically musicalized version of the radio play by Samuel Beckett using computerized voices.

Dodge has written *Any Resemblance is Purely Coincidental* for computerized operatic tenor voice and piano (1980); *Mingo's Song* for synthesized voice (1983); *Roundelay* for chorus and tape (1985); and three works for voice and tape: *The Waves* (Virginia Woolf; 1984), *Postcard from the Volcano* (Wallace Stevens; 1986), and *Hoy* (*In His Memory*; 1990).

In 1981 he composed computerized vocal music for a radio play, *Han motte henne I parken* by Richard Kostelanetz, translated by S. Hanson, transmitted in the following year in Venice. It was repeated in 1983 on Warsaw Radio as *He Met Her in the Park*. *The Village Child*, music for a puppet show, dates from 1992.

With Thomas A. Jerse, Dodge is the author of a book, *Computer Music: Synthesis, Composition and Performance*, published in 1985 (2nd edition 1997).

DONATO, ANTHONY

b. Prague, Nebraska, 8 March 1909
d. 1990

Donato was educated at the Eastman School of Music, Rochester, New York (B.Mus.,1931; M.Mus., 1937;

Anthony Donato.
Courtesy Northwestern University Archives.

Ph.D., 1947). His teachers were Howard Hanson, Edward Royce, and Bernard Rogers for composition, Gustave Tinlot for violin, and Eugene Goossens for conducting. He began his musical career as a violinist in chamber music and with the Rochester Philharmonic Orchestra (1927–31). Donato was appointed head of the violin department and conductor of the University Symphony Orchestra at Drake University, Des Moines, Iowa in 1931. He held similar posts at Iowa State Teachers' College (1937–39) and the University of Texas, where he also taught composition (1939–46). From 1947 to 1976 he was professor of theory and counterpoint at Northwestern University, Evanston, Illinois and was later named professor emeritus. He also conducted the University Chamber Orchestra there (1947–50).

Donato is best known as a composer for two overtures, *Prairie Schooner* (1947) and *The Plains* (1953). Also for orchestra he has written two symphonies (1944, 1945); two sinfoniettas (1936, 1959); *Elegy for Strings* (1938); *Divertimento* (1939); *Mission San José de Aguaya* (1945); *Cotton Pickers* (1946); *Suite for Strings* (1948); *Solitude in the City* for narrator and orchestra (1954); *Episode* (1954); *Serenade for Small Orchestra* (1961); *Centennial Ode* (1967); *Improvisation* (1968); and *Discourse* for flute and strings (1969).

Donato produced a large number of short choral pieces, both religious and secular. The extended compositions are an anthem, *The Last Supper* (1952); *Thou Art My God* for female voices (1953); *Prelude and Choral Fantasy* for men's voices, brass, and timpani (1961); and *Blessed is the Man* for chorus, brass quartet, and organ (1970). For chorus and orchestra he wrote *March of the Hungry Mountains* (1949) and *The Congo* (Vachell Lindsay; 1957). For wind band he composed *The Lake Shore* (1950); *The Hidden Fortress* (1950); *Cowboy Reverie* (1955); and *Concert Overture* (1958). An opera, *The Walker Through Walls*, was completed in 1964.

Among his instrumental works are four string quartets (1941, 1947, 1951, 1974); two violin sonatas (1938, 1949); *Prelude and Dance* for four clarinets; *Sonatine* for three trumpets (1949); *Drag and Run* for clarinet, two violins, and cello (1950); a Wind Quintet (1955); *Suite for Brass* (1956); *Prelude and Allegro* for trumpet and piano (1957); a Piano Trio (1959); Clarinet Sonata (1966); *Discourse I* for flute and piano (1969) and *II* for saxophone and piano (1974); and Nonet for brass and percussion. Donato wrote a number of works for piano solo, including *African Dominoes* (1948), *Recreations* (1948), *Three Preludes* (1948), a Sonata (1951), and many teaching pieces.

Donato was also the author of a useful book, *Preparing Music Manuscript,* published in 1963.

Richard Donovan.
Photo: Crosby Studio; MSS 7, The Richard Donovan Papers in the Irving S. Gilmore Library of Yale University.

DONOVAN, RICHARD FRANK
b. New Haven, Connecticut, 29 November 1891
d. Middletown, Connecticut, 22 August 1970

Donovan studied at Yale University (1912–14, 1922) and at the Institute of Musical Art, New York (1914–18). He was also a pupil of Charles-Marie Widor in Paris. Donovan was appointed music director at the Taft School, Watertown, Connecticut (1920–23) and taught at Smith College, Northampton, Massachusetts (1923–28). In 1928 he joined the music faculty at Yale University where he succeeded David Stanley Smith as Dean of the Faculty in 1940. He was made a full professor in 1947, becoming Battell Professor in 1954; he retired in 1960. He also taught at the Institute of Musical Art (1925–28) and at Finch College, New York City (1926–40).

In 1928, Donovan was appointed organist at Christ Church, New Haven, retiring in 1965; he was also conductor of the Bach Cantata Club (1933–44) and the New Haven Symphony Orchestra (1936–51). For the 1936 season he was conductor of the New York Symphony Orchestra. Donovan took a leading part in the organization of the Yaddo Music Festival at Saratoga

Springs, New York. He was a director of the American Composers' Alliance and its President (1961–62).

Donovan's best-known work is the overture *New England Chronicle*, composed in 1946. Donovan described it as "an account of the adventures of a few musical ideas on one section of the country." It was given its first performance by the NBC Symphony Orchestra on 17 May 1947 under Alfred Wallenstein.

Donovan's first important composition was *Woodnotes* for chamber orchestra, composed in 1926. His symphonic poem *Smoke and Steel,* based on Carl Sandburg's poem, dates from 1932. In 1937 he composed a Symphony for chamber orchestra. Later orchestral works are *Passacaglia on Vermont Folk Tunes* (1949); Symphony in D (1956); and *Epos* (1963). He also wrote *Ricercare* for oboe and strings (1938); Suite for oboe and strings (1944–45); *Design for Radio* for 26 players (1945); and *Music for Six* for chamber ensemble (1961).

Among his various instrumental pieces are two serenades, one for oboe and string trio (1939), the other for flute, violin and cello; Sextet for piano and winds (1932); Piano Trio in one movement (1937); *Terzetto* for two violins and viola (1950); Woodwind Quartet (1953); *Soundings* for trumpet, bassoon, and percussion (1953); *Fantasia* for bassoon and seven players (1960, rev. 1961); and Piano Trio no. 2 (1963). For organ he composed *Two Choral Preludes on American Folk Hymns* (1947) and *Antiphon and Chorale* (1955). His piano music includes two suites (1932, 1953).

Donovan wrote five important works for female voices: *How Far Is It to Bethlehem?* with organ (1927); *Chanson of the Bells of Oseney,* with piano (1930); *Hymn to the Night* (1947); *How Should I Love?,* with piano (1947); and *Four Songs of Nature,* with piano (1953). For men's voices he wrote *Fantasy on American Folk Ballads,* with tenor solo and orchestra (1940); *Good Ale,* with piano (1947); a Mass with organ, three trumpets, and timpani (1955); and the *Magnificat* (1961).

His vocal compositions include *Five Elizabethan Lyrics* for high soprano and string quartet (1932–57); *Four Songs* for soprano and string quartet (1933); and *Four Songs on English Texts* for medium voice and piano (1930).

DORAN, MATT (HIGGINS)
b. Covington, Kentucky, 1 September 1921

Doran studied at flute and composition at the Los Angeles College and the University of Southern California (B.M., 1947; D.M.A, 1953) where he was a pupil of Ernst Toch, Gail Kubik, and Hanns Eisler. He was a flutist in the Corpus Christi (Texas) and Muncie (Indi-

ana) Symphony Orchestras while teaching at Del Mar College, Corpus Christi (1953–55) and Ball State University, Muncie (1956–57), respectively. In 1957 he was appointed to the music faculty of Mount St. Mary College, Los Angeles, serving as professor from 1966 until his retirement in 1986.

Doran has composed ten operas, including *The Little Hand* (1950); *The Committee* (1953), staged in Corpus Christi in 1955; the three-act *Obstinate* (1969); and *The Marriage Counselor,* produced in Los Angeles in 1977.

Among Doran's orchestral works are four symphonies (1946, 1959, 1977, 1979) and two chamber symphonies (1980, 1984). Other orchestral works are *Dramatic Overture; Merry Overture;* a Flute Concerto (1953); Horn Concerto (1954); *Essay* (1955); *Overture 1957*; *Youth Overture* (1964); a Piano Concerto (1970, rev. 1975); Cello Concerto (1975); Double Concerto for flute, guitar, and strings (1976); Concerto for marimba and chamber orchestra (1986); and Double Concerto for piano, flute, and strings (1991).

Doran's instrumental music makes much use of his own instrument, the flute, including three wind quintets; Suite for flute and string quartet; *Four Movements* for four flutes and piano; Trio for flute, oboe, and guitar; *Four Short Pieces* (1963); *Poem* for flute and piano (1965); Sonatina for flute and cello (1968); Trio for flute, clarinet, and piano (1979–80); Flute Sextet (1987); Octet for flutes (1989); *Face of Jazz* for flute and piano (1990); Flute Sonata (1993); Trio for flute, viola, and harp (1998); and Trio for flute, oboe, and clarinet (2003). Other chamber works are *Seven Short Pieces* for clarinet (1966); Clarinet Sonata (1967); Quartet for oboe, clarinet, bassoon, and viola (1970); Sonatina for oboe and piano (1982); and *Four Movements* for double bassoon and piano. Among his keyboard compositions are four piano sonatas (1960, 1981–82, 1993. 1994) and *Pastorale* for organ.

Doran has written two oratorios, *Song of Mercy and Judgment* (1953) and *Eskaton* for soloists, chorus, and orchestra (1976), as well as three vocal pieces: *To March* (Emily Dickinson) for soprano and piano; *To the Moon* for soprano, horn, and piano (1979); and *Three Sonnets* (Shakespeare) for soprano and flute (1984).

DRAKE, EARL ROSS
b. Aurora, Illinois, 26 November 1865
d. Chicago, Illinois, 6 May 1916

After studying violin in Chicago and Cincinnati, Drake became a pupil of Joachim at the Berlin Hochschule für Musik. He was appointed head of the violin department of the Gottschalk Lyric School in Chicago (1893–97), and in 1900 founded his own school of music in Chicago.

Drake composed two operas, *The Blind Girl of Castel-Cuille* (Chicago, 1914), and *The Mite and the Mighty* (Chicago, 1915). His orchestral works include *Brownie Suite* (1905); *Dramatic Prologue* (1915); *Ballet*; and *Gypsy Scenes* for violin and orchestra.

DRUCKMAN, JACOB (RAPHAEL)
b. Philadelphia, Pennsylvania, 26 June 1928
d. New Haven, Connecticut, 24 May 1996

Druckman's early studies in violin, counterpoint, and composition were with Louis Gesensway and in solfège and score-reading with Renée Longy. He attended the Juilliard School (1949–54, 1955–56), where he was a pupil of Bernard Wagenaar, Vincent Persichetti, and Peter Mennin. During the summers of 1949 and 1950 at Tanglewood he studied with Aaron Copland. On a Fulbright Fellowship in 1954 he went to Paris, where he received composition lessons from Tony Aubin at the Ecole Normale de Musique.

Upon graduation from the Juilliard School in 1956, Druckman joined the faculty there, remaining until 1972. During the years 1961–65 he also taught at Bard College. From 1965 to 1976 he worked at the Columbia-Princeton Electronic Music Center. In 1972 he assumed the directorship of the Brooklyn College Electronic Music Studio. In 1976 he assumed directorship of the Yale University School of Music's Electronic Music Studio, in addition to being professor of music and coordinator of composition studies. He was Composer-in-Residence with the New York Philharmonic Orchestra from 1982 to 1986. Druckman was the recipient of two Guggenheim Fellowships (1957, 1968) in addition to a Fulbright Fellowship (1954). In 1981 he was appointed President of the Koussevitzky Foundation.

Druckman's early orchestral works include *Music for the Dance* (1949); *Concerto for Strings* (1951); a ballet, *Spell* (1951); *Volpone Overture* (1953); *Suite* (1953); a Violin Concerto (1956); a ballet, *Performance*, for José Limón (1966); and *Odds and Ends,* a game for children's orchestra (1966). *Windows,* commissioned by the Koussevitzky Foundation and performed by the Chicago Symphony Orchestra, won the Pulitzer Prize in 1972. An orchestral version of *Incenters* (1968) for trumpet, horn, trombone, and orchestra was completed in 1973 and performed that year by the Minnesota Orchestra, conducted by Stanislaw Skrowaczewski. *Mirage* received its premiere in St. Louis, Missouri, on 4 February 1976 by the St. Louis Symphony Orchestra under Leonard Slatkin.

In November 1977 the New York Philharmonic Orchestra conducted by Lorin Maazel performed *Chiaroscuro,* a Bicentennial commission. In 1978, Druckman received two major commissions from the New York Philharmonic Orchestra: a Viola Concerto, first performed on 3 December 1978 with Sol Greitzer as soloist, Joseph Levine conducting; and *Aureole,* premiered on 9 June 1979 , conducted by Leonard Bernstein.

Other orchestral pieces include *Prism* (1980); *A Birthday Bouquet* (1986); *Athanor* (1986); *Paean* (1986); *Maga* (New York, 1986); *In Memory: Vincent Persichetti* (1987); *That Quickening Pulse* (1988); *Variations on Bernstein's "New York, New York"* (1988); *Brangle* (Chicago, 1989); *Nor Spell, Nor Charm* for chamber orchestra (1990); *Summer Lightning,* performed by the Boston Symphony Orchestra at Tanglewood in 1991; *Shog* (1991); *Demos* (1992); *With Bells On* for symphonic winds and percussion (1994); and a Piano Concerto (1996).

Among Druckman's vocal compositions are *Laude* for baritone, alto flute, viola, and cello (1952); *Dark Upon the Harp* for mezzo-soprano, brass quintet, and percussion (1962); *The Sound of Time* for soprano and orchestra to a text by Norman Mailer (1964); and *Lamia* for soprano and orchestra (1974), performed by Jan de Gaetani with the New York Philharmonic Orchestra under Pierre Boulez on 17 October 1975. *Bo* for marimba, harp, bass clarinet, and three women's voices (1979) was premiered at the Juilliard Theater, New York on 3 March 1980. A third piece for soprano and orchestra,

Jacob Duckman.
Courtesy The Juilliard School.

Counterpoise, dates from 1994. *Nor Spell,* for mezzo-soprano and English horn, dates from 1990.

Druckman's choral music includes *The Simple Gifts* for chorus and piano (1954); *Four Madrigals* (1958); *Antiphonies I, II,* and *III,* all for a cappella voices; three works for chorus, organ, and percussion: *Psalm 89, Hymnus Referamus*; and *Dance of the Maidens* (1965); and a setting of the *Sabbath Evening Service* for tenor and six instrumentalists (1967). The major choral work is *Vox Humana* for chorus and orchestra, premiered at the Kennedy Center in Washington, D.C. in 1983.

Many of Druckman's instrumental works use pre-recorded tape, including *Animus I* for trombone (1966); *Animus II* for soprano and two percussionists (1968); *Animus III* for clarinet (1969); *Orison* for organ (1970); *Delizie contente che l'alme Beate* (after Francesco Cavalli) for wind quintet (1973); and *Animus IV* for tenor and six instruments (1979). He also used tape in two film scores, *Traite du Rossignol* (1970) and *Look Park* (1970); for tape alone he composed *Synapse* (1971).

Instrumental pieces without tape include three string quartets (1948, 1966, 1981); *Duo* for violin and piano (1949); Divertimento for clarinet, horn, harp, and string trio (1950); *Interlude* for flute, clarinet, and timpani (1953); *Incenters* for 13 players (1968); *Other Voices* (1976) composed for the American Brass Quintet; *Tromba Marina* for four double basses (1981); *Dance With Shadows* for brass quintet (1989); *Come Round* for chamber ensemble (1992); *Dark Wind* for violin and piano (1994); *Duo* for violin and cello (1994); and *Glint* for clarinet, horn, harp, and string trio (1995).

In addition to the two early ballets, Druckman adapted four works as dance scores for Gerald Arpino and the City Center Joffrey Ballet: *Valentine, Solarwind* (from *Animus III*), *Animus* (from *Animus I*), and *Synapse.*

DUBENSKY, ARCADY
b. Viatka, Russia, 15 October 1890
d. Tenafly, New Jersey, 14 October 1966

Dubensky received musical training from an early age and was a violinist in a theater orchestra when only 11. From 1904 to 1909 he studied at the Moscow Conservatory and in 1911 became a member of the Moscow Imperial Opera Orchestra, a post he held until 1919. It was during this time that he achieved his first success as a composer, with a one-act opera, *Romance With a Double Bass* (1916), performed by the Imperial Opera Company.

In 1921, Dubensky settled in America, joining the New York Philharmonic Orchestra in the following year. His long practical experience as an orchestral player enabled him to write expertly for all instruments. He retired from playing in 1953. Dubensky's music is composed in a conservative idiom, avoiding modernity of harmony and embracing a tuneful, if somewhat academic, style. Stokowski and the Philadelphia Orchestra gave the first performance of several Dubensky works, and it was for them that he wrote *Fugue* for eighteen violins (1932). The same orchestra gave the premiere of his *Tom Sawyer Overture* in 1935 and the *Suite "Anno 1600"* for strings in 1937.

Dubensky's best-known orchestral work is *Stephen Foster: Theme, Variations and Finale,* a symphonic treatment of Foster songs. It was first performed by the Indianapolis Symphony Orchestra in 1941. Dubensky's other important orchestral compositions are the Symphony in G minor (1916); *Suite Russe* (1921); *Intermezzo and Complement* (1927); *From Old Russia* (1927); a symphonic poem, *Russian Bells* (1928); *Gossips* for string orchestra (1928); *Three Compositions* (1928); *Rajah* (1930); *The Raven* (with narrator) (1931); *Prelude and Fugue* (1932); *Russian Soldier's Song* (1932); *American Dance* (1935); *Political Suite* (1936); *Serenade* (1936); *Oriental, song and dance* (1945), *After the Rubaiyat of Omar Khyyam*; *Overture to a Comedy*; a Concerto Grosso for strings; and *Ballade* for viola and orchestra.

Dubensky is perhaps best remembered for compositions involving multiple instruments of the same kind. In addition for the *Fugue* for eighteen violins, he wrote *Variations* for eight clarinets (1932); *Theme and Variations* for four horns (1932); *Prelude and Fugue* for four bassoons (1933); *Prelude and Fugue* for four double basses (1934); a Suite for four trumpets (1934); a Suite for nine flutes (1935); and a *Fugue* for 34 violins (1948).

Among his pieces for neglected instruments are a *Capriccio* for piccolo and orchestra (1930) and a *Fantasy on a Negro Theme* for tuba and orchestra (1938). For brass he wrote a Concerto Grosso for three trombones, tuba, and orchestra (1950); a *Prelude, Toccata and Fugue* for three trombones, tuba, and strings; and a Trombone Concerto (1953). A curiosity is his *Trumpet Overture* for 18 toy trumpets, three trombones, tuba, and two bass drums (1949). On more conventional lines are two string quartets (1932, 1954) and a String Sextet (1933).

Dubensky's later operas have American settings: the three-act *Downtown* (1930) and two one-act operas, *On the Highway* (1936) and *Two Yankees in Italy* (1944).

DUKE, JOHN WOODS
b. Cumberland, Maryland, 30 June 1899
d. Northampton, Massachusetts, 26 October 1984

Duke attended the Peabody Conservatory, Baltimore (1915–18), where he studied piano with Harold

(1944), and a one-act operetta, *The Yankee Pedlar* (1962), both to libretti by his wife. His choral music includes *Pole Star for This Year*, a setting of words by Archibald McLeish for a cappella chorus; *Psalm 23* for female voices; *O Sing Unto the Lord a New Song* for female voices and strings (1955); *Magnificat* for unison voices and organ (1961); *Three River Songs* (texts from the Chinese) for women's voices and piano (1963); and *A Christmas Hymn* for chorus (1972).

It is as a composer of art songs that Duke is best known. In all he wrote about 260 songs, many of which continue to appear in concerts throughout the United States. Towards the end of his life he completed two six-poem song cycles, one setting works of Emily Bronte (for mezzo-soprano), the other Emily Dickinson (for soprano).

DUKELSKY, VLADIMIR (PSEUD. VERNON DUKE)

b. Parfianova, near Pskov, Russia, 10 October 1903
d. Santa Monica, California, 16 January 1969

Dukelsky studied at the Kiev Conservatory (1916–19) where he was a pupil of Reinhold Glière. After the Revolution he left Russia with his family to live in Constantinople. He moved to Paris in 1924 and in that year his First Piano Concerto sufficiently impressed Serge Diaghilev to commission a ballet from him. This score, *Zephyre et Flore,* was performed in 1925 with choreography by Léonide Massine. The association with Diaghilev continued; in 1926, with Francis Poulenc, Georges Auric, and Vitturio Rieti, he was one of the four pianists in the Ballet Russe production of Stravinsky's *Les Noces* in London. He remained in London until 1929, writing songs for musicals. In 1929 he went to the United States where he settled in New York. He became an American citizen in 1936. From 1934–35 he studied with Joseph Schillinger.

Dukelsky's Symphony no. 1 in F was composed in 1928. The Second Symphony in D-flat, written in the following year, was heard at the I.S.C.M. Festival in London in 1931. In addition to a Third Symphony in E (1946), he composed two piano concertos; *Ballade* for piano and orchestra (1931, rev. 1943); a Violin Concerto, premiered in Boston in 1943 by Ruth Posselt; *Ode to the Milky Way* (1946); a Cello Concerto (1946); *Variations on an Old Russian Chant* for oboe and strings (1955); and *Dédicaces* for soprano, piano solo, and orchestra (1935).

After his arrival in the United States, Dukelsky's style was much affected by his meeting with George Gershwin, who persuaded him to use the name "Vernon Duke" for his songs. This influence is seen especially in his music for revues and films. He provided songs

John Woods Duke.
Courtesy Smith College Archives.

Randolph and composition with Gustav Strube. He spent the following four years in New York as a pupil of Howard Brockway and Bernard Wagenaar in composition and Franklin Cannon in piano. In 1920 he began a promising career as a pianist and in 1923 joined the music faculty of Smith College, Northampton, Massachusetts, as an assistant professor, becoming a full professor in 1938. He retired as professor emeritus in 1967. In 1929 he went to Europe for a year where he worked with Artur Schnabel in Berlin and Nadia Boulanger in Paris.

In addition to an Overture in D minor for strings (1928), now withdrawn, Duke's orchestral music includes a Concerto in A for piano and strings (1938) and *Carnival Overture* (1940). His important instrumental compositions are two string quartets (1941, 1967); a Suite for solo viola (1933); a Suite for solo cello (1934); *Fantasy* for violin and piano (1936); String Trio (1937); a Piano Trio in D (1943); and *Dialogue* for cello and piano (1943).

Duke composed two one-act operas: *Captain Lovelock*, to his own libretto, performed in New York in 1953; and *The Sire of Maledroit* (1957) to a text by his wife, Dorothy, performed in Schroon Lake, New York in 1958. Also for the stage he wrote a musical fantasy for children, *The Cat That Walked by Himself* for a number of musicals: *Yvonne* (1926); *The Yellow Mask* (1928), both produced in London; and Broadway shows including *Ziegfeld Follies of 1934; Ziegfeld Follies of 1936; The Show is On* (1936); *Open Your Eyes* (1939); *Banjo Eyes* (1941); *The Lady Comes Across* (1942); *Dancing in the Streets* (1943); *Jackpot* (1944); *Tars and Spars* (1944); *Sadie Thompson* (1944); *Sweet Bye and Bye* (1946); *Two's Company* (1952); *The Littlest Revue* (1956); and *Time Remembered* (1957). Duke's most famous song, *April in Paris,* was written for the musical *Walk a Little Faster* (1932); his most lasting success, the musical *Cabin in the Sky* (1940), was made into a film. He provided songs and dances for Gershwin's incomplete score for the film *Goldwyn's Follies* (1937).

Among his other works for the stage are three operas: the two-act *Damoiselle Paysanne* (1928), *Mistress into Maid* (Santa Barbara, 1963), and *Zenda* (San Francisco, 1963). In addition to *Zephyr et Flore* (1925), he composed six other ballets: *Public Gardens* (Chicago, 1934); *Field Day* (1936), based on music by John Field; *Bal de Blachisseuses* (1946); *Souvenir de Monte Carlo* (1949-56); *Emperor Norton* (San Francisco, 1957); and *Lady Blue* (1961).

Dukelsky's important chamber music includes two violin sonatas, no. 1 in D (1948) and no. 2 (1960); Trio for flute, bassoon, and piano (1930); *Capriccio mexicano* for violin and piano (1939); *Etude* for violin and bassoon (1939); *Three Pieces* for wind quartet and piano (1946); *Nocturne* for six wind instruments (1947); a String Quartet (1956); and many pieces for piano.

Among his vocal music are the song cycle *Triolet of the North* to words by Feodor Sologub (1922); *Ogden Nash's Musical Zoo* (20 songs; 1946); and *A Shropshire Lad* (A. E. Housman; 1949). His best known choral works are *Epitaph* (*on the Death of Diaghilev*), a setting of a text by Osip Mandelstamm for soprano, chorus, and orchestra (1931); an oratorio, *The End of St. Petersburg,* performed in New York in 1937; and a cantata, *Paris, Aller et Retour* for soprano, tenor, chorus, and orchestra (1948).

Dukelsky was the author of two lively books, an autobiography, *Passport to Paris,* published in 1955; and *Listen Here* (1963).

DUNN, JAMES PHILIP
b. New York, New York, 10 January 1884
d. Jersey City, New Jersey, 24 July 1936

After graduating from City College of New York in 1903, Dunn studied with Edward MacDowell and Cornelius Rybner at Columbia University. He held various organ appointments in New York, Jersey City, and Bayonne, New Jersey.

For orchestra he wrote a symphonic poem, *Lovesight* (1919); an *Overture on Negro Themes* (1922); *The Confessions of Saint Augustine* (1925); a tone poem, *We,* commemorating Lindburgh's flight in 1927; a Symphony in C (1929); *Choral* (1930); and *Passacaglia and Theme Fugatum* (1930).

His major works were an opera, *The Galleon* (1918); a Mass in C; and a cantata, *The Phantom Drum* (1917). Among his chamber music are two string quartets (1913); a Piano Quintet in G minor (1910); a Violin Sonata in G minor (1912); a Piano Trio in B-flat (1913); and *Variations* for violin and piano (1915). Among his choral works are *It Was a Lover and His Lass* for female voices and orchestra (1918); *The Music of Spring* for female voices and orchestra (1918); *Song of the Night* for double chorus (1923); and *Missa Choralis* for chorus and organ (1925).

E

EATON, JOHN CHARLES
b. Bryn Mawr, Pennsylvania, 30 March 1935

Eaton began composing at the age of seven and was studying harmony and counterpoint a year later. At Princeton University (1953–59) he was a pupil of Milton Babbitt, Edward T. Cone, Earl Kim, and Roger Sessions. In 1970 he joined the music faculty at Indiana University, Bloomington, where he was appointed professor of music (composition) and artistic director of the Center for Electronic and Computer Music. In 1991 he left to become professor of music at the University of Chicago, retiring in 2001. From 1976 to 1977 he was Composer-in-Residence at the American Academy in Rome. He was awarded three Rome Prizes (1959, 1960, 1961), two Guggenheim Fellowships (1962, 1965), and a 1990 MacArthur Foundation "genius award." Eaton has received commissions from the Koussevitzky and Fromm Foundations, the Santa Fe Opera, the National Endowment for the Arts, and the Public Broadcasting Corporation. As a performer of electronic and microtonal music, he has appeared in Europe, the Soviet Union and North and South America.

Eaton is best known for his work in electronic music and as the composer of operas. The first of these, *Ma Barker* in one act to a libretto by Arthur Gold was written in 1957. *Herakles* (1964), a grand opera in three acts (libretto by Michael Fried), was performed at Indiana University in 1974 and televised nationally in the following year. In 1971 he completed an opera *Myshkin* for television and a chamber opera, *The Lion and Androcles,* dates from 1973.

Danton and Robespierre in three acts, libretto by Patrick Creagh, was also staged by the Indiana University Opera Theater in 1978. *The Cry of Clytaemnestra* (1979), in one act, again to a text by Patrick Craegh, was premiered by the same group in March 1980. The latest operas are *The Tempest* (Shakespeare) (1983–85) for Santa Fe Opera; *The Reverend Jim Jones* (1988); *Let's Get This Show on the Road: An Alternative View of Genesis* (1993); *Golk* (1995); *Antigone* (1999); *Inasmuch* (200); and *King Lear* (2003–04). In addition, Eaton has composed four theater pieces, *Peer Gynt* (1990); *Don Quixote* (1994); *Salome's Flea Circus* (1994); and *Travelling with Gulliver* (1997).

In his electronic compositions, he has made extensive use of the Syn-Ket, a portable sound system designed and built by Paul Ketoff in Rome. Works using electronic processes include *Songs for R.P.B.* for voice, piano and Syn-Ket (1964); *Prelude for Myshkin* for solo Syn-Ket (1966); *Concert Piece No. 2.* for solo Syn-Ket (1966); *Thoughts on Rilke* for soprano, Syn-Ket, Syn-mill, vibrator and reverberation plate (1966); *Soliloquy* for Syn-Ket (1967); *Duet for Syn-Ket* for Syn-Ket and Moog synthesizer (1968); *Blind Man's Cry* for soprano and electronic music synthesizers (1968); *The Three Graces,* a theater piece for three voices, electronic ensemble and dancer (1972); *Oro* for voice and synthesizer (1974); *Lord of Lampedusa* for soprano, mezzo-soprano, piano and synthesizer (1974); *Mass 69* for soprano, clarinet, an orchestra of electronic sound synthesizers and tape presented at the Library of Congress, Washington, D.C. in January 1979, a cantata *El Divino Narciso* (1998); a dramatic cantata *Youth* (2000); and *Vespers* for two sopranos, mezzo-soprano, tenor, baritone, bass and ensemble with digital display (2002). *Concert Piece* for Syn-Ket and orchestra was premiered under Gunther Schuller at the Berkshire Music Festival, Tanglewood in 1966. Other pieces in this medium include *A Packet for Emily and Dill* for mezzo-soprano, clarinet and electronics (1991) and *Genesis* for Eaton-Moog multiple touch-sensitive keyboard (1992.

Eaton has composed much music for conventional forces. His orchestral works include *Tertullian Overture*

(1958); *Adagio and Allegro* for flute, oboe and strings (1960); *Ajax* for baritone and chamber ensemble (1972); Symphony no. 2 (1980–81); *Remember Rome,* a sinfonietta for strings (1987); and *Thenody for Paisan* (2003).

Among his instrumental compositions are a Flute Sonata (1955); *Concert Piece* for flute, two oboes and two clarinets (1956); *Piano Variations* (1957); 3 string quartets (1958, 1989, 2003), Trumpet Sonata (1958); *Encore Piece* for flute and piano (1959); *Concert Piece* for clarinet and piano (1960); *Three Epigrams* for clarinet and piano (1960); *Concert Music* for solo clarinet (1961); *Theme and Variations* for solo flute, *Vibrations* for flute, two oboes and two clarinets (1967); *Thoughts for Sonny* for solo trumpet (1968); *Sonority Movement* for flute and nine harps (1971); *Trio in Memory of Mario Cristini* for piano trio (1971); *Two Plaudits for Ralph Shapey* for flute, oboe and cello (1991); *Salome's Flea Circus* for clarinet and piano (1994); and *Golk Sonatina* for oboe and piano (1995).

Vocal music without electronics instruments includes *Song Cycle on Holy Sonnets of John Donne* for soprano and orchestra(1956); *Ajax* for baritone and instruments (1972); *Guillen Songs* for mezzo-soprano and piano(1974); *Lullaby for Estela* (1977); all for voice and piano, his only choral work, *Duo* for mixed voices commissioned for the Cork Festival, Ireland in 1977, *Songs of Despair* (James Joyce) for mezzo-soprano and instrumental ensemble (1986); *Notes on Moonlight* for soprano, mezzo-soprano and chamber ensemble (1991); *Trumpet Voluntary* for soprano and brass quintet (1991); *Songs of Desperation and Comfort* for mezzo-soprano and chamber orchestra (1993); *Lettere* for mezzo-soprano, flute, harp and string quartet (1995); *Tocotin* for mezzo-soprano and guitar (1998); and *Elegy for Jane* (Roethke) for mezzo-soprano, harp, guitar and mandolin (1999).

Eaton is the author of *Involvement with Music: New Music Since 1950* (1976).

ECKHARD, JACOB, SR.
b. Eschwege, Hesse, Germany, 24 November 1757
d. Charleston, South Carolina, 10 November 1833

Eckhard arrived in America in 1776 as a musician with the Hessian troops during the War of Independence, settling first in Richmond, Virginia. In 1786 he was appointed organist at St. John's Lutheran Church in Charleston, moving in 1809 to St. Michael's Episcopal Church, where he was succeeded on his death by son George Eckhard. He published a collection of hymns, *Eckhard's Choral Book,* in Boston in 1816. He was also the composer of two patriotic naval songs, *The Pillar of Glory* and *Rise, Columbia, Brave and Free* published in Philadelphia in 1813.

EDMUNDS, JOHN
(REAL NAME CHARLES STERLING)
b. San Francisco, California, 10 June 1913
d. Berkeley, California, 9 December 1986

Edmunds studied at the University of California, Los Angeles, and at the Curtis Institute, where he was a pupil of Rosario Scalero. His other teachers included Walter Piston at Harvard (1941), Roy Harris at Cornell, and Otto Luening at Columbia University. In addition he went to England to study continuo playing with Arnold Goldsborough and Thurstan Dart. He was awarded a Fulbright Fellowship (1951) and a Guggenheim Fellowship (1969). After teaching at Syracuse University, New York, and the University of California at Berkeley, he was in charge of Americana at the New York Public Library (1957–61). He spent the years from 1968 to 1976 in England transcribing English songs and poetry of the 17th century. His 12-volume *The Major Epoch of English Songs* (1940–76), 300 English songs arranged from lute tablature for voice and piano, remains unpublished. Edmunds was also widely known for his editing the songs of Purcell and vocal music by Alessandro Scarlatti and Benedetto Marcello. He also edited the *Sandison Hymnal* (1957–62) and the *Adams Book of Carols* (1957–72).

Edmunds's own music is predominantly vocal. For chorus he wrote a masque, *The Pastoral Kingdom* (*The Shepherd's Maze*) (1963, rev. 1974); *Twelve Choral Hymns and Carols* (1966); a *Choric Requiem* (*Dance Requiem*) for solo voices, chorus, organ and percussion (1968); *Rites of Christmas* (1968); *Hymns Sacred and Profane* for narrator, mezzo-soprano, chorus, organ and percussion (1966, rev. 1975); and *Toward the Western Hills* for male narrator, female narrator, chorus, organ and percussion (1984). Among his songs are numerous settings of English poets.

For the stage Edmunds composed three ballets for children, *Jehovah and the Ark* (1968), rev. 1973 and retitled *The Voyage to Ararat*; *The Parliament of Fowls* (1974, rev. 1976); and *The Council of Rooks* (1983).

He was the author of a book, *History of American Music in Pictures,* and the coauthor with Gordon Boelzner of *Some Twentieth Century American Composers: A Selective Bibliography* (1959).

EFFINGER, CECIL
b. Colorado Springs, Colorado, 22 July 1914
d. Boulder, Colorado, 22 December 1990

Effinger studied the violin and oboe and was first oboe in the Denver Symphony Orchestra from 1937 to 1941.

He was a pupil of Bernard Wagenaar in New York (1938) and studied in France with Nadia Boulanger (1939). He taught at Colorado College (1936-41, 1946-48). In 1948 he was appointed professor of composition at the University of Colorado, Boulder, retiring in 1981 but remaining as Composer-in-Residence until 1984. Although he used atonal methods at times, his choral music in particular is in an American traditional idion.

Effinger composed five symphonies (1946, 1947, 1952, 1954, 1958); two *Little Symphonies* (1945, 1958); and many other orchestral pieces, including *Nocturne* (1938); Concerto Grosso (1940); *Prelude and Fugue* (1940); *A Western Overture* (1942); *Tennessee Variation* (1946); an *Orchestral Suite* (1946); *Lyric Overture* (1949); *Symphony Concertante* for harp, piano and orchestra (1954); *Tone Poem on the Square Dance* (1955); *Trio Concertante* for trumpet, horn, trombone and chamber orchestra (1964); *Landscape* (1966); *Quiet Evening* (1972); *Capriccio* (1975); *Toccata* for chamber orchestra (1980); and *Landscape II* (1984).

Effinger composed a Concertino for organ and small orchestra (1945); a Piano Concerto (1946); and a Concerto for violin and chamber orchestra (1972).

His major choral compositions are three oratorios: *The Invisible Fire* (1957), *Paul of Tarsus* (1968), and *This We Believe* (1975); three cantatas: *The St. Luke Christmas Story* (1953), *Cantata for Easter* (1971), and *Cantata from Ancient Prophets* (1983); and *American Men* for male chorus and band (1942); *Set of Three* for chorus and brass (1961); *The Long Dimension* for chorus and orchestra, *Let Your Mind Wander Over America* for chorus, string orchestra and band (1969); *In Praise of Musicke* for chorus, piano, double bass and drums (1984); and *An American Hymn* for chorus and band.

For the stage Effinger wrote a short opera for young people, *Pandora's Box* (1961), a three-act opera *Cyrano de Bergerac* (1965); and a music drama, *The Gentleman Desperado and Miss Bird* (1976).

Of his many works for band, important items are *Interlude on a Blues Tune* (1944); a *Suite* (1944); *Little Symphony* (1957); *Silver Plume* (1961); and *They That Mourn* (1966). Among his chamber music pieces are six string quartets (1943, 1944, 1944, 1948, 1963, 1985); a Viola Sonata (1944); three piano sonatas (1946, 1949, 1968); a Woodwind Quintet(1947); *Divertimento* for piano trio (1950); a Piano Trio (1975); *Rondo* for piano trio (1975); *Intrada* for brass quintet (1982); and a Flute Sonata (1985).

Effinger was also the inventor of the Musicwriter, a special music typewriter.

EICHHEIM, HENRY
b. Chicago, Illinois, 3 January 1870
d. Montecito, near Santa Barbara, California, 22 August 1942

Eichheim studied violin at the Chicago College of Music and joined the Theodore Thomas Orchestra, in which his father was a cellist. From 1890 to 1912 he was a member of the Boston Symphony Orchestra.

Eichheim visited the Far East on five occasions from 1915 through the mid-1930s, collecting ethnic instruments, and Oriental music had a deep effect upon his compositions. *Impressions of Pekin* for chamber orchestra and oriental percussion was performed at the I.S.C.M. Festival in Vienna in 1925. The exoticism of Asia can be heard in most of his works: *Oriental Sketches* (1921), revised in 1927 and retitled *Oriental Impressions*; *Malay Mosaic* (1924); *Korean Sketch* (1925); the suite *Burma* (1927); *Java* (1929); *Japanese Nocturne* (1930); and *Bali* (1933), all for orchestra.

He composed two ballets, *Chinese Legend,* subtitled *The Rivals* (1924), and *A Burmese Pwe* (1926). Among Eichheim's other instrumental works are *Six Etudes* for violin (1890); two violin sonatas (1892–95, 1934); a String Quartet (1895); and two piano pieces, *Gleanings from Buddha's Fields* (1906) and *Oriental Impressions* (1918–22).

ELKUS, ALBERT ISRAEL
b. Sacramento, California, 30 April 1884
d. Oakland, California, 19 February 1962

After graduating from the University of California, Berkeley in 1907, Elkus studied piano with Harold Bauer in Paris, and with Josef Lhevinne in Berlin. In Vienna he took conducting lessons from Franz Schalk and later in Berlin was a composition pupil of Robert Fuchs. At the Music theory department of the San Francisco Conservatory, he was head (1923–25) and director (1931–37), returning there in 1951, and he taught piano at Dominican College, San Rafael, California (1924–31), and at Mills College, Oakland, California (1929–44). In 1931 he was appointed to the faculty of the University of California, Berkeley, becoming Head of the music department in 1935 and chairman from 1937 to his retirement in 1951. From 1951 to 1957 he was director of the San Francisco Conservatory.

Among Elkus's orchestral works are a *Concertino on Lezione III of Ariosto* for cello and strings (1917); *Impressions from a Greek Tragedy* (1920), which won the Juilliard Award; and *On a Merry Folk Tune* (1922). Elkus also composed a *Serenade* for string quartet (1921); a Violin Sonata (1914); and three choral pieces:

Synagogue Service (1914), *Sir Patrick Spens* (1915), and *I Am the Reaper* for men's chorus and piano (1917).

ELKUS, JONATHAN (BRITTON)
b. San Francisco, California, 8 August 1931

Jonathan Elkus is the son of the composer Albert Elkus. He studied at the University of California, Berkeley (B.A., 1953) with Charles Cushing and William Denny, at Stanford University (M.A., 1954), where he was a pupil of Ernst Bacon and Leonard Ratner, and at Mills College, Oakland (1957), where he received lessons from Darius Milhaud. From 1955 to 1957 he was assistant director of the bands at Stanford before moving to Lehigh University, Bethlehem, Pennsylvania where he taught until 1973. In 1979 he was appointed director of music at Cape Cod Academy in Osterville, serving as chairman of the Humanities department from 1985 to 1989. In 1989 he became chairman of the hhstory department at Stuart Hall School, Staunton, moving to the University of California, Davis to be a lecturer in music (1991–2003).

Elkus is widely known for his works for the stage. These include four operas: *The Outcast of Poker Flat* (Bret Harte) (Bethlehem, 1960); *Medea* (1963), performed in Milwaukee in 1970; *The Mandarin* (New York, 1967); and *Helen in Egypt* (Milwaukee, 1970). His musicals have also been widely produced throughout the United States and the United Kingdom: *Tom Sawyer* (San Francisco: 1953); *Treasure Island* (1961); *A Little Princess* (Cambridge, England: 1980); and *Act Your Age* (Osterville, 1983).

Among his compositions for band are *Camino Real* (1955); *Serenade* for horn, baritone horn and band (1957); *C.C. Rag* (1974); *The Apocalypse Rag* (1974); *Pipers on Parade* (1976); *Chiaroscuro Suite* (1977); and *Cal Band March* (1978).

Elkus has written much vocal music, including *The Oxen* (Thomas Hardy) for high voice and piano (1956); *Four 3-Part Catches* for chorus (1958); *The Dorados* (W. Smith) for male voices (1961); *Triptych* (H.D.) for mezzo-soprano and four bassoons (1964); *In the Time of Your Life* (William Saroyan) for countertenor and piano (1963); *Two Sonnets* (E. St. V. Millay) for medium voice and piano (1964); *After Their Kind* (F.J. Arnstein) for medium voice, violin and piano (1965); *Of Players to Come* (Lengyel) for chorus and piano (1974); and *The Age of Fable* (Thomas Bullfinch) for chorus (1978). Among a handful of instrumental pieces are *Five Sketches* for two clarinets and bassoon (1954); *Three Medieval Pieces* for organ (1959); *The Charmer,* a rag for clarinet, trombone and piano (1972); *Laurel* for harpsichord (1973); and many piano rags.

Elkus is the author of *Charles Ives and the Ameri-can Band Tradition: A Centennial Tribute* (1974). In 1983 he established the publishing group Overland Music Distributors.

ELLINGTON, DUKE (EDWARD KENNEDY)
b. 29 April 1899: Washington, D.C.
d. 24 May 1974: New York, New York

Duke Ellington is considered widely to be the greatest jazz musician of all time. His skill as a pianist and the innovatory approach he had to everything he undertook made him a man apart. He composed prolifically for the concert hall, theater, films, nightclubs and recording studio. For almost 50 years he maintained a steady flow of pieces for his band, often tailor-made for the outstanding individuals who loyally stood by him for decades. During this time he constantly took the band on lengthy tours throughout the world.

Ellington began piano lessons at the age of seven, dropping out of school at 17 to become a professional musician. His five-piece band, the Washingtonians, was founded in New York; its number gradually increased to ten and was renamed The Kentucky Club in 1926. From 1927 to 1931 his resident band at the Cotton Club in Harlem gained a reputation far beyond New York. Phonograph record sales mounted with the notable successes of "Creole Love Call" (1927), "Black and Tan Fantasy" (1927), and "Mood Indigo" (1930). A tour to the West coast of the United States in 1930 was the first of many that enhanced his position as the leading jazz composer-performer. Frustrated by the limitations of 10-inch 78-rpm records, he was the first jazz musician to compose more extended pieces for two sides of a 12-inch disc. The first of these works was *Creole Rhapsody* (1931).

In 1939 the brilliant arranger-composer Billy Strayhorn (1915–1967) joined with Ellington, resulting in the most remarkable collaboration in jazz history. His contribution lifted their creations to a level of excellence unknown before or since. By 1946 the Ellington orchestra numbered 18 players, a figure generally maintained thereafter. It survived the difficult financial time of the 1950's, when so many other bands could not afford to continue. The orchestra's tour of Europe in 1958 marked a significant revival, culminating in the ground-breaking visit in 1971 to the U.S.S.R., during the height of the Cold War. In the same year it toured Europe, South America, and Mexico.

A new development took place on 16 September 1965 when the first of Ellington's "Sacred Concerts," *In the Beginning, God* was performed in Grace Cathedral, San Francisco. Scored for orchestra, soloists, chorus and dancer, it was followed by two others in 1968 and 1973.

For the stage he wrote five musicals: *Jump for Joy* (Los Angeles, 1941), concerning civil rights; *Beggar's Holiday*, based on *The Beggar's Opera* (New York, 1946); *Sugar City* (Detroit, 1965); *My People* (Chicago, 1963); and *The Blue Angel, Pousse Café* (1966). He also worked for several years on an opera, *Boola* (left unfinished).

One of his most ambitious scores is the ballet *The River*, composed for the American Ballet Theater and produced in New York in June 1970. He also composed incidental music for the 18th-century French play *Turcaret* by Alain R. le Sage (1960) and Shakespeare's *Timon of Athens* (Stratford, Ontario: 1963).

Ellington's most substantial works are a sequence of suites, mostly for jazz band: *Reminiscin' in Tempo* (1935); *Diminuendo and Crescendo in Blue* (1937); *Black, Brown and Beige* (1943); *Blue Belles of Harlem* (a Paul Whiteman commission; 1943); *Blutopia* (1944); *Perfume Suite* (1944); *New World A'Comin* (1945); *Deep South Suite* (1946); *Liberian Suite* (1947); *The Tattooed Bride* (1948); *Harlem* (*A Tone Parallel to Harlem*; 1950); *Night Creature*, a radio commission for jazz band and orchestra (1955); *Newport Jazz Festival Suite* (1955); *A Drum is a Woman* (1957); *Such Sweet Thunder* (1957); *Nutcracker Suite* (after Tchaikovsky; 1960); *Suite Thursday* (1932); *Far East Suite* (1964); *The Golden Broom and the Green Apple* (New York Philharmonic Orchestra, 1965); *Virgin Islands Suite* (1965); *La plus belle africaine* (1967); *Murder in the Cathedral* (1967); *Latin American Suite* (1968); *Afro-Eurasian Eclipse* (1971); *New Orleans Suite* (1971); and *Togo Bravo ! Suite* (1971).

Among his film scores are *Black and Tan* (1929); *Symphony in Black* (1935); *Hit Parade* (1937); *New Faces* (1937); *Reveille With Beverly* (1943); *The Asphalt Jungle* (1950); *Jonas* (1957); *Anatomy of a Murder* (1959); *Paris Blues* (1960); *Austro-Freight* (documentary) (1966); *Assault on a Queen* (1966); *Change of Mind* (1968); and *Racing World* (1968).

ELMORE, ROBERT HALL
b. Ramapatnam, India, 2 January 1913
d. Ardmore, Pennsylvania, 22 September 1985

With his American parents, Elmore moved to the United States in 1914. He graduated from the Royal Academy of Music in London in 1933; he also studied at the University of Pennsylvania (1934–37) with Harl McDonald (composition) and Pietro Yon (organ). He was professor of piano and organ at the Clarke Conservatory, Philadelphia (1936–53) and taught at the Philadelphia Music Academy from 1939 and the University of Pennsylvania from 1941.

For orchestra he wrote an Organ Concerto in C minor

(1938); a tone poem, *Valley Forge 1777* (1937); performed by Stokowski and the Philadelphia Orchestra; *Three Colors* for strings (1941); *The Legend of Sleepy Hollow*; *Prelude to Unrest*; *Music for Autumn*; and *Narrative* for horn and orchestra.

His choral works include *Psalm of Redemption*; *The Prodigal Son* for men's voices and orchestra; a cantata, *Out of the Depths* (1972); and two pieces for mixed chorus and orchestra, *All Ye Servants of the Lord* and *Vocalise*.

Elsmore was the composer of the first American opera seen on television: *It Began at Breakfast* (1941).

ELWELL, HERBERT
b. Minneapolis, Minnesota, 10 May 1898
d. Cleveland, Ohio, 17 April 1974

Elwell was educated at the University of Minnesota, Minneapolis and studied with Ernest Bloch in New York in 1919. From 1921 to 1926 he was in Europe, where he became a pupil of Nadia Boulanger in Paris (1921–24). He was in Rome on an American Academy Award (1924–27). In 1928, Elwell settled in Cleveland, where he was music critic for *The Plain Dealer* (1932–64). He was appointed head of the department of theory and composition at the Cleveland Institute, from which he retired in 1945 to devote himself to composition.

As a composer he is best known for the ballet *The Happy Hypocrite* (1925), based on the story by Max

A famous 1925 photograph showing (from the left) Virgil Thomson, Walter Piston, Herbert Elwell, and Aaron Copland at Nadia Boulanger's Paris apartment.
Aaron Copland Collection, Music Division, Library of Congress.

Beerbohm. Elwell's important works for orchestra are *The Centaur* (1924); *Orchestral Sketches* (1937); *Introduction and Allegro* (1942); *Ode* (1950); *Concert Suite* for violin and orchestra, commissioned by the Louisville Orchestra in 1957; and *Symphonic Sketches* for small orchestra (1966). His chamber music includes a Piano Quintet (1924); Divertimento for string quartet (1926); a Piano Sonata (1926); a Violin Sonata (1927); two string quartets, no.1 (1929) and no.2 in E minor (1937); and *Variations in E* for violin and piano (1951).

The *Lincoln Requiem* for baritone, chorus and orchestra won the Paderewski Prize in 1945. Among his vocal music are three works for voice and orchestra: *Blue Symphony* (1944), *Pastorale* (1947), and *The Forever Young* (1953); and a cantata, *I Was With Him* (1937).

ENGEL, A. LEHMAN

b. *Jackson, Mississippi, 14 September 1910*
d. *New York, New York, 29 August 1982*

Engel studied at the Cincinnati College Conservatory (1926–29) and at the Juilliard School (1930–34), where he was a pupil of Rubin Goldmark. In 1935 he also received composition lessons from Roger Sessions. From 1949 to 1952 he was musical director of the State Fair Musicals, Dallas, Texas. He earned an enviable reputation as an expert in music for the theater, especially Broadway musicals.

Among Engel's orchestra works are *Jungle Dance* (1930); *Introduction and Allegro* (1932); *Scientific Creation* (1935); two symphonies (1939, 1945); a Viola Concerto (1945); a Violin Concerto (1945); *Overture for the End of the War* (1946); *The Creation* (with narrator; 1946); and *Jackson Overture* (1961). His choral music includes a cantata, *The Chinese Nightingale* (1928); *Rain* (1929); *Excerpts from Job* (1932); *Rest* (1936); and *Let Us Now Praise Famous Men* (1955).

For the stage Engel composed three operas: *The Pierrot of the Minute* (1927), *Malady of Love* (1954), and *The Soldier* (1955); an opera-ballet, *Medea* (1932); and two musicals, *Golden Ladder* (1953) and *Serena* (1956). In addition to incidental music, especially for Shakespeare plays, Engel provided many dance scores: *Phobias* (Gluck Sandor, Felicia Sorel; 1932); *Driver of the Storm Winds* (Edwin Strawbridge; 1932); *Ekstasis* (Martha Graham; 1933); *Ceremonials* (Graham); *Transitions* (Graham; 1934); *Crystal* (Tashimira; 1934); *Song of the Night* (Harry Losee; 1935); *Marching Song* (Graham; 1935); *Parade* (Gene Martel; 1935); *Traditions* (Charles Weidman, Jose Limon, William Matons; 1935); *Imperial Gesture* (Graham; 1935); *The Shoebird* (Rex Cooper; 1967); and *Jackson* (1968).

Engel composed music for a feature film, *Boogie's*

Bump (1954), and ten World War Two documentaries: *Honduras*; *National Defense*; *Strategic Attack*; *Berlin Powderkeg*; *The Hedgerow Story*; *Unconditional Surrender* (1945); *The Fleet That Came To Stay* (1945); *Fury in the Pacific* (1945); and *Well Done* (1945). Engel's other instrumental music includes a String Quartet (1933); a Piano Sonata (1936); *The Garden of Paradise* for violin and piano (1941); a Cello Sonata (1945); *Dialogue* for violin and viola (1950); a Violin Sonata (1953); and a Viola Sonata (1955).

He was also the author of several books: an autobiography, *This Bright Day* (1956, rev. 1974); *Planning and Producing the Musical Show* (1957, rev. 1966); *The American Music Theater: A Consideration* (1967, rev. 1975); *The Musical Book* (1971); *Words with Music* (1972, rev. 1981); *Getting Started in the Theater* (1973); *The Making of the Musical* (1977); and *Getting the Show On: The Complete Guidebook for Producing a Musical in Your Theater* (1983). He was editor of a seven-volume series of music, *Renaissance to Baroque: Three Centuries of Choral Music*, issued between 1931 and 1969.

EPPERT, CARL

b. *Carbon, Clay County, Indiana, 5 November 1882*
d. *Milwaukee, Wisconsin, 1 October 1961*

Eppert studied at the American Conservatory in Chicago and in Berlin (1907–14), where he was a pupil of Hans Kaun, Arthur Nikisch, and Ernst Kunwald. He was the founder and conductor of the Terre Haute (Indiana) Symphony Orchestra (1903–07) and Milwaukee Civic Orchestra (1921–25), as well as conductor of the Milwaukee Symphony Orchestra (1926) and the Grand Opera of Seattle. In 1922 he was appointed head of the department of music theory and composition at the Wisconsin Conservatory; he also taught at the Wisconsin College of Music and the Milwaukee Institute of Music.

Eppert wrote copiously for orchestra. Among his output are seven symphonies, the first of which, *Symphony of the City Traffic,* won an NBC contest in 1932. Other orchestral pieces include *Arabian Suite* (1915); *Serenade for Strings* (1917); a tone poem, *The Pioneer* (1925); *Concert Waltz* (1930); a tone poem, *The Wanderer's Night Song* (1933); *Argonauts of '49* (1934); *City Shadows* (1935); *Speed* (1935); *Vitamins Suite* (1937); *Escapade* (1937); *Escort to Glory, a Concerto Grosso* (1940); *Two Symphonic Impressions* (1941); and *Image of America*. He also produced two items for concert band: *The Road to Mecca* (1933) and *Symphonic Tonette* (1934).

An opera, *Kaintuckee*, was completed in 1915. Most of his choral music is scored for men's voices and orchestra: *Mississippi* (with mixed voices; 1916); *Fog Bell* (1916); *The Candle* (1931); *The Ballad of Beowolf* (1934); and *The Road Song of the Bandar-Log* (1935).

Eppert's instrumental works include a Violin Sonata (1912); two string quartets, no. 1 in E minor (1927) and no. 2 in G minor (1935); *Theme and Variations* for wind quintet (1935); two suites for wind quintet (1935, 1936); and a Quartet for woodwind (1937).

EPSTEIN, DAVID MAYER
b. New York, New York, 3 October 1930
d. Concord, Massachussetts, 15 January 2002

After graduating from Antioch College, Yellow Springs, Ohio, in 1952, Epstein earned a M.F.A. degree (1954) from Brandeis University, Waltham, Massachusetts, where he was a pupil of Irving Fine and Arthur Berger. Subsequently he earned a Ph.D. from Princeton University (1968), where he had studied with Roger Sessions, Edward T. Cone, and Milton Babbitt. He was also a private pupil of Darius Milhaud in composition and studied with Carl McKinley at the New England Conservatory, Boston.

Epstein studied conducting under George Szell, Max Rudolf, and Izler Solomon, and later conducted many of the major orchestras in America and Europe. He was music director of the Harrisburg Symphony Orchestra (1974–78) and music director of the Worcester (Massachusetts) Festival and Worcester Orchestra from 1976 to 1980. After teaching at Antioch College (1957–1962) and Sarah Lawrence College, Bronxville, New York, he became music director of Channel 13/WNDT (now WNET), New York City's public broadcasting station. He joined the music faculty of Massachusetts Institute of Technology, Cambridge in 1965, becoming a professor in 1971, then retiring in 1998. During his time there he conducted the MIT Symphony Orchestra for 33 years.

Epstein's principal orchestral works are *Movement for Orchestra* (1953); Symphony no. 1 (1958); *Sonority-Variations* (1967); and a Cello Concerto (1979). Among his instrumental music are two string quartets (1952, 1971); a Piano Trio (1953–55); *Piano Variations* (1961); *Fantasy Variations* for solo violin or viola (1963); String Trio (1964); and *Ventures* for wind ensemble (1971).

In 1974 he composed *Night Voices* for narrator, children's chorus and orchestra, commissioned by the Boston Symphony Orchestra. Other choral works include *Five Scenes* (Carl Sandburg) (1955); *Concord Psalter,* commissioned by the Concord Chorale in New Hampshire in 1979; and *Lament of Job* for three narrators, chorus, piano, cello and percussion (1980), written for the Illinois Wesleyan University, Bloomington.

Epstein's vocal music includes *Song of Isaiah* for voice, violin and piano (1953); *Four Songs* for soprano, solo horn and string orchestra (1960); and two song cycles on poems of Emily Dickinson, *The Seasons* (1956) and *Fancies* (1966).

Epstein's major honors include Ford and Rockefeller Foundation grants and awards from the Massachusetts Arts Foundation. He was the author of *Beyond Orpheus: Studies in Musical Structure* (1979) and *Shaping Time: Music, the Brain and Performance* (1995). Epstein died from complications of lung and liver disease in early 2002.

ERB, DONALD (JAMES)
b. Youngstown, Ohio, 17 January 1927

After war service in the U.S. Navy, Erb studied with Kenneth Gaburo at Kent State University, Ohio (1947–50) and at the Cleveland Institute of Music with Marcel Dick (1950–53). He also received lessons from Nadia Boulanger in Paris in 1952. From 1953 to 1961 he taught at the Cleveland Institute of Music. In 1961 he moved to Indiana University, where he completed a doctorate (1964) and worked with Bernhard Heiden. Following this he was at Bowling Green University, Ohio (1964–65), then returned in 1970 to the Cleveland Institute as Composer-in-Residence. He was Meadows Professor of Music at Southern Methodist University (1981–84) and taught again at Indiana University (1985-87). From 1987 to 1996 he was Distinguished Professor of Composition at the Cleveland Institute of Music. Erb has won many honors for his work, including a Ford Foundation Award in 1962 and a Guggenheim Fellowship in 1965. He was Composer-in-Residence at the Dallas Symphony Orchestra in 1968 under a grant from the Rockefeller Foundation.

Erb's musical style embraces atonality, and in some compositions he has made use of aleatoric and electronic devices. For orchestra he has written a *Chamber Concerto* for piano and strings (1958); *Bakersfield Pieces* for trumpet, percussion, piano and strings (1962); *Symphony of Overtures* (1964); Concerto for solo percussionist (1966); *Christmasmusic,* performed in Cleveland in 1967, *The Seventh Trumpet* (1969); *Autumnmusic,* with electronics (1973); *Treasures of the Snow* (1973); *Music for a Festive Occasion,* also with electronics (1975); Concerto for trombone (1976); Cello Concerto (1976); Concerto for keyboards (1978); Trumpet Concerto (1980); *Sonneries* (1981); *The Devil's Quickstep* for 12 instruments and tape (1983); and *Prismatic Variations* (1983). Later orchestral pieces include a Concerto for clarinet and orchestra (1984); Double Bassoon Concerto (1984); *Dreamtime* (1984); Concerto for Orchestra (1985); Concerto for brass and orchestra

(1987); *Solstice* for chamber orchestra (1988); *Ritual Observances* (1991); Violin Concerto (1992); and *Evensong* (1995).

Erb has composed several works for concert band, including *Compendium* (1962); *Space Music* (1962); *Reticulation* (with tape; 1965); *Concert Piece* for alto saxophone and band (1966); *Stargazing* (with tape; 1966); *The Purple-Roofed Suicide Parlor* for wind ensemble and tape (1972); *Cenotaph for E.V.* (1979); and *Symphony for Winds* (1989).

Among his numerous instrumental works are *Dialogue* for violin and piano (1958); three string quartets (1960, 1989, 1995); *Music* for brass choir (1960); *Music* for violin and piano (1960); *Sonneries* for brass choir (1961); Quartet for flute, oboe, alto saxophone and double bass (1962); Sonata for harpsichord and string quartet (1963); *Hexagon* for six instruments (1963); *Dance Pieces* for violin, trumpet, piano and percussion (1963); *Phantasma* for flute, oboe, string quartet and harpsichord (1965); Trio for violin, electric guitar and cello (1966); *Diversion for Two (other than sex !)* for trumpet and percussion (1966); *Reconnaissance* for violin, double bass and electronics (1967); *Three Pieces* for brass and piano (1968); *Trio for Two,* scored for double bass, flute, timpani and triangle (1968); *Harold's Trip to the Sky* for viola, piano and percussion (1972); *Music for Mother Bear* for solo alto flute (1972); Quintet for clarinet, violin, cello and electric piano (1976); *Mirage* for flute, double bass, trumpet, trombone, percussion, electric piano, electric harpsichord and electric organ (1977); and Trio for violin, percussion and keyboard (1977).

In the next decade he wrote a Sonata for clarinet and piano; *Déjà-vu* for double bass (1981); *Three Pieces* for harp and percussion (1981); *The Last Quintet* for wind quintet (1982); *Brass Quintet: St. Valentine's Day* (1982); *Aura* for string quintet (1982); *Fantasy* for cellist and friends (1982); *Rainbow Snake* for trombone, percussion, keyboards and tape (1984); *Views of Space and Time* for violin, keyboards, harp and two percussion (1987); *A Book of Fanfares* for brass quintet (1987); *Three Poems* for violin and piano (1987); *Watchman Fantasy* for amplified piano with digital delay and synthesizer (1988); *Five Red Hot Duets* for two contrabassoons (1989); *Four for Percussion* for celesta, harp, piano, four timpani and percussion (1989); and *Four Timbre Pieces* for cello and double bass (1989).

Recent instrumental music includes *Celebration Fanfare* for 13 instruments (1990); *Drawing Down the Moon* for piccolo and percussion (1991); Sonata for solo violin (1994); *Remembrances* for two trumpets (1994); *Changes* for clarinet and piano (1994); Harp Sonata (1995); *Sunlit Peaks and Dark Valleys* for violin, clarinet and piano (1995); *Dance, You Monster to My Soft Song* for solo trumpet (1998); *Three Pieces* for

solo double bass (1999); and *Three Pieces for Enterprising Young Flutist* (2000).

In many works Erb has employed pre-recorded tape. These include *Kyrie* for chorus and tape (1967); *In No Strange Land* for trombone, double bass and tape (1968); *Basspiece* for string bass and four-track prerecorded string bass (1969); *Klangfarbenfunk I* for orchestra, rock band and electronic sounds, performed in Detroit in 1970; *Z Milsci Do Warszawy* for piano, clarinet, trombone, cello and electronic sound (1971); and *Towers of Silence* for electronic quartet. Two multimedia creations are *Fission* for tape, soprano, saxophone, piano, dancers and lighting (1968) and *Souvenir* for tape, instruments and lighting (1970). *Suddenly It's Evening* for electronic cello dates from 1998.

In 1974, Erb was commissioned to write a work to celebrate the centenary of the Cincinnati May Festival. In response he composed *New England's Prospect* for narrator, triple chorus, children's choir and orchestra. Other choral pieces are *Cummings Cycle* for chorus and orchestra (1963); *Fallout* for chorus, narrator, string quartet and piano (1964); *N 1965* for chorus, viola, cello, double bass and piano (1965); and *God Love You Now* (T. McGrath) for speaker, chorus, harmonicas and percussion (1971).

ERICKSON, ROBERT
b. Marquette, Michigan, 7 March 1917
d. Encinitas, California, 24 April 1997

As a child Erickson learned to play the piano and violin, and he began to compose in his early teens. He studied with Wesley La Violette at the Chicago Conservatory. From 1938 to 1948 he took composition lessons from Ernst Krenek at Hamline University, St. Paul (B.A., 1943; M.A., 1947). He was also a pupil of Roger Sessions at the University of California, Berkeley (1950). Erickson taught at St. Catherine College, St. Paul, Minnesota (1947–53), San Francisco State College (1953–54), University of California, Berkeley (1956–58), San Francisco College of Music (1957–66), and the University of California, San Diego as professor of music (1967–87).

In his early works, Erickson made extensive use of serialism and counterpoint. After 1957 he experimented with a new approach to rhythm, combining different tempi and at times adopting improvisatory techniques. During the 1960s he worked with musique concrète on tape, both with and without instruments and voices.

For orchestra he wrote *Introduction and Allegro* (1949); Divertimento for flute, clarinet and strings (1953); *Fantasy* for cello and orchestra (1953); *Variations for Orchestra* (1957); a *Chamber Concerto* that employs both strict notation and improvisation (1960);

Sirens and Other Fliers (1965); *Rainbow Rising* (1979); *East of the Beach* (1980); *Auroras* (1982); and *Music* for trumpet, strings and harp (1997).

Instrumental works include two string quartets (1953, 1955); Piano Sonata (1948); Piano Trio (1953); *Duo* for violin and piano (1959); *Ramus,* a toccata for piano (1962); Concerto for piano and seven instruments (1963); *High Flier* for amplified flute (1969); *General Speech* for trombone (1969), which use a text by General Douglas MacArthur intoned down a trombone; *Oceans* for trumpet and tape (1970); *Loops* for Flute, clarinet, trumpet, saxophone, bassoon and marimba (1973); *Summer Music* for violin and tape (1974); *Taffytime* for large ensemble (1983); and *Solstice* for string quartet (1984–85).

Ricercar à 5 for trombone and tape (1966) combines the solo trombone with four trombones on tape. *Ricercar à 3* for double bass and tape (1967) similarly combines one live double bass with two on tape. *Down in Piraeus* (1967) is scored for soprano, chorus and tape. *Pacific Sirens* (1968) uses the sound of the sea electronically filtered and remixed with live instruments. For tape alone he composed *Roddy* (1966), with sounds produced by rods, and *Birdland* (1967).

Important vocal compositions are *Rilke Songs* (1940); *The End of the Mime of Mick, Nick and the Maggies* (James Joyce) for chorus (1963); *Cardenitas 68* for singer and six instruments (1968); *Do It* for double chorus, speaker, gongs and drone (1968); *The Idea of Order at Key West* to words by Wallace Stevens (1980) for voice and instruments; *Mountain* for mezzo-soprano and chamber orchestra (1983); and *Sierra* for tenor (or baritone) and chamber orchestra (1984).

Erickson wrote two books: *The Structure of Music: The Listener's Guide* (1957) and *Sound Structures in Music* (1975). For the last fifteen years of his life he suffered from polymyositis.

ETLER, ALVIN (DERALD)
b. Battle Creek, Iowa, 19 February 1913
d. Northampton, Massachusetts, 13 June 1973

Etler studied at the University of Illinois, Urbana; Western Reserve University (1931–36); and Yale University (1942–44). His teachers included Arthur Shepherd, Melville Smith, and Paul Hindemith. In addition to being a composer, Etler was an accomplished oboe player. From 1938 to 1940 he was a member of the Indianapolis Symphony Orchestra. He was awarded Guggenheim Fellowships in 1940 and 1963. In 1942 he taught at Yale before moving to Cornell University in 1946. The following year he joined the music faculty of the University of Illinois. From 1949 until his death in 1973, he was a professor at Smith College.

Alvin Etler.
Courtesy Smith College Archives.

For orchestra he composed *Music for Chamber* Orchestra (1938); two sinfoniettas (1940, 1941); *Passacaglia and Fugue* (1947); a Symphony (1951); *Dramatic Overture* (1956); *Elegy* (1959); *Triptych* (1961); and *Convivialities* (1968).

Etler wrote eight concertos: for string quartet and strings (1948); *Concerto in one movement*, commissioned to celebrate the 40th anniversary of the Cleveland Orchestra (1958); for violin and wind quintet (1958); for wind quintet and orchestra, performed in Tokyo (1962); for clarinet, brass and double bass (1962); for string quartet and orchestra (1967); for brass quintet, strings, and percussion (1967); and for cello (1970).

Etler's ability as an oboist led to the composition of many works for that instrument: Suite for oboe and string trio (1936); Sonata for oboe, clarinet and viola (1944); Quartet for oboe, clarinet, viola and bassoon (1949); *Introduction and Allegro* for oboe and piano (1952); *Duo* for oboe and viola (1954); two wind quintets (1955, 1957); Sextet for oboe, clarinet, bassoon and string trio (1959); Suite for flute, oboe and clarinet (1960); and *Six From Ohio* for oboe and string trio. Other instrumental works include two string quartets (1963, 1965); two clarinet sonatas (1952, 1969); a Sonata for bassoon and piano (1952); a Sonata for viola and harpsichord (1959); a Cello Sonata (1956); Concerto for violin and wind quintet (1958); Brass Quintet (1963); and *Sonic Sequence* for brass quintet (1967).

Ode to Pothos (1961) is a setting of the composer's words for a cappella double chorus. Also using his own text is *Onomatopoesis* (1965) for men's voices, wind and percussion.

Etler wrote a valuable book entitled *Making Music, an Introduction to Theory,* published in 1974.

EVETT, ROBERT
b. Loveland, Colorado, 30 November 1922
d. Tacoma Park, Maryland, 3 February 1975

Evett studied at Colorado College (1941–46), where he was a pupil of Roy Harris. In 1951 at the Juilliard School he received composition lessons from Vincent Persichetti. He was chairman of the music department, Institute of Contemporary Arts, Washington, D.C. (1947–50). In addition to his work as a composer, he was a music critic for the *New Republic* (1952–68) and wrote articles for several magazines. From 1970 to his death he was music journalist and book editor for the *Washington Star News.*

Evett's principal works are three symphonies (1960, 1965, 1965); five concertos, two for cello (1954, 1970) and one each for piano (1957), harpsichord (1961), and bassoon (1969); *Concertino for orchestra* (1952); *Variations* for clarinet and small orchestra (1955); *Anniversary Concerto 75* for orchestra (1963); and *The Windhover* for bassoon and orchestra (1971). His last completed composition was a dance score, *Monadnock* (1975). Evett also composed a Clarinet Sonata (1948); a Piano Quintet (1954); a Sonata for cello and harpsichord (1955); *Duo* for violin and piano (1955); a Viola Sonata (1958); a Violin Sonata (1960); a Piano Quartet (1961); a Harpsichord Sonata (1961); an Oboe Sonata (1964); *Fantasia on a Theme by Handel* for piano trio (1966); *Mary Dyer* for piano trio and percussion, performed at the University of Maryland in 1968; four piano sonatas (1945, 1952, 1953, 1956); and an incomplete Violin Sonata no. 2 (1975).

Evett's important choral works include a setting of the Mass for two voices and organ (1950); *Lauds in Honor of St. Ignatius Loyala* for men's chorus and orchestra (1964); *Office of Compline* for 8-part chorus (1966); *The Liturgical Office of Prime* for chorus (1968); and a *Requiem* for unaccompanied chorus (1973). Among his solo vocal music are *The Mask of Cain* for soprano, two baritones and harpsichord (1949); *Billy in the Darbies* for baritone, clarinet, string quartet and piano (1958); and *The Five Books of Life* for soprano, baritone and harpsichord (1960).

F

FAIRCHILD, BLAIR
b. Belmont, Massachusetts, 23 June 1877
d. Paris, France, 23 April 1933

After studying at Harvard University with John Knowles Paine and Walter Spalding (1896–99), Fairchild went to Florence where he was a pupil of the pianist Giuseppe Buonamici. He temporarily abandoned a career in music to enter the diplomatic service and acted as attaché in Constantinople and Teheran. In 1903 he settled in Paris as a music teacher, where he studied briefly with Widor, returning to the United States for the duration of the First World War. He spent the rest of his life in Paris.

For orchestra Fairchild composed a poem, *East and West* (1908); three symphonic poems inspired by his time in Persia, *Tamineh* (1913), *Zal* (1915), and *Shah Feridoun* (1915); *Three Symphonic Tableaux*; and three pieces for violin and orchestra: *Légende* (1912), *Etude Symphonique* (1922), and *Rhapsody on Old Hebrew Melodies* for violin and orchestra (1924). For the stage Fairchild wrote three ballets, *Dame Libellule* (1919), performed in Paris at the Opera Comique in 1921; *Le Songe d'Isfendier*; and *A Bel-ebat*, which was completed after the composer's death by Louis Aubert.

His choral music includes *Six Psalms* (1911) and *In Memoriam,* both for solo voices and chorus, and *Requiem* for tenor and male chorus. Among his instrumental works are three string quartets (1907, 1908, 1931); two violin sonatas (1908, 1919); a Cello Sonata (1907); *Concerto de Chambre* for violin, piano, and string quartet (1911); and a Piano Trio (1912).

FARBERMAN, HAROLD
b. New York, New York, 2 November 1929

Farberman received his musical education at the Juilliard School and the New England Conservatory,

Boston. From 1951 to 1963 he was a percussionist-timpanist with the Boston Symphony Orchestra under such eminent conductors as Pierre Monteux and Charles Munch. As a composer he has naturally taken a great interest in writing for percussion instruments.

For orchestra he has composed a Double Concerto for jazz trumpet, classical trumpet, and orchestra (1956); Symphony for percussion and strings (1956–57); *Impressions* for oboe, strings, and percussion (1959–60); *Elegy, Fanfare and March* (1964); *The Paramount Concerto* for piano and orchestra (1974); *The "You Name It' March* (1981); *Shapings* for English horn, strings, and percussion (1983); *A Summer's Day in Central Park* (1987); *Extended Progressions* for flute, percussion, and strings (1997); *The Little Boy (or Girl) and the Tree Branch* for narrator and orchestra (1998); and *Time Travel* for cello and orchestra (2000). In addition he has written concertos for bassoon (1956), timpani (1958), alto saxophone (1965), violin (1972), piano (1980), cello (*Millenium Concerto*; 2000), and oboe (*Concerto for Cathy*; 2001).

Many of his other works employ percussion: *Variations* for percussion and piano (1954); *Evolution* for seven percussion, soprano, and French horn (1954); *Variations on a Familiar Theme* for percussion (1955); *Greek Scene* for soprano, piano, and percussion (1957); *Music Inn Suite* for six percussion (1958); *Progressions* for flute and percussion (1959–60); Trio for violin, piano, and percussion (1962); *For Eric and Nick* for alto saxophone, tenor saxophone, trumpet, trombone, drums, vibraphone, cello, and double bass (1964); *The Preacher* for electric trumpet and four percussion (1969); *Alea,* a game of chance for six percussionists (1976); *Duo* for English horn and percussion (1981); *Combinations* for six percussionists (1984); *D'Obe* for timpani and marimba (1986); and *Early Hudson Valley Scenes* for two pianos and two percussion (2002).

As might be expected of a percussionist, Farberman has been influenced by jazz, reflected by works written for the medium: *There's Us, There's Them* (1967) for jazz orchestra; Concerto for jazz drummer (1986); Concerto for jazz vibes and orchestra (1991); *The Princess* for singer, narrator, and jazz orchestra (1989); and two pieces for jazz percussion ensemble, *The Dancers Suite* (1990) and *Ground Zero Paradiddle* (1990). Instrumental pieces without percussion include Quartet for flute, oboe, viola, and cello (1956); a String Quartet (1960); *Quintessence* for wind quintet (1961); *Five Images* for brass quintet (1964); *Three States of Mind* for six players (1964); and Trio for clarinet, trombone, and cello (1973).

Three musical curiosities are a setting of an extract from a newspaper entitled *New York Times, August 30th, 1964* for solo voice (1964); *Then Silence* for jazz ensemble, written in the same year as a memorial to the jazz saxophonist Eric Dolphy; and *If Music Be* for voice, rock group, orchestra, film, and audience (1969).

Farberman's two-act opera, *The Losers,* commissioned by the Juilliard School, is the story of a motorcycle gang in California. The plot describes uncontrolled violence that leads to meaningless destruction and death. It was performed at the Juilliard School American Opera Center in March 1971. An earlier one-act opera, *Medea* was performed in 1961 at the Boston Conservatory of Music. Currently he is writing a two-act opera *The Song of Eddie* for production in September 2004.

In 1985 he wrote a play with music, *The Mind on Trial,* performed in the following year in Colorado Springs. In addition he has composed music for two ballets, *Frankel Ballets* for the Dance Drama Company and *Crumble Ballet* for the Murray Louis Ballet Company, produced in New York as a double bill in 1964.

Solo vocal music includes *His Hero* for soprano and piano (1953); *Medea Suite* for mezzo-soprano and orchestra (1965); *The Lindsay Swing* (or *Fun City*) for soprano, baritone, and orchestra (1971); and *War Cry on a Prayer Feather,* based on Taos Indian poems for soprano, baritone, and orchestra (1975). He also wrote the music for the 1974 Academy Award-winning documentary film *The Great American Cowboy.*

Farberman has gained a reputation as an orchestral conductor and early in his career promoted concerts and recordings of contemporary American music. He has been conductor of the New Arts Orchestra, Boston (1955–63), music director of the Colorado Springs Orchestra (1967–68), Principal Guest Conductor of the Denver Orchestra, musical director of the Oakland Symphony Orchestra (1971–79), and Principal Guest Conductor of the Bournemouth Sinfonietta, England (1986). He has recently been awarded the Charles Ives Medal by the Charles Ives Society. He was founder and first chairman of the Conductors' Guild, the first organization for conductors in the United States. He has appeared with most of the leading orchestras in America and Europe and recorded the complete Mahler symphonies with the London Symphony Orchestra.

FARWELL, ARTHUR (GEORGE)
b. St Paul, Minnesota, 23 April 1872
d. New York, New York, 20 January 1952

Farwell studied electrical engineering at the Massachusetts Institute of Technology, Cambridge, and did not take up music until he had graduated from the Institute in 1893. He received composition lessons from Homer Norris and George Chadwick in Boston, and in 1897 went to Europe for two years where he was a pupil of Humperdinck and Pfitzner for composition in Berlin and Guilmant in Paris for organ. On his return to America in 1899, Farwell became a lecturer in music history at Cornell University, Ithaca, New York. In 1909 he was made supervisor of municipal music in New York and chief critic of *Musical America.* He was appointed director of the New York Music School Settlement in 1915. From 1918 he was acting head of the music department of the University of California, Berkeley and in the following year took over as director of the Santa Barbara Chorus. In 1927 he was elected head of the music theory department of Michigan State College, East Lansing, a post he held until his retirement in 1939.

Farwell's most important contribution to music was his study of American Indian music and his encouragement of American composers. His interest in Indian music began about 1900, after which date he spent much time traveling throughout the United States lecturing and making a through investigation of the music of different tribes. His large-scale works have Indian music as their basis: *The Domain of Hurakan* (1902); *Dawn* (1904); the popular *Navajo War Dance* (1923), originally for piano, but later orchestrated; and the suite *The Gods of the Mountain* (1927). Also for orchestra are three works inspired by folk songs: the symphonic hymn *March, March* (1922) and the symphonic song *Old Black Joe* (1923), both with optional chorus, and *Spanish Songs of Old California* (1923).

Farwell's other important composition, not founded on Indian music, is the *Rudolf Gott Symphony* (1934), which has its origin in a fragment of a symphony by a friend of the composer who died before that work could be completed. His other orchestral works include *The Death of Virginia* (1894); *Academic Overture: Cornell* (1900); *Symbolistic Study no. 2. "Perthelion'* for piano and orchestra (1904); *Symbolistic Study no. 4.* (1906); *Symbolistic Study no. 5.* (1906); *Chant for Victory* (1919); *Symbolistic Study no. 3.* after Walt Whitman (1905, rev. 1922); *Symbolistic Study no. 6. "Mountain*

Arthur Farwell.
Courtesy the Ruth T. Watanabe
Special Collections, Sibley Music
Library, Eastman School of Music,
University of Rochester.

Vision' for two pianos and orchestra (1931); the suite *Mountain Song* for chorus and orchestra (1931); *Prelude to a Spiritual Drama* (1935); and *The Heroic Breed: in memoriam General Patton* (1946).

For the tercentenary commemoration of the death of Shakespeare in 1916, he composed music for a masque by Percy MacKaye entitled *Caliban*, produced in New York. Among his other community-oriented stage works are a Christmas masque, *The Evergreen Tree* (1917); *Grail Song* (1925); and *Mountain Song* (1931).

Farwell composed *Fugue Fantasy* for string quartet (1914); a String Quartet in A (*The Hako*) (1922); a Sonata for violin and piano (1927, rev. 1935); a Sonata in G minor for solo violin (1934); a Piano Quintet in E minor (1937); a Cello Sonata (1950); and various piano pieces.

His strong support for the music of American composers led him to found the Wa-Wan Press, named after a ceremony of the Omaha Indians, which from 1901 to 1912 published many works by such composers as Gilbert, Stillman Kelley, Buᵗlinghame Hill, Shepherd, and himself. The project was financed by Farwell through lecturing, since the large music publishers were unwilling to risk printing new music. In 1912 he passed the Wa-Wan catalog over to G. Schirmer of New York.

Farwell's collected writings were published in 1995 under the title *Wanderjahre of a Revolutionist*

FELCIANO, RICHARD JAMES
b. Santa Rosa, California, 7 December 1930

After graduating from San Francisco State College in 1952, Felciano attended Mills College, Oakland, California, where he was a pupil of Darius Milhaud who subsequently took him to Paris here he spent two years at the Conservatory. Following private study with Luigi Dallapiccola in Florence (1958–59), he received his Ph.D. in 1959 from the University of Iowa, Iowa City, and in the same year was appointed professor at San Francisco College for Women. In 1967 he became the first resident composer at the National Center for Experiments in Television in San Francisco. That same year he joined the music faculty at the University of California, Berkeley in 1967. From 1971 to 1973 he was Composer-in-Residence to the City of Boston. In 1975 he served as resident fellow at the Rockefeller

Richard Felciano.
Courtesy the composer.

Foundation's International Study and Conference Center, Bellagio, Italy. From 1976 to 1980 he was Arts Commissioner for the City of San Francisco. In 1982 he moved to Paris, where he worked for a year at IRCAM. In 1987 he returned to the University of California, Berkeley where he founded the Center for New Music and Audio Technologies.

Felciano's work comprises four general areas: concert music, experimental video, environments, and liturgical music. In the latter he has pioneered the use of prerecorded electronic tape in conjunction with more conventional forces.

On Pentecost Sunday 1967, St. John Fisher Church in Pittsburgh was the scene of the premiere of two of his earliest liturgical works: *Double Alleluia for Pentecost Sunday* for unison men's voices, organ, and tape; and *Glossolalia,* a phonetically manipulated setting of Psalm 150 for baritone, organ, percussion, and tape. These pieces led to the subsequent compositions in the same medium: *Sic Transit* for boys' voices, organ, tape, and light sources (1970); *Out of Sight (The Ascension That Nobody Saw)* for chorus, organ, and tape (1971); and *Three-in-One-in-Three* for antiphonal choruses, two

organs, and tape (1971). Also in 1971 for Trinity Church, New York, he composed *Signs* for chorus, tape, and three filmstrip projectors. *Hymn to the Universe,* a setting of a text by Teilhard de Chardin for chorus and tape, was written for Westminster Choir College in 1973. To a commission from the Church of St. John the Divine, New York, in 1974 he composed *Te Deum* for mixed voices, three solo boys' voices, organ, piano, percussion, and three antiphonal trumpets. *Two Public Pieces* for unison voices and tape were composed in 1972. *Window in the Sky* for chorus, organ, and tape dates from 1975.

Dating from the same years are several works for organ and tape: *God of the Expanding Universe* (1969), *Litany* (1971), and *Stops* (1972). To a commission from the University of Hartford in 1972 he wrote *Ekagrata* for organ, two drummers, and tape. In 1980 he composed *Lumen,* a virtuoso duo for the American soprano Phyllis Bryn-Julson and her husband, the organist Donald Sutherland. *A Japanese Songbook* for soprano and electronics was written in 1992. Religious choral works without tape include *Short Unison Mass* (1966); *Songs of Darkness and Light* (1970); *Alleluia to the Heart of the Matter* for choir and organ (1976); *The Seasons* (1978); *Mad With Love* for chorus, organ, and handbells (1978); and *Mass for Catherine of Siena* for chorus and organ (1981).

In addition to many pieces for mixed chorus and several items for children's voices, Felciano has composed a number of significant secular choral works, including *Four Poems from the Japanese* for women's voices, five harps, and percussion to translations by Kenneth Rexroth (1964); *The Captives,* a setting of words by Thomas Merton for chorus and orchestra (1965); and *The Passing of Enkidu* for chorus, piano, percussion, and tape, based on the *Epic of Gilgamesh* (1976).

Felciano's important orchestral works are *Mutations* (1966); *Galactic Rounds* for large orchestra, based on Doppler shifts (1972); *Orchestra,* commissioned by the National Endowment for the Arts (1980); an Organ Concerto (1986); *Camp Songs* for chamber orchestra (1992); *Symphony for Strings* (1993); and *Overture Concentante* for clarinet and orchestra (1995). Among his many instrumental compositions are *Evolutions* for clarinet and piano (1962); *Gravities* for piano duet (1965); *Contractions* for wind quintet (1965); *Aubade* for string trio, harp, and piano (1966); *Spectra* for flutes and double bass (1967); *from and to, with* for violin and piano (1980); *Crystal* for string quartet (1981); *Of Things Remembered* for flute, violin, and harp (1982); *Salvadore Allende* for string quartet, clarinet, and percussion (1983); *Volkan* for five flutes (one player) (1983); *Introduction and Allegro* for double bass and organ (1984); *Dark Landscape* for English horn (1985);

and *Lontano* for harp and piano (1986). More recent chamber music includes *Constellations* for multiple brass (1987); *Shadows* for six players (1987); *Masks* for flute and trumpet (1989); *Palladio* for violin, piano, and percussion (1989); *Primal Balance* for flute and double bass (1991); *Cante Jondo* for clarinet, bassoon, and piano (1993); a String Quartet (1995); and a Wind Quintet (1996).

Instrumental pieces with tape include *Noosphere I* for alto flute (1966); *Crasis* for seven instruments (1967); *Background Music*, a theater piece for harp, sympathetic piano, and radios (1969); *Lamentations for Jani Christou* for 12 players, commissioned by the Fromm Foundation in 1970, *Frames and Gestures* (*Quintet Vineyards Music*) for string quartet and piano (1970); *. . . and from the abyss* for tuba (1976); and *Come Away With Me* for recorder (1984). Works including live electronics are *Sound Space for Mozart* for flute (1970); *The Angels of Turtle Island* for soprano, flute, violin, percussion, and live electronics on four channels (1972), commissioned by the Rhode Island State Council on the Arts; and *Chod* for violin, cello, double bass, piano, and percussion (1975).

Sir Gawain and the Green Knight, a chamber opera in two acts based on the anonymous fourteenth-century English poem, won the Fromm Foundation Prize at the Aspen Music Festival in 1964. In 1968 he produced a number of video works including *Linearity* for harp and live electronics, the first musical work ever to be conceived of video materials, and Trio for speaker, screen, and viewer for audience-participation.

Since 1967 Felciano has taken an increasing interest in the musical implications of the time-space continuum; the first piece to reflect this was *Nooshere II* for tape alone (1967). It was subsequently manifested in environments: *Sound Garden I* (1971), conceived for Boston's City Hall, uses 14 electronic sound channels and light sculptures by the composer. *Islands of Sound* (1975), commissioned by the Fort Worth Art Museum, is written for any number of carillons in close proximity or distant locations.

His interest in the music of the orient, already apparent in works such as *Crasis* and *Four Poems from the Japanese,* took its most substantial and challenging form in a work written for the International Musicological Society's Twelfth World Congress in 1977. *In Celebration of Golden Rain* (1977) combines Indonesian gamelan and occidental pipe organ, each in its respective tuning. Feliciano's more recent vocal music includes *Responsory* for male voice and interactive live electronics (1991); *A Japanese Songbook* for soprano and tape (1992); *Streaming/Dreaming* for soprano (1994); *Vac* for woman's voice, clarinet, violin, viola, cello, and piano (1995); and *Walden* for soprano and organ (or string quartet) (1998).

FELDMAN, MORTON
b. *New York, New York, 12 January 1926*
d. *Buffalo, New York, 3 September 1987*

Feldman studied composition with Wallingford Riegger and Stefan Wolpe. From 1950 he was strongly influenced by John Cage and the abstract expressionist painters who lived in New York. At this time, he incorporated into his works a considerable element of choice for the performers. He adopted a system of notation on a graph, beginning with the *Projection* series (1950–51), abandoning it three years later to readopt the method in a different form he called "free rhythm notation," which controlled pitch and duration, dynamics, and tempo, evident in *Piano* (*Three Hands*; 1957) and *Piano Four Hands* (1958). In most of his earlier works, Feldman indicates only approximate notation with freedom of interpretation regarding pitch and rhythm. Of his music, he wrote, "To me my score is my canvas, my space. What I do is try to sensitize this area, this time space." He developed what he termed "race-course notation," where each instrumental part is precisely notated but durations and vertical co-ordination remain undetermined. The *Duration* series of five scores for various instrumental groups (1960–62) is an example of this technique.

Feldman described his music as "being—existing in the eternal present! It often has no structure in a conventional sense; the tempo is usually slow and at a dynamic low." His great interest in abstract art produced a parallel in his own works. Through the 1950s and 1960s, he provided his compositions with totally abstract titles: *Intermissions I – VI* (1951); *Projections I – V* (1951); *Intersections I – IV* (1951–53); *Extensions I – V* (1951–53); *Directions I–V* for various ensembles (1960–61); and *Vertical Thoughts* for instrumental ensemble, two with solo soprano (1968). Most of his compositions are for instrumental groups, often with voices, although he wrote a few orchestral works: *Marginal Intersections* (1951); *Atlantis* for chamber orchestra (1959); *Structures* (1960–62); *In Search of an Orchestration* (1967); and *On Sound and the Instrumental Factor* (1969).

Other instrumental pieces include *Four Structures* for string quartet (1951); *Eleven Instruments* for 11 players (1953); *Three Pieces* for string quartet (1954–56); *Two Instruments* for cello and horn (1958); *Numbers* for nine instruments (1964); *Four Instruments I* (1965); *First Principles* (1966–67); *Between Categories* for two pianos, two chimes, two violins, and two cellos (1969); and *Four Instruments II* (1975).

Some pieces have comparatively exotic titles: *The Straits of Magellan* for seven instruments (1962) and *De Kooning* for piano, violin, cello, horn, and percussion (1965). *Out of "Last Pieces"* for piano and instruments (1961) is partly composed with details of pitch and duration left to the players. Each square on the notated paper represents one-eigthieth of a minute. The result is haphazard and explosive with kaleidoscopic effects of sound. *False Relations and The Extended Ending* was performed at the Palermo Festival in 1968. In essence, the two groups of instruments—piano, trombone, and violin, balanced against two pianos and chimes—perform two separate works, beginning together but later diverging.

From 1969, Feldman returned to comparative conventional notation with *On Time and the Instrumental Factor,* where pitches are fully notated but there is a free balance between the parts, producing a general blurred aural effect. He also began to undertake longer duration for his works: String Quartet no. 1 (1979) lasts one hour and forty minutes, while Quartet no. 2 (1968) is intended to last six hours. *Three Voices* (1982) for solo soprano and three sopranos on pre-recorded tape is an unbroken hour in length. Other instrumental pieces include *The King of Denmark* for solo percussion (1964); *The Viola in My Life I– IV* for solo viola and six instruments (1970–71); *Madame Press Died Last Week at 90* (1970); *I Met Heine on the Rue Furstenberg* (1971); *Three Clarinets, Cello and Piano* (1972); *For Frank O'Hara* (1973); and *Instruments I* (1974), *II* (1975), and *III* for flute, oboe, and percussion (1977).

Feldman's vocal music includes *Four Songs to e.e.cummings* for soprano, cello, and piano (1951); a cantata, *The Swallows of Salangan* for chorus and instruments (1960); *Intervals* for baritone and instruments (1961); *The O'Hara Songs* for bass-baritone and five instruments (1962); *For Franz Kline* for soprano, violin, cello, horn, chimes an d piano (1962); *Rabbi Akiba* for soprano and ten instruments (1963); *Christian Wolff in Cambridge* for chorus (1963); *Journey to the End of the Night* for soprano and four wind instruments (1965); *Chorus and Instruments I and II* (1963); *Chorus and Orchestra I and II* (1971–72); and *Voices and Instruments I and II* (1972). Also dating from 1972 is a choral work, *The Rothko Chapel,* written for the Institute of Religious and Human Development, Houston, Texas. Consisting of text-less choral chords, it was performed in a room devoted to the paintings of Marc Rothko.

The close similarity of titles has caused some confusion among Feldman's piano compositions. In addition to the early *Piano Piece,* he wrote five other works with the same title, distinguished only by their dates: 1952, 1955, two in 1956, and 1963. In addition he composed *Illusions* (1949), *Two Intermissions* (1950), *Intermission V* (1952), *Three Pieces* (1954), *Last Pieces* (1959), *Piano* (1977), and *Triadic Memories* (1981), all for piano solo. He also wrote *Two Pieces* (1954) and *Two Pianos* (1957) for two pianos and *Two Pieces* for three pianos (1966).

Orchestra, commissioned by the Scottish National Orchestra and performed in Glasgow in September 1976, became the first item of a trilogy completed by *Elemental Procedures* for chorus and orchestra, premiered in Cologne in January 1977, and *Routine Investigation* for six instruments (1976). *Oboe and Orchestra, Voice and Piano* was commissioned for the Holland Festival in 1976. On 13 May 1977 Rome Opera presented the one-act opera *Neither.* It is scored for solo soprano and orchestra to an original text by Samuel Beckett. Feldman also composed music for a radio play, *Samuel Beckett: Words and Music* (1987), with two narrators and ensemble.

Among his last works are five pieces for his friends: *For John Cage* for violin and piano (1982); *For Philip Guston* for flute, alto flute, percussion, piano, and celeste (1984), lasting four hours; *For Bunita Marcus* for piano (1985); *For Christian Wolff* for flute, piano, and celeste (1986), lasting three hours; and *For Stefan Wolpe* for chorus and two vibraphones (1986).

Feldman served at professor of music, holding the Edgard Varèse Chair at the State University of New York in Buffalo from 1972 to his death. He exerted a profound influence on composers of the next generation.

FETLER, PAUL
b. Philadelphia, Pennsylvania, 17 February 1920

In 1922, Fetler's family moved to Riga, Latvia, where he received his first music lessons. In 1936 he settled briefly in Amsterdam, spending the following year in Stockholm. In 1938 he studied in Switzerland before returning to the United States in 1939. He enrolled at the Chicago Conservatory prior to attending Northwestern University, Evanston, Illinois (1940–43), where he had been a pupil of David van Vactor. At this time he composed his first major work, *Symphonic Fantasy and Passacaglia* for organ and orchestra.

After the Second World War, Fetler acted as a Russian interpreter in Berlin and studied conducting with Sergiu Celibadache. Back in America in 1946 he became a student at Yale University, where his teachers included Quincy Porter and Paul Hindemith. He joined the music faculty of the University of Minnesota, Minneapolis in 1948 as an instructor in theory and composition, becoming professor of composition, and retired as professor emeritus in 1991. In 1952 he returned for a year to Berlin where he studied with Boris Blacher. He retired in 1990. He has received many awards, including one from the Society for the Publication of American Music (1953), two Guggenheims (1953, 1960), and two from the National Endowment for the Arts (1975, 1977).

Paul Fetler.
Courtesy the composer.

For orchestra he has composed four symphonies (1948, 1951, 1954, 1968). Other orchestral pieces include *Passacaglia* (1942); *Dramatic Overture* (1943); *Berlin Scherzo* (1945); *Prelude* (1945); *Orchestral Sketch* (1950); *Comedy Overture* (1952); *Gothic Variations* (1953); *Contrasts,* an ebullient four-movement work commissioned by the Minneapolis Symphony Orchestra in 1958; *Soundings* (1962); and *Cantus Tristis,* composed in 1964 in memory of John F. Kennedy.

Among his later orchestral works are two violin concertos (1971, 1980); *Three Poems of Walt Whitman* for narrator and orchestra (1975); *Celebration,* written to commemorate the Bicentennial (1976); Serenade (1981, rev. 1982); a Piano Concerto (1984); *Capriccio* for flute and small orchestra (1985); *Three Excursions,* a concerto for percussion, piano, and orchestra (1987); and Serenade for flute and strings (1994).

Among his choral music are *Six Songs* for mixed chorus (1952); the cantata *Nothing But Nature* (Ogden Nash) for soloists, chorus, and orchestra, written in 1961; and *Lamentations* for narrator, chorus, organ, and percussion, presented in Minneapolis in 1974. Other choral works include *Of Earth's Image* (1958); *Te Deum* (1963); *Jubilate Deo* for chorus and brass (1963); *A Contemporary Psalm* (1968); a sacred cantata, *This Was the Way* (1969); *The Words From the Cross* for chorus (1971); *Songs of the Night* (1975); *Song of the Forest Bird* (1978); *Missa de Angelis* for three choruses, organ, and handbells (1980); *The Hour Has Come* for two choruses, brass, and organ (1981); *The Garden of Love* for solo voice and orchestra (1983); *December Stillness* for voices, flute, and harp (1994); and *Up the Dome of Heaven* for chorus and flute (1996). A setting of Poe's poem *The Raven* for bass, clarinet, percus-

sion, and strings dates from 1998. Fetler's opera for young people, *Sturge Maclean,* was premiered in St. Paul in 1965.

His instrumental compositions include Sextet for clarinet, horn, and string quartet (1942); two string quartets (1947, 1989); two violin sonatas (1950, 1952); *Three Pieces* for violin and piano (1952); *Cycles* for percussion and piano (1970); *Dialogue* for flute and guitar (1973); *Pastoral Suite* for piano trio (1976); *Five Piano Games* (1981); *Rhapsody* for violin and piano (1985, rev. 1987); *Three Pieces* for flute and guitar (1985, rev.1987); String Quartet (1989); *Toccatas* for organ (*I*,1990; *II*, 1998); *Twelve Hymn Settings* for organ and instruments (1994); a Suite for oboe, clarinet, and bassoon (1995); and *Saraband Variations* for guitar (1999).

Fetler has taken a particular interest on the guitar, for which he has written several solo pieces: *Six Pastoral Sketches* (1974); *Three Venetian Scenes* (1974); *Five Pieces* (1974); *Six Autumn Songs* (1979); and *Folia Lirica* (1999). He has also composed *Three Impressions* for guitar and orchestra (1977).

FINE, IRVING GIFFORD
b. Boston, Massachusetts, 3 December 1914
d. Natick, near Boston, Massachusetts, 23 August 1962

Fine was educated at Harvard University (1933–39), where he was a pupil of Walter Piston, Edward Burlingame Hill, and Archibald Davison. He also studied conducting with Serge Koussevitzky and later went to Paris, where he attended the classes of Nadia Boulanger (1938–39). In 1939 he was an assistant and teaching fellow at Harvard, becoming an instructor in 1942 and an associate professor in 1947. In 1950 he was appointed assistant professor and chairman of the School of Creative Arts at Brandeis University, Waltham, Massachusetts, a position he held at his death in 1962. From 1946 to 1957 he also taught during the summer at Tanglewood. In 1950 he was a Fulbright Scholar in France and in 1951 and 1958 he was awarded Guggenheim Fellowships.

Fine's early works reveal a strong neo-classical influence from Stravinsky and Hindemith. These include *The Choral New Yorker* for chorus and piano (1944); *Toccata Concertante* for orchestra (1948); *Partita* for wind quintet (1948); and *Music for Piano* (1948). Fine's String Quartet of 1952 makes use of the 12-tone system. The song cycle *Mutability* for mezzo-soprano and piano, composed in the same year, has proved to be one of his most enduring works. The set of songs *Childhood Fables for Grown-ups* was commissioned in 1956 for the 50th anniversary of the Juilliard School.

Darius Milhaud, Irving Fine, and
Aaron Copland at Tanglewood, 1948.
*Irving Fine Collection, Music Division,
Library of Congress.*

In addition to the neo-Romantic *Notturno* for strings and harp (1951) and *Serious Song*, a lament for strings (1955), Fine composed two major works for orchestra, *Diversions* (1960) and his last work, *Symphony in Three Movements* (1962) for large orchestra, an extensive percussion section, and an important piano part; it was performed in Boston in March 1962. In addition he wrote a short piece for the Boston "Pops' Orchestra entitled *Blue Towers* (1959).

Fine was an experienced choral conductor; thus his writing for voices reveals a particular expertise and fluency. For choir and orchestra he composed *Chorus from Alice in Wonderland* (1942) and *Hymn: Ingrato Jubilate* (1949). In many respects his outstanding work in this medium is the cycle of settings of Ben Jonson poems entitled *The Hour Glass* (1949). It ranks as a masterpiece of a cappella choral writing and deserves wide recognition. He also wrote *An Old Song* (1953) for unaccompanied chorus.

Two important chamber works are a Violin Sonata (1946), in a Stravinskian neo-classical idiom, and *Fantasy String Trio* (1957), which combines serialism and the language of Bartók. He also composed a *Romanza* for wind quintet (1961).

Fine's sudden death at the age of 47 was a serious loss to music in the United States.

FINE, VIVIAN

b. Chicago, Illinois, 28 September 1913
d. Bennington, Vermont, 20 March 2000

Born of Russian-Jewish immigrant parents, Fine studied from the age of six at the Chicago Musical College (1919–22) and at the American Conservatory in Chicago (1925–31), where she was a pupil of Ruth Crawford Seeger and Adolf Wedig. After receiving lessons from Roger Sessions in New York (1934–42), she moved away from her former radically dissonant style. In addition to being a composer, she was a proficient pianist, a pupil of Abby Whiteside. She taught at New York University (1945–48), the Juilliard School (1948), and the State University of New York, Potsdam (1951–64). From 1964 to her retirement in 1987 she was a member of the faculty of Bennington College, Vermont. Among the honors she received were grants from the National Endowment for the Arts (1974, 1976), two Guggenheim Fellowships (1980, 1994), and election to the National Academy and Institute of Arts and Letters (1980). From 1961 to 1965 she was vice-president of the American Composers' Alliance.

For orchestra Fine composed *Prelude and Elegiac Song* for strings (1937); *Dance Suite* (1938); *Concertante* for piano and orchestra (1944); *Romantic Ode* for string trio and strings (1976); *Drama*, commissioned by the San Francisco Symphony Orchestra in 1982; *Poetic Fires* for piano and orchestra (1984); *Dancing Winds* (1987); and *After the Tradition* (1988) for chamber orchestra.

Her instrumental music includes her first performed composition, *Solo* for solo oboe, heard in New York in 1929; String Trio (1930); *Three Pieces* for two flutes (1930); *Prelude* for string quartet (1937); *Lyric Piece* for cello and piano (1937); a Sonatina for oboe and piano (1939); *Capriccio* for oboe and string trio (1946); Divertimento for cello and percussion (1951); Violin Sonata (1952); a String Quartet (1957); *Three Pieces* for flute, bassoon, and harp (1961); *Fantasy* for cello and piano (1962); *Dreamscapes* for three flutes, cello, piano, and percussion (1964); *Chamber Concerto* for cello and six instruments (1966); Quintet for trumpet, harp, and string trio (1967); Quartet for brass (1978); *Lieder* for viola and piano (1979); *Nightingales* for flute, oboe, violin two violas, and double bass (1979); *Music* for flute, oboe, and cello (1980); Quintet for oboe, clarinet, and piano trio (1984); and a Cello Sonata (1986).

As a pianist Fine wrote extensively for her instrument. Important works include a Suite in E-flat (1940); *Sinfonia and Fugato* (1963); *Momenti* (1978); Concertino for piano and percussion (1965); and Concerto for piano, percussionist, and strings (1972).

For the stage she composed *A Guide to the Life Expectancy of a Rose* for soprano, tenor, and instrumental ensemble, commissioned in 1956 by the Rothschild Foundation and later choreographed by Martha Graham. For a number of years she was pianist to various dance companies for which she provided scores, including *The Race of Life* after drawings by James Thurber, for piano and percussion, completed in 1937 for Doris Humphrey, and orchestrated in the following year; *Opus 51* (1938) for Charles Weidman; *Tragic Exodus* (1939) and *They Too Are Exiles* (1939) for Hanya Holm; *Alcestis* (1960) for Martha Graham, and *My Son, My Enemy* (1965) for the José Limón Company. Fine wrote two operas, *The Women in the Garden* (1977) and *Memoirs of Uliana Rooney* (1994).

Among her most attractive works are a number of songs, including *Four Elizabethan Songs* (1937–41); *The Great Wall of China* for soprano, flute, cello and piano (1947); *The Confession* for soprano, flute, violin, viola, cello and piano (1963); *Two Neruda Poems* for voice and piano (1971); *Three Sonnets* (Keats) for baritone and orchestra (1976); and *Ode to Purcell* for medium voice and string quartet (1984). *Missa Brevis* for four cellos and taped mezzo-soprano voice dates from 1972.

Fine's major choral compositions are *Psalm 13* for baritone, women's chorus, and piano (1953); *Valedictions* for soprano, tenor, chorus, and chamber orchestra (1958); *Epitaph (My Sledge and Hammer Lay Reclining)* for chorus and orchestra (1967); *Paean* (Keats) for narrator, female chorus, and brass (1969); *Soundings of the Nightingale* for soprano, women's chorus and nonet (1971); *Teisho* for small chorus and string quartet (1975); and *Meeting for Equal Rights, 1866* for narrator, solo voice, chorus, and orchestra (1976).

FINNEY, ROSS LEE

b. Wells, Minnesota, 23 December 1906
d. Carmel, California, 5 February 1997

As a child Finney learned to play the piano and cello. He was educated at the University of Minnesota, Min-

neapolis (1924–25), where he was a pupil of Donald Ferguson, and at Carleton College, Northfield, Minnesota (1925–27). In 1927 he worked his way to Europe, playing in a jazz orchestra so that he could receive lessons from Nadia Boulanger. On his return to the United States the following year he attended Harvard University. Back in Europe in 1931 he studied with Alban Berg. In 1936 he received lessons from Roger Sessions and spent the following year in Asola, Italy, where he studied with Gian Francesco Malipiero.

After his year at Harvard (1929), Finney was appointed to the faculty of Smith College, Northampton, Massachusetts where he taught until 1949. Later he was on the faculty of Mount Holyoke College, South Hadley, Massachusetts (1938–40), Hartt School of Music, Hartford University (1941–42), and Amherst College, Massachusetts (1946–47). From 1949 to 1973 he was professor of music and Composer-in-Residence at the University of Michigan, Ann Arbor. Finney was awarded Guggenheim Fellowships in 1937 and 1947 and a Pulitzer Traveling Scholarship for his Second String Quartet, composed in 1937.

Finney's important early compositions are a Violin Concerto (1933, rev. 1952) and several chamber works, including a Violin Sonata (1934); Piano Trio (1937); Viola Sonata (1937); three piano sonatas (1933, 1939, 1942); and two string quartets (1935, 1937). The principal influences on his music at this time were the composers Roger Sessions and Walter Piston.

Finney grew up in North Dakota singing folk songs to guitar accompaniment. This background has always been a part of his musical language. During the 1940s it found expression, due partly to his acquaintance with the music of Charles Ives, in his Third String Quartet (1941, rev. 1956). *Hymn, Fuguing and Holiday* for orchestra (1943) is a tribute to William Billings and is based on the hymn tune "Berlin." A third work reflecting the American musical heritage is *Pilgrim Psalms* for soprano, tenor, chorus, and organ (1945), a setting of 14 psalms from the Ainsworth Psalter of 1612. Also dating from this time is his Quartet Symphony, subtitled *Communique 1943,* completed in that year but not performed until 1962 by the Louisville Orchestra.

During the 1940s several of Finney's works were strongly influenced by the seventeenth-century concept of the circle, including *Spherical Madrigals* (1947), which has been widely performed, and *Three Love Songs to Words of John Donne* (1948).

Reacting belatedly to his work with Berg, Finney felt the need for greater chromatic integration in his music during the late 1940's. Though he never abandoned the concept of tonal orientation (pitch polarity) in the larger form of his works, the small details were determined by a serial technique. He called this process a "system of complementarity." His adoption of the 12-tone system is certainly not the product of a sterile academic dogmatism. The major work of his transitional period, leading to total serialism, is the Fourth String Quartet in A minor (1948). The Fifth Quartet (1948) and the Second Cello Sonata (1950) are highly chromatic but have a strong tonal organization. All his works after this time, with the exception of the song cycle *Chamber Music* (1951) and the choral piece *Immortal Autumn* (1952), have a serial basis.

Finney continued to write copiously for chamber ensembles, often for performance by the resident musicians at the University of Michigan. Important among these compositions are two piano quintets (1953, 1961); String Quartet no. 6 (1950); Quartet no. 7 (1955); Quartet No. 8. (1960); and a String Quintet commissioned by the Elizabeth Sprague Coolidge Foundation in 1958. Wider recognition came to him with the commission by Yehudi Menuhin of *Fantasy in Two Movements* for unaccompanied violin, presented at the World's Fair in Brussels in June 1958.

Except for a Piano Concerto (1948), Finney had written no orchestral music since 1943; he returned to the medium with the *Variations for Orchestra* (1957), based on a tone-row of Dallapiccola, to whom the work is dedicated. This impressive composition was premiered by the Minneapolis Orchestra in 1965. Symphony no. 2. was commissioned by the Koussevitzky Foundation in 1959 and was first performed by the Philadelphia Orchestra under Eugene Ormandy in the same year. In the following year, Finney completed his Third Symphony which also received its premiere with the Philadelphia Orchestra. His next orchestral was a Concerto for Percussion and Orchestra, commissioned for the centennial of Carleton College and composed in 1965 for the Minneapolis Symphony Orchestra. This is a brilliant exercise in virtuosity for four solo percussion players who are taxed to their limits in a remarkable range of musical effects. His *Three Studies in Fours* for percussion orchestra dates from the same year.

Finney's next orchestral composition was a *Symphony Concertante* commissioned for the Kansas City Philharmonic, completed in 1966 and performed in February 1968. Piano Concerto no. 2. (1968) was first performed in November 1972 by William Doppmann and the University of Michigan Symphony Orchestra. Symphony no. 4. (1972) was premiered under Sergio Comissiona in 1973 by the Baltimore Symphony Orchestra, which had commissioned it.

In several works composed at this time, the composer admitted to "memory-orientation." The first of these, *Divertissement,* written in 1964, recalls life in Paris in the 1920s. *Summer in Valley City* for concert band (1969) is based on the memory of summer festivities in the small North Dakota town of Valley City where Finney lived from the age of 6 to 13; it was first performed by the University of Michigan Band in April 1971. *Skating on the Cheyenne* (1977), commissioned by the Brooklyn College Band, was premiered in 1978. *Two Acts for Three Players* (clarinet, piano, and percussion), commissioned by G. Leblanc, Inc. and performed in 1970, was inspired by the memory of the early cinema. A work of this sequence, *Landscapes Remembered* for chamber orchestra (1971), was premiered at Cornell University in November 1972. It presents a collage of pictures that fade in and out and is based on folk songs that the composer had sung to his own guitar accompaniment.

Spaces for large orchestra (1971), commissioned by the North Dakota Arts Council for the Fargo Symphony, has three movements: *The Valley* (closed space), *The Prairie* (open space), and *The Sky* (outer space). Like the Fourth Symphony, it makes use in certain passages of indeterminate notation. A Concerto for alto saxophone and wind instruments (1974) was premiered by Donald Sinta and the University of Michigan Band in 1975.

The poetry of Archibald McLeish, a close friend, exercised a strong influence on Finney's music for voices. It first appeared in *Poems by Archibald McLeish* for voice and piano (1935) and again in the song cycle *Bleheris* for tenor and orchestra (1937). Three choral works make use of McLeish poems: *Pole Star for This Year* (1939); *Words to be Spoken* (1946); and *Edge of Shadow* (1959), commissioned by Grinnell College, Iowa and premiered in 1960.

Finney's major choral work is a trilogy, *Earthrise,* commissioned by the University of Michigan to celebrate its bicentennial, the building of Hill Auditorium, and the centennial of the founding of the School of Music. The first part is *Still Are New Worlds* (1962), using texts from Kepler, Harvey, Marlowe, Donne, Milton, Fontenelle, Henry More, Akenside, and Camus. It deals with man's fear once he realized that his world was not the center of the universe. It was premiered at the 1963 May Festival by the Philadelphia Orchestra and the Choral Union. The second part, *The Martyr's Elegy* (1967), is based on Shelley's "Adonais." It is concerned with man's persecution of man. The premiere was given at the 1967 May Festival by the same performers. The third part, *Earthrise,* using texts by Lewis Thomas and Teilhard de Chardin, tells of man's fear when he saw the earth as a living cell, rising in view from the moon. It was performed by the University of Michigan Choir and Symphony Orchestra on 11 December 1979 under Gustav Meier. Each work may be given separately or as part of the trilogy.

Finney organized the electronic music studio at the University of Michigan in 1963 after working at the Columbia-Princeton Studio in New York under Mario Davidovsky. *Three Pieces* for strings, winds, percussion, and tape was composed at that time and premiered in New York City in 1963. Except for an electronic tape to be used in the performance of *Still Are New Worlds,* he did not continue to work in this medium.

Later compositions include Violin Concerto no. 2. (1975), commissioned for the American Bicentennial and premiered by Robert Gerle and the Dallas Symphony Orchestra in 1976; *Variations on a Memory* for ten instruments, also commissioned for the Bicentennial by the Baltimore Chamber Music Society and premiered under Sergio Comissiona in 1975; *Two Ballades* for flutes and piano (1973); *Tubes I* for one to five trombones (1974); *Narrative* for cello and 14 instruments (1976); *Concerto for Strings* (1977); Quartet for oboe, cello, percussion, and piano (1979); and *Two Studies* for saxophone and piano (1981). At the end of his composing career Finney turned to a hitherto unexplored area, the stage. He wrote two operas, *Weep Torn Land* (1984) and *Computer Marriage* (1987), and three ballets: *Heyoka* (New York, 1981), *The Joshua Tree* (New York, 1984), and *Ahab* (1985).

Ross Lee Finney was the teacher of many of America's most distinguished composers, including William Albright, Robert Ashley, Leslie Bassett, George Crumb, and Roger Reynolds. Although Finney has not attracted the attention accorded many of his contemporaries—Barber, Copland, Harris, and Schuman, for example—there is an increasing awareness among performers and the musical public that he was a composer of considerable significance whose merit will soon be acknowledged. Of his many compositions, the *Orchestral Variations,* Second and Third Symphonies, Concerto for Percussion, and several of his instrumental and choral works deserve wider recognition.

FLAGELLO, NICOLAS (ORESTE)

b. New York, New York, 15 March 1928
d. New Rochelle, New York, 16 March 1994

Flagello was educated at the Manhattan School of Music (1946–50), where he was a pupil of Vittorio Giannini, and at the Accademia di Santa Cecilia in Rome under Ildebrando Pizzetti. He also studied conducting privately with Dimitri Mitropoulos. From 1950 to 1977 he was professor of composition and conducting at the Manhattan School of Music; from 1964 to 1965 he was also head of the composition department at the Curtis Institute in Philadelphia. In addition to his teaching commitments he was conductor of the Chicago Lyric Opera in 1961, the New York City Opera in 1967, and the Salerno Music Festival Orchestra. From 1977 he devoted himself to composition and orchestral conducting.

Flagello composed five operas: *Mirra* (1953), a three-act tragedy on a story by Alfieri; *The Wig* (1953)

in one act; *The Sisters* (1958), a one-act opera to a text by D. Mundy set in America in 1800; *The Judgment of St. Francis,* also in one act, performed at the Manhattan School of Music in 1966; and *Beyond the Horizon* (1983). He also wrote two operettas for children, *Rip Van Winkle* (1957) and *The Piper of Hamelin* (1970).

His output of orchestral music was considerable, including *Beowolf* (1949), four piano concertos (1950, 1955, 1962, 1975), *Concerto for Amber* (1951), *Symphonic Aria* (1951), *Overture giocosa* (1952), *Concerto Antoniano* for flute (1953), Serenade for small orchestra (1955); *Theme, Variations and Fugue* (1955); a Violin Concerto (1956); *Missa Sinfonica* (1957); a *Concerto for Strings* (1959); *Capriccio* for cello (1961); *Lautrec Suite* (1965); two symphonies (1967, 1971); *Serenata* (1968); *A Goldoni Overture* (1969); *Credendum* for violin and orchestra (1973); and Concerto for saxophone quartet (1985).

Flagello contributed many useful works to the repertory of wind instruments: *Lyra* for brass sextet (1945); *Episode and Chorale* (1945); Concertino for piano, brass, and timpani (1963); *Philos* for brass quartet (1968); *Ricercare* for 19 brass instruments and percussion (1971); *Prisma* for seven horns (1974); *Diptych* for brass trio (1979); and *Odyssey* for wind band (1981). His other instrumental music includes a *Divertimento* for piano and percussion (1960); a Sonata for harp (1961); *Burlesca* for flute and guitar (1961); a Violin Sonata (1963); Suite for harp and string trio (1965); *Electra* for piano and percussion (1966); and *Declamation* for violin and piano (1967). Among his many piano pieces are *Three Dances* (1945), *Three Episodes* (1957), *Prelude, Ostinato and Fugue* (1960), Sonata (1962), *Petits Pastels* (1968); and *Notturno* (1969).

Flagello's principal choral works are *Pentaptych* (1951); *Tristis Est Anima Mea* (1959); *Te Deum for All Mankind* (1968); an oratorio, *The Passion of Martin Luther King* (1968); and *Psalmus Americanus* (1976), all for chorus and orchestra. He also composed several pieces for solo voice and orchestra: *The Land* (Tennyson) for bass baritone (1956); *Five Songs* for soprano (1955); *L'Infinito* (text: Leopardi) for bass-baritone (1956); *Dante's Farewell* (1962); *The Contemplations of Michaelangelo* (1964); *Island in the Moon* (William Blake); and *Canto* for soprano (1979). *Remembrance* (Emily Bronte) for soprano, flute, and string quartet was completed in 1971.

FLANAGAN, WILLIAM (JR.)

b. Detroit, Michigan, 14 August 1923
d. New York, New York, 31 August 1969

Flanagan studied at the Eastman School of Music, Rochester, New York, with Burrill Phillips and Bernard

Rogers, and at Tanglewood with Arthur Honegger, Arthur Berger, and Aaron Copland. He also received composition lessons from David Diamond in New York. He became a perceptive writer on musical subjects and was a critic for the *New York Herald Tribune* (1957–60) and *Stereo Review*.

For orchestra he wrote a Divertimento for classical orchestra (1948), not performed until 1960, *Concert Overture* (1948); *Concert Ode* (1951); *Notations* for large orchestra (1960); and *Narrative* (1964).

His one-act opera *Bartleby*, based on a story by Herman Melville, was composed between 1952 and 1957 and performed in New York in 1961. He collaborated with Edward Albee on several works, providing incidental music for four of Albee's plays: *The Sandbox* (1961), *The Death of Bessie Smith* (1961), *The Ballad of the Sad Café* (1963), and *Malcolm* (1966). He chose Albee as librettist for his major composition, the opera *Ice Age*, commissioned by the New York City Opera for its 1966–67 season, but the score was left unfinished. Flanagan also set Albee poems in *Song for a Winter Child* (1950) and *The Lady of Tearful Regret* (1958) for coloratura soprano and ensemble.

Flanagan's other songs include *Times Long Ago* (1951), to poems by Herman Melville; *The Weeping Pleiades* for voice, flute, clarinet, and piano trio (1953), using a selection of verses from A. E. Housman's *Last Poems*; and *King Midas* for voice and orchestra (1961). Among his other songs are a group of five to words by Howard Moss (1959–62); a setting of Whitman's *Goodbye My Fancy* (1959); and *Another August* (James Merrill) for soprano and orchestra (1967). He completed four choral pieces: *The Waters of Babylon* for voices and string quartet (1947); *Billy in the Darbies* for chorus and piano (1949); *A Woman of Valor* for unaccompanied chorus (1949); and *Chapters from Ecclesiastes* for chorus and string orchestra (1962). At the time of his death he was working on *Silences* for female chorus and orchestra.

Flanagan wrote only three extended chamber works: *Divertimento* for string quartet (1947), a *Chaconne* for violin and piano (1948), and a Piano Sonata (1950). He wrote scores for two documentary films: *The Climate of New York* (1949) and *See Naples and the Island of Ischia* (1951).

A suicide, he left incomplete a book on American composers.

FLETCHER, H(ORACE) GRANT

b. Hartsburg, Illinois, 25 October 1913
d. Tempe, Arizona, May 4, 2002

Fletcher studied at the Illinois Wesleyan University (1932–35); the University of Michigan, Ann Arbor, where he was a pupil of Ernst Krenek; and in Toronto with Healey Willan. At the Eastman School of Music, Rochester, New York (1947–51), he was a pupil of Bernard Rogers and Howard Hanson, and in Cleveland he received lessons from Herbert Elwell. From 1945 to 1948 he conducted the Akron (Ohio) Orchestra. He taught at the Chicago Musical College (1949–51) and Arizona State University, Tempe from 1956 until his retirement in 1978; he held the title of professor emeritus there until his death.

For orchestra he has composed three symphonies (1950, 1982–83, 1994) and four concertos: no. 1 for piano (1953), no. 2, *Regency Concerto* for piano and strings (1966), no. 3 for winds (1969), and no. 4, *Multiple Concerto* for five winds and wind ensemble (1990). Other orchestral pieces include *Rhapsody* for flute and strings (1935); *Nocturne* (1935); *A Rhapsody of Dances* (1935); *Sailors' Songs and Dances* for strings (1941); *Musicke for Christening* for strings (1944); *A Song for Warriors* (1945); *An American Overture* (1945); *Panels for a Theater Wall* (1949); *A Pocket Encyclopedia of Orchestral Instruments* (1952); *Sumare and Wintare* (1956); *Dictionary for Orchestra* (1959); *Seven Cities of Cibola* (1961); *Retrospection (Rhapsody III)* for flute, strings, and tape (1965); *Dances From the Southwest* for strings and piano (1966); *Diaphony* (1968); *Diversion III* for strings (1971); *Celebration of Times Past* (1976); *Saxson II* for saxophone and strings (1977); Serenade (1979); *Symphonic Suite* (1980); and *Partita* for chamber orchestra (1985). For wind band he has composed *Diaphony* (1968), *Dyad* (1970), *Glyphs* (1970), *Aubade* (1974), and *A More Proper Burial Music for Wolfgang* (1977).

Fletcher's major choral work, *The Crisis,* with words by Tom Paine, dates from 1945. In addition he wrote a set of four sacred cantatas: no. 1, *O Childe Swete* (1965); no. 2 (1967); no. 3, *The Branch* (1970); and no. 4, *Judas* (1978). He has also set *Psalm 1* for chorus and organ (1979) and *The Time For Making Songs Has Come* for double chorus (1981). *Song of America* (1955) is scored for chorus and band. For the stage, he wrote two operas, *The Carrion Crow* (1946) for children and *The Sack of Calabasas* (1964–66), and two ballets, *Lomatawi* (1957) and *Cinco de Mayo (The Fifth of May)* (1972).

Fletcher's instrumental music includes five string quartets; sonatas for clarinet (1958), cello (1972), saxophone (1974), solo viola (1977), and solo violin (1983); *Caprice Argentine* for violin and piano (1934); *Nocturnes* for piano (1935); *Heralds* for brass and timpani (1949); *Tower Music* for brass choir (1957); *Prognosis 1 – 3* for brass quintet (1963–67); two pieces for percussion ensemble, *Uroboros* (1969) and *Quadra* (1976); *TR – IO* for flute, guitar, and piano (1971); *Ottocelli* for eight cellos (1971); a Cello Sonata (1972); Trio for flute, guitar, and piano (1973); *Saxson I* for saxophone

(1977); *Trio Bulgarico* for flute, clarinet, and bassoon (1980); *Palimpset* for flute choir (1980); and *Madrigals* for clarinet choir (1981). In addition there is a set of pieces entitled *Zortzicos* for various instruments: no. 1 for saxophone (1967), no. 2 for double bass and piano (1977), no. 3 for bassoon and piano (1979), no. 4 for cello and piano (1979), no. 5 for clarinet and piano (1980), and no. 6 for viola and piano (1980).

FLORIO, CARYL (REAL NAME WILLIAM JAMES ROBJOHN)
b. Tavistock, Devon, England, 2 November 1843
d. Morganton, South Carolina, 21 November 1920

At the age of 14, Robjohn was taken to the United States by his parents. He changed his name to Caryl Florio in 1870 in response to the objection of his family to his musical career. In New York he acquired a reputation as a singer and organist. He settled in Asheville, North Carolina in 1903, where he taught and conducted the church choir.

Florio composed two operas to his own texts, *Gulda* (1879) and *Uncle Tom's Cabin,* which was not a success at its premiere in Philadelphia in 1882. In addition he wrote two operettas, *Les Tours de Mercure* (1869) and *Suzanne* (1879), and a burlesque, *Inferno* (1870), based on the music of Offenbach. Among his choral works are five cantatas—*Song of the Elements* (1872), *The Bridal of Triermain* (1874), *The Crown of the Year* (1887), *Christmas Past and Present* (1889), and *The Night at Bethlehem* (1891)—and a quantity of church music.

He composed two symphonies, no. 1 in G (1887) and no. 2 in C minor (1887); *Marche der Feés* (1870); *Marche Triomphale* (1878); and a Piano Concerto in A-Flat (1875, rev. 1915). Most of his other compositions are chamber works, including a Piano Trio in D (1866); a Piano Quintet (1870); four string quartets (1872, 1877, 1878, 1886); four violin sonatas; two piano sonatas; Quartet for four horns (1877); *Réverie and Scherzo* for two clarinets, violin, and cello (1972); a Saxophone Quartet (1877); and a Quintet for four saxophones and piano (1879).

Florio was the author of *A Textbook of Practical Harmony,* published in 1892.

FLOYD, CARLISLE (SESSIONS, JR.)
b. Latta, South Carolina, 11 June 1926

Floyd began piano lessons at the age of ten. His principal musical training was received at Converse College, Spartanburg, South Carolina (1943–45) and Syracuse University, New York (1945–46, 1948–49), where he was a pupil of Ernst Bacon. He was also a piano pupil of Rudolf Firkusny at Aspen (1952, 1955). In 1947, he joined the music faculty of Florida State University, Tallahassee, where he taught piano and composition (1947–76). In 1976 he was appointed professor of music at the University of Houston, Texas, retiring in 1996. He was inducted into the American Academy of Arts and Letter in 2001.

Floyd has earned wide recognition for two important operas, *Susannah* and *Of Mice and Men.* His first work for the stage, the one-act musical play *Slow Dusk,* was performed in 1949 while he was still a student at Syracuse University. A second opera, *Fugitives,* was withdrawn by the composer after its premiere at Florida State University in 1951.

The two-act *Susannah* is a version of the story from the Apocrypha concerning the woman wrongfully accused of evil. The opera takes place in the present time in the Tennessee Mountains. As with all his operas, Floyd wrote his own libretto. After the first performance on 24 February 1955 at Florida State University, it quickly gained wider acclaim; the New York City Opera production the following year won the New York Critics' Circle award. It remained in the repertory for many years and was produced at the Brussels World's Fair in June 1958.

Floyd's *Wuthering Heights* is the second opera by an American composer to be based on Emily Bronte's novel; the first, by Bernard Herrmann, was composed in 1950. Floyd's opera was commissioned by the Santa Fe Opera Company and first performed by them on 16 July 1958. It was produced the following year by the New York City Opera.

Since 1960 he has composed seven more operas. *The Passion of Jonathan Wade* was produced by New York City Opera on 11 October 1962. The setting is post-Civil War South Carolina. The composer made extensive revisions to the work and the new version was performed in Houston in January 1991. *The Sojourner and Mollie Sinclair,* a comic opera in one act set in colonial America, was commissioned to celebrate the North Carolina Tercentenary. It was premiered on 2 December 1963 in Raleigh, North Carolina. A short story by Robert Louis Stevenson provided the basis for his next opera, *Markheim,* in one act, staged in New Orleans on 31 March 1966. It tells of a man tormented by his conscience and goaded to murder.

Of Mice and Men, a setting in three acts of John Steinbeck's famous novel, received much critical praise after the premiere in Seattle on 22 January 1970. The three-act music drama, *Bilby's Doll,* is based on Esther Forbes' 1928 novel, *Mirror for Witches.* The music was composed in 1975 and the work staged by the Houston Grand Opera Company in February 1976. *Willie Stark,* a music drama based on Robert Penn Warren's book, *All the King's Men,* was produced and co-commissioned by the Houston Grand Opera and the Kennedy Center in April 1981. Floyd's most recent opera is a comedy, *Cold Sassy Tree,* set in 1900. It is based on the novel by Olive Ann Burns, published in 1984, and was premiered in Houston in 2000.

Although he is best known for his operas, Floyd has written a number of important works in other media. Among his vocal works are *Pilgrimage,* a cantata for low voice and orchestra (1955) and the song cycle *The Mystery (Five Songs of Motherhood)* for voice and orchestra, on poems by Gabriella Mistral, commissioned in 1960 by the Ford Foundation for Phyllis Curtin. The monodrama *Flower and Hawk,* for soprano and orchestra to words of the composer, was completed in 1972. In 1983 he composed the song cycle *Citizen of Paradise,* settings of poems by Emily Dickinson for mezzo-soprano and piano or chamber orchestra. Floyd has also written *Death Came Knocking* for male chorus and *The Martyr* for chorus and orchestra. A large-scale choral work, *A Time to Dance* for bass, chorus, and orchestra, was commissioned by ACDA and premiered by the Westminster Chorus and the San Antonio Symphony Orchestra in March 1993.

Floyd's two orchestral works are *Introduction and Dance* (1967) and *In Celebration,* commissioned in 1971 by the Triennial Committee for South Carolina. Instrumental pieces include the ballet *Lost Eden* for two pianos (1952); *Theme and Variations,* also for two pianos, and a Piano Sonata composed in 1957 for Rudolf Firkusny.

FOOTE, ARTHUR (WILLIAM)
b. Salem, Massachusetts, 5 March 1853
d. Boston, Massachusetts, 8 April 1937

At the age of 15, Foote attended the New England Conservatory in Boston. Two years later he entered Harvard University, where he studied with John Knowles Paine. After graduating (B.A., 1874; M.A., 1875), he settled in Boston, where for the next 60 years he was a much-respected teacher of piano and composition. Briefly in 1883 he received piano lessons from Stephen Heller in Paris. From 1921 to 1937 he taught piano at the New England Conservatory. He was the first recipient of a master's degree in music from Harvard in 1875.

Foote was a professional organist, a pupil of B. J. Lang; he held the post of organist at the First Unitarian Church in Boston until 1910. He also appeared in public as a pianist, especially with the Kneisel Quartet from 1890 to 1910.

Although he attended the Bayreuth Festival in 1876, he received all his musical training in America, the first

composer of significance to do so. His own compositions were much influenced by the French tradition; his chamber music shows a strong affinity with Brahms and Dvořák.

The first of Foote's three orchestral suites, no. 1 in E major op. 12, was performed in 1886 by the Boston Symphony Orchestra. Suite no. 2 in D, op. 21 for strings and Suite no. 3 in D minor, op. 36 were composed in 1889 and 1896, respectively. Also for orchestra are a *Serenade for Strings in E,* op. 25 (1886); an overture, *In the Mountains,* op. 14 (1887, rev. 1910); *Symphonic Prelude to Francesca da Rimini* (after Dante), op. 24 (1891); a Cello Concerto (1894); *Suite in E for Strings* op. 63 (1909); and *Four Character Pieces after Omar Khayyam,* op. 48 (1912).

The only one of Foote's many compositions to have survived in performance to the present day is *Night Piece* for flute and string quartet (1914), which the composer arranged for flute and string orchestra on the advice of Pierre Monteux.

His chamber music includes three string quartets: no. 1. in G minor, op. 4 (1883), no. 2 in E, op. 32 (1893), and no. 3 in D minor, op. 70 (1911); a Piano Quintet in A minor, op. 36, performed by the composer and the Kneisel Quartet in 1898, a Piano Quartet in C, op. 23 (1891); two piano trios—no. 1 in C minor, op. 5 (1883), and no. 2 in B-flat, op. 65 (1908)—a Violin Sonata in G minor, op. 20 (1890); and a Cello Sonata, op. 76 (1915). Among Foote's piano pieces are *Five Poems After Omar Khayyam,* op. 41 (1898), *24 Preludes,* op. 52 (1904), three suites, and a number of pieces for the left hand alone. He also wrote music for the organ and over 150 songs.

For his three choral compositions, Foote set words by Longfellow: *The Farewell of Hiawatha,* op. 11 for baritone, men's chorus, and orchestra (1885), *The Wreck of the Hesperus* op. 17 (1888), and *The Skeleton of Armor* op. 28 (1891).

Foote wrote *Modern Harmony in its Theory and Practice* (with Walter R. Spalding, 1905); *Some Practical Things in Piano Playing* (1909); *Modulation and Related Harmonic Questions* (1919); and *An Autobiography* (1927, published in 1947).

FOSS, LUKAS (ORIGINALLY FUCHS)
b. Berlin, Germany, 15 August 1922

Foss began writing music at the age of seven and had his first published work issued when he was only 15. He studied piano and theory with Julius Herford-Goldstein in Berlin before the rise of Hitler forced his family to move to France in 1933. In Paris he attended the Lycée Pasteur and studied at the Paris Conservatory,

Lucas Foss, 2000.
Photo: Irene Haupt, courtesy Music Library, State University of New York, Buffalo.

receiving piano lessons from Lazare Levy and composition from Noel Gallon. He also studied the flute with Louis Moyse and orchestration with Felix Wolfes.

In 1937 he went with his parents to America, becoming a naturalized citizen in 1942. He attended the Curtis Institute in Philadelphia where his teachers included Rosario Scalero and Randall Thompson for composition, Isabel Vengerova for piano, and Fritz Reiner for conducting. He also studied conducting with Serge Koussevitzky at the Berkshire Summer Music Center, Tanglewood. From 1940 to 1941 he was a pupil of Paul Hindemith at Yale, but he soon adopted a personal style of a distinctly American flavor. He was a pianist with the Boston Symphony Orchestra (1944–50). In 1945 he became the youngest composer to be awarded a Guggenheim Fellowship. In 1950 he went to Europe for two years on a Fulbright Fellowship and Prix de Rome.

On his return to the United States early in 1953, he was appointed professor of composition at the University of California, Los Angeles, succeeding Schoenberg in the post. He continued to appear as a soloist and conductor with leading American orchestras. From 1963 to 1970 he was conductor and musical director of the Buffalo Philharmonic Orchestra, where he introduced many modern works into concerts each season. In Buffalo in 1963 he founded the Center for Creative and Performing Arts to encourage young musicians to pursue a career in new music. From 1972 to 1976 he was chief conductor of the Kol Israel Orchestra, renamed in 1974 the Jerusalem Symphony Orchestra. From 1972 to 1990 he was conductor of the Brooklyn Philharmonia, later renamed the Brooklyn Philharmonic Orchestra. He was also conductor of the Milwaukee Symphony Orchestra (1981–86). In 1986 he was the Mellon Lecturer at the National Gallery of Art in Washington, D.C. Over the last decades, Foss has appeared as a guest conductor for many major U.S. and world orchestras, including the Boston Symphony, Chicago Symphony, Cleveland Orchestra, Los Angeles Philharmonic, New York Philharmonic, Philadelphia Orchestra, San Francisco Symphony, Berlin Philharmonic, Leningrad Symphony, London Symphony Orchestra, and Tokyo Philharmonic

Foss's early works include *Four Two-part Inventions* for piano (1938); incidental music for Shakespeare's *The Tempest* (1939–40); *Set of Three Pieces* for two pianos (1940); and *Passacaglia* for piano (1941). His Piano Concerto no. 1 dates from 1941–42; it was originally scored as a Concerto for clarinet. In 1944 he completed a Symphony in G, which he conducted himself with the Pittsburgh Symphony Orchestra.

It was with the cantata *The Prairie* (1942–44) to words by Carl Sandburg that Foss first came to public notice. In this work, with its distinctly American character, Foss expressed his love for his new country. During 1944 he composed three ballets scores: *The Heart Remembers* for Doris Humphrey and Charles Weidman, *Within These Walls* for Virginia Johnson, and *The Gift of the Magi* for American Ballet Theater. Also written in 1944 was *Ode* for orchestra, performed by George Szell and the New York Philharmonic Orchestra; the work was revised in 1958.

In 1945 Foss composed the first of his two biblical cantatas, *Song of Anguish* for baritone and orchestra, a setting of verses from the Book of Isaiah. In 1946 he completed the second cantata, *Song of Songs* for soprano and orchestra, which betrays some influence of the neo-classicism of Stravinsky. In the second movement, "Come My Beloved," Foss deliberately imitates the pastoral form of a Bach aria with an obbligato oboe. The last movement is written entirely in quarter notes with no counterpoint, a surprisingly simple yet bold step for a young composer. *Song of Songs* was commissioned by the League of Composers and first performed on 7 March 1947 by Ellabelle Davis and the Boston Symphony Orchestra conducted by Koussevitzky.

Pantomime for orchestra, excerpted from *The Gift*

of the Magi, received its first performance in Baltimore in November 1946. The assassination of Gandhi was the inspiration for *Ricordare,* heard in Boston in December 1948. A neo-classical Oboe Concerto, written in 1947-48, was performed on radio in February 1950. Chamber music of this decade includes *Composer's Holiday* for violin and piano (1946), String Quartet no. 1. in G (1947), and *Capriccio* for cello and piano (1948). Foss was himself the soloist in the premiere of his Piano Concerto no. 2 in Venice in 1951. He revised the score in 1953 and the work won the New York Music Critics' Circle Award in the following year.

The one-act opera *The Jumping Frog of Calaveras County* indicates the composer's ability to respond to the humorous story by Mark Twain with witty music. It was first produced at Indiana University, Bloomington on 18 May 1950. In *A Parable of Death,* on poems of Rilke for narrator, tenor solo, chorus, and orchestra (1952), Foss reveals a more personal voice. It was commissioned by the Louisville Orchestra and performed in March 1953. An opera in three acts, *Griffelkin* (libretto: Alastair Reid), was commissioned by NBC and performed on television in November. (In 1986 the composer extracted an orchestral suite from the score.) *Psalms* for chorus and two pianos (or orchestra), composed in 1957, is further evidence of the composer's interest in setting texts from the Old Testament. *A Symphony of Chorales,* based on Bach chorales, was written in 1958 as a tribute to Albert Schweitzer.

The miniature opera *Introductions and Goodbyes* marks the last of Foss' purely tonal works. Composed for the Spoleto Festival in 1960, it is a setting of a single-page libretto by Gian-Carlo Menotti evoking a cocktail party where no conversation takes place except the introductions of the host and the hellos and goodbyes of the guests. The whole piece lasts only nine minutes.

At this time Foss altered his entire approach to music composition and performance. He abandoned the classical forms and tonality that had served in his previous works. The principal influence upon this change was his formation of an ensemble in 1957 at the University of California, Los Angeles, which toured the United States and Europe to demonstrate his method of improvisation for chamber music players. Through this experiment he hoped to free performers from being rigidly linked to the printed notes.

Partly from this system came *Time Cycle,* a setting of four texts concerned with time, clocks, and bells: W. H. Auden's "We're Late," A. E. Housman's "When the bells justle in the tower," extracts from Kafka's *Diaries,* and Nietzsche's "O Man Take Heed" from *Thus Spake Zarathustra.* In its first version (1960), the songs were composed for soprano and orchestra. Between the songs, the Foss Ensemble provided optional improvisations. It was in this version that *Time Cycle* won the New York Music Critics' Circle Award in 1961. In 1963 the composer rescored the song accompaniment for the ensemble, omitting the interludes and improvisations.

Another major creation, *Echoi,* was composed for the group between 1960 and 1963. It is an instrumental tour de force, incorporating the use of prerecorded tapes of the Ensemble. The title *Echoi* is intended to imply the imitation of musical ideas among the performers. Each instrumentalist is provided with a full score so that he can follow what the others play. *Echoi* proved to be a pivotal composition in Foss' musical development. The music was used for a ballet performed by Ballet Rambert at the Warwick Arts Centre, England on 18 January 1979.

In *Elytres,* Foss expanded his instrumental forces while preserving the techniques used in *Time Cycle* and *Echoi.* The title refers to the heavy exterior wings that protect the lighter translucent wings of certain insects. The work is scored for solo flute, two violins, distant violins, percussion, harp, vibraphone, and piano. The choice elements produce different results in each performance. *Elytres* was first heard in the Hollywood Bowl in December 1964.

Fragments of Archilochus (1965) extends Foss's improvisational procedures to include voices and makes much use of speech. The work randomly sets scraps of ancient Greek by the satirist Archilochus (714–675 B.C.) dealing with life, death, love, and war. It is scored for four choruses, two speakers with megaphones, countertenor, guitar, mandolin, and percussion. Foss composed *Fragments of Archilochus* to a commission from the Spring Arts Festival at the State University of New York at Potsdam, and it was performed there on 3 February 1967. *For 24 Winds* was composed in 1966 for the Institute of Culture and Fine Arts, Caracas, Venezuela, and performed there in April 1966.

Foss's next work, *Phorion,* was commissioned by the Association of Women's Committees and first performed in April 1967 by the New York Philharmonic Orchestra under Leonard Bernstein. The title, from the Greek, means "stolen goods," a reference to its thematic origin. Here the choice method is applied to the Prelude from Bach's Partita in E major for unaccompanied violin. The original music is played complete against a manipulation of the same material by the other instruments in an ingeniously virtuoso manner. The intricate scoring is for strings, electric organ, amplified harpsichord, amplified harp, electric harp, winds, and percussion. *Phorion* later became the third movement of *Baroque Variations,* where the other two movements are based in a similar way on the Larghetto from Handel's Concerto Grosso op. 6, no. 12 and Scarlatti's Sonata no. 23 in E for keyboard.

For Mstislav Rostropovich, Foss composed *Concert*

for cello and orchestra. As with *Baroque Variations,* music of an earlier period provides material for part of the work. The last movement is based on the Sarabande from Bach's Cello Suite no. 5. Pre-recorded tape is also employed in places. *Concert* was first performed at Carnegie Hall, New York in March 1967 by Rostropovich with the London Symphony Orchestra conducted by the composer.

Non-Improvisation, Foss's next composition, is scored for electronic organ and electronic tape. It contains long dissonant drones that drown out scraps of Bach's D minor Concerto for keyboard. It was first heard at the Warsaw Festival in 1967. Also dating from 1967 is *Etudes* for organ, commissioned for the new organ at Cornell College, Mount Vernon, Iowa. It was premiered by Robert Triplett in November of that year.

Paradigm "for my friends" (1968) employs five musicians: percussion/director, electric guitar, violin, clarinet, and cello, with a sixth part provided by tape recorder. The performers have musical notes to play and words to speak, whisper, and shout. They are given cues and instructions but within these there is a large degree of choice. The words are often used as musical notes. *Geod* for orchestra is scored for four separate instrumental groups, each with its own music and conductor. In some respects it resembles Stockhausen's *Gruppen* with its interplay of forces. The principal conductor indicates to the directors of each group when their music should be audible. Foss has described this work as "a musical action without end, without development, without rhetoric, without events." It was first performed under the composer's direction in December 1969. *MAP* (Musicians at Play), composed in 1970, is a musical game for four instrumentalists, lasting an entire evening. It uses tape with thematic reiterations as a stimulus for musical reactions from the players. It was first performed on 16 June 1970 in St. Paul de Vence and revised in 1973.

In 1972 Foss produced four important works. *Cave of the Winds* was composed in Italy for the Dorian Quintet, which had commissioned it and gave the first performance at Hunter College, New York, on 14 December 1972. It makes use of multiphonics on the woodwind instruments. *Ni Bruit, Ni Vitesse* is scored for two percussionists who play their instruments inside two grand pianos. *Three Airs for Frank O'Hara's Angel* is a setting of O'Hara's poems for soprano, female chorus, and instrumental ensemble. The poet Frank O'Hara, a friend of Foss, died tragically on 24 July 1966. This work was written for a concert in his memory given at the Whitney Museum, New York. The fourth composition dating from 1972 is *Orpheus,* described as a concerto for cello (or viola or violin) and an orchestra comprising strings, piano strings, oboes,

harps, and chimes. It is dedicated to a friend, the cellist Gregor Piatigorsky.

For the 50th anniversary of the Turkish Republic in 1973, Foss composed *Fanfare.* In this piece the orchestral players are required to walk about on the stage and among the audience while playing. Two other works dating from the same year are *Divertissement pour Mica* (String Quartet no. 2) and *Lamdeni* (*Teach Me*) for chorus and keyboard or plucked instruments. In 1974 the Ford Foundation commissioned a Percussion Concerto. As in *Paradigm,* the percussionist is called upon to be more than soloist. In the words of the composer: "Anything he does affects the rest of the ensemble (a full orchestra or a group of 26 musicians). Wherever he turns or walks, a musical activity comes to pass, as if he held a magic wand. Sounds emerge, submerge; percussive machine-like fragments form around him. He walks to various areas on the stage, entering into a dialogue now with the violins, now with the strings or woodwind or brass. He battles with the timpanist, playing simultaneously with him (on the same timpani)." The concerto is subtitled "All the Angels Have Big Feet," a quotation from Ezra Pound.

String Quartet no. 3 (1975), written for the Concord Quartet, is described by the composer as his most extreme work. In his view, "it is themeless, tuneless and restless." It was premiered at Alice Tully Hall, New York on 15 March 1976. Two orchestral works followed in 1975, *Folk Song* and *Salomon Rossi Suite* for small orchestra, the latter based on music by a sixteenth-century Italian composer. *American Cantata* was commissioned in 1976 by the American Choral Directors' Association to celebrate the Bicentennial. Arieh Sachs provided a collage text from American poetry, political speeches, and other sources, including an extract from the Wall Street Journal, to create a drama. The protagonist is a tenor "put on trial" by the chorus. In this work Foss employs a potpourri of styles, ranging from Renaissance music to modern rock and from his early works to the latest experiments. It was first performed at Interlochen, Michigan, on 24 July 1976 by the American Choral Directors' Association Chorus with the World Youth Orchestra under the composer.

Curriculum Vitae for solo accordion was commissioned in 1977 by the American Accordionists Society. In the same year Foss composed *Music for Six* for any six instruments, for which there are separate written parts and instructions but no score. In 1978 he completed a Brass Quintet which he adapted first as a choral work entitled *. . . And then the rocks on the mountain began to shout* (a quotation from Charles Ives) and in 1979 as *Quintet for Orchestra,* performed by the New York Philharmonic under Leonard Bernstein. *Thirteen Ways of Looking at a Blackbird,* a setting of the poem by Wallace Stevens, was commissioned by radio

WFMT in Chicago in 1978. It is scored for mezzo-soprano, flute, piano, and a percussionist who plays the strings of the piano with various instruments.

Later orchestral works include *Night Music for John Lennon* for brass quintet and orchestra (1979–80); *Dissertation* (1981), revised a year later as *Exeunt*; *Renaissance Concerto* for flute and orchestra (1985–86); *For Lenny* (*Variations on New York, New York*) for piano and orchestra (1989); *Guitar Concerto: American Landscapes* (1989); *Celebration* (*American Fanfare*), commissioned for the 50th anniversary of the Berkshire Summer Music Center (1990); Symphony no. 3, *Symphony of Sorrows* (1991–92); Concerto for piano, left-hand for Leon Fleisher (1993); and Symphony No 4, *Window to the Past,* commissioned by the City College of New York in 1994 and performed by the Boston University Symphony Orchestra in the following year.

More recent instrumental pieces include *Round a Common Center* for piano quartet or piano quintet, with or without a solo mezzo-soprano (1979); *Solo Observed* for piano, electric organ, cello, and vibraphone (1982); *Percussion Quartet* (1983); Trio for violin, horn, and piano (1983); *Saxophone* Quartet (1985); *Embros* for three winds, three brass, percussion, strings, and electric instruments (1985); *Tashi* for clarinet, string quartet, and piano (1987); *Central Park Reel* for violin and piano (1987); *Chaconne* for guitar (1987); and String Quartet no. 4 (2003).

Among Foss's vocal compositions are *Measure for Measure*, for tenor and chamber orchestra (1980), derived from the *Salomon Rossi Suite*; *De Profundis* for chorus (1982); and *With Music Strong* for chorus and orchestra (1988).

FOSTER, STEPHEN COLLINS
b. Laurenceville, Pittsburgh, Pennsylvania, 4 July 1826
d. New York, New York, 13 January 1864

Although he learned to play the flute when young, Foster had no formal musical training. After leaving school he went into business and in 1846 moved to Cincinnati to become an accountant. However, he soon gave up any intention of a career in this direction. His first song to be published, *Open Thy Lattice, Love,* appeared in 1844 when he was only 17 years old. Despite family opposition, Foster soon began to devote his energies to composing. His fluency in this respect resembles that of Schubert. Like Schubert, Foster seems to have adopted a casual attitude towards his music at first. At the age of 20 he gave a number of his songs, including *Oh Susanna,* as a present to a Pittsburgh publisher. The publisher subsequently earned over $10,000 from them, but the composer received nothing.

Many of Foster's songs were written for minstrel shows. Among these was *Old Folks at Home* (*Way Down Upon the Swanee River*), which has been accepted into the corpus of American folk music. It was written for E. P. Christy of the Christy Minstrels and it was Christy's name, not that of Foster, which appeared as its composer on the first printed copies in 1851, although this time the royalties came to Foster. Not until 1879 did Foster's' name appear on the music. Foster's careless attitude to business caused him to give away manuscripts of his songs that were later published by others as their own work. In 1849 he signed a contract with Firth, Pond and Co., which finally gave him some financial stability.

Among his 189 songs, for which he also wrote the words, about 20 are still heard frequently today, one hundred and fifty years after they were composed. These include *Jeanie With the Light Brown Hair, Massa's in the Cold, Cold Ground, Camptown Races* and *Old Black Joe. Beautiful Dreamer* dates from 1863, only a few months before his death.

Although he received quite considerable sums of money from royalties and outright payments, probably at least $15,000, Foster became increasingly in debt, and took to drink. In the last few months of his short life, he was a pathetic figure; his wife and child left him, he owed money, and he was ill. In January 1864, while in poor health, he had an accident in his cheap lodging house; he died a few days later in Bellevue Hospital, New York, aged 37.

FRACKENPOHL, ARTHUR (ROLAND)
b. Irvington, New Jersey, 23 April 1924

At the Eastman School of Music, Rochester, New York (B.A., 1947; M.A., 1949), Frackenpohl studied with Bernard Rogers. In 1950, he also received composition lessons from Darius Milhaud at Tanglewood and Nadia Boulanger in Fontainebleau, France. In 1957 he received his doctorate from McGill University, Montreal. In 1949 he joined the Music Faculty of Crane School of Music, State University of New York at Potsdam, becoming professor in 1961 and retiring in 1985.

Frackenpohl's one-act chamber opera *Domestic Relations* (*To Beat or Not to Beat*), completed in 1964, is based on an O. Henry novel, *Harlem Tragedy.*

For orchestra Frackenpohl has composed *A Jubilant Overture* (1957); *Allegro Scherzando* (1957); Overture in D (1957); Symphony no. 1 (1957); *Symphony for Strings* (1960); *Largo and Allegro* for horn and strings (1962); *Short Overture* (1965); Concertino for tuba and strings (1967); Suite for trumpet and strings (1970); *Flute Waltz* for three flutes and orchestra (1979); and

Arthur Frackenpohl.
Courtesy the composer.

Concerto for brass quintet and orchestra (1986). He has also written three pieces for concert band: *Allegro Giocoso* (1956), *American Folk Song Suite* (1973), and *Variations* for tuba and winds (1973); *Academic Processional March*; *On the Go*; *Cantilena*; *Chorale Episode*, *Rondo Marziale*; and *Seaway Valley*.

Among Frackenpohl's many instrumental works are a *Brass* Quartet (1950); *March of Peace* for brass ensemble and keyboard (1960); two brass quintets (1963, 1972); Trombone Quartet (1967); Brass Trio (1967); Suite for wind quintet (1969); *Two Short Pieces* for string quartet (1970); String Quartet (1971); *Introduction and Rag* for four pianos (16 hands) (1972); *Breviates* for brass ensemble (1973); Trio for oboe, bassoon, and horn (1982); Tuba Sonata (1983); Sonata for clarinet and piano (1997); *Woodwork by Pastiche*, for clarinet, trumpet, percussion, and piano (1999); and *Au Sable Valley Suite* for wind ensemble (2000).

Frackenpohl's choral music comprises a cantata, *The Natural Superiority of Men* (J. Pearson) for female voices and piano (1962); *Make a Joyful Noise* for chorus, brass quartet, and organ (1963); *Seven Essays on Women* (Ogden Nash), a cantata for solo voices, men's chorus, and piano (1967); *Winter Celebration* for mixed voices and piano (1968); *Meet Job* for mixed voices and winds (1978); a cantata, *A Child This Day* for solo voices, chorus, narrator, brass, and organ (1980); Mass for chorus and orchestra (1990); and *Te Deum* for chorus and orchestra. His solo vocal music includes *Recent Rulings*, to words from the *New York Times* (1965); *Odd Owls* (1966); and *First Corinthians* (1980). His other vocal music includes *Two Songs for Soprano and Organ* (1999)

Frackenpohl is the author of a book, *Harmonization at the Piano,* first published in 1962 (6th edition, 1990).

FRANCO, JOHAN HENRI GUSTAV
b. Zaandam, Holland, 12 July 1908
d. Virginia Beach, VA, April 14, 1988

Franco studied privately with Willem Pijper from 1928 to 1933. In 1934 he went to America and served in the U.S. Army in the Second World War, becoming a naturalized citizen in 1942. On his marriage to the writer Eloise Bauder Laurischeff in 1948, he settled in Virginia Beach, Virginia where he devoted himself solely to composition.

He composed five symphonies: 1933, 1939, 1939, 1950 (tenor and orchestra), and 1958 (*The Cosmos*). Also for orchestra he wrote two symphonic poems, *Peripetie* (1935) and *Baconiana* (1942); an *Elegy* for strings (1933); a *Suite for Strings* (1945); and six *Concerti Lirici:* no. 1 for violin (1937), no. 2 for cello (1962), no. 3 for piano (1967), no. 4 for solo percussion (1970), no. 5 for guitar (1971), and no. 6 for flute (1974), all with orchestral accompaniment. Other works for solo instruments are *Serenata Concertante* for piano and chamber orchestra (1938) and *Fantasy* for cello and orchestra (1951).

To words by his wife, he composed a cantata, *As the Prophets Foretold* (1955) for soloists, chorus, brass, and carillon, and an oratorio, *The Stars Look Down* (1957). Among his other vocal works are *The Virgin Queen's Dream Monologue* for soprano and orchestra (1947, orchestrated in 1952) and the song cycles *Songs of the Spirit* for soprano and wind quintet (1959), *Twelve Words* (1965), and *Sayings of the Word* (1968). *Ode* for men's voices and symphonic band (1968) won the 1974 Delius Composition Contest in Jacksonville, Florida.

Franco provided incidental music for five dramatic productions of the Everyman Players: *Romans by Saint*

Paul (1963), *The Book of Job* (1967), *The Pilgrim's Progress* (1967), *Electra* (1971), and *The Tempest* (1972).

His instrumental compositions include six string quartets (1931-60)—the Sixth is subtitled *The Prodigal* (*Six Aphorisms*)—Suite for violin and piano (1946); Divertimento for flute and string quartet (1947); and sonatas for solo instruments: violin (1944), cello (1950), viola (1951), and tenor saxophone (1964). *Diptych* for flute and electronic tape dates from 1972; *Trittico Capricioso* for saxophone and tape was completed in 1975. For his own instrument, the piano, he wrote a *Concert Piece* (1940); six *Partitas* (1940-52); *Canticle* (1958); *Redemption Triptych* (1960); *Twelve Preludes* (1975); and a work for piano duo, *Hymn* (1940).

Franco took a keen practical interest in the carillon; however, he did not appreciate the carillons of his native country, as they were apparently extremely out of tune. His enthusiasm was aroused when he heard the finely tuned Taylor carillons in Luray, Virginia and Lake Wales, Florida in the 1950's. For this instrument he composed over 150 pieces, including *Seven Biblical Sketches* (1978), *California Suite* (1981), and numerous partitas, toccatas, variations, and nocturnes. In 1978 he completed a carillon ballet, *The Ways of Water*, for carillon, narrator, and dancers to a text by his wife. In the following year he was commissioned to compose a Suite for the new Wake Forest University carillon in Winston-Salem, North Carolina.

FREED, ISADORE

b. Brest Litovsk, Russia, 26 March 1900
d. Rockville Centre, Long Island, New York, 10 November 1960

At the age of three, Freed was taken by his parents to the United States. From 1914 to 1918 he attended the University of Pennsylvania and the Philadelphia Conservatory. He studied piano with Adele Margulies in New York (1918–20), George Boyle in Philadelphia (1920–23), Joseph Weiss in Berlin (1924), and Josef Hofmann in Philadelphia (1924). He received composition lessons from Ernest Bloch in New York (1918–21) and at the Schola Cantorum in Paris (1929–30), where his teacher was Vincent d'Indy.

Freed's first musical appointment was for one year at the Curtis Institute, Philadelphia in 1924. In 1935 he joined the music faculty of Temple University of Fine Arts in Philadelphia. From 1944 to 1950 he was professor of composition at the Julius Hartt College of Music, Hartford University. For the last ten of his life he was professor of sacred music at Hebrew Union College, New York. In 1934 he founded the Philadel-

Isadore Freed.
Courtesy American Jewish Archives, Cincinnati, OH.

phia Chamber Orchestra and was its conductor for the first two years. Freed also held several important organ posts; from 1937 to 1947 at the Temple Keneseth Israel, Philadelphia, and from 1947 to 1960 at Temple Israel, New York.

For orchestra Freed composed a symphonic rhapsody, *Pygmalion* (1926); three suites, *Vibrations* (1928, from a ballet of the same name), *Jeux de Timbres* (1931), and *Pastorales* (1936); *Tryptique* for strings (1932); *Music for Strings* (1936); *Appalachian Sketches* (1938); *Horizons* (1941); and *Festival Overture* (1944). His two symphonies (1937, 1942) show an affinity with the music of Borodin. For solo instruments and orchestra he wrote *Ballade* for piano (1925); *Concertante* for piano (1953); *Rhapsody* for viola (1939); a Violin Concerto (1939); *Rhapsody* for trombone (1951); a Cello Concerto (1952); and Concertino for English horn (1953).

Freed composed three operas: *Homo Sum* in one act (1930), *The Princess and the Vagabond* (1946), and *The Taming of the Shrew*. His major choral works are a sacred cantata, *Songs of Praise* (1937); *Sacred Service for the Sabbath* (1937); an oratorio, *The Prophecy of Micah* (1957); and settings of *Psalm 103* and *Psalm 118* for chorus and orchestra.

Among his large quantity of instrumental music are three string quartets (1925, 1930, 1936); a Violin Sonata (1925); a Piano Sonata (1933); a Piano Quintet (1937); a Trio for flute, viola, and harp (1940); a Piano Quartet (1946); a Wind Quintet (1949); and an Oboe Sonatina (1954).

Freed was the author of *Harmonizing the Jewish Modes*, published in 1958.

FREER, ELEANOR (NÉE EVEREST)
b. Philadelphia, Pennsylvania, 14 May 1864
d. Chicago, Illinois, 13 December 1942

Eleanor Freer studied singing in Paris with Mathilde Marchesi (1882–83) and was a composition pupil of Benjamin Godard. On her return to the United States she taught singing at the National Conservatory of Music, New York (1889–91). After her marriage in 1891, she lived in Leipzig for eight years. In 1899 she settled in Chicago, where she studied theory with Bernard Ziehn (1902–07).

Ten of her operas were performed: *The Legend of the Piper* (South Bend, Indiana, 1924); *Massimiliano, The Court Jester* (Lincoln, Nebraska, 1926); *The Chilkoot Mandarin* (Alaska, 1926); *A Christmas Tale* (Houston, Texas, 1929); *Joan of Arc* (1929); *Frithiof* (1929); *The Masque of Pandora* (1930); *A Legend of Spain* (1931); *Scenes from Little Women* (Chicago, 1934); and *The Brownings Go to Italy* (Chicago, 1936).

Freer composed two orchestral works, *Four Modern Dances* (1931) and *Spanish Ballet Fantasy* (1935).

Among her 150 songs is a complete setting of the *Sonnets from the Portuguese* by Elizabeth Barrett Browning (1939).

Her autobiography, *Recollections and Reflections of an American Composer*, was published in Chicago in 1929.

FRY, WILLIAM HENRY
b. Philadelphia, Pennsylvania, 19 August 1813
d. Santa Cruz, Virgin Islands, 21 September 1864

Fry learned to play the piano when a child and was one of the first American composers to be taught exclusively in the United States. After leaving school he entered journalism, becoming editor of the *Philadelphia Ledger* in 1844. Two years later he continued his career as a pioneering music critic by traveling to Europe as correspondent for the *New York Tribune* and various Philadelphia newspapers.

On his return to America in 1852, as music critic for the *Tribune,* Fry became a champion of American music, seeking to counteract the dominating influence of Europe upon all cultural and artistic activities in the United States. Of particular impact was a series of ten lectures entitled "The Science and Art of Music' in the Metropolitan Hall, New York. At his own expense, these lectures were illustrated with live performances from a group of Italian singers, a chorus of 100, a full orchestra, and a military band. Fry hoped to change popular taste towards a more serious acceptance of music by living American composers.

Fry began writing music at the age of 14 and won some success with an overture that was played in Philadelphia before he was 20. After attempting two early operas, *Cristiana e Pagani* (1838) and *Aurelia the Vestal* (1841), he became a great opera enthusiast. In 1844 he composed his first full-scale opera, *Leonora,* based on the novel *The Lady of Lyons* by Lord Edward Bulwer-Lytton. This three-act lyrical drama was produced in Philadelphia on 4 June 1845. Since it was founded upon the popular Italian operas, especially those of Bellini and Donizetti, *Leonora* enjoyed a fair degree of success, with 12 performances, although most music critics were condescending in their praise, taking pains to reveal the origin of the music. This major undertaking was financed by the composer himself, who must have found it an expensive way of promoting his own work, since it involved an orchestra of 60 players and a chorus of 80. For the first performance it was sung in English, but at its revival in New York 13 years later, musical taste required the text to be translated into Italian.

In 1864, the year of Fry's death from tuberculosis, his second opera, *Notre Dame de Paris,* based on Victor Hugo's novel *The Hunchback of Notre Dame*, was performed in Philadelphia under the direction of Theodore Thomas, who repeated it in New York.

Fry composed at least seven symphonies. Four of them, each with an illustrative title, were performed by the Jullien Orchestra in the 1853–54 season in New York: *The Breaking Heart* (1852); *Santa Claus* (1853); *A Day in the Country* (1853), now lost; and *Childe Harold* (1854), also lost. The composer claimed *Santa Claus* was the longest unified instrumental composition written on a single subject, an opinion hardly sustainable since it lasts under half an hour. Three other symphonies survive: the one-movement *Niagara Symphony* (1854); a sacred symphony, *Hagar in the Wilderness* (1854); and a dramatic symphony, *The Dying Soldier.* Also for orchestra are three overtures: *The World's Own* (1857, lost), *Evangeline* (1860), and *Macbeth* (1862), the latter probably his most original work.

Fry's choral music includes a *Stabat Mater* (1855) and an unfinished Mass in E-Flat.

FULEIHAN, ANIS

b. Kyrenia, Cyprus, 2 April 1900
d. Palo Alto, California, 11 October 1970

Fuleihan was educated at the English School in Nicosia, Cyprus. Although he came to the United States in 1915, he left soon afterwards to tour the East, settling for two years in Cairo. He returned to America in 1928, where he became a pianist, conductor and composer. From 1932 to 1939 he worked for the publisher G. Schirmer, Inc. In 1947 he was appointed a professor at Indiana University, moving to become director of the Beirut Conservatory, Lebanon from 1953 to 1960. For the U.S. State Department he went to Tunisia in 1962 to organize musical activities, and founded the Orchestre Classique de Tunis, returning to the United States in 1965. Fuleihan was awarded a Guggenheim Fellowship in 1939.

Fuleihan is best known for the *Mediterranean Suite* for orchestra composed in 1932 and first performed in Cincinnati in 1935. For orchestra he also wrote two symphonies (1936, 1962); *Preface to a Child's Story Book* (1932); *Invocation to Isis* (1933); *Fiesta* (1939); *Three Cyprus Serenades* (1941); *Etude* (1942); *Six Concert Etudes* (1941–43); *Overture to the Five Winds* (1947); a symphonic poem, *The Pyramids of Giza* (1952); and a symphonic suite, *Islands* (1961).

Fuleihan wrote a large number of concertos: three for piano (1936, 1936, 1963); three for violin (1930, 1965, 1967); and one each for two pianos (1940), violin and piano (1943), Ondes Martenot (1944), Theremin (1945), flute (1962), viola (1963), and cello (1963). In 1962 he composed a Concerto for Oud and chamber orchestra.

Other works for solo instrument and orchestra are *Fantasy for Viola* (1938); *Symphonie Concertante* for string quartet (1940); *Epithalamium* for piano and strings (1941); *Divertimento* for oboe, bassoon, horn, trumpet, and strings (1942); *Rhapsody* for cello and strings (1945); *Toccata* for piano (1960); Concertino for bassoon (1965); and *Le Cor Anglais s'Amuse* for English horn and strings (1969).

Fuleihan composed one opera, *Vasco,* completed in 1960.

He wrote many instrumental works, producing five string quartets (1940, 1949, 1957, 1960, 1965); *Pastorale Sonata* for flute (1940); Overture for five winds (1947); a Horn Quintet (1959); a Piano Quintet (1964); a Clarinet Quintet; a Piano Trio (1968); *Suite Concertante* for flute and piano; a Woodwind Quartet; sonatas for violin (1961), cello, and viola; and 14 piano sonatas (1940–74).

FUSSELL, CHARLES C(LEMENT)

b. Winston-Salem, North Carolina, 14 February 1938

After receiving piano lessons as a child, Fussell entered the Eastman School of Music in 1956 where he studied piano, composition, and conducting. Among his teachers were Thomas Canning, Wayne Barlow, and Bernard Rogers. On a Fulbright Fellowship he was a pupil of Boris Blacher in Berlin (1962). He has taught at the University of Massachusetts, Amherst (1966–76), North Carolina School of Arts, Winston-Salem (1976–77), and Boston University (from 1983). In 1992, he received a citation and award from the American Academy of Arts and Letters. Fussell has received Fulbright, Ford, and Copland Foundation grants; grants from the Massachusetts Council on the Arts and Humanities; and numerous commissions.

Among his works are five symphonies: no. 1 in one movement (1963); no. 2 for soprano and orchestra (1964–67); no. 3 (*Landscapes*) for chorus and orchestra (1978–81); no. 4 (*Wilde*) for baritone and orchestra (1989; nominated for a Pulitzer Prize in 1991); and no. 5 (1996). Other orchestral works include *Three Processionals* (1972–73); *Northern Lights* for chamber orchestra (1977–79); *Three Portraits* for chamber orchestra: *I. Virgil Thomson Sleeping* (1981), *II. Maurice Grosser Cooking* (1982–83), and *III. Jack Larson* (1986); *Four Fairy Tales after Wilde* (1980–81); *High Bridge* (1999); *Right River* for cello and strings (2001); and Triple Concerto (2002).

Fussell's chamber music includes two piano trios (1962, 1998); *Dance Suite* for flute, trumpet, viola, and two percussionists (1963); *Ballade* for cello and piano (1968, rev. 1976); *Greenwood Sketches: Music for String Quartet* (1976); *Free Fall* for 7 players (1988); *Last Trombones* for six trombones, five percussion, and two pianos (1990); *Song and Dance* for violin and piano (1993); and *Sonata-Duo* for violin and piano (1994).

His choral music includes two "dramas," *Saint Stephen and Herod* for speaker, chorus, and winds (1964) and *Julian* for soprano, tenor, chorus, and orchestra (1969–71); *Voyages* for soprano, tenor, women's chorus, piano, and winds with a recorded speaker (1970); *The Gift* for soprano and chorus (1986); *A Song of Return* (Auden) for chorus and orchestra (1989); a cantata, *Specimen Days* (Whitman) for baritone, chorus, and orchestra (1991–92); two pieces for mixed voices, *Invocation* (1993) and *Mists* (Hart Crane) (1997); *From a Pioneer Songbook* for chorus (1998–99); *A Whitman Sampler* for chorus and piano (2000);

Infinite Fraternity for baritone chorus, flute, and viola (2001–02); and *The Bridge* (Hart Crane) for soloists, chorus, and orchestra (2004).

For solo voices he has written *Poems* (1965) for voices and chamber orchestra; *Eurydice* for soprano and chamber ensemble (1973–75); *Resume,* 9 songs for soprano, clarinet, double bass, and piano (1975–76); *Cymbeline,* a romance for soprano, tenor, narrator, and chamber ensemble (1984); *Five Goethe Lieder* for so-prano or tenor and piano (or orchestra; 1987); *Wilde,* two monologues for baritone and orchestra (1989–90); *Being Music* (Whitman) for baritone and string quartet (1992–93); and *November Leaves* for mezzo-soprano and orchestra (1997–98).

An opera, *Caligula*, was completed in 1962. A chamber opera, *The Astronaut's Tale* (1996–97) for soprano, tenor, baritone, narrator, and seven instruments, was premiered in Boston in 1998.

G

GABURO, KENNETH (LOUIS)
b. Somerville, New Jersey, 5 July 1926
d. Iowa City, Iowa, 26 January 1993

Gaburo studied with Bernard Rogers at the Eastman School of Music, Rochester, New York (1943, 1946–49); at the Accademia di Santa Cecilia, Rome under Goffredo Petrassi (1954–55); and at the University of Illinois with Burrill Phillips (1955–62). He taught at Kent State University, Ohio (1949–50), McNeese State College, Louisiana (1950-54), and at the University of Illinois (1955–68). In 1968 he was appointed professor of music at the University of California, San Diego, becoming founder-director of the Studio of Cognitive Studies in 1975. From 1983 to 1991 he was professor of music at the University of Iowa. Gaburo received many awards, including a Fulbright Scholarship (1954), a Guggenheim Fellowship (1967), a UNESCO Creative Arts Award (1962), and commissions from the Koussevitzky and Fromm Foundations.

Although he was considered one of the more "extreme" composers, Gaburo wrote two "traditional" operas: *The Snow Queen* in three acts for children (1952) and a trilogy of one-act operas, *The Widow*, *The Hermit*, and *The Dog King* (1959). Less conventional operas are *Blur* (1956) and *Bodies* (1956–57) for actors and musique concrète. He also provided music for a play, *Tiger Rag* (1956).

Gaburo's orchestral music includes *Three Interludes* for strings (1949); Concerto for piano and orchestra (1949); *On a Quiet Theme* (1950); *Elegy* for small orchestra (1954–56); *Antiphony I* for three string groups and tape (1958); *Shapes and Sounds* (1964) and *Antiphony IX* (*—a dot is no small a thing—*) for orchestra, children's chorus, and tape (1984–85). Among his numerous instrumental works are *Four Inventions* for clarinet and piano (1954); *Music for Five Instruments*

(1954); *Ideas and Transformations no. 1* for violin and viola, *no. 2* for violin and cello, *no. 3* for viola and cello, and *no. 4* for violin, viola, and cello (1955); String Quartet (1956); *Line Studies* for flute, clarinet, trombone, and viola (1956–57); and *Music for Harry Partch* for ensemble (1965).

After 1960 Gaburo made an increasing use of prerecorded tape, as evidenced by his *Antiphonies*: *I* for voices and tape (1958); *II* on a poem by Cavafy for soprano solo, chorus, and tape (1962); *III* (*Pear-White-Moment*) for voices and tape (1962–63); *IV* "Poised" for piccolo, trombone, double bass, and tape (1966-67); *V* for piano, and tape (1968-71); *VI* for string quartet, tape, and projection (1971); *VII* for four video systems (1974–75); and *VIII* (*Revolution*) for percussion and tape (1984).

As early as 1959 Gaburo developed a persistent interest in language, which led to his creation of the term "compositional linguistics." In 1965 at the University of Illinois he founded the first of his New Music Choral Ensembles (NMCE 1) to perform his works in this medium and to foster the production of experimental pieces by other composers. His later group, New Music Choral Ensemble IV, was based at the University of San Diego, California. Their programs included twentieth-century choral music by Schoenberg, Messiaen, and later composers; music theater works and theater (Beckett, Albee); and Gaburo's linguistic compositions. His works for the group are *Privacy One, Words Without Song* (graphics and text; 1950–74); *Collaboration One* (graphics, text, live and taped performance, and slides (1972); *Dwell* (graphics and text; 1973) and *Privacy Two* (*My, My, My, What a Wonderful Fall*; graphics, text, and live and taped performance) with dancers (1974). Other works for tape include *The Wasting of Lucretzia* (1964); *Fat Millie's Lament* (1964); *Lemon Drops* (1965); *For Harry* (*Partch*) (1965); *Dante's Joynt*

(1965); *Rerun* for 8-track tape (1983); *Of Metal* (1983); *Few* (1985); and *Tapestry* for 4-channel tape (1986). Music for instruments and tape are *Antiphon* for percussion (1984) and *Antiphony X "Winded"* for organ (1985–89).

Gaburo's a cappella choral music includes *Two Madrigals: Snow and The Willow* (1950) and *Alas! Alack!* for women's chorus (1954); *Three Dedications to Lorca* (1953); *Four Sacred Motets: Ave Maria, Ad te Domine, Laetantur Coeli,* and *Terra Tremuit* (1956); Mass for male voices (1958); *Psalm* (1965); *Never* for four groups of male singers (1966); *December 8th* for 40 male voices (1967); and *Dirige (Antiphonae) in Memory of Igor Stravinsky* (1971). Among his other vocal music are *The Night Still* for soprano and piano (1952); *Stray Birds,* five songs for soprano and piano (1959); *Lingua: I (Poems and Other Theaters), II Maledetto, III In the Can,* and *IV The Flow* for various vocal ensembles and instruments (1965–70); *Cantilena IV* (G.M. Hopkins) for soprano and trombone (1975); *Subito* for voice, trumpet, viola, and double bass (1977–78) and *Two* for mezzo-soprano, alto flute, and double bass (1982).

GALLICO, PAOLO
b. Trieste, Italy, 13 May 1868
d. New York, New York, 6 July 1955

Gallico studied at the Vienna Conservatory, where he was a pupil of Anton Bruckner (composition) and Julius Epstein (piano). After establishing a reputation in Europe as a pianist, he came to America in 1892 where he became a much-respected soloist and teacher of piano, composition, and orchestration. Frederick Jacobi and Jerome Kern were two of his pupils.

Gallico's principal work is the dramatic oratorio *The Apocalypse* for six soloists, chorus, and orchestra. In 1921 it was awarded a prize of $500 from the National Federation of Music Clubs. For orchestra he wrote *Euphorion* (1922); *Rhapsodie Mondiale* (1927); and *Rhapsodie Montereyan* (1929). The Septet for piano, horn, string quartet, and contralto (1924) and a Piano Quintet (1936) were once widely performed. Gallico composed a three-act lyric opera, *Harlequin,* produced in 1926. The writer Paul Gallico was his son.

GEHOT, JOSEPH (OR JEAN) BAUDOIN
b. Liege, Belgium, 8 April 1756
d. Philadelphia: Pennsylvania, ca. 1820

Gehot settled in London in 1780, making a living as a violinist and composer of operas. He played in Haydn's orchestra in 1791. The following year he emigrated to America, living first in New York before he made his home in Philadelphia as a violinist and orchestral leader.

All his published music is instrumental: two sets of six string quartets, op. 1 and op. 7; *String Trios,* op. 2; two sets of *Six Duets* for violin and cello; *Six Trios* for two violins and cello; and *24 Military Pieces* for two clarinets, two horns, and bassoon. His *Overture in Twelve Movements, expressive of a Voyage from England to America* was performed in New York in September 1792.

In London he published three books on music: *Treatise on the Theory and Practice of Music in Three Parts* (1784); *Complete Instructor for Every Instrument* (1790); and *The Art of Bowing the Violin* (1790).

GERSCHEFSKI, EDWIN (PETER)
b. Meriden, Connecticut, 10 June 1909
d. Athens, Georgia, 17 December 1992

Gerschefski studied at Yale University with David Stanley Smith and Richard Donovon (1926–31). On a Charles Ditson Fellowship he was a pupil at the Matthay School in London (1931–33). He also received piano lessons from Artur Schnabel in Italy (1935). On his return to the United States he studied with Joseph Schillinger in New York (1936–38). Gerschefski taught in the music schools of Yorkville (1933–37) and Turtle Bay (1937–40) sections of Manhattan. In 1940 he was appointed instructor in piano, theory, and composition at Converse College, Spartanburg, South Carolina. From 1945 to 1959 he was Dean of the Converse School of Music. He also taught at the University of New Mexico, Albuquerque (1959–60) and the University of Georgia, Athens (1960–80).

For orchestra Gerschefski wrote *Saugatuck Suite* (1931); a *Classic Symphony* (1931); a Piano Concerto in one movement (1931); *Test Tubes* (1936); *Fanfare, Fugato and Finale* (1937); *Nocturne* (1942); a Violin Concerto (1951–52); *Toccata and Fugue* (1953–54, rev. 1957–58) and *Celebration* for violin and orchestra (1964). Gerschefski contributed several works to the repertory of the wind band: *Streamline* (1935); Symphony (1937); *Discharge in E* (1937); *Music for a Stately Occasion* (1968) and *Guadalcanal Fantasy.*

Among his choral works are a cantata *Half Moon Mountain* (1947–48); *The Lord's Controversy with His People* (1947–48); *The Salutation of the Dawn* (1952); *Psalm 100* (1965); *Border Raid* (1965) and *Letter from BMI* (1981).

Gerschefski's instrumental pieces include *Statement, Aria and Development* for violin and piano (1933); *Workout* for two violins and two violas (1933); Piano Quintet (1935); *Eight Variations* for string quartet (1937); Brass Septet (1938); *100 Variations* for solo violin (1952); Clarinet Sonatina (1952); Piano Trio (1955–56, rev. 1959-60); *Variations "America"* for winds (1962); Suite for solo trombone (1963); *Rhapsody* for piano trio (1963); *24 Variations* for solo cello (1963); *The Alexander Suite* for two cellos (1971) and *Poem* for cello and piano (1973).

For piano he wrote *Preludes* (1931); *The Portrait of an Artist* (1934); *Eight Variations* (1934); Sonata no. 1 (1936); *New Music* (1937); *Nocturne* (1942); *Seven Pieces* (1963); *Twelve Etudes* (1966); Sonata no. 2 (1967–68); *Homage a Chopin* (1966) and *Six Pieces* (1971).

GERSHWIN, GEORGE
b. Brooklyn, New York, 26 September 1898
d. Hollywood, California, 11 July 1937

Like Aaron Copland's parents, Gershwin's mother and father were Russian-born Jews who had settled to Brooklyn. The family name was Gershovitz. In 1912 George received his first serious piano lessons from the composer Charles Hambitzer, with whom Gershwin studied the Classical and Romantic composers and new music of the time, Debussy, Ravel, and others. It was Hambitzer that Gershwin always acknowledged as the principal influence upon him. In 1915 he began to study harmony and composition with Edward Kilenyi, remaining with him for four years.

Still seeking to widen his technique as a composer, Gershwin became a pupil of Rubin Goldmark in 1923. In that year he acted as accompanist to the singer Eva Gauthier when, in addition to his own pieces, they performed songs by Bartók, Milhaud, Hindemith, and Schoenberg. In 1926 he studied counterpoint with Henry Cowell. On a visit to Europe in 1928 he asked Ravel for lessons. Although the two men became friends, the French composer declined to give Gershwin formal tutoring. As late as 1932 he became a pupil of Joseph Schillinger and studied with him for the next four years. This persistent seeking after technical improvement contrasts with the extrovert confidence that Gershwin exuded in his public piano playing. It emphasizes his ambition to find a way that would lead to serious composition.

Meanwhile, Gershwin's popular music career was underway. A *Tango* which he played at a concert in New York in March 1914 seems to have been the earliest of his compositions. At the age of 15 Gershwin began to write his own songs and at this early time became a pianist and songplugger for the New York publisher J. H. Remick and Co. However, life as a songplugger eventually produced frustration. Tired of having to play so much inferior music and fired by an admiration for the songs of Jerome Kern in particular, Gershwin be-

George Gershwin.
Photo: Nicholas Haz, from the Collections of the Library of Congress.

gan to write his own. His first published song was "When You Want 'em, You Can't Get 'em; When You Got 'em, You Don't Want 'em," written when he was 17. In 1917 he gave up his post with Remick and freelanced as a pianist at rehearsals and in nightclubs. He continued writing songs and sought ways of promoting them, with little success. Salvation came when he was approached by Max Dreyfus, head of the publishing firm of Harms, Inc. Dreyfus offered him $35 per week to write music for him. This arrangement lasted for 12 years to the benefit of both composer and publisher.

Various songs found their way into revues and shows, and in 1918 Gershwin was asked to write the music for an entire production. *Half Past Eight* was a failure more through inadequate staging than because of the quality of the music. Not disheartened, Gershwin began work on *La, La Lucille*. This was produced on Broadway in May 1919 and ran for 104 performances.

Gershwin's first successful song, "Swanee," owes something in idiom to the music of Stephen Foster and the minstrel tradition. When introduced into the revue *Sinbad* by Al Jolson, it was greeted with tumultuous applause. Musical comedies and individual songs occupied him for the next five years, including contributions to George White's *Scandals* (1920–24); *Our Nell* (1923); *Sweet Little Devil* (1923), which received 120 performances after the first night in Boston; and *Blue Monday* (1922), a short Negro opera, a forerunner of *Porgy and Bess.*

In 1923 Paul Whiteman, popularly known as "The King of Jazz," was at the height of his fame as a bandleader. He planned a concert of symphonic jazz and invited several composers, including Irving Berlin and Victor Herbert, to contribute works. Although the concert had been discussed between Whiteman and Gershwin, the composer was astonished to read in the *New York Tribune* in January 1924 that he was said to be writing a jazz concerto for Whiteman. With only a month before the concert, he began *Rhapsody in Blue,* leaving the orchestration to Whiteman's arranger, Ferde Grofé, in view of the shortage of time and his own lack of expertise.

On 12 February at Aeolian Hall, in the presence of Rachmaninoff, Heifetz, Mischa Elman, Efrem Zimbalist, Godowsky, Stokowski, Stravinsky, and Sousa, the now-legendary concert took place. The evening was somewhat pretentiously called "An Experiment in American Music." The 26 items on the program included a symphonic suite by Irving Berlin, *An Orange Grove in California,* and Victor Herbert's *Serenades,* conducted by the composer; it ended strangely with a *Pomp and Circumstance March* by Elgar. *Rhapsody in Blue* lay next-to-last in the marathon concert; but in spite of the tedium engendered in the audience by the overabundance of music, the *Rhapsody* was received with warm enthusiasm. Gershwin had composed the embryonic score in only ten days and many of the passages for solo piano were improvised at the time. Although definitely American, the *Rhapsody* is not jazz; its roots lie in popular song and dance music. After the *Rhapsody,* Gershwin returned to the theater, completing scores for *Scandals of 1924*; *Lady Be Good* (which included "Fascinatin' Rhythm"); *Tell Me More,* and *Tip Toes* (with "That Certain Feeling" and "The Song of the Flame"), all in 1924.

Also in the audience at Aeolian Hall for Whiteman's concert was Walter Damrosch, conductor of the New York Symphony Orchestra, who commissioned Gershwin in 1925 to compose a piano concerto, originally to be called *New York Concerto.* Gershwin began work on it at his summer retreat in Chautauqua and, with some assistance from Rubin Goldmark, completed the orchestration himself. Feeling a little unsure of his talents in this respect, he hired an orchestra before the first performance to try out the music. After a few revisions to the string parts, he delivered the score to Damrosch. The premiere of the Piano Concerto in F with the composer as soloist took place in Carnegie Hall on 3 December 1925. The Concerto shows a greatly increased professionalism about the writing of large-scale works. The loosely improvisatory piano part of the *Rhapsody* had given way to more inventive music, development of thematic material, and a greater range of harmony and color. For many years it remained overshadowed by the earlier work but its importance has recently become more widely recognized.

The speed with which Gershwin could write popular songs and musical comedies produced for him not only great fame but also considerable wealth. Before he was 30 he had become the best-known American composer and the toast of New York society. He again turned to musicals: *Oh Kay!* (1925) with Gertrude Lawrence and Victor Moore, including such songs as "Clap Yo' Hands" and "Someone to Watch Over Me," and *Funny Face* (1927), which introduced "'S Wonderful." Both shows had over 200 performances. Also in 1927 he wrote *Strike Up the Band.* In that year he visited London where his music was as great a success as it was in America.

He also took up painting, for which he possessed a distinct talent, especially as a portraitist. He became a discerning collector of modern art with special respect for Rouault. His own collection included Picasso's *The Absinthe Drinker* and works by Chagall, Gauguin, Kandinsky, Leger, Modigliani, and Rousseau. In 1928 Gershwin again went to Europe where in Paris he met Ravel, Poulenc, Prokofiev, and Stravinsky. Here he began the sketches for *An American in Paris.*

Back in America he wrote the music for another show, *Treasure Girl* (1928). *An American in Paris* was performed at Carnegie Hall on 13 December 1928 by Walter Damrosch and the New York Symphony Orchestra; it was described in the program as "a rhapsodic ballet." The critics were lukewarm in their praise but the scoring, entirely by Gershwin, shows an expert hand and was praised by several writers. In *Show Girl* (1929), a ballet sequence was based on parts of *An American in Paris.* It was followed by *Girl Crazy* (1930) which included "I've Got Rhythm" and "Embraceable You," and a film musical, *Delicious* (1930), composed in Hollywood. From *Delicious* he extracted an orchestral work with piano solo given a number of titles but eventually called *Second Rhapsody.* It was first performed on 29 January 1932 by the Boston Symphony Orchestra under Koussevitzky with the composer as soloist. After a brief vacation in Cuba, Gershwin wrote *Rumba,* an attractive orchestral work not often heard today. It was premiered at the Lewisholm Stadium, New York on 16 August 1932, and was later retitled *A Cuban Overture.* In December 1933 he completed his fourth piece for piano and orchestra, the lively *Variations on "I've Got Rhythm."*

In 1931 Gershwin composed music for a political satire of a Presidential election campaign, *Of Thee I Sing*. The play's writers, Ira Gershwin, George Kaufman, and Morris Ryskind, were awarded a Pulitzer Prize, but the composer was not included in the commendation. It received 441 consecutive performances. A sequel, *Let 'em Eat Cake* (1933) was unsuccessful. Gershwin's last important stage score, *Pardon My English*, also dates from 1933.

At the age of 35 and at the peak of his powers and fame, Gershwin began work on his masterpiece, the opera *Porgy and Bess*. He had long admired DuBose Heyward's 1925 novel, *Porgy*. The title character was based on a true-life figure, Samuel Smalls, a black cripple who travelled in a goat cart. DuBose Heyward was crippled by polio, and to some extent Porgy is a self-portrait. Heyward himself was a Southerner and therefore aware of the plight of the blacks he describes in the story, although his attitude to them in real life was somewhat ambivalent.

The setting is Catfish Row, a Negro slum area of Charleston. In the first act, Crown, the man living with Bess, kills another black, Robbins, in a quarrel. Bess goes to live with Porgy, but Crown, who is now running from the police, returns to look for her. He is killed by Porgy. While Porgy is being questioned by the police, Bess is persuaded by Sportin' Life, the slippery confidence man, to go to New York. In despair at the loss of Bess, Porgy sets out in his goat cart to look for her in New York. Violence and death are ever-present in the story; the hurricane that hits the community is another manifestation of the elemental darkness that surrounds the scene.

Porgy had been dramatized by the author and his wife in 1927. In 1933 negotiations had been started for a musical version by Jerome Kern and Oscar Hammerstein II after the great success of *Show Boat*. It was, however, Gershwin who eventually secured the musical rights. The composer and his librettist, Heyward, worked remarkably well together, with only minor disagreements. Ira, George's older brother and lyricist for many Gershwin songs, was co-lyricist for this work. In the summer of 1934, Gershwin went to live near Charleston to learn something of the life and music of the Southern black. After only eight weeks he had written a substantial part of the score. The entire opera took little more than a year of concentrated effort and was finished on 2 September 1935.

Lasting nearly three hours, the opera contains almost continuous music with brilliant orchestration entirely by Gershwin. After six weeks of rehearsal, *Porgy and Bess* opened in Boston on 30 September 1935 and ten days later premiered in New York. Critics were divided in their assessment, although most agreed that there were some fine songs. The show ran for only 124 performances and was a commercial failure. Many of the separate songs have entered American music history and have become some of the best-known tunes composed in the twentieth century. That so many fine songs should be contained in one work is a measure of its stature: "Summertime," "A Woman is a Sometime Thing," "I Got Plenty of Nuttin'," "Bess, You is my Woman Now," "It Ain't Necessarily So," and "O Lawd, I'm on My Way." However, the work's failure depressed the composer; not until 1941, with its revival four years after the composer's death, did it begin to establish its place in the annals of American music. Since then it has been produced all over the world, including even Moscow, where it was staged in 1945.

Although he had planned another operatic collaboration with Heyward, based on the latter's novel *Star-Spangled Virgin*, Gershwin went instead to Hollywood. There he recovered his usual optimism and wrote music for three films: *Shall We Dance*, *Damsels in Distress*, and *The Goldwyn Follies*, the last of them completed by Vernon Duke after Gershwin's death. Gershwin planned a ballet with George Balanchine on *American in Paris* and began composing a String Quartet. Unfortunately none of the Quartet survives, although a *Lullaby* for string quartet dating from 1920 was discovered after the composer's death and published in 1968. His only other instrumental music is the set of *Three Preludes* for piano, composed in 1928. Originally there were five *Preludes* for violin and piano, but two were omitted and the others adapted for piano alone in the following year.

In 1937 in California Gershwin appeared in many concerts of his music, both as pianist and conductor. During the performance of the Piano Concerto in Hollywood he suffered uncharacteristic lapses of memory and soon afterwards began to have severe headaches. His health began to deteriorate and one day at the film studio, while working on *The Goldwyn Follies*, he collapsed. A brain tumor was diagnosed, but it was inoperable. He died in the Cedars of Lebanon Hospital, Hollywood, aged 38.

GESENSWAY, LOUIS
b. Dvinsk, Latvia, 19 February 1906
d. Philadelphia: Pennsylvania, 11 March 1976

After training as a violinist, Gesensway moved to Canada to study at the Toronto Conservatory. Later he was a composition pupil of Tibor Serly at the Curtis Institute, Philadelphia (1926–29) and Zoltán Kodály in Budapest (1930–31). In 1926 he joined the Philadelphia Orchestra, retiring in 1971

In his music, Genseway employed a scale of 41 degrees and a system of color harmony. His major orchestral works were performed by the Philadelphia Orchestra: *Five Russian Pieces* (1935); Suite for strings and percussion (1939); Flute Concerto (1946); *Suite on Jewish Themes* (1948); *Dance Portrait* (1953); *The Four Squares of Philadelphia* (with narrator) (1955); *Ode to Peace* (1960); *March* (1963); *Revery* for strings (1964); *Commemoration Symphony* (1966–68); *A Pennsylvania Overture* (1972); and a Cello Concerto (1973).

Among his instrumental compositions are a Piano Sonata (1937); two string quartets (1938, 1954); *Fantasy* for organ (1941); *Duo* for violin and viola (1941, rev. 1967); Quartet for English horn, flute, violin, and cello (1942); Concerto for 13 brass instruments (1942); *Eight Miniatures* for flute and percussion (1949); *Ana* for cello and piano (1950); Quartet for clarinet and strings (1950); Quartet for oboe, bassoon, violin, and viola (1951); *Duo* for flute and clarinet (1952); Quartet for timpani, percussion, violin, and cello (1957); Sonata for solo bassoon (1959); *Duo* for oboe and guitar (1959); *Duo* for viola and bassoon (1959); *Dance Suite* for harp (1968); Divertimento for flute, two violins, and viola (1969); Divertimento for wind quintet (1969); *Duo* for two cellos (1970); and *Duo* for violin and cello (1970).

He wrote a one-act children's opera, *The Great Boffo and His Talking Dog* (1973).

Vittorio Giannini.
Courtesy The Juilliard School.

GIANNINI, VITTORIO

b. Philadelphia, Pennsylvania, 19 October 1903
d. New York, New York, 28 November 1966

Giannini's father, Ferrucio (1869–1948), was an Italian tenor of some repute, and the soprano Dusolina Giannini (1900–1986) was his sister. Following four years of study at the Milan Conservatory (1913–17), he entered the Juilliard School in 1925, where he was a pupil of Rubin Goldmark. In 1932 he won the Prix de Rome scholarship and spent four years in Italy. In 1939, he was appointed a teacher of composition at the Juilliard School and also taught at the Manhattan School of Music (1941). He was appointed the first director of the North Carolina School of the Arts, Winston-Salem in 1965, a post he held until his death.

It is natural that coming from a family of Italian opera singers, Giannini should make opera his main form of musical expression. The first of these operas, *Lucedia*, with a prologue and three acts, composed in 1932, was given its premiere in Munich in October 1934. Another opera of this period, *Not All Prima Donnas are Ladies*, remained unstaged. Giannini completed another three-act opera, *Flora*, in 1937. The following year saw the production of two further operas. In June 1938 in Ham-

burg, *The Scarlet Letter*, based on the novel by Hawthorne, was staged; it had been completed three years earlier. A one-act opera for radio, *Beauty and the Beast*, was broadcast by CBS in November 1938. A second one-act radio opera, *Blennerhasset*, concerns the conspiracy of Aaron Burr, the American statesman. It was broadcast by CBS in February 1939.

Giannini chose Shakespeare's *The Taming of the Shrew* for his next three-act opera. It was given a concert performance in Cincinnati in January 1953 and a staged production on NBC television in March 1954. The New York City Opera production was presented on 13 April 1958. *Christus* composed in 1956 was unperformed. A three-act opera, *The Harvest*, set in the rural America of 1900, was produced in Chicago on 25 November 1961. *The Rehearsal Call*, a three-act opera buffa, was staged in New York in 1962. *The Servant of Two Masters*, a setting of Goldoni's comedy, was performed by the New York City Opera on 9 March 1967, after the composer's death. His last projected opera, *Oedipus Rex*, remained unfinished.

Giannini's six symphonies mark his main achievement in orchestral music. The first of these, in one movement, unnumbered but subtitled *In Memoriam Theodore Roosevelt*, was composed in 1935 and performed in January of the following year in New York by the NBC Symphony Orchestra under the direction of the composer. Another unnumbered symphony, subtitled *IBM*, was commissioned for the New York World's Fair and performed there in 1939. Symphony no. 1 for woodwind, brass, and percussion received its premiere in Cincinnati in 1951. Symphony no. 2, first performed in St. Louis, dates from 1956. Symphony no. 3 for band was first performed in 1958 and has been widely performed throughout the United States. Symphony no. 4 was completed in 1960.

His other orchestral music includes a *Prelude and Fugue* for strings (1926); a Suite for orchestra (1931); *Prelude, Chorale and Fugue* (1939); *Concerto Grosso* for strings (1946); *Frescobaldiana* (1948); a suite, *Love's Labours Lost* (1958); three divertimenti (1953, 1961, 1964); *Dedication Overture* (1964); and *Variations and Fugue* (1964). Giannini composed several pieces for solo instrument and orchestra: Piano Concerto (1935); an Organ Concerto, commissioned by the Gesellschaft der Musikfreunde of Vienna and performed in that city in 1937; a Concerto for two pianos (1940); a Violin Concerto (1945); a Trumpet Concerto (1945); and *Psalm 130* for cello or double bass and orchestra (1963).

The first of his choral works is a large-scale setting of *Stabat Mater* for soloists, chorus and orchestra, written in 1919 when he was aged only 16. It was followed by *Madrigal* for four solo voices and string quartet (1931) and *Cantata Primavera* for soprano, tenor, chorus, and orchestra, completed in 1933

Giannini's Requiem Mass for soloists, chorus, and orchestra is massive in concept, lasting over two and a half hours. It was first performed in Vienna in May 1937 and earned the composer considerable fame. Another cantata, *The Lament for Adonis*, dates from 1940. In 1951 he composed *Canticle for Christmas* for baritone, chorus, and orchestra. In 1957 he was commissioned to write *Canticle of the Martyrs* for the 500th anniversary of the founding of the Moravian Church. It is scored for baritone, chorus, and orchestra and was premiered in Winston-Salem, North Carolina in that year. For solo voice and orchestra he composed *Triptych* (1937), *The Medead*, a monodrama (1960), and *Antigone* (1962).

Among his many instrumental works are two violin sonatas (1926, 1940); a String Quartet (1930); Piano Quintet (1930); Piano Trio (1931); Wind Quintet (1934); Piano Sonata (1934); a Sonata for two violins (1940–45); a Sonata for unaccompanied violin (1945); and a Flute Sonata (1958).

GIDEON, MIRIAM
b. Greeley, Colorado, 23 October 1906
d. New York, New York, 18 June 1996

Miriam Gideon graduated from Boston University in 1926 and studied composition privately with Lazare Saminsky (1931–34) and Roger Sessions (1935–43). In addition, she was a piano pupil of Hans Barth in New York. She held a master of arts degree in musicology from Columbia University (1946) and a doctorate of sacred music in composition from the Jewish Theological Seminary in New York (1970). Formerly a member of the music faculty of Brooklyn College (1944–55), she was appointed professor of music at the Jewish Theological College in 1955. From 1967 she also taught at the Manhattan School of Music. She was visiting professor of music at City College of New York (1971–77). Her honors and awards she received included a grant from the National Endowment for the Arts for an orchestral work with voice (1974), election to the American Academy and Institute of Arts and Letters (1975), and a commission from the Library of Congress, Music Library Association for a chamber work (1980).

Among Gideon's dramatic works are a three-scene opera, *Fortunato*, completed in 1958, and *The Adorable Mouse* (1960), a French folktale after La Fontaine for singer-narrator and chamber orchestra.

Her orchestral works include *Allegro and Andante* (1939), later withdrawn; *Lyric Piece* for string orchestra (1941); *Epigrams* for chamber orchestra (1941); *Symphonia Brevis* (1953); and *Songs of Youth and Madness*, on poems of Friedrich Holderlin, for high voice and orchestra (1977). Compositions using chamber ensembles are *Three Cornered Pieces* for flute, clarinet, and piano (1936); Quartet for strings (1946); Divertimento for wind quartet (1948); *Fantasy on Irish Folk Motives* for oboe, bassoon, vibraphone, glockenspiel, tam-tam, and viola (1975); and Trio for clarinet, cello, and piano (1978).

For solo instruments and piano she wrote sonatas for flute (1943), viola (1949), and cello (1961); *Incantation on an Indian Theme* for viola and piano (1940); *Fantasy on a Javanese Motive* for cello and piano (1948); *Biblical Masks* for violin and piano (1960); Suite for clarinet (or bassoon) and piano (1972); and *Eclogue* for flute and piano (1988). Her works for piano include three suites; *Canzona* (1945); *Of Shadows Numberless*, based on Keats' "Ode to a Nightingale" (1966); and a Piano Sonata (1977).

Gideon composed many songs and several vocal works with instrumental accompaniment, among which are settings of Francis Thompson's poem *The Hound of Heaven* for voice, oboe, and string trio (1945); *Sonnets from Shakespeare* for voice, trumpet, and string quartet (1950); *Sonnets From "Fatal Interview"* (Millay) for voice and string trio (1952); *The Condemned Playground* for soprano, tenor, flute, bassoon, and string quartet (1963); *Questions on Nature* for voice, oboe, piano, and percussion (1965); *Rhymes From the Hill* for voice, clarinet, cello, and marimba (1965); *The Seasons of Time* for voice, flute, cello, piano, and celeste (1969); *Nocturnes* for voice, flute, oboe, violin, cello, and vibraphone (1975); *Voices From Elysium* on ancient Greek poetry, for voice, flute, clarinet, violin, cello, and piano (1979); *Spiritual Airs* for voice and chamber ensemble (1979); *The Resounding Lyre* for high voice and ensemble (1979); *Spirit Above the Dust* for voice, flute, oboe, bassoon, horn, and string quartet (1980); *Wing'd Hour* for medium voice and ensemble (1983); and *Creature to Creature*, six songs for medium voice, flute, and harp (1985). Songs with piano accompaniment include *Epitaphs from Robert Burns* (1952); *Songs of Voyage* (1961); *Ayelet Hashakhat* (*Morning Star*) in Hebrew (1980); and *A Woman of Valor* (1981).

Gideon's choral music includes *Slow, Slow Fresh Fount* (Ben Jonson) for chorus (1941); *Sweet Western Wind* (Herrick) (1943); *How Goodly Are Thy Tents* for female or male voices, and organ (1947); *The Habitable Earth*, a cantata based on the *Book of Proverbs* for soloists, chorus, oboe, and piano (1965); *Spiritual Madrigals* for male voices, viola, cello, and bassoon (1965); settings of the *Saturday Morning Sacred Service* (1971) and the *Friday Evening Sacred Service* (1974); and *Where Wild Carnations Blow* (Christopher Smart) for soloists, chorus, and ensemble (1983).

GILBERT, HENRY FRANKLIN BELKNAP

b. *Somerville, Massachusetts, 26 September 1868*
c. *Cambridge, Massachusetts, 19 May 1928*

Gilbert studied French literature before attending the New England Conservatory in Boston (1886–87). He was later the first American pupil of Edward MacDowell (1889–92). He became a businessman but gave up his career in 1902 to devote himself to composition. Throughout his life he suffered a congenital cardiac defect, tetralogy of Follot (blue babies disease). The Boston heart specialist Dr. Dudley White wrote an important medical book on Gilbert's unique condition (1929).

Gilbert was one of the principal composers of his time to turn away from European influences in favor of American themes. His interest in African and Native American musics led to his best-known work, *Comedy Overture on Negro Themes*. Composed in 1905 and

Henry Gilbert.
Belknap MSS 35, The Henry Gilbert Papers in the Irving S. Gilmore Music Library of Yale University.

intended for an operetta based on Joel Chandler Harris' *Uncle Remus Tales*, it made use of jazz almost before jazz itself had become established. It was even performed in Russia under the direction of Reinhold Glière. Orchestral works in the same vein are *Two Episodes* (1895–97); *Humoreske on Negro Minstrel Tunes* (1903); *Americanesque* (1903); *Three American Dances* (1911); *Shout* (1912); *Negro Rhapsody* (1912); and *Dance for jazz band* (1924). *Dance in the Place Congo* (1916), named after a square in New Orleans, was produced as a ballet at the Metropolitan Opera House in New York. It was heard at the I.S.C.M. Festival of 1927 in Frankfurt and has been described as "Scriabin with a Latin-American beat." Gilbert composed *Hymn to America* (1915) and *Six Indian Sketches* (1921) for chorus and orchestra, and several piano pieces in African and Native American idiom, *Indian Scenes* (1912) and *Negro Dances* (1914). He also edited over one hundred American folk songs.

Among his few works not derived from American influences are the orchestral works *Orlamonde*, a symphonic poem (1897); *Summer Day Fantasie* (1899), a symphonic prologue to Synge's *Riders to the Sea* (1904); *Symphonic Piece* (1925); *Nocturne* (after Whitman) (1925–26); Suite for chamber orchestra (1928); *Salammbo's Invocation to Tanith* (Flaubert) for soprano and orchestra (1902); and *Island of the Fay* (Poe) for piano (1909, orchestrated 1923). His two operas, *Uncle Remus* (1906) and the one-act *Fantasy in Delft* (1915–20), were never staged. Gilbert also provided incidental music for a number of plays, including

GILLIS, DON

Cathleen ni Houlihan (W. B. Yeats) (1903); *Pot of Broth* (1903); *Riders to the Sea* (1904, rev. 1913); *The Twisting of the Rope* (1904); and *The Redskin or the Land of His Race* (1906).

GILCHRIST, WILLIAM WALLACE

b. Jersey City, New Jersey, 8 January 1846
d. Easton, Pennsylvania, 20 December 1916

Gilchrist spent most of his life in Philadelphia, first studying at the University of Pennsylvania and later leading an active life as a conductor of choirs and orchestras and as an organist and singing teacher, first in Cincinnati in 1871, returning to Pennsylvania in the following year. He was conductor of the Mendelssohn Club, Tuesday Club of Wilmington, and the Philadelphia Symphony Society.

He won prizes for several of his choral works, which include a setting of *Psalm 46* (*God is Our Refuge*; 1882); *The Rose* (J.R. Lowell; 1887); *Legend of the Bended Spear* (Felicia Hemans; 1888); *Prayer and Praise* (1888); *The Syrens* (Lowell) for female voices (1904); *An Easter Idyll* (1907); an oratorio, *The Lamb of God* (1909); *The Knight of Togganberg* for female voices (1911); *Ode to the Sun*; *Journey of Life*; and *The Uplifted Gates*. In 1895 Gilchrist compiled the *Hymnal for the Presbyterian Church of the United States*, followed by *The Hymnal for Use in Congregational Churches* (1902).

Gilchrist composed two symphonies, no. 1 in C (1891) and no. 2 in D, completed after the composer's death by William Happich and performed in Philadelphia in 1937; *Symphonic Poem* (1910); a Suite for piano and orchestra; and a quantity of chamber music: Nonet in G minor for piano, wind, and strings, a Piano Quintet in C minor, a String Quartet, and a Piano Trio. His many songs were at one time very popular.

GILLIS, DON

b. Cameron, Missouri, 17 June 1912
d. Columbia, South Carolina, 10 January 1978

At school Gillis learned to play trumpet and trombone. After graduating from the Texas Christian University, Fort Worth in 1936, he taught there as an instructor and band director. He was also on the faculty of the Southwestern Baptist Seminary School (1935–42). In 1942 he became chief of productions with WBAP radio, Fort Worth, Texas, moving in 1944 to New York as producer for Arturo Toscanini and the NBC Symphony Orchestra, a post he held for ten years. From 1956 to 1962 he was vice-president for development at the National Music Camp, Interlochen, Michigan. In 1967

he was appointed chairman of the music department at Southern Methodist University, Dallas. He was chairman of the art department at Dallas Baptist College (1969–73) and director of the Center for Media Arts Studies at the University of South Carolina, Columbia (1973–78).

Almost all of Gillis's music is in a popular American style, as the titles suggest. He composed 12 symphonies, two of them unnumbered: *Star-Spangled Symphony* for strings, and his best-known work, *Symphony for Fun* (Symphony 5-1/2), first performed in April 1945 by Arthur Fiedler (not Toscanini as often reported) and the Boston "Pops" Orchestra. All but one of the other symphonies have programmatic titles: no. 1, *American* (1941); no. 2, *Symphony of Faith* (1940); no. 3, *Symphony of Free Men* (1940–41); no. 4, *The Pioneers* (1943); no. 5, *In Memoriam* (1944–45); no. 6, *Midcentury U.S.A.* (1947); no. 7, *Saga of a Prairie School* (1948); no. 8, *Dance Symphony* (1949); no. 9 (1956); and no. "X," *Big D* (1967).

American pioneering history and pastoral life provide the source of many of Gillis's orchestral works: *The Panhandle Suite* (1937); *Portrait of a Frontier Town* (1940); *Prairie Poem* (1943); *The Alamo* (1944); *Thomas Wolfe, American* for narrator and orchestra (1950); *The New Frontier* (1961); *Paul Bunyan, Portrait of a Legend* (1964); *Dude Ranch Suite* (1967); and a Bicentennial commission, *The Secret History of the Birth of a Nation* (1976) for narrator, chorus, and orchestra. Other orchestral pieces include *Four Moods in Three Keys* (1936); *The Woolyworm* (1937); *Thoughts Provoked on Becoming a Prospective Papa* (1937); *Intermission: Ten Minutes* (1940); *A Short Overture to an Unwritten Opera* (1944); *To an Unknown Soldier* (1945); *Rhapsody* for harp and orchestra (1947); *Tulsa, Portrait in Oil* (1950); two piano concertos (1956, 1967); *Toscanini, a Portrait of a Century* (1967); and one of his last commissions, *One Giant Step*, commemorating the landing on the moon, written for the International Festival of Youth Orchestras in 1971

Gillis wrote several pieces for narrator and orchestra, including a setting of Edgar Allan Poe's poem *The Raven* (1938); *The Man Who Invented Music* (1950); *Alice in Orchestralia*; and three religious works for choir and orchestra: *The Crucifixion* (1937); *The Night Before Christmas* (1941); and *The Coming of the King* (1954). He also composed an enormous quantity of instrumental music, including six string quartets (1936–47) and three wind quintets (1935–39); much of this was for amateur performance.

For the stage Gillis wrote nine operas: *The Park Avenue Kids* (1957); *The Libretto* (1958); *The Legend of Star Valley Junction* (1961–62); *World Premiere* (1966–67); *The Gift of the Magi* (1966); *The Nazarene* (1967–68); *Miss Martha B and the Heavenly Flop* (1971);

171

Behold the Man (1972); and *Instant Replay* (1976). He also composed two ballets, *Shindig* (1949) and *Twinkletoes* (1956).

His works for concert band include *Pep Rally* (1956); *America's Gifted Youth* (1958); *Dialogue* for trombone and band (1958); *The Land of Wheat* (1959); *Saga of a Pioneer* (1961); *Abe Lincoln – Gettysburg 1863* (1963); *Ceremony of Allegiance* (with narrator) (1964); and *Portrait of a City Made in Steel* (1966).

Gillis was the author of two books, *The Unfinished Symphony Conductor* (1967) and *The Art of Media Instruction* (1973).

GIORNI, AURELIO
b. Perugia, Italy, 15 September 1895
d. Pittsfield, Massachusetts, 23 September 1938

After studying with Giovanni Sgambati at the Accademia di Santa Ceccilia, Rome (1909–11) and with Englebert Humperdinck and Ferruccio Busoni in Berlin (1911–1913), Giorni came to the United States at the age of 20. He was an active pianist, especially in chamber music as a member of the Elshuco Trio. He taught at the Juilliard School, the Philadelphia Conservatory, and finally at Smith College, Northampton, Massachusetts.

For orchestra Giorni composed a symphonic poem, *Orlando Furioso* (1926); a *Sinfonia Concertante* for piano and orchestra (1931); and a Symphony in D minor (1936). His important chamber music compositions are sonatas for cello (1924), violin (1924), flute (1932), and clarinet (1933); a Piano Quartet (1926); a Piano Quintet (1927); a Piano Trio (1934); and a String Quartet (1936).

In reaction against hostile criticism of his music, he committed suicide by jumping into the Housatonic River.

GLANVILLE-HICKS, PEGGY
b. Melbourne, Australia, 29 December 1912
d. Sydney, Australia, 25 June 1990

After receiving several awards at home, Glanville-Hicks won a scholarship to the Royal College of Music in London (1932–36), where she studied with Ralph Vaughan Williams (composition) and Arthur Benjamin (piano). Later in Vienna she was a pupil of Egon Wellesz (1936–38) and in Paris she received lessons from Nadia Boulanger. She went to the United States in 1939 and became an American citizen in 1948. From 1938 to 1948 she was married to the English composer Stanley Bate. In 1959 she settled in Athens, Greece, returning to Australia in 1976. Glanville-Hicks was twice the recipient of Guggenheim Fellowships (1956–57, 1957–58) and was awarded a Fulbright Fellowship (1961–63) for research into Aegean Demotic music. From 1948 to 1960 she was director of the Composers Forum concerts in New York.

Her most important works are operas. After the early *Caedmon*, now withdrawn, Glanville-Hicks wrote *The Transposed Heads*, based on the novel by Thomas Mann. Commissioned by the Louisville Orchestra, it was premiered in 1954 and presented in New York in 1958. *The Glittering Gate* is a one-act comedy set outside the gates of Heaven, where two burglars are seeking entry. To a text by Lord Dunsany, it received its first performance in New York in 1959.

Nausicaa is based on Robert Graves' story "Homer's Daughter." It was produced at the Athens Festival in August 1961. *Carlos Among the Candles* was completed in 1962. Her next opera, *Sappho*, also with a Greek setting, is in three acts to a libretto by Lawrence Durrell. It was commissioned in 1963 by the San Francisco Opera for Maria Callas, through a grant from the Ford Foundation. Her last opera, *Beckett*, dates from 1990.

Glanville-Hicks composed nine ballets: *Hylas and the Nymphs* (1935); *Postman's Knock* (1938); *Killer-of-Enemies* (1946); *The Masque of the Wild Man* and *Triad*, performed at the first Festival of the Two Worlds in Spoleto, Italy in 1958; *Saul and the Witch of Endor* (CBS Television), *Saul* (1964), *A Season in Hell*, based on Arthur Rimbaud's poem (1965); and *Tragic Celebration* (*Jephthah's Daughter*) (1966). A *Choral Suite* for women's voices, oboe, and strings was conducted by Sir Adrian Boult at the I.S.C.M. Festival in London in 1938.

For orchestra Glanville-Hicks composed *Meditation* (1933); *Three Gymnopedies* (1934); two sinfoniettas (1934, 1938); *Scherzo* (1937); *Sinfonia da Pacifica* (1952); *Etruscan Concerto* for piano and orchestra (1955); *Concerto Romantico* for viola and orchestra (1956); *Tapestry* (1964); and *Drama* (1966). Her instrumental music includes a String Quartet (1937); Sonatina for flute (or recorder) and piano (1939); *Concertino da Camera* for piano and woodwind (1943); Concertino for flute, clarinet, bassoon, and piano (1946), performed at the I.S.C.M. Festival in Amsterdam in 1948; a Harp Sonata, written in 1950 for Nicanor Zabeleta; a Sonata for harp, flute, and horn (1950); a Sonata for piano and percussion (1951); *Concertino Antico* for harp and string quartet (1955); *Musica Antiqua* for two flutes, harp, marimba, timpani, and two percussion (1957); *Prelude and Presto for Ancient American Instruments* (1959); and *Girondelle for Giraffes* for six instruments (1978).

Two unusual vocal compositions are *Thomsoniana* for soprano, flute, horn, string quartet, and piano, which uses texts from music reviews of Virgil Thomson (1949), and *Letters from Morocco* for tenor and chamber orchestra, dating from 1952, which is a setting of letters from the composer Paul Bowles. Other vocal items are *Pastoral* for female voices and orchestra (1933) and *In Midwood Silence* for soprano, oboe, and string quartet (1935). Choral works include two pieces for chorus and orchestra, *Poem* (1933) and *Song in Summer* (1935); *Aria Concertante* for tenor, women's voices, chorus, oboe, piano, and gong (1945); and *Dance Cantata* for tenor, narrator, speaking chorus, and orchestra (1947).

Glanville-Hicks composed scores for eight documentary films: *Robot* (1936); *Clouds* (1938); *Glacier* (1938); *Tulsa* (1949); *Tel* (1950); *The African Story* (1956); *All Our Children* (1956); and *A Scary Time* (1958).

Blindness after an operation in 1969 severely curtailed her composing career.

GLASS, PHILIP
b. Baltimore, Maryland, 31 January 1937

Glass learned to play the violin at six and the flute at eight, attending the Peabody Institute, Baltimore (1945–52). He entered the University of Chicago in 1952 at the age of fifteen, studying philosophy, mathematics, and music, graduating in 1956. In 1955 he took harmony lessons with Louis Cheslock. At the Juilliard School (1956–61) he was a pupil of Victor Persichetti and William Bergsma; his fellow students included Peter Schickele and Steve Reich. During the summer of 1960 he joined the composition class of Darius Milhaud at Aspen. His first appointment was as Composer-in-Residence in Pittsburgh, Pennsylvania, high schools (1962–64). A Fulbright Fellowship enabled him to study in Paris with Nadia Boulanger (1963–64) where he also assisted Ravi Shankar in writing film scores.

In 1965 Glass married the actress and theater director Jo Anne Akalaitis, with whom he collaborated in providing incidental music for stage productions in Paris, initially with the Mabou Mines Company. Together they traveled in India, North Africa, and Central Asia (1965–66). On his return to New York in 1966 Glass worked with Steve Reich and several visual artists, notably Richard Serra. In 1968 he established the Philip Glass Ensemble for the performance of his works.

Glass's early compositions, all now withdrawn, include an *Essay* for orchestra; two Ariosi for strings; several string quartets; a Brass Sextet; and choral settings of Carl Sandburg and Walt Whitman. In 1966 he abandoned conventional music to adopt a repetitive style, close to the minimal music of Reich and Terry Riley. In 1971 and 1973 he again visited India, where

Philip Glass.
Courtesy the composer.

he studied oriental modes that affected his own work at this time. Other influences were serialism, rock music, and the piano pieces of Erik Satie.

The first of Glass's characteristic minimalist pieces, *1 + 1* (1968), is for amplified table-top in contact with a microphone, amplifier, and loudspeaker. Like Reich's *Clapping Music*, the rhythms patterns tapped out are concentrated solely on rhythm without pitch considerations. It was followed by *Two Pages* for electric keyboards (1968); *600*, an "open score' (1968); *Music in Eight Parts* (1969); *Music in Contrary Motion* (1969); *Music in Fifths* (1969); *Music in Similar Motion* (1969); *Music With Changing Parts* (1970); *Music in 12 Parts* (1971–74), which lasts four hours; *Another Look at Harmony* (1975); and *Music for Fourth Series III* (1978), culminating in *Glassworks* (1981).

The major works of Philip Glass comprise the sequence of operas and theater pieces. The first of these, *Einstein on the Beach*, was premiered in Avignon, France in 1976 and subsequently performed throughout Europe in that year. Lasting five hours, it is scored for five instrumentalists and sound engineer. The music and libretto are by Glass, décor and direction by Robert Wilson. There is no plot as such, with the separate numbers sung or spoken to sol-fa syllables.

The madrigal opera *The Panther* dates from 1980. In the same year the city of Rotterdam commissioned for the Netherlands Opera *Satyagraha*, based on the life of Gandhi in South Africa. It was premiered in

Amsterdam in the summer of 1981 and performed in Brooklyn, New York in October 1981. The chamber opera *The Philosopher* was also first staged in Amsterdam in 1982 The three-act opera *Akhnaten*, set among the pharaohs of Egypt, uses a combination of ancient languages and English. Following a successful premiere in Stuttgart in March 1984, it was staged in Houston in October of that year and in New York and London in 1985.

Glass's sixth opera, *The Civil Wars: A Tree is Best Measured When It is Down*, described as a musical theater piece, was produced in Rome in 1983. *The Juniper Tree* dates from the same year. Houston Grand opera commissioned *The Making of the Representative for Planet 8* (1985–88), based on a story by Doris Lessing. Edgar Allen Poe's *The Fall of the House of Usher* provided the plot for his next opera, produced in Cambridge, Massachusetts in 1988.

There followed *1000 Airplanes on the Roof* (Vienna, 1988); *Hydrogen Jukebox* (Philadelphia, 1990); and *White Raven*, composed in 1991 and produced in Lisbon in 1998. To mark the 500th anniversary of the discovery of America, Glass composed *The Voyage* in 1992 to a commission from the Metropolitan Opera in New York. His next two operas are *Orphée* (Cambridge, Mass., 1993) and *La Belle et La Bête* (Gibellina, Sicily, 1994). The dance opera *Les Enfants terribles* was premiered in Zug, Switzerland in 1996. His most recent operas are *The Marriages Between Zones Three, Four and Five* (Heidelburg, 1997) and *Monsters of Grace* (Los Angeles, 1998).

In the 1980s, Glass turned to writing orchestral music: *The Olympian Lighting the Torch and Closing the 23rd Olympiad* (1984); *Phaedra* for strings (1985); *The Upper Room* for chamber orchestra, composed in 1986 for the dancer Twyla Tharp; Violin Concerto (1987) for Paul Zukovsky; *The Light* (Cleveland: 1987); *The Canyon* (1988); *Passages* for chamber orchestra (1990); *Concerto Grosso* (1992); six symphonies: no. 1, *Low Symphony* after David Bowie and Brian Eno (1992), no. 2 (1994), no 3 for strings (1994), no. 4, *Heroic Symphony* after David Bowie and Brian Eno (1996), no. 5 for five soloists, chorus, and orchestra (2000), and no. 6 (New York: 2002); *Echorus* for two violins and strings (1994–95); Concerto for Saxophone Quartet (1995); *Music from "The Secret Agent"* for chamber orchestra (1995); Double Concerto for timpani and orchestra, composed for Evelyn Glennie (New York: 2000); *Dancissimo* (Milwaukee: 2001); Cello Concerto (2001) for Julian Lloyd-Webber; and *Concerto Fantasy* for two timpanists and orchestra (2002).

The instrumental music of Glass includes five string quartets: no. 1, (1966), *Company* (1983), *Mishima* (1985), *Buczak* (1989), and no. 5 (1991); *In Again and Out* for two pianos (1967); *Head On* for piano trio (1967); *Pieces in the Shape of a Square* for two flutes (1967); *Strung Out* for amplified violin (1967); *Gradus* for soprano saxophone (1968); *How Now* for piano or ensemble (1968); *Another Look at Harmony III* for clarinet and piano (1975); *Fourth Series Part II* for flute and harmonica (1978); *Facades* for two soprano saxophones or two flutes and strings (1981); *Changes* for string quartet (1983); *Prelude to Endgame* for trumpet and double bass (1984); *Arabesque: in memoriam* for flute (1988); and *France: From the Screens* for violin (1991).

Glass's works for voices includes *Fourth Series Part I* for chorus and organ (1978); *Habeve Song* for soprano, clarinet, and bassoon (1983); *Three Songs* for chorus (1984); *Six Songs From Liquid Days* for voice and instruments (1986); *Itaipu* for chorus and orchestra (1988); and *Planctus* for voice and piano (1997).

Among the incidental music he has written, mostly for the Mabou Mines Company, are *Play* (Beckett) (1965); *Red Horse Animation* (Lee Breuer) (1968); *Music for Voices* (1972); *The Last Ones* (1975); *The Saint and the Football Player* (1975); *Dressed Like an Egg* (1977); *Cascando* (Beckett) (1979); *Mercier and Carnier* (1979); *Dead End Kids* (1980); *Company* (Beckett) (1983); *Pages From Cold Harbor* (1983); and *Endgame* (Beckett) (1984).

Following his collaboration on film music with Ravi Shankar in Paris in 1964, Glass has devoted an increasing amount of time to the medium. To date he has provided almost a hundred scores for features and documentaries, including films of his own music. Important among these are *North Star* (1977); *Koyaanisqatsi* (1981); *Hamburger Hill* (1987); *Powaqqatsi* (1988); *The Thin Blue Line* (1988); *Candyman* (1992); *The Secret Agent* (1996); *Kundun* (1997); *The Truman Show* (with Burkhard Dallwitz) (1998); and *The Hours* (2002), which won an Academy Award nomination.

GLEASON, FREDERICK GRANT
b. Middletown, Connecticut, 17 December 1848
d. Chicago, Illinois, 6 December 1903

After writing a Christmas Oratorio at the age of 16 without formal training, Gleason was taught by Dudley Buck. In 1869 he went to Germany, where he was a pupil of Ignaz Moscheles in Leipzig. The following year he moved to study in Berlin and London. It was in Europe that he first became familiar with the music of Wagner, and he himself composed several operas, only one of which, *Otho Visconti* (1877–90), was produced; it received one performance in Chicago in 1907. Another opera, *Montezuma*, is constructed on Wagnerian proportions and makes use of leitmotifs.

At the age of 28 Gleason settled in Chicago as an organist and composer. He taught at the Hershy School of Musical Art (1877–91) and the Chicago Conservatory (1891–1903). From 1884 to 1889 he was music critic of the *Chicago Tribune*. A number of his orchestral works were performed by Theodore Thomas, including *Processional of the Holy Grail*; a symphonic poem, *Edris* (1896); the tone poem *The Song of Life* (1900); and a Piano Concerto in G minor. His major choral work, *The Culprit Fay*, is a setting of Joseph Rodman Drake's poem. He also composed a *Te Deum* and *Auditorium Festival Ode* (1889). In addition he wrote three piano trios.

GOEB, ROGER (JOHN)

b. Cherokee, Iowa, 9 October 1914
d. Rockville Centre, New York, 3 January 1997

Goeb began his formal musical education after graduating from the University of Wisconsin with a degree in agricultural sciences. Following a stay in Paris (1939–39), where he was for a short time a pupil of Nadia Boulanger, he attended the Cleveland Institute of Music, where he studied with Herbert Elwell (M.M., 1942). He also received tuition from Otto Luening and attended New York University and Iowa State University, where he was awarded his Ph.D. (1945). In 1942 Goeb was appointed an instructor in music at the University of Oklahoma. Two years later he joined the music faculty of the University of Iowa. In 1945 he taught at Bard College, Annandale-on-Hudson, New York before moving two years later to the Juilliard School, where he stayed for three years. He taught for a year each at Columbia University and Stanford University, California. From 1957 to 1963 he was executive secretary of the American Composers Alliance. He was awarded two Guggenheim Fellowships (1950, 1952). For many years in the 1960's and 1970's, Goeb's career as a composer was seriously interrupted by the illness of his wife and son, who both suffered from multiple sclerosis.

Goeb's reputation rests mainly on his instrumental works and six symphonies. The First Symphony, composed in 1941 and later withdrawn, was followed four years later by Symphony no. 2 (1950). Symphony no. 3, written in 1952, was performed by Stokowski, who also recorded it. This piece, his most performed work, is characterized by strong rhythmical impulses and vigorous melodic lines. His Fourth Symphony, dating from 1956, was performed by William Steinberg and the Pittsburgh Symphony Orchestra. Symphonies no. 5 and no. 6 were written in 1981 and 1989.

Goeb's other orchestral works include *Lyric Piece* for trumpet and strings (1942); *Prairie Songs* for small orchestra (1947); *Fantasy* for oboe and strings (1947);

Romanza for strings (1948); and two concertinos, no. 1 (1950) and no. 2, commissioned by the Louisville Orchestra in 1956. He also wrote four *Concertants*: no. 1 for flute, oboe, clarinet and strings (1948), no. 2 for bassoon (or cello) and strings (1951), no. 3 for viola and chamber orchestra (1951), and no. 4 for chamber orchestra (1951); *Fantasy* for piano and strings (1952); *Five American Dances* for strings (1952); a Violin Concerto (1953); a Piano Concerto (1954); two *Sinfonias* (1957, 1962); *Encomium* (1958); and *Iowa Concerto* for small orchestra (1959). In 1982 he returned to orchestral music with *Divertissement* for strings, *Memorial*, and *Caprice*. His last works in this medium include *Fantasia* (1983), *Essay* (1984), and *Gambol* (1984).

Goeb composed much instrumental music: four string quartets (1942, 1948, 1954, 1980); four woodwind quintets (1949, 1955, 1980, 1982); Sonata for solo viola (1942); a String Trio (1945); Suite for wind trio (1945); Piano Quintet (1948); Brass Septet (1949); Quintet for trombone and strings (1949); two Divertimenti for solo flute (1950); *Three Processionals* for organ and brass quintet (1951); Divertimento for cello and piano (1951); *Three Processionals* for brass and organ (1953); Sonata for solo violin (1957); *Declarations* for cello and woodwind quintet (1961); *Running Colors* for string quartet (1961); Oboe Quartet (1964); Brass Trio (1979); String Quintet (1979); Octet (1980); Brass Quintet (1980); Flute Quartet (1983); *Imagery* for viola and piano (1984); *Black on White* for clarinet and strings (1985); and *Nuances* for clarinet and viola (1986).

GOLDMAN, RICHARD FRANKO

b. New York, New York, 7 December 1910
d. Baltimore, Maryland, 19 January 1980

Richard Franko Goldman was the son of Edwin Franko Goldman (1878–1956), the famous bandmaster. He studied with Ralph Leopold, Clarence Adler, and Wallingford Riegger, and graduated from Columbia University in 1931. He was a pupil of Nadia Boulanger in Paris in the mid-1930s. On his return to the United States, he became associate conductor of the Goldman Band in 1937, succeeding his father as conductor in 1956, a post he held until 1979. From 1952 to 1960 he was chairman of the literature and materials department at the Juilliard School and editor of the *Juilliard Review* (1953–58). In addition he was New York critic of *Music Quarterly* (1948–68). He was also a visiting professor at Princeton University (1952–56). In 1968 he became head of the Peabody Conservatory, Baltimore, and in the following year was named to the post of president there. He retired in 1977.

Goldman's works for concert band include *A Curtain*

Richard Franko Goldman.
Courtesy The Juilliard School.

Raiser and Country Dance; *Hymn* for brass choir; and *A Sentimental Journey* (1941). For orchestra he wrote *Le Bobino Suite* and *The Lee Rigg*. Instrumental music includes *Three Duets* for clarinets (1944) and a Violin Sonata (1952). He also wrote two operas, *Athalia* and *The Mandarin*.

In 1943, Goldman edited *Landmarks of Early American Music*, an important collection of songs and instrumental pieces from 1760–1800. His other books are *The Band's Music* (1938), *The Concert Band* (1946), *The Wind Band: Its Literature and Technique* (1961), and *Harmony in Western Music* (1965).

GOLDMARK, RUBIN
b. New York, New York, 15 August 1872
d. New York, New York, 6 March 1936

Goldmark was the nephew of the Austrian composer Karl Goldmark (1830–1915). After studying with Dvořák at the New York National Conservatory (1891–93) and at both the University and Conservatory in Vienna, he was appointed a teacher of piano and composition at the College Conservatory, Colorado Springs (1895–1901), moving to a similar post at the National Conservatory in 1902 In 1924 he joined the faculty of the Juilliard School as head of the department of composition, a post he held until his death.

Although he was considered in his time a composer of some significance, it is as a teacher that Goldmark is remembered today. Among his pupils were George Gershwin, Aaron Copland, Frederick Jacobi, Paul Nordoff, Bernard Wagenaar, Vittorio Giannini, and Nicolai Berezowsky. Goldmark's own compositions reflect his patriotic admiration for American life and culture. For orchestra he wrote an overture, *Hiawatha* (1900); a tone-poem, *Samson*, performed in Boston in 1914; *The Call of the Plains* (1915, orchestrated 1922); and *A Negro Rhapsody* (1923). His Requiem (1918) is based on Lincoln's Gettysburg Address. His instrumental music includes a String Quartet in A; a Piano Trio in D minor (1892); a Piano Quartet (1910); and a Violin Sonata. A Piano Quintet won the Paderewski Prize in 1909.

GOTTLIEB, JACK
b. New Rochelle, New York, 12 October 1930

Gottlieb was first encouraged to be a composer by Max Helfman, a noted composer of music for the synagogue. He received his bachelor of arts degree from Queens College, New York (1953), where he was a pupil of Karol Rathaus; a master of arts degree from Brandeis University, Waltham, Massachusetts (1955) as a pupil of Irvine Fine; and a D.M.A. from the University of Illinois, Urbana (1964). His teachers of composition included Robert Palmer and Burrill Phillips. He also studied with Aaron Copland and Boris Blacher at the Berkshire Music Center, Tanglewood.

From 1958 to 1966 he was Leonard Bernstein's assistant at the New York Philharmonic. He taught at Loyola University, New Orleans, Louisiana in 1966; from 1970 to 1973 he served as music director at Temple Israel, St. Louis, Missouri.

In 1967 his sacred service *Love Songs for Sabbath* was performed at the College of St. Catherine in St. Paul, Minnesota, probably the first time in history that a full-length Jewish liturgical service had ever been given under Roman Catholic auspices. In 1973 he was named Composer-in-Residence at Hebrew Union College, Jewish Institute of Religion, and in 1975 he was appointed the first professor of music at its New York School of Sacred Music.

In 1977 he assumed the position of publications director of Amberson Enterprises, Inc., a company which managed the various music activities of Leonard Bernstein. In 1978 he formed his own publishing company, Theophilous Music Enterprises, Inc. in association with G. Schirmer, Inc. From 1991 to 1997 he was President of the American Society for Jewish Music.

Jack Gottlieb.
Courtesy Theophilous Music, Inc.

Gottlieb has composed an orchestral overture, *Pieces of Seven* (1962, later withdrawn) and *Articles of Faith* for orchestra and memorable voices (tapes of famous statesmen; 1965). He has written two one-act operas: *Tea Party* (libretto: Erik Johns; 1955), winner of the Ohio University Opera Competition and Nadworney Memorial Award of the National Federation of Music Clubs; and *Public Dance* (1964), later withdrawn. Other dramatic works are the "operatorio" *The Song of Songs, Which is Solomon's*, a setting of the biblical text, completed in 1976 with the assistance of a grant from the National Endowment for the Arts; *The Movie Opera*, a music drama for torch soprano and chorus (1982); and two further operas, *Death of a Ghost* (New York, 1988) and *Belwether* (New York, 1989), the latter also withdrawn. Gottlieb's most recent stage works are a musical fable in two acts, *After the Flood* (1990–91, rev. 1995, 2001) for six voices; and *Monkey Biz'niz* (1991–93), described as a musical diversion, performed in December 1998.

Choral works include *Kids' Calls* (1957), a first-prize winner in a National Federation of Music Clubs Choral Contest; *In Memory of . . .* , a cantata, first-prize winner in a Brown University Choral Contest and his first published work (1960); *Shout for Joy*, psalm settings for choir, piano, two flutes, and three drums (1967); *New Year's Service for Young People* (1973); *Verses (from Psalm 118)* for chorus and organ (1973); *Sharing the Prophets* for chorus, piano, percussion, and bass (1975); *Four Affirmations* for chorus and brass quintet (1976); *Set Me as a Seal* for chorus, violin, and piano (1976, rev. 1991); and *Psalmistry* for four singers and 11 jazz players (1979, rev. 2000). More recent choral works are *Presidential Suite* for chorus (1989); a cantata, *Scenes From the Song of Songs* (1997); *Grant Us Peace* for soloists, chorus, and organ (1999); *Your Hand, O God, Has Guided* (1999); and *May the Words* (1999).

Among his chamber compositions are *Pastorale and Dance* for violin and piano (1953); a Clarinet Quintet (1952), later withdrawn; a String Quartet (1954), prize winner in a Broadcast Music Inc. competition; Piano Sonata (1960); a wind quintet with narrator, *Twilight Crane* (1961, rev. 2000); *Flickers* for winds, percussion, and cello (1967); *Fantasy on High Holy Day Themes* for unaccompanied cello (1998); *Sessionals* for brass quintet (1998); and *Rick's Place* (*Piano Trio*) (2002).

In addition to a considerable body of solo liturgical music written for the synagogue, there are Gottlieb's secular songs: *Hoofprints* (Tennessee Williams) (1954); *Two Blues* for voice and clarinet (1954); *Songs of Loneliness* (Cavafy) (1962); *Haiku Souvenirs* (Bernstein) (1967); *Downtown Blues for Uptown Halls* for voice, clarinet, and piano (1967, rev. 1999); three "night' songs: *May We Lie Down* (1973), *Acquainted with the Night* (1975), and *It is Evening* (1975); three songs to Hebrew texts, *Tefilor sheva* (1974), *Veahavta* (1977),

177

and *Hashkiveinu* (1977); *I Think Continually* (Stephen Spender; 1978); *Torch Song*, a concert mad scene (1980); *Light and Splendor* (Leonard Cohen) for voice, flute, and clarinet (1981); and three song cycles, *Solitaire* (1988-91); *Scrapbook* (1989–91); and *yes is a pleasant country* (e.e. cummings; 1993).

Gottlieb is a lecturer and reviewer as well as the author of numerous articles on musical subjects for program and record notes and scholarly journals. His lecture-entertainment entitled "From Shtetl to Stage Door' has been performed throughout the United States.

GOTTSCHALK, LOUIS MOREAU

b. New Orleans, Louisiana, 8 May 1829

d. Tijuca, Rio de Janiero, Brazil, 18 December 1869

Gottschalk's father was a Jewish businessman of English origin; his mother, a Creole, came from a family of plantation owners in San Domingo. From an early age he had shown remarkable musical talent; as a child he was able to play on the piano tunes by Rossini, Donizetti, and Meyerbeer he heard at the French Opera House in New Orleans. In his hometown he had become familiar with the dances of the African-American slaves and the music of the Spanish and French settlers. In addition, the folk music of Latin America and the Creoles exerted a strong influence upon him as a composer. He was one of the first to use genuine African-American tunes in serious works for the concert hall.

In 1842, at the age of 13, Gottschalk was sent to France to study the piano and composition. His first piano teacher in Paris was Charles Hallé. This unusual child with such original musical ideas soon gained an enviable reputation. He was a great favorite in the salons of Paris society and was highly praised by Chopin, who hailed him as a future king of the keyboard. He also impressed Berlioz, who taught him composition, as did Liszt. In 1850 he toured France and Switzerland and the following year went to Spain, where he resided until 1852

After a short stay in Paris, Gottschalk returned to America in 1853 and became one of the first musicians to undertake extensive tours throughout the United States. His season in New York was a social and musical triumph. Even the Civil War did not interrupt his career, as he continued to play his own compositions and newly acquired works from Europe in every part of the country. In the winter of 1855–56 he gave 80 concerts in New York, and between 1862 and 1865 he played in 1,100 concerts across the United States and Canada. His flamboyant manner charmed the ladies but aroused animosity in some men. Oliver Wendell Holmes

described him and being "something between a remembrance of the Count D'Orsay and an anticipation of Oscar Wilde."

Gottschalk's striking personality and Lisztian virtuosity created a sensation wherever he went. In 1857 he visited Cuba with the 14-year old Adelina Patti and spent the next six years traveling in the Caribbean. It was at this time that he took a personal role in opposing slavery, although his maternal grandparents had been slave-owners. He himself freed three slaves he had inherited on San Domingo. On these extended tours, Gottschalk indulged his extravagance by arranging concerts with choirs and orchestras numbering several hundred performers.

Most of his compositions in their original form were for piano or piano duet, and typical of their time, often possess little intrinsic value. Others, considering the early date of composition (before 1860), reveal great originality. *Le Bananier* (*The Banana Seller*), *Danse des Nêgres*, *Chanson Nêgre*, *La Savane*, and *La Bamboula*, written when Gottschalk was only 15, are not only brilliant displays of virtuosity but are quite unlike any comparable music from Europe. *Souvenir de Porto Rico* (*Marche des Gibaros*) uses a musical language of the Caribbean not encountered again in any composer until the early years of the next century. It is constructed in the form of a patrol that begins in the distance, rises gradually to a powerful climax, and moves away into the distance. Many of these works exist in several forms, for piano solo, piano duet, two pianos, or for orchestra, and it is often difficult to detect which version is the original.

Gottschalk composed two so-called symphonies, though neither is precisely symphonic in form or stature. The First, in two movements, subtitled *La Nuit des Tropiques*, was completed in Guadeloupe in 1859. The opening Andante recalls Berlioz and early 19th-century opera composers, even Wagner at times, with an abundance of expressive melody. The second movement has its roots firmly in Latin America, although the ghost of Rossini hovers over the closing pages. The Afro-Cuban percussion instruments that maintain an ostinato rhythmical background are amazingly innovative for the time. Symphony no. 2, *À Montevideo*, is in one movement, has seven sections, and is in essence an orchestral rhapsody. As the title suggests, it was composed in Uruguay. Anticipating Charles Ives, Gottschalk combines Uruguayan tunes with "Hail Columbia" and "Yankee Doodle" in the final part.

For each country he visited, Gottschalk composed a musical tribute of some kind. On his arrival in Havana in 1859 he wrote an opera in one act, *Escenas Campestres* (*Cuban Country Scenes*), a *Triumph Hymn*, and a *Grand March*. These were performed at a giant festival on 17 February 1860. The orchestra numbered

Louis Moreau Gottschalk.
*Courtesy the Rare Book, Manuscript,
and Special Collections Library,
Duke University.*

650, with 50 drums and 80 trumpets; the event was a great success. His piano piece *Ojos Criollos* (*Creole Eyes*; 1859) was arranged for 39 pianists and performed at another Havana "festival gigantica" in 1861. Later for a concert in Rio de Janiero, he wrote *Marche Solennelle*, dedicated to the Emperor of Brazil, Juan Carlos, ending with a setting of the Brazilian national anthem for orchestra, brass bands, and cannons, some years before Tchaikovsky composed his *Overture 1812* for similar forces. No doubt his lessons with Berlioz in Paris had given Gottschalk a taste for enterprises on such a huge scale.

Most of the other surviving extended works, such as *Fantasia Triomphale sur l'Hymne Nationale Brésilien* (1862); *"The Union,"* a *Concert Paraphrase on National Airs* (1862); the delightfully ebullient *Grande Tarantelle* (1868); and *Variations on the Portuguese National Hymn* (1869), all for solo piano and orchestra, are the best examples of Gottschalk's fluent if somewhat facile technique for writing popular music. At times they border on the banal and absurd, but their jaunty, infectious humor still endear them to listeners.

Many of his works have only recently been rediscovered and prepared from their original editions and manuscripts for performance today. Their revival has helped illustrate the musical scene in America during the 19th century. Although often providing greater curiosity than musical value, these works do reveal a strikingly individual talent with a refreshing directness of expression. His diary, published after his death as *Notes of a Pianist*, gives a vivid picture of the abundance of music-making in both North and South America at the time when it might be thought that little notable activity was taking place.

Among his pupils was the pianist Maria Teresa Carreño (1853–1917), who was an ardent advocate of the piano music of MacDowell. Gottschalk died in Rio de Janiero, probably of yellow fever, although some stories suggest he was murdered by a jealous husband. He was buried in Greenwood Cemetery, Brooklyn where an appropriately large monument marks the grave.

GOULD, MORTON

b. Richmond Hill, Queens, New York, 10 December 1913

d. New York, New York, 21 February, 1996

Gould received his first piano lessons at a very early age and at six had his first piece of music published, a *Waltz* for piano. He was a student at the Institute of Musical Art (later the Juilliard School) and New York

179

University, from which he graduated at the age of 15. He became a staff pianist with NBC and in 1936 was conductor of the WOR Radio Orchestra. He was later on the network and on Columbia and RCA records, and was guest conductor with all the major orchestras in America. From 1986 to 1994 he was president of ASCAP.

Gould's compositions reflect the very strong influence of "Americana," in which American history and legend play a great part in providing musical inspiration.

To his credit are two Broadway musicals, *Billion Dollar Baby* (1945) and *Arms and the Girl* (1950). The ballet *Fall River Legend* tells the story of Lizzie Borden and the famous axe-murders of 1892. Commissioned for Agnes de Mille, it was produced at the Metropolitan Opera House in New York by Ballet Theater in 1948. Another ballet, *Fiesta*, was staged in Cannes in 1957. *Interplay*, with choreography by Jerome Robbins, has been in the repertory of leading ballet companies. He composed two further ballets, *Clarinade* (Ballanchine, 1964) and *I'm Old Fashioned* (Robbins, 1983).

Gould's output of orchestral works was enormous. He wrote four numbered symphonies: no. 1, performed in Pittsburgh under Fritz Reiner in 1943; no. 2, *On Marching Tunes* (1944) for the New York Philharmonic Orchestra under Vladimir Golschmann; no. 3 (Dallas, 1947), an ambitious work on the scale of a "Great American Symphony," revised with a new finale and re-premiered by Mitropoulos in 1948; and no. 4 for band, commissioned by West Point and performed there in 1952.

Other principal orchestral compositions include three *American Symphonettes* (1933, 1935, 1937); *Little Symphony* (1936); *Spirituals* (1937); *A Homespun Overture* (1939); *Serenade of Carols* (1939); a *Foster Gallery* on Stephen Foster songs, commissioned by Fritz Reiner in 1940; *Latin American Symphonette* (1940); *A Lincoln Legend*, commissioned for the NBC Symphony Orchestra in 1942; *Cowboy Rhapsody* (1942); *American Salute* (1943); *Harvest* for vibraphone, harp, and strings (1945); Concerto for Orchestra (1945); *Minstrel Show* (1946); *Philharmonic Waltzes* (1948); *Big City Blues* (1950); *Showpiece* (1954); *Jekyll and Hyde Variations* (1955); and *Rhythm Gallery* for narrator and orchestra (1958).

Later orchestral works are *Festive Music* (1963); *Calypso Souvenir* (1964); *Venice*, commissioned by the Seattle Symphony Orchestra in 1966, scored for double orchestra and brass choirs; *Columbia: Broadsides for Orchestra* (1967), composed for the National Symphony Orchestra of Washington, D.C.; *American Ballads* (1968); *Concerto Grosso* (1969); and *Soundings* (1969), commissioned by the Junior League of Atlanta for Robert Shaw and the Atlanta Symphony Orchestra.

In 1970 Gould wrote four short orchestral pieces: *Fire Music: Toccata*, *Indian Attack*, *Night Music*, and *Serenade*. For the 1976 Bicentennial he composed *Symphony of Spirituals*. His last orchestral pieces were *Cheers!*, a celebration march (1979); *Burchfield Gallery* (1980); *Housewarming* (1982); *Apple Waltzes* (1983); *Flourishes and Galop* (1983); *Classical Variations on a Colonial Theme* (1986); *Flares and Declamations* (1987); and *Minute + Waltz Rag* (1990).

Gould composed two concertos for piano (1937, 1944) and one each for violin (1938), viola (1943), tap dancer (1952), four guitars (1968), and flute (1984). Other works with solo instruments are *Chorale and Fugue in Jazz* for two pianos (1932, orchestrated 1934); *American Concertette*, subtitled *Interplay*, for piano (1943); *Dance Variations* for two pianos (1952); *Inventions* for four pianos (1953); *Dialogues* for piano and strings (1956); *Vivaldi Gallery* for string quartet and divided orchestra (1968); *Troubadour Suite* for four guitars (1969); and *Diversions* for tenor saxophone (1990). In 1954 for Benny Goodman he composed *Derivations* for clarinet and jazz band.

Gould contributed several significant items to the repertory of the concert band including *Jericho* (1939); *Fanfare for Freedom* (1942); *Concertante* for viola and band (1943); *Ballade* (1945); *Family Album Suite* (1951); *Folk Suite* (1955); *Santa Fe Saga* (1956); *St Lawrence Suite* (1958); *Prisms* (1962); *Mini Suite* (1968); *American Ballads* (1976); *Gala* (1983); and *Centennial Symphony* (1983), in addition to the Fourth Symphony.

An early choral work, *Cantata* for chorus and 24 instruments, was completed in 1931. Other pieces for voices are *Song of Freedom* for narrator, chorus, and orchestra; *Of Time and the River* (Thomas Wolfe) for chorus (1946); *Declaration*, a symphonic narrative for two speakers, speaking chorus, and orchestra (1957); a cantata, *Something to Do* for soloists, narrator, chorus, and orchestra (1976); and *Quotations* for double chorus and orchestra (1984).

Gould composed film scores for cinema and television including *Ring of Steel* (1941); *Delightfully Dangerous* (1945); *San Francisco Conference* (1945); *Cinerama Holiday* (1955); *Windjammer* (1957); *War World I* (1964); *Scott Fitzgerald and Hollywood* (1976); *Holocaust* (1977); *Turn of the Century*; and *The Secret of Freedom*.

Among his instrumental pieces are a Suite for violin and piano (1945); *Benny's Gig* for clarinet and double bass (1962); Tuba Suite (1971); Suite for cello and piano (1981); *Concerto Concertante* for violin, wind quintet, and piano (1981-82); *Duo* for flute and clarinet (1982); and two works for brass and percussion completed in 1991, *Festive Fanfare* and *Hail to the First Lady*. His piano pieces include three sonatas

(1930, 1933, 1936) and popular short items such as *Boogie Woogie Etude* (1943).

GRANT, WILLIAM PARKS

b. Cleveland, Ohio, 4 January 1910
d. Oxford, Mississippi, 5 April 1988

Grant received his initial musical training at Capital University, Columbus, Ohio (1929–32) and Ohio State University (1932–33). At the Eastman School of Music (Ph.D., 1948), he was a pupil of Howard Hanson, Herbert Elwell, Wayne Barlow, Bernard Rogers, and Harold Gleason. He taught at the Tarleton State College (1937–43), Northeast Junior College branch of Louisiana State University (1943–47), Temple University (1947–53), and the University of Mississippi from 1953 until his retirement in 1973.

Grant's only work for the stage is a ballet, *The Dream of the Ballet Master* (1934). His orchestral music includes three symphonies: no. 1 in D minor (1930–38), no. 2 (1941–43), and no. 3 in one movement (1961); *Poeme Elegiaque* (1928); *Overture: Macbeth* (1929-30); *Masque of the Red Death* (1931–41); a Horn Concerto (1940); a Clarinet Concerto (1942–45); *Autumn Woodland Poem* for strings (1945–46); a Double Bass Concerto (1946); three *Suites for Strings* (1946, 1952, 1959); *Rhythmic Overture* (1947); *Scherzo* for flute and small orchestra (1949); *Homage Ode* (1949); *Dramatic Overture* (1949); two overtures (1955); *A Musical Tribute* (1955, rev. 1959); and *Characteristic Sketches* (1963).

Among his instrumental pieces are *Night Poem* for string quartet (1940–42); two piano sonatas (1940, 1953); *Poem* for horn (or cello) and organ (1945); *Gothic Triptych* for organ (1947); *Essay* for horn (or cello) (1948); two string quartets (1948–49, 1963); *Laconic Suite* for brass quartet (1949); *Prelude and Dance* for brass ensemble (1951); *Soliloquy and Jubilation* for wind quintet (1952); *Brevities* for brass quartet (1952); *Concert Duo* for tuba and piano (1954); and *Lento and Allegro* for brass quintet (1954–55).

Grant was the author of two educational books, *Music for Elementary Teachers* (1951, rev. 1960) and *Handbook of Musical Terms* (1967).

GRANTHAM, DONALD

b. Duncan, Oklahoma, 9 November 1947

Grantham studied at the University of Oklahoma (1967–70) and at the University of Southern California, Los Angeles (1970–73) with Halsey Stevens and Robert Linn. He spent the summers of 1973 and 1974 as a pupil of Nadia Boulanger in Paris. He returned in 1974

Donald Grantham.
Courtesy the composer.

to teach at the University of Southern California, moving in the following year to the University of Texas at Austin, where he became a professor in 1991.

For orchestra he has composed *En album de los duendecitos* (1983); *Invocation and Dance* (1988); *To the Wind's Twelve Quarters* (1993); *Fantasy on Mr Hyde's Song* (1993), *Southern Harmony* (2000); and *Exhilaration and Cry* (2000). For wind ensemble he has provided several major works, including a Concerto for bass trombone (1979); *Bouncer* for brass quintet (1991); *Bum's Rush* (1994); *Fantasy Variations* (1995); *J'ai ete un bal* (1999); and *Kentucky Harmony* (2000). Among his many instrumental compositions are a Piano Trio (1971); *Chamber Concerto* for harpsichord and string quartet (1974); Sonata in one movement for bass trombone and piano (1979); *Duendecitos!* for flute and piano (1981); and *Fantasy Variations* for two pianos (1996).

His vocal music includes *La noche en la isla* (Neruda) for baritone and orchestra (1980); *To the King Celestial* for soprano and chamber orchestra (1981); *Four Choral Settings of e.e. cummings* (1985); *Seven Choral Settings of Emily Dickinson* (1983); *Three Choral Settings of W.B. Yeats* (1986); *You Shall Go Out in Joy* for chorus and organ (1989); *Lascivious Love Songs* for mezzo-soprano and wind quintet (or piano; 1990); and *On This Day*, a Christmas cantata for soprano, chorus, children's chorus, percussion, and harp (1993). His opera *The Boor* dates from 1989.

GREEN, RAY BURNS
b. Cavendish, Missouri, 13 September 1908
d. New York, New York, April 16, 1997

Green studied with Ernest Bloch at the San Francisco Conservatory (1927–33) and at the University of California, Berkeley (1933–35) with Albert Elkus. He was a pupil of Darius Milhaud in Paris (1936), where he also studied conducting with Pierre Monteux. He succeeded Bloch as head of composition at the San Francisco Conservatory. From 1939 to 1941 he was supervisor and director of the Northern California Federal Music Project in San Francisco. He was musical director of the May O'Donnell Dance Company in New York (1940–61) and from 1948 to 1961 served as executive secretary of the American Music Center. In 1951 he founded the American Music Edition.

Although Green was noted primarily as a teacher, he composed a large quantity of music. For orchestra he is best known for the incidental music he wrote for Aristophanes' play *The Birds* (1934); Symphony no. 2 (1945); and the lively *Sunday Sing Symphony* (1946). Other orchestral pieces include *Prelude and Fugue* (1937); *Jig Tune* (1944); three *Short Symphonies*: no. 1 in A (1945–53), no. 2 in F (1970), and no. 3 in C (1974); *Three Pieces for a Concert* for chamber orchestra (1947); and *Country Dance Symphony* Among his works for solo instrument and orchestra are a Concertino for piano (1937); *Three Inventories for Casey Jones* for piano (1939); *Concertante* for viola (1946); *Rhapsody: Lonesome Valley* for harp (1950); a Violin Concerto (1952); and a Piano Concerto (1981). He also wrote two suites, no. 1 for violin and piano (1929) and no. 2 for viola and piano (1930); a String Quartet and a Wind Quintet, both dating from 1933; *Five Epigrammatic Portraits* for string quartet (1933); Piano Sonata (1933); *Holiday for 4* for viola, clarinet, bassoon, and piano (1935); *Concert Set* for trumpet, piano, and drums (1941); *Duo Concertante* for violin and piano (1950); and *Twelve Short Sonatas* for piano (1949–80).

For the O'Donnell Company, Green composed numerous dance scores, including *Hymn Tune Set* (1937); *Of Pioneer Women* (1937); *Jig for a Concert* (1937–39); *Rondo Running Set* (1939); *Dance Theme and Variations* (1940); *So Proudly We Hail: American Dance Saga* (1940); *On American Themes* (1941); *Forsaken Garden* (1949); *Dance Energies* (1950–73); *Ho-*

rizon Song (1951); *Suspension – at a Still Point in a Turning World* (1952); *The Queen's Obsession* (1952–59); and *Dance Sonatas* no. 1 (1953) and no. 2 (1957). He also provided two scores for other ballet companies, *American Document* (Martha Graham, 1938) and *Beachcomber* (R. Jonay, 1938). His contribution to the band repertory includes *Processional Dance* (1938); *Walkaround* (1938); *Kennedy Mountain Running Set* (1946); *Jig Theme and Six Changes* (1948); and *Folksong Fantasies* for trumpet and band (1949).

Green was the author of a book, *Bibliography on Musical Theory* (1952).

GRIFFES, CHARLES TOMLINSON
b. Elmira, New York, 17 September 1884
d. New York, New York, 8 April 1920

Griffes began to study the piano with his sister Katherine. In 1889 he undertook lessons with Mary Selina Broughton, who discovered his talent as a composer. After graduating from school in 1903, on the advice of Broughton, he went to Germany, arriving in Berlin in late August. He enrolled at the Stern Conservatory where he studied piano with Ernst Jedliczka and Gottfried Galston. After a year he left to work privately, receiving composition lessons from Englebert Humperdinck.

Although piano was intended to be his principal subject, composition occupied an increasing amount of Grifes's time. In Berlin he wrote his first published work, *20 Songs* to German texts, and two orchestral pieces, an *Overture* (1905) and *Symphonische Phantasie* (1907). Griffes returned to the United States in 1907 and took up the post of director of music at the Hackley School for Boys, Tarryrown, New York, where he remained until his death.

In spite of the teaching of Humperdinck, Griffes felt his musical leanings were definitely toward the French School of Debussy and Ravel. These influences are clearly marked in his most significant orchestral work, the symphonic poem *The Pleasure Dome of Kubla Khan*, inspired by Coleridge's poem. This piece conjures up the exotic world of the orient, beginning with a peaceful picture of the flowing river, building to a climax of orgiastic revelry, which is later interrupted by a return of the opening music. *The Pleasure Dome of Kubla Khan*, begun in 1912 as a piano piece, was completed for orchestra in 1916. This work of masterly orchestration received its first performance by the Boston Symphony Orchestra under Pierre Monteux on 28 November 1919, a few months before the composer's death.

Another orchestral work, *Clouds*, is closely modeled on *Nuages*, the first of Debussy's *Nocturnes*, and opens with a chordal sequence played by the woodwinds that certainly had its origin in the Debussy piece. *Poem* for flute and orchestra (1918) is an attractive concert item which deserves to be more widely known.

Griffes's piano music, including *The White Peacock* (1915), which he orchestrated for a ballet in 1919, and his songs appear from time to time today in recital programs. They too reveal the very strong French characteristics of his music. His last work, the Piano Sonata (1917–19), shows that the composer had transcended the influence of Debussy and was forging a more personal language, although certain features of the music of another composer, Scriabin, appear in the piano writing itself.

His interest in oriental music, evident in *The Pleasure Dome of Kubla Khan* and the Piano Sonata, is further reflected in two compositions for the stage: *Sho-jo,* a Japanese music and dance drama for small orchestra of exotic instruments, written in 1917; and the dance drama *The Kairn of Koridwen,* composed in 1916 and produced in the following year in New York by Adolf Bolm for Ballet Intime.

Griffes's other important works are *Three Tone Pictures,* op. 5 (1910–12), *Notturno* (1918), *Nocturne* (1919), and *Bacchanale* (1919), all for orchestra; *Two Sketches* for string quartet, based on Indian themes (1918–19); and a setting of J. A. Symonds' poem *These Things Shall Be* for unison choir (1916).

His later songs are somewhat eclectic in style, relying on the French *melodie* as their source of inspiration. Important among them are *Two Rondels,* op. 4 (1914); *Five Poems of Ancient China and Japan,* op. 10. for medium voice and orchestra (1916–17); *Three Poems of Fiona MacLeod,* op. 11 for voice and orchestra (1918); *German Songs* (1909–10), *Tone Images,* op. 3 (1912), *Four Impressions* (1912–15), settings in the original French of poems by Oscar Wilde; and the unpublished *Song of the Dagger* (1916).

In addition to the Piano Sonata, Griffes composed many piano pieces, a number of which were orchestrated by the composer (see above). The *Four Roman Sketches,* op. 7 (1915–16) are entitled *The White Peacock, Nightfall, The Fountain of Acqua Paolo,* and *Clouds.* The first piece derives its name not from the D.H. Lawrence novel but from a lesser-known poem by William Sharp (Fiona MacLeod). *Four Preludes* for piano were completed in 1910.

Had he lived another 30 years, Griffes might have become the most influential composer of his generation in the United States. His last important work, the Piano Sonata, shows that he had absorbed the initial influences of his earlier music and had begun to establish his own style. Technical mastery of form and orchestration is evident even in his first compositions.

His death at such a crucial time in the development of American music robbed the nation of her most promising protégé. He died of empyema at the age of 35.

GRIFFIS, ELLIOT

b. Boston, Massachusetts, 28 January 1893
d. Los Angeles, California, 8 June 1967

Griffis studied at Ithaca College (1910–13) and with Horatio Parker at Yale (1915–16). He was also a pupil of George Chadwick at the New England Conservatory, Boston (1917–18). In 1920 he began teaching at Grinnell College, Iowa, moving to the Brooklyn Settlement School in 1923. He also taught at St Louis School of Music (1935–36) and Westchester Conservatory, White Plains, New York (1942–43). Following the Second World War he spent two years in Vienna before settling in Los Angeles, where he worked on film music.

For the stage Griffis composed an operetta, *The Blue Scarab* (1934), and an opera, *Port of Pleasure,* produced in Los Angeles in 1963. His orchestral music includes *Variations* for strings (1924); *A Persian Fable* (1925); a symphonic poem *Paul Bunyan, Colossus* (1926, rev.34); Symphony *No.* 1 (1931); Symphony no. 2 *Fantastic Pursuit* for strings (1941); *Yon Green Mountain Suite* (1943); and *Montevallo: Concerto Grosso* for organ, piano, and strings (1945). His music followed neo-Romantic models.

Among his instrumental compositions are a Piano Sonata (1919); three string quartets, no. 1 (1926), no. 2 (1930), and no. 3 (1937); a Violin Sonata (1931); *To the Sun* for piano trio (1940); Suite for piano trio (1940); *The Aztec Flute* for flute and piano trio (1942); and *The Fox and the Crow* for chamber ensemble (1950). He also wrote many songs and piano solos.

GRIMM, CARL HUGO

b. Zanesville, Ohio, 31 October 1890
d. Cincinnati, Ohio, 25 October 1978

Grimm studied in Cincinnati and with Frank Van Der Stucken. He taught at the Cincinnati Conservatory from 1907, becoming head of the composition department in 1931 and retiring in 1952. In addition he held several posts as organist in the city from 1907 to 1952.

For orchestra he composed *Erotic Poem* (1927); *Thanatopsis* (1928); *Abraham Lincoln* (1930); a *Byzantine Suite* (1930); a symphonic poem *Montana* (1943); *An American Overture* (1946); a Trumpet Concerto (1948); and *Pennsylvania Overture* (1955). His instrumental music includes a String Quartet; *Fantasia* for two clarinets, cello, and piano; a *Little Serenade* for wind instruments (1934); and a Cello Sonata (1945).

His *Gothic Mass* for mixed voices, composed in 1970, was his last work.

GROFÉ, FERDE (FERDINAND RUDOLPH VON)

b. New York, New York, 27 March 1892
d. Santa Monica, California, 3 April 1972

Grofé was born into a family of musicians. At 17 he joined the Los Angeles Symphony Orchestra as a viola player and remained there for ten years. In 1917 he became a pianist and arranger for Paul Whiteman's band in Los Angeles and achieved a certain fame as the orchestrator of Gershwin's *Rhapsody in Blue*. For the Whiteman Band he composed *Russian Rose* (1922); *Broadway at Night* (1924); *Three Shades of Blue* (1927); *Blue Flame* (1928); *Digga, Digga Da* (1928); *Musette* (1928); *Knute Rockne* (1931); *Metropolis: A Blue Fantasia* (1932); and *Trylon and Persiphere* (1939). From 1939 to 1942 he taught at the Juilliard Graduate School, New York.

The popularity of *Grand Canyon Suite* (1931), frequently played by Toscanini, earned Grofé a wide reputation. Most of his other orchestral works are of a similar pictorial nature: *Mississippi: a tone journey* (1925); *Mark Twain Suite* (1925); *Tabloid Suite* (1933); *Killarney (An Irish Fantasy)* (1934); *Hollywood Ballet* (1935); *Rudy Vallee Suite* (1935); *A Day on the Farm* (1936); *Hollywood Ballet 2* (1937); *Kentucky Derby Suite* (1938); *Tin Pan Alley (The Melodic Decades)* (1938); *Going to Press* (1938); *Wheels Suite* (1939); *Biography of an American* (1943); *Aviation Suite* (1946); *Atlantic Crossing* (with chorus) (1950); *Lincoln's Gettysburg Address* (1954); *Hudson River Suite* (1956); *Death Valley Suite* (1957); *Valley of Enchantment* (1959); *San Francisco Suite* (1960); *Niagara Falls Suite* (1960); *Hollywood Suite* (1965); and *Virginia City, Requiem for a Ghost Town* (1968). *Symphony in Steel*, composed in 1937, employs four pairs of shoes, two brooms, locomotive bell, pneumatic drill, and compressed air tank in addition to an orthodox symphony orchestra. *The World's Fair Suite* was composed for the New York World's Fair in 1964.

Grofé wrote a Piano Concerto in D minor (1960) and a ballet, *Café Society*, for the Catherine Littlefield Ballet Company produced in Chicago in 1938. In addition he provided many scores for films: *The King of Jazz* (1930); *Diamond Jim* (1935); *Yankee Doodle Rhapsody* (1936); *Knute Rockne: All American* (1940); *Minstrel Man* (Academy Award nomination, 1944); *The Return of Jesse James* (1950); and *Rocketship X-M* (1950).

Grofé is reported to have said at one time, " I make more money than all American symphonic composers put together."

GRUENBERG, LOUIS

b. Brest Litovsk, Russia, 3 August 1884
d. Beverly Hills, California, 9 June 1964

When Gruenberg was a one-year-old, his family moved to America. He soon revealed a considerable musical talent as a pianist, and in 1903 he went to Berlin to become a pupil of Ferruccio Busoni. In 1912 he attended the Vienna Conservatory, making his debut as a pianist in that year. After establishing a reputation as a concert pianist, he gave up his career to devote himself to composition. This decision was prompted by his winning the Flagger Prize in 1919 with a symphonic poem, *The Hill of Dreams*.

Gruenberg made his name as a composer in the 1920s through his concentration on symphonic jazz. During these years he wrote *The Daniel Jazz* (1924), a setting of Vachel Lindsay's poem, and *The Creation* (1924), a Negro sermon, both for voice and eight instruments. *The Daniel Jazz* was performed at the I.S.C.M. Festival in Venice in 1925. Other works in this idiom are *Jazzberries* for piano (1924), *Jazz Suite* for orchestra (1925), and *Jazzettes* for violin and piano (1926).

After these directly jazz-inspired works, he turned his attention in the next decade to the stage. He already had three operas to his credit. The first, *The Witch of Brocken*, was composed in 1912 for children. The following year, to a libretto by Busoni, he wrote *The Bride of the Gods*. His third opera, written in 1921, was based on Anatole France's story *The Dumb Wife*. Through a dispute with the owners of the original copyright, this opera was never performed. In addition Gruenberg provided the music for lighter stage works including two operettas, *Signor Formica* (E.T.A. Hoffmann) (1910) and *Piccadillymadel* (1913), and three musicals: *Rolyboly Eyes* (1919); *Lady X* (1927); and *Hallo! Tommy!*, which was staged in New York in 1931.

On 19 November 1931, his fourth opera, a satirical setting of *Jack and the Beanstalk*, was produced at the Juilliard School. Its success encouraged the composer to write another work for the theater. The result was Gruenberg's masterpiece, *Emperor Jones*, based on the play by Eugene O'Neill. To some extent this mirrored a return to the African American idiom in which he had worked nearly ten years earlier. The story concerns a Pullman car attendant who makes himself emperor of a West Indian island. In keeping with the character of the play, Gruenberg's music is often violent. with outburst of dramatic emotion and impassioned cries. Much of the music uses speech-like declamation with very little lyrical melody. Preparations were made for its premiere in Berlin under Erich Kleiber, but the political climate of the time caused the production to be abandoned. After the first performance on 7 January 1933 at the Metropolitan Opera House, New York, under Tullio Serafin, the work remained in the Metropolitan's repertory for two years. It was also staged in Amsterdam in 1934.

Gruenberg composed seven more operas, but none achieved any lasting success: *Helena's Husband* (1936); *Green Mansions*, performed on CBS radio in 1937; *Volpone* (1945); *One Night of Cleopatra* (1953); *The Miracle at Flanders* (1954), a musical legend based on Balzac; *The Delicate King* (Dumas) (1955); and *Antony and Cleopatra* (1955, rev. 1958, 1961).

Besides these operas, Gruenberg's output of music, especially for orchestra, was considerable. He wrote five symphonies: no. 1 (1919, rev.1928), performed in Boston in 1934; no. 2 (1941, rev. 1959, 1963); no. 3 (1941–42, rev. 1964); no. 4 (1946, rev 1964); and no. 5 (1948); a Sixth Symphony remained incomplete. His concertos include two for piano (1914; 1938, rev. 1963); a Violin Concerto written in 1944 for Jascha Heifetz; and a Cello Concerto (1946, rev. 1963).

Orchestral music includes two symphonic poems, *Vagabondiana* (1920) and *Enchanted Isle* (1919, rev. 1928); *Prairie Song* (1930, rev. 1954); *Serenade to a Beauteous Lady* (1933); *Music for an Imaginary Ballet* (1945); *Americana* (1945); *Pastoral Variations* (1947); *Music to a Legend* (1948); *Country Music* (*Five Country Sketches*) (1949); *Dance Rhapsody* for violin and orchestra (1949); *Poem* for viola and orchestra (1951); *Harlem Rhapsody* (1953); and Concerto for strings and piano (1953, rev. 1955).

From his chamber music, notable items include two piano quintets (1929, 1937); two string quartets (1937, 1941); three violin sonatas (1912, 1919, 1948); a Suite for violin and piano (1914); *Four Bagatelles* for cello and piano (1922); *Poeme* for cello and piano (1924); *Four Indiscretions* for string quartet (1924); *Four Diversions* for string quartet (1930); Divertimento no. 1 for two pianos and percussion (1930); Divertimento no. 2 for violin, horn, cello, and piano (1955); *Poem* for viola and piano (1959); and a Piano Trio.

Gruenberg's single choral work, an oratorio, *A Song of Faith*, for speaker, soloists, chorus, dancers and orchestra, was completed in 1962. He composed much vocal music published in collections: *Eleven Songs*, op. 4 (1904–12); *Three Love Songs* (1917); *Eleven Songs*, op. 42 (1939–40); *Seven Songs*, op. 77. (1962); and *Prose Songs* (1963). He also set Coleridge's *Kubla Khan* for voice and orchestra (1940, rev. 1947).

In his later years Gruenberg lived in California and provided scores for a number of films. Three of these, *The Fight for Life* (1940), *So Ends Our Night* (1941),

and *Commandos Strike at Dawn* (1942) were nominated for Academy Awards. His other film scores are *Stagecoach* (co-composer) (1939); *An American Romance* (1944); *Counterattack* (*One Against Seven*) (1945); The Gangster (1946); *Smart Woman* (1948); *The Arch of Triumph* (1948); *Quicksand* (1949); and *All the King's Men* (1950).

GUION, DAVID (WENDELL FENTRESS)
b. *Ballinger, Texas, 15 December 1892 (not 1895)*
d. *Dallas, Texas, 17 October 1981*

Guion was of French Huguenot descent. He studied in Texas and Illinois before going to Vienna in 1911, where he was a piano pupil of Leopold Godowsky for three years. As a composer he was almost entirely self-taught. On his return to America in 1914 he taught in New York, at Southern Methodist University, Dallas, Texas, and at the Chicago Musical College. From 1920 he devoted his time to collecting and arranging American folk songs.

Guion achieved a wide reputation with his arrangements of cowboy and African American songs, originally for voice and piano but later orchestrated. The best known of these are *The Arkansas Traveler*, *Turkey in the Straw*, and *Home on the Range* (1930). His original songs number over 250, many of which are still heard today: *At the Cry of the First Bird*, *White Clouds*, and *Wild Geese*. The last of these include *My Lord and My God* (1972) and *Songs to be Sung by Children* (1980).

Among his large-scale works for orchestra are two ballets, *Shingandi* (1929) and *Mother Goose* (1930); *Alley Tunes* (1926); a Suite for orchestra (1931); *Texas Suite*, composed in 1950 for the Houston Symphony Orchestra; and *Prairie Suite*, performed by the Stuttgart Symphony Orchestra in 1952

GUTCHË, GENE
(REAL NAME: ROMEO MAXIMILLIAN EUGENE LUDWIG GUTSCHË)
b. *Berlin, Germany, 3 July 1907*
d. *White Bear Lake, Minnesota, 15 November 2000*

Born of Polish and French parents, Gutchë was educated in Italy, Switzerland, and Germany, where he studied with Ferruccio Busoni. He went to America in 1925 and at first worked in an export business in New York. Later he settled in Minnesota, obtaining his M.A. at the University of Minnesota as a pupil of Donald Ferguson (1950) and his Ph.D. at the University of Iowa (1953), where he studied with Philip Greeley Clapp. Thereafter he has devoted himself entirely to composition, living in isolation near White Bear Lake,

Minnesota. He was the recipient of two Guggenheim Fellowships (1961, 1964) and many awards, including the City of Trieste Prize in 1969 and 1972, the Oscar Espla Composition Prize (1962), the Louis Moreau Gottschalk Gold Medal (1970), and four grants from the National Endowment for the Arts (1974, 1975, 1976, 1978). In certain works he made use of microtones, produced by different tuning of string instruments. He also adopted both strict and modified 12-tone row techniques in some compositions.

Gutchë's important music was written for orchestra. This includes six symphonies: no. 1, op. 7 (1950), no. 2, op. 14 (1950), no. 3, op. 19 (1952), no. 4 in one movement, op. 30 (1960), no. 5 for strings, op. 34 (1962), and no. 6, op. 45 (1970). Many of his orchestral compositions have exotic literary titles: *Holofernes Overture*, op. 27, no. 1 (1959); *Judith Prologue*, op. 27, no. 2 (1959); *Genghis Khan*, op. 37 (1963); *Raquel*, op. 38 (1963); *Rites of Tenochtitlan*, op. 39 (1965); *Hsiang Fei*, op. 40 (1965); *Gemini*, op. 41 (1965); *Aesop Fables Suite*, op. 43 (1968); *Epimetheus USA*, op. 41 (1969); and *Cybernetics XX*, op. 47 (1972).

For the Bicentennial, the National Symphony Orchestra of Washington, D.C. commissioned *Icarus*, op. 48. (1974). For the same occasion Gutchë composed *Bi-Centurion*, op. 49 (1975) for the Rochester Symphony Orchestra. Other commissions are *Perseus and Andromeda XX*, op. 50 (1977) for the Cincinnati Symphony Orchestra; *Helios Kinetic*, op. 51 (1978) for the Florida Philharmonic Orchestra; and *Akhenaten* (*Eidetic Images*), op. 52 (1978) for chorus and orchestra for the Milwaukee Symphony Orchestra. Also for orchestra are *Utilitarian Dance*, op. 9 (1950); *Rondo Capriccio*, op. 21 (1953); *Asymmetric Dance*, op. 22 (1953); Concertino for small orchestra, op. 28 (1962); *Bongo Divertimento*, op. 35 with solo percussion (1962); and *Classic Concerto* for chamber orchestra, op. 44 (1967).

For solo instruments and orchestra he wrote concertos for piano, op. 24 (1956), cello, op. 26 (1957), violin, op. 36 (1962), and piano duo, op. 42 (1966), and a *Concertante* for timpani, op. 31 (1962). His instrumental music includes four string quartets and three piano sonatas. For the stage he composed an opera, *Judith*, as yet unperformed.

He was the author of two books, *Essays: Come Prima* (1970) and *Music of the People* (1978).

H

HADLEY, HENRY KIMBALL

b. Somerville, Massachusetts, 20 December 1871

d. New York, New York, 6 September 1937

Hadley studied with George Whitefield Chadwick in Boston, Eusebius Mandyczewski in Vienna (1894–95), and Ludwig Thuille in Munich (1905–07). At the age of 22 he became a violinist in James Henry Mapleson's Opera Company Orchestra; later he took over as its conductor. He spent the years from 1904 to 1909 in Europe as a conductor and as a pupil of Ludwig Thuille, returning to the United States to direct the Seattle Symphony Orchestra. In 1911 he was appointed conductor of the newly-formed San Francisco Orchestra, resigning in 1915. Hadley settled in New York in 1920, where he conducted the New York Philharmonic Orchestra (1920–27) and founded the Manhattan Orchestra in 1929; he also established the Berkshire Music Festival in 1934. As the founder of the National Association of American Composers and Conductors, Hadley devoted much of his time to the promotion of music by his fellow composers.

Hadley's early works were strongly influenced by Wagner. His first opera, *Safie*, was performed in Mainz, Germany, in 1909. This was followed by *Azora, the Daughter of Montezuma* (1915), performed in Chicago on 26 December 1917, and the one-act *Bianca*, completed in 1916. His most successful opera, *Cleopatra's Night*, was produced at the Metropolitan on 31 January 1920 and remained in the repertory for two seasons. In 1925 he composed another one-act opera, *A Night in Old Paris*, performed on radio in 1933. In lighter vein he wrote a number of operettas including *Happy Jack* (1897); *Nancy Brown* (1903); *The Pearl Girl* (1913); *The Fire Prince* (1917); and *The Red Flame*. He provided incidental music for a pageant *The Masque of Newark* (1916).

None of Hadley's numerous orchestral works has established any lasting reputation, although between the two World Wars his music was widely performed in the United States. He composed five symphonies: no. 1, *Youth and Life* (1897), no. 2 *Four Seasons* (1901), no. 3 in B minor (1906–07), no. 4 in D minor (1911), subtitled *North, East, South, West*, and no. 5 in C minor (1935), commissioned for the Connecticut Tercentenary. His first orchestral work, *Hector and Andromache*, was composed in 1894. He composed three symphonic poems, *Salome* (1905), *Lucifer* (1910), and *The Ocean* (1916); several overtures, including *Herod* (1901), *In Bohemia* (1902), *Othello* (1919), *Aurora Borealis* (1931), *Alma Mater* (1932), and *The Enchanted Castle*; and many other orchestral pieces: *Festival March* (1887); *Ballet Suite* (1895); *Oriental Suite* (1903); a rhapsody *The Culprit Fay* (1909); *Symphonic Fantasia* (1910); *The Atonement of Pan* (1912); *Youth Triumphant* (1931); *Silhouettes Suite* (1918); *Suite Ancienne* (1924); *October Twilight*, *The Garden of Allah*, *San Francisco Suite* (1931); *The Legend of Hani* (1933); and *Scherzo Diabolique* (1934). His *Chinese Suite: The Streets of Pekin* was written in 1930 while on a visit to the East. A *Konzertstück* for cello and orchestra, composed for his brother Arthur, dates from 1907. He also wrote a Piano Concertino (1937).

Hadley's important choral works are *The Fairies* for soprano, chorus, and orchestra (1894); *In Music's Praise* for soloists, chorus, and orchestra (1898); *Lelawala* for chorus and orchestra (1898); *The Princess of Ys* for women's voices and orchestra (1903); *A Legend of Grenada* for soloists and female voices (1904), a lyric drama *Merlin and Vivian* (1906); *The Fate of the Princess Kiyo* for women's voices and orchestra (1907); *The Nightingale and the Rose* for soprano, women's voices, and orchestra (1911); *The Golden Prince* a cantata for soprano, baritone, female voices, and orchestra (1914); *Ode to Music* (1915); *The Fairy Thorn* for female voices and orchestra (1917); *Ode: The New Earth* (1917); *Ode: Music in Arcady* for chorus and orchestra (1919); an oratorio *Resurgam* (1922); a Christmas cantata *Prophesy and Fulfillment* for soloists, chorus, and orchestra (1922); *Mirtil in Arcadia* (1927), which includes a part for narrator; *The Admiral of the Seas*, a cantata for tenor, chorus, and orchestra (1928); and a cantata, *Belshazzar* (1932).

Among his chamber compositions are a Piano Quintet in A minor (1920); two piano trios (1896, 1933); two string quartets (1896, 1934); a Violin Sonata (1895); and *Elegy and Gavotte* for cello and piano (1910). He also wrote over 150 songs.

HAGEMAN, RICHARD

b. Leeuwarden, Holland, 9 July 1882
d. Beverly Hills, California, 6 March 1966

Hageman studied at the Amsterdam Royal Conservatory, of which his father was director, and later at the Brussels Conservatory. He was appointed conductor of the Netherlands Opera (1899–1903) and acted as accompanist to the singer Mathilde Marchesi de Castrone in Paris in 1903. Hageman traveled to America in 1906 as accompanist to Yvette Guilbert, and in 1907 was appointed assistant conductor at the Metropolitan Opera House. He became an American citizen in 1915. From then until 1926 he appeared regularly as an opera conductor and accompanist to singers. Later he conducted the Chicago and Los Angeles Opera Orchestras and taught at the Chicago Musical College and the Curtis Institute, Philadelphia, where he was head of the opera department.

Hageman is remembered as a composer of songs, which still appear from time to time in recital programs. The best known of these are *Do Not Go, My Love* (1917) and *At the Well* (1919). Hageman wrote one opera, *Caponsacchi* (1931), which was first produced in Germany in 1932 and staged at the Metropolitan on 4 February 1937. In 1943 he composed a concert drama, *The Crucible*.

In 1938 he moved to Hollywood where he conducted at the Hollywood Bowl. From the late 1930s he was associated with Paramount Pictures in Hollywood, for which he composed many film scores, including *If I Were King* (1938); *Hotel Imperial* (1939); *Stagecoach* (1939; Academy Award); *Rulers of the Sea* (1939); *The Howards of Virginia* (1940); *The Long Voyage Home* (1940); *This Woman is Mine* (1941); *Paris Calling* (1942); *The Shanghai Gesture* (1942); *Angel and the Badman* (1947); *The Fugitive* (1947); *Mourning Becomes Electra* (1947); *Fort Apache* (1948); *Three Godfathers* (1948); *She Wore a Yellow Ribbon* (1949); and

Wagonmaster (1950). He received six nominations for an Academy Award.

HAGEN, FRANCIS FLORENTINE

b. Salem, North Carolina, 30 October 1815
d. Lititz, Pennsylvania, 7 July 1907

Hagen was one of the last of the Moravian composers of Pennsylvania. His Christmas carol *Morning Star* is still performed today. He edited *The Church and Home Organist's Companion* and composed many anthems. For orchestra he wrote an Overture in F (1835).

HAIEFF, ALEXEI (VASILIEVICH)

b. Blagovestchensk, Siberia, Russia, 25 August 1914
d. Rome, Italy, 1 March 1994

Raised in Manchuria from the age of six, Haieff went to the United States in 1931. He received piano lessons privately from Alexander Siloti and studied at the Juilliard School (1934–38) under Rubin Goldmark and Frederick Jacobi. From 1938 to 1939 he was a pupil of Nadia Boulanger in Paris and Cambridge, Massachusetts. He won several major awards including the Lili Boulanger Prize in 1942, Guggenheim Fellowships in 1946 and 1949, and the American Prix de Rome in 1947. Haieff was Composer-in-Residence at the American Academy in Rome from 1952 to 1953 and again from 1958 to 1959. He held professorships at the State University of New York, Buffalo (1962, 1964), the Carnegie-Mellon Institute of Technology, Pittsburgh, Pennsylvania (1963) and Brandeis University, Waltham, Massachusetts (1965). From 1967 to 1970 he was Composer-in-Residence at the University of Utah, Salt Lake City.

Haieff's first important composition, Divertimento for chamber orchestra (1944), was used by George Ballanchine for a ballet produced in 1946 by the New York Ballet Society. Another ballet, *Princess Zondilda and Her Entourage*, was written for Merce Cunningham in 1946. The composer later arranged the music as a *Dance Suite* for flute, bassoon, trumpet, violin, cello, and piano. He composed a third ballet, *Beauty and the Beast* (1947).

Haieff's most widely performed work is his Piano Concerto, commissioned in 1950. It won the New York Music Critics' Circle Award in 1952 and represented the United States at the I.S.C.M. Festival in 1956. A Second Piano Concerto, based on the Sonata for two pianos, was completed in 1976. His other orchestral works include three symphonies: no. 1 (1942), no. 2, first heard in Boston in 1958 and awarded a UNESCO prize, and no. 3 (1961). He also composed a Violin Concerto (1948); *Eclogue*; *La Nouvelle Heloise* for harp and strings (1953); *Ballet in B flat* and *Ballet in E* (1955); *Eloge* for chamber orchestra (1967); and *Caligula* (Robert Lowell) for baritone and orchestra (1970).

Among his chamber music compositions are Sonatina for string quartet (1937); two string quartets (1951, 1960); *Three Bagatelles* for oboe and bassoon (1939–55); *Serenade* for oboe, clarinet, bassoon, and piano (1940); Suite for violin and piano (1941); Sonata for two pianos (1945); *Eclogue* for cello and piano (1945); Piano Sonata (1955); Cello Sonata (1963); *Rhapsodies* for guitar and harpsichord (1980); *Duet* for two flutes (1982); Wind Quintet (1983); *Three Pieces* for violin and piano; and many piano solos.

Of Haieff's few vocal works, *Cantata on Russian Folk Texts* (1939) and the song cycle *In the Early Hours* are the best known. For chorus he composed *Holy Week Liturgy* (1968–69).

HAILSTORK, ADOLPHUS (CUNNINGHAM) III

b. Rochester, New York, 17 April 1941

After graduating from Howard University, Washington, D.C., in 1963, Hailstork spent that summer in Paris as a student of Nadia Boulanger. At the Manhattan School of Music (1963–65) he was a pupil of Nicholas Flagello, Vittorio Giannini, and David Diamond. He completed his musical education at Michigan State University, East Lansing (Ph.D., 1971) with H. Owen Reed. From 1969 to 1971 he taught at Michigan State University before moving to Youngtown (Ohio) State University. From 1977–2000 he was a member of the music faculty at Norfolk (Virginia) State University, and then moved to Old Dominion University, where he is currently Eminent Scholar and Professor of Music.

For the stage Hailstork has written *The Race for Space* for singers, speaker, dancers and piano (1963); an opera, *Paul Laurence Dunbar: Common Ground* (1994); and *Joshua's Boots* (1999) for Kansas Lyric Opera. His orchestral works include a tone poem, *Phaedra* (1966); *Statement, Variation and Fugue* (1966); *SA-1* for jazz ensemble (1971); *Bellevue* (1974); *Celebration* (1974); Concerto for violin, horn, and orchestra (1975); *Epitaph* (1979) in memory of Martin Luther King Jr.; *American Landscape no. 3* (1982); *Sport for Strings* (1982); *American Landscape no. 4* (1984); Symphony no. 1 (1988); *My Lord What a Morning* for chamber orchestra (1989); *Sonata da Chiesa* for strings (1991); *Intrada* (1991); a Piano Concerto (1992); a *Festival March* (1992); Sonata for trumpet and strings (1996); *Two Romances* for viola and strings

Adolphus Hailstork.
Courtesy of Old Dominion University Libraries, Diehn Composers Room.

(1997); Symphony no 2 (Detroit 1999); *Baroque Suite* for strings (1999); and Symphony no 3 (2001).

To the wind band repertory Hailstork has contributed *Out of the Depths* (1974); *American Landscape No. 1* (1977); *American Guernica* for piano and band (1982); a march, *Norfolk Pride* (1980); and *And Deliver Us From Evil* (1994).

Hailstork's catalog of vocal and choral music is extensive: *In Memoriam Langston Hughes* for chorus (1967); a song cycle, *A Charm at Parting* for mezzo-soprano and piano (1969); *Lament for the Children of Biafra* for voice, narrator, jazz ensemble, and percussion (1969); *Spartacus Speaks* for male voices, brass, and percussion (1970); *Serenade* for soprano, female chorus, violin, and piano (1971); *My Name is Toil* for chorus, brass, and percussion (1972); *Oracle* for tenor, female chorus, three flutes, two percussion, and tape (1977); *Set Me as a Seal* for chorus (1979); *Psalm 72* for chorus, brass, and organ (1981); *Look to This Day* for chorus and band (1982); *Songs of Isaiah* for chorus and orchestra (1987); *I Will Lift Up Mine Eyes*, a cantata for tenor, chorus, and ensemble (1989); *Break Forth* for chorus, brass, timpani, and organ (1990); *Hodie:*

Christus Natus Est for chorus (1994); *Out of the Stars* for chorus, brass, timpani, and organ (1998); *Songs of Innocence* for soloists, chorus, and orchestra (2000); and *Missa Brevis* (2003).

Among his instrumental works are a Horn Sonata (1966); *Capriccio for a Departed Brother: Scott Joplin* for strings (1969); *From the Dark Side of the Sun* for three flutes, soprano saxophone, strings, and percussion (1971); String Sextet (1971); Violin Sonata (1972); *Bagatelles* for brass quartet (1973); *Pulse* for percussion ensemble (1974); *Spiritual* for brass octet (1975); *Scherzo* for solo piano and wind octet (1975); *Processional and Recessional* for brass quartet (1977); *American Landscape No. 2* for violin and cello (1978); Piano Sonata no. 1 (1978–81); *Variations* for trumpet (1981); *Music for 10 Players* (1982); Piano Trio (1985); *Essay* for string ensemble (1986); Sonata for two pianos (1987); Piano Sonata no. 2 (1989); *Arabesques* for flute and percussion (1991); *Consort Piece* for ensemble (1993); *Sanctum* for viola and piano (1995); *As Falling Leaves: Bassoon Set* for solo bassoon (1996); String Quartet (2002); and *Trio* for flute, viola, and harp (2002).

HANNAY, ROGER (DURHAM)
b. Plattsburgh, New York, 22 September 1930

Hannay studied at Syracuse University with Ernst Bacon and Franklin Morris (1948–52), Boston University with Gardner Read and Hugo Norden (1952–53), and at the Eastman School with Howard Hanson and Bernard Rogers (1954–56). He was also a pupil of Aaron Copland and Lukas Foss at the Berkshire Center (1959), and worked with Roger Sessions, Milton Babbitt, and Elliott Carter at Princeton (1960). From 1958 to 1966 he was associate professor at Concordia College, Moorhead, Minnesota, becoming head of theory and composition at the University of North Carolina, Chapel Hill (1966–1995), where he established the Electronic Music Studio, the U.N.C. New Music Ensemble, and Composer's Concerts. Since 1995 he has been a professor emeritus.

Hannay's early works made use of twelve-note techniques, but from 1955 he adopted a freer atonality. After 1966 he explored electronic and mixed media idioms. His stage and mixed media works include a chamber opera, *Two Tickets to Omaha* (*The Swindlers*) (1960); *The Fortune of St. Macabre* (1964); *America, Sing!* for tape and visuals (1967); *Live and in Color!* for announcer, painter, percussion, tape, and visuals (1967); *The Interplanetary Aleatoric Serial Factory* for ensemble, tape, audience, and visuals (1969); *Squeeze Me* for ensemble and visuals (1969); *Glass and Steel* for tape and film (1970); *Cabaret Voltaire* for tape, fe-

male reciter, soprano, saxophone, percussion, and visuals (1971, rev.1978); *Tuonela Journey* (after Sibelius) for English horn, tape, and optional film (1971); *Arp-Dances* for film and dance (1977); *Fantasy* for tape and film (1980); and an opera, *The Journey of Edith Wharton* (1983).

At the center of his orchestral music are eight symphonies: no. 1 (1953, rev. 1973); no. 2 (1956); no. 3 (*The Great American Novel*) with optional chorus (1976–77); no. 4 (*American Classic*) with solo vocal quartet and optional tape (1977); no. 5 (1987–88); no. 6 for large string orchestra (1992); no. 7 in one movement (1994–95); and no. 8 (2002–03). He has also composed a Symphony for band (1963). Also for orchestra are *Music for Strings* (1954, rev. 1994); *A Dramatic Overture* (*Homage to Arnold Schoenberg*) (1951, rev. 1981); *Summer Festival Overture* (1958); *Prelude and Dance* (1959, rev. 1974); *Sonorous Image* (1968); *Listen* (1971); an overture, *Celebration* (1975, rev. 1980); *Pastorale – from Olana* for horn and strings (1982); *The Age of Innocence* (1983); *Rhapsody* (*Serenade*) for piano and orchestra (1991); *Arriba!* (1992); *Vikingrwest* (1992); and *Consortium* (1994).

Among Hannay's numerous instrumental compositions are *Rhapsody* for flute and piano (1952); Divertimento for wind quintet (1958); three string quartets: no. 1 (1962); no. 2, *Lyric* (1963); and no. 3, *Designs* (1963); Piano Sonata (1964); *Structure* for percussion ensemble (1965, rev. 1975); *Fantome* for clarinet, viola, and piano (1967); *The Fruit of Love* for chamber ensemble (1969); *Piano Episodes* (1971, rev. 1991); *Four for Five* for brass quintet (1973); String Quartet no. 4 (*Quartet of Solos*) (1974); *Festival of Trumpets* for 10 trumpets (1978); *Nocturnes* for wind quintet (1979); Trumpet Sonata (1980); Suite for flute, clarinet, cello, and piano (1981); *Souvenirs* for flute, clarinet, violin, cello, percussion, and piano (1984); *Trio-Rhapsody* for flute, cello, and piano (1984); *Modes of Discourse* for flute, violin, and cello (1988, rev. 1994); and *A Farewell to Leonard Bernstein* for chamber ensemble (1990).

Hannay's choral music includes a cantata, *Doth Not Wisdom Cry* for chorus and orchestra (1952, rev. 1994); *Christmas Tide* for men's voices (1956); Requiem for soprano, chorus, and orchestra (1961); *Shakespeare Songs* for men's voices and orchestra (1961); *Sayings of Our Time* for chorus and orchestra (1968); *Two Choral Fantasias* for chorus and orchestra (1970, rev. 1984); *The Prophesy of Despair* for male chorus and percussion (1972); *Emerging Voices* for unaccompanied chorus (1984); *Hold the Fort* for chorus and piano (1989); and *Make We Joy* for chorus and organ (1991).

For solo voice Hannay has written *The Fruit of Love* (Millay) for soprano and piano (1964); *Marshall's Medium Message* for girl announcer and four percussion; *Vocalise* for soprano, tape, and optional brass (1972); *Songs of Walden* (Thoreau) for tenor and piano (1980); *The Nightingale and the Rose* for soprano, flute, guitar, and double bass (1986); and a monodrama, *Dates and Names* for soprano and piano (1991).

Hannay is the author of *My Book of Life*, published in 1997.

HANSON, HOWARD (HAROLD)
b. Wahoo, Nebraska, 28 October 1896
d. Rochester, New York, 26 February 1981

Hanson was born of Swedish parents. He was educated at Luther College, Wahoo, Nebraska (1911); the Institute of Musical Art in New York (1912–14), where he was a pupil of Percy Goetschius; and Northwestern University, Evanston, Illinois (1914–16). In 1916 he was appointed an Instructor at the College of the Pacific in San Jose, California, becoming Dean in 1919. In 1921 a Prix de Rome Fellowship took him to Italy for three years.

At the age of 27 in 1924 he was appointed director of the Eastman School of Music in Rochester, New York, a post he held until retirement in 1964. It was here that he devoted the greater part of his time to teaching, conducting, and administration. Musical life in America today owes a considerable debt to Hanson for fostering the early works of so many composers who later became famous. The American Music Festivals and the numerous recordings he made have given the widest encouragement and publicity to young composers of every style. Hanson also conducted American music outside the United States. In 1940 he was co-founder with Marion Bauer, Aaron Copland, Quincy Porter, and Otto Luening of the American Music Center in New York. He was awarded many honorary doctorates from leading American universities for his services to music.

Hanson's own music is richly romantic, the early works showing the influence of Sibelius and other Scandinavian composers. He wrote in every musical form and was unusually prolific for one so deeply committed to teaching. The influence of nineteenth-century music is evident in the titles and form of Hanson's early works: *Symphonic Prelude* (1916); *Symphonic Legend* (1917); *Symphonic Rhapsody* (1919); Concerto for organ, strings, and harp (1921); and five symphonic poems: *Before Dawn* (1920), *Exaltation* (with piano obbligato; 1920), *North and West* (obbligato chorus; 1923), *Lux Aeterna* (obbligato viola; 1923), and *Pan and Priest* (obbligato piano; 1926). The Concerto for Organ of 1926 is based on themes from *North and West*.

His seven symphonies occupy an important place in his orchestral output. Symphony no. 1 in E minor, *"Nor-*

Howard Hanson.
Courtesy Northwestern University Archives.

dic," Op. 21, was composed in 1922 in Rome, where the composer conducted it in the following year. Symphony no. 2, Op. 30, *"Romantic,"* was commissioned by the Boston Symphony Orchestra for its 50th anniversary in 1930. Roussel's Third Symphony and Stravinsky's *Symphony of Psalms* were also commissioned for the orchestra at this time. Symphony no. 3 in A minor, Op. 33 (1936) was intended as a tribute to the early Swedish pioneers who settled in Delaware. The first three movements were performed by the NBC Symphony Orchestra in 1937 under Hanson's direction. The premiere of the complete work was given in December 1939 by the Boston Symphony Orchestra under Serge Koussevitzky. Symphony no. 4, Op. 34., subtitled *"Requiem,"* is dedicated to the memory of the composer's father. Hanson conducted the premiere in Boston in 1943 and the work was awarded a Pulitzer Prize the following year. Symphony no. 5, *"Sinfonia Sacra,"* written at the request of Eugene Ormandy, was performed in Philadelphia in 1955. Symphony no. 6 was commissioned by the New York Philharmonic Orchestra and performed them under the composer in March 1968. Symphony no. 7, *"Sea Symphony"* for chorus and orchestra to words by Walt Whitman (1977), was written to mark the 50th anniversary of the National Music Camp, Interlochen, Michigan.

As a wedding present for his wife, Hanson composed a Serenade for flute, strings, and harp in 1945. Three years later, to a commission from UNESCO, he added a companion piece, *Pastorale* for oboe, strings, and harp. In the same year, 1948, to a commission from the Koussevitzky Music Foundation, he wrote his Piano Concerto in G. Another work for piano and strings, *Fantasy on a Theme of Youth*, followed in 1951. In memory of Serge Koussevitzky, who had done so much to encourage him, Hanson composed *Elegy* for the 75th anniversary of the Boston Symphony Orchestra in 1955. For the 40th anniversary of the Cleveland Orchestra in 1958, he wrote *Mosaics*. Other orchestral works are *Bold Island Suite* (1961); *Summer Seascape No. 1*, commissioned by the New Orleans Philharmonic Orchestra; *For the First Time*, completed in 1962; *Summer Seascape No. 2* (1966); *Dies Natalis* (1967); and *Rhythmic Variations for Strings* (1978).

Hanson produced several impressive choral works that have been widely performed. *The Lament of Beowolf* (1925) was heard the following year in Ann Arbor, Michigan. For the centenary of the death of Beethoven in 1927 he wrote *Heroic Elegy* for wordless chorus and orchestra. The words of Walt Whitman were set in *Three Songs from "Drum Taps,"* dating from 1935. *The Cherubic Hymn* (1949), *Centennial Ode* (1950) for the 100th anniversary of Rochester University, and *The Song of Democracy* (1957) are all scored for chorus and orchestra. A cantata, *Song of Human Rights*, was performed in Washington, D.C. in 1963. In addition to *Four Psalms* for baritone, cello, and orchestra (1964), Hanson has set *Two Psalms* for baritone, chorus, and orchestra (1968). Other works for chorus include *How Excellent Thy Name* (1952), *Psalm 150* (1965), and *Streams in the Desert* (1969), all for chorus and orchestra; *The Mystic Trumpeter* (Whitman) for narrator, chorus, and orchestra (1970); *Lumen in Christo* for chorus and small orchestra (1975); and *New Land, New Covenant* for soloists, narrator, chorus, and small orchestra (1976).

Hanson's most extended work is the three-act opera *Merry Mount*, commissioned by the Metropolitan Opera in 1933 and given a tumultuous reception at its premiere on 10 February 1934. To a libretto by Richard Stokes, it describes love, death, and destruction in a Puritan village in Massachusetts in the seventeenth century. The composer extracted an orchestral suite from the music, which he used as a demonstration piece in an outstanding illustrated lecture on the orchestra. Both this and a recording of the original production have been reissued on compact disc. He wrote two other works for the stage: a ballet with voices, chorus and orchestra, *California Forest Play of 1920*, performed in that year; and a second ballet, *Nymphs and Satyr*, produced by the Chautauqua Ballet in 1979.

Among his instrumental music are an early Piano Quintet in F minor (1916); *Concerto da Camera*, also for piano quintet (1917); and a String Quartet (1923). Later items include *Seascape No. 2* for string quartet

(1966), dedicated to his friend Edwin Hughes, and *Elegy* for viola and string quartet (1966). Hanson wrote many piano pieces including *Four Poems* (1917–18); a Sonata in A minor (1918); *Scandinavian Suite* (1919); *Three Etudes* (1920); and *Prelude and Double Fugue* for two pianos (1915). For concert band he composed *Chorale and Alleluia* (1954); *Centennial March* (1966); *Four French Songs* (1972); *Dies Natalis II* (1972); *Young Person's Guide to the Six-Tone Scale* for piano and wind ensemble (1972); *Laude* (1975); and *Variations on an Ancient Hymn* (1977).

Hanson was the author of a book, *Harmonic Materials of Modern Music: Resources of the Tempered Scale*, published in 1960.

HARBISON, JOHN
b. Orange, New Jersey, 20 December 1938

John Harbison's father was a distinguished history professor at Princeton University and an amateur musician and composer. As a youngster Harbison studied violin and piano, playing in jazz bands. After graduating from Harvard in 1960 where he studied with Walter Piston, he spent a year at the Berlin Hochschule fur Musik as a pupil of Boris Blacher. In addition he studied conducting in Salzburg with Dean Dixon. He earned an M.F.A. degree in 1963 at Princeton, working with Roger Sessions, Earl Kim, and Milton Babbitt. He conducted the Princeton University Orchestra and the Cantata Singers, Boston and served as Composer-in-Residence at Reed College, Portland, Oregon (1968–69) and with the Los Angeles Philharmonic Orchestra (1986–88). After teaching briefly at Harvard and Brandeis University, in 1969 he joined the music faculty of Massachusetts Institute of Technology. He was awarded a Guggenheim Fellowship in 1978.

Among Harbison's orchestral works are three symphonies: no. 1 written in 1984 for the centennial of the Boston Symphony Orchestra, no. 2 commissioned in 1987 for the San Francisco Symphony Orchestra, and no. 3 written in 1990 for the Baltimore Symphony Orchestra and dedicated to his friend and fellow composer Christopher Rouse. Other orchestral pieces include *Descant – Nocturne on a Lullaby of Shifrin* (1976); a Piano Concerto (1978); *Snow Country* for oboe and strings (1979); and a Violin Concerto, written for his wife Rose Mary Pedersen, who performed it in 1980 (the score was revised in 1987). Later orchestral items include a Concerto for oboe, clarinet, and strings (1985); *Fanfare for Foley's* (1986); *Remembering Gatsby: Foxtrot* (1986); Viola Concerto (1989); Concerto for double brass quintet and orchestra (1989–90); Oboe Concerto composed for William Bennett and the San Francisco Symphony Orchestra (1990–91);

for *Calvin Simmons* for ensemble (1982); *Overture: Michael Kohlhaus* for brass ensemble (1982); *Twilight Music* for horn, violin, and piano (1985); and *Four Songs of Solitude* for solo violin (1985).

Later chamber music includes *Magnum Mysterium* for brass quintet (1987); *Two Chorale Preludes for Advent* for brass quintet (1987); *Fantasy Duo* for violin and piano (1988); *November 19, 1828* for piano quartet, written in 1988 as a tribute to Schubert who died on that date; *Little Fantasy on the Twelve Days of Christmas* for brass quintet (1988); *Nocturne* for brass quintet (1989); *Fanfare and Reflections* for two violins (1990); *Fourteen Fabled Folksongs* for violin and marimba (1992); *Variations* for string quartet (1993); Suite for solo cello (1997); and *Six American Painters* for flute, oboe, and string quartet (2000).

Among Harbison's many choral works are two pieces for female voices, *He Shall Not Cry* (1957) and *Ave Maria* (1959); *Music When Soft Voices Die* (Shelley) for chorus (1966); *Five Songs of Experience* (William Blake) for soloists, chorus, string quartet, and percussion (1971); a cantata, *The Flower-Fed Buffaloes* for baritone, chorus, and instruments (1977); *Nunc Dimittis* for male voices (1980); a cantata, *The Flight into Egypt*, which won the Pulitzer Prize in 1987; *Recordare*, one of 14 contributions from different composers for a composite setting of the Requiem Mass, performed in Stuttgart, Germany in 1995; and a Requiem, premiered in March 2003 by the Boston Symphony Orchestra under Bernard Haitink.

For unaccompanied choir he has composed *Two Emmanuel Motets* (1990); *Ave Verum* (1991); two settings of *O Magnum Mysterium* (1991, 1992); *Concerning Them Which Are Asleep* (1993); and *Communion Words* (1994). These pieces were composed for performance at Emmanuel Church in Boston, as was *Four Psalms* for soloists, chorus, and orchestra in 1999. Vocal music includes *Autumnal* for mezzo-soprano and piano (1965); *Shakespeare Series* for mezzo-soprano and piano (1965); *Elegiac Songs* (Emily Dickinson) for mezzo-soprano and piano (1974); *Book of Hours and Seasons* (Goethe) for mezzo-soprano, flute, cello, and piano (1975); *Moments of Vision* (Thomas Hardy) for soprano, tenor, recorder, gamba, and lute (1975); *Three Harp Songs* for tenor and harp (1975); *Samuel Chapter* (Bible) for soprano (or tenor), flute, clarinet, viola, cello, piano, and percussion (1978); *Motelli di Montale*, a cycle for soprano and 9 instruments or piano (1980); *Mirabai Songs* for voice and eight instruments (1982); *The Natural World* for soprano (or mezzo-soprano) and five instruments (1987); *Rot und Weiss* for voice and four instruments (1987); *Christmas Vespers* and *Three Wise Men* for reader and brass quintet (1988); *Im Spiegel* for voice, violin, and piano (1988); *Simple Daylight* for soprano and piano (1988); *Words from*

John Harbison.
Photo: Katrin Talbot, Madison WI, courtesy the composer.

Fantasia on a Ground (1993); *David's Fascinating Rhythm Method* (1991); *Gli Accordi Piu Usati* (*The Most Often Used Chords*) (1992); a Cello Concerto (1993); Flute Concerto (1994); and *Partita*, written in 2001 for the Minnesota Orchestra centenary. For wind band he has written *Music for 18 winds* (1986); *Olympic Dances* (1996); *Three City Blocks*, commissioned by the U.S. Air Force band; and a novelty piece, *Deep Potomac Bells* for 250 tubas (1983).

Harbison has composed prolifically for instruments: four string quartets (1985, 1987, 1993, 2002); *Duo* for flute and piano (1961); Sonata for solo viola 1961; *Confinement* for 12 players (1965); *Four Preludes* for ensemble (1967); Serenade for flute, clarinet, bass clarinet, and string trio (1968); *Parody Fantasia* for piano (1968); Piano Trio (1969); *Bermuda Triangle* for amplified cello, tenor saxophone, and electric organ (1970); *Die Kurze* for flute, clarinet, violin, cello, and piano (1970); *Amazing Grace* for solo oboe (1972); Wind Quintet (1979); *Organum for Paul Fromm* for chamber ensemble (1981); Piano Quintet (1981); *Variations* for clarinet, viola, and piano (1981); *Exequiem*

Peterson for baritone and chamber ensemble (1989); *Between Two Worlds* for soprano, two cellos, and two pianos (1991); *The Flute of Interior Time* for baritone and piano (1991); *The Reawakening* for soprano and string quartet (1991); *La Primavera de Sottoripa* for soprano and ensemble (1999); and *Chorale Cantata* for soprano, oboe, violin, and strings.

In 1974 Harbison completed a two-act opera, *A Winter's Tale*, produced by the San Francisco Opera in 1979. A second opera, *Full Moon in March*, was performed in 1979 by Boston Musica Viva; the text is based on poems by W. B.Yeats. His third opera, *The Great Gatsby,* to his own libretto based on F. Scott Fitzgerald, was commissioned by the Metropolitan Opera, New York, where it was premiered on 20 December 1999 and revived for the 2001–2002 season. Also for the stage he has written two ballets, *Ulysses' Bow* (Pittsburgh 1984) and *Ulysses' Raft* (New Haven 1984), and incidental music for Shakespeare's *The Merchant of Venice* (1971).

HARLING, WILLIAM FRANKE
b. London, England, 18 January 1887
d. Santa Monica, California, 1 October 1958

Harling was brought to the United States as an infant. After studying in Boston, Brussels, and at the Royal Academy of Music in London, he returned to America where he served as a church organist before settling in Hollywood.

For orchestra he wrote *Chansons Populaires* (1932); a *Jazz Concerto*, a Piano Concerto in C minor, a symphonic poem, *Monte Cassino* (1944); *Three Elegiac Poems* for cello and orchestra (1946); *Venetian Fantasy*; a symphonic poem, *At the Tomb of the Unknown Soldier*; a tone poem, *Captain, My Captain*; and *Nocturne* for strings.

For the stage he composed three operas: *A Light for St. Agnes* (Chicago, 1925); *Deep River*, a "native opera" with jazz set in New Orleans (Lancaster, Pennsylvania, 1926); and *Alda*; a marionette opera, *Wake Up, Jonathan*; and a ballet, *Columbine's Dream*. Among his many choral works are *The Miracle of Time* (1916); *Bible Trilogy*; *Before the Dawn*; *The Death of Minnehaha (An Indian Pastorale)*; *Requiem (O My Captain)*; *23rd Psalm*; and *Two Angels*.

He collaborated on the film *Stagecoach*, which won an Academy Award in 1939. Between 1930 and 1946 he composed a further 56 scores for Hollywood movies, including *Interference* (1929); *Monte Carlo* (1930); *Winner Takes All* (1932); *Shanghai Express* (1932); *Trouble in Paradise* (1932); *Bill of Divorcement* (with Max Steiner, 1932); *Farewell to Arms* (1932); *The Invisible Man* (1933); *By Candlelight* (1934); *Golden Arrow* (1936); *Adventure in Washington* (1941); *The Lady is Willing* (1942); and *When the Lights Go On Again* (1944).

HARRIS, DONALD
b. St Paul, Minnesota, 7 April 1931

Harris studied with Ross Lee Finney at the University of Michigan, Ann Arbor (1949–52) before spending a year in Paris, where he received lessons from Nadia Boulanger and Max Deutsch. He was also a pupil of Boris Blacher and Lukas Foss at the Berkeley Center during the summers of 1954 and 1955, and of André Jolivet in Aix-en-Provence. From 1968 to 1977 he was an administrator at the New England Conservatory, Boston, moving to a teaching post at the Hartt School of Music, University of Hartford. From 1988 to 1997 he was Dean of the College of Arts, Ohio State University, Columbus, and then stepped down to rejoin the music faculty as a professor, a position he holds today.

For the stage he has composed an opera, *The Little Mermaid* (1988–95); two ballets, *The Legend of John Henry* (1954, rev. 1979) and *The Golden Deer* (1955); a dance piece, *Intervals* (1959); and incidental music for *Twelfth Night* (1989).

Donald Harris.
Photo: Barb Stimpert, courtesy the composer.

His orchestral works include a symphony in two movements (1958–61); *On Variations* for chamber orchestra (1976); *Prelude to a Concert in Connecticut* (1981); and *Mermaid Variations* for chamber orchestra (1992). For concert band he has written *A Fanfare for the Seventies* (1978). Among his instrumental works are *Fantasy* for violin and piano (1957); a Piano Sonata (1957); String Quartet (1965); *Ludus I* for 10 instruments (1966); *Ludis II* for five instruments (1973); *Balladen* for piano (1979); *Three Fanfares* for four horns (1984); *A Birthday Card for Gunther* (*Schuller*) for solo violin (1985); and *Canzona and Carol* for double bass quartet and timpani (1986).

For voice, Harris has composed *Charmes* for soprano and orchestra (1971–80); *For the Night to Wear* for mezzo-soprano and chamber ensemble (1978); *Of Hartford in a Purple Light* (1979); *Les Mains* (1983); and *Pierrot Lieder* for soprano and chamber ensemble (1988).

HARRIS, ROY (LEROY) ELLSWORTH
b. Chandler, Lincoln County, Oklahoma, 12 February 1898
d. Santa Monica, California, 1 October 1979

Harris was born of Scottish and Irish parents in a log cabin built by his father who, as a farmer, had moved into pioneer land. His grandfathers had both been stagecoach drivers, so that Harris could claim an almost legendary background for himself. It is appropriate that he shared his birthday with Abraham Lincoln. While he was still young, the family moved to San Gabriel Valley in Southern California. Here at the age of five he began piano lessons with his mother. Following a brief spell of farming, he spent a year in the army during World War I.

In 1919 Harris turned to serious study and became a student at the University of California, taking philosophy and economics as his principal subjects. After one year he left to become a pupil of Arthur Farwell, from whom he received lessons in composition. He also worked on orchestration with Arthur Bliss. The performance of an *Andante for Strings* in 1926 led the composer to move first to New York and then to Paris, to study more thoroughly as a musician. In Paris he attended the classes of Nadia Boulanger, and a Guggenheim Fellowship in 1927 enabled him to devote all his time to composing. A serious accident in 1929 damaged his back, forcing him to lie in hospital for many months. Thus deprived of the use of a piano, Harris found new freedom in composing away from the keyboard and at this time wrote his First String Quartet.

In 1930 he was awarded a fellowship from the Pasadena Music and Arts Association, which again allowed him to compose unhindered. From 1931 to 1938 he

taught at the Westminster Choir College in Princeton, New Jersey. After a year on the faculty of the Juilliard School, he became Composer-in-Residence, first at Cornell University (1941–43) and then at Colorado College, Colorado Springs (1943–45). He spent three years (1945–48) in the U.S. Office of War Information as chief of the music section's radio program. Harris subsequently taught at Utah State College (1948–49); George Peabody College for Teachers, Nashville, Tennessee (1949–51); Pennsylvania College for Women, Pittsburgh (1951–56); Southern Illinois University, Carbondale (1956–57); and Indiana University, Bloomington (1957–60). After two years at the Inter-American University of San German in Puerto Rico, he joined the music faculty of the University of California, Los Angeles in 1962. He retired in 1973.

Of all composers, Harris was one of the most deeply American in character, not only because of the circumstances of his early life, but because of his whole outlook on music. Folk songs, hymn tunes, the poetry of Walt Whitman, and American history (the impact of Lincoln in particular) are at the very center of everything he wrote. His musical language is strongly personal, based on a modality with polytonal implications at times. In his harmony he employs a juxtaposition of major and minor triads that step from key to key but preserve a tonal structure. The frequent use of fugato is derived not from academic European sources but from the "fuging tunes" of early American hymnody. Harris expressed his aesthetic purposes in many articles he wrote for various publications. He felt that his music should be a part of a specifically American artistic expression. He was extremely prolific, producing music in every field except opera. The greater part of his works were orchestral and choral. In many of these he used titles or texts on American subjects.

Harris wrote a monumental set of symphonies. Symphony no. 1 is subtitled *1933* to avoid confusion with a four-movement work composed in 1929 that remained in manuscript. It was performed by the Boston Symphony Orchestra under Serge Koussevitzky in 1934 and became widely known through a phonograph recording. The Second Symphony followed a year later and was heard on Boston in 1936.

The year 1938 marked the completion of Harris's best-known work, the legendary Third Symphony. After the premiere in Boston in 1939, its success was outstanding, with performances under many conductors, including Arturo Toscanini, throughout the United States and Europe. Although a "late starter" as a composer, by his early forties Harris had achieved worldwide fame; his Third Symphony has taken its place in the American musical heritage. Its single-movement form is related to the Seventh Symphony of Sibelius but the language is wholly American. Such powerful character established Harris's name, but inevitably this single work has tended to overshadow the remaining symphonies.

Folk Symphony (no. 4) for chorus and orchestra, completed in 1940, fuses traditional songs with abstract musical thought. The five choral movements are settings of "The Girl I Left Behind Me," " Western Cowboy," "I'm Going Away," "De Trumpet Sounds It in My Soul," and "When Johnny Comes Marching Home." He had already arranged the last song for orchestra in an Overture commissioned by RCA Victor in 1934 and in a choral version in 1937. The two interludes of this symphony are dance movements based on fiddle tunes. Written at a time when the world was becoming deeply involved in war, the work no doubt gained some popularity from its patriotic spirit. Today there seems to be something of a dichotomy between the charm and simplicity of the material and the serious treatment of the themes. The premiere was given at the American Spring Festival in Rochester, New York on 26 April 1940, conducted by Howard Hanson.

Symphony no. 5 was commissioned by Koussevitzky and performed in 1945. Its three movements show a stronger reliance on formal structure than is the case with the Third Symphony. The chorale-like second movement and the three fugal sections of the finale possess a tight control of form. Like its predecessor, Symphony no. 6 is scored for a large orchestra. The inspiration was Lincoln's Gettysburg Address, but the piece is purely instrumental with no direct reference to Lincoln's words. It is dedicated to "the Armed Forces of Our Nation" and was conducted by Koussevitzky in Boston in April 1944. Symphony no. 7 (1951), in one extended movement, was commissioned by the Koussevitzky Foundation. Although it bears some similarity to the Third Symphony, the material is more unified. Like Sibelius, Harris begins with a sense of searching for a solution that is eventually found in the ecstatic final section. The work was first performed by the Chicago Symphony Orchestra under the direction of Rafael Kubelik in November 1952.

Ten years and the death of Koussevitzky separate the Seventh and Eighth Symphonies. Again designed as a single movement, divided into five related parts, Symphony no. 8 was commissioned to celebrate the 50th anniversary of the founding of the San Francisco Symphony Orchestra, which performed it in January 1962. Symphony no. 9 (1962) received its premiere by the Philadelphia Orchestra under Eugene Ormandy in January 1963. The inspiration here was the Preamble to the American Constitution and the poetry of Walt Whitman. The dense textures of scoring make this one of the composer's most complex works. Symphony no. 10, *Abraham Lincoln*, scored for chorus, brass, and two amplified pianos, departs from the purely symphonic

and orchestral character of the other symphonies. It was performed at Long Beach, California in April 1965.

Harris conducted the premiere of his Symphony no. 11 on his 75th birthday in 1968 with the New York Philharmonic Orchestra, which had commissioned the work for its 125th anniversary. In 1968 Marquette University, Milwaukee, Wisconsin, commissioned Symphony no. 12 to celebrate the 300th anniversary of the exploration of the Midwest by Jacques Marquette (1637–1675), a Jesuit missionary. For reasons of superstition, Harris omitted a Symphony no. 13, giving the next in order, a commission from the National Symphony Orchestra to celebrate the American Bicentennial, the number 14. This work, for speaker, chorus, and orchestra, sets passages from the United States Constitution and words of Abraham Lincoln and the composer. It was first performed under the direction of Antal Dorati in Washington in February 1976. Following the composer's death, it has been renumbered 13, which has caused some confusion. Rumors of a Symphony no. 15 seem to be unfounded.

Harris's other orchestral works are extensive. His earliest compositions include *Our Heritage*, performed by Howard Hanson in Rochester, New York, in 1926; *American Portraits* (1929); *Toccata* (1931); *Andantino* (1931); *Chorale for Strings* (1933); *Overture: When Johnny Comes Marching Home* (1934); *Prelude and Fugue* for strings (1935); a symphonic elegy, *Farewell to Pioneers* (1936); *Time Suite* (1936); *Three Symphonic Essays* (1938); and *Prelude and Fugue* for four trumpets and strings (1939). The war years stimulated the writing of several patriotic pieces: *Ode to Truth* (1940); *American Creed* (with chorus) (1940); *Acceleration* (1941); *Evening Piece* (1941); *March in Time of War* (1943); and *Ode to Friendship* (1944). These were followed by *Memories of a Child's Sunday* (1945); *Celebration: Variations on a Theme by Hanson* (1946); *Quest* (1948); and *Kentucky Spring* (1949), a Louisville Orchestra commission. The next decade produced *Cumberland Concerto* (1950); *Fantasia* (1954); *Concert Piece* (1954); *Symphonic Epigram* (1954); *Ode to Consonance* (1957); and *Elegy and Dance* (1958). His later orchestral works include *Epilogue to Profiles of Courage, J.F.K.* (1964); *Horn of Plenty* (1964); *Salute to Death* (1963); *Rhythm and Spaces* for strings (1965); and *Fantasy* for organ, brass, and timpani (1966).

For solo instruments and orchestra Harris composed two violin concertos, no. 1 (1938; later withdrawn) and no. 2 (1949); Concerto for piano and band (1941); Concerto for organ and brass (1943); Concerto for accordion and orchestra (1946); Concerto for two pianos (1947); four works for piano and orchestra: two concertos (1945, 1953), *Fantasy* (1954), and Concerto for amplified piano, brass, and percussion (1968); and *Folksong Suite* for harp (1973).

Harris produced a prodigious and valuable output of choral music. Here again, texts by American writers, especially Whitman, expressing national and folk sentiments predominate. Whitman's poems are set in *Triptych* for female voices and piano (1927); the eight-part *A Song of Occupations*, performed in Moscow in 1934; the *Symphony for Voices* in three movements, also for eight-part chorus (1936); and *The Whitman Suite* for chorus, strings, and two pianos (1944). His religious music includes *The Story of Noah* for unaccompanied double chorus (1933); *Sanctus* (1935); *Alleluia* for chorus, brass, and organ (1945); *Israel*, a motet for tenor, chorus, and organ (1946); *An Easter Motet* for men's voices and organ (1947); and *Jubilation* for chorus, brass, and piano (1964). Secular choral works are *Puena Hueca* for chorus and piano trio (1920); *Song Without Words* for chorus and two pianos (1922); *Railroad Man's Ballad* for male voices (1938); *Challenge* (1940) and *American Creed* (1940), both for choir and orchestra; *The Red Bird in the Green Tree* (1940); *Freedom's Land* (Archibald McLeish) for baritone, chorus, and orchestra (1941); *Blow the Man Down* for chorus, band, and strings (1946); *Madrigal* for a cappella chorus (1947); and *The Brotherhood of Man* (Abraham Lincoln) for chorus and organ (1966).

Impressive among his solo vocal music is the cantata of lamentation, *Abraham Lincoln Walks at Midnight* (1953). Vachel Lindsay's poem, set for mezzo-soprano with piano trio, is treated in a natural declamatory style. *Give Me the Splendid Silent Sun* (1959) is a setting of the Whitman poem for baritone and orchestra. His last two vocal items are *Canticle of the Sun* for coloratura soprano and orchestra (1961) and *Rejoice and Sing* for baritone, string quartet, and piano (1976).

In addition to the Piano Concerto of 1941, Harris composed several important pieces for concert band: *Cimarron*, a symphonic overture (1941); *Rhythms of Today* (1943); *Conflict (War Piece)* (1944); *The Sun From Dawn to Dusk* (1944); *Take the Sun and Keep the Stars* (1944); *Fruit of the Gold* (1949); *Dark Devotion* (1950); and *Symphony for Band: West Point* (1952).

Harris's early chamber music includes *Impressions of a Rainy Day* for string quartet (1926) and Concerto for clarinet, piano, and string quartet, performed in Paris in 1927. His String Quartet no. 1 was also heard in Paris, in 1930. The *Fantasy* for piano and wind quintet and a Sextet for strings were composed while he was in Pasadena in 1932. Quartet no. 2 (*Three Variations on a Theme*) dates from 1933. In 1934 he wrote a work with the title *Four Minutes, Twenty Seconds* for flute and string quartet. By pure coincidence, it predates John Cage's legendary curiosity *4'33"* by almost 20 years. A radio broadcast was four minutes, twenty seconds short, so Harris produced this piece to fill the time, which was probably unknown to Cage.

After the Piano Trio (1934), Harris composed a Piano Quintet as a wedding present for his wife in 1936. String Quartet no. 3 (*Four Preludes and Fugues*) (1939) and a String Quintet (1940) both received their premieres in Washington, D.C. Other instrumental works include *Soliloquy and Dance* for viola and piano (1939); a lyrical Violin Sonata (1941); *Duo* for cello and piano (1964); Cello Sonata (1964, rev. 1968); and a Piano Sextet (1968). Among his many piano pieces are a Sonata (1928); *Variations on an Irish Theme* (1938); *Little Suite* (1938); *Toccata* (1939, rev. 1949); and *American Ballads* (1945).

Harris composed little for the stage. There are four ballets—*Western Landscape* (1940), *From This Earth* (1941), *What So Proudly We Hail* (1942), and *War* (1945)—but no operas. His single film score, *One Tenth of a Nation*, was produced in 1941.

HARRISON, LOU (SILVER)
b. Portland, Oregon, 14 May 1917
d. Lafayette, Indiana, 2 February 2003

Harrison was educated at San Francisco State College (1934–35), where he was a pupil of Henry Cowell. He also studied with Arnold Schoenberg in 1942. He was a member of the faculty of Mills College, Oakland, California (1937–40); the University of California, Los Angeles (1942); Reed College, Portland, Oregon (1949–50); and Black Mountain College, North Carolina (1951–52). From 1945 to 1948 he was a music critic for the *New York Herald Tribune*, a protégé of Virgil Thomson. He taught at San Jose State University (1967–80), then returned to Mills College, where he occupied the Darius Milhaud Chair of Music until 1985. In 1983 he was a senior Fulbright scholar at four universities in New Zealand. He was awarded two Guggenheim Fellowships in 1952 and 1954.

Throughout his life Harrison was an eclectic composer. It is impossible to classify him since his music ranges from neo-classical and modal to atonality, oriental music influences, and the aleatoric devices of the avant-garde. Each new musical experience he encountered became a part of his style. From his first teacher, Cowell, he absorbed both experimental and traditional elements. After studying with Schoenberg he adopted atonal practices that survived from time to time in his music.

Working with John Cage on percussion, Harrison began to build and adapt instruments, notably the tack piano, an upright with drawing pins in the hammer heads producing a sound similar to a dry harpsichord. In 1953 he met Harry Partch in California, who encouraged him to further instrumental experiments. Another potent influence was a visit to Japan, Taiwan, and

Korea in 1961, which opened up a whole new world of orchestral sounds involving different scales, pitch relationships, and microtones. This led to an interest as a composer, constructor, and performer of gamelan music and instruments (from Indonesia).

Harrison composed two operas, *The Only Jealousy of Emer* (after Yeats) (1949) and *Rapunzel*, based on a poem by William Morris (1954). A third opera for puppets, *Young Caesar*, was completed in 1970. The ballet *Solstice* (1949) shows the strong influence of Indian music. Other ballets include *Changing World* (San Francisco:1936); *Green Mansions* (San Francisco: 1939); *Something to Please Everyone* (1939); *Johnny Appleseed* (San Francisco: 1940); *Omnipotent Chair* (Oakland, California: 1940); *The Perilous Chapel* (New York: 1948); *Western Dance* (for Merce Cunningham) (1948); *The Marriage at the Eiffel Tower* (Jean Cocteau) (Portland: Oregon: 1949); *Almanac of the Seasons* (Portland: 1950); *Io and Prometheus* (New York: 1951); *Praises for Hummingbirds and Hawks* (1951); and *Rhythms with Silver* (1997) for Max Morris, based on the playing of the cellist Yo-Yo Ma. He also provided incidental music for plays: *Peter Pan* (J. M. Barrie; 1934); *Choephore* (Aeschylus; 1937); *Electra* (Euripides;1938); *The Trojan Women* (Aeschylus; 1938); *A Winter's Tale* (Shakespeare; 1938); *The Beautiful People* (William Saroyan; 1941); and *Cinna* (Corneille; 1957). In addition he wrote four film scores: *Nuptiae* (with James Broughton; 1969), *Discovering Korean Art* (1979), *Beyond the Far Blue Mountains* (1981–82), and *Devotions* (1983).

With the exception of *Alleluia* (1946), which uses dissonant counterpoint reminiscent of Carl Ruggles, Harrison's early works for orchestra are comparatively conservative in character, as their titles imply: *Prelude and Sarabande* (1937), two suites for strings (1936–60, 1948), and *Symphony on G* (1948–54). This last work, serially composed but based on the note G, was revised after the premiere in 1964. With a new finale it was performed in 1966 by the Oakland Symphony Orchestra.

In the Suite for violin, piano, and small orchestra (1957), he introduced Javanese gamelan effects. From 1976 to 1984 he composed some 36 works with a gamelan, with titles that combine Far Eastern and Western elements, such as *Scenes from Cavafy* for baritone and gamelan (1972); *Ladrang Epikuros* (1981); *Ladrang Samuel* (1981); and *Ketawang Wellington* (1983).

After the *Symphonic Suite for Strings* (1960), his orchestral were scored for very unorthodox collections of instruments. *Symfony [sic] in Free Style* (1956, rev. 1980) employs 17 flutes (four players), five harps, eight violas, trombone, piano, celeste, drum, and bells. *Pacifika Rondo* (1963) makes use of oriental instruments in addition to the conventional orchestra. Later orchestral pieces include *Pastorales* (1969); Concerto for organ, multiple percussion, and orchestra (1972–73); *Elegiac Symphony* (1975, rev. 1981–82); performed by the Oakland Youth Symphony Orchestra, Double Concerto for violin, cello, and large Javanese gamelan orchestra (1981–82); Symphony no. 3 (1937–82); and a Piano Concerto (1985). *Last Symphony* (no. 4), composed in 1990 and performed in that year by the Brooklyn Symphony Orchestra, was revised several times between 1991 and 1995.

Harrison had a great interest in percussion instruments. In 1940 he composed the first of three *Canticles* for percussion, which evoke a sense of primitive tribal music but also possess a melodic quality which justifies the rather ambiguous title. Three later works make extensive use of percussion. The Concerto for Violin (1959) has a colorful accompaniment of a vast assemble of exotic percussion that, in addition to the more usual instruments, introduces a washtub, suspended pipe lengths or flower pots, and coffee cans. *Concerto in Slendro* (1961) is scored for solo cello, celeste, two pianos (with tacks in the hammer heads), and percussion. Suite for violin and gamelan orchestra dates from 1974.

Important among Harrison's instrumental works are six sonatas for harpsichord (1934–35); *Schoenbergiana* for string quartet (1945); a String Trio (1946); Suite for cello and harp, influenced by Stravinsky (1949); Suite for ensemble (1950); *Scenes from William Morris* for flute, string trio, harp, and percussion (1955); *At the Tomb of Charles Ives* for ensemble (1963); *In Memory of Victor Jowers* for clarinet and piano (1968); *String Quartet Set* (1978–79); and Serenade for guitar and percussion (1979).

Among Harrison's relatively few choral pieces are a *Mass for St. Anthony* for mixed voices, trumpet, harp, and strings (1939–49), written for liturgical use; *Easter Cantata* for solo voices, chorus, and orchestra (1943–46); *Nova odo* for chorus and orchestra (1962); *Four Strict Songs* for eight baritones and orchestra (1968); *Peace Pieces* for chorus, soloists, and orchestra (1968); *Orpheus* for baritone, chorus, and large percussion orchestra (1969); and *Lo Koro Sutra*, a setting of an Esperanto text for chorus, gamelan, and percussion (1972).

Harrison was an early champion of the music of Charles Ives and acted as editor of several of his works, including the Fourth Symphony. In New York in 1946 he conducted the world premiere of Ives's Symphony no. 3. Harrison was the author of several pioneering books, including *About Carl Ruggles* (1946); *Music Primer: Various Items About Music to 1970* (1971); *Soundings: Ives, Ruggles, Varèse* (1975); *A Lou Harrison Reader* (ed. P. Garland; 1987); and a volume of poetry, *Joys and Perplexities* (1992).

HART, FREDERIC PATTON

b. Aberdeen, Washington, 5 September 1894
d. Los Angeles, California, May 10, 1983

Hart studied with Ernest Hutcheson at the American Conservatory in Chicago and at the Chicago Art Institute. In New York he attended the Diller-Quaile School and was a pupil of Rubin Goldmark. In addition he received composition lessons from Nadia Boulanger in Paris. Back in the United States he taught at Sarah Lawrence College, Bronxville, New York (1929–47) and the Juilliard School (1947–60) before retiring to Los Angeles.

For the stage Hart composed two operas, the three-act *The Wheel of Fortune* (1934) and *A Farewell Supper*, premiered in New York in 1984, a year after his death. An opera-ballet in one act *The Romance of the Robot* was staged in New York in 1937. His orchestral works include a *Concert Overture* and *Three Pastorales* for wind quartet and orchestra. Among his instrumental music are an *Adagio and Scherzo* for string quartet (1931), a String Quartet (1937), and a Suite for string trio.

HART, WELDON

b. Place-Bear Spring, Tennessee, 19 September 1911
d. East Lansing, Michigan, 20 November 1957

Hart studied in Nashville, at the University of Michigan, Ann Arbor, and at the Eastman School of Music, Rochester, New York (with Howard Hanson and Bernard Rogers). He was head of the department of music at Western Kentucky State College (1946–49) and director of the School of Music, University of West Virginia, Morgantown (1949–57). In 1957, the year of his death by suicide, he was appointed head of the music department at Michigan State University, East Lansing.

For orchestra Hart wrote a symphonic poem, *The Dark Hills* (1939); a Sinfonietta (1944); a Symphony (1945); *Symphonic Movement* (1945); a Violin Concerto (1951); *John Jacob Niles Suite*; *Darling Cory*; *Pennyrile Overture*; and *Stately Music* for strings (1955).

Among his choral works are *Three West Virginia Folk Songs* (1954) and a setting of *O Sing Unto the Lord.*

HARTKE, STEPHEN (PAUL)

b. Orange, New Jersey, 6 July 1952

Hartke studied at Yale University (1970–73) and with George Rochberg at the University of Pennsylvania (1974–76). At the University of California, Santa Barbara he was a pupil of Edward Applebaum. He later taught there (1981–83, 1985–87) and at the University

Stephen Hartke.
Photo: Robert Millard, courtesy the composer.

of S[tilde]ao Paolo, Brazil (1984–85). Since 1987 he has been a member of the music Faculty of University of Southern California, Los Angeles and was Composer-in-Residence with the Los Angeles Chamber Orchestra (1988–92). He has been the recipient of the Rome Prize (1991–92) and a Guggenheim Fellowship (1998).

For orchestra, Hartke has written *The Bull Transcended* for strings (1970); *Passion, Poison and Petrification: a chamber symphony* (1973); Symphony no. 1 (1974–76); *Alvorada Madrigals* for strings (1983); *Maltese Cat Blues* (1986); *Pacific Run* (1988); Symphony no. 2 (1990); a Violin Concerto (1992); *The Ascent of the Equestrian in a Balloon* (1995); and Symphony no. 3 premiered by the New York Philharmonic Orchestra in 2003. His many instrumental pieces include *Caoine* for violin (1980); *Sonata-Variations* for violin and piano (1984); *Oh These Rats Are Mean in My Kitchen* for two violins (1985); *Precession* for 13 instruments (1986); *The King of the Sun* for piano quartet (1988); *Wir küssen Ihnen tausendmal die Hände – Homage to Mozart* for clarinet, horn, string trio, and fortepiano (1991); *Wulfstan at the Millennium* for 10 instruments (1995); *The Horse With the Lavender Eye* for violin, clarinet, and piano (1997); *The Rose of the Winds* for string octet (1998); and a Piano Sonata (1999).

Among Hartke's vocal compositions are a cantata, *Alysoun*, for contralto and eight instruments (1971);

The Hunting of the Snark (Lewis Carroll), a chamber cantata for baritone solo, chorus, and small orchestra (1972); *Two Songs for an Uncertain Age* for soprano and orchestra (1981); *Four Madrigals on Old Portuguese Texts* for soloist and chorus (1981); *Cancoes modernistas* for high voice, clarinet, bass clarinet, and viola (1982); *Inglesia abanonada* for soprano and violin (1982); *Sons of Noah* for soprano, four flutes, four guitars, and four bassoons (1996); and *Tituli* for five solo men's voices, violin, and two percussion (1999).

HASTINGS, THOMAS
b. *Washington, Connecticut, 15 October 1784*
d. *New York, New York, 15 May 1872*

Hastings settled first in Clinton, New York, in 1796 before moving in 1828 to Utica, New York. From 1832 to his death he lived in New York City, earning a living as teacher and choirmaster. In 1858 he was awarded an honorary doctorate in music at New York University.

Hastings composed over 1,000 tunes and 600 verses for hymns. In this work he was assisted by Lowell Mason. Among his published collections of music are *Musica Sacra* (Utica, 1815), which went into 12 editions; *The Musical Reader* (1817); *The Union Minstrel* (1830); *Spiritual Songs for Social Worship* (with Mason; 1831); *Musical Miscellany* (New York, 1836); *Manhattan Collection* (New York, 1836); *The Sacred Lyre* (New York, 1840); *Sacred Songs for Family and Social Worship* (1842); *Indian Melodies* (1845); *Devotional Hymns and Religious Poems* (1850); *Selah: Sacred Poems* (1850); and *Songs of Zion* (1851). Hastings is remembered today for the tune *Toplady*, sung to the words of *Rock of Ages*.

He also published several books, including *Dissertation on Musical Taste* (Albany, 1822, rev. 1853) and *A History of Forty Choirs* (New York, 1853).

HAUBIEL, CHARLES TROWBRIDGE (ORIGINAL NAME: PRATT)
b. *Delta, Ohio, 30 January 1892*
d. *Los Angeles, California, 26 August 1978*

Haubiel was educated at the Mannes College, New York (1919–24), where he was a pupil of Rosario Scalero. In addition he received piano lessons from Rudolf Ganz in Berlin (1911–13) and Josef and Rosina Lhevinne in New York (1920–26). In 1913 he joined the faculty of Kingfisher College, Oklahoma, as a teacher of piano and composition. Two years later he was appointed to the Musical Arts Institute in Oklahoma City. From 1922 to 1930 he taught at the Institute of Musical Art in New York and at New York University from 1923 to 1947.

Charles Trowbridge Haubiel.
Courtesy New York University Archives.

Haubiel's musical language is clearly derived from nineteenth century romantic composers and reflects an age that had passed. Although several of his works won important prizes, this did not lead to frequent performances of his music.

The symphonic variations *Karma* won the Columbia Record Company Schubert Competition in 1928. It was retitled *Of Human Destiny* in a new version dating from 1968. *Ristratti* (*Portraits*) was given the first prize in the Swift Symphonic Competition in 1935. *Passacaglia in A minor*, now named *The Plain Beyond*, won a New York Philharmonic Orchestra prize in 1938. This work, *Pastoral* (*Dawn Mists*) (1935), and *Meridian* (*Fugue*) (1942) were gathered together under the collective title *Solari*.

Other major orchestral works are *Mars Ascending* (1923); *Vox Cathedralis* (1934); Symphony no. 1 *in Variation Form* (1937); *Miniatures* for string orchestra (1939); *Passacaglia Triptych* (1937–40); *Pioneers*, a symphonic saga of the composer's own home state, Ohio (1943); *Nuances* for flute and strings (1943); *Gothic Variations* for violin and orchestra (1961); *He-*

roic Elegy (in honor of General Douglas MacArthur) (1946); a symphonic poem, *1865 A.D.* (1943, rev. 1958 and 1962); and *Mississippi Story* for strings (1959).

American Rhapsody for high voice and chorus (1948), a setting of Raymond Duncan's poem "Oh You 48 States," also exists as an orchestral piece (1962) and in a version for piano solo (1963). *Suite Passacaille,* originally a piano piece composed in 1915, was orchestrated in 1931 and rescored for chamber orchestra in 1974.

For solo voice and orchestra he wrote *Portals* (1935), a triple triptych (*Three Nature Songs, Three Love Songs, Three Philosophical Songs*); *The Cosmic Christ* (1940); and *A Browning Cycle* for baritone and soprano.

For chorus and orchestra, Haubiel composed several cantatas: *Serenade* (1924); *L'Amore Spirituale* for six-part female chorus in canonical form (1924–32); *The Vision of St. Joan* (1941); *Father Abraham* (1944); *Both Grave and Gay* for female voices (1948); and *Flight into Egypt* for high voice, chorus, and orchestra (1968 rev. 1974). In addition there is *The Astronaut's Lunar Christmas* for female voices, piano, and percussion (1971). For unaccompanied voices he composed a Passion motet, *Christ Crucified* (1924), and *Stay With Me For God* for men's chorus and boys' voices (1970).

For the stage Haubiel composed a musical satire in the style of Gilbert and Sullivan, *Brigand's Preferred* (1925, rev. 1946); three operas: *The Witch's Curse* (1946), *Sunday Costs Five Pesos* (1947), a Mexican folk opera later renamed *Berta,* and *The Enchanted Princess* (1955); an operetta, *The Birthday Cake* (1942); and an opera for children, *Adventures on Sunbonnet Hill* (1971). He wrote incidental music for *The Passionate Pilgrim* (Henry James; 1932) and a film score for Paramount, *Swanee River Goes Hi-Hat* (1936).

Haubiel composed much chamber music: *Duoforms* (1929–32); *Gay Dances and Romanza* (1932) for piano trio; *In Praise of Dance* for oboe and piano trio (1932); *Ecchi Classici* for string quartet (1931 and 1939); *Masque* for oboe and string trio (1937); *In the French Manner* (1942); String Trio (1943); *Pastoral Trio* (1944) for flute, cello, and piano; *Gothic Variations* for violin and piano (1919, 1943); *String Duo* in D minor (1943); Cello Sonata (1944); *Shadows* for violin and piano (1947); Violin Sonata *in D minor* (1948); Oboe Sonata (1968); Trio in D minor for clarinet (or viola), cello, and piano (1968); and *Suite Concertante* for clarinet (or viola) and string quartet (1973).

In 1935 Haubiel founded the Composers Press, Inc., to publish music by American composers. In addition he sponsored competitions and recordings to encourage performance of these publications. When the catalog was taken over by Seesaw Music Corporation in 1971, 135 composers were represented by over 500 works.

HAUFRECHT, HERBERT
b. New York, New York, 3 November 1909
d. Albany, New York, 23 June 1998

Haufrecht studied piano and composition at the Cleveland Institute of Music with Quincy Porter and Herbert Elwell (1926–30) and at the Juilliard Graduate School with Rubin Goldmark (1930–34). In addition to his work as a composer, he was an editor and arranger for Mills Music Inc. (1945–49), Associated Music Publishers, and Broadcast Music Inc, (1951–59). From 1959 to 1966 he was national music director of Young Audiences Inc. He was again an editor for Belwin-Mills Publishing Corporation from 1968 to 1977.

For orchestra Haufrecht wrote *Overture for an American Mural* (1939); *Three Fantastic Marches* (1939); a Symphony for brass and timpani (1956); and several works for string orchestra, including a Suite (1934), *Square Set* (1941), and *Ballad and Country Dance* (1967). Amongst his music for band is *Prelude to a Tragedy* (1967–68). He also wrote a number of pieces for children's audience for narrator and orchestra—*The Story of Ferdinand* (1939), *Peter Rabbit* (1944), *Little Red Hen* (1949), *Whoa, Little Horses* (1950), *A Walk in the Forest* (1951) and others—all of which have been recorded. For the Humphrey-Weldman Dance Company he composed *When Dad was a Fireman* (1946).

Among Haufrecht's many instrumental solos and chamber music are *Sicilian Suite* (1944); *Caprice* for clarinet and piano (1950); *Etude in Blues* (1954); *A Woodland Serenade* for wind quintet (1955); *Nocturnes* for piano (1956); a Piano Sonata (1956); *From Washington's Time* for flute and harpsichord (or piano) (1958); *Air on a Ground* for flute or oboe and guitar (1961); *Fantasy on Haitian Themes* for clarinet, viola (or cello), and percussion (1974); and a Suite for brass quintet.

Haufrecht composed two folk operas: *Boney Quillen* (1951) and *A Pot of Broth* (1961–63). In 1974 he wrote *Benjamin Franklin's Poor Richard's Almanac* for a cappella chorus. Several of his works deal with the folklore of New York's Catskill Mountains, where he lived for many years: *Folk Songs of the Catskills* for voice and piano or for a cappella chorus (1943); *We've Come from the City,* a cantata (1945); and *Walkin' the Road* for band (1945).

He also edited a number of books including *Folk Sing* (1960); *Round the World Folk Sing* (1963); *Travelin' On with the Weavers* (1966); *Laura Ingalls Wilder Songbook* (1968); *Judy Collins Songbook* (1969); and *Folk Songs in Settings by Master Composers* (1970).

HAUSSERMANN, JOHN (WILLIAM JR.)
b. Manila, Philippines, 21 August 1909
d. Denver, Colorado, 5 May 1986

Haussermann moved with his family to Ohio in 1915 where he learned piano. From 1924 to 1927 he studied organ and theory at the Cincinnati Conservatory. In 1930, at the Schola Cantorum in Paris, he was a pupil of Marcel Dupré (organ) and Paul Le Flem (composition). On his return to the United States he devoted most of his time to composition, as his activities as a performing musician were limited by cerebral palsy. Haussermann composed three symphonies (1938, 1941, 1947), all first performed in Cincinnati, and several other orchestral pieces, including *Nocturne and Dance* (1933); *The After Christmas Suite* (1938); *Rhapsodic Overture* for piano and chamber orchestra (1939–41); a Concerto for voice and orchestra (1941); *Etude Romanesque* (1943); *Rondo Carnavalesque* (1949); *Stanza* for violin and orchestra (1956); and Concerto for organ and strings (1985).

Among his instrumental works are a Piano Quintet (1934); a Quintet for wind and harpsichord (1935); a String Quartet (1936); *Suite Rustique* for flute, cello, and piano (1937); *Divertissements* for string quartet (1940); *Poeme et Claire de Lune* for violin and piano (1940); a Violin Sonata (1941); and *Serenade* for theremin and string quartet (1945). Haussermann wrote copiously for piano: *24 Preludes symphoniques* (1932–33); *Sonata fantastique* (1932); *Ballade, Burlesque et Légende* (1936); *Seven Bagatelles* (1948); *Nine Impromptus* (1958); and *Five Harmonic Etudes* (1968).

His vocal music includes *Five Singing Miniatures* for soprano and piano (1933–34); *Three Moods* (1939); *On the River* (5 Songs; 1945); *Three Psalms* for tenor and piano (1959); and *Four Haiku for Nelge* for soprano and piano (1982). For chorus he composed *St. Francis' Prayer* (1968).

HEIDEN, BERHARD
b. Frankfurt-am-Main, Germany, 24 August 1910
d. Bloomington, Indiana, 30 April 2000

From 1929 to 1933 Heiden was a pupil of Paul Hindemith at the Berlin Hochschule für Musik. In 1935 he went to the United States and settled in Detroit, where he was an arranger for WWJ radio (1938–39). He conducted the Detroit Chamber Orchestra (1942–43) and studied musicology with Donald Grout at Cornell University. He became an American citizen in 1941. Following war service in the U.S. Army, he was appointed professor of composition at Indiana University in 1946, retiring in 1981. He was awarded the Mendelssohn Prize (1933) and a Guggenheim Fellowship (1966–67) and

Berhard Heiden.
Courtesy Indiana University Archives.

received a grant from the National Endowment for the Arts (1976).

For orchestra he composed two symphonies (1938, 1954); *Euphorion: Scene for Orchestra* (1949); Concerto for small orchestra (1949); *Memorial* (1955); *Philharmonic Fanfare* (1958); *Variations* (1960); *Envoy* (1963); *Concertino for Strings* (1967); *Partita* (1970); and *Salute* (1989). Heiden composed concertos for piano trio (1956), cello (1967), horn (1969), tuba (1976), trumpet and winds (1981), recorder (1987), and bassoon (1990). There are several other works for solo instruments: *Recitative and Aria* for cello and chamber orchestra (1985); *Fantasia Concertante* for alto saxophone, wind, and percussion (1987); and *Symfonietta Concertante* for flute, cello, and chamber orchestra (1995).

Heiden's opera, *The Darkened City*, completed in 1961, was performed in 1963 and revived in 1978 by the Indiana University Opera Theatre. Choral works include *Two Songs of Spring* (S. Yellen) for female voices (1949); *Divine Poems* (John Donne; 1949); *In Memoriam* (Hal Borland; 1964); *Advent Song* (1965); and *Riddles* (Jonathan Swift) for women's voices (1975).

Most of his important works are for chamber ensembles. He is best known for the Sonata for alto saxophone and piano (1937); Sonata for horn and piano (1939); and a Horn Quintet (1952). In addition Heiden composed three string quartets (1947, 1951, 1963); *Sinfonia* for wind quintet (1949); a Violin Sonata

(1954); Clarinet Quintet (1955); Serenade for bassoon and string trio (1955); Piano Trio (1956); Cello Sonata (1958); Flute Sonatina (1958); Viola Sonata (1959); *Intrada* for string quartet (1962); Quintet for oboe and strings (1963); *Seven Pieces* for string quartet (1964); Wind Quintet (1965); *Four Dances* for brass quintet (1967); *Inventions* for two cellos (1967); *Intrada* for wind quintet and alto saxophone (1970); *Variations* for tuba and nine horns (1974); Quintet for flute, violin, viola, bassoon, and double bass (1975); *Variations on Lilliburlero* for solo cello (1976); *Four Movements* for saxophone quartet and timpani (1976); *Sonata for Louise Labe* for soprano and string quartet (1977); *Terzetto* for two flutes and cello (1979); Quartet for horns (1981); Sextet for brass and piano (1983); Quartet for horn, violin, cello, and piano (1985); *Trio Serenade* for violin, clarinet, and piano (1987); Trio for oboe, bassoon, and piano (1992); *Encounters* for brass quartet (1994); and Clarinet Trio (1995).

Heiden's keyboard works include two piano sonatas (1941, 1952), *Variations* (1959), and *Hommage a Scarlatti* (1971) for piano solo; Sonata for piano duet (1946); and *Fantasia* for two pianos (1971).

Heiden was also a noted teacher, numbering Easley Blackwood and Donald Erb among his pupils.

HEILMAN, WILLIAM CLIFFORD

b. Williamsport, Pennsylvania, 27 September 1877
d. Williamsport, Pennsylvania, 20 December 1946

Heilman studied at Harvard University (B.A., 1900), and in Europe with Charles-Marie Widor and Joseph Rheinberger. He taught at Harvard (1905–30). He composed a symphonic poem, *Porta Catania* (1916), a Piano Trio, and a *Romance* for cello and piano. His choral music includes *Night Song, Among the Garden*, and *Knew Not the Sun*.

HEINRICH, ANTHONY PHILIP (ANTON PHILIPP)

b. Schönbüchel, Bohemia (now Krasny Buk, Czech Republic), 11 March 1781
d. New York, New York, 3 May 1861

Heinrich was the son of a rich banker. He came to America in 1810, settling first in Philadelphia where he was a violinist, pianist, and conductor. A year later, his father went bankrupt, forcing him to earn a living through music. He moved to Lexington, Kentucky, where he taught and played the violin. It was there that Heinrich led an orchestra in the first known performance of a Beethoven symphony in America, no. 1 in C, given on 12 November 1817. Even at this time he was striving to be accepted as an American musician. He thought that his work would revolutionize music in America, but almost all his persistent efforts at having his pieces performed met with failure. His life seems to have been full of disappointments and misfortune, resulting from the constant rejection of his large-scale compositions and ill health.

In the spring of 1818 Heinrich withdrew from society to a log cabin in the woods near Bardstown. The natural beauty of this wild scenery provided inspiration for much of his music. In 1820 he published a vast collection of miscellaneous pieces for piano and violin entitled *Dawning of Music in Kentucky or the Pleasures of Harmony in the Solitude of Nature*. In the preface, he states: "The many and severe animadversions so long and repeatedly cast on the talent for Music in this Country has been one of the motives of the Author; in the exercise of his abilities, and should he be able by this effort to create but one single Star in the West, no one would ever be more proud than himself to be called an American Musician."

In the same year Heinrich issued a second collection of music, *The Western Musician*. In 1823 in Boston he published a miscellany of seven piano pieces and songs, *The Sylviad: or Minstrelsy of Nature in the Wilds of North America*, dedicated to the Royal Academy of Music in London, no doubt to gain favor with them prior to a visit he had planned to London. Some of these items reveal an Ivesian extravagance of dissonance. *The Minstrel's Catch* is a canon for eight to 40 voices, an early example of indeterminacy.

Heinrich went to London in 1827, returning to America in 1832, where he became an organist in Boston. Back in London two years later, he played in the orchestra at the Drury Lane Theatre. His reputation in Europe was such that four of his works were performed at a concert in Graz, Austria, in 1836. Two years later he finally settled in New York City.

One might compare the curiously complex mind of Heinrich with that of Charles Ives, but, unlike that composer, Heinrich would not accept the indifference of musicians and the public towards his compositions. His orchestral works were all planned on a grand scale, often of great length with impressive, if pompous, titles: *Grand Symphony: The Ornithological Combat of Kings, or The Condor of the Andes and the Eagle of the Cordilleras* (1847/1856); *The Colombiad, a Grand American National Chivalrous Symphony* (1837); *Yankee Doodliad* (c. 1855); *Jenny Lind and the Septinarian* (c.1850); *The Wildwood Troubadour, a Musical Autobiography* (1834/1853); *National Memories: a Grand British Symphony* (1844/1852); *Schiller, Grande Sinfonia Dramatica* (1847); *The Tomb of Genius, to the Memory of Mendelssohn Bartholdy, Sinfonia Sacra* (c. 1847); *The War of the Elements and the Thundering of Niagara; The Jubilee, a Grand National Song of Triumph* for chorus and orchestra; and many others.

American history was fully commemorated and documented in such works as *The Treaty of William Penn with the Indians, a Concerto Grosso, an American National Dramatic Divertissement* for full orchestra (1834, rev. 1847), "successively in six different characteristic movements united as one." Heinrich was not modest in the titles selected for his pieces. He was possibly the first composer to make use of the music of the American Indians as the basis for certain works. As early as 1831 he wrote *Pushmataha, a Venerable Chief of a Western Tribe of Indians*, and by 1845 he had composed *Manitou Mysteries, or the Voice of the Great Spirits, a grand sinfonia misteriosa indiana*, both of which claim to be based on American Indian melodies.

In 1842 he was chairman of the meeting that founded the New York Philharmonic Society. In the same year, the Heinrich Grand Musical Festival in New York presented seven of his works to great acclaim from a large audience. In 1843, for a projected choral symphony entitled *Poem on the Emancipation of the Slaves*, he vainly sought a text from John Quincy Adams. A benefit concert of his music given in New York on 6 May 1846 was also well-received. One critic commented, "Much of the music is truly magnificent and grand; but in the midst of this sublimity and grandeur, we are sometimes startled by the quaintest and oddest passage we ever heard. There are certainly a wonderful deal of originality in all of Mr H's compositions, and the most fantastic parts are always artistically correct, and perfectly descriptive of their subject."

The great moment of recognition came to "Father" Heinrich, as he became known, toward the end of his life. For years he had struggled to have his music performed; on 21 April 1853, when he was 72, a concert was given in Metropolitan Hall, New York that included a number of his works. All the important musicians in the city took part and, judging from the program, the concert must have lasted several hours, since at least four of his large-scale orchestra pieces were played. An advance newspaper notice of the event described Heinrich's long struggle to be heard: "He has gone on in his solitary attic, composing oratorios, operas, symphonies and songs, merely composing, not publishing till he had accumulated several large chests full of original compositions, his only wealth. May the devoted old servant of St. Cecilia be cheered by a full house, and may some of that inspiration which has sustained his long labors appear in his works and be felt by his audience." After this brief success, in 1857 Heinrich visited Europe for the last time, where three concerts were given in his honor in Prague. For the occasion he wrote several pieces reflecting his own national origin, including *Bohemia, sinfonia romantica* (c. 1853); *Hom-*

age à la Bohème (1855), and a march, *Austria: Heil dir ritterlicher Kaiser*. He returned to New York in 1859.

Heinrich had tried hard to establish himself as an American composer. For many of his works he had taken specific American themes of a national and patriotic nature. Music of the Indians had served as inspiration for works mentioned above and for two other orchestral pieces, *Indian Carnival* and *Indian Fanfares*, both published as piano solos. His output was enormous: 36 orchestral scores, 150 songs (of which over one hundred were published), 40 choral items, six chamber works, and at least a hundred piano solos. In *Our American Music*, John Tasker Howard paid tribute to Heinrich: "We must respect him for what he tried to do, and never forget that he was the first to make the attempt. That he failed to accomplish his ends was unfortunate, in many ways tragic, but the important fact is that Heinrich was the first to attempt American nationalism in the larger forms of musical composition."

Heinrich died in poverty in New York; he was buried in the family vault of his friend John James Audubon, the naturalist and artist.

HELFER, WALTER
b. Lawrence, Massachusetts, 30 September 1896
d. New Rochelle, New York, 16 April 1959

Helfer studied in Boston with Daniel Gregory Mason, at Harvard University (BA), Columbia University (MA), and at the Paris Conservatory. From 1925 to 1928 he was a pupil of Ottorino Respighi in Rome. Helfer was director of music at Deane School, Santa Barbara, California (1924–25), and later taught at Hunter College, New York, where he was chairman of the music Department (1938–50).

Helfer's orchestral works include a *Fantasy on Children's Tunes* (1935); *A Water Idyll* (1936); *Concert Overture* (1937); *Symphony on Canadian Airs* (1937); *Prelude, Intermezzo and Fugue* for chamber orchestra (1937); *Overture: A Midsummer Night's Dream* (1939); Concertino for piano and chamber orchestra (1947); *In Modo Giocoso*; and Suite for chamber orchestra. Among his instrumental works are a String Quartet *in G* (1923); String Trio *in F* (1928); a Violin Sonata (1928); *Elegiac Sonata* for piano (1931); and *Soliloquy* for cello and piano (1947).

HELM, EVERETT (BURTON)
b. Minneapolis, Minnesota, 17 July 1913
d. Berlin, Germany, 25 June 1999

Helm studied at Carleton College, Northfield, Minnesota (1930–34) and Harvard University (1934–36,

1938–39), where he was a pupil of Walter Piston. In Europe he received lessons from Gian Francesco Malipiero (1936–37) and Vaughan Williams (1937–38). At Mills College, Oakland, California (1941) he was a pupil of Darius Milhaud. Helm held various teaching posts: at the Longy School, Cambridge, Massachusetts (1939–41), Mills College (1941), and as head of music at Western College, Oxford, Ohio from 1942 to 1944. He spent two years in Latin America (1944–46), and after the Second World War he lived mostly in Europe, acting as correspondent for a number of newspapers and magazines (*New York Times*, *Christian Science Monitor*, *Musical Times*, *Music Review*, *Neue Zeitschrift für Musik* and others). From 1961 to 1963 he was editor-in-chief of *Musical America*. He also taught at the University of Ljubljana, Yugoslavia (1966–1968). Thereafter he was resident in Europe, first in Asola, Italy, moving in the 1980s to live in Germany.

Among Helm's major orchestral compositions are *Three Gospel Hymns* (1942, rev 1953); *Brasitiana* (1946); Concerto for string orchestra (1950); two piano concertos (1951, 1956); Concerto for five solo instruments (1953); Symphony for string orchestra (1955); *Sinfonia da Camera* (1961); a Concerto for double bass and strings (1968); *Cambridge Suite*; *Kentucky Sonata* for violin and orchestra; and *Three American Songs*. Instrumental works include a Violin Sonata (1938); two sonatas for flute and piano; Divertimento for flutes (1957); two string quartets (1962, 1970); a Wind Quintet (1966); and piano pieces.

Helm composed four works for the stage: *Adam and Eve*, a setting of a twelfth-century mystery play, produced in Wiesbaden in 1951; a three-act opera *The Siege of Tottenburg*, commissioned by Suddeutscher Rundfunk in 1956; a singspiel, *500 Dragons-Thalers* (1956); and a ballet, *Le Roy fait battre tambour* (1956). For the last two decades of his life he concentrated on his activities as a music critic.

Helm was the author of several books: *Béla Bartók* (1965); *Composer, Performer, Public: A Study in Communication* (1970); *Franz Liszt* (1972); *Tchaikovsky* (1976); and *Music and Tomorrow's Public* (1981), and contributed to the *New Oxford History of Music* and other musical dictionaries and encyclopedias.

HELPS, ROBERT (EUGENE)

b. Passaic, New Jersey, 23 September 1928
d. Tampa, Florida, 24 November 2001

Helps studied at the Juilliard School (1937–43), Columbia University (1947–49), and the University of California, Berkeley (1949–51). He also received private lessons in composition from Roger Sessions (1944–57) and with Abby Whiteside for piano (1943–

57). He was awarded a Guggenheim Fellowship in 1966. As well as being a composer, Helps was a pianist of concert standard, appearing with leading orchestras in the United States. He was an active advocate of American music, which he frequently performed in concerts and on recordings. He taught at the San Francisco Conservatory (1967–69), Stanford University (1967–68), the University of California, Berkeley and Davis (1968–70), the New England Conservatory, Boston (1970–72), the Manhattan School of Music (1972–78), and Princeton University (1972–78). In 1980 he was appointed professor of music at the University of South Florida in Tampa, where he continued to teach until his death from cancer.

The slow movement of his First Symphony was premiered by Stokowski and the Symphony of the Air in 1956. Later the Symphony won the Naumburg Award and was recorded by Columbia Records. It contains music of considerable energy in the outer movements with a lyrical slow movement (*Adagio for Orchestra*) of great beauty. Other orchestral pieces are *Cortège* (1963) and two piano concertos (1968, 1972), the second a commission from the Ford Foundation and the pianist Richard Goode.

Among Helps's chamber works are a String Quartet (1951); two piano trios (1957, 1996); Serenade in three movements, to be performed as such or as separate pieces: *Fantasy* for violin and piano, *Nocturne* for string quartet, and *Postlude* for horn, violin, and piano, finished in 1966; Quintet for flute, clarinet, violin, cello, and piano (1976); and *Second Thoughts* for solo flute (1981). Helps wrote much vocal music, including *Two Songs* to texts by Herman Melville (1950); *The Running Sun* to words by James Purdy (1972), and *Gossamer Noons* for soprano and orchestra (1974).

For his own instrument, the piano, he composed extensively: *Fantasy* (1952); *Three Etudes* (1956); *Image* (1958); *Recollections* (1959); *Solo* (1961); *Saccade* (4 hands; 1967); *Quartet for Piano* (1970); *Three Homages* (1972); *Nocturne* (1973); *Music for the Left Hand* (1975); *Valse mirage* (1977); and *In Retrospect* (1981).

HERBERT, VICTOR (AUGUST)

b. Dublin, Ireland, 1 February 1859
d. New York, New York, 26 May 1924

Herbert was the grandson of the Irish poet and novelist Samuel Lover. He showed musical talent when very young and was sent to Stuttgart at the age of eight to study the cello. While in Europe he played in many famous orchestras including that of Johann Strauss. After marrying an Austrian singer, he settled in New York in 1886 as first cellist in the Metropolitan Opera Orchestra, while his wife was a member of the chorus.

From 1889 to 1891 he was associate conductor of the Worcester (Massachusetts) Festival and from 1891 to 1898 was a bandmaster in New York. He was appointed conductor of the Pittsburgh Symphony Orchestra in 1896, a post he resigned in 1904 to devote himself to composition.

Although he is remembered today as the composer of operettas, Herbert began as a writer of choral and orchestral works. For himself as soloist he composed a Suite for cello and orchestra (1883) and a Cello Concerto (1885). A dramatic cantata, *The Captive*, was commissioned by the Worcester Festival in 1891. Three years later, his Second Cello Concerto was warmly praised by Dvořák after its premiere in New York. (Dvořák is thought to have considered writing his masterpiece for the same instrument after hearing Herbert's work.) Also for orchestra he composed a *Serenade for Strings* (1888), an *Irish Rhapsody* (1892); *American Fantasia* (1898); a symphonic poem, *Hero and Leander* (1901); *Woodland Fancies*, an orchestral suite (1901); *Suite Romantique* (1901); *Columbia Suite* (1902); *Soixante-neuf* for strings (1902); and, at the end of his life, a *Suite of Serenades* for Paul Whiteman (1924).

Herbert's first success on the stage, *Prince Ananais*, was performed in Boston in 1893. Thereafter he composed about 40 more operettas at a rate of more than one a year. These include *The Wizard of the Nile* (1895); *The Gold Bug* (1896); *The Serenade* (1897); *The Idol's Eye* (1897); *The Fortune Teller* (1898); *Cyrano de Bergerac* (1899); *The Ameer* (1899); *The Singing Girl* (1899); *The Viceroy* (1900); *Babes in Toyland* (1903); *It Happened in Nordland* (1904); *Mademoiselle Modiste* (1903); *Babette* (1903); *Miss Dollar Dollies* (1905); *Wonderland* (1905); *Dream City* (1906); *The Magic Knight* (1906); *The Red Mill* (1906); *The Tattooed Man* (1907); *The Prima Donna* (1908); *The Rose of Algeria* (1908); *Little Nemo* (1908); *Old Dutch* (1909); *When Sweet Sixteen* (1910); *Naughty Marietta* (1910); *Mlle. Rosita* (revised as *The Duchess*; 1911); *The Enchantress* (1911); *The Lady and the Slipper* (1912); *The Madcap Duchess* (1913); *Sweethearts* (1913); *The Debutante* (1914); *The Only Girl* (1914); *The Princess Pat* (1915); *The Century Girl* (1916); *Her Regiment* (1917); *Eileen* (1917); *My Golden Girl* (1919); *The Velvet Lady* (1919); *Angel Face* (1919); *The Girl in the Spotlight* (1920); *Oui, Madame* (1920); *Orange Blossoms* (1922); and *The Dream Girl* (1924). Although the Second Cello Concerto has been revived in recent years, Victor Herbert's name will always be associated with operetta, and such tunes as "Ah, Sweet Mystery of Life" from *Naughty Marietta*.

Herbert attempted two grand operas, but the weakness of the libretti prevented their becoming popular. *Natoma* (1910), in three acts, which makes use of American Indian melodies, was declined by the Metropolitan Opera but was later performed by the Philadelphia-Chicago Opera in Philadelphia on 25 February 1911. Three days later it was heard at the Metropolitan. The one-act *Madeleine* was staged in January 1914 in New York.

Herbert was an early and ardent fighter for composer's rights. His lawsuit against Shanley's Restaurant in New York City, which was profiting by playing his popular melodies during dinner hours, established the idea of "performance rights" as a source of income for composers. In 1914, Herbert was a founding member of the American Society of Composers, Authors and Publishers (ASCAP), which was formed to police these rights and to collect and distribute income to composers.

HERBST, JOHANNES
b. Kempten, Germany, 23 July 1735
d. Salem, North Carolina, 15 January 1812

Herbst came to America in 1786, settling first in Lancaster, Pennsylvania. From 1791 to 1811 he was a preacher at Lititz, a nearby settlement. In 1811 he was appointed bishop to the church at Salem, North Carolina.

He composed about 180 anthems, of which *I Will Go in the Strength of the Lord* and *O Sacred Head, New Wounded*, based on the Hassler chorale, are notable examples. He also published a book of chorales in four parts and made an extensive collection of music by Moravian composers.

HERRMANN, BERNARD
b. New York, New York, 29 January 1911
d. Los Angeles, California, 24 December 1975

Herrmann studied with Albert Stoessel, Philip James, and Percy Grainger at New York University (1929–30) and at the Juilliard School with Bernard Wagenaar (1930–32). He soon established a reputation as a talented conductor and in 1940 was appointed chief conductor of the Columbia Broadcasting System Orchestra. He was always an enthusiastic promoter of modern music by both British and American composers and he gave the first American performances of major works, including compositions by Charles Ives. It is however for his film music that he is most widely remembered.

Herrmann's own compositions are basically neo-romantic in idiom. Of these the most important is the four-act opera *Wuthering Heights*, begun in 1941 and completed in 1950. It possesses great dramatic strength and lyrical beauty with a fine feeling for nature. Although recorded in 1966 it has been staged only once, with drastic cuts, in Portland, Oregon in November 1982. The cantata *Moby Dick* for solo voices, men's chorus, and orchestra (1940) is an impressive setting of Herman Melville's story. The score contains several pre-echoes of Britten's *Billy Budd*, which was not composed until 1951.

Also for the stage Herrmann composed a musical comedy, *The King of Schnorrers* (1968); a ballet, *The Skating Rink* (1934); ballet music for *The American Revue* (1932); and a play, *The Body Beautiful* (1935). He also composed two short operas for television, *A Christmas Carol* (1954) and *A Child is Born* (1955).

A cantata, *Johnny Appleseed* for soloists, chorus, and orchestra begun in 1940, remained unfinished. The song cycle *The Fantasticks* (1942) comprises settings of poems by the Elizabethan, Nicolas Breton (1545–1626), for solo voices, chorus, and orchestra.

Among his orchestral works are two tone poems, *The Forest* (1929) and *November Dusk* (1929); *Marche Militaire* (1932); *Prelude to Anathema* for chamber orchestra (1933); *Aubade (Silent Noon)* (1933); *Variations on Deep River and Water Boy* (1933); a symphonic poem *The City of Brass* (1934); *Sinfonietta for Strings* (1935); *Currier and Ives Suite* (1935); *Nocturne and Scherzo* (1935); an incomplete Violin Concerto (1937–40); a tough, hard-grained Symphony (1940), and an elegiac berceuse *For the Fallen* (1943), commissioned by the New York Philharmonic Orchestra.

His chamber music includes *Twilight* for violin and piano (1929); *Aria* for flute and harp (1932); a String Quartet (1932); *Aubade* for 14 instruments (1933); a *Clarinet Quintet: Souvenirs de Voyage* (1963), and *Echoes* for string quartet (1965).

Herrmann was particularly successful in providing musical scores of distinction for many films. From the two he composed for Orson Welles, *Citizen Kane* (1940) and *The Magnificent Ambersons* (1942), he produced the *Suite: Welles Raises Kane*, performed in New York in 1942 under the composer's direction. He reworked the material from his next film score, *The Devil and Daniel Webster* (1941), to produce another orchestral suite, performed in 1943 by Eugene Ormandy and the Philadelphia Orchestra.

Herrmann collaborated with Alfred Hitchcock on many films, including *The Trouble with Harry* (1955), *The Man Who Knew Too Much* (1956), *Vertigo* (1958), *North by Northwest* (1959), *Psycho* (1960), *The Birds* (1963), and *Marnie* (1964); he also collaborated with Francois Truffaut on *Fahrenheit 451* (1966) and *The Bride Wore Black* (1967). His other notable scores are *Jane Eyre* (1942); *Hangover Square* (1945); *Anna and the King of Siam* (1946); *The Ghost and Mrs Muir* (1947); *The Day the Earth Stood Still* (1951); *On Dangerous Ground* (1952); *Five Fingers* (1952); *The Snows of Kilimanjaro* (1953); *White Witch Doctor* (1953); *Beneath the Twelve-Mile Reef* (1953); *King of the Khyber Rifles* (1954); *Garden of Evil* (1954); *The Egyptian* (1954); *The Kentuckian* (1955); *A Christmas Story* (1955); *Prince of Players* (1955); *The Man in the Gray Flannel Suit* (1956); *The Wrong Man* (1957); *A Hatful of Rain* (1957); *Williamsburg; the Story of a Patriot* (1957); *The Seventh Voyage of Sinbad* (1958); *The Naked and the Dead* (1958); *Journey to the Center of the Earth* (1959); *Blue Denim* (1959); *The Three Worlds of Gulliver* (1961); *Cape Fear* (1961); *Tender is the Night* (1961); *Mysterious Island* (1961); *Jason and the Argonauts* (1963); *Joy in the Morning* (1964); *Torn Curtain* (1966; not used); *Twisted Nerve* (1969); *Battle of Neretva* (1970); *Endless Night* (1971); *The Night Digger* (1971); *Sisters* (1972); *It's Alive* (1973); and *Obsession* (1975). He died in Hollywood while recording his last film score, for Martin Scorsese's *Taxi Driver* (1975).

HEWITT, JAMES
b. Dartmoor, England, 4 June 1770
d. Boston, Massachusetts, 1 August 1827

Hewitt was the son of a naval officer. As well as being a composer, he was an expert violinist who played in concerts in London under the direction of Haydn and Pleyel. With several other musicians, he went to America in 1792. In 1797 Benjamin Carr sold him the New York branch of his music business. Until 1812 Hewitt lived in New York, where he was conductor of various orchestras and military bands. In 1798 he founded his own publishing business, which was continued by his son into the middle of the nineteenth century. In 1812 he moved with his family to Boston, where he soon took an active part in musical affairs, returning to New York in 1816.

Among Hewitt's many compositions are three programmatic overtures of curiosity value, the first of which, probably written in England, bears the title *Overture in nine movements expressive of a Battle*. The other two are *The New Federal Overture* (1797) and *Overture Demophon*.

Of his operas, *Tammany*, first produced in New York on 3 March 1794, is his major work. It caused a stir because of the political satire contained in the libretto. His ballad operas include *The Patriot or Liberty Asserted* (1794); *The Mysterious Marriage* (1799); *Columbus* (1799); *Pizarro or the Spaniards in Peru* (1800); *Robin Hood* (1800), *The Wild Goose Chase* (1800); and *The Tars From Tripoli* (1806–07). His comic opera *The Spanish Castle, or The Knights of Guadalquivir* was performed in New York on 5 December 1800. Hewitt also provided incidental music for several plays.

Hewitt was organist at Trinity Church, Boston, and composed a number of patriotic works for organ: *Yankee Doodle with Variations* (1807–10); *The Fourth of July* (*A Grand Military Sonata*); and *The Battle of Trenton* (1797). In addition he published three piano sonatas.

HEWITT, JOHN HILL
b. New York, New York, 11 July 1801
d. Baltimore, Maryland, 7 October 1890

John Hill Hewitt was the eldest son of James Hewitt. After attending West Point (1818–22), he began a career as a travelling musician. Although he had a permanent home in Baltimore (1825–40, 1874–90), he spent much of his life as a performer touring throughout the United States. Through his songs he became known as the "Father of the American Ballad."

Although he composed a number of choral works, including two cantatas—*Flora's Festival* (1838), performed in Washington, D.C. in 1846, and *The Fairy Bridal* (Boston 1845)—and an oratorio, *Jeptha* (Baltimore 1845), Hewitt's reputation rested on his songs. For the stage he wrote four ballad operas—*Rip Van Winkle*, *The Vivandiere*, *The Prisoner of Monterey*, and *The Artist's Life*—and much other theater music. His most widely performed songs were *The Minstrel's Return From the War* (1828) and *All Quiet on the Potomac* (1863).

HIER, ETHEL GLENN
b. Cincinnati, Ohio, 25 June 1889
d. Winter Park, Florida, 14 January 1971

Hier studied with Stillman Kelley at the Cincinnati Conservatory (BM., 1911) and with Percy Goetschius at the Institute of Musical Art, New York (1917). She was also a pupil of Ernest Bloch (1918–21). In Europe she received tuition from Alban Berg, Egon Wellesz, and Gian Francesco Malipiero. In 1926 she was co-founder of the Association of American Women Composers, actively working to promote music by women composers. In 1930 she was awarded a Guggenheim Fellowship. In New York in 1948 she established the Composers Concerts, and frequently lectured on contemporary music.

She composed a handful of orchestral works, including *Carolina Christmas Suite* (1926, orch. 1939); *Three Symphonic Pieces* (1938); *Asola Bells* (*Campane d'Asola*; 1939); *Badinage* (1954); a *Scherzo* ; and a ballet, *Choreographie*. Among her chamber music are a Sextet for flute, oboe, string trio, and piano (1925); three quintets for flute, viola, cello, harp, and voice (1936); *Rhapsody* for violin and piano (1940); a String Quartet; a Suite for string quartet; and a *Suite: A Day in the Peterboro' Woods* for piano (1924).

Hier's major choral works are *America, the Beautiful* and a cantata, *Mountain Preacher* (1941).

HILL, EDWARD BURLINGAME
b. Cambridge, Massachusetts, 9 September 1872
d. Francestown, New Hampshire, 9 July 1960

After graduating from Harvard University in 1894, where he was a pupil of Paine, Hill studied in Boston with George Chadwick and in Paris with Charles-Marie Widor. He returned to Harvard in 1908 as an instructor during the absence of W. R. Spalding, becoming assistant professor in 1918 and a full professor in 1928. He retired in 1940. Among his pupils were Leonard Bernstein, Arthur Berger, Elliott Carter, Ross Lee Finney, Walter Piston, Randall Thompson and Virgil Thomson. His music shows strong affinities with that of the French Impressionists composers. In 1924 he published a book, *Modern French Music*, which was a further indication of his Gallic leanings.

Hill composed three symphonies: no. 1 in B flat

Edward Burlingame Hill.
Courtesy James P. Murphy Collection, Georgetown University Library

(1928); no. 2 in C (1930); and no. 3 in G, performed in Boston in 1937. Also for orchestra he wrote two *Stevensonia Suites*, inspired by the poems of Robert Louis Stevenson: no. 1 in 1917, and no. 2 in 1922, which were widely performed in the 1930s; a tone poem, *Jack Frost in Midsummer* (1908); three symphonic poems: *The Parting of Lancelot and Guinevere* (1915), *The Fall of the House of Usher* (1920), and *Lilacs* (1926); *Prelude to "The Trojan Women"* (1920); *Scherzo* for two pianos and orchestra (1924); Sinfonietta (1932); *Sinfonietta for Strings* (1936); which is an arrangement of his String Quartet *in C* (1935); a Piano Concertino in one movement (1931), which adopts a mildly jazzy idiom; and Concertino for strings (1940). His Violin Concerto (1933–34, rev. 1937) was first performed by Ruth Posselt and the Boston Symphony Orchestra in 1938.

Hill's last orchestral works were *Music for English Horn and Orchestra* (1943); *Diversions* for small orchestra (1947); Concerto for two flutes and small orchestra (1947); and a *Prelude* commissioned by the Koussevitzky Foundation in 1953.

His choral work *Nuns of the Perpetual Adoration* was written in 1907. For the 50th anniversary of the Boston Symphony Orchestra in 1930 he composed an *Ode* for chorus and orchestra to a text by Robert Hillyer.

The one work by Hill that is still frequently played is the Sextet for woodwind and piano, completed in 1934. His other instrumental pieces include a Flute Sonata (1926); a Clarinet Sonata (1927); a String Quartet *in C* (1935); a Piano Quartet (1938); a Clarinet Quintet (1945); and a Bassoon Sonata (1948). He also wrote many songs and piano pieces.

HILLER, LEJAREN (ARTHUR JR.)
b. New York, New York, 23 February 1924
d. Buffalo, New York, 26 January 1994

Hiller studied at Princeton University, where he obtained a doctorate in chemistry in 1947. At that time he was also a pupil of Milton Babbitt and Roger Sessions. From 1947 to 1952 he worked as a research chemist for E. I. du Pont de Nemours before moving in late 1952 to the University of Illinois to teach chemistry. In 1958 he made the remarkable change to becoming a professor of music and director of the Experimental Music Studio. In 1968 he was appointed the Frederick B. Slee Professor of Music at the State University of New York, Buffalo. From 1968 to 1974 he was co-director with Lukas Foss of the Center for the Creative and Performing Arts, an organization devoted to the performance of new music. He retired in 1989.

Hiller used his knowledge of science and engineering in his approach to composition. The early works,

almost all instrumental, are traditional. These include three string quartets (1949, 1951, 1953); three violin sonatas (1949, 1955, 1970); the first four piano sonatas (1946, rev. 1968, 1947, 1950, 1950); and *Artifacts* for piano (1948, rev. 1973). Serialism and variation form combine in his first important serial work *Twelve-Tone Variations* for piano written in 1954. Also dating from this time are a Piano Concerto (1949); Suite for small orchestra (1951); and Symphony no. 1 (1953).

In 1955 with Leonard Isaacson he began to experiment with computer programs for creating music. The first product of this system was *Illiac Suite* (Quartet no. 4) for string quartet (1957). During the next several years he also began composing extensively for the theater, providing incidental music for not only standard plays (Aristophanes, Ibsen, Pirandello, Strindberg) but also music for experimental works, exploiting the then-new electronic medium. This interest foreshadows his later work in multimedia.

His next major instrumental works are Symphony no. 2 (1959); Piano Sonata no. 5 (1960); and String Quartet no. 5 (1962), which uses both serialism and quarter-tones. These were followed by *Amplifications* for jazz band and tape (1962); *Music for Man With the Oboe* (1962); *Music for Spoon River Anthology* (1962); and *Seven Electronic Music Studies* (1963).

In collaboration with Robert A. Baker he produced *Computer Cantata* in 1964, the first work to be created by a computer; *Machine Music* of the same year is scored for piano, percussion, and tape. It possesses a mathematical precision regarding not only the musical material but also the precise timing of sections in 30- and 60-second units. Other works include *Triptych for Hieronymus* (1960) for actors, dancers, acrobats, projections, tape, and antiphonal groups; Suite for two pianos and tape (1966); *The Avalanche* for pitchman, prima donna, player piano, percussion, and tape (1968); and *Algorithms I* for nine instruments (1968). A further collaboration in 1968, this time with John Cage, gave rise to *HPSCHD*, a work scored not only for one to seven harpsichords but also one to 51 tape-recorders with 58 amplifiers and loudspeakers.

Violin Sonata no. 3 (1970) in three movements marks a return to more orthodox music. String Quartet no. 6, composed in 1972, was performed early in the following year by the Concord Quartet. String Quartet no. 7 dates from 1979.

Other compositions include *Three Rituals* for percussion, film, and lights (1969); *A Cenotaph* for two pianos; and *Algorithms II* for nine instruments and tape, written in co-operation with Ravi Kumra. During a stay in Warsaw (1973-74) as the first Fulbright-Hays Lecturer in Music in Poland, he completed *A Portfolio for Diverse Performers and Tapes*, commissioned by Polskie Radio. (He also served as Fulbright-Hays

Lecturer in Music in Brazil in 1980.) Early in 1975 he finished *Malta* for tuba and tape, which reflects a stay of several months on the island. In 1975 he also completed a computer composition commissioned by the Buffalo Philharmonic Orchestra, called *A Preview of Coming Attractions.*

In 1976 Hiller finished his largest electronic composition. It exists in two forms: an "indoor version" called *Electronic Sonata*, lasting 53 minutes on four-channel tape; and an "outdoor version" entitled *Midnight Carnival,* lasting many hours and made up of several tapes and theatrical events. It was an American Bicentennial commission for the city of St. Louis, and an estimated 50,000 people witnessed the premiere.

Later works are on a more modest scale. These include *Ponteach*, a melodrama for narrator and piano dealing with the American Indians (1977); *Persiflage* for flute, oboe, and percussion (1977); and two pieces involving folk instruments, *Dialelskie Skrzypce* for stringed instruments and harpsichord (1978) and *An Apotheosis of Archeopterix* for piccolo and berimbau (1979).

Music for tape alone include *Nightmare Music* (1961), *Elec Sonata* (1976), and *Three Compositions* (1983). For instruments and tape are a Suite for two pianos (1966), *Computer Music* for percussion (1968, rev. 1981), and *Quadrilateral* for piano (1981).

In addition to a book on chemistry, Hiller wrote two books on music: *Experimental Music* (with L. M. Isaacson; 1959) and *Informationstheorie und Computermusik* (1964).

HIVELY, WELLS

b. San Joaquin Valley, California, November 2, 1902

d. Palm Beach, Florida, June 1969

Hively studied at the Paris Conservatory and at the Brussels Royal Conservatory. On his return to the United States he attended the Juilliard School. He settled in Palm Beach where he followed a career as pianist and teacher.

His training in France is clearly evident in his best-known work, *Tres Himnos* for orchestra, composed in 1946 in Mexico and performed in 1954 by the Eastman Orchestra under Howard Hanson.

Hively composed two operas, *The Sleeping Beauty* in one act and *Junipero Serra*; a ballet, *Adolescents*; and a musical play, *Canek*, scored for chorus, actors, and orchestra. His orchestral works include *Habanera Suite*; a symphonic poem, *Salomy Jane*; a suite, *Pandora*; *Priscilla Variations* for piano and orchestra (1939); *Summer Holiday (Rive Gauche)* (1944); an orchestral portrait, *Icarus* (1961); and a Piano Concerto.

HODKINSON, SYDNEY PHILLIP

b. Winnipeg, Manitoba, Canada, 17 January 1934

Hodkinson studied at the Eastman School of Music, Rochester, New York (1953–58) where he was a pupil of Louis Mennini and Bernard Rogers. At Princeton University (1960) he received composition lessons from Elliott Carter, Roger Sessions, and Milton Babbitt. In 1968 he was awarded a D.M.A. from the University of Michigan, Ann Arbor, where he studied with Leslie Bassett, Niccolo Castiglioni, Ross Lee Finney, and George B. Wilson. He was also a conducting pupil of Max Rudolf.

After teaching woodwinds in Rochester and Brighton, New York schools (1955–58), he taught at the University of Virginia, Charlottesville (1958–63), Ohio University, Athens (1963–66), and the University of Michigan (1968–73). He served as Artist-in-Residence for Minneapolis-St. Paul, Minnesota under a grant from the Ford Foundation-sponsored Contemporary Music Project, Washington, D.C. (1970–72). In 1973 he was appointed professor of conducting and ensembles and composition at the Eastman School of Music, retiring in 1998. From 1984 to 1986 he was visiting professor at Southern Methodist University, Dallas, Texas. Hodkinson has received awards from the National Institute of Arts and Letters (1971), National Endowment for the Arts (1975, 1977) and Canada Council Senior Arts Award (1977) and a Guggenheim Fellowship (1978-79). In addition to his activities as a composer, Hodkinson is a professional clarinetist and conductor.

Of major significance among his works is the set of ten symphonies: no. 1, *Fresco, music in five panels* (1965–68), performed in Buffalo in 1974; no. 2, *Sinfonie Fantastique* for organ, brass, and percussion (1974–82); no. 3, *The Celestial Omnibus* (1975); no. 4, *Horae Canonica* for soprano, baritone, two choruses, solo cello, and orchestra (1977–83); no. 5, *Sinfonia concertante* for chamber orchestra (1980); no. 6, *Sonata quasi una fantasia* for violin and large orchestra (1982–83); no. 7, *The Vanishing Hand* for wind ensemble (1992); no. 8 (1994–96); no. 9, *Epiphanies* for orchestral winds (1994); and no. 10 (1994–97).

For orchestra he has written *Threnody* (1957); *Diversions* for strings (1964); *Caricatures* (five paintings; 1966); *Drawings 7 & 8* for strings (1970); *Valence* for chamber orchestra (1970); *Stabile* (1970); *Epigrams* (1971); *Celestial Calendar* for strings (1976); *Edge of the Olde One* for electric English horn, strings, and percussion, commissioned in 1977 by the New York Philharmonic Orchestra (1977); *Bach Variations* for winds, piano, harp, and percussion (1977); *Bumberboom (Scherzo diabolique)* for English horn, orchestra, and electronics (1982); *The Burning Bell*, a

Sydney Hodkinson.
Photo: Laurie Beck, courtesy the composer.

symphonic poem for youth orchestra (1985); *Tango, Boogie and Grand Tarantella* for double bass and orchestra (1987); and *Tilt* (1997). Hodkinson has also provided a number of items for the band repertory: *Litigo* for winds and percussion (1959); *A Contemporary Primer* (1972); *Blocks* (1972); *Tower* (1974); *Pillar* (1974); *Monalith: Megalith VI* (1974); *Cortege: Dirge Canons* (1975); and *Palisade: Megalith VIII* for brass and percussion (1975).

Among his many instrumental works are *Stanzas* for piano trio (1959); *Drawings*, ten sets for various instrumental groups (1960–79); *Mosaic* for brass quintet (1964); *Quartet no. 1* (for 5 players; 1967); *The Dissolution of the Serial* for clarinet and piano (1967); *Imagin'd Quartet* for four percussionists (1967); *One Man's Meat* for solo double bass (1970); *Another Man's Poison* for brass quintet (1970); *Taula* (*Magalith IV*) for double wind quintet (1974); *Stone Images*, four instrumental pieces (1974); *Dance Variations* for piano trio (1977); *Five Absurdities* (after Lewis Carroll) for five trombones (1978); and *Two Fanfares for a Festival* for brass (1978). More recent instrumental works include a Double Bass Sonata (1980); *String Trio: Alla marcia* (1983); *Introit, Elegie et Danse Macabre* for

viola and piano (1983); *Echo Preludes* for brass choir and cello (1983); *Sonata: Das Leberwohl* for piano trio (1984); *The Steps of Time*, an elegy for cello (or trombone), string quartet and percussion (1984); and *Trauermusik* for trombone (or cello), piano, and percussion (1984).

Hodkinson's important choral compositions are *Ritual* (1970); *Sea Chanteys* (1970); *Menagerie* (1970); *Vox Populous*, an active oratorio for teo actors, electronics technician, four vocal soloists, and chorus (1971–72); *Daydreams* for speaker, chorus, and instruments (1974); *Menagerie Set 2* for speaking chorus (1977); *Maxims and Minims* for chorus (1977); *Missa Brevis* for chorus and bells (1978); and *Divine Poems* (John Donne) for chorus, string quartet, horn, and percussion (1985–88). Other vocal music includes *Arc*, an aria with interludes for soprano, flute, piano, and two percussion (1969); *Lengeren* (*Megalith V*) for voice and double quintet (1973); *November Voices* for voice, speaker, and small ensemble (1975); *Chansons de Jadis* (*Six Songs of Loneliness*) for high voice and orchestra (1979); *Alte Liebeslieder* for medium voice and instruments (1981); and *Nuevas Canciones: I The Hidden Ocean, II The Sea Hours* for soprano and ensemble (1982).

For the stage Hodkinson has composed five operas: *The Swinish Cult* (1969-75), *The Wall* (1980), *In the Gallery* (1981), *Catsman* (1985), and *Saint Carmen of the Main* in two acts (1984–87); *Taiwa*, a myth for actors, dancers, and musicians with choreography by F. Coggan (1965); *Armistice*, a truce for dancers and musicians (1966); and *Interplay*, a histrionic controversy for four musicians (1966).

HOIBY, LEE

b. Madison, Wisconsin, 17 February 1926

Hoiby studied at the University of Wisconsin (1941–47) and at Mills College, Oakland, California, where he was a piano pupil of Egon Petri and composition pupil of Darius Milhaud (1947). At the Curtis Institute, Philadelphia (1948–52) he was taught by Gian Carlo Menotti. He was awarded a Guggenheim Fellowship (1958) and a Fulbright Fellowship (1953), which allowed him to study in Rome. In 1975 he undertook a career as a concert pianist.

Hoiby's valuable contribution to American music has been in the area of opera. The first of his operas, *The Scarf*, based on a short story by Anton Chekhov, is his best known work. It was commissioned by Mary Curtis Zimbalist and first performed at the Festival of the Two Worlds in Spoleto, Italy in 1957 and staged by the New York City Opera in April 1959. *Beatrice*, to a text derived from Maeterlinck, was commissioned by WAVE radio and television company in 1959 and performed by the Louisville Orchestra. Hoiby's next opera, *Natalia Petrovna*, based on Turgenev's *A Month in the Country*, was completed in 1964 and performed in October that year by the New York City Opera, which had commissioned it.

Hoiby's fourth opera, *Summer and Smoke* in two acts, based on the play by Tennessee Williams, was produced in Minnesota by the St. Paul Opera Company. It was staged in New York in the following year. A one-act opera buffa, *Something New For the Zoo*, was completed in 1979. It was followed in 1980 by two monodramas, *The Italian Lesson* (text: Ruth Draper) and *Bon Appetit!* for mezzo-soprano and chamber orchestra.

The Tempest, with a libretto based on Shakespeare by Mark Shulgasser, was composed in 1986 for the Des Moines Opera. Hoiby's latest opera, *This is the Rill Speaking*, dates from 1993. He has also provided incidental music for 15 New York stage productions. Also for the theater he has composed three ballet scores, *Hearts, Meadows and Flags* (1952), *After Eden* (1967), and *Landscapes* (1968). Currently he is composing an opera on *Romeo and Juliet*.

For orchestra he has written a Suite (1953); a Flute Concerto (1956); two piano concertos (1958, 1979); *Design* for strings (1965); an overture, *Music for a Celebration* (1975); and Serenade for violin and orchestra.

Important among his choral works are *A Hymn to the Nativity* for soloists, chorus, and orchestra (1960), performed in Washington Cathedral in December 1961; an oratorio, *Galileo Galilei*, composed in 1974 for the Von Braun Arts Center, Huntsville, Alabama; *Magnificat and Nunc Dimittis* for choir and organ (1983); and Psalm 93 for large choir, organ, brass, and percussion, premiered in the Church of St. John the Divine, New York in May 1985. Recent works in this medium include an oratorio *For You, O Democracy* (Whitman; 1992); *Rain Forest* (Elizabeth Bishop) for voices, wind quintet, and piano (1996); and *Measureless Love* (Whitman) for baritone and chorus (1996).

His solo vocal music includes *The Tides of Sleep* for low voice and piano (1961); *Bemudas* (Andrew Marvell) for soprano, mezzo-soprano, and piano (1982); *Trois Poemes de Rimbaud* for baritone and piano (1982); *The English Painter* for mezzo-soprano and piano (1983); *What is Light?* for narrator and piano (1994); *I Was There*, five Whitman songs for baritone and orchestra (1995); and *Free at Last*, retitled *I Have a Dream* (Martin Luther King) (1995).

His few instrumental pieces are a Cello Sonata; a Violin Sonata (1951, rev. 1980); *Diversions* for woodwind quartet (1953); a Sextet for piano and winds (1974), commissioned by the Dorian Quintet; a Piano Quintet (1974); Serenade for violin and piano (1988);

and a Piano Quartet, commissioned by the American Piano Quartet in 2001. Solo piano music includes a *Toccata* (1949); *Nocturne* (1950, rev. 1980); *Five Preludes* (1952, rev. 1977); *Capriccio on Five Notes* (1962); *Ten Variations on a Schubert Ländler* (1981); and *Narrative* (1983).

HOLDEN, OLIVER
b. Shirley, Massachusetts, 18 September 1765
d. Charlestown, Massachusetts, 4 September 1844

In 1788 Holden settled in Charlestown, where he worked as a carpenter. He became an extensive landowner and a member of the Massachusetts House of Representatives (1818–33). With William Billings, he should be considered as one of the most important composers of his day. With Daniel Read he established a periodical, *The Massachusetts Musical Magazine* in 1793, although it did not seem to have survived many issues.

Holden's first book, *The American Harmony*, was published in Boston in 1792. The hymn tune that has secured his reputation, *Coronation* (*All Hail the Power of Jesus' Name*), was printed in his *Union Harmony* (1793). Its survival for over a century is proved by its appearance in the opening movement of Charles Ives' First String Quartet. Holden compiled three other books: *Plain Psalmody* (1800), *Sacred Dirges, Hymns and Anthems* (1800), and *Charlestown Collection* (1803). He also edited the revised versions of the *Worcester Collection of Sacred Harmony* from 1797 to 1803.

Holden marked the death of George Washington with two choral works, *From Vernon's Mount Behold the Hero Rise*, and a cantata, *Dirge, or Sepulchral Service*, performed in Boston in 1800. He was one of the editors of *The Massachusetts Compiler* (1795), an important contribution to the literature of psalmody.

HOLLINGSWORTH, STANLEY
b. Berkeley, California, 27 August 1924
c. Rochlin, California, 29 October 2003

Hollingsworth studied at San Jose State College, California (1941–44), with Darius Milhaud at Mills College, Oakland, California (1944–46), and with Gian-Carlo Menotti at the Curtis Institute, Philadelphia (1948–50). He was awarded a fellowship at the American Academy in Rome (1955–57) and received a Guggenheim Fellowship in 1958. From 1961 to 1963 he taught at San Jose State College, California and was a member of the faculty of Oakland University, Rochester, Michigan from 1976 until retiring in 1993.

Hollingsworth's 1954 opera, *La Grande Bretèche*,

Stanley Hollingsworth.
Courtesy Oakland University.

based on Balzac, was performed on NBC television in 1957. Another opera, *The Mother*, in one act, was completed in 1949. In 1981 he composed two operas for children, *The Selfish Giant* (1933) and *Harrison Loved His Umbrella.* Important choral works are *Dumbarton Oaks Mass* for chorus and string orchestra; *Stabat Mater* for chorus and orchestra (1957); *A Song of David* for tenor, chorus, and orchestra (1962); and *Death Be Not Proud* (John Donne) for chorus and orchestra (1978).

His orchestral works include a Piano Concerto (1979); Divertimento (1982); *Three Ladies Beside the Sea* for narrator and orchestra (1983); and a Violin Concerto (*Concerto Lirico*; 1991). Among his instrumental music are an Oboe Sonata (1954); a Quintet for harp and woodwind; *Ricordanza* for oboe and string trio (1981); and *Reflections and Diversions* for clarinet and piano (1987).

HOLYOKE, SAMUEL (ADAMS)
b. Boxford, Massachusetts, 15 October 1762
d. East Concord, New Hampshire, February 1820

Holyoke, a graduate of Harvard College (1789), endeavored to improve on the church music of William Billings and the other "primitives." He published *Harmonia Americana* in Boston in 1791 and a large collection of church music, *The Columbian Repository of Sacred Music* in 1802. With Oliver Holden he published another collection of sacred music, *The Massachusetts Compiler* in 1795. Two further compilations of tunes, *The Christian Harmonist* and *The Vocal Companion*, were issued in 1804 and 1807. His hymn tunes still sung today include *Arnheim*, *Andover*, and *Hinsdale*.

Holyoke also composed instrumental music and published *The Instrumentalist's Assistant* (1800), a volume of band music, one of the first of its kind in America, followed in 1807 by a second volume. He wrote many secular songs, including a tribute to George Washington, *Hark from the Tombs* (1800).

In 1814 he moved to Boston, but the opposition of European musicians in the city forced him to retire to the country where, embittered, he turned to drink.

HOMER, SIDNEY
b. Boston, Massachusetts, 9 December 1864
d. Winter Park, Florida, 10 July 1953

Homer studied with George Chadwick in Boston and with Joseph Rheinberger in Munich. In 1895 he married Louise Beatty, who as Louise Homer earned a worldwide reputation as a singer; she was also the aunt of Samuel Barber. In 1900 they settled in New York.

At one time Homer's songs were widely heard in the United States. Particularly popular were *Banjo Song*, *The Song of the Shirt*, *Sing to Me*, and *Sweet and Low.* His instrumental works include two string quartets, two violin sonatas, an Organ Sonata (1922), a Piano Quintet (1932); and a Piano Trio (1937).

Homer was the author of a book of memoirs, *My Wife and I* (1939).

HOMMANN, CHARLES
fl. early 19th century, Philadelphia, Pennsylvania

Little is known of Hommann, a teacher of violin and piano in Philadelphia. An *Overture in D*, composed for the Bethlehem Philharmonic Society won a prize in 1835. Among his surviving works are a Symphony in E-flat, an Overture in C, *and* three string quartets.

213

HOPKINS, (CHARLES EDWARD) JEROME

b. Burlington, Vermont, 4 April 1836
d. Athenia (now Clifton), New Jersey, 4 November 1898

Although Hopkins was a leading organist in New York and a composer of popular church music, his most important contribution to American music was his work as a lecturer and journalist who helped to foster new composers. In 1856 he founded the American Musical Association, the first organization to promote American music. Hopkins led an active life as a propagandist in this respect. He was founder and editor of the *New York Philharmonic Journal* (1868–85).

Among his 700 compositions are a Symphony (*Life*); a *Child's Symphony* for strings; Serenade in E (1880); a Piano Concerto (1857); and a Concerto for piano trio and orchestra (1892). He composed two operas, *Samuel*, produced in New York in 1877, and *Dumb Love* (1878), as well as a children's opera, *Taffy and the Old Munch* (1880).

Hopkins's choral works include an oratorio, *Samson*; *Victory Te Deum* (1862); and *Easter Festival Vespers* for three choirs, echo-choir, two organs, and orchestra (1875). His once-popular piano piece, *The Wild Demon* (*Rhapsodie caracteristique*), op. 11 (1859) is in the tradition best expressed in the music of Gottschalk. Hopkins also composed a Piano Trio (1858).

HOPKINSON, FRANCIS

b. Philadelphia, Pennsylvania, 21 September 1737
d. Philadelphia, Pennsylvania, 9 May 1791

Hopkinson's place in the history of American music is assured by his song *My Days Have Been So Wondrous Fair*, dating from 1759, which makes him probably the first American to compose music. Like his contemporaries, he was an amateur musician; by profession he was a lawyer and politician, holding several offices such as U. S. Secretary of the Navy (the first to hold this position) and, from 1779, Judge of the Admiralty in Philadelphia. He was also a noted writer of political satire. A personal friend of George Washington, he was one of the signatories of the Declaration of Independence and may have designed the American flag.

Hopkinson graduated from the College of Philadelphia in 1757 and later gained the degrees of master of arts and doctor of laws. His musical studies were conducted in Philadelphia, and in 1766 he visited England, where he was greatly impressed by a performance of Handel's *Messiah* in Gloucester. In 1780 he is known to have composed an *Ode* in memory of his teacher, James Bremner, who had died that year. Hopkinson was also a capable harpsichord player and organist, and he invented a new method for quilling the harpsichord. In addition he created the Bellarmonic, a set of tuned bells. He also helped to organize the important subscription concerts in Philadelphia

Hopkinson's first important composition, *Ode to Music*, may have been written in 1754 when he was only 17 years old. In 1781 he composed *The Temple of Minerva*, an opera or dramatic oratorio celebrating the alliance between America and France. Only the libretto has survived. Among Hopkinson's other works are *Seven* (actually eight) *Songs*, dedicated to George Washington and published in Philadelphia in 1788, and *A Collection of Psalm Tunes with a few Anthems*, published in 1763. In 1930 a number of manuscript of songs attributed to Hopkinson were discovered but these were later proved to be forgeries.

His son Joseph wrote the words for *Hail Columbia*.

HORN, CHARLES EDWARD

b. London, England, 21 June, 1786
d. Boston, Massachusetts, 21 October 1849

Horn was the son of a German musician, Karl Friedrich Horn, who had settled in England in 1782. The young Charles was highly successful in London as the composer of operas and in providing music for Vauxhall Gardens.

Horn first went to America in 1827, where he organized a season of Italian opera in New York; his second visit in 1833 was equally successful. On this occasion he produced his own opera *Nadir and Zuleika*, written in England the previous year, and an adaptation of Mozart's *The Magic Flute*. His *Ode to Washington* was performed in Boston in 1828, and he composed an oratorio, *The Remission of Sin* (1836), later intriguingly retitled *Satan*.

In 1842 he was one of the founders of the Philharmonic Society in New York. In 1843 he returned to London to direct music at the Princess's Theatre. He was back in America in 1847, settling in Boston where he became conductor of the Handel and Haydn Society. With his wife, a singer, he gave numerous concerts in New York and Boston. These comprised a mixture of orchestral, piano, instrumental, and vocal items that seemed to have been very popular at the time.

Although he wrote several large-scale oratorios, including *Daniel's Prediction* (1848), and a widely used song book, *National Melodies of America*, published in 1839, he is best remembered today as the composer of the song *Cherry Ripe*.

HOSMER, LUCIUS
b. *South Acton, Massachusetts, 14 August, 1870*
d. *Jefferson, New Hampshire, 9 May 1935*

Hosmer was a pupil of George Chadwick at the New England Conservatory in Boston.

For orchestra, Hosmer composed *Southern Rhapsody, Northern Rhapsody, Ethiopian Rhapsody, On Tiptoe,* and *Chinese Wedding Procession.* His stage works include two operas, *The Rose of the Alhambra* (1905), and a comedy, *The Walking Delegate*, revised and retitled *The Koreans.*

HOVHANESS (CHAKMAKJIAN), ALAN (VANESS SCOTT)
b. *Somerville, Massachusetts, 8 March 1911*
d. *Seattle, Washington, 21 June 2000*

Hovhaness was the son of an Armenian father, a professor of chemistry, and a Scottish mother. He later dropped his original name in favor of his second. After learning the piano, he entered the New England Conservatory in Boston in 1932, where he studied with Frederick Converse. From 1940 to 1947 he lived in a small room in Boston, devoting his time to composition and earning a living as a teacher and accompanist. In 1942 he won a scholarship to Tanglewood, where he was a pupil of Bohuslav Martinů, who encouraged him to follow his own path. In 1948 he was appointed to the music faculty of the Boston Conservatory of Music. He left in 1951 to live in New York.

A world tour in 1959 on a Fulbright fellowship took Hovhaness on an extended visit to India and Japan, where he came into direct contact with a musical culture very much in sympathy with his own. In 1962 a Rockerfeller Grant allowed him to study music in Japan and Korea. In 1967 he became Composer-in-Residence with the Seattle Symphony Orchestra. After this for a while he lived in Lucerne, Switzerland before returning to settle in Seattle. Hovhaness was granted Guggenheim Fellowships (1953–54, 1958), and in 1951 won an award from the National Institute of Arts and Letters.

His earliest enthusiasm was for music of the Renaissance; he was attracted by its modal harmony and melodic lines. This influence is evident in contrapuntal writing throughout his life, emphasized by his preference for using large note values. His classical music training is also reflected in the rigorous use of fugue. He explained: "Fugue form I use strictly. I apply it to the modes. I like to develop those principles because I feel they're universal. I've always been a great admirer of Bach and Handel."

In 1936 Hovhaness heard for the first time music of the East when a group of musicians from North India performed in Boston. Their non-Western scales (ragas) and elaborate rhythms (talas) were to have a strong impact on his later compositions. During the 1940s he undertook an intense study of Armenian religious music, inspired by the Armenian composer-priest Komitas (Gomidas Vartabed), who died in 1936. From 1940 to 1947 Hovhaness played the organ at the Armenian Church in Watertown, near Boston, where he had the opportunity to study Armenian religious music closely.

With this new dimension to his compositions, Hovhaness destroyed over almost 1000 of his earlier works, including seven symphonies, five string quartets, operas, and other extended pieces. Nevertheless he continued to compose prolifically, his opus numbers passing the 400 mark in the 1980s, including 67 symphonies. His music possesses a curious personal idiom with exotic melodies and complex rhythmic patterns, not allowing much variety but containing many unusual instrumental effects. These is little contrast in the music, which relies on percussive effects and iteration of short rhythmical or melodic phrases that are often related to the ritualistic music of the Armenian Church. It is primarily monodic with modal harmony.

A typical work, Concerto no. 1 for orchestra, op. 88 (1951), subtitled *Arevakal*, shows well how Hovhaness retains the simplicity of oriental music without giving it a sophisticated Western presentation, while still forging a personal language out of these Eastern features. There is in much of what he has written the timeless serenity of Indian music.

"Symphony" is a term Hovhaness used for almost any large-scale composition. Six are scored for wind band, three include chorus, and four have important parts for solo singers. Five are in effect concertos: no. 29 (baritone horn), no. 34 (bass trombone), no. 36 (flute), no. 39 (guitar), and no. 51 (trumpet). His earliest surviving symphony, subtitled *Exile*, dating from 1936, was performed in London on 26 May 1939 by the BBC Symphony Orchestra conducted by Leslie Heward.

The first work to bring Hovhaness's name to wider attention was Symphony no. 2, *Mysterious Mountain*, commissioned by the Houston Symphony Orchestra, which gave its premiere on 31 October 1955 conducted by Leopold Stokowski. It is the first of six symphonies which have the word "mountain" in the title. The composer explained: "Mountains represent symbols, like pyramids, of man's attempt to know God. Mountains are symbolic meeting places between the mundane and spiritual worlds." In the music of Hovhaness there is an implied religious content. The tranquility, mystery, sublimity, and ecstasy have a parallel with the works of Messiaen, but for Hovhaness it is unspecific, neither Christian nor Eastern, maybe pantheistic or even pagan in its reverence for the natural world.

Symphony no. 3 (1956) was performed in Japan in 1960. Symphony no. 4 (1959) is scored for large wind symphony orchestra, with up to six of each instrument. Symphony no. 5 (1953, rev. 1963) uses an average-size orchestra. Symphony no. 6 (1959) in one movement for chamber orchestra is subtitled *Celestial Gate*.

Symphony no. 7 (1959), like the Fourth Symphony, is for wind orchestra and is subtitled *Nanga Parvat*. Symphony no. 8 (1947), originally a symphonic poem, *Arjanu*, was first performed in Madras, India in 1960. Symphony no. 9 (*St. Vartan Symphony*; 1949–50) comprises 24 short movements. It was composed to commemorate the 1,500th anniversary of the death of the Armenian Christian martyr Vartan Marmikonian. Symphony no. 10 (*Vahaken*; 1959), like the *St. Vartan Symphony*, employs a small orchestra.

Symphony no. 11, *All Men Are Brothers*, was commissioned for the 25th anniversary of the New Orleans Philharmonic Symphony Orchestra in 1961. It was revised in 1969 and performed in its new version by the same orchestra in 1970. Symphony no. 12 (1960) is a choral setting of Psalm 23, *The Lord is My Shepherd*. The sound of a mountain waterfall is added on tape to the orchestral score. Symphony no. 13 in one movement is for chamber orchestra; it was premiered in Paris in 1961. Symphony no. 14 (*Ararat*) (1960) is scored for wind orchestra. Symphony no. 15 for full orchestra is subtitled *Silver Pilgrimage* and named after a novel by the Indian writer M. Anantanarayan. It was composed in the Far East and was first performed in Hawaii in 1963.

Symphony no. 16 is written for Korean instruments with string orchestra. It was first performed by the Korean Broadcasting Orchestra in January 1963. In the previous year, Hovhaness had made a detailed investigation of *gagaku*, the ancient court music of Japan. He took the opportunity to visit neighboring countries, making a study of *ah-ahk*, the court music of Korea. He explained that the symphony had been inspired by the beauty of the Korean mountains.

Symphony no. 17 (*Symphony for Metal Orchestra*; 1963) derives its title from the use Hovhaness makes of six flutes, three trombones, and percussion as the instrumental forces. Symphony no. 18 (*Circe*; 1963) was used as the basis of a ballet with that name. Symphony no. 19 (*Vishnu*) was originally a symphonic poem, *To Vishnu*, commissioned by the New York Philharmonic Orchestra, which performed it in the Lincoln Center in 1967. Symphony no. 20 (1968) for band is entitled *Three Journeys to a Holy Mountain*. Symphony no. 21 (*Symphony Etchmiadzin*; 1968) uses two trumpets with strings, harp, and percussion. Symphony no.

22 (1970) is subtitled *City of Light*. Symphony no. 23 (1972) for large symphonic band is subtitled *Ani*. Symphony no. 24 (*Majnun*) composed in 1973, is scored for tenor solo, chorus, trumpet, and strings. Symphony no. 25 (*Odysseus*), dating from the same year, was first performed in London by the Polyphonia Orchestra in March 1974. Symphony no. 26 was premiered by the San Jose Symphony Orchestra in October 1975.

Of the remaining symphonies, no. 34 was performed by the St. Luke's Chamber Orchestra, New York in January 1980. Symphony no. 35 is scored for two orchestras, the first a full symphony orchestra, the second a group of Korean *ah-ahk* instruments. It was performed in Seoul, South Korea to mark the opening of the New-Art Center in June 1978. Symphony no. 36 was premiered by the National Symphony Orchestra in Washington, D.C. in 1979. Symphony no. 38 was first performed in Seattle in September 1978 by the North West Chamber Orchestra. Symphony no. 46 (*Walla Walla, Land of Many Waters*) for coloratura soprano and orchestra was commissioned for the 75th anniversary of the Walla Walla (Washington) Symphony Orchestra and first performed in November 1981.

On the morning of 18 May 1980 in Hovhaness's home state of Washington, Mount St. Helens erupted violently, causing massive destruction as the side of the mountain was blown away. This cataclysmic event prompted the composer to devote a symphony to describing his impressions. Symphony no. 50 (*Mount St. Helens*), completed in 1983, explicitly relates the music to the landscape and the eruption. Symphony no. 65 was perfomed in Carnegie Hall, New York on 6th October 1991 to mark the composer's 80th birthday.

Among Hovhaness's many other orchestral works are eight concertos for orchestra, some including solo instruments (1951–53); *Vision from High Rock* (1954); *Meditation on Orpheus* (1958); *Mountain of Prophesy* (1960); *Meditation on Zeami* (1963); *Variations and Fugue* (1963); *Ukiyo* (*Floating World*; 1965); *Fantasy on Japanese Prints* (*Han-ga Genso*; 1965) with solo xylophone; *Ode to the Temple of Sound*, commissioned by the Houston Symphony Orchestra in 1965; *The Holy City* (1967); *Fra Angelico* (1969), commissioned by the Detroit Symphony Orchestra; and *God Created Great Whales* (1970), commissioned by the New York Philharmonic Orchestra, which includes a tape recording of the humpback whale.

A number of works with oriental titles are virtually concertos for solo instruments and strings. Thus *Lousadzak* (1944) is a piano concerto, as is *Zartik Parkim* (1949); *Tzaikerk* (1945) is a concerto for flute, violin, and timpani; *Krimian Hairig* (1944) and *Haroutiun* (*Resurrection*; 1949) are both for trumpet; *Diran* (1948) is for baritone horn; *Sosi* (*Forest of Prophetic Sounds*; 1949) is for flute, piano, and percussion; *Artik* (1950) is a horn concerto; *Elibris* (*God of Dawn*; 1950) is for flute; and *Talin* (1951–52) is for viola. A Cello Concerto, dating from 1936, did not receive its premiere until 1975.

For the stage Hovhaness composed *Blue Flame* (1959), a musical fairy tale in four scenes, and four one-act operas: *The Burning House* (1959, rev. 1962), *Pilate* (Los Angeles, 1966), *The Spirit of the Avalanche* (1966), and *The Travellers* (Los Altos Hills, 1967). In 1946 he completed his first full-length opera, *Etchmiadzin*. A second opera, *Pericles*, dates from 1975. His last opera, *The Tale of the Sun Goddess Entering the Stone House*, to a libretto by his wife, Hinako Fujihara, was performed in Salinas, California in 1978.

His ballets include *Is There Survival?* (*King Vahaken*; 1949); *Circe* (1963), based on Symphony no. 18; *A Rose for Miss Emily* (1968); *Killer of Enemies* (1983); and *God the Revenger* (1986). He composed two dance-dramas: *Wind Drum*, commissioned by the East-West Center, Hawaii and performed at the University of Hawaii in May 1962, and *The Leper King*, staged at the University of Wisconsin, Milwaukee in May 1968.

Almost all Hovhaness's choral music and many of his solo songs are settings of religious texts. These include *The Thirtieth Ode of Solomon* for baritone, chorus, trumpet, trombone, and strings (1947); *Triptych* for soprano, chorus, and instruments (1952–55); *Glory to God* for soloists, chorus, brass, and percussion (1954); *Anabasis* for narrator, soloists, chorus, and orchestra (1955); *Magnificat* for four soloists, chorus, and orchestra (1959), written to a commission from the Koussevitzky Foundation; *In the Beginning Was the Word* for soloists, chorus, and orchestra (1963); *Praise the Lord With the Psaltery* for chorus and large orchestra (1968); and *Lady of Light* for soprano, chorus, and chamber ensemble (1969).

Hovhaness's last choral works included an oratorio, *The Way of Jesus* for soloists, chorus, and orchestra, completed in 1974. It received its premiere at St. Patrick's Cathedral, New York City on 23 February 1975 under the direction of Laszlo Halasz. There followed *A Simple Mass* for chorus and organ (1975) and an oratorio, *Revelations of St. Paul* for soloists, chorus, and orchestra, first performed in Avery Fisher Hall, New York in January 1981. In addition there are over 60 shorter works for chorus, mostly for a cappella voices.

Hovhaness's chamber works are as extensive in number for almost every combination of instruments. As well as pieces for standard ensembles such as five string quartets (1936, 1950, 1968, 1970, 1976) and two piano quintets (1926, rev. 1962, 1964), there are sonatas for koto (Japanese psaltery; 1962), ryuteki (Japanese flute) and sho (mouth organ; 1962), and hichiriki (Japanese oboe) and sho (1971). Later works include a Cello

Sonata (1974) and a Suite for brass quintet (1977). He also produced over 50 works for keyboard.

The unusual quality of the music of Hovhaness is difficult to define; at times the effect is one of startling originality, with exotic textures, but other works are restricted in variety of melodic and harmonic invention, so the result can seem monotonous. Long before Henryk Górecki, Arvo Pärt, and John Taverner, he was producing what has been defined as "holy minimalism." Detractors draw attention to the four basic recurring ingredients of Hovhaness's music: chorales on divisi strings or brass, relentlessly worked out mechanical fugues, modal solo incantation against slow moving harmonies and a walking bass, and what the composer himself called "spiritual murmurs": uncoordinated repetition short figures, a forerunner of aleotoric devices. These mannerisms risk becoming tiresome clichés from one piece to another.

To a listener not familiar with this music, Symphony no. 2 (*Mysterious Mountain*) or Symphony no. 50 (*Mount St. Helens*) would serve as an ideal introduction to this extraordinarily sensitive composer. For those wishing to explore further the haunting timbres of the more oriental works, *St. Vartan Symphony*, one of his finest compositions, presents a clear idea of his very personal idiom.

HOWE, MARY (CARLISLE)
b. Richmond, Virginia, 4 April 1882
d. Washington, D.C., 14 September 1964

Mary Howe came from a Scots-Welsh ancestry. After studying the piano in Europe, she entered the Peabody Conservatory in Baltimore, where she was a composition pupil of Gustave Strube. Later she studied with Nadia Boulanger. She undertook a career as a concert pianist and made frequent tours with Anne Hull as a piano duo (1920–35). In addition, she was one of the first directors on the board of the National Symphony Orchestra of Washington, D.C. (1931).

Howe wrote many pieces for her instrument, of which the best known is *Castellana* for two pianos and orchestra (1935), based on Spanish folk songs. Her two short tone poems, *Sand* (1926) and *Stars* (1934), reveal an effective impressionistic gift with light scoring for the instruments. Her other orchestral works include *Fugue* for strings (1922); *Poeme* (1924); *Dirge* (1931); *Free Passacaglia with Fugue* for chamber orchestra (1932); *American Piece* (1933, rev. 1940); *Coulennes* (1936); *Spring Pastoral* (1936); *Potomac Suite* (1940); *Paean* (1940); *Polka, Waltz and Finale* (1946); *Agreeable Overture* (1949); and *Rock* (1955).

For the stage she composed two ballets, *Cards* (1930) and *Le Jongleur de Notre Dame* (1959).

The first of her three string quartets was performed at the Yaddo Festival in 1940. Among her other chamber works are a Violin Sonata (1922), a Suite for piano quintet (1923), and a *Scherzo and Fugue* (1936) for string quartet.

HOWLAND, WILLIAM LEGRAND
b. *Asbury Park, New Jersey, 1873*
d. *Douglas Manor, New York, 26 July 1915*

Howland studied with Philip Scharwenka in Berlin and subsequently lived most of his life in Europe.

His opera *Sarrona*, to his own libretto, received its premiere in Italian in Bruges, Belgium in August 1903. It was performed in English in New York in February 1910. He wrote a second opera, *Nita*. Howland also composed two oratorios, *Ecce Homo* and *The Resurrection*.

HUGO, JOHN ADAM
b. *Bridgeport, Connecticut, 5 January 1873*
d. *Bridgeport, Connecticut, 29 December 1945*

After studying at the Stuttgart Conservatory (1888–97), Hugo toured England, Germany, and Italy as a concert pianist. He returned to the United States in 1899.

Hugo's one-act opera, *The Temple Dancer*, was produced at the Metropolitan Opera House, New York in 1919 and in Chicago in 1922. He composed two other operas, *The Hero of Byzanz* and *The Sun God*. He also wrote a Symphony, two piano concertos, and a Piano Trio.

HUSA, KAREL
b. *Prague, Czechoslovakia, 7 August 1921*

After graduating from the Conservatory and Academy of Music in Prague in 1946, where he had been a pupil of Jaroslav Ridký, Husa went to study in Paris at the Ecole Normale du Musique and the Conservatory. There his teachers included Arthur Honegger, Nadia Boulanger, André Cluytens, and Eugene Bigot.

Since 1954 Husa has lived in the United States, where he has established a reputation as a composer, conductor, and teacher. He became an American citizen in 1959. He was awarded Guggenheim Fellowships in 1964 and 1965, and in 1974 was elected a member of the Belgian Royal Academy of Arts and Science. He was elected a member of the American Academy of Arts and Letters in 1994. In 1954 he joined the music faculty at Cornell University, and in 1973 was appointed a Kappa Alpha Professor, retiring in 1992. He was also musical director of the Cornell University Symphony and Chamber Orchestras, and has appeared as guest conductor with most leading orchestras in America and Europe. From 1967 to 1986 he also taught at Ithaca College.

Husa's principal works are for orchestra. *Frescoes* (1949, rev.1963) was first performed by the Prague Radio Orchestra under Vacláv Smetacek. Symphony no. 1, composed in Paris in 1953, was premiered in the following year on Belgian Radio. *Fantasies* was commissioned in 1956 by the Friends of Music at Cornell and first performed there in April 1957. *Mosaiques* was commissioned by Hamburg Radio in 1961 and performed that year under the composer's direction.

Music for Prague, 1968, scored originally for concert band, was arranged for orchestra in 1969. Prompted by the tragic events in that city, the composer makes use of the Hussite hymn "Ye Warriors of God and His Law," which Dvořák had incorporated into his *Hussites Overture* and Smetana into his cycle *My Country*. The hymn is a symbol of national resistance against oppression. The political troubles in Prague in the summer of 1968 produced from Husa a creative work of great defiant force. In the concert band version, *Music for Prague* received 5,000 performances in the ten years following its premiere.

Subsequent orchestral works include *Two Sonnets of Michelangelo* (1972), composed for the Evanston (Illinois) Symphony Orchestra; *Al Fresco* for wind orchestra (1973); and *The Steadfast Tin Soldier*, a tale for children after Hans Christian Andersen, for narrator and orchestra (1974). For string orchestra he has written a Divertimento (1948), *Portrait* (1953), *Four Little Pieces* (1955), and *Pastoral* (1979).

Husa has composed a number of works for solo instruments and orchestra: Concertino for piano (1949); *Poem* for viola and chamber orchestra (1959), heard at the I.S.C.M. Festival in Cologne in 1960; *Elegie and Rondeau* for alto saxophone (1961); Serenade for wind quintet, strings, xylophone, and harp (1963), commissioned by the Baltimore Symphony Orchestra; Concerto for brass quintet and strings (1965); Concerto for alto saxophone and concert band (1967); Concerto for percussion and wind ensemble (1970–71); a Concerto for trumpet and wind orchestra (1973); an Organ Concerto, *The Sunlights* (1987); a Concerto for trumpet and orchestra, commissioned by the Chicago Symphony Orchestra in 1988; a Cello Concerto (1988), which won the Grawemeyer Award in 1993; and a Violin Concerto (1993).

Like *Music for Prague, Apotheosis of This Earth* exists in two forms. Completed in 1970, it was scored for concert band and first performed in April 1971 by the Michigan School Band at the University of Michigan, Ann Arbor. In 1973 the composer prepared a new

HUSA, KAREL

version for chorus and orchestra, which was premiered at Cornell University in April 1973. Especially in its original form, it is Husa's most powerful work and one of the most important items in the whole repertory of the concert band.

Husa's first ballet, *Monodrama*, was commissioned in honor of the Bicentennial by Jordan College of Music, Butler University, Indianapolis, Indiana. Inspired by James Baldwin's "The Creative Process," it was premiered on 26 March 1976 in Indianapolis by the Butler Ballet and the Indianapolis Symphony Orchestra.

More recent orchestral pieces are *Symphonic Suite* (1984); Concerto for Orchestra (1986); *Overture: Youth* (1990); *Cayuga Lake: Memories* for chamber orchestra (1992), written for the centenary of Ithaca College; *Celebration Fanfare* (1996); *Midwest Celebration* (1996); and *Celebracion* (1997).

For wind band he has composed Concerto for wind ensemble (1982), *Smetana Fanfare* (1984), and *Les Couleurs Fauves*, written in 1996 for the Northwestern University Wind Ensemble. Four string quartets are his major instrumental works. The First, dating from 1948, was performed by the Haydn Quartet at the I.S.C.M. Festival in Brussels in 1950; it was awarded the Lili Boulanger Prize in that year. The Second was commissioned by the Parrenin Quartet in 1953. Quartet No. 3 was composed for the Fine Arts Quartet, which gave the premiere in 1968. It won the Pulitzer Prize in the following year. The Fourth Quartet, *Poems*, was completed in 1990 for the Colorado Quartet.

Other chamber music includes Sonatina for violin and piano (1945); Suite for viola and piano (1945); *Poeme* for viola and piano (1950); *Evocations of Slovakia* for clarinet, viola, and cello (1951); Divertimento for brass and percussion (1959); *Two Preludes* for flute, clarinet, and bassoon (1966); Divertimento for brass quintet (1968); and a Violin Sonata, commissioned in 1972 by the Koussevitzky Foundation and first performed in New York in March 1974. In 1977 to commemorate the Bicentennial, he composed *Landscapes* for brass quintet for the Western Brass Quintet of Western Michigan University.

Other instrumental pieces of this period are *Three Dance Sketches* for percussion (1979); *Intradas and Interludes* for seven trumpets and percussion (1980); *Sonata à Tre* for violin, clarinet, and piano (1982), composed for the Verdehar Trio; *Recollections* for wind quintet and piano (1982); *Variations* for piano quartet (1984); *Intrada* for brass quintet (1984); *Tubafest* for tuba quartet (1992); *Five Poems* for wind quintet (1994); and *Postcard from Home* for alto saxophone and piano (1997).

For the centenary of Cornell University in 1965, Husa composed *Festival Ode* for chorus and orchestra. His major choral work, *An American Te Deum* for bari-

tone, chorus, and band, was written in 1976 to mark the 125th anniversary of Coe College, Cedar Rapids, Iowa, and in honor of the American Bicentennial. In addition to the words of the *Te Deum*, sung in English, the composer uses texts from various sources, including Henry David Thoreau, Paul Engle, a Moravian folk song, and a Swedish immigrant ballad. In 1978 Husa made an orchestral version of this work with chorus and baritone soloist, performed in May 1978 at the Inter-American Festival of the Arts in Washington, D.C.

Among Husa's other choral works is *Every Day* for a cappella chorus to words by Thoreau, performed by the Ithaca College Chorus in November 1981. *Three Moravian Songs* for chorus date from the same year. In 1983 he composed a *Cantata* for male chorus and brass quintet. His single vocal work is a set of *Twelve Moravian Songs* (1956).

For piano Husa has composed a Sonatina, his first published work (1943); *Elegie* (1957); and two sonatas: no. 1, written in Paris in 1949, and no. 2, commissioned by Andre-Michel Schub for the Bicentennial Piano Series at the John F. Kennedy Center in Washington, D.C. in 1975. He has also written *Eight Czech Duets* for piano duo (1958).

A ballet on the subject of *The Trojan Women* by Euripides, commissioned by the Louisville Orchestra and Ballet, was premiered on 28 March 1981 to celebrate the opening of Louisville University's new Performing Arts Center.

HUSS, HENRY HOLDEN
b. Newark, New Jersey, 21 June 1862
d. New York, New York, 17 September 1953

Huss was a descendant of Jan Hus (1373–1415), the Bohemian preacher. He was a pupil of Joseph Rheinberger at the Munich Royal Conservatory (1882–85) and became widely known as a teacher, composer, and pianist. From 1930 to his retirement in 1938 he taught at Hunter College, New York.

The music of Huss is distinctly nineteenth century in character. He was the soloist in his *Rhapsody in C* for piano and orchestra, performed when he graduated from the Munich Conservatory in 1885. He later gave the premiere in Boston of his Piano Concerto in B major, completed in 1894. The *Romance and Polonaise* for orchestra was performed at the Paris Exposition in 1889. He wrote a Violin Concerto in D minor (1906) and five other orchestral works: *Forest Idylls* (1884), *Cleopatra's Death* (1896), *Festival March* (1897), *La Nuit* (1902, orchestrated 1939), and a symphonic poem, *Life's Conflicts* (1921). Huss also composed much chamber music including four string quartets, two violin

219

sonatas, a Viola Sonata, a Cello Sonata, two piano trios, and numerous piano pieces.

For choir and orchestra he wrote an *Ave Maria* (1888) for female chorus, strings, organ, and harp, performed in Chicago in 1898 by Theodore Thomas; *Festival Sanctus, Nocturne* (1913); and his best-known composition, *The Ride of Paul Revere* for soprano, female chorus, and orchestra (1920).

I

IANNACCONE, ANTHONY (JOSEPH)
b. Brooklyn, New York, 14 October 1943

Iannaccone studied with Vittorio Giannini, David Diamond, and Nicolas Flagello at the Manhattan School of Music (1961–68) and at the Eastman School of Music, Rochester, New York, where he was a pupil of Samuel Adler and Warren Benson. He also studied privately with Aaron Copland (1959–64). After teaching at the Manhattan School of Music (1967–68), he joined the music faculty of East Michigan University in 1971, where he established the electronic music studio.

From 1967 to 1975 he adopted serial techniques, after which he developed his own musical language of a more tonal character.

Iannaccone has composed three symphonies: no. 1 (1965); no. 2 (1966); and no. 3, *Night Rivers* in one movement (1992). Other orchestral works are a Suite (1962); Concertino for violin and orchestra (1967); a concert overture, *Lysistrata* (1968); *Variations* for violin and orchestra (1969); Divertimento (1983); *Sinfonia Concertante* for flute, violin, viola, cello, piano, and orchestra (1989); *Whispers of Heavenly Death* (1989); *Concertante* for clarinet and orchestra (1994); *Al Chiaro di Luna* (1994); *Crossings* (1996); *West End Express* (1997); *Waiting for the Sunrise on the Sound* (1998); *From Time to Time* (2000); and *Escape* (2002). Iannaccone has been particularly successful in writing for wind bands: *Interlude* (1970); *Antiphonies* (1973); *Scherzo* (1976); *Of Fire and Ice* (1977); *Images of Song and Dance: I Orpheus* (1979-82) and *II Terpsichore* (1981); *After a Gentle Rain* (1980); *Plymouth Trilogy* (1981); *Apparitions* (1986); and *Sea Drift* (1993).

Iannaccone's chamber music includes *Parodies* for wind quintet (1958); Piano Trio (1959); Viola Sonata (1961); three violin sonatas (1964, 1971, 1983); three string quartets (1965, 1965, 1999); *Hades* for brass

Anthony Iannaccone.
Photo: Richard Schwatze, courtesy the composer.

quartet (1968); *Remembrance* for viola and piano (1968); *Three Mythical Sketches* for brass quartet (1971); *Anamorphoses* for two horns, trombone, and percussion (1972); *Rituals* for violin and piano (1973); *Bicinia* for flute and saxophone (1975); Sonatina for trumpet and tuba (1975); *Aria Concertante* for cello

221

and piano (1976); *Invention* for two saxophones (1978); Trio for flute, clarinet, and piano (1976); Octet (1985); *Mobiles* for eight brass and two percussion (1986); *Toccata Fanfares* for brass (1986); Piano Quintet (1996); and Quintet for clarinet and string quartet (2002). For piano he has composed *Retail Rags* (1959), *Partita* (1967), *Keyboard Essays* (1972), and *Two-Piano Inventions* (1985). *Toccata Variations* for organ dates from 1983.

His choral works include *Magnificat* for chorus and orchestra (1963); *Solomon's Canticle* for chorus (1968); *The Prince of Peace* for soprano, mezzo-soprano, baritone, bass, chorus, and orchestra (1970); *Music Strong I Come* (Walt Whitman) for chorus, two pianos, and ensemble (1974); *The Sky is Low, the Clouds Are Mean* (Emily Dickinson) for chorus (1976); *Song of Thanksgiving* for chorus (1980); *Walt Whitman Song* for solo voices, chorus, and wind (1980); *Whitman Madrigals* for chorus and piano (1984); *Autumn Rivulets* for chorus and chamber orchestra (1984); and *Chautauqua Psalms* for chorus and piano (1987). Iannaccone's vocal music includes *Five Songs on Immortality* for soprano and piano (or orchestra) (1959) and *My Comfort by Day, My Song in the Night* for high voice and piano (1985).

Among his pieces for tape alone are *Prelude* (1968), *Times Square and Forty-Second Street* (1969), and *Fission* (1971).

IMBRIE, ANDREW WELSH

b. New York, New York, 6 April 1921

Imbrie was given his first piano lessons at the age of four. Later he was a pupil of Leo Ornstein (1930–42) and Robert Casadesus (1941). He studied with Roger Sessions, first privately, then at Princeton University, and briefly with Nadia Boulanger in 1937. He graduated from Princeton (B.A., 1942), and after the war continued his studies in composition with Roger Sessions at the University of California, Berkeley (M.A., 1947). In 1947 he joined the music faculty at Berkeley, but spent the next two years in Rome as a Fellow of the American Academy there. He returned to Rome in 1953 on a Guggenheim Fellowship. A second Guggenheim Fellowship allowed him to spend 1959 in Tokyo.

Imbrie was professor of music at Berkeley from 1949 to 1991. From 1967 to 1968 he was Composer-in-Residence at the American Academy in Rome, and after 1970 he also taught at the San Francisco Conservatory. He was elected to membership of the National Institute of Arts and Letters (now the American Academy of Arts and Letters) in 1969 and to the American Academy of Arts and Sciences in 1980. He has been a visiting professor at Brandeis University (1982), University

of Chicago (1994, 1996–97), Northwestern University, Chicago (1994), New York University (1995), and Harvard University (1997). In 1991 he was Composer-in-Residence at Tanglewood.

Imbrie came to the notice of the public with a String Quartet in B-flat, composed in 1942 when he was only 21. He won the New York Music Critics' Circle Award for 1943–44. The Second and Third Quartets, written in 1951 and 1957 respectively, have fulfilled the promise of the earlier work. Two more quartets, both composed for the Pro Arte Quartet, have followed: no. 4 in 1969 and no. 5 in 1987. His other instrumental music includes two piano trios (1946, 1996); a Piano Sonata (1947); Divertimento for flute, bassoon, trumpet, violin, cello, and piano (1948); Serenade for flute, viola, and piano (1952); *Impromptu* for violin and piano (1960); a Cello Sonata (1966); *Three Sketches* for trombone and piano (1967); *Dandelion Wine* for oboe, clarinet, string quartet, and piano (1967); and *To a Traveler* for clarinet, viola, and piano (1971).

Among Imbrie's later chamber works are *Pilgrimage* for flute, clarinet, piano trio, and percussion (1983); *Dream Sequence* for flute, oboe, clarinet, violin, viola, cello, piano, and percussion (1986); *Three Piece Suite* for harp and piano (1987); *Earplay Fantasy* for flute, clarinet, piano trio, and percussion (1996); *Spring Fever* for flute, oboe, clarinet, string quartet, double bass, piano, and percussion (1996); *Chicago Bells* for violin and piano (1997); *Mukashi mukashi* (*Once Upon a Time*) for two pianos (1997); *Soliloquy* for solo violin (1998); a Piano Quartet (1998); *From Time to Time* for chamber ensemble (2000); *Four-Hand Fantasy* for piano, four hands (2001); *Duet for Friends* for bass clarinet and cello (2002); and *In Memoriam, Nathan Schwartz* for solo cello (2002). Three works for brass are *Here We Stand* (1969), *A Hawk for Peace* (1970), and *Fancy for Five* (trombones) (1973).

For orchestra Imbrie has composed *Ballad in D* (1947), *Legend* (1959), *Little Concerto* for piano (four hands) and orchestra (1960), and Symphony no. 1, commissioned in 1965 by the San Francisco Symphony Orchestra. An important work is the Violin Concerto, commissioned by the Koussevitzky Foundation, which was begun in 1951 and finished three years later in Rome. It was first performed in Berkeley, California in 1958 with Robert Gross as soloist. Later orchestral compositions are a *Chamber Symphony* (1968); Symphony no. 2 (1969), performed in San Francisco the following year; Symphony no. 3, premiered by the Halle Orchestra in Manchester, England in December 1970; a Cello Concerto (1972), presented in Oakland California in 1973; and three piano concertos (1973, 1974, 1992), the *Second* commissioned by the Ford Foundation. In 1977 he was commissioned to write a Flute Concerto for the New York Philharmonic Orchestra. It was first performed by that orchestra with Julius Baker as soloist and Erich Leinsdorf conducting in October 1977.

Imbrie has set two of Whitman's poems: *On the Beach at Night* for chorus and string orchestra (1949) and *Drum Taps* for chorus and orchestra (1960). His other choral music includes *Introit, Gradual and Offertory for All Saints Day* for chorus and organ (1956); *Psalm 42* for men's voices and organ (1962); *Three Songs* for chorus and piano (1964); *Let All the World* (George Herbert) for chorus, brass, and percussion (1971); *Prometheus Bound* (Aeschylus) for soloists, double chorus, orchestra, and dancers (1980); *Three Campion Songs* for four singers and piano (1981); *Song for St. Cecilia's Day* (Dryden) for chorus, solo flute, two violins, brass, percussion, and two pianos (1982); *Requiem in memoriam John H. Imbrie 1962–81*, in memory of his son, for soprano, chorus, and orchestra, performed in 1984 by the San Francisco Symphony Orchestra; *Adam* for soprano, chorus, and small orchestra, based on late medieval and American Civil War texts (1994); and *Songs of Then and Now* for girls' choir, flute, clarinet, piano trio, and percussion (1998). He has also written *Three Songs* for soprano and orchestra (1949), to texts by Robert Frost, Edgar Lee Masters and John Crowe Ransom, and *Five Roethke Songs* for soprano and piano (1980).

For the stage Imbrie has composed a one-act opera, *Three Against Christmas, or Christmas in Peebles Town* (1960–61), with libretto by Richard Wincor, and has provided incidental music for James Schevill's play *Voices of Mass and Capital A* (1962). For the Bicentennial celebrations in 1976, he wrote a full-length opera, *Angle of Repose,* based on the Pulitzer Prize-winning novel by Wallace Stegner. It was first performed by the San Francisco Opera Company on 6 November 1976.

INCH, HERBERT REYNOLDS
b. Missoula, Montana, 25 November 1904
d. La Jolla, California, 14 April 1988

Inch graduated from the Eastman School of Music, Rochester, New York, and the University of Rochester (BM., 1925, M.M., 1928), where he had been a pupil of Howard Hanson (1922–28). He also studied at the University of Montana. In 1931 he was awarded a Fellowship by the American Academy in Rome. From 1925 to 1928 and from 1930 to 1931 he taught at the Eastman School before joining the faculty at Hunter College, New York in 1937, retiring in 1965.

For orchestra he composed three "Symphoniettas" (1948, 1950, 1953); *Variations on a Modal Theme* (1927); a Suite for small orchestra (1929); *Two Pieces* for small orchestra (1930); a Symphony (1932); a Serenade for wind and strings (1936); a Piano Concerto (1937); *Answers to a Questionaire* (1942); *Northwest Overture* (1943); a Violin Concerto (1946); and Concertino for piano and strings (1953).

Inch's chamber music includes a Piano Quintet (1930); two string quartets (1933, 1936); *Mediterranean Sketches* for string quartet (1933); Divertimento for Brass (1934); a Cello Sonata (1934); three piano sonatas (1935, 1950, 1966); *Three Conversations* for string quartet (1944); and a Piano Trio (1963). He composed a single choral work, *Return to Zion* for female voices and piano (1945).

INGALLS, JEREMIAH
b. Andover, Massachusetts, 1 March 1764
d. Hancock, Vermont, 6 April 1828

In his early 20s, Ingalls moved to Newbury, Vermont, where he kept a tavern. Later he lived in Rochester, Vermont before settling in Hancock, where he died. He was active as a choral trainer and bass viol player.

Ingalls was one of the first musicians in the North to adapt secular tunes to the words of hymns, and published a collection of them, *The Christian Harmony or Songster's Companion* in Exeter, New Hampshire in 1805. Many of these tunes were original folk songs from England, Scotland, and Ireland, given added choruses and three-part settings. His fuguing piece *Northfield* (*How Long, Dear Saviour, O How Long*) has remained popular to the present.

IVES, CHARLES EDWARD
b. Danbury, Connecticut, 20 October 1874
d. New York, New York, 19 May 1954

An ancestor of Charles Ives, William Ives of Dorchester, England, landed in Boston in 1635 and settled in Connecticut, where the family remained for over three hundred years. Charles received his first musical training at home from his father, George, who was a teacher of violin, piano, and theory, director of the local band, and an enthusiastic experimenter in the science of acoustics. George Ives constructed a number of musical devices, including a prepared piano that produced quarter-tones. He had, with difficulty, taught members of his family to sing quarter-tones, a process his son called "hardening the ears." Of his father, Charles Ives wrote: "He had a kind of natural interest in sounds of every kind, known and unknown." In spite of his intense concern for music, George Ives did not attempt composition, confining himself to experiments and to arranging pieces for his band. Charles grew up in this lively atmosphere, so his musical education was at first entirely based upon his father's original and unorthodox approach to the phenomenon of sound, a method far removed from the more traditional music teaching of the time. The other major influences upon him were the psalm and hymn tunes which he heard and later played in church; the popular songs of Stephen Foster, who was a personal acquaintance of George Ives; and the knowledge of orchestral and instrumental music acquired at his father's rehearsals of the town band.

From the age of eight, Charles had begun his own experiments with tonality by trying to reproduce the sound of bells and drums on the piano with various combinations of dissonant notes. However, his father also gave him a thorough academic training in harmony and counterpoint, and taught him to play the piano, the organ, and the violin. He obtained a permanent post as an organist at the age of 13. For some years he had been writing pieces of music for his friends and his father's band, and by the age of 14 he had composed a number of songs and organ pieces as well. In 1891, he wrote *Variations on a National Hymn* (*America*) for organ, which includes canons in two and three different keys simultaneously and is perhaps the earliest example of deliberate polytonality. His *Fugue in Four Keys* of the same year introduces the successive entries of the subject in separate keys, which are maintained throughout: the first in C, the second in G, the third in D, and the fourth in A.

The sudden death of George Ives in 1894 deeply affected his son, who lost not only a father but also a profound musical stimulus. To this can be attributed the reticence of Charles Ives, who now had no kindred spirit to whom he could show his music for sympathetic criticism and who would understand his work. At the age of 21, Ives entered Yale University to study with Horatio Parker, and remained there for three years. It was at Yale that he came into conflict with academic precepts and became frustrated at having to go over the same harmony and counterpoint exercises he had covered as a boy with his father. After a while, Parker ignored the strange pieces his pupil brought him, considering them mere musical jokes. Ives wrote his First Symphony between August 1897 and May 1898 while he was at Yale. Parker made him rewrite the first movement to conform with the harmonic conventions of symphonic form. As a result, the work is not representative of the composer. A *Prelude and Postlude*, also written at Yale, contains a polytonal texture with major and minor chords placed on top of each other.

After three years at Yale, Ives was faced with the problem of choosing a career. He had seen the difficulties his father experienced in looking after a family while attempting to earn a living as a musician. Rather than devote a lifetime to playing music he disliked, Ives

Charles Ives.
Photo: W. Eugene Smith, MSS 14, The Charles Ives Papers in the Irving S. Gilmore Music Library of Yale University.

decided on a career in business. In 1898 he began as a clerk in the Mutual Life Insurance company. While improving his position in the company, he continued to compose music in his spare time, often writing into the early hours of the morning; he was also organist at a church in New York. He seldom went to concerts, as the works of other composers interfered with the thoughts he had of his own music. Thus his compositions were not influenced by the so-called modern tendencies of the time. He said that he had heard not a note of the music of Schoenberg or Stravinsky until long after he had ceased to compose. He continued to devote great energy to the insurance business, and by 1907 he had established his own agency with a friend, Julian Myrick. The following year the married Harmony Twitchell, and the couple settled in New York City. When Ives retired from the business in 1930, his name was respected by thousands of men who were unaware that he was anything but a brilliant businessman and a financial genius. The agency he founded continues to thrive in New York today, and one of the books he wrote on the training of insurance agents, *The Amount to Carry*, remained in print until recent times.

After leaving Yale, Ives continued to write copiously, completing a cantata, *The Celestial Country*, in 1899, as well as a setting of Psalm 67, which is the most widely performed of his choral works. In this piece, the choir is divided into two groups that sing independently, the sopranos and altos holding one tonality, the tenors and basses another.

In addition to *The Celestial Country* and Psalm 67, Ives composed several other important choral works, including *Three Harvest Home Chorales*, written in 1898 but lost and reconstructed in 1912 for chorus, brass, and organ. The most remarkable of his choral compositions are the early settings of Psalms 100 and 150 for two choirs (1896), Psalm 90 for chorus, organ, and bells (1901), and the experimental Psalm 24 (1898), which uses systematic application of "progressive intervals," starting with semitones and tones and enlarging to ninths. *Lincoln, the Great Commoner*, a setting of a text by Edwin Markham for chorus and orchestra (1912), was later adapted for voice and piano. Ives's last important work for chorus is a setting of Vachel Lindsay's poem "General Booth Enters Into Heaven," based on the Salvation Army hymn "Are You Washed in the Blood of the Lamb?," for bass solo, chorus, and band, written in 1914.

Ives constantly rewrote and revised his music to suit different forms; for example, the song *His Exaltation,* composed in 1913, was adapted from the Second Violin Sonata of 1903, and the song *The Rainbow* (1914) was arranged as an orchestral piece in 1921. The first movement of Symphony no. 2 (1897–1902) comes from an early sonata, the third movement was once an organ prelude, and the last movement is largely based on an overture, *American Woods*. This symphony reveals the childhood influences on Ives as a composer. In the last movement there is an incongruous mixture of lyrical pastoral music and a vulgar military band that repetitively blasts forth fragments of march tunes. There is no real fusion between these incompatible elements, and the result is a curious jumble of confused musical ideas which cannot exist compatibly side by side.

Ives needed at this time to hear his own works adequately performed so that he would know how they would sound. But the few occasions when his larger compositions were tried out usually roused either fierce hostility or complete bewilderment and misunderstanding. In 1951 Leonard Bernstein invited the composer to the first performance of the Second Symphony, but Ives did not attend. We can only wonder at his reaction to hearing music he had written almost half a century earlier. The last movement of the symphony may be "American" and highly patriotic in mood, but it is unsatisfactory as absolute music. One writer called the piece "an intensely nationalistic, strange, primitive, moving symphony," but none of these adjectives describes it in musical terms.

The Second and Third Symphonies, the most often performed of his larger works, are uncharacteristic of Ives's experiments and inventive powers. The Third Symphony, completed in 1904, is based on hymn tunes and organ pieces that the composer had played at his church. Forty-three years later it was awarded the Pulitzer Prize. In this work Ives uses a relatively small orchestra without any startling originality. All the movements lack rhythmic and harmonic variety and the symphony is not representative of Ives the visionary. Lionel Salter wrote of the Third Symphony: "Judged altogether dispassionately and without wishing to give offence, this symphony sounds like a not very successful effort lacking in interest, personal style and organic form, while the composer has handled his small orchestra without the slightest feeling for instrumental color" (*The Gramophone*, February 1951). This may seem damning criticism, but the elements that are wanting are those one would expect to find even in the least inspired professional composer. In this way the technical weaknesses in the larger works and Ives's disregard of practical difficulties of performance often outweigh the extraordinary imagination of the composer.

From the earliest days of his insurance agency, Ives wrote music almost every night, making sketches for chamber music and large orchestral works, often put away for several years before being completed or adapted, producing a prodigious pile of manuscripts. An example of the lapse of time between conception and completion is *Central Park in the Dark*, begun in 1898 but not finished until 1907. It is a polytonal, polyrhythmic impressionistic picture, constructed from numerous conflicting musical fragments—ragtime, popular songs, and derivations from actual sounds, both natural and man-made—which had been experienced by the composer and concentrated into a remarkable piece of music.

The Unanswered Question, composed sometime before 1908, is Ives's best-known work. The small orchestra employed is divided into three entirely independent groups. The strings play a chorale, pianissimo throughout, with very slow-moving harmony, which does not alter in tempo or mood, representing "the silence of the Druids, who know, see and hear nothing." Separate from the body strings is a solo trumpet which repeats at measured intervals a short questioning phrase, "the perennial question of existence." The third group consists of four flutes which attempt to answer the trumpet's angular melody with frenzied, dissonant outbursts in a different tempo from the strings, becoming louder and faster at each entry. The points at which the flutes enter are not precisely indicated in the score; it is left to the conductor to determine when he wishes the flutes to play. The success of *The Unanswered Question* is perhaps attributable to the avoidance of banal quotations from popular melodies and other extraneous material which often conflict with the basic musical ideas of other compositions.

In his book *Music of Our Time*, Adolfo Salazar considers that "the general significance of Ives' music has less interest than his experiments with musical material." This is abundantly clear in *Orchestral Set no. 1,"Three Places in New England,"* composed between 1903 and 1914. The second movement, *Putnam's Camp,* is one of the greatest musical curiosities of all time. In this piece Ives wishes to depict the dreams of a child who falls asleep near the Revolutionary Memorial at Redding Center, Connecticut. "Long rows of stone camp fireplaces still remain to stir the child's imagination." The aural effect is one of confused cacophony, representing a number of military bands playing different marches simultaneously in a variety of keys, which is both polytonal and polyrhythmical, with fragments of familiar tunes, including "The British Grenadiers," emerging from time to time out of the orchestral mêlée. Ives here recalls the experience he had as a boy of hearing two band marching into Danbury from opposite directions, each playing a different tune with a resultant clash of harmonies and rhythms that fascinated him. It was this episode which laid the foundation for *Putnam's Camp.* Ives's acute hearing, fostered in the early days by the attention of his father to the phenomenon of sound, enabled him to fuse a number of conflicting musical factors into one comprehensive effect. To the average musician this still remains chaos, but to Ives it was a basis for a musical work, although it is open to question how much of this combined result was clear even to him.

The third movement, *The Housatonic at Stockbridge,* is an impressionistic creation of great delicacy, revealing most vividly Ives's acute ear for particularly striking aural effects. The title is taken from a poem by Robert Underwood Johnson (1853–1937), and Ives wrote of the work : "One Sunday morning we walked in the meadows along the River (Housatonic) and heard the distant singing from the church across the River. The mist had not entirely left the river bed, and the colors, the running water, the banks and the trees were something that one would always remember." This movement is one of Ives's completely successful works and deserves to be played on its own, since it does not require the same large forces as the other two movements.

Among Ives's other important orchestral compositions is *A Set of Pieces for Theater Orchestra*; it dates from 1911, but the first and third movements have their origins in music dating from 1904 and 1906. *In the Cage* exists in a form for voice and piano, composed in 1908. *In the Inn* is derived from the second movement of the First Piano Sonata and evokes the sound of dancing coming from a tavern. *In the Night*, especially composed to complete the *Set*, quotes a minstrel song of the 1880s.

Robert Browning Overture (1918) was the only work completed of a projected series, "Men of Literature Overtures." It is a long and complex composition on the scale of a symphonic poem. After a slow introduction, the music works up to a characteristic polyrhythmically chaotic allegro; the central adagio variations have an appealingly eloquent simplicity which, like *The Unanswered Question*, reveals Ives at his best when he is not striving after over-elaboration. The final fugato restores the frenzied drive, but the work ends with a brief, quiet coda recalling the variations.

In addition to the four numbered symphonies, Ives composed four separate works that, in the words of the composer, "may be lumped together as a symphony." The first movement of this "Holidays Symphony" is entitled *Washington's Birthday* (1909) and is scored for flute, horn, bells, strings, and a Jew's harp. Shortly after completion, an attempt was made at playing it through by a theater orchestra, but the musicians refused to take the piece seriously. It was, however, performed in America and Europe in the 1930s under Nicolas Slonimsky and even in Vienna, where the conductor was Anton Webern. The second movement, *Decoration Day* (1912), quotes fragments of "Swanee River" and "Goodnight, Ladies," describing a procession to the cemetery and the noisy march home. *The Fourth of July* (1912–13) is the most complicated part of the set, making use of polymusical and polytonal textures, using a very large orchestra. Not for the first time in a work by Ives, "Columbia, Gem of the Ocean" can be heard taking its place among a sequence of popular tunes. Except for the second movement of the *Fourth Symphony,* this is the most difficult of all Ives' compositions for both conductor and players. The last movement, *Thanksgiving and/or Forefathers' Day,* was written as early as 1904 and uses a chorus in addition to the orchestra.

Orchestral Set no. 2 consists of three short movements. The first, *An Elegy for Our Forefathers,* completed in 1913 and originally entitled *An Elegy to Stephen Foster,* employs phrases from "Old Black Joe" and "Massa's in the Cold, Cold Ground." The second movement, composed in 1911, is based on one of four *Ragtime Dances* for piano of 1902. The quotations from two revivalist hymns explains in part the title, *The Rockstrewn Hills Join in the People's Outdoor Meeting.* The third movement, *From Hanover Square North at the End of a Tragic Day,* commemorates the sinking of the *Lusitania* on 7 May 1915 and evoked for the composer recollections of the effect the news had on the home-bound public in New York on that day.

Symphony no. 4 (1910–16), his last completed orchestral work, is scored for large orchestra and uses a chorus in the first movement for "Watchman, Tell Us of the Night" and in the last movement, where the wordless voices sing the hymn "Bethany." The second movement presents the most involved music, which is just within the realms of practical performance. Ives requires the players to follow 22 separate rhythmical patterns simultaneously, with numerous quotations including "Turkey in the Straw" and the hymn "Beulah Land." At one point, the upper orchestral instruments increase in speed while the lower instruments remain at the same tempo until an eventual collapse occurs. When the first two movements were performed in New York by Eugene Goossens in January 1927 there was almost a riot in the audience. By contrast, the slow fugal third movement, based on two hymn tunes, is scored for strings, organ, and three wind instruments (flute, clarinet, horn). It was first heard in a radio broadcast in 1935 under the direction of Bernard Herrmann. Of the finale Ives wrote: "The last movement is an apotheosis of the preceding content in terms that have something to do with the reality of existence and its religious experience." In the Fourth Symphony, Ives used quarter-tones and unusual time signatures: not only 7/2, 5/4, and 9/2, but also 6-1/2 over 2 which, not surprisingly, posed problems for the players. The score was laboriously reconstructed by the staff of the Edwin Fleisher Collection of Orchestral Music.

Ives composed his First String Quartet at the age of 22, while studying with Horatio Parker at Yale. Subtitled *A Revival Service*, its four movements all make use of hymn tunes. The opening fugue has "From Greenland's Icy Mountains" as its subject. The second and third movements, *Prelude* and *Offertory*, were originally organ pieces the composer had written for himself to play in church, and the *Finale/Postlude* quotes "Stand up, Stand up for Jesus." Its homespun simplicity harks back in spirit to William Billings and is a musical equivalent of the American folk paintings epitomized by Grandma Moses.

The Second Quartet, composed between 1907 and 1913, is more typical of his personal language and was described by Ives as "a string quartet for four men who converse, discuss, argue politics, fight, shake hands, shut up, then walk up the mountainside to view the firmament." Throughout, it is a more dissonant work than the First Quartet, with the quoted material absorbed into the generally atonal texture. His description of the ideas behind the music explains the significance of the titles of the three movements. The opening, *Discussion,* makes use of several popular tunes including "Dixie." *Argument*, the second movement, refers to "Columbia, the Gem of the Ocean" and "Marching Through Georgia." The Adagio finale, *The Call of the Mountains,* includes oblique references to Tchaikovsky's Symphony no. 6, Brahms' Symphony no. 2, and the appropriate hymn "Nearer My God to Thee."

Ives's other chamber work which makes a frequent appearance on concert programs is the *Largo* for clarinet, violin, and piano (1902), which was derived from the so-called Pre-First Violin Sonata and is probably the sole surviving movement of a Clarinet Trio, also composed in 1902 but now lost.

Apart from the early Pre-First Sonata, Ives composed four violin sonatas: no. 1, begun in 1903 and finished in 1908; no. 2 (1903–10), which was much revised and finally rewritten by Lou Harrison; no. 3 (1902–04), edited by Ingolf Dahl and Sol Babitz; and no. 4 (1914–15), subtitled *Children's Day at the Camp Meeting,* which uses hymn tunes in the first and last movements. Although these sonatas were greeted with total incomprehension when tried out soon after composition, they are now regarded as standard works of the modern repertory of American violinists and constitute the most consistent set of pieces by Ives.

The First Piano Sonata was composed between 1902 and 1910 and is as powerful a work as the better-known *Concord* Sonata. The pianist is faced with formidable problems that stretch technique to the limits in a way not required by any other composer until the 1950's. The first movement quotes two tunes, "Where's my wandering boy tonight?" and "I was a wandering sheep." The second movement is derived from ragtime and includes his own piece *In the Inn*, later to be orchestrated as the second part of the *Set for Theater Orchestra* (1911). The third movement is a Largo with a central allegro section quoting the hymn "What a Friend We Have in Jesus." The fourth movement, like the second, makes use of ragtime. The formidable finale falls into several sections and is the longest movement, lasting nearly 14 minutes.

The Second Piano Sonata, subtitled *Concord, Mass., 1840–60,* was composed between 1909 and 1915 and was privately printed in 1919. Ives continued to make alterations to it until the final version, edited by John Kirkpatrick, was published in 1947. It was Kirkpatrick's advocacy of the Sonata that brought the name of Ives to the attention of the musical world in the late 1930s.

The composer's own writings, *Essays Before a Sonata,* throw much light on the inspiration behind each part of this monumental work. As with the First Sonata, the problems for the performer are prodigious; even to read the notes needs much skill, and the frequent use of sequences of five-note chords in each hand will daunt all but physically strong pianists from attempting even a single movement. Although time signatures do appear briefly, most of the Sonata is written without bar lines and at times on three staves.

The first movement, *Emerson*, was planned first as a piano concerto, then as an overture in the "Men of Literature" series, but after 1912, Ives turned the sketches towards a solo piano sonata. With several different transcriptions of this section by the composer, the published version and those heard in performance often differ in detail. The music is generally rhapsodic in mood, fluctuating in tempo from the slow opening to occasional quicker outbursts. Sketches for the *Emerson Piano Concerto* dating from 1907 have been reconstructed in the 1990s by David G. Porter and performed in the United States and Europe.

The second movement, *Hawthorne,* is a very rapid scherzo; in the central, slower section, the pianist is instructed to use in the right hand a strip of wood 14-¾ inches in length to press down chords of black notes without striking the keys. The short third movement, entitled *The Alcotts,* is slow and generally relaxed. Ives quotes Scottish airs and hints at the opening of Beethoven's Fifth Symphony, a reference to Beth Alcott playing the spinet-piano given to her by Sophia Thoreau. The final movement, *Thoreau,* suggests a summer day by Walden Pond. In the closing bars there is an optional flute part to suggest the poet playing quietly to himself as the sun sets. After Kirkpatrick's performance of the Sonata in 1939, Lawrence Gillman called the work "the greatest music composed by an American."

As Ives heard hardly any of his works performed, his music became more and more complex, of such astounding imagination and virtuosity that makes some pieces almost unreadable and beyond any practical possibilities. Ives was a true pioneer in music, but his inability to organize his material and to discriminate often produced a confusion of ideas.

Ives's modesty in some ways covered a bitterness against musicians who were not capable of playing or understanding his music. In the introduction to his volume of *114 Songs,* published privately at his own expense in 1922, he wrote: "This volume is thrown, so to speak, at the music fraternity, who for this reason will feel free to dodge it on its way, perhaps to the wastepaper basket." He referred to the volume as "plenty of songs which have not been and will not be asked for." These songs cover a multitude of styles—dramatic, lyrical, religious, humorous—with folk and war songs, some adaptations of instrumental pieces, and some songs in various foreign languages. These reveal both the weakness and strength of Ives as a composer. Side by side are songs of striking originality, such as *Walking, Berceuse,* and *When the Eagle,* and others that are banal and sentimental. This lack of self-criticism, which could have been altered by the reaction of the composer to public performance, appears in many of his compositions.

From Ives's vast outpouring of music, which came to an abrupt halt in 1928, the four symphonies, *The Unanswered Question,* and *Three Places in New England* are the most approachable works of this strange, primitive, remarkable man. The four violin sonatas possess a greater unity of style than most of his pieces, but are not altogether representative of the composer.

Ives was a man of extraordinary vision and original ideas, an uninhibited eccentric whose music cut across all the conventional concepts of harmony and musical history. He was a naïve man who wrote whatever came into his head, often what he thought up during his ten-mile walk to the office each day. He felt that there could never be a final version of any pieces of music, so he was constantly revising and adapting compositions. He began his last work, *The Universe Symphony,* as early as 1911 and was still adding to it until 1952, but he intended that it should remain forever incomplete "because it represents aspects of life about which there is always more to be said." In this work Ives transcends even Mahler and Schoenberg in the intended use of several orchestras with groups of singers placed at various parts of a valley to produce a gigantic stereophonic effect. This piece seems the natural culmination of his work, which became progressively more complex and thereby less and less practical as he withdrew into his own world of music. In the words of Elliott Carter, "Ives saw the artist as a prophet living in the pure transcendent world of the spirit, above the mundane matters of money. In gradually retiring into this dream, he cut himself off from music's reality." (*Music Quarterly,* April 1960).

In 1945 in his private papers, Schoenberg paid the following tribute to Ives: "There is a great man living in this country—a composer. He has solved the problem of how to preserve one's self and to learn. He responds to neglect by contempt. He is not forced to accept praise or blame. His name is Ives."

IVEY, JEAN EICHELBERGER
b. Washington, D.C., 3 July 1923

Ivey received her musical training at Trinity College, Washington, D.C. (1941–44), Peabody Conservatory (M.Mus., piano) (1944–46). and the Eastman School of Music, Rochester, New York (M.Mus., composition) (1956). She was awarded her doctorate by the University of Toronto in 1972. In 1969 she was appointed to the composition faculty of the Peabody Conservatory and was the founder and director of the Electronic Music Studio. Ill-health forced her to give up teaching and composing in the mid-1990s.

For orchestra she has written a *Little Symphony* (1948); *Passacaglia* for chamber orchestra (1954); *Festive Symphony* (1955); *Overture* for small orchestra (1955); *Ode for Orchestra* (1965); *Forms in Motion,* a three-movement symphony (1972); *Sea Change* for large orchestra and four-channel tape (1979); and a Cello Concerto (1983-85).

Ivey has used electronic tape especially in combination with voice and instruments. Among her works in this medium are *Terminus* (Emerson) for mezzo-soprano (1970); *Three Night Songs* for soprano and five instruments (1971); *Here Hung the Sky* (Carolyn Kizer) for mezzo-soprano, seven winds, three percussion, and piano (1973); *Aldebaran* for viola (1973); *Music for Viola and Tape* (1974); *Testament of Eve* for mezzo-soprano and orchestra to texts by the composer (1976); *Prospero* for bass voice, horn, and percussion (1978); and *Ariel in Flight* for violin (1983).

Other vocal music without tape includes *Woman's Love* (1962), a song cycle to poems by Sara Teasdale; *Tribute: Martin Luther King* for baritone and orchestra (1969); *Two Songs* for high voice, flute, and piano (1977); *Solstice* for soprano, flute/piccolo, percussion, and piano (1977); *Crossing Brooklyn Bridge* (Whitman) for baritone and piano (1979); *Notes Towards Time* (three songs) for mezzo-soprano, flute/alto flute, and harp (1984); and *My Heart is Like a Singing Bird* (Christina Rossetti) for female voices and flute (1994).

Among her instrumental music are a *Scherzo* for wind septet (1953); a String Quartet (1960); Suite for cello and piano (1960); Sonatina for unaccompanied clarinet (1963); *Six Inventions* for two violins (1959); *Ode* for violin and piano (1965); *Music for Viola and Piano* (1974); and *Triton's Horn* for tenor saxophone and piano (1982). She has also written several works for piano, including *Theme and Variations* (1952), *Prelude and Passacaglia* (1955), Sonata (1957), and *Skaniadaryo* (with tape) (1973).

Ivey's activities in the field of electronic music have led to the creation of a handful of tape commissions: *Enter Three Witches* (*Macbeth*) (1964); *Montage V: How to Play Pinball,* a film score (1965); *Continuous Form* (1967); *Cortege: for Charles* (1969); and *Theater Piece* (1970).

In 1982 she completed an opera, *The Birthmark,* based on a tale by Nathaniel Hawthorne.

J

JACOBI, FREDERICK
b. San Francisco, California, 4 May 1891
d. New York, New York, 24 October 1952

Jacobi was a pupil of Rubin Goldmark in New York and studied with Bloch and Paolo Gallico. Later in Berlin at the Hochschule, he joined the composition class of Paul Juon. On his return to the United States in 1913, Jacobi was appointed assistant conductor at the Metropolitan Opera in New York, a post he held for four years. After a number of teaching positions in New York, he joined the faculty of the Graduate School of Juilliard in 1936, retiring in 1950. His pupils there included Alexei Haieff, Robert Starer, and Robert Ward. In 1939 he taught for a year at Mills College, Oakland, California.

Although Jacobi was recognized as one of the leading Jewish composers in the United States, he first became known for works based on the music of the American Indians. In the early 1920's he went to live with the Pueblo Indians in Arizona and New Mexico, carefully noting their melodies. This research produced two significant works, *String Quartet on Indian Themes* (1924) and *Indian Dances* for orchestra (1927–28). The Quartet was heard at the I.S.C.M. Festival in Zurich in 1926. He composed two other string quartets (1933, 1945). His last work, *Yeibichai* for orchestra, is a set of variations on a Navajo theme (1949).

Jacobi had already achieved some success with a symphonic poem, *The Pied Piper* (1915), which was widely performed throughout the United States. *California Suite* of 1917 was once equally popular. He also composed two symphonies: No. 1 in C, *Assyrian* (1922) and No. 2 (1947); *Night Piece* for flute and small orchestra (1926); *Three Psalms* for cello and orchestra (1932); concertos for cello (1932), piano (1935), and violin (1937); three works for piano and orchestra: *Ave*

Frederick Jacobi.
Courtesy The Juilliard School.

Rota (*Hail to the Wheel*) (1939), Concertino (1940), and *Ballade Concertante*; *Rhapsody* for harp and strings (1940); and *Nocturne and Dance* for flute and orchestra (1941). Also for orchestra are *The Eve of St. Agnes* (1919), *Ode* (1941), *Music Hall Overture* (1941), and *Two Pieces in Sabbath Mood* (1946).

Jacobi's major works are the opera *The Prodigal Son* (1943–44); *Sabbath Evening Service* for baritone and chorus (1930–31), commissioned by Temple Emanu-El, New York; *Two Assyrian Prayers* for high voice and orchestra (1923); *The Poet in the Desert* for baritone, chorus, and orchestra (1925); *Sadia* for men's voices (1942); *Ahavas Olom* for tenor, chorus, and organ (1945); and *Friday Evening Service* (1952).

Jacobi's most important chamber music composition is the Piano Quintet, *Hagiographa* (1938), based on the Old Testament stories of Job, Ruth, and Joshua. Other instrumental works include *Three Preludes* for violin and piano (1921); three string quartets (1924, 1933, 1945); a *Scherzo* for wind quintet (1936); *Fantasy* for viola and piano (1941); *Ballade* for violin and piano (1942); *Meditation* for trombone and piano (1947); and Cello Sonata (1950). He also composed many solo pieces for piano and organ.

JAMES, DOROTHY

b. Chicago, Illinois, 1 December 1901
d. St Petersburg, Florida, 1 December 1982

Dorothy James studied with Adolph Weidig and Louis Gruenberg at the Chicago Musical College and at the American Conservatory, Chicago. She was also a pupil of Ernst Krenek and Howard Hanson. From 1929

Dorothy James.
Courtesy Eastern Michigan University Archives, Ypsilanti, Michigan.

to 1969 she taught at Eastern Michigan University, Ypsilanti.

For orchestra James wrote *Three Symphonic Fragments* (1931); *Three Pastorales* (1932); *Ellyptic Poem* (1937); Divertimento for piano and small orchestra (1937); *Elegy for the Lately Dead* (1938); and a Suite for small orchestra (1940).

Choral and vocal works include *Four Preludes from the Chinese* for contralto and piano quintet (1924); *Tears* for chorus and orchestra (1930); a cantata, *The Jumblies* (Edward Lear), for children's chorus and orchestra (1934); *Paul Bunyan* for baritone, female chorus, and orchestra (1937); *Niobe* for female voices and chamber orchestra (1941); *The Golden Years* for chorus and orchestra (1953); *Nativity Hymn* for chorus (1957); *Mutability* for women's voices and chamber orchestra (1967); and *Sonnets after Michaelangelo* for mezzo-soprano, baritone, horn, and piano (1967).

Among her instrumental music are a Suite for string quartet (1926); *Rhapsody* for piano trio (1930); a String Quintet in one movement (1932); *Three Pastorales* for clarinet, strings, and celesta (1933); *Recitative and Aria* for string quintet (1943); *Morning Music* for flute and piano (1967); *Motif* for oboe and organ (1970); and *Patterns* for harp (1977).

An opera in three acts, *Paola and Francesca*, was completed in 1932.

JAMES, PHILIP (FREDERICK WRIGHT)

b. Jersey City, New Jersey, 17 May 1890
d. Southampton, New York, 1 November 1975

Among his teachers in the United States, James numbered Elliott Schenck, Rosario Scalero, Homer Norris, and Rubin Goldmark. In 1909 he went to France to study with Joseph Bonnet and Alexandre Guilmant and in London with Sir Frederick Bridge. James began his activities as a conductor after serving in the U. S. Army during the First World War. He directed several orchestras before founding in 1922 the New Jersey Symphony Orchestra, which he conducted for seven years. From 1929 to 1936 he was conductor of the Bamberger Little Orchestra. He was also guest conductor with most of the leading orchestras in America. In 1923 he was appointed professor at New York University, becoming chairman of the department of music in 1934; he retired in 1955. He also taught at Columbia University (1931–38).

Of James's large output of orchestral music, the earliest extant items are a Suite for chamber orchestra (1924) and *Overture in Olden Style on French Noels*, composed in 1926. In the same year he wrote a *Chamber Symphony* and the first of his three *Bret Harte Overtures*; the other two date from 1933 and 1935. *A Sea*

Philip James.
Courtesy New York University Archives.

Symphony for baritone and orchestra was completed in 1928, but not performed until 1960. A symphonic poem, *Song of the Night,* written in 1930, won first prize in a contest sponsored by the New York Women's Symphony in 1938. In 1932 he was awarded a prize of $5,000 offered by NBC radio for a satirical suite entitled *Station WG2BX,* portraying the chaotic activities of a radio station.

Other orchestral pieces of this period are Suite No. 1 for strings (1933), a *Welsh Rhapsody: Gwalia* (1936), *Brennan on the Moor* (1939), and a Sinfonietta (1939). Symphony No. 1, composed in 1943, was given its premiere in Vienna in 1952. There followed a Second Suite for strings (1946); two pieces for narrator and orchestra, *Miniver Cheevy* and *Richard Cory* (1947); a symphonic poem, *Chaumont* (1948); and *Overture to a Greek Play* (1952). Symphony no. 2 in one movement was completed in 1946.

James wrote much choral music. In 1917 he composed the cantata *Spring in Vienna* for female chorus and orchestra. A Christmas cantata *The Nightingale of Bethlehem* for soloists, chorus, and orchestra, dates from 1920. *The Light of God* (1920) for choir and orchestra was performed in 1928. A setting of *Stabat Mater Speciosa* was completed in 1921 but not heard until 1930. Another work for female voices and orchestra with contralto solo, *The Nun,* was completed in 1922

and premiered in New York in 1939. In 1922 he also wrote *Song of the Future* for unaccompanied double chorus. *The Victory Riders* for baritone and orchestra was completed in 1925. In 1932 James set Vachel Lindsay's poem "General William Booth Enters Heaven" for tenor solo, male voices, trumpet, trombone, percussion, and piano, a combination of voices and instruments similar to that of the version composed by Charles Ives in 1914.

Further choral pieces are the cantata *The Triumph of Israel* (1933) and *The World of Tomorrow* (1938), both for chorus and orchestra; *Founded for Freedom* (1940, rev. 1953) for soloists, chorus, brass, and percussion; and a cantata, *To Cecilia* on a text by W. H. Auden for soprano, chorus, and chamber orchestra (1966).

Among James's church music are a *Magnificat* (1910); a *Te Deum in C* (1913); *By the Waters of Babylon* (Psalm 137) (1920); *Missa Imaginum* (*Mass of the Pictures*) for chorus and orchestra (1929); settings of Psalm 150 (1940, rev. 1956) and Psalm 117 (1944); and *Mass in Honor of St. Mark* (1958).

James' instrumental music includes a String Quartet (*The Venetian*) (1924, rev. 1939); a Suite for woodwind quintet (1936); a Piano Quartet (1937, rev. 1948); and three important pieces for organ: a Sonata (1929), a Suite (1949), and *Variations on a Theme of Schubert* (1969).

For the stage James produced *Judith,* a ballet with dramatic readings based on the biblical story, performed in 1927. He also wrote incidental music for Goethe's *Iphigenia in Tauris* (1937) and *Arms of Venus* (1937).

JANSSEN, WERNER
b. New York, New York, 1 June 1899
d. Stony Brook, New York, 19 September 1990

Janssen received his education at Dartmouth College, Hanover, New Hampshire (1918–21). He studied conducting under Felix Weingartner in Basle (1920–21) and Hermann Scherchen in Strasbourg (1921–25). Despite parental opposition, he devoted himself to music after graduation, playing the piano and writing popular songs to earn a living. Later he studied at the New England Conservatory in Boston with George Chadwick and Frederick S. Converse. In 1930 he won the Prix de Rome, which enabled him to receive tuition from Ottorino Respighi. In 1934 he was awarded an honorary doctorate in music from Dartmouth, and made his conducting debut with the New York Philharmonic Orchestra.

Most of Janssen's compositions were written in the 1930s. For orchestra he composed *New Year's Eve in New York* (1928), *Louisiana Suite* (1932), *Fantasy on American Popular Melodies* (1932), *Dixie Fugue* (1932), and a *Foster Suite* (1937).

In the field of chamber music he produced *Obsequies of a Saxophone* for six instruments and snare drum (1930), *Kaleidoscope* and *Fantasy* for string quartet (1932), and two string quartets (1934, 1935). The Harvard Musical Association commissioned *Quintet for 10 (ten) instruments* in 1965.

In 1934 at Toscanini's request, Janssen became the first native New Yorker to conduct the New York Philharmonic Orchestra. He turned to conducting with such success that Sibelius declared him to be greatest interpreter of his music. He conducted most of the leading orchestras in North and South America and Europe. In Los Angeles he founded his own orchestra, which performed widely and made many recordings (1940–52).

In Hollywood Janssen worked as a film composer and conductor. Among his many scores are *The General Died at Dawn* (1936); *Blockade* (1938); *Lights Out Over Europe* (1938); *Winter Carnival* (1939); *Strictly Honorable* (1939); *Eternally Yours* (1939); *The House Across the Bay* (1940); *Guest in the House* (1944); *The Southerner* (1945); *Captain Kidd* (1945); *A Night in Casablanca* (1946); *Ruthless* (1948); *Soil* (1956); *Robin Hood* (1964); and *Uncle Vanya* (1965).

JOHNSON, HUNTER

b. Benson, North Carolina, 14 April 1906
d. Benson, North Carolina, 27 August 1998

Johnson studied at the University of North Carolina (1924–26) and the Eastman School, Rochester, New York (1927–29), where he was a pupil of Bernard Rogers. He also studied with Casella in Rome (1933). He was awarded two Guggenheim Fellowships (1941, 1954). From 1929 to 1933 he was head of composition at the University of Michigan. On a Prix de Rome scholarship he worked in Europe from 1933 to 1935. After teaching at the University of Manitoba (1944–47), Cornell University (1948–53), and the University of Illinois (1959–65), he moved to the University of Texas in 1966. He retired in 1971.

Johnson's best known work is the ballet *Letter to the World*, produced by Martha Graham in 1940. Two further ballets for Martha Graham are *Deaths and Entrances* (1943) and *The Scarlet Letter* (1975). An earlier ballet score *In Time of Armament* dates from 1939. For orchestra he has composed *Prelude* (1930); a Symphony (1931); a Piano Concerto (1935); *Elegy* for clarinet and strings (1936); *For an Unknown Soldier* for flute and strings (1938); Concerto for Orchestra (1944); *Music for Strings* (1948); *North State* (1963); and *Past the Evening Sun* (1964).

Johnson's instrumental music includes a Piano Sonata (1934, rev. 1936, 1947–48); *Elegy for Hart Crane* (Clarinet Quintet; 1936); a Violin Sonatina (1937); Serenade for flute, clarinet, and piano (1937); and a Trio for flute, oboe, and piano (1954).

JOHNSON, LOCKREM

b. Davenport, Iowa, 15 March 1924
d. Seattle, Washington, 5 March 1977

Johnson studied at the Cornish School of Music, Seattle (1931–38) and the University of Washington (1938–42), where he was a pupil of George Frederick McKay. After war service he returned to teach at the University of Washington (1947–49). At the same time he was music director of the Eleanor King Dance Company (1947–50) and pianist with the Seattle Symphony Orchestra (1948–51). He was awarded a Guggenheim Fellowship in 1952.

In 1951 he moved to New York to enter the music publishing business, first with Mercury Music (1951–54), then C. F. Peters (1954–58), becoming President of Dow Publishers in 1957. In 1962 he returned to Seattle as head of the music department at the Cornish School (1962–69), after which he taught privately. In 1970 he founded Puget Music Publishing to issue the works of American composers living in the North West.

For the stage Johnson composed a chamber opera, *A Letter to Emily* (1951), based on the life of Emily Dickinson. After the premiere in New York in 1955 it received over 50 performances. He also wrote a ballet, *She* (1948, rev. 1950).

His three orchestral works are *Lyric Prelude* (1948, rev. 1949), *Chaconne* for string quartet and string orchestra (1949), and a Symphony (1966). Among his instrumental pieces are three violin sonatas (1942, 1948 rev. 1949, 1953), two cello sonatas (1949, 1953), a Guitar Sonata (1947), and a Trumpet Sonatina (1950). For piano he composed three sonatas (1947, rev. 1983; 1949; 1954) and *Twenty Preludes* (1950).

Johnson wrote much vocal music, including *Two Songs to a Child* (1948); a cycle, *Songs in the Wind* (1949); *Four Songs*, op. 44 (1950–57); and *Songs on Leaving Winter* for low voice and piano (1951). His choral works are a Christmas cantata, *Suite of Noels* (1940) and *Lament and Mourning Dance* for female voices and chamber orchestra (1953).

JOHNSTON, BEN(JAMIN) BURWELL

b. Macon, Georgia, 15 March 1926

Johnston studied at the College of William and Mary, Williamsburg, Virginia (A.B., 1949) and at the Cincinnati Conservatory of Music (M.Mus., 1950). After a year at the University of California, Los Angeles, he attended Mills College, Oakland, California (1951–52),

Ben Johnston.
Photo: Barringer Studio, courtesy the composer.

where he was a pupil of Darius Milhaud. On a Guggenheim Fellowship he studied at the Columbia-Princeton Electronic Music Center in 1959 with Otto Luening and Vladimir Ussachevsky. Among his other teachers were John Powell (piano) (1940–43), Harry Partch (microtonal music, 1950–51), and John Cage (composition, 1959–60). From 1946 to 1948 Johnston was a dance band pianist. From 1951 he taught at the University of Illinois, Urbana, becoming professor there in 1967; he retired in 1983.

Johnston's music periodically makes use of microtonal tunings and just intonation, at times combined with serialism. These features are particularly evident in his chamber music, especially in his ten string quartets (1959, 1964, 1966, 1973, 1979, 1980, 1985, 1986, 1988, 1995). Other instrumental pieces include Concerto for brass ensemble and timpani (1951); *Dirge* for percussion ensemble (1952); Septet (1956–58); *Diversion for Four* (1959); Sonata for two violins and cello (1960); *Knocking Piece I* for two percussionists and piano (1962); *Duo* for flute and double bass (1963); *Lament* for flute, trumpet, trombone, viola, cello, and double bass (1966); *One Man* for trombone and percussion (1967); *Duo* for two violins (1978); *Diversion* for 11 instruments (1979); *Twelve Partials* for flute and microtonal tape (1980); Trio for clarinet, violin, and cello (1981); *Toccata* for solo cello (1984); *Variations on an Old French Hymn* for solo clarinet (1985); *The Demon Lover's Double* for trumpet and microtonal piano (1985); *Ponder Nothing* for clarinet or alto saxophone (1989); Sextet (1990); *Pursuit* for bassoon and tuba (1992); *Sleeping and Waking* for percussion ensemble (1994); *Alap* for double bass (1996); *Nightreach*

for saxophone quartet (1998–99); *O Waly Waly Variations* for saxophone quartet (1998–99); and Octet (1999–2000).

For piano Johnston has written *Etude* (1949), *Satires* (1953), *Celebration* (1953), *Portrait* (1953), *Variations* (1954), *Aubade* (1959), *Knocking Piece* (1962), and two works for microtonal piano, *Sonata/Grindlemusic* (1964) and Suite (1977).

Johnston's vocal music includes *Three Chinese Lyrics* for soprano and two violins (1955); *Night* (Robinson Jeffers) for baritone, women's voices, and strings (1955); *Five Fragments* (Thoreau) for mezzo-soprano, oboe, cello, and bassoon (1960); *A Sea Dirge* (Shakespeare) for mezzo-soprano, flute, oboe, and violin (1962); *In Memory* for soprano, strings, percussion, and tape (1975); *Three Songs of Innocence* (Blake) for soprano and chamber ensemble (1978); *Two Sonnets of Shakespeare* for counter-tenor, bass-baritone, and chamber ensemble (1978); *Calamity Jane to Her Daughter* for soprano, violin, and synthesized drumset (1990); *Ma Mie Qui Danse* for soprano and microtonal piano (1990); *A Man and a Woman Set Near Each Other* for baritone, clarinet, and horn (1993); *Quietness* for speaker/baritone and string quartet (1996); *Invocation* for soprano and strings (1997); and *The Tavern* for voice and microtonal guitar (1999).

Among Johnston's choral works are *Of Vanity* for chorus and piano (1964); *Prayer* for chorus (1966); *Ci Git Satie* for chorus, double bass, and drums (1967), composed for the Swingle Singers; Mass for chorus, eight trombones, and percussion (1972); *Twelve Psalms* for chorus (1977); a piece for the New Swingle Singers, *Sonnets of Desolation* (Gerard Manley Hopkins)

(1980); *On Love* for chorus (1985); *Journeys* for alto, chorus, and orchestra (1986); and *Mantram and Raga* (1993) and *Secret* (1994), both for chorus.

For the stage Johnston has composed a dance opera, *Gertrude, or Would She Be Pleased to Receive It?* for solo voices, chorus, and chamber ensemble (1965), and a chamber opera, *Carmilla* (1970), both to texts by Wilford Leach; and four dance scores: *St. Joan* (1955), *Of Burden and of Mercy* (1957) and *Gambit* (1959), choreographed by Merce Cunningham, and *Relationships* for two musicians and two dancers (1984). He also wrote five *Do-it-yourself Pieces* (1969–81), indeterminate theater pieces.

Johnston has written only a few orchestral works: *Passacaglia and Epilogue* (*St. Joan*) (1955–60); *Quintet for Groups* (1966), premiered by the St. Louis Symphony Orchestra in 1967; *Diversion* for eleven players (1979); a Symphony in A (1988); and a *Chamber Symphony* (1990). He also composed a pair of pieces for jazz band, *Ivesberg Revisited* and *Newcastle Troppo* (1960).

His electronic music includes *Knocking Piece Collage* (1969); *Kindergartenlieder* (1969); *Strata* (1978); a film score, *Museum Piece* (1968–69); and an environment, *Auto Mobile* (1968–69).

JONES, CHARLES W.

b. Tamworth, Ontario, Canada, 21 June 1910
d. New York, 6 June 1997

From 1928 Jones made his home in the United States. He studied violin at the Institute of Musical Art in New York (1928–32); at the Juilliard School he was a composition pupil of Bernard Wagenaar. After five years on the faculty of Mills College, Oakland, California (1939–44), he taught at the Music Academy of the West, Santa Barbara, California (1949–54), the Juilliard School (1954–73), and the Mannes School, New York from 1972. He also taught at the Aspen Music School for many summers after 1951.

Jones composed four symphonies: no. 1 (1939), no. 2 (1957), no. 3 (1962), and no. 4 (1965). His other orchestral works include *Galop* (1940); *Overture* (1942); *Five Melodies* (1945); *Cassation* (1945); *Hymn* (1949); *Little Symphony for the New Year* (1953); Concerto for four violins and orchestra (1963); and *Allegory* (1970).

For chamber orchestra he wrote a Suite (1937); *Suite for Strings* (1937); *Pastorale* (1940); *Cowboy Song* for oboe and strings (1941); *Introduction and Rondo* for strings (1957); and *Suite after a Notebook of 1762* (1957).

Jones's major instrumental works are ten string quartets (1936, 1944, 1951, 1954, 1961, 1970, 1978, 1984, 1988, 1994). For his own instrument, the violin, he composed several works with piano: a Sonatina (1942), Suite (1945), *Duo* (1947), Sonata (1958), *In Nomine* (1972), and *Ballade* (1986). For solo violin there is a Sonatina (1938) and *Chorale Prelude* (1958). Other string pieces are *Threnody* for viola solo (1947); *Duo* for violin and viola (1956); *Music for Two Violinists* (1966); a String Trio (1968); and *Triptychon I* for violin, viola, and piano (1975) and *II* for violin and piano (1981).

Jones's remaining chamber works include *Lyric Waltz Suite* for wind quartet (1948); *Sonata a Tre* for piano trio (1952); *Sonata Piccola* for piccolo and harpsichord (1961); a Sonata for oboe and harpsichord (1965); *Prelude and Fugue* for viola and piano (1972); Serenade for flute, violin, cello, and harpsichord (1973); Piano Trio (1982); *Meditation* for bass clarinet and piano (1982); *Capriccio* for cello and piano (1983); and *Serena* for 9 instruments (1986).

A ballet, *Down With Drink,* performed in 1943, is scored for the unusual combination of female voices, piano, and percussion. A setting of Milton's *Ode on the Morning of Christ's Nativity* for five-part chorus dates from 1953.

Jones's vocal music includes three settings of William Langland: an oratorio, *Piers the Plowman* for tenor, chorus, and orchestra (1963); *I am a Mynstral* for tenor, violin, harpsichord, piano, and percussion (1967); and *Anima,* a song-cycle for voice, viola and piano (1978). He wrote four settings of Alexander Pope: *Three Songs* (1952–53); *Masque,* to a text taken from "Rape of the Lock" for speaker and 12 players (1968); *A Winter Piece* for countertenor, cello, and harpsichord (1980); and *Four Scenes* for voice and piano (1980). Other music for voices includes *The Seasons,* a cantata for speaker, soprano, baritone, and chamber ensemble (1959); *The Fond Observer,* a cycle for voice and piano to words by Henry James (1979); and *Poemata* for voice, violin, and cello (1987).

Among Jones's many piano solos are *Three Pieces* (1943); *Album for Pianists* (1944); *Seven Holidays* (for children; 1945); two sonatas (1946, 1950); *Toccata* (1955); *Ballade* (1961); *Psalm* (1976); *A Book of Hours* (1979); a Sonata for two pianos (1947); and a Sonata for piano (four hands; 1983).

JOSTEN, WERNER (ERICH)

b. Elberfeld, Germany, 12 June 1885 (not 1888)
d. New York, New York, 6 February 1963

Josten studied in Munich and Paris and with Emile Jaques-Dalcroze in Geneva. In 1918 he was appointed assistant conductor of the Munich Opera. He went to the United States in 1920 and became a naturalized citizen in 1933. From 1923 to 1949 he was professor of

Werner Josten.
Courtesy Smith College Archives.

music at Smith College, Northampton, Massachusetts.

Josten made his name with the symphonic poem *Jungle,* composed in 1928, which was later made into a ballet entitled *Forêt Exotique,* based on the paintings of Henri Rousseau. It has an affinity with Stravinsky in its use of violent, primitive rhythms. He wrote three other ballets: *Batouala* (1931), *Joseph and His Brethren* (1932), and *Endymion* (1933).

Josten's two symphonies, the first for strings, were composed in 1935 and 1936. His *Concerto Sacro,* in two parts (Part I, 1927; Part II, 1929), was inspired by Grunewald's paintings on the altar at Isenheim. This famous triptych also forms the basis of Hindemith's *Symphony: Mathis der Maler.* Also for orchestra are *Serenade* (1934) and *Rhapsody* for violin and orchestra (1959).

Josten's vocal music includes *Hymnus to the Quene of Paradys* for contralto solo, women's chorus, strings, and organ (1921); *Ode to St. Cecilia's Day* for soloists, chorus, and orchestra (1925); and *Crucifixion* for bass and chorus, composed in 1915.

Josten's most notable instrumental works are a String Quartet in B minor (1934); Sonata for violin and cello (1938); Trio for flute, clarinet, and bassoon (1941); String Trio (1942); Trio for flute, cello, and piano (1943); *Canzona Seria* for flute, oboe, clarinet, and bassoon (1957); and sonatas for piano (1937), cello (1938) and horn (1944). The first of his two violin sonatas in A was performed at the I.S.C.M. Festival in London in 1938; the second was written in 1945.

Josten also made a special study of seventeenth- and eighteenth-century music and was responsible for the first U. S. performances of *Orfeo, The Coronation of Poppea,* and *The Combat of Tancredi and Clorinda* by Monteverdi; *Apollo and Daphne, Julius Caesar, Rodelinda,* and *Serse* by Handel; and *Costanza e Fortezza* by Fux.

K

KANITZ, ERNST (ERNEST)
b. Vienna, Austria, 9 April 1894
d. Menlo Park, California, 7 April 1978

Kanitz studied in Vienna with Richard Heuberger (1912–14) and Franz Schreker (1914–20), From 1922 to 1938 he taught at the Neues Konservatorium in Vienna. He emigrated to the United States in 1938, becoming an American citizen in 1944. Kanitz taught at Winthrop College, Rock Hill, South Carolina (1938–41), and Erskine College, Due West, South Carolina (1941–44). He was professor of music at the University of Southern California, Los Angeles (1945–59) and Marymount College (1960–64).

For orchestra Kanitz composed three symphonies: no. 1, *Sinfonia Breve* (1963), no. 2, *Sinfonia Seria* (1965), and no. 3; *Sinfonia Concertante* for violin, cello, and orchestra (1967); *Heitere Overture* (1918);a Concerto for theremin (1938); *Intermezzo Concertante* for saxophone and orchestra (1948); *Concerto Grosso* (1949); *Concert Piece* for trumpet and orchestra (1951); Concerto for Chamber Orchestra (1957); Bassoon Concerto (1964); *Motion Picture Suite*; and *Ballet Music*.

For the stage Kanitz composed six one-act operas: *Kumana* (1953), *Room 12* (1958), *Royal Auction* (1958), *The Lucky Dollar* (1959), *Perpetual* (1960), and *Visions at Midnight* (1964).

Kanitz's vocal and choral music includes an oratorio, *Das Hohelied* (1921); a cantata, *Zeitmusik* (1931); an oratorio, *Life Song of a Common Man* for soloists, chorus, boys'chorus, and orchestra; *Cantata* for chorus and two pianos (1961); and *Four Songs* for soprano and orchestra.

Among his instrumental music are *Dance Sonata* for flute, clarinet, trumpet, bassoon, and piano (1932); *Quintettino* for piano and wind (1945); Sonata for violin and cello (1947); two violin sonatas (1947, 1951); Divertimento for viola and cello (1949); *Notturno* for flute, violin, and viola (1950); two string quartets (1951); a String Trio (1951); *Sonata Breve* for piano trio (1952); *Sonata California* for alto saxophone and piano (1952); Sonata for solo cello (1956); Viola Sonatina (1958); Suite for brass quintet (1960); and *Little Concerto* for saxophone and piano (1970).

KASTLE, LEONARD (GREGORY)
b. New York, New York, 11 February 1929

Kastle studied composition with George Szell and piano with Paul Wittgenstein. He also attended the Institute of Musical Art, New York (1939–40), the Mannes School of Music, New York (1940–42), and Columbia University (1947–50). He received piano lessons from Paul Wittgenstein (1942–45). At the Curtis Institute, Philadelphia (1944–50) he was a pupil of Isabelle Vengerova (piano) and Rosario Scalero, and Samuel Barber and Gian-Carlo Menotti (composition). Kastle was active as a conductor on Broadway and NBC Television and in 1978 joined the music faculty of the State University of New York, Albany, retiring in 1989.

Kastle's two operas, *The Swing*, in one act (1956) and *Deseret*, in three acts with text by Anne Howard Bailey (1961) were produced on NBC television. A third opera, *The Pariahs*, dates from 1976. Two parts of *The Passion of Mother Ann: A Sacred Festival Play*, an opera trilogy about the Shakers, were performed: *The Calling of Mother Ann* in Albany, N.Y. in 1985 and *The Journey of Mother Ann* in Potsdam, N.Y. in 1987. He also wrote a musical play, *The Birdwatchers* (1980–88), and a one-act children's opera, *Professor Lookalike and the Children* (Albany: 1988).

Among his vocal music are *From a Whitman Reader* for mezzo soprano and orchestra (1954); *Whispers of*

Heavenly Death (Whitman) for chorus (1956); a song cycle, *Acquainted With the Night* (Robert Frost) (1957); *Three Songs from Moby Dick* (Herman Melville) for chorus (1963); *Poontoosuc* (Melville) for baritone and orchestra (1974–75); and a setting of the Mass for chorus, organ, and piano (1977).

Kastle was the soloist in the premiere of his Piano Concerto in Albany in 1981. His instrumental music includes a Piano Sonata (1950), Violin Sonata (1955, rev. 1986), and a Suite for piano (1957).

Kastle also wrote and directed the film *The Honeymoon Killers*, released by Cinerama in 1970. It was successfully re-released in 1992 and shown at the San Francisco Film Festival and in Italy and Finland.

KAY, HERSHY

b. Philadelphia, Pennsylvania, 17 November 1919
d. Danbury, Connecticut, 2 December 1981

Although he studied with Randall Thompson at the Curtis Institute (1936-40), Kay was mostly self-taught. He was best known as an expert orchestrator for the theater and worked in collaboration with George Balanchine, Leonard Bernstein (*On the Town*, 1944; *Candide*, 1954; *Mass*, 1971; *1600 Pennsylvania Avenue*, 1976), and Marc Blitzstein. He also orchestrated the musicals *A Chorus Line* (1975), *Evita* (1979), and *Barnum* (1980).

Kay's own ballet scores, often based on the music of other composers, include *The Thief Who Loves a Ghost* (Weber; 1951); *Cakewalk* (Gottschalk; 1951); *Western Symphony* (American folk songs; 1954); *The Concert* (Chopin; 1956); *Stars and Stripes* (Sousa; 1958); *Tarantella* (Gottschalk; 1961); *L'Inconnu* (Poulenc; 1961); *The Clowns* (1968); *Meadowlark* (1969); *Cortege Burlesque* (1969); *Who Cares?* (Gershwin; 1970); *Grand Tour* (Noel Coward; 1971); *Winter's Court* (1972); and *Union Jack* (English popular music; 1975).

For concert band he wrote *Variations on "Joy to the World."*

KAY, ULYSSES (SIMPSON)

b. Tucson, Arizona, 7 January 1917
d. Englewood, New Jersey, 20 May 1995

Kay, a nephew of the jazz musician King Oliver, studied at the University of Arizona (1934–38), the Eastman School of Music, Rochester, New York (1938–41) with Howard Hanson and Bernard Rogers, at Yale University under Paul Hindemith (1941–42), and Columbia University with Otto Luening (1946–49). During World War II he was a bandsman in the U.S. Navy. He was awarded two Prix de Rome scholarships (1949, 1951), a Guggenheim Fellowship (1964–65) and two Rosenwald Fellowships. In 1953 he was appointed music consultant to Broadcast Music Inc. From 1968 to 1988 he was professor of music at the Herbert H. Lehman College of the City University of New York.

Kay withdrew several of his early works, including three orchestral pieces, Sinfonietta (1939), an Oboe Concerto (1940), and a suite, *Evocations* (1944); and *Five Mosaics* for chorus and orchestra (1940). His most important surviving music is for orchestra. These works include *Of New Horizons* (1944); *Suite in Five Movements* (1945); *A Short Overture* (1946); *Brief Elegy* for oboe and strings (1946); *Ancient Saga* for piano and strings (1947); two suites for strings (1947, 1949); *Portrait Suite* (1948); Concerto *for Orchestra* (1948); *Pieta* for English horn and strings (1950); *Sinfonia in E* (1950); and *Six Dances* (*America Dances*) for string orchestra (1954). Kay's Serenade was composed in 1954 for the Louisville Orchestra. This was followed by *Fantasy Variations* (1963), commissioned by the Portland (Maine) Symphony Orchestra; *Reverie and Rondo* (1964); *Umbrian Scene* (1964), recollections of a holiday in Italy in 1950; and *Markings*, a symphonic essay dedicated to the memory of Dag Hammerskjöld (1966).

Later works for orchestra are an unpublished Symphony (1967); *Theater Set* (1968); *Scherzi Musicale*, first performed by the Princeton Chamber Orchestra in February 1969; *Aulos* for flute and chamber orchestra (1971); *Harlem Children's Suite* (1973); *Quintet Concerto* for brass quintet and orchestra (1974); *Southern Harmony* (1975); *The Western Paradise* (with female narrator) (1975); *Chariots* (1979); and *String Triptych* (1987).

Kay was also active in the field of choral music. He composed three cantatas: *Song of Jeremiah* for baritone, chorus, and orchestra (1945, rev. 1947), *Phoebus, Arise* (1959), and *Inscriptions from Whitman* for chorus and orchestra (1963), and *Once There Was a Man* for narrator, chorus, and orchestra (1969). For a cappella choirs are *Triumvirate* for men's voices (1953), *How Stands the Glass Around* (1954), *What's in a Name?* (1954), and *Pentagraph* for female voices (1972). Four further works for voices are *A Choral Triptych* for chorus and strings (1962); *Stephen Crane Set* (1967) for chorus and 13 players; *Parables* for chorus and orchestra (1971), written for Kansas State University; and *Epigrams and Hymn* for chorus and organ (1975). Among Kay's solo vocal works are a cantata, *Song of Ahab* for baritone and orchestra (1950); *Three Pieces After Blake* for mezzo-soprano and small orchestra (1955); *Fugitive Songs* for mezzo-soprano and piano (1950); and *Triptych on Texts of Blake* for soprano and piano trio (1962).

Kay's chamber music includes three string quartets (1953, 1956, 1961); Suite for brass choir (1943); *Suite in B* for oboe and piano (1943); Suite for flute and oboe (1943); Piano Quintet (1949); *Partita in A* for violin and piano (1950); a Brass Quartet (1952); Serenade for four horns (1957); *Facets* for wind quintet and piano (1971); *Five Portraits* for violin and piano (1972); *Tromba* for trumpet and piano (1983); *Five Winds* for wind quintet (1984); and *Guitarra* for guitar (1973/1985); and several pieces for piano solo, including *Ten Essays* (1939), a Sonata (1940), *Four Inventions* (1946), *Two Nocturnes* (1973), and *Two Impromptus* (1986).

To the repertory of the concert band he contributed six items: a *Short Suite* (1949); *Solemn Prelude* (1949); *Trigon* (1961); *Forever Free: A Lincoln Chronicle* (1962); *Concert Sketches* (1965); *Four Silhouettes* (1972); and *Prologue and Parade* (1977).

For the stage Kay composed a ballet, *Danse Calinda* (1941), and five operas: *The Boor* (1955), based on a play by Chekhov; *The Juggler of Our Lady* (1956); *Capitoline Venus*, produced at the University of Illinois in March 1971; *Jubilee*, a three-act opera commissioned and premiered by Opera South in 1976; and *Frederick Douglass* (1980–85), staged in Newark, New Jersey in 1991.

For the screen Kay provided music for several films: *The Quiet One* (1948); *The Lion, Griffin and Unicorn* (1951); *New York, City of Magic* (1958); *Going Home* (1962); *Nosotros* (1962); and *A Thing of Beauty* (1966). His television scores include *F.D.R.: From Third Term to Pearl Harbor* (1958); *Submarine* (1959); *The Fall of China* (1959); *Admiral Byrd* (1960); *The Shape of Things* (1960); *The Three Musketeers* (1960); *The Land* (1962); and *Essay on Death* (1964).

KEATS, DONALD HOWARD
b. 27 May 1929: New York, New York

After studying at the Manhattan School of Music, Keats entered Yale University where he was a pupil of Quincy Porter and Paul Hindemith (Mus., B.A. 1949). At Columbia University (M.A., 1952) he studied with Otto Luening, Douglas Moore, and Henry Cowell. He also specialized in musicology with Alfred Einstein and Leo Schrade at Yale and with Paul Henry Lang at Columbia University. He was awarded his doctorate at the University of Minnesota (1962), where he had been a pupil of Paul Fetler and Dominick Argento. On a Fulbright Fellowship in 1954 Keats went to Hamburg where he worked with Philipp Jarnach. He was also awarded two Guggenheim Fellowships (1964, 1972). From 1957 to 1975 he taught at Antioch College, Yellow Springs, Ohio, moving in 1975 to take up an appointment at the University of Denver; he retired in 1999. He was also a visiting professor at the University of Washington, Seattle (1969–70).

Keats's orchestral works include two symphonies, no. 1 (1955–57) and no. 2, *An Elegiac Symphony* (1960–62); *Concert Piece* (1951); *Elegy* (1959); *Branchings* (1976); and a Piano Concerto (1990). Instrumental pieces constitute a major part of his output. He has written a Clarinet Sonata (1948); a String Trio (1949); Divertimento for winds and strings (1949); three string quartets (1951, 1965, 2001); *Piano Theme and Variations* (1954–55); a Piano Sonata (1960); *Polarities* for violin and piano (1968-70); *Dialogue* for piano and winds (1973); *Diptych* for cello and piano (1973–74); *Musica Instrumentalis* for ten players (1980); and *Revisitations* for piano trio (1992).

For chorus Keats has written *The Naming of Cats* (T. S. Eliot) for vocal quartet and piano (1951); *The Hollow Men* (T. S. Eliot) for chorus and piano (1952); and *anyone lived in a pretty how town* (e.e. cummings) for unaccompanied mixed voices (1965). His solo vocal music includes *A Love Triptych* (W. B. Yeats) for soprano and piano (1973); *Upon the Intimation of Love's Mortality* for soprano and piano (1974); and *Tierras del Alma* (*Poemas de amor*) for soprano, flute, and guitar (1977). A ballet. *The New Work*, dates from 1967.

KECHLEY, GERALD
b. Seattle, Washington, 18 March 1919

Kechley was educated at the University of Washington, Seattle and received private lessons from George McKay and Aaron Copland. He was awarded two Guggenheim Fellowships (1949, 1951). He taught at the University of Michigan (1950–51) and was director of music at Centralia Junior College, Washington (1953–54); in 1955 he became a member of the composition faculty of the University of Washington School of Music, retiring in 1989.

For the stage Kechley has composed two operas, *The Beckoning Fair One* (1954) and *The Golden Lion* (1959). His orchestral music includes two symphonies (1956, 1988); *Eight Variations on an Original Theme* (1947); *Prelude and Allegro* for chamber orchestra (1948); *Suite for a Decade* (1959); *Prologue, Enactment and Epilogue* for violin, oboe, and strings (1972); and *Aria and Scherzo* for violin and orchestra (1999). For wind band he has written a Suite for brass and percussion (1950); *Introduction and Fanfare* (1952); *Antiphony for winds* (1958); *Introduction and Passacaglia* (1960); *Mosaic* for winds (1969); and a Suite *for Concert Band*.

Within Kechley's catalog of instrumental pieces are a Wind Quintet (1941); *Dances in Four Rhythms* for

Gerald Kechley.
Courtesy University of Washington Libraries, MSCUA, Neg. 7611-B.

wind quintet (1941); *Rhapsody* for clarinet, string quartet, and piano (1945); *Two Moods* for oboe and piano (1945); *Music for flute and piano* (1945); *Duo Delicios* for flute and cello (1962); Piano Trio (1964); *Variants* for wind quartet (1978); *Suite Marigaux* for oboe and piano (1979); *March Slightly Incognito* for piano and percussion (1984); Piano Quartet (2001); and Sonatina for flute and piano (2002). Piano solo music includes *Seven Preludes* (1940); *Foggy Morning* (1946); *Six Neuroses* (1949); *Variants II* (1987); *A Quotable Scherzo* (1992); *BEA Variations* (1994); *Celebrity Variations* (2000); Piano Sonata (2001); *Baroquial Suite* (2002); and two works for two pianos, a Sonata (1961) and *Three Dances* (2000).

Among Kechley's choral compositions are *Dwelling of Youth* for chorus and orchestra (or band; 1960); *I Will Lift My Eyes Unto the Hills* for chorus and organ (1960); *Cantata for St. Cecilia's Day* (1962); a dramatic oratorio, *Daedalus and the Monotaur* for soloists, chorus, and orchestra (1962); *For Men Yet Unborn* (1969); *Drop, Slow Tears* for chorus, oboe, strings, and harpsichord (1971); and a setting of Psalm 150 for male voices, organ, and brass (1966). More recent pieces include *Carol of the Birds* for chorus, flute, oboe, and double bass (1977); *Three Love Lyrics* for chorus and three horns (1980); *Invitation* for chorus and English

horn (1987); *Reconciliation* for chorus and piano (1993); and two items for chorus and oboe, *Quiet Sun* and *Silent Snow*, both dating from 2001.

For unaccompanied mixed voices Kechley has written *Sing No Sad Songs* (1946); *O Lord Increase My Faith* (1959); Psalm 121 (1959); *Maker of All the Earth* (1959); *In the Lonely Midnight* (1970); *Thank We Now the Lord of Heaven* (1970); *Pleasure It Is* (1971); *Res Miranda* (1979); *At a Concert of Music* (1982); *The Good Morrow* (1988); and *Now in the Tomb is Laid* (1992). Solo vocal music includes *Fog* for voice and piano (1939); *Will You Not Weep?* for voice, clarinet, and strings (1948); *Carol: I Sing of a Maiden* for voice and violin (1969); and three songs for voice and piano: *Little Elegy* (1989), *Little Flower* (2002), and *Lonely I Wandered* (2002).

KELLER, HOMER T(ODD)
b. Oxnard, California, 17 February 1915
d. Montclair, California, May 12, 1996

Homer studied at the Eastman School of Music, Rochester, New York (1934–38), where he was a pupil of Howard Hanson and Bernard Rogers. On a Fulbright Fellowship he received lessons from Honegger and Nadia Boulanger in Paris (1950–51). He taught at the University of Michigan (1947–54) and the University of Oregon (1958–77).

For orchestra Keller composed three symphonies (1939, 1950, 1956) and a *Chamber Symphony* (1941). His *Serenade* for clarinet and strings (1937) is an unpretentious but useful addition to the repertory of the instrument. Among his other works are an *Overture* (1947), a Piano Concerto (1949), *Sonorities* (1971), and *Little Suite* for violin and orchestra. Instrumental pieces include a Viola Sonata, a Flute Sonata, *Five Pieces* for clarinet and bassoon, and a Brass Quintet. For chorus, brass, and timpani he composed a cantata, *The Raiders*.

KELLEY, EDGAR STILLMAN (EDGAR STILLMAN-KELLEY)
b. Sparta, Wisconsin, 14 April 1857
d. New York, New York, 12 November 1944

Kelley studied in Chicago (1874–76) and in Stuttgart (1876–80). On his return to the United States he became an organist, teacher, and music critic in San Francisco. In 1890 he moved to New York, where he taught at the New York College of Music (1891–92) and was a lecturer in music for the University Extension of New York University (1896–97). For one year, 1901, he was a member of the faculty at Yale University, and then went to Berlin where he taught until 1910. From 1911 to 1934 he taught theory and composition at the Cincinnati Conservatory.

Kelley's operetta, *Puritania*, was successfully premiered in Boston in 1892 and ran for one hundred performances. An earlier operetta, *Pompeiian Picnic* dates from 1887. While in Berlin he wrote two important chamber works, a Piano Quintet (1904) and a String Quartet *in D* (1907).

Most of Kelley's compositions were written during his time in Cincinnati. The cantata, *The Pilgrim's Progress*, completed in 1918, was performed widely throughout America and heard at the Three Choirs Festival in England. This was followed in 1919 by the suite *Alice in Wonderland*, derived from music he had composed for a pantomime performed at the Norfolk (Connecticut) Festival. The orchestral suite *The Pit and the Pendulum* received its premiere at the Cincinnati Festival in 1925.

Kelley's other major compositions are a dramatic version of *Ben Hur* (1899), which was given over two thousand performances; incidental music for *Macbeth* (1885) and *Prometheus Bound* (1891); *Suite on Chinese Themes* (*Aladdin*; 1887–89); *Confluentia* for strings (1913); *New England Symphony* (1913–22); and *Gulliver Symphony* (1914–35). His instrumental music includes a *Theme and Variations* for string quartet (1980) and a Piano Quintet (1898–1901).

In addition to *The Pilgrim's Progress*, he composed several vocal works: a *Wedding Ode* for tenor, male chorus, and orchestra (1882); *O Captain! My Captain!* (Whitman) (1918); *America's Creed* (1919), and *The Sleeper* (Poe), all for chorus and orchestra; and four songs, *Phases of Love* (1988), *A California Idyll, Israfel*, and *Eldorado* (Poe) (1918) for soprano and orchestra.

Kelley was the author of two books, *Chopin the Composer* (1913) and *Musical Instruments* (1925).

KELLY, ROBERT

b. Clarksburg, West Virginia, 26 September 1916

Kelly was a student of violin at the Juilliard School, New York with Samuel Gardner and at the Cincinnati College of Music before entering the Curtis Institute, Philadelphia where he studied composition with Rosario Scalero, receiving his Bachelor's degree. He was later awarded his Master's degree from the Eastman School of Music where he was a composition pupil of Herbert Elwell. During the Second World War he served in the U.S. Army. In 1946 he joined the composition department of the music faculty of the University of Illinois, Urbana; since 1976 he has been professor Emeritus.

Kelly's important orchestral works include Symphony no. 1, *A Miniature Symphony* (1950); Symphony no. 2 (1958); Symphony no. 3, *Emancipation Symphony* (1961), composed for the centenary of the Emancipation Proclamation in 1963; Symphony no. 4, *A Symphony of Rose Sonnets* for soprano, baritone, and orchestra (1993); Symphony no. 5 (*Choral*) for chorus, brass, and percussion (1996); and concertos for violin and cello (1961), violin (1968), cello (1974), viola (1977), and violin and viola (1980). Also for orchestra are *Adirondack Suite* (1941); *Rounds for Strings* (1947); *An American Diptych* (1963); *Colloquy* for chamber orchestra (1965); Concertino for chamber orchestra (1977); *Garden of Peace: A Meditation for Strings* (1979); *A Heavenly Rhapsody* for flute, celesta, percussion, and strings (1988); *Sinfonia Concertante* for chamber orchestra (1997); and *Variations on a Theme of Franz Schubert*.

Kelly's major work is the three-act opera *The White Gods*, commissioned by the University of Illinois Center for Advanced Study and completed in 1966. The plot concerns the conquest of Mexico seen from the Aztec point of view. Also for the stage he has composed the one-act folk opera *Tod's Gal* (1950) and a ballet, *Paiyatuma* (1946).

His chamber music includes four string quartets (1944, 1952, 1963, 1982); a Clarinet Quintet (1956); Piano Quintet (1999); sonatas: two violins (1943), two for viola (1950, 1997), two for violin (1952, 1995), trombone (1952), oboe and harp (1955), and two for cello (1958, 1988); a Suite for solo cello or viola (1955); and a Sonata for two cellos (1998). Other instrumental pieces are *Theme and Variations* for violin, viola, and piano (1947); *Passacaglia and Fugue* for wind quintet (1949); *Introduction and Dialogue* for horn, cello, and piano (1967); *Diacoustics* for piano and percussion (1970); *Three Expressions* for violin and cello (or viola) (1971); *Fluctuations* for organ and percussion (1979); *Shenandoah Variations* for cello ensemble (1981); *Fantasia* for harp, alto flute, oboe, and string quartet (1984); *Oriental Gardens* for cello and piano (1990); *Variations on Five Moods* for oboe and harp (1991); *Serenades* for saxophone quartet and percussion (1995); *An Irish Fantasy* for viola and harp (1998); and *Memories* for string trio (1999). His last compositions dating from 2000 are three *Chamber Concertos*: no. 1 for viola (or cello), wind quartet and percussion; no. 2 for violin, brass quartet, and percussion; and no. 3 for piano and chamber orchestra.

Five important contributions to the wind band repertory are *Chorale and Fugue* for antiphonal brass choirs and timpani (1951); Concertino for winds and percussion (1953); *Hillbilly Serenade* (1975); *Tubulations*, a concerto for solo tuba, winds, and percussion (1973); and *The Celestial Trumpet: A Trinity* for solo trumpet and symphonic brass ensemble (1982).

Kelly's principal choral works are the cantata *The*

Word of God for soprano, baritone, chorus, brass and strings (1957); *The Sounding of the Seven Trumpets* for narrator, chorus, trumpet and percussion (1958); *The Torment of Job* for men's chorus, brass, piano and percussion (1960); *Walden Pond* (Thoreau) for narrator, soprano, chorus, flute, piano and percussion (1975); *Christmas Poem* for chorus and piano (or organ; 1990); and *Humorous Songs* for soprano (or tenor) and chorus (1999).

For solo voice he has written the cantata *Patterns* (1953), to texts by Amy Lowell, with orchestral accompaniment; *Song Cycle* (1954) to words by Edna St. Vincent Millay; *Rural Songs* for soprano and orchestra (1980); and two songs for soprano and piano, *Night Sky* (1997) and *What Do You See So Far Away?* (1998).

Kelly is the author of a book, *The Evolution of an American Composer*, published in 1998.

KENNAN, KENT WHEELER
b. *Milwaukee, Wisconsin, 18 April 1913*
d. *Austin, Texas, 1 November 2003*

Kennan was educated at the University of Michigan (1930–32) where he was a composition pupil of Hunter Johnson, and at the Eastman School of Music, Rochester, New York (1932–34, 1935–36) where he studied with Howard Hanson and Bernard Rogers. After winning the Prix de Rome in 1936, he spent three years in Italy where he studied briefly with Ildebrando Pizzetti. On his return to the United States in 1939 he taught theory and piano at Kent State University, Ohio. The following year he joined the faculty of the University of Texas, Austin, but his career was interrupted in 1942 when he undertook war service as an army bandmaster. In 1947 he was appointed professor of Theory at Ohio State University, Columbus, moving in 1949 to become professor of music at the University of Texas, Austin; he retired in 1983.

Kennan's best-known work is the short *Night Soliloquy* for flute and strings composed in 1936. His other orchestral pieces are a Symphony (1938); *Promenade* (1938); *Dance Divertimento* (1938); *Air de Ballet* (1939); *For an American Going to War: Lament* (1941); and a Concertino for piano and wind ensemble (1946, rev. 1963). He has also written a *Nocturne* for viola and orchestra (1937), *Il Campo dei Fiori* for trumpet and orchestra (1937), and an *Andante* for oboe and small orchestra (1939).

For chorus and orchestra, Kennan composed a setting of *Blessed Are They That Mourn* (1939). *The Unknown Warrior Speaks* (1944) is scored for male voices.

The important items of his chamber music are *Sea Sonata* for violin and piano (1939); *Scherzo, Aria and Fugato* for oboe and piano (1948); Sonata for trumpet and piano (1956); and three piano works: *Three Preludes* (1939), Sonatina (1945, rev. 1979), and *Two Preludes* (1951).

Kennan is also the author of two widely used text books, *The Technique of Orchestration* (1952; 5th edition, 1997) and *Counterpoint Based on 18th Century Practice* (1959; 4th edition, 1999).

KERNIS, AARON JAY
b. *Philadelphia, Pennsylvania, 15 January 1960*

After attending the San Francisco Conservatory (1977–78), where he was a pupil of John Adams, Kernis studied at the Manhattan School of Music with Charles Wuorinen (1978–81). At Yale University (1981–83) he received composition lessons from Jacob Druckman, Gilbert Amy, Bernard Rands, and Morton Subotnick. He was awarded the Rome Prize (1984–85) and a Guggenheim Fellowship (1985–86).

For orchestra, Kernis has composed *Mirror of Heat and Light* (1985); *Invisible Mosaic III* (1988), inspired by the mosaics at Ravenna; *Symphony in Waves* (1989); *New Era Dances* (1992); a Concerto for English horn, *Colored Field* (1994), written in response to visits to Nazi concentration camps; Symphony no. 2 (1995); *Lament and Prayer* for violin and orchestra (1996); and Symphony no. 3, *Garden of Light* for soloists, chorus, boys' chorus, and orchestra, a Disney commission (1999). A Double Concerto for violin and guitar was completed in 1999. His latest orchestral pieces are a Cello Concerto: *Colored Fields* (2001), written for Truls Mork and the Minnesota Orchestra, which won the Grawemeyer Award; and *Color Wheel*, performed by the Philadelphia Orchestra in 2001. A Toy Piano Concerto was premiered in Singapore in January 2003 by Margaret Leng Tan.

Kernis's instrumental music includes *Meditation in memory of John Lennon* for cello and piano (1981); *Music for Trio: Cycle IV* for flute, cello, and piano (1981); *Passacaglia Variations* for viola and piano (1985); *Invisible Mosaics I* for clarinet, violin, cello, and piano (1986); String Quartet no. 1 *Musica Celestis* (1990); *Harlem River Reveille* for brass quintet (1993); *Still Movement with Hymn* for piano and string quartet (1993); *100 Greatest Dance Hits* for guitar and string quartet (1993); *Invisible Mosaics II* for chamber ensemble (1997); and String Quartet no. 2, *Musica Instrumentalis* written for the Lark Quartet in 1997, which won the Pulitzer Prize in the following year.

Kernis has composed two choral works, *Stein Times Seven* for chorus and piano (1980) and *How God Answers the Soul* for chorus, commissioned by the Cheltenham Festival, England in 1996. His vocal music includes *Cycle III* for soprano, baritone, and chamber ensemble (1981); *Dream of the Morning Sky: Cycle V* for soprano and orchestra (1982); *Morningsongs* for baritone and orchestra (1982–83); *America(n) (Day) Dreams*, settings of poems by May Swenson, for mezzo-soprano and chamber ensemble (1984); *Love Scenes* for soprano and cello (1987); *Songs of Innocents* for high voice and piano (1989); *Brilliant Sky, Infinite Sky* for baritone, viola percussion, and piano (1991); *Simple Songs* for soprano or tenor and orchestra (1991); and *Goblin Market* for narrator and orchestra (1995). Kernis is composing an opera based on the novel *Bel Canto* by Ann Patchett scheduled for production by the Santa Fe Opera in 2006.

KERR, HARRISON
b. Cleveland, Ohio, 13 October 1897
d. Norman, Oklahoma, 13 August 1978

In Cleveland, Kerr was a pupil of James Hotchkiss Rogers and Claus Wolfram; in France at the Fontainebleau Conservatory he was a fellow student of Aaron Copland and Herbert Elwell. There he studied with Nadia Boulanger and received piano lessons from Isadore Philipp; he was also a pupil of Paul Vidal for composition and Albert Wolff for conducting. In 1927 he was appointed director of music at Greenbriar College, Lewisburg, West Virginia. The following year he moved to the Chase School in Brooklyn where he remained as director of music and art until 1935. From 1937 to 1949 he held various positions in music publishing and promotion and as secretary of the American Composers' Alliance. In 1940 he became the first secretary of the American Music Center in New York. Kerr joined the music faculty of the University of Oklahoma as Dean of Fine Arts in 1949, becoming Composer-in-Residence in 1960 and emeritus professor in 1968.

Kerr's very strong self-criticism prevented his becoming a prolific composer, and except for a few songs, he withdrew all his compositions written before 1929. His early works were conservative in idiom, but gradually he adopted a more chromatic language which eventually embraced a use of 12-tone techniques in a Romantic manner.

Kerr's earliest surviving composition of significance is the single-movement Symphony no. 1 in C minor, composed in 1928–29, revised in 1938 and first performed by the Rochester Symphony Orchestra in 1945. A Second Symphony, completed in 1939, was withdrawn, and replaced by another in E minor, written between 1943 and 1945, and performed by the Oklahoma City Symphony Orchestra in 1951. Symphony no. 3 in D minor followed in 1953. A Fourth Symphony

remained unfinished at his death. His other orchestral works are *Movement* for strings (1936); the important Violin Concerto (1950–51, rev. 1956); *Variations on a Ground Bass* (1966); and *Sinfonietta da Camera*, completed in 1968 for the Oklahoma University Chamber Orchestra.

Except for the four-act opera *The Tower of Kel*, composed in 1958, but never staged, *Wink of Eternity* for chorus and orchestra (1937), and *In Cabin'd Ships at Sea* for chorus, organ, and piano (1971), most of Kerr's other music is for chamber ensembles. Kerr's two trios, the first for clarinet, cello, and piano (1936), the second for piano trio (1938), are his most frequently performed works. The first evidence of his use of the 12-tone system is heard in the Second String Quartet of 1937. The Third String Quartet was completed in 1973. The *Dance Sonata* for two pianos and percussion (1938) was written only one year after Bartók's sonata for the same forces, but Kerr was quite unaware of the earlier work. It was intended as a ballet score. He also wrote two piano sonatas (1928, 1943); a Suite for flute and piano (1940–41); *Eight Preludes* for piano (1943–73); *Overture, Arioso and Finale* for cello and piano (1944–51); a Sonata for solo violin (1954); a Sonata for violin and piano (1956); *Quasi Quodlibet* for eight trombones (1974); and *Three Duos* for two flutes (1976), his last completed work.

Among Kerr's vocal music are *Three Songs* with chamber orchestra (1924–28), *Six Songs* to poems by Adelaide Crapsey (1924–28), and *Notations on a Sensitized Plate* for voice, clarinet, string quartet, and piano (1935).

KESSNER, DANIEL (AARON)
b. Los Angeles, California, 3 June 1946

At the University of California, Los Angeles (1964–69), Kessner studied with Henri Lazarof. He has taught at the California State University, Northridge since 1970, becoming a professor in 1980.

Kessner's stage works include a monodrama, *The Tell-Tale Heart* for tenor and chamber orchestra (1975–78); *The Masque of the Red Death*, a theater piece that combines music, dance and light for a dancer and seven instruments (1979); and *Texts for Nothing*, described as a "musical-literary-theatrical stream" for soprano, flute, trombone, viola, and cello (1980–82).

Kessner's orchestral music includes *Strata* (1971); *Mobile* (1973); *Romance: Orchestral Prelude No. 1* (1979); *Raging: Orchestral Prelude No. 2* (1981); a Piano Concerto (1984–86); *Breath* for cello and orchestra (1991); *Lyric Piece* for piano and orchestra (1994); *Icoane Romanesti* (*Images of Romania*) for narrator and orchestra (1996); *Celebrations* for flute and orchestra

Daniel Kessner
Photo: Kim Ramseyer, courtesy the composer.

and tape (1972); a String Quartet (1990); and a Sonata for four timpani (1999).

Kessner's choral music includes *Madrigals* for chorus and organ (1970); *Alea-luia* for chorus (1978); *Tre Solfeggi, per Coro* for chorus (1990); and *On a Mountain, Cantata No. 2*, for soprano and baritone soloists, mixed choir, and organ (2001).

KIM, EARL
b. Dinuba, California, 6 January 1920
d. Cambridge, Massachusetts, 19 November 1998

Kim was born of Korean parents; his first name was really Eul. At the University of California (1939–40) he was a pupil of Arnold Schoenberg. He moved to the University of California, Berkeley in 1940 where he studied with Ernest Bloch before his course was interrupted in the following year by war service in the U.S. Army. On his return there after the war he was taught by Roger Sessions, graduating in 1952. He also won the Prix de Rome. From 1952 to 1967 he was an assistant professor at Princeton University, moving to Harvard University where he taught until 1990. In 1971 he received the Brandeis University Creative Arts Award.

Kim was not a prolific composer, producing only a handful of works. At times using 12-note techniques, his compositions are economical in scale and abstract in character. Most of them employ the voice, both

(1998); and *River of Time* (2001) for orchestra. For the repertory of the wind band, he has contributed several major works: *Wind Sculptures* (1973), *Variations* (1977), *Sky Caves* (1984–85), *Symphonic Mobile II* (1996), and *Balkan Dance* (1999).

Most of his instrumental compositions have been gathered into two categories: *Equali I* for four flutes, string trio, and double bass (1968–69), *II* for piano, celesta, and three percussionists (1970), *III Nebulae* for string trio, two guitars, and harpsichord (1972), *IV* for brass quintet (1977), *V* for six horns (1977–82), and *VI* for marimba ensemble (1978); and *Chamber Concertos*: no. 1 for high voice, recorder, oboe, string quartet, piano, and percussion (1972), no. 2 for marimba and percussion ensemble (1978), no. 3 for piano, alto flute, English horn, bass clarinet, bassoon, and string quintet (1980), no. 4 for wind quartet and string quintet (1989), no. 5 for clarinet, bassoon, horn, and string quintet (1992), no. 6 for flute, English horn, string trio, and piano (1994–45), and no. 7 for brass ensemble (1997). He has also written *Ensembles* for violin, clarinet, and harp (1968); *Intersections* for flute, cello, piano, and tape (1971); *Intercurrence* for harp

Earl Kim.
Courtesy Harvard University Archives.

speaking and singing. One of the earliest, *Letters Found Near a Suicide* (F. Horne), is a song cycle for soprano and piano dating from 1954.

Exercises en Route: Dead Calm, Rattling on, Gooseberries she said, They are far out for soprano, flute, oboe, clarinet, violin, cello, percussion, actors, dancers, and film (1961–71) sets texts by Samuel Beckett. The Irish writer was also the inspiration for *Narratives: Monologues Melodrama 1 Lines Eh Joe Melodrama 2 Duet Earthlight (Romanza)* for actress, female narrator, high soprano, two trumpets, trombone, two violins, two cellos, piano, and television lights (1973–76).

Now and Then: On the Meadow, Thither, Roundelay is a song cycle on words by Chechov for soprano, flute, viola, and harp (1981). Other vocal music includes *When Grief Slumbers* (Apollinaire, Rimbaud), seven songs for soprano, harp, and strings (1983); *Cornet* for narrator and orchestra (1983); *The Seventh Dream* (1986) and *The Eleventh Dream* (1988), both for soprano, baritone, violin, cello, and piano (1986); *Three Poems in French* for soprano and string quartet (1989); *Four Lines From Mallarme* for voice, flute, vibraphone, and percussion (1989); *Some Thoughts on Keats and Coleridge "In Memoriam Roger Sessions"* for chorus (1990); *The 26th Dream* for baritone, chorus, and strings (1991–92); and *Dear Linda* for woman's voice, cello, marimba, and percussion (1992).

Kim composed one work for the stage, a one-act opera, *Footfalls* (1983).

His few instrumental pieces are *Two Bagatelles* for piano (1948–50), *Dialogues* for piano and orchestra (1959), a Violin Concerto, written in 1979 for Itzhak Perlman, *12 Caprices* for solo violin (1980), and *Scenes From Childhood* for brass quintet (1984).

KIMBALL, JACOB JR.
b. Topsfield, Massachusetts, 22 February 1761
d. Topsfield, Massachusetts, 26 February 1826

The son of a blacksmith, Kimball became a drummer boy in the American Revolution. He studied law at Harvard University, graduating in 1780, and was admitted to the bar in Stratford, New Hampshire. He later gave up legal practice to become a musician in his home town.

Kimball published *The Rural Harmony* (1793) and *Village Harmony* (1800), and with Samuel Holyoke was co-editor of *The Essex Harmony* (1800); together they contain all his known compositions. After almost a century and half of neglect, a number of his hymn tunes were reissued under the title *Down East Spirituals* in 1949. These include some fine melodies such as *Bradford, Uxbridge*, and *Swanzey* and the more elabo-

rate settings *Lancaster, Come My Beloved*, and *Hark What News the Angels Bring*.

Kimball taught in singing schools throughout New England, but was discouraged by the lack of interest in his books. He died an impoverished drunkard in the Topsfield almshouse.

KIRCHNER, LEON
b. Brooklyn, New York, 24 January 1919

Kirchner was born of Russian parents. At the age of nine he and his family moved to California. He graduated from the University of California, Berkeley in 1940 and was a composition pupil of Ernest Bloch, Roger Sessions, and Arnold Schoenberg. He taught at Berkeley (1946–47) and the University of Southern California (1950–54), and was Luther Brusie Marchant Professor of Music at Mills College, Oakland, California from 1954 to 1960. In 1961 he succeeded Walter Piston as Walter Bigelow Professor of Music at Harvard University, retiring in 1989. He was Composer-in-Residence at the American Academy in Rome (1973–74).

Kirchner is a fine pianist and gave the first performance of his Piano Concerto no. 1 in 1956. He has played a number of his other piano works in public and has appeared as a soloist in Europe. For 12 years he was conductor at the Marlboro Music Festival in Vermont and has conducted most of the leading orchestras in the United States. As a composer, Kirchner is an admitted Romantic. Although not a serialist, he is a follower of Berg and Schoenberg with, in his earlier works, traces of the influence of Bartók. His music is highly dissonant but powerful in expression.

For orchestra he has written *Piece* for piano and orchestra (1946); a *Sinfonia in two parts* (1950), commissioned by Rodgers and Hammerstein; *Toccata* for strings, winds, and percussion (1956); a Concerto for violin, cello, ten wind instruments, and percussion (1960), commissioned by the Baltimore Chamber Society; a Second Piano Concerto, commissioned in 1963 by the Ford Foundation for Leon Fleisher; *Music for Orchestra*, commissioned in 1967 by the New York Philharmonic Orchestra to celebrate its 125th anniversary; *Music for Flute*, commissioned in 1978 for Paula Robison; *Music* for cello and orchestra (1992), written for Yo-Yo Ma and premiered in Philadelphia in 1995; and *Music for Orchestra II* (1996). Young-Uck Kim gave the first performance of Kirchner's Violin Concerto in Los Angeles in 2002.

Kirchner's earliest extant work is a setting of words by Federico Garcia Lorca, *Dawn* for chorus and orchestra (1943–46). Other choral items are *Words from Wordsworth* (1968) and *Of Things Exactly as They Are* for soprano, baritone, chorus, and orchestra (Boston,

1997). Solo vocal music for soprano and piano includes *Letter* (1943); *The Times Are Nightfall* (Gerard Manley Hopkins; 1943); *Of Obedience* (1950); *The Runner* (Whitman; 1950); and a cycle to words by Emily Dickinson, *The Twilight Stood* (1983). His opera *Lily* (1973–74) is based on Saul Bellow's novel *Henderson, the Rain King.*

Most of Kirchner's remaining compositions are instrumental. Important among these are three string quartets. The First, composed in 1948, won the New York Music Critics' Circle Award in 1949. The Second Quartet (1958) won the Critics' Award for 1959–60. The Third Quartet (1966) makes use of electronic tape; it won the Pulitzer Prize in the following year. Other chamber music includes *Sonata Concertante* in one movement for violin and piano; *Fanfare* for brass trio (1965); *Fanfare* for brass (1985); *Music for 12* (1985); *Illuminations*, a fanfare for the 350th anniversary of Harvard University (1986); *For Solo Cello* (1986); *Two Pieces* for violin (1986–88); *Two Duos* for violin and cello (1988); *Triptych* for violin and cello (1988); and Piano Trio no. 2 (1993). Among his piano solo works are a Sonata (1948), *Little Suite* (1949), *A Moment for Roger* (1978), *Five Pieces* (1984), *Interlude* (1989), and *For Left Hand* (1995).

KOHN, KARL (GEORGE)

b. Vienna, Austria, 1 August 1926

Kohn was brought to the United States in 1939, becoming an American citizen in 1945. He studied at the New York College of Music (1940–44) and Harvard University (B.A., 1950; M.A., 1955), where he was a pupil of Walter Piston, Irving Fine, Randall Thompson, and Edward Ballantine. In 1950 he joined the music faculty at Pomona College and Claremont Graduate School, California where he remained until 1994. He taught at Tanglewood in the summers of 1954, 1955, and 1957. He was awarded a Fulbright Fellowship (1955–56) and a Guggenheim Fellowship (1961–62). In his music he combines serialism with medieval polyphonic devices. Recent works sometimes make use of extracts from specific pieces from the past.

For orchestra Kohn has written a *Sinfonia Concertante* for piano and orchestra (1951); *Overture for Strings* (1953); a suite for children, *Castles and Kings* (1958); *Scenes* (1960); *Concerto Mutabile* for piano and chamber orchestra (1962); *Interludes* (1964); *Episodes* for piano and orchestra (1966); *Centone* (1973); Horn Concerto (1974); *Waldmusik*, a concerto for clarinet (1979); *Time Irretrievable* (1985); *Return*, a symphonic essay for brass, percussion, and strings (1990); *Ode* for strings (1991); *Concert Music* for strings (1993); and *Memory and Hope: Essay* (1997).

Among his pieces for wind band are *Innocent Psaltery* (1976), *Serenade II* (1977), *Wind Chamber* (1981), and *An Amiable Piece* for two pianos, winds, and percussion (1987).

Kohn's principal choral works are *Three Songs* for treble voices (1956); *Three Descants* (Ecclesiastes) for chorus (1957); *Sensus Spei* (Lamentations) for chorus and piano (1961); *Madrigal* for chorus and piano (1966); *Esdra: Anthems and Interludes* for chorus and small orchestra (1970); *Only the Hopeful* for men's voices (1971); *What Heaven Confers* for chorus and vibraphone (1981); *Alleluia (Militant Praise)* for chorus and brass (1982); and *Three Proverbs* for a cappella chorus (2003).

Instrumental music includes a String Trio (1949); Piano Quartet (1952); Wind Quartet (1955); Violin Sonata (1956); *Concert Music* for 12 winds (1956); Quartet for horns (1957); Divertimento for wind quintet (1959); *Capriccios* for harp, cello, flute, clarinet, and piano (1962); *Kaleidoscope* for string quartet (1964); *Encounters I -V* for solo instruments and piano (1965–73); *Introductions and Parodies* for clarinet, bassoon, horn, string quartet, and piano (1967); *Rhapsodies* for percussion (1968); *Impromptus* for eight winds (1969); Trio for horn, violin, and piano (1972); *Paronyms* for flute and piano (1974); *The Prophet Bird* for chamber ensemble (1976); Brass Quintet (1976); *Son of Prophet Bird* for harp (1977); *Paronyms II* for saxophone and piano (1978); *Prophet Bird II* for piano and chamber ensemble (1980); and *Recreations* for two guitars (1980).

Later chamber works are *Capriccios II* for chamber ensemble (1983); *San Gabriel Set* for clarinet, violin, viola, cello, and piano (1984); *Entr'acte* for string quartet (1985); *Senza Sordino* for horn and viola (1985); *Choice Wood, Precious Metals* for flute, trumpet, marimba, and glockenspiel (1986); *Concords* for violin, flute, and guitar (1986); *Colla voce* for viola and guitar (1986); *Before Beethoven* for clarinet, cello, and piano (1989); *Soliloquy* for guitar (1989); *Cassation* for wind quintet (1990); *Ternaries* for flute and piano (1993); *Accords* for two guitar (1993); *Tripartita* for vihuela or guitar (1993); *Set of Three* for flute, viola, cello, marimba, vibraphone, and piano (1993–95); *Reconnaissance* for 11 players (1995); *SAX for 4* for saxophone quartet (1996); *More Reflections* for clarinet and piano (1997); *Capriccio* for violin, alto and soprano saxophones, and piano (1998); *Toccata*, and *Virelais* for accordion, and harp (1998); *Trio 2K* for piano trio (1999); *Violaria* for viola, and piano (2000); and *Night Music I* (2000), and *II* (2001) for six guitars.

Among Kohn's compositions for piano are *Three Rhapsodies* (1960, 1971, 1977); *Recreations* for piano duet (1968); *Adagio and Allegro for Dancing* (1995–96); three pieces for two pianos, *Shadow Play* (1981),

Dream Pieces (1983), and *Number Play* (1999); and one item for piano four-hands, *Again, Again* (2000). For organ Kohn has written a *Prelude* (2000) and *Grand Fantasia* (2002).

KOHS, ELLIS BONOFF
b. Chicago, Illinois, 12 May 1916
d. Los Angeles, California, 17 May 2000

Kohs studied at the San Francisco Conservatory and at the University of Chicago (1933–38) under Carl Bricken. He was a pupil of Bernard Wagenaar at the Juilliard School (1938–39) and studied with Willi Apel, Hugo Leichtentritt, and Walter Piston at Harvard University (1939–41). He taught for one year at the University of Wisconsin before undertaking was service in the U.S. Army and Army Air Force where he was a bandleader. In 1946 he took up a post at the Wesleyan University, Connecticut, moving in 1948 to teach at the College of the Pacific in Stockton, California. In 1950 he was appointed to the music faculty of the University of Southern California where he became professor of theory and composition. He retired in 1985.

Kohs's music possesses a dramatic tension that arises from an emphasis on the importance of counterpoint. In general he maintained classical forms and was first influenced by his teachers, but his later works became more dissonant than those of either Wagenaar or Piston and perhaps owe a little to Hindemith. He used serial techniques in a quasi-tonal context in some compositions.

Kohs's major compositions are two symphonies (1950, 1956), the second with chorus; a Concerto for Orchestra, performed at the San Francisco I.S.C.M. Festival in 1942; and a *Chamber Concerto* for viola and string nonet (1949). He also wrote a *Passacaglia* for organ and string nonet (1946), a Cello Concerto in C (1947), and *Legend* for oboe and strings (1947). His last orchestral piece, a Violin Concerto, was commissioned for the University of Southern California centenary and performed by Eunice Shapiro and the U.S.C. Symphony Orchestra in April 1981.

Among his choral compositions are *The Automatic Pistol* for men's chorus (1943); settings of Psalm 25 (1947) and Psalm 23 (1957–58); *Lord of the Ascendant* for soloists, chorus, dancers, and orchestra, based on *Gilgamesh* (1956); *Three Greek Choruses* for female voices (1957); and *Three Songs from the Navajo* for chorus (1957). Kohs composed a song cycle, *Fatal Interview* to words by Edna St. Vincent Millay (1951); *Epitaphs* for tenor and piano (1959); *Four Orchestral Songs* for low voice; and two pieces for narrator and percussion, *Men* (Gertrude Stein) (1982) and *Subject Cases* (1983).

Kohs's instrumental music includes three string quartets (1940, 1948, 1984); *Night Watch* for flute, horn, and timpani (1943); Sonatina for violin and piano (1948); *Three Chorale Variations on Hebrew Themes* for organ (1952); a Brass Trio (1957); *Studies in Variation* in four parts: *I* for wind quintet, *II* for piano quartet, *III* Piano Sonata no. 2, and *IV* Sonata for solo violin (1962); Suite for cello and piano (1970); sonatas for bassoon (1944), violin (1948), clarinet (1951), and snare drum (1966); *Duo* for violin and cello (1971); Concerto for Percussion Quartet (1979); and a String Trio (1983).

Kohs composed one opera, *Amerika*, on the novel by Kafka, completed in 1969. Also for the stage he wrote *Lohiau and Hiiaka*, a Hawaiian legend for narrators, flute, cello, percussion, and dancers (1987), and incidental music for a production of *Macbeth* at Wesleyan University (1947).

Kohs was the author of three valuable textbooks: *Music Theory* in two volumes (1961), *Musical Form* (1968), and *Musical Composition: Projects in Ways and Means* (1980).

KOLB, BARBARA (ANNE)
b. Hartford, Connecticut, 10 February 1939

Kolb studied clarinet and composition at the Hartt College of Music, Hartford, Connecticut (1957–64), and at Tanglewood during the summers of 1960, 1964, and 1968, where she was a pupil of Lukas Foss and Gunther Schuller. In addition she played in the Hartford Symphony Orchestra (1960–66), and from 1965 to 1969 earned her living as a music copyist in New York. On a Fulbright Fellowship she went to Vienna in 1966. In 1969 she was the first woman to win the Prix de Rome. In 1973 she studied electronic music at Mills College, California. Kolb taught at the Marlboro Festival (1973), Brooklyn College, CUNY (1973–75), the American Academy in Role (1975), and Temple University, Philadelphia (1978). From 1979 to 1982 she was director of the "Music New to New York" concert series and served on the faculty of the Eastman School, Rochester, New York (1984–85). She has held MacDowell Colony Fellowships in 1968, 1969, 1971–72, 1980, 1983, and 1987–89. Currently she is working in Providence, Rhode Island on a Meet the Composer residency.

Kolb's principal works are for chamber ensemble and include *Seguela* (1966); *Crosswinds* for alto saxophone, winds, and percussion (1968); *Trobar Clus* (*Closed Creation*, 1970), *Soundings* for small orchestra and tape (or large orchestra without tape; 1972); *Millefoglie* for ensemble and computer-generated tape (1984–85, rev. 1987); *Yet That Things Go Round* for chamber orchestra (1986–87); *Voyants* for piano and chamber orchestra (1991); and *New York Moonglow* for chamber ensemble, commissioned in 1995 by the Scottish Chamber Orchestra. For full orchestra she has written *Grisaille* (1979); *The Enchanted Loom* (1988-89, rev. 1992), commissioned by the Atlanta Symphony Orchestra; *All in Good Time* (1993); and *Criss Cross*, a percussion concerto for Evelyn Glennie and the Buffalo Philharmonic Orchestra (2001).

Among Kolb's instrumental works are *Rebuttal* for two clarinets (1964); *Figments* for flute and piano (1966, rev. 1969); *Toccata* for harpsichord and tape (1971); *Solitaire* for piano and tape (1971); *Looking for Claudio* for guitar and tape (1974); *Spring River Flowers Moon Night* for two pianos, percussion, and tape (1974–75); *Homage to Keith Jarrett and Gary Burton* for flute and vibraphone (1976, rev. 1977); *Appello* for piano (1976); *Musique pour vernissage* for flute, guitar, violin, and viola (1977); *Related Characters* for E-flat clarinet (or alto saxophone, or viola, or trumpet) and piano (1980); *Three Lullabies* for guitar (1980); *Cavatina* for violin or viola (1983, rev. 1985); and *Time . . . and Again* for oboe, string quartet, and tape (1985). Later instrumental pieces include *Umbrian Colors* for violin and guitar (1986); *Extremes* for flute and cello (1989); *Cloudspin* for organ and tape (or organ and brass; 1991); *Introduction and Allegro* for guitar (1992); *Monticello Trio* for piano trio (1992); *In Memory of David Huntley* for string quartet (1994); *Turnabout* for flute and piano (1994); *Sidebars* for bassoon and piano (1995); and *Web Spinner* (2003).

Kolb's vocal music includes *Chansons bas* (Mallarmé) for voice, harp, and two percussionists (1965); *Three Place Settings* for narrator, clarinet, violin, double bass, and percussion (1968); *Frailties* for tenor and four-channel tape (1971); *Songs Before an Adieu* for soprano, flute (or alto flute), and guitar (1976-79); *Chromatic Fantasy* (Howard Stern) for narrator and chamber ensemble (1979); *Poem* for chorus (1980); *The Point That Divides the Wind* for three solo male voices, organ, and percussion (1982); a jazz song, *The Sundays of My Life* (1982); and *Virgin Mother Creatrix* for chorus (1998). A tape collage for a film by James Herbert on the life of St Francis of Assisi, *Cantico* (1982), was used in 1995 as a dance score.

KORN, PETER JONA
b. Berlin, Germany, 30 March 1922
d. Munich, Germany, 14 January 1998

Korn studied at the Berlin Hochschule für Musik (1932–33) before going to London, where he received composition lessons from Edmund Rubbra (1934–36). At the Jerusalem Conservatory (1936–38) he studied with Stefan Wolpe. After coming to the United States in 1941 he became a pupil of Arnold Schoenberg at the University of California, Los Angeles (1941–42). He was also taught by Ernst Toch and Hanns Eisler at the University of Southern California (1946–47) and studied film composition with Miklós Rózsa and Ingolf Dahl (1946–47). He became an American citizen in 1944. Korn was musical director of the Coronet Theater, Los Angeles (1947–48) and conductor of the New Orchestra of Los Angeles (1948–56). From 1964 to 1965 he was a lecturer at the University of California, Los Angeles, after which he returned to Germany and served as director of the Richard Strauss Conservatory of Music in Munich until he retired in 1987.

For orchestra Korn wrote four symphonies: no. 1 (1940, rev. 1957), no. 2 (1951), no. 3 (1956, rev. 1969), and no. 4, *Ahasver* (1989–90); *Romantic Overture*; *Idyllwild Overture* (1947, rev.1957); a *Tom Paine Overture* (1950); *Rhapsody* for oboe and strings (1951); Horn Concertino (1952); *Overture: In Medias Res* (1953); *Adagietto* for small orchestra (1954); *Variations on a Theme from the Beggar's Opera* (1954–55); Saxophone Concerto (1956, rev. 1982); *Berolina Suite* for small orchestra (1959); *Variations on a German Folksong* for cello and orchestra (1960); Violin Concerto (1964–65); *Semi-Symphony* (1966); Divertimento (1966); *Toccata* (1966); *Exorcism of a Liszt Fragment* (1966–68); Serenade for strings (1968); *Four Pieces* for strings (1970); *Morgenmusik* for trumpet and strings (1973); *Overture* for strings (1976); *Beckmesser Variations* (1977); *Trumpet* Concerto (1979); *Romanza concertante* for oboe and small orchestra (1987); and *Concerto classico* for harpsichord and orchestra (1988).

A three act opera, *Im Fremde Haus*, based on the book *Heidi* by Johanna Spyri, was completed in 1963 and first staged in Saarbrücken in 1978.

Instrumental music includes a Cello Sonata (1949); Oboe Sonata (1949); String Quartet no. 1 (1950); *Passacaglia and Fugue* for eight horns (1952); Horn Sonata (1953); *Aloysia Serenade* for flute, viola, and cello (1953); *Prelude and Scherzo* for brass quintet (1953); *Phantasy* for horn, violin, cello, and piano (1955); Serenade for four horns (1957); Quartet no. 2 (1963); *Quintetto* for flute, clarinet, bassoon, cello, and piano (1964); Wind Quintet (1966); *Eine Kleine Popmusik* (1972); Piano Trio (1975); Wind Octet (1976); *Siesta* for 12 cellos (1976); *Fantasia* for oboe and organ (1981); and *Toccata* for organ (1981).

For a cappella chorus, Korn wrote four works: *The Merry Bachelor* (1951), *Three Scottish Epigraphs* (Burns) (1955), *Three Graces* (1956), and *Three Songs of Autumn* (1964). Other choral pieces are a cantata, *Munich* for solo voices, narrator, chorus, and orchestra (1979) and *Psalm of Courage* for baritone, chorus, and orchestra (1983). He also wrote a cantata, *Eine kleine Stadt* for tenor, harpsichord, and orchestra (1980–81).

KORNGOLD, ERICH WOLFGANG

b. Brno, Austria (now Czech Republic), 29 May 1897

d. Hollywood, California, 29 November 1957

Korngold studied first with his father, Julius, a noted music critic in Austria, before going to Vienna, where he became a pupil of Alexander Zemlinsky and Robert Fuchs. By the age of 12 he had composed much music, including a pantomime, *Der Schneemann*, which was orchestrated by Zemlinsky and performed in Vienna in October 1910, when the composer was only 13 years old. At the time he had already published a Piano Trio in D (1909). In 1911 his overture *Schauspiel* was performed by Nikisch in Leipzig. Weingartner conducted his Sinfonietta, op. 5 with the Vienna Philharmonic Orchestra in 1913; it was heard in Chicago under Frederick Stock the following year.

In 1916 two operas, *Der Ring des Polykrates*, op. 7 and *Violanta*, op. 8, were staged in Munich. Korngold's major opera, *Die Tote Stadt*, op. 12 was produced in Cologne and Hamburg in 1920 and at the Metropolitan Opera House, New York in 1921. Three more operas followed: *Das Wunder der Heliane*, op. 20 (Hamburg, 1927), *Die Kathrin*, op. 28 (Stockholm, 1939), and *Die stumme Serenade*, op. 36 (1946), performed in Dortmund in 1954. In Vienna in 1919 two orchestral works received their premieres: *A Suite: Much Ado About Nothing*, op. 11 and an overture, *Sursum Corda*, op. 13.

In 1929 Korngold worked with the producer Max Reinhardt on several stage productions. After a spell of teaching at the Vienna Academy of Music (1927–34), he went to Hollywood to escape Nazi Europe and to work with Reinhardt again, this time on films. He became an American citizen in 1943.

Korngold was a pioneer composer of film scores before the Second World War, providing music for many classics of the cinema: *A Midsummer Night's Dream* (1935); *Captain Blood* (1935); *Another Dawn* (1936); *Anthony Adverse* (1936); *The Story of Louis Pasteur* (1936); *Give Us This Night* (1936); *The Green Pastures* (1936); *Rose of the Ranch* (1936); *The Prince and the Pauper* (1937); *The Adventures of Robin Hood* (1938); *Juarez* (1939); *The Private Lives of Elizabeth and Essex* (1939); *The Sea Hawk* (1940); *King's Row* (1941); *The Sea Wolf* (1941); *The Constant Nymph* (1942); *Devotion* (1943); *Between Two Worlds* (1944); *Of Human Bondage* (1945); *Deception* (1946); *Escape Me Never* (1946); and *Magic Fire* (1954). For two films, *Anthony Adverse* and *The Adventures of Robin Hood*, Korngold won Academy Awards.

In addition to his film music, Korngold is remembered for a Symphony in F# minor, op. 40 (1950), a Cello Concerto in C, op. 37 (1946), taken from music

Erich Korngold, 1947.
Courtesy Brendan G. Carroll/The Korngold Society.

for the film *Deception*, and an impressive, lyrical Violin Concerto in D, op. 35 (1945), composed for Huberman but first performed by Heifetz in St. Louis in February 1947; the thematic material again came from music originally written for the screen. At the time of his death he was working on a Second Symphony. He also composed a Piano Concerto for the left hand, op. 17 (1923) for Paul Wittgenstein; *Symphonic Serenade* in B for strings, op. 39 (1947); and *Theme and Variations*, op. 42 (1953) and *Straussiana* (1953), both for orchestra.

Korngold's choral works include *Passover Psalm*, op. 30 for soprano, chorus, and orchestra (1941); *Tomorrow When You Have Gone*, op. 33 for soprano, female chorus, and orchestra (1942); and *Prayer* for tenor, chorus, and orchestra (1942).

Most of Korngold's instrumental music was composed before he went to the United States. These works include a Violin Sonata in G, op. 6 (1914); a String Sextet in D, op. 10 (1917); a Piano Quintet in E, op. 15 (1921); and a String Quartet in A, op. 16, performed at the I.S.C.M. Festival in Venice in 1925. String Quartet no. 2 in E-flat, op. 26 (1935) and String Quartet no. 3 in D, op. 34 (1945) were written in Hollywood.

Korngold also composed piano music and several important works for voice, including *Einfache Lieder* (1911–16); *Lieder des Abschieds*, op. 14 (1920); *Drei Gesänge* (1924); a song cycle, *The Eternal*, op. 27 (1935); *Three Shakespeare Songs* (1937); *Songs of the Clown* (Shakespeare), op. 29 (1939); *Five Songs*, op. 38 (1946); and *Sonett für Wien*, op. 41 (1952).

After half a century of neglect, Korngold's music has been revived though modern recordings of his film scores and related orchestral pieces.

KORTE, KARL (RICHARD)
b. Ossining, New York, 23 June 1928

After studying at the Illinois Wesleyan University (1948–49), Korte moved to the Juilliard School, where he was taught by Vincent Persichetti, Peter Mennin, and William Bergsma (B.S., 1952; M.S., 1956). In addition he received composition lessons from Aaron Copland, Otto Luening, and Petrassi. He received a Fulbright Fellowship and two Guggenheim Fellowships (1960, 1970). He taught at Arizona State University (1963–64), State University of New York at Binghampton (1964–70) and at the University of Texas, Austin (1971–96).

For orchestra Korte has written three symphonies: no. 1, no. 2 in one movement (1961), and no. 3 (1968); Concertino for brass, strings, and percussion; *Concertato on a Choral Theme* (1955); *Music for a Young Audience* (1958); *Song and Dance* for double string orchestra; *Southwest* (*Dance Overture*) (1963); and a Concerto for piano and winds (1976). *Metamorphosis* for strings and jazz band was written for Clark Terry in 1976.

His concert band pieces include *Ceremonial Prelude and Passacaglia* (1962); *Nocturne and March* (1962); *Prairie Song* for trumpet and band (1963); *I Think You Would Have Understood* for trumpet, tape, and band (1971); *Fibers* (1977); Concertino for bass trombone, winds, and percussion (1978); and *Texarcana—Variations on a Texan Folk Songs* for wind ensemble (1992).

Korte's choral works include an oratorio, *Pale is this Good Prince* (1973); *Mass for Youth* (*Missa St. Dominick*) for double chorus and chamber orchestra (1963); *Songs of Innocence* (William Blake) for women's voices and piano (1964); *Aspects of Love* for chorus and piano (1968); *May the Sun Bless Us* (Tagore) for men's voices, brass, and percussion (1968); Psalm 23 for chorus and tape (1970); *Libera Me* (1972); *Sappho Says* for mezzo-soprano, female chorus, flute, and piano (1981); *Music for a New Easter* for chorus and brass (or piano; 1982); *Of Time and Season* for solo voices, chorus, piano, and marimba (1982); *Three*

Psalm Settings for chorus (1989); *Four Songs of Experience* for female voices and piano (2001); and *Holy Thursday* for chorus and piano (2001).

For solo voice, Korte has written *Four Blake Songs* for female voice and piano (1961), *Song of Wen I-to* for high voice and piano (1973), *The Whistling Wind* for mezzo-soprano and tape (1982), and *Five New Zealand Songs* for voice and piano (1989).

Among his instrumental pieces are two string quartets (1948, 1969); *Fantasy* for violin and piano (1958); Oboe Quintet (1960); *Introductions* for brass quintet (1962); *Matrix* for wind quintet, saxophone, percussion, and piano (1967); *Facets* for saxophone quartet (1969); *Gestures* for wind ensemble, piano, and percussion (1970); *Remembrances* for flutes and tape (1971); *Symmetries* for saxophone and percussion (1974); a Piano Trio (1977, rev. 1982); Double Concerto for flute, double bass, and tape (1984); *Vochi*, a trio for clarinet, violin, and piano (1984); *Demiola* for bassoon and tape (1984); *Colloquy* for flute and tape (1987); *Evocation and Dance* for trombone and tape (1988); *Extensions* for percussion and tape (1994); *The Freda Variations* for wind quintet (1997); *Wired Dance* for piano and tape (1998); *Viola Dance* for viola and piano (2000); and *Distant Pentachords* for flute and wind chimes (2000).

For tape and slides he has written *Hill Country Birds* (1982); there are two pieces for computer, *Birds of Aotearoa* (1986) and *Meeting the Enemy* (1994–95).

KOUTZEN, BORIS
b. Uman, near Kiev, Ukraine, 1 April 1901
d. Pleasantsville, New York, 10 December 1966

Before emigrating to the United States in 1923, Koutzen studied with Reinhold Glière at the Moscow Conservatoire (1918–22) and was a violinist with the Moscow Symphony Orchestra. In the United States he joined the Philadelphia Orchestra (1922–27) and became head of the violin department of the Philadelphia Conservatory of Music in 1930. He later played in the NBC Symphony Orchestra under Toscanini (1937–45) and taught at Vassar College, Poughkeepsie, New York (1944–66).

Koutzen composed a *Symphonic Movement* for violin and orchestra (1929); a Concerto for five instruments (1934); a *Concert Piece* for cello and strings (1940); a Viola Concerto (1949); a Concertino for piano and strings (1957); and *Concertante* for two flutes and orchestra (1965). His daughter Nadia was the soloist in the premiere of his Violin Concerto with the Philadelphia Orchestra in 1952. His orchestral works include two symphonic poems, *Solitude* (1927) and *Valley Forge* (1931); Symphony in C (1939); an over-

Boris Koutzen.
Courtesy Special Collections, Vassar College Libraries.

ture, *From the American Folklore* (1943); Sinfonietta (1947); *Morning Music* for flute and strings (1950); *Eidolons* (1953); Divertimento (1956); *Fanfare, Prayer and March* (1961); and *Elegiac Rhapsody* (1961).

Koutzen's opera *The Fatal Oath* (1938-54) is based on a story by Balzac. A second opera in one act, *You Never Know,* was composed in 1960. He wrote two chorale works, *An Invocation* for female voices and orchestra (1948) and *Words of Cheer From Zion* for chorus (1962).

Koutzen composed three string quartets (1922, 1936, 1944); two violin sonatas (1928, 1951); a Trio for flute, cello, and harp (1933); *Duo Concertante* for violin and piano (1943); a Piano Trio (1948); a Sonata for two pianos (1944); a Sonata for violin and cello (1952); *Landscape and Dances* for wind quintet (1953); *Poem* for violin and string quartet (1963); and *Pastorale and Dance* for violin and piano (1964).

KRAFT, LEO (ABRAHAM)

b. Brooklyn, New York, 24 July 1922

Kraft was educated at Queens College, New York (1940–45), where he was a pupil of Karol Rathaus. From 1945 to 1947 he studied with Randall Thompson at Princeton University. In 1954 he received a Fulbright Fellowship and went to Paris where he was a pupil of Nadia Boulanger. From 1947 to 1989 he was a member of the department of music at Queens College where he held the rank of professor. In addition he was Distinguished Composer-in-Residence at New York University (1988–92).

Kraft has long been active in organizations that support contemporary music and music in higher education. He served as President of the American Music Center from 1976 to 1978 and has been on the governing bodies of the College Music Society, the League of Composers, International Society for Contemporary Music, the Society for Music Theory and the National Association of Composer U.S.A.

For chamber orchestra Kraft has written six concertos: no. 1 for flute, clarinet, trumpet, and strings (1951), no. 2 for 13 players (1966, rev. 1972), no. 3 for cello, wind quintet, and percussion (1967), no. 4 for piano and 14 instruments (1978), no. 5 for oboe and strings (1986), and no. 6 for clarinet and orchestra (1986); *Larghetto in Memory of Karol Rathaus* for strings and timpani (1954); and *From the Hudson Valley* for flute, harp, and strings (1997). For full orchestra he has composed *Overture in G* (1947); *Variations* (1958); *Three Pieces for Orchestra* (1963); *Music for Orchestra* (1975); *Chamber Symphony* (1980); Symphony in one movement (1985); *A New Ricercare* for strings (1985); *Pacific Bridges* for strings with clarinet obbligato (1989); *Tableaux* for 10 wind instruments and piano (1989); *Symphonic Prelude* (1993); *Chamber Symphony no. 2* (1994); and *Symphonic Prelude* (1998).

Kraft's many instrumental works include four string quartets (1951, 1954, 1966, 1994); Suite for brass (1947); *Short Suite* for flute, clarinet, and bassoon (1951); Sextet for clarinet, string quartet, and piano (1952–53); Cello Sonata (1954); Violin Sonata (1956); Wind Quintet (1956); *Two's Company* for two clarinets (1957); *Partita* no. 2 for violin and viola (1961); *Fantasy* for flute and piano (1963); *Ballad* for clarinet

Leo Kraft.
Photo: Carol Lager, courtesy the composer.

and piano (1963); *Partita* no. 3 for wind quintet (1964); *Trios and Interludes* for flute, viola, and piano (1965); *Dialogues* for flute and tape (1968); *Dualities* for two trumpets (1970); *Pentagram* for alto saxophone (1971); *Line Drawings* for flute and percussion (1972); *Diaphonies* for oboe and piano (1975). *Partita* no. 4 for flute, clarinet, violin, and double bass was commissioned in 1975 by the National Endowment for the Arts. In 1976 to a commission from the Chamber Music Society of Baltimore, he wrote *Dialectica* for flute, clarinet, violin, cello, and tape. Other instrumental items include *Three Pieces* for alto saxophone and piano (1977); *Strata* for eight instruments (1979); *Conductus novus* for four trombones (1979); *Episodes* for clarinet and percussion (1979); *Fantasy* no. 2 for flute and piano (1980); *Partita* no. 5 for flute and guitar (1982); *Interplay* for trumpet and percussion (1983); *Primavera* for flute, oboe, and clarinet (1984); *Inventions and Airs* for clarinet, violin, and piano (1984); *New Songs for Old* for clarinet (1988); *Cloud Studies* for 12 flutes (1989); *Tableaux* for double wind septet (1989); *Cinque Fantasies* for violin and cello (1990); *Six Pieces* for violin and piano (1991); *Green Mountain Notes* for oboe, clarinet, bassoon, horn, violin, and piano (1991); *Cape Cod Sketches* for flute and string trio (1992); *Omaggio* for flute, clarinet, and string trio (1992); *Four Dialogues* for clarinet and piano (1993); *For Two* for alto saxophone and clarinet (1995); *Strata* for nine instruments (1997); *Second Fantasy* for flute and piano (1997); *Five Short Pieces* for wind quartet (1997); *Music for Sunday Afternoon* for flute and clarinet (1997)

and *Inventions and Arias* for clarinet, violin, and piano (1997).

Kraft has composed several pieces for piano: *Scherzo* (1949); *Variations* (1951); Sonata (1956); *Allegro Giocoso* (1957); *Partita* no. 1 (1958); *Statements and Commentaries* (1965); *Easy Animal Pieces* (1968); *Sestina* (1972); *Ten Short Pieces* (1975); *Venetian Reflections* (1989); and *Antiphonies* (1969) for piano duet and tape.

Among his choral and vocal compositions are *Festival Song* for chorus (1951); *Let Me Laugh* for chorus and piano (1951); *A Proverb of Solomon* for chorus and small orchestra (1953); *Thanksgiving* for female voices (1958); *When Israel Came Forth* (Psalm 114) for mixed voices (1961); *Four English Love Songs* for high voice and piano (1961); Psalms 89 and 90 for men's voices (1963–68); *Fyre and Yse* for chorus and tape (1966); *Spring in the Harbor* (1969), a chamber cycle for soprano, flute, cello, and piano (1969); *Eight Choral Songs* to poems by Moses Ibn Ezra (1974); *Four Songs from the Chinese* for soprano, flute, and percussion (1990); *Set Me As a Seal* for chorus, cello, and harp (1993); *October 1864* for high voice and piano (1994); and *cummingsong* for tenor, flute, oboe, violin, viola, and cello (1995).

Kraft is the author of three books: *Gradus: An Integrated Approach to Harmony, Counterpoint and Analysis* (1976, rev. 1987), *A New Approach to Ear Training* (1967), and *A New Approach to Keyboard Harmony* (1978).

KRAFT, WILLIAM
b. Chicago, Illinois, 9 June 1923

Kraft first studied music at San Diego State College and the University of California, Los Angeles before serving in the U.S. forces during World War II where he acted as pianist, drummer and arranger. During this time he also took courses at Cambridge University in England. At Columbia University (1949–53) he was a pupil of Normand Lockwood, Henry Cowell, Jack Beeson, Otto Luening, Seth Bingham, and Vladimir Ussachevsky. During this time he also studied timpani with Morris Goldenberg and Saul Goodman at the Juilliard School. At the Berkshire Music Center, Tanglewood in 1948 he received lessons in composition from Irving Fine and in conducting from Leonard Bernstein. He was awarded two Guggenheim Fellowships (1967, 1972).

After a season playing in the Dallas Symphony Orchestra Kraft joined the Los Angeles Philharmonic Orchestra in 1955 as a percussionist, becoming principal timpanist in 1963. He resigned in 1981 to concentrate on composition. He has also taught at the

University of Southern California and the California Institute of Arts. From 1981 to 1985 he was Composer-in-Residence with the Los Angeles Philharmonic and director of the Los Angeles Philharmonic New Music Group. He served as visiting professor at the University of California, Los Angeles from 1988 to 1990.

Many of Kraft's works have prominent parts for percussion. Important among these are *Theme and Variations* for percussion (1956); *Three Miniatures* for percussion and orchestra (1958); Nonet for brass and percussion (1958); Suite for four percussionists (1958); Symphony for strings and percussion (1960); Concerto for four percussionists and orchestra (1964); *Configurations* (1966), a concerto for four percussionists and jazz orchestra; *Momentum* for eight percussionists (1966); *Double Trio* for prepared piano, piano, electric guitar, tuba, and two percussionists (1966); *Morris Dance* for solo percussionist (1967); *Triangles*, a concerto for percussion and ten instruments (1968); *Games: Collage No. 1* for two antiphonal choruses of brass and percussion (1969); *English Suite* for percussion (1973); *Des Imagistes* for two reciters and six percussionists (1974); *In the Morning of the Winter Sea* for cello and percussion (1975); *Images* for solo timpani (1978); *Variations on King George* for solo timpani (1980); *Weavings* for percussion and string quartet (1984); *Quintessence*, a concerto for five percussionists and band (1985); Quartet for percussion (1988); and Timpani Concerto no. 2 (San Francisco, 2005).

Other orchestral works are *A Simple Introduction to the Orchestra* (1958); *Variations on a Folksong* (1959); *Concerto Grosso* for flute, bassoon, violin, cello, and orchestra (1961); *American Carnival Overture* (1962); *Derivations* (1962–64); *Contextures: Riots—Decade '60* (1967); a Piano Concerto, written for Mona Golabek (1973); *Tintinnabulations: Collage III* (1974); and *The Dream Tunnel: A Magical Journey Through the Music of America* for narrator and small orchestra (1976).

In 1977 Kraft composed *Andirivieni*, a concerto for tuba, three chamber groups, and orchestra performed in the 1977–78 season by the Los Angeles Philharmonic with Roger Bobo as soloist. Later orchestral pieces include *Interplay* (1984); *Of Ceremonies, Pageants and Celebrations* (1986, rev. 1987); *A Kennedy Portrait* for narrator and orchestra to commemorate the 25th anniversary of the assassination of President Kennedy in 1988; *Veils and Variations* for horn and orchestra (1988); *Vintage Renaissance* (1989); *Vintage 1990–91* (1990); and Concerto for English horn and orchestra, commissioned by the Los Angeles Philharmonic Orchestra and premiered in January 2003.

Kraft's non-percussion instrumental music includes *Six Pieces* for strings trio (1963); *Mobiles* for three chamber groups (1970); *Cadenze* for seven instruments (1971); *Colorations*, a graphic score with slides for any

instruments (1972); *In Memoriam Igor Stravinsky* for violin and piano (1972–74); *Melange* for flute, clarinet, violin, cello, piano, and percussion (1985); and *Quartet for the Love of Time* for clarinet, violin, cello, and piano (1987). Two keyboard pieces are *Ombra* for piano and *Requiescat* for electric piano (1975).

Kraft has produced a series of works entitled *Encounters*, for which there are nine to date: *I* for solo percussion and tape (1975), revised and retitled *Soliloquy*; II for solo tuba (1966); *III*, a duel for trumpet and percussion (1971); *IV*, a duel for trombone and percussion (1972); *V*, *Homage to Scriabin* for cello and piano (1975); *VI*, concertino for roto-toms and percussion quartet (1976); *VII* for two percussionists (1977); *VIII* for solo percussion (1979); and *IX* for saxophone and percussion (1982).

Kraft's single opera, *Red Azelia* (1997-98), was premiered at the University of California, Santa Barbara on 7 February 2003. A song cycle, *Silent Bough* for soprano and strings, was composed in 1963 for Marilyn Horne. Other vocal music includes *The Sublime and the Beautiful* for tenor, flute, clarinet, violin, cello, piano, and percussion (1979); *Contextures II: The Final Beast* for soprano, tenor, and chamber orchestra (1984); *Feerie* for mezzo-soprano, flute, clarinet, viola, cello, and piano (1987); and *Mein Brude* for soprano, flute, clarinet, violin, cello and piano (1988).

Kraft has composed four film scores: *Desire in the Dump* (1958), *Psychic Killer* (1975), *Avalanche* (1978), and *Fire and Ice* (1982).

KRAMER, A(RTHUR) WALTER
b. New York, New York, 23 September 1890
d. New York, New York, 8 April 1969

Kramer studied the violin from the age of 11. He graduated from City College of New York in 1910. Although he was most active in the field of literature on music and was a publisher, he also found time to compose a large number of works. He joined the staff of *Musical America* in 1910, becoming editor-in-chief in 1929. From 1936 to 1956 he was managing director of Galaxy Music.

Kramer is best remembered as the composer of songs, including the cycle *Beauty of Earth* to poems of C. H. Towne.

For orchestra Kramer wrote two symphonies, *Night Song, Symphonic Rhapsody* in F minor for violin and orchestra (1912), *Elizabethan Days* for strings, and a symphonic poem, *The Tragedy of Man*. His choral works include *In Normandy* for soprano, female chorus, and orchestra (1925), a cantata *The Lady of Ceret*, and *Before the Paling of the Stars* for chorus and small orchestra.

KRENEK, ERNST
b. Vienna, Austria, 23 August 1900
d. Palm Springs, California, 23 December 1991

Krenek studied with Franz Schreker in Vienna (1916) and Berlin (1920–23). He spent two years in Zurich before becoming an opera coach in Kassel in 1925, moving to Wiesbaden in 1927. In 1928 he returned to Vienna and, in addition to continuing his compositional work, he undertook literary activities. In 1937 he visited the United States to supervise the production of his own edition of Monteverdi's *Coronation of Poppea*. In view of the political situation in Europe, the following year he decided to settle in the United States, taking citizenship in 1945.

Krenek taught for a time at the Malkin Conservatory of Music in Boston, and from 1939 to 1942 he was professor of music at Vassar College, Poughkeepsie, New York. In 1942 he was appointed head of the department of music at Hamline University, St. Paul, Minnesota, a post he held until 1947. After that time he settled in Palm Springs, California.

Krenek's earliest works reflect the Viennese late Romantic tradition, especially that of Mahler, to whose daughter Anna he was briefly married. In the 1920's he was influenced by the jazz scene which also affected Kurt Weill; later he became associated with the composers under Schoenberg's guidance. The premiere of his jazz-inflected opera *Jonny Spielt Auf* (*Jonny Strikes Up*), op. 45 in Leipzig on 11 February 1927 brought immediate fame. Performances followed in over one hundred opera houses throughout the world. The American premiere was given at the Metropolitan Opera House on 19 January 1929.

Krenek's first work adopting 12-tone techniques was the opera *Karl V*, completed in 1933. Excerpts were heard in concert form in Barcelona in 1936; the entire work was staged in Prague in 1938. Although he wrote extensively in all genres, his operas are his most important works. Except where noted, he provided his own texts.

Besides *Jonny Spielt Auf* and *Karl V*, Krenek's works composed in Europe are a scenic cantata in one act *Die Zwingburg* (*The Tyrant's Castle*), op. 14 (Berlin, 1924); *Der Sprung über den Schatten* (*The Leap Over the Shadow*), op. 17 (Frankfurt, 1924); *Orpheus und Eurydike*, op. 21, after a drama by Oscar Kokoschka (Kassel, 1926); *Leben des Orest* (*Life of Orestes*), op. 60 (Leipzig, 1930); and three one-act operas: *Der Diktator*, op. 49 (1926), *Das geheime Königreich* (*The Secret Kingdom*), op. 50 (1926–27), and *Schergwicht* (*Die Ehre der Nation*) (*Heavyweight, or The Pride of the Nation*), op. 53, all performed in Wiesbaden in 1928. His last operas from the European era (besides *Karl V*) are *Kehraus um St. Stephan* (*Last Dance at St.*

Ernst Krenek.
Courtesy Ernst Krenek Archive, Palm Springs, California.

Stephen's), op. 66 (1930) and *Cefalo e Procris*, op. 77 (Venice, 1934).

In America Krenek composed *Tarquin*, op. 90 (1941) to a libretto by Emmet Lavery; *What Price Confidence?* (*Vertrauenssache*), op. 111 (1946); *Dark Waters*, op. 125 (1951) and *Pallas Athene weint* (*Pallas Athena Weeps*), op. 144, produced in Hamburg on 17 October 1955 to open the new opera house. These were followed by *The Bell Tower*, op. 153, based on a story by Herman Melville. Commissioned by the Fromm Foundation, it was staged at the University of Illinois, Urbana on 17 March 1957.

His first opera for television, *Ausgerechnet und Verspielt* (*Computed and Confounded*), op. 179 was produced in Vienna in 1962. *Der Goldene Bock* (*The Golden Ram*), op. 186 was staged in Hamburg on 6 June 1964. A second opera for television, *Der Zauberspiegel* (*The Magic Mirror*), op. 191, dates from 1967 and was first produced in Munich. *Sardakai*, op. 206 (1967-69) was performed in Hamburg in 1970. A third television opera *Flaschenpost vom Paradies*, op. 217, was composed in 1973.

Also for the stage Krenek wrote several ballets including *Mammon*, op. 37 (1926); *Der Vertauschte Cupido* (*The Exchanged Cupid*), op. 38 after Rameau

(1926); *Eight Column Line*, op. 85 (1939); *Sargasso* (1946); *Jest of Cards* (*Spass mit Karten*), op. 162 (1957); and *Alpbach Quintet*, op. 180 (1962).

Krenek provided incidental music for a large number of plays: *Cyrano de Bergerac* (1917); *Napoleon* (1922); *Fresco* (1922); *Das Leben ein Traum* (1925); *Von Lieben Augustin*, op. 40 (1925); *Die Rache des Verhohnten Liebhabers* (*The Spurned Lover's Revenge*), op. 41 (1925); *Das Gottenskind* (*God's Child*), op. 42 (1925); *Der triumph der Empfindsamkeit* (*The Triumph of Sensitivity*), op. 43 after Goethe (1925); *A Midsummer Night's* Dream, op. 46 (1926); *Marlborough s'en-va'-t'en guerre* (1927); *Das Kaiser von Neufunflung* (1927); *Herr Reinecke Fuchs* (1931) and *Oedipus*, op. 188 after Sophocles (Salzburg, 1965). In 1960 he composed the score for a film of Hofmannsthal's *Jedermann* (*Everyman*), op. 176.

Krenek's orchestral works occupy a significant place in his output. Important among these are nine symphonies: the first four unnumbered (1920–26), no. 1, op 7 (1921), no. 2, op. 12 (1922), no. 3, op. 16 (1922), no. 4, op. 113 (1947) and no. 5, op. 119 (1949). Other compositions for orchestra include a Concerto Grosso, op. 25 (1924); Symphony for wind and percussion, op. 34 (1924–25); *Three Merry Marches*, op. 44 (1926); *Kleine Symphonie*, op. 58 (1928); *Theme and Variations*, op. 69 (1931); *Little Suite* for wind orchestra, op. 70 (1931); *Symphonic Piece* for strings, op. 86 (1939); and *Variations on a Folk-tune from North Carolina "I Wonder as I Wander,"* op. 94 (1942). The tragic death of Anton Webern deeply moved Krenek and inspired the *Symphonic Elegy* for strings, op 105 (1946), dedicated to Webern's memory.

In 1955 the Louisville Orchestra commissioned *Eleven Transparencies*, op. 142. Also for orchestra are *Kette, Kreis und Spiegel* (*Circle, Chain and Mirror*), op. 160 (1957) and *From Three Make Seven*, op. 177 (1961). *Perspectives*, op. 199 (1968) was commissioned for the sesquicentennnial of Illinois. *Horizon Circled*, op. 196 and *Six Profiles*, op. 203 date from the same year. *Fivefold Enfoldment*, op. 205 was composed in 1969. Pieces for chamber orchestra are *Hexaeder*, op. 167 (1958); *Quaestio Temporis*, op. 170 (1959); *Static and Ecstatic*, op. 214 (1972); *Von vorn herein* (*From the Outset*), op. 219 (1974); and *The Art of Life*, op. 234 (1981).

For solo instruments and orchestra Krenek composed four piano concertos: no. 1 in F#, op. 18 (1923), no. 2, op. 81 (1938), no. 3, op. 107, in which Dimitri Mitropoulos was the soloist in the premiere (1946), and no. 4, op. 123 (1950). He also wrote two violin concertos, no. 1, op. 29 (1924) and no. 2, op. 140 (1955); a Harp Concerto, op. 126 (1952); a Concerto for two pianos, op. 127 (1953); two cello concertos, no. 1, op. 133 (1954) and no. 2, op. 236 (1982); and four works

for groups of soloists: Concertino for flute, violin, harpsichord, and strings, op. 27 (1924); *Little Concerto* for piano, organ, and chamber orchestra, op. 88 (1940); *Double* Concerto for violin, piano, and chamber orchestra, op. 124 (1951); and *Kitharaulos* for oboe, harp, and chamber orchestra, op. 213 (1972). A Concerto for organ and strings, op. 230 was composed for the Carinthian Summer Festival, Ossiach, Austria in 1979; a second Organ Concerto, op. 235 was premiered in Melbourne, Australia in 1983.

Krenek wrote a considerable amount of choral music, including *The Seasons*, op. 25 (1925); *Lamentations of Jeremiah the Prophet*, op. 93 (1941); *The Santa Fe Timetable*, op. 102 (1945), a setting of all the names of the railroad stations from Albuquerque to Los Angeles; and *Veni Sanctificator*, op. 141 (1955); all of these are for a cappella chorus. Choral works with orchestra include an oratorio, on his own words, *Glauben und Wissen* (*To Believe and Know*), op. 192 for solo voices and chorus; *Deutsches Proprium fur das Dreifaltigkeitsfest* (*German Proper of the Mass for Trinity Sunday*), op. 194 for soprano, chorus, organ, two trumpets, and timpani (1968); *Deutsche Messgesange zum 29 Sonntag im Jahreskrieg* for narrator, chorus, and organ, op. 204 (1968); *Fiertags-Kantate* (*Holiday Cantata*), op. 221 for speaker, solo voices, chorus, and orchestra (1974); and *Opus sine nomine*, an oratorio (1980-88). For female chorus he wrote *Cantata for War Time*, op. 95 (1944) on poems of Herman Melville.

Krenek's considerable output of instrumental music includes eight string quartets dating from 1921 to 1981; two sonatas for violin and piano, no. 1 in F# minor, op. 3 (1919) and no. 2, op. 99 (1945), two sonatas for solo violin, no. 1, op 33. (1924) and no. 2, op. 115 (1948); Trio for violin, clarinet, and piano, op. 108 (1946); *Fibonacci Mobile*, op. 187 for string quartet and piano duet (1964); and many other pieces for solo instruments and ensembles.

Krenek himself was a fine pianist who appeared in concerts as an accompanist. For piano he composed seven sonatas (1913–51). A later keyboard work, *Piano Piece in Eleven Parts*, op. 197 was commissioned by the Chicago Music College in April 1968. *Doppelt beflügeltes Band*, op. 207 for two pianos and tape was premiered in Graz in 1970. In 1975 he composed an important work for organ, *Four Winds Suite*, op. 223. He also provided two pieces for accordion, *Toccata*, op. 183 (1962) and *Acco-Music*, op. 225 (1976). For mezzo-soprano and orchestra he wrote a dramatic monologue, *Medea*, op. 129 (1953). Also for voice and orchestra are *O Lacrimosa*, op. 48 (1926); *Konzertarie* (*Monolog der Stella*), op. 57 (1928); a song cycle, *Durch die Nacht* (*Through the Night*), op. 67 (1931); *La Corona* (seven sonnets by John Donne), op. 91 (1941) for mezzo-soprano, baritone, organ, and percussion; *Sestina*, op. 161 (1957) to his own works for soprano, violin, guitar, flute, clarinet, trumpet, and percussion; *Instant Remembered*, op. 201 (1968); *Zeitlieder* for mezzo-soprano and string quartet (1972); *Spätlese* (*Late Harvest*), op. 218, a song cycle (1973); and *The Dissembler* for baritone and ensemble (1978).

In later years Krenek took an interest in the use of electronic tape, usually with instruments and voices. In this new medium he wrote *Exercises for a Late Hour* (*Übungen der späten Stunde*), op. 200 for chamber orchestra and tape; *Quintina*, op. 189 for soprano, flute, viola, guitar, percussion, and tape (1966); a pentecostal oratorio, *Spiritus Intelligentiae, Sanctus*, op. 152 for voices and electronic sound (1956); *Tape and Double*, op. 207 for two pianos and tape (1969); and *Orga-Nastro*, op. 212 for organ and tape (1971). He composed two pieces for tape alone: *San Fernando Sequence*, op. 185 (1964) and *Quintona*, op. 188 (1965).

In addition to arranging Monteverdi's *Coronation of Poppea*, Krenek edited the Adagio of Mahler's unfinished Tenth Symphony and in 1922 completed Schubert's Piano Sonata in C. Krenek also found time to write a number of valuable books on music. These include *Music Here and There* (1939); *Studies in Counterpoint, based on the Twelve-tone Technique* (1940); *Selbstdarstellung* (*Self-Analysis*; 1948); *Musik im Goldenen Westen* (1949); *Johannes Ockeghem* (1953); *De Rebus Prius Factis* (1956); *Tonal Counterpoint of the 18th Century* (1958); *Modal Counterpoint of the 16th Century* (1959); *Komponist und Hörer* (1964); *Prosa, Drama, Verse* (1965); *Horizons Circled: Reflections on My Music* (1974); *Das musikdramatische Werk* (1982); *Im Zweifelsfälle: Aufsäatze uber Musik* (1984); *Franz Schubert: Ein Portrait* (1990); and *Dokumente aus dem Exil* (1992). He also wrote a defense of the 12-tone system entitled *Über Neue Musik* (1936). He published two collections of essays, *Zur Sprache gebracht* (1958) and *Gedanken unterwegs* (1959). A selection of these essays has appeared in English as *Exploring Music* (1966).

KREUTZ, ARTHUR

b. La Crosse, Wisconsin, 25 July 1906
d. Oxford, Mississippi, 11 March 1991

Kreutz was educated at the University of Wisconsin, Columbia University's Teachers College and the Royal Conservatory, Ghent. He was a pupil of Cecil Burleigh (violin) and Edwin Stringham and Roy Harris (composition). He taught at Georgia State College for Women, Milledgeville (1940–46), Rhode Island State College, Providence (1946–52), and the University of Mississippi (1952–64). He was awarded the Prix de Rome (1940) and a Guggenheim Fellowship (1944–46).

For orchestra he wrote two symphonies: no. 1, *Music for Orchestra*, performed by the NBC Symphony Orchestra in 1940, and no. 2 (1946); *Paul Bunyan Suite* (1940), which won the Prix de Rome; *Symphonic Sketches* (1941); a symphonic poem, *Winter of the Blue Snow* (1942); *Triumphant Overture* (1942); *Three American Dances* (1946); *Mosquito Serenade* for strings (1948); and *Scenes from Hamlet* (1949).

Five orchestral pieces reflect his interest in jazz: *A Study in Jazz* (1943), *Symphonic Blues* (1945), Concerto for Dixieland band and orchestra (1949), *Jazz Fugue* (1965), and *Concert Jazz* (1988).

Works for solo instruments and orchestra include two violin concertos (1942, 1965); a Concertino for oboe, horn, and strings (1944–45); *Dance Concerto* for clarinet and orchestra (1950); a Clarinet Concerto (1958); *Concertino in Blue* for violin and orchestra (1963); a Saxophone Concerto (1963); and a Piano Concerto (1970).

Kreutz composed four operas: *Acres of Sky* (two acts), produced at Columbia University in 1952; *The University Greys* (Clinton, Missouri: 1953); *Sourwood Mountain* (Clinton, Missouri, 1959); and *Verbena*. His ballet *Litany of Washington* (*Land Be Bright*) was commissioned by Martha Graham in 1942.

Among his choral and vocal music are three pieces for chorus and orchestra: *New England Folk-sing* (1946), *Gettysburg 1863*, and *Three Rhode Island Folk Songs*; and two sets of songs, *Three Shakespeare Love Lyrics* for soprano and orchestra (1943) and *Four Poems by Robert Burns* for high voice and chamber orchestra (1944).

His instrumental works include three *Jazzsonatas* for violin and piano (1961, 1968, 1984); *Song and Dance* for violin and piano (1977); *Jam Session* for saxophone quartet (1978); *Saxonata* for alto saxophone and piano (1979–80); and *Fantasy* for alto saxophone and piano (1983).

KUBIK, GAIL (THOMPSON)

b. South Coffeyville, Oklahoma, 5 September 1914
d. Covina, Claremont, California, 20 July 1984

Kubik studied violin with Samuel Belov and composition with Bernard Rogers and Edward Royce at the Eastman School of Music, Rochester, New York (1930–34). By the age of 19 he had acquired two degrees, one in violin and one in composition. He obtained a Master's degree in 1936 while a pupil of Leo Sowerby at the American Conservatory of Music in Chicago. He later worked with Walter Piston at Harvard University (1937–38) and in Paris with Nadia Boulanger (1937).

Kubik was appointed an Instructor at Monmouth College, Illinois in 1934, moving to Dakota Wesleyan

University (1936–37) and the Teachers' College, Columbia University (1938–40). In 1940 he joined NBC as a staff composer and music program adviser, in which capacity he wrote several scores for radio. In 1942 he became director of music for the Bureau of Motion Pictures, U.S. Office of War Information. During this time he was awarded his first Guggenheim fellowship (1944); a second Guggenheim was awarded in 1967.

After the Second World War Kubik was guest professor at various universities in America. He won the American Prix de Rome in 1950 and from 1950 to 1955 he lived in Rome and Paris; from 1959 to 1967 he was again in France and Italy. In 1970 he was appointed Composer-in-Residence at Scripps College, Claremont, California, retiring in 1980.

Kubik's first work of note, *American Caprice* for piano and small orchestra, dates from his student days and was completed in 1933. Two other large-scale works, Suite for orchestra and Violin Concerto no. 1, were also written in this student period. In 1936 the cantata *In Praise of Johnny Appleseed*, a setting of Vachel Lindsay's poem for baritone, chorus, and orchestra, brought his name to a wider musical public. Later choral works include *Choral Profiles: Folk Song Sketches* for chorus (1938); *Litany and Prayer* for men's chorus, brass, and percussion (1943–45); *A Christmas Offering* for a cappella chorus (1967); *A Christmas Set* for chorus and orchestra (1968; written for Nadia Boulanger's 80th birthday); and *A Record of Our Time* (*A Protest Piece*), for narrator, soloists, chorus, and orchestra, composed in 1970 and premiered in November of that year by the combined choirs of Kansas State University (which commissioned it) and the Minnesota Symphony Orchestra, with Ray Milland as narrator. The Roger Wagner Chorale gave the West Coast premiere in Los Angeles in 1976. In 1972 Kubik wrote *Scholastica: A Medieval Set* for a cappella chorus, and in 1976 was commissioned by the State of Texas to write *Magic, Magic, Magic* for chamber chorus and small orchestra to celebrate the American Bicentennial.

Kubik's many orchestral works include three symphonies: no. 1 in E-flat (1947–49); no. 2 in F, commissioned by the Louisville Orchestra and the Rockefeller Foundation in 1955; and no. 3, composed in 1956 for Dimitri Mitropoulos and the New York Philharmonic Orchestra. Kubik's *Second* Violin Concerto in D minor won a $1,000 prize offered by Jascha Heifetz in 1941. Kubik conducted the premiere in 1953 with Ruggiero Ricci as soloist with the Symphony Orchestra of Rome Radio. The *Symphony Concertante* for viola, piano, trumpet, and orchestra won the Pulitzer Prize in 1952. Other orchestral items include the Suite (1935, rev. 1937); *Variations on a Thirteenth Century Troubadour Song* (1935); *Puck* for narrator and orchestra (1940); *Scherzo* (1941); *Music for Dancing* (1940–46); *Folk Song Suite* (1941–46); *Toccata* for organ and strings (1946); *Bachata* (*Cuban Dance Piece*; 1947); *Symphonie Concertante* (1952); *Thunderbolt Overture* (1953); *Scenario for Orchestra* (1957); *Scenes for Orchestra* (1964); *Prayer and Toccata* for organ and chamber orchestra (1969), revised as a work for two pianos and organ in 1979; and *Pastorale, Spring Valley Overture* (1972). His last major work was a Piano Concerto, *Four Nocturnes*, completed in 1983.

Kubik's reputation as a composer of wide appeal has been gained through films, radio, and television. While serving with the U.S. Office of War Information, he provided music for a number of documentary films including, *Men and Ships* (1940), *Paratroops* (1941), *The World at War* (1942), and *Air Pattern Pacific* (1944).

The entertaining score *Gerald McBoing Boing* for narrator, nine instruments, and percussion soloist (1950) was animated by John Hubley of United Productions of America for Columbia Pictures, and in that form won an Academy Award in 1952. For William Wyler he wrote the music for *The Memphis Belle* (1944), which won the New York Film Critics' Award for that year; *Thunderbolt* (1945); and *The Desperate Hours* (1955). Other film scores include *C-Man* (1949); *The Miller's Daughter* (1950); *Two Gals and a Guy* (1951); *Transatlantic* (1952), which received the Edinburgh Film Festival Award in 1954; *Down to Earth* (1959); *I Thank a Fool* (1962); and two scores for CBS television, *Hiroshima* (1958) and *The Silent Sentinel* (1959).

For the stage, Kubik composed three operas: a one-act farce, *Boston Baked Beans* (1950), a two-act folk opera, *A Mirror in the Sky* (1946–47), and the incomplete *Ondine*, based on a play by Jean Giraudoux, which was commissioned by the Venice Music Festival.

Kubik's large output of chamber music includes *Two Sketches* for string quartet (1932); a Piano Trio (1934); *Trivialities* for flute, horn, and string quartet (1934); Wind Quintet (1937); Piano Sonatina (1941), dedicated to his former teacher Walter Piston; Sonatina for violin and piano (1941); *Little Suite* for flute and two clarinets (1947); Piano Sonata (1947); *Soliloquy and Dance* for violin and piano (1948); Clarinet Sonatina (1959); and three divertimenti: no. 1 for 13 players (1959), no. 2 for eight players (1959), and no. 3, *Five Theatrical Sketches* for piano trio (1971).

KUPFERMAN, MEYER
b New York, New York, 3 July 1926
d. New York, New York, November 26, 2003

Kupferman was educated at New York's High School of Music and Art and from 1944 to 1946 he studied at Queen's College, New York. In composition he was self-

Meyer Kupferman.
Courtesy Jeffrey W. James Arts Consulting.

taught. In 1951 he joined the music faculty at Sarah Lawrence College, Bronxville, New York becoming chairman of the music department and director of the Sarah Lawrence Improvisation Group, and retiring in 1994. In 1986 he founded his own recording and publishing company Soundspells Productions. Kupferman's first works to gain recognition were the Divertimento for chamber orchestra (1948) and *Chamber Symphony* (1950). The latter is neoclassical, although atonal in a way that suggests a deliberate intention to adopt the emotional and structural characteristics of Mozart and Beethoven.

At the center of his orchestral works are 11 numbered symphonies: no. 1 (1950), no. 2 (*Chamber Symphony*; 1950), no. 3 (*Little Symphony*; 1952, rev. 1983), no. 4 (1956), no. 5 (*Lyric Symphony*; 1956), *No.6* (*Yin-Yang*; 1972), no. 7 (1974), no. 8 (*Sinfonia Brevis*; 1975), no. 9 (1980), no. 10 (*FDR*), composed in 1981 to mark the centenary of the birth of Franklin D. Roosevelt, and no. 11 (1983). In addition there is a *Jazz Symphony* for mezzo-soprano, alto saxophone, and orchestra (1988).

Also for orchestra are three piano concertos (1948, 1978, 1999); *Libretto* (1949); *Ostinato Burlesco* (orchestrated from a piano piece in 1954); *Variations for Orchestra* (1959); *Sculptures* (1971); Concerto for cello, tape, and orchestra (1974); *Steps* (1975); Concerto for

six instruments and orchestra (1976); *Passage* for strings (1976), revised as *Flight Alone* in 1995; *Atto* (1976); Violin Concerto (1976, rev. 1995 as *Fantasy Concerto*); *Richter 7* (1979), described as "a musical earthquake"; *Sound Objects 10* for small orchestra (1979); *Phantom Rhapsody* for guitar and small orchestra (1980); *Sound Phantoms No.8.* (1980); *Tuba* Concerto (1983); *Challenger* (1983); Clarinet Concerto (1984); *Quasar Symphony* (1984); *Wings of the Highest Tower* (1988); *Overture for Double Orchestra* (1988); *Savage Landscape* (1989); *Symphonic Odyssey* (1990); Double Concerto for two clarinets and orchestra (1991, rev. 2000); *Hot Hors D'Oeuvres* for small orchestra (1993); Concerto for amplified guitar and orchestra (1993); *Hexagon Skies* for amplified guitar and small orchestra (1994); and *Banners* for small orchestra (1995). Recent orchestral pieces include *Three Faces of Electra* (1995); *Winter Symphony* (1997); *Lunar Symphony* (1998); *Tinker Hill* (1999); *Speculum Symphony* (1999); *Quantum Symphony* (2000); *Icon Symphony* (2000); *Structures for Orchestra* (2001); and *Into the Breach* (2002).

Kupferman's later works for solo instruments and orchestra are *Rhapsody* for guitar (1990); *The Moor's Concerto* for piano (1993); *Concerto Brevis* for flute (1997); Concerto for four guitars (1998); Clarinet Concertino: *Fly By Night* (2001); Violin Concerto: *The Voyager* (2001); Concerto for guitar and strings (2001); and *Elegy for the Vanished* for guitar, dedicated to the victims of September 11th (2001).

Kupferman's large catalog of ensemble music includes nine string quartets (1946–93); Concertino for 11 brass instruments (1948); *Chamber Concerto* for flute, piano, and strings (1955); Wind Quintet (1958); *Curtain Raiser* for wind quintet (1960); Brass Quintet (1970); *Jazz Concerto: Tunnels of Love* for clarinet (1971); *The Flames of Abracadabra* for piano and string trio (1976); *Icarus* for guitar, viola, and cello (1976); *Masada*, a chamber symphony for flute, clarinet, violin, cello, double bass, and piano (1977); *New Songs for Old Instruments* for medieval and Renaissance instruments (1979); *Poems '83* for flute, violin, cello, and harp (1984); *Symphony for Six* (1984); Piano Quintet (1985); Clarinet Quintet (1986); *Rock Shadows* for brass quintet (1986); *A Little Licorice Concerto* for clarinet and clarinet choir (1986); *A Little Ivory Concerto* for piano, string quartet, and wind quintet (1986); *Summer Music* for two guitars, flute, and cello (1987); *Top Brass 5* for five trumpets (1989); *Ice Cream Concerto*, concerto grosso for 11 instruments (1992); *Acrobats of Apollo* for guitar, marimba, and chamber orchestra (1996); and *A Faust Concerto* for horn and chamber ensemble (1997).

Instrumental pieces include *Duo Divertimento* for clarinet and bassoon (1948); *Evocations* for cello and piano (1950); *Four Pieces* for cello and piano (1963); *Four on a Row* for clarinet and piano (1965); *Available Forms* for trumpet and trombone (or clarinet and bassoon) (1966); *Pierrot* for violin and piano (1966); *Five Singles* for solo clarinet (1967); *Three Ideas* for trumpet and piano (1967); *Superflute* for taped alto flute and taped piccolo (1972); *Fantasy Sonata* for violin and piano (1972); *Angel Footprints* for violin and tape (1973); *The Last Blue Zeppelin* for cello and horn (1973); *Fiddle Energizer* for violin and piano (1973); *The Garden of My Father's House* for violin and clarinet (1975); *Premeditations* for clarinet and guitar (1975); *Invisible Timepiece* for guitar and tape (1975); *Echoes of Barcelona* for guitar (1975); Sonata for two cellos (1987); *Chaconne Sonata* for flute and piano (1994); and *Duo Arsenalas* for flute and viola (1996).

For piano Kupferman wrote the serial *Variations* (1948); *Partita* (1949); *Sonata on Jazz Elements* (1958); *Infinities Fantasy* (1962); *Little Sonata* (1964); *Thoughts* (1972); *Second Thoughts* (1973); *Sonata Mystikos* (1973–79); *Sonata Occulta* (1979); *Erasmus* (1979); *Distances* (1988); *Red Sonata* (1989); *Twilight Sonata* (1989); *The Canticle of Ulysses* (1991); *Five Moons* (1994), *Celestial Gate* for piano and tape (1973); and a Sonata for two pianos (1956).

A major series of pieces composed in the 1960's, entitled *Circle of Infinities*, comprise 26 different works, all based on the same tone-row: no. 1 (1961) is for flute; no. 3 (1961), for saxophone, double bass, and drums; no. 4 (1961), for soprano who sings settings of Rimbaud as a duet with herself on tape; no. 5 (1962, rev 1982), for cello, double bass, jazz-band, and tape; no. 6 (1963), another setting of Rimbaud for chorus; no. 8 (1963), a string quartet; nos. 12 (1964), 14 (1966), and 21 (1968), all for chamber ensembles; no. 13 (1965), for four performers who play eight instruments; no. 20 (1968), *Schemata*, for orchestra; and no. 26, *Moonchild and the Doomsday Trombone* (1968), for voice, oboe, and chamber and jazz ensembles. There is also an *Infinities Concerto* for three saxophones, cello, and double bass.

Kupferman took a direct interest in jazz and made numerous arrangements for leading jazz bands, contributing to what is known as "Third Stream." From 1975 until his death, he directed and performed, as a clarinetist, with a group called "Music by My Friends," comprising clarinet, cello, piano, and percussion. More than 30 international composers have provided works for the group's annual series at the Carnegie Recital Hall. He himself wrote *The Red King's Throw* for the group in 1977. Other jazz-influenced pieces include a Concerto for cello and jazz band (1962) and *Tunnel of Love* for jazz ensemble (1971).

In the 1970s Kupferman adopted an approach to composition which he calls "gestalt musical forms." Essentially, this is the free interchange or mixture of styles and techniques within the same composition, whereby one may encounter both tonal and atonal, classical and jazz styles, Baroque and late-Romantic overtones, and internal structures such as passacaglia and sonata form. Works in this idiom include the Concerto for cello, tape, and orchestra (1975) and two sets of pieces: *Sound Objects I to X* (1978–79), all for different and unusual ensembles (trumpet, tuba, and piano, or guitar and harp, or violin and double bass); and *Sound Phantoms I* to *X* (1980–81), based on "dream images," also for odd combinations such as eight guitars with flute, violin, and bass.

Kupferman wrote nine operas: *In a Garden* (1948), to a text by Gertrude Stein; *The Curious Fern* (1957); *Voices for a Mirror* (1957); *Draagenfut Girl* (1958); *Dr. Faustus Lights the Lights* (1952, rev. 1963), also to a libretto based on Gertrude Stein; *The Judgment* (*Infinities No.18*; 1966–67), a three-act opera for unaccompanied voices; *Prometheus Condemned* (1975); *The Proscenium* (1991); and *The Waxing Moon* (1993). Also for the stage there are four ballets: *Persephone* (1968), with choreography by Pearl Lang; *The Possessed* (1974); *O Thou Desire Who Art About to Sing* (1977); and *Icarus* (1980). The humorous cantata *Comicus Americus* was premiered in 1969 by the Kansas City Symphony Orchestra. In 1985 he completed a cantata, *Ode to Shreveport* for solo voices, chorus, and orchestra.

Kupferman's principal vocal compositions are *Mask for Electra* for mezzo-soprano, oboe, and electric keyboard; two song cycles on Nietzsche, *A Nietzsche Cycle* for soprano, horn, and piano (1979) and *Dem unbekannten Gott*, for soprano and seven instruments (1982); a monodrama, *Antigonae* for soprano and chamber orchestra (1973); two pieces for soprano and clarinet, *Three Blake Songs* and *Gnats* (1975); *The Conceptual Wheel* (Michael Benedikt) for soprano, clarinet, and piano (1980); and *Torchwise* for soprano, basset horn, and piano (1983). More recent are *A Crucible for the Moon* for soprano, alto saxophone, and percussion (1986); a song cycle, *Wicked Combinations* for mezzo-soprano and piano (1989); *The Shadows of Jerusalem* for mezzo-soprano, clarinet, cello, and piano (1992); and *Miro, Miro on the Wall*, a solo cantata for soprano, piano, alto saxophone, vibraphone, and double bass (1995).

Kupferman's film music includes scores for documentaries: *Chinese Dressmaking* (1959); *Chinese Firecrakers* (1959); *Nanking* (1959); *Peking* (1959); *Tsientsien* (1959); *Cool Wind* (1961); *Faces of America* (1965); and *High Arctic* (1965). Feature film scores include *Blast of Silence* (1960); *Hallelujah the Hills* (1963); *Goldstein* (1963); *Black Like Me* (1964); *The Double-Barreled Detective Story* (1965); *A Christmas Memory* (1966); *Frank's Greatest Adventure* (*Fearless*

Frank) (1967); *Among the Paths of Eden* (1968); *Truman Capote's Trilogy* (1969); and *Zamrok* (1982).

KURKA, ROBERT (FRANK)
b. Cicero, Illinois, 22 December 1921
d. New York, New York, 12 December 1957

Kurka was born of Czech parents. After graduating from Columbia University in 1948, where he had been a pupil of Otto Luening, he studied briefly with Darius Milhaud. He taught at the City College of New York, Queens College, and Dartmouth College. In 1951 he was awarded a Guggenheim Fellowship. Kurka is remembered for his opera *The Good Soldier Schweik*, based on the novel by Jaroslav Hasek, which he completed in 1957. It received its premiere after his death at the New York City Opera on 23 April 1958.

Kurka's orchestral music includes two symphonies (1951, 1953); a *Chamber Symphony* (1946); a Symphony for brass and strings (1948); a Violin Concerto (1948); *Music for Orchestra* (1949); Serenade for small orchestra (1954); *John Henry*, a portrait (1954); *Julius Caesar*, a symphonic epilogue (1955); Concertino for two pianos, trumpet, and strings (1955); Marimba Concerto (1956); *Ballad* for horn and strings (1956); and *Chamber Sinfonietta* (1957).

Among his chamber music are five string quartets (1945, 1947, 1949, 1950, 1954); four violin sonatas (1946, 1949, 1953, 1955); Sonata for solo violin (1947); *Music* for violin, clarinet, horn, trumpet, and double bass (1951); Piano Trio (1951); *Seven Moravian Folksongs* for wind quintet (1951); and Cello Sonatina (1953). Keyboard pieces include a Piano Sonata (1952) and *Dance Suite* for piano duet (1953).

Kurka wrote only two choral pieces, *Who Shall Speak to the People?* to words by Carl Sandburg for male voices and orchestra (1952) and *Song of the Broad-Axe* for men's chorus (1956).

L

LABUNSKI, FELIX (RODERYK)

b. Ksawerńow, Poland, 27 December 1892
d. Cincinnati, Ohio, 28 April 1979

Labunski studied at the Warsaw Conservatory with Lucian Marczewski (1922–23) and Witold Maliszewski (1923–24). At the Ecole Normale, Paris (1927–30) he was a pupil of Nadia Boulanger and Paul Dukas. Labunski worked for Polish Radio (1934–36) before going to the United States in 1936. He became an American citizen in 1941. He taught at Marymount College, New York (1940–41), Cincinnati College Conservatory (1945–55), and the University of Cincinnati from 1955 to his retirement in 1964.

For orchestra Labunski composed *Danse Fantastique* (1926); *Triptyque Champêtre* (1931); Symphony no. 1 in G minor (1937); a ballet, *God's Man* (1937); *Suite for Strings* (1938); *Elegy in Memory of Ignaz Paderewski* (1941); *Variations for Orchestra* (1947); *Elegy* (1954); Symphony no. 2 in D (1954); *Xaveriana* for two pianos and orchestra (1956); *Symphonic Dialogues* (1960); *Canto di Aspirazione* (1963); *Music for Piano and Orchestra* (1966); *Polish Renaissance Suite* (1967); *Nocturne* (1967); a ballet, *Salut à Paris* (1968); and *Primavera* (1973).

Choral works include *Polish Cantata* (1932); an Easter cantata, *There is No Death* (1950); a cantata, *Images of Youth* (1956); Mass for treble voices and organ (1958); *Two Madrigals* (1960); and *Five Polish Carols* (1966).

Among Labunski's chamber music are *Cycle of Infinities* for string quartet; two string quartets (1935, 1962); Divertimento for flute and piano (1936); *Three Bagatelles* for brass quartet (1955); Divertimento for wind quartet (1956); Piano Sonata no. 2 (1957); *Diptych* for oboe and piano (1958); and *Intrada Festiva* for brass (1967).

LABUNSKI, WIKTOR

b. St Petersburg, Russia, 14 April, 1895
d. Kansas City, Missouri, 26 January 1974

Wiktor Labunski was the brother of Felix Labunski. He studied piano with Vasili Safonov at the St. Petersburg Conservatory. From 1919 to 1928 he was head of the piano department at the Krakow Conservatory. Labunski emigrated to the United States in 1928 and made his debut as a pianist in Carnegie Hall the same year. He taught at the Nashville Conservatory (1928-31), and was director of the Memphis College of Music (1931–37). In 1937 he was appointed director of the Kansas City Conservatory, retiring in 1971.

For orchestra Labunski wrote a Piano Concertino (1932); Symphony in G minor (1936); a Piano Concerto in C (1937), Variations on a Theme by Paganini for piano and orchestra (1945); and a Concerto for two pianos (1951). Among his solo piano pieces are *Toccata* (1923) and *Variations* (1923).

LADERMAN, EZRA

b. Brooklyn, New York, 29 June 1926

Laderman first studied at the High School of Music and Art in New York before serving in the U.S. Army during World War II. He entered Brooklyn College (1946–49) where he was a pupil of Miriam Gideon. At Columbia University (1950–52), his teachers included Otto Luening and Douglas Moore. He also received composition lessons privately from Stefan Wolbe (1945–48). Laderman taught at Sarah Lawrence College, Bronxville, New York from 1960 to 1961 and again from 1965 to 1966. From 1971 to 1981 he was Composer-in-Residence at the State University of New York, Binghampton. He was president of the American Music

Center (1972–75) and director of the music program of the National Endowment for the Arts (1979–82). From 1982-83 he worked at the American Academy in Rome. He was president of the American Music Council (1987–89) and Dean of the Yale School of Music (1989–95). He has won many awards for his music including three Guggenheim Fellowships (1955, 1958, 1964) and the Prix de Rome (1963–64).

Laderman has composed seven operas: *Jacob and the Indians* (1957); *Sarah,* broadcast on NBC television in 1959; *Goodbye to the Clowns* (1960); *The Hunting of the Snark* (1961); *Shadows Among Us* (1965–69) for the New York City Opera; *Galileo Galilei* (1978); *Marilyn* (1993); and a musical, *Dominique* (1962). He also provided a dance score *Esther* for Anna Sokolow in 1960. Other dance pieces are *Duet* for flute and dancer (1956), *Dance Quartet* for flute, clarinet, cello, and dancer (1957), *Solos and Chorales* (1960) for Jean Erdman, and *Luther* (1968) for José Limón.

In addition to the *Leipzig Symphony,* composed while he was serving in the U.S. Army in Germany in 1945, Laderman has composed eight numbered symphonies: no. 1 (1963–64), no. 2, *Luther* (1968), no. 3, *Jerusalem* (1973), no. 4 for brass orchestra (1980), no. 5, *Isaiah* for soprano and orchestra (1982), no. 6 (1982, rev. 1988), no. 7 (1984), and no. 8 (1993). His other orchestral works include *Concerto for Orchestra: Satire* (1968); *Theme, Variations and Finale* (1957); *Stanzas:* five pieces for chamber orchestra (1960); *Double Helix* for flute, oboe, and strings (1968); *Celestial Bodies* for flute and strings (1972); and *Cadence* for two flutes and strings (1977). Also for full orchestra he has written *Organization I* (1952); *Sinfonia* (1956); *Identity* (1959); *Summer Solstice* (1980); *Sonore* (1983); *Pentimento* (1985); *Sanctuary: An Original Theme and Variations,* written in 1986 for the Louisville Orchestra; *Sinfonia Concertante* (1988); *A Play Within a Play – Concerto for Double Orchestra* (1989); Concerto for Chamber Orchestra (1989); *Citadel* (1990); and *Israel* (1998).

In addition to two unnumbered piano concertos (1939, 1957), Laderman has composed two others, no. 1 (1978) and no. 2 (1989). There are also two violin concertos (1951, rev. 1963, 1979); a Concerto for bassoon and strings (1955); a Viola Concerto (1978); a Concerto for string quartet and orchestra (1980); a Flute Concerto (1984); a Cello Concerto (1986); a Concerto for violin and cello (1986); a Concerto for clarinet and strings (1995); and Concerto for bass clarinet (2002).

Important works for soloist, chorus, and orchestra are the oratorios *The Eagle Stirred* (1960–61) and *The Trials of Galileo* (1967); two cantatas, *And David Wept* (1971) and *The Questions of Abraham* (1973), both produced on CBS television; a cantata, *A Handful of Souls* (1975); *Thrive Upon the Rock* (Norman Rosten) for chorus and piano (1975); and an oratorio, *A Mass for Cain* (1979). For the opening of the Lincoln Center in 1967, Laderman composed *Magic Prison* for two narrators and orchestra, setting poems by Emily Dickinson. The work was conducted by André Kostelanetz, who had commissioned it.

Laderman has concentrated especially on chamber music. Among these instrumental works are 12 string quartets, the first unnumbered (1953), no. 1 (1959), no. 2 (1962), no. 3 (1966), no. 4 (1974), no. 5 (1976), no. 6 (1980), no. 7 (1983), no. 8 (1985), no. 9 (1998), no. 10 (2001), and no. 11 (1999). In addition there are a Cello Sonata (1948); two flute sonatas (1951, 1957); a Piano Quintet (1951); *Theme and Variations* for violin and piano (1954); a Woodwind Quintet (1954); *Duo* for violin and cello (1955); *Music* for winds, strings, and harpsichord (1955); Piano Trio (1955, rev. 1959); *Three Pieces* for clarinet, cello, and piano (1956); Violin Sonata (1956); *Cello Partita* (1957), Wind Octet (1957); Clarinet Sonata (1958); *Portraits* for violin and piano (1959); a Piano Trio (1959); and Sextet for wind quintet and double bass (1959). Later works in this field are an Oboe Quartet (1960); *Duo no. 2* for violin and cello (1963); *Nonette* for piano, strings, wind, and brass (1968); *Priorities* for jazz band, rock band, and string quartet (1969); *Duo* for violin and piano (1971); *Five Trios and a Fantasy* for wind quintet (1972); *Elegy* and *Other Voices* for solo viola (1974); *Double String Quartet* (1983); *Duo* for cello and piano (1984); *Remembrance* violin, cello, clarinet, and piano (1982); Clarinet Quintet (1987); *Introduction, Barcarolle and Allegro* for flute and harp (1987); and *Partita* for solo violin (1990).

Laderman's solo vocal music includes *Songs for Eve* (Archibald McLeish) for soprano and piano (1966); *Songs from Michaelangelo* for baritone and piano (1968); *From the Psalms* for soprano and piano (1970); *Visions – Columbus* (Kazantzakis) for bass-baritone and orchestra (1975); *Worship* for soprano, tenor, and piano (1976); and *Song of Songs,* a cantata for soprano, flute, viola and cello (1977).

Laderman has provided music for the following documentary films: *The Charter* (1958); *The Invisible Atom* (1958); *The Black Fox* (1962); *The Question Tree* (1962); *The Image of Love* (1963); *Odyssey* (1964); *The Eleanor Roosevelt Story* (1965); *Magic Prison* (1966); *The Meaning of Modern Art* (1967); *The Bible as Literature* (1972); and *The Burden of Mystery* (1972). Among his scores for television are *Herschel* (1959); *The Invisible City* (1961); *The Voice of the Desert* (1962); *Eltanin* (1963); *Grand Canyon* (1964); *The Forgotten Peninsula* (1967); *Our Endangered Wildlife* (1967); *California the Most* (1968); *Before Cortez*

(1970); *In the Fall of 1844* (1971); *Cave People of the Philippines* (1972); and *Lamp Unto My Feet* (1978). He also wrote incidental music for two plays, *Machinal* (1960) and *The Lincoln Mask* (1971).

LA MONTAINE, JOHN

b. Oak Park, Illinois, 17 March 1920

La Montaine was a piano pupil of Margaret Parker, Margaret Farr Wilson, and Rudolph Ganz in Chicago, and received his first composition lessons from Stella Roberts. He attended the American Conservatory in Chicago (1935–38) and the Eastman School of Music, Rochester, New York (1938–42), where he studied under Howard Hanson, Max Landau, and Bernard Rogers. After serving in the U.S. Navy (1942–46) he received lessons from Bernard Wagenaar at the Juilliard School. He was also a pupil of Nadia Boulanger in Fontainbleau. From 1950 to 1954 he was a pianist with the NBC Symphony Orchestra under Toscanini. He was awarded two Guggenheim Fellowships (1959, 1960) and in 1962 was Composer-in-Residence at the American Academy in Rome. He taught briefly at the Eastman School of Music (1961, 1964–65).

La Montaine's first important work was the Piano Concerto, op. 9, commissioned by the Ford Foundation in 1958, which won the Pulitzer Prize the following year. The soloist at its premiere was Jorge Bolet with the National Symphony Orchestra of Washington, D.C. Also for piano and orchestra is *Birds of Paradise*, op. 34. Written in 1964, it was inspired by bird song from throughout the world and was used by Gerald Arpino for the ballet *Nightwings,* produced in 1966. He has composed three further piano concertos: no. 2, *Transformations* (1987); no. 3, *Children's Games* (1987); and no. 4 (1989).

La Montaine's orchestral music include *Canons*, op. 10a (1957); *Ode* for oboe and strings, op. 11 (1957); *Six Sonnets*, op. 12a (1957); *Recitative, Aria and Finale* for strings, op. 16a (1958); *Jubilant Overture*, op. 20 (1958); *Colloquy* for strings, op. 21 (1957); *Passacaglia and Fugue*, op. 21a (1958); Symphony No. 1, op. 28 (1957); *Overture: From Sea to Shining Sea*, op. 30, commissioned in 1961 for the inauguration of President John F. Kennedy; *A Summer Day,* a sonnet for orchestra, op. 32 (1962); *Canticle for Orchestra*, op. 33 (1963); *Overture: An American Sampler* (Be Glad then America), op. 43a (1974); a Flute Concerto, op. 48 (1979); *Two Scenes From the Song of Solomon* for flute and orchestra (1979); *Symphonic Variations* for piano and orchestra, op. 50 (1982); Concerto for strings, op. 51 (1981); and *Of Age, After Euripides* (1990). He has also composed *Incantation*, op. 39

(1968) for jazz band, commissioned by the Repertory Dance Theater of Utah.

Washington National Cathedral commissioned a trilogy of Christmas operas: *Novellis Novellis*, op. 31 (1960), *The Shephardes Plays*, op. 38 (1967), and *Erode the Greate*, op. 40 (1969). In addition to the *Christmas Trilogy,* he has also composed a cycle of carols, *Wonder Tidings*, op. 23 (1957) for soloists, chorus, harp, and percussion; *The Nine Lessons of Christmas*, op. 44 for chorus, harp, and percussion (1975); *The Whittier Service*, op. 45 for chorus, guitar, and organ (1979); and *The Lessons of Advent*, op. 52 for solo voices, narrator, double chorus, and instrumental ensemble (1983). Other choral works include *God of Grace and Glory*, op. 22 for chorus and organ (1958); *Sanctuary*, op. 17 for baritone, chorus, and organ (1961); *Te Deum*, op. 35 for chorus, wind, and percussion (1964); *Three Psalms*, op. 36 for chorus and small orchestra (1965); *Missa Naturae*, op. 37 for narrator, chorus, and orchestra (1966); *The Marshes of Glynn*, op. 53 for baritone, chorus, and orchestra (1984); a cantata, *The Birth of Freedom* (1988); and *In Praise of Britain's Queen and Elgar's Enigma* for chorus (1994).

La Montaine has composed several vocal works, usually on religious texts. The best known of these are *Songs of the Rose of Sharon*, op. 6 (1948), a biblical cycle for soprano and orchestra; and *Songs of the Nativity*, op. 13, originally for a cappella chorus, but later arranged for mezzo-soprano, organ, and small percussion ensemble. Other pieces for voice and orchestra include *Fragments from the Song of Songs* (Second Biblical Cycle), op. 29 for soprano (1959); and *Wilderness Journal*, op. 41 for bass baritone, organ, and orchestra, based on texts from Thoreau, which dates from 1972, perhaps his most significant work to date.

Among La Montaine's instrumental compositions are a Cello Sonata, op. 8 (1956); a String Quartet, op. 16 (1960); Woodwind Quartet, op. 24a (1958); Sonata for solo flute, op. 24 (1959); *Conversations*, op. 42 (1973); originally for clarinet and piano but subsequently arranged for several solo instruments including violin, viola, flute, saxophone, trombone, and marimba, each with piano accompaniment; *Twelve Studies*, op. 46 for two flutes (1975); and *Canonic Variations* for flute and clarinet, op. 47 (1980). His piano music includes a *Toccata*, op. 1; a Sonata, op. 3; *Twelve Relationships*, op. 10 (1959); *Six Dance Preludes*, op. 18; and a Sonata for piano, four hands, op. 25 (1960).

Besides the Christmas church pageants, La Montaine has written two operas, *Spreading the News*, op. 27 in one act (1957) and *Be Glad Then America*, op. 43, commissioned by the Institute for the Arts and Humanistic Studies, Pennsylvania State University for the American Bicentennial and performed on 6 February 1976.

265

LANSKY, PAUL
b. New York, New York, 18 June 1944

After studying at Queens College of the City University of New York with George Perle and Hugo Weisgall, Lansky moved to Princeton, where his teachers included Milton Babbitt, Edward Cone, and Earl Kim. He was a professional horn player with the Dorian Wind Ensemble (1965–66). Since 1969 he has taught at Princeton.

Except for one choral work, *Three Campion Choruses* (1992), most of his music has been instrumental or computer-generated. His chamber music includes *Modal Fantasy* for piano (1970); a String Quartet (1972–77); *Fanfare* for two horns (1976); *Crossworks* for piano, flute, clarinet, violin, and cello (1974–75); *Dance Suite* for piano (1977); Serenade for violin, viola, and piano (1978); *As If* for string trio and tape (1981–82); *Values of Time* for string quartet, wind quintet, and tape (1987); *Stroll* for piano, flute, cello, marimba, and tape (1988); *Hop* for marimba and violin (1993); and *Dancetracks for an Improvising Guitarist* for electric guitar and tape (1994).

Among his works for computer are *milde und leise* (1973); *Artifice (on Ferdinand's Reflection)* (1975–76);

Paul Lansky.
Photo: Kareem Black, courtesy the composer.

Six Fantasies on a Poem by Thomas Campion (1978–79); *Folk-Images* (1980–91); *As It Grew Dark* (1983); *Guy's Harp* for computer-processed harmonica (1984); *Idle Chatter* (1985); *Wasting* (1985); *Just-More-Idle-Chatter* (1987); *Notjustmoreidlechatter* (1988); *Smalltalk* (1988); *The Lesson* (1989); *Talkshow* (1989); *Not So Heavy Metal* for computer-processed guitar (1989); *Late August* (1989); *QuakerBridge* (1990); *NightTraffic* (1990); *The Sound of Two Hands* (1990); *Table's Clear* (1990); *Now and Then* (1991); *Word Color* (1992); *Memory Pages* (1993); *Still Time* (1994); and *Things She Carried* for computer-processed voice and sounds (1995–96).

LARSEN, LIBBY (BROWN)
b. Wilmington, Delaware, 24 December 1950

Larsen studied at the University of Minnesota (B.A., 1971; M.M., 1975; Ph.D., 1978), where her teachers included Dominick Argento, Paul Fetler, and Eric Stokes. In 1973 with Stephen Paulus she founded the Minnesota (now American) Composers' Forum in Minneapolis. From 1983 to 1987 she was Composer-in-Residence with the Minnesota Orchestra.

For the stage she has composed eleven operas: *The Words Upon the Windowpane* (W. B. Yeats) in one act, produced in Minneapolis in 1978; a one-act children's opera, *The Silver Fox* premiered in St Paul in 1979; *Tumbledown Dick* in two acts (St. Paul, 1980); *Moondoor* (3 acts; 1976, 1980); the three-act *Claire de Lune* (1984) performed in the following year in Little Rock, Arkansas; *Frankenstein: The Modern Prometheus* (1989), first heard in St. Paul in 1990; *A Wrinkle in Time* (one act; 1991); a chamber opera, *Mrs Dalloway* (1992); *Eric Hermannson's Soul* (1997); a chamber opera *Barnum's Bird* (2000); and the one-act *Dreaming Blue* (2002).

Larsen is widely known for her five symphonies. The First, subtitled *Water Music*, was commissioned by the Minnesota Orchestra, which gave the premiere in New York on 30 January 1985. Symphony no. 2, *Coming Forth Into Light* for soprano, tenor, chorus, and orchestra (1985) sets words by Jehan Sadat, the widow of the Egyptian President. Symphony no. 3, *Lyric* was first performed in 1991 by the Albany Symphony Orchestra. Symphony no. 4 (1998) is scored for string orchestra. Symphony no. 5 (*Solo Symphony*) was commissioned by the Denver Symphony Orchestra in 1999. Other orchestral works include *Tom Twist* (W.A. Butler) for narrator, mime, and orchestra (1975); *Weaver's Song and Jig* for string band and string orchestra (1978); *Three Cartoons* (1979); *Black Roller* for winds, strings, and piano (1981); *Pinions* for violin and chamber orchestra (1982); *Deep Summer Music* (1983); *Overture:*

Libby Larsen.
Photo: Ann Marsden, courtesy the composer.

Parachute Dancing, performed in 1984 by the American Composers Orchestra; *Seven Sneezes* (1985); *Carolis* (1986); *What the Monster Saw* (1987); *Collage Boogie* (1988); Trumpet Concerto (1988); *Three Summer Scenes* (1989); *Cold, Silent Snow,* a concerto for chamber orchestra (1989); a Piano Concerto*: Since Armstrong* (1989); *Ghosts of an Old Ceremony* for dancers and orchestra (1991); *Tambourines!* (1991); *Marimba Concerto: After Hampton* (1992); *Overture for the Ending of a Century* (1994); and a symphonic poem, *Ring of Fire* (1995).

Later orchestral pieces are *Happy Birthday to David* (1996); *Fanfare: Strum* (1996); *Blue Fiddler* (1996); *Cartoon Dance* (1997); *Roll Out the Thunder* (1997); *A Spell on Me That Holy Hour: Overture to Tsvetaeva* (1997); *All Around Sound: A Young Person's Introduction to Orchestral Sound* (1999); and *Still Life With Violin* for violin and orchestra (2000).

Larsen has contributed several items to the band repertory: *Grand Rondo: Napoleon Dances the Can-Can Across Italy, Hungary and Poland* (1988); *Sun Song* (1991); *Short Symphony* (1996); *Brass Flight* (1996); *Concert Dances* (1996); and *Hambone* (1999).

Larsen has composed a considerable number of instrumental works. Among these are *Theme and Deri-*

vations for harp (1972); *Three Pieces* for treble instrument and guitar (1973–74); *Four on the Floor* for violin, cello, double bass, and piano (1977); *Bronze Veils* for trombone and percussion (1979); *Ulloa's Ring* for flute and piano (1980); *Scudding* for cello (1980); *Triage* for harp (1982); *Jazz Variations* for bassoon (1984); *North Star Fanfare* for chamber ensemble (1984); *The Astonishing Flight of Gump* for chamber ensemble (1986); *Song Without Words* for clarinet and piano (1986); *Juba* for cello and piano (1986); *Love and Hisses* for double wind quintet (1986); *Vive* for flute quartet (1988); *Corker* for clarinet and percussion (1989); and *Xibalba* for bassoon and two percussionists (1989).

More recent chamber works include *Aspects of Glory* for organ (1990); *Schoenberg, Schenker, Schillinger* for string quartet (1991); *Concert Pieces* for tuba and piano (1993); *Slang* for clarinet, violin, and piano (1994); *Dancing Solo* for clarinet (1994); *Three Blue Third Pieces* for clarinet and guitar (1996); *A Child's Garden of Monsters: Dracula's Blues* for wind ensemble (1997); *Brazen Overture* for brass quintet (2000); *Ballet Deux* for two clarinets (2001); *Barn Dances* for flute, clarinet, and piano (2001); *The Book of Rhythm* for winds and Orff instruments (2001); Piano Trio no. 3 (2001); and Viola Sonata (2001).

Among Larsen's choral music are *Lachrimosa Christe* for solo voices, chorus, and orchestra (1974); *Dance Set* for chorus, clarinet, cello, piano, and percussion (1980); *In a Winter Garden* (Hampl) for soprano, tenor, chorus, and chamber orchestra (1982); *Ringeltanze* for chorus, strings, and bells (1983); *A Creeley Collection* (R. Creeley) for tenor, chorus, flute, and percussion (1984); *Three Summer Scenes* for chorus and orchestra (1988); *Song-Dances to the Light* for female voices, Orff instruments, and orchestra (1988); *Missa Gaia: Mass for the Earth* for unaccompanied voices (1991–92); *Ways of Spreading Light* (*Celebration of Light*) for chorus and orchestra (1994); and *Rag Rhythm Kid* for children's chorus and orchestra (1997). In addition she has composed numerous shorter works for a cappella chorus.

For solo voice, she has written *Saints Without Tears* (Phyllis McGinley) for soprano, flute, and bassoon (1976); *Three Rilke Songs* for soprano, flute, guitar, and harp (1977); *Eurydice* (H.D.) for soprano and string quartet (1978); *Cowboy Songs* for soprano and piano (1979); *Black Birds, Red Hill* for soprano, clarinet, and piano (1987); *Me* (Brenda Ueland) for soprano and piano (1987); *Sonnets from the Portuguese* (Elizabeth Barrett Browning) for soprano and piano (1991); *Mary Cassatt* for mezzo-soprano, trombone, and orchestra (1993); *Beloved Thou Hast Brought Me Many Flowers* for mezzo-soprano, cello, and orchestra (1994); *Margaret Songs* for soprano and piano (1996); *Songs of*

Love and Light for soprano and ensemble (1998); *Try Me, Good King* (*Last Words of the Wives of Henry VIII*) for soprano and piano (2000); *Notes Slipped Under the Door* for soprano, flute, and orchestra (2001); *If I Can Stop One Heart From Breaking* for soprano and orchestra (2001); *Hell's Bells* for soprano and handbells (2001); and *Raspberry Island Dreaming* for mezzo-soprano and orchestra (2002). *I It Am* for soprano, chorus, and orchestra was premiered at the London Promenade Concerts in July 2003.

LATHAM, WILLIAM PETERS
b. Shreveport, Louisiana, 4 January 1917

Latham studied at the Cincinnati College of Music, University of Cincinnati (1936–38) and at the Eastman School of Music, Rochester, New York with Eugene Goossens, Herbert Elwell, and Howard Hanson. Following service in the U.S. Army during World War II, he taught at Iowa State Teachers' College, Cedar Falls (1946–65). From 1965 to 1984 he was professor of music at North Texas State University, Denton. At his retirement, he was designated professor emeritus of music there.

For orchestra he has written a symphonic poem, *The Lady of Shalott* (1939); *Suggestions* (1939); *Fantasy Concerto* for flute, strings, and harp (1941); *Fantasy* for violin and orchestra (1946); *And Thou America* (1947); Symphony no. 1 (1950); Suite for trumpet and strings (1951); Symphony no. 2 (Sinfonietta) (1953); *Concerto Grosso* for two saxophones and wind ensemble (1960, rev. 1962); Concertino for saxophone and symphonic winds (1968, rev. 1969); *American Youth Performs* (1969); *Jubilee 13/50* (1978); *Supernova* (1983); and *Excelsior K-2* for piano and orchestra (1994).

Latham has written extensively for concert band: two marches, *Brighton Beach* (1954) and *Proud Heritage* (1955); *Three Chorale Preludes* (1956); *Court Festival* (1957); *Honors Day* (1959); *Passacaglia and Fugue* (1959); *Plymouth Variations* (1962); *Escapades* (1965); *Dionysian Festival* (1965); *Dodecaphonic Set* (1966); *Prayers in Space* (1971); *Dilemmae* (1973); *Prolegomena* (1974); *Revolution!* (1975); *Fusion* (1975); *March 6* (1979); *Drones, Airs and Games* (1983); *Suite Summertime* (1995); and *Y2K – The New Millenium March* (1999).

His choral works are equally numerous: *Peace* (Rupert Brooke) for chorus and orchestra (1943); *Prayer After World War* for chorus (1945); *A Prophesy of Peace* for chorus, organ, piano, and cymbals (1951); a cantata, *The Ascension of Jesus* (1952); Psalm 130 (1954); Psalm 148 (1954); *Music for Seven Poems* for chorus and orchestra (1958); *Blind With Rainbows* for

William P. Latham.
Courtesy Carol Latham.

chorus (1962); *Te Deum* for chorus, wind ensemble, and organ (1964); *The Music Makers* for chorus, rock group, tape, guru, and band (1972); *St. David's Mass* for chorus (1977); *Epigrammata* for chorus (1978); *Gaudeamus Academe* for tenor, chorus, announcer on tape, and percussion (1981); *Bitter Land* for chorus, brass quintet, and piano (1985); *My Heart Sings* for chorus and organ (1987); *Missa Novella* for young chorus (1988); and *Only in Texas* for chorus, piano, and percussion (1994).

Among Latham's vocal music are *River to the Sea* for baritone and orchestra (1942); *A Lenten Letter* for soprano, strings, and percussion (1974); *Te Deum Tejas*, eight poems for soprano, flute, and percussion (1981); *Metaphors*, three songs for soprano, tenor, and piano (1989); *A Green Voice*, a cantata for soprano, tenor, and piano (1989); *The Sacred Flame* for baritone and orchestra (1990); and *Requiem for My Love* (Mary Coleridge) for high voice (1996).

Latham's instrumental music includes three string trios (1938-39); three string quartets (1938-40); a Flute Sonatina (1937); an Oboe Sonata (1947); a Violin Sonata (1949); *Suite in Baroque Style* for flute and piano (1954); Sonata for recorder and harpsichord (1959); *Sisiphus 1971* for alto saxophone and piano (1971); *Preludes Before Silence* for piccolo and flute (1974); *Eidolons* for euphonium and piano (1977); *Ex Tempore* for alto saxophone (1978); and *Ion, the Rhapsode* for clarinet and piano (1984). For the stage Latham has composed three works: an opera, *Orpheus in Pecan Springs* (Denton, 1980); a ballet, *A Modern Trilogy* (Cincinnati, 1941); and a scenic cantata-ballet, *Orpheus in Cow Town* (1997).

LA VIOLETTE, WESLEY
b. St James, Minnesota, 4 January 1894
d. Escondido, California, 29 July 1978

La Violette graduated from Northwestern University, Evanston, Illinois in 1917 and received a D.Mus. from the Chicago Musical College in 1925. He taught at the Chicago Musical College (1923–33), De Paul University, Chicago (1933–40), and at the Los Angeles Conservatory from 1946. His influence on the West Coast extended to several jazz musicians, including Milt Rogers and Jimmy Giuffre.

For orchestra La Violette wrote *Requiem* (1925); *Chorale* (1926); *Penetrella* for strings (1928); *Osiris* (1929); *Festival Ode* (1930); *The Spook Hour* for small orchestra (1931); *Scherzo* for chamber orchestra (1931); *Nocturne* (1932); *Ode to an Immortal* (1934); Symphony no. 1 (1936); *Collegiana* (1936); *Prelude and Aria* (1937); *San Francisco Overture* (1939); Symphony no. 2, *Tom Thumb* for children (1940); *Music for the High Sierras* (1935); and Symphony no. 3 (1952). Works for solo instruments and orchestra include two violin concertos, no. 1, *Dedication* (1929) and no. 2 (1938); a Piano Concerto (1937); Double Concerto for string quartet and orchestra (1937); and a Concertino for flute (1943).

The three-act opera *Shylock,* completed in 1927, was awarded the David Bispham Medal in 1929. In 1955 he completed a second opera, *The Enlightened One*, on the life of Buddha. A ballet, *Schubertiana*, was performed in 1935 by Chicago Opera Ballet.

Among La Violette's choral works are *The Broken Vine* (1921); *Anima Mundi* (1933); the cantata *The Road to Calvary* (1952); a choral symphony, *Song of the Angels* (1952); and *Delphic Psalm* for chorus and brass (1964).

La Violette composed much chamber music including three string quartets (1926, 1933, 1936); a Piano Quintet (1927); Sonatina for two violins (1931, rev. 1951); Octet (1934); two violin sonatas (1934, 1937); *Evocation* for violin and piano (1936); *Three Pieces for string quartet* (1937); Sextet for piano and winds (1940); *Filigree Quartet* for flour flutes (1940); *Masquerade* for wind quintet (1940); a Flute Sonata (1941); *Largo Lirico* for string quartet (1942); a Flute Quintet (1943); and Serenade for flute and string quartet (1945).

He wrote a book, *Music and Its Makers*, published in 1937, and three volumes on religion: *The Creative Light* (1940), *The Bhagavad Gita* (1944, rev. 1955), and *The Crown of Wisdom* (1949).

LAW, ANDREW
b. Milford, Connecticut, 21 March 1749
d. Cheshire, Connecticut, 13 July 1821

Law graduated from Brown University, Providence, Rhode Island in 1778 and was ordained a minister at Hartford in 1787. He became a preacher and singing teacher in Philadelphia and Baltimore. He saw himself as a reformer of church music, who sought to improve standards in every way. His own compositions are simple, deliberately avoiding decorative extravagance. He also broke with tradition in his hymn settings by giving the melody to the soprano, not the tenor as had been the practice hitherto.

Today Law is remembered for the hymn tunes *Archdale* and *Blendon* and the patriotic song *Bunker Hill*. His first published book, *Select Number of Plain Tunes*, appeared in Boston in 1777. This was followed by four publications of greater importance: *Select Harmony* (New Haven 1778), *Collection of Best Tunes and Anthems* (1779), *A Collection of Hymns for Social Worship* (Cheshire 1782), and *The Musical Primer* (1793). In these he introduced the "shape-note" system, whereby normal musical notation was replaced by differently shaped note-heads: a triangle, oval, square, and diamond represented Fah, Soh, Lah, and Mi respectively in the sol-fa scale.

Law also published *Rudiments of Musick* (Cheshire 1783), which ran to four editions during the next ten years; *The Art of Singing* (Cheshire 1793); *Harmonic Companion and Guide to Social Worship* (Philadelphia 1807); and *The Art of Playing the Organ and Pianoforte* (Philadelphia 1809). He was one of the earliest writers on music in America, publishing *Essays on Music* in Philadelphia in 1814.

LAYTON, BILLY JIM
b. Corsicana, Texas, 14 November 1924

After studying with Carl McKinley at the New England Conservatory in Boston (1945–48), Layton attended Yale University (1948–51) where he was a pupil of Quincy Porter, and Harvard University (1951–54, 1957–60) as a pupil of Walter Piston. In 1954 on a Prix de Rome scholarship he went to Europe for three years.

After a year of teaching at the New England Conservatory, he joined the Harvard faculty in 1960. From 1968 to 1972 he was chairman of the department of music at the State University of New York at Stony Brook. Although initially a follower of Charles Ives and Elliott Carter, Layton has been influenced by Anton Webern; this is evident in the pointillistic instrumentation of his later works. He is so self-critical that only seven of his works have been published.

Layton's most widely successful composition is the Divertimento, op. 6 for violin, clarinet, bassoon, cello, trombone, harpsichord, and percussion (1958–60). Among his other pieces are *Five Studies* for violin and piano, op. 1 (1952); *Three Dylan Thomas Poems* for chorus and brass sextet, op. 3 (1954–56); and *Three Piano Studies*, op. 5 (1957). A String Quartet in two movements, op. 4, written in Rome in 1956, makes slight use of quarter tones in a manner derived from jazz. For orchestra he has composed an *Overture: An American Portrait*, op. 2 (1953) and *Dance Fantasy*, op. 7 (1962–64), a ballet score without scenario.

LAZAROF, HENRI

b. Sofia, Bulgaria, 12 April 1932

Lazarof studied at the Academy of Music in Sofia before moving to Israel in 1948; he attended the New Conservatory of Music in Jerusalem (1949–52), where he was a pupil of Paul Ben-Haim. From 1955 to 1957 he studied with Goffredo Petrassi at the Academy of St. Cecilia in Rome. He went to America in 1957 and was a pupil of Arthur Berger and Harold Shapero at Brandeis University, Waltham, Massachusetts (1957–59). In 1962 he joined the music faculty at the University of California, Los Angeles, where he was a professor until his retirement in 1987. In 1971 he spent a year as Composer-in-Residence in West Berlin at the invitation of the West German Government.

Most of Lazarof's compositions are instrumental and atonal in an idiom that in the early works shows some influence of both Bartók and Schoenberg. Pride of place in his music is the set of seven symphonies: no. 1 (1978), no. 2 (1992), no. 3, *Choral Symphony* for alto, bass-baritone, chorus, and orchestra (Seattle 1994), no. 4, *In Celebration* for chorus and orchestra (1998), no. 5 for chorus, winds, brass, and percussion (1999), no. 6, *Winds of Sorrow* (2000); and no. 7 (2001). His other orchestral works include *Piccolo Serenata* (1959); *Odes* (1963); *Structures Sonores* in five movements, performed by the Los Angeles Philharmonic Orchestra under Zubin Mehta in 1966; *Mutazione* (1967) for the Utah Symphony Orchestra; *Omaggio* for a chamber ensemble of 19 players (1968); *Koncordia* for strings (1972); *Ritratto* (1973); Concerto for Orchestra no. 1 (1977); *Chamber Symphony* (1977); Sinfonietta (1981); Concerto for Orchestra no. 2, *Icarus* (1984); *Poema*

(1985); *Concertante I* for 16 strings and two horns (1988); and *Three Pieces* (1995).

For solo instruments and orchestra Lazarof has written a Piano Concerto (1956); a Viola Concerto (1959–60); Concerto for piano and 20 instruments (1960-61); *Tempi concertati,* a double concerto for violin, viola, and chamber orchestra (1964); two cello concertos (1968, 1991); *Ricercar* for viola, piano, and orchestra (1968); *Textures* for piano and five instrumental groups (1970); two flute concertos composed for James Galway (1973, 2002); *Spectrum* for solo trumpet (doubling flugelhorn), orchestra, and tape (1972–73); *Chamber Concerto no. 3* for 12 instrumentalists (1974); *Volo (Canti da Requiem)* for viola and two string ensembles (1976); Violin Concerto no. 2 (1985); *Tableaux* for piano and orchestra (1987); a Clarinet Concerto (1989); *The Summit Concerto* for solo trumpet, brass, and percussion (1996); Concerto for oboe and chamber orchestra (1997); *Fantasia* for horn (1997); *Viola Rhapsody* (1998); *Partita Madrigali*; a double concerto for violin and cello (2000); *Symphonia Concertante* for four winds (2000); and Violin Concerto no. 3 (2002).

Lazarof's large output of instrumental music includes eight string quartets (1956, 1962, 1980, 1996, 2000, 2001, 2002, 2002); a String Trio (1957); Sonata for solo violin (1958); *Concertino da Camera* for wind quintet (1959); *Asymptotes* for flute and vibraphone (1959); *Inventions* for viola and piano (1962); Trio for winds (1962); *Quantetti* for four pianos (1964); *Espaces* for instrumental ensemble (1966); *Rhapsody* for violin and piano (1966); Octet for wind instruments (1967); *Intonazione* for two pianos (1967); Divertimento for five players (1969); *Cadence I* for cello (1969); *Cadence II* for viola and tape (1969); *Cadence III* for violin and two percussion (1970); *Continuum* for string trio (1970); *Partita* for brass quintet and tape (1971); *Cadence V* for flute and tape (1972); *Cadence VI* for tuba and tape (1973); *Duo* for cello and piano (1973); *Concertanzioni* for trumpet, six instruments, and tape (1973); *Adieu* for clarinet and piano (1974); Suite for solo percussion and five instruments (1975); *Fanfare* for six trumpets (1980); Wind Trio no. 2 (1981); *Lyric Suite* for violin (1983); Serenade for string sextet (1985); *La Laurenziana* for string octet (1987); *Concertante II* for octet (1988); a Piano Trio (1989); *Prayers* for ten players (1990); Divertimento no. 1 for clarinet, viola, cello, and vibraphone (1990); Divertimento no. 2 for clarinet, horn, string trio, and piano (1992); *Offrande* for clarinet, violin, viola, and piano (1996); *Inventione Concertata* for brass quintet (1997); *Six Bagatelles* for solo violin (1997); String Quintet (1997); Violin Sonata (1998); *Variants* for horn quartet (1998); *Intermezzi* for cello and piano (1999); and Quintet for oboe and strings (1999).

Although most of Lazarof's works are for instruments, he has written four choral items: *Cantata* for narrator, mixed chorus, and instruments (1958), *The First Day* for a cappella choir (1959), *Canti* for large chorus (1973); and *Legends From the Bible* for chorus, four horns, and two vibraphones (2000). For soprano and chamber ensemble he has composed a setting of poems by Dylan Thomas, *Encounters* (1997).

For the stage he has written three ballets: *Events* (1973), *Canti* (1980), and *Mirrors, Mirrors* (1980).

LEAUMONT, CHEVALIER MARIE ROBERT DE

b. France, 18th century
d. Charleston, South Carolina, 1812

The Chevalier de Leaumont was one of the many refugees from the French Revolution who sought safety in America. At that time every aristocrat was taught to be a competent musician as part of his normal education. When faced with earning a living in the New World, these gentlemen found music to be the only practical training they had received which could be used to gain a livelihood. Leaumont was a nobleman and former officer who seems to have found little difficulty in establishing himself as a violinist and "leader of the band." In 1790 he was directing an orchestra and playing chamber music in Boston. It is recorded that he performed symphonies by Haydn and Pleyel on 1 June 1796. On 20 April 1798 he gave a benefit concert for himself, one of the few direct ways in which to earn money through music.

Although only an amateur musician, he gained a reputation as a violinist, and one of his compositions, a *Duo Concertante pour clavecin ou la forte-piano et violoncello* (1781), although closely modeled on the instrumental music of Haydn, has great charm. In 1800 he moved to Charleston, South Carolina, where he died.

LEE, DAI-KEONG

b. Honolulu, Hawaii, 2 September 1915

Lee was born of Chinese parents. At first he studied medicine at the University of Hawaii, but in 1937 he went to the United States, where he became a pupil of Roger Sessions at Princeton University and of Otto Luening at Columbia University (1951). Later, on a Juilliard Fellowship, he worked with Frederick Jacobi and took lessons from Aaron Copland at Tanglewood (1941). During the Second World War he served in the U.S. Air Force. He was awarded two Guggenheim Fellowships (1945, 1951). His whole life has been devoted to composition.

Lee has composed seven one-act operas: *The Poet's Dilemma* (New York, 1940); *Open the Gates* (New York, 1951); *Phineas and the Nightingale* (1951), a comedy concerning Jenny Lind and P.T. Barnum, the circus owner; and *Night People.* This last work, about gang warfare in Greenwich Village, has certain parallels with *West Side Story.* A fifth opera, *Speakeasy,* was performed in New York in February 1957. It was revised in 1979 with a new title, *Ballad of Kitty the Barkeep.* Also dating from 1957 are a pair of one-act operas, *Two Knickerbocker Tales* (1957).

His most popular work is the incidental music for the comedy *Teahouse of the August Moon,* which was staged in 1954 and later made into a successful movie. He composed two other musical plays, *Noa Noa* (1972) and *Jenny Lind* (1981), based on *Phineas and the Nightingale,* and a ballet, *Waltzing Matilda* (1951).

Lee's principal orchestral works are two symphonies, no. 1 in one movement (1941, rev. 1947) and no. 2 performed in San Francisco in 1952. Other orchestral pieces are *Prelude and Hula* (1939); *Introduction and Scherzo* for strings, a CBS commission (1941); *Hawaiian Festival Overture* (1942); *Golden Gate Overture* (1942); *Pacific Prayer* (1942); *Festival Ode* (1942); *Overture in C* (1945); Violin Concerto (1947, rev. 1955); *Concerto Grosso* for strings (1952); *Polynesian Suite* (1958); *Three Pieces for the Pacific* (1959); *The Golden Lotus* (1961); *The Gold of Their Bodies* (1963); and *Music for Naupaka..* For children he has written *Peter and His Magic Flute* (*Variations on a Theme of Prokofiev*) for narrator and orchestra.

Lee's major choral works are *Mele Olili* for solo voice, chorus, and orchestra (1961) and *Canticle of the Pacific* for choir and orchestra (1968).

Among his instrumental music are a Piano Sonatina (1943), a String Quartet (1944), *Introduction and Allegro* for cello and piano (1947), and *Incantation and Dance* for violin and piano (1948).

LEES, BENJAMIN

b. Harbin, China, 8 January 1924

Lees went with his Russian parents to the United States when he was very young. After serving in the U.S. Army in the Second World War, he attended the University of Southern California (1946–48) where his teachers included Halsey Stevens and Ingolf Dahl. His most important mentor was George Antheil, with whom he worked for five years (1949–54). A Guggenheim Fellowship in 1954 and a Fulbright Fellowship in 1956 enabled him to spend five years in France, one year in Vienna and one year in Finland. He was awarded a second Guggenheim Fellowship in 1966. He has taught at the Peabody Conservatory (1962–64, 1966–68), Queen's College, New York (1964–66), the Manhattan School of Music (1972–74), and the Juilliard School (1976–77). Since then he has concentrated solely on composition. His music shows some influence of his long stay in France with an emphasis on classical forms and counterpoint.

Lees has written five symphonies. No. 1 was composed in 1953; no. 2, commissioned and premiered by the Louisville Orchestra in 1958; no. 3, commissioned by the Detroit Symphony Orchestra, was premiered in Detroit in 1969. Symphony no. 4, subtitled *Memorial Candles*, is a commemoration of the Holocaust, scored for mezzo-soprano, solo violin and orchestra; it sets poems by Nelly Sachs. Its premiere was given in 1985 by the Dallas Symphony Orchestra, which had commissioned it. Symphony no. 5, *Kalmar Nyckel* (1986), was premiered by the Delaware Symphony Orchestra in Wilmington in 1988.

In 1962 the Rochester Philharmonic Orchestra introduced the Concerto for Orchestra written in 1959. Another significant composition, Concerto for String Quartet and Orchestra, was commissioned by the Kansas City Philharmonic Orchestra and performed by them with the Paganini Quartet in January 1965. The Concerto for Chamber Orchestra was commissioned by the Chamber Symphony of Philadelphia in 1964. Other orchestral works include *Profile* (1952); *Declamation* for piano and strings (1953); *Divertimento Burlesca* (1957); *Prologue, Capriccio and Epilogue* (1959); *Interlude* for string orchestra (1960); *Spectrum* (1964); *Concertante Breve* (1959); *Silhouettes* (1967); and *The Trumpet of the Swan* for narrator, trumpet, and orchestra (1972).

Lees has written a Violin Concerto (1958), first performed by Henryk Szeryng and the Boston Symphony Orchestra under Erich Leinsdorf in 1963, and an Oboe Concerto, commissioned in 1963 by John de Lancie and performed in Philadelphia. His Piano Concerto no. 1 received its premiere with Alexander Jenner as soloist in Vienna in 1956. The Second Piano Concerto (1966) was first performed by Gary Graffman and the Boston Symphony Orchestra under Erich Leinsdorf in March 1968.

Etudes for piano and orchestra was commissioned by the Houston Symphony Orchestra and performed in 1974 by James Dick with Lawrence Foster conducting. *Variations* for piano and orchestra was commissioned in 1976 by the Music Teachers National Association and performed by Eugene List with the Dallas Symphony Orchestra under Louis Lane. Other orchestral works include *Fanfare for a Centennial* for brass and percussion (1974); *Passacaglia* (1976), commissioned for the National Symphony Orchestra of Washington, D.C.; and Concerto for Woodwind Quin-

Benjamin Lees.
Courtesy Boosey & Hawkes.

tet and Orchestra for the Detroit Symphony Orchestra (1977). *Mobiles* was performed by the Fort Worth Symphony Orchestra under John Giordano at Carnegie Hall, New York on 12 April 1980. The *Double* Concerto for cello, piano, and orchestra was performed in New York on 7 November 1982 by Harry Clark and Sanda Schuldmann with the New York Philharmonic Orchestra, conducted by Sergiu Comissiona.

Lees's most recent compositions for orchestra are Concerto for brass choir and orchestra (1983); *Celebration* (1983); *Portrait of Rodin,* commissioned by the Dallas Symphony Orchestra (1984); a Horn Concerto (1992), premiered by the Pittsburgh Symphony Orchestra conducted by Lorin Maazel; *Borealis,* performed in 1993 by the Wichita Symphony Orchestra; *Constellations* (1996–97); and a Percussion Concerto, performed in Monte Carlo in 1999.

For the stage Lees has written two operas, the one-act *The Oracle* (1955) to his own text, and *Medea in Corinth,* performed in London in 1971. The ballet *Scarlatti Portrait,* based on seven Scarlatti keyboard sonatas, was performed by San Francisco Ballet on 15 March 1979; an orchestral suite was premiered in 1982 by the Vienna Chamber Orchestra under Philippe Entremont. Lee's dramatic cantata *Visions of Poets* for soprano, tenor, chorus, and orchestra is his only extended choral work. It was composed in 1961 to a commission from the Seattle Symphony Orchestra and dedicated to the new Seattle Opera House. The premiere in 1962 was conducted by Milton Katims.

Lees has written several extended pieces for solo voices, including *Songs of the Night* to poems of Richard Nickson (1952); *Three Songs* for contralto and piano to words by Blake and Nickson, premiered in New York in 1960 by Maureen Forrester; *Cyprian Songs* for baritone and piano (1960); *Staves* (Richard Nickson) (1977–78); *Omen* (Nickson) for soprano and piano (1980); *Paumanok* (Whitman) for mezzo-soprano and piano (1980); *Echoes of Normandy* for tenor, tape, organ, and orchestra, commissioned in 1994 by the Dallas Symphony Orchestra to commemorate the D-Day landings in World War II; and *The Golden Net* for soprano, tenor, countertenor, and baritone (1997).

Lees's chamber music comprises five string quartets (1952, 1955, 1980, 1990, 2002), the second of which won a UNESCO prize; three violin sonatas (1953, 1973, 1989); *Evocation* for flute (1953); *Movement da camera* for flute, clarinet, cello, and piano (1954); *Three Variables* for piano and wind quartet (1955); a Horn Sonata (1958); *Invenzione* for unaccompanied violin written for Ruggiero Ricci in 1965; *Duo* for flute and clarinet (1967); *Study No. 1* for solo cello (1969); *Collage* for wind quintet, string quartet, and percussion (1973); and *Soliloquy Music for King Lear* for flute (1975). Later instrumental music includes *Dialogue* for cello and piano (1977); Cello Sonata (1981); two piano trios, no. 1 (1983) and no. 2, *Silent Voices* (1998); *Contours* for violin, cello, clarinet, horn, and piano (1994); and *Night Spectres* for solo cello (1999).

Lees has contributed a number of important items to the repertory of contemporary piano music including four sonatas (1949, 1950, 1956, 1963), the first two now withdrawn; *Toccata* (1953); *Fantasia* (1954); *Ten Pieces* (1954); *Sonata Breve* (1956); *Six Ornamental Etudes* (1957); *Kaleidoscopes* (1958); *Epigram* (1960); *Three Preludes* (1962); *Odyssey I* (1970); *Fantasy Variations* (1984); *Odyssey II* (1986); *Mirrors* (1992); and a work for two pianos, *Tableau* (2002).

LESSARD, JOHN AYRES

b. San Francisco, California, 3 July 1920

Lessard learned to play the piano and trumpet, and received his first lessons in composition from Henry Cowell. At the age of 17 he went to study in Paris with Alfred Cortot at the Ecole Normale (1937–39). Nadia Boulanger was his teacher at this time and also later at the Longy School of Music in Cambridge, Massachusetts (1940). He was awarded two Guggenheim Fellowships (1946, 1953) and an Alice M. Ditson Award (1946). From 1962 until his retirement in 1990, he was

on the music faculty of the State University of New York at Stony Brook. Lessard is one of the original members of the so-called Stravinsky school, which included Berger, Irving Fine, Haieff, and Foss. His music is fundamentally neo-classical in style. After 1959 he gradually incorporated serial techniques of pitch, rhythm and timbre into his compositions.

The Piano Sonata (1940), performed in New York in 1941 by Joanna Harris, and the Quintet for flute, clarinet, and string trio (1943) are his first important works. Lessard's interest in wind instruments is reflected in many of his compositions: Concerto for wind instruments (1949); *Partita* for wind quintet (1952); Octet for wind (1953); *Quodlibets* for two trumpets and trombone (1967); Wind Quintet no. 2 (1970); Brass Quintet (1973); and *Fantasy* for trumpet and piano (1974). Other instrumental pieces include *Three Movements* for violin and piano (1948); a Cello Sonata (1953–54); *Trio of Consanguinity* for flute, viola, and cello (1957); Trio for flute, violin, and piano (1959); *Duo Sonata* for violin and piano (1962); String Trio (1963); and Piano Trio (1966). From 1975 to 1978 Lessard occupied himself with chamber music for trumpet in a work entitled *Movements for Trumpet and Various Instruments*: *I*, with vibraphone, *II*, viola, *III*, violin, *IV*, percussion, V, violin and cello, *VI*, viola, cello and percussion, *VII*, cello, and *VIII*, flute, harp, and two cellos.

At the request of Sylvia Marlowe he has made a significant contribution to the limited repertory of modern music for harpsichord. These include a solo *Toccata in four movements* (1951), *Perpetual Motion* (1952), and a Concerto for harpsichord and chamber ensemble (1959). In 1980 he completed a large-scale piece for piano, *Threads of Sound Recalled,* premiered by Dwight Peltzer. Also for piano are a Piano Sonata (1945), *For Aaron* (1981), and four *Bagatelles* (1986, 1988, 1990, 1991).

Later chamber music has focused on the guitar: *Concert Duo* for viola and guitar (1981); Divertimento for guitar (1981); *Music 1–3* for guitar and percussion (1983); *Concert Duo* for two guitars (1984); and *Four Pieces* for viola, guitar, and cello (1987). His most recent instrumental works include *Drift, Follow, Persist* for horn, piano, and percussion (1988); Quintet for flute, clarinet, violin, cello, and piano (1993); and *Gather and Disperse* for chamber ensemble (1994).

Outstanding among his 50 songs are the early *Ariel's Song* (Shakespeare; 1941); *Orpheus* (Shakespeare; 1943); *Full Fathom Five* (Shakespeare; 1948); *The Bag of a Bee* (1949); *When as in Silks My Julia Goes* (1951); *Six Mother Goose Songs* (1953); *Don Quixote and the Sheep* for baritone and orchestra (1955); and *Rose Cheekt Laura* (1960). His most extended vocal work is *Fragments from the Cantos of Ezra Pound* for baritone and nine instruments, composed in 1969. His recent sets of songs are *Stars, Hill, Valley* for soprano and piano, dating from 1983; *The Pond in a Bowl* for soprano, piano, marimba, and vibraphone (1984); and *The Seasons* for soprano, two percussionists, and piano (1992).

Lessard has composed three concertos: for violin (1941), for flute, clarinet, bassoon, and strings (1952), and for harp (1963). His other orchestral works are *A Box Hill Overture* (1946); *Cantilena* for oboe and strings (1946); *Little Concert* (1947); Wind Concerto (1949); *Serenade for Strings* (1953); Serenade (1957); *Suite for Orchestra* (1959); *Sinfonietta Concertante* (1961); and *Pastimes and an Alleluia* (1974).

LEVANT, OSCAR

b. Pittsburgh, Pennsylvania, 27 December 1906
d. Beverly Hills, California, 14 August 1972

Levant studied piano with Sigmund Stojowski and composition with Joseph Schillinger and Arnold Schoenberg. He was a gifted pianist and close friend of George Gershwin. Levant is best remembered today for his aphorisms and musical portraits of his contemporaries in three autobiographical books: *A Smattering of Ignorance* (1940), *The Memoirs of an Amnesiac* (1965), and *The Unimportance of Being Oscar* (1968).

Levant was the soloist in his own Piano Concerto (1936), performed in 1942 with the NBC Symphony Orchestra. His orchestral works include a *Sinfoniette* (1934), *Nocturne* (1936), Suite (1937), and an overture, *1912* (1942). Among his chamber works are a String Quartet (1937) and a Piano Sonata (1931).

Levant provided scores for a number of films, including *Tanned Legs*; *Street Girl*; *Leathernecking* (1930); *Crime Without Passion* (1934); *Charlie Chan at the Opera* (1936); *Nothing Sacred* (1937); and *Fellow Americans* (1943). He also performed both musically and dramatically in over a dozen films, including *The Dance of Life* (1929), *In Person* (1935), *Rhythm on the River* (1947), *Rhapsody in Blue* (1945), and *An American in Paris* (1951).

LEVY, MARVIN DAVID

b. Passaic, New Jersey, 2 August 1932

At New York University, Levy was a pupil of Philip James; he later studied with Otto Luening at Columbia University. From 1952 to 1958 he was archivist for the American Opera Society. He has also been a music critic for several leading publication including *Musical America*, *New York Herald Tribune*, *American Record Guide*, and *Opera News*. He was the recipient of two Prix de Rome Fellowships (1962–63, 1965) and two Guggenheim Fellowships (1960, 1964). From 1989 to 1994 he was artistic director of the Fort Lauderdale (now Florida Grand) Opera.

Levy's principal activities as a composer have been in the field of opera. Important among his works for the stage are three one-act operas: *The Tower,* an opera buffa composed in 1955 for the Santa Fe Opera; *Sotoba Komachi,* based on a fourteenth-century Japanese Noh play, for two dancers, four singers, and chamber ensemble performed in New York in 1957; and *Escorial* (1958), based on a play by Michel de Ghelderode.

Levy's best-known work is the three-act opera *Mourning Becomes Electra,* from the play by Eugene O'Neill. It was commissioned by the Ford Foundation in 1966 and performed at the Metropolitan Opera, New York on 17 March 1967. In 1978 he completed *The Balcony,* an opera based on the play by Jean Genet, commissioned by the Metropolitan Opera. To his own libretti and lyrics Levy has composed a musical, *The Grand Balcony* (2 acts; 2003), and *The Zachary Svar,* an opera in one act for children (2001).

His vocal music includes *Echoes* for soprano and chamber ensemble (1956); a Christmas oratorio, *For the Time Being* (Auden) for soloists, narrator, chorus, and orchestra (1959); a cantata, *One Person* for contralto and orchestra (1962); and *Masada* (1973, rev. 1987 and 2000), a large-scale oratorio for narrator, tenor, chorus, and orchestra, composed to celebrate the 25th anniversary of the founding of the state of Israel. It was premiered at the John F. Kennedy Center for the Performing Arts, Washington, D.C. in October 1973 under the direction of Antal Dorati.

Levy has also written *In Memoriam: W. H. Auden* for voice and chamber orchestra, premiered in New York in February 1974; *Canto de los Marranos* for soprano and orchestra (1977); *Since Nine O'Clock* for voice and orchestra (1984); and *A Winter's Tale* (Dylan Thomas) for mezzo-soprano and orchestra. He has also set the *Sacred Service Sabbath Eve: Shir Shel Mushe,* composed in 1964 for the Park Avenue Synagogue in New York City.

For orchestra he has composed *Caramoor Festival Overture* (1959); a Symphony (1960); *Kyros,* a dance poem for chamber orchestra (1961); a Piano Concerto (1970); *Sonata strofico* for chamber orchestra (1970); *Trialogues I* for the Chicago Symphony Orchestra, performed in 1972; *Trialogues II* (1972); *Pascua Florida* (1987); and *Arrows of Time* (1988). Among his instrumental pieces are a String Quartet (1955), *Rhapsody* for violin, clarinet, and harp (1956), and *Chassidic Suite* for horn and piano (1956).

Levy provided incidental music for George Farquhar's play *The Recruiting Officer* (1955) and the film score for *The Neighboring Shore* (1960).

LEWIS, ROBERT HALL
b. Portland, Oregon, 22 April 1926
d. Baltimore, Maryland, 22 March 1996

Hall studied at the Eastman School of Music with Bernard Rogers and Howard Hanson (1946–51); Princeton University; and, in Paris, with Nadia Boulanger and Eugene Bigot (1952–53). In addition he was a pupil of Hans Erich Apostel and Ernst Krenek in Vienna (1955–57). He also received conducting lessons from Pierre Monteux and Hans Swarowsky. From 1958 he taught at Goucher College and the Peabody Conservatory and was a member of the music faculty of Johns Hopkins University (1969–80). He was the recipient of two Fulbright Fellowships (1955, 1957) and two Guggenheims (1966, 1980).

In his music Lewis used a mixture of serialism and free atonality. For orchestra he wrote *Poem* for strings (1949); *Concert Overture* (1951); *Sinfonia: Expressions for Orchestra* (1955); *Prelude and Finale* (1959); *Designs* (1963); Symphony no. 1 (1964); *Music for 12 Players* (1965); *Three Pieces* (1965, rev. 1966); Concerto for chamber orchestra (1967, rev. 1972); Symphony no. 2 (1971); *Intermezzi* (1972); *Nuances II* (1975); *Ossevazioni II* for winds, keyboard, harp, and percussion (1978); *Moto* (1980); *Atto* for strings (1981); Symphony no. 3 (1982–85); Concerto for strings, four trumpets, harps, and piano (1984); *Destini* for winds and strings (1985); *Invenzione* (1988); *Three Movements on Scenes of Hieronymous Bosch* (1989); Symphony no. 4 (1990); *Images and Doalogues* (1992); *Ariosi* (1995); and *Siena* for strings (1995).

Lewis composed four string quartets (1956, 1962, 1981, 1993); *Music for 12 players* (1965); Brass Quintet (1966); Trio for clarinet, violin, and piano (1966); *Monophonies I – IX* for solo winds (1966–77); *Tangents* for double brass quartet (1968); Sonata *for solo violin* (1968); Divertimento for six instruments (1969); *Inflections I* for double bass (1969) and *II* for piano trio (1970); *Serenades I* for piano (1970), *II* for flute and piano (1970), and *III* for brass quintet (1982); *Fantasiemusik I* for cello and piano (1973), *II* for clarinet and piano (1978); *III* for saxophone, piano, and percussion (1984); *Combinazioni I* for clarinet, violin, cello, and piano (1974), *II* for eight percussion and piano (1974), *III* for narrator, oboe/English horn, and percussion (1977), *IV* for cello and piano (1977), and *V* for four violas (1982); *Nuances I* for violin and piano (1974); *Osservazioni I* for flute; piano, and percussion; *Facets* for cello and piano (1978); *A due I* for flute/alto flute/piccolo and harp (1981), *II* for oboe/English horn and percussion (1981), *III* for bassoon and harp (1985), *IV* for soprano and piano (1985), and *VII* for bassoon and trumpet (1986); a Wind Quintet (1983); *Diptychon* for nine players (1984); *Duo* for cello

and percussion (1987); *Dimensioni* for clarinet, string trio, and piano (1988); *9 Visions* for piano trio (1992); and *Ottetto* (1994).

Among Lewis's vocal works are *Acquainted with Night* (Robert Frost) for soprano, chorus, and orchestra (1951); *Five Songs* (R. Felmayer) for soprano, clarinet, horn, cello, and piano (1957); *Due Madrigali* for chorus and percussion (1972); *Prayers of Jane Austen* for chorus, piano, and percussion (1977); *Kantaten* for chorus and piano, based on 16th century chorales with German, English and Italian texts (1980); and *Monophony X* for solo soprano (1983).

LIEBERMANN, LOWELL
b. New York, New York, 22 February 1961

Liebermann began piano lessons at the age of eight, making his concert debut in 1977 at the Carnegie Recital Hall, New York. He studied with David Diamond, at first privately, later with him at the Juilliard School (1979–84), where he also received lessons from Jacob Lateiner (piano) and Vincent Persichetti (composition). While attending Juilliard, he studied conducting privately with Laszlo Halasz.

Among his orchestral works are Concertino for cello and chamber orchestra (1982); two symphonies, no. 1 (1982) and no. 2 for chorus and orchestra (1999),

Lowell Liebermann.
Photo: Christopher Beane, courtesy the composer.

premiered in the following year in Dallas; two piano concertos (1983, 1992); *The Domain of Arnheim* (1990); two concertos for James Galway, flute (1992) and flute and harp (1995); and a *Piccolo* Concerto (1996) for Jan Gippo. Also for orchestra are *Revelry* (1995); *Kontapunktus* for Japanese drums and orchestra (1996); *Loss of Breath* (1997); a Trumpet Concerto (1999); *Pegasus* for narrator and orchestra (2000); a Violin Concerto composed in 2001 for Chantal Juillet; *Rhapsody on a Theme of Paganini* for piano and orchestra (2001); Concerto for Orchestra (Toledo, Ohio, 2002); and *Dorian Gray: A Symphonic Portrait* (2000). His opera *The Picture of Dorian Gray* (1993–94) was produced in Monte Carlo in 1996.

Liebermann's chamber music includes two cello sonatas (1978, 1998); *Two Pieces* for violin and viola (1978); two string quartets (1979, 1998); a Viola Sonata (1984); a Flute Sonata (1987); a Double Bass Sonata (1987); a Sonata for flute and guitar (1988); a Quintet for clarinet, piano, and string trio (1988); *Fantasy on a Fugue by J.S. Bach* for wind quintet and piano (1989); Concerto for violin, piano, and string quartet (1989); *Fantasy* for bass koto (1989); a Piano Trio (1990); a Piano Quintet (1990); a Violin Sonata (1994); Sonata for flute and harp (1996); *Eight Pieces* for flutes (1997); *Nocturne Fantasy* for two guitars (2000); and Trio no. 1 for flute, cello, and piano (2002).

Of Liebermann's many works for piano, the most important are three sonatas, no. 1 (1977), no. 2 *Sonata Notturna* (1983), and no. 3 (2002); *Eight Nocturnes* (1990–03); *Three Impromptus* (2000); and *Variations on a theme of Mozart* for two pianos (1993; orch. 2001). His most performed piano work is *Gargoyles*, op. 29 (1989).

For voices Liebermann has written *War Songs* for baritone and piano (1980); *Three Poems of Stephen Crane* for baritone and small orchestra (1985); *Sechs Gegange nach Gedichten von Nelly Sachs* for soprano and piano (1986); *Final Songs* for baritone and piano (1987); *Night Songs* for baritone and piano (1987); *A Poet to His Beloved* for tenor, flute, string quartet, and piano (1993); *Out of the Cradle* for mezzo-soprano and string quartet (1993); *Appalachian Liebeslied* for soprano, baritone, and piano duet (1996); *Struwwelpeterlieder* for soprano, viola, and piano (1996); *Three Dream Songs* for tenor and piano (1996); *Six Songs on Poems of Longfellow* for tenor and piano (1997); *Six Songs on Poems of Raymond Carver* for tenor and piano (2002); and *Two Songs on Poems of Anthony Hecht* for tenor and piano (2003). His three works for choir are *Two Choral Elegies* (1977), *Missa Brevis* for tenor, baritone, chorus, and organ (1985); and *Three Elizabethan Songs* for a cappella chorus (1999).

LIEBERSON, PETER
b. New York, New York, 25 October 1946

Peter Lieberson is the son of the recording executive and composer Goddard Lieberson (1911–1977) and the ballet dancer and actress Vera Zorina. He is married to the mezzo-soprano Lorraine Hunt Lieberson. He studied English at New York University (1964–68) and received informal composition lessons from Milton Babbitt. At Columbia University (1972–74) he was a pupil of Charles Wuorinen and Harvey Sollberger. Since 1974 he has made an extensive study of Tibetan Kajnagana Buddhism in Boulder, Colorado, where he was a pupil of the late Chogyam Trungpa Rinpochee. During his work on a doctorate at Brandeis University (1981) he was guided by Donald Martino. Before settling in Halifax, Nova Scotia as director of a center for training in Shambhala Buddhism, he taught at Harvard University (1984–88). He has received a number of awards from the National Institute of Arts and Letters and a Guggenheim Fellowship (1984).

Lieberson is best known for two piano concertos, no. 1 written for Peter Serkin (1980–83) and no. 2, *Red Garuda* (1998–99), and *Drala* (1986), all premiered in Boston. Among his other orchestral works are *The Gesar Legend* (1988); *World's Turning* (1993); a Viola Concerto (1993); *Fire* (1995) composed for the 150th anniversary of the New York Philharmonic Orchestra; *Free and Easy Wanderer*, commissioned in 1998 by the London Sinfonietta; Horn Concerto (1998); *Six Realms*, a Cello Concerto written in 2000 for Yo-Yo Ma; and *AH* (2002).

Among his many instrumental works are *Variations* for solo flute (1971); Concerto for four groups of instruments (1972–73); Concerto for cello and four trios (1974); *Accordance* for eight instruments (1975–76); *Tashi Quartet* for clarinet, violin, cello, and piano (1978–79); *Lalita: Chamber Variations* for ten instruments (1983–84); *Feast Day* for flute, oboe, cello, and piano (or harpsichord) (1985); *Ziji* for six instruments (1987); *Raising the Gaze* for eight instruments (1988); *Elegy* for violin and piano (1990); *Wind Messengers* for 13 instruments (1990); two *Little Fanfares*, *I* for flute, trumpet, violin, and harp (1991) and *II* for clarinet, violin, viola, cello, and piano (1993); *Variations* for violin and piano (1993); *Rumble* for viola, double bass, and percussion (1994); a String Quartet (1994); Piano Quintet (2003); and a Violin Sonata, composed in 2003 for Pamela Frank and Peter Serkin.

For piano solo Lieberson has composed *Piano Fantasy* (1975), *(3) Bagatelles* (1985), *Scherzo No. 1* (1989), *Fantasy Pieces* (1989), *Garland* (1994), *Variations* (1996), and *The Ocean That Has No West and East* (1997).

Lieberson's opera *Ashoka's Dream* was performed by Santa Fe Opera in July 1997. His other vocal music includes *Motetti di Eugenio Montali* for soprano, alto, and four instruments (1971–72); *Double Entendre* (Shelley, Swift) for soprano and three instruments (1972); *Three Songs* (Penick) for soprano and 13 instruments (1981); and *King Gesar* for narrator and eight instruments (1991–92). In 2001 he completed the *Rilke Songs* for his wife.

LIEURANCE, THURLOW (WEED)

b. Oskaloosa, Iowa, 21 March 1878
d. Boulder, Colorado, 9 October 1963

Lieurance learned to play the cornet and later became a bandmaster. He was awarded a D.M. from the Cincinnati College, and he received further tuition in Paris. In 1903 he undertook a study of the Crow Indians, notating their music and making recordings. He toured the United States, giving lectures; the results of his research are now in the Archive of Folk Culture at the Library of Congress in Washington, D.C. He taught at the University of Nebraska, Lincoln (1927–40) and the

Thurlow Lieurance.
Courtesy: Special Collections, University of Iowa Libraries.

Municipal University, Wichita, Kansas, serving as dean of the music department (1940–47).

As many of the titles suggest, American Indian culture is reflected strongly in Lieurance's music. He composed one stage work, *Drama of the Yellowstone*, and several orchestral pieces, including *Minisa* (1930); *Paris: France* (1931); *Trails Southwest* (1932); *The Conquistador* (1934); *Colonial Exposition Sketches*; *Prairie Sketches*; *Medicine Dance*; and *Water Moon Maiden*.

Lieurance was best known for his songs, one of which, *By the Waters of Minnetonka* (*Moon Deer*) (1917), gained him an international reputation. Among his other vocal music are *Five Songs* (1907); *Nine Indian Songs* (1913); *Songs of the North American Indian* (1920); *Songs from the Yellowstone* (1920–21); *Eight Songs from Green Timber* (1921); *Forgotten Trails* (1923); *Three Songs*; *Each to His Own Tongue* (1925); *Six Songs from Stray Birds* (1937); *From the Land in the Sky* (1941); and *Singing Children of the Sun* (1943). In addition he wrote several choral pieces, including an oratorio, *Queen Esther* (1897), *Eleven Indian Love Songs* (1925); and *Ten Indian Songs* (1934).

At one time his many piano solos were popular, but all have long fallen out of fashion.

LINN, ROBERT

b. San Francisco, California, 11 August 1925
d. Los Angeles, California, 28 October 1999

Linn studied at Mills College, Oakland, California, with Darius Milhaud (1947, 1949) and at the University of Southern California, Los Angeles (1947–51), where he was a pupil of Halsey Stevens, Ingolf Dahl, and Roger Sessions. In 1958 he was appointed professor of music theory at the Thornton School of Music at the University of Southern California, serving as chairman from 1973 and retiring in 1990.

For orchestra Linn wrote an Overture that won a Louisville Award in 1952; *Adagio and Allegro* for chamber orchestra (1956); Symphony in one movement (1956–60); *March for the Olympians* for the Winter Olympic Games in 1960; *The Hexameron,* an arrangement of music by Liszt, Thalberg, Pixis, Herz, Czerny, and Chopin for three pianos and orchestra (1962); *Sinfonia for Strings* (1967–68); Concerto for clarinet, strings, and percussion (1970), Concertino for oboe, horn, strings, and percussion (1972); *Fantasia* for cello and strings (1975–76); a Concerto for woodwind quintet and strings (1981–82); and a Piano Concerto (1990). In 1952 he composed a film score, *The Story Tellers of the Canterbury Tales.*

Linn composed several pieces for concert band: *Four*

277

Pieces (1954), *Concerto Grosso* for brass trio and wind orchestra (1961), *Elevations* (1963), *Propagula* (1970), Concerto for flute and winds (1980), *Partita* (1980), and Concerto for piano and winds (1984).

Among his choral works are *Three Madrigals* (1951); *Five Children's Songs* (1954); *An Anthem of Wisdom* (Book of Proverbs) for chorus and orchestra (1958); *Three German Folk Songs* for men's voices (1959); an oratorio, *The Pied Piper of Hamelin* (1968); *John Burns of Gettysburg* (Bret Harte) for narrator, chorus, and piano (1976); *Home From the Sea* (R. L. Stevenson) for solo voices, chorus, and piano (1976); and *Songs of William Blake* for unaccompanied chorus (1981). His vocal music includes *Cantata Jovialis* for soprano and ensemble (1996).

Linn's many instrumental compositions include a Clarinet Sonata (1949); *Five Pieces* for flute and clarinet (1950); a String Quartet (1951); String Trio (1950); Quartet for saxophones (1953); two piano sonatas (1955, 1964); Quartet for four horns (1957); *Duo* for cello and piano (1959); *Duo* for clarinet and cello (1959); *Prelude and Dance* for saxophone quartet (1960); Suite for viola and cello (1962); Brass Quintet (1963); Wind Quintet (1963); *Dithyramb* for eight cellos (1965); Concertino for violin and wind octet (1965); *Fanfares* for three clarinets (1972); *Five Piano Preludes* (1973); *Vino* for violin and piano (1975); *Twelve* for chamber ensemble (1976–77); *Diversions* for six bassoons (1979); *Trombosis* for 12 trombones (1979); Serenade for flute, clarinet, cello, and guitar (1982); *Three Pieces* for flute, alto saxophone, and guitar (1983); and *Variations for Piano* (1997).

LO PRESTI, RONALD

b. Williamstown, Massachusetts, 28 October 1933
d. Tempe, Arizona, 25 October 1985

Lo Presti received his musical education at the Eastman School of Music, Rochester, New York where he was a pupil of Louis Mennini and Bernard Rogers. He graduated in 1955, receiving his master's degree in the following year. From 1959 to 1960 he was an instructor in music theory at Texas Technological College, Lubbock. After two years as Composer-in-Residence at the public schools of Winfield, Kansas (1960–62), he was appointed an assistant professor of music at Indiana University of Pennsylvania. From 1964 until his death he was professor of theory and composition at Arizona State University, Tempe.

Lo Presti's best known orchestral work, *The Masks* (1955), received a Koussevitzky award. Among his other orchestral compositions are two symphonies (1960, 1968); *Nocturne* for viola and strings (1955–56); *Kansas Overture* (1960); *Kansas Suite* (1961);

Llana Estacado (*The Staked Plain*) (1961); *Port Triumphant* (1952); *From the Southwest* (1967); and *Rhapsody* for marimba, vibraphone, and orchestra (1975). His many pieces for band include *Pageant Overture* (1956); *Prelude* (1956); *Introduction, Chorale and Jubilee* (1961); *Elegy for a Young American* (1964); *Tundra* (1966); and *A Festive Music* (1968). In 1976 he composed the scores for six documentary films entitled *Southwestern Indian Artists* for KAET-TV, Tempe, Arizona.

Lo Presti wrote many choral works including *Alleluia* for chorus, brass, and timpani (1960); *Kanza* for four narrators, chorus, and orchestra (1961); *Two Civil War Songs* for male chorus and ensemble (1961); *Tribute* (Whitman) for chorus and orchestra (1962); *Elegy* (Vachel Lindsay) for chorus and orchestra; *Ode to Independence* for baritone solo, chorus, and symphonic band (1974), written under a grant from the National Endowment for the Arts and premiered at Arizona State University in 1976; Requiem for chorus and orchestra (1975); and *Memorials* for chorus and orchestra (1975).

For the stage he composed an opera, *The Birthday* (Winfield 1962); a one-act opera for children, *Playback,* premiered at Arizona State University in 1970, which won a Phi Mu Alpha Award that year; and a ballet, *Scare-crow* (1973), scored for mixed voices and an orchestra of cellos.

Lo Presti was a prolific writer of instrumental music, especially for brass and percussion; among many pieces in this medium are suites for four horns (1958), eight horns (1960), and five trumpets (1961); *Sketch* for percussion ensemble (1959); *Chorale* for three trombones (1960); *Fanfare* for 38 brass (1960); *Requiescat* for brass ensemble (1961); *Miniature* for brass quintet (1962); *Duo* for two horns (1966); Trombone Trio (1968); *Rondo* for timpani and piano (1969); Trio for three percussionists (1971); and *Fantasy* for five horns (1972). Among his other instrumental works are *Five Pieces* for violin and piano (1960), *Scherzo* for four violins (1960), a String Quartet (1970), Suite for six bassoons (1971), *Cantalena* for cello orchestra (1972); and a Wind Quintet (1975).

LOCKWOOD, NORMAND

b. New York, New York, 19 March 1906
d. Denver, Colorado, 9 March 2002

Lockwood studied at the University of Michigan (1921–24) and was a pupil of Ottorino Respighi in Rome from 1925 to 1926. During the following two years he received composition lessons from Nadia Boulanger in Paris. In 1929 a Priz de Rome Fellowship enabled him to continue his work in Italy. He was awarded Guggenheim Fellowships in 1943 and 1944. On his

Normand Lockwood.
Courtesy American Music Research Center, Music Library, University of Colorado at Boulder.

return to America in 1932, he joined the faculty of the Oberlin Conservatory, Ohio, becoming an associate professor in 1938. From 1945 to 1953 he taught at Columbia University and at the Sacred School of Music, Union Theological Seminary, New York, leaving in 1953 to take up a post at Trinity University, San Antonio, Texas. After 1955 he taught at the universities of Wyoming (1955–57), Oregon (1957–59), and Hawaii (1960–61), and from 1961 to his retirement in 1975 he was Composer-in-Residence at the University of Denver, Colorado.

Although Lockwood composed music in almost every form, he is most widely known for his choral works. Many of these are based on religious texts: Psalm 150 (1937); *The Birth of Moses* for female voices and flute (1947); *The Closing Doxology* (1952); Psalm 114 (1954); a *Magnificat* (1954); *The Old Hundredth* (1956); *Children of God,* an oratorio performed in Cincinnati in 1957; and an oratorio, *Light Out of Darkness* (1957), all for choir and orchestra; and *Love Divine* for soprano, alto, chorus, children's choir, and orchestra (1969). His setting of Whitman's poem, *Out of the Cradle Endlessly Rocking,* won a 1938 G. Schirmer, Inc. prize ($500) for a work suitable for high school choirs. For unaccompanied voices he composed a further Whitman setting, *Dirge for Two Veterans* (1934). Three other major choral works are *Elegy for a Hero,* based on Whitman's "Memories of President Lincoln"

(1951); *Carol Fantasy* (1952); and *Prairie,* a setting of Carl Sandburg's famous poem, performed in 1953 at the Ann Arbor May Festival.

Later choral compositions are *Shine, Perishing Republic* for chorus, brass, two violas, organ, and percussion (1968); *Choreographic Cantata* (1968); an oratorio, *For the Time Being* (Auden; 1971); *Life Triumphant* for chorus, flute, and brass (1976); two works for children's voices and orchestra, Mass (1976) and *Thought of him I Love* (Whitman; 1982); *Donne's Last Sermon* for chorus and organ (1978); *A Child's Christmas in Wales* (Dylan Thomas) for children's voices and piano (1984); *University* Anthem for chorus and band (1996); *Mass of the Holy Ghost* for chorus and organ (1998); Psalm 98: *O Sing Unto the Lord* for a cappella chorus; and Psalm 30 for chorus and organ. In addition to many choral items and arrangements especially for school choirs, Lockwood also wrote a number of works for children's records including *Hiawatha, The Travels of Babar, Mickey Goes to School, Animal Super Market*, and *Riddle-Me-This.*

Lockwood composed five operas: *The Scarecrow,* produced at Columbia University in May 1945; *Early Dawn* (Denver, 1961); *Wizards of Balizar* (Denver, 1962); *The Hanging Judge* (1964); and *Requiem for a Rich Young Man* (Denver, 1964). He also wrote a staged oratorio, *Land of Promise* (1959). In addition he provided incidental music for 16 plays, including *Elektra, Medea, Tamburlane, The Emperor Jones, The Crucible, The Devils, A Midsummer Night's Dream*, and *Macbeth.*

For orchestra Lockwood composed a *Suite: Odysseus* (1929); *A Year's Chronicle* (Symphony) (1934); Symphony (1941); *Moby Dick* (1946); *Chateau Overture*; *Symphonic Sequences* (1966); *Goin' to Town,* a piano concerto (1974); two concertos for organ and brass (1950, 1978); *From an Opening to a Close* for winds and percussion (1967); Oboe Concerto (1968); a Concerto for organ and chamber orchestra (1973); *Symphony for Strings* (1975); *Panegyric* for horn and strings (1978–79); *Symphony for large orchestra* (1978–79); Concerto for two harps and strings (1981); *Prayer and Fanfare* for brass, strings, and percussion (1982); and *Symphony in four movements and a coda* (1993). An early Symphony (1928–29) was withdrawn. Lockwood's instrumental music includes seven string quartets (1933–50); a Piano Quintet (1940); Trio for flute, viola, and harp (1940); a Piano Sonata (1944); *Six Serenades* for string quartet (1945); a Clarinet Quintet (1959); a Sonata for four cellos (1968); a Flute Sonata (1971); *Excursions for four string basses* (1976); *Valley Suite* for violin and piano (1976); *Eight Organ Preludes* (1979–80); *Tripartito* for flute and guitar (1980); *Three Chorale Voluntaries* for trumpet and organ (1982); and a Piano Trio (1985).

Among Lockwood's vocal compositions are *Mary*

Who Stood in Sorrow for soprano and orchestra (1946); a song cycle, *Five Quatrains* (1948); *Four Songs from James Joyce's Chamber Music* for medium voice and string quartet (1948); *Prelude to Western Star* (Stephen Vincent Benet) for bass and piano (1948); Psalm 23 for soprano and organ (1955); *The Dialogue of Abraham and Isaac* for tenor and piano (1965); *Fallen is Babylon the Great! Hallelujah!* for mezzo-soprano and piano (1967); *To Margaret Debayle* for soprano and piano (1977); *Four Songs on Whitman Poems* for soprano, violin, and organ (or piano accompaniment) (1979); *Four Poems of Liu Chang-Ch'ing* for mezzo-soprano, flute, and piano (1984); and Psalms 17 and 114 for mezzo soprano and organ (1985).

LOEFFLER, CHARLES MARTIN (TURNOW)

b. Schöneberg, near Berlin, Germany (according to records) or Mulhouse, Alsace, France (according to Loeffler), 30 January 1861
d. Medfield, Massachusetts, 19 May 1935

While very young, Loeffler was taken by his parents to live in Smela, near Kiev in Russia. Some years later, the family moved to Debreczin in Hungary, and then on to Switzerland. His remembrance of Russia is portrayed in the orchestral work *Memories of Childhood,* subtitled *Life in a Russian Village,* which he wrote in 1923. After a short period as a pupil of Joseph Joachim in Berlin, he studied the violin at the Paris Conservatory. He also received lessons in composition from Ernest Guiraud, a friend of Bizet. After leaving the Conservatory, Loeffler became a violinist in the Pasdeloup Orchestra in Paris, and later in the private court of Baron Paul von Derweis in Switzerland.

In 1881 Loeffler went to the United States to play in Damrosch's orchestra. The following year he was invited to join the Boston Symphony Orchestra, where he was deputy concertmaster until he gave up playing in 1903 to devote himself to farming and composition. He had already become an American citizen in 1887. Not unnaturally, the diverse musical influences Loeffler encountered in the various countries he lived in had an effect upon his style of composition. He became an authority on Gregorian chant and frequently in his music, especially the orchestral works, the melodies are modal in harmonic implications with the flavor of plainsong. The orchestral pieces also betray a strong admiration for the music of Scriabin, although Loeffler's harmonic language is simpler, often naively primitive.

Loeffler's complete withdrawal into a hermit-like existence on his farm at Medfield, Massachusetts, affected the music he wrote. As with Ives, the lack of contact with the outside world led him into a kind of mysticism which disregards the listener and performer, and corresponds only to the composer's inner world. He did not engage in the experiments and explorations of Ives, although his best-known piece, *Pagan Poem,* op. 14, written in 1901, is scored for an unconventional combination of instruments: three obbligato trumpets, heard at first off-stage, coming nearer and nearer until they join the small orchestra of piano, two flutes, oboe, English horn, clarinet, two horns, viola, and double bass. Based on the Eighth Eclogue of Virgil, *Pagan Poem* conjures up a mysterious world of dark, brooding sounds and textures, strongly reminiscent of Scriabin.

Also in 1901 he wrote *Poem for Orchestra,* subtitled *La Bonne Chanson,* which was first performed in the following year by the Boston Symphony Orchestra. Loeffler withdrew the work to re-orchestrate it; the revised version was given by the same orchestra under Pierre Monteux in 1918. The inspiration for *La Bonne Chanson* came from the fifth poem of the cycle of that name by Paul Verlaine. It is a warmly romantic work, betraying certain passages of Franckian harmony with expansive gestures, again derived from Scriabin.

Loeffler's other works composed before his retirement from the concert world include a suite for violin and orchestra, *Les Veillées de l'Ukraine* (1891, rev. 1899); a *Fantastic Concerto* for cello and orchestra (1894); and *Divertissement* in A minor for violin and orchestra (1895). He also wrote two large-scale orchestral pieces, the dramatic poem *Le Mort de Tintagiles* (after Maeterlinck), op. 6 for viola d'amore and orchestra (1897, rev. 1900), and *La Villanelle du Diable,* op. 8 for organ and orchestra, composed in 1901. Also dating from this time is *Divertimento Espagnole* for saxophone and orchestra (1901).

The *Symphony: Hora Mystica,* commissioned for the Norfolk (Connecticut) Festival in 1916, reveals Loeffler's interest in the ritual of Christianity. He described the work as a "religious meditation and adoration of nature." In it are portrayed processions of monks and nuns, the tolling of bells, and other symbolic representations of medieval religious rites. The Symphony is in one long movement and makes use of a men's chorus.

Memories of My Childhood (*Life in a Russian Village),* composed in 1923, won first prize in a competition in Chicago, where it was subsequently performed by the Symphony Orchestra under Frederick Stock. The music recalls for the composer peasant songs from his days in Russia, with the liturgical music of the Orthodox Church and other nostalgic associations.

The Elizabeth Sprague Coolidge Foundation commissioned *Canticum Fratris Solis,* a setting for solo voice and small orchestra of St Francis' "Canticle of the Sun." It received its first performance in a concert at the Library of Congress, Washington, D.C. in 1925. In this work the composer uses plainsong. His last important composition, written in 1930, was *Evocations* for narrator, female chorus, and orchestra. It was given for the first time in 1931 by the Cleveland Orchestra, which had commissioned it to mark the opening of Severence Hall. For the theater he composed three operas: *The Passion of Hilarion* (1912–13), *Les Amants jaloux* (1918), and *The Peony Lantern* (1919).

Loeffler, not a prolific composer, took considerable pains over all his works before he allowed them to be performed. In addition to the music already mentioned, he wrote several instrumental pieces and songs. He composed a setting of Psalm 137, *By the Waters of Babylon* for female chorus and orchestra (1902); *For One Who Fell in Battle* for eight-part chorus (1911); and *Beat, Beat Drums* (Whitman) for men's chorus and orchestra (1917). *Five Irish Fantasies* for voice and orchestra (1922) are settings of poems by W. B. Yeats.

Loeffler's chamber music includes a Violin Sonata (1986); String Quartet (1889); String Sextet (1885–92); Octet for two clarinets, string quartet, double bass, and harp (1896); a Quintet in one movement for three violins, viola, and cello (1897); *Le Passeur d'eau* (String Sextet; 1900); two *Rhapsodies* for oboe, viola, and piano (1905); *Music for four stringed instruments* (1923), influenced strongly by Gregorian chant; *Partita* for violin and piano (1930); and *Studies* for violin (1935). In 1922, Fauré dedicated his Cello Sonata in G minor, op. 117 to Loeffler.

Loeffler was an eccentric, similar in some respects to the reclusives Ives and Ruggles; he died on his farm in Medfield after 30 years of almost total seclusion from the outside world.

LOOMIS, CLARENCE

b. Sioux Falls, South Dakota, 13 December 1889
d. Aptos, California, 3 July 1965

Loomis was educated at Dakota Wesleyan University, Mitchell, South Dakota; he then attended the American Conservatory in Chicago as a pupil of Heniot Levy (piano) and Adolph Weidig (composition). On leave of absence in Vienna he studied with Godowsky and Franz Schreker (1918–19). He taught at the American Conservatory, Chicago (1914–29), the Chicago Musical College (1929–30), the Arthur Jordan Conservatory, Indianapolis (1930–36), Highlands University, Las Vegas, New Mexico (1945–55), and Jamestown College, North Dakota (1955–56) before retirement.

For the stage Loomis composed eight operas: *Yolanda of Cyprus* (Chicago, 1929); *A Night in Avignon* (1932); *The White Cloud* (1935); *The Fall of the House*

of *Usher* (Indianapolis, 1941); *Revival* (1943); *The Captive Woman* (1953); *The Castle of Gold*; and *The Songs of David*. He also wrote a musical, *Susannah, Don't You Cry* (New York 1939), based on Stephen Foster songs; and a comic ballet, *The Flapper and the Quarterback*, first performed in Kyoto, Japan in 1928 at the coronation of the Emperor Hirohito. A second ballet is entitled *Oak Street Beech*.

For orchestra Loomis composed the symphonic prelude *Gargoyles* (1936); *Gaelic Suite* for strings (1953); *Fantasy* for piano and orchestra (1954); *Macbeth* (1954); *The Melting Pot* (American Dances); and the symphonic poem *Potaganissing*.

Loomis wrote many choral works, including *Dream Fantasy* (1930), *Albado Sea* (1933), *The Passion Play* (1955), *Song of the White Earth* (1956), *America the Eleventh* (1957), and the choral cycle *Erin, The Harp and the Willow* (1958).

His major instrumental works are three string quartets (1953, 1963, 1965).

LOOMIS, HARVEY WORTHINGTON

b. Brooklyn, New York, 5 February 1865
d. Roxbury, Massachusetts, 25 December 1930

Loomis studied at the National Conservatory in New York (1891–93), where he was a pupil of Dvořák. He became a specialist in American Indian music, and his arrangements of such melodies as songs and piano pieces were at one time very popular. Among these are *Lyrics of the Red Man*, op. 76 (1903–04).

Loomis composed a one-act opera, *The Traitor Mandolin* (1898), and four burlesque operas: *The Maid of Athens, The Burglar's Bride, Going Up*, and *The Bey of Baba*. In addition to Indian melodies, his vocal music includes *22 Shakespeare Lyrics, Scottish Songs, Song Flowers for Children*, and a cantata for children, *Fairy Hill* (1895). Other works include a melodrama, *Sandalphon* (1896), a dramatic recitation, *The Song of the Pear Tree* (1913), an early Piano Concerto, a Piano Sonata, and a Violin Sonata.

LOPATNIKOFF, NICOLAI (LVOVICH)

b. Reval (now Tallin), Estonia, 16 March 1903
d. Pittsburgh, Pennsylvania, 7 October 1976

Lopatnikoff studied at the Petrograd Conservatory (1914–17) before leaving Russia in 1918 after the Revolution to live in Finland. He attended the Helsinki Conservatory (1918–20), moving to Mannheim where he was a pupil of Ernst Toch (1921). In 1927 he graduated from the Karlsruhe Technological College as a civil engineer and left Germany in 1933 to settle in London.

Nicolai Lopatnikoff (in overcoat) with a group of colleagues, c. 1946.
Courtesy the Carnegie Mellon University Archives.

He went to the United States in 1939 to be head of the theory and composition at Hartt College for Music, Hartford, Connecticut, and later at the Westchester Conservatory in White Plains, New York. From 1945 to 1968 he was professor of composition at the Carnegie Institute of Technology in Pittsburgh. In 1944 he took American citizenship. He was twice awarded Guggenheim Fellowships (1945, 1953) and in 1963 was elected a member of the National Institute of Arts and Letters.

For orchestra Lopatnikoff composed four symphonies, no. 1 (Berlin, 1929), no. 2 (Boston, 1939), no. 3 (Pittsburgh, 1954), and no. 4 (Pittsburgh, 1971); *Prelude to a Drama* (1920); *Introduction and Scherzo* (1928); *Short Overture* (1932); *Opus Sinfonicum* (1933–41); *Deux Nocturnes* (1940); Sinfonietta (1942); Concertino (1945), commissioned by the Koussevitzky Music Foundation; *Two Russian Nocturnes* (1945); Divertimento (1951); and *Variazioni Concertanti,* commissioned in 1958 for the Pittsburgh Symphony Orchestra. In 1958 the Louisville Orchestra commissioned *Music for Orchestra,* performed the following year. The premiere of *Festival Overture* was given by the Detroit Symphony Orchestra in October 1960. The American

Wind Symphony commissioned a Concerto for Wind Instruments for its 1963 season, and a Concerto for Orchestra was completed in 1964. *Partita Concertante* for orchestra dates from 1966.

Lopatnikoff composed two piano concertos, the first in 1921, the second completed in 1930 and heard at the I.S.C.M. Festival in Vienna in 1932. He also wrote a Violin Concerto (1941) and a Concerto for two pianos (1950–51).

His last work, the ballet *Melting Pot,* was commissioned by the Indianapolis Ballet Theater in 1975. Among his chamber works are three string quartets (1920, 1928, 1955); two violin sonatas (1926, 1948), the first with optional side drum; two piano trios (1918, 1935); a *Duo* for violin and cello (1926); a Cello Sonata (1928); a Piano Sonata (1943); and *Fantasia Concertante* for violin and piano (1962).

Lopatnikoff's single opera, *Danton* (1930–33), is based on the play *Danton's Death* by Georg Büchner.

LUCIER, ALVIN (AUGUSTUS, JR.)
b. Nashau, New Hampshire, 14 May 1931

Lucier received his musical education at Yale University (1950–56) from David Kraehenbuhl, Quincy Porter, Richard Donovon, and Howard Boatwright; at Tanglewood with Lukas Foss; and at Brandeis University, Waltham, Massachusetts, (1958–60) where he was a pupil of Harold Shapero, Irving Fine, and Arthur Berger. At the Darmstadt summer course in 1961 he sat in on David Tudor's piano class. In 1960 on a Fulbright Scholarship he studied with Giorgio Ghedini in Venice, settling for two years in Rome. From 1962 to 1969 he was choral director and director of the Electronic Music Studio at Brandeis University. In 1970 he joined the faculty of Wesleyan University, Middletown, Connecticut, becoming chairman of the department.

Except for a few early works including *Action Music* for piano (1962) and *Composition for Pianist and Mother* for pianist and actress (1963), most of Lucier's compositions employ some elements of electronics. Among a handful of orchestral and instrumental pieces without electronics are *Sonata da Camera* for brass and percussion (1956); a Concerto for trumpet and chamber orchestra (1959); *Music* for bassoon and strings (1959); *Festival Music* for five winds (1960); *Fragments* for strings (1961); and *Memory Space* for orchestra (1970).

In *Music for Solo Performer* (1965), electrodes are placed on the scalp of the performer. The alpha brain waves picked up are modified by amplifiers and filters to activate a number of sympathetic percussion instruments. *Shelter* (1967) uses vibration pick-ups activated by environmental sounds. *Whistlers* (1967) captures electro-magnetic disturbances in the ionosphere, which are then processed electronically. In *Chambers* (1968) the performers are instructed to make sounds with resonant resources, sea-shells, cupped hands, et al. *Hymn* (1970) uses "the building and amplification of a web-like structure"; the length, weight, and density of strands determine pitch and timbre.

Other electronic works include *Elegy for Albert Anastasia* (1965); *Vespers* (1965); *The Fires in the Mind of the Dancers* (1974); *Bird and Person Dyning* (1975); *Music on a Long Thin Wire* (1977); *Ghosts* (1978); *Clocker* (1978); *Solar Sounder* (1979); *Reflection of Sound from the Wall* (1980); *Sferics* (1981); and three pieces for sound installation: *Seesaw* (1983), *Spinner* (1984), and *Sound on Paper* (1985).

Vocal music includes *Song* for soprano (1963); *North American Time Capsule* for voices and vocoder (1967); *The Only Talking Machine of its Kind in the World* for speaker and tape (1969); *I am Sitting in a Room* for voice and taped voice (1970); *The Duke of York* for voice(s) and synthesizer (1971); *Lullaby* for unamplified or amplified voice (1979); *Intervals* for chorus and sound-sensitive lights (1983); and *Salmon River Valley Songs* for soprano, English horn, xylophone, and oscillators (1986). Further works for various ensembles include *Gentle Fire* for synthesizers and related equipment (1971); *The Queen of the South* for players, responsive surfaces, strewn material, and closed circuit television system (1972); *Still and Moving Lines of Silence in Families of Hyperbolas* for singers, dancers, and unattended percussion (1974); *Outlines of Persons and Things* for microphones, loudspeakers, and

electronic sounds (1975); *Tyndall Orchestrations* for female voice, Bunsen burners, glass tubes, and recorded bird calls (1976); *Job's Coffin* for performer and amplified chest of drawers (1979); *Shapes and Sounds from the Board* for amplified piano (1979); and *Music for Men, Women and Reflecting Walls* for oscillators (1986).

Lucier has combined instruments and electronics in *Directions of Sound from the Bridge* for string instrument, audio oscillation, and sound-sensitive light (1978); *Music for Pure Waves* for percussion and oscillator (1980); *Crossings* for symphony orchestra and oscillator (1982–84); *In Memoriam Jon Higgins* for clarinet and slow-sweep, Pure Wave oscillator (1984); Serenade for 13 instruments and oscillator (1985); *Septet* for three strings; four winds, and oscillator (1985); and *Kettles* for five timpani and two oscillators (1987).

Three more recent works are for instruments alone: *Fideliotrio* for viola, cello, and piano (1988), *Carbon Copies* for saxophone, piano, and percussion (1988), and *Navigations* for string quartet (1991). Also dating from 1991 is an unclassifiable piece, *Amplifier and Reflector I* for open umbrella, ticking clock, and glass oven dish.

Inspired by the work of John Cage, Lucier continues to explore natural sounds. Among his latest creations are *Opera With Objects* for performers with resonant objects, composed for Sam Ashley (1997); *Heavier Than Air* for any number of players with carbon dioxide-filled balloons (1999); and *What Day is Today?*, eight short works on tape based on natural radio waves and other data from the sun, moon, Mars, Mercury, Jupiter, Venus, and Saturn (1999).

Other pieces of this period are *Music for Gamelan Instruments, Microphones, Amplifiers and Loudspeakers* (1994); *Q* for quintet and pure wave oscillators (1996); *40 Rooms* for quintet and LARES system (1996); *Two Twenty-Two* for violin, clarinet, trombone, cello, and double bass (1996); *Sweepers* for orchestra (1997); *Cassiopeia, Five Stars in the Shape of a 'W'* for orchestra (1999); and *On a carpet of leaves illuminated by the moon* for koto with wave oscillator (2000).

Alvin Lucier.
Photo: Amanda Lucier, courtesy the composer.

LUENING, OTTO (CLARENCE)
b. Milwaukee, Wisconsin, 15 June 1900
d. New York, 2 September 1996

Luening studied at the State Academy of Music in Munich (1915–17) and at the Zurich Municipal Conservatory (1917–20) with Phillip Jarnach for composition and Volkmar Andreae for conducting. He was also a private pupil of Busoni. For several years in Europe he worked as a conductor, accompanist, and flute player. On his return to the United States, he was co-founder and conductor of the American Grand Opera Company

Otto Luening.
Photo: Irene Haupt, courtesy Music Library, State University of New York, Buffalo.

in Chicago in 1920. From 1923 to 1928 he was executive director of the opera department at the Eastman School of Music, Rochester, New York. In 1932 he was appointed associate professor at the University of Arizona, moving in 1934 to Bennington College, Vermont, where he was chairman of the music division for ten years. In 1944 he joined the music faculty of Barnard College, New York. In 1947 he became a professor at Columbia University, and from 1966 to 1970, was music chairman of the School of Arts there; he was named emeritus professor in 1968. He also served on the faculty of the Juilliard School from 1971 to 1973. In the spring of 1975 he was Hadley Fellow at Bennington College.

Luening was the recipient of many honors, including Guggenheim Fellowships from 1930 to 1932 and from 1974 to 1975. He was granted an award by the National Institute of Arts and Letters in 1946. In 1940, with Bauer, Copland, Hanson, and Porter he was a founder of the American Music Center, remaining chairman until 1960.

In 1933 his four-act opera *Evangeline*, based on a narrative poem by Longfellow, won the David Bispham Medal for American opera. The opera was firstly produced under the composer's direction at the Columbia University Festival in May 1948. In 1974 he revised the work into three acts. Also for the stage he wrote incidental music for Maeterlinck's play *Sister Beatrice* (1926) and Lorca's *Blood Wedding* (1940).

Early in his career Luening was a prolific composer of orchestral and instrumental music and songs. For orchestra he wrote a Concertino for flute, harp, celesta, and strings (1923); *Music for Orchestra* (1923, rev. 1951); *Symphonic Poem* (1924), retitled *Symphonic Fantasia I*; Serenade for three horns and strings (1927); *Symphonietta* (1933; rev. in 1979 and retitled *Short Symphony*); *Two Symphonic Interludes* (1936); *Suite for Strings* (1937); *Prelude on a Hymn Tune by William Billings* (1937); and *Fantasia Brevis* for strings (1939).

After the Second World War, Luening returned to orchestral music with *Symphonic Fantasy II* (1939–49); *Prelude* and *Pilgrim's Hymn* for chamber orchestra (1946); *Kentucky Concerto,* commissioned by the Louisville Orchestra in 1951; *Legend* for oboe and strings dating from the same year; *Kentucky Rondo* (1951); *Wisconsin Suite* (1954); Serenade for flute and strings (1957); *Lyric Scene* for flute and orchestra (1958); *Fantasia* for solo strings quartet and orchestra (1959); and *Fantasia* for strings (1966). His early instrumental works are equally abundant: Violin Sonata no. 1 (1917); *Gavotte and Minuet* for cello and piano (1917); Sextet (1918); Sonatina for flute (1919); String Quartet no. 1 with clarinet obbligato (1920); Piano Trio (1922); Violin Sonata no. 2 (1922); Quartet no. 2 (1922); Cello Solo Sonata (1923); *Legend* for violin and piano (1924); Quartet no. 3 (1928); *Fantasia Brevis* for flute and piano (1929); *Fantasia Brevis* for clarinet and piano (1936); *Fantasia Brevis* for string trio (1936); *Fuguing Tune* for wind quintet (1941); Suite for cello and piano (1946); Violin Sonata no. 3 (1943–51); three suites for solo flute (1947, 1953, 1961); and *Elegy* for solo violin (1963).

For keyboard, Luening also wrote extensively, including a Piano Sonata (1929), *Sonata in Memoriam Ferruccio Busoni* (1971), and several works for organ, including *Choral Fantasy* (1922), *Fantasia* (1932), and *Fugue* (1971).

Also dating from the early years are a pair of choral pieces, *Two Choruses to Words by Byron* for female voices (1928) and *Christ is Arisen* for chorus, organ and strings (1929). His solo vocal music includes *The Soundless Song* for soprano, string quartet, flute, clarinet, and piano (1922); Trio for soprano, violin, and flute (1923); *Five Songs on Poems of Whitman* (1927–36); *Ten Songs* (1930); Suite for soprano and flute (1936–

37); an *Emily Dickinson Song Cycle* (1942–51); and *Six Proverbs* for mezzo-soprano and piano (1973).

In 1952 Luening turned his attention to electronic music and thereafter devoted much of his composing energy in that direction. He made a particular study of combining live instruments and orchestras with pre-recorded music and electronic sounds on tape, especially in collaboration with Vladimir Ussachevsky. In 1959 with Sessions and Babbitt (Princeton University) and Ussachevsky (Columbia University), he was co-founder of the Columbia-Princeton Electronic Music Center in Manhattan, which has become the leading electronic music studio in the United States. Many other composers have since been associated with the center.

For tape alone he composed *Low Speed* (1952); *Invention* (1952); *Fantasy in Space* (1952); *Dynamophonic Suite* (1958); *A Study in Synthetic Sounds* (1961); *Sonority Canons* (1962); and *Moonflight* (1967). For tape and orchestra he composed *Rhapsodic Variations* (1954) with Ussachevsky for the Louisville Orchestra (the first work of its kind); *A Poem in Cycles and Bells* (1954), commissioned by the Los Angeles Philharmonic Orchestra; *Concerted Piece* (1960), commissioned by the New York Philharmonic Orchestra; and *Carlsbad Caverns* (1955) and *Incredible Voyage* (1968) both for CBS television. Other pieces include *Incantation* (1952), a ballet, *Of Identity* (1955), and incidental music for *King Lear* (1955) and *Back to Methuselah* (Shaw) (1958).

His solo compositions in this sphere are *Theater Piece no. 2* (New York, 1956), a ballet for Doris Humphrey and José Limón; *Synthesis* for electronic sound and orchestra (1960); *A Day in the Country* for violin and tape (1961); *Gargoyles* for violin and synthesized sound (1961); and *Fugue and Chorale with Electronic Doubles* for organ and tape (1975). In 1970 he composed *In the Beginning* for taped voice and electronic sound.

Luening continued to write copiously for orthodox instruments without electronic enhancement. His other chamber music includes three solo sonatas for violin (1958–70); a Sonata for solo viola (1958); Sonata for solo double bass (1958); *Sonority* for two to 37 flutes (ad lib.; 1962); Trio for flute, cello, and piano (1963); *Duo* for violin and viola (1963); two suites for solo flute (1965, 1969); Trio for three flutes (1966); *Introduction and Allegro* for trumpet and piano (1970); *Short Suite* for flute, clarinet, and bassoon (1974); a Trio for trumpet, horn, and trombone (1974); *Three Short Sonatas* for flute and piano (1976); *Seven Short Sonatas* for piano (1940–80); Serenade for piano trio (1983);

Opera Fantasia for violin and piano (1985); *Canons* for two flutes (1985); *Duo* for flute and viola (1985); *Fantasie* for baroque flute (1987); Divertimento for brass quintet (1988); Divertimento for oboe (or flute), clarinet, and bassoon (1990); Cello Sonata (1992); *Canonical Variations* for string quartet (1992); and Divertimento for clarinet, violin, and piano (1994).

Two late choral pieces are a cantata, *No Jerusalem But This* for narrator, chorus, and orchestra (1982), and *Lines From the Book of Urizen and Vala* (Blake; 1982).

His later orchestral works included *Sonority Forms I* (1973) and *Fantasia for Strings* (1973). In 1974 he was commissioned by the National Endowment for the arts to compose *A Wisconsin Symphony* for the Milwaukee Symphony Orchestra. Also in that year he was commissioned to write *Two Mexican Serenades* by the National University of Mexico for performance in March 1975. His final burst of composing for orchestra produced *Third Symphonic Interlude* (1976); *The Hook Fantasia* (1979); *Symphonic Fantasias III* (1969–82), *IV* (1969–82), *V* (1979–85), *VI* (1985), *VII* (1986), and *VIII* (1986); *The Triffin Fantasia* (1979); *Potawatomi Legends* for chamber orchestra, commissioned by the University of Wisconsin in 1980; *Sonority Forms II* (1983); *Symphonic Interlude IV* (1985); and *Fanfare for Those We Have Lost* for wind orchestra (1993).

Luening was co-author of *The Development and Practice of Electronic Music,* published in 1975. *The Odyssey of an American Composer: The Autobiography of Otto Luening* was published in 1980.

LYON, JAMES
b. Newark, New Jersey, 1 July 1735
d. Machais, Maine, 12 October 1794

In 1759, while studying at Nassau Hall in Newark, now Princeton University, Lyon composed the first known ode by an American composer; this is perhaps the first original composition by an American musician. He was ordained a Presbyterian minister in 1764 and the following year went to Nova Scotia. After considerable difficulties, he returned with his family to New England, settling in Machais, Maine in 1772.

Lyon was much respected as a musician, and in 1761 in Philadelphia he published *Urania,* a choice collection of psalm tunes, anthems, and hymns that included six of his own compositions. *Urania* was reissued at least twice, in 1767 and 1773, which gives some indication of its popularity.

M

MACDOWELL, EDWARD (ALEXANDER)
b. New York, New York, 18 December 1861
d. New York, New York, 23 January 1908

MacDowell's paternal grandparents, themselves of Scottish origin, had come to the United States from Ireland. This factor helps to explain the Celtic influences on the titles of some of his piano music. His father, Thomas MacDowell, settled in New York as a businessman, but was also a keen amateur artist. Edward began piano lessons at the age of eight and later studied with Paul Desvernine and Teresa Carreño. In April 1876, at the age of 15, he was taken by his mother to Paris where he was accepted at the Conservatory. His teachers were Antoine-François Marmontel for piano and Augustin Savard for composition; one of his fellow students was Claude Debussy. At first he experienced considerable difficulty in understanding the classes, which were conducted in French. Dissatisfied with the standard of teaching, he seriously considered devoting himself to painting. His few extant drawings and paintings from this time show that he had inherited a certain talent as an artist from his father.

In 1878 Edward attended a concert in Paris where Nicholas Rubinstein performed a concerto by Tchaikovsky. So impressed was MacDowell that he urged his mother to allow him to give up lessons in Paris to go to Germany or Russia where he could find more dynamic teaching. After a short, unsuccessful time at the Stuttgart Conservatory, he moved to Frankfurt in 1879, where he remained at the Conservatory for two years. His teachers were Carl Heymann for piano and

Edward MacDowell and his wife.
From the Collections of the Library of Congress.

Joachim Raff for composition. During this time he began to compose his first serious works. Disappointed at not being offered a post in Frankfurt, he went to the Darmstadt Conservatory as a teacher of piano. He soon returned to Frankfurt to begin a concert career and to teach privately. It was while playing in Weimar that he met Liszt, who was much impressed by the young American, and it was on Liszt's recommendation that MacDowell performed his First Piano Suite in Zurich in July 1882. This work proved a considerable success for the unknown composer, and the Suite was published as his op. 10 by Breitkopf and Härtel in 1883.

The years 1882 to 1885 mark a highly creative period in his life. Between active concert tours throughout Germany, MacDowell composed his First Piano Concerto in A minor op. 15. (1885) and a number of important piano pieces: Suite no. 2, op. 14 (1883); Serenade, op. 16 (1882); *Four Piano Pieces*, op. 19 (1885), which include the once popular *Hexentanz,* and two works for piano duet, *Drei Poesien*, op. 20 and *Mondbilder*, op. 21 (1885). He also published the first of his songs, opp.11 and 12. The German influence on his music, especially that of Liszt and Joachim Raff, is seen in the two tone poems, *Hamlet* and *Ophelia, op.* 22 (1885), dedicated respectively to Henry Irving and Ellen Terry.

In 1884 MacDowell married Marian Nevins, and the following year the couple settled in Wiesbaden. Here he continued to compose, completing a Second Piano Concerto in D minor op. 23 (1885), more piano pieces including *Six Idylls*, op. 31 and *Four Little Poems*, op. 32, and songs. The tone poem *Lancelot and Elaine* op. 25, written in 1886, was dedicated to a fellow American composer in Germany, George Templeton Strong. MacDowell's music was becoming known throughout Germany, and his fame had spread to England and America. After completing the two orchestral fragments *Die Sarazenan (The Saracens)* and *Die Schöne Alda (The Beautiful Alda),* parts of an abandoned *Song of Roland Symphony,* he returned to the United States in 1888. He settled in Boston as a respected teacher and pianist, and the following year added to his increasing reputation as a composer when he performed his Second Piano Concerto in New York under Theodore Thomas.

In 1896 MacDowell accepted the newly created chair of music at Columbia University. Although his academic duties took up much of his time, MacDowell continued to compose. Since his return to the United States, he had written an *Orchestral Suite*, op. 42 (1891–93) and the first of his four piano sonatas, *Sonata Tragica*, op. 45, published in 1893, which owes little to the classical tradition of the sonata, and is modeled on Liszt's Piano Sonata. Liszt is also the inspiration for the *Twelve Virtuoso Studies*, op. 46, performed by the composer in Boston in 1894.

Further critical acclaim greeted the *Second "Indian" Suite* for orchestra, op. 48, dedicated to the Boston Symphony Orchestra and performed by them in 1897. Although each movement possesses a title with American Indian associations, today we detect the stronger flavor of European music.

MacDowell's other piano sonatas have romantic titles. *Eroica Sonata*, op. 50 was written in 1895 and, like *Lancelot and Elaine*, takes its inspiration from Arthurian legend. Both the *Norse Sonata*, op. 57 (1900) and *Keltic Sonata*, op. 59 (1901) were dedicated to Grieg, to whom MacDowell owed much in his pianistic style. These titles also reveal national legend as a background to their composition.

Belonging to this period are the two sets of piano pieces that brought the greatest renown to the composer in his lifetime and which find a place in concert programs today. The poetic imagery of nature with impressionistic implications lies behind the *Woodland Sketches*, op. 51 (1896), which contains the ever-popular "To a Wild Rose," as well as *Sea Pieces*, op. 55 (1898). The world of Thoreau with its forests and rivers is closely related to these musical evocations and mood paintings. The titles of the movements may seem naïve today but the composer's feelings for his subjects were quite genuine. Towards the end of his life he produced two more collections of piano pieces inspired by the environment of his country home in New Hampshire: *Fireside Tales*, op. 61 (1902) and *New England Idylls*, op. 62 (1903).

MacDowell was not temperamentally suited to university life. The administrative duties and regular timetable of lectures proved increasingly irksome to him. He was a Romantic composer and pianist, not an academic musician. Friction arose between him and the authorities, and by 1903 he felt compelled to resign from Columbia. It was reported that he wished to devote himself to composition but an indiscreet newspaper interview led to the disagreement being published in the press. In spite of attempts by President Nicholas Murray Butler of Columbia University to avoid publicity, MacDowell revealed his feelings of disappointment in a letter to the *New York Post*. Unpleasant recriminations followed, which had a disastrous effect upon the composer.

From this time MacDowell suffered a gradual mental decline, and his condition was aggravated by his being knocked down by a cab in a New York street. Within a year of his resignation in January 1904, he had ceased to compose and subsided into a state of acute melancholia. He died in the Westminster Hotel, New York at the age of 46. Mrs. MacDowell fulfilled her husband's wishes by establishing a colony at their home in Peterborough, New Hampshire, where composers, writer, artists, and poets could work during the summer. She took an active interest in the project until her death in 1956 at the age of 99.

MacDowell's position in the development of American music has been underestimated by many critics. He was the first composer of Romantic music in the United States to produce works that enjoyed a wide reputation outside his native country. He influenced the next generation of composers and proved to the musical establishment in Europe that the United States had a musician of significance. In his longer works, the four piano sonatas, the two piano concertos, and his early orchestral pieces, he reveals his debt to the European masters—Grieg and Liszt in the piano music, Wagner and Raff in the orchestral items. His visit to Germany also produced a deep understanding of the European literary culture. In several piano pieces he was inspired by the writings of Virgil, Dante, Goethe, Heine, Byron, Victor Hugo, and others.

In many other instances he was his own musical poet. Occasionally he tried to transcend the heights with loftily titled sonatas, sometimes falling to near banality with "From a Wandering Iceberg" in *Sea Pieces*. Nevertheless, in many of his shorter piano works, for example "A. D. 1620" from the same set, and some of the 42 songs, now sadly neglected, he speaks with the distinctive voice of an American who has absorbed the near-stifling influences of Europe and allowed a New England simplicity to be heard. MacDowell's importance is not merely historical; seen more clearly in their context, many of his works deserve a generous treatment from concert artists today.

MACERO, TEO (ATTILIO JOSEPH)
b. Glen Falls, New York, 30 October 1925

Macero studied at the Juilliard School (1947–53), where he was a pupil of Henry Brant. After teaching there (1951–52) and at the Institute for the Education of the Blind (1953–55), he became a producer for Columbia Records, where he remained until 1975; while there, he became famous for his production work on Miles Davis's jazz-rock albums of the late 1960s and early 1970s. Since 1976 he has been president of M. Productions, Inc., a recording company, and Teo Records. He is also a saxophonist and conductor of various ensembles. He has appeared as conductor, composer, and performer with the New York Philharmonic, Kansas City Symphony, Buffalo Symphony, and Santa Clara Symphony Orchestras. Macero has been the recipient of two Guggenheim Fellowships (1953–54, 1958) and a grant from the National Endowment for the Arts (1974).

His principal activities as a composer have been in the field of ballet and films for television and the screen.

Teo Macero.
Courtesy the composer.

He has provided over 80 scores for the Pennsylvania Ballet Company, Anna Sokolow Ballet Company, Winnipeg Ballet Company, Robert Joffrey Ballet Company, and the Juilliard School of Music Ballet Company. Among these are *Ride the Culture Loop* (Sokolow, 1970), *Mr. B* (Joffrey, 1983), and *Jamboree* (Joffrey, 1984).

Macero's documentary film music includes *The Miracle Months*; *Frank Lloyd Wright*; *Eugene O'Neill*; *Bridges-Go-Round* (1958); *Skyscrapers* (1958); *Faces and Fortunes* (1960); *Opus Op* (1967); *The Transplanters* (1969); *AKA Cassius Clay* (1970); *The Body Human* (Emmy Award:1978); *Life Line* (Emmy Award: 1979); and *The Magic Scene* (Emmy Award: 1980). Among his feature film scores are *End of the Road* (1970), *Jack Johnson* (1971), *Top Secret* (1979), *Virus* (1980), and *Omni* (1982). He has also written three operas: *The Heart* (1970), *The Share* (1978), and *Twelve Years a Slave* (1986).

Macero's important orchestral works are *Fusions* (1956); *C* for alto saxophone, violin, viola, and orchestra (1957); *Polaris* (1960); *Torsion in Space* (1961–62); *Time Plus Seven* (1963); *Pressure* (1964); *One and Three Quarters* (1968); *Paths* for chamber orchestra

(1971); *Overture: Le grande spectacle* (1975); *Timeless Viewpoint* for string orchestra (1980); *Virgo Clusters – M87* for chamber orchestra (1981); and *The Jupiter Effect* for alto saxophone and chamber orchestra (1983). Instrumental music includes *Wi* for piano (1973); *Adieu mon amour* for cello and tape (1974); *Pagoda Sunset* for violin and piano (1974); *Violent,·Non Violent* for alto saxophone and two pianos (1976); *Rounds* for two percussionists and piano (1976); *Butter and Big Horn* for tuba and tape (1977); *Goodbye Mr. Good Bass* for chamber ensemble (1979); *A Jazz Presence* for narrator and jazz ensemble (1980); and *Theme for the Uncommon Man* for brass and percussion (1981).

MACHOVER, TOD
b. New York, New York, 24 November 1953

Machover received his principal music training at the University of California, Santa Cruz (1971–73), Columbia University (1973–74), and the Juilliard School of Music, New York (B.M.,1975; M.M., 1977). He later studied computer music at Massachusetts Institute of Technology, Cambridge (MIT) and Stanford University, California. He was also a pupil of Luigi Dallapiccola (1973), Roger Sessions (1973–75), and Elliott Carter (1975–78). From 1978–79 he was principal cello in the National Opera of Canada Orchestra in Montreal. In 1980 he was appointed director of IRCAM in Paris; he then joined the music faculty of MIT (1985), where he became director of the Experimental Media Facility in the following year.

Machover made an extensive study of computer music and has invented musical instruments adapted by technology. His best-known work, *Toy Symphony,* was created at the MIT Media Laboratory, intended to introduce children to creative music-making. It makes use of a hyperscore, an electronic musical sketch pad that allows anyone to create music compositions which can be played by a live orchestra. Also employed are a hyperviolin, a violin driven by software to make complex rhythms, and "shapers," squeezeable soft toys that produce sounds. The unofficial premiere with Joshua Bell as soloist was given in Berlin in 2001, followed by the official first performance in Dublin.

Other orchestral music includes a Concerto for amplified guitar and orchestra (1978); *Nature's Breath* for chamber orchestra (1984–85); *Desires* for large orchestra (1985–89); *Forever and Ever,* a concerto for hyperviolin and orchestra (1993); *Hyperstrung Trilogy* for hyperviolin, hyperviola, hypercello, and chamber orchestra (1991–93, rev. 1996–97); and *Sparkler* for hyperorchestra (electronic instruments), first performed

Tod Machover.
Photo: Webb Chappell, courtesy MIT Media Lab.

in Carnegie Hall in October 2001. Machover has composed four operas: *Twelve Looney Tones* (*Schoenberg in Hollywood*) for Opera Monte Carlo; *Valis* (Paris, 1989); *Brain Opera* (New York, 1999); and *Resurrection*, in two acts (libretto: Laura Harrington), staged in 1999 by Houston Opera.

Among his chamber works are *Yoku Mireba* for flute, cello, and piano (1977); *With Dadaji in Paradise* for cello (1977–78, rev. 1983); *Light* for 15 instruments (1979); String Quartet no. *1* (1981); *Winter Variations* for nine instruments (1981); *Chansons d'amour* for piano (1982); and *Hidden Sparks* for solo violin (1984).

He has also combined electronics with instruments: *Deplacements* for guitar and computer electronics (1979); *Fusione Fugace* for 4-track tape and computer (1981); *Electronic Etudes* for cello, tape, and electronics (1983); *Spectres Parisiens* for flute, horn, cello, synthesizer, 18 instruments, and computer (1983–84); *Flora* for computer tape (1989); *Bug-Mudra* for two guitars, percussion, and live computer (1989–90); *Song of Penance* for hyperviola, computer voice, and large ensemble (1992); *Bounce* for hyperkeyboards (1992); and *Meteor Music* for electronics and computer interactive music (1998).

Machover's vocal music includes *Fresh Spring*

MAILMAN, MARTIN

(Edmund Spenser) for baritone and ten instruments (1977); *Ye Gentle Birds* (Spenser) for soprano, mezzo-soprano, two flutes, oboe, horn, bassoon, and contra-bassoon (1977); *Two Songs* (R. Moss) for soprano, flute, clarinet, viola, double bass, and harp (1978); *Soft Morning City* (Joyce: *Finnegans Wake*) for soprano, double bass, and computer tape (1980); *Epithalamion* for vocal soloists, 25 players, and live and recorded computer electronics; and *He's Our Dad* for soprano, keyboard, and computer-generated sounds (Boston: 1997).

Machover is the author of four books: *Le Compositeur et l'Ordinateur* (Paris, 1984); *Musical Thought at IRCAM* (London, 1984); *Quoi, Quand, Comment? La Recherche Musical* (*The Concept of Musical Research*) (Paris, 1985; London, 1988); and *Microcomputers and Music* (New York, 1988).

MAGANINI, QUINTO
b. Fairfield, California, 30 November 1897
d. Greenwich, Connecticut, 10 March 1974

Maganini trained as a flute player with George Barrère in New York and joined the San Francisco Symphony Orchestra in 1917, later becoming a member of the New York Symphony Orchestra (1919–26). In 1926–27, he attended the American School in Fontainebleau as a pupil of Nadia Boulanger, and was awarded a Guggenheim Fellowship in 1929. In 1930 he became conductor of the New York Sinfonietta and two years later founded his own orchestra. After that, Maganini gave up orchestral playing to concentrate upon teaching and composition. He also devoted himself to conducting and appeared with most of the leading orchestras of the United States. He was conductor of the Norwalk (Connecticut) Symphony Orchestra (1941–67). He helped young composers through his work with the publishers Carl Fischer Inc., and Editions Musicus, New York, which he himself founded. He was for a time a member of the faculty at Columbia University as a teacher of composition. In 1953 he was elected president of the American School in Fontainebleau, where he had been a pupil.

Maganini's major work is the four-part opera cycle *The Argonauts* which concerns the history of California. It was completed in 1934 after 14 years' work. A second opera *Tennessee's Partner* was written in 1942. His only ballet, *Even Hours,* dates from 1928.

For orchestra he composed a rhapsody, *Tuolumne* with solo trumpet (1920); *South Wind* (1922); *La Rumba: Cuban Rhapsody* (1925); *An Ornothological Suite* (1928); Concerto in D minor for strings (1935); *Napoleon,* a symphonic portrait (1935); *Genevieve (Rhapsody in Symphonic Form)* (1935); *The Royal*

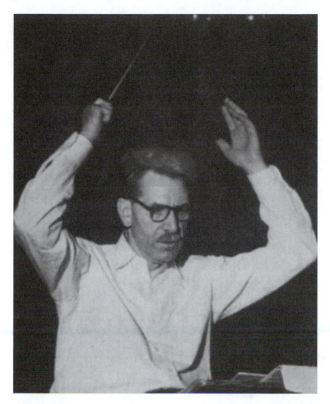

Quinto Maganini.
Courtesy the Norwalk Symphony Orchestra.

Ladies (1940); *Americanese Suite* (1940); *Peaceful Land* (1946); and *Tanglewood Tales.* His Symphony no. 1 in C minor and *Sylvan Symphony* for 13 instruments both date from 1932.

Maganini's choral works include *Songs of the Chinese* for female voices, two pianos, and percussion (1925) and *The Cathedral at Sens* for chorus, cello, and orchestra (1931).

MAILMAN, MARTIN
b. New York, New York, 30 June 1932
d. Denton, Texas, 18 April 2000

Mailman studied at the Eastman School, Rochester, New York (1951–54, 1956–60), where he was a pupil of Wayne Barlow, Howard Hanson, Louis Mennini, and Bernard Rogers. He was Composer-in-Residence at Jacksonville University College, Florida (1959–61) and head of theory at the Brevard Music Center, North Carolina (1960–61). He was professor of music at East Carolina University, Greenville (1961–66), moving in 1966 to become professor of composition at North Texas State University, Denton, where he taught until his death.

For orchestra Mailman wrote three symphonies (1969, 1979, 1983); *Dance in Two Moods* (1952);

291

Martin Mailman.
Courtesy the University of North Texas.

Autumn Landscape (1954); *Jubilate* (1955); *Elegy* (1955); *Cantiones* (1957); *Christmas Music* (1958); two *Preludes and Fugues* (1959, 1963); *Partita* for strings (1960); *Gateway City Overture* (1960); *Suite in Three Movements* (1961); Sinfonietta (1964); *Concepts* (1966); *Generations 2* for three string orchestras and percussion (1969); a Violin Concerto (1982); *Elegy* for strings (1985); *Mirror Music* (1987); and *Dance Imageries* (1999).

Mailman wrote extensively for concert band including *Commencement March* (1960); *Four Miniatures* (1960); *Geometrics I – V* (1961–76); *Associations Overture* (1962); *Alarums* (1962); Concertino for trumpet and band (1963); *Liturgical Music* (1964); *Associations I* (1968–69); *In Memoriam Frankie Newton* (1970); *Shouts, Hymns and Praises* (1972); *Decorations: Music for a Celebration* (1974); *Night Vigil* (1980); *Exaltations* (1981); *For Precious Friends Hid in Death's Dateless Night* (1988); *Toward the 2nd Century* (1989); Clarinet Concertino (1990); *Bouquets* (1991); *Secular Litanies* (1993); Concerto (1993); and *Pledges* (1998).

Among his choral works are five pieces for voices

and band: *Alleluia* (1960); *Genesis Resurrected* with narrator (1960); *Leaves of Grass* (Whitman) with narrator (1963); *Let Us Now Praise Famous Men* for men's voices and narrator (1975); and *Generations 3: Messengers* for children's chorus (1977). Other choral pieces include *Three Madrigals* (Shakespeare; 1960); *Music for Moby Dick* for chorus and ensemble (1965); *Shakespeare Serenade* for chorus and four instruments (1968); *Requiem, Requiem* (R. Sale) for solo voices, chorus, and orchestra (1970); *Soft Sounds for a Wordless Night* (1979); *Secular Hours* (1982); *Cantata* for soloists, jazz choir, and large jazz ensemble (1984); *Agnus Dei* (1994); *Colleagues Remembered* (1995); and *Choral Greetings* (1998).

Mailman also made a significant contribution to the song repertory: *West Wind* (Shelley) for soprano and piano (1956); *Wind Across the Nations* for voice, piano, percussion, flute, and guitar (1975); and *Love Letters from Margaret* for soprano and orchestra (1991).

Mailman's instrumental works include two string quartets (1962, 1995); *Promenade* for brass and percussion (1953); *Four Divisions* for percussion ensemble (1966); *Variations on a Short Theme* for piano (1966); *Partita* no. 4 for nine performers (1967); *In Memoriam Silvio Scionti* for piano (1974); *Clastics I – III* for ensemble (1977–80); Piano Trio (1985); *Surfaces* for wind quintet (1991); and *Fanfare Folio* (1997). His one-act opera, *The Hunted,* was composed in 1959.

MAMLOK, URSULA
b. Berlin, Germany, 1 February 1928

Mamlok began piano lessons at the age of nine in Berlin. In 1939 the rise of the Nazis forced her family to escape to Ecuador. In 1942, aged 13, she enrolled at the Mannes School of Music in New York, where she was taught by George Szell. Later she was a private pupil of Roger Sessions, Stefan Wolpe, Edward Steuermann, and Ralph Shapey. She became an American citizen in 1945. In 1955 she was awarded a scholarship to the Manhattan School of Music where she studied with Vittorio Giannini, obtaining her M.M. in 1958. Mamlok has taught at New York University (1967–76) and Kingsborough Community College, New York (1972–75); from 1968–2003 she was on the faculty of the Manhattan School of Music. Especially in her early compositions she employed serial techniques influenced by the music of Schoenberg.

Mamlok has concentrated on writing instrumental music. Amongst her works are a Wind Quintet (1955); *Sonatina* for two clarinets (1957); *Variations* for solo flute (1961); *Composition* for cello (1962); two string quartets (1962, 1998); *Designs* for violin and piano (1962); *Concert Piece for 4* for flute, oboe, viola, and percussion (1964); *Music* for viola and harp (1965); *Capriccio* for oboe and piano (1967); *Polyphony* for clarinet (1968); *Sintra* for alto flute and cello (1969); *Variations and Interludes* for percussion quartet (1971); *Polyphony II* for English horn (1972); Sextet (1977); *When Summer Sang* for flute, clarinet, violin, cello, and piano (1980); String Quintet (1981); *Panta Rhei* (*Time in Flux*) for piano trio (1981); *Fantasie Variations* for cello (1982); and *From My Garden I*, for violin and crotales (1983), *II*, for oboe, horn, piano, and crotales (1984), and *III*, for viola and crotales (1984).

Recent chamber music includes *Alariana* for recorder (or flute), clarinet, bassoon, violin, and cello (1985); *Bagatelles* for clarinet, violin, and cello (1988); *Rhapsody* for clarinet, viola, and piano (1989); a Violin Sonata (1989); *Rhapsody* for clarinet, viola, and piano (1989); *Girasol*, a sextet for flute, clarinet, violin, viola, cello, and piano (1990); *Music for Stony Brook* for flute, violin, and cello (1990); *Five Intermezzi* for guitar (1991); and *Polarities* for flute, violin, cello, and piano (1995). Her single work for tape, *Sonar Trajectory,* dates from 1966.

For orchestra Mamlok has composed a *Concerto for Strings* (1950); *Grasshoppers* (*Six Humoresques*; 1956); a Symphony in E-flat (1956), later withdrawn; an Oboe Concerto commissioned in 1976 by the City University of New York, Concertino for wind quintet, two percussionists, and strings (1987); and *Constellations,* commissioned by the San Francisco Symphony Orchestra in 1994. Among her vocal compositions are *Daybreak* for soprano and piano (1948); *Four German Songs* for medium voice and strings (1957); *Stray Birds* (Tagore) for soprano, flute, and cello (1963); *Haiku Settings* for soprano and flute (1967); and *Der Andreas Garten* (Dwight Mamlok), nine poems set for voice and piano (1986).

MANA-ZUCCA (GIZELLA AUGUSTA ZUCKERMANN)

b. New York, New York, 25 December 1887
d. Miami Beach, Florida, 8 March 1981

Mana-Zucca studied piano with Alexander Lambert in New York and Godowsky and Busoni in Berlin before embarking on a concert career in 1907. She was also a singer in light opera who toured widely as a soloist. In 1921 she settled in Florida, where she devoted herself to composition.

She composed two operas, *Hypatia* (1920) and *The Queene of Ki-Lu* (1920), and a ballet, *The Wedding of the Butterfly.* For orchestra she wrote *Novelette and Fugato Humoresque* (1917), a Piano Concerto (1917), a Violin Concerto (1955), *Cuban Dance*, and *Havana Night.* Instrumental pieces include a Violin Sonata, a

Cello Sonata, a Piano Trio, and many piano solos. She was best known for her song *I Love Life* (1923).

MARTIN, VERNON

b. Guthrie, Oklahoma, 15 December 1929

Martin was educated at the University of Oklahoma with Harrison Kerr, at the Juilliard School with Henry Brant, and Columbia University with Henry Cowell. From 1964 to 1966 he was a cataloguer of music and records at the New York Public Library. He was music librarian at North Texas State University, Denton (1966–70), moving in 1970 to become director of library services, Morningside College, Iowa. From 1974 until retirement in 1993 he was head of the art and music department at Hartford Public Library, Connecticut. Martin has withdrawn all the music he wrote before 1968. The earliest surviving piece is *Orchestral Piece with Birds* (with tape; 1968).

For the theater he has composed four chamber operas: *Ladies Voices* (Gertrude Stein), *What Happened* (Gertrude Stein), *Waiting for the Barbarians* (Constantine Cavafy), and *Fables of Our Time* (James Thurber), in addition to a ballet, *Dancing Back the Buffalo.* His instrumental music includes *New England Fandango* for salsa band; *Liber Contrapunctum* for flute, clarinet, and bassoon; two pieces for piano, *Toccata and Fugue* and *Bagatelle*; and *Soundpiece* for two pianos.

Among Martin's vocal compositions are two works for mixed chorus and piano, *God's Trombone* and *The Lord's Prayer*; a song cycle, *We have met the enemy and he is us*; and *Seven Pogo Songs.*

MARTINO, DONALD (JAMES)

b. Plainfield, New Jersey, 16 May 1931

Martino studied composition with Ernst Bacon at Syracuse University and with Milton Babbitt and Roger Sessions at Princeton University. A Fulbright Fellowship enabled him to receive lessons from Luigi Dallapiccola in Florence from 1954 to 1956. He taught at Princeton University from 1957 to 1959 and was associate professor of theory of music at Yale University (1959–69). In 1971 he was visiting lecturer at Harvard. From 1965 to 1980 he served as chairman of the composition department at the New England Conservatory in Boston. From 1980 to 1983 he was professor of music at Brandeis University, Waltham, Massachusetts. In 1983 he was appointed professor of music at Harvard University, retiring in 1993. Martino has been the recipient of many commissions and awards. In addition to the Fulbright Fellowship he

Donald Martino.
Photo: Lourdes Awad, courtesy the composer.

received three Guggenheim Fellowships (1967, 1973, 1982), an award from the National Institute of Arts and Letters (1967), a Brandeis Creative Arts Citation (1967), and the Pulitzer Prize (1974).

In his music Martino has adopted serial and arithmetical techniques. He has taken a particular interest in writing for unaccompanied instruments; he himself is a clarinet player. Among the solo pieces are *Suite of Variations on Medieval Melodies* for cello (1952); *Set* for clarinet (1954); *Quodlibets* for flute (1954); *Fantasy Variations* for violin (1962); *Parisonatina Al'Dodecafonica* for cello (1964); *B.A.B.B.I.T.T.* for clarinet (with C extension; 1966); *Strata* for bass clarinet (1967); *Quodlibets II* for flute (1980); and *Piccolo Studio* for alto saxophone (1999); and Sonata for violin (2002).

Other instrumental pieces include a Clarinet Sonata (1950–51); *Setti Canoni Enigmatici* for various instruments (1955); String Trio (1955); Quartet for clarinet and strings (1957); Trio for clarinet, violin, and piano (1959); String Quartet no. 3 (1962); *Cinque Frammenti* for oboe and double bass (1962); Concerto for wind quintet (1964); *Notturno* for flute, clarinet, violin, cello, percussion, and piano (1973), which received the Pulitzer Prize; String Quartet no. 4 (1983); *Canzone e tarantella sul nome Petrassi* for clarinet and cello

(1984); *From the Other Side* for flute, cello, piano, and percussion (1988); *Three Sad Songs* for viola and piano (1993); and *Serenata Concertante* for octet (1999).

Martino's piano music includes a *Fantasy* (1958); *Pianississimo* (Sonata) (1971); *Impromptu for Roger* (Sessions; 1977); *Fantasies and Impromptus* (1980); *Suite in Old Form* (*Parody Suite*; 1982); and *Twelve Preludes* (1991).

For orchestra Martino has written *Contemplations* (original title: *Composition*), commissioned in 1957 by the Paderewski Fund; a Piano Concerto, commissioned by the New Haven Symphony Orchestra in 1965; *Mosaic* (1967), commissioned by the University of Chicago; a Cello Concerto (1972); *Ritorno* (1975); Triple Concerto for clarinet, bass clarinet, contrabass clarinet, and chamber orchestra (1977); *Diversions for Youth Orchestra* (1981); Concerto for alto saxophone and chamber orchestra (1987); and a Violin Concerto (1995).

Martino's vocal music includes *Separate Songs* (James Joyce and A. E. Housman; 1952); *The Bad Child's Book of Beasts* (Hilaire Belloc; 1952); a cantata, *Portraits* for soloists, chorus, and orchestra (1955); *Two Rilke Songs* (1961); *Seven Pious Poems* to poems by Robert Herrick for a cappella chorus (1971); *Paradiso Choruses* for soloists, chorus, tape, and orchestra (1974); and *The White Island* (Herrick) for chorus and chamber orchestra (1985).

In 1972 Martino composed *Augenmusik,* described as "A Mixed Mediocritique" for actress, danseuse or uninhibited female percussionist, and electronic tape. He has also written two film scores, *The White Rooster* (1950) and *The Lonely Crime* (1958).

MARTIRANO, SALVATORE
b. Yonkers, New York, 12 January 1927
d. Urbana, Illinois, 17 November 1995

Martirano served as a bandsman in the U.S. Marine Corps and toured as a jazz pianist (1946–47). He was a pupil of Herbert Elwell at Oberlin Conservatory, Ohio (1947–51), Bernard Rogers at the Eastman School of Music, Rochester, New York (1952), and Luigi Dallapiccola at the Cherubini Conservatory in Florence (1952–54). In addition he was a Prix de Rome Fellow from 1956 to 1959. In 1963 he joined the music faculty at the University of Illinois, Urbana-Champaign, becoming professor of composition, retiring in 1995. His early music was influenced by serialism, and from 1968 he took a great interest in computer-generated music.

Martirano was widely known for two choral works: a Mass for a cappella chorus (1952–53), composed in Florence and first performed on West German Radio, Hamburg, under Max Thurm in 1959; and *O, O, O, O,*

Salvatore Martirano working in his home studio in Champaign, playing the SalMar Construction, c. 1972. *Courtesy Dorothy and John Martirano.*

That Shakespeherian Rag for chorus and chamber orchestra (1958). In the latter, the chorus is required to speak, trill, hiss, whisper, and shout.

Martirano's early orchestral pieces are *Prelude* (1950), *Piece* (1952), and *Contrasts* (1954). A chamber opera, *The Magic Stone* (1951), based on a story from the *Decameron,* was produced at the Oberlin (Ohio) Conservatory. He also provided incidental music for *The Cherry Orchard* (Chehkov; 1949) and *Richard III* (Shakespeare; 1950). *Chansons Innocentes* for soprano and piano (1957) sets poems by e. e. cummings.

His instrumental music includes a Sextet for winds (1949); *Variations* for flute and piano (1950); a String Quartet (1951); a Violin Sonata (1952); *Cocktail Music* for piano (1962); *Octet* (1963), commissioned by the Koussevitzky Foundation; *Selections* for alto flute, bass clarinet, viola, and cello (1969); and *LON/dons* for chamber orchestra (1989).

In the 1960s Martirano turned to electronic music and composed *Three Electronic Dances* for tape (1963), *123–456* for computer (1964), and a sequence of theater pieces, including *Underworld* for four actors, four percussionists, two double basses, tenor saxophone, and tape (1964–65); *Buffet* for tape (1965); *Ballad* for amplified nightclub singer and instrumental ensemble (1966); *L's GA* for gas-masked actor who breathes helium, three movie projectors, and tape, using as text the Gettysburg Address (1967–68); *The Proposal* for tape and slides (1968); *Election Night Diversion* (1968), an evening's entertainment created in collaboration with

Edwin London; *Action Analysis* for 12 people (1968); and *Bunny and Controller* (1968).

After 1968 he mostly abandoned conventional composition with instruments in favor of the Sal-Mar, a computer-generated electronic machine, and other electronic devices. Resulting compositions are *Sal-Mar Construction Recordings* (1971–75); *Shoptalk* (1974); *Fast Forward* (1977); *Fifty One* (1978); *In Memoriam Luigi Dallapiccola* (1978); *She Spoke* (with narrator) (1979); and *Fantasy* (with violin) (1980). A few works of this period marked a brief return to instrumental music, *Stuck on Stella* for piano (1979) and *Thrown* for five winds and percussion (1984).

Martirano created four music videos: *Omaggio a Sally Rand* (1982), *Look at the Back of My Head Awhile* (1985), *L's GA Update* (1985), and *Dance/Players I & II* (1986). Other instrumental pieces include *Sampler: Everything Goes When the Whistle Blows* for amplified violin and live electronics (1985); and *Phleu* for amplified flute and live electronics (1988).

MASLANKA, DAVID (HENRY)
b. New Bedford, Massachusetts, 30 August 1943

Maslanka received his musical education at the New England Conservatory, Boston (1959–61) and Oberlin College Conservatory, Ohio (1962–65), where he was a pupil of Joseph Wood. In 1963 he spent a year at the Salzburg Mozarteum studying conducting with Gerhardt Wimberger. From 1965 to 1970 he was a pupil of H. Owen Reed at the Michigan State University. He taught at Geneseo College of the State University of New York (1970–74), Sarah Lawrence College (1974–80), and New York University (1980–81). From 1981–90 he was on the music faculty of Kingsborough Community College, CUNY. He then retired from teaching and moved to Missoula, Montana, to focus on composing.

Maslanka's orchestral works include a Symphony (1970); a ballet, *Fragments* (1971); *Intermezzo* for chamber orchestra (1979); *A Child's Garden of Dreams, Book II* (1982); and *Music for Strings* (1992). Maslanka has made a major contribution to the repertory of the concert band. Among his many pieces in this category are Concerto for piano, winds, and percussion (1974–76); *A Child's Garden of Dreams, Book I* (1981); *Prelude on a Gregorian Tune* (1981); Symphony no. 2 (1985); *In Memoriam* (1989); *Golden Light* (1990); Concerto for marimba and band (1990); Symphony no. 3 (1991); *Montana Music: Chorale Variations* (1993); Symphony no. 4 (1993); *Tears* (1994); *Laudamus Te* (1994); *A Tuning Piece: Songs of Fall and Winter* (1995); *Hell's Gate* for saxophone trio and symphonic band (1996); *Morning Star* (1997); *Sea Dreams,* a concerto for two horns and winds (1997); *UFO Dreams,* a concerto for euphonium and wind ensemble (1998); Concerto for saxophone and winds (1999); and Symphony no. 5 (2001).

Among his many instrumental works are a String Quartet (1968); Trio for violin, clarinet, and piano (1971); *Duo* for flute and piano (1972); Trio for viola, clarinet, and piano (1973); *Pray for Tender Voices in the Darkness* for harp and piano (1974); *Four Pieces* for clarinet and piano (1975–79); *Variations on "Lost Love"* for marimba (1977); *Cello Songs* for cello and piano (1978); *Piano Song* (1978); *Music for Dr. Who* for bassoon and piano (1979); *Fourth Piece* for clarinet and piano (1979); *Orpheus* for two bassoons and marimba (1979); *My Lady White* for marimba (1980); *Heaven to Clear When Day Did Close* for tenor saxophone and string quartet (1981); *Meditation on "Dr. Affectionata" by Gunther Grass* for guitar (1981); three *Wind Quintets* (1981, 1986, 1999); *Arcadia* for four cellos (1982); *Arcadia II,* a concerto for marimba and percussion ensemble (1982); Saxophone Sonata (1988); *Little Concerto* for six players (1990); *Crown of Thorns* for keyboard percussion ensemble (1991); Oboe Sonata (1992); *Montana Music: Three Dances* for percussion (1992); *Montana Music: Fantasy on a Chorale Tune* for violin and viola (1993); a Horn Sonata (1996, rev. 1999); *Mountain Roads* for saxophone quartet (1997); and *Song Book* for saxophone and marimba (1998).

Maslanka has composed a chamber opera, *Death and the Maiden,* commissioned in 1974 by the State University of New York. His choral music includes *The Nameless Fear or the Unanswered Question Put Yet Another Way* for chorus, speakers, guitars, harpsichord, flute, bassoon, and percussion (1973); *A Litany of Courage and the Seasons,* six songs for chorus, clarinet, and vibraphone (1988); and Mass for soprano, baritone, chorus, organ, and symphonic winds (1992–94). For solo voice he has written *Five Songs* for soprano, baritone, and chamber orchestra (1975–76); *Anne Sexton Songs* for soprano and piano (1975); *Hills of May* (Robert Graves) for soprano and string quartet (1978); and *Lincoln Speaks at Gettysburg* for tenor, alto flute, and double bass (1984).

MASON, DANIEL GREGORY
b. Brookline, Massachusetts, 20 November 1873
d. Greenwich, Connecticut, 4 December 1953

Mason was the grandson of Lowell Mason. He studied at Harvard University (1892–95) under John Knowles Paine, with George W. Chadwick in Boston, and Percy Goetschius in New York. He was a piano pupil of Ethelbert Nevin. After attending Vincent d'Indy's composition classes in Paris in 1913, he returned to the United States and joined the music department at Columbia University in 1914, becoming MacDowell Professor of Music in 1929; he retired in 1942. All of Mason's music is deeply rooted in the Romanticism of the nineteenth century, taking little account of any stylistic changes after 1900.

His Symphony no. 1 in C minor was performed by Stokowski and the Philadelphia Orchestra in 1916. It was revised in 1924 and given a new premiere by Koussevitzky and the Boston Symphony Orchestra in 1928. Symphony no. 2 in A was composed in 1928 and played the following year by the Cincinnati Symphony Orchestra under Fritz Reiner. Mason's *Lincoln Symphony* (1935–36) received its premiere by the New York Philharmonic Symphony Orchestra, conducted by John Barbirolli in 1937. For orchestra he also wrote *Scherzo-Caprice* (1917), *Chanticleer Overture* (1928), and a *Suite After English Folk Songs* (1931), performed by Bruno Walter and the New York Philharmonic Orchestra in 1934. *Prelude and Fugue* for piano and orchestra (1914) was dedicated to and performed by John Powell in 1921.

Almost all of Mason's other compositions are for instrumental ensembles. These include a Sonata for violin and piano (1907–08); Piano Quartet (1911); *Pastorale* for clarinet, violin, and piano (1912); *Three Pieces* for flute, harp, and string quartet (1912); Clarinet Sonata (1913); *Quartet on Negro Themes* (1919); *Variations on a Theme of John Powell* for string quartet (1924); Divertimento for wind quintet (1926); *Fanny*

Blair, a folk song fantasy for string quartet (1927); Serenade for string quartet (1931); and *Four Sentimental Sketches* for piano trio (1935). Mason's *Country Pictures* for piano were at one time widely played by Josef Hofmann, Percy Grainger, and other leading pianists. Also for piano are a Sonata (1895) and *Elegy* (1896).

Among his few vocal and choral works are *Six Love Songs* (1914); the song cycle *Russians* for baritone and orchestra (1918); and *Songs of the Countryside* (1923), settings of poems by A. E. Housman for soprano, baritone, chorus, and small orchestra.

As a writer on a wide range of subjects, Mason made valuable contributions to the literature on music. He wrote 18 books: *From Grieg to Brahms* (1902); *Beethoven and His Forerunners* (1904); *The Romantic Composers* (1906); *The Appreciation of Music* (with T.W. Surette; 1907); *The Orchestral Instruments and What They Do* (1908); *A Guide to Music* (1909); *A Neglected Sense in Piano Playing* (1912); *Great Modern Composers* (with Mary Mason; 1916); *Short Studies of Great Masterpieces* (1917); *Contemporary Composers* (1918); *Music as a Humanity* (1920); *From Song to Symphony* (1920); *Artistic Ideals* (1925); *The Dilemma of American Music* (1928); *Tune In, America!* (1931); *The Chamber Music of Brahms* (1933); *Music in My Time* (1938); and *The Quartets of Beethoven* (1947).

MASON, LOWELL

b. Medfield, Massachusetts, 8 January 1792
d. Orange, New Jersey, 11 August 1872

Mason was the descendant of an English settler, Robert Mason, who had come to Salem, Massachusetts in 1630. As a musician, Lowell Mason was mostly self-taught, and began his working life as a bank clerk in Savannah, Georgia, in 1812. He received some harmony and counterpoint from Frederick Abel. He was a composer of hymn tunes, many of which are found in hymn books today, including *Olivet* (*Nearer My God to Thee*), *From Greenland's Icy Mountains*, *Hebron*, *Olmutz*, *Boylston*, *My Faith Looks Up to Thee,*, and *O Jesus I Have Promised* (the last also found in the current English hymnal). He continued the tradition of New England church music, adopting a more musical and professional approach to his work.

In Boston in 1822, in collaboration with F. L. Abel, Mason compiled a book of hymn tunes adapted from melodies by Mozart, Haydn, and Beethoven, entitled *The Handel and Haydn Society's Collection of Church Music.* The success of this publication led in 1827 to Mason's appointment as supervisor of music in Boston churches. In 1832, with George J. Webb, he established the Boston Academy of Music. This marked the

beginning of his major contribution to the musical history of America. He turned his attention to musical education. After a year in Germany studying teaching methods, he served as superintendent of music (1838–45), authorized to introduce music into the curriculum of all Boston schools; his work made Mason' reputation as a pioneer educator. He continued to compile several collections of music. From 1844 until retirement in 1851, Mason was choirmaster and organist of the Central Church in Boston.

With Webb, Mason wrote a history of the Boston Glee Club, published in Boston in 1838. In 1853 he published in New York an account of his experiences in England and Germany, entitled *Musical Letters From Abroad.* Although he had gone to Europe to study music education, he took a great interest in English church music and concert life in Germany. In 1853, he settled in Orange, New Jersey, where he worked on several books and articles for periodicals. In 1855, New York University awarded Mason an honorary doctorate in music, only the second person so honored in America.

The next two generations of Masons also achieved success as composers. Mason's son William (1829–1908) was a performing pianist, piano pedagogue, and composer; another son, Henry (1831–1890), co-founded the well-known Mason & Hamlin piano manufacturing company in 1854. Henry's son Daniel Gregory (1873–1953) was a composer and educator, teaching for many years at Columbia University (1905–1942).

MAYER, WILLIAM (ROBERT)

b. New York, New York, 18 November 1925

Mayer studied at Yale University (1944–48) with Richard Donovan and at the Mannes School of Music, New York City (1949–52), where he was a pupil of Felix Salzer. At the Juilliard School, New York he studied with Roger Sessions. He was also a pupil of Otto Luening and Izler Solomon. He has taught at Boston University and conducted lectures and seminars at Yale University, Columbia University, the New School of Social Research, New York, and the Juilliard School.

Mayer's first important works were *Concert Piece* for trumpet and strings (1955) and the orchestral *Overture for an American,* composed to mark the Theodore Roosevelt Centennial in 1958. Also for orchestra are an *Andante for Strings* (1955); *Hebraic Portrait* (1957); *Two Pastels* (1960); *Scenes from the Snow Queen* (1966), derived from a ballet composed in 1963; *Octagon* for piano and orchestra, introduced by Stokowski in 1971; *Inner and Outer Strings* for string quartet and string orchestra (1982); *Of Rivers and Trains* (1988); and *Good King Wenceslas* for narrator and orchestra (1994).

William Mayer.
Courtesy Music Associates of America.

Mayer has been particularly successful in composing for the stage. He began his theater career with two operas for children, *The Greatest Sound Around* (1954) and *Hello World!* (1956).The latter, a musical trip around the world, was recorded with Eleanor Roosevelt as the narrator and was chosen by the Philadelphia Orchestra for the first "Year of the Child." In 1962 he wrote the one-act opera *Christmas Long Ago* and a six-minute choral opera, *Brief Candle,* produced by the New School Opera Workshop in 1967. His next stage work was a full-length opera based on James Agee's Pulitzer Prize novel *A Death in the Family,* premiered in Minneapolis in March 1983. The opera received a special citation from the National Institute for Music Theater. Subsequent productions were mounted by Opera Theater, St. Louis and the Manhattan School of Music. This was followed by *A Sobbing Pillow of a Man,* an extended scene relating to *A Death in the Family* but not included in the opera; it was staged in New York in 1995.

An impressive choral piece, *Letters Home* for soloists, narrator, chorus, and orchestra was performed in May 1968. Dedicated to the memory of Martin Luther King, Jr., it comprises settings of texts from letters written by soldiers fighting in Vietnam. Other choral works include *Four Madrigals*; *The Eve of St. Agnes* (1968), based on the poem by Keats, commissioned by East Illinois University Choir and Orchestra in 1969; and *Lines of Light,* on poems by Coleridge and Dylan Thomas, for female voices and piano (1970). *Spring Came on Forever* (1975), a cantata celebrating romantic love through the ages, was first performed by the New York Choral Society in Avery Fisher Hall. Mayer's more recent choral compositions include a setting of Keats' *La Belle Dame sans Merci* (1977); *Ae Fond Kiss* (Robert Burns) (1992), commissioned for the 70th birthday of choral conductor Robert De Cormier; and *The Negro Speaks of Rivers* (Langston Hughes;1998).

Mayer has composed 12 attractive works for voice and instrumental ensemble: *Always, Always, Forever, Again* to a text by Eugene O'Neill (1964); *Eight Miniatures* to texts by Dorothy Parker (1967); *Two News Items* (1967); *Khartoum* (1968); *Enter Ariel* (1980), to texts by Hart Crane, Sara Teasdale, e. e. cummings, and Langston Hughes; *Fern Hill* (Dylan Thomas; 1981); *Passage* a song cycle for mezzo-soprano (1981); *First Song* (Galway Kinnell; 1991); *Distant Playing Fields* for tenor and four players (1994); *Last Song,* derived from *A Death in the Family* (1998); *Zoom-bah* (1998); and *Summer Glints* for countertenor, flute, oboe, string quartet, and harpsichord.

Mayer has composed a wide variety of art and theater songs, some to his own texts. *That Purple Bird* (1951)*, Lover's Lament* (1974)*, Paradox* (1952), and the duet *Barbara, What Have You Done?* are among the most frequently performed.

His instrumental music includes five pieces for winds: *Essay* for brass and winds (1954); *Country Fair* (1957); Brass Quintet (1964); *Yankee Doodle Fanfare* (1976); and *Unlikely Neighbors* (1991). Other chamber pieces are *Celebration Trio* for flute, clarinet, and piano (1956); *Back Talk* for 15 players (1970); *Messages* for flute, string trio, and percussion (1973); *Dream's End* for oboe, clarinet, horn, violin, cello, and piano (1976); and a chamber version of *Of Rivers and Trains* (1998). Among shorter pieces are *Song* for oboe (1952); *Two Moods* for clarinet (1960); *Three for Three* for two percussionists and piano (1960); *Appalachian Echoes* for harp (1976); and *Wedding Romp* for violin and bassoon (1982).

For piano Mayer has written a partly-serial Sonata (1959); *Pepper and Salt* (1968); *A Most Important Train* (1970); a *Toccata* (1972), to a commission from the Musicians Club of New York; *Abandoned Bells* (1985); and *Subway in the Sunlight and Other Memories* (1970–96).

In addition to composing, Mayer has been chairman of Composers Recordings Inc., and frequently writes on musical subjects for various publications, including the *New York Times* and *Horizon*.

MCBRIDE, ROBERT GUYN
b. Tucson, Arizona, 20 February 1911

At the University of Arizona, Tucson (1928–35), McBride studied with Otto Luening, becoming a teaching fellow there himself (1933–35) and obtaining a M.Mus. degree in composition. In addition he played in the Tucson Symphony Orchestra (1928–35). From 1935 to 1945 he was on the music faculty of Bennington College, Vermont. He returned to the University of Arizona in 1957, becoming professor emeritus in 1976.

As a schoolboy, McBride played clarinet, saxophone, and organ in theaters and dance bands. Much of his music reveals this early interest in jazz and popular music with titles that are light-hearted, reflecting the jazzy nature of the pieces: *Workout* (1936); *Swing Stuff* (1938); *Strawberry Jam* (1941); *Jam Session* for wind quintet (1941); *Stuff in G* for orchestra (1942); *Wise Apple Five* and *Aria and Toccata in Swing* for violin and piano (1946); and *Swing Foursome* for string quartet (1957). His best known works in this vein are the colorful *Mexican Rhapsody* (1934), *Pumpkin Eater's Little Fugue* (1952), and *Panorama of Mexico* (1960).

In contrast McBride's more serious compositions have appropriately more serious titles: *Prelude to a Tragedy* for orchestra (1935) and a Violin Sonata, sub-

Robert McBride, 2001.
Courtesy Carol McBride.

titled *Depression* (1934). Other works for orchestra are *Fugato on a Well Known Theme* (1935); *Concerto for Doubles* for clarinet, bass clarinet, and saxophone (one player; 1947); *Variety Day* (1948); a Violin Concerto (1954); *Symphonic Melody* (1968); *Folk-Song Fantasy* (1973); and *Light Fantastic* (1976–77).

McBride's chamber music includes a Piano Quintet (1934); *Prelude and Fugue* for string quartet (1936); Oboe Quintet (1937); *Five Winds Blowing* for wind quintet (1957); *Variations on Various Popularisms* for clarinet, English horn, and bassoon (1965); and *Lament for the Parking Problem* for trumpet, horn, and trombone (1968).

His ballet *Show Piece* was performed by Ballet Caravan in 1937. Four other ballets originally with piano accompaniment are *Punch and the Judy* (1941), composed for Martha Graham; *Furlough* (1945); *Jazz Symphony* (1954); and *Brooms of Mexico* (1970).

For wind band he has written *A Sherlock Holmes Suite* (1946); *Hollywood Suite* (1950); *Sunday in Mexico* (1963); *A Hill Country Symphony* (1964); *Country Music Fantasy* (1965); *Sportmusic* (1976–77); and the march *Sonora,* commissioned in 1979 by the Ohio State University Marching Band, his last completed work.

McBride has provided film scores for travelogues and documentaries, including *Magazine Magic* (1946) and *Sea-Going Smoke Eaters* (1953). Among his feature film scores are *Farewell to Yesterday* (1950), *The Man With My Face* (1951), and *Garden of Eden* (1957), as well as a cartoon, *Rodney* (1951).

MCDONALD, HARL
b. Boulder, Colorado, 27 July 1899
d. Princeton, New Jersey, 30 March 1955

At the age of 22, McDonald made his debut as soloist in his own Piano Concerto with the San Francisco Symphony Orchestra. Later he studied at the University of Southern California (1918–21) and the Leipzig Conservatory (1921–23). At the University of Redlands, California he was awarded a doctorate in music. After touring Europe and the United States as a pianist, he settled in Philadelphia in 1926 as a conductor and teacher. In 1930 he began a serious study of acoustics, and three years later published a book, *New Methods of Measuring Sound.* From 1924 to 1926 he taught at the Philadelphia Academy of Music. He served as director of music at the University of Pennsylvania (1926–46) and was manager of the Philadelphia Orchestra (1939–55).

As a composer, McDonald was both prolific and successful in receiving performances of his music. His five symphonies were at one time frequently heard: no. 1, *The Santa Fe Trail* (1932); no. 2, *Rumba* (1934); no. 3, *Tragic Circle* for soprano, chorus, and orchestra, also subtitled *The Lament of Fu Hsuan* (1935); no. 4, *Festival of Workers* (1938); and no. 5, *Children's Symphony on Familiar Themes* (1948).

Of McDonald's many orchestral works, only the *Suite from Childhood* for harp and orchestra (1940), based on six English nursery rhymes, is at all widely known today. Other orchestral pieces are the symphonic fantasy *Mojave* (1922); *Three Poems on Aramaic Themes* (1935); *San Juan Capistrano* (1938); *Miniature Suite* (1938); *Legend of the Arkansas Traveler* (1939); *Chameleon Variations* (1940); *My Country at War* (1942); *Bataan* (1943); *Saga of the Mississippi* (1943); *Two Concert Pieces* (1947); and *Overture for Children* (1950). In addition to the Piano Concerto, he composed a Concerto for two pianos (1935) and a Violin Concerto (1943).

Among his 50 choral works are *Missa de Battale*, based on Spanish chants; *Missa ad Patrem* for chorus and orchestra (1937); *Songs of Conquest* (1937–39); *Lament to the Stolen* for female voices and orchestra (1939) in memory of the Lindbergh kidnapping; *Wind in the Palm Trees* for female voices and strings (1940); *Dirge for Two Veterans* (Whitman) for female voices and orchestra (1940); and a setting of Psalm 84. For soprano and orchestra he composed *Song of the Nations* (1945).

The first of his two string quartets, composed in 1933, makes use of African-American melodies. He also composed two piano trios (1931, 1932) and a *Fantasy* for string quartet (1932).

MCKAY, GEORGE FREDERICK
b. Harrington, Washington, 11 June 1899
d. Stateline, Nevada, 4 October 1970

McKay studied at the University of Washington and later at the Eastman School of Music, Rochester, New York, where he was a pupil of Christian Sinding (1921–22) and Selim Palmgren (1923). (In 1923 he became the school's first composition graduate.) He returned to the University of Washington in 1927, becoming a professor in 1943 and retiring in 1968.

Among McKay's large number of orchestral works are four sinfoniettas (1925, 1929, 1933, 1942); a *Symphony for Seattle* (1951); a Symphony, *Evocations* (1951); and two *Symphonic Miniatures* (1930, 1967). Many of the orchestral pieces have descriptive titles such as *A Prairie Portrait* (1932); *Fantasy on a Western Folk Song* (1933); *From a Mountain Town* (1934); *Westward* (1935); *Machine Age Blues* (1935); *Harbor Narrative Suite* (1935); *To a Liberator: A Lincoln Trib-*

George Frederick McKay.
Courtesy Fred McKay and The George Frederick McKay Estate.

ute (1940); *A Pioneer Epic* (1942); *Music of the Americas* (1947–50); *Song Over the Great Plains* (1954); *Down to the Sea Again*; *From a Moonlit Ceremony*; and *The Big Sky*. Others are scored for string orchestra: *Port Royal 1861* (1939); *Introspective Poem* (1941); *Rocky Harbor and Sandy Cove* (1950); *Sky Blue and Meadow Green* (1950); *Halyard and Capstan* (1950); *From the Maine Woods* (1951); and *Buffalo and Crow,* songs and dances of the Oklahoma Indians (1951). McKay wrote concertos for violin (1940) and cello (1942) and a Suite for viola and orchestra.

McKay's many choral works include *A Lanier Pastorale* for female voices and orchestra (1935); *Choral Rhapsody* for chorus and brass (1936); *Pioneers* (Whitman) for chorus and orchestra (1942); Concerto for chorus and orchestra (1944); and a cantata, *Lincoln Lyrics* (1949).

He composed a large quantity of chamber music, including a Violin Sonata (1923); a Woodwind Quintet (1930); an Organ Sonata (1930); a Piano Trio (1931); a String Quartet (1936); *American Street Scenes* for wind quartet and piano (1936); *Bravura Prelude* for brass (1936); Sonata for organ and piano (1937); Trombone Sonata (1951); Suite for chamber ensemble (1958); and Suite for flute and harp (1960). Of his works for the stage, the best known is the dance drama *Epoch,* composed in 1935.

McKay was the author of a textbook, *Creative Orchestration*, published in 1963.

MCKINLEY, CARL

b. *Yarmouth, Maine, 9 October 1895*
d. *Boston, Massachusetts, 24 July 1966*

McKinley studied at Knox College and Conservatory, Galesburg, Illinois, and at Harvard University, where he was a pupil of Edward Burlingame Hill. From 1917 to 1918 he received lessons from Rubin Goldmark and Walter Rothwell. He was later a pupil of Nadia Boulanger. Among the awards he received were the Boott Prize from Harvard (1916), a Naumburg Traveling Fellowship (1917), a Flagler Prize of the New York Symphony Society (1921), and two Guggenheim Fellowships (1927, 1929). From 1928 to 1929 he was a stage assistant at the Munich Opera. On his return to the United States in 1929 he taught organ, history, and composition at the New England Conservatory, Boston until his retirement. He was also an organist in Hartford, Connecticut and New York.

Carl McKinley.
Courtesy The New England Conservatory of Music.

McKinley is best known for his orchestral works. The first of these, *Indian Summer Idyll* (1917), was first performed by the New York Philharmonic Orchestra in 1919. *The Blue Flower* won the Flagler Prize in 1921 and was premiered by the same orchestra in 1924. *Masquerade* (*American Rhapsody*) was performed by the Chicago Symphony Orchestra in May 1926. Also for orchestra are *Chorale, Variations and Fugue* (Rochester, 1939) and *Caribbean Holiday* (Boston, 1948). His many instrumental compositions include a String Quartet (1941), a Cello Sonata (1951), a *Suite for Five* (Wind Quintet), and *Cantilena* for organ.

MCKINLEY, WILLIAM THOMAS

b. *New Kensington, Pennsylvania, 9 December 1938*

McKinley began piano lessons at the age of five. His musical education continued at the Carnegie-Mellon University, Pittsburgh (B.A., 1960), where his teachers included Nicolai Lopatnikoff and Alexei Haieff. At Yale University (M.A., 1968; M.F.A., 1969) he studied with Gunther Schuller, Mel Powell, Yehudi Wyner, and Lawrence Moss. In the summer of 1963 at Tanglewood he received lessons from Aaron Copland, Lukas Foss, and Gunther Schuller. He taught at the University of Chicago (1969–73) and at the New England Conservatory, Boston (1973–92), specializing in composition and jazz. In 1991, he founded the Master Musicians Collective to release recordings of works by contemporary composers. Among his awards is a Guggenheim Fellowship (1985–86). He has also performed and recorded as a jazz pianist.

Among his orchestral works are six symphonies: no. 1 (1977), premiered in Minneapolis in 1979; no. 2, *Of Time and Future Monuments* (1978); no. 3, *Romantic,* performed in New York in 1984; no. 4 (1985); no. 5, *Irish* (1989); and no. 6, first performed in St. Lucia, Australia in 1990. Other orchestral compositions include *October Night* (1976); two concertos for Orchestra (1977, 1993); a tone poem, *The Mountain* (1982); *Poem of Light* for piano and chamber orchestra (1983); *SinfoNova* for strings (1985); *Boston Overture* (1986); *Tenor Rhapsody* for tenor saxophone and orchestra (1988); *Curtain Up* for chamber orchestra (1988); *New York Overture* (1989); *Silent Whispers* (1992); *Andante and Scherzo*, both for piano and orchestra; *Chamber Concerto no. 3* (1991); *Fantasia Variazioni* for harpsichord and orchestra (1993); *Concert Variations* for violin, viola, and orchestra (1993); *Patriotic Variations: Reading Festival Overture* (1993); *Lightning Overture* (1993); and *Freedom Dreams* (2002), a work dedicated to Martin Luther King, Jr. and premiered on the anniversary of his birth date (21 January) by the Indianapolis Symphony Orchestra.

In addition to works for orchestra alone, McKinley has written many concertos: three for piano (1973, 1987, 1994); three for clarinet (1977, 1990; 1994, *The Alchemist*); three for viola; piano, double bass, drums, and orchestra (1970); cello (1977); Double Concerto for double bass, bass clarinet, and chamber ensemble (1984); *Summer Dance* for violin and chamber ensemble (1984); flute and strings (1986); *Huntington Horn Concerto* (1989); *Jubilee Concerto* for brass quintet (1990); *Concerto for the New World* for wind quintet, strings, and percussion (1991); *Concerto Domestica* for trumpet, bassoon, and orchestra (1992); and clarinet and violin.

His numerous instrumental works include nine string quartets (1959–92); *Attitudes* for flute, clarinet, and cello (1967); *Studies* for string trio (1968); *For One* for solo clarinet (1971); *Tashi* for clarinet, violin, cello, and piano (1977); *August Symphony* for flute, clarinet, violin, cello, and piano (1982–83); *Paintings I – VIII* for ensemble (1972–86); *Duo Concertante* for clarinet and piano (1983); *Two Entratas* for clarinet (1983); *Two Nocturnes* for clarinet and cello (1983); *Trio appassionata* for clarinet, viola and piano (1983); *Duo* for flute and piano (1984); *Romances* for violin, clarinet, and piano (1984); *Three Romances* for flute and piano (1984); *Golden Portals* for clarinet (1985); *Quintet Romantico* (1987); Piano Quartet no. 1 (1988); *Ancient Memories* for viola and chamber ensemble (1989); *Glass Canyons* for clarinet, piano, and percussion (1990); *Der Baum des Lebens* for string quartet (1993); *Elegy* for solo flute (1993); and *Tango Variations* for violin and piano (2001).

For solo voice he has composed *New York Memories* for soprano and piano (1987); *When the Moon is Full* for mezzo-soprano, baritone, and seven instruments (1989); *Emsdettener Totentanz* for soprano, alto, baritone, and chamber ensemble (1991); *Westfälischer Pan* for mezzo-soprano, clarinet, and piano (1991); *Jenseits der Mauer* for baritone, trumpet, and organ (1992); *Three Poems of Pablo Neruda* for mezzo-soprano and orchestra (1992); and *Dallas 1963* (W. Bezanson) for baritone and orchestra (1995). His oratorio *Deliverance: Amen* for chorus, chamber ensemble, and organ was completed in 1983.

MCPHEE, COLIN (CARHART)

b. Montreal, Canada, 15 March 1901
d. Los Angeles, California, 7 January 1964

McPhee graduated from the Peabody Institute, Baltimore in 1921 where he had been a pupil of Gustav Strube. He studied piano with Arthur Friedheim in Toronto (1921–24) and composition privately with Varèse in New York. From 1925 to 1927 he lived in Paris, where he was a pupil of Isador Philipp (piano) and Paul le Flem (composition).

Success came with the performance in Baltimore of his First Piano Concerto, *Mort d'Arthur* in 1920 when he was still a student. The scores of this work and his Second Piano Concerto (1923) are now lost, as is his First Symphony in one movement, dating from 1930. Other early works include *Sarabande for Orchestra* (1927); Concerto for piano and wind octet (1928); *Sea Shanty Suite* for baritone, men's chorus, two pianos, and two timpani (1929); and two experimental film scores, *Mechanical Principles* and *H20*, both dating from 1931.

In 1931 McPhee went to Bali, now part of Indonesia; planning to stay for six months, he remained there for almost seven years, becoming an expert on the music of the island. The influence of Balinese music had a profound effect upon McPhee, giving rise to two orchestral works, *Bali* and *Tabuh-Tabuhan*, both composed in 1936 and first performed in Mexico City, and *Balinese Ceremonial Music* for flute and two pianos (1942). *Tabuh-Tabuhan* makes use of varied rhythmic and metrical forms directly related to Balinese music. It is scored for two pianos, celeste, xylophone, marimba, glockenspiel, Balinese gongs, and cymbals to re-create the gamelan orchestra of Bali. Also at this time McPhee completed *From the Revelations of St, John the Divine* for men's chorus, three trumpets, two pianos, and two timpani (1936).

McPhee returned to New York in 1939, becoming an American citizen in that year and working for the Office of War Information, a post he held from 1940 to 1947. He taught at the Institute of Ethnomusicology, University of California, Los Angeles (1958–64).

Other orchestral works without Balinese influences include *Four Iroquois Dances* (1944), *Transitions* (1951), *Nocturne* (1958), and *Concerto for Wind Orchestra* (1959). His Second Symphony, *Pastoral* was commissioned by the Louisville Orchestra and first performed in 1957. A Third Symphony, begun in 1962, remained unfinished.

McPhee wrote three books about his musical discoveries. The first, entitled *A House in Bali*, was published in 1947, followed a year later by *A Club of Small Men*. His monumental volume, the authoritative *Music of Bali*, a study of form and instrumental organization in Balinese orchestral music, was begun in 1942 but not completed until 1963, shortly before his death, and published posthumously in 1966.

MECHEM, KIRKE (LEWIS)
b. Wichita, Kansas, 16 August 1925

Mechem studied at Stanford University, California

(B.A., 1951) and at Harvard University (M.A., 1953), where his teachers included A. Tillman Merritt, Walter Piston, and Randall Thompson. He taught at Menlo College, California (1953–56) and Stanford University (1953–56), then lived in Vienna (1956–57, 1961–63). He has been Composer-in-Residence at San Francisco State College (1965–66) and Lone Mountain College, University of San Francisco (1966–72).

His opera *Tartuffe* (1977–80), based on the play by Moliere, was staged in San Francisco in 1980, subsequently receiving over 200 performances. His other operas are *John Brown* (1988–89) and *The Newport Rivals* (2000), derived from *The Rivals* by Sheridan.

His principal orchestral works are two symphonies, no. 1 (1958–59), premiered in San Francisco in 1965, and no. 2 (1966, rev. 1968). Also for orchestra he has written *Haydn's Return: Variations and Fugue on a Theme of Haydn* (1960) and an overture, *The Jayhawk* (1976).

Among his instrumental music are a Suite for two violins (1952–53); Trio for oboe, clarinet, and bassoon (1955); Trio for violin, cello, and piano (1956–57); Divertimento for flute and string trio (1958); a String Quartet (1962–63); and three pieces for piano, Suite (1954), Sonata (1964–65), and *Whims* (1967).

Mechem has written several major choral compositions, including two cantatas, *Songs of Wisdom* for four soloists and chorus (1958–59) and *The King's Contest* for soloists, chorus, and orchestra (1960–61, rev. 1972); *Five Centuries of Spring* for chorus (1960); *Seven Joys of Christmas*, a sequence of carols for soprano, chorus, and harp (1964); a cantata, *Singing in So Good a Thing: An Elizabethan Recreation* for soprano or tenor, chorus, and chamber orchestra (1970–71); *Speech to a Crowd* for baritone, chorus, and orchestra (1974); *American Madrigals* for chorus and instruments (1975); *Songs of the Slaves* for bass-baritone, chorus, and orchestra (1993); *Three Motets* for chorus (1993–94); *Barter* for women's voices, trumpet, and piano duet (1994); *Choral Variations on American Folk Songs* for chorus and piano (1995); *Earth My Song* for chorus and piano (1996); *Winging Wildly* for unaccompanied chorus (1996); and *To Music* for chorus and piano (1998).

MENNIN, PETER

b. Erie, Pennsylvania, 17 May 1923
d. New York, New York, 17 June 1983

Mennin was of Italian descent; the family name is Mennini but he changed it to avoid confusion with his brother Louis, also a composer. He began piano lessons at the age of five and wrote his first piece of music for the instrument two years later.

Peter Mennin.
From the collection of Mrs. Mennin, courtesy The Juilliard School.

He studied with Normand Lockwood at the Oberlin Conservatory, Ohio (1940–42) and at the Eastman School of Music, Rochester, New York under Howard Hanson and Bernard Rogers (1945–47). He was awarded a doctorate for his Symphony no. 3. From 1947 to 1958 he taught at the Juilliard School in New York. In 1958 he was appointed director of the Peabody Conservatory in Baltimore, but in 1962 he returned to the Juilliard School, succeeding William Schuman as its president.

Mennin's First Symphony was composed in 1942 when he was only 19 years old. Symphony no. 2, completed two years later, won the George Gershwin Award and received its premiere by Leonard Bernstein and the New York Philharmonic Orchestra.

Mennin's most remarkable work is probably the Third Symphony, completed in May 1946 on the composer's 23rd birthday. This three-movement work was performed by the New York Philharmonic on 27 February 1947 under Walter Hendl. Subsequently it was played throughout the United States and later recorded by the New York Philharmonic under Mitropoulos. The first movement of the Third Symphony has something in common with the Sixth Symphony of Vaughan Williams, but predates that work by over a year. The last movement reveals an affinity with another English symphony, Walton's First, but it is unlikely that the music of either composer acted as even an indirect influence upon Mennin.

The Fourth Symphony, *The Cycle* (1949), is a setting for chorus and orchestra of philosophical texts written by the composer. Commissioned for the Dallas Symphony Orchestra, the Fifth Symphony appeared in 1950 and was followed three years later by the Sixth Symphony, commissioned by the Louisville Orchestra.

By the age of 30, Mennin had six symphonies to his credit. Ten years later he completed his Seventh Symphony, subtitled *Variations* (1964), written for the Cleveland Orchestra. Symphony no. 8 was premiered by the New York Philharmonic and Daniel Barenboim on 21 November 1974. Although completed before the onset of the composer's final illness, Symphony no. 9 (*Sinfonia capricciosa*) has a valedictory air, especially in the dignified central Adagio, which ends with a tolling bell. Commissioned by the National Symphony Orchestra of Washington, Symphony no. 9 was written in 1981.

Mennin's other orchestral works include a Concerto for Orchestra (1944); Concertino for flute, strings, and percussion (1945); *Folk Overture* (1945); *Sinfonia* for chamber orchestra (1946); *Fantasie for Strings* (1947); a Violin Concerto (1950); and a *Concertato for Orchestra* (1956), based on Herman Melville's *Moby Dick*. The Piano Concerto (1947), composed for the 40th anniversary of the Cleveland Orchestra, is a work calling for considerable virtuoso powers from the soloist. He has also written a Cello Concerto (1956), commissioned for the 50th anniversary of the Juilliard School. His last composition, a Flute Concerto, was completed in 1983. The neo-Romantic *Canto for Orchestra* dates from 1963. *Symphonic Movements*, retitled *Sinfonia for Orchestra in two movements*, was commissioned in 1971 and first heard in St. Paul by the Minnesota Orchestra under Stanislaw Skrowacewski.

Among Mennin's choral works is *The Christmas Story* (1949), scored for soloists, chorus, brass, strings, and timpani. *Cantata de Virtute*, a setting of Browning's poem "The Pied Piper of Hamelin" for soloists, chorus, narrator, and orchestra, was presented at the Cincinnati May Festival in 1969. For a cappella voices he wrote *Four Choruses on Chinese Texts* (1948). His final choral work, *Reflections of Emily Dickinson* for boys' voices, harp, piano, and percussion, was commissioned in 1978 by the National Endowment for the Arts.

His instrumental music includes two string quartets (1941, 1950); an Organ Sonata (1941); *Canto and Toccata* for piano (1950); *Sonata Concertante* for violin and piano (1956); a Piano Sonata (1967); and *Cadenza Capricciosa* for harp.

MENNINI, LOUIS ALFRED
b. Erie, Pennsylvania, 18 November 1920
d. Naples, Florida, 22 February 2000

Mennini was the older brother of Peter Mennin. He studied at the Oberlin Conservatory, Ohio (1939–42). After three years in the U.S. Air Force, he entered the Eastman School of Music, Rochester, New York, where he was a pupil of Bernard Rogers and Howard Hanson; he graduated in 1947. (He was awarded a doctorate there in 1961.) He taught at the University of Texas (1948–49) and at the Eastman School (1949–65). He was founder and dean of the School of Music, North Carolina School of Arts, Winston-Salem (1965–71). From 1973 to 1983 he was director of music at Maryhurst College, Pennsylvania. In 1983 he founded the Virginia School of Arts, Lynchburg, retiring in 1988.

For orchestra he wrote two symphonies (*Da Chiesa*, 1960; *Da Festa*, 1963); *Andante and Allegro* for strings (1946); *Ariosa* for strings (1948); *Canzona* for chamber orchestra (1949); *Cantilena* (1950); *Overture Breve* (1952); *Credo* (1955); *Tenebrae* (1963); and *Concerto Grosso* (1975).

His major works for the stage are two operas, *The Well* (1951) and *The Rope*, a Koussevitzky Foundation commission (Tanglewood, 1955), in addition to a ballet, *Allegro Energico* (1948). Choral compositions include *Tenebrae* for chorus (1948) and *The Proper of the Mass* (1953). Among his instrumental pieces are a Violin Sonata (1947), a Cello Sonata (1952), and a String Quartet (1961).

MENOTTI, GIAN-CARLO
b. Cadigliano, Italy, 7 July 1911

Menotti received his first musical training from his mother, and wrote an opera entitled *The Death of Pierrot* when he was only ten years old. After studying at the Milan Conservatory from 1923 to 1927 he went to the United States where he studied at the Curtis Institute in Philadelphia (1927–33). Among his teachers were Rosario Scalero, himself an Italian by birth. Menotti taught composition there from 1948 to 1955.

Although he made his home in America from 1927 to 1973, Menotti retains his Italian citizenship. More than any other composer in the United States, he has established a sequence of operas that have been performed and revived throughout the world. Indeed, he and Benjamin Britten are the only composers of the second half of the 20th century to have their stage works constantly in the repertory of opera companies in both Europe and America. Although some of these operas have American settings, the plots and characters seldom

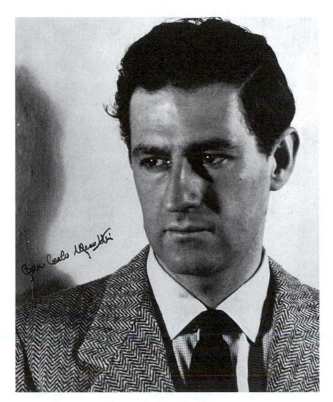

Gian Carlo Menotti.
Courtesy Music Library, State University of New York, Buffalo, J. Warren Perry Collection of Photographs, Box 10, Item 6.

have narrow national characteristics and thereby hold a universality which ensures wide appeal.

From the beginning, Menotti has written his own libretti. His remarkable understanding of the theater and an inherent feeling for combining words and music have assured the dramatic success of his works for the stage. Except for *Amelia Goes to the Ball* (*Amelia al Ballo*) and *The Last Savage*, he has always used English, a language he feels most suited in its range of expression for contemporary situations. His musical style is derived from the "verismo" style of Puccini and the early twentieth-century Italian composers and the simple direct declamation of Mussorgsky, but with an updating of harmony and orchestration appropriate to the present.

Menotti's first opera, *Amelia Goes to the Ball,* begun in 1933, was produced at the Curtis Institute on 1 April 1937 under the direction of Fritz Reiner. The following year it was staged at the Metropolitan Opera House in New York. Particularly in its original Italian version, it resembles *Susanna's Secret* by Wolf-Ferrari. Both operas reveal the problems facing certain married women. Amelia wishes to go to the ball, but neither her husband nor her lover will take her, so she is accompanied there by the Police Inspector. In some

respects the action resembles a Feydeau farce. In 1938 NBC commissioned *The Old Maid and the Thief,* a comedy in 14 scenes, performed on radio on 22 April 1939 and staged in Philadelphia on 11 February 1942. His third opera, *The Island God,* a one-act tragedy, received its premiere at the Metropolitan on 20 February 1942.

Wide critical acclaim greeted Menotti's next opera, *The Medium,* first performed in New York on 8 May 1946. This two-act tragedy tells of a fraudulent spiritualist who begins to believe the voices she hears. Its macabre atmosphere produces moments of fear that create perhaps the most frightening experiences in the realm of opera, showing the composer-librettist at his best. It was followed the next year by a complete contrast, the one-act comedy *The Telephone,* produced on 18 February 1947 by New York's Ballet Society. In this charming two-character story a young man finds the only way he can propose to his young lady without interruptions from her friends, who constantly call her on the telephone, is to pop the question to her over the telephone. *The Medium* and *The Telephone* have frequently been performed with great success as a double bill.

Menotti's reputation was further enhanced by his sixth opera, *The Consul.* It is unlikely that anyone who saw the original production staged in New York in May 1950 and later taken to London will ever forget the impact on the audience. Set in an unnamed totalitarian state, the plot tells of the ordeal of a family of political fugitives and their difficulties in obtaining visas to leave the country. John Sorel has escaped over the border but his wife and child have not been permitted to follow him. He returns to help his wife but is captured. His wife, Magda, commits suicide by gassing herself after her child and her mother-in-law have died. The frustrations of waiting at the consulate and the inhuman lack of concern of the Consul, who does not appear in the opera, bring home to the listener the horrors of the refugee situation. Magda Sorel is one of the most moving tragic heroines of twentieth-century opera. The sense of fear and political oppression and the deep compassion for the victims are conveyed with astounding power. Like *Fidelio* and *Tosca,* which it echoes in some respects, the subject is as relevant today as when it was written.

For Christmas Eve 1951, NBC commissioned the television opera *Amahl and the Night Visitors.* It was composed in a very short time and Menotti acknowledges the inspiration of the painting *The Adoration of the Magi* by Hieronymus Bosch. In the opera, the Three Kings on their way to Bethlehem stay for a night at the humble abode of Amahl, a poor cripple, and his mother. When he expresses a desire to go with them and give his crutch to the Christ Child, he is cured of his lameness. This delightful opera, with its appropriately captivating music, is deservedly popular and regularly received performances at Christmas around the world, both on television and on stage.

Menotti's eighth opera, described as a music drama in three acts, *The Saint of Bleecker Street,* won the New York Drama Critics' Award in 1954 and the Pulitzer Prize in 1955. It was also produced on television. In a poor Italian community in New York City, Annina, the invalid heroine, has the stigmata and is treated with awe by her brother Michele, who tries to prevent her from becoming a nun. The deep religious faith of the girl is set against the doubts held by her brother. At the end of the opera she dies, shortly after taking the veil.

New avenues were explored in Menotti's next work for the stage. *The Unicorn, the Gorgon and the Minotaur* is a madrigal fable with the action mimed by dancers while the instrumental ensemble and chorus tell the story from the orchestra pit. Stylistically there are deliberate similarities to the madrigal operas of Banchieri and Vecchi, but the basic idiom, especially in the instrumental interludes, is modern. The composer satirizes the desire of certain people to keep up with fashion. The work was commissioned by the Elizabeth Sprague Coolidge Foundation and was first performed at the Library of Congress, Washington, D.C. on 21 October 1956.

For the World's Fair in Brussels in August 1958, Menotti composed *Maria Golovin.* Of all his works, this three-act tragedy most closely resembles the operatic world of Puccini in its dramatic and musical elements. The principal characters are Donato, a war-blinded young man, and Maria Golovin, a married woman with whom he falls in love. The opera contains some of the composer's most extended dramatic scenes with a number of impressive musical moments. It is an undeservedly neglected composition.

Almost five years elapsed before Menotti's next opera. *The Labyrinth* was produced on NBC television on 3 March 1963. It is a symbolic music drama depicting a bride and bridegroom searching through the Grand Hotel for their room and their key to it. After meeting several strange and foreboding figures, the bridegroom finds the manager who is Death and in death he discovers what he has been seeking. That same year Menotti completed *The Last Savage,* an opera buffa commissioned by the Paris Opera, begun originally with an Italian text but given in French at its premiere in Paris on 21 October 1963. The first performance in the Unites States, in English, took place at the Metropolitan Opera on 23 January 1964. It is a three-act contemporary satire set in India and Chicago. For the Bath Festival in England, Menotti wrote a short church opera,

Martin's Lie, performed in Bristol Cathedral on 3 June 1964. It concerns the religious persecution of an orphan boy who dies under interrogation.

The one-act children's opera *Help! Help! The Globolinks!* presents creatures from space who can be frightened off only by music. Appropriately the work makes use of electronic effects. It received its world premiere in Hamburg, Germany on 19 December 1968; the first American performance took place in Santa Fe, New Mexico on 1 August 1969. Menotti's 14th adult opera, *The Most Important Man,* was produced by the New York City Opera on 7 March 1971. It exposes the hypocrisy of the attitude of white people towards black nations with a doctor and his daughter who have settled in a "white" African state to conduct scientific experiments.

Menotti's next opera, *Tamu-Tamu,* was commissioned by the 9th International Congress of Anthropological and Ethnological Sciences in Chicago. It was presented in that city in September 1973. "Tamu-tamu" is an Indonesian word meaning "guests," and the work is a sociological and political morality tale about a refugee Indonesian family who arrive unexpectedly at the home of an American couple. Toward the end of the opera, when the two families have begun to understand each other, a group of soldiers bursts in and takes the Indonesian family to kill them. The American couple then settle back into their mundane life with the audience left to draw its own conclusion about what has happened.

On 1 June 1976 his comic opera *The Hero,* a political satire in three acts, was produced in Philadelphia. In the same year the church opera *The Egg,* describing an incident in the life of St. Simeon Stylites, was presented in Washington Cathedral. It was followed by another opera for children, *Chip and His Dog,* first performed in Guelph, Ontario on 5 May 1979. Menotti's next opera, *La Loca,* recounts the life of Joanna La Loca of Castille, who married the Duke of Burgundy in the sixteenth century. The daughter of Ferdinand and Isabella of Spain, she was imprisoned as mad for 48 years, first by her father, later by her son. The opera was performed by the San Diego Opera on 3 June 1979 with Beverly Sills in the title role. The European premiere took place on 26 April 1981 at the Geissen Stadttheater, Germany.

Two operas for children followed: *A Bride from Pluto,* staged in Washington, D.C. on 14 April 1982; and *The Boy Who Grew Too Fast*, performed in Wilmington, Delaware on 24 September 1982. The next opera, *The Wedding*, commissioned for the Olympic Games, was staged in Seoul, South Korea on 16 September 1988.

From its first planning in 1977, Menotti's opera *Goya*

was intended for Placido Domingo, who sang in the premiere at Washington Opera on 15 November 1986. The three-act work is designed on a grand scale worthy of Verdi, dealing with the painter's final years and the court scandal involving the Queen of Spain and the Duchess of Alba. It was produced at the Spoleto Festival in Italy on 26 June 1991. He has composed one more opera for children, *The Singing Child,* staged in Charleston, South Carolina on 31 May 1993. Menotti has also written two non-musical plays, *The Copy of Madame Aupic* (New Milford, Connecticut, 1947), and *The Leper* (Tallahassee, Florida, 1970).

The strength of Menotti's characterization is evident in the sympathy he arouses for those who suffer. The pathos produces an emotional appeal that is sadly lacking in much modern opera. Such sympathy is often felt for those who are seen as misguided or destructive. In *The Saint of Bleecker Street,* Michele is a pitiable figure from whom everyone, even his sister, turns. He is a violent man who commits murder because he deeply loves his sister. Similarly in *Maria Golovin,* the motives of Agata, the jealous maidservant, are revealed with understanding, since she fears losing the blinded Donato whom she has tended with complete devotion.

Although opera has been his chief interest throughout his career, Menotti has composed works in other media. He has written two ballets: *Sebastian,* performed by the Original Ballet Russe in New York in 1944, and *Errand into the Maze*, with choreography by Martha Graham, also staged in New York in 1947. In addition he wrote the scores for two unperformed ballets: *L'Ombre des Jeunes Filles en Fleurs* (1947) and *The Days of the Shepherd* (1974). He has provided incidental music for three plays: *La Poète et sa muse* (Cocteau), produced by Zefferelli in Spoleto in 1959; *Medee* (Anouilh; 1966); and *Romeo and Juliet* (Shakespeare; 1968).

For orchestra Menotti has composed *Pastoral* for piano and strings (1935); two piano concertos (1945, 1983); a symphonic poem, *Apocalypse* (1951); a Violin Concerto written for Efrem Zimbalist in 1952; and a Triple Concerto, first performed in October 1970 by Stokowski and the American Symphony Orchestra. A *Fantasia* for cello and orchestra was completed in 1975, and the following year the Philadelphia Orchestra commissioned a Symphony, *The Halcyon*, performed on 4 August 1976. His most recent orchestral piece, a Concerto for Double Bass, was written in 1983 for J. VanDemark and the New York Philharmonic Orchestra.

Menotti's first choral work, *The Death of the Bishop of Brindisi* to his own text, tells of the dying cleric who is haunted by the memories of the Children's Crusade, which had left Brindisi with his blessing for the Holy Land in the thirteenth century. This dramatic cantata was performed at the Cincinnati Festival on 10 May 1963. A cantata, *Landscapes and Remembrances*, dates from 1976. A children's cantata, *The Trial of the Gypsy*, was premiered in New York on 24 May 1978. In 1979 he composed *Missa O Pulchritudo* for soloist, chorus, and orchestra performed in Milwaukee in May 1979. *Miracles* for boys' voices was completed in the same year.

The next decade produced further choral works: *The Song of Hope (An Old Man's Soliloquy)* for baritone, chorus, and orchestra (1980); *Mary's Mass,* a setting in English for choir, congregation, and organ performed in Baltimore in 1984; and *Moans, Groans, Cries and Sighs,* written in 1987 for the King's Singers.

Two late cantatas set Spanish texts. *Muero porque no muero* (St. Teresa of Avila) for soprano, chorus, and orchestra was written in 1982 for the Catholic University of America, Washington, D.C. Words of St. John of the Cross are used in *Oh llama de amor viva,* composed for the same institution in 1991. Menotti set his own text for a third cantata, *The Death of Orpheus* for tenor, chorus, and orchestra, commissioned by the Atlanta Symphony Orchestra in 1990. In 1995 he completed a *Gloria.* His most recent work, the cantata *Jacob's Prayer* (1997) for chorus and orchestra, recounts the story of Jacob and the Angel. For Elizabeth Schwarzkopf he composed a song cycle, *Canti di Lontananza* (1967). Other solo vocal items include *The Hero* (Robert Horan; 1952), *Four Songs* for tenor and piano (1981), and *Notturno* for voice, harp, and string quartet (1982).

Among Menotti's instrumental music are two pieces for string quartet, *Variations and Fugue* (1932) and *Italian Dance* (1935); *Trio for a Housewarming Party* for flute, cello, and piano (1936); Suite for two cellos and piano, commissioned by Piatigorsky in 1973; *Cantilena and Scherzo* for harp and string quartet (1977); and Trio for violin, clarinet, and piano (1996), commissioned by the Verdehr Trio. For piano he has written *Variations on a Theme of Schumann* (1930), *Poemetti* (1937), and *Ricercare su nove toni* (1956).

From 1958 to 1968 he was president of the Festival of Two Worlds, Spoleto, Italy and Charleston, South Carolina, where he was responsible for some of the most enterprising productions, especially for the stage, although he would not allow any of his own works to be performed there during that time. Since 1968 he has continued to take an active interest in the Spoleto Festival and still tours the world supervising productions of his works. In addition to writing the texts of all his operas, he has provided libretti for Samuel Barber's operas *A Hand of Bridge* and *Vanessa* and Lukas Foss's *Introductions and Goodbyes*. In 1974 he moved to Gifford near Edinburgh, Scotland.

MEYEROWITZ, JAN (HANS-HERMANN)
b. Breslau, German (now Wroclaw, Poland), 23 April 1913
d. Colmar, near Labaroche, France, 15 December 1998

In 1930 Meyerowitz entered the Berlin Hochschule für Musik, where he studied with Walter Gmeidl and Alexander von Zemlinsky. He left Germany in 1933 and went to Rome, where he was a pupil of Ottorino Respighi and Alfredo Casella for composition and Bernardino Molinari for conducting at the Academy of Santa Cecilia. From 1938 to 1946 he lived first in Belgium and then in the south of France. In 1946 he married the French singer Marguerite Fricker. In that year he went to the United States, where he became a naturalized citizen in 1951. He taught at Tanglewood (1948–51), Brooklyn College (1954–61), and the City College of New York (1962–80). He was awarded Guggenheim Fellowships in 1956 and 1958.

After going to America, Meyerowitz concentrated upon writing vocal music with a particular emphasis on opera. Two of his early operas were produced at Tanglewood: *Simoon* (1949) and *Bad Boys in School* (1953). In 1950 a music drama, *The Barrier* to a libretto by Langston Hughes, was performed at Columbia University and received its European premiere at the Teatro San Carlo, Naples, in 1971. Meyerowitz's fourth opera, *Emily Dickinson,* originally titled *Eastward in Eden,* was staged in Detroit in 1953.

Esther, based on a story by Langston Hughes and completed in 1956, was performed at the University of Illinois in the same year. Hughes also provided the text for Meyerowitz's next opera, *Port Town,* in one act, performed at Tanglewood in 1960. *Godfather Death,* his seventh opera, to a text by P. J. Stephens, dates from 1961. His last opera, *Winterballade* (original name *Die Doppelgängerin),* to a text in German by Gerhardt Hauptmann, was produced in Hannover, Germany in 1967.

Meyerowitz's many choral works receive regular performances in the United States. These include *Music for Christmas* (1952); the Easter cantata *The Glory Around His Head* (1953), to words by Langston Hughes; *Missa Rachel Plorans* (1953); *The Five Foolish Virgins* (1953); *New Plymouth Cantata* (1956); *Stabat Mater* (1957); *Hebrew Service* (1962); and *I Rabbini* (1965), to a text from the Talmud, commissioned by RAI (Italian State Radio). For solo voice and orchestra Meyerowitz wrote *An Emily Dickinson Cantata* (1954) and *Robert Herrick Cantata* (1954), both for soprano; *e.e. cummings cantata* for baritone (1956); and *Six Songs on Poems by August von Platen* (1976).

Meyerowitz also wrote a few works for orchestra: *Silesian Symphony* (1957); *Symphony: Midrash Esther* (1957); *Flemish Overture* (1959); Oboe Concerto (1962); Flute Concerto (1963); *Six Pieces* (1965); *Sinfonia Brevissima* (no. 3; 1967); and *Seven Pieces* (1973), as well as two items for band, *Three Comments on War* (1957) and *Four Romantic Pieces* (1978). His chamber music includes a Cello Sonata (1946); a Trio for flute, cello, and piano (1946); a Woodwind Quintet (1954); a String Quartet (1955); a Piano Sonata (1958); a Violin Sonata (1960); a Flute Sonata (1961); and many songs, among them three cycles to poems by the sixteenth-century poet Maurice Scève.

He is the author of two books, a monograph on Schoenberg (1967) and *Der echte jüdische Witz* (Berlin, 1971).

MICHAEL, DAVID MORITZ
b. Einhausen, near Erfurt, Germany, 21 October 1751
d. Neuwied-am-Rhein, Germany, 26 February 1827

In Germany, Michael was an opera orchestra musician. He arrived in America in 1795, living first in Nazareth, Pennsylvania, before moving to Bethlehem in 1808. There he is believed to have conducted the first complete performance of Haydn's *The Creation* in the New World. Michael composed a number of anthems, including *Hearken, Stay Close to Jesus Christ* for soprano, chorus, and strings (1800), and *I Love to Dwell in Spirit* for soprano and strings, in addition to a setting of Psalm 103 for soprano, chorus, and orchestra. Michael also wrote much instrumental music, of which 16 *Parthien* (suites) for wind, a Suite for wind quintet, and *Die Wasserfahrt (The Boat Ride)* for wind sextet are extant.

After retiring as a church musician, he returned to Germany in 1815, where he remained until his death.

MICHALSKY, DONAL
b. Pasadena, California, 13 July 1928
d. Newport Beach, California, 31 December 1975

After learning to play the clarinet, Michalsky entered the University of Southern California, Los Angeles, where he was a pupil of Halsey Stevens and Ingolf Dahl. In 1958 he went to Germany where he studied with Wolfgang Fortner in Freiberg. In 1960 he was appointed professor of composition at the California State University at Fullerton, where he remained until his death.

In most of his compositions Michalsky employed serial techniques. For orchestra he wrote three symphonies: no. 1, *The Wheel of Time* (choral; 1967), no. 2, *Sinfonia Concertante* for clarinet, piano, and orchestra (1969), and no. 3 (1975). His other works are primarily instrumental. These include a Quintet for

Donal Michalsky, 1966.

brass and piano (1951); Divertimento for two clarinets and bass clarinet (1952); *Partita* for oboe d'amore, string trio, and string orchestra (1956); a Cello Sonata (1958); *Morning Music* for ensemble (1959); *Trio Concertino* for flute, oboe, and horn (1961); *Trio Allegro* for two clarinets and piano (1961); *Variations* for clarinet and piano (1962); *Partita Piccola* for flute and piano (1962); *Fantasias* for brass quartet (1963); Concertino for 19 wind instruments and percussion (1964); and *3 x 4* for saxophone quartet (1972). Among his keyboard works are a Sonata for two pianos, *Sonata Concertante* for piano solo (1961), *Fantasias* for clavichord (1961), and *Song Suite* for piano (1970). Michalsky composed several works for band, including a Concerto for trombone and band (1953) and a *Little Symphony* (1959).

Michalsky died with his wife, two small children, and two house guests when his home was destroyed by fire on New Year's Eve 1975. The manuscript of an opera, *Der Arme Heinrich*, was lost in the fire.

MILBURN, ELLSWORTH

b. Greensburg, Pennsylvania, 6 February 1938

Milburn studied with Scott Huston and Paul Cooper at the University of Cincinnati College-Conservatory of

Music (1968–70). At the University of California, Los Angeles (1959–62), he was a pupil of Roy Travis and Henri Lazarof. At Mills College, Oakland, California he received composition lessons from Darius Milhaud. From 1963–68, he was music director for The Committee, San Francisco's improvisational-satirical theater company. From 1970 to 1975 he taught at the Cincinnati College Conservatory of Music, moving in 1975 to take up a position at Rice University, Houston, Texas; he retired from this position in January 2000. He currently lives in Hunlock Creek, Pennsylvania.

Milburn has composed three orchestral works: *Voussoirs* (1970), *Chiaroscuro* (1984), and *Salus . . . esto* (1984). Milburn's instrumental pieces include *Five Inventions* for two flutes (1965); a String Trio (1968); *Soli I* for five players on ten instruments (1968), *II* for two players of flutes and double bass (1970), *III* for clarinet, cello, and piano (1971) and *IV* for flute, clarinet, double bass, and harpsichord (1972); String Quintet (1968); Violin Sonata (1972); *Lament* for harp (1972); three string quartets (1974, 1988, 2003); *Menil Antiphons* for eight players (1989) two piano solos, *Scherzo* (1989) and *The Stone Forest* (1989); *Entre nous* for violin, cello, and piano (2002); and *Bagatelles* (2003) for piano and percussion.

Among Milburn's vocal compositions are *Menage* (C. E. Cooper) for soprano, mezzo-soprano, viola, and chamber ensemble (1982), *Two Love Songs* (Edna St. Vincent Millay) for mezzo-soprano and piano (1970), and *Spiritus Mundi* for mezzo-soprano and five instruments (1974).

Ellsworth Milburn.
Courtesy the composer.

MILLS, CHARLES (BORROMEO)

b. Asheville, North Carolina, 8 January 1914
d. New York, New York, 7 March 1982

Mills spent his childhood in Spartanburg, South Carolina, where he was raised amid sounds of jazz and the blues. By the age of 17 he was earning his living playing saxophone, clarinet, and flute in jazz bands. At 19 he set out for New York to pursue a career as a symphonic composer. He enrolled at the Greenwich Music School and subsequently studied privately for six years with Aaron Copland, Roger Sessions, and Roy Harris. He was music critic for the radio program "Modern Music" for eight years and served as head of the composition department of the Manhattan School of Music (1954–55). Thereafter he devoted himself entirely to composition.

Among his orchestral works are six symphonies: the First in E minor, composed in 1940; no. 2 in C (1942); no. 3 in D minor (1946); the Fourth, entitled *Crazy Horse Symphony*, first performed in Cincinnati in 1958; no. 5 for full string orchestra, completed in 1980 under a grant from the National Endowment for the Arts; and no. 6 (1981). Other orchestral items are *Theme and Variations* (1951), commissioned by Mitropoulos for the New York Philharmonic Orchestra; *Prologue and Dithyramb* for strings (1951, rev. 1954); *Prelude and Fugue* (1952); *Toccata* (1952); Serenade for wind and strings (1960); *In a Mule-Drawn Wagon* for strings (1968); and *Symphonic Ode* for string orchestra (1976), on a grant from the National Endowment for the Arts. Mills wrote a Concerto for piano and orchestra (1948) and a Concertino for oboe and strings (1956). For smaller ensembles he wrote a *Chamber Symphony* (1935), now withdrawn; *Chamber Concertino* for wind quintet (1941); *Chamber Concerto* for ten instruments (1942); and a *Concerto Grosso* (1949).

Mills took a particular interest in composing pieces for the recorder, an instrument he played professionally. These include a Sonata for treble recorder solo; two sonatas with piano, one for alto, one for tenor recorder (1964); *Breezy Point Pipings*, eight pieces for two recorders; *Welcome Blues* for solo alto recorder (1961); *Cocobolo Canticle* for solo tenor recorder (1969); *Sonata di Chiesa* for tenor recorder and piano (1972); *The Five Moons of Uranus* for tenor recorder and piano (1972); and *Duo Eclogue* for tenor recorder and organ (1976). Other woodwind instruments have also been provided with useful additions to the repertory. For flute he has written two unaccompanied sonatas, a *Sonatine* for flute and string quartet, and a Suite for two solo flutes (1952). In 1960 the jazz flautist Yusef Lateef commissioned him to compose *The Centaur and the Phoenix* and *Summer Song*. He composed a Sonata for oboe and piano (1942), a Sonata for English horn and piano (1945, commissioned by Josef Marx), and *Chant and Hymn* for solo oboe (1955). He also wrote a Serenade for flute, horn, and piano (1946).

Mills possessed an acute understanding of string instruments. Among his numerous pieces of chamber music are five string quartets (1939, 1942, 1943, 1950,1958); six violin sonatas (1940, 1942, 1945, 1956, 1970, 1977); a Piano Trio in D minor (1941); *The Fourth Joyful Mystery* for two violins and piano (1946); and *Prelude and Allegro* for violin and piano (1966). Two sonatas for cello and piano date from 1940 and 1942. For unaccompanied violin there are two sonatas (1942, 1944), *Four Stanzas* (1958), and *Sonata Fantasia* (1973). Other instrumental music includes *Concerto Serena* for woodwind octet (1948), a Brass Quintet in three movements (1962), and Brass Sextet (1964). Among his many solo piano pieces are two sonatas (1941, 1942), four suites, eleven sonatinas (1942–45), and *30 Penitential Preludes* (1945).

Mills's vocal works are equally numerous and include *Ars Poetica* (1940); *Canticle of the Sun* for voice and piano (1945); *The Dark Night* for female chorus and string orchestra (1946); *The True Beauty* (1950); *The Ascension Cantata* for unaccompanied chorus (1954); *The First Thanksgiving* for chorus and organ (1956); *Ballad of Trees and the Masters* (1958); and many songs for solo voice and piano.

Mills composed two ballets, *John Brown* (1945) and *Divine Dances of the Apocalypse* (1960). He also provided the scores for four films: *Greenwich Village Sunday* (1958), *Tracks in the Sand* (1961), *Whitey* (1962), and *On the Bowery* (1956), which was awarded first prize at the Edinburgh Film Festival for best film score.

MOEVS, ROBERT WALTER

b. La Crosse, Wisconsin, 2 December 1920

Service in the U.S. Air Force (1942–47) interrupted Moevs's studies at Harvard (1938–42, 1951–52), where he was a pupil of Walter Piston. He also received composition lessons at the Paris Conservatory from Nadia Boulanger (1947–51). He was a fellow at the American Academy in Rome (1952–55). In 1955 he returned to Harvard to teach. He joined the music faculty at Rutgers University, New Brunswick in 1964 where, from 1974 until his retirement in 1991, he was chairman of the department of music. He was awarded a Guggenheim Fellowship in 1963. Most of his music is serial, based on a systematic chromaticism of his own and influenced by the work of Pierre Boulez.

For orchestra Moevs has composed *Passacaglia* (1941); *Introduction and Fugue* (1949); an Overture (1950); *Fourteen Variations* (1952); *Three Symphonic Pieces* (Symphony in three movements; 1954–55); a *Concerto Grosso* for piano, percussion, and orchestra (1960–68, rev. 1977); *Main-Traveled Roads* (*Symphonic Piece no. 4*) (1973); *Prometheus: Music for Small Orchestra I* (1980); *Pandora: Music for Small Orchestra II* (1983); *Symphonic Piece no. 5* (1984); and *Symphonic Piece no. 6.* (1986).

Moevs established his reputation in 1950 with the performance of his Piano Sonata. Other instrumental works include *Spring* for four violins and trumpets (1950); *Pan* for solo flute (1951); *Fantasia sopra uno motivo* for piano (1951); *Duo* for oboe and English horn (1953); a Violin Sonata (1956); three string quartets (1957, 1989, 1994–95); *Variazioni sopra una melodia* for viola and cello (1961); *In Festivitate* for winds and percussion (1962); *Musica da Camera I* (1965), *II* (1972), *III* (1992), *IV* (1996), *V* (1998), and *VI* (2001) for chamber ensemble; *Fanfare Canonica* for six trumpets (1966); *Piece for Synket* (1969); *Heptachronon* for cello (1969); *Paths and Ways* for dancer and saxophone (1970); *Phoenix* for piano (1971); *Games of the Past* for two pianos (1976); *Una Collana Musicale* for piano (1977); *Crystals* for solo flute (1979); a Piano Trio (1981); *Three Pieces* for violin and piano (1984); *Dark Litany* for wind ensemble (1987); Wind Quintet (1988); *Echo* for guitar (1992); and *Conundrum* for five percussionists (1993).

Moevs has also written a number of choral works: *Great Nations of This Earth* for female voices (1942); *The Bacchantes* (Euripides; 1947); *Cantata Sacra* (*Easter Liturgy*) for baritone, men's chorus, flute, four trombones, and timpani (1952); *Attis I* (1958) and *II* (1963; Catullus) for soprano, tenor, chorus, and orchestra; *Itaque ut* for mixed voices (1959); *Et nunc, reges* for female chorus, flute, and two clarinets (1963); *Et occidentum illustra* (Dante) for chorus and orchestra (1964); *Ave Maria* (1966); *Alleluia for Michaelmas* for congregation and organ (1967); *A Brief Mass* for chorus, organ, vibraphone, guitar, and double bass (1968); and *The Aulos Player* for two choruses and two organs (1975). His solo vocal music includes *Youthful Song* (1940–51); *Villanelle* (1950); *Time* for mezzo-soprano and piano (1969); *Epigram* (1978); *Ode to an Olympic Hero* for voice and orchestra (1963); and *Six Songs on Poems by Ungaretti* (1990–92). Moevs' only work for the stage is a ballet, *Endymion*, dating from 1948.

For piano he has composed a Sonatina (1947), *Pentachronon* (1993), and *Rondo* (1993); a harpsichord solo, *Sarabande* (1986); and an organ piece, *BACH – Est ist genug* (1990).

MOHAUPT, RICHARD ERNEST EDWARD
b. Breslau, Germany (now Wroclaw, Poland), 14 September 1904
d. Reichenau, Austria, 3 July 1957

After receiving his musical education at the University of Breslau, Mohaupt became an opera conductor, performing throughout Germany and Russia. In 1939 he left Germany to settle in the United States. He taught privately in New York, returning to Europe in 1955.

Mohaupt's works for the stage include five operas: *The Landlady of Pinsk* (1938); *Boleslav the Bashful* (1944); *Die Bremer Stadtmusikanten* (*The Bremen Town Musicians*) (1949); *Double Trouble* (1954), a Louisville Orchestra commission; and *The Green Cockatoo* (1958). He also composed two ballets: *Die Gaunerstreiche der Courasche* (1936) after Grimmelshausen; and *Lysistrata* (1946) after Aristophanes (rev. 1955 as *Der Weiberstreik von Athen*). He also composed a dance-burlesque, *Max und Moritz* (1945), and a mimodrama, *The Legend of the Charlatan* (1949).

Mohaupt's best known work is *Town Piper Music*, composed in 1939. It is based on a mural by Albrecht Dürer, "Nurnberger Stadtpfeifer," and was heard at the I.S.C.M. Festival in London in 1946. Also for orchestra he wrote a Symphony (*Rhythm and Variations*) (1942); *Three Episodes* (1938); a Piano Concerto (1938, rev. 1942); *Overture: Much Ado About Nothing* (1941); Concerto for Orchestra (1942); a Violin Concerto (1945); a work for narrator and orchestra, *Max and Moritz* (1946, derived from the ballet); and *Offenbachiana* (1955). He also wrote several pieces for band, including an *Overture in B-flat in Modo Classico* and a *Paganini Overture*. Among his vocal and choral music are a *Trilogy* for alto and orchestra (1951) and *Bucolica* for four soloists, chorus, and orchestra (1955).

MOLLER, JOHN CHRISTOPHER (JOHANN CHRISTOPH)
b. Germany, c. 1755
d. New York, New York, 21 September 1803

From 1775 to 1790 Moller was a musician in London. He went to New York in 1790, moving the following year to Philadelphia, where he organized concerts and founded a school of music. With Capron he established a music printing press in 1793, probably the first in America. He was organist at the Zion Lutheran Church and a noted performed on the glass harmonica. He returned to New York in 1795 and became organist at Trinity Episcopal Church and a concert organizer in the city.

Moller's surviving works include a set of six string quartets (c. 1775) in the style of Haydn; a *Duetto* for viola or clarinet and piano, published in 1796; a Quartet for glass harmonica, two violins, and cello; and 12 sonatas for piano with violin or cello accompaniment (1775–82). He also composed two books of teaching pieces, *Progressive Lessons for the Harpsichord* and *Compleat Book of Instruction for the Pianoforte*. For orchestra he composed a *Sinfonia* (1793), an Overture, and two keyboard concertos. A cantata, *Dank und Gebet*, was performed in Philadelphia in 1794.

MONK, MEREDITH

b. Lima, Peru, 20 November 1943

Meredith Monk was born in Peru, where her mother, the singer Audrey Marsh, was on tour. Her great-grandfather had been a cantor in a Moscow synagogue; her grandparents founded the Zellman Conservatory of Music in New York. She was taught piano and singing and the Dalcroze method of music and movement before entering Sarah Lawrence College, Bronxville, New York, where she graduated in 1964. Working with the avant-garde Judson Dance Theater allowed her to develop her personal approach to music-theater, based on her own singing voice. Her approach to vocal technique broadened the usual singing range, incorporating overtones and making use of sighs, sobs, moans, and wailing, often wordless and integrated with movement. She has stated: "I have always thought of my music as being part of the aural tradition."

Monk has established herself as one of the most highly respected performance artists in the United States and the creator of strikingly original and ambitious projects. In 1978 she established the Meredith Monk Vocal Ensemble, initially with six singers, but expanded to much larger numbers when required. She also formed a group, The House (now The House Foundation of the Arts), based in New York.

Among the solo vocal items she has made for herself to perform are *Candy Bullets and Moon* for voice, electric organ, electric double bass, and percussion (1967); *Blueprint: Overload/Blueprint 2* for voice, tape, and live electronics (1967); *Dying Swan with Sunglasses*, performed at Expo'67 in Montreal; *A Raw Recital* for voice and electric organ (1970); *Our Lady of Late* for voice and wine glass (1972–73); *Songs From the Hill* (1976–77); *View no. 1* (1980) and *no. 2* (1982) for voice and synthesizer; *I Don't Know* for voice and piano (1986); *Double Fiesta* for voice and two pianos (1986); *String* for solo voice (1986); and *Volcano Songs* for voice, piano, and tape (1994).

On a larger scale Monk has composed six operas: *Vessel*, described as an opera epic or a performance tapestry, for 75 solo voices (1971); *Education of the Girlchild* (1972–73), which won first prize at the Venice Biennale in 1975; *Quarry* for 38 voices (1976); *Specimen Days* for 14 voices (1981); *Atlas*, an opera in three parts commissioned by the Houston Grand Opera in 1991; and *Magic Frequencies*, a chamber opera (1998). Her other theater pieces include *Cartoon* (1964); *Duet for Cat's Scream and Locomotive* (1967); *Juice* for 85 voices and 85 jew's harps, performed in the Guggenheim Museum, New York in 1969; *Needle-brain Lloyd and the Systems Kid* for 150 solo voices (1970); *Key: An Album of Invisible Theater* for solo voice, electric organ, vocal quartet, percussion, and jew's harp (1970); *Plainsong for Bill's Bojo*, incidental music for a play by W. Dumas (1971); *Paris* for two voices (1972); *Chacon* for 25 voices (1974); *Venice/Milan* for 15 voices and piano (four hands) (1976); *The Plateau*

Meredith Monk in performance.
Photo: Massimo Agua, courtesy the composer.

Series for five voices (1977); *Recent Ruins* for 14 voices (1979); *The Games* for 16 voices (1983); and *Facing North* (in collaboration with Robert Een) (1990–91), originally conceived as a concert work.

For her own vocal ensemble she has written *Dolmen Music* (1979); *Tokyo Cha-cha* (1983); *Two Men Walking* (1983); *Panda Chants I & II* (1984); *Graduation Song* for 14 voices (1984); *Book of Days* for 25 voices (1985), later adapted as a film, *Duet Behavior* (1987); *The Ringing Place* for nine voices (1987); *Do You Be* for ten voices (1987); *Fayum Music* (1988); *Light Songs* (1988); *Cat Song* (1988); *Three Heavens and Hells* (1992); *American Anthology No. 1: Roosevelt Island* (1994); *Nightfall* (1995); *Denkai Krikiki Chants* (1995); *The Politics of Quiet*, eleven pieces for ten voices (1996); and *Astronaut Anthem* (1997).

Among her few purely instrumental works are three piano solos, *Window in 7's* (1986), *Raven* (1988), and *Steppe Music* (1997); and three pieces for two pianos, *Parlour Games* (1988), *Waltz* (1986), and *Phantom Waltz* (1990). Monk's single orchestral work, *Possible Sky*, was written over a four-year period and first performed by the New World Symphony Orchestra under Michael Tilson Thomas in April 2003.

Monk's most recent compositions are *Micki Suite* for four voices (2000); *Mercy* for six voices, two keyboards, percussion, violin, and theremin (2001); *When There Were Work Songs* for vocal ensemble (2002); and *Last Song* (James Hillman) for voice and piano (2003).

In addition to *Book of Days*, Monk has directed and scored two films, *16 millimeter earrings* (1966) and *Ellis Island* (1981–82).

MONTANI, NICOLA ALOYSIUS
b. Utica, New York, 6 November 1880
d. Philadelphia, Pennsylvania, 11 January 1948

After receiving private music lessons in the United States, Montani studied with Lorenzo Perosi in Rome. On his return to America he was organist at St. John the Evangelist, Philadelphia (1906–23) and St. Paul the Apostle, New York (1923–25). In 1914 he founded the Society of St. Gregory of America to encourage the singing of Gregorian chant. He was founder and editor of *The Catholic Choirmaster* (1914–41) and editor of the *St. Gregory Hymnal* and *The Catholic Choir Book*. He also published *Essentials of Sight-Reading* and *The Art of A Cappella Singing*.

All of Montani's works were choral settings of religious texts: eight Masses (including *Missa Festiva*, *Missa Solemnis*, and *St. Nicholas Mass* for three voices), *Stabat Mater*, and many motets.

MOORE, DOUGLAS (STUART)
b. Cutchogue, Long Island, New York, 10 August 1893
d. Greenport, Long Island, New York, 25 July 1969

At Yale University (1911–17), Moore studied with Horatio Parker and David Stanley Smith. In Paris (1921), he was a pupil of Vincent d'Indy and Nadia Boulanger. On his return to the United States he received lessons from Ernest Bloch in Cleveland. In 1921 he was appointed director of music at the Cleveland Art Museum. A Pulitzer Fellowship in 1925 enabled him to spend a further year in Europe. In 1926 he began teaching at Barnard College. He joined the faculty of Columbia University, becoming head of the department of music, succeeding Daniel Gregory Mason (1940); he retired in 1962. He was awarded a Guggenheim Fellowship in 1934 and was elected president of the National Institute of Arts and Letters in 1946.

Moore's music is workmanlike and characteristically American. His Symphony no. 2 in A, completed in 1945, received lavish praise from the critics and was widely performed throughout the United States. It received honorable mention from the Music Critics' Circle of New York City.

His first significant instrumental piece, a Violin Sonata, was performed at a League of Composers concert in 1930. A String Quartet was completed in 1933. Among his other chamber works are a Wind Quintet (1942, rev. 1948); *Down East Suite* for violin and piano (1944); an attractively neo-Romantic Clarinet Quintet (1945); and a Piano Trio (1953).

Moore's most important contribution to music in America was in the field of opera. His first opera, *White Wings*, a setting of a play by Philip Barry, was written in 1935 and performed in Hartford, Connecticut in 1949. For children he composed an operetta, *The Headless Horseman*, produced by the schools of Bronxville, New York in 1937.

His third opera, *The Devil and Daniel Webster*, composed in 1938, has proven to be his most popular stage work. It is based on an American folk tale by Stephen Vincent Benet, derived from the Faust legend. In this opera, spoken dialogue separates the set musical pieces. The plot concerns a New Hampshire farmer, Jabez Stone, who sells his soul to the Devil in exchange for material wealth so that he can marry. Only the intervention of the statesman Daniel Webster, who delivers a speech to the jury of the most infamous scoundrels in history, saves Stone from damnation. Much of the melodic material is pseudo-folk song of lyrical charm, handled in a conversational, *parlando* manner. The opera was staged by the American Lyric Theater at the Martin Beck Theater, New York in May 1939.

Moore's next two stage works were operettas for children: *The Emperor's New Clothes* (1948), a setting of the story by Hans Christian Andersen (New York, 1949), and *Puss in Boots* (1949), also performed in New York (1950).

In 1950, he completed a three-act tragedy, *Giants in the Earth*, based on a novel by O. E. Rolvaag (1876–1931), which portrays the sufferings of a Norwegian pioneer family in the Dakota Territory. The opera was awarded a Pulitzer Prize in 1951. To celebrate the 25th anniversary of the Opera House Association, Central City, Colorado in 1956, Moore wrote *The Ballad of Baby Doe*, an opera set near Denver and based on a true story. Baby Doe Tabor was the second wife of a mine owner who became the richest man in Colorado through mining silver. After abandoning his first wife for Baby Doe, he lost all his wealth in 1895 and died four years later. Baby Doe survived until 1935, dying in poverty only a few miles from the mine which had previously provided her extravagant living. The opera was commissioned by the Koussevitzky Foundation and was first produced by the Central City Opera Association on 7 July 1956. The New York premiere was given by the City Center Opera Company on 3 April 1958; the opera received the New York Music Critics' Circle Award for that year.

Moore's next opera, *The Wings of a Dove*, based on the novel by Henry James, was first produced in New York on 12 October 1961. *The Greenfield Christmas Tree* in one act, to a text by Arnold Sundgaard, was composed in 1962. Sungaard had previously provided the libretto to *Gallantry*, described by the composer as a "soap opera in one act," performed in New York in March 1958.

Moore's last opera, *Carrie Nation*, also based on a true story, was commissioned for the centennial of the University of Kansas in 1966. It received its premiere in Kansas on 28 April 1966. After the title character's husband dies of alcoholism, she begins a crusade to break up drinking saloons; the action takes place shortly before the Prohibition era in America. The deep psychological problems of the character that imbue the libretto are seldom matched by music of equal intensity; in addition, the composer was unable to introduce the folk element which was so much a part of his previous operatic style. The New York City Opera presented the work in New York on 28 March 1968.

Moore's work at the Cleveland Art Museum no doubt inspired his first orchestral work, *Four Museum Pieces*, portraying items in that collection; it was first performed in Cleveland in 1923. *The Pageant of P.T. Barnum*, composed in 1924, has proved to be his most widely played work. As with his operas, Moore took his subject from American history. The first movement describes the birth of the showman; the second movement depicts an elderly African-American woman whom Barnum displayed as George Washington's nurse; the third movement is entitled "Tom Thumb," the fourth, "Jenny Lind," after the singer engaged by Barnum in 1850 to sing for two seasons. Moore used several folk songs, each appropriate to the subject.

Moore's other orchestral works include a symphonic poem, *Moby Dick* (1928); *Symphony of Autumn* (1928); a ballet score, *Greek Games* (1930); *Overture on an American Tune* (1931), inspired by Sinclair Lewis's novel *Babbitt*; *Village Music* (1942); *In Memoriam* (1943); Symphony no. 2 (1945); *Farm Journal* (1947), for a film entitled *Power in the Land* (1940); and *Cotillion Suite* for strings (1952). Other film scores include *Youth Gets a Break* (1941), *Bip Goes to Town* (1941), and *Village Music* (1941).

Moore's only large-scale choral work is *Prayer for the United Nations* for contralto, chorus and orchestra, setting words by Stephen Vincent Benet, composed in 1943. Benet had earlier provided the text for Moore's *The Ballad of William Sycamore* for baritone, flute, trombone and piano (1926).

Moore wrote two books on music, *Listening to Music* (1931) and *From Madrigal to Modern Music* (1942, rev. 1962).

MOORE, MARY (LOUISE) CARR
b. Memphis, Tennessee, 6 August 1873
d. Ingleside, California, 9 January 1957

After studying at Chapman College, Los Angeles, Moore began teaching in Lemoore, California in 1895, moving to Seattle in 1901 and San Francisco in 1915 before returning to Los Angeles (1926). She taught at the Olga Steeb Piano School (1926–43) and at Chapman College (1928–47).

For the stage she composed ten operas. Moore herself sang the leading role in her first opera, *The Oracle*, performed in San Francisco in 1894. *Narcissa*, or *The Cost of Empire* (1909–11), staged in Seattle in 1912, was awarded the David Bispham Medal. Thereafter followed *The Leper* (1912); *Memories* (Seattle, 1914); *Harmony* (San Francisco, 1917); *The Flaming Arrow* or *The Shaft of Ku'pish-ta-ya* (*An Indian Romance*; 1919–20; San Francisco, 1922); *David Rizzio* (1927–28; Los Angeles, 1932); *Los Rubios* (Los Angeles, 1931); *Flutes of Jade Happiness* (1932–33; Los Angeles, 1934); and *Legende Provencale* (1929–35).

Moore's orchestral works include *Ka-mi-a-kin* (1930), a Piano Concerto in F minor (1933–34), and *Kidnap* (1937–38). Among her chamber music are three piano trios (1895, 1906, 1941); a Violin Sonata (1918–19); two string quartets, no. 1. in G minor (1926) and no. 2 in F minor (1930); a String Trio in G minor (1936);

Mary Carr Moore.
Courtesy Mary Carr Moore Estate.

and a Piano Quintet, subtitled *Brief Furlough* (1942).

Moore composed over 250 songs, including a cycle, *Beyond These Hills*, for mixed voices and piano (1923–24).

MORGAN, JUSTIN

b. West Springfield, Massachusetts, 28 February 1747

d. Randolph, Vermont, 22 March 1798

In 1788 Morgan settled in Randolph, Vermont, where he became town clerk. He was in turn schoolmaster, tavern keeper, and a famous breeder of horses. Eight of his nine known compositions were published in Benham's *Federal Harmony* (1790). Among these are *Montgomery* and *Amanda*, which make use of remarkable "false-relation" dissonances. His most extended composition is *Judgment Anthem* in eight parts, which contains some intricate harmonic features. An anthem, *Despair*, is a lament on the death of his wife.

MOROSS, JEROME

b. Brooklyn, New York, 1 August 1913

d. Miami, Florida, 25 July 1983

Moross began playing piano at age five and was composing by the time he was eight. A brilliant student, he graduated from public school in 1924, and entered New York University's School of Music in 1929, remaining there from 1932; during his senior year he also held a Juilliard conducting fellowship. Initially he supported himself by writing for the theater, acting as assistant conductor and pianist for George Gershwin. He was awarded two Guggenheim Fellowships (1947, 1948).

Although he is best known for his ballets and film scores, Moross composed music in most other forms. His first two ballets were *Paul Bunyan: American Saga* (1935) and *American Patterns* (1936). This last work was commissioned by Ruth Page, who two years later presented in Chicago his most popular success, *Frankie and Johnny* (1938). It was revived in 1945 by Ballets Russes and has been widely performed since.

Moross wrote four ballet-operas, or "ballet ballads," to libretti by John Latouche: *Guns and Castanets* (1939), *Willie the Weeper* (1945), *The Eccentricities of Davy Crockett* (1946), and *Red Riding Hood Revisited* (1946). Another ballet is *The Last Judgement* (1953). Also for the stage he wrote a revue, *Parade* (1935), and four operas. *Susanna and the Elders* was staged in 1940. *The Golden Apple* (1949–50), first presented on Broadway, contains the song "Lazy Afternoon"; it received the New York Drama Critics' Award in 1954. *Gentlemen, Be Seated* (1955–57), in two acts, was produced by the New York City Opera on 10 October 1963. In 1977 he completed a one-act opera, *Sorry, Wrong Number*.

Jerome Moross.
Courtesy Moross.com.

In 1940 Moross went to Hollywood as an arranger and orchestrator. He contributed a number of effective and impressive scores of his own for films. These include *Close-up* (1950); *When I Grow Up* (1950); *Captive City* (1951); *Hans Christian Andersen* (1952); *Seven Wonders of the World* (1955); *The Sharkfighters* (1956); *The Proud Rebel* (1957); *The Big Country* (1958, a score that virtually created the "classic western" idiom); *Jayhawkers!* (1959); *The Adventures of Huckleberry Finn* (1960); *The Mountain Road* (1961); *Five Finger Exercise* (1961); *The Cardinal* (1963); *The War Lord* (1965); *Forget Me Not* (1965); *Rachel, Rachel* (1967); *The Valley of Gwangi* (1968); and *Hail, Hero!* (1969). He also wrote the music for two television serials, *Wagon Train* and *Lancer.*

Among his orchestral works are *Paeans* (1931); *Biguine (1934); A Tall Story*, commissioned by CBS in 1938; a Symphony (1940–41); *Variations on a Waltz* (1946, orch. 1968); and *Music for the Flicks* (1965). His instrumental compositions include *Recitative and Aria* for violin and piano (1943) and four sonatinas: no. 1 for clarinet choir (1967), no. 2 for string bass and piano (1968), no. 3 for woodwind quintet (1970), and no. 4 for brass quintet (1969). In 1975, he completed a Sonata for piano duet and string quartet; a Concerto for flute and string quartet dates from 1978.

For mezzo-soprano and small orchestra he wrote a cantata, *Those Everlasting Blues* (1932), a setting of words by Alfred Kreymborg.

MORRIS, HAROLD

b. San Antonio, Texas, 17 March 1890
d. New York, New York, 6 May 1964

Morris studied at the University of Texas and later at the Cincinnati Conservatory, where he was a pupil of Edgar Stillman Kelley and Leopold Godowsky. He lectured at Rice Institute in Houston, Texas, before taking up a post at the Juilliard School in 1921. In 1939 he was awarded a doctorate from the Cincinnati Conservatory and in the same year joined the faculty of Columbia University; he retired in 1946.

Morris first came to prominence with his *Poem (Gitanjali)* for orchestra (1918), based on a story by Rabindranath Tagore. In 1931 he was the soloist in the first performance of his Piano Concerto (1929), with the Boston Symphony Orchestra under Serge Koussevitzky. The first of his four symphonies, *Prospice* (1925), was inspired by Robert Browning's poem. Symphony no. 2, *Victory* was completed in 1936; no. 3, *Amaranth* was composed in 1946; no. 4 dates from 1952.

Morris composed a large quantity of orchestral music, including *Variations on a Negro Spiritual, "I Was Way Down Yonder"* (1925); a Suite for small orchestra (1927); two suites for strings (1927); an overture, *Joy of Youth* (1935); a Violin Concerto (1938); Suite for small orchestra (1938); *Passacaglia and Fugue* (1939); *American Epic* (1942); *Overture Heroic* (1943); a Second Piano Concerto; *Dramatic Overture* (1950); *Lone Star (A Texas Saga)*; *Passacaglia, Adagio and Finale* (1955); *Still Dews of Quietness*; and *Sam Houston Suite.*

Morris's output of chamber music was equally large, including two piano trios (1917, 1933); a Violin Sonata (1919); two string quartets (1928, 1937); two piano quintets (1929, 1937); a Suite for flute, violin, cello, and piano (1943); and *Ballet Music* for wind instruments. His four piano sonatas (1910, 1915, 1920, 1939) reveal the strong influence of Scriabin.

Morris was the author of a book, *Contemporary American Music*, published in 1934.

MOSS, LAWRENCE (KENNETH)

b. Los Angeles, California, 18 November 1927

Moss studied at the University of California, Los Angeles (B.A., 1949), and the Eastman School of Music, Rochester, New York (M.A., 1950). At the University of Southern California, Los Angeles he was a pupil of Ingolf Dahl and Leon Kirchner (Ph.D., 1957). He has taught at Mills College, Oakland, California (1956–59), Yale University (1960–69), and the University of Maryland (from 1969). Among the awards he has received are a Fulbright Fellowship (1953–54) and two Guggenheim Fellowships (1959–60, 1968–69). He has also been given the Distinguished Scholar/Teacher Award by the University of Maryland.

For the stage he has written two operas: a one-act comedy, *The Brute*, based on Chekhov (1960), and *The Queen and the Rebels*, composed in 1965 (rev. 1981). In addition to his credit is a series of theater pieces: *Unseen Leaves* (Whitman) for soprano, oboe, tapes, slides, and lights (1975); *Nightscape* for soprano, flute, clarinet, violin, percussion, dancer, tape, and slides (1978); *Dreamscape* for dancer, tape, and lights (1980); *Images* for dancer, clarinet, and tape (1983); *Rites* for dancer, slides, and tape (1983); *Song to the Floor* for dancer and tape (1984); *That Gong-Tormented Sea* for dancers and tape (1985); *Lesbia's Sparrow* for soprano, dancer, and tape (1985); *Incidental Music* for dancers, mime, and percussion (1986); *Blackbird* for clarinet, dancer, mime, and tape (1987); and *Summer Night on the Yogahenney River* for soprano, dancer, and tape (1989).

Moss's orchestral music includes a Suite (1950); *Scenes* for chamber orchestra (1961); *Paths* (1970); *Symphonies* for brass quintet and chamber orchestra (1977); *Clouds* for chamber ensemble (1989); and a

Lawrence Moss.
Courtesy the composer.

tone poem, *New Dawn* (2001). In addition he has written two pieces for band, *Chinese Lullaby* (1994) and *Dragon and Phoenix* (1997). Among his extensive catalogue of instrumental works are Trio for flute, violin, and cello (1953); three string quartets (1958, 1975, 1980); a Violin Sonata (1959); *Music for Five* for brass quintet (1963); *Remembrances* for eight instruments (1964); *Windows* for flute, bass clarinet, and double bass (1966); *Patterns* for flute, clarinet, viola, and piano (1967); *Exchanges* for two flutes, oboe, two trumpets, trombone, and percussion (1968); *Elegy* for two violins and viola (1969); *Timepiece* for violin, piano, and percussion (1970); *Tootsweet* for oboe and two percussionists (1976); *Little Suite* for oboe and harpsichord (1978); *Flight* for brass quintet (1979); *Chanson* (*Omaggio III*) for eight flutes (1979); *Espressivo* for solo cello (1981); *Apresludes* for flute and percussion (1983); *Music of Changes* for seven performers (1986); *Various Birds* for wind quintet (1987); *Through a Window* for flute, clarinet, and contrabassoon (1991); *Quartet* for flute, cello, percussion, and piano (1992); *Six Little Pieces* for saxophone and piano (1993); *Fantasy* for harp (1996); *River Music* for saxophone quartet (1996); *Conversations* for oboe and string trio (1998); *Dao Ditties* for clarinet, violin, percussion, and piano (1998); *The Swan* for cello and piano (2000); and *Nature Studies* for piano trio (2000).

Moss has composed many pieces combining instruments and tape: *Auditions* for wind quintet (1971); *Evocation and Song* for alto saxophone (1972); *B.P.: a Melodrama* for trombone and piano (1976); *Omaggio II* for piano four hands (1977); *Hands Across the C* for piano (1979); *Variation/Aria* for viola (1984); *Violaria, una dramma per musica* for viola (1988); *Saxpressivo* for alto saxophone (1992); *Into the Woods* for flute (1996); *Life Lines* for clarinet (1998); and *Harried* for bass clarinet (1999). For piano he has written *Fantasia* (1952), *Four Scenes* (1961), *Fantasy* (1973), *Ballad* (1979), and *Racconto* (1996), and two pieces for piano four hands, *Omaggio* (1966) and *A Musical Trip* (1984).

Moss has been equally prolific in the choral and vocal repertory. His choral works include *A Song of Solomon* for female voices and piano (1956); *Exercise* for chorus and tape (1973); *Grand is the Seen* for six soloists and chorus (1989); and two pieces for chorus and piano, *A Bird . . . A Sleep . . . A Thought* (1998) and *I Hear America Singing* (2002). Among his solo vocal music are *Song of Myself* (Whitman) for baritone and chamber orchestra (1957); *Three Rilke Songs* for soprano and piano (1963); *Ariel* (Sylvia Plath) for soprano and orchestra (1969); *Hear This Touch* for soprano and tape (1976); *Tubaria* (Requiem) for bass-baritone and tuba (1979); *Loves* (Catullus) for soprano, flute, clarinet, viola, harp, and piano (1982); *Dark Harbor* for soprano and tape (1983); *Portals* (Whitman) (1983) and *Voyages* (1985), both for tenor, flute, clarinet, violin, viola, cello, and percussion; *Love Songs* for tenor and harp (1990); *Songs of the Earth and Sky* for mezzo-soprano, clarinet, violin, and piano duet (1990); *Two Songs to Poems of Emily Dickinson* for soprano and piano (1993); *Ten Miracles*, a cycle for tenor, oboe, and harp (1993); *From Dawn to Dawn* for baritone, oboe, and orchestra (1994); *Three Chinese Poems* for soprano and cello (1999); and *New Dawn* for soprano and large chamber ensemble (2002).

MOURANT, WALTER
b. Chicago, Illinois, 29 August 1910
d. San Luis Obispo, California, May 1995

Mourant studied at the Eastman School of Music, Rochester, New York, with Howard Hanson and Bernard Rogers (1931–34), and with Bernard Wagenaar at the Juilliard School in New York City (1934–35).

Mourant was a composer of a number of attractive orchestral works, generally on a small scale. The best known of these, the *Sleepy Hollow Suite* for strings and harp, was written in 1955. Dating from the same year is *The Valley of the Moon* for string orchestra, performed by André Kostelanetz and the New York Philharmonic Orchestra, and *Air and Scherzo* for oboe, harp, and strings.

For full orchestra he composed *Five Inhibitions* (1937) and *Three Dances* (1939), performed at concerts at the Eastman School of Music and the Juilliard School. His Overture was premiered by the NBC Symphony in 1940. A later work to achieve wide success is *Aria for Orchestra: Harpers Ferry, West Virginia*, first performed in 1960. Other orchestral pieces include *Spiritual* (1940), *Three Acts From Punch and Judy* (1941), and *Fantasia* for trumpet and orchestra (1969). Mourant also composed a number of short items for solo clarinet and orchestra—*Blue Haze, Ecstasy, Concertino, Pied Piper*, and *Burlesque*—written between 1950 and 1960. His chamber music includes a String Quintet (1939), a Saxophone Quartet (1967), *Prelude and Dance* for clarinet and harp (1969), piano pieces, and many songs to words by James Stephens.

Mourant made a setting of the *Preamble to the Constitution of the United States* for chorus and orchestra (1939), first performed by the CBS Symphony Orchestra.

Robert Muczynski, 1983.
Courtesy the composer.

MUCZYNSKI, ROBERT
b. Chicago, Illinois, 19 March 1929

Muczynski studied at De Paul University, Chicago (B.M., 1950; M.M., 1952), where he was a pupil of Alexander Tcherepnin. He was director of the piano department at Loras College, Iowa (1956–59) and taught at Roosevelt University (1964–65). From 1965 to 1988 he was professor of music and resident composer at the University of Arizona, Tucson, becoming professor emeritus of composition upon retiring.

Muczynski's orchestral music includes a Divertimento for piano and orchestra, composed in 1952 as his graduation work; a Symphony, commissioned by the Fromm Foundation in 1953; a Piano Concerto, commissioned by The Louisville Orchestra, for which the composer was soloist at its first performance in 1955; a suite, *Galena: A Town* (1958); *Dovetail Overture* (1960); *Dance Movements*, commissioned in 1963 by Thor Johnson and the Chicago Little Orchestra; *Symphonic Dialogues*, commissioned by Howard Mitchell and the National Symphony Orchestra of Washington, D.C. (1965); *Charade* (1971); *A Serenade for Summer*, performed by the Arizona Chamber Orchestra in 1978; and *Cavalcade: A Suite* (later renamed *Symphonic Memoir*), commissioned in 1979 for the 50th anniversary of the Tucson Symphony Orchestra. In 1981 he completed a Concerto for alto saxophone and chamber orchestra, nominated for the Pulitzer Prize.

Among Muczynski's chamber works are *Allegro deciso* for brass sextet and timpani (1952); *Fragments* for wind trio (1958); *Trumpet* Trio (1959); *Three Designs* for timpani (1960); Sonata for flute and piano (1961); *Movements* for wind quintet (1962); *Three Preludes* for solo flute (1962); *Gallery*, a suite for solo cello (1966); three piano trios (1967, 1975, 1986–87); *Fantasy Trio* for clarinet, cello, and piano (1969); *Voyage*, seven pieces for trumpet, horn, and trombone (1969); Sonata for alto saxophone (1970); String Trio (1972); *Impromptus* for solo tuba (1972); *Duos* for two flutes (1973); *Time Piece* for clarinet and piano (1983); a Wind Quintet (1985); and *Movements* for flute and piano (1992).

Muczynski has written many works for piano solo, including a Sonatina (1950); *Five Sketches* (1952); *Variations on a Theme of Tcherepnin* (1955); three sonatas (1957, 1966, 1974); a Suite (1960); *Toccata* (1961); *A Summer Journal* (1964); two collections of teaching pieces, *Fables* (1965) and *Diversions* (1967); *Seven* (1971); *Maverick Pieces* (1976); *Dream Cycle* (1983); and *Desperate Measures, Variations on a Theme of Paganini* (1994). The one-movement *Masks* (1980) was composed for the Gina Bachauer Piano Festival and Competition. For unaccompanied voices he has written *Alleluia* (1961) and a setting of Emily Dickinson's "I Never Saw a Moor" (1967).

Muczynski provided the music for documentary films produced by the University of Arizona Film Department: *The Great Unfenced* (1963); *Yankee Painter* (1963); *American Realists* (1964); *Cajititlan* (1965); *Charles Burchfield: His Art* (1966); *Terra Sancta* (1967); *Bellota: Story of Roundup* (1969); and *Journey Thru Eden* (1975).

MUMMA, GORDON
b. Framingham, Massachusetts, 30 March 1935

Mumma studied the horn and piano in Detroit (1949–52) and was a student of composition at the University of Michigan (1952–53). In 1958 at Ann Arbor he was co-founder of the Electronic Music Studio and director of the ONCE Group (1960–68); he also co-founded Space Theater with Robert Ashley and the artist Milton Cohen. From 1959 to 1962 he attended the Institute of Science and Technology at Ann Arbor, where he was a research assistant the following year, studying acoustics and seismics.

In 1966 he began his collaboration with Merce Cunningham, providing electronic scores for the Cunningham Dance Company. He has also organized the ONCE Festival and taken part with the Sonic Arts Group in ensemble performances with electronic equipment. He has taught at Brandeis University, Waltham, Massachusetts (1966–67), the State University of New York at Buffalo (1968), University of Illinois (1969–70), University of California, Berkeley (1971), Dartmouth College (1972), University of California, San Diego (1973–78, 1985, 1987), Mills College (1981, 1989), and University of California, Santa Cruz (1975–94).

Mumma, a former professional horn player, has com-

Gordon Mumma.
Courtesy the composer.

posed several pieces for his own solo performance, including *Hornpieces* (1964) and three works for horn and cybersonic console: *Horn* (1965), *Hornpipe* (1967), and *Second Horn* (1969).

Mumma's creations for electronic tape alone include *Vectors* (1959); *Densities* (1959); *Mirrors* (1960); *Epoxy* (*Sequence I*; 1962); *Truro Synodicle* (1962); *Megaton for William Burroughs* (1963); *The Dresden Interleaf 13 February 1945* (1964); *Music for the Venezia Space Theatre* (1964); *Diastasy, As in Beer* (1965); *Digital Processes* (1967–69); *Runway* (1969); *Cybersonic Catilevers* (1973); *Echo D* (1978); *Echo Synodial* (1978); *Retrospect* (1962–82); and *Epifont* (*Spectral Portrait in memoriam George Cacioppo*; 1984). *Communication in a Noisy Environment* was produced at Automation House in New York in November 1970. Other works in this medium are *Medium Size Mograph* (1962), *Large Size Mograph* (1962), *Very Small Mograph* (1963), *Mesa* for cybersonic bandoneon (1966), and *Ambivex* (1971).

Works for purely conventional instruments are *Gestures II* for two pianos (1958–62); Piano Suite (1959); *Mographs* for combinations of pianos and pianists (1962–64); *Quartet of four pieces* for four instruments (1963); *Faisandage et galimafree*, a divertimento for trios of diverse instruments (1984); *Aleutian Displacement* for chamber ensemble (1987); and *Menages a deux* for violin, piano, vibraphone, and marimba (1989).

Mumma has combined instruments with electronic tape. Principal compositions in this sphere are *Meanwhile* for percussion and tape (1961); *Sinfonia* for 12 instruments and tape (1961); *Than Particle* for percussion and computer (1965); *Mesa* for bandoneon and cybersonic console (1966); *Swarmer* for violin, concertina, bowed saw, and cybersonic modification (1968); *Beam* for violin, viola, and cybersonic modification (1969); *Than Particle* for percussion and digital computer (1985); and *Peasant Boy* for jazz trio and tape.

Conspiracy 8 (1969–70) is scored for bowed cross-cut saw, gate-controlled amplifiers with controlled oscillation teletype and cathode-ray tube display, time-sharing digital computer with link, and seven auxiliary performers. Later works in this idiom include *I Saw Her Dance* for cross-cut saw, dancer, slides, and tape (1970); *Schoolwork* for cross-cut saw, bowed psaltery, and piano-melodica (1970); *Telepos* for dancers, telemetry belts, and accelerometers (1971); *Phenomenon Unarticulated* for frequency-modulated untrasonic oscillators (1972); *Passenger Pigeon* (1976); and *Equale: Zero Crossings* for violin, flute, clarinet, saxophone, bassoon, cello, and bandoneon (1976).

Mumma's theater works include *Temps* for live electronics (Space Theater: 1963); *Some Voltage Drop* (1974); *Earheart: Flights, Formations and Starry Nights* for dancers and electronics (1977); *Echo-BCD* for the same forces (1978); *Pontpoint* for dancers and tape (1979); and *Orait* for dancers and vocal ensemble (1988).

MYROW, FREDERIC
b. Brooklyn, New York, 16 July 1939
d. Hollywood Hills, California, 14 January 1999

Myrow was the son of the film composer Josef Myrow. He was educated at the University of Southern California and was a pupil of Darius Milhaud and Ingolf Dahl. In Rome on a Fulbright Fellowship he studied with Goffredo Petrassi at the Academy of Saint Cecilia. In addition to his achievements as a composer, Myrow made many public appearances as a pianist in the United States, Canada, and Italy.

Myrow's orchestral music includes *Symphonic Variations* (1960), a *Chamber Symphony* (1963), *Ode to a Marine*, and *Music for Orchestra*. His songs reveal a deep interest in oriental music, especially that of Japan: *Four Songs in Spring* (1959), *In Twilight* (*Japanese Songs*; 1960), and *Songs from the Japanese* for soprano and nine instruments (1964–65). For keyboard he wrote *Six Preludes in Six Styles*, *Theme and Variations*, and a *Triple Fugue* for two pianos.

Myrow's reputation rests on his film music, much of it for horror movies. Among his 22 scores are *Leo the Last* (1969), *The Steagle* (1971), *Soylent Green* (1973), and *Phantasm I – IV* (1979–1998).

Frederic Myrow, c. 1964–66.
Courtesy Music Library, State University of New York, Buffalo.

N

NABOKOV, NICHOLAS

*b. Lyubcha, Novogrudok, near Minsk, Belarus, 17
April 1903*

d. New York, New York, 6 April 1978

Nabokov studied with Vladimir Rebikoff in Yalta (1920)
and in Berlin (1921–23) with Paul Juon and Busoni.
From 1923 to 1933 he lived in Paris, where he attended
the Sorbonne (1926) and came into contact with
Diaghilev, who commissioned a ballet from him. In
1933 he settled in the United States, becoming naturalized in 1939. He was head of music at Wells College,
Aurora, New York (1935–40) and taught at St. John's
College, Annapolis, Maryland (1940–44). For the next
two years he was cultural advisor to the U.S. Military
Government in Berlin. On his return to America he
became professor of composition at the Peabody Conservatory, Baltimore (1948–50), and taught at the
American Academy in Rome (1950–51). In 1952 he
went to Paris as secretary-general of the Congress of
Cultural Freedom. He was cultural advisor to German
chancellor Willy Brandt (1963–66) and directed the
Berlin Festival in 1968. In that year he returned to the
United States to teach briefly at City College of New
York. In 1968 he joined the faculty of the State University of New York in Buffalo, moving to New York University in 1972.

Nabokov first came to prominence with his ballet
Ode: Meditation at Night on the Majesty of God, performed in 1928 in Paris by the Ballets Russes of
Diaghilev. In addition to the orchestra there are important parts for two solo voices and chorus in the score.
Before going to America, he composed a second ballet, *Aphrodite* (1930). Three more ballets date from
1934: *Les Valses de Beethoven, La Vie de Polchinelle*
(Paris), and *Union Pacific*, performed in Philadelphia
by Ballets Russes with scenario by Archibald McLeish

and choreography by Serge Lifar. James Thurber's illustrated parable provided the inspiration and title for
his next ballet, *The Last Flower* (1941), performed in
Berlin in 1958. A choral work, *Symboli Chrestiani* for
bass-baritone and orchestra (1953), was produced as a
one-act ballet in Nice in 1962. Nabokov's last ballets
were *Don Quichotte*, performed at the New York City
Ballet in 1965 with choreography by Balanchine, and
The Wanderer (1966).

Nabokov composed two operas. The first, *The Holy
Devil*, is set in Russia in 1916 and is based on a libretto
by Stephen Spender and the composer. Revised and
renamed *Rasputin's End*, it was performed by the Cologne Opera in November 1959. For his second opera,
he chose Shakespeare's *Love's Labours Lost*, with a
libretto adapted by W. H. Auden and Chester Kallman.
Presented in English, it was first staged in Brussels by
the Deutsche Oper of Berlin in February 1973.

One of Nabokov's early choral works, *Chants à la
Vièrge Marie*, was heard at the I.S.C.M. Festival in
Geneva in 1929. The oratorio *Job* was performed in
1933. Other vocal and choral works are *Collectionneur
d'Echos* for soprano, bass, chorus, and orchestra (1933);
The Return of Pushkin for high voice and orchestra, an
elegy in three movements, performed in Boston in 1948;
a cantata, *America Was Promises* for alto, baritone, and
men's voices (1950); *La Vita Nuova,* a cantata based
on Dante for soprano, tenor, and orchestra (1951); and
Four Poems of Boris Pasternak for baritone and orchestra (1959).

Nabokov's major orchestral works are three symphonies. The First, the *Lyrical Symphony,* was performed in Paris in 1930. The Second, *Sinfonia Biblica*,
received its premiere in New York in 1941. Leonard
Bernstein introduced the Third Symphony (*A Prayer*)
in New York in 1968. He wrote a Piano Concerto
(1932); a *Concerto Corale* for flute, strings, and piano

(1948), based on the chorale *Herzliebster Jesu*; and a Cello Concerto. subtitled *Les Hommages*, performed in Philadelphia in 1953. Other orchestral pieces include *La Vie du Polichinelle Suite* (1934); an overture, *La Fiancé* (1934); *Studies in Solitude,* composed in 1961 for the Philadelphia Orchestra; *Symphonic Variations* (1967); and *Variations on a Theme by Tchaikovsky* for cello and orchestra (1968). Among Nabokov's instrumental works are a String Quartet (1937); a Sonata for bassoon and piano (1941); and *Canzone, Introductione e Allegro* for violin and piano, written in 1947 for Nathan Milstein. He also composed two piano sonatas (1926, 1940).

As an administrator, Nabokov was responsible for three important music festivals, Masterpieces of the Twentieth Century (Paris, 1952), Music in Our Time (Rome, 1954), and East-West Music Encounter (Tokyo, 1961). At the time of his death he was planning a large-scale Stravinsky Festival for 1980 in Venice.

Nabokov, a cousin of the the writer Vladimir Nabokov, was the author of three books: *Old Friends and New Music* (1951), *Igor Stravinsky* (1964), about one of his closest friends, and an autobiography, *Bagazh*: *Confessions of a Russian Cosmopolitan* (1975).

NAGINSKI, CHARLES
b. Cairo, Egypt, 29 May 1909
d. Lenox, Massachusetts, 4 August 1940

Naginski took piano lessons as a child and began to compose at the age of ten. He went to the United States in 1927 and studied composition at the Juilliard School (1928–33) under Rubin Goldmark; he was also a pupil of Roger Sessions. In 1938 he was awarded an American Academy Fellowship to study in Rome. Naginski's promising career was brought to a sudden and tragic end; while attending the Berkshire Music Festival he drowned while swimming in a lake near Lenox, Massachusetts.

Naginski composed a Suite for orchestra (1931); two symphonies (1935, 1937); a symphonic poem, *1936*; *Three Movements* for chamber orchestra (1937); a Sinfonietta (1937), performed at the I.S.C.M. Festival in New York in 1941; *Children's Suite* (1938); and *Nocturne and Pantomime* (1938). For the Ballet Caravan he wrote a ballet, *The Minotaur* (1938). His chamber music includes two string quartets (both 1933) and a Piano Sonatina.

NANCARROW, CONLON
b. Texarkana, Arkansas, 27 October 1912
d. Mexico City, Mexico, 10 August 1997

After learning to play the trumpet in jazz ensembles, Nancarrow studied at the Cincinnati Conservatory (1929–32). In Boston (1933–36) he was a pupil of Nicolas Slonomsky, Walter Piston, and Roger Sessions. After fighting in the Spanish Civil War, he returned to the United States in 1939. Finding himself ostracized because of his socialist political views (and denied a U. S. passport), he emigrated in 1940 to Mexico City, becoming a Mexican citizen in 1956. He did not return to the United States until 1981. In 1982 he was Com-

Conlon Nancarrow.
Photo: Irene Haupt, courtesy Music Library, State University of New York, Buffalo.

poser-in-Residence at the Cabillo Music Festival in Aptos, California.

With remarkable single-mindedness Nancarrow concentrated almost exclusively on composing for the Ampico player piano. He perfected a technique for composing directly onto the piano rolls by punching holes for the notes. His major compositional accomplishment is a set of 52 *Studies for Player Piano* (1948–93); nos. 39, 40, 41, 43, and 44 make use of two instruments.

At the beginning and end of his career he composed a few works for conventional forces. He wrote an orchestral Suite (1943) and *Piece* for large orchestra (1943, rev. 1945). Instrumental works include *Sarabande* for oboe, bassoon, and piano (1930); *Toccata* for violin and piano (1935); *Septet* (1940); Trio for clarinet, bassoon, and piano (1942) and three string quartets: no.1 (1945), no. 2 (unfinished), and no. 3 (1993). Among a handful of pieces for a standard piano are *Prelude* (1935), *Blues* (1935), a Sonatina (1941), *Tango* (1983), and *Canons for Ursula* (*Oppens*) (1988).

NEIKRUG, MARC (EDWARD)
b. New York, New York, 24 September 1946

From 1964 to 1968 the composer and pianist Marc Neikrug studied with Giselher Klebe at Nordwestliche Musikakademie in Detmold, Germany. He continued his musical education at the State University of New York, Stony Brook (M.M., 1971) and was a pupil of Gunther Schuller at the Berkshire Music Center. He has been advisor for contemporary programs for the St. Paul Chamber Orchestra (1979–87), director of the Melbourne Summer School (1986, 1988, 1991), and artistic director of the Santa Fe Chamber Music Festival (1998–2006). He has followed a career as a pianist, especially in concerts with the violinist Pinchas Zuckerman. In 1972 he served as Composer-in-Residence at the Marlboro Music Festival.

Among his orchestral works are *Eternity's Sunrise* (1979–80); *Mobile* (1981); *Chetro Ketl*, composed in 1988 for the St. Paul Chamber Orchestra; Symphony no. 1 (1991); *Flamenco Fanfare* (1994); and *Suite* from *Los Alamos* (1998). He has concentrated on writing for solo instruments and orchestra, producing two piano concertos (1966, 1995); a Clarinet Concerto (1967); a Viola Concerto, premiered in Boston in 1979, two violin concertos, no. 1 (1982) and no. 2, *Departures and Remembrances*, composed in 1999 for Pinchas Zukerman; a Concerto for string quartet and chamber orchestra (1987); and a Flute Concerto performed in Pittsburgh in 1989.

Neikrug's chamber music includes a Sonata for solo cello (1967); two string quartets (1969, 1972); Suite for cello and piano (1974); *Rituals* for flute and harp

Marc Neikrug.
Photo: Stacia Spragg, courtesy the composer.

(1976); Concertino for flute, oboe, clarinet, violin, viola, cello, and piano (1977); *Three Fantasias* for violin and piano (1977); *Continuum* for cello and piano (1979); *Cycle of Seven* for piano (1978); *Kaleidoscope* for flute and piano (1979); *Duo* for violin and piano (1983); *Voci* for clarinet, violin, cello, and piano (1988); *Stars the Mirror* for string quartet (1989); *Take Me t' Susan's Gift* for percussion (1989); *Sonata Concertante* for violin and piano (1994); String Quintet (1995); *Fast Forward* for violin and piano (2001); *Petrus* for cello and piano (2001); and a Piano Quintet (2003).

For the stage Neikrug has composed a theater piece, *Through Roses* for actor and eight instruments (1979–80), and an opera, *Los Alamos*, staged in Berlin in 1988. Among his vocal compositions are *Nachtlieder* for soprano and orchestra (1988) and *Pueblo Children's Songs* for soprano and piano (1995).

NELHYBEL, VACLAV
b. Polanka nad Odrou, Czechoslovakia, 24 September 1919
d. Scranton, Pennsylvania, 22 March 1996

Nelhybel studied composition and conducting with Jaroslav Ridký at the Prague Conservatory (1938–42) and musicology at the University of Prague (1938–42). In 1946 he moved to Switzerland, where he attended the University of Fribourg. From 1947 to 1950 he worked for Swiss National Radio and was director of

Vaclav Nelhybel.
Courtesy: Dorothy Nelhybel.

music for Radio Free Europe, Munich (1950–57). He went to the United States in 1957, becoming an American citizen in 1962. Based in New York City, he worked as a composer, conductor, lecturer, and teacher until the mid-1970's, then moved to Connecticut. He held several academic appointments, including teaching at the University of Massachusetts, Lowell (1978–79); from 1994 to his death he was Composer-in-Residence at the University of Scranton, Pennsylvania.

A large number of Nelhybel's compositions are for instrumental groups, especially wind ensembles, including three wind quintets (1948, 1958, 1960). For brass he wrote a Quartet for horns (1957); Quartet for piano and brass (1959); a Trio (1961); *Numismata* for seven brass (1961); two quintets (1961, 1965); a Quintet for piano and brass; *Twelve Concert Pieces* for three trumpets; *Motet and Pavane* for brass septet and percussion; *Grand Intrada* for six trumpets and four trombones; *Three Pieces* for four trombones (1966); Suite for two trumpets and piano (1966); *Music for Six Trumpets* (1975); *Ludus* for four trombones or tubas (1978); and *Music* for 12 trumpets and wind (1980). Other instrumental pieces include two string quartets (1949, 1962); *Golden Concerto on a Twelve-Tone Row* for trumpet and piano (1960); *Impromptus* for six winds (1965); *Quintetto Concertante* for trumpet, trombone, xylophone, violin, and piano (1965); *Oratio No. 2* for oboe and string trio (1976); and a *Concertante* for two violins and vibraphone (1978).

Nelhybel's orchestral works include an early Symphony (1942); *Two Movements* for chamber orchestra; *Ballade* (1946); *Three Movements* for strings (1949); *Etude Symphonique* (1949); *Five Modes* (1960); *Sinfonia Concertante* (1960); *Passacaglia* (1965); *Music for Orchestra* (1966); *Polyphonies* (1972); and *Slavonic Triptych* (1976). For solo instruments and orchestra Nelhybel wrote a Concertino for piano and chamber orchestra (1949); a Viola Concerto (1962); *Passacaglia* for piano (1965); *Houston Concerto* for string quartet and orchestra (1967); *Concertino da Camera* for cello, winds, and percussion (1971); *Toccata* for harpsichord, winds, and percussion (1972); *Cantus and Ludus* for piano, winds, and percussion (1973); *Oratio No. 1* for piccolo, trumpet, chimes, and strings (1974); *Polyphonic Variations* for trumpet and strings (1975); and *Cantus Concertante* for soprano, violin, viola, cello, and orchestra (1979).

Nelhybel provided several major pieces for the concert band repertory: *Caucasian Passacaglia* (1964); *Concerto Antiphonale* for brass (1964); *Symphonic Requiem* (with bass-baritone solo) (1965); *Estampie* (1965); *Trittico* (1965); *Suite from Bohemia* (1969), *Yamaha Concerto* (1971); *Introit* (1971); *High Plains* (1972); *Concert Piece* (1973); *Dialogue* (with piano) (1976); *Sinfonia Resurrectionis* (1980); *Psalm XII* for wind and percussion (1981); *Concerto Grosso* (1981); Clarinet Concerto (1982); and *Prelude and Chorale* (1999).

Later instrumental pieces include three *Sonate di Chiesa*: no. 1 for violin and organ, no. 2, *Sequence* for trumpet and organ, and no. 3, *Variations on "Our God Almighty"* for trombone and organ; and four *Concerti Spirituale*: no. 1 for 12 flutes, electric harpsichord, and voice (1974), no. 2 for 12 saxophones, electric keyboard, and percussion (1973), no. 3 for electric violin, English horn, horn, tuba, vibraphone, winds, percussion, and voice (1975), and no. 4 for voice, string quartet, and chamber orchestra (1977). He also composed *Praeambulum* for organ and timpani (1977).

Among his many choral works are *Caroli Antiqui Varii* for unaccompanied voices (1962); *Epitaph for a Soldier* for soloists and chorus (1964); *Peter Piper* for chorus and clarinet choir (or piano) (1965); *Cantata Pacis* for solo voices and chorus with winds, percussion, and organ (1965); *Dies Ultima* for three soloists, chorus, speaking chorus, orchestra, and jazz band (1967); *Sine Nomine* for soloists, chorus, and tape (1968); *America Sings* for baritone, chorus, and band (1974); *Estampie Natalis* for double chorus, piccolo, viola, cello, and percussion (1976); *Adoratio* for chorus (1979); *Fables for All Time* for narrator, chorus, and orchestra (1980); *Let There Be Music* for baritone, chorus, and orchestra (1982); and *Pages From a Girl's Diary* for female voices.

For the stage Nelhybel wrote three operas, *A Legend* (1951–54; winner of the Ravitch Foundation Award in 1954), *Everyman,* a morality play (Memphis, 1974), and *The Station* (1978); and three ballets, *Fêtes de Feux* (1942), *In the Shadow of a Lime Tree* (1946), and *The Cock and the Hangman* (Prague, 1947).

NELSON, LARRY ALAN
b. Broken Bow, Nebraska, 27 January 1944

Nelson graduated in 1967 from the University of Denver, Colorado, where he had been a pupil of Normand Lockwood. He later studied with Will Bottje at Southern Illinois University (M.Mus., 1968) and at Michigan State University (Ph.D., 1974) with H. Owen Reed. He was director of the electronic music studio at Michigan State University (1970–71). Since 1971, he has taught at the West Chester State College, Pennsylvania, where he is currently professor of music theory and composition, director of the Center for Music Technology, co-director of the Concerts of New Music concert series, and co-director of the West Chester University New Music Ensemble. He has won numerous awards, including fellowships from the MacDowell Colony and the Norlin Award, and grants from the National Endowment for the Humanities, ASCAP, Meet the Composer, and other organizations.

For large ensemble he has written *Variations* (1973–74); *Catena* (1986); *Loose Leaves* (1989); *In Silence In Memory* (1994); and *Dance in the Prism* (1998). Nelson's chamber music includes *Watch* for twelve players (1970); *Duo* for cello and piano (1972); *Nocturne* for cello and piano (1975); *Poem of Soft Music* for flute, cello, and piano (1975); *Cadenzas and Interludes* for clarinet and percussion (1975); *Strider* for oboe and string quartet (1989); *String Quartet: Excelsior* (1992); *The Starry Messenger* for flute and piano (1996); and *Danceable Haze* for violin, viola, cello, and piano (2003). *Dance In The Prism,* composed for the West Chester University Wind Ensemble, was premiered in April of 1999. He is currently working on a new composition for flute, saxophone, cello, and piano. His solo piano works include *Music of Twelve Centers* (1980). Nelson's vocal works include *Creeley Songs* (1993) and *Seven Clay Songs* (2003).

Works including electronics and/or computer processing are *Flute Thing* (1970); *Music* for clarinet and tape (1973); *Consequences* for performers, tapes, slides, and lights (1973); *Music for Flute and Electronic Sounds* (1987); *Order and Alliance* for piano and tape (1991); and *Dulcet Mimicry* for soprano saxophone and interactive sounds (2002).

NELSON, RON(ALD JACK)
b. Joliet, Illinois, 14 December 1929

Nelson studied at the Eastman School of Music, Rochester, New York (1947–56; B.Mus., 1952; M.A., 1953; D. Mus., 1956), where he was a pupil of Howard Hanson, Bernard Rogers, Wayne Barlow, and Louis Mennini. In 1954 he went to Paris on a Fulbright Fellowship to receive composition lessons from Tony Aubin at the Ecole Normale du Musique and Paris Conservatory. In 1956, he joined the faculty at Brown University, Providence, Rhode Island, where he served as department chairman from 1963 to 1973, retiring in 1993.

For orchestra Nelson has written *Savannah River Holiday* (1957); *Jubilee* (1960); *Overture for Latecomers* (1961); *Toccata* (1961); *This is the Orchestra* with narrator (1963); *Sarabande for Katherine in April* (1964); a *Trilogy* (*JFK, MLK, RFK*) with soprano (1969); *Rocky Point Holiday* (1969); *A Guide to the Elements of Music* (1969); *Five Pieces for Orchestra,* after paintings by Andrew Wyeth (1976); *Meditation and Dance* (1976); *Epiphanies I: Fanfares and Chorales* (1993); *Epiphanies II: Panels* (1996); and *Resonances III* for orchestra and brass (1997).

Nelson is widely known as a choral conductor, and works for voices constitute his most important compositions. These include *The Christmas Story* for narrator, chorus, and orchestra (1958); *Glory to God* (1958) for chorus, organ, and brass (1958); *Fanfare for a Festival: All Praise to Music* for chorus, brass, and timpani (1960); *Five Anthems for Young Choirs* for female voices and piano (1961); *Three Ancient Prayers* for chorus and organ (1962); *Triumphal Te Deum* for double chorus, brass, and percussion (1962); *What is Man?* for soloists, chorus, narrator, tape, and orchestra (1964); *Vocalise* for female voices (1965); *God, Show Thy Sword* for chorus, organ, and percussion (1968); *Meditation on the Syllable OM* for men's chorus (1970); and *Alleluia! July 20th 1969* (1970) and *Hear, O Israel,* both for mixed voices.

Later choral works for mixed voices and orchestra are *Psalm XCV* (1971); *Prayer for the Emperor of China on the Altar of Heaven* (1972); *Prayer of St. Francis of Assisi* (1975); *Four Pieces After the Seasons* (1979); *Three Autumnal Sketches* (1979); *Mass of St. La Salle* (1980); *For Freedom of Conscience* (1980); *Three Nocturnal Pieces* (1981); *Three Seasonal Reflections* (1982); *Make Music in the Lord's Honor* for chorus, organ, and brass (1982); *Te Deum Laudamus* for chorus and wind ensemble (1985); *Festival Anthem* for chorus, organ, and brass (1985); *Prime: The Hour of Sunrise* for chorus, organ, and brass (1985); *Another Spring* for chorus and string quartet (1987); *Invoking the Powers* for chorus, piano, and percussion (1990); *And This Shall be for Music* for chorus and brass (1990); and *Songs of Praise and Reconciliation* for chorus, piano, and percussion (1991).

Nelson has written two one-act operas, *The Birthday of the Infanta* (1956) and *Hamaguchi* (1980); a ballet, *Dance in Ruins* (1957), with scenario by Eugene Berman; and several film scores, including *Before the Day* (1962), *The Social Security Story* (1962), and *The Long Haul* (1963).

Among his instrumental music are *Six Pieces* for chamber ensemble (1977); *Kristen's Song* for violin, flute, and organ (1982); *Pebble Beach Sojourn* for organ, brass, and percussion (1982); *Dance Capriccio* for alto saxophone and wind ensemble (1988); *Elegy II* for strings (1988); *Fanfare for the Hour of Sunrise* for wind and percussion (1989); and *Resonances I* for wind and percussion (1990). For wind band he has composed a Piano Concerto (1948); *Mayflower Overture* (1958); *Medieval Suite* (1983); *Aspen Jubilee* (1984); *Morning Alleluias* (1989); *Lauds: Praise High Day* (1991); *To the Airborne* (1992); *Passacaglia: Homage on B-A-C-H* (1993); *Chaconne In Memoriam* (1994); *Sonoran Desert Holiday* (1994); *Courtly Airs and Dances* (1995); *Fanfare for Kennedy Center* (1996); *Nightsong* (1998); and *Fanfare for the New Millennium* (1999).

NEVIN, ARTHUR (FINLEY)
b. Edgeworth, Pennsylvania, 27 April 1871
d. Sewickley, Pennsylvania, 10 July 1943

Arthur Nevin was the younger brother of Ethelbert Nevin, and although his music was of a more serious nature, his reputation did not rival that of his brother, whose *Narcissus* and *The Rosary* are still heard today.

Nevin was educated in Pittsburgh and at the New England Conservatory in Boston (1889–93). He continued his studies in Berlin with Klindworth and Humperdinck (1893–97). On his return to the United States he taught and conducted in various cities throughout the country. For a while he was professor of music at the University of Kansas (1915–20).

During the years 1903 and 1904 he made a special study of the music of the Blackfoot Indians in Montana. Arising directly from this work came the opera *Poia,* based on an Indian story he had heard. It was first produced at the Royal Opera House in Berlin on 23 April 1910. A second opera, the one-act *Twilight,* was composed in 1911, but it did not receive its premiere until 5 January 1918, when it was performed in Chicago under the title *A Daughter of the Forest,* with the composer conducting. The influence of American Indian music is found in a number of his other works including the masque *A Night in Yaddo Land* (1900). His orchestral pieces of importance are *Lorna Doone Suite* (1897); a *Miniature Suite* (1902); *Springs of Saratoga* (1911); *Love Dreams Suite* (1914); *Symphonic Poem* (1930); *Arizona* (1935); *Bakawali Dances*; and a Piano Concerto.

Among his other works are a String Quartet in D minor (1929); *At the Spring* for string quartet; a Piano Trio; piano pieces; songs; and two cantatas, *The Djinns* (New York, 1913) and *Roland* (1914).

NEVIN, ETHELBERT (WOODBRIDGE)
b. Edgeworth, Pennsylvania, 25 November 1862
c. New Haven, Connecticut, 17 February 1901

Nevin was the son of Robert Peebles Nevin, a friend of Stephen Foster. As a child he showed marked musical talent and was taught the piano from an early age. In

Ethelbert Nevin.
Courtesy: Ethelbert Nevin Collection, Center for American Music, University of Pittsburgh Library System.

1876 he went to Western University in Pittsburgh. At first his father, who was an amateur musician of some standing, opposed his son's intention of making a living through music, but relented when it became clear how eager the boy was.

After leaving school, Nevin studied in Boston under Benjamin J. Lang and Stephen Emery (1881–83). In 1884 he went to Germany and spent two years in Berlin as a pupil of Karl Klindworth and Hans von Bülow. There he achieved great success as a solo pianist, and on his return to the United States he settled in Boston in 1887 to begin a concert career. At this time, Nevin's early songs and piano pieces were beginning to earn him a reputation as a composer of salon pieces. The most popular of all his compositions, *Narcissus,* was published in 1891 as the fourth of a suite, *Water Pieces*. Later he was to see it choreographed by the 20-year old Isadora Duncan.

Nevin spent the years 1891 to 1897 in Europe, living for a while in Italy in 1895. He continued to compose evocatively titled piano suites that enjoyed considerable popularity in his day: *In Arcady* (1892), *May in Tuscany* (1895), and *A Day in Venice* (1896). Back in the United States in 1897, Nevin lived mostly in New York, but he was suffering at this time from serious ill-health. His best-known songs date from the final years of his life: *The Rosary* (1898) and *Mighty Lak' a Rose* (1901). He composed a song cycle, *Captive Memories*, for baritone, chorus, and piano (1899).

Nevin was essentially a miniaturist; in all he composed 46 songs and 33 piano pieces. He attempted only two large-scale works: a pantomime, *Lady Floriane's Dream* (1898), and an unfinished opera, *Nathan Hale*, along Wagnerian lines. A cantata, *The Quest*, was completed after his death by Horatio Parker.

He died after a long illness at the age of 39.

NEWLIN, DIKA
b. Portland, Oregon, 22 November 1923

Newlin studied at Michigan State University, East Lansing (B.A., 1939), the University of Southern California, Los Angeles (M.A., 1941), and Columbia University (Ph.D., 1945), and later studied privately with Arthur Farwell, Roger Sessions, and Arnold Schoenberg. She was also a piano pupil of Rudolf Serkin and Artur Schnabel. Newlin taught at Western Maryland College, Westminster, Maryland (1945–49) and was a member of the faculty at Syracuse University, New York for the next two years. In 1951 she spent a year in Vienna on a Fulbright Fellowship. On her return to the United States in 1952 she established the music department at Drew University, Madison, New Jersey. In 1965 she was appointed professor of music at North Texas University, Denton. In 1977 she joined the faculty of the New School of Social Research, New York City, moving in the following year to teach at the Virginia Commonwealth University, where she continues to be a professor of music.

She has composed a *Chamber Symphony* for 12 instruments (1949); a Piano Concerto, a Symphony for chorus and orchestra, a Piano Trio (1948); two works for piano, *Sinfonia* (1947) and *Fantasy on a Row* (1958); *Study in 12 tones* for viola d'amore and piano (1958); *Atones* for chamber ensemble (1976); and *Second Hand Rows* for voice and piano (1977–78).

Newlin is well-regarded as a writer on musical subjects. In 1947 she published a valuable book, *Bruckner, Mahler, Schoenberg* (rev. 1977). She has also translated Schoenberg's *Style and Idea* (1951) and Rufer's *The World of Arnold Schoenberg* (1962), and edited *Schoenberg Remembered: Diaries and Recollections (1938–76)*, published in 1980.

NEWMAN, ANTHONY
b. Los Angeles, California, 12 May 1941

In addition to his achievements as a composer, Newman is a highly respected performer on harpsichord and organ. In Paris (1959–60) he studied organ with Pierre Cochereau and composition with Nadia Boulanger at the Ecole Normale du Musique. Back in the United States he continued his musical education at the Mannes College, New York (B.S., 1962), at Harvard University, with Leon Kirchner and Luciano Berio (M.A., 1963), and at Boston University (D.M.A., 1966). He has taught at the Juilliard School, New York (1968–73), State University of New York at Purchase (1968–75), and Indiana University (1978–81). He is also music director at St. Matthew's Church in Bedford, New York.

For orchestra Newman has written a Violin Concerto (1979); a Viola Concerto, composed for the 1985 Viola Congress in Boston; a symphonic poem, *On Fallen Heroes* (*Sinfonia no. 1*; 1988), performed by the Milwaukee Symphony Orchestra under Lukas Foss in 1989; a Piano Concerto (1989); two symphonies, no. 1, *American Classic* (1991) and no. 2 (1999); and an Organ Concerto (1994).

Newman's instrumental works include a Cello Sonata (1978); a Violin Sonata (1980); *Introduction and Toccata* for flute and piano (1983); Piano Quintet (1983, rev. 1995); Suite for flute and guitar (1985); Sonata for viola (or clarinet) and piano (1986); *Prelude and Grand Contrapunctus* for guitar (1989); Suite for guitar (1990); *Ride the Wild Horse* for guitar (1992); a String Quartet (1994); *Variations and Toccata* for violin (1994); a Piano Trio (1995); Bassoon Sonata (1995) and Sonata for oboe (or clarinet) and piano (1997).

Anthony Newman.
Courtesy The Juilliard School.

For his own performance, he has written works for piano: *Variations and Fugue in B-A-C-H* (1992), *Sonata of the Americas* (1992), *The Equal Tempered Piano: 12 Preludes and Fugues* (1992), and *Toccata and Fugue* (1995); for harpsichord, *Chimeras* (1968) and a Suite (1989); and for organ, two symphonies (1985, 1991); *Concert Etude* (1990); two volumes of *Preludes and Fugues* (1991, 1994); and *Toccata and Fugue on BACH* (1999).

Among his choral works are *Grand Hymns of Awakening* for soloists, chorus, and orchestra (1984); *Absolute Joy* for chorus and orchestra (1995–97); and an oratorio, *Lives and Times of Angels* (1998). Newman's single stage work, the opera *Nicole and the Trial of the Century,* was completed in 1998.

NILES, JOHN JACOB
b. *Louisville, Kentucky, 28 April 1892*
d. *Lexington, Kentucky, 1 March 1980*

Niles was educated at the Cincinnati Conservatory (1919), where he was later awarded an honorary doctorate of music, one of five he held. He studied at the Schola Cantorum in Paris and at the University of Lyons. He was also a pupil of Edgar Stillman Kelley in America. He was one of the most outstanding collectors of American folk songs, especially the Anglo-American ballads of the southern Appalachians, and established a reputation both as a performer and arranger. Among his numerous published collections of American songs are *Singing Soldiers* (1927), *Seven Kentucky Mountain Songs* (1929), *Songs My Mother Never Taught Me* (1929), *Seven Negro Exaltations* (1929), *Songs of the Hill Folk* (1934), *Ten Christmas Carols* (1935), *More Songs of the Hill Folk* (1936), *Ballads and Tragic Legends* (1937), and *The Anglo-American Ballad Study Book* (1945).

Niles's best known compositions are the songs "Go 'Way From My Window," "I Wonder as I Wander," "The Carol of the Birds," "Black is the Color of My True Love's Hair," and "Venezuela," which have come to be accepted as folk songs. His last collection, *The Niles-Merton Song Cycles,* contain 22 songs for voice and piano to poems by Thomas Merton, composed in the late 1960s and early 1970s and first performed in Lexington, Kentucky in 1975 by Jacqueline Roberts and later given in Washington, D.C. (1979) and New York (1980).

On a larger scale Niles wrote an oratorio, *Lamentation* (1951); a cantata, *Rhapsody for the Merry Month of May* (1954); a Christmas miracle play, *Mary, the Rose*; *Golgotha* (1971); and *The King and the Common Man* (1976). He also composed a ballet, *Indian Summer Suite.*

He was the author of *The Ballad Book of John Jacob Niles* (1961) and a book of poems, *Brick Dust and Buttermilk* (1978).

NIXON, ROGER
b. *Tulare, California, 8 August 1921*

Nixon first learned to the play the clarinet. He studied with Arthur Bliss at the University of California, Berkeley (1940). Following U.S. Navy service during the Second World War (1942–46), he returned to Berkeley (1947–52). He also received composition lessons from Arnold Schoenberg (1948) and Roger Sessions (1952). He taught at Modesto Junior College, California (1951–59) before joining the faculty of the San Francisco State University in 1960; he retired in 1991.

For orchestra Nixon composed *Air for Strings* (1952), *Elegiac Rhapsody* (with solo viola; 1962), *Three Dances* (1963), Viola Concerto (1969), Violin Concerto (1976), and *San Joaquin Sketches* (1982). He has made a significant contribution to the concert band repertoire: *Elegy and Fanfare-March* (1958); *Fiesta del Pacifico* (1960); *Reflections* (1962); *Nocturne* (1965); *Prelude* and Fugue (1966); Centennial Fanfare-March (1970); A Solemn Procession (1970); Dialog (1972); Festival Fanfare-March (1972); Music for a Civic Celebration (1975); Pacific Celebration Suite (1976); Psalm (1979); Chamirato! (1980); Academic Tribute (1982); California Jubilee (1982); Golden Jubilee (1985); Flower of Youth (1989–90); A Centennial Overture (1993); Monterey Holidays (1999); A Millenium Fanfare (2000); and Mondavi Fanfare (2002).

Among Nixon's many choral works are a cantata, The Wine of Astonishment (1960), and several pieces for unaccompanied mixed voices, including Summer Rain (1958); Swallows (Stevenson; 1964); Bye Bye Baby (1965); Christmas Perspectives (1980); Festival Mass (1980); The Canterbury Tales (1986); The Daisy (1987); Wonders of Christmas (1988); Long, Long Ago (1998); Cradle Song (1999); Carol (1999); Christmas Bells (2000); Our Joyful Feast (2000); Glad Sight (2001); The Queen of Night (2001); The Rainbow (2001); Visions (2001); Cradle Hymn (2001); A Christmas Remembrance (2001); and A Perfect Woman (2002). For male voice choir he has written Love's Secret (Blake; 1960) and Chaunticleer (Chaucer; 1984).

Nixon has composed four song cycles: Chinese Scenes (1942), Six Moods of Love (1950), Five Transcendental Songs (Whitman) (1979), and A Narrative

of Tides for soprano, flute, and piano (1984). He has composed a chamber opera, The Bride Comes to Yellow Sky (1968, rev. 1969).

Nixon's output of instrumental music includes a String Quartet (1949); Nocturne for flute and piano (1960); Duos I for violin and viola (1960), II for flute (or oboe) and clarinet (1960), III for flute and alto flute (1978), IV for piccolo and flute (1978), V for flute and clarinet (1978), and VI for piccolo and flute (1978); Movement for clarinet and piano (1975); Ceremonial Piece for brass (1976); Lament for solo cello and six cellos (1978); Conversations for violin and clarinet (1981); Music for clarinet and piano (1986); Variations for clarinet and cello (1991); and 24 Piano Preludes (1946–2001).

NORDOFF, PAUL
b. Philadelphia, Pennsylvania, 4 June 1909
d. Herdecke, Germany, 18 January 1977

Nordoff was educated at the Philadelphia Conservatory of Music (1923–27) and at the Juilliard School (1928–33), where he was a pupil of Rubin Goldmark and Olga Samaroff. In 1933 and again in 1935 he was awarded Guggenheim Fellowships. From 1938 to 1943 he was head of composition at the Philadelphia Conservatory.

Paul Nordoff, teaching in April 1961. *Courtesy Clive Robbins/Nordoff-Robbins Music Therapy.*

After a brief time as associate professor at Michigan State College (1945–49), he was appointed professor of music at Bard College in 1949, a post he held for nine years.

Nordoff composed a considerable quantity of music. His orchestral works include two symphonies, subtitled *Winter* (1954) and *Spring* (1956); *Prelude and Three Fugues* for chamber orchestra (1932–36); two piano concertos (1934, 1936); Suite for orchestra (1938); a Concerto for two pianos (1939); a Violin Concerto (1940); a Concerto for violin and piano (1948); a Suite for chamber orchestra (1958); *Gothic Concerto* for piano and orchestra (1959); *Landscape with Figures*; *Little Symphony*; and *The Frog Prince* for narrator and orchestra (1954).

Among his many chamber music compositions are two string quartets (1932, 1935); a Piano Quintet (1936), which won him a Pulitzer Traveling Scholarship in 1940; a Quintet for piano and wind (1948); a *Little Concerto* for string trio, double bass, and small orchestra, written for a children's concert; a Violin Sonata (1932); a Cello Sonata (1941); a *Lyric Sonata* for violin and piano (1950); and a *Dance Suite* for flute and piano (1953).

For the stage Nordoff wrote three operas: *Timothy Fortune* (1937–38, rev. 1956–57), based on the story "Mr. Fortune's Maggot" by Sylvia Townsend Warner; *The Masterpiece* (1941); and *The Sea Change* (1951). He also composed three ballets, *Every Soul is a Circus* (1938), *Salem Shore* (1943), and *Tally Ho* (1943). Notable among his 300 songs are two cycles, *The Path of Love* (1943), and *The Story of Sweeney* (1943). *Secular Mass* for soloists, chorus, and orchestra (1934) is his best-known choral work. He also composed a dance-cantata, *The Sun* (1945).

Nordoff took a great interest in music therapy for handicapped children, and after 1959 focused entirely on this area. From 1967 to 1974 he traveled widely in Europe, Australia, New Zealand, and the United States, demonstrating his principles, techniques, and materials with his colleague Clive Robbins. Together they set up Nordoff-Robbins Music Therapy Institutes throughout the world. For these children he composed numerous pieces of music, including two volumes of *Children's Play Songs* and musical plays such as *The Story of Artaban* and *The Children's Christmas Play*. Other works in this medium are a musical adventure, *The Three Bears*; *Pif-Paf-Poltrie*, a working game; a setting of Psalm 23 for singers, speech chorus, chime-bars, and piano; and *A Message for the King* for narrator, singers, percussion, and piano.

Nordoff and Robbins co-authored three books: *Music Therapy for Handicapped Children* (1965, rev 1971), *Music Therapy in Specia Education* (1971), and *Creative Music Therapy* (1977).

NORTH, ALEX
b. Chester, Pennsylvania, 4 December 1910
d. Pacific Palisades, California, 8 September 1991

North studied the piano at the Curtis Institute, Philadelphia before attending the Juilliard School (1929–32), where he was a pupil of Bernard Wagenaar. He spent two years in Russia (1933–34) studying at the Moscow Conservatory and directing the orchestra of the Latvian State Theatre. In New York (1935–39) he received composition lessons from Ernst Toch and Aaron Copland. During this time he composed a number of ballet scores for Martha Graham, Hanya Holm, and Agnes de Mille, including *Ballad in a Popular Style* (1935); *Case History* (1935); *War is Beautiful* (1936); *Slaughter of the Innocents* (1937); *American Lyric* (1938); *Exile* (1941); and *The Golden Fleece* (1941). Later ballets are *Clay Ritual* (1942); *A Streetcar Named Desire* (1952); *Daddy Long Legs* (1955); and *Mal de siècle* (1958). In 1939 he traveled to Mexico with the Anna Sokolow Ballet Company. During the next two years he came into contact with Carlos Chávez and attended the composition class of Silvestre Revueltas. After serving in the U.S. Army during the Second World War, he settled in New York.

The success of the incidental music he wrote for Elia Kazan's stage production of Arthur Miller's *Death of a Salesman* (1948) led to the beginning of his career as a writer of Hollywood film scores. The first of these was for Kazan's screen version of *A Streetcar Named Desire* (1950). There followed a sequence of distinguished scores for major films at regular intervals, including *Death of a Salesman* (1950); *Viva Zapata!* (1951); *A Member of the Wedding* (1953); *Desiree* (1954); *The Rose Tattoo* (1955); *Unchained* (1955, including "Unchained Melody"); *The Bad Seed* (1956); *The Rainmaker* (1956); *I'll Cry Tomorrow* (1956); *South Seas Adventure* (1958); *The Long Hot Summer* (1959); *The Sound and the Fury* (1959); *Spartacus* (1960); *Sanctuary* (1961); *Cleopatra* (1962); *Cheyenne Autumn* (1964); *The Agony and the Ecstasy* (1965); *Who's Afraid of Virginia Woolf?* (1966); *The Shoes of the Fisherman* (1968); *Willard* (1970); *Under the Volcano* (1984); *Prizzi's Honor* (1985); and *Good Morning, Vietnam* (1988).

North continued to write incidental music for Broadway: *The Innocents* (W. Archibald; 1950), *Coriolanus* (1953), *Richard III* (1954), and *The American Clock* (Arthur Miller; 1984).

North's concert works include a cantata, *Negro Mother* (Langston Hughes; 1940); *Ballad of Valley Forge* for baritone, chorus, and orchestra (1941); *Rhapsody U. S. A.* for chorus and orchestra (1942); *Holiday Set* for orchestra (1945); a cantata, *Morning Star* (1946); *Revue* for clarinet and orchestra (1946), performed by

Benny Goodman with Leonard Bernstein and the New York Philharmonic Orchestra; a cantata, *Morning Star* (1946), commissioned by the *New York Herald Tribune*; Symphony no. 1 (1947); *Rhapsody* for piano and orchestra (1953); Symphony no. 2, *Africa* (1968), based on music written for a television documentary of the previous year; *Homage to Vaudeville* for orchestra; *Names on the Land* for baritone; chorus, and orchestra; and Symphony no. 3 (1971).

He also wrote several attractive works for children: an opera, *Hither and Thither of Danny Dither* (1940), and four pieces for narrator and orchestra: *The City Sings for Michael* (1940), *The Waltzing Elephant* (1945), *The Little Indian Drum* (1946), and *Christopher Columbus* (1948).

North's chamber music includes *Quest* for chamber ensemble (1938), Suite for flute, clarinet, and bassoon (1938), Woodwind Trio (1938), and a Wind Quintet (1942).

NOVÁČEK, OTTOKAR (EUGEN)

b. *Weisskirchen (now Bela Crkva), Hungary, 13 May 1866*

d. *New York, New York, 3 February 1900*

Nováček was a Hungarian violinist of Czech descent. After initial training with his father, Martin Josef Nováček, he studied the violin with Jakob Dont in Vienna (1880–83) and with Henry Schradieck and Adolf Brodsky in Leipzig (1883–85). He played in the Leipzig Gewandhaus Orchestra and was a member of Brodsky's quartet. In 1891 he went to America to play in the Boston Symphony Orchestra under Arthur Nikisch. In 1892 he was appointed principal viola in the Damrosch Orchestra in New York. A serious heart condition forced him to retire in 1899.

Nováček's fame rests on a single work, *Perpetuum Mobile* (1895) for violin and orchestra, still performed as a virtuoso recital item. He also composed a Piano Concerto in C in one movement (*Eroica*), first performed in 1894 by Busoni; three string quartets, published in 1890, 1898, and 1904; a Sinfonietta for woodwind; and *Bulgarian Dances* for violin and piano.

NOWAK, LIONEL (HENRY)

b. *Cleveland, Ohio, 25 September 1911*

c. *North Bennington, Vermont, 4 December 1995*

Nowak studied at the Cleveland Institute of Music (1929–36), where he was a pupil of Herbert Elwell, Roger Sessions, and Quincy Porter. He was a piano pupil of Edwin Fischer and Beryl Rubinstein and made his concert debut in Cleveland in 1924. In 1944 he was

Lionel Nowak, 1986.
Courtesy Alison Nowak

the soloist in his own Piano Concerto. He taught at Fenn College, Cleveland (1932–38). From 1938 to 1942 he was composer and musical director of the Humphrey-Weidmann Dance Company. He joined the faculty at Converse College, Spartanburg, South Carolina (1942–46) and Syracuse University (1946–48), moving in 1948 to Bennington College, Vermont.

For the Humphrey-Weidmann Dance Company Nowak composed six ballets: *Square Dance* (1938), *On My Mother's Side* (1939), *The Green Land* (1941), *Flickers* (1942), *House Divided* (1944); and *The Story of Mankind* (1946). He also provided a dance score for José Limón, *Danzas Mexicanas* (1939).

Nowak's instrumental pieces include a Suite for four winds (1945); an Oboe Sonata (1949); three cello sonatas (1950, 1951, 1960); *Diptych* for string quartet (1951); Trio for clarinet, violin, and cello (1951); Quartet for oboe and strings (1952); Sonata for solo violin, subtitled *Orrea Pernel*, after the dedicatee (1952); Piano Trio (1954); *Fantasia* for piano (1954); *Duo* for viola and piano (1960); *Concert Piece* for timpani and strings (1961); *Soundscape* for three woodwinds (1964); a String Quartet (1970); *Soundscape* for bassoon and piano (1971); *Soundscape* for violin, piano, and percussion (1971); Wind Trio (1973); *Four Fancies* for five players (1980); Suite for two cellos (1981); *Four Green Mountain Sketches* for flute and cello (1981); *Games* for four flutes (1984); Suite for baroque flute and harpsichord (1989); and *Three Movements* for chamber orchestra.

Nowak's vocal music includes *Poems for Music* for tenor and clarinet (1951); *Wisdom Exalteth Her Children* for female voices (1952); *Four Songs from Vermont* for tenor and piano (1953); *Cowboys and the Songs They Sang* (1967); and *Seven Songs From the Diary of Izumi Shikibu* (1982).

O

O'HARA, GEOFFREY

b. Chatham, Ontario, 2 February 1882
d. St. Petersburg, Florida, 31 January 1967

O'Hara settled in the United States in 1904, becoming a naturalized citizen in 1919. He studied composition with Homer Norris and J. Volger. Although he entered banking as a career, he later became a singer and pianist. A deep interest in the music of the American Indian led him to lecture throughout the United States. He taught at Teachers College, Columbia University (1936–37) and Huron College (1947–48).

O'Hara composed ten operettas: *Peggy and the Pirate* (1927), *Riding Down the Sky* (1928), *The Count and the Co-ed* (1929), *The Smiling Six-pence* (1930), *Lantern Land* (1931), *Harmony Hall* (1933), *The Princess Runs Away* (1936), *Our America* (1934), *Puddinhead the First* (1936), and *The Christmas Thieves* (1943). His many songs, especially *K-K-K-Katy* and *Your Eyes Have Told Me*, were at one time widely popular.

OLDBERG, ARNE

b. Youngstown, Ohio, 12 July 1874
d. Evanston, Illinois, 17 February 1962

Oldberg studied in Chicago with Wilhelm Middelschulte, in Vienna with Theodor Leschetizky (1893–95), and in Munich with Joseph Rheinberger. On returning to the United States in 1899 he was appointed head of the piano department at Northwestern University, Evanston, Illinois; he retired in 1941.

Oldberg's work was championed by Chicago Symphony Orchestra conductor Frederick Stock, who made his symphonic works a regular part of the orchestra's programs. For orchestra Oldberg composed five sym-

Arne Oldberg.
Courtesy Welles Library, Northwestern University.

phonies: no. 1 (1910), no. 2 (1918), no. 3 in F minor (1927), no. 4 in B minor (1942), and no. 5 in E minor (1950). Other orchestral works include the overture *Paola and Francesca,* op. 21 (1908), *Academic Overture* (1909); *At Night* (1917); a symphonic poem, *The Sea* (1934); two piano concertos; a Violin Concerto (1933); a Horn Concerto; and two pieces for organ and orchestra, a Concerto and *Variations* (1938).

His vocal music includes St. *Francis of Assisi* for baritone and orchestra (1954). Among his instrumental works are a String Quartet; two piano quintets, no. 1 in B minor (1905) and no. 2 in C# minor (1908); and a Quintet in E-flat for piano and wind.

OLIVER, HENRY KEMBLE
b. Beverly, Massachusetts, 24 November 1800
d. Salem, Massachusetts, 12 August 1885

After graduating from Dartmouth College in 1818, Oliver became an organist in Salem. In 1826 he founded the Salem Mozart Society. From 1844 to 1859 he lived in Lawrence, Massachusetts where he served as mayor (1859). He was also mayor of Salem (1861–65). He was awarded an M.A. from Harvard University in 1862 and a doctorate from Dartmouth College in 1883.

Oliver was a notable writer of hymn tunes and is remembered for *Federal Street*, *Morning*, *Harmony Grove*, *Beacon Street*, *Hudson*, and *Merton*. On 25 June 1872, he conducted a chorus of 20,000 voices in his choral work *Federal Street* as part of Boston's World Peace Jubilee. He published three books: *The National Lyre* (with Tuckerman and Bancroft, 1848), *Oliver's Collection of Hymns and Psalm Tunes* (1860), and *Oliver's Original Hymn Tunes* (1875). He also composed a setting of the *Te Deum*.

OLIVEROS, PAULINE
b. Houston, Texas, 30 May 1932

At the age of thirteen Oliveros learned to play the accordion, an instrument that became integral to her music thereafter. She studied accordion and composition at the University of Houston (1949–52). From 1954 to 1957 she attended San Francisco State College and received private composition lessons from Robert Erickson. In 1963 she collaborated with David Tudor and the choreographer Elizabeth Harris, producing works using a variety of sounds. Later she worked extensively with the performance artist Linda Montano. Oliveros was director of the Tape Center at Mills College, Oakland, California (1966–67) and from 1967 to 1981 taught composition and experimental studies at the University of California, San Diego, where she was director of the Center for Musical Experiment (1976–79). Currently she is Distinguished Research Professor in Music at the Rensselaer Polytechnic Institute, Troy, New York and Darius Milhaud Composer-in-Residence at Mills College. She won a Guggenheim Fellowship in 1973.

Oliveros's early music includes a freely atonal Sextet (1959–60); *Sound Patterns* for chorus (1961); Trio

Pauline Oliveros.
Photo Gisela Gamper, courtesy Deep Listening/the composer.

for flute, piano and page turner, who silently depresses keys on the piano (1961); and *Outline* for flute, piano and string bass (1963). After this time she abandoned conventional notation of her music.

In 1961 she formed an improvisation group, Sonics, with Morton Subotnick and Roman Sender. The same year marks the completion of her first electronic work, *Perspectives*. From 1963 to 1970 she made extensive use of tape and electronic techniques in many of her creations. These include *Pieces of Eight* for wind octet and tape (1965); *George Washington Slept Here Too* for amplified violin, tape, projections, film and staging (1965); *The C(s) for Once* for flutes, trumpets, vocalists and tape delay system (1966); *Double Basses at Twenty Paces* for two double basses, tape, slides, conductor/referee and two seconds (1968); *Night Jar* for viola d'amore, tape, film and lighting (1968); and a dance piece for Merce Cunningham, *In Memoriam Nicola Tesla: Cosmic Engineer* (1968–69).

Among her works for tape alone at this period are *Bye Bye Butterfly* (1965), *Big Mother is Watching You* (1966), *I of IV* (1966), and *Beautiful Soop* (1967). Two works without tape are *Aeolian Partitions* for flute, violin, clarinet, cello, and piano (1968) and *Meditations on the Points of a Compass* for solo voices, chorus, and percussion (1970).

In 1970 Oliveros developed a deep interest in Asian culture and Tibetan Buddhism. Meditation techniques became integral to her music, evident in *To Valerie Solanas and Marilyn Monroe in Recognition of Their Desperation* for orchestra, chorus, electronics and lights (1970); *24 Sonic Meditations* for voices, instruments and unspecified performers (1971–72); and *The Wheel of Life* for vocal ensemble (1974).

The ceremonial theater piece *Crow Two* was commissioned in 1975 by the State University of New York, Buffalo. It was followed in 1977 by a similar work, *Rose Moon,* in which the performers move in circles for two hours playing bells and other percussion instruments. It was commissioned by Wesleyan University, Middletown, Connecticut. Other pieces at this time include *Willow Brook Generations and Reflections* for winds, brass and vocalists (1976) and *To Those in the Gray Northwestern Rainforests* for unspecified ensemble (1976). In 1977 Oliveros won first prize from the city of Bonn for *Bonn Feier,* an environmental theater piece composed in 1971.

Works from the later 1970's include *The Yellow River Map,* a ceremonial meditation for a large group of 50 or more people, commissioned in 1977 by the Experimental Intermedia Foundation, New York; *The Witness* for solo, duo and ensemble virtuoso instrumentalists (1977); *El Relicario de Los Animales* for the singer Carol Plantamura and 20 instruments (1979); and *MMM (Lullaby for Daisy Pauline)* (1980), in which the audience participates by humming.

She moved to Mount Tremper, New York, in 1981 where she set up the Oliveros Foundation. In 1988 she formed the group Deep Listening with composer and trombonist Stuart Dempster and composer Paniotis. The theater piece *Njinga: The Queen King,* performed at Brooklyn Academy of Music in 1993, places African musicians on stage. Recent dance pieces are *Contenders* (1991); *Skin* (1991); *Walter's Finest Hours* (192); *Hommage a Serafina* (1994); *Ghost Dance*, performed at the Lincoln Center, New York in 1996; and *Antigone Dreams* (1999).

Recent compositions include *Portrait of Malcolm* for violin (1989); *Lion's Tale* for digital sampler (1989); *In Memoriam, Mr Whitney* for voice, accordion and vocal ensemble (1991); *Shape Shifting,* commissioned in 1995 by the American Accordion Association; *Portrait of the Quintet of America* for wind quintet (1996); *Saxual Orientation* for saxophone quartet (1997); *Primordial/Lift* for ensemble (1998); *Out of the Dark* for chamber orchestra (1998); *Six For New Time* for four guitars and two percussion (1999); *The Heart of Tones* for trombone and oscillators (1999); *Elemental Gallop* for voice, flute, cello and piano (2000); *Lunar Opera: Deep Listening for Tunes,* premiered at the Lincoln Center in 2000; *Rabbit in the Moon* (2000); *For Solo Drummer* (2001); and *Sound Patterns and Tropes* for chorus and percussion (2001).

Among her film scores are two documentaries, *4 H Clubs* (1958) and *Art in Woodcut* (1963), and three features, *Covenant* (1965), *Events* (1965), and *Paulina* (1997).

Oliveros is the author of three books: *Initiation Dream* (1983), *Software for People: Collected Writings 1963–80* (1984), and *The Roots of the Moment: Collected Writings 1980–96* (1998).

ORNSTEIN, LEO
b. Kremenchug, Ukraine, 11 December 1892
d. Green Bay, Wisconsin, 24 February 2002

Ornstein's father was a cantor in Kiev; as a child prodigy, he received lessons from Anna Essipova (not Alexander Glazunov, as often stated) at the St. Petersburg Conservatory. His family left Russia for the United States to escape the pogroms against Jews; his arrival in America is usually dated 1907, but his wife claimed that 1901 is correct. He continued his musical education in New York at the Institute of Musical Arts with the pianist Bertha Fiering Tapper. Ornstein's career began in 1911 when he appeared as piano soloist with many of the leading American orchestras, including those in New York, Philadelphia, and Boston . In the following year he undertook a successful tour of Europe performing many of his own works.

Ornstein's first compositions were conventional pieces for piano, but in 1911 he wrote *Danse Sauvage* (*Wild Man's Dance*), which makes use of dissonant tone clusters similar to those used by Henry Cowell in his piano music of the same period. The violence of the piano writing branded Ornstein as a radical, and he was for a decade the "enfant terrible" of modern music, prior to George Antheil's accession to the title. In his more sentimental pieces, Ornstein seems to have followed Scriabin as his model. He was one of the first pianists to introduce the music of Scriabin, Schoenberg, and Satie into the United States.

Ornstein's works for the piano include eight sonatas; *Three Moods* (1914); *Suicide in an Airplane* (1914); *A la Chinoise* (1918); *Arabesques* (1918–20); and *A Morning in the Woods* (1971). He performed the first three sonatas in concerts from memory but was unable to remember them when he later tried to write down the music. The Fifth Sonata, subtitled *Biography in Sonata Form,* was completed in 1973. Of the remaining sonatas, no. 6 dates from 1981, no. 7 from 1988; and no. 8, probably his final work, from 1990, when he was aged 98.

As a composer, Ornstein was most active between the two World Wars. In addition to several hundred other piano pieces, he composed a Piano Concerto (1923), a Piano Quintet (1929), which he played with both the

Leo Ornstein, age 103.
Courtesy Severo Ornstein.

Pro Arte and Stradivarius quartets, and a String Quartet (1929). Other compositions include a symphonic poem, *Fog* (1915); a Second Piano Concerto; two violin sonatas (1915, 1917); two cello sonatas (1918, 1920); a pantomime, *Lima Beans* (1931); incidental music for Aristophanes's *Lysistrata* (1930); a Symphony (1930); and *Nocturne and Dance of the Fates* (1935), commissioned by the League of Composers for the St. Louis Symphony Orchestra, his last significant work before a long period of silence.

In 1920 Ornstein retired from a performing career, emerging only to play his Piano Concerto in 1925 with Leopold Stokowski and the Philadelphia Orchestra. Anticipating Antheil by a decade, Ornstein faded from the musical scene in the 1920's. After a spell of teaching at the Philadelphia Musical Academy, he and his wife Pauline Mallet-Prevost founded the Ornstein School of Music in Philadelphia in 1940, from which he retired in 1955.

After withdrawing from public life, Ornstein returned to composition towards the end of his very long life. In 1975 he completed a Second String Quartet. String Quartet no. 3 received its premiere at Brandeis University, Waltham, Massachusetts in February 1979. Other late instrumental pieces include *Hebriac Fantasy*

for violin and piano (1975); *Intermezzo* for flute and piano (1978); *Ballade* for alto saxophone and piano (1978); and *Poem* for flute and piano (1979). Among his final piano compositions are *Just Fun Piece* (1977), *An Autumn Improvisation* (1978), *Valse Diabolique* (1978), and *The Deserted Garden* (1982).

OTEY, ORLANDO
b. Mexico City, Mexico, 1 February 1925

Otey gave his first piano recital in his native Mexico City at the age of 4; he subsequently toured as a child prodigy pianist in Mexico and Europe. At age 17, he joined the faculty of the National School of Music at the University of Mexico. He emigrated to the United States in 1945. After graduating from the Curtis Institute, Philadelphia in 1948, Otey undertook a career as a concert pianist. He was also director of the Otey Music School, Wilmington, Delaware.

Otey's orchestral works include *Arabesque* (1950); *Sinfonia Breve* (1956); *Suite for Strings* (1957); *Alacran: Sinfonia breve* (1957); *Tzintzuntzan* for strings (1958); and *Poetica* for trumpet and orchestra. For piano, he has composed two sonatas, no. 1, *Tenochtitlan* and no. 2, *Adelita*; *Mexican Fantasy*; *Preludio y Toccata "Alacrán"*; *Arabesque*; *The Sea of Galilee*; and several etudes.

Otey has developed an elaborate system of music theory that he describes in *Otey Music Teaching Method* (1973) and a book on "non-septonic musical keys."

OTT, DAVID
b. Crystal Falls, Michigan, 5 July 1947

Ott received his musical education at the University of Wisconsin, Platteville (B.S. in Mus. Ed., 1969), Indiana University School of Music, Bloomington (M.M., 1971), and the University of Kentucky, Lexington (D.M.A., 1982). He joined the music faculty of Houghton College, New York in 1972, moving to the University of Kentucky in 1976. He taught at Catawba College, Salisbury, North Carolina (1977–78) and at Pfeiffer College, Misenheimer, North Carolina (1978–82). In 1982 he moved to De Pauw University, Greencastle, Indiana, remaining there through 1999. From 1991–97, He was Composer-in-Residence with the Indianapolis Symphony Orchestra (1991–97) and Evansville (Indiana) Philharmonic (2003–04).

Since 1999, Ott has been conductor/music director of the Northwest Florida Symphony Orchestra and has taught at the University of West Florida. He is the recipient of many awards and fellowships, including the 1986 Fisher Fellowship, the 1995 Lancaster Symphony

Composer of the Year Award, and the 2003 Music Alive Award.

Ott's principal compositions are for orchestra, with four symphonies taking pride of place: no. 1, *Short Symphony* for chamber orchestra (1984), no. 2 (1990), no. 3 (1991), and no. 4 (1994). Other orchestral works are *Genesis II* (1980); *Water Garden* (1986); *Celebration at Vanderburgh* (1987); *Vertical Shrines* (1989); *Music of the Canvas* (1990); *String Symphony* (1990); *Overture on an American Hymn* for chamber orchestra (1992); *Indianapolis Concerto for Orchestra* (1992–93); *The Four Winds* (1993); and *Improvisation on "Freudvoll und Liedvoll" (Egmont)* (1993).

Ott has been particularly prolific in writing concertos for solo and groups of instruments. These include a Piano Concerto (1983); Percussion Concerto (1984); Cello Concerto (1985); Saxophone Concerto (1987); Viola Concerto (1988); Concerto for two cellos (1988); *Triple Brass Concerto* for trumpet, horn and trombone (1990); Violin Concerto (1992); Trombone Concerto (1992); Triple Concerto for clarinet, violin and piano (1993); and Double Concerto for violin and cello (1995). Among his instrumental works are a Viola Sonata (1982); *Sabado* for wind quintet (1985); Trombone Sonata (1986); *DodecaCelli* for twelve cellos (1988); a String Quartet (1989); and *Five Interludes* for cello and piano (1990). In April 2003, his Concerto for alto saxophone and winds, commissioned by the University of Wisconsin, Platteville, was premiered.

Ott has composed two operas, *Lucinda Hero* (1985) and *Visions: The Isle of Patmos* (1988).

OVERTON, HALL (FRANKLIN)
b. Bangor, Michigan, 23 February 1920
d. New York, New York, 24 November 1972

Overton studied at Aquinas College, Grand Rapids, Michigan (1938–40) and at the Chicago Musical College (1940–42). After serving in the U. S. Army, he settled in New York, where he became a pupil of Vincent Persichetti at the Juilliard School (1948–50); he later studied with Wallingford Riegger in New York (1951) and Darius Milhaud at the Aspen Summer School (1953). He taught at the Juilliard School (1960–71), the New School for Social Research, New York (1962–66), and at Yale University (1970–71). From 1967 to 1969 he was president of the American Composers' Alliance.

Like Gunther Schuller, Overton worked extensively in the field of jazz as well as serious music. His first success came with the production of his opera *The Enchanted Pear Tree*, at the Juilliard School in 1950. A second opera, *Pietro's Petard*, was completed in 1963. The one-act opera *Huckleberry Finn*, performed at the Juilliard American Opera Center in May 1971, was one of his last works. He also composed a ballet, *Nonage* (1951).

Overton wrote two symphonies, no. 1 for strings, dating from 1955, no. 2, in one movement, to a commission from the Louisville Orchestra in 1962. Also for orchestra are *Symphonic Movement* (1950); Concertino for violin and strings (1958); *Dialogues* (1963); *Rhythms* for violin and orchestra (1963); *Sonorities* (1964); *Interplay* (1964); and *Pulsations* for chamber orchestra (1972).

Overton's most important compositions are two sonatas, one for viola and piano, the other for cello and piano, both written in 1960. They make considerable demands upon the technical skill of the performers. Among other instrumental are three string quartets (1950, 1954, 1966); a Trio for clarinet, cello and piano; a String Trio (1957); *Fantasy* for brass quintet, piano and percussion (1957); a Piano Sonata (1963); and *Processional* for brass quartet and percussion (1965).

P

PACHELBEL, CARL THEODORE

b. Stuttgart, Germany, 24 November 1690
d. Charleston, South Carolina, 14 September 1750

Carl Theodore Pachelbel was the son of Johann Pachelbel (1653–1706), the famous German organist and composer. He emigrated to America in 1732 or 1733, living first in Boston. After only a short time there, he went to Newport, Rhode Island, as organist at Trinity Church. It is recorded that he was given a benefit concert in New York on 21 January 1736, the earliest account of formal music making. He finally settled in Charleston, South Carolina, where he held the post of organist at St. Philip's Church (1737–50).

Only one work of his survives, a *Magnificat in C* for eight voices and continuo in a style more appropriate to the seventeenth century. It was probably composed in Germany before he emigrated.

PAINE, JOHN KNOWLES

b. Portland, Maine, 9 January 1839
d. Cambridge, Massachusetts, 25 April 1906

John Knowles Paine.
Courtesy Harvard University Library.

Paine's ancestor Thomas Paine (1612–1706) emigrated from England in 1636, settling in Yarmouth. Cape Cod. John K. H. Paine (1787–1835), the composer's grandfather, was an organ builder in Portland whose three sons all became musicians. John Knowles Paine studied in America under Hermann Kotzschmar (1829–1909), a German émigré. From 1858 to 1861 he attended the Hochschule in Berlin where he was a pupil of Karl August Haupt. After a successful tour of England and Germany as an organist he returned to the United States in 1861.

Paine was appointed Instructor of music at Harvard in 1862, becoming Assistant professor in 1873. In 1875 he was awarded the first chair in music to be established at any university in America when he was elected a full professor at Harvard. In 1890 he received an honorary Doctorate of music. He retired in 1905, one year before his death. His pioneering attempt to bring music into the realm of serious academic study deserves a lasting tribute. His pupils included John Alden Carpenter, Frederick Converse, Arthur Foote, Edward Burlingame Hill, Daniel Gregory Mason, and William Spalding.

Paine's first significant achievement was the performance of his Mass in D under his direction at the Singakademie in Berlin on 16 February 1867. This substantial work, which shows the influence of Beethoven and Schubert, had been started as early as 1859 when he was a student in Germany. The Mass was first heard in the United States in Boston in 1868. In Portland, Maine, in 1873 he conducted the premiere of the oratorio *St. Peter.* The popularity of these works led him to compose four cantatas: *Phoebus Arise* (words by William Drummond; 1882), *The Realm of Fancy* (Keats; 1882), *The Nativity* (Milton; 1883), and *A Song of Promise,* performed at the Cincinnati Festival in 1888.

The premiere of Paine's Symphony no. 1 *in C minor* in Boston on 26 January 1876 under the direction of Theodore Thomas confirmed the composer's position as a vital pillar of musical society in New England. Symphony no. 2 *in A,* subtitled *In Springtime,* was premiered in Boston on 10 March 1880 to great acclaim. In the same year the full score was issued by Arthur P. Schmidt, the first symphony by an American to be published. Paine composed two symphonic poems, *The Tempest* (1877) and *An Island Fantasy* (1882); an overture, *As You Like It* (1876); *Duo Concertante* for violin, cello, and orchestra (1877); *Columbus March and Hymn* (1892); and an unfinished work, *Lincoln: a Tragic Tone Poem* (1904–06). His *Centennial Hymn* for the U. S. Centennial was heard at the Philadelphia Exhibition in 1876. (Wagner wrote his *Centennial March* for this same exhibition.)

For performances at Harvard of Sophocles's *Oedipus Tyrannos* in 1881 and Aristophanes' *The Birds* in 1901, Paine provided incidental music, each with an extended overture of impressive character. His opera *Azara,* a setting of the Aucassin and Nicolette legend, was completed in 1901 but never staged, although a concert performance was given in Boston in 1907. An earlier opera, *Il Pesceballo,* completed in 1862, was never performed; the score is lost. He also composed a String Quartet, written when he was only 16 years old, a Piano Trio (1874), and a Violin Sonata (1875, rev. 1905), as well as several works for organ including *Fantasia on "Ein Feste Burg"* (1860), *Concert Variations on the Austrian Hymn* (1860), and *Variations on "The Star-Spangled Banner"* (1861).

Paine was the author of a book, *The History of Music to the Death of Schubert,* published posthumously in Boston in 1907.

PALMER, ROBERT MOFFAT

b. Syracuse, New York, 2 June 1915

After graduating from the Eastman School of Music, Rochester, New York, in 1939 where he had been a pupil of Howard Hanson and Bernard Rogers, Palmer studied privately with Roy Harris, Aaron Copland, and Quincy Porter. He was awarded two Guggenheim Fellowships (1952, 1960) and a Fulbright Fellowship (1960). From 1940 to 1943 he taught at the University of Kansas. In 1943 he was appointed to the faculty of Cornell University, Ithaca, New York, retiring in 1980.

Palmer's first significant work was *Poem* for violin and orchestra, composed in 1938. In 1942 his Concerto for small orchestra (1940) was performed at the I.S.C.M. Festival in San Francisco and was awarded a prize by the National Institute of Arts and Letters. Also for orchestra are a Concerto (1943); *Symphonic Variations* (1945); *Variations, Chorale and Fugue* (1945, rev. 1954); *Symphonic Elegy "K 19" for Thomas Wolfe* (1945); *Chamber Concerto* for violin, oboe, and string orchestra (1949); Symphony no. 1 (1953); *Memorial Music* (1957); a *Centennial Overture* (1965); Symphony no. 2 (1966); *Choric Song and Toccata* for winds (1968–69); a Piano Concerto (1970); *Overture on a Southern Hymn* for band (1979); and a Concerto for two pianos, two percussion, strings, and brass (1984). Palmer has composed one work for the stage, the ballet *Irish Legend.*

Palmer's important choral pieces are a setting of Vachel Lindsay's *Abraham Lincoln Walks at Midnight* for chorus and orchestra (1948); *Slow, Slow Fresh Fount* for unaccompanied mixed voices (1953); *The Trojan Women* (Euripides) for female voices, wind, and percussion (1953, rev. 1959); a dramatic oratorio, *Nabuchodonosor* for tenor, baritone, men's chorus, brass, and percussion (1960–64); *Portents of Aquarius* for narrator, chorus, and organ (1975); and *Of Night and Sea,* a chamber cantata for four solo voices and instrumental ensemble (1956). His solo vocal music includes *Two Whitman Songs* for voice and piano (1940) and *Carmona amoris* (Sappho) for soprano, clarinet, violin, and piano (1951).

Among Palmer's numerous instrumental compositions are four string quartets (1937, 1943, 1954, 1959); two string trios (1937, 1942); two piano quartets (1947, 1975); Concerto for five instruments (1943); Piano Quintet (1950); Wind Quintet (1951); Quintet for clarinet, piano, and strings (1952, rev. 1953); a Piano Trio (1958); and *Symphonia Concertante* for nine instruments (1972). In addition he has written sonatas for violin (1942), viola (1951), trumpet (1972), and two for cello (1976–78, 1983), all with piano. Palmer composed three sonatas for solo piano (1938, 1948, 1978), one for two pianos (1944), and one for piano duet (1952).

PARKER, HORATIO WILLIAM

b. Auburndale, Massachusetts, 15 September 1863
d. Cedarhurst, New York, 18 December 1919

Parker did not take an interest in music until the age of 14, but within two years he had made remarkable progress as a pianist and had composed a number of

Horatio Parker.
MSS 32, The Horatio Parker Papers in the Irving S. Gilmore Music Library of Yale University.

songs. After studying with George Chadwick who had recently returned from Europe, Parker went to Germany in 1882 to become a pupil of Joseph Rheinberger in Munich. On his return to America in 1885 he taught at the National Conservatory in New York. In 1893 he moved to Boston and the following year was appointed Battell Professor of Music at Yale University, a post he occupied until his death. At Yale he organized the New Haven Symphony Orchestra, which, through its connection with the University, was used at times by student composers to enable them to hear their compositions. His work schedule was such that he had little time for composing himself. He retained his position as a church organist and took an active part as a conductor of choirs and orchestras, in addition to his teaching and administrative work.

Parker's reputation as a composer rests on his choral compositions. His greatest success, the oratorio *Hora Novissima,* was written in 1891, based on the Latin poem "De Contemptu Mundi" by Bernard of Cluny. He submitted *Hora Novissima* to a competition for which one of the judges was Dvořák, but the prize was awarded to another of his choral works, *The Dream King and His Love,* composed in the same year. *Hora Novissima* can be considered the most important American choral work of its time. After the first performance

in New York on 3 May 1893 under the composer, it was heard in Boston and Cincinnati. In 1899 it was performed at the Three Choirs Festival in Worcester, England, with such notable success that Parker was commissioned to compose two further works for England, *A Wanderer's Psalm* for Hereford Cathedral in 1900, and *Star Song* for the Norwich Festival in 1902.

Another oratorio, *The Legend of St. Christopher,* was produced in New York in 1898 and at Bristol, England in 1902, and the composer was given a doctorate of music at Cambridge the same year. This gives some indication of the reputation he had earned outside the United States in so short a time. His other choral works include three oratorios, *The Holy Child* (1893), *Morven and the Grail* (1915), and *The Dream of Mary* (1918); *Redemption Hymn* (1877); *The Ballad of the Knight and His Daughter* (1884); *King Trojan* (1885); *King Gorm the Grim* (1907); and a quantity of church music. Works for solo voice and orchestra include *Cáhal Mór of the Wine-red Hand,* a rhapsody for baritone (1893), and an aria, *Twilight* for mezzo-soprano (1907).

In response to a competition sponsored by the Metropolitan Opera Company with a prize of $10,000 for an opera by an American composer with a text in English, Parker composed *Mona* to a libretto by a Yale professor of English, Brian Hooker. The panel of judges, which included Chadwick, his former teacher, selected Parker's score. The story, like that of Bellini's *Norma,* is set in Roman Britain and tells of Mona, a British princess who falls in love with the son of a Roman general. *Mona* was first produced at the Metropolitan on 14 March 1912. Although the production was inadequate and ran for only four nights, critical acclaim was considerable; some who know the music have claimed it worthy of comparison with the operas of Richard Strauss. The following year Parker composed a opera to another libretto by Hooker, *Fairyland.* This, too, won a prize of $10,000 and was produced in Los Angeles in 1915, where it received six performances.

Parker's orchestral works, mostly composed while he was in Germany, include a *Concert Overture* (1884); *Venetian Overture* (1884); *Overture: Regulus* (1884); a *Symphony in C* (1884); a *Scherzo in G minor* (1886); *Overture: Count Robert of Paris* (1890); *A Northern Ballad* (1899); an *Organ Concerto in E flat* (1902); a symphonic poem, *Vathek* (1903); and several other overtures, all now long gone from the repertory. He also composed a *String Quartet* (1885), *String Octet in F* (1888), a *String Quintet* (1894), an *Organ Sonata* (1908), and many songs and piano pieces.

Parker is remembered today not so much for his music as for his long tenure at Yale and as a teacher of a distinguished group of pupils, including Seth Bingham, Charles Ives, Douglas Moore, Quincy Porter, Roger Sessions, and David Stanley Smith.

PARRIS, ROBERT

b. Philadelphia, Pennsylvania, 21 May 1924
d. Washington, D.C., 5 December 1999

Parris began piano lessons at the age of 12. He studied at the University of Pennsylvania (1941–46) and at the Juilliard School (1946–48), where he was a pupil of Peter Mennin and William Bergsma. At Tanglewood in the summers of 1950 and 1951 he received lessons from Aaron Copland and Jacques Ibert. In 1952 on a Fulbright Fellowship he spent a year at the Ecole Normale du Musique in Paris, where he was a pupil of Arthur Honegger. Parris taught at Washington State University, Pullman (1948–49) and the University of Maryland (1961–62). In 1963 he was appointed to the music faculty at George Washington University, Washington, D.C., becoming a full professor and head of the theory and composition department in 1976. From 1958 to 1979, he also served as a music critic for the *Washington Post* and *Washington Star*. He was active as a performer on piano and harpsichord.

For orchestra Parris composed two *Symphonic Movements* (1948, 1956); *Harlequin's Carnival* (1949); concertos for piano (1954), five timpani (1955), viola (1956), violin (1958), flute (1960), trombone and chamber orchestra (1964), and timpani (*The Phoenix*; 1969); *Sinfonia* for brass (1963); *The Golden Net* for chamber orchestra (1968); *The Messengers* (*Angels*; 1974, rev. 1978); *Rites of Passage* for clarinet and chamber orchestra (1978); *The Unquiet Heart* for violin and orchestra (1981); *Chamber Music,* commissioned in 1984 by the Royal Scottish National Orchestra, and *Symphonic Variations* (1987), commissioned and premiered by the National Symphony Orchestra under Mstislav Rostropovich.

Parris's choral music includes *The Hollow Men* for men's voices and chamber ensemble (1949); *Alas for the Day,* a cantata for chorus and organ (or orchestra) (1954); *Hymn for the Nativity* for chorus, brass, timpani, and percussion (1962); *Reflections on Immortality* for chorus and brass (1966); *Dirge for the New Sunrise* for mixed voices (1970); and *Walking Around* (Pablo Neruda) for chorus, violin, clarinet, piano, and percussion (1973). Among Parris's vocal works are *Three Songs* for baritone, piano, and celeste (1947); *Night* (R. Jeffers) for baritone, clarinet, and string quartet (1951); *Three Passacaglias* for soprano, violin, cello, and harpsichord to texts by W. J. Smith and Gerard Manley Hopkins (1957); *The Leaden Echo and the Golden Echo* (Hopkins) for baritone and orchestra (1960); *The Raids: 1940*, to words by Edith Sitwell for soprano, violin, and piano (1960); *Mad Scene* for soprano, two baritones, and chamber orchestra (1960); *Dreams* for soprano and seven instruments (1976), and *Cynthia's Revels* (Ben Jonson) for baritone and guitar (or piano; 1979).

Parris's instrumental compositions, a significant part of his overall output, include a Cello Sonata (1946); Sonatina for brass quintet (1948); two string trios, no. 1, *Lament for Joseph* (1948) and no. 2 (1952); two string quartets (1951, 1952); *Variations* for piano (1953); *Fantasy and Fugue* for solo cello (1954); Sonatina for winds (1954); Violin Sonata (1956); Quintet for violin, cello, flute, oboe, and bassoon (1957); Viola Sonata (1957); Trio for clarinet, cello, and piano (1959); *Cadenza, Caprice and Ricercar* for cello and piano (1961); *Lamentations and Praises* for nine brass instruments and percussion (1962); Sonatina for recorder quartet (1964); *Duo* for flute and piano (1965); Sonata for solo violin (1965); Concerto for percussion, violin, cello, and piano (1967); *St. Winifred's Well* for flute, violin, two cellos, piano, and percussion (1967); and *Book of Imaginary Beasts I* for flute, violin, cello, and piano (1972) and *II* for clarinet, violin, cello, and two percussion (1983).

Later pieces are *Three Duets* for electric guitar and amplified harpsichord (1984); *Metamorphic Variations* for flute, clarinet, violin, cello, and percussion (1986); *Thirteen Pieces* for trumpet, violin, viola, cello, and percussion (1989); and *Nocturnes I* for flute, violin, viola, cello, and percussion (1992) and *II* for clarinet, violin, viola, cello, double bass, and percussion (1994).

PARTCH, HARRY

b. Oakland, California, 24 June 1901
d. San Diego, California, 3 September 1974

Partch was brought up in southeastern Arizona, then Albuquerque, New Mexico. He began composing at the age of 14; after graduating high school, he moved to northern California, where he began to formulate a system of music based on the acoustical theories of Hermann Helmholtz. During the 1920s he devised a 37-tone-to-the-octave scale of "just" intonation, in which intervals were tuned to their simplest acoustical relationships (whole-number ratios). After experimenting with paper coverings on string fingerboards, from 1928 Partch began reworking instruments to perform the music he conceived, creating the Adapted Viola (1928) and Adapted Guitar I (1934, by which time his scale had reached 43 tones). Although he would later adapt a reed organ (Chromelodeon I, 1941), from 1938 he invented his own, more elaborate and often beautifully designed string and percussion instruments with exotic names such as Kithara, Harmonic Canon, Diamond Marimba, Cloud-Chamber Bowls, Spoils of War,

Boo, Zymo-Xyl, Quadrangularis Reversum, Ektara, and Mbira Bass Dyad.

In 1934 he was awarded a year-long Carnegie Award (traveling to Europe to do research, he met William Butler Yeats and Ezra Pound, among others), and later received Guggenheim Fellowships in 1943, 1945, and 1950. Tirelessly anti-academic, Partch nonetheless received semi-official support over the years from universities; these "residencies" contributed in the composition of five major stage works (*Oedipus*, 1950–52; *The Bewitched*, 1955; *Revelation in the Courthouse Park*, 1960; *Water Water* 1961; and *Delusion of the Fury*, 1965–66). His music began receiving attention because of these works; nonetheless, none of his works was published until 1967, and his only recordings before 1964 were self-produced.

Partch's early life in the Southwest, financial poverty during the 1920s and Depression era (he hoboed in the U.S. from 1935 to 1943), and a fiercely independent personality contributed to his isolation from the contemporary world of art music; these factors, plus dissatisfaction with the tempered scale, led him to devise a new elemental musical language. He endeavored to combine "just'" intonation with increasingly multi-layered textures and unencumbered monody, far removed from the mainstream music of the tempered scale.

As an ensemble, the instruments Partch built are reminiscent of the Balinese gamelan orchestra. The Adapted Viola has a lengthened neck, is tuned an octave below the violin and is played on the knees (like a viola da gamba). The Chromelodeon I (he adapted three more) produces the 43-tone scale and serves to tune the ensemble. The Diamond Marimba (1946), Bass Marimba (1949–50), Marimba Eroica (1951), Bamboo Marimba (Boo I; 1955), Zymo-Xyl (1963), Eucal Blossom (1964–67), Quadrangularis Reversum (1965), Boo II (1971), and Mbira Bass Dyad (1972) are all forms of marimba with wooden blocks. The three Harmonic Canons are elaborate dulcimers played with plectra or the fingers. Cloud-Chamber Bowls, originally the tops of Pyrex glass carboys (discarded by the physics laboratories at the University of California at Berkeley), are struck with soft mallets on the rim or the top to produce pitched bell-sounds.

Partch's music (almost exclusively vocal) is based on speech rhythms ("intoning"), generally allied to a text with careful control of material and texture; except where noted, he used the untempered 43-tone scale, although he occasionally expanded it when it suited his purpose. He was much influenced by classical Greek philosophy and Zen Buddhism.

Partch's earliest surviving works are *While My Heart Keeps Beating Time* for voice and piano (conventional song in tempered scale, 1929); *Seventeen Lyrics by Li Po* (1930–33); *The Lord is My Shepherd* (1930); *The Potion Scene* (from Shakespeare's *Romeo and Juliet*) (1931); *By the Waters of Babylon* (1931); and *Bitter Music* for voice(s) and piano (tempered scale, part of a "diary" of his early hoboing years; 1935–36). All the untempered works of this period were written for intoning voice and Adapted Viola; these as well as later compositions were gradually revised to take advantage of his growing ensemble.

After a virtual musical silence during his hoboing days, Partch produced *Barstow* (voice and Adapted Guitar, 1941), the first untempered piece to reflect his "own Great Depression"; its subtitle, *Eight Hitch-hiker Inscriptions From the Highway Railing at Barstow, California,* explains its inspiration. His personal experiences of traveling on American railroads were behind *U. S. Highball* (voice and Adapted Guitar, 1943). The text centers on the random thoughts of "Mac," a stand-in for Partch, conjuring passing railroad station names and the words of fellow travelers; the accompaniment imitates railroad sounds. Partch considered this the most original work he ever composed. *San Francisco* (1943) sets 1920s newsboy cries; *The Letter* (1943) brings to life a humorous letter from a fellow hobo, accompanied by plucked strings and Chromelodeon. (These four "hobo" works were reorchestrated and combined by the composer under the heading *The Wayward* in 1955.) Also from this period are *Dark Brother* (after Thomas Wolfe; 1942–43), the satirical *Yankee Doodle Fantasy* for soprano, flexatones, flute and oboe (1944), and *Two Settings from Joyce's Finnegan's Wake* (1944).

From 1944 to 1947 Partch served as a "research assistant" at the University of Wisconsin, Madison; here he wrote *Two Studies in Ancient Greek Scales* in anticipation of the completion of his theoretical and historical treatise *Genesis of a Music* (begun ca. 1927, finished 1947) and continued work on *Eleven Intrusions*, parts of which date back to 1942. Returning to northern California, Partch completed the *Intrusions*, the last of which, *Cloud Chamber Music* (1950), evokes (and quotes) the music of southern California Indians. He composed a setting of Sophocles' *Oedipus* to fulfill a commission by Mills College, Oakland, where it was premiered in 1952; it features monodic recitative relieved by hints of Japanese and Balinese music. He completed the tripartite *Plectra and Percussion Dances* (1949–52), which includes *Castor and Pollux*, an allegory of rebirth with symbolic reference to Partch's own outlook on music.

Partch moved to Sausalito in 1953 and founded his Gate 5 Ensemble for the performance and recording of his works. He built several new instruments and completed two Lewis Carroll settings (*O Frabjous Day* and

The Mock Turtle Song, 1954) as well as *Ulysses Returns to the Edge (of the World)* for two saxophones and instrumental ensemble (1955). Partch's next stage work, *The Bewitched* (1955), is a dance satire in ten scenes and an epilogue. He spent the late 1950's and early 1960's in Illinois and Ohio. After *The Bewitched* received its premiere at the University of Illinois, Urbana-Champaign (1957); he went to Evanston, Illinois, to compose the score for the film *Windsong* (1958, revised as *Daphne of the Dunes*, 1967), a retelling of the Daphne and Apollo myth directed and produced by Madeline Tourtelot; this was the first of several collaborations between the two. In 1959 he returned to Urbana-Champaign; where he wrote *Revelation in the Courthouse Park*, produced at the University of Illinois Contemporary Art Festival in 1961. This work is a parallel retelling of *The Bacchae* of Euripides, alternating a traditional presentation with a contemporary parody combining tumblers, majorettes, cheerleaders, fireworks, clog dancers, and a brass band, a spectacle not too far removed from the worlds of Gottschalk and Ives. His last important work in Urbana-Champaign, *Water Water – An Intermission,* was a commission fulfilled in a timely but unsatisfactory manner, and he soon returned to California.

In 1963 Partch moved to Petaluma, California, where he began work on what would become his last major work, *Delusion of the Fury*, by composing a set of 32 instrumental studies, or "verses," *And on the Seventh Day Petals Fell in Petaluma* (1963–66). In 1966, now in southern California, he completed *Delusion of the Fury*, a pair of mimed dramas (based on a Noh play and an African folktale) separated by a dance-song; it was premiered in Los Angeles (1969) to great acclaim. In 1966 he received an award from the National Institute of Arts and Letters for his pioneering work. His last composition, *The Dreamer That Remains* (1972), was written in Encinitas. This rather nostalgic score for a biographical film has a text for narrating and intoning voices, chorus, and instruments.

The specially constructed instruments required for the performance of his music has confined Partch's works to a relatively small audience of admirers, but recordings issued in the last three decades have enabled a wider audience to become acquainted with his original musical language. Toward the end of his life he was recognized as a prophet of the avant-garde, but his own integrity and personal idiosyncrasies kept him outside the realms of passing fashion or general acceptance. His individual genius and single-minded exploration of a new musical world could not produce a school of disciples, nor did he want one. Dean Drummond, who played with Partch in the 1960s, is now custodian to the instruments and organizes Partch

performances. Partch's work was a model for those who sought alternatives to tempered tuning (e.g., Lou Harrison, Ben Johnston) and especially for inventors of new instruments (as opposed to the sound sculptures of Europeans like the Baschet brothers). Partch's book *Genesis of a Music* was finally published in 1949; a second, expanded edition was issued in 1974, just a few months before his death.

PASATIERI, THOMAS
b. New York, New York, 20 October 1945

Pasatieri began studying piano at age nine, and a year later gave his first public performance. At the age of 16, Pasatieri won a scholarship to the Juilliard School where he was a pupil of Vittorio Giannini and Vincent Persichetti. In 1964 he began teaching at Juilliard, and five years later he was the first recipient of a doctorate in composition there. In 1965, he studied with Darius Milhaud at Aspen, Colorado. In 1969, Pasatieri joined the faculty of the Manhattan School of Music, where he remained for the next two years. He then focused on his composing work. From 1980-84, he was artistic director of the Atlanta Opera. From 1980–82, he also taught at the Cincinnati College-Conservatory of Music. In 1984, Pasatieri moved to Los Angeles, working as an orchestrator and conductor for film scores while continuing to compose. In 2003, he returned to New York City.

Pasatieri has been especially prolific in the field of opera, writing in a style clearly derived from Puccini and Menotti. To date he has composed fifteen operas. The first three, all in one act to his own texts—*La Divina,* opera buffa (1965; New York, 1966), *The Women,* chamber opera (1965; New York, 1966), and *Padrevia,* lyric tragedy (1966; Brooklyn, 1967)—can be performed as a group under the title *Triptych.* Pasatieri's first full-length opera was *The Penitentes,* composed to a text by Anne H. Bailey in 1967, but not performed until 1974 at the Aspen Festival. Another one-act opera, *Calvary,* with text by the composer after W. B. Yeats, was premiered in Bellevue, Washington (1971).

Pasatieri had two works produced in 1972. *The Black Widow*, a three-act opera based on Miguel de Unamuno's novella *Dos Madros*, was staged in Seattle, Washington. The television opera, *The Trial of Mary Lincoln,* with a libretto by Bailey, was commissioned and broadcast by public television station WNET, New York; a stage version was premiered at the San Francisco Conservatory of Music in 1987.

In March 1974, the Houston Opera premiered *The Seagull* in three acts, based on Chekhov's play (libretto:

Thomas Pasatieri.
Courtesy the composer.

clarinet, and piano (1976); *Day of Love* for soprano and piano (1979); *Permit the Voyage,* setting excerpts of works by James Agee for soprano, chorus, and orchestra (1976); and Mass for solo voices, chorus, and orchestra (1983). More recent choral works include *A Joyful Noise* (1985), *Three Mysteries* (1991), *The Harvest Frost* (1993), *Bang the Drum Loudly* (1994), and *Canticle of Praise* and *Morning's Innocent* (1995). Among Pasatieri's 400 songs are three song cycles: *Canciones del Barrio* (1983), *Sieben Lehmannlieder* (*Seven Lehmann Songs*; 1988), and *The Rustling of Angels* (12 songs; 2003).

He has also written three piano sonatas (1966, 1969, 1999); *Theatrepieces* for violin, clarinet, and piano (1987); a Sonata for viola and piano (1995); a Sonata for flute and piano (1997); and Quartet for flute, viola, cello and piano (1995). His first work for orchestra, *Invocation,* dates from 1968; later orchestral works include Serenade for violin and chamber orchestra (1992), *Concerto for Piano and Orchestra* (1993), and a Concerto for two pianos and strings (1994).

PATTISON, JOHN NELSON
b. Niagara Falls, New York, 22 October 1845
d. New York, New York, 27 July 1905

Pattison studied the piano in Germany with Sigismond Thalberg, Adolf Henselt, Hans von Bülow, and Franz Liszt. On his return to the United States he undertook a career as an accompanist for famous singers and instrumentalists. His principal composition is a symphonic poem, *Niagara*, for orchestra and military band. He also wrote a *Comedy Overture*, performed in Germany, and a *Concert Fantasia* for piano and orchestra. For his own instrument he composed over two hundred pieces.

PATTISON, LEE
b. Grand Rapids, Wisconsin, 22 July 1890
d. Claremont, California, 22 December 1966

Pattison was educated at the New England Conservatory, Boston where he was a pupil of George Chadwick. Later he went to Berlin to study the piano with Artur Schnabel and composition with Paul Juon. He was known equally as a pianist, teacher, and administrator. He made his debut as a concert pianist in Boston in 1913, and from 1921 to 1935 devoted much time to concert work. He formed a two-piano team with Guy Maier (1919–31). From 1914 to 1918 he taught at the New England Conservatory. In 1932 he joined the faculty of Sarah Lawrence College, Bronxville, New York,

Kenward Elmslie); that same year, the one-act *Signor Deluso*, based on a play by Moliere, with text by the composer, was premiered at the Wolf Trap in Vienna, Virginia. Two new operas were premiered in 1976: the three-act *Inez de Castro* (text: Bernard Stambler; Baltimore) and *Washington Square* (two acts, after the Henry James novella, adapted by Elmslie; Detroit). Pasatieri worked again with Elmslie on an adaptation of Chekov's *Three Sisters*, completing the one-act work in 1979; it remained unstaged until a 1986 premiere in Columbus, Ohio. The New York City Opera premiered *Before Breakfast,* (one act; text: Frank Corsaro), in 1980, followed a year later by a children's opera, *The Goose Girl* (text: composer, based on fairy tales by the Brothers Grimm), premiered in Fort Worth, Texas. Pasatieri's last opera to date is the one-act *Maria Elena* (text: composer; Tucson, 1983). Two "student" operas have been withdrawn: *The Trysting Place* (1964) and *Flowers of Ice* (1965).

Apart from his operas, most of Pasatieri's music is for voice: *Heloise and Abelard* for soprano, baritone, and piano (1971); *Rites of Passage* for medium voice and orchestra (1974); *Three Poems of James Agee* for voice and piano (1974); *Far From Love* for soprano,

Lee Pattison (seated at the piano).
Courtesy Scripps College Archives,
Ella Strong Denison Library.

which he left in 1937 to accept an appointment to Columbia University. From 1938 he was musical director of the American Lyric Theatre in New York. In 1941, he joined the faculty of Scripps College in Claremont, California, as professor of piano and music, where he remained through his retirement. Two recital halls on the campus now bear his name

Among his few compositions are the piano suites, *Florentine Sketches* and *Told in the Hills.* He also wrote a Violin Sonata and orchestrated Liszt's *Concerto Pathetique* for two pianos and orchestra, performed in 1921 by the Chicago Symphony Orchestra under Frederick Stock.

PATTON, WILLARD
b. *Milford, Maine, 26 May 1856*
d. *Minneapolis, Minnesota, 12 December 1924*

After studying composition with Dudley Buck, Patton established a career as a tenor and teacher of singing. Except for an oratorio, *Isaiah* (1897), and a symphonic fantasy, *The Spirit of 1861* (1915), his principal works were for the stage: a grand opera, *Pocahontas* (Minneapolis, 1911); two operettas, *The Gallant Garroter* (1882) and *La Fiesta* (1889); and two music epics, *The Star of Empire* (1900) and *Foot-stone of a Nation* (1906).

PAULUS, STEPHEN (HARRISON)
b. *Summit, New Jersey, 24 August 1949*

Paulus studied at the University of Minnesota (B.M., 1971; M.M., 1974; Ph.D., 1978), where his teachers included Paul Fetler and Dominick Argento. He has served as Composer-in-Residence with the Minnesota Orchestra (1983–87), Santa Fe Chamber Music Festival (1986), Atlanta Symphony Orchestra (1988–92), and Aspen (Colorado) Music Festival (1992).

Paulus has made a particular mark as the composer of opera. The first of these, *The Village Singer* (1977), was premiered in St. Louis in 1979. He is best-known for *The Postman Always Rings Twice* (1981), based on the novel by James Cain, first staged in St. Louis (1982). The production was taken to the Edinburgh International Festival in 1983. He has completed four more operas: *The Woodlanders,* after the novel by Thomas Hardy, performed in St Louis in 1985; *Harmonia,* an opera for children (1991); *The Woman at Otowi Crossing* (1995); and *Summer* (1997–99), based on Edith Wharton's novel (Pittsfield, Massachusetts, 1999).

Among his many orchestral works are *Spectra* for small orchestra (1980); *Translucent Landscapes* (1982); *Seven Short Pieces* (1983); Concerto for Orchestra (1983); *Ordway Overture* (1984); *Reflections: Four Movements on a Theme by Wallace Stevens* (1985); Symphony in Three Movements (*Soliloquy*; 1985);

Grand Barrier Overture (1987); *Night Speech* (1989); *Concertante* (1989); *Symphony for Strings* (1989); *Street Music* (1990); Sinfonietta (1991); and *Manhattan Sinfonietta* (1995). He has written a Divertimento for harp and chamber orchestra (1983); two violin concertos (1987, 1992); *Ice Fields* for guitar and orchestra (1990); Trumpet Concerto (1991); Organ Concerto (1982); *The Veil of Illusion,* a concerto for violin, cello, and orchestra (1994); and *Three Places of Enlightenment,* a concerto for string quartet and orchestra (1995).

Paulus has composed much instrumental music: *Duo* for clarinet and piano (1974); four pieces for chamber ensemble, *Exploration* (1974), *Village Tales: A Tree of Life* (1975), *Graphics* (1977), and *Lunar Maria* (1977); *Colors* for brass quintet (1974); Wind Suite for wind quartet (1975); *Indefinite Images* for clarinet and bassoon (1976); *Seven Translucent Landscapes* for piano (1978); two string quartets, no. 1, *Music for Contrasts* (1980) and no. 2 (1987); *Courtship Songs for a Summer's Eve* for flute, oboe, cello, and piano (1981); *Banchetto musicale* for cello and piano (1981); *Partita* for violin and piano (1986); *American Vignettes* for cello and piano (1988); *Fantasy in Three Parts* for flute and guitar (1989); *Bagatelles* for violin and piano (1990); *Quartessence* for string quartet (1990); Concerto for brass quintet (1991); *Air on Seurat: The Grand Canal* for cello and piano (1992); and *Music of the Night* for piano trio (1992).

Paulus has been equally prolific in writing for voices. His choral music includes *Three Chinese Poems* for chorus (1973); *Personals* for chorus, flute, and percussion (1975); *Canticles: Songs and Rituals for Easter and the May* (Thomas Browne) for soprano, mezzo-soprano, chorus, and orchestra (1977); *North Shore* for soloists, chorus, and orchestra (1977); *Letters for the Times* for chorus and chamber ensemble (1980); *So Hallow'd is the Time,* a Christmas cantata for treble, soprano, tenor, baritone, chorus, chamber orchestra, and organ (1980); *Echoes Between the Silent Peaks* for chorus and instrumental ensemble (1984); *Madrigali di Michelangelo* for chorus (1987); *Voices* (Rilke), a cycle for chorus and orchestra (1988); *Canticum Novum* for chorus, flute, oboe, percussion, and harp (1990); *Sacred Songs* for chorus, flute, oboe, percussion, and organ (1990); *Visions of Hildegard* for chorus and instruments (1992–95); *Whitman's Dream* for double chorus and instrumental ensemble (1994); and *The Earth Sings* for women's voices, percussion, and piano (1995). Among his works for solo voices are *Three Elizabethan Songs* for soprano and piano (1973); *Mad Book, Shadow Book: Michael Morley's Songs* (Thomas Browne) for tenor and piano (1976); *Letters From Colette* for soprano and chamber ensemble (1986); *Artsongs* for tenor and piano (1983); and two cycles, *All My Pretty Ones* (1983) and *Bitter Suite* (1987).

Paulus has written two pieces for tape, *Dance a Line* (1976) and *Prison Songs* (1976).

PELISSIER, VICTOR
b. France, c. 1740–50
d. New York, New York or New Jersey, c. 1820

Pelissier was one of many French musicians who left France after the French Revolution. A horn player and composer, he settled in Philadelphia in 1792, where he played in orchestras under Alexander Reinagle. From 1793 to 1811 he lived in New York, where he joined the orchestra of the American Company and provided much incidental music and songs for the stage, including *The Mysterious Monk* (William Dunlap; 1796, lost) and *Virgin of the Sun*, after Kotzebue (1800, lost). Other stage works performed in New York include the operas *Edwin and Angelina, or The Banditti* (1796) and *Sterne's Maria or the Vintage* (1799); the melodramas *Ariadne Abandoned by Theseus in the Isle of Naxos* (1797, lost) and *A Tale of Mystery* (with James Hewitt; 1803); the pantomimes *The Fourth of July, or Temple of American Independence* (1799, lost) and *Raymond and Agnes, or The Bleeding Nun* (1804, lost).

Pelissier composed a String Quartet and published *Pelissier's Columbian Melodies*, 12 volumes of piano arrangements of vocal and instrumental music (Philadelphia, 1811–12). He was last heard of in New York, where a benefit concert was given for him on 18 March 1817.

PERLE, GEORGE
b. Bayonne, New Jersey, 6 May 1915

Perle attended DePaul University, Chicago (1934–38) and the American Conservatory, Chicago. He was also a private pupil of Wesley LaViolette (1934–38) and Ernst Krenek; at New York University he studied musicology with Curt Sachs and Gustave Reese. In 1947 he joined the faculty of Brooklyn College. He was next appointed lecturer in musical history at the University of Louisville (1949–57); it was during this time that the Louisville Orchestra commissioned his Second Symphony (1950). From 1957 to 1961 he taught at the University of California, Davis. In 1961 he became a member of the music faculty of Queens College of the City of New York, retiring in 1984. He was visiting professor at the University of Southern California (1965), Yale (1965–66), State University of New York, Buffalo (1971–72), the University of Pennsylvania (1976, 1980), and Columbia University (1979).

Perle has been awarded two Guggenheim Fellowships (1966–67, 1974–75). His Wind Quintet no. 4 won

George Perle.
Photo: William Johnston.

the Pulitzer Prize in 1986. He is an atonalist whose personal musical language uses key as a fundamental point of reference. His book *Serial Composition and Atonality: An Introduction to the Music of Schoenberg, Berg and Webern,* first published in 1962 (6th ed., 1991), has become one of the standard publications on the theoretical aspect of modern music. His two-volume study *The Operas of Alban Berg* was issued in 1980 and 1985. His intensive study of the music of Berg led to his discovery of Berg's own annotated score of the *Lyric Suite,* leading to a new insight into the life and work of this composer. Another book, *Twelve-tone Tonality,* was published in 1977 (rev. ed., 1995). This has been followed by *The Listening Composer* (1990), *The Right Notes*: *23 Selected Essays on Twentieth Century Music* (1994), and *Style and Idea in the "Lyric Suite"* (1995).

Perle has composed three symphonies (1948, 1950, 1952); *Rhapsody for Orchestra,* a commission from the Louisville Orchestra in 1953, *Three Movements for Orchestra* (1960); *Six Bagatelles* for orchestra (1965); and a Cello Concerto (1966). Later orchestral works are Concertino for piano, winds, and timpani (1979); *A Short Symphony,* premiered on 16 August 1980 by the Boston Symphony Orchestra under Seiji Ozawa; Serenade no. 3 for piano and chamber orchestra (1983); *Dance Overture,* revised as *Dance Fantasy* (1986); two sinfoniettas (1987, 1990); two piano concertos (1990, 1991); *Adagio* (1992); and *Transcendental Modulations*

(1993), commissioned to mark the 150th anniversary of the New York Philharmonic Orchestra.

Perle has concentrated particularly on instrumental music, writing several works for unaccompanied instruments: Sonata for Viola (1942); three clarinet sonatas (1943); *Hebrew Melodies* (cello) (1945); Sonata for Cello (1947); two sonatas for violin (1959, 1963); *Monody I* for flute (1960); *Monody II* for double bass (1962); and *Three Inventions* for bassoon (1962). In addition he has composed eight string quartets (1942–88); four wind quintets (1959, 1959, 1967, 1984); *Lyric Piece* for cello and piano (1946); Sonata for Viola and Piano (1949); String Quintet (1958); *Introduction and Rondo Capriccioso* for violin and piano (1959); *Solo Partita* for violin and viola (1965); *Sonata Quasi una Fantasia* for clarinet and piano (1972); *Sonata a quattro* for flute, clarinet, violin, and cello (1982); *Sonata a cinque* for bass trombone, clarinet, violin, cello, and piano (1986); *New Fanfares* for brass ensemble (1987); *Lyric Intermezzo* for 15 players (1987); *For Piano and Winds* (1988); *Nightsong* for flute, clarinet, violin, cello, and piano (1988); *Duos* for horn and string quartet (1995); and *Critical Moments* for flute, clarinet, violin, cello, piano, and percussion (1996). He has also written two serenades for chamber ensemble (1962, 1968), the first with a solo viola.

In 1974 he completed a major work for chorus and orchestra, *Songs of Praise and Lamentation,* dedicated to the memory of the conductor and scholar Noah Greenberg. Dating from the same year is *Sonnets to Orpheus* (Rilke) for chorus and orchestra. For voice and piano he has composed *Three Rilke Songs* (1941) and *Thirteen Dickinson Songs* (1978).

Perle's piano music includes a *Little Suite* (1939); *Piece* (1945); *Six Piano Preludes* (1946); Sonata (1950); *Three Inventions* (1957); *Short Sonata* (1964); *Toccata* (1969); *Suite in C* (1970); *Six Etudes* (1975); *Ballade* (1980–81); *Six New Etudes* (1984); *Lyric Intermezzo* (1987); *Phantasieplay* (1994); *Celebratory Inventions* (1995); *Chansons cachées* (1997); *Musical Offering* (left hand alone) (1999); and *Nine Bagatelles* (1999).

PERSICHETTI, VINCENT (LUDWIG)
b. *Philadelphia, Pennsylvania, 6 June 1915*
d. *Philadelphia, Pennsylvania, 15 August 1987*

The son of Italian immigrants, Persichetti received piano lessons as a child and by the age of 11 was performing professionally. He gained his first appointment as an organist when only 15. After graduating from Combs College in Philadelphia in 1936, he studied conducting under Fritz Reiner at the Curtis Institute, Philadelphia. In 1939 he attended the Philadelphia

Conservatory and studied with Olga Samaroff and Paul Nordoff. Later he was a pupil of Roy Harris at Colorado College, Colorado Springs.

Persichetti was appointed head of the composition department at Combs College in 1939, moving in 1941 to a similar post at the Philadelphia Conservatory. In 1947 he joined the faculty of the Juilliard School, becoming chairman of the composition department in 1963; he remained on Juilliard's faculty until the year of his death. In 1952 he was appointed director of publications for Elkan-Vogel, Inc, which later became a part of the Theodore Presser company, where Persichetti was an executive until the mid-1980s. Persichetti was the recipient of three Guggenheim Fellowships and many other honors.

Persichetti chose classical forms for many of his works; indeed, a major part of his output falls into the three "S's": symphonies, serenades, and sonatas. He composed nine symphonies: no. 1 (1942); no. 2 (1943); no. 3 (1947); no. 4 (1951); no. 5 for strings (1953), commissioned by the Louisville Orchestra; no. 6 for band (1956); no. 7, *Liturgical*, commissioned by the St. Louis Symphony Orchestra in 1959; no. 8 (1967), commissioned by the Baldwin-Wallace Conservatory (Berea, Ohio); and no. 9, *Sinfonia Janiculum*, performed by the Philadelphia Orchestra in March 1971.

Vincent Persichetti.
William Schuman Photo Collection #24, neg #158. Courtesy The Juilliard School.

Persichetti's serenades are scored for various instrumental forces: no. 1 is for ten wind instruments (1929); no. 2 for piano (1929); no. 3 for piano trio (1941); no. 4 for violin and piano (1945); no. 5 for orchestra (1950); no. 6 for trombone, viola, and cello (1950); no. 7 for piano (1952); no. 8 for piano duet (1954); no. 9 for soprano and alto recorders (1956); no. 10 for flute and harp (1957); no. 11 for band (1960); no. 12 for solo tuba (1961); no. 13 for two clarinets (1963); no. 14 for solo cello; and no. 15 for harpsichord (1984).

Persichetti made an impressive contribution to the keyboard repertory with 12 piano sonatas (1939–80), six sonatinas (1950–56), eight sonatas for harpsichord (1951–84), a Sonata for two pianos (1940), and Concerto for piano duet (1952). *Three Toccatinas* for piano were commissioned by the University of Maryland for the 1980 International Piano Competition. For organ he composed a Sonata (1960); *Shimah B'koli* (Psalm 130; 1962); *Chorale Prelude: Drop, Drop Slow Tears* (1966); and *Parable VI* (1961). There are also four works for pedals alone: *Sonatine* (1940), *Do Not Go Gentle* (1974), *Dryden Liturgical Suite* (1979), and *Auden Variations* (1977).

Persichetti's orchestral music includes a *Dance Overture* (1942); *Fables* for narrator and orchestra (1943); *The Hollow Men* for trumpet and strings (1944); *Fairy Tale* (1950); *Introit* for strings (1964); *Night Dances* (1970); and *A Lincoln Address* for narrator and orchestra (1972). He also wrote a Piano Concertino (1940), a Piano Concerto (1962), and a Concerto for English horn, composed in 1977 for the New York Philharmonic Orchestra and winner of the first Kennedy Center Friedheim Award (1978). For the stage he composed an opera, *The Sibyl* (1976), performed in Philadelphia in 1985; a ballet, *Then One Day* (1944), later withdrawn; and *King Lear*, composed for Martha Graham (1948).

Persichetti wrote a number of important choral items. Among these are *Magnificat* for chorus and piano (1940); *Stabat Mater* (1963) and *Te Deum* (1963) for chorus and orchestra; *Spring Cantata* (1963) and *Winter Cantata* (1964), both for female voices; *Celebration* for chorus and wind ensemble (1966); *The Pleiades* for chorus, trumpet, and strings (1967); *The Creation* for soloists, chorus, and orchestra (1969); *Glad and Very* for chorus and piano (1964); and *Flower Songs* (Cantata No. 6) for chorus and strings (1984). There are also a number of pieces for a cappella voices, including *Proverbs* (1948), a Mass (1960), and *Four Cummings Choruses* (1964).

Among his chamber music are four string quartets (1939, 1944, 1961, 1972); two piano quintets (1940, 1955); a Suite for violin and cello (1940); Sonata for solo violin (1940); *Fantasy* for violin and piano (1941); *Pastoral* for wind quintet (1943); a Sonata for solo cello (1952); and *Infanta Marina* for viola and piano (1960).

Persichetti later composed a sequence of pieces entitled *Parables,* mostly for unaccompanied instruments: I for flute (1965); II, brass quintet (1968), III, oboe (1968); IV, bassoon (1969); V, carillon (1969); VI, organ (1971); VII, harp (1971); VIII, horn (1972); IX, band (1972); X, string quartet no. 4 (1972); XI, alto saxophone (1972); XII, piccolo (1973); XIII, clarinet (1973); XIV, trumpet (1973); XV, English horn (1973); XVI, trombone (1974); XVII, double bass (1974); XVIII, viola (1974); XIX, piano (1974); XX, *The Sibyl* (opera) (1975); XXI, guitar (1978); XXII, tuba (1981); XXIII, piano trio (1981); and XXIV, harpsichord (1982).

Besides the Sixth Symphony, Serenade no. 11, and *Parable IX,* there are several major works for band, including Divertimento in five movements (1950); *Psalm* (1952); *Pageant* (1953); *Bagatelles* (1961); *Chorale Prelude*: *So Pure the Star* (1962); *Masquerade* (1963); *Chorale Prelude*: *Turn Not Thy Face* (1966); *O Cool is the Valley* (1971); and *Chorale Prelude*: *O God Unseen* (1984).

Persichetti's vocal music includes the song cycle *Harmonium* to words by Wallace Stevens (1951); *Sara Teasdale Songs* (1957); *James Joyce Songs* (1957); *Hilaire Belloc Songs* (1957); *Carl Sandburg Songs* (1957); *Robert Frost Songs* (1957); *Emily Dickinson Songs* (1957); and *A Net of Fireflies* (1970), 17 songs on Japanese texts.

Persichetti was the author of a textbook, *Twentieth Century Harmony: Creative Aspects and Practice,* published in 1961, and, with Flora Rheta Schreiber, a study of the music of William Schuman, published in 1953.

PETER, JOHANN FRIEDRICH

b. Heerendijk, Holland, 19 May 1746
d. Bethlehem, Pennsylvania, 13 July 1813

Peter was born in Holland of German parents. He received thorough training in music at a seminary in Barby, Saxony, and in May 1770 crossed the Atlantic to join the Moravian community in Nazareth, Pennsylvania, settling in 1773 in the neighboring community of Bethlehem. Although himself not a Moravian, he became one of the most distinguished musicians of that sect. At the age of 24 he was appointed music director at Nazareth; he later acquired a similar position in Bethlehem. He also spent several years in North Carolina, Maryland, and New Jersey.

Peter's vocal and instrumental compositions are numerous, including over one hundred anthems with organ and orchestral accompaniment. Notable among these are several for soprano and strings: *I Will Make an Everlasting Covenant* (1782), *The Days of All Thy Sorrows Shall Have an Ending, Lead Me in Thy Truth,*

and *The Lord is in His Temple. It is a Precious Thing,* for soprano, baritone, chorus, and strings was composed in Nazareth in August 1772.

Six string quintets written in 1789 in Salem, North Carolina, where Peter had been living for ten years, are his most important surviving instrumental works. They are probably the earliest chamber music composed in America. Peter adopted classical models for his compositions, and although expressing no great originality, these quintets are particularly well written for the instruments and reveal a decorative character in the melodic lines, akin to the colorful Moravian folk art, which adds a particular charm to the music.

PHILE, PHILLIP

b. Germany, c. 1734
d. Philadelphia, Pennsylvania, between 1 August and 9 November 1793

During the Revolutionary War, Phile served in the Pennsylvania German Regiment. From 1784 he lived in Philadelphia, where he was active as a violinist and composer. He is credited with the composition of the *President's March* to which Joseph Hopkinson, son of Francis Hopkinson, added the words of "Hail Columbia." It was first published by Benjamin Carr in *The Gentleman's Amusement,* issued in Philadelphia in 1793. His only other known composition is a Violin Concerto, performed in Philadelphia on 12 April 1787. He died of yellow fever.

PHILLIPS, BURRILL

b. Omaha, Nebraska, 9 November 1907
d. Berkeley, California, 22 June 1998

Phillips was educated at the Denver College of Music, Colorado (1924–28) with Edwin Stringham and at the Eastman School of Music, Rochester, New York (1928–33), where his teachers were Howard Hanson and Bernard Rogers. After graduating in 1933 he joined the faculty at the Eastman School. In 1949 he took up a post at the University of Illinois, where he was professor of music and director of the division of theory and composition until he resigned in 1964 to devote himself to composition. He was later a visiting professor at the University of Hawaii, the Eastman School, the Juilliard School (1968–69), and Cornell University (1972–73). He was granted Guggenheim Fellowships in 1942 and 1961, and received an award from the American Academy of Arts and Letters in 1944. A Fulbright Grant in 1960 allowed him to be at the University of Barcelona, Spain.

Phillips is best remembered for his valuable work

as a teacher. His first success as a composer came with *Selections from McGuffey's Readers*, written in 1933. This entertainment in three movements derives its title from a set of American school books published between 1836 and 1857. The last movement in particular, *The Midnight Ride of Paul Revere,* possesses a vivid pictorial character that will ensure its continued popularity.

Phillips's many orchestral works include *Grotesque Dance for a Projected Ballet* (1932); *Sinfonia Concertante* (1933); *Dance Overture* (1935); *Courthouse Square* (1935), produced as a ballet in 1937; a Concerto for piano and chamber orchestra, first performed in 1943; *Music for Strings* (1938); a *Concert Piece, "American Dance"* for bassoon and strings (1940); *Three Satiric Fragments* (1941); *Scherzo* (1945), commissioned by the League of Composers; a *Tom Paine Overture,* commissioned by the Kousssevitzky Foundation in 1946; *Scena* for small orchestra (1946); *Concerto Grosso* for string quartet and chamber orchestra (1949); Divertimento for strings (1950); and Triple Concerto for viola, clarinet, and piano (1953). Three later orchestral compositions are *Perspectives in a Labyrinth* for three string orchestras (1962), *Soleriana Concertante* (1965), and *Theatre Dances* (1966). He also wrote two works for band, *Fantasia* (1968) and *Yellowstone, Yates and Yosemite* for tenor saxophone and band (1972).

The chamber opera *Don't We All* dates from 1947. In 1981 he completed a three-act opera, *The Unforgiven,* with libretto by Alberta Phillips. He composed five ballet scores: *Katmanusha* (1932–33), *The Princess and the Puppet* (1935), *Play Ball* (1938), *Step Into My Parlor* (1942), and *La Pinata,* commissioned in 1968 by the Juilliard for José Limón. He also provided incidental music for *Dr Faustus* (Marlowe) (1957).

Phillips's major choral works are *Declaratives* for female voices and small orchestra (1943); *What Will Love Do?* and *The Hag* (Herrick) for female voices (1949); a cantata, *The Return of Odysseus* for baritone, narrator, chorus, and orchestra, commissioned by the Fromm Foundation in 1956; *Nine Latin Motets* for unaccompanied voices (1958); *The First Day of the World* for male voices and piano (1958); and *Canzona V* for chorus and piano (1971). For solo voices and instruments he wrote *Canzona III* (1964); *Canzona IV* (1967); *Eva Learns a Little* (1974); *The Recesses of My House* (1978); and *Letters From Italy Hill* to texts by Alberta Phillips (1984).

Among Phillips's many instrumental compositions are two string quartets (1939, 1958); a Trio for three trumpets (1937); *Piece* for six trombones (1940); a Violin Sonata (1942); a Cello Sonata (1946); a *Partita* for piano quartet (1947); *Conversations and Colloquies* for two violins and two violas (1950); *Four Figures in Time* for flute and piano (1953); *Music for This Time of Year*

for wind quintet (1954); *Dialogues* for violin and viola (1954); Quartet for oboe and strings (1967); *Intrada* for wind ensemble (1975); *Scena da Camera* for violin and cello (1978); and *Canzona VI* for wind quintet (1985). He also composed many piano pieces, including four sonatas (1942, 1949, 1953, 1960); *Suite: A Set of Informalities* (1935); *Toccata* (1944); *Three Divertimenti* (1946); *Commentaries* (1983); and a Serenade for piano duet (1956).

PICKER, TOBIAS
b. New York, New York, 18 July 1954

While still a teenager Picker gained musical experience as a pianist at the Martha Graham School for Contemporary Dance. Later he studied with Charles Wuorinen at the Manhattan School of Music (M.B., 1976), the Juilliard School with Elliott Carter (M.M., 1978), and with Milton Babbitt at Princeton University. He was awarded a Guggenheim Fellowship in 1981 and was Composer-in-Residence with the Houston Symphony Orchestra (1985–87).

Picker has composed three symphonies: no. 1 (1982), performed in San Francisco in the following year; no. 2, *Aussöhnung* (*Reconciliation*) for soprano and orchestra, on texts by Goethe (1984); and no. 3 for strings (1989). Among his works for solo instruments and

Tobias Picker.
Photograph © Xavier Guardans, courtesy the composer.

orchestra are three piano concertos: no. 1 (1980), no. 2, *Keys to the City,* written in 1983 to mark the centenary of the Brooklyn Bridge, and no. 3 (1986), performed in Honolulu, Hawaii in 1988; a Violin Concerto (1981); *Romances and Interludes* (after Schumann) for oboe and orchestra (1990); *Bang* (1992) for piano and orchestra, written for the 150th season of the New York Philharmonic Orchestra; a Viola Concerto (1992–94); and a Cello Concerto, commissioned in 2000 by the B.B.C. in London for Paul Watkins. His orchestral works include *The Encantades* (Henry Melville) for narrator and orchestra (1983), recorded by Sir John Gielgud; *Old and Lost Rivers* (1986); *Two Fantasias* (1991); and *Séance* (1991).

In recent years Picker has earned a reputation in the field of opera. His first essay in the medium, *Emmeline,* staged by the Sante Fe Opera in 1996, is on the subject of a young single mother who gives away her baby, only to marry him twenty years later. *Fantastic Mr Fox,* based on a story by Roald Dahl, was performed by Los Angeles Opera in 1998. His greatest success has been *Thérèse Raquin,* a setting of the Emile Zola novel, commissioned jointly by Dallas Opera, L'Opera de Montreal and San Diego Opera. It was premiered in Dallas on 28 November 2001. Currently he is writing an opera based on Theodore Dreiser's novel *An American Tragedy* for the New York Metropolitan season of 2004–05.

Among Picker's instrumental compositions are four sextets: no. 1 (1973), no. 2 (1976), no. 3 (1977), and no. 4, *The Blue Hula* (1981); *When Soft Voices Die* for piano (1977); *Rhapsody* for violin and piano (1978); *Octet* (1978); *Nova* for violin, viola, cello, double bass, and piano (1979); *Romance* for violin and piano (1979); *Pian-o-rama* for two pianos (1981); Serenade for piano and wind quintet (1983); String Quartet: *New Memories* (1986–87); Piano Quintet (1988); and a Violin Sonata, *Invisible Lilacs* (1992). *Tres sonetos de amor* for baritone and orchestra was premiered in Houston, Texas in October 2002.

PINKHAM, DANIEL (ROGERS JR.)

b. Lynn, Massachusetts, 5 June 1923

Pinkham studied with Walter Piston, Archibald Davison, and Aaron Copland at Harvard University and was later a pupil of Arthur Honegger, Samuel Barber, and Nadia Boulanger. He also received lessons in harpsichord from Wanda Landowska and organ from E. Power Biggs. He is a noted conductor, organist, and harpsichord player in addition to his activities as a composer. After a brief spell of teaching at Simmons College, Boston University, he was appointed director of music at King's Chapel, Boston in 1958, retiring after 42 years of service in 2000 and joining the faculty of

the New England Conservatory of Music the following year.

Much of Pinkam's early music is neo-classical in idiom with a particular emphasis on sonorities, exemplified by his frequent use of unusual instrumental combinations such as are found in his *Concerto for Celesta and Harpsichord Soli* (1954). His own extensive experience as a keyboard player of Baroque music has left an impression upon his compositions.

Choral music has a particular importance in Pinkham's output. These works include *Glory to God* for double chorus (1951); a *Wedding Cantata* (1956); a *Christmas Cantata* (*Sinfonia Sacra*; 1957); an *Easter Cantata* for chorus, brass, timpani, celesta, and percussion (1961); *An Emily Dickinson Mosaic* for female voices and chamber orchestra (1962); *Festival Magnificat and Nunc Dimittis* for chorus and organ (1962); a Requiem Mass for soloists, chorus, and brass (1963); *Stabat Mater* (1965); *St. Mark Passion* (1966); *Lamentations of Jeremiah* (1967); and a dramatic cantata, *Jonah,* for soloists, chorus, and orchestra (1967). The titles alone in many cases reveal Pinkham's debt to music of earlier times.

From 1970 Pinkham began combining voices, instruments, and recorded tape. He produced several important short choral works incorporating this technique, including *In the Beginning of Creation* for chorus and tape (1970); *Seven Last Words* for tenor, baritone, bass, chorus, organ, and tape (1971); *To Troubled Friends* for chorus, strings, and tape (1972); *Daniel in the Lion's Den* for soloists, chorus, two pianos, percussion, and tape (1973); *Four Elegies* for tenor, chorus, small orchestra, and tape (1975); and *The Call of Isaiah* for chorus, organ, percussion, and tape (1977). Other choral works of this period are *Magnificat* for soprano, female chorus, and instrumental ensemble (1967); *Ascension Cantata* for chorus and wind ensemble (1970); *Hezekiah* for chorus (1979); *Before the Dust Returns* for chorus and orchestra (1981); and *The Conversion of St. Paul* (1981).

Pinkham's most recent choral pieces are *Lauds* for two voices, two horns, double bass, organ, and percussion (1984); *In Heaven Soaring Up* for alto, tenor, chorus, oboe, and harp (1985); a second setting of *Stabat Mater* (1990); *Advent Cantata* (1991); *The Creation of the World* for narrator, chorus, brass quintet, and organ (1994); *The Guiding Star* for tenor, chorus, brass quintet, and organ (1994); *The White Raven* for soprano, chorus, and orchestra (1995); *Jubilee and Psalm* (1999); *Christmas Jubilations* for choir and wind quintet (2001); *Covenant Motets* for chorus and organ (2001); and *Revelation Motets* for chorus and organ (2002).

Pinkham has written four symphonies (1960, 1963, 1985, 1990); a Piano Concertino (1950); two violin concertos (1956, 1968); three organ concertos (1970,

1995, 1997); Divertimento for oboe and strings; and *Concerto Piccolo* for piccolo and orchestra (1989). Other orchestral pieces include *Catacoustical Measures,* composed in 1962 to test the acoustics of the Lincoln Center's Philharmonic Hall; *Signs of the Zodiac* in 12 short movements, with an optional part for narrator (1964); and *The Seven Deadly Sins* for organ, orchestra, and tape (1974). His latest works include *Overture Concertante* (1992); *Music for an Indian Summer* for harp and woodwind (1997); *Evening Music* for brass and glockenspiel (1998); Triple Concerto for violin, viola, cello, and strings (2000); and *Make Way for Ducklings* for narrator and orchestra (2002).

Other ensemble compositions are those for original instrumental groupings: *Concertante* for violin and harpsichord soloists, celesta, and strings (1955); *Concertante* for organ, celesta, and percussion (1958); *Concertante* for organ, brass quartet, and percussion (1964); and *Concertante* for harpsichord, guitar, strings, and percussion (1968). He has also written three sonatas for organ and strings (1943, 1954, 1986). For more orthodox combinations there are *Cantilena and Capriccio* for violin and harpsichord (1956); *Fanfare, Aria and Echo* (1967); two brass quintets (1968, 1983); a Brass Trio (1969); *Variations* for oboe and organ (1969); *Masks* for harpsichord and chamber ensemble (1977); Serenade for trumpet and wind ensemble (1979); a String Quartet (1990); a Reed Trio (1994); and a String Trio (1998).

Other instrumental works include *Eclogue* for flute, harpsichord, and off-stage handbells (1965); *Toccatas for the Vault of Heaven* for organ and tape (1972); two organ sonatas, no. 1, with two violins and cello and no. 2, with string quartet; *Liturgies* for timpani and organ (1974); *Diversions* for organ and harp (1980); *Sonata da chiesa* for viola and organ (1988); *Morning Music* for organ and brass quintet (1994); *Sagas* for guitar and cello (1997); *Odes* for English horn and organ; two pieces for piano, four hands, *Quarries* (1999) and *Weather Report* (2000); and Brass Trio no. 2 (2002). Among Pinkham's works for organ solo are *Revelations*; *The Four Winds*; *Four Epigrams: Flute Soliloquy, Interlude, Reminiscence, and Acclamation*; *Blessings* (1977); *Epiphanies* (1978); *Proverbs* (1979); *Psalms* (with tape) (1983); and *A Proclamation* (1984). Pinkham has written many songs, including four song cycles: *Eight Poems of G. M. Hopkins* for baritone and viola (1964); *Letters from St. Paul* for voice and organ (1963); *Charm Me Asleep* for voice and guitar (1977); and *Transitions* for voice and bassoon or piano (1979). Among his solo vocal works are *The Song of Jephtha's Daughter* for soprano and piano (1963); *Safe in Their Alabaster Chambers* (Emily Dickinson) for mezzo-soprano and tape (1972); *Manger Scenes* for soprano and piano (1980); *The Death of the Witch of Endor* for alto,

harpsichord, and percussion (1981); *Music in the Manger* for soprano and harpsichord (1981); and *The Wellesley Hills Psalm Book* for medium voice and organ (1983).

For the stage Pinkham has composed an opera, *The Dreadful Dining Car* (after Mark Twain) (1982); a chamber opera, *The Garden of Artemis* (1948); two chancel operas, *The Passion of Judas* (1976) and *The Descent into Hell* (1980); a comic opera, *Garden Party* (1977); the one-act opera *The Cask of Amontillado* (Poe; 2001); and a version of John Gay's *The Beggar's Opera* (1953).

PISK, PAUL AMADEUS
b. Vienna, Austria, 16 May 1893
d. Los Angeles, California, 12 January 1990

Pisk studied with Guido Adler at the University of Vienna, where he wrote a doctoral thesis on the music of Jacob Handl (1910). He graduated in 1919 from the Vienna Conservatory, where he had been a pupil of Franz Schreker. He also received private lessons from Arnold Schoenberg. He was a founder member of the I.S.C.M. and editor of *Wiener Arbeiterzeitung* (1921–34). From 1922 to 1934 he was director of music at the Volkshochschule in Vienna. Pisk emigrated to the United States in 1936; in 1937 he was appointed to the music faculty of the University of Redlands, California, where he served as head of the department of music

Paul Pisk.
Courtesy Paul Pisk Collection, Washington University Libraries, Gaylord Music Library Special Collections.

(1948–51). He taught at the University of Texas, Austin (1951–63) and at Washington University, St. Louis (1963–72). From 1972 until his death he lived in Los Angeles as a teacher and musicologist. He became an American citizen in 1941.

In his music Pisk combined atonality with classical forms. For orchestra he wrote a *Symphonic Overture* (1918); *Partita* (1924), performed at the I.S.C.M. Festival in Prague in 1925; Divertimento (1933–35); *Passacaglia* (1944); *Suite on American Folk Songs* (1944); *Bucolic Suite* for strings (1946); *Adagio and Fugue* (1948–54); *Rococo Suite* for viola and orchestra (1953); *Baroque Chamber Concerto* (1953); *Elegy* for strings (1958); *Three Ceremonial Rites* (1958); and *Sonnet* for chamber orchestra (1960).

Pisk's considerable output of instrumental pieces includes four violin sonatas (1921, 1927, 1939, 1977); a String Quartet (1924); a Piano Trio (1933–35); a Wind Quartet (1945); a Clarinet Sonata (1947); a Horn Sonata (1953); a Flute Sonata (1954); a String Trio (1958); a Wind Quintet (1958); *Music* for violin, clarinet, cello, and bassoon (1962); *Envoi* for oboe, clarinet, bassoon, and string trio (1964); *Perpetuum Mobile* for organ and brass (1968); *Discussions* for oboe, clarinet, bassoon, viola, and cello (1974); a Brass Quintet (1976); *Three Movement* for violin and piano (1978); Trio for oboe, clarinet, and bassoon (1979); *Music* for oboe and piano (1982); and a Suite for solo cello (1983).

Pisk composed an opera, *Schattenseite* (1930–31) and a ballet, *American Suite* (1948). His vocal music includes two cantatas, *Die Neue Stadt* (1926) and *The Trail of Life* (1956); Requiem for baritone and orchestra (1942); *A Toccata of Galuppi* (Browning) for soprano and orchestra (1947); a song cycle, *The Labyrinth* to poems by Borges and Updike for voice and piano; and a work for narrator and orchestra, *Der grosse Regenmacher* (1931).

PISTON, WALTER (HAMOR JR.)

b. Rockland, Maine, 20 January 1894
d. Belmont, Massachusetts, 12 November 1976

On his father's side, Piston was of Italian descent, the family name originally being Pistone. He studied at the Massachusetts Normal Art School; later he turned to music and learned to play piano and violin, thereafter earning a living performing in hotels and restaurants. After serving as a bandsman in the U.S. Navy during the First World War, he entered Harvard University. In 1924, a John Knowles Paine Fellowship enabled him to study in Paris, where he was a pupil of Nadia Boulanger for two years. He also received lessons from Paul Dukas at the Ecole Normale de Musique. On his return to the United States in 1926, he joined the music faculty at Harvard, becoming professor of music in 1944, later succeeding E. B. Hill as chairman of the music department; he retired in 1960.

Piston's European training is evident in the emphasis upon counterpoint and classical forms in much of his music. Almost all of his output was orchestral and instrumental, with no opera or songs and few choral compositions. He was awarded a Guggenheim Fellowship in 1935 and two Pulitzer Prizes (1948, 1961). He was elected a Fellow of the American Academies of Arts and Sciences and Arts and Letters.

A major part of his talent was devoted to orchestral music: the eight symphonies form the backbone to his work. All are scored for large orchestra with triple woodwind. Symphony no. 1 was commissioned by the League of Composers in 1936 and performed by the Boston Symphony Orchestra under the composer's direction in 1938. Symphony no. 2, commissioned by the Alice M. Ditson Fund, was heard in Washington, D.C., in 1944. It won the New York Critics' Circle Award the following year. Symphony no. 3 (1947), performed in 1948 by Koussevitzky and the Boston Symphony Orchestra, received the Pulitzer Prize. It is dedicated to the memory of Nadia Koussevitzky. Symphony no. 4 (1949–50) was commissioned by the University of Minnesota and performed by the Minneapolis Symphony Orchestra under Antal Dorati in 1951. Symphony no. 5 was commissioned to celebrate the 50th anniversary of the Juilliard School. It received its premiere by the Juilliard Orchestra under Jean Morel in New York in 1956. Symphony no. 6 was commissioned to celebrate the 75th anniversary of the Boston Symphony Orchestra, which performed it under the direction of Charles Munch in 1955. Symphony no. 7, composed for the Philadelphia Orchestra in 1960, received the Pulitzer Prize in 1961. Symphony no. 8, first performed in Boston under Erich Leinsdorf, marks a change in Piston's style with a use of the 12-note system in melodic development.

Piston's first success came with the performance of his *Symphonic Piece* (1927) by the Boston Symphony Orchestra, under Piston's direction in March 1928. Suite no. 1 (1929) for orchestra received its premiere in March 1930 by the Philadelphia Orchestra, again led by the composer. The Boston Symphony Orchestra introduced the Concerto for Orchestra in 1934, conducted by the composer. His next orchestral work, *Prelude and Fugue* (1934), was played by the Cleveland Orchestra in March 1936. The Sinfonietta, performed by the Zighera Chamber Orchestra in 1941, was later heard at the I.S.C.M. Festival in Amsterdam in 1948.

The events of the Second World War provided the stimulus for two short pieces: *Fanfare for the Fighting French*, one of a set of fanfares commissioned by the Cincinnati Symphony Orchestra in 1942, and *Fugue on a Victory Tune,* performed in New York in 1944. A *Symphonic Suite* (Suite no. 2), commissioned by the Dallas Symphony Orchestra, dates from 1948. Also in 1948, *Toccata for Orchestra* was performed by the Orchestre Nationale de Paris under Charles Munch in Bridgeport, Connecticut, while the orchestra was touring the United States.

In 1956 the Louisville Orchestra commissioned *Serenata. Three New England Sketches* were first heard at the Worcester (Massachusetts) Music Festival in October 1959. *Symphonic Prelude* (1960) was commissioned by the Association of Women's Committees for Symphonic Orchestras and performed by the Cleveland Orchestra in April 1961. *Lincoln Center Overture,* commissioned for the opening of the New York performing arts center, was first performed there in September 1962. *Ricercare* for orchestra was also given its premiere in New York in March 1968, to celebrate the 125th anniversary of the New York Philharmonic Orchestra. Two other short orchestral works are *Variations on a Theme by E. B. Hill* (1963) and *Pine Tree Fantasy* (1965). Piston's final purely orchestral work was *Bicentennial Fanfare,* performed by the Cincinnati Symphony Orchestra on 14 November 1975.

Piston wrote several compositions for solo instruments and orchestra. The first of these, a neo-classical Concertino for piano and orchestra, was commissioned by CBS and performed by Jesus Maria Sanroma in June 1937. Violin Concerto no. 1 received its premiere in March 1940 with Ruth Posselt as soloist. A *Prelude and Allegro* for organ and strings was performed in Boston in 1943. *Fantasy* for English horn, strings, and harp (1952) was also first heard in Boston in 1954. The Viola Concerto, completed in 1958 and performed in Boston, won the New York Music Critics' Circle Award for that year. There followed a Concerto for two pianos (1959); Violin Concerto no. 2, commissioned by the Ford Foundation for Joseph Fuchs, who performed it in Pittsburgh in 1960; and a *Capriccio* for harp and strings (1963). *Variations* for cello and orchestra (1966) was written for Mstislav Rostropovich, who was the soloist in New York in March 1967. The Concerto for Clarinet received its first performance at Dartmouth College, Hanover, New Hampshire in August 1967. Piston's last works for solo instruments were *Fantasia* for violin and orchestra (1970), first heard in March 1973; a Flute Concerto (1971), premiered in September 1972 by Doriot Anthony Dwyer with the Boston Symphony Orchestra; and a Concerto for string quartet, wind instruments, and percussion, completed in 1976 for the Portland (Maine) Symphony Orchestra.

Piston wrote only two choral works: *Carnival Song* (1938), a setting of Italian words by Lorenzo de Medici for male voices and brass, performed by the Harvard Glee Club in 1940; and *Psalm and Prayer of David* for mixed voices and seven instruments, which dates from 1958.

Piston's best-known composition is the score he wrote for the ballet *The Incredible Flutist,* presented by the Boston "Pops" Orchestra in 1938. The concert suite adapted two years later has been played throughout the world. For symphonic band he wrote an intermezzo, *Tunbridge Fair* (1950).

Piston's earliest instrumental items were *Three Pieces* for flute, clarinet, and bassoon (1926); a Flute Sonata (1930), performed at the I.S.C.M. Festival in Barcelona in 1936; and a Suite for oboe and piano (1931). These were followed by String Quartet no. 1 (1933); Piano Trio no. 1 (1933); Quartet no. 2 (1935); a Violin Sonata (1939); *Interlude* for viola and piano (1942); Quintet for flute and strings (1942); *Partita* for violin, viola, and organ (1944); Sonatina for violin and harpsichord (1945); Divertimento for nine instruments (1946); Quartet no. 3 (1947); Piano Quintet (1949); *Duo* for viola and cello (1949); Quartet no. 4 (1951); Wind Quintet (1956); Quartet no. 5 (1961); String Sextet (1964); Piano Quartet (1964); and Piano Trio no. 2 (1966). His last instrumental works were a *Duo* for cello and piano (1972); *Three Counterpoints* for string trio (1973); *Nonet* for brass; and *Study in Sonority* for ten violins.

Piston's keyboard works are few in number. His earliest extant piece is a Piano Sonata, dating from 1926. A *Piano Passacaglia* was published in 1943. He also wrote a *Chromatic Study on BACH* for organ (1940).

Piston was widely known as the author of four textbooks used by musicians throughout the world: *Principles of Harmonic Analysis* (1933), *Harmony* (1941, rev. 1948), *Counterpoint* (1947), and *Orchestration* (1955).

PLESKOW, RAOUL

b. Vienna, Austria, 12 October 1931

Pleskow was taken to the United States as a child in 1939, becoming an American citizen in 1945. He received his musical education at the Juilliard School (1950–52), Queens College, New York (1952–56), where he was a pupil of Karol Rathaus, and at Columbia University (1956–58), where he received composition lessons from Otto Luening. In 1959 he joined the music faculty at C. W. Post College, Greenvale, New York where he was later appointed chairman of the music department; he retired from teaching in 1984, although he remained Composer-in-Residence there. He has won numerous awards and honors, including awards from the Ford Foundation (1972) and the Guggenheim Foundation (1977).

Pleskow was much influenced by the music of Stefan Wolpe, suggested by similarities in the titles of many of his works. For orchestra Pleskow has written *Two Movements* (1968), *Music for Orchestra* (1968), *Bagatelles* (1981), *Six Epigrams* (1985), *Consort* for strings (1988), and *Epigram* for piano and strings (1996). Most of his other compositions are for various instrumental groups, sometimes with voices. These include *Movements* for flute, cello, and piano (1962); *Music* for two pianos (1965); *Movement* for oboe, violin, and piano (1966); *Music* for seven players (1966); *Bagatelles* for solo violin (1967); *Three Pieces* for piano, four hands (1968); *Movement* for nine players (1968); *For Five Players and Baritone* (1969); *Duo* for cello and piano (1969); *Three Movements* for quintet (1975); *Per Vege Viene* for violin and piano (1970); *Pentimento* for piano (1974); Trio for flute, cello, and piano (1978); a String Quartet (1979); *Four Pieces* for flute, cello, and piano (1979); *Variations on a Lyric Fragment* for cello and piano (1980); *Four Short Pieces* for seven players (1981); *Divertimento: Sua sei canzoni* for five players (1984); *Intrada* for flute, clarinet, violin, and cello (1984); and *Composition* for four instruments (1987).

Pleskow's few vocal works include two cantatas for soloists, chorus, and orchestra (1975, 1979); *Motet and Madrigal* for soprano, tenor, and ensemble; *Six Brief Verses* for two sopranos or female voices, strings, and piano (1983); *Paumanok* for soprano, chorus, and chamber ensemble (1985); Serenade for chorus and orchestra (1988); *Chamber Setting* for soprano, flute, violin, cello, and piano (1998); and *Tre Ballati* for two sopranos and two string quartets (2001).

POLIN, CLAIRE

b. *Philadelphia, Pennsylvania, 1 January 1926*
d. *Merion, Pennsylvania, 6 December 1995*

In addition to her activities as a composer, Polin was a flutist. She was educated at the Philadelphia Conservatory of Music; Temple University, Philadelphia; and the Juilliard School. She studied composition with Vincent Persichetti, Peter Mennin, Roger Sessions, and Lukas Foss and flute with William Kincaid. She taught at the Philadelphia Musical Academy (1949–64) and was a professor at Rutgers University, Camden (1962–91). She died of complications from Parkinson's disease and cancer.

Polin's principal orchestral works are two symphonies, no. 1 (1961) and no. 2, *Korean* (1976); *Scenes from Gilgamesh* for flute and strings (1972); *Amphion* (1978); and *Mythos* for harp and strings (1982). Most of her other compositions are instrumental, often incorporating a part for her instrument. These include

three string quartets (1953, 1959, 1969); a Sonata for flute and piano (1954); *Structures* for flute and piano (1964); *Consecutivo* for flute, clarinet, violin, cello, and piano (1964); *Summer Setting* for harp (1966); *Cader Idris* for brass quintet (1970); *The Journey of Owain Madoc* for brass quintet and percussion (1971); *Makimono I* for flute, clarinet, violin, cello, and piano (1972); *Makimono II* for brass quintet (1972); Sonata for flute and harp (1972); *Aderyn Pur* for flute, alto saxophone, and bird tape (1973); *Tower Sonata* for flute, clarinet, and bassoon (1974); *The Death of Procris* for flute and tuba (1974); *Serpentine* for viola solo (1974); *Telemannicon* for oboe and tape (1975); *Klockwork* for alto saxophone, bassoon, and horn (1977); *Synaulia* for flute, clarinet, and tape (1977); *Vigniatures* for harp and violin (1980); *Felina* for harp and violin (1982); *Res naturae* for wind quintet (1982); *Kuequenaku-Cambriola* for piano and percussion (1982); *Walum Olum* for clarinet, viola, and piano (1984); *Freltic Sun* for violin and piano (1986); *Garden of Earthly Delights* for wind quintet (1987); *Regensburg* for flute, guitar, and dancer (1989); *Phantasmagora* for piano duet (1990); and *Taliesin* for flute, oboe, and cello (1993).

Polin's vocal music includes *Welsh Bardic Odes* for soprano, flute, and piano (1956); *Canticles* for men's voices (1959); *Lorca Songs* for voices and piano (1965); *Infinito* for soprano, narrator, chorus, and alto saxophone (1973); *Biblical Madrigals* for chorus (1974); *Windsongs* for soprano and guitar (1974); *Isaiah Syndrome* for chorus (1980); *Mystic Rondo* for voice, violin, and piano (1987–88); and *Paraselene* for soprano, flute, and piano.

With William Kincaid, she published several books on flute playing, including *The Art and Practice of the Modern Flute* (3 volumes, 1967) and *The Advanced Flutist* (2 volumes, 1974). She also wrote two books on musicology, *Music of the Ancient East* and *The Ap Huw Manuscript*.

POND, SYLVANUS BILLINGS

b. *Milford, Vermont or Worcester County, Massachusetts, 5 April 1792*
d. *Brooklyn, New York, 12 March 1871*

Pond was conductor of the New York Sacred Music Society and director of the New York Academy of Music. In 1832 he joined the publishing house of Firth and Hall; in 1842 the firm became Firth, Pond and Company, which published the songs of Stephen Foster. Pond himself composed hymn tunes, including *Armenia* (1835) and *Franklin Square* (1850). He issued three collections, *Union Melodies* (1838), *The U. S. Psalmody* (1841), and *The Book of Praise* (1866).

PORTER, (WILLIAM) QUINCY

b. New Haven, Connecticut, 7 February 1897
d. Bethany, Connecticut, 12 November 1966

Porter's father and grandfather were professors of divinity at Yale University. He himself graduated from Yale in 1921, where his teachers had been Horatio Parker and David Stanley Smith. He went to Paris, where he received composition lessons from Vincent d'Indy at the Schola Cantorum (1920–21) and studied violin with Lucien Capet. On his return to the United States Porter became a pupil of Ernest Bloch in Cleveland (1921–22) and earned his living by playing the violin in various theater orchestras. In 1922 he was appointed to the faculty of the Cleveland Institute of Music. A Guggenheim Fellowship enabled him to be in Paris from 1928 to 1931.

After a further year at the Cleveland Institute, he moved to Vassar College, Poughkeepsie, New York, where he remained as professor and conductor of the orchestra until 1938. That year he succeeded Frederick Converse as Dean of the New England Conservatory in Boston, becoming director in 1942. In 1946 he returned to Yale as Battell Professor of Music; he retired in 1965. With Bauer, Copland, Hanson, and Luening, he was one of the founders of the American Music Center in New York in 1940.

Porter's compositions betray the characteristics of works by a teacher, always workmanlike in construction and usually based on classical forms. Porter's first orchestral work, *Ukranian Suite* for strings, was performed in Rochester, New York in 1925. It was followed in 1926 by Suite in C minor. He conducted the premiere of *Poem and Dance* in Cleveland in 1932. *Dance in Three Time* for chamber orchestra was heard in St. Louis in 1937. Symphony no. 1, written in 1934, was also directed by the composer in a New York concert in 1938. *Four Dances for Radio* (1938) was commissioned by CBS. Porter's next orchestral works were *Music for Strings* (1941), *Fantasy on a Pastoral Theme* for organ and strings (1942), and *The Moving Tide* (1944).

As a performer himself, Porter took special care over what is probably his finest orchestral composition, the Concerto for Viola. Dedicated to William Primrose, it was given its first performance in 1948 with Paul Doktor as soloist. There followed three more works for solo instruments: *Fantasy* for cello and small orchestra (1950); *Concerto Concertante* for two pianos and orchestra, commissioned by the Louisville Orchestra in 1954 and recipient of a Pulitzer Prize; and Concerto for harpsichord and chamber orchestra (1959). The symphonic suite *New England Episodes* was commissioned by the International American Festival held in Washington, D.C. in 1958. It was followed by a Con-

Quincy Porter.
Courtesy Manuscript and Archives, Yale University Library.

certo for wind orchestra, completed in 1959. Symphony no. 2 (1962) was commissioned by the Louisville Orchestra and performed in January 1964. Porter's last orchestral work was the *Ohio Overture* (1963).

The experience gained as a string player led Porter to instrumental music as his principal means of expression. His outstanding contribution to American music is the set of ten string quartets, composed at regular intervals throughout his career (1923, 1925, 1930, 1931, 1935, 1936, 1943, 1950, 1955, and 1965). Other instrumental works are *Andante* for string quartet (1917); *In Monasterio* for string quartet (1927); a Piano Quintet (1927); *Little Trio* for flute, violin, and viola (1928); Clarinet Quintet (1929); *Quintet on a Childhood Theme* for flute and strings (1940); *String Sextet on Slavic Folk Themes* 1947); Divertimento for wind quintet (1960); and Oboe Quintet (1966). Appropriately for one who excelled in chamber music, his last composition, completed only a few months before his death, was a Quintet for oboe and strings. As if to signify his long association with university life, he quotes the student song "Gaudeamus Igitur" at the end of the third movement. Somewhat prophetically he gave the piece the subtitle *Elegie*.

Porter also composed two violin sonatas (1926, 1929); a Suite for solo viola (1930); a Piano Sonata

(1930); a Horn Sonata (1946); *Four Pieces* for violin and piano (1947); and two *Duos*, no. 1 for violin and viola (1954) and no. 2 for flute and harp (1957). He wrote an impressive *Toccata, Adagio and Finale* for organ (1929–32) and many piano solos.

Porter produced no choral music and only three extended works for the voice: *Three Mimes* for voices, string quartet, and percussion (1933), from the incidental music for T.S. Eliot's *Sweeney Agonistes*; *This is the House That Jack Built* for soprano and chamber orchestra (1938); and *The Desolate City* for baritone and orchestra (1950). He also composed incidental music for Shakespeare's *A Midsummer Night's Dream* (1926), *Antony and Cleopatra* (1935), and *The Merry Wives of Windsor* (1954); *The Sunken Bell* (Hauptmann; 1926); *Song for a Broken Horn* (H. M. Mills; 1952); and *The Madwoman of Chaillot* (Giraudoux; 1957).

He was the author of two short books: *The Study of Sixteenth Century Counterpoint Based on Lassus* and *The Study of Fugue Based on the "Well-Tempered Clavier."*

POWELL, JOHN
b. Richmond, Virginia, 6 September 1882
d. Charlottesville, Virginia, 15 August 1963

When very young, Powell showed signs of marked musical ability. He studied at the University of Virginia. In Vienna he studied piano with Theodor Leschetizky and composition with Karl Navrátil (1902–07). In 1907 he made his debut as a concert pianist in Berlin, and later toured Europe and the United States. Throughout his career he was primarily a concert pianist rather than a composer.

Powell came to prominence with *Rhapsodie Nègre* for piano and orchestra, given its premiere in Carnegie Hall in March 1918. It was inspired by Joseph Conrad's novel *Heart of Darkness*. This was one of the first attempts by an American composer to write a serious piece in an African-American idiom and was therefore a precursor of *Rhapsody in Blue*, although it lacked the sophistication and jazz influence that affected Gershwin's work. *Rhapsodie Nègre* enjoyed considerable success throughout the United States and Europe, often with the composer playing the solo part.

In 1906, Powell composed the first of his three violin sonatas, *Sonata* Virginianesque; in 1921, he wrote an overture, *In Old Virginia,* which showed his continued interest in the music of the American South. Later he turned to American folk songs of Anglo-Scottish origin, and made a particular study of the music of the Appalachian Mountains. He considered folk music of basic importance to the artistic life of the country. In 1931 he wrote *Natchez-on-the-Hill* for orchestra, based on three dance tunes. In this and a later work, *A Set of*

Three (1935), Powell maintained the essential characteristics of the original melodies in a way that resembles the treatment of folk songs by Vaughan Williams and other English composers. He retained also the modal implications of the themes he used.

In addition to the works mentioned, Powell composed a Violin Concerto in E (1910); a Piano Concerto in B minor (138); a Symphony in A, *The Virginian,* first performed in 1947 by the Detroit Symphony Orchestra; and several shorter orchestral pieces, including a Suite, *At the Fair* for chamber orchestra (1925). He also wrote a Christmas cantata, *The Babe at Bethlehem* (1934), and an opera, *Judith and Holofernes.* His other instrumental music includes two string quartets (1907, 1922); three piano sonatas: no. 1, *Psychologique* (on the sermon of St. Paul on "the wages of sin"; 1905), no. 2, *Sonata Nobile* (1907), and no. 3, *Sonata Teutonica* (1913); and many piano pieces, including *Suite: In the South* (1906), *At the Fair* (1907), and *Dirge,* a sextet for two pianos, 12 hands (1928).

POWELL, MEL(VIN EPSTEIN)
b. New York, New York, 12 February 1923
d. Valencia, California, 24 April 1998

Powell began his career as a jazz pianist and arranger with Benny Goodman's band in 1941. He was also associated with the Glenn Miller Band and other jazz ensembles of the 1940's. He studied with Bernard Wagenaar and Joseph Schillinger in New York (1937–39) and Ernst Toch in Los Angeles (1946–48). Later he was a pupil of Paul Hindemith at Yale University. He taught at Mannes School of Music and Queens College, New York, and was appointed to the Yale faculty in 1957. There he founded the Electronic Music Studio and was its director from 1960 to 1969. From 1972 to 1976 he was provost of the California Institute of Arts at Valencia, becoming professor in 1978; he retired in 1998.

Most of Powell's works are for small instrumental ensembles. His few compositions for orchestra employ expanded ensembles. These include *Cantilena concertante* for English horn and orchestra (1948); *Symphonic Suite* (1949); *Intrada and Variants* (1956); *Stanzas* for chamber orchestra (1957); *Setting* for cello and orchestra (1961); *Immobiles I to IV* for orchestra and/or tape (1967); *Setting II* for cello and orchestra (1968); *Immobiles V* for orchestra and tape (1969); *Modules: An Interlude* for chamber orchestra (1985); and *Duplications,* a concerto for two pianos and orchestra, performed in Los Angeles, which won the Pulitzer Prize in 1990. *Capriccio* for symphonic band dates from 1950.

Powell's early instrumental music is neo-classical

Mel Powell.
Courtesy The California Institute of the Arts; MSS 70, The Mel Powell Papers in the Irving S. Gilmore Music Library of Yale University.

in character: String Quartet no. 1, *Beethoven Analogs* (1949); *Recitative and Toccata Percossa* for harpsichord (1953); Piano Trio (1954); Divertimento for violin and harp (1955); and Divertimento for five wind instruments (1955). Over the next two years he progressed towards atonality. This transition is seen clearly in a Piano Quintet (1957) and the *Eight Miniatures* for flute, oboe, string trio, and harpsichord (1958), in essence a Baroque ensemble piece fusing Schoenbergian serialism with Hindemith-like tonality.

After these pieces he wrote *Filigree Setting* for string quartet (1959) and *Improvisations* for clarinet, violin, and piano (1962). His other instrumental pieces include *Setting* for wind instruments, violin, and tape (1972); *Cantilena* for trombone and tape (1982); String Quartet no. 2 (1982); *Intermezzo* for piano (1984); Wind Quintet (1985); *Setting* for guitar (1986); *Invocation* for solo cello (1987); *Amy-abilities* for percussion (1987); *Three Madrigals* for solo flute (1988); Sextet (1996); and Sonatina for solo flute (1996).

Electronic Setting (1960) was Powell's first electronic composition; this led to the foundation of the Electronic Music Studio at Yale. *Second Electronic Setting* (1961), *Events* (1963), and *Analogs I to IV (Machine Music)* (1966) are further explorations of this medium. Also for tape are *Variations* (1976), a ballet,

Inscape (1976), *Three Synthesizer Settings* (1970–80), and *Computer Prelude* (1988).

Powell's vocal compositions include *Sweet Lovers Love the Spring* (Shakespeare) for female voices and piano (1953); *Haiku Settings* for voice and piano (1961); *Six Love Songs* for voice and piano (1961); *Two Prayer Settings* for tenor, oboe, violin, and cello (1963); *Cantilena* for soprano, violin, and tape (1970); *Settings* for soprano and chamber ensemble (1979); *Little Companion Pieces* for soprano and string quartet (1979); *Strand Settings: Darker,* a song cycle for mezzo-soprano and tape (1983); *Letter to a Young Composer* for soprano and piano (1987); *Die Violine* for soprano, violin, and piano (1987); a song cycle, *Levertov Breviary* (1997); and *Seven Miniatures: Women Poets of China* for voice and harp (1998).

PRATT, SILAS G(AMALIEL)
b. Addison, Vermont, 4 August 1846
d. Pittsburgh, Pennsylvania, 30 October 1916

After leaving school Pratt worked as a clerk in order to earn money to travel to Germany (1868), where he studied for three years with Theodor Kullak and Friedrich Kiel in Berlin. He returned to Chicago, where his First Symphony was performed in 1871. Back in Europe in 1875, he became a piano pupil of Liszt at Weimar and Bayreuth. While there he composed a *Centennial Overture,* which he conducted in Berlin in 1876, and a Second Symphony, *The Prodigal Son* (1876), which he conducted at the Crystal Palace in London in 1885.

Pratt's first two operas, *Lucille* (original title: *Antonio,* 1870–71; rev. 1887) and *Zenobia, Queen of Palmyra* (1882), were produced in Chicago. His third opera, *Ollanta,* was never staged. A cantata, *The Last Inca,* dates from 1879.

From 1888 to 1902 Pratt taught at the Metropolitan School of Music in New York. In 1905, he published a tutor, *The Pianist's Mental Velocity.* In 1906 he settled in Pittsburgh, where he founded the Pratt Institute of Music and Art.

Pratt's compositions were usually conceived on a grand scale, but he was essentially unsuccessful in his desire to become an important nationalistic composer. Most of his works reflect a pride in American history, as their titles indicate: *The War in Song* (1891), a choral fantasy representing the battles fought during the American Civil War; *The Triumph of Columbus* for choir and orchestra (1892); *America,* a scenic cantata (1894); *A Lincoln Symphony*; and *The Tragedy of the Deep* (in memory of the *Titanic* disaster) (1912).

Although Pratt was a dynamic personality, little of his work survived. An anecdote indicative of his self-esteem relates that Wagner said to him, "You are the

Richard Wagner of the United States," to which Pratt replied, "and you are the Silas G. Pratt of Germany."

PREVIN, ANDRÉ (GEORGE) (ANDREAS LUDWIG PRIWIN)
b. Berlin, Germany, 6 April 1930

At the age of six Previn received piano lessons at the Berlin Hochschule für Musik. In 1938 the family moved to Paris, where the young André was a pupil of Marcel Dupre. The political situation in Europe forced them to emigrate to Los Angeles, where his father's cousin, Charles Previn, was music director at the Universal film studios. In Los Angeles he studied composition with Mario Castelnuovo-Tedesco, Joseph Achron, and Ernst Toch.

While only 16 years old, Previn joined the M.G.M. film studios as a composer and arranger. During his years in the film industry he served as musical director for 19 movies, winning the Academy Award four times for *Gigi* (1958), *Porgy and Bess* (1959), *Irma la Douce* (1963), and *My Fair Lady* (1964). Notable among his 38 original film scores are *Kim* (1950), *Elmer Gantry* (1960), *The Four Horsemen of the Apocalypse* (1961), *Long Day's Journey into Night* (1962), *Inside Daisy Clover* (1965), *Valley of the Dolls* (1967), and *Six Weeks* (1982). He collaborated with Alan Jay Lerner on the musical *Coco* for Broadway (1970) and with Johnny Mercer on *The Good Companions* for London's West End (1974).

In the late 1960s, Previn left the world of the cinema where he had earned an enviable reputation to concentrate on conducting symphony orchestras. He became conductor of the Houston Symphony Orchestra in 1967 in succession to Sir John Barbirolli. During his two years there he showed remarkable talent and in 1968 he was appointed musical director of the London Symphony Orchestra, a post he held until 1979; he was created Conductor Emeritus when he left. Other orchestras he directed were the Pittsburgh Symphony (1976–84), Royal Philharmonic Orchestra, London (1985–92), and Los Angeles Philharmonic (1985–90). He took over the Oslo Philharmonic in 2002. From time to time Previn has also continued to perform jazz, for which he has an outstanding natural gift, especially as a pianist in small groups.

Among his orchestral works are an *Overture to a Comedy*; a *Symphony for Strings* (1962); a Cello Concerto (1967); a Guitar Concerto, written for John Williams in 1971; *Principals* for the Pittsburgh Symphony Orchestra (1980); *Reflections* for English horn, cello, and orchestra, composed in 1981 for the Philadelphia Orchestra; Divertimento (1982); a Piano Concerto for Vladimir Ashkenazy (1995); *Diversions*, a Vienna Phil-

harmonic Orchestra commission; and a Violin Concerto, written for his wife, Anne-Sophie Mutter, performed in San Francisco in 2002.

Previn's many instrumental pieces include *Two Little Serenades* for violin and piano (1970); a Wind Quintet (1973); a Brass Quintet (1974); *Four Outings*, composed in 1976 for the Philip Jones Brass Ensemble; *Peaches* for flute and piano (1978); *Triolets* for brass ensemble (1985); *A Wedding Waltz* for two oboes and piano (1986); a Cello Sonata for Yo-Yo Ma (1993); Trio for oboe, bassoon, and piano (1994); *Violin Sonata: Vineyard* (1994); Bassoon Sonata (1997); *Hoch soll er Leben* for brass quintet (1997); *Tango, Song and Dance* for violin and piano (1998); a Clarinet Sonata (2002); and *Quartet with Soprano* (2002). His piano music includes *Paraphrase on a Theme of William Walton* (1973), *Six Preludes* (1974), *The Invisible Drummer* (1975), *Five Pages from My Calendar* (1977), *Matthew's Piano Book* (1979), and *Variations on a Theme of Haydn* (1990).

Especially in recent years, Previn has composed a number of important solo vocal items: *Five Songs to Poems by Philip Larkin*, performed in London in October 1977; *Honey and Rue*, a cycle to poems by Toni Morrison, for soprano and orchestra, performed by Kathleen Battle in 1992; *Sallie Chisum Remembers Billy the Kid* (Michael Ondantje) for soprano and piano (or orchestra; 1994); *Four Songs* (Toni Morrison) for soprano, cello, and piano (1994); *Vocalise* for soprano, cello, and piano (1995); *Two Remembrances* for soprano, alto flute, and piano (1995); *The Magic Number* for soprano and orchestra (1995); *Three Dickinson Songs* for soprano and orchestra (1999); and *The Giraffes Go to Hamburg* (Karen Blixen) for soprano, alto flute, and piano (2000).

On 1 July 1977 at the Royal Festival Hall, London, Previn conducted the first performance of his score for Tom Stoppard's play *Every Good Boy Deserves Favour*, which concerns a Russian dissident who is imprisoned in a mental hospital. The music is more than incidental, providing an integral part of the story. A version for theater orchestra was produced at the Mermaid Theatre, London, in the following year. The American premiere was given at the Metropolitan Opera House, New York in the summer of 1978 with the composer conducting the Pittsburgh Symphony Orchestra.

Previn's opera *A Streetcar Named Desire*, based on Tennessee Williams's play, was premiered on 19 September 1998 by the San Francisco Opera, with Renee Fleming in the leading role. It was first heard in Europe in December 2001 at the Oper der Rhin, Strassburg, Germany. He is currently writing a second opera, based on the novel *Silk* by Alessandro Baricco.

In addition to successful television programs presenting music, Previn is the author of four books: *Music Face to Face* (1971), *Orchestra* (1979), *André*

Previn's Guide to the Orchestra (1983), and an entertaining and perceptive insight into the film music industry, *No Minor Chords*: *My Days in Hollywood* (1991).

PRICE, FLORENCE (BEATRICE) (NÉE SMITH)
b. Little Rock, Arkansas, 9 April 1888
d. Chicago, Illinois, 3 June 1953

Price was the first African-American female composer to have her music performed by professional musicians. She studied piano, organ, and composition at the New England Conservatory, Boston (1902–06), where her teachers included George Chadwick, Frederick Converse, and Benjamin Cutter. After graduating at the age of 18 she undertook teaching at Shorter College, North Little Rock, Arkansas. In 1910 she was appointed head of music at Clark College, Atlanta, Georgia. After her marriage to a lawyer in 1912, she gave up teaching. Faced with racial hostility, the Prices settled in Chicago in 1927, where she resumed her studies, taking lessons with Leo Sowerby at the American Conservatory of Music and with Carl Busch and Wesley LaViolette at the Chicago Musical College.

The score of an early Symphony composed in Boston has been lost. In 1932 her Symphony no. 1 in E minor, composed in 1925, won the Wanamaker Competition in 1932; it was performed in the following year by the Chicago Symphony Orchestra under Frederick Stock. She composed at least four other symphonies: no. 2 in D minor, *Mississippi River* (1934); no. 3 in C minor, performed in Detroit in 1940; no. 4 in G minor; and *Colonial Dance Symphony*. Also for orchestra Price wrote *Ethiopia's Shadow in America* (1932); Piano Concerto in F minor in one movement (1934); two violin concertos, no. 1 and no. 2 (1952); *Chicago Suite*; *Dances in the Canebrakes*; two *Concert Overtures*; *Rhapsody* for piano and orchestra; *Songs of the Oak*, a tone poem; and a *Suite of Dances*.

Price was highly regarded for her solo songs, which were taken up by leading singers of the day. Among these are *Dreamin' Town* (1934), *Songs to the Dark Virgin* (Langston Hughes; 1941), *Night* (1946), *Out of the South Blew a Wind* (1946), *An April Day* (1949), and *Dawn's Awakening*. Her arrangements of spirituals were also widely popular. Among her choral works are four pieces for female voices: *The Moon Bridge* (1930), *Witch of the Meadow* (1947), *Sea Gulls* (1951), and *Nature's Music* (1953); a setting of Vachel Lindsay's poem *Abraham Lincoln Walks at Midnight* for chorus and orchestra; *After the First and Sixth Commandments* for chorus; *Communion Service in F* for choir and organ; and *The Wind and the Sea* for chorus and orchestra.

Florence Price.
Photo: G. Nelidoff, Chicago. Florence Beatrice Smith Price Collection, MC 988, Box 1, Folder 12, Item 1, Special Collections, University of Arkansas Libraries, Fayetteville.

For piano she wrote *At the Cotton Gin* (1928), a Sonata in E minor (1932), *Bayou Dance* (1938), *Dance of the Cotton Bottoms* (1938), and *Three Little Negro Dances* (1939). She also composed two piano quintets.

PROTHEROE, DANIEL
b. Gwngiedd, near Ystradgynlais, Wales, 5 November 1866
d. Chicago, Illinois, 25 February 1934

Before leaving Wales to settle in the United States in 1886, Protheroe had established himself as a conductor of men's choirs. From 1886 to 1894 he was a choral conductor in Scranton, Pennsylvania. In 1894 he settled in Milwaukee, where he undertook a career as a teacher and singer. From 1909 to his death in 1934, he lived in Chicago.

Protheroe is remembered for his original compositions and arrangements for men's chorus. In addition he wrote a symphonic poem, *In the Cambrian Hills*, and a String Quartet in A minor. He compiled a hymnal for the Welsh Presbyterian Church and wrote a book, *A Course in Harmony and Choral Conducting*.

R

RAPHLING, SAM

b. Fort Worth, Texas, 19 March 1910
d. New York, New York, April 1988

After studying at the Chicago Musical College under Rudolf Ganz and at the Berlin Hochschule für Musik, Raphling followed a career as composer, pianist, and teacher. He taught at the Chicago Musical College (1937–45) and was a piano soloist with the Chicago Symphony Orchestra (1940–44).

Among his orchestral works are four symphonies (1946, 1947, 1960, 1960); four piano concertos; a Symphony for chamber orchestra; a Symphony for brass; a Concerto for piano and percussion; a Trombone Concerto; a Timpani Concerto; a Concerto for tuned percussion; a *Concertante* for glockenspiel; *Passacaglia* (*Abraham Lincoln Walks at Midnight*); *Cowboy Rhapsody* for violin and orchestra; *Suite for Strings* (1946); *Lively Overture*; Trumpet Concerto; *Ticker-tape Parade Overture*; *Israel Rhapsody* (1957) and *Minstrel's Rhapsody* (1962), both for piano and orchestra; *Kibbutz*; *Carnival of the Mind*; *The Mystic Trumpeter*; and *Rhapsody* for Ondes Martenot.

Raphling's many instrumental works include three violin sonatas; six piano sonatas; two string quartets; two suites for solo percussion and piano; a Horn Sonata; *24 Etudes* for piano; and *Warble for Lilac Time* for flute and strings.

For the stage Raphael wrote five operas: *President Lincoln* (four acts); *Nathan the Wise* (one act); *Johnny Pye and the Fool Killers* (two acts); *Feathertop* (one act); and an opera for children, *Liar, Liar* (one act). His many songs include three cycles: *Dream Keeper* (Langston Hughes), *Four Poems of Carl Sandburg*, and *Spoon River Anthology* (Edgar Lee Masters).

RATHAUS, KAROL

b. Tarnopol, Galicia, Poland, 16 September 1895
d. New York, New York, 21 November 1954

Rathaus studied in Vienna with Franz Schreker (1919, 1921–22) and in Berlin (1920–21, 1922–23). From 1925 to 1933 he taught at the Berlin Hochschule, but resigned because of Nazi pressure. He went first to Paris

Karol Rathaus.
Courtesy Queens College Archives.

(1933–34), then to London (1934–38), before settling in New York in 1938, where he taught at Queens College (1940–54). His musical language, derived from Schreker, is tonal but very chromatic, making some use of polytonality.

For orchestra Rathaus composed three symphonies (1922, 1923, 1942) and numerous shorter pieces, including *Four Dance Studies* (1923); *Intermezzo Giocoso* (1928); Suite for violin and orchestra (1929); Serenade (1931); *Notturno,* subtitled *Jacob's Dream* (1938); *Prelude and Gigue* (1939); *Music for Strings (Adagio)* (1941); *Polonaise Symphonique* (1943); *Vision Dramatique* (1945); and a work with the impressive title *Contrapuntal Tryptich.* A Suite for Orchestra was performed at the I.S.C.M. Festival in Liège (1930); a Piano Concerto (1939) was heard at the I.S.C.M. Festival in San Francisco (1942).

Among Rathaus's last compositions are *Salisbury Cove* for orchestra (1949), inspired by the coastline of Maine; *Sinfonia Concertante* (1950); and a *Prelude* (1953), commissioned by the Louisville Orchestra. Rathaus also provided incidental music for a number of plays including 's *The Merchant of Venice* (Shakespeare), *Herodes and Marianne* (Hebbel), and *Uriel Acosta* (Gutzkow) (1936, rev. 1947).

Before going to America, Rathaus composed four film scores in Europe: *Film Record of the Eucharistic Congress* (1926), *The Trunks of Mr. O. F.* (1932), *The Loves of a Dictator* (1935), and *Broken Blossoms* (1936).

His instrumental music includes five string quartets (1921, 1925, 1936, 1946, 1954); the Third Quartet was given at the 1938 I.S.C.M. Festival in Oxford, England. He also wrote four piano sonatas (1922, 1924, 1927, and 1946); two violin sonatas (1924, 1938); *Little Serenade* for clarinet, bassoon, trumpet, horn, and piano (1927); Trio for clarinet, violin and piano (1944); *Rapsodia Notturna* for cello and piano (1950); and *Trio Serenade* for piano trio (1953).

Among his few vocal compositions are a Requiem for chorus and piano (1941); *Lament* from *Iphigenia in Aulis* (Euripides), for chorus and instruments (1947); a cantata, *O Juvenes* (1947); *Diapason* for baritone, chorus, and orchestra (1950); and *Choral Songs* (1952).

For the stage Rathaus composed an opera, *Strange Soil* (1930), and two ballets, *The Last Pierrot* (Berlin, 1927) and *Le Lion Amoureux* (1934; Covent Garden, London).

READ, DANIEL

b. Attleborough, Massachusetts, 16 November 1757
d. New Haven, Connecticut, 4 December 1836

Read began in business as a publisher and bookseller, but later became a successful manufacturer of ivory combs in Hartford, Connecticut. He compiled and published *The American Singing Book* in 1785, followed three years later by *An Introduction to Psalmody.* He issued two further volumes of church music, *The Columbian Harmonist* (1793) and *The Litchfield Collection* (1806). He was also the editor of *The New Haven Collection of Sacred Music* (1818). In 1786 he began a monthly journal, *The American Musical Magazine,* which included music by American and European composers.

Read's own compositions were mainly hymn tunes; notably *Amity; Calvary; Greenwich; Judgment; Lisbon; Madison; Mortality; Russia;* and *Stafford,* and "fuging pieces," notably *Sherburne* to the words of *While Shepherds Watched Their Flocks.*

READ, GARDNER

b. Evanston, Illinois, 2 January 1913

Read studied privately at Northwestern University, Evanston (1930–32) while still a high school student, and at the Eastman School of Music, Rochester, New York (1932–37), where his teachers included Bernard Rogers and Howard Hanson. In 1938 on a Cromwell Fellowship he went to Europe, where he received lessons from Ildebrando Pizzetti in Rome and Jean Sibelius in Finland. However, the outbreak of the Second World War caused him to return home earlier than intended. After studying with Aaron Copland at the Berkshire Music Center in 1941, he served as head of composition at the St. Louis Institute of Music (1941–43). From 1943 to 1945 he headed the composition department of the Kansas City Conservatory of Music, followed by a similar position at the Cleveland Institute of Music (1945–48). From 1948 to 1978 he was professor of composition and Composer-in-Residence at the Boston University School for the Arts; he is now professor emeritus.

Read's Symphony no. 1 in A minor won a $1,000 prize offered by the New York Philharmonic Orchestra which performed it under Barbirolli in Novemebr 1937. Symphony no. 2 in E-flat minor, given its premiere in Boston in November 1943, was awarded the Paderewski Prize. He has completed two other symphonies, no. 3 (1948) and no. 4 (1958). Among his many orchestral scores are *The Lotus Eaters* (1932); *The Painted Desert* (1933); *Sketches of the City,* after poems by Carl Sandburg (1933); *Prelude and Toccata* (1937); *Suite for Strings* (1937); *Petite Pastorale* for small orchestra (1940); *Pan e Dafni* (1940); *Three Satirical Sarcasms* (1941); *American Circle* (1941); *Night Flight,* after Antoine de St. Exupéry (1942); *First Overture* (1943); *A Bell Overture* (1946); *Partita* for small orchestra (1946); *Quiet Music* for strings (1946); *The Tempta-*

tion of St. Anthony, a dance symphony after Flaubert (1947); *Pennsylvania Suite* (1947); *Dance of the Locomotives* (1948); *Ariosa Elegiaca* for strings (1951); *Toccata Giocosa* (1953); *Vernal Equinox* (1955); *Jeux de Timbres* (1963) and *Astral Nebulae* (1983).

Read's works for solo instruments and orchestra including *Poem* for horn, viola, harp, and strings (1934); a *Fantasy* for viola (1935); a Cello Concerto (1945); *Music* for piano and strings (1946); *Threnody* for flute and strings (1946); and a Piano Concerto (1977).

Read has composed an opera, *Villon* (1967), to a text by James Forsyth. Choral works include *The Golden Journey to Samarkand* (J. E. Flecker) (1936–39) for soloists, chorus, and orchestra; an oratorio, *The Prophet* for contralto, baritone, chorus, and orchestra (1960); *Though I Speak With the Tongues of Men* for chorus and organ (1960); *Chants D'Auvergne* for mixed voices and instrumental ensemble (1962); and *By-Low My Babe* for chorus, flute, English horn, and harp (1978–79). For voice and orchestra Read has written *Four Nocturnes* (1934), *From a Lute of Jade* (1936), and *Songs for a Rainy Night* (1942). His other vocal music includes *Songs to Children* (1947–49) and *A Sheaf of Songs* (1949–50), both for mezzo-soprano and piano; *Petite Suite* for soprano, alto recorder, and harpsichord (1975); and *The Hidden Lute* for soprano, alto flute, harp, and percussion (1979).

Read's output of instrumental music is enormous, embracing almost every medium, including a Suite for string quartet (1935); *Six Intimate Moods* for violin and piano (1935–37); a Piano Quintet (1945); *Sonata Brevis* for violin and piano (1948); *Sound Piece* for brass and percussion (1949); *Nine by Six* for wind sextet (1950); String Quartet (1957); *Los Dioses Aztecas* for percussion (1959); *Sinfonia di Chiesa* for organ and brass (1969); *Haiku Seasons* for speakers and instrumental ensemble (1970); *Hexadic: A Game of Musical Chairs* for ensemble (1972); and four *Sonoric Fantasias*: no. 1 for celesta, harpsichord, and harp (1958), no. 2 for violin and orchestra (1965), no. 3 for five flutes, harp, and percussion (1968), and no. 4 for organ and percussion (1975).

More recent chamber music includes *Music for Chamber Winds* (1980); *Phantasmagoria* for oboe, oboe d'amore, English horn, and organ (1985–87, rev. 1988); *Five Aphorisms* for violin and piano (1991); and *Invocation* for trombone and organ (1997).

Read has composed several important works for organ: *Passacaglia and Fugue* (1936); a Suite (1949); *Fourteen Preludes on Old Southern Hymns* (1950, 1960); *Variations on a Chromatic Ground* (1964); and *Galactic Novae* (with percussion; 1978). His many piano pieces include a Sonata (1945), *Touch Piece* (1949), *Five Polytonal Etudes* (1961–64), and *Motives* (1980). Although Read has an impressive number of works

to his credit, his reputation as a composer has not traveled widely outside the United States. He is, however, known throughout the musical world as the author of the *Thesaurus of Orchestral Devices*, published in 1953, an enormous compendium of musical examples that illustrate the use of orchestral instruments, especially by twentieth-century composers. Read has written ten other books: *Music Notation: A Manual of Modern Practice* (1964); *Twentieth Century Notation* (1971); *Contemporary Instrumental Techniques* (1976); *Modern Rhythmic Notation* (1978); *Style and Orchestration* (1978); *Genesis of an Opera* (1979); *Source Book of Proposed Music Notation Reform* (1987); *Twentieth-Century Microtonal Notation* (1990); *Compendium of Modern Instrumental Techniques* (1993); and *Pictographic Score Notation* (1995).

REED, H(ERBERT) OWEN
b. Odessa, Missouri, 17 June 1910

Reed studied at the University of Missouri, Columbia (1929–33) under James Quarles and Scott Goldthwaite; at Louisiana State University, Baton Rouge (1933–37) with Helen Gunderson; and at the Eastman School of Music, Rochester, New York (1937–39) with Howard Hanson, Bernard Rogers, and Burrill Phillips. At the Berkshire Music Center, Tanglewood, he studied composition with Martinů (1942) and Copland and Bernstein (1947). In Colorado Springs he also received private lessons from Roy Harris. In 1948–49 and 1960 he visited Mexico to study folk music, and in 1976 spent two weeks in the Caribbean on a similar project. He has received several awards, including a Guggenheim Fellowship (1948–49). Read taught at Michigan State University, East Lansing (1939–76), where he was chairman of theory and composition, then chairman of music composition (1967–75). He retired as a professor emeritus.

For orchestra Reed has written a symphonic poem, *Evangeline* (1938); a Symphony (1939); an Overture (1940); *Symphonic Dance* (1942); a Cello Concerto (1949); *La Fiesta Mexicana* for band (1949; orchestral version, 1964); *Overture for Strings* (1960); *The Turning Mind* (1968); and *Ut Re Mi*, variations on "Ut queant laxis" for orchestra and men's voices (1979).

In addition to *La Fiesta Mexicana*, Reed has composed a number of other works for band: *Spiritual* (1947); *Missouri Shindig* (1951); *Theme and Variations* (1954); *Renascence* (1959); *Che-Ba-Kuh-Ah* (*Road of Souls*) (1959); *The Touch of the Earth* with chorus (1971); *For the Unfortunate* for band and chorus (or tape; 1975); *The Awakening of the Ents* (1985); *Fanfare for Remembrance* for narrator, brass, and percussion (1986); and *Of Lothlorien* (1988).

For the stage Reed has written a ballet-pantomime, *The Masque of the Red Death* (1936); a two-act folk opera, *Peter Homan's Dream* (1955, rev. 1959), commissioned by Michigan State University for its centennial celebrations; and three dance operas: *Earth Trapped* (1960), based on an Indian spirit legend; *Living Solid Face* (1974); and *Butterfly Girl and Mirage Boy* (1980).

Reed's important instrumental works are a Piano Sonata (1934), a String Quartet (1937), *Scherzo* for clarinet and piano (1947), *Symphonic Dance* for piano and wind quintet (1954), *El Muchacho* for seven handbells and three percussionists (1965), and *El Son de la Negra* for piano (1975).

His choral music includes an oratorio, *A Tabernacle for the Sun* for contralto, chorus, men's speaking chorus, and orchestra (1963); *Ripley Ferry* for female chorus and wind septet (1958); and *Rejoice! Rejoice!* for soloist, chorus, taped chorus, bells, and double bass (1977). In addition he has composed *A Psalm of Praise* for soprano and seven instruments (1937) and *Wondrous Love* for tenor and wind quintet (1948).

Reed has written a number of important textbooks: *A Workbook in the Fundamentals of Music* (1947); *Basic Music* (1954); *Scoring for Percussion* (with Joel T Leech; 1969, rev. 1979); *The Materials of Music Composition* (with Robert G. Sidnell; 1978–80); and *Basic Contrapuntal Technique* (rev. ed. with Greg Steinke; 2003).

REICH, STEVE (STEPHEN MICHAEL)

b. New York, New York, 3 October 1936

As a child Reich learned to play the piano, and at the age of 14 began Western rudimentary drumming with Roland Kohloff. After studying Wittgenstein's philosophy at Cornell University (1953–57), he returned to music, taking composition lessons privately from Hall Overton in New York (1957–58) before entering the Juilliard School, where he was a pupil of William Bergsma and Vincent Persichetti (1958–61). At Mills College, Oakland, California (1961–63) he studied composition with Luciano Berio and Darius Milhaud, receiving his M.A. in music (1963). From 1969 to 1971 he taught at the New School for Social Research in New York.

In 1970, on a grant from the Institute of International Education, Reich studied drumming at the Institute of African Studies at the University of Ghana in Accra. During the summers of 1973 and 1974 he studied Balinese gamelan music at the American Society for Eastern Arts in Seattle, Washington and Berkeley, California. During 1976–77 he explored the cantillation (chanting) of the Hebrew scriptures in New York and Jerusalem.

Steve Reich.
Photo: Alice Arnold, courtesy Howard Stokar Management.

Reich occasionally presented his own works at the San Francisco Tape Music Center (1964–65), and has used tape in several of his compositions. In 1966 he founded his own performing group, Steve Reich and Musicians (or the Steve Reich Ensemble), which has performed widely. He believes strongly in the combination of composing and performing. Between 1971 and 1979 his ensemble undertook 11 American and European tours, totaling over two hundred concerts.

Some of his early compositions with tape make use of speech, with phrases made into repeating loops: *It's Gonna Rain* (1965); *Come Out* (1966); *Melodica* (1966); *My Name Is* (1967); *Slow Motion Sound* (1967); *Pendulum Music* for microphones, loudspeakers, amplifiers, and performers (1968); and *Pulse Music*, for an instrument invented by Reich, the "phase-shift pulse gate." This led to a sequence of works using the technique of "phasing," a form of staggered repetition in which certain rhythmic patterns are repeated with slight increases in tempo in different parts so that co-ordination moves in and out of phase. This effect is demonstrated in *Reed Phase* for soprano saxophone and tape (1967); *Piano Phase* for two pianos and two marimbas (1967); *Violin Phase* for violin and tape (1967); *Four*

Organs for four electric organs and marimbas (1970); and *Phase Patterns* for four electric organs (1970). With these innovations, Reich became associated with Terry Riley and Philip Glass in the foundation of what is now termed "minimalism." The discipline of phasing is evident in three works that concentrate exclusively on repeated rhythm patterns that gradually shift apart from one section to another: *Four Log Drums* (1969), *Clapping Music* for two performers, and *Music for Pieces of Wood* for five pairs of differently pitched claves (both 1973).

Reich's name first came to international attention in 1971 with his ensemble piece, *Drumming*, scored for two wordless female voices, piccolo, four pairs of tuned bongo drums, three marimbas, and three glockenspiels. This 90-minute work resulted from his direct experience of West African drumming. Unlike his earlier phasing pieces, an unvarying pulse is maintained throughout, against which the performers elaborate a single rhythmic motif in a massive percussive ritual. It was followed in 1973 with *Music for Mallet Instruments, Voices and Organ* for three wordless female voices, three marimbas, three glockenspiels, vibraphone, and electric organ. It is based on two alternating chords that begin slowly and imperceptibly increase in tempo. In the same year he composed *Six Pianos*, adapted in 1986 as *Six Marimbas*.

The success of *Drumming* was exceeded by *Music for Eighteen Musicians*, premiered in The Town Hall, New York in April 1976. Subsequent television broadcasts throughout America and Europe led to huge sales of its recording. The scoring for four female voices, two clarinets and bass clarinet, three marimbas, two xylophones, vibraphone, four pianos, maracas, violin, and cello offers more opportunity for exploitation than its predecessors. Its intricate structure is based on a sequence of eleven chords with cumulative repetition, set out in eleven linked sections against an unvaried pulse. A ballet entitled *Rain*, performed in Brussels in 2001, was based on this score.

In similar vein is *Music for Large Ensemble* (1978) for two female voices, four woodwind, four trumpets, five tuned percussion, and ten strings. *Octet* (1979) was also produced as a ballet, *Embarque*, by Ballet Rambert in London in 1999. The score was revised in 1983 as *Eight Lines*, also adapted as a ballet, *Feast* (Amsterdam, 1999).

Variations for Winds, Strings and Keyboard (1979) was premiered by the San Francisco Symphony Orchestra under Edo de Waart in 1980. A revised version for ensemble was performed by the Steve Reich Ensemble in New York in the same year. His next work, *Tehillim*, is the first Reich ensemble piece to set text. In the original version for four solo female vocalists (singing Psalm texts in Hebrew), flute, piccolo, oboe,

English horn, six percussion, two electric organs, and strings, it was first heard complete in a broadcast on West German Radio, Cologne in September 1981. An orchestral arrangement followed in 1982. *Vermont Counterpoint* (1982) for piccolo, flute, alto flute, and tape also exists in a version for eleven flutes. *Sextet* for four percussionists and two pianos was completed in 1985.

The Desert Music, commissioned in 1982 by West German Radio, Cologne, sets a poem by William Carlos Williams for amplified choir and large orchestra. Peter Eötvös conducted the first performance in Cologne in March 1984; the United States premiere followed in July 1984 under Michael Tilson Thomas in Richmond, Virginia. The opening movement conjures up the wasteland caused by the two atom bombs that fell on Japan in August 1945. In a further departure, Reich composed two works for standard large orchestra: *Three Movements* (1986) for the St. Louis Symphony Orchestra, and *The Four Sections* (1987) for the San Francisco Symphony Orchestra.

Working in collaboration with the enterprising Kronos Quartet in 1988, Reich wrote *Different Trains* for string quartet and tape. This autobiographical exercise recalls the composer's experiences as a child of divorced parents, frequently taking the four-day trip by railroad between his father's home in New York and his mother's in Los Angeles; the tape is made up of sounds associated with the journey.

In 1976 Reich married Beryl Korot, an expert in multichannel video. With her co-operation he created the first of two video operas, *The Cave*. Using texts from the Torah, the Qur'an, and documentary material, the three-act theater piece was presented at the Vienna Festival in May 1993. Also dating from this period are *Typing Music I* (Genesis XVI, after *The Cave*) for five percussionists (1989); *Typing Music* (Genesis XII) for keyboards and percussion (1991); *Duet* for two violins and string ensemble (1993); and *Nagoya Marimbas* for two marimbas (1994).

Reich and Korot collaborated on a second documentary video opera, *Three Tales*, using solo voices, film, stills, video, instruments, and electro-acoustic manipulation. Act I: *Hindenburg* traces the history of the ill-fated zeppelin from its construction to its destruction at Lakehurst, New Jersey, in 1937. This part was premiered at the Spoleto USA Festival in Charleston, South Carolina, in May 1998. Act II: *Bikini* is based on the atomic bomb tests in the Pacific (1946–54) and the effect on the people who lived there. Act III: *Dolly* comments on the cloning of an adult sheep in Scotland in 1997. The world premiere of the complete *Three Tales* took place at the Vienna Festival on 12 May 2002 and was followed by twenty five performances throughout Europe and the United States.

Three later compositions are *City Life* for ensemble (1995); *Proverb* (Ludwig Wittgenstein) for voices and ensemble, premiered in Alice Tully Hall, New York in February 1996; and *Triple Quartet* for three quartets (one live, two on tape), commissioned by the Kronos Quartet and first performed by the Smith Quartet in Washington, D.C. in May 1999. A version for string orchestra was played at the Juilliard School in January 2000. Reich's most recent composition, *Cello Counterpoint*, was premiered in October 2003 in Poland by Maya Beiser.

Reich is the author of a book of essays, *Writings on Music,* published in 1974.

REINAGLE, ALEXANDER
b. Portsmouth, England, 23 April 1756
d. Baltimore, Maryland, 21 September 1809

Reinagle was born in England of Austrian parents. He studied music under Raynor Taylor in Edinburgh and became a close friend of C. P. E. Bach in Hamburg in 1785. He arrived in New York in 1786, where he gave lessons in piano and violin. By the end of the year he had moved to Philadelphia, where he organized concerts for his own benefit. Such concerts were often the

Alexander Reinagle.
Courtesy University of Pennsylvania Library, Special Collections.

only way practical musicians could earn money with their music.

Reinagle returned to New York as a performer (1788–89) and was more successful than he had been earlier. He subsequently organized the Philadelphia City Concerts (1791–92) and became a partner with Thomas Wignell in the New Company, a theatrical organization that erected theaters in Philadelphia and in Baltimore. Reinagle directed the theaters' orchestras and contributed incidental music and songs to numerous stage productions.

Reinagle composed or adapted at least five operas: *Robin Hood*, or *Sherwood Forest* (1794); *The Spanish Barber, or The Fruitless Precaution* (with Benjamin Carr; 1794); *The Volunteers* (1795); *Auld Robin Gray, or Jamie's Return from America* (1795); and *The Travellers*, or *Music's Fascination* (1807). He also provided music for pantomimes, including *The Witches of the Rock, or Harlequin Everywhere* (1796); and plays, melodramas, and ballets.

Reinagle's range of compositions was enormous, including a *Federal March Overture* (1788); two string quartets (1791); a Piano Concerto (1794); four piano sonatas (1786–94); *Masonic Overture* (1800); two sets of keyboard *Variations*; and numerous vocal and piano works, including *America: Commerce and Freedom*, a set of seven songs published in 1794. He published two collections of *Scots Tunes with Variations* for keyboard.

REYNOLDS, ROGER (LEE)
b. Detroit, Michigan, 18 July 1934

At first Reynolds studied engineering at the University of Michigan, but after graduating in 1957, he stayed there to study music (B.M., 1960; M.M., 1961). He was a pupil of Ross Lee Finney and Roberto Gerhard. In 1962 on a Fulbright Fellowship he pursued his interest in electronic music in Cologne (1962), continuing this work in France and Italy on Guggenheim and Fulbright Fellowships (1963–66). In 1966 he began a three-year fellowship in Japan under the auspices of the Institute of Current World Affairs. Upon his return to the United States in 1969 Reynolds was appointed professor of music at the University of California, San Diego, where he created the Center for Music Experiment and Related Research in 1971. He has also served as a visiting professor at IRCAM in Paris (1981–83), Yale University (1982), Brooklyn College, New York (1985), and the Peabody Conservatory of Music, Baltimore (1992–93).

Reynolds has been a long-time member of the group of composers representing the avant-garde in America. He acknowledges the music of Ives, Cage, and Varèse as the principal influences upon his early work. With

Roger Reynolds.
Photo © Malcolm Crowthers, courtesy the composer.

Robert Ashley, Gordon Mumma, and others, he was a founder-member of the ONCE group at Ann Arbor, Michigan (1960), which explored the use of magnetic tape and other media in experimental performances. His music has always shown aspects of serialism, often combining instruments with electronic and computer-generated sounds for live performance. In many works he makes use of graphic notation to suggest sounds.

Reynolds's early works won him acclaim, including *Wedge* for chamber ensemble (1961), *The Emperor of Ice Cream*, a theater piece for eight voices, piano, percussion, and double bass (1962, rev. 1974), and *Quick Are the Mouths of the Earth* for chamber orchestra (1965). This last piece, inspired by a quotation from Thomas Wolfe, is scored for the unusual combination of three flutes, oboe, trumpet, two trombones, three cellos, and piano (doubling harmonica) as well as two percussion players who cover 21 instruments.

Graffiti for large orchestra, a Rockefeller Foundation commission, was performed in May 1965 by the Seattle Symphony Orchestra under Milton Katims and produced as a ballet by the Netherlands Dance Theater in Amsterdam in October 1969. Four other large-scale works are *Blind Men* for chorus of 24 voices, brass,

piano, percussion, and tape, a Fromm Foundation commission (1966); *Masks* for eight-part chorus and orchestra (1965); *Threshold* for orchestra (1967), premiered by Seiji Ozawa at the "Orchestral Space '68" Festival in Tokyo; and *Only Now and Again* for 20 winds, piano, and percussion (1977), another Fromm commission.

Reynolds has written extensively for instrumental ensembles: a String Quartet (1960); *Acquaintances* for flute, double bass, and piano (1961); *Four Studies for Flute Quartet* (1961); *Mosaic* for flute and piano (1962); *Gathering* for woodwind quintet (1964), premiered by the Danzi Quintet; and *Ambages* for solo flute (1965). During his time in Japan he composed *Traces* for piano, flute, cello, and six channels featuring taped sound, signal generator, and ring modulator (1969).

In 1968 Reynolds began to write multimedia works in earnest. First came *Ping*, inspired by the Samuel Beckett story, for flute, piano, harmonium, bowed cymbal, tam-tam, electronic sound, film, and slides. In 1970 he produced *Again* for pairs of sopranos, flutes, trombones, double basses, percussionists, amplification, and four-channel tape. *I/O, A Ritual,* for nine female vocalists, nine male mimes, two flutes, clarinet, projections, and electronics (1971), is based on Buckminster Fuller's conception of complementary opposition. In 1973 he composed *Compass* (Jorge Luis Borges) for cello, double bass, tenor, bass, four-channel tape, and projections.

"*. . . from behind the unreasoning mask*" (1975) is written for trombone, percussion, and four-channel tape, while its complementary work, "*. . . the serpent-snapping eye*" (1978), is scored for trumpet, percussion, piano, and four-channel computer-generated sound. *Fiery Wind* (1977) is an elaborate search for orchestral sonorities, based on the enigmatic Japanese novelist Kobo Abe and the phenomenon of solar wind. *Less Than Two* (1977–79) is for two pianists, two percussionists, and computer-generated sound.

From 1975 Reynolds began exploring the combination of unusual means of vocal production, and the spatial attributes of sound, in a series of works entitled *Voicespace*. The first, *Still* (1975), sets a Coleridge poem; the second, *A Merciful Coincidence* (1977), is taken from Beckett's novel *Watt*; the third, *Eclipse* (1984), setting texts by several authors, is excerpted from music for a media collaboration with Ed Emshwiller; the fourth, *The Palace*, for baritone, four-channel tape, and lighting (Borges, 1980), involves computer-processed voice and live vocalist. *Voicespace V: The Vanity of Words* for voice and computer-processed tape dates from 1986.

Later orchestral pieces include *Archipelago* for chamber orchestra and computer-processed tape (1982);

Transfigured Wind II and *III* for solo flute, chamber orchestra, and computer-generated tape (1984); *Le Mistral* for harpsichord, brass, and strings (1985); *Dream of the Infinite Rooms* for cello, orchestra, and computer-generated tape (1987); three symphonies, *Vertigo* (San Francisco, 1987), *Myths* (Tokyo, 1990), and *The Stages of Life* (1991–92; Los Angeles, 1993); and *Dreaming* (1992).

Reynolds's instrumental works include *The Promises of Darkness* for 11 players, written in memory of his teacher, Roberto Gerhard (1975); *Shadowed Narratives* for chamber quartet (1977–82); *Borrowed Time* for chamber ensemble (1985); *Sextet* (1988); *Versions/Stages I – V* for ensemble and computer-processed sound (1986–91); *Personae* for violin, chamber ensemble, and computer-generated tape (1990); *Dionysus* for eight instruments (1990); *Kokoro* for violin (1992); *Visions*, composed for the Arditti String Quartet (1985–94); and *Ariadne's Thread* for string quartet and computer-generated sound (1994). In 1989 he won the Pulitzer Prize for *Whisper Out of Time* for violin, viola, cello, double bass, and strings.

Among his most recent works are an as yet unstaged opera, *Odyssey* for mezzo-soprano, baritone, two reciters, 16 instruments, and computer sound (1989–1993); *last things I like to think about* (John Ashbery) for bass-baritone, piano, and computer sound (1994); *Watershed I – IV* for solo percussion, chamber ensemble, and real-time computer sound (1995); *Two Voices*, an allegory for orchestra and stereo sounds (1996); *The Red Act Arias* for chorus, orchestra, computer-processed sound, performed at the London Promenade Concerts in the Royal Albert Hall in the summer of 1997; *On the Balance of Things* for chamber ensemble and computer-processed sound (1996–98); *brain-ablaze*, for up to three piccolos and processed tape (2000); *Justice* (Aeschylus) for actress, soprano, percussion, and computer sounds (1999–2001); *A Common Past* for cello and piano (2001); *The Angels of Death*, a concerto for piano, chamber orchestra, and six-channel computer sound (2001); *Process and Passion* for violin, cello, and computer sound (2002); and *Elegy for Toru Takemitsu* for flute, percussion, and strings.

His compositions for solo piano make use of certain effects inside the instrument. These pieces include *Epigram and Evolution* (1959), *Fantasy for Pianist* (1964), and *Variations* (1988).

Reynolds has written numerous articles for music journals and four books: *Mind Models*: *New Forms of Musical Experience* (1975); *A Searcher's Path*; *A Composer's Ways* (1987); *A Jostled Silence*: *Contemporary Japanese Musical Thought* (1993); and *Form and Method*: *Composing Music* (2002).

RHODES, PHILLIP
b. Forest City, North Carolina, 6 June 1940

Rhodes was educated at Duke University, North Carolina (1958–62), where he was a composition pupil of Iain Hamilton, and at Yale University (1963–66), where he studied with Donald Martino and Mel Powell. He also received tuition from Gunther Schuller and George Perle, and attended the Berkshire Music Center, Tanglewood. From 1966 to 1968 he was Composer-in-Residence for the public schools in Cicero-Berwyn, Illinois, sponsored by the Ford Foundation. After teaching at Amherst College, Massachusetts (1968–69), he was appointed Composer-in-Residence for the City of Louisville (1969–71). From 1972 to 1974 he was Composer-in-Residence with the Kentucky Arts Commission. Since 1974 he has been Composer-in-Residence and Andrew W. Mellon Professor of the Humanities at Carleton College, Northfield, Minnesota.

For orchestra he has composed *Four Movements* (1962); *Madrigal* (1968); *Three B's* (1971); Divertimento for small orchestra (1971); *Concerto* (*Bluegrass Festival Suite*) for fiddle, banjo, mandolin, guitar, double bass, and orchestra (1974); *Ceremonial Fanfare and Chorale* for two brass groups and orchestra (1977); and *Reels and Reveries* (1991). His contribution to the concert band repertory include *Remembrances* (1966–

Phillip Rhodes.
Photo: Bachrach Studios, courtesy the composer.

67), *Three Pieces* (1967), *Devil's Advocate* (1972), *Adventure Fantasies for Young Players* (1983), and *Cosmic Fantasies* (1984, rev. 1999).

For the stage Rhodes has composed two operas, *The Gentle Boy* (1979–80) and *The Magic Pipe* (1983), and a ballet, *About Faces* (1970). Choral works include an opera-oratorio, *From Paradise Lost* (Milton) for narrator, soprano, tenor, baritone, chorus, and orchestra (1972); *Witticisms and Lamentations from the Graveyard* for mixed voices (1972); *On the Morning of Christ's Nativity* (Milton), a cantata for soprano, tenor, chorus, and five instruments (1976); *Wind Songs* (1979) and *Dancing Songs* (1985), both for treble choir and Orff instruments; *Ad Honorem Stravinsky* (1981); *In Praise of Wisdom* for chorus, brass, and winds (1982); *Nets to Catch the Wind* for chorus and percussion (1986); *Chorale and Meditation* for women's voices and organ (1994); and *Three Appalachian Settings* for chorus and violin (2000).

Among Rhodes's vocal compositions are *Three Scenes* for mezzo-soprano and piano (1965); *Autumn Setting* for soprano and string quartet (1969); *The Lament of Michal* for soprano and orchestra (1970); *Five Songs on Children's Poems* for high voice and piano (1972); *Mountain Songs* for voice and piano (1976); *Visions of Remembrance* for two sopranos and orchestra (1979); *The Face I Carry With Me* (Emily Dickinson) for soprano, flute, violin, cello, and piano (1981–82); and *Mary's Lullaby* for soprano, violin, and organ (1993).

Rhodes is best known for his instrumental music: String Trio (1964, rev. 1973); *Three Pieces* for cello (1966); *Duo* for violin and cello (1968); *Museum Piece* for clarinet and string quartet (1973); Quartet for flute, violin, cello, and harp (1975); *Reflections* for piano (1977); *Partita* for solo viola (1979); and *Fiddletunes* for violin and tape (1996).

RICHTER, MARGA

b. Reedsburg, Wisconsin, 21 October 1926

Marga Richter's paternal grandfather, Richard Richter, was a composer and conductor of the municipal orchestra of Einbeck, Germany, a post occupied earlier by Gustav Mahler. Her mother, Inez Chandler Richter, was a noted soprano. Richter was educated at the MacPhail School of Music, Minneapolis. Later, at the Juilliard School (1945–51), she was a piano pupil of Rosalyn Tureck; her composition teachers were Vincent Persichetti and William Bergsma. With Herbert Deutsch, she co-founded the Long Island Composers Alliance in 1972 and has at various times served as its co-director, president, and vice-president.

Marga Richeter.
Photo: Alan Skelly, courtesy the composer.

For orchestra Richter has composed two piano concertos, no. 1 1955 (and) no. 2; *Landscapes of the Mind I* (1968–74); *Lament for Strings* (1956); *Aria and Toccata* for viola and strings (1957); *Variations on a Sarabande* (1959); *Eight Pieces for Orchestra* (1961); *Blackberry Vines and Winter Fruit* (1976); *Fragments* (1976); *Spectral Chimes/Enshrouded Hills* for three orchestral quintets and orchestra (1980); *Düsseldorf Concerto* for flute, viola, harp, piano, and strings (1981–82); *Out of the Shadows and Solitude* (1985); *Quantum Quirks of a Quick Quaint Quark* (1991); and *Variations and Interludes on Themes of Monteverdi and Bach*, concerto for violin, cello, piano, and orchestra (1992). For band she has written *Country Auction* (1977).

In 1964 the Harkness Ballet commissioned *Abyss*, with choreography by Stuart Hodes. A second ballet, *The Servant* (later renamed *Bird of Yearning*), another Harkness commission, received its premiere in Cologne in 1969. A chamber opera in one act, *Riders to the Sea* (J. M. Synge), was completed in 1996.

Richter's vocal music includes a song cycle on Chinese poems, *Transmutation* (1949), *Two Chinese Songs* for mezzo-soprano and piano (1953), and *Lament for Art O'Leary* for soprano and piano (1983). Among her choral pieces are *Three Songs of Madness and Death* to texts by John Webster (1955); Psalm 91 (1962); *Seek Him*, a setting of a verse from the Book of Amos (1965); *To Whom*, to texts by Virginia Woolf and the Kyrie from the Mass (1980); *Do Not Press My Hands* for vocal sextet (1981); *Into My Heart* for chorus, oboe, violin, brass, timpani, and percussion (1990); *Erin Odyssey*, 14 limericks by the composer, for voice and piano (2000); *Dew-drops on a Lotus Leaf*, a setting of 10 poems by the Japanese poet Taigu Ryokan for countertenor (or contralto) and string quartet (or piano) (2002); and *Testament Song*, eight poems by Anne M. Lindbergh, for medium voice and piano (2002).

Among Richter's numerous instrumental compositions are two string quartets (1950, withdrawn; 1958); Sonata for clarinet and piano (1948); *Ricercare* for brass quartet (1958); *Darkening of the Light*, a suite for solo viola (1961) or solo cello (1976); Suite for violin and piano (1964); *Landscapes of the Mind II* for violin and piano (1971); *Variations on a Theme by Neithart von Reuenthal* for organ (1971); *Landscapes of the Mind III* for piano trio (1979); *Sonora* for two clarinets and piano (1981); *Seacliff Variations* for piano quartet (1984); *Qhanri* for cello and piano (1988); and *Obsessions* for solo trombone (1990).

Richter's keyboard works include *Soundings* for harpsichord (1965) and several piano pieces: Sonata (1954); *Eight Pieces* (1961); *Fragments* (1963); *Remembrances* (1971); Requiem (1978); *Melodrama* for two pianos (1952, rev. 1958); and *Variations on a Theme by Latimer* for piano duet (1964).

RIEGGER, WALLINGFORD (CONSTANTIN)

b. Albany, Georgia, 29 April 1885
d. New York, New York, 2 April 1961

Riegger received his first musical training from his parents: his mother was a pianist, his father a violinist and choral conductor. After the family moved to New York in 1900 he studied theory with Percy Goetschius, and spent one year (1904) at Cornell University. From 1905 to 1907, he attended the Institute of Musical Art (now the Juilliard School). In 1907 he went to Germany, where he studied at the Hochschule für Musik in Berlin and received private lessons from Max Bruch and Edgar Stillman Kelley. In 1910 he returned to America to become a cellist with the St. Paul Symphony Orchestra. He was in Germany again in 1914 to conduct operas in Würzburg and Königsberg.

Returning to the United States for good in 1917, Riegger taught at Drake University, Des Moines (1918–22) and at the Institute of Musical Art, New York (1924–25). In 1926 he joined the music faculty of Ithaca Conservatory, New York. He finally settled in New York in 1929, where he taught at the New School for Social Research and the Metropolitan Music School.

Although Riegger's early works are tonal, he made use of the 12-tone system after 1926 in most of his large-scale works, adapting it to suit his own needs in each composition. For orchestra he wrote four symphonies: no. 1 (1944, withdrawn), no. 2 (1944, withdrawn), no. 3, which won the 1948 New York Music Critics' Circle Award, and no. 4, performed at the University of Illinois in 1957. Other important orchestral works are *Elegie* for cello and orchestra (1916); *American Polonaise* (1923); *Rhapsody (Second April)* (1924–26); *Holiday Sketches* for violin and orchestra (1927); *Fantasy and Fugue* for organ and orchestra (1930–31); *Rhapsody* (1931); *Dichotomy* (1931); *Scherzo* (1932); *New Dance* (1934); *Canon and Fugue* for strings (1941), performed at the I.S.C.M. Festival in San Francisco in 1942; *Passacaglia and Fugue* (1942); *Variations* for two pianos and orchestra (1952–54); *Dance Rhythms* (1955); *Music for Orchestra* (1956); an Overture (1956); *Preamble and Fugue* (1956); *Festival Overture* (1957); *Quintuple Jazz* (1959); and Sinfonietta (1959). The Louisville Orchestra commissioned *Variations* for piano and orchestra (1952–53) and *Variations* for violin and orchestra (1959). His last important work was *Duo* for piano and orchestra (1960).

Riegger's setting of Keats' *La Belle Dame Sans Merci* for four voices and chamber orchestra won the Elizabeth Sprague Coolidge Prize in 1924. Other vocal music includes *Eternity* for female voices and four instruments (1942); *Who Can Revoke* for chorus and piano (1948); a cantata, *In Certainty of Song* for soloists, chorus, and chamber orchestra (1950); and *A Shakespeare Sonnet* (no. 138) for baritone, chorus, and orchestra (1956).

In addition to *New Dance*, choreographed by Doris Humphrey (1935), Riegger wrote many dance scores, including *Bacchanale* (Martha Graham, 1930); *Frenetic Rhythms* (Graham, 1933); *Theatre Piece* (Humphrey, 1935); *The Cry* (Hanya Holm, 1935); *With My Red Fires* (Humphrey, 1936); *Chronicle* (Graham, 1936); *City Nocturne* (Holm, 1936); *Four Chromatic Eccentricities* (Holm, 1936); *Candide* (Charles Weidman, 1937); *Festive Rhythm* (Holm, 1937); *Trend* (Holm, 1937), *Case History No. . . .* (Anna Sokolow, 1937); *Trojan Incident* (Helen Tamiris, 1938); and *Pilgrim's Progress* (Erick Hawkins, 1941).

Among his instrumental works are a Piano Trio in B minor, which won the Paderewski Prize in 1922; *Study in Sonority* for ten violins or multiples of ten (1927); Suite for solo flute (1929); *Three Canons* for flute, oboe, clarinet, and bassoon (1930); Divertimento for flute, harp, and cello (1933); three string quartets (1938–39, 1945–47, 1948); *Music for Brass Choir* (1948); Piano Quintet (1951); *Nonet* for brass (1951–52); Wind Quintet (1952); Concerto for piano and wind quintet (1952); *Variations* for violin and viola (1956); *Movement* for two trumpets, trombone, and piano (1957); and *Introduction, Scherzo and Fugue* for cello and wind (1960).

RIETI, VITTORIO

b. Alexandria, Egypt, 28 January 1898
d. New York, New York, 19 February 1994

Born of Italian parents, Rieti studied in Milan (1912–17) and with Respighi in Rome (1919–20). From 1925 he was frequently in Paris, where he joined the cosmopolitan musical community. In 1940 he moved to the United States and became an American citizen in 1944. For two years he taught at the Peabody Conservatory in Baltimore (1948–50) before going to the Chicago Musical College (1950–53). In 1955 he joined the music department at Queens College, New York. From 1960 to 1964 he was on the music faculty of the New York College of Music.

Although he composed in every field of music, Rieti excelled in writing ballet scores. His first success came with a 1923 performance at the I.S.C.M. Festival in Prague of an orchestral suite based on *L'Arca di Noé* (*Noah's Ark*), composed in 1922 but never staged. Diaghilev was sufficiently impressed to commission two more ballets, *Barabau* (London, 1925) and *La Bal* (Monte Carlo, 1929). Rieti's other ballets include *Robinson et Vendredi* (1924); *David Triomphant* (Paris, 1937); *Hippolyte* (Paris, 1937); *Waltz Academy*, for Ballet Theater (Ballet Theater; Boston, 1944); *The Mute Wife*, after Paganini (New York, 1944); *The Night Shadow*, after Bellini (choreography by Balanchine; New York, 1946); *Trionfo di Baco e Arianna* (Ballet Theater; New York, 1948), also choreographed by Balanchine; *Conundrum* (1961); *A Sylvan Dream* (1965; Indianapolis, 1982); *Scenes Seen* (Indianapolis Ballet Theater, 1976); *Verdiana* (Indianapolis, 1985); and *Kaleidoscope* (Indianapolis, 1988).

Also for the stage Rieti composed a lyric tragedy, *Orfeo tragedia* (1928); *Teresa nel bosco*, a chamber opera performed at the Venice Festival in September 1934; a one-act opera, *Don Perlimplin*, based on a story by Lorca (Theatre des Champs Elysee, Paris, 1952); *The Pet Shop*, also in one act, completed in 1958; *The Clock* (1960); and *Maryam the Harlot* (1966). An opera for radio, *Viaggio d'Europa*, dates from 1954. Rieti provided incidental music for many plays, including Moliere's *L'Ecole des Femmes* (1936), Corneille's *L'Illusion* (1937), and Giraudoux's *Electre* (1937).

Among Rieti's orchestral works, eight symphonies take pride of place: no. 1 (1929); no. 2 (1930); no. 3, *Sinfonietta* (1932); no. 4, *Sinfonia Tripartita* (1944); no. 5 (1951); no. 6, premiered by the New York Musica Aeterna (1974); no. 7 (1977); and no. 8, *Sinfonia Breve* (1987). For chamber orchestra he composed *Two Pastorales* in 1925. The *Concerto du Loup*, named after a river in southern France, was performed in Paris (1936) and by the Los Angeles Chamber Orchestra at the I.S.C.M. Festival in San Francisco (1942). The

Vittorio Rieti.
Courtesy James P. Murphy Collection, Georgetown University Library.

Louisville Orchestra commissioned *Introduzione e Gioco della Ore*, which received its premiere in 1954. A symphonic suite, *La Fontaine* (1972), was performed in New York in 1977.

For solo instruments and orchestra Rieti composed Concerto for five wind instruments, performed at the I.S.C.M. Festival in Prague in 1924; three piano concertos (1926, 1937, 1955); two violin concertos (1928, 1969); two cello concertos (1934, 1935); Concerto for two pianos (1951); and a Harpsichord Concerto (1955, rev. 1972). A Triple Concerto for violin, viola, and cello, completed in 1973, was premiered in New York. A Concerto for string quartet and orchestra (1976) was performed in New York in 1977. Other solo pieces include *Concerto Novello* for ten instruments (1986) and *Enharmonic Variations* for piano and chamber orchestra (1988). Among his choral works are a cantata, *Ulysses Wandering* (1939), and *Missa Brevis* for choir and organ (1973).

Rieti's output of instrumental works for various ensembles is considerable. These include four string quartets (1926, 1941, 1953, 1958); a Sonata for flute, oboe, bassoon, and piano (1924), performed at the I.S.C.M. Festival in Venice in 1925; *Madrigals* for 12 instruments (1927); Serenade for violin and 11 instruments, heard at the I.S.C.M. Festival in Vienna in 1932; a Woodwind Quintet (1958); Concertino for flute, viola, cello, harp, and harpsichord (1963); *Capriccio* for violin and piano (1966); *Sonata a Cinque* for flute, oboe, clarinet, bassoon, and piano (1966); *Sonata Breve* for violin and piano (1967); Octet for piano, wind, and strings (1971); *Sicilienne e Tarantella* for cello and piano (1971); Piano Trio (1972); Piano Quintet no. 1 (1973); and *Sestetto pro Gemini* for flute, oboe, violin, viola, cello, and piano (1975). He also wrote *Silografie* (*Woodcuts*) for wind quintet and *Incisioni* (*Engravings*) for brass quintet (1977).

Among his later chamber music are *Sonata a 6* (1980); *Spiccata* for flute, strings, and piano (1981); *Allegretto alla croma* for flute, oboe, clarinet, bassoon, and strings (1981); *Sonata a 10* (1982–83); *Elegia* for flute, cello, and piano (1983); *Romanza lidica* for clarinet and piano (1984); *Concertino pro San Luca* for woodwind, trumpet, string quartet, and piano (1984); *Congedo* for 12 instruments (1987) and Piano Quintet no. 2 (1989).

Rieti took a great interest in writing for the harpsichord. In addition to the Concerto, he composed a *Partita* for flute, oboe, string quartet, and harpsichord (1945) and *Sonata all' antica* for harpsichord and strings, both at the request of Sylvia Marlowe, and *Variations on Two Cantigas de Santa Maria* (Medieval Spanish) for flute, oboe, bassoon, cello, and harpsichord (1978). Among his many piano pieces are *Poema Fiesolano* (1921), a Sonata in A-flat (1938), *Variations Academiques* (1950), *Medieval Variations* (1962), *Chironomos* (1972), and *Twelve Preludes* (1979). He also wrote several entertaining works for two pianos: *Second Avenue Waltzes* (1942); *Chess Serenade* (1944; set as *Pasticcio* for the Winnipeg Ballet, 1956); *Suite Champêtre* (1945); *Chorale, Variations and Finale* (1970); *Three Vaudeville Marches* (1971); *Introduzione e Bagatella* (1978); and *Moonlight Dance* (1979). For piano duet he composed *Improvviso* (1979).

Rieti's vocal music includes *Four Italian Poems* (1945), *Two Songs Between Waltzes* (Yeats) (1957), *Four D.H. Lawrence Poems* (1960), *Five Elizabethan Songs* (1967), and *Sappho Poems* (1974).

RILEY, JOHN ARTHUR
b. Altoona, Pennsylvania, 17 September 1920

Riley studied with Wayne Barlow and Bernard Rogers at the Eastman School of Music, Rochester, New York (1948–51), with Quincy Porter at Yale University (M.Mus, 1955), and at the Paris Conservatory with Arthur Honegger (1952–53). He was also a cellist in the San Antonio Symphony Orchestra (1947–49), Rochester Philharmonic (1949–51), the Hartford Symphony

(1953–56), and the New Haven Symphony Orchestra (1953–62). He taught cello, music history, and composition at the Hartt School of Music, Hartford and Connecticut State College, New London.

Among his compositions are *Rhapsody* for cello and orchestra (1951); *Apostasy* for orchestra (1954); two string quartets (1954, 1959); *Fantasy* for oboe and strings (1955); Sinfonietta (1955); and a *Divertimento* for wind quintet.

RILEY, TERRY (MITCHELL)
b. Colfax, California, 24 June 1935

Riley studied at San Francisco State College (1955–57) and at the University of California, Berkeley (1960–61) with William Denny and Seymour Shifrin; he also studied privately with Robert Erickson. In addition to his work as a composer, he played the saxophone for a living. He traveled to Spain, Morocco, and Russia during 1962, where he was much affected by the folk music he encountered. In 1970 he became a disciple of the Indian musician Pandit Pran Nath, with whom he studied raga singing in San Francisco and India. From 1971 to 1980 Riley was assistant professor of music at Mills College, Oakland, California. He led the ensemble Khayal (1989–93); in 1992, he formed a company, Travelling-Avantt-Gaard, to perform his chamber opera, *The Saint Adolf Ring*. In 2000 he established the group Terry Riley and the All-Stars.

Riley's music contains a considerable degree of indeterminacy of an advanced character. As with Steve Reich, he makes extensive use of repeated formulas, with "phasing" of separate rhythmic patterns against a constant pulse. His early compositions include a Trio for clarinet, violin, and cello (1957, now lost); *Spectra* for six instruments (1959); *Two Piano Pieces* (1959); String Trio (1961); String Quartet (1961); and two works for two pianos and tape, *Concert* (1960) and *Earpiece* (1961). In addition there are two compositions for electronic tape: *I Can't Stop No Mescalin Mix* (1972–63) and *She Moves She* (1963). A theatrical extravaganza, *The Gift*, based on a play by Ken Deway, was performed in San Francisco in 1962 by Anna Halprin and her Dance Company. The jazz trumpeter Chet Baker and his band provided the musicians.

Riley's international reputation rests on a single work, *In C* (1964). The score comprises a single page with 53 modules, short melodic and rhythmic fragments which are intended to instigate improvisation. Against an unvaried pulse, each player decides what to play from the patterns offered. The work became the foundation of the American minimalist school. Originally designed for 13 players, it is now playable by any number and has no fixed duration. Its success led to a commission of Riley by Swedish Radio, resulting in *Olson III* for any instrument and voices (1966).

Riley followed *In C* with a sequence of improvisation pieces, mostly not notated as such. These include *Dorian Reeds* for winds, brass, strings, and tape loops (1964); *Poppy Nogood and the Phantom Band* for soprano saxophone, electric keyboard, tape delay, and feedback (1967); *A Rainbow in Curved Air* for electronic keyboards and tambourines (1968); *Persian Singing Dervishes* (1971) and *Descending Moonshine Dervishes* (1975) both for electric keyboards; *Happy Ending* (film score for *Les Yeux Fermés*) for piano, electric keyboard, soprano saxophone, and tape delay (1972); *Le Secret de la Vie* (*Lifespan*), film score (1975); *Shri Camel* for electronic organ and tape delay (1976); and *Do You Know How It Sounds?* for voice, piano, and tabla (1983). Other instrumental pieces of this period are *Keyboard Studies* for amplified keyboard instruments (1965), *Untitled Organ* for amplified reed organ (1966), *Music for Balls* (1969); and a ballet, *Genesis '70* (1970).

In the late 1980s Riley concentrated on combining instruments with tape: *Chanting the Light of Foresight* for saxophone quartet (1987); *The Room of Remembrance* for vibraphone, marimba, piano, and soprano saxophone (1987); *Cactus Rosary* for ensemble (1990); *Wolfli Portraits* for flute, clarinet, piano, two percussion, violin, and cello (1992); *El Hombre* for piano quintet (1993); *Ritmos and Melos* for violin, piano, and percussion (1993); *Night Music* for piano (1996); *Remember This...* for voice and ten instruments (1997); *DeepChandi* for string orchestra and pre-recorded percussion (1998); *MissiGono* for mixed ensemble (1998); and *Vieux Chateaux* for piano (1998).

Riley's close collaboration with the Kronos Quartet began in 1980, when he composed *G-Song*. There followed *Sunrise of the Planetary Dream Collector* (1980); *Cadenza on the Night Plain* (1983); two pieces for voice, piano, sitar, tabla, string quartet, and synthesizer, *The Medicine Wheel* and *Song of the Emerald Runner* (both 1983); *Salome Dances for Peace* (1985–87); *The Crow's Rosary* for keyboard, string quartet, and tape (1988); and *Three Requiem Quartets*, including *Requiem for Adam*, composed in memory of Adam Harrington, son of Kronos Quartet leader David Harrington, who died in 1995 at age 16. Their most recent project, *Sun Rings*, a joint commission by NASA and the University of Iowa, is scored for string quartet and 80 voices. Performed in 2003, it is intended that the sounds should be projected into space.

Among Riley's vocal compositions are *Chorale of the Blessed Day* for voice and two synthesizers (or voice, piano, and sitar; 1980); *Songs From the Old Country* for voice, piano, sitar, tabla, and soprano saxophone (1980); *Remember This, O Mind* for voice and

synthesizer (1982); and five pieces for voice and two synthesizers: *Eastern Man* and *Embroidery* (both 1980) and *The Ethereal Time Shadow, Offering to Chief Crazy Horse*, and *Rites of the Imitators* (all 1982).

Three works of 1991 show Riley employing more conventional musical forces: Concerto for string quartet and orchestra, subtitled *The Sands*, commissioned by the Salzburg Festival; *June Buddhas*, a concerto for chorus and orchestra, setting words by Jack Kerouac; and *Jade Palace* for orchestra and synthesizers, commissioned for the centenary of Carnegie Hall, New York.

Recent compositions include three pieces for double bass and synthesizer, *Diamond Fiddle Language*, *Tritono*, and *Shiv-Ji-Ki-Rung* (1998); *Mandala Miniature* for saxophone quartet (1998); *Josephine the Mouse Singer*, incidental music for a play by Michael McClure (2000); *The Dream*, an evening-length piece for microtonal piano (2000); *Two Fairy Tales* for strings (2001); *The Book of Abbeyozzud*, 24 pieces for guitar and guitar ensemble (2001); *Assassin Reverie* for saxophone quartet (2001); *Y Bolanzero* for large guitar ensemble (2001); *Piedad* (*Pity*) for solo guitar (2001); a Piano Concerto (*Banana Humberto*) (2002) for the composer to perform with the Paul Dresher Ensemble; and *The Heaven Ladder* for one or more pianos, an ongoing work begun in 1994.

ROBERTSON, LEROY (JASPER)
b. Fountain Green, Utah, 21 December 1896
d. Salt Lake City, Utah, 25 July 1971

Robertson studied with George Chadwick and Frederick Converse at the New England Conservatory, Boston (diploma, 1923). He then traveled to Europe, studying with Ernest Bloch (Switzerland) and Hugo Leichtentritt and Ernst Toch (Berlin). Returning to the United States, he was professor and chairman of the music department at Brigham Young University, Provo, Utah (1925–48), at the same time studying at the University of Utah (M.A., 1932). He was appointed in 1948 to the chair of the music department at the University of Utah, Salt Lake City; during this time he obtained a Ph.D. at the University of Southern California, Los Angeles (1954). He retired from teaching in 1963.

For orchestra Robertson wrote an Overture in E minor, which won the Endicott Prize (1923); *Prelude, Scherzo and Ricercare* (*Variations on Two Western Themes;* 1940); *Rhapsody* for piano and orchestra (1944); *American Serenade* for strings (1944); *Punch and Judy Overture* (1945); *Trilogy* (1947); a Violin Concerto (1948); *Passacaglia* (1955); *University of Utah Festival Overture* (1965); a Cello Concerto (1966); and a Piano Concerto (1966). Chamber works include

Leroy Robertson.
Courtes: Special Collections Dept., J. Willard Marriott Library, University of Utah

a Piano Quintet (1933) and a String Quartet (1940), which won the New York Music Critics' Circle Award in 1944.

His best-known work, the oratorio *The Book of Mormon*, dates from 1953.

ROBINSON, EARL (HAWLEY)

b. Seattle, Washington, 2 July 1910
d. Seattle, Washington, 20 July 1991

Robinson studied piano, violin, and viola as a child. He entered the University of Washington in 1929, studying composition with George McKay (B.M., 1933). He moved to New York City in 1934, where he received lessons from Aaron Copland, Hanns Eisler, and George Antheil. During this period, he worked for the Federal Theater Project of the WPA, and wrote several topical songs addressing labor and racial issues. He was awarded a Guggenheim Fellowship in 1940. Radio work led to opportunities in Hollywood in the latter 1940's and early 1950's, but Robinson's liberal background caused him to be blacklisted during the McCarthy era. From 1958 to 1965 he was head of music at the Elizabeth Irwin School in New York. He continued to compose music through the 1980's, returning to his hometown of Seattle in 1989.

Robinson was essentially a man of the theater. He composed two folk operas, *Sandhog* (1951–54) pro-

duced in New York, and *David of Sassoon* (1978), and a music drama, *Song of Atlantis* (1983). He made his reputation with a series of musicals: *Processional* (1938), *Sing for Your Supper* (1939), *One Foot in America* (1962), *Earl Robinson's America* (1976), and *Listen for the Dolphin* (1981). In addition he provided incidental music for a play, *Dark of the Moon* (1947), and composed a ballet, *Bouquet for Molly*, staged in Los Angeles in 1949.

Among his orchestral works are *Good Morning* (1949); *A Country They Call Puget Sound*; a tone poem for tenor and orchestra (1956, rev. 1961); *Banjo* Concerto (1966–67); a Piano Concerto entitled *The New Human* (1973); and *To the Northwest Indians* for narrator, folk instruments, and orchestra (1974).

His choral music reflects his strong social and political views. His best-known work, *Ballad of Americans* for bass, chorus, and orchestra, was first performed with Paul Robeson as soloist in 1938. Other works include *The People, Yes* (Carl Sandburg; 1938-41); *The Lonesome Trail* (1942); *Battle Hymn* (1942); *The Lonesome Train* for speakers, soprano, chorus, and orchestra (1942); *The Town Crier* for solo voices, chorus, and orchestra (1947); *When We Grow Up* for children's voices and instruments (1954); *Preamble to Peace* for narrator, chorus, and orchestra (1960); *Giants in the Land* for soloists, chorus, and orchestra (1968); *Strange Unusual Evening: The Santa Barbara Story* (1970); and *Ride the Wind* for speakers, chorus, and orchestra (1974).

Robinson composed a number of popular songs; the most popular are "Abe Lincoln" (1936), "Joe Hill" (1936), "The House I Live In" (1942), and "Hurry Sundown" (1963). He wrote music for many feature films, including *California* (1937); *People of the Cumberland* (1937); *A Walk in the Sun* (1945); *The House I Live In*, which won an Academy Award in 1946; *The Romance of Rosy Ridge* (1947); *The Man From Texas* (1948); and *The Adventures of Huckleberry Finn* (1975). He provided scores for several documentaries: *United Action* (1939); *It's Up to You* (1941); *The Negro Soldier* (with Dmitri Tiomkin; 1944); *Hell Bent for Election* (1944); *Muscle Black* (1948); *When We Grew Up* (1951); *Giants in the Land* (1956); *Something New Under the Sun* (1959); and *The Concept of Intensive Coronary Care* (1969).

Robinson died in an automobile accident shortly after completing an autobiography, *Ballad for Americans* (published 1998).

ROBYN, ALFRED G(EORGE)

b. St. Louis, Missouri, 29 April 1860
d. New York, New York, 18 October 1935

At the age of ten, Robyn succeeded his father, William

Robyn (1814–1905) as organist at St. John's Church, St. Louis. After touring the U. S. and Europe as an accompanist and solo pianist (1876–84), he returned to St. Louis to open a piano studio, serve as organist at several religious institutions, and form the Apollo Club, a men's singing group (1894–1902). In 1910 he moved to New York, where he founded the Marion English Opera Company. His light operas were extremely successful, and he became a wealthy man.

For orchestra Robyn composed the symphonic poem *Pompeii*, a Symphony in D, and a Piano Concerto in C. His choral works include the oratorio *The Ascension*, *Mass of the Sacred Heart*, *Love Unending*, and *Praise and Thanksgiving*.

Robyn wrote 28 light operas (1883–1928), including *The Yankee Consul* (1903), *The Gypsy Girl* (1905), *The Yankee Tourist* (1907), *Fortune Land* (1907), and *All For the Ladies* (1912). He also wrote many piano pieces and songs.

His brother Henry Robyn (1830–1878) was a performer, conductor, and educator in the St. Louis area. His *Thorough Description of the Braille System for the Reading and Writing of Music* (1867) was highly praised and very influential.

ROCHBERG, GEORGE

b. Paterson, New Jersey, 5 July 1918

Rochberg studied at the Mannes School of Music in New York (1939–41) with George Szell and Hans Weisse. After serving in the U. S. Army during the Second World War, he was a pupil of Rosario Scalero and Gian-Carlo Menotti at the Curtis Institute, Philadelphia; graduating in 1948; he taught there until 1954. In 1950, he held Fulbright and American Academy fellowships, living in Rome. From 1951 to 1960 he worked for the Theodore Presser Music Co. in Philadelphia, first as music editor, later as director of publications. He became chairman of the music department of the University of Philadelphia (1960–68); he remained a professor there, receiving an appointment as Annenberg Professor of the Humanities in 1979; he retired in 1982.

Prior to 1965, Rochberg's music was atonal, following the tradition of Schoenberg with an emphasis on melodic line. He has commented: "From start to finish, I have been a natural 'singer' in my music, only embracing a more abstruse, abstract approach when the emotional situation dictated." A few of his works written between 1957 and 1960 were influenced by Webern.

Rochberg's earliest major extant composition, Symphony no. 1, written in 1948–49 (five movements) and performed as a three-movement work in Philadelphia in 1958, shows a Stravinsky-like neo-classicism; a 1977 revision restored the original five-movement form.

Night Music (1948), one of his best-known orchestral works, was initially one of two slow movements of the Symphony. *Concert Piece* for two pianos and orchestra dates from 1950. The *Twelve Bagatelles* for piano (1952) was his first 12-tone composition; in 1965 he orchestrated them as *Zodiac*.

George Szell and the Cleveland Orchestra gave the first performance of Rochberg's Second Symphony (1956) on 26 February 1959, a major work that established his reputation further. All of its four movements are based on the same tone row. *Time-Span* (1960, withdrawn) marks an interesting exploration of Webern-like serialism and instrumentation. It was revised in 1962 and retitled *Time Span II*.

After 1965 Rochberg explored ways of combining atonality with tonality, progressing toward a universal language that resulted from a gradual withdrawal from serialism. This musical journey caused outrage in certain academic circles, but subsequent stylistic developments toward the end of the 20th century have vindicated his prophetic decision. *Music for the Magic Theater* for 15 players marks Rochberg's return to tonality, acting as a bridge between atonality and re-embraced tonality; it was composed in 1965 for the 75th anniversary of the University of Chicago. Symphony no. 3, later subtitled *A Passion According to the Twentieth Century*, for soloists, double chorus, chamber choir, and orchestra was commissioned by the Juilliard School and first performed there on 24 November 1970 under Abraham Kaplan. This large-scale work incorporates quotations from Schütz, Bach, Mahler, and Ives.

Imago Mundi (1973) was commissioned by the Baltimore Symphony Orchestra and premiered on 8 May 1974, conducted by Sergio Comissiona. In 1974 the Pittsburgh Symphony Orchestra commissioned a Violin Concerto for Isaac Stern, who gave the first performance on 4 April 1975. In time this impressive work should prove to be a major contribution to the concert repertory. *Transcendental Variations* for strings (1975) is based on the third movement of his third string quartet (1972). Symphony no. 4 was composed in 1976 for the Seattle Youth Orchestra, which performed it in November 1976 under Vilem Sokol. An Oboe Concerto commissioned by the New York Philharmonic Orchestra in 1983 was performed the following year.

Symphony no. 5 was commissioned in 1984 by the Chicago Symphony Orchestra to mark the 150th anniversary of the founding of the city of Chicago. Cast in one long movement, this turbulent score represents the composer's response to the political situation in the world at the time. The Symphony no. 6 is intended to form the central part of a trilogy, beginning with Symphony no. 5 and to be concluded in the future with a Symphony no. 7. Symphony no. 6 was commissioned by the Pittsburgh Symphony Orchestra in 1986 and performed by that ensemble in the following year under Lorin Maazel, who took the work on tour in October 1989 to the Soviet Union. Rochberg's most recent orchestral works are a Clarinet Concerto (1994–95) and *Eden: Out of Time and Out of Space*, a concerto for guitar and small ensemble (1997).

Rochberg's music for chamber ensembles includes a *Chamber Symphony* (1953), *Cantio Sacra* (1954), based on music by Samuel Scheidt, *Serenata d'Estate* for six players (1955), *Cheltenham Concerto* (1958) and *Music for "The Alchemist"* (B. Jonson) for eleven players, composed for a production at New York's Lincoln Center in October 1966.

Among his many instrumental compositions are the important set of seven string quartets. The First (1952) was performed in New York in 1953. The Second (1959–61), with soprano solo, uses four basically different tempi simultaneously throughout. It received its premiere in 1962 by the Philadelphia Quartet with Janice Harsanyi. Quartet no. 3 (1972) was performed in New York in May 1972 by the Concord Quartet, the first work marking his return to tonality; it was awarded the Naumberg Chamber Composition Prize. The next three quartets–no. 4 (1977), no. 5 (1978), and no. 6 (1978)—are collectively known as the "Concord" Quartets, after the name of the commissioning ensemble. They received their premieres as a group on 20 January 1979 at the University of Pennsylvania.

Rochberg's other works include several major instrumental pieces: *Duo Concertante* for violin and cello (1953), *Dialogues* for clarinet and piano (1956), *La Bocca della Verita* for oboe (or violin) and piano (1958–59), a Piano Trio (1963), *Contra Mortem et Tempus* for flute, clarinet, violin, and cello (1965), *Caprice Variations* for solo violin (1970), *Electrikaleidoscope* for amplified ensemble of flute, clarinet, cello, piano, and electric piano (1972), *Ricordanza (Soliloquy)* for cello and piano (1972), *Ukiyo-e (Pictures of the Floating World)* for solo harp (1973) and a Piano Quintet (1975), written for Jerome Lowenthal and the Concord String Quartet; they gave the first performance on 15 March 1976 in New York City.

Other chamber works are *Slow Fires of Autumn: Ukiyo-e II* for flute and harp (1978–79), Viola Sonata (1979) written to celebrate the 75th birthday of William Primrose; String Quartet no. 7 with baritone solo, commissioned by the University of Michigan (1979) and *Octet: A Grand Fantasia* for flute, clarinet, horn, piano, violin, viola, cello, and double bass (1979–80) commissioned by the Chamber Society of the Lincoln Center and first performed in April 1980. A String Quintet dating from 1982 was also written for the Concord Quartet.

His most recent instrumental compositions include a Piano Quartet (1983), Piano Trio no. 2 commissioned in 1985 by the Elizabeth Sprague Coolidge Foundation for the Beaux Arts Trio, a Violin Sonata (1988), two pieces for flute and guitar, *Ora Pro Nobis* (1989–90) and *Music of Fire* (1990), *Rhapsody and Prayer* for violin and piano (1990), Piano Trio no. 3 entitled *Summer* (1990), *Sonata – Aria* for cello and piano (1994), also for the Beaux Arts Trio, *American Bouquet: Version of Popular Music* for guitar (1998), and *Circle of Fire* (1996–97) for two pianos.

For wind ensemble he has composed *Apocalyptica* (1964) for the Montclair (New Jersey) State College Band, *Black Sounds* (1965), music for a ballet, *The Act*, with choreography by Anna Sokolow, commissioned by the Lincoln Center for performance on television, and *Fanfares* for massed brass (1968).

In addition to Symphony no. 3, Rochberg has composed two choral works, *Three Psalms* for chorus (1954) and *Behold, My Servant* for chorus (1973). For solo voice and orchestra he has written *David, the Psalmist* for tenor, completed in 1954 and first performed in 1965, *Blake Songs* for soprano and chamber ensemble (1961), *Tableaux* for soprano, two actors, men's chorus, and 12 players (1968), *Sacred Song of Reconciliation (Mizmor l'Piyus)* for bass baritone (1970), and *Phaedra* (1973–74), a monodrama for mezzo-soprano, based on Robert Lowell's version of Racine's *Phèdre*. It was commissioned by the New Music Ensemble, Syracuse, New York and first performed in January 1976 by the singer Neva Pilgrim.

Rochberg has been a prolific writer of songs. Important among these are an unpublished book of *35 Songs* (1937–69), *Cantes Flamencos* (1969), *Eleven Songs* to poems by Paul Rochberg (1969), *Songs in Praise of Krishna* (1970), *Fantasies* (1971), and *Songs of Inanna and Dumuzi* (1977).

Rochberg's piano music includes *Variations on an Original Theme* (1941), his earliest extant work; *Three Elegiac Pieces* (1950); *Twelve Bagatelles* (1952); *Sonata Fantasia* (1956); *Nach Bach Fantasia* (1966), a commentary on Bach's Partita no. 6, written for Igor Kipnis for harpsichord or piano; *Carnival Music* (1971); *Partita-Variations* (1976); composed for the Performing Arts Bicentennial Series in Washington, D.C.; *Book of Contrapuntal Pieces* (1979), a compilation of pieces, some dating from 1940; *Four Short Sonatas* (1984); and *Sonata Seria* (1999), derived in part from a withdrawn Sonata of 1950.

Rochberg's only opera, based on Herman Melville's satirical novel *The Confidence Man*, to a libretto by his wife, Gene, was commissioned for production in July 1982 by the Santa Fe Opera.

He is also the author of three books: *The Hexachord and Its Relation to the 12-Note Row* (1953); a collection of essays, *The Aesthetics of Survival: A Composer's View of Twentieth Century Music* (1984); and an unpublished treatise on symmetry in chromaticism, atonal and tonal, entitled *Chromaticism.* Currently he is writing a memoir of his music, *Five Lines, Four Spaces, and the People Who Have Played It.*

ROGERS, BERNARD

b. New York, New York, 4 February 1893
d. Rochester, New York, 24 May 1968

After attending the Institute of Musical Art in New York (1919–21), where he was taught by Percy Goetschius, Rogers became the first American pupil of Ernest Bloch in Cleveland. His other teachers included Arthur Farwell, in New York, Frank Bridge in London, and Nadia Boulanger in Paris, the latter two on a Guggenheim Fellowship (1927–29). Rogers was editor and chief critic of *Musical America* (1913–24). He taught at the Cleveland Institute of Music (1922–23) and the Hartt School of Music, Hartford, Connecticut (1926–27), before joining the faculty of the Eastman School of Music, Rochester, New York in 1929, where he was elected professor and chairman of the composition department in 1938. He retired in 1967. His pupils included William Bergsma, David Diamond, Gail Kubik, Peter Mennin, Burrill Philips, and Gardner Read.

Rogers's music possesses a strong Romantic strain. His first orchestral work, *For the Fallen,* composed in 1916, was a tribute to the American dead of the First World War. This was followed in 1918 by an overture, *The Faithful.* An earlier visit to the Orient led to the composition of *Japanese Landscapes* (*Fuji in the Sunset Glow*) for orchestra with mezzo-soprano solo (1933), *Three Japanese Dances* (1933), and *New Japanese Dances* (1961).

Several of his orchestral pieces have specific American themes: *Two American Frescoes* (1933), *The Plains* (1940), and *Elegy for F.D.R.* (1945). The Second World War inspired four compositions: a ballet, *The Colors of War* (1940), *Invasion* (1943), *Hymn to the Free French* (1943), and *Anzacs* (1944).

Most of Rogers' remaining orchestral works bear programs derived from literary or artistic subjects: *In the Gold Room* (1924); *Prelude to Hamlet* (1925); *The Supper at Emmaus* (1937), based on the painting by Rembrandt; *The Dance of Salome* (1938); *The Sailor of Toulon* (1942); and the overture *Amphitryon* (1946).

Rogers wrote many works for children, beginning in 1934 with *Once Upon a Time,* followed by *Five Fairy Tales* (1935); *Characters from Hans Christian Andersen* (1944); *Leaves From the Tale of Pinocchio* (1950); *The Musicians of Bremen,* a setting of the Grimm story for narrator and 13 players (1958); and *Pictures From the Tale of Aladdin* for wind band (1965).

His other orchestral compositions include five sym-

phonies: no. 1, *Adonis* (1925), no. 2 in A-flat (1928), no. 3 in C, *On a Thanksgiving Song* (1936), no. 4 in G minor (1945), and no. 5, *Africa* (1959). He also wrote *The Song of the Nightingale* (1939); *Elegy* for small orchestra (1947); *The Colors of Youth* (1951); *Dance Scenes* (1953); *The Silver World* for chamber orchestra (1958); *Variations on a Child's Song by Mussorgsky* (1960); and *Apparitions* (1967). Although Rogers composed no concertos as such, he wrote a number of works for solo instrument and orchestra: *Soliloquy* for flute and strings (1922); *Soliloquy* for bassoon and strings (1938); *Fantasy* for flute, viola, and orchestra (1938); *Portrait* for violin and orchestra (1952); *Fantasia* for horn, timpani, and strings (1956); and *Allegory* for two flutes, marimba, and strings (1963).

The first of his five operas, *Deirdre,* dates from 1922. *The Marriage of Aude,* completed in 1931, was performed in May of that year in Rochester; it was awarded the David Bispham Medal. *The Warrior,* a setting of the Samson story, was produced at the Metropolitan Opera House on 11 January 1947; it received the Ditson Award. His other operas are *The Veil* (1950) and *The Nightingale* (1954).

All but one of Rogers's choral works make use of religious texts, including three cantatas, *The Raising of Lazarus* (1927), *The Exodus* (1931), and *The Passion* (1941–42), performed at the Cincinnati Festival in 1944; two oratorios, *The Prophet Isaiah* (1950) and *The Light of Man* (after St. John) (1966), the latter commissioned for the Methodist Conference in Lincoln, Nebraska; Psalm 99 (1945); Psalm 89 (1963); and Psalm 114 (1968) for chorus and organ. His secular cantata, *A Letter From Pete* (1947), is based on texts by Walt Whitman.

Rogers's few chamber works include two string quartets, no. 1 (1918) and no. 2 in D minor (1925); *Mood* for piano trio (1918); *Pastorale* for eleven instruments (1924); *Music for an Industrial Film* for two pianos (1937); a String Trio (1953); *Ballade* for viola, bassoon, and piano (1959); and a Violin Sonata (1962).

He was the author of a valuable book, *The Art of Orchestration,* published in 1951.

ROHE, ROBERT KENNETH

b. New York, New York, 22 August 1916

Rohe graduated from the Peter Cooper School of Fine Arts, New York, in 1939. By profession he is a double bass player, a pupil of Fred Zimmermann. He was a member of several leading orchestras, including the NBC Symphony Orchestra. From 1944 he was principal bassist and assistant conductor of the New Orleans Symphony Orchestra.

Rohe's works for orchestra are *Louisiana Sketches;*

Two Preludes (1958); *Mainescape*, which won the Edward Benjamin Tranquil Music Award in 1966; *Yerma* (1972), a suite inspired by the tragedy by Lorca; *Remembrance*, in memory of the conductor Werner Torkanowsky (1994); *The Blue Spruce* for strings (2000); *Orpheus in Hell* (2001); *Kaleidoscope Russia* (2001); and *Elegy 9-11-01* for strings (2001). He has also written incidental music for *A Midsummer Night's Dream* (1968) and *Twelfth Night* (1969).

Rohe is widely known for pieces written for young audiences. One of these, *Land of Bottles* (1957), is a fantasy describing a rocket trip to the dark side of the moon, where all the inhabitants are bottles. It is scored for narrator, four soloists who blow on tuned bottles filled with water, and a small orchestra. Performances have taken place in many countries. *Dee Tee Dum and the Vegetable Patch* (1959), also a fantasy, uses eight soloists playing toy bird instruments with full symphony orchestra. Other compositions for young audiences are *Variations on Happy Birthday* (1958), *Musical Journey Through Time* (1964), and *The House in the Bend of Bourbon Street* (1966).

Among Rohe's chamber music are two brass quintets; a Wind Quintet (1957); String Quartet in C (1958); Suite for guitar (1961); Quartet for double basses (1964); Trio for violin, harp, and double bass (1980); and *Quartet 99* for string quartet (1999). For his own instrument he has written a Sonatina for double bass and piano (1945); a tone poem, *Yohanan*, for double bass and orchestra (1968); *Program of Christmas Carols* for narrator and four double basses (1976); a Double Bass Concerto; and numerous transcriptions of music by Bach and others.

For chorus Rohe has composed two motets, *Ave Maria* (1958) and *Glory to God* (1958). He has also made a setting of Psalm 150 for tenor and piano.

ROREM, NED

b. Richmond, Indiana, 23 October 1923

Rorem was brought up in Chicago where he received lessons in theory from Leo Sowerby (1938–39).He studied at Northwestern University, Evanston, Illinois (1940–42), the Curtis Institute, Philadelphia (1943), and with Aaron Copland at the Berkshire Music Center, Tanglewood (summers of 1946 and 1947). He also took private lessons with Virgil Thomson in New York in 1944. In 1948 he received his Master's degree from the Juilliard School where he had been a pupil of Bernard Wagenaar. From 1949 to 1958 he lived in France and Morocco. In Paris he was briefly a pupil of Arthur Honegger. From 1959 to 1961 he was Composer-in-Residence at the State University of New York, Buffalo. In 1965 he was appointed professor of composition

at the University of Utah, Salt Lake City, a post he held for two years. He has also taught at the Curtis Institute since 1980.

Rorem has been the recipient of many honors: Gershwin Memorial Award (1949), Lili Boulanger Award (1950), a Fulbright Fellowship (1951), two Guggenheim Fellowships (1957, 1977), and an award from the American Academy of Arts and Letters (1968) of which he was elected a member in 1979. In 1976 he won the Pulitzer Prize for *Air Music*.

Rorem has written many works for the stage. The one-act opera *A Childhood Miracle*, composed in Marrakesh in 1952, was performed in New York in 1955. Another one-act opera, *The Robbers* (1956), received its premiere in New York in 1958 at the Mannes School of Music. A musical comedy, *The Ticklish Acrobat*, dates from the same year. In 1959 for Opera Workshop he wrote a "mini-opera," *Last Day*.

After *The Anniversary*, completed in 1962, Rorem was commissioned to compose a full-length opera by the Ford Foundation. *Miss Julie*, with a libretto by Kenneth Emslie based on Strindberg's play, was first staged by the New York City Opera on 4 November 1965. *Bertha*, to a text by Kenneth Koch, dates from 1969. His next opera, *Three Sisters Who Are Not Sisters* (1969), is based on a play by Gertrude Stein. It was performed by the Student Opera Workshop at Temple University, Philadelphia on 24 July 1971.

Fables, five very short operas with piano accompaniment, to poems by La Fontaine, translated by Marianne Moore, was premiered at the University of Tennessee at Martin on 21 May 1971. *Hearing*, five scenes for four singers and seven instruments, performed in March 1977 by the Gregg Smith Singers, is a dramatization of the 1965 song cycle to a scenario by James Holmes using poetry by Kenneth Koch.

Rorem has written music for seven ballets: *Lost in Fear* (1945), *Death of the Black Knight* (1948), *Melos* composed in Morocco in 1951, *Ballet for Jerry* (1951), *Dorian Gray,* produced in Barcelona in 1952, *Early Voyagers* (1959) and *Excursions* (1965). In 1967 Martha Graham choreographed the *Eleven Studies* as a ballet entitled *Dancing Ground*.

Rorem's reputation rests principally on his songs which have passed the 400 total with 30 song cycles. Among these are *Mourning Scene from Samuel* for voice and string quartet (1947), continuing with *The Lordly Hudson* (1948), *Flight From Heaven* (1950), *Six Irish Poems* (1951), *Cycle of Holy Songs* (1951), *The Resurrection* (1952), *Poemes pour la Paix* (1953) and *Six Songs* for high voice. Later settings are *Three Poems of Paul Goodman* (1952–56), *Three Poems of Demetrios Capetanaki* (1954, 1957), *King Midas* (Howard Moss) for two voices and piano (1961), *Poems of Love and Rain* (1963), two versions each of nine poems by W. H. Auden, Emily Dickinson, Theodore Roethke, e. e. cummings for mezzo-soprano, a cycle, *Hearing* (Kenneth Koch) performed by Carolyn Reyer in New York in May 1967, *War Scenes* (Whitman; 1969), *Gloria* for soprano and mezzo-soprano (1970) and *Ariel* (Sylvia Plath) for soprano, clarinet, and piano (1971). *Sun* for soprano and orchestra was performed by Jane Marsh and the New York Philharmonic Orchestra under Karel Ancerl at Lincoln Center in 1967. There followed *Last Poems of Wallace Stevens* for voice, cello, and piano (1971–72), Serenade for voice and piano trio (1975), *Women's Voices,* 11 songs for soprano and piano (1975–76) and *Nantucket Songs,* performed by Phyllis Bryn-Julson with the composer at the piano on 30 October 1979 at the Library of Congress, Washington, D.C. A cycle of ten songs, *The Santa Fe Songs* for baritone, piano, violin, viola, and cello, written for the Santa Fe Chamber Music Festival, was performed in July 1980. *After Long Silence* for soprano, oboe, and chamber ensemble was premiered at the Miami New World Festival in June 1982. More recent song cycles include *The Schuyler Songs* for voice and orchestra (1988), *The Auden Poems* for tenor and string trio (1989), *Swords and Ploughshares* for four solo voices and orchestra (1990), *Their Lonely Betters* (1992), *Songs of Sadness* for voice, guitar, clarinet, and cello (1994), *More Than a Day* (Jack Larson) for voice and chamber orchestra (1995), *Evidence of Things,* 36 songs for four voices and piano (1996) and *Another Sleep* for baritone and piano (2002).

Rorem's important orchestral works are four symphonies. The First, composed in Morocco in 1950 was premiered in Vienna in 1951. The Second was written in 1955 for the La Jolla Orchestra and performed there in 1956. The Third Symphony (1957) was premiered by the New York Philharmonic Orchestra in Carnegie Hall in 1959 under the direction of Leonard Bernstein. The *String Symphony* was first performed in Atlanta, Georgia under the direction of Robert Shaw. The Overture in C, a student work composed in 1948 and now withdrawn, won the Gershwin Memorial Prize in 1950 and was performed by the New York Philharmonic Orchestra in that year conducted by Michel Piastro. Other orchestral works include *Design,* commissioned by the Louisville Orchestra in 1953, *Sinfonia* for 15 woodwind instruments and percussion, commissioned by the American Wind Society in 1957, *Pilgrims* for string orchestra (1958), *Eagles* (Philadelphia, 1958), *Ideas* (1961), *Lions* (1963), *Water Music* for violin, clarinet, and orchestra, composed for the Oakland Youth Orchestra, California (1966), and *Air Music* (1974), awarded the Pulitzer Prize in 1976.

Later orchestral works are *Assembly and Fall* for oboe, trumpet, timpani, viola, and orchestra, commissioned by the North Carolina Symphony Orchestra in 1975, *Sunday Morning,* performed by the Philadelphia Orchestra in 1978 and a *Concerto: Remembering Tommy* for piano, cello, and orchestra, commissioned in 1977 by the Cincinnati Symphony Orchestra for Jeanne and Jack Kirstein. Among his other concertos are three for piano, no. 1 (1950, withdrawn), no. 2 (1951), and no. 3 in six movements (1955); a Violin Concerto (1984), an Organ Concerto (1985), Horn Concerto (1992), Concerto for piano, left hand, written in 1993 for Gary Graffman, Concerto for English horn, commissioned in 1993 to celebrate the 150th anniversary of the New York Philharmonic Orchestra, Double Concerto for violin, cello, and orchestra (1998), Flute Concerto (2000) and Cello Concerto (2003).

More recent orchestral pieces include *Frolic: Fanfare,* commissioned in 1986 for the Houston Symphony Orchestra; *Fantasy and Polka* (1988); *Fanfare and Flourish* (1988); *Triptych* for chamber orchestra (1993); and *Waiting* (1996).

Rorem's large-scale choral works are *The Poet's Requiem* for soprano solo, chorus, and orchestra (1955; New York, 1957); *Little Prayers* (Paul Goodman) for soprano and baritone soloists, chorus, and orchestra (1973); *An American Oratorio* for tenor, chorus, and orchestra (1984); *Te Deum* for chorus, brass, and organ (1987); and an oratorio, *Goodbye, My Fancy* for cello, baritone, chorus, and orchestra (1989). Other choral compositions are Psalm 70 for chorus and organ (or chamber ensemble; 1943); *Sermon on Miracles* for soloists, chorus, and string orchestra (1947); *Miracles of Christmas* for chorus and organ (1959); *Lift Up Ye Heads* for chorus and wind instruments (1963), dedicated to the memory of Poulenc; *Letters From Paris* for chorus and orchestra (1966); *Praises for the Nativity* for double chorus and orchestra (1970); and *Whitman Cantata* for men's voices, brass, and harp (1985).

For unaccompanied voices he has written *Four Madrigals* (1946), *From an Unknown Past* (seven choruses; 1951), two sets of *Canticles* (1972), *Five Prayers for the Young* (1973), *Missa Brevis* (1973), *Three Choruses for Christmas* (1978), and *Pilgrim Strangers* (Whitman) composed in 1984 for the King's Singers.

Rorem's instrumental music includes five string quartets (1947, 1950, 1990, 1998, 2002); a Violin Sonata (1949); *Eleven Studies for Eleven Players* (1962), commissioned in 1959 by the State University of New York at Buffalo; Trio for flute, cello, and piano (1960); *Lovers* for harpsichord, oboe, cello, and percussion (1964); *Day Music* (1971) and *Night Music* (1972), both for violin and piano; *Book of Hours* for flute and harp (1975); *Sky Music* for harp (1976); *Romeo and Juliet* for flute and guitar (1977); and *Star Child* for guitar, premiered at the Blossom Music Festival, Cuyahoga Falls, Ohio in July 1980. Among his later chamber music are *Winter Pages* for clarinet, bassoon, and piano trio (1981); *After Reading Shakespeare* for solo cello (1983); *Dances* for cello and piano (1984); *Scenes from Childhood* for septet (1985); *End of Summer* for clarinet, violin, and piano (1986); *Bright Music* for flute, two violins, cello, and piano (1987); *Diversions* for brass quintet (1989); *Spring Music* for piano trio (1990); Quintet for clarinet, piano, and strings (2001); *United States* for string quartet (Quartet no. 5) (2002); *Pas de Trois* for oboe, violin, and piano (2002); and *The Unanswered Question* for chamber ensemble (2003).

Rorem has contributed three important sonatas to the repertory of the piano, no. 1 (1948), no. 2 (1950), and no. 3 (1954). Also for piano are *A Quiet Afternoon*, a set of nine pieces (1948); *Three Bagatelles* (1949); *Burlesque* (1955); *Eight Etudes* (1976); *Song and Dance* (1986); and *Soundpoints* (2003). He composed *Spiders* for harpsichord (1968). For organ he has written *Fantasy and Toccata* (1946); *Pastorale* (1950); a massive 11–movement suite, *A Quaker Reader* (1977); *Views From the Oldest House* (1981); and three *Organbooks* (1989).

Rorem is a prolific writer of essays and diaries; his outspoken opinions have often ruffled feathers in the musical world. These include *The Paris Diary of Ned Rorem* (1966) and *The New York Diary* (1967), revised and combined in 1983; *Music From the Inside Out* (1967); *Music and People* (1968); *Critical Affairs: A Composer's Journal* (1970); *Pure Contraption* (1974); *The Final Diary* (1974); *An Absolute Gift* (1980); *Setting the Tone: Essays and a Diary* (1983); *The Nantucket Diary 1973–1985* (1987); *Settling the Score: Essays on Music* (1988); *Knowing When to Stop: A Memoir* (1994); *Other Entertainment: Collected Pieces* (1996); *Lies: A Diary 1986–1999* (1999); and *A Ned Rorem Reader* (2002).

ROSEN, JEROME WILLIAM
b. Boston, Massachusetts, 23 July 1921

Rosen studied at the New Mexico State University, Las Cruces, the University of California, Berkeley, with Roger Sessions and William Denny. In Paris (1949–51) he was a pupil of Darius Milhaud. From 1952 to 1988 he taught at the University of California, Davis, where he was professor of music and director of the Electronic Music Studio. He was also active as a clarinetist. Rosen has been awarded three From Foundation Awards (1953, 1954, 1960) and two Guggenheim Fellowships (1958, 1959).

Although most of Rosen's compositions are for instrumental ensembles, he has written several orchestra works, including a Saxophone Concerto (1949–57); *Sounds and Movements* (1963); a Concerto for clarinet, trombone, and band (1964); *Synket Concerto*

(1968), *Three Pieces* for two recorders and orchestra (1971); and a Clarinet Concerto (1973). For concert band he has composed *Five Pieces* (1960) and *Three Waltzes* for saxophone and band.

For the stage Rosen has written a musical play, *Emperor Norton Lives!* (1976), a chamber opera, *Calisto and Melibea* (1978), and an opera, *Emperor Norton of the U.S.A.* (1980). Two ballet scores, described as "dance satires," are *Search* (1953) and *Life Cycle* (1954).

Among his many instrumental works are *Two Pieces* for piano (1949); a Wind Quintet (1949); Sonata for clarinet and cello (1949); *Overture and Dance* for clarinet, bassoon, and cello (1950); *A Birthday Piece* for string trio (1951); *Prelude to a Dance* for clarinet, bassoon, and cello (1951); Serenade for violin, clarinet, and piano (1951); two string quartets (1953, 1965); *Duo* for clarinet and piano (1955); *Petite Suite* for four clarinets (1959); Clarinet Quintet (1959); *Five Pieces* for wind quintet and piano (1960); *Elegy* for solo percussion (1963), *Five Pieces* for clarinet and piano (1964); Viola Sonata (1970); *Serenade for Basses* for bass clarinet and double bass (1972); *Play Time* for cello and double bass (1981); *Play Time II* for clarinet and string quartet (1981); *Fantasy* for solo violin (1983); and *Concertpiece* for clarinet and piano (1984).

Rosen's choral music includes *Three Songs* (Gerard Manley Hopkins) (1952); *The Friendly Beasts* for chorus and two clarinets (1954); *Three Songs* for chorus and piano (1965); *Chamber Music* for female voices and harp (1975); and *Campus Doorway* for chorus and orchestra (1978). For solo voice he has written a song cycle, *Thirteen Ways of Looking at a Blackbird* (Wallace Stevens) for soprano and piano (1951); *Recollection* (Emily Dickinson; 1952); *Five Songs* (medieval Latin) for soprano and piano (1954); Serenade for soprano and saxophone (1964); *White-Haired Love*, a cycle for baritone, flute, clarinet, string quartet, and piano (1985); and *Love Poems*, a cycle for male and female speaking voices, flute, clarinet, string quartet, and piano (1988).

ROSENBOOM, DAVID
b. Fairfield, Iowa, 9 September 1947

Rosenboom studied at the University of Illinois, Urbana (1965–67) with Gordon Binkerd, Salvatore Martirano, Kenneth Gaburo, and Lejaren Hiller. He was Composer-in-Residence at the Center for Creative and Performing Arts of the State University of New York at Buffalo (1967–68). From 1970 to 1971 he studied Indian music with Pandit Pran Nath. In 1971 he was appointed director of Electronic Music at York University, Toronto. He joined the faculty of Mills College in 1979, becoming Darius Milhaud Professor of Music. In addition he taught at the San Francisco Arts Institute

David Rosenboom.
Photo: Steve Gunther, courtesy the composer.

(1981–84) and California College of Arts and Crafts. Since 1990 he has been dean of the School of Music and co-director of the Center for Experimental Art, Information and Technology at the California Institute of the Arts.

Rosenboom's works without electronics include *Contrasts* for violin and orchestra (1963); *Septet* for strings, brass, and piano (1964); Sextet for flute, bassoon, and strings (1965); *Caliban upon Setebos* (Browning) for orchestra (1966); Trio for clarinet, trumpet, and double bass (1966); *Pocket Piece* for flute, alto saxophone, viola, and percussion (1966); *To That Predestined Dancing Place* for percussion quartet (1967); *Suitable for Framing* for two pianos and *mrdangam* (South Indian drum; 1975); *Champ Vital (Life Field)* for violin, piano, and percussion (1987); *Bell Solaris* for piano (1997–98); and *Seeing the Small in the Large* for large orchestra (1998–99). In 1980 he completed a set of five *Etudes*: *I* (trombones), *II* (keyboards, mallets, and harps), *III* (piano and two oranges), *IV* (electronic), and *V, The Story* for chamber orchestra and film.

Since 1967 Rosenboom has concentrated on multimedia works with unusual titles. These include *The Thud, Thud, Thud of Suffocating Blackness* for two percussionists, alto saxophone, electric cello, piano, tape, and lights (1966–67); *Then We Wound Our Way Through an Aura of Golden Yellow Gauze* for musicians and actress, *The Brandy of the Damned*, a theater piece for electronic tape (1967); *She Loves Me, She Loves Me Not,* a theater piece for four–channel tape, two actors, musicians, percussion, and projectors (1968); *Urboui* for tape and film (1968); *And Came Up Dripping* for oboe and analog computer (1968); *How Much Better if Plymouth Rock Had Landed on the Pilgrims* for live electronics and traditional instruments (1969–71); and *Ecology of the Skin*, an environmental piece (1970).

Later multimedia creations are *It is About to . . . Sound, It is About . . . Vexations* for two interactive media installations, celebrating the life and work of John Cage (1993) and *On Being Invisible II (Hypatia Speaks to Jefferson in a Dream)*, an interactive multimedia piece premiered at the University of Illinois in 1995.

Among his compositions combining instruments and electronics are *Precipice in Time* for quintet with computer processing (1966); *The Seduction of Sapientia* for viol da gamba and electronics (1974); *And Out Came the Night Eyes* for piano and electronics (1978); *In the Beginning* for soloists, chamber ensemble, orchestra, and electronics (1978–81); *Future Travel* for computer and acoustic instruments (1982, rev. 1987); *Zones of Influence* for percussion solo and electronics (1984–85); *Roundup*, an anthology of live electronic and acoustic works (1987); *Systems of Judgement* for various instruments and computer processing (1988); *Extended Trio* for instruments and electronics (1992); and *Predictions, Confirmations and Disconfirmations* for piano and computer (1991).

Rosenboom is the editor of a book, *Biofeedback and the Arts* (1976), and the author of *Extended Musical Interface with the Human Nervous System* (1990).

ROUSE, CHRISTOPHER (CHAPMAN)
b. Baltimore, Maryland, 15 February 1949

Rouse studied at the Oberlin College Conservatory, Ohio (1967–71) with Richard Hoffmann and Randolph

Coleman. From 1971 to 1973 he took private composition lessons with George Crumb in New York. At Cornell University (1973–77) he was a pupil of Karel Husa and Robert Palmer (M.F.A.; D.M.A.). Rouse taught at the University of Michigan, Ann Arbor (1978–81) before being appointed to the music faculty of the Eastman School of Music in 1981, becoming a professor in 1991. He was responsible for introducing the first rock music course there; as a youngster he had been a drummer in a rock band. Since 1997 he has also taught at the Juilliard School, New York. He has been Composer-in-Residence with the Indianapolis Symphony Orchestra (1985–86) and Baltimore Symphony Orchestra (1986–89). In 1990 he was awarded a Guggenheim Fellowship.

Most of Rouse's compositions written before 1979, including a Symphony dating from 1967, have been withdrawn. Rouse's earliest surviving orchestral work, *The Infernal Machine*, was commissioned in 1981 by the League of Composers and premiered in France. Later orchestral scores include *Gorgon* (1984), a Rochester Philharmonic commission; *Phantasmata* (1981, 1985), incorporating *The Infernal Machine* (its third movement, *Bump*, has also been performed as an independent work); *Phaeton*, performed by the Philadelphia Orchestra in 1986; *Jagannath* (1987), premiered in 1990 by the Houston Symphony Orchestra; Symphony no. 1 in one movement (1988); *Iscariot* for chamber orchestra (1989); *Concerto per Corde* (1990); Symphony no. 2 (Houston, 1995), whose slow movement was written in memory of the composer Stephen Albert; *Envoi* (1996); and *Rapture* performed in 1999 by the Pittsburgh Symphony Orchestra.

For solo instruments and orchestra Rouse has written a Double Bass Concerto (1985), first performed in Buffalo; Violin Concerto, introduced at the Aspen Summer Festival in 1991; Trombone Concerto, composed in 1992 for the New York Philharmonic Orchestra in memory of Leonard Bernstein and winner of the Pulitzer Prize in 1993; a Flute Concerto (Detroit, 1993); Cello Concerto composed in 1994 for Yo-Yo Ma; *Der gerettete Alberich*, a concerto for percussion written for Evelyn Glennie and the Los Angeles Philharmonic Orchestra in 1998; *Seeing* for piano and orchestra, for Emmanuel Ax (1998); *Concerto de Gaudi* for guitar and orchestra, performed in Hamburg in 1999; and Clarinet Concerto (Chicago, 2001).

The instrumental music of Rouse covers a wide variety of forms: *Morpheus* for solo cello (1975); *Ogoun Badagnis* (named after a Haitian voodoo deity) for percussion ensemble (1976); *Ku-Ka-Ilimoku* for percussion ensemble (1978); *Thor* for wind ensemble (1980); *Rotae passionis* (*Passion Wheel*), describing the Seven Stations of the Cross, for chamber ensemble (1982); two string quartets (1982, 1988); *Lares hercii* for vio-

lin and harpsichord (1983); *The Surma Ritornelli* for chamber ensemble (1983); *Artemis* for brass quintet (1988); *Bonham* for eight percussionists (1988), a tribute to Led Zeppelin drummer John Bonham; *Deploration* for string quartet (1994); *Goldberg Variations* for cello and piano (1995); *Compline* for flute, clarinet, harp, and string quartet (1996); *Valentine* for solo flute (1996); and *Rapturedux* for 145 cellos, composed in 2001 for a cello festival in Manchester, England. His *The Nevill's Feast* was commissioned by the Boston "Pops" Orchestra and premiered in May 2003.

For voices Rouse has written *Four Madrigals* for double chorus (1976); and *Karolju* for choir and orchestra performed in 1990 by the Baltimore Symphony Orchestra. He is currently composing a Requiem, commissioned by Sol Deo Gloria for the 2003–2004 season. His solo vocal music include *Eight Songs* for soprano and ensemble; *Mitternachtlieder* (Georg Trakl) for baritone and chamber ensemble (1979); *Nuit d'ivresse* (after Berlioz) for mezzo-soprano, baritone, oboe d'amore, and piano (1981); and *Kabir Padavali* for soprano and orchestra (1997).

RÓZSA, MIKLÓS
b. *Budapest, Hungary, 18 April 1907*
d. *Los Angeles, California, 27 July 1995*

Rózsa studied at both the University and Conservatory in Leipzig (1925–29), then settled in Paris in 1932. In 1935 he moved to London, where he studied conducting at Trinity College of Music with Kennedy Scott and John Fry. It was in England that he began his career as a writer of film music. He emigrated to the United States in 1940, making his home in Hollywood. From 1945 he taught at the University of Southern California in Los Angeles.

Although Rózsa earned a wide reputation as a composer of music for the screen, he wrote a substantial number of works for the concert hall. Many of these were influenced by Hungarian folk music: *Variations on a Hungarian Peasant Song* for violin and orchestra, op. 4 (1929); *North Hungarian Peasant Songs and Dances*, op. 5 (1929), also for violin and orchestra; the ballet *Hungaria*, written for the Markova-Dolin Company (London, 1935); *Three Hungarian Sketches*, op. 14 (1937); and *Notturno Ungherese*, op. 28 (1961).

Rózsa's orchestral works include Serenade for small orchestra, op. 10 (1932; rev. 1946 as *Hungarian Serenade*, op. 25); Symphony in three movements, op. 11 (1930, rev. 1993); *Theme, Variations and Finale*, op. 13 (1933); *Concerto for Strings*, op. 17 (1943); *Kaleidoscope* for small orchestra, op. 19 (1948); *The Vintner's Daughter* (*Variations*), op. 23 (1952); *Overture for a Symphony Concert*, op. 26 (1956–57);

Tripartita, op. 33 (1970); and *Fantasy* for brass, organ, and timpani, based on the score for *Young Bess* (1982).

For solo instruments and orchestra he wrote an early Violin Concerto (1928–29), subsequently withdrawn; *Rhapsody* for cello, op. 3 (1928); Violin Concerto, op. 24 (1954) received its premiere in January 1956 with Jascha Heifetz as soloist; and Leonard Pennario played Rozsa's Piano Concerto, op. 31 (1965) in Los Angeles in 1967. Other concertos include *Sinfonia Concertante*, op. 29 for violin and cello, composed in 1963 for Heifetz and Piatigorsky; and a Cello Concerto, op. 32 written for János Starker, a fellow Hungarian, who performed it at the Berlin Festival in September 1972. In 1979 he completed a Viola Concerto, op. 37 for Pinchas Zukerman. For the American Bicentennial in 1976, Rózsa wrote a *Festive Flourish* for brass and percussion.

Among his vocal and choral works are *Two Vansittart Songs*, op. 16 for alto and piano (1940); *Two Madrigals*, op. 18 for female voices (1944); *To Everything There is a Season*, op. 21 a motet for double chorus and organ (1946); *The Vanities of Life*, op. 30, a motet for mixed voices (1966); *Five Songs*, op. 33 (1972); Psalm 23, op. 34 for mixed voices (1973); and *Three Chinese Poems*, op. 35 for mixed voices (1973).

Rozsa composed many instrumental works: String Trio, op. 1 (1928); Piano Quintet in F minor, op. 2 (1928); *Duo* no. 1, op. 7 for violin and piano (1931); *Duo* no. 2, op. 8 for cello and piano (1932); Sonata for two violins, op. 15 (1933, rev. 1973); String Quartet no. 1, op. 22 (1950); Clarinet Sonatina, op. 27 (1960); *Toccata Capricciosa*, op. 36 for cello and piano (1978); String Quartet no. 2, op. 38 (1981); Flute Sonata, op. 39 (1983); and a Sonata for solo clarinet (1987).

A capable pianist, he wrote several works for that instrument: *Piano Variations*, op. 9 (1932), *Bagatelles*, op. 12 (1932), *Kaleidoscope*, op. 19 (1948), Sonata, op. 20 (1948), and *Valse Crepusculaire* (1976).

Rózsa composed over 100 full-length film scores; among the most significant are including *Knight Without Armor* (1937); *Thunder in the City* (1937); *The Four Feathers* (1939); *The Thief of Bagdad* (1940); *Lady Hamilton* (1942); *Jungle Book* (1942); *Sahara* (1943); *Blood on the Sun* (1944); *Double Indemnity* (1944); *The Red House* (1945); *The Lost Weekend* (1945); *Spellbound* (1945); *The Killers* (1946); *Brute Force* (1947); *The Naked City* (1948); *A Double Life* (1948); *Madame Bovary* (1949); *Adam's Rib* (1949); *Young Bess* (1949); *Quo Vadis?* (1951); *Ivanhoe* (1952); *Julius Caesar* (1953); *The Asphalt Jungle* (1954); *Diane* (1955); *Bohwani Junction* (1956); *Lust for Life* (1956); *Ben-Hur* (1959); *King of Kings* (1960); *The Green Berets* (1968); *The Power* (1968); *The Private Life of Sherlock Holmes* (1969); *The Golden Voyage of Sinbad* (1973); (1970); *Providence* (1976); *Fedora* (1978); *The Last Embrace* (1978); *Time After Time* (1979); *The Eye of the Needle* (1981); and *Dead Men Don't Wear Plaid* (1982).

In 1982, he published his autobiography, *Double Life*.

RUDHYAR, DANE
(BORN DANIEL CHENNEVIÈRE)
b. Paris, France, 23 March 1895
d. San Francisco, California, 13 September 1985

In Paris, Chennevière studied law and philosophy at the Sorbonne and briefly attended the Conservatory. In composition he was largely self-taught. His book, *Claude Debussy and the Cycle of Musical Civilization*, was published by Durand in Paris in 1913 when he was only 18 years old; some piano pieces were also published at that time. He went to New York in November 1916 for the performances in April 1917 of his *Poems Ironiques* and *Vision Vegetale* at a festival of dance at the Metropolitan Opera House conducted by Pierre Monteux. This was the first polytonal music ever heard in America. That year he changed his name from Daniel Chennevière to Dane Rudhyar. In 1920 he visited Hollywood on a commission to write music for *The Pilgrimage Play*. In 1922, his *Soul Fire* won a $1,000 prize offered by the newly formed Los Angeles Philharmonic Orchestra for a symphonic poem. He became an American citizen in 1926. His music was composed mostly between 1920 and 1935.

After 1925, Rudhyar's music was entirely atonal, based on what he called the principles of dissonant harmony and the free rhythm of speech, rather than the classical patterns derived from dance. It is a very personal, inward, and expressive language based on the power of tone and resonance. He aimed at inducing psychological states and inner transformation in the hearer, as the "spiritual" titles of his pieces imply. From 1912, he believed that the old Euro-American culture had been disintegrating, and his many creative activities were polarized by an attempt to formulate basic principles on which a new culture and society could be built.

His orchestral compositions include *Dithyramb* (1919); *Syntony No. 1* (1920–21); *To the Real* (1921); *Syntony No. 2* (1921); *The Warrior* for piano and orchestra (1921); *The Surge of Fire* (1921); *To the Real* (1922); *Syntony No. 3, Ouranos* (1927); *The Human Way* (1927); *Threnody* (1927); Sinfonietta (1927); *Five Stanzas* for strings (1928); *Hero Chants* (1930); *Desert Chants* (1932); *Emergence* for strings (1948); *Tripthong* for piano and orchestra (1948, rev 1977); and *Thresholds* (1955). His last orchestral works were *Encounter* for piano and orchestra (1977), *Dialogues* (1977), and *Cosmic Cycle* (1977).

Rudhyar's chamber music includes *Three Melodies* for flute with piano and cello accompaniment (1918); *Three Poems* for violin and piano (1920); a Violin Sonata (1920); two "miniature string quartets," *Solitude* (1926, performed 1951) and *Dark Passage* (1941); Piano Quintet (1950); a Quintet for alto flute, piano, and strings, subtitled *Nostalgia* (1977); and two string quartets of "normal" duration, *Advent* (1977) and *Crisis and Overcoming* (1979) for the Kronos Quartet.

He wrote extensively for the piano; particularly noteworthy are *Four Pentagrams* (1924–26), *Paeans* (1927), *Syntony* (1929), *Granites* (1929), and *Nine Tetragrams* (1920–67). His final keyboard works include two "tone rituals," *Transmutation* (1976) and *Theurgy* (1976); *Three Cantos* (1977); *Autumn* (1977); *Epic Poem* (1978); and *Rite of Transcendence* (1981).

After many years of limited recognition and few performances, Rudhyar's music was rediscovered at the end of his life and warmly received by the younger generation. In this respect he had much in common with Charles Ives. This late discovery led to a new burst of creative energy in his eighties. In 1976 and 1977 Rudhyar received successive grants from the National Endowment for the Arts, and in 1978 he was honored with the Marjorie Peabody Waite Award from the American Academy and Institute of Arts and Letters.

Rudhyar was very active as an author and lecturer, having written thousands of articles and several books on non-academic philosophy, aesthetics, and social criticism, and around 20 volumes dealing with the psychological reformulation of astrology. One of his books, *The Rebirth of Hindu Music*, was published in 1928. He also published several books of poetry, took the part of Christ in Cecil B. De Mille's silent movie *The Ten Commandments* (1923), and exhibited a number of non-objective paintings.

RUGER, MORRIS HUTCHINS

b. Superior, Wisconsin, 2 December 1902
d. San Diego, California, July 1974

After graduating from Columbia University in 1924, where he had been a pupil of Seth Bingham, Ruger went to Paris, where he became a pupil of Isador Philipp and André Bloch. On his return to the United States he attended Northwestern University, Evanston, Illinois and the Juilliard School. In 1945 he was appointed assistant director of the Los Angeles Conservatory.

His opera *Gettysburg* was produced at the Hollywood Bowl in 1938. Other works include a Violin Concerto, a Piano Quintet, and a String Quartet. In 1947 he published a book, *Harmony: A Creative Approach to Four-part Writing.*

RUGGLES, CARL (CHARLES SPRAGUE)

b. Marion, Massachusetts, 11 March 1876
d. Bennington, Vermont, 24 October 1971

As a child, Ruggles learned to play the violin, and later studied at Harvard University under John Knowles Paine. He moved to Winona, Minnesota where he founded and conducted the Winona Symphony Orchestra. From 1923 to 1933 he lived in New York, where he was a member of the International Composers Guild and was an active colleague of Edgar Varèse in promoting music with the Pan-American Association of Composers. From 1933 to his death he lived in reclusion with his wife in a converted schoolhouse in Arlington, Vermont. He was fortunate in acquiring a patron, Harriet Miller, so that he could devote all his energies to composition and to painting, at which he was equally adept.

As with Ives, Ruggles's almost legendary isolation from the world of professional music allowed him to evolve his own musical language without external influences, in his case adopting a 21-note scale comprising the seven white notes, seven sharps, and seven flats. For him a sustained melodic line was all-important, with complex, rhythmical grouping of lines. In sharp contrast with Ives, however, the total number of Ruggles' surviving compositions hardly reached double figures, and most of these last only a few minutes in performance. In his music a striving for the sublime caused him constantly to revise his few works in an attempt to achieve perfection and compactness of form. He is said to have spent 20 years searching for a musical system and then discarded all his works written before 1916, including an opera, *The Sunken Bell,* based on a play by Gerhart Hauptmann.

Ruggles came to the notice of the public when *Angels,* for six muted trumpets, was performed at the first I.S.C.M. Festival, held in Venice in 1925 . In his account of the problems that arose during that festival, Edward J. Dent describes the hostility aroused by *Angels*: "It was very slow, but mercifully short, and the trumpets were all muted and playing pianissimo; every note was an agony, and sounded if it cost the players agony too; I never heard anything so excruciating in all my musical experience, though it awoke childhood memories of slate-pencils on slate. The audience was too bewildered to either demonstrate or to applaud." In 1939 Ruggles revised the scoring for four trumpets and three trombones, all muted.

Angels was intended as the second part of a larger work in three sections, *Men and Angels,* first completed in 1921. The opening piece, *Men,* was revised in 1924 to become an independent composition, *Men and Mountains,* performed in 1936. It is cast in three sections

Carl Ruggles.
*MSS 26, The Carl Ruggles Papers
in the Irving S. Gilmore Library of
Yale University.*

and scored for large orchestra. The first movement, *Men, a Rhapsodic Proclamation* for horns and orchestra, has a dense texture of solid orchestration, and its 40 measures contain frequent changes of time signature. *Lilacs* for string orchestra, the second movement, is sometimes played separately, although it lasts only 30 measures. Its elegiac mood evokes the poem by Whitman, "When lilacs last by the dooryard bloom'd"; once again, the writing for the instruments produces a thick texture of dark harmonies, "to be played with deep feeling." The final section, *Marching Mountains,* is for full orchestra with a pervading drumbeat that seems to recall the fatalistic opening of Brahms' First Symphony. The score is prefaced with a quotation from William Blakes's *Gnomic Verses*: "Great things are done when men and mountains meet."

The proposed third part of *Men and Mountains* set was *Sun-treader*; the title is taken from Browning's tribute to the poet Shelley. This "magnum opus" for large orchestra took the composer six years to complete, but consists of only 50 pages of score lasting about 16 minutes. It was finished in 1926 and given its premiere in Paris under Nicolas Slonimsky in 1932 and performed at the I.S.C.M. Festival in Barcelona in 1936. For this work, Ruggles constructed a continuous sheet of music paper 20 feet long from butcher's wrapping paper so that a double and triple canon could be seen all at once. Like *Men and Mountains*, it is heavily scored with slow-moving, massive grandeur of considerable harmonic complexity. *Sun-treader* was not heard in the

United States until 24 January 1966, when it was played by the Boston Symphony Orchestra at Bowdoin College (Portland, Maine) under Jean Martinon. Ruggles himself never attended a performance of his masterpiece.

Ruggles's other works for orchestra are *Portals* for 13 string instruments, composed in 1925 (rev. 1930, 1950); *Organum* (1943–49); and his last composition, *Affirmations* (1957). For voice and orchestra he wrote *Toys* (1919) and *Vox Clamans in Deserto* (1922). *Evocations* for piano (1937–43, rev. 1954), subtitled *Four Chants*, found a champion in John Kirkpatrick, who had brought Charles Ives' *"Concord" Sonata* to the public.

Like Ives, Ruggles wrote in a vacuum, completely withdrawn from the world, entirely uninfluenced by contemporary trends, and without regard for audiences or, it seems, even public performance. The mythical aura which surrounded the reputation of Ruggles while he was alive has given rise to a misguided and uncritical reverence that has been applied to all his compositions. His ardent supporters regarded him as a high priest of music, treating every utterance as of oracular significance, partly because the works are so complicated and unusual, and partly because they are so few in number.

Seen against the background of both American and European music, Ruggles and Ives have no counterparts, although the self-conscious music of Ruggles viewed objectively has something in common with that of Schoenberg and Alban Berg, but lacks the variety and interest of these two composers. He was too limited by his self-imposed abstruse musical theories.

RUSSO, WILLIAM (JOSEPH)

b. Chicago, Illinois, 25 June 1928
d. Chicago, Illinois, 11 January 2003

Russo studied English at Roosevelt University, Chicago, graduating in 1955. He was a private composition pupil of John J. Becker (1953–55) and Karel Jirák (1955–57). He also studied with the jazz pianist Lenny Tristano. In Chicago in 1947 he founded a rehearsal orchestra, "An Experiment in Jazz." As a trombonist and composer-arranger he worked for Stan Kenton (1950–54), with his own orchestra in New York (1959–61), and as director of the London Jazz Orchestra (1962–64). He taught at the Lenox School of Music, Massachusetts (1957–60) and the Manhattan School of Music (1959–61). From 1965 to 1975 he was director of the Center for New Music at Columbia College, Chicago and conductor of the Chicago Jazz Ensemble. He taught at the Peabody Conservatory, Baltimore (1969–71) and at Antioch College, Yellow Springs, Ohio (1971–72) and was Composer-in-Residence to the City and County of San Francisco (1975–76). Until the early 1990s he was Composer-in-Residence at Columbia College.

In his compositions, Russo attempted to fuse jazz and blues with the symphonic orchestra. Among his large-scale symphonic jazz works are Symphony no. 1 (1957); Symphony no. 2 in C, *Titans* (1958), a Koussevitzky Foundation commission; Cello Concerto (1962); *English Concerto* for violin and jazz orchestra (1963), commissioned by Yehudi Menuhin; *Variations on an American Theme* (1964); *America 1966*, a concerto grosso for jazz orchestra (1966); *Three Pieces for Blues Band and Orchestra* (1968), danced as a ballet, *Mother Blues*, by the San Francisco Ballet in 1974; *Street Music: A Blues Concerto* for harmonica player, piano, and orchestra (1975); and *Carousel Suite* for narrator, chamber orchestra, and dancers (1975). For orchestra Russo wrote *Solitaire* for strings (1949), *Newport Suite* (1958; arr. for jazz orchestra, 1960), and *Urban Trilogy* (1981).

In addition to numerous arrangements, Russo composed much for jazz orchestra: two suites, no. 1 (1952, rev. 1962), and no. 2 (1951–54, rev. 1962); *Four Pieces* (1953–57); *Seven Deadly Sins* (1960); *The New Age Suite* (1984); *For My Friend* (1991); *The Horn Blower* (1991); and *The Garden of Virtue* (1993).

For the stage he wrote two ballets, *The World of Alcina* (1954, rev. 1962) and *Les Deux Errants,* commissioned by the London Festival Ballet in 1955. He

has also composed several operas: *John Hooton* (1961) in three acts to his own libretto, broadcast on B.B.C. London radio in 1983; *The Island* (1964) in one act to a text by Adrian Mitchell, commissioned by the B.B.C. as its entry for the Italia Prize; *Antigone* (1967), in one act; *Land of Milk and Honey* (1964); *The Alice B. Toklas Hashish Fudge Revue* (1970), which had a lengthy run in New York. (Retitled *Paris Lights*: *The All-Star Literary Genius Expatriate Revue*, it was revived at the American Place Theater in New York in 1980.) *Aesop's Fables*, a rock opera with a text by Jon Swan, received almost two hundred performances in New York, including an off-Broadway run in 1972.

Two one-act comic operas, *Isabella's Fortune* and *Pedrolina's Revenge*, were produced in New York in 1974. *A General Opera*, a chamber opera in one act with libretto by Arnold Weinstein (1976), was completed under a grant from the National Endowment for the Arts. More recent operas include *The Shepherds' Christmas*, staged in Chicago in 1979; *The Pay Off*, a cabaret opera (1984); *Dubrovsky* (1988); and *The Sacrifice* (1990). In 1984 he composed a musical, *The Golden Bird* for narrator, singers dancers, and small orchestra, staged in Chicago.

Russo composed several rock cantatas for soloists, chorus, and band, including *The Civil War* (1968), *David* (1968), *Joan of Arc* (1970), *The Bacchae* (1972), and *Song of Songs* (1972). Other choral pieces include *In Memoriam* (1966), *Songs of Celebration* for solo voice, chorus, and orchestra (1972), and *Touro Cantata* (1988).

Among a handful of instrumental pieces are *21 Etudes* for brass instruments (1959), a Violin Sonata (1986), *Memphis* for alto saxophone and nine instruments (1988), and *Women* for harmonica, piano, and string quartet (1990). Vocal music includes a song cycle, *Talking to the Sun* (1989); *Listen Beneath* for soprano, jazz contralto, and orchestra (1992); and *In memoriam, Hermann Conaway* for mezzo-soprano, tenor, baritone, and 11 instruments (1994). Russo also composed a number of film scores, including *Everybody Rides the Carousel* (1976), *Women of the World*, and *The Second Chance*.

He was the author of three significant books: *Composing for Jazz Orchestra* (1961, rev. 1973); *Jazz: Composition and Orchestration* (1968, rev. 1974); and *Composing Music*: *A New Approach* (1983).

RZEWSKI, FREDERIC (ANTHONY)

b. Westfield, Massachusetts, 13 April 1938

At Harvard University (1954–58) Rzewski was a pupil of Randall Thompson (composition) and Claudio Spies (orchestration). He studied Greek literature and philosophy and the music of Wagner at Princeton University (1958–60), and received tuition from Milton Babbitt and Roger Sessions. On a Fulbright Fellowship he studied with Luigi Dallapiccola in Florence (1960–62). In addition he was a pupil of Elliott Carter in Berlin (1963–65) and Walter Piston at Harvard. Rzewski taught in Cologne (1964–65); in 1966, he founded the Musica Elettronica Viva Studio in Rome. Since 1977 he has been professor of composition at the Liège Conservatory, Belgium. He has also taught at Yale School of Music, University of Cincinnati, State University of New York at Buffalo, Mills College, California, University of California at San Diego, and the Hochschule der Künste in Berlin and Karlruhe. As a pianist Rzewski has played a leading part in the promotion of new music. Several of his works reveal a deep involvement with contemporary social and political issues.

Rzewski's instrumental music includes an Octet (1961–62); *For Violin* (solo) (1962); *Composition for 2* for any two instruments (1964); *Speculum Dianae* for any eight instruments (1964); *Self-Portrait* for one person, any instrument (1964); *Nature Morte* for chamber ensemble (1965); *Spacecraft* (1967); *Prose Pieces* for ensemble (1967–68); *Symphony for Several Performers* (1968); *Les Moutons de Panurge* for any ensemble (1969); *Last Judgment* for trombone (1969); *Second Structure* for improvisation ensemble (1972); *What is Freedom?* for six instruments (1974); *Seven Instrumental Studies* (1977); *Song and Dance* for ensemble (1977); *Moonrise with Memories* for bass trombone and six instruments (1978); *To the Earth* for percussion (1985); *Spots* for percussion, keyboards, and winds (1986); *The Lost Melody* for percussion, keyboards, and winds (1989); *WhangDoodles*, a trio for violin, piano, and percussion (1990); and *Shtick* for clarinet and soprano saxophone (1990).

More recent chamber works are *Knight* for solo cello (1992); *Crusoe* for 4–12 performers (1993); *Holes* for 4–8 players (1993); *Histories* for four saxophones (1993); *Whimwhams* for string quartet and marimba (1993); *Family Scenes* for ensemble (1995); *When the Wind Blows* for ensemble (1996); *Spiritus* for four recorders and percussion (1997); *For Hanns* for flute, clarinet, cello, and piano (1998); Piano Trio (1998); *Man Drag* for nine players (1999); *Cradle Rock* for ensemble (1999); and *Pocket Symphony* for six instruments (2000).

For larger forces Rzewski has composed *A Long Time Man* for piano and orchestra (1979); *Satyrica* for jazz band (1983); *Una breve storia d'estate* for three

flutes and small orchestra (1983); *Scratch Symphony* (1997); and *Movable Type* (1999).

Rzewski has composed many piano pieces for his own use: *Preludes* (1957); *Poem* (1959); *Dreams* (1961); *Falling Music* (with tape) (1971); *The People United Will Never Be Defeated* (1975), his best-known work; *Variations on "No Place to Go But Around'* (1976); *Four Pieces* (1977); *Four North American Ballads* (1978–79); *Squares* (1978); *Eggs* (1986); *Steptangle* (1986); *The Turtle and the Crane* (1988); *Mayn Yingele*, Twenty-four Variations on a Jewish Theme (1989); *Bumps* (1990); *Ludes* (1990–91); *De Profundis* (1991); a Sonata (1991); *A Life* (1992); *Fouges* (1994); *Fantasia* (1999); and four works for two pianos, Sonata (1960), *Winnsboro Cotton Mill Blues* (1980), *A Machine* (1984), and *Night Crossing With Fisherman* (1994). Since 1996 he has been working on *The Road*, an extended piece for piano in eight sections.

Among Rzewski's vocal works are a Requiem for chorus and ensemble (1963–67); *Work Songs* (1967–69); *Moments* for voice and piano (1970); *Freud* for any voice (1970); *Old Maid* for soprano and chorus (1970); *Jefferson* for voice and piano (1970); *Attica* for speaker and ensemble (1972); *Coming Together* for voice and low instrumental ensemble (1972); *Apolitical Intellectuals* for voice and piano (1973); *No Progress Without Struggle* for bass and orchestra (1974); *Nothing Changes* for baritone and piano (1976); *Le silence des espaces* for female chorus, orchestra, and tape (1980); *The Price of Oil* for two sopranos, wind, and percussion (1980); *Pablo Neruda in Exile* for voice and piano (1983); *Music for Antigone* (Brecht) for mezzo-soprano and piano (1984); *Mayakovsky* for speaker, string quartet, and piano (1984); *Mary's Dream* for soprano, clarinet, cello, double bass, piano, and percussion (1984); *The Invisible Persian Army* for voice and prepared piano (1984); *The Waves* for speaker and ensemble (1988); and *Logique* (Paul Verlaine) for voice, flute, cello, and piano (1997). In 1995 Rzewski composed two political pieces for chorus, *Stop the War!* and *Stop the Testing!*

Five music theater works are *Impersonation* for two soloists and four stereo tapes (1966); *Projector Piece* for musician, dancer, and slide projector (1966); *Portrait* for actor, lights, slides, film, photoresistors, and tapes (1967); *The Persians* (1985); and *The Triumph of Death* (1987–88). Rzewski's works for tape alone include *Zoologischer Garten* (1965) and *Music for Children* (1971).

S

SALZEDO, (LÉON) CARLOS
b. Arcachon, France, 6 April 1885
d. Waterville, Maine, 17 August 1961

Salzedo studied at the Bordeaux and Paris Conservatories before going to the United States in 1909 on the recommendation of Arturo Toscanini to take up the position of solo harpist with the Metropolitan Opera House in New York (1909–13). In 1917 he established his harp ensemble; three years later, he was elected president of the National Association of Harpists. Although he is remembered today as a virtuoso harpist, his work as a composer, conductor and promoter of modern music is equally worthy of tribute. In 1921 he was co-founder with Edgar Varèse of the International Composers Guild, one of the first organizations to promote regular concerts of twentieth-century music in America. It was at one of these events that Salzedo conducted the premiere of Varèse's *Offrandes* in 1922. Salzedo became an American citizen in 1924, the year in which he created the harp department at the Curtis Institute in Philadelphia. He later taught at the Juilliard School in New York.

Almost all of Salzedo's compositions are for harp, adding valuable contributions to a very limited repertory. These include *The Enchanted Isle* for harp and orchestra (1918); Harp Sonata (1922); a Harp Concerto (1925–26); *Preamble and Jeux* for harp, wind, and strings (1929); *Music for harp, brass and strings* (1937); and Suite for harp (1943). A second Harp Concerto was completed by Robert Russell Bennett in 1966. In 1919 he composed settings of three poems by Sara Jarrow for soprano, six harps, and three wind instruments. *Three Poems by Mallarmé* for soprano and harp date from 1924.

Among Salzedo's numerous solo pieces are *Five Poetical Studies* (1918), a single-movement Sonata for harp and piano, and a *Suite of Eight Dances* (1937). All these works exploit every device available to the skilled player. Salzedo's considerable knowledge of the instrument led him to invent new techniques, and in 1928 he created a new design for a harp.

Salzedo published three pedagogical books for harp: *Modern Study of the Harp* (1921), *Method of the Harp* (1929), and *The Art of Modulating* (with L. Lawrence; 1950).

SALZMAN, ERIC
b. New York, New York, 8 September 1933

Salzman studied composition with Mark Lawner before entering Columbia University (1950–54), where he was a pupil of Otto Luening, Vladimir Ussachevsky, and Jack Beeson. He also studied at Princeton University under Roger Sessions, Earl Kim, and Milton Babbitt (1954–56). In 1957 on a Fulbright Fellowship he went to Europe for two years, where he worked at the Academy of Saint Cecilia, Rome and privately with Goffredo Petrassi. He also spent some time at Darmstadt. On his return to America he was a music critic with the *New York Times* (1958–62) and the *New York Herald Tribune* (1963–66). From 1962 to 1963 and again from 1968 to 1971 he was music director of WBAI-FM, a non-commercial radio station in New York. He began writing for *Stereo Review* in 1966 and was editor of *Musical Quarterly* (1984–91). From 1966 to 1968 he was on the music faculty of Queens College, New York and since 1982 has taught at Yale University and Hunter College, New York. He was founder and artistic director of the American Music Theater Festival (1982–94).

Salzman's early works include *cummings set* for voice and orchestra (1952–53, rev. 1963); *Indian Set* for violin and piano (1952); String Quartet (1954–55); Piano Suite (1954–55); Flute Sonata (1956); *Inventions for Orchestra* (1956–57); and a *Partita* for solo violin (1958).

After *In Praise of the Owl and the Cuckoo* (1963) for voice, guitar, and chamber ensemble, a number of his compositions have used magnetic tape. These include *Verses I to IV* for voices, instruments, and tape (1967), *Queens Collage* for tape (1968), and music for a multimedia environment with film, *Feedback* (1967), devised with Stan Vanderbeek. Other tape works include *Wiretap* (1968), *Strophe/Antistrophe* for keyboard and tape (1969, rev.1971), and *Birdwalk* for tape and optional keyboard (1986).

Salzman has explored music drama with several important works: *Foxes and Hedgehogs* to a text by John Ashbery for voices, instruments, and tape (1967); a dance drama, *The Peloponnesian War* (1967–68); *Can Man Survive?* (1968–69), a multi-media walk-through environment, composed for the Museum of Natural History in New York; and *The Nude Paper Sermon*, tropes for actors, Renaissance consort, and electronics, commissioned by Nonesuch Records in 1969.

In 1970 Salzman founded the multimedia ensemble Quog, of which he is musical director. For them he has written *Helix* (1971), *Saying Something* (1972), *Biograffiti* (1973), and *Lazarus* (1973–74), in which the original 12th century music drama is followed by a contemporary version of the same events.

Since 1975 he has collaborated with Michael Sahl on words and music for a series of theater pieces or theater operas which have been produced off-Broadway in association with Quog and recorded for National Public Radio. These include *The Conjurer* (1975), *Stauf* (an American *Faust*) (1976, rev. 1987), *Civilization and Its Discontents* (1977), *Noah* (1978), and *The Passion of Simple Simon* (1979).

Other works of this period include *Accord* for solo accordion, written for William Schimmel (1977), *Variations* for solo harpsichord, composed for Igor Kipnis (1979), and *Variations on Sacred Harp Hymn Tunes* for harpsichord (1982).

More recent theater pieces include *Big Jim and the Small-time Investors* (in collaboration with Ned Jackson; 1984–85), *Toward an American Opera* (1985), *The Last Words of Dutch Schultz* (1995–96), and *Body Language* for singers, dancers, violin, piano accordion (with Sahl; 1995–96). *La Prière du Loup* was performed in France in 1997.

Among his vocal music are *Songs* (Whitman) for voice and piano (1955–57), *Larynx Music* for soprano, guitar, and four-track tape (1966–67), and *The Ten Qualities and Three Madrigals* (John Ashbery) for chorus (197–71). In collaboration with Sahl, Salzman has composed two radio operas for a cappella choir, *Voices* (1971) and *Boxes* (1981–82).

His latest theater pieces are *Abel Gance à New York*, commissioned by Chants Libres, Montreal in 2000; *Cassandra*, a solo piece for soprano to a text by the composer's daughter Eva, premiered by Kristin Norderval at the National Opera, Oslo (2001; Vienna, 2002; New York, 2003); and *Jukebox in the Tavern of Love*, a contemporary madrigal comedy commissioned the Western Wind Vocal Ensemble (2002).

Salzman is the author of three books: *Twentieth Century Music* (1969; 4th ed., 2002), *Making Changes: A Practical Guide to American Vernacular Harmony* (with Michael Sahl; 1971), and *The New Music Theater* (2003).

SAMINSKY, LAZARE
b. *Valegotsulova, near Odessa, Russia, 27 October (new date 8 November) 1882*
d. *Port Chester, New York, 30 June 1959*

Saminsky attended the Conservatory in St. Petersburg (1906–09), where he was a pupil of Anatoli Liadov, Nicolai Tcherepnin, Alexander Glazunov, and Nicolai Rimski-Korsakov. At the same time he studied mathematics and philosophy at the University of St. Petersburg. After three years as a conductor, teacher, and eventually director of the Conservatory in Tiflis, he left Russia in 1918, moving first to Paris, then to London, before settling in the United States in 1920 where he became a naturalized citizen in 1926. Saminsky was one of the founder-directors of the League of Composers instituted in 1923. The following year he was appointed director of the Temple Emanu-el in New York, a post he held until 1958. His conducting career took him to Italy and Vienna from 1927 to 1930, and he toured North and South America extensively.

For the stage, Saminsky composed an opera, *Julian, the Apostate Caesar* (1933–38), and three opera-ballets or mime dramas: *The Vision of Ariel* (1915), *The Gagliarda of the Merry Plague* (1924), based on Edgar Allan Poe's "The Masque of the Red Death," and *Jeptha's Daughter* (1928). He also wrote a ballet, *The Lament of Rachel* (1913, rev. 1920), which reveals the influence of folksong.

Saminsky's six symphonies constitute the backbone of his orchestral music: no. 1, *Of the Great Rivers* (1914); no. 2, *Of the Summits* (1918); no. 3, *Of the Seas* (1924); no. 4 (1926); no. 5, *Jerusalem, City of Solomon and Christ* for chorus and orchestra (1930); and no. 6 (1948). Also for orchestra he composed *Vigiliae*, a symphonic triptych (1910); *Orientalia* (1912); *Hassidic Suite* for violin and orchestra (1922);

Lazare Saminsky.
Courtesy James P. Murphy Collection,
Georgetown University Library.

Hebrew Rhapsody for violin and orchestra (1923); *Venice* for chamber orchestra (1928); a symphonic poem, *Ausonia* (*Italian Pages*; 1930); *To the New World* (1932); a symphonic poem *Three Shadows* (1935); *Pueblo, a Moon Rhapsody* (1936); *Stilled Pageant* (1937); and a suite for violin and orchestra, *From East to West* (1940).

In addition to providing music for the synagogue, including *Sabbath Evening Service* (1925, rev. 1947), *Sabbath Morning Service* (1925–28), and the *Holiday Service* (1927–29), Saminsky wrote several choral works: *Four Sacred Choruses* (1913); *Three Sacred Songs of Jemmen and Palestine* (1913); Psalm 137, *By the Waters of Babylon* (1926); *King Saul* (1929); Psalm 93, *De Profundis* (1933); *The Lord Reigneth* for soprano, baritone, chorus, piano, and organ (1933); and Serenade (1946). He composed a song cycle, *The Dying Day* (1914); two sets of *Hebrew Songs* (1909, 1914); *The Songs of the Three Queens* for soprano and orchestra (1924); *Litanies of Women* (1925); and *Six Russian Songs* for voice and chamber orchestra (1925–26).

Although as a writer Saminsky was a specialist in oriental and early Hebrew music, his best-known books concern twentieth-century music: *Music of Our Day* (1932, rev. 1939) and *Living Music of the Americas* (1949). On Jewish music he wrote *Music of the Ghetto and the Bible* (1934). His other publications were *Physics and Metaphysics and Essays on the Philosophy of Mathematics* (1957) and *Essentials of Conducting* (1958). In Russia he had written *Jewish Music Past and Present* (1914); at his death he left an unpublished autobiography, *Third Leonardo.*

SANDERS, ROBERT L(EVINE)
b. *Chicago, Illinois, 2 July 1906*
d. *Delray Beach, Florida, 29 December 1974*

Sanders studied at the Bush Conservatory in Chicago (Mus.B., 1924; M.A, 1925), and later went to Rome on a Fellowship at the American Academy where he was a pupil of Respighi. In 1929 he joined the faculty of the Juilliard School. In 1938 he was appointed Dean of the School of Music at Indiana University, Bloomington. In 1947 he became professor at the music department at Brooklyn College; until 1954 he served as its chairman, and retired in 1972.

Sanders's first important work, *Suite for Large Orchestra*, was composed in Rome between 1926 and 1928 and performed there in 1929. One movement, *Barn Dance,* was heard in New York in 1934. *Saturday Night,* another barn dance, was also performed in 1934 by the Chicago Symphony Orchestra. In 1938, the *Little Symphony* in G won joint first prize in a competition sponsored by the New York Philharmonic Orchestra. *Little Symphony* no. 2 in B-flat (1953), was performed by the Louisville Orchestra in 1954. *Little Symphony* no. 3 in D dates from 1963. Sanders's other orchestral works are *Scenes From Poverty and Toil* (1935); a Violin Concerto in A minor (1935); Symphony in A (1955), a Knoxville Symphony Orchestra commission; and Concerto for brass and orchestra (1962). A Symphony for concert band dates from 1943. A ballet, *L'Agyga,* was produced at the Hollywood Bowl in 1944.

In the field of chamber music Sanders wrote a String Quartet in A minor (1929); a Piano Trio in C-sharp minor (1926); two violin sonatas, no. 1 in C minor (1928), and no. 2 in B-flat (1961); a Cello Sonata in one movement (1932); Quintet for brass (1942); a Trombone Sonata in E-flat (1945); Suite for brass quartet (1950); a Horn Sonata in B-flat (1958); a Brass Trio (1958); and a Clarinet Sonata in G minor (1969).

Among his choral compositions are Psalm 23 for unaccompanied chorus (1928); *The Mystic Trumpeter,* a setting of Whitman's poem for narrator, chorus, and orchestra (1939–40); a cantata, *The American Psalm* for female chorus and chamber orchestra or organ (1945); *The Hollow Men* for men's chorus and piano (1950); and the cantata *A Celebration of Life* for soprano solo, chorus, and chamber orchestra (1956). A later important work is the setting of Whitman's poem *Song of Myself,* presented in Brooklyn in 1970. It is a musical treatment of the entire poem, lasting over three hours, scored for male narrator and soprano with accompaniment by 12 brass instruments and five percussionists.

Sanders was the author of *A Manual for Melody Writing* and co-editor of a *Dictionary of Hymn Tunes in the United States.*

SATUREN, DAVID HASKELL
b. Philadelphia, Pennsylvania, 11 March 1939

The first public performance of a Saturen composition took place when, at the age of eleven, he won a composition contest sponsored by the Philadelphia Orchestra. He subsequently studied at the University of Pennsylvania (B.A. 1960; M.A. 1962) and Temple University (D.M.A., 1967). Saturen taught at Fairleigh Dickinson University (1968–85; 1987–88) and Moravian College (1988–94); he joined the piano faculty in 1994 at the Community Music School, Allentown, Pennsylvania, where he currently teaches.

David H. Saturen.
Courtesy the composer.

Saturen has composed one symphony (1990). For chamber orchestra, he has composed *Expression: Lyric Piece for Small Orchestra* (1962); *Exposition for 16* (1965); *Largo for Strings* (1966); *Largo and Allegro* for violin, cello, and strings (1967); *Ternaria* for organ, timpani, and strings (1969; full orchestra version, 1970); *Dialogue* for harpsichord and strings (1972); *Evolution* for viola, harpsichord, and strings (1977); *Lyric Progression* for double bass and string orchestra (1981); and *Spring on Rittenhouse Square* (1996); and two fanfares (1997, 2001). All chamber orchestra works beginning with *Exposition for 16* were commissioned by the Chamber Orchestra of Philadelphia.

Among his solo chamber works are a sonata for clarinet (or viola) and piano (1966); Trio for clarinet, mallet percussion, and piano (1977); Trio for clarinet, timpani, and piano (1980); and *Music of the Wind* for mezzo-soprano, flute, and piano (2003; text by Emma Wolf-Saxon). His pieces for piano are *Five Moods in Miniature* for piano (1971) and two sonatas (1964, 1996). For electronic tape, Saturen composed *Form in White and Brass* (1968). Saturen arranged two popular melodies, *Arkansas Traveler* and *Tennessee Waltz*, for performance by the Chamber Orchestra of Philadelphia at the celebration of President Clinton's first inauguration.

SAYLOR, BRUCE STUART
b. Philadelphia, Pennsylvania, 24 April 1946

At the Juilliard School on a Rogers and Hammerstein scholarship (1964–69), Saylor studied with Hugo Weisgall and Roger Sessions. A Fulbright Fellowship (1969–70) enabled him to receive lessons from Goffredo Petrassi in Rome; he also studied with George Perle. After teaching at Queens College, New York (1970–76), he was appointed to the music faculty of New York University. In 1979 he returned to Queens College, also teaching at the Graduate School of the City University of New York from 1983.

His orchestral works include *Cantilena* for strings (1965); *Notturno* for piano and orchestra (1969); *Conductus* for winds, strings, and percussion (1970); *Turns and Mordants,* a Flute Concerto (1977); *Paeans to Hyacinthus* (1980); Symphony in two parts (1980); *Archangel* for antiphonal brass and orchestra (1990); and *Supernova* for concert band (1992).

For the stage Saylor has composed two operas: *My Kinsman, Major Molineux* in one act (1976), and *Orpheus Descending* (1994), while he was Composer-in-Residence with Chicago Opera. In addition he has written four dance scores: *Cycle* (1978), *Inner World Out* (1978), *Wildfire* (1979), and *Spill* (1984).

Among his many choral compositions are *To*

Autumn, To Winter (William Blake) for chorus and orchestra (1968); *Two Yiddish Folksongs* for tenor, chorus, and piano duet (1969); *Benedictus es* for choir and organ (1969); *Jesu, Thou Joy of Loving* for soprano, choir, and organ (1970); *Te Deum* for choir and organ (1982); *Mass of the Holy Trinity* for congregation, choir, organ, and brass (1987); *Jubilate Fantasy* for soprano, chorus, and orchestra (1990); *Star of Wonder,* a Christmas cantata for children's choir, string quartet, and harp (1990); *Three Spirituals* for soprano and chorus (1990); *The Star Song* for mezzo-soprano, chorus, and orchestra (1992); *Honor, Honor* for soprano and chorus (1993); *Canticle of Blessing* for chorus, brass, percussion, and organ (1994); *In Praise of Jerusalem* for choir, three brass ensembles and organ (1994); *Song of Ascent* for choir, three trumpets, and organ (1994); and *By the Power of Your Love* for women's voices and mixed chorus (1995).

Among Saylor's solo vocal music are *Five Songs of Whispers of Heav'nly Death* (Whitman) for soprano and string quartet (1965–67); *Three Collects* for mezzo-soprano and organ (1968); *Lyrics* for soprano and violin (1971); *Loveplay* for mezzo-soprano, flute, viola, and cello (1975); *Four Psalms* for voice and flute (1976–78); *Songs of Water Street* for mezzo-soprano, viola, and piano (1976–80); *Swimming by Night* for mezzo-soprano, viola, and piano (1980); *The Waves* (Virginia Woolf), a dramatic monologue for mezzo-soprano, flute, clarinet, viola, and cello (1981); *Five Old Favorites* for voice, flute, and piano (1985); *It Had Wings* for voice and piano (1984); Psalm 23 for voice and oboe (1985); *See You in the Morning* for soprano and six instruments (1987); *Behold That Star* for soprano and string quartet (1990); *Angels* for mezzo-soprano, flute, cello, and piano (1993); and *Magnificat* for voice, flute, and guitar (1995).

Saylor's instrumental catalog is equally varied and impressive: *Ricercare* for organ (1965); Wind Quintet (1965); Suite for solo viola (1967); *Sinfonia* for organ (1969); *Conductus* for three winds, three strings, and percussion (1970); *Duo* for violin and viola (1970); *Firescreen* for flute, cello, and piano (1979); *St. Ulmo's Fire* for flute and harp (1980); *Fire-flaught* for flute, bassoon, and harp (1982); *State Trumpets* for organ and brass (1982); *Fanfares* for double bass quartet (1983); *Sogetti I* for flute (1985) and *II* for flute and harpsichord (1986); *Electra: A Translation* for viola, double bass, and piano (1986); Trio for clarinet, viola, and piano (1989); and *Fanfare and Echoes* for horn and string trio (1992). For piano he has composed *Five Short Pieces* (1965–67), *Ricercare* (1972), *Saltarello* (1981), and Quattro Passi (1991).

As a writer he has contributed to *Musical America* and *Music Quarterly* and is the author of a monograph, *The Writings of Henry Cowell*, published in 1977.

Rosario Scalero.
Courtesy The Milton R. Rock Resource Center, The Curtis Institute of Music.

SCALERO, ROSARIO
b. Moncalieri, near Turin, Italy, 24 December 1870
d. Settimo Vittone, near Turin, 25 December 1954

Scalero studied violin at the Turin Liceo Musicale and with Camillo Sivori in Genoa and August Wilhelmj in London. He was also a pupil of Eusebius Mandyczewski in Vienna. In 1896 he was appointed a violin teacher in Lyons, France, moving in 1904 to a similar post at the Academy of Saint Cecilia in Rome. He also taught at the Parma Conservatory before going to the United States in 1919. He taught violin and composition at the Mannes School of Music in New York (1919–28). In 1924 he also joined the composition department at the Curtis Institute in Philadelphia, retiring in 1946. His pupils included Samuel Barber, Marc Blitzstein, Carl Bricken, Lukas Foss, Charles Haubiel, Robert Kelly, Gian-Carlo Menotti, George Rochberg, and Hugo Weisgall.

Scalero composed a Violin Concerto, *La Divina Foresta* for orchestra, a Suite for string quartet and string orchestra (1921), *Neapolitan Dances* for violin and piano, *Romantic Pieces* for violin and piano, and two sets of motets for chorus.

SCARMOLIN, ANTHONY LOUIS

b. Schio, Italy, 30 July 1890

d. Wyckoff, New Jersey, 13 July 1969

Scarmolin was taken to the United States in 1900, settling in New Jersey. He graduated from the New York College of Music in 1907 and served in the U.S. Army during the First World War. After the war he lived for a while in Philadelphia, settling eventually in Union City, New Jersey, where he served as director of the Schools System (1919–49) until a heart condition enforced his retirement.

Scarmolin was a compulsively prolific composer, completing over 1,150 full-scale works. His early music is chromatic, at times atonal, but in the 1930s he adopted a more impressionistic whole-tone-scale language, influenced by Debussy and Puccini. Among his many orchestral pieces are three symphonies: no. 1 in E minor in one movement (1937), no. 2 (1946), and no. 3, *Sinfonia Breve* (1952). Other orchestral compositions include *Two Symphonic Fragments* (1928); *The Clockmaker* (1932); *Nostalgic Retrospect* (1936); a symphonic poem, *Night* (1937); *Overture on a Street Vendor's Ditty* (1938); *Dramatic Overture* (1938); *The Ambassador Overture* (1938); *Mercury Overture* (1939); *Visions,* a symphonic poem (1939); *Dramatic Tone Poem* (Chicago, 1939); *Three Miniatures* (1940); *Miniature Symphony* no. 1 in C (Cleveland, 1940); *Miniature Symphony* no. 2 in D minor (1942); *The Tower Prince* (1941); *Variations on a Folk-song* for strings (1942); *Pastorale* (1943); *Poeme Pathétique* (1944); *Six Symphonic Fragments* (1944); *Invocation* (1947), *Symphonietta* in A for strings (1948); *The Sunlit Pool* (1951); *Arioso* for strings (1953); and a symphonic poem, *The Break of Day* (1956). Scarmolin composed two works for band: *Reuben and Rachel Sight-seeing in New York* (1945) and *Mexican Holiday* (1946).

His choral music includes three cantatas: *O Wisest of Men* (1938); *The Gifts of Bethlehem* for women's voices, organ, and orchestra (1938); and *The Temptation on the Mount.* For the stage he composed three operas, *The Oath* (1945), *The Caliph* (1948), and *The Interrupted Serenade,* performed in Union City, New Jersey on 26 May 1974.

SCHELLING, ERNEST (HENRY)

b. Belvidere, New Jersey, 26 July 1876

d. New York, New York, 8 December 1939

Schelling showed considerable musical promise when very young, making his debut as a pianist at the age of four in a concert at the Philadelphia Academy of Music. He studied at the Paris Conservatory (1882–85)

Ernest Schelling.
Courtesy the University of Maryland College Park Foundation.

before moving to the Vienna Conservatory, where his teachers included Theodor Leschetizky for piano and Bruckner for composition; he was also a pupil of Paderewski and Moskowski. As a composer he had his first success in Europe with *Légende Symphonique* (1904), performed in 1906 by the Berlin Philharmonic Orchestra, and a *Fantastic Suite* for piano and orchestra, which received its premiere by the Amsterdam Concertgebouw Orchestra under Willem Mengelberg in 1907.

On his return to the United States, Schelling devoted his time to composition, conducting, and piano playing. An automobile accident in Switzerland in 1919 put an end to his career as a concert pianist, so he turned to orchestral conducting as his principal activity. A music educator, he established the Saturday morning children's concerts of the New York Philharmonic Society in 1924, which introduced a wide range of music to his young audiences. From 1935 to 1937 he was conductor of the Baltimore Symphony Orchestra.

Schelling continued to compose during this time; in 1913 his *Impressions of an Artist's Life,* a set of variations for piano and orchestra, was performed in Boston under the direction of Karl Muck with the composer as soloist. Fritz Kreisler gave the premiere of Schelling's Violin Concerto in B minor in one movement in 1916, also in Boston.

Schelling's most widely performed work was *A Victory Ball,* a fantasy for orchestra inspired by the poem by Alfred Noyes, which contrasts the luxury of the ball with the horrors of war. Stokowski conducted the premiere with the Philadelphia Orchestra in 1923. Three years later it became the first American orchestral work to be issued on record. In 1925 he composed a Divertimento for piano quintet; his last important work, the tone poem *Morocco,* was heard in New York in 1927. He also wrote a Symphony in C# minor, a Violin Sonata, piano pieces; and songs. Excerpts from his opera *Moloch* were performed in Boston in 1909.

SCHICKELE, PETER
b. Ames, Iowa, 17 July 1935

Schickele studied at Swarthmore College (B.A., 1957) and at the Juilliard School under Vincent Persichetti and William Bergsma (M.S., 1960). He also received composition lessons from Roy Harris in Pittsburgh and from Darius Milhaud at Aspen, Colorado (1959). From 1961 to 1965 he taught at the Juilliard School and at Aspen.

Although he has acquired wide popularity for his creation of the "composer" P. D. Q. Bach, Schickele is a serious composer with a considerable number of works to his credit, although some pieces possess bizarre features with strong pop and jazz influences. For orchestra he has written *Invention* (1958); Serenade (1959); *Fantasy* for strings (1959), *Celebration With Bells* (1960), *A Zoo Called Earth* for taped narrator and orchestra (1970), *Requiem Mantras* for rock group and orchestra (1972), *Pentangle,* five songs for horn and orchestra (1976); *Five of a Kind* for brass quintet and orchestra (1978); *Far Away From Here* for bluegrass band and orchestra (1984); *Scenes From Brueghel* for Renaissance group and orchestra (1986); *The View From the Roof* for three orchestras (1989); *Elegy* for strings (1992); *Legend* (1992); *Thurber's Dogs Suite* (1994); *What Did You Do Today at Jeffrey's House?* (1994); a Symphony (1995),*One for the Money* (1999); and *New Century Suite* for saxophone quartet and orchestra (2000). Schickele has composed four concertos: flute (1990), oboe (1994), bassoon (1999), and cello (2000).

Instrumental pieces include five string quartets: no. 1, *American Dreams* (1983); no. 2, *In Memoriam* (1987); no. 3, *The Four Seasons* (1988); no. 4, *Inter-Era Dance Suite* (1992); and no. 5, '*A Year in the Country* (1998); *Sequiturs* for solo cello (1959); a String Trio (1960); *Diversions* for oboe, clarinet, and bassoon (1963); *Three Scenes* for five instruments (1965); *Summer Trio* for flute, cello, and piano (1965); *Windows* for viola, flute, clarinet, and guitar (1966); *Elegies* for clarinet and piano (1974); *Trio Serenade* for two flutes and piano (1979); Quartet for clarinet and string trio (1979); *Spring Serenade* for flute and piano (1983);

Divertimento for two clarinets and bassoon (1984); *Serenade for Six* (1988); *Dream Dances* for flute, oboe, and cello (1988); and *Summer Serenade* for bassoon and piano (1989). Among more recent chamber music are a String Sextet (1990); *Serenade for Three* (clarinet, violin, and piano) (1992); Octet (1992); *River Music* for viola and piano (1993); and two piano quintets (1996, 1997). For piano he has written three sonatinas (1957–64) and *Epitaphs* (1979).

Schickele's many choral works include a Mass for men's voices (1957); *The Birth of Christ* for chorus and piano (1960); *After the Spring Sunset* for chorus (1961); *In This Year,* a cantata on Anglo-Saxon poems for two tenors, female chorus, chorus, band, and strings (1961); *Songs for The Knight of the Burning Pestle* for voices and instruments (1974); *Three Pirate Songs* for men's voices and piano (1978); *Summer Music* for choir and recorder (1979); *Ceremony,* a cantata for baritone, chorus, and jazz ensemble (1985); and *Concerto: The Twelve Months* for piano and chorus (1987). Vocal music includes *Songs From Shakespeare* (1954, rev. 1992); *The Flow of Memory* for voice and instruments (1963); *Three Strange Cases* (Ogden Nash) (1972); *Maiden in the Moor* for counter-tenor and chamber orchestra (1975); *Three Girls, Three Women* for male singer/pianist and orchestra (1972); *The Lowest Trees Have Tops,* a cantata for soprano, flute, violin, and harp (1974); *Three Songs for a Wedding* for voice and guitar (1981); and *If Love is Real* for two voices and chamber orchestra (1991).

Schickele has composed several film scores. Documentaries include *Poland* (1964), *Israel* (1965), *Big People, Small People* (1967), *Someday* (1967), and *Film for the Texas Pavillion at the Hemisfair* (1968). Among his feature films are *The Crazy Quilt* (1965), *Funnyman* (1967), *Silent Running* (1971), *A Likely Story* (1974), and *Where the Wild Things Are* (1988). For television he has provided music for *The Sound of Alienation* (1966), *Three Riddle Films* ("Sesame Street"; 1969), *Where the Garbage Goes* (1969), and *Sweet Visions* (1970).

SCHIFRIN, LALO (BORIS)
b. Buenos Aires, Argentina, 21 June 1932

Schifrin was born into a musical family; his father was concertmaster of the Buenos Aires Symphony Orchestra for 30 years. After a formal musical training in Argentina he went to Paris in 1950 where he experienced European jazz and attended the Paris Conservatory. There he was advised by Charles Koechlin and received composition lessons from Olivier Messiaen. On his return to Argentina in 1956 he established a reputation as a composer, arranger, conductor, and pianist. Fol-

Lalo Schifrin.
Courtesy the composer.

lowing a meeting with Dizzy Gillespie in Buenos Aires, in 1958 he became an arranger in New York for the jazz bands of Gillespie, Count Basie, Stan Getz, and others. Since the early "60s, he has primarily worked as a film and television composer in Hollywood. From 1968 to 1971 he taught at the University of California, Los Angeles.

Schifrin's work with jazz bands led to the composition of several pieces for jazz band and related ensembles: *Gillespiana* (1961); a ballet, *Jazz Faust* (1963); *Jazz Suite on the Mass Texts* (1965); *Dialogues* for jazz quintet and orchestra (1969); *Improvisations* for jazz soloists and orchestra (1969); *Rock Requiem* (1970); and *Pulsations* for electric keyboards, band, and orchestra (1971).

His other orchestral pieces include a *Variations on a Madrigal by Gesualdo* for chamber orchestra (1969); *Tropicos* for chamber orchestra (1983); Guitar Concerto (1984); two piano concertos, the second subtitled *Concerto of the Americas* (1992); Concerto for trumpet, percussion, and wind; and Double Concerto for violin and cello. Other pieces include a Suite for trumpet and brass (1961), *The Ritual of Sound* for 15 instruments (1962); and *Canons* for string quartet (1969).

His vocal works include an oratorio *The Rise and Fall of the Third Reich* (1967), *Madrigals for the Space Age* for narrator, chorus, and orchestra (1976), and *Songs of the Aztecs* for soloist and orchestra (1988).

In 1963 Schifrin began his Hollywood career with the film score for *Rhino*. Among his subsequent scores,

numbering over 160, are *The Cincinnati Kid* (1965); *The Liquidator* (1965); *The Fox* (1967); *Bullitt* (1968); *Coogan's Bluff* (1968); *Eye of the Cat* (1969); *Kelly's Heroes* (1970); *Pussycat, Pussycat, I Love You* (1970); *The Master Gunfighter* (1975); *The Four Musketeers* (1975); *The Eagle Has Landed* (1978); *The Amityville Horror* (1979); *The Dead Pool* (1988); and *Tango* (1999). He also composed the well-known theme music for the television series "Mission Impossible."

SCHILLINGER, JOSEPH (MOISEYEVICH)
b. Kharkov, Russia, 31 August 1895
d. New York, New York, 23 March 1943

Schillinger was educated in St. Petersburg at the Conservatory under Nicolai Tcherepnin and at the University (1914–18). From 1918 to 1922 he taught at the State Academy of Music in Kharkov and was Conductor of the Ukraine Symphony Orchestra (1920–21). From 1925 to 1928 he was composer at the Leningrad State Academic Theater. At the end of 1928 he went to the United States to lecture at Columbia University, and two years later settled permanently in New York, taking American citizenship in 1936. He also taught at the New School for Social Research in New York.

Extant compositions from his time in Russia are *March of the Orient* for orchestra (1924), Sonata for Violin and Piano (1922), *Excentriade Suite* for piano (1924), *Sonata Rhapsody* for piano (1925), and *Symphonic Rhapsody October* for piano and orchestra, to a commission from the U.S.S.R. to celebrate the tenth anniversary of the Russian Revolution (1927). In the United States Schillinger wrote *Airphonic Suite* (1929) for the Cleveland Orchestra, an experimental piece using the theremin, a recently invented electronic instrument . Both the *North Russian Symphony*, for accordion and orchestra, and a ballet, *The People and the Prophet*, were composed in 1931.

Schillinger's most significant achievement was his work as a teacher and the author of five remarkable books on music. These were *The Mathematical Basis of the Arts*, published in 1933, *Kaleidophone, New Resources in Melody and Harmony* (1940), *Electricity, a Liberator of Music*, and the monumental two-volume *Schillinger System of Musical Composition* (1941; reissued 1946). *Encyclopaedia of Rhythm* was issued posthumously in 1966. In these publications he sets out scientific techniques for composing music, where strict formulae are applied to harmony, counterpoint, and the creation of melodies. Among Schillinger's pupils were many successful popular song-writers and important musicians such as Oscar Levant, Vernon Duke, Benny Goodman, Glenn Miller, and Tommy

Dorsey. George Gershwin was one of his orchestration students; at the time Gershwin was composing the *Cuban Overture* and the opera *Porgy and Bess* (1931–35).

Schillinger's wife wrote *Joseph Schillinger: Memoir*, published in 1949.

SCHMIDT, WILLIAM JOSEPH

b. Chicago, Illinois, 6 March 1926

Schmidt was educated at the U.S. Naval School of Music (1944–46), Chicago Music College with Max Wald (1946–49), and the University of Southern Califonia (1955–60), where he was a pupil of Halsey Stevens and Ingolf Dahl.

For many years he was a freelance woodwind player, and most of his compositions are for wind instruments. These include concertos for clarinet and trumpet, both with wind ensembles; Concertino for piano and brass quintet; *Variations on a Negro Folk Song* for brass quintet (1955); *Chorales* for brass (1966); a Chamber Concerto for organ and brass quintet (1969); and four suites for brass quintet.

Other instrumental pieces are *Septigrams* for flute, piano, and percussion (1956); *The Percussion Rondo* for percussion quartet (1957); Viola Sonata (1959); *Ludus Americanus* for narrator and percussion (1971); Sonatina for bass clarinet and piano (1977); *Spirituals* for cello and percussion; *Prelude and Fugue* for wind trio; Suite for saxophone quartet; and sonatas for saxophone, horn, and trumpet. Schmidt has written three works for band, *The Natchez Trail* (1957), *Concerto Breve* (1957), and *Sakura Variations* (1968).

SCHULLER, GUNTHER ALEXANDER

b. New York, New York, 22 November 1925

Schuller studied at the St. Thomas Choir School (1937–40) and Manhattan School of Music (1938–44). The son of a violinist with the New York Philharmonic Orchestra, he began his musical career at the age of 16 as a horn player, first with Ballet Theater, then with the Cincinnati Symphony Orchestra (1943–45); from 1945 to 1959 he was a member of the Metropolitan Opera House Orchestra, the last eight years as principal horn. From 1950 he was appointed to the faculty of the Manhattan School of Music. He was an associate professor at Yale University (1964–66) before becoming president of the New England Conservatory, a position he held until 1977. He was also long associated with the Berkshire Music Center, Tanglewood (1963–84), first as head of compositional activities, then as artistic director (from 1974). In 1984 he was Composer-in-Residence with the Lyric Opera, Chicago. Schuller has been the recipient of an award from the National Institute of Arts and Letters (1960), two Guggenheim Fellowships (1962, 1963), and a Pulitzer Prize (1994).

In 1964 at the age of 19 Schuller was soloist in his own Concerto for Horn, performed with the Cincinnati Symphony Orchestra under Sir Eugene Goossens. In the following year he completed *Vertige d'Eros* for orchestra and a Cello Concerto. *Symphonic Study* (1947–48) was also premiered by the Cincinnati Symphony Orchestra. His Symphony for Brass and Percussion (1949–50) was performed at an I.S.C.M. concert in New York City in 1951; it was later set to choreography by José Limón as a ballet on the story of Jesus and Judas, *The Traitor*. Three other orchestral compositions from this period are *Dramatic Overture* (1951), *Recitative and Rondo* for violin and orchestra (1952), and *Contours* for chamber orchestra (1956).

One of Schuller's best-known works, *Seven Studies on Themes of Paul Klee,* was commissioned by the Ford Foundation for the Minneapolis Symphony Orchestra and was premiered and recorded in November 1959. *Spectra* (1956–58) uses spatial effects with the orchestra re-seated and divided into seven complementary ensembles. It was commissioned by the New York Philharmonic Orchestra and performed under Mitropoulos in January 1960. *Contrasts* for wind quintet and large orchestra (1961) was first heard at Donaueschingen, Germany in October 1961. His Piano Concerto was composed in 1962 and premiered in Cincinnati that year.

Other orchestral works include a Symphony commissioned by the Dallas Symphony Orchestra in 1965; *American Triptych (Three Studies in Texture),* composed in 1965 for the New Orleans Symphony Orchestra; Concerto for Orchestra, commissioned for the 75th anniversary of the Chicago Symphony Orchestra in 1966; *Diptych* for brass quintet and orchestra, performed in Boston in 1967; *Triplum I* (1967), commissioned for the 125th anniversary of the New York Philharmonic Orchestra; and Concerto for Double Bass (1968), composed for Gary Karr and commissioned by the Koussevitzky Foundation. Shorter orchestral pieces include *Movements* for flute and strings (1961); *Journey Into Jazz* for narrator, jazz quintet, and orchestra (1962); *Journey to the Stars* (1962); *Threnos* for oboe and orchestra (1963), in memory of Mitropoulos; *Composition in Three Parts* (1963); *Five Bagatelles* (1964); *Colloquy* for two pianos and orchestra, premiered by the Berlin Philharmonic Orchestra in 1966; *Fanfare for St. Louis* for the opening of Powell Hall, the new home of the St. Louis Symphony Orchestra (1968); *Shapes and Designs* (1968); and *Consequents* (1969).

Schuller's interest in music of earlier times has produced *Museum Piece* for symphony orchestra and a large ensemble of Renaissance instruments, including recorders, shawms, crumhorns, racket, cornetti, viols, lutes, regal, and harpsichord (1970). Subsequent orchestral works are *Capriccio Stravagante,* performed by the San Francisco Symphony Orchestra in December 1972; *Three Nocturnes* (1973); a Violin Concerto premiered at the Lucerne Festival in August 1976 with Zvi Zeitlin as soloist; *Four Soundscapes* (*Hudson Valley Reminiscences*; 1974); *Triplum II* (1975); a *Second* Horn Concerto (1976); Concerto for Orchestra no. 2 (1977); Concerto for Contrabassoon (1978); Concerto for Trumpet (1979); *Eine Kleine Posaunenmusik* for solo trombone and large wind ensemble (1980); *Music for a Celebration* (with chorus; 1980); and *In Praise of Winds* for wind orchestra (1980).

Schuller has continued to compose copiously for orchestra: Piano Concerto no. 2 (1981), Concerto for alto saxophone performed in Pittsburgh in 1983; *Concerto Festivo* for brass quintet and orchestra (1984); *Concerto Quarternio* for four soloists and four instrumental groups (1984); *Jubilee Musik* (1984); a Bassoon Concerto, *Eine kleine Fagottmusik* (1985); *Farbenspiel* (Concerto for Orchestra no. 3; 1985); Viola Concerto (1985); Concerto for string quartet and orchestra (1988); Flute Concerto (1988); *Chamber Symphony* (1989); Concerto for two pianos (three hands) (1989); Violin Concerto no. 2 (1991); *Ritmica Melodica Armonica* (1992); *And They All Played Ragtime* (1992); *Of Reminiscences and Reflections,* a Louisville Orchestra commission in 1993; *The Past is in the Present* (1993); an Organ Concerto (1994); and *An Arc Ascending* (1996).

Schuller has composed several pieces for band, including *Meditation* (1963); *Study in Textures* (1966); *Dyptich* for brass quintet and band (1967); *On Winged Flight* (1989); *Song and Dance* for violin and band (1990); *Festive Music* (1992); and *Blue Dawn into White Heat* (1995). In addition to *The Traitor,* he has composed the ballet *Variants,* produced in New York in January 1961 by the New York City Ballet with choreography by Balanchine.

The opera *The Visitation* was greeted with considerable critical acclaim after the premiere in Hamburg on 12 October 1966. It was performed by the Hamburg Opera Company at Lincoln Center on 28 June 1967. The plot, based on Kafka's novel *The Trial,* is adapted so that Josef K. becomes a black man, Carter Jones, a victim of racial prejudice. A second opera, *The Fisherman and His Wife,* written for children, is a setting of the Grimm fairy tale to a libretto by John Updike. It was produced in Boston on 8 May 1970. His most recent opera, *A Question of Taste,* was staged in Coopertown, New York in 1989.

Schuller has composed several important choral works: *O Lamb of God* (1941) and *O Spirit of the Living God* (1962), both for double chorus; *Sacred Cantata,* a setting for chorus and orchestra of Psalm 98

(1966); *Poems of Time and Eternity* (Emily Dickinson) for chorus and nine instruments (1972); an oratorio, *The Power Within Us,* premiered in Atlanta, Georgia in March 1972; *Thou Art the Son of God,* a cantata for chorus and chamber ensemble (1987); *Magnificat and Nunc Dimittis* for choir and organ (1994); and *Mondrian's Vision* for chamber choir and instruments (1994). He has written three sets of solo songs: *Six Early Songs* on German texts by Klabund for soprano and piano (or orchestra; 1944–45), *Six Renaissance Lyrics* for tenor and seven instruments (1962), and *Five Shakespearean Songs* for baritone and orchestra (1964). *Deaï* (*Encounters*) for seven voices and three orchestras was performed in Tokyo in 1978.

Schuller's chamber works constitute an important part of his output, in particular the Sonata for clarinet, horn, and piano (1941), the partly jazz-influenced Suite for wind quintet (1945), and a Cello Sonata (1946). He wrote two *Fantasies Concertante* (1947), the first for three oboes and piano, the second for three trombones and piano; both were later orchestrated and incorporated into his Concerto for Orchestra no. 2.

In 1947 he composed the remarkable *Quartet for Four Double Basses,* a tour de force deemed unplayable at the time and not performed until 1960. With its ingenious exploitation of every possible technical device, it has become one of the most outstanding works in the double bass repertory. This was followed by a Trio for oboe, horn, and viola (1948); *Duo Sonata* for clarinet and bass clarinet (1949); Sonata for oboe and piano (1948–51); *Perpetuum Mobile* for four horns and bassoon (1949); *Fantasy* for solo cello (1951); *Two Movements* for flute and string trio (1952); *Five Pieces* for five horns (1952); and *Recitative and Rondo* for violin and piano (or orchestra) (1953).

Music for violin, piano and percussion and String Quartet no. 1 date from 1957. Other instrumental pieces include a Woodwind Quintet (1958); *Fantasy* for harp (1959); *Lifelines* for flute, guitar, and percussion (1960); *Lines and Contrasts* for 16 horns (1960); *Music for Brass Quintet* (1961); *Double Quintet* for woodwind and brass (1961), commissioned by the University of Southern California; *Automation* for ten instruments (1962); *Episodes* for solo clarinet (1964); String Quartet no. 2 (1965); *Aphorisms* for flute and string trio (1967); *Concerto da Camera,* commissioned for the 50th anniversary of the Eastman School of Music in 1971; *Five Moods* for tuba quartet (1972); and *Tre Invenzioni* (1972), commissioned for the 20th anniversary of the Fromm Foundation.

More recent Schuller chamber works are *Sonata Serenata* for clarinet, violin, cello, and piano (1978); Octet for clarinet, horn, bassoon, string quartet, and double bass (1979); *Duologue* for violin and piano (1982); Piano Trio (1984); *On Light Wings* for piano quartet (1984); Sextet for bassoon, piano, and string quartet (1986); *Chimeric Images* for chamber ensemble (1988); Horn Sonata (1988); *Five Impromptus* for English horn and string quartet (1989); *Impromptu and Cadenza* for six instruments (1990); *Hommage a Rayechka* for eight cellos (1990); *Trio Setting* for violin, clarinet, and piano (1990); *Sonata-Fantasia* for piano (1992); Brass Quintet no. 2 (1993); *Lament to M* for tenor saxophone and ensemble (1994); Sextet for piano (left hand) and wind quintet (1994); Sonata for alto saxophone and piano (1999); and *Quodlibet* for oboe, horn, violin, cello, and harp (2001).

In his desire to bridge the gap between "serious" music and jazz with John Lewis and the Modern Jazz Quartet, Schuller founded the Jazz and Classical Music Society in New York in 1955. He coined the term "Third Stream" to denote the fusion of these two musical worlds. His first composition in this medium, *12 by 11,* written in 1955, is scored for jazz group and chamber ensemble. His interest in jazz had appeared earlier in the *Atonal Jazz Study* of 1948, but from 1955 he concentrated upon a pioneering venture to bring together leading jazz and "straight" musicians. His association with John Lewis and the Modern Jazz Quartet produced several important works: *Transformation* for jazz chamber ensemble (1956), *Conversation* for string quartet and jazz quartet (1959), Concerto for jazz quartet and orchestra (1960), and *Passacaglia* for jazz quartet with an orchestra of winds and percussion (1962). In 1960 he wrote three "Third Stream" pieces: *Abstraction* for alto saxophone (Ornette Coleman), string quartet, two double basses, guitar, and percussion; *Variants on John Lewis'* "*Django*"; and *Variants of Thelonius Monk's* "*Criss Cross*" (1960). Other works in this

sphere are *Symphonic Tribute to Duke Ellington* (1955), *Night Music* for bass clarinet, guitar, two double basses, and drums (1962), and *Journey into Jazz* for narrator, jazz ensemble and orchestra (1962).

For his score for a Polish film, *Yesterday in Fact* (1963), Schuller won the Darius Milhaud Award. His other scores are *Automation* (1962), *Journey to the Stars* (1962), and *The Gift* (1962).

In yet another field, Schuller has revealed his talents as a writer. He has produced three outstanding and authoritative books: *Horn Technique* (1962), *Early Jazz: Its Roots and Musical Development* (1968), and *The Compleat Conductor* (1997).

SCHUMAN, WILLIAM
b. New York, New York, 4 August 1910
d. New York, New York, 14 February 1992

Schuman entered the School of Commerce, New York University, in 1928 and studied business administration and advertising for two years. He was attracted to "Tin Pan Alley" and composed his own popular songs, one of which, *Lovesick,* to lyrics by his friend Eddie Marks, was published. He also collaborated with Frank Loesser in writing approximately 40 songs. In 1930 he turned to serious music and undertook harmony lessons with Max Persin, a teacher at the Malkin Conservatory in New York, who had been a pupil of Anton Arensky. The following year he studied counterpoint with Charles Haubiel. In the summers of 1932 and 1933 he attended the Juilliard School, where his teachers were Bernard Wagenaar for harmony and Adolf Schmid for orchestration. After graduating from the Teachers

William Schuman, 1943, seated at the piano with the score for *Symphony for Strings* on the easel.
William Schuman Photo Collection #88, neg #222. Rizolla Photo Service, courtesy The Juilliard School.

College of Columbia University in 1935 he went to Europe where, during the summer, he studied conducting at the Mozarteum Academy in Salzburg.

On his return to the United States later that year, he began teaching at Sarah Lawrence College, Bronxville, New York. He received composition lessons from Roy Harris for the next two years. In 1945 he left teaching to become director of publications with G. Schirmer, Inc., succeeding Carl Engel. That year he was also appointed president of the Juilliard School of Music. He resigned from G. Schirmer in 1952 and in 1962 left the Juilliard School to become president of the new Lincoln Center for the Performing Arts in New York, a post he held until 1969.

Schuman's first important work, *American Festival Overture,* was performed in October 1939 by the Boston Symphony Orchestra. In that year he was awarded a Guggenheim Fellowship, receiving another in 1940.

Symphony no. 1 for 18 instruments, composed in 1935, was performed by the Gotham Symphony Orchestra in 1936. Symphony no. 2 (1937) received its premiere in May 1938 by the Greenwich Orchestra and was subsequently performed by Koussevitzky and the Boston Symphony Orchestra in February 1939, to a hostile reception from the critics. The composer withdrew both works. Symphony no. 3 (1941) also received its premiere under the direction of Koussevitzky with the Boston Symphony Orchestra on 17 October 1941. One of the most powerful and impressive works to be written in the United States, it won the New York Music Critics' Circle Award in 1942. In January 1942, Artur Rodzinski conducted the first performance of Schuman's Fourth Symphony in Cleveland. These two works quickly established the composer's name throughout America. *Symphony for Strings* (no. 5), another work of dynamic energy, was heard in Boston on 12 November 1943 under Koussevitzky, who had commissioned it. It was an immediate success, being performed widely and recorded. In 1946 it represented the United States at the I.S.C.M. Festival in London.

Symphony no. 6, in one movement, was completed in 1948 and first performed in Dallas under Antal Dorati in February of the following year. Probably the finest of the cycle of symphonies, it contrasts dark brooding passages with aggressively vigorous music of exciting rhythmical complexity.

Twelve years elapsed before Schuman wrote his next symphony. The Seventh, Eighth, and Ninth Symphonies form a set related in character. Symphony no. 7 was commissioned by the Koussevitzky Musical Foundation to celebrate the 75th anniversary of the Boston Symphony Orchestra, which performed it under Charles Munch in October 1960. Symphony no. 8 (1961–62), scored for large orchestra, was commissioned by the New York Philharmonic for the opening of Philhar-

monic Hall (now Avery Fisher Hall) at Lincoln Center on 4 October 1962, conducted by Leonard Bernstein. Symphony no. 9, subtitled *Le Fosse Ardeatine,* was inspired by the composer's visit to a cave near Rome, where the Germans had murdered 335 Italian civilians in retaliation for resistance activities in the Second World War. The Symphony was performed by the Philadelphia Orchestra in January 1969. It is dedicated to the memory of Alexander Hilsberg, concertmaster of the orchestra from 1926 to 1953, whose friends had commissioned the work. Symphony no. 10 (*American Muse*; 1975) was commissioned to celebrate the Bicentennial and performed by the National Symphony Orchestra of Washington, D.C. under Antal Dorati in April 1976.

For solo instruments and orchestra Schuman composed a Concerto for piano and orchestra (1938, rev. 1942); a Violin Concerto (1947), first performed by Isaac Stern (Boston, 1950; rev. 1954, 1958); *Song of Orpheus,* a fantasy for cello and orchestra (1962), commissioned by the Ford Foundation and based on his own song, "Orpheus and His Lute" (from a production of Shakespeare's *Henry VIII*, 1944); and *To Thee Old Cause* for oboe solo, brass, timpani, piano, and strings (1968). In 1978, in response to a commission from Zubin Mehta for a horn concerto for the New York Philharmonic Orchestra, Schuman wrote *Three Colloquies,* first performed on 24 January 1980 with Philip F. Myers as soloist.

Schuman's other orchestral works include *Prayer in Time of War* (1943); *Circus Overture* (1944); *Credendum, Article of Faith* (1955); *New England Triptych* (1956; also for band), based on music by William Billings; *The Orchestra Song* (1963); and *In Praise of Shahn* (1969), a canticle in memory of the artist Ben Shahn. *Concerto on Old English Rounds* for viola, women's chorus, and orchestra (1973) was first performed on 29 November 1974 by the Boston Symphony Orchestra under Michael Tilson Thomas. *Voyage,* composed in 1972 for the American Symphony Orchestra is an orchestration of a piano piece dating from 1953. His final orchestral work, *American Hymn,* was written for the St Louis Symphony Orchestra in 1980. Schuman also provided scores for two documentary films, *Steeltown* (1944) and *The Earth is Born* (1959).

For concert band he composed several important pieces, including *Newsreel* (1941; later orchestrated), *George Washington Bridge* (1950), *Philharmonic Fanfare* (1965), *Dedication Fanfare* (1968), *Anniversary Fanfare* (1969), and *Prelude for a Great Occasion* for brass and percussion (1974).

Schuman's strong enthusiasm for baseball is reflected in the one-act opera *The Mighty Casey* to a libretto by Jeremy Gury. It was produced in Hartford, Connecticut, on 4 May 1953. He composed four ballets.

The first of these, *Undertow* (Antony Tudor), was performed by Ballet Theater at the Metropolitan Opera House, New York (April 1945). For Martha Graham he wrote *Night Journey* (1947), staged on 3 May 1947; *Judith* (1949), performed in Louisville, Kentucky in January 1950; and *The Witch of Endor*, staged in November 1965.

Schuman's choral music comprises *Four Canonic Choruses* (1932); *Pioneers!* (1937), a setting of Whitman's words for eight-part chorus; *Choral Etude* for wordless voices (1937); *Prologue* (Thomas Wolfe) for chorus and orchestra (1939); *This is Our Time,* a secular cantata for chorus and orchestra (1940); *Requiescat* for female voices (1942); *Holiday Song* for female or mixed voices (1942); *A Free Song* (Whitman; 1942), winner of the Pulitzer Prize; *Te Deum* (1944); *Truth Shall Deliver* for men's voices (1946); *The Lord Has a Child* (Langston Hughes) for chorus and piano (1956); *Five Rounds on Famous Words* (1957); and *Carols of Death* (Whitman) for mixed voices (1958), his most frequently performed choral work.

There followed *Deo Ac Veritati* for men's voices (1963); *Declaration Chorale* (1971); *Mail Order Madrigals* (1971); *Casey at the Bat,* a cantata for soprano, baritone, chorus, and orchestra (1976); *Esses: Short Suite for Singers on Words Beginning with S* for soprano and chorus (1982); *Perceptions* (Whitman; 1982); and *On Freedom's Ground* (Richard Wilbur), a cantata for baritone, chorus, and orchestra (1983).

In 1975 Schuman composed *The Young Dead Soldiers,* a setting of words by Archibald McLeish for soprano, horn, eight woodwinds, and nine strings. It was performed by the National Symphony Orchestra, Washington, D.C. on 6 April 1976, conducted by Antal Dorati. Other vocal music includes *In Sweet Music* for voice, flute, viola, and harp (1978) and *Time to the Old,* three songs to words by McLeish, completed in 1979.

Among his instrumental works are five string quartets (1936, 1937, 1939, 1950, 1988); *Quartettino* for four bassoons (1939); *Amaryllis Variations* for string trio (1964); *XXV Opera Snatches* for solo trumpet (1978); *American Hymn* for brass quintet (1980); and *Dances* for wind quintet and percussion (1984). For piano solo he wrote *Three-Score Set* (1943), *Voyage,* five pieces (1953), and *Three Piano Moods* (1958).

SCHWANTNER, JOSEPH C.

b. *Chicago, Illinois, 22 March 1943*

Schwantner was educated at Chicago Conservatory College (B.A., 1964) and Northwestern University, Evanston, Illinois (M. Mus., 1966; D. Mus., 1968). He taught at Northwestern University School of Music (1966–68), Chicago Conservatory College (1968–69),

Joseph C. Schwanter.
Courtesy the composer.

and Ball State University, Muncie, Indiana (1969–70). Since 1970 he has taught composition at the Eastman School of Music, Rochester, N.Y., where he became associate professor (1975) and professor of composition (1980). He has received many awards, including a Guggenheim Fellowship (1978) and the Pulitzer Prize (1979). His first compositions are serial but after 1975 he adopted a freer style with a wider range of expression. In spite of a heavy teaching schedule he has remained remarkably prolific.

For orchestra Schwantner has composed *Sinfonia Brevis* (1963) and *August Canticle* (1968). *Aftertones of Infinity* (1978), commissioned by the American Composers' Orchestra, performed in January 1979 at Lincoln Center, New York under Lukas Foss; it won the Pulitzer Prize. Later works include *Distant Runes and Incantations* for piano and chamber orchestra (1983); *A Sudden Rainbow* (1984); *Someday Memories* (1984); *Toward Light* (1986); *From Afar,* a fantasy for guitar and orchestra (1987); a Piano Concerto (1988); *Freeflight, Fanfares and Fantasy* for the Boston "Pops" Orchestra (1989); and *A Play of Shadows* for flute and orchestra (1990)

More recent orchestral compositions are a Percussion Concerto, written in memory of Stephen Albert for the New York Philharmonic Orchestra in 1994; a Horn Concerto; *Beyond Autumn* (1998); a Violin Concerto (2000); *Angelfire,* a fantasy for amplified violin and orchestra (2001); and *September Canticle* a fantasy for organ, brass, percussion, amplified piano, and strings commissioned in 2002 for the Dallas Symphony Orchestra to commemorate the tragedy of 9/11.

Works for large ensembles include a Concertino for alto saxophone and three chamber ensembles (1964); *Diaphonia Intervallum* (1965); *Consortium* (1970); *Consortium II* (1971); *Modus Caelestis* (*Consortium III*) for 12 flutes, 12 strings, three percussionists, piano, and celeste (1972); *Canticle of the Evening Bells* for flute and 12 players (1975), written in memory of Dallapiccola and performed by the Contemporary Chamber Players under Arthur Weisberg; *And the Mountains Rising from Nowhere* for amplified piano, winds, brass, and percussion (1977), *From a Dark Millenium* for percussion group, winds, and brass (1980), *Through Interior Worlds* (1980), staged as a ballet in Seattle in 1992; and *In Evening Stillness* for winds (1996).

Among Schwantner's instrumental pieces are *Entropy* for soprano saxophone, bass clarinet, and cello (1966); *Chronicon* for bassoon and piano (1967); *Enchiridion* for violin and piano (1968); *In Aeternum II* for organ (1972); *Shadows I* for piano quartet (1973); *In Aeternum* (*Consortium IV*) for cello and four players (1973); *Autumn Canticles* for piano trio (1974); *Gossamer Song* for amplified double bass and amplified piano (1977); *Elixir* for flute and five players (1975), performed at the I.S.C.M. Festival in Helsinki in 1978; *Veiled Autumn* (*Kindertotenlied*) for piano (1987); *Wind, Willow, Whisper* for flute, clarinet, violin, cello, and piano (1980); *Music of Amber* for flute, clarinet, violin, cello, piano, and percussion (1981); and *Velocities* for marimba (1990).

Schwantner's important vocal works are *Music for Soprano, Brass and Percussion* (1964); *Shadows II* for baritone and eight players (1973); *Wild Angels of the Open Hills* for soprano, flute, and harp (1977); *Sparrows* for soprano and eight players (1979); *Two Poems of Agueda Pizarro* for soprano and piano (1980); *New Morning for the World Daybreak of Freedom,* a setting of words by Martin Luther King Jr. for narrator and orchestra (1982); *Magabunda* (*Witchnomad*) (Agueda Pizarro), a song cycle for soprano and orchestra (1983); *Dreamcaller* for soprano and orchestra (1984); and *Evening Land,* a symphony for chorus and orchestra, composed in 1995 for the St. Louis Symphony Orchestra.

SCHWARTZ, ELLIOTT (SHELLING)

b. Brooklyn, New York, 19 January 1936

Schwartz studied at Columbia University with Otto Luening and Jack Beeson (1953–57; B.A., 1957; M.A.,

1958) and at Columbia Teachers College (1957–60; Ed.D., 1962). He was also a private pupil of Paul Creston. In addition, at Bennington (Vermont) Composers Conference during the summers (1961–66) he received lessons from Hugo Aitken, Henry Brant, Chou Wen-Chung, Morton Feldman, Roger Goeb, Ralph Shapey, Edgar Varèse, and Stefan Wolpe. From 1960 to 1964 he was an instructor in music at the University of Massachusetts, Amherst. In 1964 he joined the music faculty at Bowdoin College, Brunswick, Maine, first as an assistant professor (1975–78) and as chairman of the music department (1980–87). He was visiting professor at Ohio State University (1985–86, 1989–92), vice-president of the American Music Center (1982–88), and National President of the College Music Society (1989–91). In 1996 he became a director of the American Composers Alliance.

Schwartz has been a resident fellow at the College of Creative Studies, University of California, Santa Barbara (1970, 1974, 1978), Harvard (2001), and the London College of Music (2002), and visiting fellow at Trinity College of Music, London (1967), the Center for Music Experiment, University of California, San Diego (1978–79), and Robinson College, Cambridge, England (1993, 1999).

With Earle Brown, Roger Reynolds, Lukas Foss, Morton Subotnick, and Larry Austin, Schwartz represented the strong avant-garde in the later part of the twentieth century. Although most of his works are instrumental, he has written several orchestral pieces: *Music for Orchestra with Electronic Tape* (1966); *Magic Music* for piano and orchestra (1967–68); *Island* (1970); *Dream Overture* for orchestra and recorded orchestra (1972); *The Harmony of Maine,* based on four tunes from Supply Belcher's 1794 collection and scored for synthesizer and orchestra (1974); *Janus* for piano and orchestra (1976); and *Zebra* for youth orchestra and tape (1980). Later orchestral works include *Celebrations/ Reflections: A Time Warp* (1985); *Four Ohio Portraits* (1986); *Sinfonia Juxta* (1991); *Timepiece 1794* for chamber orchestra (1994); *Equinox: Concerto for Orchestra* (1994); *Rainbow* (1996); *Jack o' Lantern* for orchestra and lights (2000); *Mehitabel's Serenade* for alto saxophone and orchestra (2001); *Voyager* (2002); and *Water Music* for string orchestra and water sounds (2002).

For large chamber ensembles he has composed *Concert Piece* for ten players (1965); Symphony in two movements (1965); *Texture* for strings, wind, and brass (1966); Septet (1969); Octet (1971); *Eclipse I* for ten players (1971); *Eclipse III* (1975); and five chamber concertos: no. 1 for double bass and 15 players (1977), no. 2 for clarinet and nine players (1977), no. 3 for piano and small orchestra (1977), no. 4 for saxophone and ten players (1981), and no. 5 for bassoon, strings, and piano (1992).

Elliott Schwartz, 1996.
Photo: Bowdoin College News Service, courtesy the composer.

Schwartz's works for wind ensembles include *Memorials 1963* for band and organ (1963); *Voyage* for winds, brass, and percussion (1969); *Eclipse II* for band (1974); *Scatter* for 12 players (1979); *Chiaroscuro: Zebra Variations* for wind ensemble (1995); and *Rain Forest with Birds* for symphonic winds, with bird song and music by William Byrd on tape (2001).

Among the many pieces Schwartz has written for solo instruments are *Romance* for bassoon and piano; Sonata for solo oboe; *Aria no. 1* for clarinet and piano; Suite for viola and piano (1965); *Dialogue no. 1* for solo double bass (1966–67); *Decline and Fall of the Sonata* for violin and piano (1972); *Archeopteryx* for trombone and piano (1976); Divertimento no. 3 for organ and percussion (1977); *Souvenir* for clarinet and piano (1979); *Dream Piece* for violin and piano (1980); *Second Thoughts* for oboe and piano (1983); *Reading Session* for clarinet and piano (1984); *Flame* for tuba and piano (1988); *Palindromes* for cello and percussion (1989); and *Spaces* for piano and percussion (1995).

Works for solo instrument and tape include *Dialogue no. 2* for clarinet; *Aria no. 4* for bassoon; *Interruptions* for wind quintet (1965); *Music for Prince Albert* for piano (1969); *Music for Napoleon and Beethoven* for trumpet and two pianos (1969); *Memorabilia* for cello (1970); *Options I* for trombone (1970); *Mirrors* for piano (1973); *Grand Concerto* for piano (1973); *Prism* for organ (1974); *Extended Oboe* (1975), *Extended Clarinet* (1975); *Pentagonal Mobile* for piano (1976); *Ziggurat* for flute (1976); and *Extended Piano* (1977).

Schwartz's chamber works include *Three Short Scenes* for two cellos; *Music* for oboe, trumpet, and cello; Sonata for violin and double bass; Divertimento no. 1 for clarinet, horn, and piano; Serenade for flute, double bass, and percussion; *Graffiti* for violin and cello; *Three Movements* for brass quintet; *Multiples* for three percussionists and piano; *Sibling Suite* for two flutes; Oboe Quartet (1963); *Four Studies* for two clarinets (1964); *Soliloquy* for flute, clarinet, violin, and piano (1965); *Essay* for trumpet and trombone (1966); *Aria no. 2* for violin and drums (1966); *Aria no. 3* for viola and wood blocks (1967); Divertimento no. 2 for two horns, harpsichord, piano, and celesta (1968); *Signals* for trombone and double bass (1968); *Mini concerto* for flute, oboe, and string trio (1969); *Ballagio Variations* for string quartet (1980); Divertimento no. 4 for flute, double bass, and piano (1981); *Jet Pieces* for keyboards and three instruments (1980); and *Cleveland Doubles* for clarinet, saxophone, and winds (1981).

Among more recent instrumental pieces are *Dream Music with Variations* for piano quartet (1983), *Octagon* for eight percussionists (1984), *Spirals,* commissioned in 1984 by Speculum; *Northern Pines* for two oboes, clarinet, two horns, and piano (1988); *A Garden for RKB* for violin, clarinet, and piano (1990); *Elan* for wind quintet (1993); *Reflections* for six bassoons (1995); *Tapestry* for violin, cello, and piano (1997); *Vienna Dreams* for viola, clarinet, and piano (1998); *Kaleidoscope* for violin, contrabassoon, and piano (1999); *Downeast Fanfare* for three trumpets (2001); *Hall of Mirrors* for saxophone quartet and piano (2002); *Riverscape* for clarinet, string quartet, and piano (2002); and *A Riot of Reeds* for nine clarinets (2003).

Chamber compositions that use tape are *Ninas* for

flute and oboe; *Music for Napoleon and Beethoven* for trumpet and two pianos (1969); *Options II* for clarinet and percussion (1970); *Rip* for brass trio (1970); *Echo Music I* for viola and clarinet (1973); *Echo II* for flute, oboe, clarinet, and bassoon (1974); *Cycles and Gongs* for trumpet and organ (1975); and *Five Mobiles* for flute, organ, and harpsichord (1975).

Theatrical mixed-media works by Schwartz include *Elevator Music* (1967), to be performed in a multi-story space outside elevator doors; *Areas* for 2 to 4 dancers, flute, clarinet, violin, cello, trombone, and piano (1968); *Gibson Hall* for keyboards to be staged in a music building; *Music for Audience and Soloist* (1970), where the audience is divided into four sections, each with a conductor; *Scales and Arpeggios* for tape (1973), to be played in lobbies and public places; *A Dream of Bells and Beats* for piano, audience performers with radios, metronomes, music boxes, audience chorus, and alarm clocks (1977); *California Games* for 4 to 6 players, audience performers, and audience chorus (1978); and *Radio Games,* a duet for performers on radio (1980). *Telly* for nine players has optional parts for television sets, radios, and tape (1972).

His works for voices include *Music for the Ascension* for chorus, organ, percussion, and narrator, *Songs from Brecht* for soprano, oboe, clarinet, and double bass, and *Though I Speak* for men's chorus.

Schwartz has written five books: *The Symphonies of Ralph Vaughan Williams* (1964), *Contemporary Composers on Contemporary Music* (with Barney Childs; 1967, rev. 1998), *Electronic Music: A Listener's Guide* (1973, rev. 1976), *Music: Ways of Listening* (1982), and *Music Since 1945: Issues, Materials and Literature* (with D. Godfrey; 1993).

SCOTT, TOM (THOMAS JEFFERSON)
b. Campbellsburg, Kentucky, 28 May 1912
d. New York, New York, 12 August 1961

Scott learned the violin from his uncle and as a boy played in jazz bands. For a number of years he worked in Hollywood. Among his teachers were George Antheil, Harrison Kerr, and Wallingford Riegger.

For orchestra he wrote *Song with Dance* (1932); *Plymouth Rock* (1938); *Hornpipe and Chantey* (1944); a Symphony, performed by the Rochester Symphony Orchestra in 1946; *From the Sacred Harp* (1946); *Johnny Appleseed* (1948); *Binorie Variations* (1953); *Lento* for saxophone and strings (1953); *Fanfare and Cantilena,* and three pieces for strings: *From the Southern Highlands, Colloquy,* and *Music for Strings.* Scott composed two works for narrator and orchestra, *Ballad of the Harp Weaver* (1947) and *Sophocles and the Hyena* (text: Jim Moran). An opera, *The Fisherman,*

was completed in 1936. His instrumental works include two string quartets (1944, 1956) and *Emily Dickinson Suite* for violin and harp (1955).

SELBY, WILLIAM
b. London, 1738
d. Boston, Massachusetts, 12 December 1798

Selby settled in Boston in 1771, where he was a harpsichord player and organist at King's Chapel. He soon took a leading part in organizing the musical life in his adopted city. He was organist at Trinity Church, Newport, Rhode Island (1773–74), returning to Boston in 1776. Like almost all other composers at the time in America, he was an amateur musician, earning his living for a while selling groceries. He performed and taught music in his spare time. Although hardly any of his compositions survive, contemporary accounts reveal that Selby wrote mainly instrumental music, including a Concerto for organ, a Sonata for two violins and cello, and several *Voluntaries* and *Fugues* for organ or harpsichord.

In 1782 he attempted to launch a musical magazine to be called *The New Minstrel,* but there is no evidence that his plans ever reached fruition. In later years he composed choral music and songs with such titles as *Ode in Honor of George Washington, Ode on the Anniversary of Independence,* and *Ptalaemon and Patora.* He published *9 Psalms* and *9 Pieces for guitar.* When George Washington visited Boston in 1789, Selby arranged concerts in his honor, in which he included several of his own works.

SEMEGEN, DARIA
b. Bamberg, Germany, 27 June 1946

Daria Semegen emigrated to the United States in 1950 as a child of Ukranian parents, becoming an American citizen in 1957. She studied composition with Otto Miller and David Holden at the Chautauqua Institution. At the Eastman School of Music, Rochester, New York, from which she graduated in 1968, she was a pupil of Samuel Adler and Burrill Phillips. After a year of study in Poland with Witold Lutoslawski, she attended Yale University, where she worked with Bulent Arel in electronic music and with Alexander Goehr in composition. In 1971 she studied with Vladimir Ussachevsky at the Columbia-Princeton Electronic Music Center, where she also taught until 1976. She joined the music faculty at the State University of New York at Stony Brook in 1974, where she is currently an associate professor and a director of the Electronic Music Studios.

Although she is widely recognised as a composer of

electronic music, Semegen has composed much instrumental and vocal music. For orchestra she has written *Fantasia* (1963), *Triptych* (1966), and *Study for 16 strings* (1968). Her instrumental pieces include two string quartets (1963, 1964); a Suite for flute and violin (1965); *Three Piano Pieces* (1965); *Composition for string quartet* (1965); *Quattro* for flute and piano (1967); *Three Pieces* for clarinet and piano (1968); *Jeux de Quatres* for clarinet, trombone, cello, and piano (1970); *Music for Violin Solo* (1973); *Music for Clarinet Solo* (1979); *Music for Doublebass Solo* (1981); *Music for Violin and Piano* (1988); and *Vignette* for piano (1997).

Semegen's vocal music includes *Silent, Silent Night* (Blake) for tenor and piano (1965); *Lieder auf der Flucht* (text: I. Bachmann) for soprano and eight players (1967); *Poem: For* (R. Sward) and Psalm 43, both for chorus (1967); *Prayer for Hannah* for soprano and piano (1968); and *Poème Premiere: Dans la Nuit* (Henri Michaux) for baritone and instrumental ensemble (1969).

Her principal electronic music compositions are *Six Plus* for tape and five instruments (1965); *Out of Into,* a film score (1971); *Trill Study* (1971); *Electronic Composition no. 1* (1972); *Spectra Studies* (1974–75); *Arc: Music for Dancers* (1977); *Electronic Composition no. 2: Spectra* (1979); *Music for Viola and Tape* (1980); commissioned by the National Endowment for the Arts, *Rhapsody* for Yamaha MIDI piano (1990); and *Arabesque* for two-channel tape, a tribute to Bulent Arel (1992).

SERLY, TIBOR

b. Losonc, Hungary, 25 November 1900
d. London, England, 8 October 1978

Serly was taken to the United States in 1905, becoming an American citizen in 1911. After initial musical training from his father, a pupil of Liszt, he went to Hungary in 1922 to study with Kodály and Leo Weiner at the Royal Academy of Music, Budapest. He was also a violin pupil of Jenö Hubay. On his return to the United States he became a viola player in the Cincinnati Symphony Orchestra (1926–27); he then played violin in the Philadelphia Orchestra (1928–35) and the NBC Symphony (1937–38). From 1938 he taught privately.

For orchestra he wrote *Transylvanian Rhapsody* (1926); a Viola Concerto (1929), first performed in Budapest in 1935; Symphony No 1 in B minor (1931); Symphony no. 2 for winds, brass, and percussion (1932); *Six Dance Designs* (1935); *Sonata Concertante* for strings (1935–36); three symphonic poems: *Colonial Pageant* (1936), *Alarms and Excursions* (1937), and *Pagan City* (1938); *Midnight Madrigal* for trum-

pet and orchestra (1939); *American Elegy* (1945); *Rhapsody* for viola and orchestra (1948); *Fantasy on Quodlibets* (*on American Folk-Songs*; 1950); Concerto for two pianos (1948–52); Trombone Concerto (1952); *Lament: Homage to Béla Bartók* for strings (1955); *Variations* for audience and orchestra (1956); Concerto for violin and winds (1953–58); *String Symphony* (1956–58); *Symphony in Four Cycles* for strings (1960); *Piano Concertino 3 x 3* (1967); *Canonic Fugue in ten voices on ten tones* for strings (1972); and *Music* for two harps and strings (1976).

For concert band he wrote *Contrapuntal Divertissement* for wind and percussion (1931), *Four Centuries Suite* (1953), and *Three Variations on an Old Hungarian Song* (1964). Serly composed three ballets: *Mischchianza* (1936), *Ex Machina* (1943), and *Cast Out* (1973).

Instrumental pieces include a Violin Sonata (1923); a String Quartet (1924); *Innovations* for two harps and string quartet (1933–34); *Sonata Lascivus* for solo violin (1947); Trio for clarinet, violin, and piano (1949); *Chorale* for three harps (1967); *Adagio and Scherzo* for solo flute (1968); *Rondo Fantasy in Stringometrics* for violin and harp (1971); and *Threnody* for four cellos (or four horns) (1935–73). For piano he wrote a Piano Sonata (1946), a Suite for two pianos (1946), and *40 Etudes in Modus Lascivus* (1946–60).

Serly's vocal music includes *Four Songs from "Chamber Music"* (James Joyce) for soprano and orchestra (1926); *Strange Story* (Elinor Wylie) for mezzo-soprano and orchestra (1927); *A Little Christmas Cantata* for chorus, audience, and orchestra (1957); *Anniversary Cantata on a Quodlibet* for voices and small orchestra (1966); *Consovowels I* for soprano (1968), *II & III* for soprano and clarinet (1970–71), and *IV & V* for soprano and violin (1974); and *The Pleiades,* a cantata for solo voices, chorus and orchestra (1975).

He was the author of three books: *A Second Look at Harmony* (1965), *Modis Lascivus: The Road to Enharmonicism* (1976), and *The Rhetoric of Melody* (1978). Serly was also responsible for the completion of Bartók's Third Piano Concerto and Viola Concerto. He died as a result of a road accident in London.

SESSIONS, ROGER

b. Brooklyn, New York, 28 December 1896
d. Princeton, New Jersey, 16 March 1985

At the age of four, Sessions began to receive piano lessons from his mother, herself a graduate of the Leipzig Conservatory. When only 12, he composed his first piece of music, followed in the next year by an opera, *Lancelot and Elaine*. At the remarkably early age of 14, he went to Harvard University, where his teachers included Archibald Davison and Edward Burlingame Hill. He graduated in 1915 at the age of 18. He continued his studies at Yale University (1915–17), where he was a pupil of Horatio Parker and received his bachelor's degree in music. Later he studied with Ernest Bloch (1919–21). His first teaching position was at Smith College, Northampton, Massachusetts where he joined the faculty in 1917. In 1921 he moved to the newly founded Cleveland Institute of Music as an assistant to his former teacher, Bloch, who had been chosen as the Institute's first director.

From 1925 to 1933 Sessions lived mostly in Europe, dividing his time between Florence, Rome and Berlin. He was awarded two Guggenheim Fellowships in 1926 and 1927, and won a Prix de Rome scholarship (1928–31) and a Carnegie Fellowship (1931–32). On his visits to America he assisted Aaron Copland from 1928 to 1931 to organize the Copland-Sessions Concerts where new music by American composers was presented. When he finally returned from Europe he taught at Boston University (1933–35) and at the New Jersey College for Women (1935–37). In 1935 he was also appointed to the music faculty of Princeton where he remained for ten years. From 1945 to 1952 he was a professor at the University of California at Berkeley. He returned to Princeton in 1953, retiring in 1965. He taught at the Juilliard School of Music in New York (1965–85). He was president of the American section of the I.S.C.M. from 1936 to 1941 and always played an active part in the promotion of new music.

Sessions's music is generally rhapsodic in character with an extensive use of counterpoint. His harmonic language in the early works is diatonic. After 1940 it became more chromatic, and by the mid-1950's he was making use of tone-rows in most of his early compositions, though never in a dogmatic sense. His first significant piece was the incidental music for a production of Leonid Andreiev's play *The Black Maskers* at Smith College in 1923. In 1928 he arranged a suite from the score, still his best known piece; it is dedicated to Ernest Bloch.

The set of nine symphonies is the core of Session's music: Symphony no. 1 in E minor, composed in 1927, was performed in Boston under Koussevitzky, and heard at the I.S.C.M. Festival in Geneva in 1929. The Second Symphony (1944–46) was premiered in San Francisco in 1947. Dedicated to the memory of Franklin D. Roosevelt, it was performed at the I.S.C.M. Festival in Amsterdam in 1948.

Symphony no. 3 was composed to celebrate the 75th anniversary of the Boston Symphony Orchestra. It is dedicated to the memory of Serge and Natalie Koussevitzky and first performed under Charles Munch in December 1957.

Symphony no. 4, completed in 1958, was first performed in Minneapolis in 1960. Symphony no. 5 received its premiere in Philadelphia in 1964. Symphony no. 6, completed in 1966, was first performed in that year in Newark, New Jersey. Symphony no. 7 (1967) was performed in Ann Arbor, Michigan by the Chicago Symphony Orchestra under Jean Martinon as a part of the University of Michigan's Centennial Celebrations. Symphony no. 8 was one of 18 works commissioned to celebrate the 125th anniversary of the New York Philharmonic Orchestra. It was for performed under the direction of William Steinberg in May 1968. Symphony no. 9 was completed in 1978 and performed in January 1980 by the Syracuse Symphony Orchestra, which had commissioned it. In addition, Sessions composed three other unpublished symphonies (in D, 1917; 1929; 1934–35, lost).

Sessions's other orchestral works are *Nocturne* (1922); *Strophes* for piano and orchestra (1927–29); *Ballata* (1929–30); *Waltzes* (1929–31); *Three Dirges* (1933); Divertimento (1959); *Rhapsody* (1970); Concertino for chamber orchestra (1972), commissioned by the Fromm Foundation; and Concerto for Orchestra, commissioned by the Boston Symphony Orchestra and performed under Seiji Ozawa in October 1981; it was awarded the Pulitzer Prize. He also provided incidental music for *Turandot*, staged in Cleveland in 1925.

The impressive Violin Concerto (1933–35) had its first performance in Colorado Springs in 1939 by Robert Gross, accompanied at the piano by Sessions; its orchestral premiere came in 1940, with Gross and the Illinois Symphony Orchestra conducted by Izler Solomon. A Piano Concerto, dedicated to the memory of Artur Schnabel, was completed in 1956. In 1971 Sessions composed a Double Concerto for violin, cello, and orchestra, first performed at the Juilliard School to celebrate the composer's 75th birthday, with Paul Zukovsky and John Sessions, the composer's son and a former cello pupil of Gaspar Cassado.

In addition to his childhood work, *Launcelot and Elaine* (1910) and the unfinished *The Fall of the House of Usher* (1925), Sessions composed three operas. The one-act *The Trial of Lucullus,* a musical setting of a radio play by Brecht, translated by H.R. Hays, was first staged at the University of California, Berkeley in 1947. The three-act *Montezuma,* to a text by G. Antonio Borgese, was begun as early as 1947. Completed in 1962, it was produced by the Deutsche Oper in West Berlin in 1964. It received its American premiere in Boston in March 1976 and was revived in 1982. His last opera, *The Emperor's New Clothes* (1978–84), remains unstaged.

His choral works include *Turn, O Libertad* (Whitman; 1943), scored for chorus and piano duet. The Mass for unison voices and organ dates from 1955.

In 1970 he completed a large-scale work, *When Lilacs Last at the Dooryard Bloom'd* (Whitman) for chorus and orchestra, dedicated to the memory of Martin Luther King, Jr. and John F. Kennedy. Composed to mark the centenary of the University of California, Berkeley, it was premiered on 23 May 1971 by the UCB Symphony and Chorus, conducted by Michael Senturia. *Three Biblical Choruses* for chorus and orchestra were composed in 1971 to a commission from Amherst College, Massachusetts for its sesquicentennial and performed there in 1975.

For soprano and orchestra he composed *Romualdo's Song* (Andreiev; 1923); *On the Beach at Fontana* (Joyce; 1930); Psalm 140 (1953); and *Idyll of Theocritus,* performed in Louisville, Kentucky in 1956.

His many chamber works include two string quartets, no. 1 in E minor (1936) and no. 2 (1951); three violin sonatas (1916, 1953, 1981); a Piano Trio (1916); *Duo* for violin and piano (1942); Sonata for unaccompanied violin (1953); a String Quintet (1957); *Six Pieces* for unaccompanied cello (1966), composed for John Sessions; *Canons* for string quartet (1971), written in memory of Igor Stravinsky; and *Duo* and violin and cello (1978).

For piano he composed three sonatas: no. 1 (1930), performed at the I.S.C.M. Festival in Oxford, England (1931), no. 2 (1946), and no. 3 (1964); a suite, *From My Diary* (1940); *Five Pieces for Piano* (1975); and *Waltz* (1977–78). *Three Chorales* for organ appeared in 1926.

As an extension to his teaching, Sessions wrote five valuable books: *The Musical Experience of the Composer, Performer, Listener* (1950), *Harmonic Practice* (1951), *Reflections on the Musical Life in the United States* (1956), *Questions About Music* (1970), and *Roger Sessions on Music* (collected essays; 1980).

SHACKFORD, CHARLES REEVE

b. New York, New York, 18 April 1918

d. New London, Connecticut, 21 April 1979

Shackford studied with Hindemith at Yale University (B.A., 1941), with Walter Piston at Harvard University (Ph.D., 1954), and at the Juilliard School. He taught at Bennett Junior College (1944–46), Harvard University (1949–50), Wellesley College, Cambridge, Massachusetts (1952–53), School of Nursing, Newton, Massachusetts (1956–62), and Wilson College, Chambersburg, Pennsylvania (1962–65). He was appointed professor of music at Connecticut College, New London in 1965, where he remained until his death.

Shackford's works include Serenade for piano and chamber orchestra (1942); Trio for oboe, violin, and viola (1942); String Trio (1942); *Duo* for two clarinets

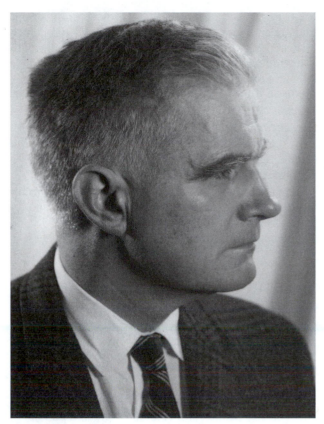

Charles Reeve Shackford.
MSS 38, The Charles Shackford Papers in the Irving S. Gilmore Music Library of Yale University.

(1948); *Duo* for horn and cello (1949); *Fantasy* for cello and piano (1951); Wind Trio (1952); *Toccata* for brass (1967); *Fantasy on Vysehrad* for two pianos and orchestra (1969); Sonata for solo viola (1970); Quintet for clarinet, horn, and string trio (1973); and *Overture Concertante* for band (1973).

SHAHAN, PAUL W.

b. Grafton, West Virginia, 2 January 1923

d. Murray, Kentucky, 2 February 1997

Shahan was educated at West Virginia University, Morgantown under Weldon Hart and the Peabody College, now part of Vanderbilt University in Nashville. At the Eastman School of Music, Rochester, New York he studied with Bernard Rogers and Howard Hanson. He also received private lessons from Roy Harris and Kent Kennan. He was appointed professor of theory and brass at Murray State College, Kentucky in 1957, retiring in 1988.

For orchestra he wrote *Three Portraits* (1950), *Two Symphonic Miniatures* (1953), a Symphony (1955), *Two Maskers, Nocturne* for horn and strings; and *Soliloquy* for trumpet and strings (1953). Other compositions include an opera, *The Stubblefield Story* (1963), and a cantata, *Lazarroth* for voice and orchestra. To the concert band repertory he contributed a Concerto for double bass and band (1953); *Spring Festival* (1955); *Holiday in Spain* (1959); *The Fountain Head* for brass and percussion (1963); *The Lincoln Heritage Trail* (1966); *A Speech Splendor* (1966); and *Mosaics in Motion* (1968).

Among his choral works are *Sing, Rejoice in the Lord* (1960), *How Excellent are Thy Works* (1962), and a setting of Psalm 150 (1963).

Shahan's instrumental music includes *Spectrums* for brass choir (1952), *The City of David* for brass and organ (1956), *Leipzig Towers* for brass choir (1957), and *The Solemn Sea* for tuba and piano (1960).

SHAPERO, HAROLD SAMUEL

b. Lynn, Massachusetts, 29 April 1920

Shapero began taking piano lessons at the age of seven and in his teens developed a great enthusiasm for jazz through playing in dance bands. This interest continued as can be seen in *On Green Mountain* for 13 jazz instruments, composed in 1957 and based on a chaconne by Monteverdi (literally, "green mountain"). Aged 16, he went to Boston to study with Nicolas Slonimsky at the Malkin Conservatory (1936–37). During 1937 he studied with Ernst Krenek, who was visiting the United States. At Harvard (1938–41) he received composition lessons from Walter Piston; at the Berkshire Music Center, Tanglewood he was a pupil of Hindemith (1940–41). He also spent two years attending the classes of Nadia Boulanger at the Longy Music School, Cambridge, Massachusetts (1942–43).

Shapero was the recipient of many awards, including the Gershwin Prize in 1948, Guggenheim Fellowships (1947, 1948), and Naumberg and Paine Fellowships. In 1952 he joined the music faculty of Brandeis University, Waltham, Massachusetts, becoming an associate professor in 1960, He was also chairman of the music department and director of the University Electronic Music Studios. He retired in 1988.

Shapero's musical language is predominantly contrapuntal; the various influences of his teachers have been absorbed into a personal style, although the neoclassicism of Stravinsky is strongly evident in the early works. He is not a prolific composer, and from 1970 tp 1980 almost entirely ceased writing music.

While still a student at Harvard, he completed his String Quartet in 1940 which he dedicated to Piston, his teacher. This work, along with the *Nine Minute Overture,* performed by the CBS Orchestra in 1941, won him the Prix de Rome in 1941. Shapero's other important early orchestral pieces are Serenade in D for strings (1945), *Sinfonia: The Travellers* (1948), and *Symphony for Classical Orchestra* (1948), all closely modeled on musical forms of the eighteenth century, and a ballet, *Lyric Dances* (1956–58). Also for orchestra are *Credo,* commissioned in 1955 by the Louisville Orchestra; Concerto for Orchestra (1950–58); and *Partita* in C for piano and small orchestra (1960). In 1958 he provided the score for a television film, *Woodrow Wilson* (1958).

In addition to the String Quartet, his instrumental music includes *Three Pieces for Three Pieces* (flute, clarinet, bassoon; 1938); a String Trio (1938); Trumpet Sonata in C (1939); a Violin Sonata (1942); a Sonata

Irving Fine (left) and Harold Shapero, 1948.
Photo: Irving Fine Collection, Library of Congress, Music Division.

for piano duet (1941); and several works for piano solo, including three *Amateur Sonatas* (1944), *Variations* in C minor (1947), a Sonata in F minor (1948), and *American Variations* (1950).

His choral items are *Two Psalms* for chorus (1952) and *Cantata on Hebrew Texts,* for soloist, choir, and ensemble, composed for the American Jewish Tercentenary in 1955. For voice and piano he has written *Four Baritone Songs* (e.e. cummings; 1942) and *Two Hebrew Songs* (1970, orch. 1980).

Among Shapero's compositions are works using a Buchla synthesizer and piano; including *Three Improvisations in B* (1968), *Three Studies in C#* (1969), and *Four Pieces in B-flat* (1970). Recent compositions include *Six for Five* for wind quintet (1994) and four works for orchestra: Trumpet Concerto (1995), *Fantasy* for trumpet and orchestra (1995), *Credo II* (2002), and Sinfonietta (2003).

SHAPEY, RALPH

b. Philadelphia, Pennsylvania, 12 March 1921
d. Philadelphia, Pennsylvania, 13 June 2002

Shapey began his musical studies in violin at the age of seven and was later a pupil of Emanuel Zeitlin for violin and Stefan Wolpe for composition. After teaching at the University of Pennsylvania, Philadelphia (1963–64) he was appointed professor of composition at the University of Chicago, retiring in 1985. After a year at Queens College, New York he returned to the University of Chicago, teaching there until 1991. He was founder and musical director of the Contemporary Chamber Players, a group specializing in the music of twentieth-century composers. Shapey conceived music in terms of concrete images created by dense textures and complex counterpoint. From 1969 to 1976 he imposed a moratorium on the performance of his music, although he continued to compose. This action was in part a protest against the performing conditions regarding new music, in part, he explained, "for personal and religious reasons."

For orchestra he wrote *Fantasy* (1951); Symphony (1952); Concerto for clarinet and chamber orchestra (1954), performed at the I.S.C.M. Festival in Strasbourg in 1958; *Challenge – The Family of Man* (1955), a symphonic poem commissioned by Mitropoulos; and *Ontogeny* (1958) performed in Buffalo, New York in 1965. His Violin Concerto, *Invocation* received its premiere in 1959 at the University of Chicago with Esther Glazer as soloist and the composer conducting. Other orchestral pieces include *Rituals* (1959); *Chamber Symphony* (1962); *Partita* for violin and 13 instruments (1966), commissioned for the 75th anniversary of the University of Chicago in 1967; and *Partita Fantasy* for cello and 16 players, commissioned 1967 by the Koussevitzky Music Foundation.

Orchestral pieces written after the composer lifted his self-imposed ban include Double Concerto for violin, cello, and orchestra, composed in 1983 for the New York Philharmonic Orchestra in 1983; *Grotou* for youth orchestra (1984); *Symphonie concertante* (1985); *Concerto Fantastique*, conducted by the composer in Chicago in 1991; Concerto for cello, piano, and strings (1986); and two works for chamber orchestra, *Stony Brook Concerto* (1996) and *Gamper Festival Concerto* (1998).

Shapey's vocal music includes a cantata for soprano, tenor, bass, narrator, and chamber orchestra (1951); *Walking Upright,* eight songs for female voice and violin (1958); *This Day* (V. Klement) for voice and piano (1960); *Dimensions* for soprano and ten instruments (1961); *Incantations* for soprano and ten instruments, premiered in New York in 1961 by Bethany Beardslee; and *Songs of Ecstasy* for soprano, piano, percussion, and tape (1967), commissioned by the Fromm Foundation.

Praise, an oratorio on religious texts for bass-baritone, double chorus, and chamber orchestra, was begun in 1962 but not completed until 1971. Other works of this period include *O Jerusalem* for soprano and flute (1975); *Songs of Eros* for soprano, orchestra, and tape (1975); *The Covenant* for soprano and 16 players (1977); and *Song of Songs I, II,* and *III* for soprano, bass, 14 players, and tape (1979–81). Among his later vocal compositions are *25 Songs* for soprano and piano (1982); *Psalm II* for soprano, chorus, and chamber ensemble (1984); *In Memoriam Paul Fromm* for soprano, baritone, and nine performers (1987); *Songs of Life* for soprano, cello, and piano (1988); *Centennial Celebration* for soprano, mezzo-soprano, tenor, baritone, and 12 players (1991); *12 Goethe Songs* for soprano and piano (1995); *Celebration* for soprano, tenor, baritone, bass-baritone, chorus, dancers, and orchestra (1997); *Ode a la Cuore* for bass-baritone, violin, viola, cello, and piano (1998); *The Voice*: *The Coming of the Second Flood* for narrator, soprano, mezzo-soprano, tenor, bass-baritone, chorus, and orchestra (1999); and *Lul-La-By no. 2* for three sopranos, three flutes (one player), and tape (2001). His only opera, *The Quatogonists*, was completed in 1997.

The greater part of Shapey's output was instrumental music. He composed ten string quartets (1946, 1949, 1950–51, 1953, 1957–58, 1963, 1972, 1993, 1995, 2000); Violin Sonata (1946); Piano Quintet (1946–47); Oboe Sonata (1951–52); Oboe Quartet (1952); Cello Sonata (1953–54); Piano Trio (1953–55); *Duo* for viola and piano (1957); *Rhapsodie* for oboe and piano (1957);

Evocation for violin, piano, and percussion (1959); *Movements* for wind quintet (1960); *Five* for violin and piano (1960); *De Profundis* for double bass and instruments (1960); *Discourse* for four instruments (1961); *Piece* for violin, seven instruments, and percussion (1962); Brass Quintet (1963); *Partita* for solo violin (1966); *Poème* for viola and piano (1966); *Reyem* (*Musical Offering*) for flute, violin, and piano (1967); *Evocations II* for cello, piano, and percussion (1979); *Three for Six* for six players (1980); *Movements II* (*Concerto Grosso*) for wind quintet (1981); *Evocation III* for viola and piano (1981); and *Discourse II* for violin, clarinet, cello, and piano (1981).

Shapey remained amazingly prolific through the last two decades of his life. Among the late chamber works are *Fantasy* for violin and piano (1983); *Krosnick Soli* for solo cello (1983); *Mann Duo* for violin and piano (1984); *Concertante* for trumpet and ten instruments (1984); *Gottlieb Duo* for percussion and piano (1984); *Kroflifh Sonata* for cello and piano (1985); *Variations* for viola and nine performers (1987); *Intermezzo* for dulcimer and piano (or celesta) (1990); *Duo* for two winds (1991); *Movement of Varied Moments for Two* for flute and vibraphone (1991); Piano Trio (1992); *Trio Concertante* for violin, piano, and percussion (1992); *Inventions* for clarinet and percussion (1992); *Dinosaur Annex* for violin and vibraphone-marimba (1993); *Constellations for Bang on a Can All-Stars* for ensemble (1993); *Rhapsody* for cello and piano (1993); *Evocations IV* for piano trio and percussion (1994); *Sonata appassionata* for cello and piano (1995); *Interchange* for percussion quartet (1996); *Discourse Encore* for violin, clarinet, cello, and piano (1996); *Inter Two* (*Between Two*) for percussion duo (1997); three violin sonatas (1998); *Solo – Duet – Trio* for cello and tape (1998); *Images* for oboe, piano, and percussion (1998); *Millenium Designs* for violin and piano (2002); *Night Music I* for flutes and tape (2001); *Night Music II* for violin (or viola) and tape (2001); *Night Music III* for two violas, two oboes, and piano (2001); *Prelude and Scherzando* for cello and piano (2001); *Night Music IV* for three clarinets (one player) and tape (2002); *Two for Five* (*Concerto Grosso*) for clarinet and string quartet (2002); and a Piano Quintet (2002).

For piano he composed a Sonata (1946); *Three Essays on Thomas Wolfe* (1948–49); *Five Little Piano Pieces* (1951); Suite (1952); *Sonata-Variations* (1954); *Mutations I* (1956); *Form* (1959); *Mutations II* (1966); *Thirty-one Variations* (*Fromm Variations*; 1973); *Twenty-one Variations* (1978); *Passacaglia* (1982); *Tango Variations on a Tango Cantus* (1984); and *Sonata Profundo* (1995); two pieces for piano duet, *Seven* (1963) and *Deux* (1967); and *Passacaglia* for two pianos (one player) with a player-piano and tape, composed in 1997 for Gilbert Kalish.

SHAW, OLIVER
b. *Middleboro, Massachusetts, 13 March 1779*
d. *Providence, Rhode Island, 31 December 1848*

An accident while he was at school lost Shaw the use of an eye, and an attack of yellow fever when he was 21 eventually blinded him totally. These catastrophes forced him to abandon a nautical career and to turn to music, one of the few professions possible for a person in his condition. He studied with Gottlieb Graupner in Boston and learned to play the clarinet. He taught piano in Dedham, Massachusetts (1805–07) before settling in Providence in 1807, where he earned a living as organist at the First Congregational Church (1809–32). Two years later he founded the Psallonian Society to promote improved knowledge and practice of church music.

Shaw's popular hymns, such as *Bristol, Taunton,* and *Weybosset,* are among those published in collections he edited, notably *Columbian Sacred Harmonist* (1808), *Providence Selection of Psalm and Hymn Tunes* (1815), *Melodia Sacra* (1819), *Sacred Songs, Duets, Anthems* (1823), and *Social Sacred Melodist* (1835). He wrote a quantity of secular music, including the popular ballads *Mary's Tears, Sweet Little Ann,* and *The Death of Percy.* For military band he composed *The Bangor March, The Bristol March, For the Gentlemen* (1809), *The Battle of the Nile*, and *Bonaparte's Grand March.*

Shaw published two teaching books: *A Plain Introduction to the Art of Playing the Pianoforte* (1811) and *O. Shaw's Instructions for the Piano* (1831).

SHELLEY, HARRY ROWE
b. *New Haven, Connecticut, 8 June 1858*
d. *Short Beach, Connecticut, 12 September 1947*

Shelley studied with Gustav J. Stoeckel at Yale and with Dudley Buck and Dvoøák in New York. After further study in London and Paris, he returned home to become a noted organist in New York.

Although best known for his church music, he composed three operas: *Romeo and Juliet* (1901), *Leila,* and *Lotus Sun.* His orchestral works include two symphonies; a suite, *Souvenir de Baden-Baden;* an overture, *Francesca da Rimini;* a symphonic poem, *The Crusaders;* Violin Concerto (1891); an overture, *Santa Claus* (1900); and *Fantasia* for piano and orchestra (1900). Among his extended choral pieces are a cantata, *Vexilia Regis* (New York, 1894), *The Inheritance Divine* (1895), *Death and Life* (1898), *The Pilgrims* (1903), *The Soul Triumphant* (1905), and *Lochinvar's Ride* (New York, 1915).

Among his pupils were Charles Ives, Charles Sandford Skilton, and Timothy Spelman.

Arthur Shepherd.
Courtesy Special Collections Dept., J. Willard Marriott Library, University of Utah.

SHEPHERD, ARTHUR

b. Paris, Idaho, 19 February 1880
d. Cleveland, Ohio, 12 January 1958

From the age of 12, Shepherd studied the piano at the New England Conservatory, Boston, where he studied composition from George Chadwick. From 1897 to 1908 he lived in Salt Lake City, Utah, where he was active as a conductor and teacher. In 1908 he returned to the New England Conservatory as a teacher, remaining there until 1920. In that year he became assistant conductor of the Cleveland Orchestra. In 1928 he was appointed to the faculty of Western Reserve University in Cleveland, becoming chairman of the music division in 1933; he retired in 1950. He was also an active music critic.

Shepherd's *Overture Joyeuse* (1901) won the Paderewski Prize in 1905. His other orchestral compositions include *The Nuptials of Attila* (1902); an overture, *Festival of Youth* (1915); *Fantasy Humoresque* for piano and orchestra (1916); *Overture to a Drama* (1919); Symphony no. 1, *Horizons,* based on cowboy songs (1927); *Dance Episodes on an Exotic Theme,* a choreographic suite (1931); Symphony no. 2 in D minor (1938), conducted by the composer in Cleveland in March 1940; *Praeludium Salutorum* for strings and woodwinds, performed in New York in 1942; *Fantasia Concertante on The Garden Hymn* (1943); *Fantasy on Down East Spirituals* (1946); Violin Concerto (1946–47); and *Variations* (1952).

For chorus and orchestra he composed two cantatas, *The City in the Sea* (1913) and *The Song of the Pilgrims* (1937); *The Song of the Sea Wind* for female chorus and orchestra (1915); *Deck Thyself My Soul* for choir and organ (1918); *Ballad of the Trees and the Master* for chorus (1935); *Invitation to the Dance* (1936); *Grace for Gardens* for mixed voices (1938); a setting of *Psalm XLII* (1940); and *A Psalm of the Mountains* (1956). He composed numerous arrangements of English and American folk songs. *Triptych* for high voice and string quartet, settings of poems by Tagore, was completed in 1925.

Shepherd wrote six string quartets: G minor (unnumbered, 1926), no. 1 in E minor (1935), no. 2 in D minor (1936), no. 3 in D (1944), no. 4 (1955), and no. 5 (1955); a Piano Quintet in F#, first performed in 1940 with the composer as pianist; two violin sonatas (1914, 1927); two piano sonatas (1907, 1929); and *Divertissement* for winds (1945).

Shepherd was the author of an influential book, *The String Quartets of Beethoven* (1937).

SHIFRIN, SEYMOUR [JACK]

b. Brooklyn, New York, 28 February 1926
d. Waltham, Massachusetts, 26 September 1979

Shifrin attended the High School of Music and Art in New York City. He graduated from Columbia University in 1949, where he studied with Otto Luening. He also received composition lessons privately from William Schuman (1942–45). On a Fulbright Fellowship he studied with Darius Milhaud in Paris (1951–52). He taught briefly at Columbia University and at the City College of New York before moving to the University of California at Berkeley in 1952. In 1966 he joined the music faculty of Brandeis University, Waltham, Massachusetts where he remained a professor until his death in 1979. He received many commissions and awards in addition to the Fulbright, including two Guggenheim Fellowships (1956, 1959).

Shifrin's music cannot be easily classified into the usual categories. He employed distinctive techniques of voice leading and harmonic rhythm that helped shape and guide his highly inflected phrase structures. For orchestra he composed *Music for Orchestra* (1948), a *Chamber Symphony* (1952–53), and *Three Pieces*, commissioned in 1958 for the Minneapolis Symphony Orchestra and winner of a Naumburg Recording Award.

Seymour Shifrin.
MSS 36, The Seymour Shifrin Papers in the Irving S. Gilmore Music Library of Yale University.

Most of his works are for smaller instrumental ensembles including five string quartets (1949, 1962, 1965–66, 1966–67, 1971–72); a Violin Sonata (1948); Serenade for five instruments (1954), commissioned by the Juilliard School; *In Eius Memoriam* for flute, clarinet, violin, cello, and piano (1967–68); *Duo* for violin and piano (1968–69); a *Duettino* for violin and piano (1972); and a Piano Trio (1974).

Shifrin's solo instrumental music appears frequently in concerts of contemporary music: Cello Sonata (1948); *Concert Piece* for solo violin (1959); five works for piano: *Four Cantos* (1948), *Composition* (1950), *Trauermusik* (1956), *Fantasy* (1961), and *Responses* (1973); and *The Modern Temper* for piano duet (1959).

Unlike many of his fellow composers, Shifrin took a deep interest in word setting. The most widely heard of his works is *Satires of Circumstance* to poems of Thomas Hardy for soprano and chamber ensemble (1963–64), commissioned by the Fromm Foundation. The cantata *A Renaissance Garland* (1975) is scored for soprano, tenor, recorders, lute, viols, and percussion. For solo voice and piano he set *Two Poems of Rainer Maria Rilke* (1947) and *No Second Troy* (Yeats) (1953).

Choral music also occupies a significant place in his output. He set Helen Waddell's translation of a poem by Ausonius as *A Medieval Latin Lyric* (1954) for unaccompanied voices. His other choral works are *Cantata to Sophoclean Choruses* for chorus and orchestra (1957–58), *Give Ear, O Ye Heavens* for chorus and orchestra (1959), and *Odes of Shang* for chorus, piano, and percussion (1963). *Chronicles* (1970) was written to celebrate the 120th anniversary of the Temple Emanuel, San Francisco; however, this setting of Hebrew words for soloists, chorus, and orchestra received its premiere in Boston in October 1976.

Shifrin's last two compositions were *The Nick of Time* for eight instruments (1978) and *Five Last Songs* for soprano and piano (1979).

SHULMAN, ALAN M.
b. New York, New York, 15 January 1909
d. New York, New York, 10 July 2002

Shulman studied the cello at the Peabody Conservatory, Baltimore and in New York with Felix Salmond and Emanuel Feuermann. In 1937 he graduated from the Juilliard School, where he had been a composition pupil of Bernard Wagenaar. He also received lessons from Hindemith. From 1938 he was the cellist in the Stuyvesant Quartet; he also played in the NBC Symphony Orchestra (1937–54), except for a period of war service (1942–45). He taught at the Sarah Lawrence College, Bronxville, New York and at the Juilliard School.

For orchestra he wrote two symphonies; *Nocturne* for strings (*1938*); *Pastorale and Dance* for violin and orchestra (1941); *Theme and Variations* for viola and orchestra (1941); *Rendezvous* for clarinet and strings (1946); a Cello Concerto (1948); *Waltzes* (1949); *A Laurentian Overture* (1952); a symphonic poem, *Popacatapetl* (1952); *Four Moods* for strings; a Suite for strings (1963); and *Theme and Variations* (1966) and *Suite Parisienne* (1972), both for cello and chamber orchestra.

His chamber music compositions often included his own instrument: *Threnody* for string quartet (1950); Suite for solo cello (1950); *Suite Miniature* for eight cellos (1956); *Elegy in Memory of Felix Salmond* for eight-part cello ensemble (1971); and *Five Diversions* "for a pride of cellos" (1975). He also composed *Top Brass* for 12 brass instruments (1958).

SIEGMEISTER, ELIE
b. New York, New York, 15 January 1909
d. Manhasset, New York, 10 March 1991

At the age of 15 Siegmeister entered Columbia University, where he was a pupil of Seth Bingham (1924–

27). He also studied privately with Wallingford Riegger in New York. In Paris (1927–1932) he was a pupil of Nadia Boulanger. At the Juilliard School (1935–38) he studied conducting with Albert Stoessel and fugue with Bernard Wagenaar. He taught at Brooklyn College (1934), the New School of Social Research, New York (1937–38), and the University of Minnesota (1948). From 1949 to 1960 he was associate professor at Hofstra University, Hempstead, Long Island, New York, becoming professor and Composer-in-Residence in 1966, retiring in 1977. During this time he also directed the Hofstra Symphony Orchestra.

Siegmeister was widely known for his research on early American music and as a collector and arranger of folk songs. In 1939 he founded the American Ballad Singers to perform American folk music. Among his other contributions to American musical life was the founding of the American Composers Alliance (1938); service as vice-president of the American Music Center (1964–67) and of the Composers and Lyricist Guild (1965–68); the founding of the Kennedy Center's National Black Music Competition and Colloquium (1979–80); the founding and chairmanship of the Council of Creative Artists, Libraries and Museums (1971–80); and membership on the board of directors of ASCAP (1977–80). Although his first compositions are modernist in style, those written up to 1940 reflect a profound interest in folk music and jazz. After 1940 he developed a more personal musical language, although one still American in character.

Many of Siegmeister's important works are orchestral: eight symphonies: no. 1 (1947, rev. 1971), no. 2 (1950, rev. 1971), no. 3 (1957), no. 4 (1970), no. 5, *Visions of Time* (1971), no. 6 (1983), no. 7 (1986), and no. 8 (1989); *American Holiday* (1933, rev. 1971); *Rhapsody* (1937); *A Walt Whitman Overture: For You, O Democracy* (1939); *Ozark Set* (1943); *Prairie Legend* (1944); *Wilderness Road* (1944); *Western Suite* (1945); *Lonesome Hollow* (1946); *Sunday in Brooklyn* (1946); *Summer Night* (1947); *From My Window* (1949); Divertimento (1953); *Theater Set* (1957); *Dick Whittington and His Cat*, with narrator (1966); *Five Fantasies of the Theater* (1966); *Shadows and Light* (1975); a ballet, *Fables From the Dark Woods* (1976); *Fantasies in Line and Color* (1981); *From These Shores: Homage to Five American Authors* (1986); and *Figures in the Wind* (1990).

Siegmeister composed five concertos: clarinet (1956), flute (1960), piano (1974), violin (1978), and a Double Concerto for violin and piano (1976). He also contributed a number of works to the band repertory: *Summer Day* (1946), *Five American Folk Songs* (1949), *Riversong* (1951), *Hootenanny*, (1955), *Ballad* (1968), *Front Porch Saturday Night* (1977), and *Celebration* (1977).

Of his eight operas, five are in one act: *Darling Corie* (1952), *Miranda and the Dark Young Man* (1955), *The Mermaid in Lock no. 7* (1958), *Angel Levine* (1985), and *The Lady of the Lake* (1985). Three are full-length: *Dublin Song* (1963), revised as *The Plough and the Stars* (1969), after the Sean O'Casey play; *Night of the Moonspell* (1974–76), a version of *A Midsummer Night's Dream*; and *The Marquesa of O* (1979–80), based on a Heinrich von Kleist story. He also composed two musicals, *Doodle Dandy of the USA* (1942) and *Sing Out, Sweet Land* (1944). Siegmeister also wrote the score for the film *They Came to Cordura* (1959).

He composed many choral works, including *Heyura, Ding, Dong, Ding* (1935–70); *John Henry* (1935); *Abraham Lincoln Walks at Midnight* (Vachel Lindsay) (1937); *American Ballad Singer Series* (1943); *As I Was Going Along* (1944–67); *A Tooth for Paul Revere*, a musical folk tale for young people to a text by Stephen Vincent Benet (1945); *Lazy Afternoon* (1946); *The New Colossus* (1949); *American Folk Song Choral Series* (1953); and *Christmas is Coming* (1957).

Siegmeister's strong commitment to social issues is reflected in *The Face of War*, setting a text by Langston Hughes for voice and orchestra (1967–68) and a cantata, *I Have a Dream* for baritone, narrator, chorus, and orchestra (1967), inspired by the words of Martin Luther King, Jr. Both received their premieres in 1968. His last choral works were *A Cycle of Cities* for soloists, chorus, and orchestra (1974), *Cantata for FDR* (1981), and *Sing Unto the Lord a New Song* (1981).

The range of Siegmeister's compositional character can be demonstrated by, on one hand, a work for baritone and orchestra, *The Strange Funeral in Braddock* (1933–38, orch. 1972), a macabre song about the death of a steel-worker trapped in molten metal and buried within a three-ton block of steel; and, on the other hand, *Funnybone Alley*, a musical fantasy for children for voices and strings (1941–46).

Among his many songs for voice and piano are *Four Robert Frost Songs* (1930); *Three Elegies for Garcia Lorca* (1938); *Johnny Appleseed* (Benet; 1940); *Nancy Hanks* (Benet; 1941); *Madam to You* (Langston Hughes; 1964); *Songs of Experience* (Blake; 1968); *Five Cummings Songs* (1970); *Six Cumming Songs* (1970); *Songs of Innocence* (Blake; 1972); *City Songs* (Norman Rosten; 1977); *Ways of Love* (1983); *Bats in My Belfry* (1990); *Four Langston Hughes Songs* (1990); and *Outside My Window* (1990).

Siegmeister's extensive chamber music included three string quartets: no. 1 (1935, rev. 1968), no. 2 (1960), and no. 3, *on Hebrew Themes* (1973); six violin sonatas (1951–59, 1965–70, 1965, 1971, 1975, 1988); *Nocturne* for flute and piano (1927); *Prelude* for clarinet and piano (1927); *Contrasts* for bassoon and piano (1929, rev. 1970); *Down River* for alto saxophone and piano (1939); *Song for a Quiet Evening* for violin and piano (1955); *Fantasy and Soliloquy* for solo cello (1964); Sextet for brass and percussion (1965); *American Harp* for harp (1966); *Declaration* for brass and harp (1976); *Summer* for viola and harp (1978); and *Ten Minutes* for four players (1989). Siegmeister was equally prolific in writing for the piano, including five sonatas: no. 1, *American* (1944), no. 2 (1964), no. 3 (1979), no. 4, *Prelude, Blues and Toccata* (1980), and no. 5 (1987); *Theme and Variations* no. 1 (1932); *Sunday in Brooklyn* (1946); *Three Moods* (1959); *Theme and Variations* no. 2 (1967); and *Three Studies* (1980).

Siegmeister was the author of a short study, *Music and Society,* published in 1938 for the Critics' Group of New York. His other books are *A Treasury of American Song* (with Olin Downes; 1940, rev. 1984), *The Music Lover's Handbook* (1943, rev. 1973), *Invitation to Music* (1961), and *Harmony and Melody* (two volumes, 1965–66).

SIMONS, NETTY

b. New York, New York, 26 October 1913
d. New York, New York, 1 April 1994

Simons was educated at New York University's School of Fine Arts and at the Juilliard School. She also studied with Stefan Wolpe. She taught at the Third Street Settlement School in New York (1928–33); from 1966 to 1977, she worked for various radio stations.

Among Simons' compositions are an opera, *Bell Witch of Tennessee* (1958); three theater pieces: *Buckeye has Wings* (1971), *Too Late, the Bridge is Closed* (1972), and *Puddintame* (1972); and two ballets, *Variables* (1967) and *Scipio's Dream* (1968).

She wrote two string quartets (1950); two violin sonatas (1954); *Duo* for violin and cello (1938); Quartet for flute and strings (1951); *Design Group I and II* (1966) and *Silver Thaw* (1969), for solo double bass (1966); *Wild Tales Told on the River Bed* for clarinet and percussion (1973); *The Great Stream Silent Moves* for piano, harp, and percussion (1973); and *Facets* for violin, horn, and piano.

Simons wrote four orchestral works: *Piece for orchestra* (1940), *Pied Piper* for narrator and orchestra (1955), *Lamentations I* (1961) and *II* (1966), and *Illuminations in Space* for viola and orchestra (1972). Her vocal music includes *Diverse Settings* for soprano and chamber group (1959) and *Three Trialogues* (Dylan Thomas) for mezzo-soprano, baritone, and viola (1963–73).

SIMS, EZRA

b. Birmingham, Alabama, 16 January 1928

Sims studied at the Birmingham Conservatory, Alabama (1945–48), Yale University (1950–52) with Quincy Porter, and Mills College, Oakland, California (1953) with Leon Kirchner and Darius Milhaud. From 1958 to 1962 he was a librarian at the Loeb Music Library, Harvard University. In 1962 on a Guggenheim Fellowship he spent a year in Tokyo, researching electronic music at the NHK Studio. He returned to the Loeb Library in 1965. From 1968 to 1978 he was music director of the New England Dinosaur Dance Theater. He also taught at the New England Conservatory, Boston (1976–78). With Rodney Lister and Scott Wheeler he was co-founder of the new music ensemble Dinosaur Annex in 1974, serving as its president (1977–81) and on its board of directors (through 2003).

Sims employs microtones. He first worked with quarter-tones in the early 1960's. He then took a 72-note (sixth-tone) equal division of the octave and extracted an asymmetrical 18-pitch-per-octave scale in most of his non-tape music after 1971. He has been composing works with tape since the late 1960's, incorporating computerized elements from the late 1980's on.

For orchestra he has written *Le Tombeau d'Albers* (1959) and a dance score, *Masque.* His works for microtonal orchestra are *Longfellow Sparrow* (1976); *Yr Obedt Servt* (1977, rev. 1981); *Pictures for an Institution* for chamber orchestra (1983); *Night Unto Night* (1984); and *Concert Piece* for viola, flute, clarinet, cello, and small orchestra (1990).

A large proportion of Sims's compositions are instrumental. These include five string quartets (1959; 1961; 1962; 1984; 2000); *The Trojan Women,* incidental music for chamber ensemble (1955); *Sonate Concertante: 1–5* for oboe, viola, cello, and double bass; and *6– 0* for string quartet (1961); Octet for strings (1964); Oboe *Quartet* (1971–76); *Midorigaoka* for string quintet (1978); *Two for One* for violin and viola (1980); *All Done From Memory* for violin (1980); *Ruminations* for clarinet (1980); Sextet (1981); *Phenomena* for flute, clarinet, and string trio (1981); *Quartet* for flute and string trio (1982); *This Way to the Egress* for string trio (1983); *Tune and Variations* for one or two horns (1983); Wedding *Winds* for three clarinets (1986); Clarinet Quintet (1987); and *AEDM in memoriam* for cello (1988).

Later works include *Flight* for flute and electronics (1989); *Night Piece: In Girum Imus Nocte et Consumimur Igni* for flute, clarinet, viola, cello, and electronics (1989); *Duo* for flute and cello (1992); *Stanzas* for flute, three clarinets, viola and cello (1995); *Duo* for viola and cello (1996); *Duo '97* for clarinet

Ezra Sims.
Photo: Roland Knobe, courtesy the composer.

and viola (1997); and *Musing and Reminiscence* for flute, clarinet, violin, viola, and cello (2003).

Vocal music occupies a significant part of his output: *Chanson d'aventure* for tenor and harpsichord (1951, rev. 1975); *Cantata on Chinese Poems* for tenor and chamber ensemble (1954); *Brief Glimpses into Contemporary French Literature* for four countertenors and piano (1958); *Two Folk Songs* for baritone and piano (1958); *Three Songs* for tenor and orchestra (1960); *A Passion* for narrator, tenor, baritone, four clarinets, and marimba (1963); *Cantata III* for soprano and percussion, commissioned for Cathy Berberian (1963); *In Memoriam Alice Hawthorne* (Edward Gorey) for tenor, baritone, narrator, four clarinets, horn, and two marimbas (1967); *Celebration of Dead Ladies* for voice, alto flute, basset clarinet, viola, cello, and percussion (1976); *Elegie – nach Rilke* for soprano, flute, clarinet, and string trio (1976); *Come Away* (five songs) for mezzo-soprano, viola, alto flute, clarinet, horn, trombone, and double bass (1978); *Five Songs* for alto and viola (1979); *Song* (W. H. Auden) for mezzo-soprano, clarinet, and viola (1980); *Invocation* for voice, three flutes, viola, double bass, and quarter-tone guitar (1992); *If I Told Him* (Gertrude Stein; 1996); *Two En-*

cores (1997) for alto and cello; *and Encores: Three Parlour Songs* (2000), for alto and cello.

Among Sims's choral pieces are a Mass for chorus (1955); *The Bewties of Futeball* for children's chorus, optional recorders, and piano (1974); *What God is Like to Him I Serve?* for chorus (1976); *Aeneas on the Saxophone* for chorus, alto flute, basset clarinet, horn, trombone, viola, and double bass (1977); and *The Conversions* (Harry Matthews) for chorus (1985).

In his tape compositions, Sims often makes use of musique concrète: *Kubla Khan* no. 1 for speaker, gamelan, and chamber orchestra and no. 2 for speaker and tape (1958); *Antimatter* (1968); *Alec* (1968); *McDowell's Fault* (1968); *A Frank Overture: Four Dented Interludes and Coda* (1969); *Warts and All* (1969); *Elina's Piece* (1970); *In Memoriam* (1970); *Real Toads* (1970); *Clement Wenceslas Lothaire Nepomucene, Prince Metternich (1773–1859*; 1970); *Pastorale* (1970); *Ground Cover* (1972); *Museum Piece* (1972); *Wall to Wall* (1972); *Where the Wild Things Are* (1973); *After Lyle* (1973); and *Collage XIII* (1977).

He has lectured extensively in the United States and in Europe, and writes articles on his compositional technique for various journals.

SKILTON, CHARLES SANFORD
b. Northampton, Massachusetts, 16 August 1868
d. Lawrence, Kansas, 12 March 1941

Skilton graduated from Yale University in 1889, where he had been a pupil of Dudley Buck. Two years later he attended the Hochschule für Musik in Berlin. On his return to the United States in 1893, he became director of music at Salem College, Winston, North Carolina, moving in 1897 to teach at the State Normal School, Trenton, New Jersey. In 1903 he was appointed professor of music at the University of Kansas, Lawrence, a post he held until his death in 1941.

From 1915 Skilton took a great interest in the music of the American Indians. More than half his own compositions are inspired by Indian legend or music. Important among these are his three operas. The three-act *Kalopin* (1927) is based on events associated with the New Madrid, Mississippi earthquake of 1811; it was awarded the David Bispham Medal in 1930, but not performed. *The Sun Bride* (1930) in one act retells a story from the Pueblo Indians of Arizona. *The Day of Gayomair* was completed in 1936.

Skilton composed several large-scale choral works, including an oratorio, *The Guardian Angel* (1925), and four cantatas: *Lenore* (1895), *Pervigilium veneris* (1916), *The Witch's Daughter* (1918), and *Ticonderoga* for men's chorus and orchestra (1933). In 1930 he

Charles Skilton.
Courtesy Kenneth Spencer Research Library, University of Kansas Libraries.

completed a Mass in D and a short piece for female voices, *From Forest and Stream.*

Skilton's most notable success came in 1915 with *Two Indian Dances* (*Deer Dance* and *War Dance*), composed originally for piano, later orchestrated and included in *Primeval Suite* (1920). These pieces achieved great popularity mainly through their monotonously insistent drum rhythms. Also for orchestra he wrote *Sioux Flute Serenade* (1920); *East and West Suite* (1921); *Legend,* composed in 1927 for the Minneapolis Orchestra; an overture, *Mount Oread* (1928); *Autumn Night* (1930); *Shawnee Indian Hunting Dance* for the Detroit Symphony Orchestra (1930); *American Indian Fantasie* for cello and orchestra (1929); an Overture in E (1931); and a symphonic poem, *A Carolina Legend.*

Skilton provided incidental music for Sophocles' *Electra,* performed at Smith College, Massachusetts (1918), and for J.M. Barrie's *Mary Rose* (1933). He composed a Violin Sonatina (1923), String Quartet in B minor (1938), a Violin Sonata in G minor, and several piano and organ pieces.

He was the author of a book, *Modern Symphonic Forms,* published in 1926.

SLONIMSKY, NICOLAS (NIKOLAI LEONIDOVICH)

b. St. Petersburg, Russia, 27 April 1894
d. Los Angeles, California, 25 December 1995

After studying piano at the Conservatory in St. Petersburg with his aunt, Isabella Vengerova, and composi-

tion with Vasili Kalafati and Maximilian Steinberg, Slonimsky went to the United States in 1923, where he joined the faculty of the Eastman School of Music, Rochester, New York as an opera coach. He also studied composition there with Selim Palmgren. Slonimsky settled in Boston in 1925, where he became noted as a writer, composer, and pianist and as a teacher at the Malkin Conservatory and Boston Conservatory. He took American citizenship in 1931. From 1955 to 1957 he taught at the Peabody Conservatory in Baltimore. In 1964 he accepted a position at the University of California in Los Angeles, from which he retired in 1967.

As a promoter of modern music Slonimsky is best known for his writings. His books include *Music Since 1900* (1937, rev. 1949, 1971, 1994, 2001); *Music of Latin America* (1945); *The Road to Music* (1947, rev. 1966); *Thesaurus of Scales and Melodic Patterns* (1947); *A Thing or Two About Music* (1948); *A Lexicon of Musical Invective* (1952); *Lexionary of Music* (1988); *Perfect Pitch,* an autobiography (1988); and *Nicholas Slonimsky: The First 100 Years* (1994). He also acted as editor of the *International Cyclopedia of Music and Musicians* (4th through 8th eds., 1946–58) and *Baker's Biographical Dictionary of Musicians* (5th through 8th eds, 1958, 1978, 1984, 1992), and was a contributor to *Encyclopaedia Britannica* and the 5th edition of *Grove's Dictionary of Music and Musicians.*

Slonimsky's own music is of an advanced nature. *Fragments from the Orestes of Euripides* (1932) makes use of quarter-tones. *Studies in Black and White* for piano (1928), orchestrated in 1983 as *Piccolo Divertimento,* derives its title from the way the right

Nicolas Slonimsky, 1979.
Courtesy Electra Yourke.

hand plays only white keys throughout while the left hand is confined to black keys. Also for piano is *51 Minitudes* (1971–77).

His *Toy Balloon* for orchestra, an arrangement of *Variations on a Brazilian Tune* for piano (1942), makes use of toy balloons that are exploded at the end. Instrumental compositions include *Four Russian Melodies*

for clarinet and piano (1937) and Suite for cello and orchestra, written in 1951.

Among his vocal music are three song cycles: *Silhouettes* and *Flight to the Moon* (1927), both to words by Oscar Wilde, and *Gravestones at Hancock, New Hampshire* (1945) to texts from tombstone inscriptions. In addition he wrote *Five Advertising Songs* (1925), setting actual advertisements from American magazines.

As a conductor Slonimsky gave the first performances of works by American composers of the avantgarde, particularly Charles Ives and Edgar Varèse. He died four months short of his 102nd birthday.

SMIT, LEO
b. Philadelphia, Pennsylvania, 12 January 1921
d. Encinitas, California, 12 December 1999

In addition to his work as a composer and teacher, Smit was a gifted pianist. After receiving his first musical training from his father, Kolman Smit, a distinguished orchestral violinist, he won a scholarship to the Curtis Institute, Philadelphia, where he studied piano with Isabella Vengerova (1930–32). In 1935 he received composition lessons from Nicolas Nabokov. In 1936, at the age of 15, Smit became a pianist for George Balanchine and the American Ballet Company. It was there that he first became acquainted with Stravinsky, whose music had a strong influence upon his early compositions.

In 1947 he taught at Sarah Lawrence College,

Leo Smit, c. 1960s.
Courtesy Music Library, State University of New York, Buffalo, Leo Smit Collection of Photographs, Item 45.

Bronxville, New York, and in 1957 was appointed to the music faculty of the University of California, Los Angeles. From 1962 to 1998 he taught piano, composition,, and history seminars at the State University of New York College at Buffalo. He held Fulbright and Guggenheim fellowships and worked in Rome (1950–52).

Symphony no. 1 in E-flat, commissioned by the Koussevitzky Foundation and premiered by the Boston Symphony Orchestra under Charles Munch in 1956, won the New York Music Critics' Circle Award. Symphony no. 2 in six movements was performed in 1966 by the New York Philharmonic Orchestra under Leonard Bernstein. In 1969, Smit himself was the soloist in the first performance of his Piano Concerto ; he revised the score in 1980. Other orchestral works include an overture, *The Parcae* (1953); *Capriccio* for strings (1958, rev. 1974); *Four Kookaburra Marches* for orchestra and tape (1972); *Symphony of Dances and Songs* (Symphony no. 3;m 1981); *Variations* for piano and orchestra (1981); and *Alabaster Chambers* for strings (1989).

While Composer-in-Residence at the American Academy in Rome (1972–73), Smit wrote *Caedmon*, an oratorio with words by Anthony Hecht, performed by the Buffalo Philharmonic Orchestra in December 1972. Also in Rome he composed *Songs of Wonder* for men's voices (1976), *At the Corner of the Sky* for male voices, flute, and oboe (1976), and *Copernicus*: *Narrative and Credo*, to a text by Sir Fred Hoyle, commissioned by the National Academy of Sciences for the 500th anniversary of the birth of the great astonomer. It was premiered on 22 April 1973 at the Academy Auditorium in Washington, D.C.

For the stage Smit composed two operas, *The Alchemy of Love* (1969), to a libretto by Hoyle, and *Magic Water* (Hawthorn; 1978), as well as a melodrama, *A Mountain Eulogy* (1975). His ballet, *Virginia Sampler*, was produced in New York by the Ballet Russe de Monte Carlo in 1947. Another ballet, *Yerma*, dates from 1946.

His many choral works include *Love is a Sickness* for female chorus and piano (1947), *A Choir of Starlings* (1951), *Four Motets* (1955), and *Four Madrigals for a Roman Lady* (1955–65). Vocal music includes *Academic Graffiti* (Auden) for voice, clarinet, cello, piano, and percussion (1959), *Sequence* (Roethke) for mezzo-soprano and ensemble (1974), and *From Banja Luka* for mezzo-soprano and orchestra (1987).

Instrumental music includes Sextet for clarinet, bassoon, and string quartet (1940); *Invention* for clarinet and piano (1943); *Love Songs Without Words* (*after Cole Porter*) for wind quintet; *In Woods* for oboe, harp, and percussion (1978); *Delaunay Pochoirs* (*Stencils*) for cello and piano (1980); *Scena Cambiata* for trombone, viola, and cello (1980); *Cock Robin* for soprano,

piccolo, and percussion (1980); Sonata for solo cello (1982); *Flute of Wonder* for flute and piano (1983); *Tzadik* for saxophone quartet (1983); a String Quartet (1984); and a Piano Trio (*Exequy*; 1985).

Smit composed six works for piano solo, including a Sonata in one movement (1955) and a *Fantasy*: *The Farewell* (1953), and a Sonata for piano duet (1987).

SMITH, DAVID STANLEY
b. Toledo, Ohio, 6 July 1877
d. New Haven, Connecticut, 17 December 1949

From his father, David Stanley Smith learned to play the organ, and he held several posts in churches in New Haven while a student at Yale University. After leaving the university in 1900, he went on the advice of Horatio Parker to Europe, where he studied with Charles Widor in Paris and Ludwig Thuille in Munich. On his return to America in 1903, he was appointed an instructor at Yale. In 1920 he succeeded Parker as professor and dean of the music faculty, a position he held until 1940, although he continued to teach composition after his retirement in 1946. He was conductor of the New Haven Symphony Orchestra from 1919 until 1946.

David Stanley Smith.
MSS 31, The David Stanley Smith Papers in the Irving S. Gilmore Music Library of Yale University.

Smith's compositions are well-constructed if somewhat lacking in personality. He composed four symphonies: no. 1 in F minor, op. 28 (Chicago, 1912); no. 2 in D, op. 42 (Norfolk Festival: 1917); no. 3 in C minor, op. 60 (1928); and no. 4 in D, op. 78, performed by the Boston Symphony Orchestra in 1939. Also for orchestra are an overture, *Prince Hal*, op. 31 (1912); a *Suite*: *Impressions*, op. 40 (1916); *A Poem of Youth*, op. 55 (1926); *Epic Poem* (1926); Sinfonietta for Strings (1932); *"1929," a Satire*, op. 66, no. 1 (1932); *Overture*: *Tomorrow*, op. 66, no. 2 (1933); *Credo* (1941); and a symphonic poem, *The Apostles* (1944). For solo instruments and orchestra he wrote *Fête Galante*, op. 48 for flute (1920, rev. 1930); *Cathedral Prelude*, op. 54 for organ (1926); a Violin Concerto (1933); *Rondo Appassionata*, op. 73 for violin (1935); and *Requiem* for violin (1939).

Smith's opera *Merrymount* was completed in 1914, ten years before Howard Hanson's work on the same subject, but it was never produced on stage. Smith's choral works are *Ode to Commemoration Day* (1900); *L' Allegro e Il Penseroso* (1906); *The Fallen Star*, op. 26 (1909); *Rhapsody of St. Bernard*, op. 38, performed in Chicago in 1915; *The Vision of Isaiah*, op. 58 (1926); Requiem (1942); *Daybreak* (New York, 1945); and *The Ocean* for bass solo, chorus, and orchestra (1945).

Smith's considerable output of chamber music includes ten string quartets (1900–38); *Sonata Pastorale*, op. 43 for oboe and piano (1918); a Piano Quintet, op. 56, (1927); two violin sonatas; a Cello Sonata, op. 69 (1928); a Piano Sonata in A-flat, op. 61 (1929); a String Sextet, op. 63 (1933); and a Viola Sonata, op. 72 (1934).

SMITH, HALE
b. Cleveland, Ohio, 29 June 1925

During his service in the U.S. Army, Hale Smith played piano and bass in various bands. Later he studied with Ward Lewis and Marcel Dick and graduated from the Cleveland Institute of Music (1952). After 1958 he worked in New York as an arranger for several groups, including those of Chico Hamilton, Oliver Nelson, and Quincy Jones. In 1970 he was appointed associate professor of music at the University of Connecticut, Storrs, retiring in 1984.

For orchestra Smith has written *Orchestral Set* (1952, rev. 1968); *Contours 61* (Louisville Orchestra, 1961); *By Yearning and By Beautiful* for strings (1964); *Music for harp and orchestra* (1967); *Concert Music* for piano and orchestra (1972); *Rituals and Incantations* (1974); *Innerflexions* (1977); *Feria* for chamber orchestra; and *Variations on a Quasi Classical Tune* for strings (1992). He has composed several pieces for concert band, including *Somersault* for large wind band (1964),

Hale Smith.
Courtesy Archives & Special Collections of the Thomas J. Dodd Research Center, University of Connecticut Libraries.

Trinal Dance (1965), *Expansions* (1967), *Exchanges* for solo trumpet and band (1978), *March and Fanfare for an Elegant Lady* (1986), and *Riverrain* (1996).

For the stage Smith has written a jazz music theater piece, *Joplin's Dirty Rags* (Freeport, New York, 1973) and provided incidental music for *Yerma* (Lorca; 1951), *Lysistrata* (Aristophanes; 1952), and *Blood Wedding* (Lorca; 1953). It was in 1953 that he wrote his first choral work, *In Memoriam Beryl Rubinstein*. Other compositions for choir include *Toussaint L'Ouverture 1803* for chorus and piano (1970); a jazz cantata, *Comes Tomorrow* (1972, rev. 1977); and *Ayobami*, an African folk tale for children's chorus, timpani, percussion, and chamber ensemble (2000).

Vocal music includes *Three Songs* for contralto (1949); *Beyond the Rim of Day* (Langston Hughes) for high voice and piano (1950); *The Valley Wind* for soprano and piano (1955); *Five Songs* for voice and violin (1956); *Two Love Songs of John Donne* for soprano and nine instruments (1958); *Come Back, My Youth* (1972); *Symphonic Spirituals* for soprano and orchestra (1979); *Meditations in Passage* for soprano, baritone, and piano (or orchestra) (1980); *Five Patterson Lyrics* (1985); *I'm Going to Sing* for tenor and piano (1991); and *Music for Martyrs* for bass, piano, and drum (1997).

Among Smith's instrumental music are *Duo* for violin and piano (1953); Cello Sonata (1955); *Epicedial Variations* for violin and piano (1956); *Three Brevities* for solo flute (1960); *Introduction, Cadenzas and*

Interludes for eight players (1974); *Variations* for six players (1975); *Solemn Music* for organ and brass (1979); *Variations a due* for cello and alto saxophone (1984); *Dialogues and Commentaries* for seven players (1991); and *A Ternion of Seasons* for wind quintet, brass quintet, percussion, and narrator (1996).

For piano Smith has composed *Four Mosaics* (1948), *Faces of Jazz* (1965), *Evocations* (1966), *Anticipations, Introspections and Reflections* (1971), *For One Called Billy* (1975), and *Breaking Bread for Egbert* (1997).

SMITH, JULIA FRANCES (BORN JULIA FRANCES VIELEHR)
b. Denton, Texas, 25 January 1911
d. New York, New York, 27 April 1989

Julia Smith studied at North Texas State University, Denton (1926–30) and at the Juilliard School (1930–32, 1937–39), where she was a composition pupil of Rubin Goldmark and Frederick Jacobi. She also studied orchestration with Bernhard Wagenaar. At New York University (1932–37) she received her M.A. degree. From 1947 to 1952 she studied for her doctorate and attended classes with Marion Bauer (composition) and Virgil Thomson (music criticism) at New York University. She was awarded her doctorate in 1952 for a thesis on the music of Aaron Copland, which became the basis for a book published in 1955. From 1940 to 1942 she taught theory and counterpoint at the Juilliard School. She was a member of the faculty of New Britain State Teachers College, Connecticut (1944–46) and founder and head of the department of musical Education at Hartt College of Music, University of Hartford (1941–46).

Smith's major contribution to American music was in the sphere of opera. Her first opera, *Cynthia Parker* (1935–38, rev. 1943–45) in two acts with libretto by Jan Isbel Fortune, was produced by the North Texas State University Opera Workshop on 16 February 1939. *The Stranger of Manzano* (1941–43), in one act to a libretto by John W. Rogers, is based on an old New Mexico tale; it was staged by the same company on 1 May 1946. Her third opera, *The Gooseherd and the Goblin* (1945–46) in one act (libretto: Josephine Fetter Royle), was broadcast by the New York Municipal Broadcasting Station on 22 February 1947.

Cockcrow, a fairy tale in one act with libretto by C. D. Mackay, was completed in 1953. *The Shepherdess and the Chimney Sweep* (1962–63), a Christmas opera in one act adapted from Hans Christian Andersen's story by Mackay, was staged by the Fort Worth Opera Association on 28 December 1966. Her last opera, *Daisy* (1971–73) in two acts, is an account of the life of Juliette

Gordon Low, the founder of the Girl Scouts of America. To a libretto by Bertita Harding, it was produced on 3 November 1973 by the Florida Family Opera of Miami Greater Opera Association.

Smith's orchestral works include *American Dance Suite* (1935–36, rev. 1962–63) and *Episodic Suite* (1936). The latter was arranged for ten instruments as a ballet in 1966 and staged by the Modern Dance Group in Denton on 12 May 1967. *Hellenic Suite* (1940–41) is based on Greek folk songs. *Folkways Symphony* (on Western themes; 1947–48) was first performed in Toledo, Ohio on 31 January 1949. For concert band she wrote an overture, *Sails Aloft* (1966). Her Piano Concerto (1938–39, rev. 1971) received its premiere on 18 March 1939, with Vivian Rivkin as soloist and the Juilliard Orchesta led by Dean Dixon.

Two important choral works are *Our Heritage* for chorus and large orchestra (1956), performed in Oklahoma City in March 1957, and *Remember the Alamo* for narrator, chorus, and band, premiered in Washington, D.C. in 1965.

Her instrumental music includes *Sonatine* for flute and bassoon (1945); *Two Pieces* for viola and piano (1944); *Trio Cornwall* for piano trio (1955); a String Quartet (1962–64); and a Suite for wind octet (1979–80). Among her solo piano pieces are a *Sonatine* in C (1943–44) and *Characteristic Suite* (1949). *Three Love Songs* for voice and piano (1953–55) sets poems by Karl Flaster (1906–65). The song cycle *Prairie Kaleidoscope* for soprano and string quartet dates from 1982.

In addition to the biography Aaron Copland, Smith wrote *Master Pianist, the Career and Teaching of Carl Friedberg* (1963) and *Directory of American Women Composers* (1970).

SMITH, LELAND C(LAYTON)
b. Oakland, California, 6 August 1925

Leland C. Smith studied with Darius Milhaud at Mills College, Oakland, California (1941–43, 1946–47) and at the University of California, Berkeley (1946–48), where he was a pupil of Roger Sessions. From 1948 to 1949 he received composition lessons from Olivier Messiaen in Paris. After teaching at the University of California, Berkeley (1950–51) and Mills College (1951–52), he joined the music faculty at the University of Chicago (1952–58). From 1958 to 1992 he taught at Stanford University, becoming a professor in 1968. He returned to teach at Mills College for the summers of 1951 and 1961. He was awarded a Guggenheim Fellowship in 1964. Smith is an experienced player of the clarinet and bassoon, and was founder and director of the Stanford Computer Music Center.

His orchestral works include a Symphony (1951), Concerto for Orchestra (1956), and Divertimento no. 2 for chamber orchestra (1957). Chamber works include a Trumpet Sonata (1947); Trio for flute, cello, and piano (1947); Trio for violin, trumpet, and clarinet (1948); Divertimento no. 1 for five instruments (1949); Wind Quintet (1951); *Two Duets* for clarinet and bassoon (1953); String Trio (1953); Sonata for heckelphone (or viola) and piano (1954); Quintet for bassoon and strings (1956); Wind Trio (1960); Quartet for horn, violin, cello, and piano (1961); *Orpheus* for guitar, harp, and harpsichord (1967); and *Machines of Loving Grace* for computer, bassoon, and narrator (1970). For piano he has composed *Intermezzo and Caprice* (1952), a Sonata (1954), and *Six Bagatelles* (1965).

Although most of his works are instrumental, he has written one opera, *Santa Claus* (e. e. cummings) (1955). Among his vocal works are *Two Motets* (1948, 1954), *Three Pacifist Songs* for soprano and piano (1951–58), *Advice to Young Ladies* (Robert Herrick) for female voices, clarinet, violin, and cello (1965), and *Dona Nobis Pacem* for chorus and chamber ensemble (1964).

SMITH, W(ILLIAM) O(VERTON)
b. Sacramento, California, 22 September 1926

W. O. Smith learned the clarinet at the age of ten and soon founded his own jazz bands. He studied briefly at the Juilliard School, the Paris Conservatory, and with Milhaud at Mills College, Oakland, California. Later he was a pupil of Roger Sessions at the University of California, Berkeley, where he also taught (1952–53). He won the Prix de Rome in 1951. After teaching at the San Francisco Conservatory (1952–53), he moved to the University of Southern California in Los Angeles (1954–60). He spent several years in Rome on a Guggenheim Fellowship (1960–66). After returning from Rome, he became a member of the music faculty at the University of Washington in Seattle, retiring in 1988.

Among his many pieces with clarinet are a Sonata (1948); Clarinet Quintet (1950); Suite for clarinet and violin (1952), dedicated to Benny Goodman; *Three Pieces* (Trio) for clarinet, violin, and piano (1957); Quartet for clarinet, violin, cello, and piano (1958); *Variants* for solo clarinet (1958); Concerto for clarinet and jazz band, composed for Shelly Manne (1958); *Five Pieces* for solo clarinet (1959); *Mosaic* for clarinet and piano (1964); *Tangents* for clarinet and orchestra (1965); *Fancies* for solo clarinet (1966); *Elegia* for clarinet and strings (1976); *Ecco!* for clarinet and orchestra (1978); *MU* for clarinet and small orchestra (1978); *Twelve* for clarinet and strings (1979); *Five for Milan*

William Overton Smith.
Photo: Virginia Paquette, courtesy the composer.

for clarinet and jazz ensemble (1980); *Greetings!* for five or more clarinets (1982); *Musings* for three clarinets and three dancers (1983); *Pente* for clarinet and string quartet (1983); Trio no. 2 for clarinet, violin, and piano (1984); Concerto for clarinet and small orchestra (1985); *Oni* for clarinet, keyboard, percussion and electronics (1986); *Slow Motion* for electric clarinet and computer graphics (1987); Serenade for clarinet, violin, and cello (1989); *Ritual* for clarinet, viola, percussion, tape, and projections (1992); *86910* for clarinet and digital delay (1993); *Blue Shades* for clarinet and wind ensemble (1993); *Studies* for two clarinets and computers (1994); *Explorations* for clarinet and chamber orchestra (1998); *10 x 100* for clarinet violin, cello, piano, and percussion (1999); and *Ottana* for clarinet and cello (2001). Three recent works for clarinet and computer-generated sound are *Rites* (1999); *Gestures* (2000); and *Sumi-e* (2000).

Smith's other instrumental pieces include Suite for flute, clarinet, and trumpet (1947); *Five Pieces* for string quartet (1947); Serenade for flute, clarinet, trumpet, and violin (1947); *Three Pieces* for winds, strings, and piano (1947); *Schizophrenic Scherzo* for clarinet, alto saxophone, trumpet, and trombone (1947); Concertino for trumpet and jazz instruments (1948); a String

Quartet (1952); *Capriccio* for violin and piano (1952); Divertimento for jazz combo (1956); Quartet for clarinet, violin, cello, and piano (1958); *Five Pieces* for flute and clarinet (1961); *Fantasy* for flute, cello, and piano (1963); *Elegy for Eric* (1964); *International Set* for five instruments (1965); String Quartet no. 2 (1968); *Quadrodram* for clarinet, trombone, piano, percussion, dancer, and films (1970); *Straws* for flute and bassoon (1974); *Chronos* for string quartet (1975); Sonata for brass quintet (1977); *Eternal Truths* for wind quintet (1979); *Thirteen* for flute, two clarinets, horn, two trombones, cello, and piano (1982); *Mandala III* for large flute ensemble (1982); *Illuminated Manuscript* for wind quintet and computer graphics (1987); *Piccolo Concerto* for flute, clarinet, violin, cello, and piano (1991); *Jazz Set* for violin and wind quintet (1991); *Soli* for flute, clarinet, violin, and cello (1993); *Jazz Set* for flute, bassoon, and piano (1997); a Flute Concerto (1999); *Space* for flute, clarinet, violin, cello, and piano (2000); and *Trias* for flute, clarinet, and bassoon (2001).

Smith has concentrated upon the composition of instrumental music, having written for jazz combinations led by Shelly Manne, Dave Brubeck, and Red Norvo, with whom he has played the clarinet. He has often composed for specific jazz ensembles; as an example, he composed *Interplay* (1964) and *Quadi* (1968) for the Modern Jazz Quartet and orchestra. Other works involving jazz ensembles are the Concertino for trombone and jazz combo (1948); Concerto for jazz soloists and orchestra (1962); *Explorations I* for jazz combo and tape (1963); *Explorations II* for five instruments (1966); *Ambiente* for 11 jazz players (1970); *Agate* for jazz soloists and orchestra (1974); *Theona* for jazz combo and orchestra (1975); *Janus* for trombone and jazz ensemble (1982); *Quiet Please* for jazz orchestra (1982); *Jazz Fantasy* for jazz improvisors and string quartet (1992); *Jazz Set* for trombone and percussion (2002); and Concerto for Jazz Orchestra (2002). He has also been very active as an arranger.

Among his choral works are *The Hours Rise Up* for chorus, flute, clarinet, and trumpet (1947); a cantata, *Anyone* for soprano, female voices, and chamber orchestra (1948); *Five Songs* for chorus (1949); *Three Poems* for men's voices (1952); *My Father Moved Through Domes of Love* for chorus and orchestra (1955); *A Song for St Cecilia's Day* for soprano, baritone, chorus, and band (1957); *Ilios* for chorus, winds, and dancers (1977); *Mandala I* for voices and instruments (1977); *Intermission* for soprano, chorus, and instruments (1978); *Enchantments* for female voices and flute (1983); and *Alleluia* for chorus and instruments (1990). For solo voice Smith has written *Five Songs* for voice and cello (1959–60), *Songs to Myself Alone* for soprano and percussion (1970), *3* for soprano,

clarinet, trombone, and dancers (1975), and *Sappho* for voice, clarinet, and harp (1997).

SOLLBERGER, HARVEY (DENE)
b. Cedar Rapids, Iowa, 11 May 1938

Sollberger studied flute and composition at the University of Iowa with Philip Bezanson (1956–60). At Columbia University (1961–64) he was a pupil of Jack Beeson and Otto Luening. He has appeared throughout the United States as a flutist and conductor of chamber ensembles, especially in the promotion of new music. In New York with Charles Wuorinen in 1962, he founded the Group for Contemporary Music. He taught at Columbia University (1965–83), the Manhattan School of Music (1971–83), Philadelphia College of the Performing Arts (1980–82), and Indiana University, Bloomington (1983–92). Since 1992 he has been on the faculty of the University of California, San Diego. He has received two Guggenheim Fellowships (1969, 1973) and an award from the American Academy of Arts and Letters (1965). Since 1998, he has been the music director of the La Jolla Symphony Orchestra. Sollberger's music shows the influence of Milton Babbitt, with an emphasis on aspects of time and timbre. He uses what he terms "extended techniques" to exploit new ways of producing sound on wind instruments.

He has written the bulk of his music for his own instrument: *Two Pieces* for two flutes (1958, rev. 1962); Trio for flute, cello, and piano (1961); *Duo* for flute and piano (1961); *Grand Quartet* for flutes (1962); *Music* for flute and piano (1964); Divertimento for flute, cello, and piano (1970); *Elegy for Igor Stravinsky* for flute and alto flute (1971); *Riding the Wind I* for flute and chamber orchestra (1974) and *II – IV* for solo flute (1973–74); *Sunflowers* for flute and vibraphone (1976); *Flutes and Drums* for 8 flutes, 8 percussionists, and 4 double basses (1977); *Hara* for alto flute (1978); *Met Him Pike Hoses* for flute and violin (1980); *Six Quartets* for flute and piano (1981); *Angel and Stone* for flute and piano (1981); *Killapata/Chaskapata* for solo flute and 11 flutes (1983); *Double Triptych* for flute and percussion (1984); *Quodlibetudes* for solo flute (1988); and *Aurelian Echoes* for flute and alto flute (1989).

The remaining chamber music includes *Solos* for violin and five instruments (1962); *Two Oboes Troping* (1963); *Chamber Variations* for 12 players (1964); *Impromptu* for piano (1968); *As Things Are and Become* for string trio (1969, rev. 1971); *Iron Mountain Songs* for trumpet and piano (1971); *The Two and the One* for amplified cello and two percussionists (1972);

a String Quartet (1973); *Folio* for solo bassoon (1976); *The Humble Heart* for wind quintet (1983); *Interrupted Night* for five instruments (1983); *Persian Gulf* for strings (1987); *3 or 4 Things I Know About the Oboe,* a chamber concerto for oboe and 13 players (1987); *. . . from winter's frozen stillness* for piano trio (1990); *Mutable Duo* for flute, clarinet, violin, cello, piano, and percussion (1991); *Advance Moment* for flute, clarinet, violin, cello, piano, and percussion (1993); *CIAO Arcosanti!* for 8 instruments (1994); *Trickster Tales* for flute, clarinet, and piano (1995); *Into the Light* (in memoriam Samuel Boran) for solo flute (1997); *Oh Mensch! Gib Acht* for oboe (1999); *New Millennium Memo* for flute (2000); and *Tri(E)ste* for clarinet (2001). Sollberger's single composition for electronic tape, *Fanfare Mix Transpose,* dates from 1968.

In addition to *Music for Sophocles' "Antigone"* for narrator, speaking chorus, and tape (1966) and *Music for Prepared Dancers* for flute, violin, percussion, and dancers (1978), Sollberger has written *Musica Transalpina,* two motets for soprano, baritone, and nine instruments (1970); *Passages* for soloists, chorus, and orchestra (1990); *In Terra Aliena* for five soloists and orchestra (1995); and *Grandis Templum Machinae* for five solo singers, three choruses, and large ensemble (1996). His vocal music also includes *Five Songs* (J. R. Jimenez) for soprano and piano (1961), *To the Hawks* (D. Justice) for soprano and piano (1969), and *Life Study* for soprano, flute, and harp (1968).

John Philip Sousa.
Courtesy University of Illinois Archives, RS 12/9/54, http://door.library.uiuc.edu/sousa/online.htm.

SOUSA, JOHN PHILIP
b. Washington, D.C., 6 November 1854
d. Reading, Pennsylvania, 6 March 1932

Although certain legends arose over the origin of his name, especially the suggestion that it was a pseudonym derived from the initials S.O. and U.S.A., Sousa was in fact the son of a Portuguese father named Sousa and a Bavarian mother. He studied violin and theory in Washington, D.C., and learned to play most wind instruments. He was a Marine bandsman at the age of 13 and leader of a theater orchestra at 18. From 1880 to 1892 he was music director of the U. S. Marines Band. He founded his own band in 1892 and toured throughout North America with great success. With this band he made four visits to Europe between 1900 and 1905; a world tour in 1910 was probably the peak of his career. During the First World War he was a bandsmaster in the U. S. Navy (1917–19).

Sousa's reputation rests on his ever-popular marches, but he also composed in other media, especially the stage. He wrote four operas to his own libretti: *The Smugglers* (1879), *Desiree* (1884), *The Queen of Hearts* (1886), and *El Capitan* (1895). His many operettas include *Our Flirtation* (1880), *The Bride Elect* (1897), *The Charlatan* (1898), *Chris and the Wonderlamp* (1900), *The Free Lance* (1906), *The Glass Blowers* (1911), *The American Maid* (1913), and *Victory* (1915).

For orchestra he composed a symphonic poem, *The Chariot Race* (1890), inspired by Lewis Wallace's *Ben Hur.* His cantata *The Messiah of Nations* for chorus and piano (1902; rev. for band or orch, 1915) was performed at the Panama-Pacific Exposition in San Francisco (1915). At one time his songs and piano pieces were frequently heard, but today they have disappeared from the musical scene.

The popularity of the marches earned him the title "The March King." Of his more than 200 band pieces, many are performed as frequently now as they were in his lifetime, notably *The Stars and Stripes Forever, Washington Post, Semper Fidelis, El Capitan, Liberty Bell, King Cotton, On Parade, The Picador,* and *Hands Across the Sea.*

Sousa was the compiler of *National, Patriotic and Typical Airs of All Lands,* published in Philadelphia and New York in 1890. He wrote two autobiographical books, *Through the Years With Sousa* (1910) and *Marching Along* (1928).

SOWERBY, LEO
b. Grand Rapids, Michigan, 1 May 1895
d. Port Clinton, Ohio, 7 July 1968

Sowerby studied at the American Conservatory in Chicago and later served as an army bandmaster in America, England, and France during the First World War. On his return to the United States he became the first recipient (1921) of a fellowship from the American Academy in Rome, where he stayed for three years. He taught at the American Conservatory from 1925, becoming head of the department of composition. He was an active organist and choirmaster in Chicago until his retirement in 1962.

Sowerby's music shows the strong influence of two diverse musical elements, jazz and hymn tunes. In his teens he composed three unpublished concertos, one each: piano, cello (1914–16), and violin (1913). Two early orchestral works, an overture, *Come Autumn Time* (1916) and *The Irish Washerwoman* (1916), immediately established his reputation and are the pieces for which he is still remembered, although they are small in scale and hardly typical of his later, more mature compositions.

Also for orchestra are *Rhapsody on British Folk Tunes* (1915); *Sorrow of Mydath* (1915); *Set of Four* (1917); *Suite: From the Northland* (1923); *Money Musk* (1924); *Prairie* (1929), based on Carl Sandburg's poem; Sinfonietta for Strings (1934); *Passacaglia, Interlude and Fugue* (1932); *Theme in Yellow* (1938); *Concert Overture* (1941); and *All on a Summer's Day* (1954). In addition, there are five symphonies: no. 1 (Chicago, 1922); no. 2 in B minor (1928); no. 3 in F-sharp minor, for the Golden Jubilee of the Chicago Symphony Orchestra (1941); no. 4 (1947); and no. 5 (1964).

Sowerby was the soloist in the premieres of his piano concertos no. 1 in F (1919) and no. 2 in E (1932). He also wrote a Harp Concerto (1919); *Ballad of King Estmere* for two pianos and orchestra (1922); a second Cello Concerto in E minor (1933); *Poem* for viola and orchestra (1941); and a second Violin Concerto in G minor (1943). His last two solo works were *Ballade* for English horn and strings (1949) and two *Concert Pieces* for organ and orchestra (1951, 1968).

As an organist, Sowerby provided several major works for the instrument. For organ and orchestra he wrote *Medieval Poem* (1926) (dedicated to Howard Hanson, a fellow student in Rome), a Concerto in C (1937), and *Classical Concerto* (1944). For organ solo

Leo Sowerby.
Courtesy Harold Stover.

there are a Sonata (1914–17); a Symphony in G (1930); a Suite (1933); *Canon, Chaconne and Fugue* (1951); *Sinfonia Brevis* (1966); and four volumes of pieces entitled *Preludes, Interludes and Postludes.*

Sowerby also produced many choral works for church use: *Vision of Sir Launfal* for soloists, chorus, and orchestra (1925); a cantata, *Great is the Lord* (1934) and *Te Deum* in D minor (1936), both for chorus and organ; a Lenten cantata, *Forsaken is Man* (1939); and four cantatas for chorus and orchestra: *The Canticle of the Sun* (1945), winner of the Pulitzer Prize; *Christ Reborn* (1950); *The Throne of God* (1957); and *The Ark of the Covenant* (1959). His last major composition was *Solomon's Garden* for tenor, chorus, and organ (or small orchestra), completed in 1965.

An impressive catalogue of chamber music includes five string quartets; three piano trios; a Woodwind Quintet (1916); Suite for violin and piano (1916); Serenade for string quartet (1917); Trio for flute, viola, and piano (1919); String Trio (1922); two sonatas for violin and piano (1922, 1944); and four sonatas, one each: cello (1921), clarinet (1938), trumpet (1945), and piano (in D, 1964).

For some years he provided scores of original works and arrangements for the Paul Whiteman Band, and wrote two short but effective pieces for jazz band, *Synconata* (1924) and *Monotony* (1925).

SPALDING, ALBERT

b. Chicago, Illinois, 15 August 1888
d. New York, New York, 26 May 1953

Spalding was primarily a violinist, and most of his compositions are for his instrument. He studied in New York, Florence, at the Bologna Conservatory and the Paris Conservatory. He gave the first performances of several violin concertos including those of Jacobi and Samuel Barber. In 1937 he was elected to the American Academy of Arts and Letters.

He composed two violin concertos, a Violin Sonata and a Suite for violin and orchestra. He also wrote *Theme and Variations* for orchestra and a String Quartet. He published an autobiography, *Rise to Follow* (1943), and a fictional biography of Tartini, *A Fiddle, Sword and a Lady* (1953).

SPELMAN, TIMOTHY MATHER

b. Brooklyn, New York, 21 January 1891
d. Florence, Italy, 21 August 1970

Spelman studied privately with H. R. Shelley (1908) and at Harvard University (1909–13) with W. R. Spalding and Edward Burlingame Hill before going to Munich. In 1920 he settled in Italy, but returned to the United States in 1935. After the Second World War he went back to Italy and lived in Florence from 1947 until his death.

As a composer, Spelman is remembered for his choral works: *The Vigil of Venus* for soloists, chorus, and orchestra, *Litany of the Middle Ages* for soprano, female voices, and orchestra (1928); *How Fair, How Fresh Were the Roses* for chorus and orchestra; *Pervigilium Veneris* for soprano, baritone, chorus, and orchestra (1929); and a *Pagan Oratorio*.

For orchestra he wrote a symphonic poem *Christ and the Blind Man* (1918); *Barbaresques* (1923); a suite of four tone poems, *Saints' Days* (1925); a symphonic poem, *The Outcasts of Poker Flat* (1928), after the story by Bret Harte; a *Prelude* for strings entitled *In the Princess' Garden*; Symphony in G minor (1934); *Dawn in the Woods* for violin and orchestra (1937); a rhapsody, *Homesick Yankee in North Africa* (1944); *Jamboree* (1945); *Sunday Paper Suite* (1946); Divertimento; and an Oboe Concerto (1954).

Spelman composed five operas: two evening-length works, *The Sea Rovers* (1928) and *The Courtship of Miles Standish* (1943), based on a story by Longfellow; and three one-act works, *La Magnifica* (1920), *The Sunken City* (1930), and a comedy *Babakan* (1935). He also provided music for a four-act pantomime, *Snowdrop* (1911), and a one-act music drama, *The Romance of the Rose* (1913). His ballet *The Princess Who Was Bored* (Brooklyn, 1911) has a scenario by the composer's wife, Leolyn Louise Everett.

Among his chamber music are *Five Whimsical Serenades* for string quartet (1924); *La Pavillion sur l'eau* for five instruments (1925); Piano Sonata in D minor (1929); two string quartets in D and F; *Eclogue* for ten instruments (1926); and *Three Preludes* for guitar, commissioned by Segovia.

SPIEGEL, LAURIE

b. Chicago, Illinois, 20 September 1945

In addition to her activities as a composer, Spiegel is a lutenist. She studied at Shimer College, Mount Carroll,

Laurie Spiegel.
Photo: Joel Chadabe, courtesy the composer.

Illinois (1964–67); Oxford University (1966–68); with Vincent Persichetti at the Juilliard School (1969–72); and Brooklyn College (1973–74). Among her teachers were John Duarte (guitar) in London (1967–68) and Jacob Druckman (composition) (1972–73). Since 1970 she has taught guitar and electronic music.

In her works she often combines electronic and computer techniques. These include *Harmonic Spheres* (1971); *Return to Zero* (1971); *Orchestras* (1971); *Raga* (1972); *Sediment* (1972); *Sunsets* (1973); *Purification* (1973); *Appalachian Groove* (1974); *Patchwork* (1976); *The Expanding Universe* (1975); *A Voyage* (1976); *Evolutions* (1977); *Voices Within* (1979); *Progression* (1982); *Passage* (1987); *Motives* (1988); *The Hollows* and *Sound Zones* (1990); and *Lift Off* (1999).

She has provided incidental music for *The Library of Babel* (Paul Ahrens; (1972); *The House of Bernarda Alba* (Federica Garcia Lorca; 1972); *The White Devil* (John Webster; 1972); *The Clinic* (Robert Goldman; 1973); and *The Devils*. A ballet, *Waves* (1970), is scored for chamber orchestra and tape. Among her other dance pieces are *Music for Dance* (1975), *East River* (1975), *Escalante* (1977), *Nomads* (1981), *Over Time* (1984), *Ratin Pieces* (1985), *Gravity's Joke* (1985), and *Music of Signals* (1986). Several of her electronic scores have been written for films: *Emma* (1975), *Unicorn* (1982), *Point* (1984), *Precious Metal Variations* (1985), *Dissipative Fantasies* (1986), *Dryads* (1988), *Continuous Transformations* (1990), *Soundtrack for Sandin* (1990), and *Current Events* (2002).

For her own instrument, the guitar, she has composed *Five Easy Pieces* (1968); *Four Movements* (1969–72); *Passacaglia* (1970); *An Earlier Time* (1972–81); *Etude* (1973); *A Tablature Study* (1974); *A Study* (1975); *After Dowland* (1979); *After Sor* (1979); *Prelude* (1979); and *Fantasy on a Theme of John Duarte* (1990).

Music for piano solo includes *Time Clock* (1979); *Contraries* (1979); *An Album Leaf* (1980); *Winter Elegy* (1981); *A Paraphrase* (1981); *After Clementi* (1981); *Three Chromatic Retrogrades* (1981); *A Fantasy* (1982); *Fughetta* (1982/1990); *Three Movements on Descending Scales* (1982); *A 12-Tone Blues* (1982); *A Cyclic Score* (1984); *A Prelude and a Counterpoint* (1985–86); and *Returning East* and *After the Mountains* (1988). Two recent works, *Conversational Paws* (dogs; 2001) and *Anon a Mouse* (2003), use animal sounds recorded, edited, and processed by the composer.

STALVEY, DORRANCE
b. Georgetown, South Carolina, 21 August 1930

Stalvey studied at the Cincinnati College of Music (B. Mus., 1953; M. Mus., 1955). From 1972 to 1980 he

Dorrance Stalvey.
Courtesy the composer.

taught at the Immaculate Heart College, Los Angeles. He has also been a member of the music faculty of Pomona College, California and University of Southern California, Los Angeles, and is currently director of music programs at Los Angeles County Museum of Art. He is also director of the Los Angeles Monday Evening Concerts.

Many of his compositions use electronic techniques and are designed for multimedia performance: *Celebration Principium* for brass, percussion, and video (1967); *Points – Lines – Circles* for sextet and slides (1968); *Conflicts* (1970); *Togethers I* for guitar and tape (1970), *II* for tape and film (1970), and *III* for clarinet, tape, and slides (1970); *In Time and Not* (1970); *Fitan* for two-channel tape (1971); and a ballet, *Agathlon* (1978).

Instrumental pieces include a String Trio (1960); *Movements and Interludes* for octet (1964); *PLC – Extract* for clarinet solo (1968); *PLC – Abstract* for solo double bass (1968–72); *Celebrations – Sequent I* for chamber orchestra (1973); *Sequent II* for large orchestra (1976); *Sequent IV* for brass and percussion (1980); *Three Pairs and Seven* for trombone and piano (or trombone and tape; 1979); *Piece* for wind band and percussion (1981); *Ex Ferus* for six cellos or string sextet (1984); String Quartet (1989); *Exordium/Genesis/Dawn* for flute, clarinet, and piano trio (1990); *Requiem for a Dancer* for flute, clarinet, trumpet, bass trombone, percussion, violin, and double bass (1991, 2001); *A Fragment of Silence* for cello and piano (2001); and *Stream* for violin and piano (2002).

For piano he has written *Three Little Pieces* (1957), *Duets for Children* (1965), *Changes* (1966), *Jazz ca' 53* (1982), *Brief Passage* (1986), and a piece for two pianos or piano duet, *A Day Past* (1960, 1976).

Stalvey has composed a theater piece, *In Time and Not* for chorus, dancers, actors, visuals, tape, and instruments (1970). His vocal music includes *Pound Songs* for soprano, flute, clarinet, piano, percussion, violin, and cello (1985, rev. 1996), and *Dualities I* (1986) and *II* (1987) for soprano and ensemble.

STARER, ROBERT
b. Vienna, Austria, 8 January 1924
d Woodstock, New York, 22 April 2001

Starer attended the Vienna State Academy for a year before moving to Jerusalem, where he studied at the Conservatory with Oedoen Partos and Josef Tal. During the Second World War he served in Britain's Royal Air Force. He emigrated to the United States in 1947 to study at the Juilliard School under Frederick Jacobi (1947–49). He was also a pupil of Aaron Copland at Tanglewood in 1948 and became an American citizen in 1957. From 1949 to 1974 he was a member of the faculty of the Juilliard School. He also taught at Brooklyn College (1963–91). He was the recipient of two Guggenheim Fellowships (1957, 1963), a Fulbright Fellowship (1964), and an award from the American Academy and Institute of Arts and Letters (1979).

Starer's best known works are three symphonies (1950, 1951, 1969); a lively Piano Concerto, performed in 1949 with the composer as soloist; and a Concerto for viola, percussion, and strings, composed in 1958 during a stay in Vienna on a Guggenheim Fellowship; it was performed the following year in Switzerland and later by the New York Philharmonic Orchestra under Leonard Bernstein. Also for orchestra he wrote *Fantasy* for strings (1945); an *Oriental Rhapsody* (1946); *Prelude and Dance* (1949); *Prelude and Rondo Giocoso* (1953); *Concerto a Tre* for clarinet, trumpet, trombone, and strings (1954); *Ballade* for violin and orchestra (1955); *Dalton Suite* (1960); *Mutabili (Variants for Orchestra)* recorded by the Louisville Orchestra in 1965; *Six Variations with 12 Notes* (1967); *Invocation* for trumpet and strings (1972); and two more piano concertos (1953, 1972). Concerto for violin, cello, and piano was first performed in 1968 by the Boston Symphony Orchestra. Later orchestral works include a Violin Concerto (1981); *Concerto a quattro* for solo woodwind and strings (1983); *Hudson River Suite*

(1984); Serenade for trombone, vibraphone, and strings (1984); *Symphonic Prelude* (1984); Cello Concerto (1988); Concerto for two pianos (1996); and Concerto for piano duet (1997). To the concert band repertory he provided *Dirge* (1963–64).

For the stage Starer composed five operas. *The Intruder,* in one act, was performed in New York in 1956. The three-act *Pantagleize,* based on a play by Michel de Ghelderode, was produced in 1972 by the Brooklyn College Opera Theater. *The Lost Lover*, a musical morality play, in one act, was premiered in Katonah, New York. *Apollonia,* a full-length opera to a libretto by Gail Godwin, was commissioned by the Minnesota Opera in 1979. His last opera, *The Other Voice,* was completed in 1998.

Starer wrote seven ballets: *The Story of Esther* (1960); *The Dybbuk,* performed at the Berlin Festival in 1960; *The Sense of Touch* (1967); and four works commissioned by Martha Graham: *Samson Agonistes* (1961), *Phaedra* (1962), *The Lady of the House Asleep* (1968), and *Holy Jungle* (1974).

Many of his choral works are based on aspects of the Jewish faith. These include *Kohelet (Ecclesiastes*; 1952), *Ariel (Visions of Isaiah*; 1959), and *Joseph and His Brothers,* a cantata for narrator, soloists, chorus, and orchestra (1966). Also in Hebrew are *Vayechula* for cantor and mixed voices; a setting of the *Sabbath Eve Service* for baritone, chorus, and organ (1967) and *Psalms of Woe and Joy* (1977).

In addition he composed *Come Sleep* for female voices (1958), *Never Seek to Tell Thy Love* (William Blake) for men's voices, and *Two Songs from Honey*

Robert Starer.
Courtesy The Juilliard School.

and Salt (Carl Sandburg) for chorus and piano (or brass) (1964). *The People, Yes* (Sandburg) for chorus and orchestra dates from 1976.

For a cappella voices he wrote *Five Proverbs on Love* (1949), each movement in a different language. *On the Nature of Things* for eight-part chorus (1968) includes settings of words by Lucretius, Emily Dickinson, John Digby, and lines from Ecclesiastes. Also for mixed voices is *Images of Man* (1973) for vocal quartet, chorus, and instrumental quintet to a text from *The Four Zoas* by William Blake. Later choral compositions are *Voices of Brooklyn* for solo voices, chorus, and band (1980–84), *Night Thoughts* for chorus and synthesizer (1990), and *Proverbs for a Son* for chorus (1991).

Starer's solo vocal music includes *Journals of a Songmaker* for soprano, baritone, and orchestra (1976), commissioned for William Steinberg and the Pittsburgh Symphony Orchestra; *Anna Margarita's Will* to a text by Gail Godwin for soprano, flute, horn, cello, and piano (1980); and *Transformations* for soprano, flute (or clarinet), and piano (1980).

Starer's instrumental music occupies a significant place in his output. He wrote three string quartets (1947, 1995, 1996); Concertino for two instruments (1948); *Prelude* for harp (1948); *Five Miniatures* for brass (1949); *Duo* for violin and viola (1954); a Cello Sonata (1955); *Dirge* for two trumpets and two trombones (1956); Serenade for brass (1956); *Dialogues* for clarinet and piano (1961); *Variants* for violin and piano (1963); Trio for clarinet, cello, and piano (1964); a Woodwind Quartet (1970); *Profiles in Brass* (1974); *Mandala* for strings quartet (1974); *Colloquies* for flute and piano (1975); *Light and Shadow* for saxophone quartet (1979); *Relationships* for clarinet and piano; and a Sonata for four cellos. A Piano Quartet was commissioned in 1978 by "Music in the Round" and recorded by the Cantilena Chamber Players. Later instrumental works include *Annapolis Suite* for harp and brass quintet (1982); *Fanfare in Five* for brass ensemble (1984); *Six Preludes* for guitar (1984); *Kaaterskill Quartet* (1987); *Duo* for violin and piano (1988); *Angel Voices* for brass and organ (1989); a Clarinet Quintet (1992); *Episodes* for viola, cello, and piano (1992); *Dialogues* for flute and harp (1993); *Song of Solitude* for solo cello (1996); Piano Quintet (1998); and *Music for a Summer Afternoon* for flute and string trio (1999).

For piano solo he wrote three sonatas (1949, 1965, 1994); *Fantasia Concertante* (1959); *Sketches in Color I* (1963) and *II* (1973); *Four Seasonal Pieces* (1985); and *The Ideal Self* (1985).

Starer was the author of two books, *Rhythmic Training* (1969) and an autobiography, *Continuo: A Life in Music* (1987).

STEARNS, THEODORE
b. Berea, Ohio, 10 June 1880
d. Los Angeles, California, 1 November 1935

Stearns studied at the Oberlin Conservatory, Ohio, and in Germany at the Würzburg Conservatory. In New York (1922–24) he was a music critic and opera conductor. A Guggenheim Fellowship (1927–28) enabled him to return to Germany. In 1932 he joined the music faculty of the University of California, Los Angeles.

His opera-ballet *Snowbird*, produced in Chicago in 1923, won the David Bispham Medal in 1925. A lyric drama, *Atlantis*, dates from 1926. For orchestra he wrote *Before the Door of a Wigwam*, performed in Würzburg in 1897; *Hiawatha's Wedding Suite* (1897); and a symphonic poem, *Tiberio*.

Stearns was the author of *The Story of Music*, published in 1931.

STEIN, LEON
b. Chicago, Illinois, 18 September 1910
d. Chicago, Illinois, 9 May 2002

Stein studied at Crane Junior College, Chicago (1922–27) and the American Conservatory, Chicago (1927–29). At De Paul University, Chicago (B.Mus. 1931; M.M. 1935; Ph.D. 1949) he was a pupil of John J. Becker and Wesley La Violette. He also received private lessons in composition from Leo Sowerby and orchestration from Eric DeLamarter. Stein taught at De Paul University from 1931 to 1976. In addition he was director of the Institute of Music at the College of Jewish Studies in Chicago (1952–59). In 1955 he was appointed conductor of the Chicago Sinfonietta.

For orchestra Stein wrote four symphonies (1940, 1942, 1950–51, 1974); *Suite Hebraic* (1933); *Prelude, Fugue and Finale* (1936); *Passacaglia* (1936); a Sinfonietta for strings (1938); *Symphonic Suite* for strings (1938); a Violin Concerto (1938–39); *Three Hassidic Dances* (1940–41); *Triptych on Three Poems of Walt Whitman* (1943); *Great Lakes Suite* for small orchestra (1943–44); a *Festive Overture* (1950); *Rhapsody* for flute, harp, and strings (1954); *Adagio and Rondo Ebraico* (1957); *Symphonic Movement* (1959); *Then Shall the Dust Return* (1971); a Cello Concerto (1977); Concerto for clarinet and percussion (1979); *Nexus* for wind ensemble (1983); *Aria Hebraique* for oboe and strings (1984); and Concerto for oboe and strings (1986).

Stein's stage works include two operas, *The Fisherman's Wife* (1954) and *Deirdre* (W. B. Yeats) (1956), and two ballets, *Exodus* (1939) and *Doubt* (1940).

Leon Stein.
*Courtesy DePaul University Archives,
Chicago, Illinois.*

Among his instrumental are five string quartets (1933, 1962, 1964, 1964, 1967, the last with soprano); two violin sonatas (1932, 1960); three suites for saxophone quartet (1967); Sonatina for two violins (1931); *Trio Pastorale* (1932); *Invocation and Dance* for violin and piano (1938); *Twelve Preludes* for violin and piano (1942–49); Trio for three trumpets (1953); Quintet for alto saxophone and strings (1957); Sextet for saxophone and wind quintet (1958); Sonata for solo violin (1960); Trio for saxophone, violin, and piano (1961); Sonata for tenor saxophone and piano (1967); *Three Pieces* for solo clarinet (1969); a Sonata for viola and piano (1969); Sonata for cello and piano (1969); *Rhapsody* for alto saxophone (1969); eight sonatas for solo instruments: flute (1968), horn (1969), trombone (1969), trumpet (1969), bassoon (1969), oboe (1969), double bass (1970), and cello (1970); and a Wind Quintet (1970).

Later chamber music includes a Suite for brass quintet (1975); Quintet for harp and string quartet (1976); *Introduction and Rondo* for flute and percussion (1977); Suite for wind quintet (1978); Suite for solo flute (1978); *Duo Concertante* for violin and viola (1978); *Rhapsody* for solo cello (1979); a String Trio (1980); *Dance Ebraico* for cello and piano (1982); *Three for Nine* for ensemble (1983); *Duo Concertante* for bassoon (or violin) and marimba (1988); and *Trio Concertante* for violin, saxophone (or cello) and piano (1993).

Stein's choral music includes *Liederkranz of Jewish Folksongs* for children's chorus and piano (1936), *Songs of the Night* (Bialik; 1952), and *The Lord Reigneth* (Psalm 97) for tenor, female voices and orchestra (1953).

Stein was the author of three books: *The Racial Thinking of Richard Wagner* (1959), *Structure and Style: The Study of Analysis in Musical Form* (two volumes, 1962–63, rev. ed. 1979), and *Anthology of Musical Forms* (1962).

STEINER, GITTA HANA

b. Prague, Czech Republic, 17 April 1932

An American citizen since 1941, Steiner studied at the Juilliard School (B. Mus., 1963; M.S., 1969), where her teachers included Vincent Persichetti, Elliott Carter, and Gunther Schuller. From 1963 to 1965 she taught at the Brooklyn College of Music.

For orchestra she wrote *Music for Strings* (1953); a Suite (1958); a Violin Concerto (1963); *Tetrark* for strings (1965); *Movement for Eleven* for chamber orchestra (1966); and a Piano Concerto (1967). Her instrumental works include Suite for wind trio (1958); *Fantasy* for clarinet and piano (1964); Piano Sonata (1964); *Movement* for 11 instruments (1964); a Brass Quintet (1964); *Jouissance* for flute and piano (1965); *Refractions* for solo violin (1967); *Two Concert Pieces for Seven* (1968); a String Quartet (1968); and *Five Pieces* for trombone and piano (1969).

As a percussionist, Steiner has contributed several works to the repertoire: Percussion Quartet (1968); *Five*

Pieces for vibraphone (1968); Trio for piano and 2 percussionists (1969); *Percussion Music for Two* (1971); *Duo* for cello and percussion (1971); *Fantasy Pieces* for marimba (1978); Bagatelles for vibraphone (1990); Sonata for vibraphone; and *Duo* for vibraphone and marimba .

Her vocal music includes *Three Choruses of Emily Dickinson* for chorus (1965) and *Three Songs by James Joyce* for voice and piano (1960).

She is the author of *Contemporary Solos for Vibraphone and Marimba*.

STEINKE, GREG A.
b. Fremont, Michigan, 2 August 1942

Steinke studied oboe and composition at the Oberlin Conservatory of Music, Ohio (B.A., 1964); Michigan State University with H. Owen Reed, Mario Davidovsky, and Ross Lee Finney (M. Mus., 1967; Ph.D., 1976); and the University of Iowa (1968–71). He has taught at Evergreen State College, Olympia, Washington, the University of Idaho (1967–68), the University of Maryland (1968–72), and California State University, Northridge (1973–80). In 1980, he joined the faculty of Marylhurst (Oregon) University, where he rose to chair of the departments of art and music (holding The Joseph Naumes Endowed Chair in Music), and then associate dean of undergraduate studies. He retired in 2001 to enter into business.

For orchestra he has written *In Memoriam* (1963); *Threnody* (1965); *Music* for bassoon and orchestra (1967); *Duo Fantasy Concertante* for violin, cello, and chamber orchestra (1978); and *Northwest Sketches IIb* for flute, oboe, and chamber orchestra (1982). More recent orchestral works include *Movements from Native American Notes: The Bitter Roots of Peace* (*Image Music VIb*) for chamber orchestra (1994); *All In A Moment's Time* (*Image Music XIV*) for viola and orchestra (1995–96); and *Beijing Impressions: A Travel Triptych* (*Image Music XVI*) for chamber orchestra (2000).

Among his instrumental pieces are *Polymodal Sketches* (1961; rev. 1975); Trio for violin, viola, and violoncello (1962; rev. 1974); Trio for oboe, clarinet, and bassoon (1962; rev. 1975); Sonata for oboe d'amore and English horn (1963); *Music for String Quartet* (1964); *A Music* for oboe, double bass, and percussion (1967); *Music for Three* for oboe, guitar, and percussion (1972); *Tricinium* for alto saxophone, trumpet, and piano ·(1972); *Atavism* for oboe, bassoon, and wind ensemble (1973–76); *Four Desultory Episodes* for oboe and tape (1972–73); *Diversions and Interactions* for percussion trio (1976); *Music for Chief Joseph* for oboe and four trombones (1980); *Lyric Fantasy* (*A Music*

Greg A. Steinke.
Courtesy the composer.

for Dance) for flute, alto saxophone, and guitar (1980); *Image Music* from *Songs of the Fire Circles* for flute, oboe, trombone, and double bass (1982); *One by One* (*Image Music II*) for flute and harp (1985); *Wind River Country* for woodwind quintet (1986); *Native American Notes* for string quartet (1990; adapted for chamber orchestra in 1991); *Incantation, Meditation, and Dance* for trumpeter/flugelhorn and organ (1994); *Expressions on the Paintings of Edvard Munch* (Image Music XVII) for String Quartet (2002); and *Continental Drift: A Geographical Triptych* (*Image Music XVIII*) for percussion orchestra (2002).

Steinke's compositions for piano and celesta include Suite for piano (1962), *Six Pieces* for piano (1963–65), *Family Portrait, Five Vignettes for Piano* (1976–78), and *Albumblätter* (*Album Leaves*), *Acht Vignetten* for celesta (1994).

Vocal works include a setting of Psalm 23 for chorus and chamber orchestra (1962); *Three Sonnets of Shakespeare* for soprano, flute, and strings (1962); *Ein Japanisches Liederbuch* for soprano and chamber ensemble (1971); *Mother Earth* for voice and ensemble; and a musical, *Right On!* (1970).

STEVENS, HALSEY

b. Scott, New York, 3 December 1908
d. Long Beach, California, 20 January 1989

Stevens studied at Syracuse University (1926–31) and at the University of California, Berkeley (1944), where he was a pupil of Ernest Bloch. He was awarded Guggenheim Fellowships in 1964 and 1971. After teaching at Syracuse University (1935–37), he was appointed an associate professor at Dakota Wesleyan University, Mitchell, North Dakota, moving four years later to become director of music at Bradley University, Peoria, Illinois (1941–46). He was appointed professor of composition at the University of Southern California in 1946, becoming the first Andrew W. Mellon Professor there; he retired in 1979.

As a composer, Stevens has several impressive orchestral works to his credit. The first of his three symphonies was written between 1941 and 1945 and revised in 1950. In one movement, it was first performed in San Francisco in 1946 under the composer's direction. The Second Symphony, now withdrawn, received its premiere in New York in 1947 by the NBC Symphony Orchestra, conducted by Alfred Wallenstein. *Sinfonia Breve* was commissioned by the Louisville Orchestra in 1957.

Stevens's other orchestral compositions include a Piano Concertino (1936), later withdrawn; *Green Mountain Overture* (1948, rev. 1954); *Triskelion* (1953); *Allegro* for piano and orchestra (1956); *Adagio and Allegro* for strings (1957) transcribed from the *Third String Quartet*; *Overture for Strings* (1957); *Five Pieces* (1958); and *Symphonic Dances,* commissioned by the San Francisco Symphony Orchestra in 1958. Later works are a Cello Concerto (1964); *Threnos in Memory of Quincy Porter* (1968); Concerto for clarinet and strings (1968–69); Double Concerto for violin, cello, and strings (1972–73); and a Viola Concerto (1976).

Steven's choral pieces include *The Ballad of William Sycamore* (1955) to a text by Stephen Vincent Benet, *A Testament of Life* (1955) to Biblical texts, and a *Magnificat* (1962), all with orchestra; *Te Deum* (1967), written for Georgia Southern College, Statesboro; *Chansons courtoises* for unaccompanied chorus (1967); and *Songs from the Pauite* for chorus, four flutes, and timpani (1976).

Stevens composed a large quantity of instrumental music, including sonatas for the following instruments: violin (1936; 1942–44; 1959), bassoon (1949), viola (1950), horn (1952–53), trumpet (1953–56), cello (1965), trombone (1965), and oboe (1971). Other important chamber works are a Flute Sonatina (1943); Suite for clarinet and piano (1945, rev. 1953); Quintet for flute, string trio, and piano (1945); Piano Trio no. 2 (1945); Piano Quartet (1946); String Quartet no. 3 (1949); *Three Pieces* for bassoon and piano (1949); *Intermezzo, Cadenza and Finale* for cello and piano (1949, rev. 1950); *Notturno* for cello and piano (1953); Piano Trio no. 3 (1954); Suite for solo violin (1954); *Two Duos* for two cellos (1954); Septet for clarinet, bassoon, horn, two violas, and two cellos (1956–57); Cello Sonatina (1957); Suite for viola and piano (1959); Suite no. 2 for cello and piano (1959); Sonatina for bass tuba and piano (1959–60); Divertimento for two violins (1958–66); Trumpet Trio (1962); three sets of *Twelve Studies* for solo clarinet (1966), solo bassoon (1968), and solo oboe (1972); *Five Duos* for flute and clarinet (1966); *Quintetto Serbelloni* for wind instruments (1971–72); and *Dittico* for clarinet and piano. The first two string quartets (1943–44, 1949) were withdrawn, as was the Piano Trio no. 1 (1936–37).

For piano Stevens provided many items, including three sonatas (1933; 1937, withdrawn; 1948); six sonatinas (1942–59); *Ten Short Pieces* (1945–54); *Six Preludes* (1951–66); *Ritratti* (1959–60); *Fantasia* (1961); *Seventeen Piano Pieces* (1933–66); and *Partita*

Halsey Stevens.
Courtesy of the Family of Halsey Stevens.

for harpsichord (or piano) (1953–54). He also wrote a Sonata for piano, four hands (1975).

Among his vocal music are *Six Millay Songs* (1949–50); *Four Songs of Love and Death* (1951–53); *Two Shakespeare Songs* for voice, flute, and clarinet (1958–59); *Cuatro Canciones* (Antonio Machado) (1961); and *Siete Canciones* (Federico Garcia Lorca) (1964).

Stevens is probably best known to the musical world as the author of the standard book in English on the life and works of Béla Bartók, first published in 1953 and revised in 1964.

STILL, WILLIAM GRANT
b. Woodville, Mississippi, 11 May 1895
d. Los Angeles, California, 3 December 1978

Still spent most of his childhood in Little Rock, Arkansas. He studied at Wilberforce College, Ohio (1911–15) and attended Oberlin Conservatory, Ohio (1917–18; 1919–22). At the New England Conservatory (1922) he was a pupil of George Chadwick. Later he received composition lessons privately from Edgard Varèse (1922–25). After a year in the U.S. Navy, he settled in New York, where he worked as an arranger for W. C. Handy and others, earning a living playing in bands and orchestras. In 1936 he conducted the Los Angeles Symphony Orchestra and in 1955 conducted the New Orleans Symphony Orchestra, the first African-American to do so.

Almost every one of Still's work is a reflection of African-American life, as many of the titles reveal. His first orchestral compositions were *Darker America* (1924), *From the Journal of a Wanderer* (1925), and *From the Black Belt* (1926). Two major pieces for orchestra, *Africa* (1930) and the popular *Afro-American Symphony* (1930), established for him a wide reputation and helped him to earn a Guggenheim Fellowship in 1933. At this time Still turned his attention to the stage, with two ballets for the Ruth Page Company of Chicago, *La Guiablesse* (1927), set in Martinique, and *Sahdji* (1930), with an African background. A third ballet, *Miss Sally's Party*, dates from 1940.

A Second Symphony in G minor (*Song of a New Race*) was completed in 1937. Symphony no. 3, *Sunday Symphony*, dates from 1945. Symphony no. 4, subtitled *Autochthonous*, was composed in 1949 and was followed soon after by Symphony no. 5, entitled *Western Hemisphere* (1949). Still later reversed the numberings of the Third and Fifth Symphonies. Other orchestral works include *Kaintuck* with piano solo (1936); *Dismal Swamp* (1936); *Can'tcha Line 'em* (1940); *Old California,* composed in 1941 for the 160th anniversary of Los Angeles; *Fanfare for American War Heroes* (1943); *Poem for Orchestra* (1944) for the

William Grant Still.
Courtesy William Grant Still Music.

Cleveland Orchestra; *In Memoriam,* a tribute to the African-American soldiers who died for democracy (1944); *Festive Overture* (1944); *Fanfare for the 99th Fighter Squadron* for wind orchestra (1945); *Danzas de Panama* for strings (1946); *Archaic Ritual* (1946); *Wood Notes* (1947); *Little Red House* (1957); five suites entitled *The American Scene* (1958); *The Peaceful Land* (1960); *Patterns* (1960); and *Threnody in Memory of Jan Sibelius* (1965). Still also wrote several scores for the Paul Whiteman Band, including *A Deserted Plantation* (1933), *Ebon Chronicle* (1934), *The Black Man Dances* (1935), and *Beyond Tomorrow* (1936).

Still's first opera, *Blue Steel,* was completed in 1935. Three years later he wrote a second opera, *Troubled Island,* to a libretto by Langston Hughes. It is set in Haiti and concerns the tragic life of the Emperor Dessalines. Still wrote seven more operas: *A Bayou Legend* (1940), *A Southern Interlude* (1942), *Costaso* (1949), *Mota* (1951), *The Pillar* (1956), *Minette Fontaine* (1958), and *Highway No. 1 U.S.A.* (1962). In 1937 CBS commissioned *Lenox Avenue* for radio announcer, chorus, and orchestra. It was later produced as a ballet.

Still's commitment to African-American themes gave rise to three further settings of texts: *And They Lynched Him From a Tree* for speaker, contralto, two choruses, and orchestra (1940); *Plain Chant for*

America for baritone and orchestra (1941), later arranged for chorus and orchestra; and *Pages from Negro History* for narrator and orchestra (1943). Other choral pieces include *Caribbean Melodies* for chorus, piano, and percussion (1941) and *Wailing Women* for soprano and chorus (1946). He also composed a number of short instrumental pieces, including Suite (1943) and *Pastorela* (1946), both for violin and piano; and songs.

STOCK, DAVID FREDERICK
b. Pittsburgh, Ohio, 3 June 1939

Stock studied with Nicolai Lopatnikoff and Alexei Haieff at the Carnegie Institute of Technology (1956–63) and at Brandeis University, Waltham, Massachusetts with Arthur Berger and Harold Shapero (1965–68). In Paris (1960–61) he was a pupil of Nadia Boulanger Stock was trumpeter in the Pittsburgh Symphony Orchestra (1961–63) and taught at the Cleveland Institute (1964–65), Brandeis University (1966–68), and the New England Conservatory (1968–70). Later he was on the faculty of Antioch College, Ohio (1970–74), Carnegie-Mellon Institute (1976–77), and the University of Pittsburgh (1978–86). Since 1987 he has taught at Duquesne University. Stock was founder and conductor of the Pittsburgh New Music Ensemble from 1976 and conductor of the Carnegie Symphony Orchestra (1976–82).

Stock's orchestral works include Divertimento (1957); a Symphony in one movement (1963); *Capriccio* for chamber orchestra (1963); *Inner Space* (1973); *Triflumena* (1978); *Zohar* (1978); *A Joyful Noise* (1983); *American Accents* for chamber orchestra (1984); and *Back to Bass-ics* for strings (1985). More recent orchestral pieces are *On the Shoulders of Giants* (1986); *Rockin' Rondo* (1987); *Quick Opener* for chamber orchestra (1987); *Tekiah* for trumpet and chamber orchestra (1987); *Fast Break* (1988); *Kickoff* (1990); *Fanfarria* (1993); *Power Play* (1993); *String Set* for chamber orchestra (1993); *Available Light* for chamber orchestra (1994); *In the High Garden* (1996); Violin Concerto (1995); Symphony no. 2 (1996); *Drive Time* (1996); Viola Concerto (1997); *The Center Holds* for chamber orchestra (1997); Symphony no. 3, *Tikkun Olam* (1999); Symphony no. 4 (2001); and Symphony no. 5, *In Tempore Belli* (2002).

For wind band he has written *Nova* (1974); *The Silent Stomp* for wind ensemble (1985); *No Man's Land* for English horn and wind symphony (1988); *The Winds of Summer* for saxophone and band (1989); *Earth Beat* for timpani and wind orchestra (1992); *Nine-One-One* (2002); and Concerto for saxophone quartet and band (2002).

Stock has composed a considerable number of instrumental pieces which include five string quartets (1962, 1972, 1994, 1996, 2000); *Shadow Music* for five percussionists and harp (1964, rev. 1979); Serenade for flute, clarinet, horn, viola, and cello (1964); *Noro* for any two instruments (1966); Clarinet Quintet (1968); *Flashback* for chamber ensemble (1968); *Three Pieces* for violin and piano (1969); *Triple Play* for piccolo, double bass, and percussion (1970); *Night Birds* for four or more cellos (1975); *Icicles* for piccolo, oboe, and clarinet (1976); and *Brass Rubbings* for six trumpets (1976).

Later chamber works are *Pentacles* for brass quintet (1976); *The Body Electric* for amplified double bass, wind, and percussion (1977); *Starlight* for clarinet and percussion (1979); *Night* for clarinet, violin, and piano (1980); *Persona* for clarinet, violin, cello, piano, and percussion (1980); *The Philosopher's Stone* for violin and ensemble (1980); *Speaking Extravagantly* for string quartet (1981); *Dreamwinds* for brass quintet (1981); *Keep the Change* for ensemble (1984); *Sulla Spiaggia* for piccolo/alto flute, bass clarinet, horn, and electric piano (1985); *Yerusha* for clarinet and seven players (1986); *Partners* for cello and piano (1988); *Sunrise Serenade* for recorder quartet (1988); *Sax Appeal* for saxophone quartet (1990); *Sonidos de la Noche* for clarinet, violin, cello, and piano (1994); *Available Light* for ensemble (1994); and *Past Tense* for ensemble (1998).

Vocal music includes *Scat* for soprano, flute, bass clarinet, violin, and cello (1971); *Upcountry Fishing* for voice and violin (1982); *Spirits* for chorus, harp, and percussion (1976); and two pieces for unaccompanied chorus, *Dor l'Dor* (1990) and *Beyond Babylon* (1994).

STOESSEL, ALBERT (FREDERIC)
b. St. Louis, Missouri, 11 October 1894
d. New York, New York, 12 May 1943

Stoessel studied the violin with Willy Hess at the Hochschule in Berlin. On his return to the United States he made his debut as a solo violinist. During the First World War in France he was conductor of a U. S. Army Band (1917–19). In 1922 he succeeded Walter Damrosch as conductor of the Oratorio Society of New York and became director of music of the Chautauqua Institution in 1923. That year he was appointed head of the newly formed music department of New York University.

In 1927 he joined the faculty of the Juilliard School of Music as director of the orchestra and the opera department. Here he was responsible for many premieres, including the first performance in America of Richard

Albert Stoessel.
Courtesy The Juilliard School.

Strauss' *Ariadne auf Naxos.* His own three-act opera, *Garrick,* completed in 1936, was produced at the Juilliard School in February of that year. He died while conducting a performance of Walter Damrosch's *Dunkirk* at a concert of the American Academy of Arts and Letters.

For orchestra he composed a *Hispania Suite* (1921); a *Suite Antique* for two violins and chamber orchestra (1922); a symphonic portrait, *Cyrano de Bergerac* (1922); an *Early American Suite* (1935); and a *Concerto Grosso* for piano and strings (1935). His chamber music includes *Five Miniatures* for violin and piano (1917), a Violin Sonata in G (1921), and *Flitting Bats* for violin and piano (1925).

He was the author of a textbook, *The Technic of the Baton* (1920, rev. 1928).

STOKES, ERIC NORMAN
b. Haddon Heights, New Jersey, 14 July 1930
d. Minneapolis, Minnesota, 16 March 1999

Stokes was educated at Lawrence College, Appleton, Wisconsin (B.M.,1952), the New England Conserva-

tory (M.M,.1956), and the University of Minnesota (Ph.D.), where his teachers included Dominick Argento and Paul Fetler. He also taught there from 1961–88. He died in an automobile accident in Minneapolis.

He was hugely prolific, producing music in all media. For the stage he wrote three operas: *Horspfal,* produced in Minneapolis in 1969. Described as a collage, requiring no fewer than five conductors, it concerns the effect on the American Indians of the arrival of Europeans. There followed *The Jealous Cellist and Other Acts of Misconduct,* staged in Minneapolis in 1979, and *Apollonia's Circus* (1994). *Happ or Orpheus in Clover* (1977), to the composer's own libretto, is a "micro-opera" written in celebration of the well-known Minneapolis opera coach Yale Marshall's birthday; it consists of the words "Happy Birthday" and a few other sounds, and was performed on only one occasion.

In addition to a television musical, *We're Not Robots, You Know* (1986), Stokes composed several theater pieces, including *When This You See, Remember Me* (1970); *Lampyridae* (1973); *Rock and Roll (Phonic Paradigm I*; 1980); *Tag* (1982); and *The Shake of Things to Come* (1983). He also composed an oratorio, *Smoke and Steel* (Carl Sandburg) for tenor, male chorus, brass, and strings (1959).

Stokes completed five symphonies: no. 1 (1979), no. 2 (1981), no. 3, *Captions on the War Against Earth* (1989), no. 4, *The Ghost Bus to Eldorado* (1990), and no. 5, *Native Dancer* (1991). For large orchestra he wrote *Celebration for the Saint (Music for St. Cecilia's Day)*; two divertimenti (1960); *A Center Harbor Holiday* (Concerto for Tuba; 1963); *Three Sides of a Town* (1964); *Sonatas for Divided String Orchestra* (1967); *Variations on a Space and a Quest* (1973); *The Continental Harp and Band Report* for wind band (1974); *Anwatin Winter Set* (1980); *Concert Music* for piano and orchestra (1982); *Cotton Candy* (1986); *Stages (Homage to Kurt Weill*; 1988); and *Fanfare of Rings,* commissioned in 1994 for the centenary of the Cincinnati Symphony Orchestra.

Stokes's chamber orchestra compositions comprise *On the Badlands – Parables* (1972); *Five Verbs of Earth Encircled* with narrator (1973); *Pack-rat (2 step) Slow (March) Drag* (1976); *The Spirit of the Place Among the People* (1977); *Prairie Drum* (1981); *Prophet Bird* (after Schumann; 1992); and *Stripplings on Motley* (1995).

For unaccompanied chorus he wrote *Ivy is Good* (1962) and *A Doomsday Carol,* (1966). Other choral pieces include *The River's Minute by the Far Brook's Year* (Hart Crane) for narrator, chorus, and orchestra (1981); *Mata el pajaro,guarda el canto,* a multi-voiced canon for chorus with rattles and amplified narration (1982); *Peppercorn Songs* for chorus and piano (1984); *Wondrous World* for chorus and tape (1984); *Harbor*

Dawn and Proems for narrator, choir, and orchestra (1986); *Firecho* for five soloists and optional percussion (1987); *Mermaids Stand by the King of the Sea* for narrator, choir, and orchestra (1991) and *Pied Beauty* (Hopkins) for chorus, brass, and organ (1997). Among Stokes' many solo vocal pieces are *Four Hardy Songs* (1963) for high voice and oboe; *Gnomic Commentaries* for soprano (or tenor) and instrumental ensemble (1964–66); *Inland Missing the Sea,* nine songs for soprano, tenor, baritone, and ensemble (1977); *Caccia* (*Phonic Paradigm III*) for two high voices, cello, and birdcalls (1984); and *Song Circle* (1993) for soprano, flute, and harp.

Stokes amassed a large output of instrumental music, of which the following is a representative sample: Trio for clarinet, violin, and piano (1955, rev. 1963)); *Expositions on Themes by Henry David Thoreau* for flute, oboe, trumpet, horn, violin, cello, piano, accordion, and percussion (1970); *Eldey Island* for flute or recorder and tape (1971); *Circles in a Round* for piano and tape (1972); *The Bob and Marjorie Music* for clarinet and horn (1974); *Spring Song* (*Phonic Paradigm II*) for five performers, springs, and found objects (1980); Wind Quintet no. 2 (1981), *Tintinnabulary* (*Phonic Paradigm IV*) for two percussion and tape (1983); *Give and Take* for oboe and cello (1984); *Susquehannas* for clarinet, piano, and two percussion (1985); *Brazen Cartographies* for brass quintet (1988); *The Lyrical Pickpocket* for flute, oboe, bassoon, and toy piano (1990); *Neon Nocturne* for 8 trombones (1990); *Whittlings* for four players (1992); *Tantamounts* for four flutes and string quartet (1996); and *Shadows* for two also saxophones (1996).

Eric Stokes.
Courtesy Mrs. Eric Stokes.

His last work, *Out of the Cradle Endlessly Rocking,* was premiered posthumously at the University of Minnesota in 2000. It is scored for symphonic wind ensemble, concert choir, chamber singers, baritone, and soprano soloists, and narrator. It is a setting of an adaptation of the poem by Walt Whitman.

STOUT, ALAN (BURRAGE)
b. Baltimore, Maryland, 26 November 1932

Stout studied at Johns Hopkins University (1950–54) and at the Peabody Conservatory, Baltimore (1950–54), where he was a pupil of Henry Cowell. At the University of Washington (1958–59), he received composition lessons from John Verrall. He was also a pupil of Wallingford Riegger in New York and Vagn Holmboe in Copenhagen (1954–55). Since 1963 he has taught theory and composition at Northwestern University, Evanston, Illinois, becoming a professor in 1976.

Stout is a prolific composer. His major works for orchestra include four symphonies: no. 1 (1959), no. 2 (1951–66), no. 3 with soprano and male chorus (1959–62), and no. 4 for chorus and orchestra (1970). Also for orchestra are *Three Hymns* (1953–54), *Eight Movements* with solo violin (1962), *Fanfare for Charles Seeger* (1972), and *Pilvia* (1983). For chamber orchestra he has written *Antiphonal Music, Four Antiphonies, Interlude,* and *Velut Umbra.* Works for string orchestra include *Pieta* (1957), *Ricercare and Aria* (1959), and *Nimbus* (1949).

Among Stout's compositions for solo instruments are *Intermezzo* for English horn, strings, and percussion (1954); *Serenity* for cello, strings, and percussion (1959); *Movements* for clarinet and strings (1969); *Aria* for flute, strings, and percussion; and *Capriccio* for oboe, harp, and strings (1967).

Stout has composed several works for solo voice and orchestra: *Die Engel* (Rilke) (1957), *Two Ariel Songs* (1957), *Christmas Poem* (e. e. cummings) (1962), *Canticum Canticorum* (1962), and *Solo* (1968), all for soprano soloist; *Two Hymns* for tenor (1952); *George Lieder* for baritone (1962); *Laudi* for soprano and tenor (1962, rev. 1970); and two works for alto, *Nattstycken* (*Nocturnes*), with speaker (1969–70), and *Visages de Laforgue* (1977). For soprano and piano he composed *Five Songs from Afronland* (1967).

His choral music comprises a setting of the *Passion* for six soloists, chorus, and orchestra (1953–68); *The Great Day of the Lord* for chorus and organ (1956); *Prologue* for soprano, tenor, chorus, and orchestra (1963–64); *Dialogo per la pascua* for soloist, chorus, and instrumental ensemble (1973); *Gamma* for unaccompanied voices (1978); and *Triptych* for soprano, children's choir, and orchestra (1981).

Among his many instrumental works are ten string quartets (1953, 1953, 1954, 1955, 1957, 1959, 1960, 1961, 1962, 1962); *Serenity* for bassoon (or cello) and piano (1957); a Clarinet Quintet (1958); Suite for flute and percussion (1962); a Cello Sonata (1965); *Toccata* for alto saxophone and percussion (1965); *Study in Densities and Durations* for organ (1965); *Music for oboe and piano* (1966); *Music for flute and percussion* (1965); *Music for flute and harpsichord* (1967); *Capriccio, Recitative and Aria* for oboe, harp, and percussion (1967); *Movements* for clarinet and string quartet (1969); *Pulsar* for three brass choirs and timpani (1972); Suite for saxophone and organ (1973); Sonata for two pianos (1975); *Study in Timbres and Interferences* for organ (1977); *Nimbus* for strings and harp (1978); and a Brass Quintet (1984).

STRANG, GERALD
b. *Claresholm, Alberta, Canada, 13 February 1908*
d. *Loma Linda, California, 2 November 1983*

Strang graduated from Stanford University in 1928 and later studied at the University of California, Berkeley (1929) and the University of Southern California in Los Angeles (1935–36). In 1948 he received his doctorate from UCLA for his Second Symphony. His principal teachers were Charles Koechlin, Arnold Schoenberg, and Ernst Toch.

From 1935 to 1940 he was managing editor of New Music Editions. In 1935 he joined the music faculty of UCLA where he was an assistant to Arnold Schoenberg. From 1938 to 1958 he taught at Long Beach College. In 1958 he was appointed professor of music at San Fernando Valley State College. In 1965 he transferred to California State University, Long Beach, as chairman of the music department. In 1969 he returned to UCLA as lecturer in electronic music, a post he held until his retirement in 1974.

Strang's orchestral works include Suite for chamber orchestra (1934–35); *Intermezzo* (1937); *Canzonet* for strings (1942); two symphonies (1942, 1947); *Overland Trail* (1943); *Concerto Grosso* (1951); a Concerto for cello and wind instruments (1951); and a Violin Concerto.

Among his early instrumental compositions are *Mirrorrorrim* for piano (1931); *Two Piano Pieces* (1931–32); Clarinet Sonatina (1932); Clarinet Quintet (1933); two string quartets (1934, 1937); and *Percussion Music* for three players (1935). Later chamber works are Divertimento for four instruments (1948), Violin Sonata (1949), Flute Sonata (1951), and *Variations* for four instruments (1956).

In addition to an incomplete choral work, *Vanzetti in the Death House* for baritone, choir, and small or-chestra (begun 1937), Strang wrote two pieces for chorus, *Three Excerpts from Walt Whitman* (1950) and *Every Night and Every Morn* (Blake) (1960).

After 1963, he composed only tape music, using equipment at the Bell Telephone Laboratories, New Jersey and UCLA. With the assistance of a computer, he constructed a set of *Compusitions,* ten in number (1963–72). With the Moog and Buchla synthesizers at UCLA he composed a group of nine *Synthions* (1969–71) and *Four Synclavions* for tape (1983). Strang was also an acoustical consultant, contributing to the design of at least 25 buildings and auditoria.

STREET, TISON
b. *Boston, Massachusetts, 20 May 1943*

Street studied violin with Einar Hasson of the Boston Symphony Orchestra (1951–59) before entering Harvard University, where he was a pupil of Leon Kirchner and David Del Tredici (B.A., 1965; M.A., 1971). He was Composer-in-Residence at the Marlboro Music Festival (1964–66, 1972) and taught at the University of California at Berkeley (1971–72). From 1979 to 1982 he was a member of the music faculty of Harvard University.

For orchestra Street has written *Adagio in E-flat* for oboe and strings (1977), *Montsalvat* (1980), and *Variations on a Ground* for organ and orchestra (1981). His instrumental music includes a String Trio (1963); *Variations* for flute, guitar, and cello (1964); two string quartets (1972, 1984); a String Quintet (1974); *John Major's Medley* for guitar (1977); *Three Pieces* for four viols and harpsichord (1977); and *Arias* for violin and piano (1978). For piano he has written *Phantasy* (1975), *Chords from the Northeast* (1976), and *Gradus ad Parnassum* (1976).

Among his vocal pieces are *Six Odds and Ends from "So Much Depends"* (William Carlos Williams, James Joyce) for soprano, tenor, string quartet, and piano (1964–73) and *Three Sacred Anthems* for chorus (1973).

STRINGFIELD, LAMAR EDWIN
b. *Raleigh, North Carolina, 10 October 1897*
d. *Asheville, North Carolina, 21 January 1959*

Although at first Stringfield intended to go into medicine, his interest in music led him to learn the flute, and he entered the Institute for Musical Art in New York as a pupil of Georges Barrère. He also studied with Percy Goetschius and Nadia Boulanger. For many years he played the flute in various orchestras and held several conducting posts.

Much of his music was influenced by the folksongs

of the southern United States, as reflected in the titles of many works. In 1928 he was awarded the Pulitzer Prize for his symphonic poem *From the Mountains*, which makes use of folk music. Also for orchestra are *Tango* (1921); *Valse Triste* (1921); *Indian Legend* (1923); *From the Southern Mountains* (1927); *From a Negro Melody* for strings (1928); a symphonic fantasy, *At the Factory* (1929); *A Negro Parade* (1931); a symphonic ballad, *The Legend of John Henry* (1932); a symphonic suite, *Moods of the Moonshiner* (1934); the symphonic sketches *From the Blue Ridge* (1936); a symphonic poem, *Peace* (1942); and *Mountain Dawn* for flute and strings (1945). Stringfield also composed four pieces for band: *The Desert Wanderer* (1921), *Mountain Suite* (1922), *Asheville Kewana's March* (1929), and *Georgia Buck* (1949).

Many of his shorter chamber works were composed for himself to play and have evocative titles from local folklore: *Mountain Echoes* for flute and harp (1921); *Indian Sketches* for flute and string quartet (1922); *Mountain Sketches* for flute, cello, and piano (1923); *Fugue* for string quartet (1924); *The Ole Swimmin' Hole* for flute, viola, and cello (1924); Suite for flute and oboe (1925); *Elegy* for cello and piano (1930); a Wind Quintet (1932); *Mountain Episode* for string quartet (1933); and *Dance of the Frogs* for chamber ensemble (1939).

For the stage Stringfield composed an opera, *The Mountain Song* (1929), a musical comedy, *Carolina Charcoal* (1951–53), and a ballet, *The Seventh Queue* (1928). His two choral work are a cantata, *Peace* for choir and organ (1949) and *About Dixie* for choir and orchestra (1950).

Stringfield composed many solo songs, including *My Heart is Heavy* (1923); *A Song of a Tree* (1923); *The Moon* (1926); *Fly Low, Vermillion Dragon* (with orchestra) (1925); *The Vagabond's Prayer* for baritone and orchestra (1925); and *On a Moonbeam* for voice, flute and piano (1938).

He founded the Institute of Folk Music at the University of North Carolina in 1930 for the study of native American music, and was the author of two books: *America and Her Music* (1931) and *Guide for Young Flutists* (1945).

STRONG, GEORGE TEMPLETON
b. New York, New York, 26 May 1856
d. Geneva, Switzerland, 27 June 1948

Strong was born into a musical family. As a child he learned both violin and piano and later turned to the oboe, which he played in the Metropolitan Opera orchestra. In 1879 he entered the Leipzig Conservatory, where he studied piano, horn, oboe, violin, and com-

position. Among his teachers were Salomon Jadassohn, Richard Hofmann, and Carl Reinecke. In 1886 he settled in Wiesbaden, where he became a close friend of Edward MacDowell and later knew Wagner, Liszt, and Joachim Raff. Partly for health reasons he went to live in Vevey, Switzerland in 1890. On the advice of MacDowell he taught for a year at the New England Conservatory in Boston (1891–92) but returned to Switzerland, as he felt American composers could find no recognition in their own country.

Disillusioned with music he devoted the years from 1897 to 1912 to watercolor painting, for which he had some talent. In 1913 he settled in Geneva, where he began composing again with the active encouragement of two conductors, Carl Ehrenberg and Ernest Ansermet, who offered to perform his works. Still considering himself an American composer, he nonetheless remained in Geneva for the rest of his life, writing prolifically and contributing to the musical life of the city. Although he admired the works of Richard Strauss, Mahler, Debussy, and Ravel, his own compositions reflected late 19th-century romanticism devoid of any modernistic trends.

Strong's orchestral music includes two symphonic poems, *Ein Totentanz* (1878) and *Undine* (1883), which was dedicated to Liszt. He wrote three symphonies: no. 1, *In the Mountains*, no. 2, *Sintram* (*after Fouqué*) (1892), and no. 3, *An der See*, the score of which is lost. Also for orchestra are *Ein Märchen*: (*A Fairy Tale*) for violin and orchestra (1983); *Americana* (*Two American Sketches*) for violin and orchestra (1904); *The Night* (*Four Little Symphonic Poems*) conducted by Ansermet in Montreux in 1913; *Le Roi Arthur* (1891–1916), premiered by Ansermet in Geneva in 1918; *Elegie* for cello and orchestra (1917); *Un vie d'artiste* for violin and orchestra (1917), dedicated to Joseph Szigeti; *Hallali* for horn and orchestra (1923); Suite for cello and orchestra (1923); *Chorale on the O Scared Head Sore Wounded by Hans Leo Hassler* for strings (1929); *Pollainiani*, six pieces for cello and orchestra (1931); *Cortege Oriental* (1941); and *D'un cahier d'images I – III* (*From a Notebook of Sketches*(1939–43).

Among his many choral works are a cantata, *The Haunted Mill* (1887); *Knights and Dryads* for soloists, chorus, and orchestra; and two cantatas on German texts, *Wie ein fahrender Hornist sich ein Land erblies* and *Die verlassene Mühle*.

Strong's chamber works include a Wind Quintet (*Cinq Aquarelles*; 1933), a String Quartet (1935), and numerous keyboard pieces, notably *Three Symphonic Idylls* for two pianos (1887), dedicated to MacDowell, and *25 Preludes* for solo piano (1929).

A biography of Strong, *An American Romantic – Realist Abroad* by William C. Loring Jr., was published in 1996. Vera Lawrence's multi-volume *Strong on*

Music uses his diaries to survey 19th-century musical life in New York City.

STRUBE, GUSTAV

b. Ballenstedt, Germany, 3 March 1867
d. Baltimore, Maryland, 2 February 1953

After graduating from the Leipzig Conservatory, where he had received tuition from Adolph Brodsky (violin) and Carl Reinecke (composition), Strube played in the Leipzig Gewandhaus and Opera orchestras. In 1890 he emigrated to the United States, becoming a member of the Boston Symphony Orchestra (1891–1913). He also conducted the Boston "Pops" Orchestra. He left Boston in 1913 to live in Baltimore, where he taught composition at the Peabody Conservatory of Music, becoming director in 1916; he retired in 1946. Among his pupils were Mary Howe and Colin McPhee. In 1916 he helped to found the Baltimore Symphony Orchestra and was appointed its conductor, a post he held until 1930.

Strube was a prolific composer, writing four symphonies: an early unnumbered one in C minor (1896), No. 1 in B minor (1910), No. 2 in G (1921–22), and the *Lanier Symphony* (1925), a tribute to the 19th century American composer, writer, and poet Sidney Lanier. Also for orchestra are *Fantastic Overture* (1904); *Berceuse* for strings (1908); *Fantastic Dance* (1908); *Overture Puck* (1910); a symphonic poem, *The Lorelei* (1911–12); *Narcissus and Echo* (1911–12); *Four Preludes* (1920); a Sinfonietta (1922); *Little Symphony no. 1* (1922); Divertimento for chamber orchestra (1925); *Symphonic Prelude* (1925); *Americana* (1930); *Sylvan Scenes* (1930); a symphonic poem, *Harz Mountains* (1940); and *Peace Overture* (1945).

Among Strube's extensive output of chamber music are two string quartets (1923, 1936); a Sonata and Sonatina for violin and piano (both 1923); a Viola Sonata (1924); a Cello Sonata (1925); a Piano Trio (1925); a Woodwind Quintet (1930); and a Trio for clarinet, horn and piano (1936).

His three-act opera, *The Captive,* originally entitled *Ramona,* was completed in 1914. Strube wrote one choral work, a cantata, *Lazarus* for solo quartet, chorus, and orchestra, performed in 1926.

He was the author of *The Theory and Use of Chords* (1928), which was widely used at one time.

STUCKY, STEVEN (EDWARD)

b. Hutchinson, Kansas, 7 November 1949

Stucky studied with Richard Willis at Baylor University, Waco, Texas (B.M., 1971) and at Cornell University (M.F.A., 1973; D.M.A, 1978) with Karel Husa, Robert Palmer, and Burrill Phillips. In addition he was a conducting pupil of Daniel Sternberg. He taught at Lawrence University, Appleton, Wisconsin (1978–80) before joining the music faculty at Cornell University in 1980, where he continues to teach, serving as music department chair (1992–97). From 1988 to 1992 he was Composer-in-Residence with the Los Angeles Philharmonic Orchestra, serving as new music advisor (1992–2000) and consulting composer (from 2002). He was visiting professor at the Eastman School of Music, Rochester, New York (2001–02) and Ernest Bloch Professor of Composition at the University of California, Berkeley, in 2003.

For orchestra Stucky has written *Prelude and Toccata* (1969); four symphonies: no. 1 (1972), no. 2 (1974), no. 3 (1976), and no. 4, *Kennigar* (1977–78); *Transparent Things*: *In Memoriam V. N.* (1980); Double Concerto for violin, oboe and chamber orchestra (1982–85); *DreamWaltzes* (1986); Concerto for Orchestra (1986–87); *Threnos* for wind ensemble (1987–88); *Son et Lumiere* (1988); *Angelus* (1989–90); *Impromptus* (1989–91); *Anniversary Greeting* (1991); *Fanfare for Los Angeles* (1993); *Fanfare for Cincinnati* (1993); *Ancora* (1994); *Fanfares and Arias* for wind ensemble (1994); Concerto for two flutes (1994); *Pinturas de Tamayo* (1995); *Music* for saxophones and strings (1996); *Concerto Mediterraneo* for guitar and chamber orchestra (1997–98); *Etudes*, concerto for recorder and chamber orchestra (2000); Concerto for percussion and winds (2001); *Colburn Variations* for strings (2002); and *Spirit Voices* for solo percussion and orchestra (2003).

Among his instrumental compositions are Quartet for clarinet, viola, cello, and piano (1973); *Notturno* for alto saxophone and piano (1981); *Varianti* for flute, clarinet, and piano (1982); *Voyages* for cello and wind orchestra (1983–84); *Boston Fancies* for flute, clarinet, string trio, piano, and percussion (1985); Serenade for wind quintet (1989–90); *Salute* for eight players (1997); *Ad Parnassum* for flute, clarinet, violin, cello, piano, and percussion (1998); *Nell 'ombra, nella luce* for string quartet (1999–2000); and *Albumleaves* for piano (2002).

Stucky's solo vocal music includes *Three Songs* for soprano, clarinet, viola, and piano (1969); *Schneemusik* for soprano and piano (1973); *Two Holy Sonnets of Donne* for mezzo-soprano, oboe, and piano (1982); *Sappho Fragments* for mezzo-soprano, flute, clarinet, violin, cello, piano, and percussion (1982); *Four Poems of A. R. Ammons* for baritone, flute, clarinet, horn, viola, cello, and double bass (1992); *American Muse* for baritone and orchestra (1999); and *To Whom I Said Farewell* for mezzo-soprano and ensemble (2003).

Among Stucky's choral works are four pieces for

chorus: *Nature Like Us* (Emily Dickinson; 1971), *Cradle Songs* (1997), *Skylarks* (2001), and *Whispers* (2002).

He is the author of a pioneering book, *Lutoslawski and His Music,* published in 1981.

SUBOTNICK, MORTON
b. *Los Angeles, California, 14 April 1933*

Subotnick studied at the University of Southern California, the University of Denver, and Mills College, Oakland, California (1957–58), where he was a pupil of Leon Kirschner and Darius Milhaud. Until 1966 he was a professional clarinet player. In 1959 he joined the faculty at Mills College. From 1961 to 1967 he was music director of the Anna Halprin Dance Company. He moved to New York in 1966, where he taught for a year at New York University before becoming music director of the Repertory Theater of Lincoln Center. He was also music director of the original Electric Circus at St. Marks Place, New York City.

While at Mills College, he co-founded the San Francisco Tape Music Center. In 1969 he was appointed dean of music and director of the Electronic Music Studio at the California Institute of Arts in Valencia. Subotnick has been a visiting professor of composition at the University of Maryland, University of Pittsburgh, Yale University (1980, 1982), and Brooklyn College, New York (1983–84). In addition to a Guggenheim Fellowship, he has received awards from the National Endowment for the Arts, the American Academy of Arts and Letters, and D. A. A. D.

(Deutscher Akademische Austauschdienst) as Composer-in-Residence, Berlin.

Almost all of Subotnick's extant compositions use electronic and multimedia techniques. These include *Mandolin* for viola, tape, and light projection (1963); *Play! no. 1* for chamber orchestra, tape, and film (1963); *Play! no. 2* for orchestra and tape (1963); *Play! no. 3* for one player, tape, and film (1965); and *Play! no. 4,* a multimedia piece for soprano, piano, vibraphone, cello, electronic sound, and film (1965). He has also composed *Ten,* originally entitled *The Tarot,* for ten instruments and tape (1963, rev. 1976) and *Misfortunes of the Immortals,* a concerto for wind quintet, two film projectors, electronic sound, and lights (in collaboration with Joan La Barbara and Mark Coniglio; 1996).

Two major creations, *Silver Apples of the Moon* (Yeats; 1966) and *The Wild Bull* (1967), a Sumerian lament, are electronic scores commissioned by Nonesuch Records. He followed these with *Parades and Changes* (1967); *Reality I and II* (1968); *Touch* (1969); *Sidewinder* (1970); *Four Butterflies* (1973); *Until Spring* (1975); *A Sky of Cloudless Sulphur* (1978); and *Return* (1984), all for tape. In 1968 Subotnick provided an *Electronic Prelude and Interludes* for the film *2001, a Space Odyssey.*

Lamination for orchestra and electronic effects (1966) derives its title from the layering of orchestral and electrical effects. *Two Butterflies* for orchestra was composed in 1975 for the Los Angeles Philharmonic Orchestra. To a Bicentennial commission for the six major American orchestras he wrote *Before the Butterfly* for seven amplified instruments and orchestra (1975). *Place* (1978) was commissioned by the Oregon

The San Francisco Tape Center, 1963: Tony Mertin, Bill McGinnis, Ramon Sender, Morton Subotnick, and Pauline Oliveros.
Courtesy Morton Subotnick.

Symphony Orchestra. Other works include three *Serenades* for tape and instruments (1959); *Four Preludes* for piano solo and tape (1960–66); *Ritual Electronic Chamber Music* for electric lights, sound consoles, and eight players (1968); *A Ritual Game Room* for electronic sounds on tape, lights, dancer, and four game players (but no audience (1970); *Into Two Worlds* for saxophone and electronics (1987–88); *And Butterflies Began to Sing* for Yamaha Computer Assisted Music System and chamber orchestra (1988); *A Desert Flower* (1989); and *Echoes for the Silent Call of Girona* for nine instruments and CD-ROM (1998).

Subotnick has written incidental music for the stage: *King Lear* (Shakespeare) (1960), *The Balcony* (Genet) (1960), *Galileo* (Brecht) (1964), *The Caucasian Chalk Circle* (Brecht) (1965), and *Danton's Death* (Büchner) (1966). *Silver Apples of the Moon* has been choreographed by Netherlands Ballet, Ballet Rambert of London, and the Glen Tetley Dance Company. Another electronic score, *Ice Floe,* was premiered by the London Contemporary Dance Theatre in 1978. Also for the stage he has written a multimedia piece, *The Double Life of Amphibians* in three parts (1984), and an opera, *Jacob's Room*, produced in Philadelphia in April 1993.

In the 1970's Subotnick began a series of "ghost pieces" for solo instruments and tape. The tape has no audible sounds, but contains information that triggers electronic equipment. This in turn modifies instrumental sounds as they are being played; thus the soloist provides her or his own electronic accompaniment. The modifications affect pitch, timbre, volume, and direction of sounds. Works in this series are *Two Life Histories* (voice and clarinet, 1977); *Liquid Strata* (piano, 1977); *The Wild Beasts* (trombone and piano, 1978); *Passage of the Beast* (clarinet, 1978); *The Last Dream of the Beast* (female voice, 1979); *Parallel Lines* (piccolo and nine instruments, 1979); *After the Butterfly* (trumpet and seven instruments, 1979); *The First Dream of Light* (tuba and piano, 1980); *Ascent into Air* for instrumental ensemble (1981); *Axolotl* for cello and chamber orchestra (1982); *An Arsenal of Defense* for viola and eight instruments (1982); *The Fluttering of Wings* for string quartet (1982); *Trembling* for violin and piano (1983); *The Key to Songs* for chamber orchestra (1985) also produced as a ballet; and *All My Hummingbirds Have Alibis* for flute, cello, MIDI-piano, and MIDI-mallets (1991).

His works for instruments without electronics include two piano preludes, *The Blind Owl* and *The Feast* (1956); Viola Sonata (1959); a String Quartet (1960); Sonata for piano duet (1960); three serenades: no. 1 for flute, clarinet, vibraphone, mandolin, cello, and piano (1960), no. 2 for clarinet, horn, percussion, and piano (1962), and no. 3 for flute, clarinet, violin, piano, and tape (1963); *Ten* for ensemble (1963, rev. 1970); and *Intimate Immensity* for ensemble (1997).

In 1979 Subotnick married the singer Joan La Barbara.

SUDERBURG, ROBERT CHARLES

b. Spencer, Iowa, 28 January 1936

Suderburg was educated at the University of Minnesota under Paul Fetler (B.A., 1957), Yale University under Quincy Porter and Richard Donovan (M.M., 1960), and the University of Pennsylvania with George Rochberg (Ph.D., 1966). He has taught at Bryn Mawr College, Pennsylvania (1960–61), the University of Pennsylvania (1961–65), and the Philadelphia Music Academy (1963–66). He was chancellor of the North Carolina School of Arts, Winston-Salem (1974–84) and president of the Cornish Institute, Seattle (1984–85). From 1985 until his retirement in 2001, he taught at Williams College, Williamstown, Massachusetts.

Suderburg's best-known work is a Piano Concerto, subtitled *Within the Mirror of Time.* It was first performed in October 1974 by Béla Siki, for whom it was written, accompanied by the Seattle Symphony Orchestra under Milton Katims. Other orchestral works include *Orchestral Music I* (1969), *Wind/Vents* (1973), a Percussion Concerto (1977), and a Harp Concerto (1981). For concert band he has composed *Concert Sets* (1971).

His principal vocal works are two cantatas, no. 1, *Revelations of St. John the Divine* for soprano and orchestra (1963), and no. 2 for tenor and orchestra (1966); *Stevenson (Chamber Music V)* for voice, string quartet, and tape (1976); *Voyage de Nuit* (Baudelaire) for solo voice and chamber orchestra (1978); and *Chamber Music IX (Breath and Circuses)* for voice, trombone, and piano (1991). Among his choral works are a *Concert Mass* for unaccompanied voices (1960); *Composition on Traditional Carols* for chorus, congregation, and brass (1965); and *Choruses on Poems of Yeats* for soprano, tenor, chorus, and orchestra (1966).

Suderburg's instrumental works in include *Six Moments* for piano (1962); *Chamber Music I* for violin and cello (1967), *II* for string quartet (1975), *III*, *Night Set* for trombone and piano, *IV*, *Ritual Series* for percussion ensemble (1975), *IV* for viola and double bass (1980), *VIII* for brass and piano (1988), *X*, *Entertainment – Sets* for brass quintet (1992) and *XI*, *Strophes of Night and Dawn* (after Baudelaire) for brass quintet (1992); *Solo Music I* for violin (1971); *Fanfare for Bowdoin* for brass quartet (1993); and *Solo Music III* for clarinet (1996).

SUR, DONALD

b. Honolulu, Hawaii, 1 February 1935
d. Boston, Massachusetts, 24 May 1999

Sur was educated at the University of California, Berkeley under Seymour Shifrin; at the University of California, Los Angeles with Colin McPhee; at Princeton University with Earl Kim and Roger Sessions; and at Harvard University. In addition he studied in Korea (1965–70). From 1968 he taught at the Massachusetts Institute of Technology in Cambridge and worked for several radio stations.

Sur's compositions include *The Sleepwalker's Ballad* (Lorca) for soprano and chamber ensemble (1962); *Katana II* for chamber ensemble (1962); *Intonations before Sotoba Komachi* for chamber ensemble (1966, rev. 1975); *Piano Fragments* (1966); *Red Dust* for an orchestra of 29 Korean percussion instruments (1967); and *Book of Catenas*. Other works include *Il Tango di Trastevere* (for four double basses, later orchestrated for orchestra of low-pitched instruments); *New Yorker Sketches* (1980; rev. 1984); Violin Concerto; *The Unicorn and the Lady* (based upon the Cloisters Tapestries); *Kumidori Tansaeng* (violin, chorus, and orchestra); *Lacrimosa* (chamber orchestra); *Sonnet 97* (a cappella chorus; 1999); and *Berceuse* for violin and piano, a Library of Congress commission (premiered February 1999). He also scored two films, Martha Hanslanger's *Penumbra, Focus and Echo* and Sai-Shid Kim-Gimbson's *Silence Broken: Korean Comfort Women* (1999).

Sur's best-known and most ambitious work, *Slavery Documents* (1989), was commissioned by Boston's Cantata Singers and Ensemble given its world premiere performance by them in 1990. It was his largest work, scored for vocal soloists, chorus, organ, and large orchestra; Sur was working on a sequel to *Slavery Documents* when he died.

SURINACH, CARLOS

b. Barcelona, Spain, 4 March 1915
d. New York, New York 26 November 1997

Surinach attended the Municipal Conservatory in Barcelona (1929–36), where he was a pupil of Enrique Morera. He spent the years 1940 to 1943 in Germany, first at the Robert Schumann Conservatory in Düsseldorf as a student of piano and then at the Hochschule in Cologne, where he was a conducting pupil of Eugen Papst. From 1941 to 1943 he also studied composition under Max Trapp at the Prussian Academy of the Arts in Berlin. He was conductor of the Barcelona Philharmonic Orchestra from 1944 to 1947.

In Paris (1947–51) he increased his reputation as a conductor, and in 1951 he moved to New York, becoming an American citizen in 1959. He taught at Carnegie-Mellon University, Pittsburgh (1966–67).

Among Surinach's honors were the Alexander von Humboldt Fellowship, the Arnold Bax Society Medal in Great Britain (1966), and the highest artist award in Spain, Knight Commander of the Order of Isabella I of Castile (1972). Surinach's music strongly reflects his Spanish origins, emphasizing more the percussive rhythms and sharply focused melodic lines than the customary romantic atmosphere usually associated with Spanish music.

For orchestra Surinach wrote *Passacaglia Symphony* (1945); Symphony no. 2 (1949); *Sinfonietta Flamenco*, composed in 1953 for the Louisville Orchestra; *Doppio Concertino* for violin, piano, and strings (1954); *Fandango*, commissioned in 1954 for the Utica (New York) Symphony Orchestra; *Overture: Feria Mágica* (1956); *Madrid 1890* for chamber orchestra (1956); *Sinfonía Chica* (1957); Concerto for Orchestra (1958); *Paeans and Dances of Heathen Iberia* for wind and percussion (1959); *Symphonic Variations* (1963); *Drama Jondo Overture* (1965), composed for the Milwaukee Symphony Orchestra; and *Melorhythmic Dramas* (1966). In addition to *Soleriana* for concert band (1971), later orchestral works include a Piano Concerto, composed in 1973 for Alicia de Larrocha; *Las Trompetas de los Serafines* (*The Trumpets of the Seraphim*), an overture (1973); a Harp Concerto (1978); Concerto for Strings (1978); and *Symphonic Melismas* (1993).

Surinach provided several important works for the stage. His one-act opera *El mozo que caso con mujer brava* (*The Taming of the Shrew*) was composed and produced at the Gran Teatro del Liceo in Barcelona (1948). In addition to five ballets based on music written originally for the concert hall, he composed 14 ballet scores: *Monte Carlo* (Barcelona, 1945); *Ritmo Jondo* (choreogaphed by Doris Humphrey, 1953); *Embattled Garden* (1958) and *Acrobats of God* (1960), both choreographed by Martha Graham; *A Place in the Desert* (Norman Morrice, 1960); choreographed by Norman Morrice, *David and Bathsheba* (John Butler, 1960); *Apasionada* (Pearl Lang, 1961); *Los Renegados* (Juan Anduze, 1965); *Vente Quemada* (George Skibine, 1966); *Agathe's Tale* (Paul Taylor, 1967); *Suite Espagnole* (Jose de Udaeta, 1970); *Chronique* (Graham, 1974); *The Owl and the Pussycat* commissioned by Graham and performed at New York's Metropolitan Opera House; and *Bodas de Sangre* (*Blood Wedding*; 1979). *Feast of Ashes* (Alvin Ailey, 1962), based on two orchestral works, *Ritmo Jondo* and *Doppio Concertante*, has received more than one thousand performances throughout the world.

Surinach's principal choral works are *Cantata of St. John* for mixed voices and percussion (1962); *Songs of the Soul* for mixed chorus (1964); *The Missions of San Antonio,* a symphonic canticle for men's chorus and orchestra (1968); *Via Crucis* for mixed voices and guitar (1969); and *Celebraciones Medievales* for chorus and concert band (1977). His vocal music includes *Romance, Oracion and Saeta* for soprano and piano (1958); *Four Tonadillas* for three voices and chamber ensemble (1961); *Flamenco Meditations* for voice and piano (1965); and *Prayers* for voice and guitar (1972).

Among his instrumental compositions are a Piano Quartet (1944); *Flamenquerias* for two pianos (1951); *Tres Cantos Berberes* for chamber ensemble (1952); *Tientos* for harp (or harpsichord); English horn, and timpani (1953); *Flamenco Cyclothymia* for violin and piano (1967); and a String Quartet (1974).

SUSA, CONRAD (STEPHEN)
b. Springdale, Pennsylvania, 26 April 1935

Susa studied at the Carnegie Institute of Technology, Pittsburgh with Lopatnikoff (B.F.A., 1957) and at the Juilliard School of Music, New York (M.S., 1961), where he was a pupil of William Bergsma and Vincent Persichetti. He has been strongly associated with the theater and was Composer-in-Residence at the Globe Theatre, San Diego, California (1959–90) and musical director of APA-Phoenix Repertory Company, New York (1961–68), and the Shakespeare Festival, Stratford, Connecticut (1969–70). He is currently chair, for the composition, counterpoint, orchestration, and music literature divisions at the San Francisco Conservatory of Music.

Susa's own works for the stage include four operas, *Transformation* (Minneapolis, 1973), *Black River* (Minneapolis, 1975), *The Love of Don Perlimplin* (1983), and *Dangerous Liaisons* (San Francisco, 1994); and a ballet, *Love-In,* based on the music of Handel. His scores for television films include *The Good Doctor* (1978), *The Skin of Our Teeth* (1983), and *All My Sons* (1986).

For orchestra he has written four pieces, *A Sonnet Voyage* (Symphony) (1963), *Eulogy* for strings, *The Blue Hour* (2002), and *Pastorale* for string quartet and string orchestra. Among his vocal music are three choral works, *Dawn Greetings* (1976), *The Chanticleer Carol* (1982), and *Earth Song* (1988); and *Hymns for the Amusement of Children* (Christopher Smart) for mezzo-soprano (or chorus) and piano (1972). Susa's instrumental music includes Serenade no. 5 for oboe, cello, and two percussion and *Serenade for Christmas Night* for organ, harp, and vibraphone.

SVOBODA, TOMÁŠ
b. Paris, France, 6 December 1939

Svoboda is of Czech origin. He studied at the Prague Conservatory under Miloslav Kabeláč, Václav Dobiáš, and Emil Hlobil (1954–62) and at the Prague Academy (1962–64). After settling in the United States in 1964, he attended the University of Southern California, Los Angeles (1966–69), where he was a pupil of Ingolf Dahl and Halsey Stevens. From 1970 until his retirement in 2001 he was professor of composition at Portland State University, Oregon.

For orchestra Svoboda has composed six symphonies: no. 1, *Of Nature* (1957); no. 2 (1962); no. 3 with organ (1965); no. 4, *Apocalyptic* (1974); no. 5, In Unison (1978); and no. 6 for clarinet and orchestra (1991). Other orchestral works include *Scherzo* for two euphoniums and orchestra (1955); *In a Linden's Shadow* (1958); *Dramatic Overture* (1959); *Six Variations* for violin and strings (1961); *Christmas Concertino* for harp and orchestra (1961); Suite for bassoon, harpsichord, and strings (1962); *Etude* for chamber orchestra (1963); *Three Pieces* for orchestra (1966); *Reflections* (1968); Sinfonietta (1972); *Labyrinth* for chamber orchestra (1974); *Prelude and Fugue* for

Tomáš Svoboda.
Courtesy the composer.

strings (1974); two piano concertos (1974, 1989); a Violin Concerto (1975); *Overture of the Season* (1978); *Nocturne* (*Cosmic Sunset*; 1981); *Eugene Overture* (1982); and *Ex Libris,* a Louisville Orchestra commission (1983).

More recent orchestral pieces include Serenade (1984); *Returns Concerto* for chamber orchestra (1986); *Dance Suite* (1987); *Three Cadenzas* for piano and orchestra (1990); *Swing Dance* (1992); *Meditation* for oboe and strings (1993); a Marimba Concerto (1994); *Three Oriental Echoes* for strings (1999); Sonata for Orchestra (2000); *Spring Overture* (2002); and Concerto for wind quintet. To the band repertory Svoboda has contributed two items: *Lamentation* for piccolo trumpet and winds (1975) and *Pastorale and Dance* (1983).

Instrumental works include *Evening Negro Songs and Dances* for piano and two percussionists (1956); three string quartets (1960, 1995, 2002); *Baroque Quintet* for flute, oboe, clarinet, cello, and piano (1962); Trio for oboe, bassoon, and piano (1962); Trio for oboe, bassoon, and piano (1962); *Septet* for bassoon, harpsichord, and strings (1962); Concertino for oboe, brass, and timpani (1966); *Chorale and Dance* for brass quintet (1967); *Two Epitaphs* for string quartet (1967); *Parabola* for clarinet, violin, viola, cello, and piano (1971); *Double Octet* for eight flutes and eight cellos (1971); *Prologue* for clarinet, harpsichord, and percussion (1972); Concerto for horn and tape (1979); Trio for flute, oboe, and bassoon (1979); *Passacaglia and Fugue* for piano trio (1981); and a Guitar Sonata (1981).

Among Svoboda's later chamber music are Trio for electric guitar, piano, and percussion (1982); Trio Sonata for electric guitar, vibraphone, and piano (1982); Brass Quintet (1983); Piano Trio (1984); Violin Sonata (1984); *Chorale in E-flat* (*Homage to Aaron Copland*) for clarinet, violin, viola, double bass, and piano (1985); *Phantasy* for piano trio (1985); *Legacy* for brass septet (1988); *Military Movements* for guitar and harpsichord (1991); *Theme and Variations* for flute, clarinet, and piano (1992); *Duo* for xylophone and marimba (1993); Quartet for horns (1993); *Arab Dance* for synthesizer (1994); *Summer Trio* for oboe, clarinet, and bassoon (1997); *Concealed Shapes* for two pianos and two percussion (1999); *Dreams of a Dancer* for flute, clarinet, and piano (1999); Suite for solo cello (1994/2000); *Chaconne* for six violins (2000); and Clarinet Sonata (2000).

For piano Svoboda has composed two sonatas (1967, 1985); *Bagatelles: "In the Forest"* (1976); *Children's Treasure Box,* 4 volumes (1977–78); *Eulogy* (1994); *Benedictus* (1998); a Sonata for two pianos (1972); and *Four Visions* for three pianos.

Among his vocal compositions are a setting of the 44th *Sonnet of Michelangelo* for alto and 11 instruments (1967), *Three Studies* for mezzo-soprano and orchestra (1981), and *Summer Fragments* for soprano and piano (1992). His choral music includes *A Child's Dream* for children's chorus and orchestra (1973); *Separate Solitude* for chorus and two clarinets (1973); *Celebration of Life,* a cantata on Aztec poetry for soprano, tenor, chorus, ensemble, and tape (1976); *Chorale Without Words* for chorus and piano (1984); a cantata, *Journey* for mezzo-soprano, baritone, chorus, and orchestra (1987); two pieces for male chorus, *Festival* (1987) and *Haleluya* (1990); and *The Road is Turning* for alto and mixed chorus (1996).

SWAN, TIMOTHY

b. Worcester, Massachusetts, 23 July 1758
d. Northfield, Massachusetts, 23 July 1842

Swan was a hatter by trade, but attendance at a singing school in Groton, New York, gave him a basic musical training. Like his contemporaries, he wrote hymn tunes, some of which are still heard today: *China, London, Ocean, Poland,* and *Pownall.* He published *The Songster's Assistant* in 1786, followed in 1801 by *The New England Harmony. The Songster's Museum* was issued in 1803. Swan was an admirer of William Billings and composed "fuging tunes," of which *Rainbow* is perhaps the best. In 1807 he moved to Northfield, where he died.

SWANSON, HOWARD

b. Atlanta, Georgia, 18 August 1907
d. New York, New York, 12 November 1978

At the age of nine, Swanson moved with his family to Cleveland, Ohio. After leaving school, he worked as a locomotive engineer, letter carrier, and mail clerk before deciding to study at the Cleveland Institute of Music under Herbert Elwell, graduating in 1936. The award of a Rosenwald Fellowship allowed him to go to Paris, where he became a pupil of Nadia Boulanger (1938–40). He returned to the United States in 1940, but spent some time during the Second World War in Spain. From 1941 to 1945 he worked for the Internal Revenue Service. In 1952 he returned to Paris, remaining until 1966, when he settled in New York. Although much of Swanson's music has not received the attention it deserves, his songs appear in recital programs.

After its premiere in New York in 1950, his *Night Music* was performed widely throughout the United States and was heard at the 1951 Edinburgh Festival. It shows the influence upon his style of Schoenberg's early music. Swanson's other important works for orchestra are three symphonies (1945, 1965, 1970); a neo-classical *Short Symphony* (1948), first performed by Mitropoulos the New York Philharmonic Orchestra and winner of the New York Music Critics' Circle Award (1952); *Music for Strings* (1951); Concerto for Orchestra (1954); a Piano Concerto (1956); *Fantasy Piece* for soprano saxophone and strings (1969); and *Threnody for Martin Luther King Jr.* for strings (1969).

Swanson's instrumental music includes *Nocturne* for violin and piano (1948); a Suite for cello and piano (1949); *Sound Piece* for brass quintet (1952); *Vista no. 2* for string octet (1964); a String Quartet (1965); a Trio for flute, oboe, and piano (1970); and a Cello Sonata (1973). For piano he composed three sonatas (1948, 1970, 1978) and *Nocturnes* (1967).

Of his many vocal pieces, *Songs of the American Poets* was much acclaimed after its premiere in New York in 1946. Other items for solo voice include *The Negro Speaks of Rivers* (1942), *The Junk Man* (1946), *Ghosts in Love* (1950), *The Valley* (1951), and *Songs for Patricia* for soprano and strings (1951). He composed a number of settings of poems by Carl Sandburg and Langston Hughes. His two surviving choral works are *Nightingale* for men's voices (1952) and *We Delighted My Friend* for chorus (1977).

SWIFT, RICHARD [GENE]
b. Middleport, Ohio, 24 September 1927
d. Davis, California, 8 November 2003

Swift studied privately with Grover Buxton and John Sherwood before entering the University of Chicago in 1953, where he was a pupil of Grosvenor Cooper, Leonard Meyer, and Leland Smith. In 1956 Swift joined the faculty of the University of California at Davis, acting as chairman of the music department (1963–71) and chairman of integrated studies (1969–71). He retired in 1991. From 1958 to 1964 he conducted the University Symphony Orchestra. In 1977 he was a visiting professor at Princeton University.

Swift's music was influenced by the composers of the Second Viennese School. For orchestra he wrote two concertos for piano and chamber orchestra (1961, 1980); a Divertimento (1950); *A Coronal* (1954), performed by the Louisville Orchestra in 1956; *Extravaganza* (1962); *Tristia* for orchestra without strings (1967); Concerto for violin and chamber orchestra (1968); a Symphony (1970); and *Some Trees* (1982).

Among his instrumental compositions are six string quartets (1955, 1958, 1964, 1973, 1981–2, 1991–92); a Flute Sonata (1951); String Trio (1954–55); *Study* for solo cello (1955); *Serenade Concertante* no. 1 for piano and wind quintet (1956); *Stravaganzas I – XIV*

Richard Swift.
Courtesy Dept. of Music, University of California, Davis.

for various instruments (1956–2000); Clarinet Sonata (1957); Sonata for solo violin (1957); the series *Music for a While*: *1.* for violin, viola, and harpsichord (1956), *II* for three instruments (1969), *III* for violin and harpsichord (1975), *IV* for string quartet (1991), and *V* for viola and piano (1993–94); *Domains II* for percussion (1963); *Domains III* for ensemble (1963); *Bucolics* for harpsichord and ensemble (1964); *Thrones* for alto flute and double bass (1966); *Prime* for alto saxophone and ensemble (1971); Piano Trio no. 1 for violin, cello, and piano (1976); *Electric Affinities* for cello and piano (1983); *Some Versions of Paraphrase* for violin, clarinet, and piano (1987); Piano Trio no. 2, *In the Country of the Blue* (1988); *A Stitch in Time* for guitar (1989); *A Field of Light* for eight instruments (1990); *Music for a While* for violin, viola,, and piano (1993–94); and *In Arcadia* for clarinet and string trio (1994).

Solo pieces for piano include *Stravaganzas II* (1958), *IX* (1978), *X* (1985), and *XIV* (2000); *Summer Notes* (1965); *Mein blaues Klavier* (1978); *Things of August* (1985); *Domains* (1986); *Radix Matrix* (1992); *Elegies* (2002); and a work for two pianos *Two Stanzas* (2001).

Swift composed several important works for solo voice and chamber ensemble: *Eve* (1959); *Domains I* (Robert Lowell) for baritone; *Carmina Archilochi* for soprano (1965); *Specimen Days* (Whitman) for soprano and orchestra (1976–77); *The Garden* (Andrew Marvell) for mezzo-soprano (1984); and *Roses Only* for soprano and orchestra (1991). For soprano and piano he has written *Great Praises* (R. Eberhart; 1977). His one choral composition is *Thanatopsis* (Lucretius) for mezzo-soprano, chorus, and ensemble (1971).

His opera *The Trial of Tender O'Shea* was staged in Davis, California, in August 1964.

SYDEMAN, WILLIAM
b. New York, New York, 8 May 1928

After attending Duke University, Durham, North Carolina (1944–45), Sydeman graduated from the Mannes School of Music in New York City in 1947 and continued his studies at Hartt College of Music, Hartford, Connecticut. He was a pupil of Roger Sessions, whose influence can be seen in his early works. Since then, the music of Webern and Boulez has affected his compositions, which feature linear motivic material. He taught at the Mannes School (1959–70) before traveling widely for twelve years, studying philosophy and religion. From 1980 to 1982 he taught at Rudolf Steiner College, Fair Oaks, California.

Although Sydeman has concentrated on instrumental works, he has written several important pieces for orchestra: *Orchestral Abstractions* (1958); *Three Studies* (1962–65); *Oecumenicus,* an extensive concerto for orchestra (1964); *In Memoriam: John F. Kennedy* with narrator (1966); *Texture Studies for Orchestra,* commissioned by the Koussevitzky Foundation in 1969; and a Viola Concerto.

For chamber orchestra Sydeman has composed *Concert Piece* for wind, brass, and percussion; Concertino for oboe, piano, and strings (1956); three *Concerti da Camera* with solo violin (1959–61); *Concert Piece* for horn and strings (1959); Double Concerto for trumpet, trombone, and strings (1965); *Music for viola, winds and percussion* (1966); Concerto for piano duet and chamber orchestra (1967); and *Five Movements* for winds (1973).

Sydeman's large output of works for smaller instrumental ensembles includes a String Quartet (1955); two wind quintets (1955, 1959); Divertimento for eight instruments (1957); Trio for violin, clarinet, and double bass (1957); *Seven Movements for Septet* (1958); Trio for flute, violin, and double bass (1958); *Westbrook Quintet* for clarinet, horn, double bass, piano, and percussion (1959); *Variations* for oboe and harpsichord (1959); Quintet for clarinet, horn, double bass, piano, and percussion (1960); Quartet for oboe and strings (1961); Trio for oboe, viola, and piano (1961); *Music for flute, guitar, viola, and percussion* (1962); *Homage*

to "*L'histoire de soldat*" (1962); Quartet for violin, flute, clarinet, and piano (1963); Trio for flute, double bass, and percussion (1963); *Fantasy and Two Epilogues* for flute, cello, and piano (1964); Brass Quintet (1964); *Texture Studies* for wind quintet (1966); Trio for bassoon, bass clarinet, and piano (1968); *Trio Montagnana* for clarinet, violin, and piano (1971); Quartet for flute, violin, trumpet, and double bass (1973); and *Two Movements* for violin and piano (1978).

Sydeman has taken a particular interest in writing duos for a variety of instruments. Some of the pairings are unusual: flute and piano, clarinet and double bass, horn and clarinet, viola and harpsichord, violin and harpsichord (1963), violin and piano (1963), trumpet and percussion (1963), clarinet and piano (1966), xylophone and double bass (1968), two double basses (1970), horn and piano (1971), two percussionists (1971), violin and double bass (1972), two clarinets (1974), two horns (1976), *18 Duos* for two violins (1976), clarinet and tenor saxophone (1977), two clarinets (1977), xylophone and vibraphone (1977), and violin and cello (1979).

In addition he has composed sonatas for solo violin (1966), solo clarinet, and solo cello; *For Double Bass Alone* (1957); *The Last Orpheus* for bass flute (1976); and *Music for Xylophone* (1976). His keyboard music includes a Piano Sonata (1961), *Fantasy Piece* for harpsichord (1965), and *Short Piano Pieces* (1980). *Projections I* for amplified violin, tape, and slides (1968) was his first excursion into multimedia music. *Piece for clarinet and tape* dates from 1970.

Among Sydeman's vocal works are *Four Japanese Songs* for soprano and two violins; *Three Songs After Emily Dickinson* for soprano and cello; *Three Songs on Elizabethan Texts* for soprano and flute; *Songs* for soprano or tenor, flute, and cello (1959); *Maledictions* for tenor, string quartet, and tape (1970); *Full Circle* for three solo voices, clarinet, trombone, cello, percussion, and organ (1971); *Fugue* for string quartet and optional soprano (1976); *Five Short Songs* (1978); *Long Life Prayer* for voice and speaker (1978); and *Love Songs on Japanese Poems* for soprano, flute, and violin (1978). Sydeman's choral music includes *The Lament of Elektra* (Sophocles) for alto, chorus, and chamber ensemble (1964); a cantata, *Prometheus* for two male soloists, female chorus, and orchestra (1968); two pieces for unaccompanied mixed voices, *Round* (1978) and *The Lord's Prayer* (1980); and *Calendar of the Soul* (Rudolf Steiner) for multi-chorus (1982).

For the stage he has written an opera, *Aria Da Capo,* based on Edna St. Vincent Millay's play (1982); *Songs of Milarepa* (Tibetan Buddhist writings) for violin, narrator, and dancers (1980); and incidental music for *Antichrist* (Solovieff; 1981) and *A Winter's Tale* (Shakespeare; 1982).

T

TALMA, LOUISE JULIETTE
b. Arcachon, France, 31 October 1906
d. Yaddo, Saratoga Springs, New York, 13 August 1996

Louise Talma was born in France of American parents. Her mother, Alma Cecile Garrigue, was an opera singer; her father, Frank, a pianist. Following the death of her father, she and her mother settled in New York in 1914. From 1922 to 1930 she attended the Institute of Musical Art in New York where she was a pupil of Howard Brockway. She was also a student at New York University (1930–31) and Columbia University (1932–33). At Fontainebleau she studied with Isador Philipp for piano and Nadia Boulanger for composition.

Talma taught ear training and theory at the Manhattan School of Music (1926–28). In 1928 she joined the faculty at Hunter College, New York where she was appointed a professor of music in 1952. She also taught at the Fontainebleau School of Music (1936–39, 1978). She was awarded two Guggenheim Fellowships (1946, 1947). In 1974, she became the first woman composer to be elected to the National Institute of Arts and Letters, now the American Academy and Institute of Arts and Letters. She was also the first woman to receive the Sibelius Medal for Composition in London (1963).

At first, Talma belonged to the so-called Stravinsky School, and her early compositions reflected that composer's neo-classicism. After 1953 she was a serialist. Her most important work, the three-act opera *The Alcestiad*, to a libretto by Thornton Wilder, was performed in Frankfurt-am-Main, Germany in March 1962.

Orchestral music includes her first success, *Toccata* (1944), performed by the Baltimore Symphony Orchestra in 1945; *Dialogues* for piano and orchestra (1963–64), premiered in Buffalo in 1965 with Grant

Louise Talma.
From the Collections of the Library of Congress.

Johannesen as soloist; and *Full Circle* (1985).

Talma's choral compositions include *In Principio Erat Verbum* (St. John) for chorus and organ (1939); *Carmina Mariana* for female voices and piano (1943); an oratorio, *The Divine Flame* for soloists, chorus, and orchestra (1946–48); *The Leaden Echo and the Golden Echo* (G. M. Hopkins) for soprano, double chorus, and piano (1950–51); and a choral suite, *Let's Touch the Sky* (e.e. cummings) for chorus and woodwind (1952). Later choral compositions are *A Time to Remember*, to texts from the Bible and by John F. Kennedy for mixed choir and orchestra (1966–67), performed in New York in 1968; and *Voices of Peace* for chorus and strings (1973), premiered in Philadelphia in 1974. *Celebrations* for women's chorus and small orchestra was presented in Dallas, Texas in 1978. A setting of Psalm 84 for chorus dates from the same year. Her last choral setting was *Mass for the Sundays of the Year*, completed in 1984.

The song cycle *Terre de France* for soprano or tenor and piano dates from 1945. After becoming a serial composer she wrote *La Corona*, seven sonnets of John Donne for unaccompanied chorus (1955), and a cantata, *All the Days of My Life* for tenor, clarinet, cello, piano, and percussion (1963). *The Tolling Bell*, a triptych for baritone and orchestra on words by Shakespeare, Marlowe, and Donne, was performed in Milwaukee in 1969. Other vocal works include *Diadem* for tenor, violin, cello, flute, clarinet, and piano (1978–79); *Thirteen Ways of Looking at a Blackbird* for tenor, oboe, and piano (1979); and *Have You Heard? Do You Know?*, seven scenes for soprano, mezzo-soprano, tenor, and chamber ensemble (1974–76), premiered in New York in 1981.

Talma's instrumental compositions include a String Quartet (1954); a Violin Sonata (1962); *Three Duologues* for clarinet and piano (1967–68); *Summer Sounds*, a quintet for clarinet and strings (1969–73); *Lament* for cello and piano (1980); *Studies in Spacing* for clarinet and piano (1982); and *The Ambient Air* for flute, violin, cello, and piano (1980–83). For piano she wrote two sonatas (1943, 1944–55); *Sound Shots* (1944–74); *Alleluia in the Form of a Toccata* (1945); *Six Etudes* (1953–54); *Three Bagatelles* (1955); her first twelve-tone work, *Passacaglia and Fugue* (1955–62); *Dialogues* (1964); *Textures* (1977); and *Kaleidoscope* (1984).

Talma was the author of two textbooks, *Harmony for the College Student* (1966) and *Functional Harmony*, in collaboration with James S. Harrison and Robert Levin (1970).

TAYLOR, CLIFFORD OLIVER
b. Bellevue, Pennsylvania, 20 October 1923
d. Abington, Pennsylvania, 19 September 1987

Taylor studied with Nicolai Lopatnikoff at Carnegie-Mellon University, Pittsburgh (1941–45) and with Walter Piston, Irving Fine, and Randall Thompson at Harvard University (M.A., 1950). He was also a private pupil of Paul Hindemith. From 1950 to 1963 he was assistant professor at Chatham College, Pittsburgh, then moved at Temple University, Philadelphia; he directed the electronic music studio there from 1968 until his death.

For orchestra he composed three symphonies (1958, 1965, 1978); *Theme and Variations* (1952); *Introduction and Dance Fantasy* (1955); *Concerto Grosso* for strings (1957); an Organ Concerto (1963); a Piano Concerto (1974); and three concertos for strings with soloists (1977, 1978, 1978). A *Sinfonia Seria* for band dates from 1965.

Taylor's major choral works are *Commencement Suite* (1958) and *A Pageant of Characters from William Shakespeare* (1964). Among his chamber music are a Violin Sonata (1952); a String Quartet (1960); a Trio for clarinet, cello, and piano (1960); *Concert Duo* for violin and cello (1961); *Duo* for saxophone and trombone (1965); Serenade for percussion ensemble (1967); *Movement 3* for piano trio (1968); *Five Poems* for oboe and brass trio (1971); and String Quartet no. 2 (1978). He also wrote two piano sonatas (1952, 1978).

An opera, *The Freak Show*, was composed in 1975.

TAYLOR, (JOSEPH) DEEMS
b. New York, New York, 22 December 1885
d. New York, New York, 3 July 1966

At the age of 11, Deems Taylor began piano lessons. Later he studied for four years at New York University but as a composer he was mainly self-taught. While a student, he wrote four musical comedies, one of which, *The Echo*, was produced on Broadway in 1910. After graduation in 1906 he worked as a journalist for several publications, including the *Encyclopedia Britannica* and the *New York Herald Tribune*. From 1919 to 1925 he was music critic of the *New York World* and edited *Musical America* from 1927 to 1929. From 1933 to 1966 he was a director of ASCAP and worked for many years with NBC radio.

Taylor's best-known work still performed today is the *Suite: Through the Looking Glass* (1917–19; rev. 1921. Also for orchestra he composed *The Siren Song* (1912); *The Portrait of a Lady* (1918); a symphonic poem, *Jurgen*, presented in New York under Walter Damrosch in 1925; *Fantasy on Two Themes* (1925); *Suite: Circus Days*, originally scored for jazz band in 1925 (orchestrated 1934); *Processional*, commissioned by the Baltimore Symphony Orchestra in 1941; *Variations: Marco Takes a Walk* (New York Philharmonic) (1942); a *Christmas Overture*, performed in New York in 1944; *Elegy* (1944); *Fanfare for the People of Russia* (1944); and *Restoration Suite* (1950).

In 1925 the Metropolitan Opera Company commissioned Taylor to compose an opera. He asked Edna St.

Vincent Millay to write a libretto on a subject closely resembling the Tristan legend, set in pre-Norman England, concerning Aethelwold, who is sent by King Aedgar to fetch his queen, Aelfrida. The opera, *The King's Henchman*, was produced on 17 February 1927 to considerable acclaim. This success led to the commissioning of a second opera, *Peter Ibbetson*, based on a play by Constance Collier from the novel by Gerald DuMaurier. Its premiere in New York on 7 February 1931 was greeted with the same critical enthusiasm as *The King's Henchman*, and the work remained in the repertoire of the Metropoloitan for four seasons. It still holds the record for number of performances at the Metropolitan Opera House of an opera by an American composer (18).

For his third opera, *Ramuntcho*, Taylor wrote his own libretto from a novel by Pierre Loti, set in the Basque country at the end of the nineteenth century. Completed in 1938, it was produced by the Philadelphia Opera Company on 10 February 1942. His last opera, the one-act *The Dragon*, was composed in 1958. In addition to *The Echo*, other stage works include a musical comedy, *Cap'n Kidd and Co.* (1908); an operetta, *The Breath of Scandal* (*The Mistress of the Seas*; 1916); a pantomime, *A Kiss in Xanadu* (1932) for two pianos; and a ballet, *Casanova* (1937).

Two important choral works were composed in 1914: *The Highwayman* for baritone, female chorus, and orchestra, written for the MacDowell Festival in Peterborough, New Hampshire, and *The Chambered Nautilus* for chorus and orchestra.

In 1924 Taylor composed a score for the silent movie *Janice Meredith* (*The Beautiful Rebel*).

Taylor was the author of four books: *Of Men and Music* (1937), *The Well-Tempered Listener* (1940), *Music to My Ears* (1949), and *Some Enchanted Evenings*, the story of Rodgers and Hammerstein (1954).

TAYLOR, RAYNOR

b. London, England, 1747
d. Philadelphia, Pennsylvania, 17 August 1825

Taylor was a choir boy in the Chapel Royal. where he studied with James Nares (1715–93), a composer of instrumental and church music. When the boys of the Chapel Royal attended the funeral of Handel in 1759, the young Taylor lost his hat while looking into the grave and it was buried with the great composer. "Never mind," said one of his friends, "he left you some of his brains." Taylor was appointed organist in Chelmsford and director of music at Sadler's Wells Theatre, London, when only 18 years old. Later he provided music for the Haymarket Theatre in London. He settled in Edinburgh, where Alexander Reinagle was one of his

pupils. It was perhaps the success of Reinagle in the New World which prompted Taylor to emigrate to Baltimore in 1792.

When he arrived, Taylor advertised himself as "music professor, organist, and teacher of music in general," offering the public new musical entertainments called "olios." These were concerts featuring favorite songs, ballads, and mock operas burlesquing the Italian style. In these he collaborated with singers from Covent Garden, with whom he had performed in England.

In May 1793, Taylor moved to Philadelphia, where he remained for the rest of his life, as organist of St. Peter's Church (1795–1813) and conductor of concerts in which his music was often performed. These pieces included a Violin Concerto, a Divertimento for orchestra, a *New Overture*, and *Monody on the Death of George Washington* (1799). The surviving instrumental music of Taylor consists of six cello sonatas, written in the early years of the nineteenth century yet strongly Handelian in style.

Some of his church music is extant including three anthems, *The Souls of the Righteous*, *O Come, Loud Anthems Let Us Sing*, and *Hark, Hark How the Watchmen Cry* (all c. 1800), and *Gloria* (1809). There are also a number of solo songs and keyboard pieces.

With Reinagle he wrote the music of a ballad opera, *Pizzaro, or the Spaniards in Peru* (1800). His own opera, *The Ethiop, or The Child in the Desert*, was produced in Philadelphia in November 1814.

Taylor is also remembered with Benjamin Carr as one of the founders in 1820 of the Musical Fund Society of Philadelphia.

TCHEREPNIN, ALEXANDER NIKOLAYEVITCH

b. St. Petersburg, Russia, 21 January 1899
d. Paris, France, 29 September 1977

Tcherepnin's father, Nicolas Tcherepnin (1873–1945), was a respected composer, conductor, and teacher, having been a pupil of Rimski-Korsakov. His mother was a niece of Alexander Benois, the stage designer. Alexander Tcherepnin began piano lessons with his mother at an early age; while still a boy, he composed in all forms and appeared as a solo pianist. He entered the St. Petersburg Conservatory in 1917, where he was a pupil of Nikolai Sokolov. He moved to Tblisi a year later, when his father was appointed director at the Conservatory in that city.

In 1921 the family settled in Paris, where Tcherepnin studied piano with Isador Philipp and composition with Paul Vidal. At this time he began his career as a concert pianist, traveling widely in all European countries and in the United States. In the 1930s he twice toured the Far East, teaching for a while in Japan. In Shanghai he met the young Chinese pianist Lee Hsein Ming, whom he married in 1937. After a successful tour of the United States in 1948, he and his wife accepted an invitation to teach at De Paul University, Chicago, where they remained from 1950 to 1967 before moving to New York. Through this he divided his time between the United States and Europe.

Tcherepnin composed a large number of works in every sphere. For the stage he wrote three operas: *Ol-Ol* (1924–25), based on a play by Leonid Andreyev (Weimar, 1928); *Die Hochzeit des Sobeide* (1928–30), from a Hugo von Hofmannsthal play (Vienna Volksoper, 1933); and *The Farmer and the Nymph*, based on a Chinese story (Aspen Festival, Colorado, 1952). In 1935 he completed and orchestrated Mussorgsky's unfinished opera *The Marriage*, on a comedy of Gogol (Essen, Germany, 1937).

Tcherepnin's ballets include *Training* (1922; Vienna, 1934); *Aljanta's Frescoes* (London, 1923), written for Pavlova; *Der fahrende Schüler mit dem Teufelsbannen* (1938); *Trepak* (New York, 1938); *La Legénde de Razine* (1941); *Dejeuner sur l'herbe* (Paris, 1945); *La Colline des Fantômes* (1946), based on his Symphony no. 3; *L'homme a la peau de leopard* (Monte Carlo, 1946); *Jardin persan* (1946); *Nuit kurde* (1946); *La Femme et son ombre* (Paris, 1948); *Aux temps des tartares* (Buenos Aires, 1949); and *Le Gouffre* (*The Abyss*; / 1953), to a story by Andreyev, based on his Suite for Orchestra (Nürnberg, 1969).

For orchestra Tcherepnin composed five symphonies: no. 1 in E (1927), no. 2 (1945–51), no. 3 (1951), no. 4 (1957), and no. 5, commissioned in 1968 by the Koussevitzky Music Foundation. At the time of his death he was working on a Sixth Symphony for the Chicago Symphony Orchestra. Other orchestral works include two unpublished pieces, an Overture (1921) and *Pour un entrainement de boxe* (1922); *Magna Mater* (1927); *Russian Dances* (1934); *Romantic Overture* (1940); *L'enfance de Sainte Nino* (*Evocation*; 1948); *Symphonic March* (1949); Suite for Orchestra (1953); Divertimento (1957); *Georgiana* (1958); *Symphonic Prayer* (1959); *Serenade for Strings* (1964); *Russian Sketches*, composed for the Kansas City Youth Orchestra in 1971; and *Musica Sacra* for strings (1972).

For piano and orchestra, Tcherepnin composed six concertos: no. 1 in F (1919), no. 2 in A (1923), no. 3 (1933), no. 4, retitled *Fantasie* (1946–49), no. 5 (1963), and no. 6 (1965); and *Suite Georgiènne* for piano and strings (1938). He also rescored the *Bagatelles* for piano and strings (1913–18). Other works for solo instrument(s) and orchestra include *Rhapsodie Georgiènne* (1922) and *Mystère* (1926), both for cello;

Concerto da Camera for flute, violin, and chamber orchestra (1924); Concertino for piano trio and strings (1931); *Sonatine* for timpani (1939); and a Concerto for harmonica (1953).

Tcherepnin's output of instrumental music was considerable. Important among these pieces are *Ode* for cello and piano (1919); a Violin Sonata (1921); two string quartets (1922, 1926); four cello sonatas (1924, 1925, 1926, 1957); *Twelve Preludes* for cello and piano (*Le Violoncelle bien tempere*; 1924); Piano Trio (1925); Piano Quintet (1927); *Elegy* for violin and piano (1927); *Duo* for violin and cello (1933); a *Trio* and *Quartet* for flutes (both 1939); *Sonata Sportive* for saxophone and piano (1939); Sonatina for timpani (1939); *Andante* for tuba and piano (1939); *Trio and March* for three trumpets (1939); Suite for solo cello (1947); *Sonata da Chiesa* for viola da gamba and organ (1966); a Brass Quintet (1970); and a Wind Quintet (1976). His last composition, *Duo* for two flutes, was first performed on 18 April 1978 by Dominique Mutziker and Anne Utagarva. For piano accordion he provided three valuable pieces: *Partita* (1961), *Tzigane* (1966), and *Invention* (1967).

Tcherepnin's vocal music includes two cantatas, *Vivre d'amour* (1942) and *Pan Kéou* (1945); *Le Jeu de la Nativité* for two sopranos, tenor, bass, and chorus with strings and percussion (1945); and *Vom Spass und Ernst* for low voice and string orchestra (1963). Two works for narrator and orchestra are *Les Douze* (*The Twelve*), settings of poems by Alexander Blok (Paris, 1945), and *The Lost Flute,* heard at the Peninsula Festival, Wisconsin in 1954. Later choral compositions include a Mass for three equal voices (1966), *Six Liturgical Songs* (1967), *Four Russian Folk Songs* for a cappella voices (1969), and *Baptism Cantata* (1972).

Tcherepnin composed extensively for his own instrument, the piano. Of his first 24 published works, 20 were for keyboard, and he continued to produce piano pieces throughout his career. The important items are *Ten Bagatelles* (1913–18); two sonatas, no. 1 in A (1921) and no. 2 (1961); *Arabesques* (1921); *Nine Inventions* (1921); *Four Preludes* (1922); *Six Etudes de travail* (1923); *Message* (1927); *Piano Studies on the Pentatonic Scale* (1934); *Showcase* (1941); *Songs Without Words* (1952); *Twelve Preludes* (1952); and *Eight Piano Pieces* (1956).

In 1962 and 1963 Tcherepnin provided scores for the CBS television programs *Crisis in Suez, Catch the Graf Spee, Retreat from Arnhem,* and *Attack on Singapore.* For BBC Radio in London he composed music for a production of Tolstoy's story *Ivan the Fool* (1969).

Tcherepnin was the author of a book, *An Anthology of Russian Music*, published in 1966.

TCHEREPNIN, IVAN (ALEXANDROVICH)

b. Issy-les-Moulineaux, France, 5 February 1943
d. Boston, Massachusetts, 11 April 1998

A son of the noted composer Alexander Tcherepnin, Ivan Tcherepnin began piano lessons at the age of four with his mother. In 1950 he moved with the family to Chicago. Like his brother Serge, he attended Harvard University, where his teachers included Randall Thompson and Leon Kirchner. In 1965 a John Knowles Paine Traveling Fellowship took him to Europe where he studied composition with Henri Pousseur and Stockhausen and conducting with Pierre Boulez. The following year he went to study at the Electronic Music Studio in Toronto, and worked informally with David Tudor in a seminar on live electronic performance at Mills College, Oakland, California.

After receiving his M.A. in music composition from Harvard in 1968 he taught for two years at the San Francisco Conservatory of Music, where he re-instituted a Studio for Electronic Music. From 1970 to 1972 he taught at Stanford University; he then went to Harvard University, where he was associate professor and director of the Electronic Music Studio until his death. In the summers of 1979 and 1980 he and his brother taught seminars on electronic music at Dartington Summer School, England.

Tcherepnin's instrumental music includes *Suite progressive pentatonique* for flute, cello, and timpani (1959); *Deux Entourages sur un Theme Russe* for horn, Ondes Martinot, piano, and percussion (1961); *Reciprocals* for flute, clarinet, and bassoon (1962); *Cadenzas in Transition* for flute, clarinet, and piano (1963); *Mozartean Suite* for flute, clarinet, and piano (1963); *Sombres Lumiers* for flute, guitar, and cello (1964); *Work Music* for electric guitar, clarinet, horn, and cello (1965); and *Summer Brass* for brass sextet (1970).

Tcherepnin specialized in composing music integrating instrumental performance within a complex network of electronics; his first work of this type was *Rings* for string quartet and ring modulators (1968). His major works in that genre include *Globose Floccose* (1972) for four string and five brass instruments, amplified and fed into an electronic network simultaneously with a tape entitled *Clouds*; the curiously named *Set, Hold, Clear and Squelch* for oboe and electronics (1976), performed with the Merce Cunnningham Dance Company; *Five Songs* for contralto, flute, and digital delay networks (1979), commissioned by radio station WFMT in Chicago; and *Flores Musicales* for amplified oboe, violin, psaltery, and electronics, including the Serge Synthesizer and the David Wilson Organ and Analog Delay systems (1979).

Other instrumental pieces with electronics include *Grand Fire Music* for string quartet (1969); *Alternating Currents* for eight percussionists (1967); *Beethoven's Last Quartet* for string quartet (1968); *Light Music With Water* for instrumental ensemble (1970); *Flute Fantasy* for flute (1978); *New Rhythmantics* for string quartet (1983); *Cantilena/Hybrids* for violin (1984); *Explorations* for string trio and piano (1984); *New Rhythmantics IV* for string quartet and trumpet (1987); and *The Creative Act* for four percussionists (1990).

After more than a decade of combining instruments and tape, Tcherepnin returned to instruments alone with *Trio Fantasia* for piano trio (1985), *New Rhythmatics IV* for string quartet, trumpet, and celesta (1987), *Fanfare for Otto Hall* for brass (1995), and *Seven Fanfares* for three trumpets (1995).

Tcherepnin's large-scale ensemble works include *Wheelwinds* for nine wind instruments (1966); *Les Adieux* for 17 performers (including three singers), tape, and lights (1972); *La Vie et le Vient* for orchestra, which the composer conducted in 1978 at the Lucerne Festival; Concerto for oboe, winds, brass, and percussion, commissioned by the American Wind Symphony in Pittsburgh (1980; rev. 1988); *New Consonance* for strings (1983); *Solstice* for chamber orchestra (1984); *Status* for wind orchestra (1986); *Constitution* for narrator and wind orchestra (1987); *Concerto for Two Continents* for synthesizer and wind ensemble (1989); *Carillona* for wind orchestra (1993); *Dialogue Between the Moon and Venus as Overheard by an Earthling* for wind orchestra (1994); Double Concerto for violin and cello (1995); and Triple Concerto for English horn, trombone, doublebass clarinet, and wind orchestra (1996).

His works for tape alone include *Grand Fire Music* (1966), *Reverberations* (1968), *1,2,3, for KQUD* (1970), *Watergate Suite* (1973), and *Peelings* (1975), as well as three film scores: *Post Office* (1968), *Satina at 2* (1968), and *Cloud Music* (1978).

In 1976 Tcherepnin performed his full-evening work *Santur Opera*, for amplified santur, Serge Electronics, and Wilson Organ, in New York, San Francisco, Los Angeles, Chicago, Boston, and Paris. It was revised in 1994 and retitled *Santur Opera II*.

His only vocal works are a cantata, *And So It Came to Pass* for soprano, tenor, chorus, and orchestra (1991); *Les Adieux* for 17 performers (including three singers), tape, and lights (1972); and *Five Songs* for alto, alto flute, and electronics (1979).

Among his piano compositions are *Pieces From Before* (1958–62); *Beginnings* (1963); *Two Reminiscences* (1968); *Twelve Variations on Happy Birthday* (1970–77); *Fêtes* (1975); *Valse éternelle: The 45 RPM*

(1977); *Summer Nights* (1980); and three pieces for two pianos: *Silent Night Music* (1969), *Three Christmases* (1970–72), and *Three Pieces* (1971).

TCHEREPNIN, SERGE (ALEXANDROVICH)

b. Issy-les-Moulineaux, France, 2 February 1941

Tcherepnin studied first with his father, Alexander, and later with Nadia Boulanger. In 1958 he entered Harvard University where his teachers included Billy Jim Layton, Leon Kirchner, and Walter Piston. From 1963 to 1964 he attended Princeton University. After graduating he went to Europe, where he studied composition with Luigi Nono and Stockhausen, electronic music with Herber Eimert, and conducting with Pierre Boulez. Returning to the United States in 1968 he did research and taught at the New York University Intermedia Program, working in close collaboration with musicians and artists (Morton Subotnick, the Pulse Group, Charlemagne Palestine, Ingram Marshall, Marianne Amacher), primarily in the field of musical electronics and multimedia.

From 1970 to 1974 Tcherepnin was a professor at the California Institute of the Arts, Valencia, Los Angeles. By 1975 his research in musical electronics led him to form a company, Serge Modular Music Systems, now in San Francisco, which manufactures electronic musical instruments designed specifically to further the art of new music. He moved back to France in 1992, selling his interest in the firm.

His earliest important work, *Kaddish*, to a text by Allan Ginsberg for narrator and small ensemble, was performed at Harvard in 1962. *Figures-grounds* for any number of musicians from 7 to 77 was premiered at Princeton in 1964. Multimedia works include *Piece of Wood*, performed in Cologne in 1967, rearranged as *Piece of Wood with Weeping Women*; *Film* for Baschet instruments, tape, various electronic devices, and lights (Frankfurt, 1967); and *"Hat"* (Joseph Beuys) for actor and tape (1968).

Tcherepnin has written *Definitive Death Music* for amplified saxophone and large ensemble (1968). His other instrumental music includes a String Trio (1961), *Morning After Piece* for saxophone and piano (1966), *Quiet Day at Bach* for solo instrument and tape (1967); and two piano pieces, *Inventions* (1960) and *For Ilona Kabos* (1968).

From 1966 to 1968 Tcherepnin devoted his time to experimental music at the electronic studio at the Musikhochschule in Cologne. He invented a new electronic synthesizer and other electronic instruments. Among his creations for tape are *Two Tapes* (*Giuseppe's Background Music I and II*; 1966), *Two More Tapes*

(*Additions and Subtractions*; 1966), *At Bach* (1967), and *Spirals* (1967). In addition he has written electronic music scores for two films, *Paysages électroniques* (1977) and *Samba in Aviary* (1978).

TEMPLETON, ALEC (ANDREW)

b. Cardiff, Wales, 4 July, 1910
d. Greenwich, Connecticut, 28 March 1963

Although blind from birth, Templeton became a fine pianist. He received his musical training at the Royal Academy of Music and Royal College of Music in London, where he studied with John Ireland and Herbert Howells. In addition, he graduated from Worcester College, Oxford University. Templeton came to the United States in 1935 as the pianist in Jack Hylton's band and decided to stay. Over the next few years he appeared as soloist with leading orchestras throughout North America. He became a naturalized citizen in 1941.

Although Templeton's name is associated with witty pastiches of the classics such as *Bach Goes to Town*, his more serious compositions deserve to be recognized. For piano and orchestra he wrote *Concertino Lirico* (1942), *Rhapsodie Harmonique* (1954), and *Gothic Concerto*, which he performed in New York in 1954. He also composed a *Suite for Strings* and a setting of *The Pied Piper of Hamelin* for narrator and orchestra.

The remainder of his works were instrumental, including two string quartets; a Violin Sonata; a Trio for flute, oboe, and piano (1928); *Passepied* for wind quintet; two *Pocket-size Sonatas* for clarinet and piano (1949, 1963); *Suite Noel* for organ; and two piano sonatas.

He wrote a book, *Alec Templeton's Music Boxes*, with R. B. Baumel (1958).

THOMAS, AUGUSTA READ

b. Glen Cove, New York, 24 April 1964

Thomas studied with M. William Karlins and Alan Stout at Northwestern University (1983–87) and at Yale (1988), where she was a pupil of Jacob Druckman, followed by a year at the Royal Academy of Music, London. She was an associate professor of composition at the Eastman School of Music (1993–2001) and is now a professor of music at Northwestern University. She was a Bunting Fellow at Radcliffe College (1990), then a junior fellow in the Society of Fellows at Harvard University (1991–94). She was named Mead Composer-in-Residence with the Chicago Symphony Orchestra (1997–2006). In 1994 she married the composer Bernard Rands. In 1999 she withdrew all of her early works.

Augusta Read Thomas.
Courtesy the composer.

Thomas has received numerous prizes and awards, including ASCAP, BMI, the National Endowment for the Arts, the American Academy and Institute of Arts and Letters, the John Simon Guggenheim Memorial Foundation, the Koussevitzky Foundation, The Siemens Foundation, Columbia University (Bearns Prize), the Naumburg Foundation, the Fromm Foundation, and the New York State Council for the Arts.

Thomas's orchestral works include *Aurora: Concerto for Piano and Orchestra* (2000); *Ceremonial* (2000); *Prayer Bells* (2001); *Canticle Weaving*, for trombone and orchestra, (2002); *Tangle* (2003); *Galaxy Dances*, a ballet for orchestra (2004); and *Grace Notes* (2005). For instrumental ensemble, she composed *Silver Chants the Litanies*, an homage to Luciano Berio for solo horn and ensemble (2003), and *Whispers of Summer* for three cellos (2004).

Her chamber-opera *Ligeia*, based on a short story by Poe (libretto by Leslie Dunton-Downer). It was commissioned by Rencontres Musicales d'Evian and Mstislav Rostropovich, who led the premiere in the 1994 Evian Festival; the American premiere took place at the Aspen (Colorado) Music Festival in July 1995. *Ligeia* was awarded the International Orpheus Prize.

Works for vocalist and orchestra include *Song in Sorrow*, for solo soprano, six solo female voices, chorus, and orchestra (2000); *Daylight Divine*, for soprano, children's chorus, and orchestra (2001); *Chanting to Paradise* (E. Dickinson), for soprano soloist, large chorus, and orchestra (2002); and *Basho Settings* and *To the Rain* for children's chorus (both 2003)

THOMPSON, RANDALL
b. New York, New York, 21 April 1899
d. Boston, Massachusetts, 9 July 1985

At Harvard, Thompson's teachers included Walter Spalding, Archibald T. Davison, and Edward Burlingame Hill. He also received private composition lessons from Ernest Bloch. He went to Italy for three years on a Prix de Rome Fellowship (1922–25), and was awarded Guggenheim Fellowships in 1929 and 1930. From 1927 to 1929 and again in 1936 he was assistant professor at Wellesley College, Massachusetts. In 1937 he was appointed a professor at the University of California, Berkeley. From 1939 to 1941 he was director of the Curtis Institute, Philadelphia. In 1941 he became head of the music department at the School of Fine Arts at the University of Virginia in Charlottesville. After two years as professor of music at Princeton University (1946–48), he joined the music faculty at Harvard, from which he retired in 1967.

Thompson made a major contribution to twentieth-century choral music. Probably more than any other American composer he produced several works for choirs that have become firmly established in the repertory. His understanding of choral technique was gained first-hand as conductor of various college and university choirs. The deep knowledge thus gained was put to good effect in his expert writing for voices.

His principal successes came with works for unaccompanied chorus. The *Five Odes of Horace* were composed in Rome in 1924. These were followed by the eight-part *Pueri Hebraeorum* for female voices (1928) and *Rosemary* for female voices (1929). The best-known and most widely performed of all Thompson's works is *The Peaceable Kingdom*, a setting in eight movements of texts from Isaiah XI. Commissioned in 1936 by the League of Composers for the Harvard Glee Club and Radcliffe Choral Society, the work's title is taken from a famous painting by Edward Hicks (1780–1849), depicting William Penn in the company of American Indians, children, and wild animals. Early American hymnody and sixteenth-century music have exerted some influence on the work, but the effect is by no means archaic. Its dramatic power and impressive impact make it decidedly of its time.

In 1940 Thompson wished to write a piece of music to express hope during a time of world strife. After searching unsuccessfully for a suitable text, he chose the single word *Alleluia* and produced a little masterpiece of unaccompanied choral writing. Two further important compositions for a cappella voices are *Mass of the Holy Spirit* (*Communion Service*; 1955) and *Requiem*, a five-part, non-liturgical dramatic dialogue in English for double chorus (1958).

Thompson's earliest work for chorus and orchestra, *Ode to Venus* (1925), dates from his time in Rome. The burlesque *Americana* (1932) shows the composer's skill in using H. L. Mencken's satirical columns from *The American Mercury* as its source. He composed two works for men's voices, *Tarantella*, with piano (Belloc) (1937) and *The Testament of Freedom*, with orchestra (1943). The latter piece was written in honor of the 200th anniversary of the birth of Thomas Jefferson, whose writings it is based on. The text was particularly appropriate at a critical moment in the Second World War.

The Last Words of David for mixed voices and orchestra (1949) was written for Serge Koussevitzky and the Berkshire Music Center, Tanglewood. *Ode to the Virginian Voyage* is a setting of a 1606 poem by Michael Drayton (1563–1631). The work, celebrating the 350th anniversary of the journey from Kent, England to the New World as described in the poem, was performed in 1957 in Williamsburg, close to where the original voyagers landed. *Frostiana* for mixed voices and piano (1959) sets seven poems by Robert Frost about the countryside.

The Nativity According to St. Luke, an opera in seven scenes, was composed for the 200th anniversary of Christ Church, Cambridge, Massachusetts and first performed under the composer's direction on 13 December 1961. An oratorio, *The Passion According to St. Luke*, was heard in Boston in 1965. In 1969 Thompson wrote *The Place of the Blest*, a cantata for boys' voices and chamber orchestra for the centennial of the Boys' Choir of St. Thomas' Church in New York. This was followed in 1970 by *Two Herbert Songs* for unaccompanied voices.

In 1975 Thompson was commissioned to write a festive work for the town of Concord, Massachusetts, which became *A Concord Cantata* in three movements for mixed voices and orchestra. Among his last choral pieces are *The Mirror of St. Anne* (1972), *Farewell* (De la Mare) (1973), *The Morning Star* for choir and orchestra (1976), and *Five Love Songs* for baritone, mixed voices, and strings (1978).

Thompson's first orchestral work, *Pierrot and Cothurnus* (1922), was written for the Prix de Rome. He conducted the premiere in Rome in 1923, as he did for the symphonic prelude *The Piper at the Gates of Dawn* (1924). His First Symphony, also written in Rome, was originally scored for chorus and orchestra, but later arranged for orchestra alone (1929; Rochester, 1930). Symphony no. 2 in E minor, composed in 1930–31, has proved to be his most popular orchestral work. It too received its premiere in Rochester in 1932 at the American Composers' Concerts. Symphony no. 3 in A minor was first performed in New York in 1949. Other orchestral works include *Jazz Poem* for piano and orchestra, premiered in 1928 with the composer as soloist; and a fantasy for orchestra, *A Trip to Nahant* (1955).

Thompson composed a radio opera in one act, *Solomon and Balkis*, based on "The Butterfly That Stamped" from *Just-So Stories* by Rudyard Kipling. It was broadcast in March 1942 and staged in Cambridge, Massachusetts a month later. He also wrote a ballet, *Jabberwocky* (1951), and provided incidental music for four productions: *Torches* (1920), *The Italian Straw Hat* (Labiche; 1926), *The Grand Street Follies* (1926, lost), and *The Battle of Dunster Street* (1953).

Thompson's instrumental music, mostly written early in his career, includes a Sextet (1917); Quintet for flute, clarinet, viola, cello, and piano (1920); a Piano Sonata (1923); a Piano Suite (1924); *The Wind in the Willows* for string quartet (1924); a Suite for oboe, clarinet (or violin), and viola (1940); and two string quartets (1941, 1967).

He was also the author of *College Music*, published in 1935 under the auspices of the Carnegie Foundation.

THOMSON, VIRGIL GARNETT

b. Kansas City, Missouri, 25 November 1896
d. New York, New York, 30 September 1989

Thomson's boyhood musical background strongly resembles that of Charles Ives—hymns, popular songs, ragtime—but his later approach to music was altogether more professional and sophisticated. Even in his early works, Thomson was able to integrate conflicting musical elements (plainsong, country tunes, and Bach-like fugues) into a unified composition.

Thomson entered Harvard University in 1919, where he was a pupil of Edward Burlingame Hill and Archibald T. Davison. Among his fellow students were the organist Melville Smith, Randall Thompson, Leopold Mannes, and Walter Piston. In 1921 he interrupted his Harvard studies to spend a year in Paris on a John Knowles Paine Traveling Fellowship. There he became a pupil of Nadia Boulanger, both privately and at the Ecole Normale de Musique. In Paris he met Aaron Copland, who had been a student at the recently opened American Conservatory at Fontainebleau and was also a Boulanger pupil. Thomson soon became acquainted with Erik Satie and the members of "Les Six." At this time he began his career as a critic, writing reviews of musical events in Paris for the *Boston Transcript*. Contact with the European literary and artistic world in addition to the musical life in France exerted a profound effect upon him.

In the summer of 1922 Thomson returned to the United States to complete his degree. He was appointed organist at King's Chapel in Boston and taught at Harvard until 1925. He also introduced much new French music into his concerts, including the first complete performance in the United States of Satie's *Socrate*. A Juilliard Fellowship enabled him to study conducting in New York, where he also received composition lessons from Rosario Scalero and resumed his journalism, writing articles for *Vanity Fair*. In 1925 the lure of Paris enticed him back to that city, now home to a small community of American musicians, including George Antheil, Theodore Chanler, and Herbert Elwell. Thomson also came to know James Joyce and the writer who was to become the strongest influence upon him, Gertrude Stein.

In 1926 Thomson completed his first significant work, *Sonata da Chiesa* for E-flat clarinet, trumpet in D, viola, horn, and trombone; the very scoring reveals an affinity with French music of this time. It betrays a witty, satirical character that deliberately sets out to deflate the pomposity and sentimentality that still typified much that was being written in Europe and America.

Thomson first met Gertrude Stein in the winter of 1925–26. He set Stein's *Capital Capitals* for four male voices and piano (1927); it was performed the following year. In this piece, four cities in Provence, Aix, Arles, Avignon, and Les Baux, converse with each other in word associations.

He now asked her to write an opera libretto, and early in 1927 the plans for *Four Saints in Three Acts* began to take shape. The text was completed in June of that year and the music finished in July 1928. The opera concerns two Spanish saints, Teresa of Avila and Ignatius Loyola, who are surrounded by groups of young religious figures. In fact the opera has four acts and over 30 saints. A compère and commère introduce the characters and announce to the audience the progress of the action. The strangely haunting and at times repetitive poetry of Stein is declaimed by the singers in a musical language derived from many sources, including Gregorian and Anglican chant, children's songs, and Sunday School hymn singing, with a harmonious accompaniment for small orchestra. Although the setting of the words is deceptively simple and direct, there are considerable subtleties in the music to parallel the implied imagery of the words.

Four Saints in Three Acts was first heard at Hartford, Connecticut, in February 1934, produced by an organization called the Friends and Enemies of Modern Music. When the production moved to New York it created theatrical history with its all-black cast. The opera received over 60 performances within a year and Thomson's reputation was made almost overnight.

A second opera to a libretto by Stein, *The Mother of Us All*, was commissioned by the Alice M. Ditson Fund and staged in New York in May 1947. The central figure is Susan B. Anthony, the nineteenth-century pioneer of women's suffrage. Many other historical characters appear, including Daniel Webster, Ulysses S. Grant, Lillian Russell, John Adams, Andrew Johnson, and even "Gertrude S." and "Virgil T." His third opera, *Lord Byron*, with a libretto by Jack Larson, was commissioned for the Metropolitan Opera in 1966. Completed in 1968, it was premiered by the Juilliard School American Opera Center in New York on 20 April 1972.

Symphony on a Hymn Tune (1928) combines the Southern Baptist hymnody of Thomson's youth in Kansas City with the sophisticated music of Paris. The four-movement work is in essence a set of variations on "How Firm a Foundation," with fragments of "Yes, Jesus Loves Me" and, somewhat unusually, "For He's a Jolly Good Fellow." It had to wait until 1945 for its premiere by the New York Philharmonic Orchestra, Thomson himself conducting.

He returned to United States in 1928, bringing with him the Paris compositions. But he went back to Paris in 1929, turning again to composition. He set Max

THOMSON, VIRGIL GARNETT

Jacob's *Stabat Mater* for soprano and string quartet (1931, rev. 1981), and wrote two string quartets and a Violin Sonata. In 1933 he went to America for the performances of *Four Saints in Three Acts*. He spent 1934 in the United States, at which time he wrote incidental music for a number of plays and the *Missa Brevis* for female voices and percussion; he then returned to France.

During the Second World War, after the invasion of France in 1940, Thomson made his way to the United States through Spain and Portugal. He accepted the post of music critic for the *New York Herald Tribune*, succeeding the late Lawrence Gilman; he held the position until 1954 and established himself as the most influential writer on music in the United States.

In addition to the *Symphony on a Hymn Tune*, Thomson's orchestral music includes a Second Symphony (1931), a reworking of the First Piano Sonata; *Three Pictures for Orchestra*: *The Seine at Night*, written for the Kansas City Philharmonic Orchestra (1947); *Wheat Fields at Noon*, commissioned by the Louisville Orchestra (1948); *Sea Piece With Birds*, composed for the Dallas Symphony Orchestra (1952); *Fantasy: In Homage to Earlier England* (1966); and *Thought for Strings* (1981). Symphony no. 3 (1972) is an orchestration of the Second String Quartet. He wrote three concertos: for cello (1950), flute (1954), and the *Autumn Concerto* for harp, strings, and percussion (1964). For concert band he composed *A Solemn Music* (1949), in memory of Gertrude Stein; in 1961 he arranged it for orchestra, adding *A Joyful Fugue* the following year. For brass and percussion there is *Ode to the Wonders of Nature* (1965).

The larger part of Thomson's music is for voices. His principal choral works with orchestra are *Missa Pro Defunctis* (Requiem Mass) for men's chorus, women's chorus, and orchestra (1959–60); *Dance in Praise* (1962); *Crossing Brooklyn Ferry* (Whitman; 1962); and *The Nativity* (1967). For a cappella voices he wrote *De Profundis* (1920), *Scenes from the Holy Infancy* (1937), *Hymns of the Old South* (1949), and two settings of the *Missa Brevis*, the first for men's voices (1924), the second for women's voices and percussion (1934). *Cantata on Poems of Edward Lear* for soprano, baritone, chorus, and piano was composed in 1973 and revised the following year.

Among his works for solo voice and orchestra are *Oraison Funèbre de Bossuet* for tenor (1930); *Five Songs to Poems of William Blake* (1951) and *The Feast of Love* (1964), both for baritone; *Collected Poems* (Kenneth Koch) for soprano and baritone (1959); and *From Byron's Don Juan* for tenor (1968). *Five Phrases from the Song of Solomon* for soprano and percussion were completed in 1926. The song cycle *Praises and*

Prayers for voice and piano was commissioned in 1963 by the Ford Foundation for Betty Allen.

Thomson's instrumental music includes *Variations and Fugues on Sunday School Tunes* for organ (1926–27), two string quartets (1931, 1932), Serenade for flute and violin (1931), and Sonata for solo flute (1943). *Pange Lingua* (1962) was composed for the inauguration of the organ in Philharmonic Hall (now Avery Fisher Hall), Lincoln Center, New York. In 1975 he wrote *Family Portrait* for the American Brass Quintet.

In 1927 Thomson wrote the first of his large collection of musical portraits of his friends; ultimately numbering over 150; most are for piano, others for instrumental ensembles. Other piano works are *Synthetic Waltzes* for two pianos (1925), *Five Inventions* (1926), four sonatas (1929, 1929, 1930, 1940), *Ten Etudes* (1943), *Nine Etudes* (1954), and many shorter pieces.

A ballet, *Filling Station* (1937), was produced with piano accompaniment at Hartford, Connecticut in January 1938 and later in the year in New York with orchestra. A second ballet, *The Harvest According* (1954), commissioned by Agnes de Mille, uses music from *The Mother of Us All* and other works, adding new linking material. Other ballets are *Bayou* (George Balanchine, 1952), based on *Acadian Songs and Dances* (1948), a suite from the film score *Louisiana Story* (see below); *Hurrah!* (Erick Hawkins, 1975), a complete setting of Symphony no. 2 (1931, rev. 1941); and *Parson Weems and the Cherry Tree* (Hawkins, 1975) for seven players, derived from authentic American music of the Federal period.

Thomson's association with films began in 1936 when he composed the score for the Pare Lorentz documentary *The Plow That Broke the Plain*, which concerns soil erosion and deserted farmsteads. For the same director he wrote music for *The River* in the following year. In 1945 he composed the score for a government documentary, *Tuesday in November*. His best-known film music, for Robert Flaherty's *Louisiana Story*, dates from 1948. Two attractive concert suites from the score reveal Thomson's deep love of American folk music. It is the only film score to have received a Pulitzer Prize. Other music for the screen include *The Goddess* (1957) and two further documentaries, *Power Among Men* (1958) and *Journey to America* (1964). The concert suite from *Power Among Men* is published as *Fugues and Cantilenas*, the suite from *Journey to America* as *Pilgrims and Pioneers*.

Thomson provided incidental music for stage, radio, and television. These productions include *Macbeth* (1936); *Hamlet* (1936); *Antony and Cleopatra* (1937); *King Lear* (1952); two plays by Euripides, *Medea* (1934) and *The Trojan Women* (1940); *Oidipous*

Tyrannos (Sophocles; 1941); *A Bride and the Unicorn* (Dennis Johnson; 1934); *Ondine* (Giraudoux; 1954); and *The Grass Harp* (Truman Capote; 1953).

In addition to newspaper and magazine articles, Thomson published eight books that provide valuable critical insight into music of the 20th century: *The State of Music* (1939, rev. 1961), *The Musical Scene* (1970), *The Art of Judging Music* (1948), *Music Right and Left* (1951), *Virgil Thomson: An Autobiography* (1966), *Music Reviewed 1940–54* (1967), *American Music Since 1900* (1970), *A Virgil Thomson Reader* (1981), and *Music With Words: A Composer's View* (1989). Thomson's witty comments reveal many aspects of American music, including this particularly appropriate example: "The way to write American music is simple. All you have to do is to be an American and then write any kind of music you wish."

THORNE, FRANCIS BURRITT (JR.)

b. Bay Shore, New York, 23 June 1922

At Yale University (1939–42), Thorne studied composition with Paul Hindemith and Richard Donovan. He was also a private pupil of Leo Smit (1956–58) and David Diamond (1959–61). After spending eight years in banking, he turned to music. His activities as a jazz pianist in the 1950s are reflected in several of his works, which combine elements of modern jazz and modern techniques. In 1975, he was appointed executive director of the American Composers Alliance and cofounded the American Composers Orchestra, which gave its premiere performance in early 1977.

For orchestra Thorne has composed seven symphonies (1960, 1964, 1969, 1977, 1984, 1992, 1993); *Elegy* (1962); *Burlesque Overture* (1964); *Rhapsodic Variations* for piano and orchestra (1965); a Piano Concerto (1965–66); *Lyric Variations* (1966–67); Double Concerto for viola, double bass, and orchestra (1968); *Sonar Plexus* for electric guitar and orchestra (1968); *Liebesrock* for three electric guitars and orchestra (1968–69); *Fanfare, Fugue and Funk* (1972); Concerto no. 2 for piano and chamber orchestra (1973–74); a Cello Concerto (1975); and a Violin Concerto (1975–76), first performed at the Cabrillo Festival, California. Later orchestral works include *Pop Partita* for piano and chamber orchestra (1978), commissioned by Lukas Foss for the Brooklyn Philharmonic and premiered in February 1979; Divertimento no. 1 for flute, string orchestra, and percussion (1979), commissioned by the Contemporary Music Society for Paul Dunkel and the Orchestra of New York; and Divertimento no. 2 for bassoon and strings (1980).

Thorne's most recent works include an overture, *Humoresque* (1985); *Concerto Concertante* for flute, clarinet, violin, cello, and orchestra (1985); *Rhapsodic Variations no. 3* for oboe and strings (1986); Piano Concerto no. 3 (1990); Cello Concerto no. 2 (1996); a Clarinet Concerto (1997); *Flash Dances* (1998); an Oboe Concerto (2000); and Concerto for Orchestra, (2002) composed for the 25th anniversary of the American Composers Orchestra. He has composed two pieces for band, *Contra Band* (1970) and *Gems from Spoon River* (1980).

Thorne's instrumental music includes *Partita* for violin and piano (1961); *Anniversary Fanfare* for brass and percussion (1963); *Music for a Circus* for wind and percussion (1963); *Seven Set Pieces* for 13 players (1967); *Chamber Derivations* for clarinet, double bass, and percussion (1968); *Songs and Dances* for cello, keyboard instruments, and percussion (1969); *Antiphonies* for wind and percussion (1969–70); *Simultaneities* for brass quintet, electric guitar, and percussion (1971); and four string quartets (1960, 1967, 1975, 1983).

For varied instrumental forces, Thorne has embarked on a sequence of works with the title *Lyric Variations*: no. 1 for orchestra (1966–67), no. 2 for wind quintet and piano (1971–72), no. 3, piano trio (1972), no. 4, solo violin (1980), no. 5, orchestra (1981), no. 6, solo cello (1981), no. 7 for clarinet, bassoon, trumpet, horn, violin, cello, and piano (1982), and no. 8 for flute, celesta, and cello (1999). Other chamber music includes a *Chamber Concerto* for cello and ten instruments (1975); *Five Set Pieces* for saxophone quartet (1977); Divertimento no. 3 for wind quintet (1983); *Rhapsodic Variations no. 2* for clarinet, violin, and cello (1985), *Rhapsodic Variations no. 3* for oboe and string quartet (1986), *Rhapsodic Variations no. 4* for viola (1987), *Rhapsodic Variations no. 5* for violin and piano (1988); *Two Environments* for brass quintet (1990); *How Wild the Rows* for flute, clarinet, violin, and cello (1996); and *Quiet Night* for cello and piano (1997).

Thorne's first important choral works were *De Profundis* for soprano, chorus, and organ (1959) and *Song of the Carolina Low Country* for chorus and chamber orchestra (1968). *The Eternal Light* for soprano and orchestra (1979) was commissioned by the National Endowment for the Arts for Carole Farley. More recent items are *Praise and Thanksgiving* for chorus and orchestra (1983); *Echo* for soprano and chorus (1995); *Song* for medium voice and string trio (2002); *The Four Seasons* for medium voice, clarinet, and bass clarinet (2002); and *Power* for medium voice, clarinet, violin, double bass, and piano (2002).

For piano Thorne has written *Double Variations* (1965), a Sonata (1972), *Rhapsodic Variations No. 7* (1998), and a Suite for two pianos, *Broadway and 52nd* (1958).

For the stage he has composed three operas: *Fortuna* (1961), *Opera Buffa for Opera Buffs* (after Mozart) (1965), and *Mario the Magician* (1991–93); and two ballets, *After the Teacups* (1974) and *Echoes of Spoon River* (1976).

TILL, JOHANN CHRISTIAN

b. Gnadenthal, near Nazareth, Pennsylvania, 18 May 1762

d. Bethlehem, Pennsylvania, 19 November 1844

Till taught in Hope, New Jersey from 1793 to 1808. In 1813 he settled in the Moravian community in Bethlehem where he spent the remainder of his life. He was the organist for the Moravian church there. Among his surviving anthems for chorus and strings are *Praise and Laud and Honor* and *Rejoice Thou Lamb's Beloved Bride.*

TIMM, HENRY CHRISTIAN

b. Hamburg, Germany, 11 July 1811

d. Hoboken, New Jersey, 5 September 1892

Timm came to the United States in 1835 and settled in New York. He was primarily a conductor and virtuoso pianist, but also played horn and trombone and was one of the founders of the New York Philharmonic Orchestra in 1842. He wrote a *Grand Mass* and a number of songs and made numerous transcriptions for two pianos of popular works by other composers.

TOCH, ERNST

b. Vienna, Austria, 7 December 1887

d. Los Angeles, California, 1 October 1964

At the University of Vienna, Toch studied medicine and philosophy, but in 1909 he turned to music; from 1910 to 1913 he was a student of piano at Zuschneid's Hochschule, Mannheim and the Hoch Conservatory, Frankfurt. In 1913 he was appointed a teacher of piano at the Mannheim Hochschule. He then taught piano and composition privately in Berlin (from 1929), but with the rise of the Nazis, he left Germany, first for Paris (1933) and then for the United States (1934). He became an American citizen in 1940.

Toch taught at the New School for Social Research in New York (1934–36). In 1937 he went to Hollywood to write film music, and in 1940 he was appointed to the music faculty of the University of Southern California in Los Angeles, a post he retained until 1948.

Although he experimented with speech rhythms and occasionally made use of the 12-tone system, most of Toch's music is in a traditional Romantic idiom. He composed extensively in every medium.

Toch wrote five operas: *Wegwende* (1925; unfinished; lost), *Die Prinzessin auf der Erbse* (*The Princess and the Pea*; 1927), *Egon und Emelie* (1928), *Der Fächer* (*The Fan*; 1930), and *The Last Tale* [*of Scheherazade*] (1960). He provided incidental music for *Bacchantes* (Euripides), *As You Like It* (Shakespeare), and *Die Heilige aus U. S. A.* (Stefan Zweig). Among his film scores are *Filmstudie* (1928); *Catherine the Great* (1934); *The Private Life of Don Juan* (1934); *Little Friend* (1934); *Peter Ibbetson* (1935); *Heidi* (1937); *One Such Night* (1937); *Outcast* (1937); *Four Men and a Prayer* (1938); *The Cat and the Canary* (1939); *The Ghost Breakers* (1940); *Dr Cyclops* (1940); *Ladies in Retirement* (1941); *First Come Courage* (1943); *None Shall Escape* (1944); *Address Unknown* (1944); and *The Unseen* (1945).

Toch's major orchestral works are seven symphonies: no. 1 (Vienna, 1950); no. 2, dedicated to Albert Schweitzer (Vienna 1952); no. 3, which won the Pulitzer Prize (Pittsburgh, 1955); no. 4 (Minneapolis, 1956); no. 5, subtitled *Jeptha*, a symphonic rhapsody (Boston, 1958); no. 6 (1962); and no. 7 (1964). Also for orchestra are *Fantastische Nachtmusik* (1921); *Tanz Suite* (1923); *Funf Stücke* for chamber orchestra (1924); *Piece* for wind orchestra (1926); *Narziss* (1927); *Gewitter* (1927); *Komodie fur Orchester* (1927); *Bunte Suite* (1929); *Kleine Theater Suite* (1931); *Tragische Musik* (1931); *Big Ben, Variations on the Westminster Chimes* (1934); *Orchids* (1936); *Pinocchio, a Merry Overture* (1936); *The Idle Stroller Suite* (1938); *Hyperion*, a dramatic prelude (1948); *Miniature Overture* (1951); *Notturno*, commissioned by the Louisville Orchestra in 1954; *Circus Overture* (1954); *Peter Pan*, a fairy tale (1956); *Epilogue* (1959); *Capriccio* (1963); *Puppetshow* (1963); *The Enamoured Harlequin* (1963); *Symphony for Strings* (1964); *Three Pantomimes* (1964); and Sinfonietta for wind and percussion (1964). For solo instruments and orchestra he compose a Cello Concerto (1925); a Piano Concerto (1926), performed at the I.S.C.M. Festival in Stuttgart the following year; *Fanal* for organ and strings (1928); and Symphony for piano and orchestra (1932).

In addition to the operas, Toch wrote several works using voices. These include *An Mein Vaterland* for soloists, chorus, and organ (1915); an oratorio *Das Wasser*, performed in Berlin in 1930; *Cantata of the Bitter Herbs* for narrator, soloist, chorus, and orchestra (1938); and *Vanity of Vanities* for soprano, tenor, and five instruments (1954). His *Gesprochene Musik*, composed in 1930 for speaking chorus and percussion, includes the famous *Geographical Fugue*. For soprano and chamber orchestra he wrote *The Chinese Flute* (1923); in 1946 he composed *Poems for Martha* for voice and strings.

His chamber music includes thirteen string quartets (1902–53); Serenade for string quartet (1917); two violin sonatas (1926, 1928); a Cello Sonata (1929); a String Trio (1937); a Piano Quintet (1938); *Three Improvisations* for string trio (1963); and Quartet for oboe, clarinet, bassoon, and viola (1964). For piano he wrote three sonatas and a set of *Fifty Studies* (1931).

Toch was the author of a book, *The Shaping Forces of Music*, based on a lecture series at Harvard, published in 1948 (rev. 1977).

TORKE, MICHAEL
b. Milwaukee, Wisconsin, 21 September 1961

Torke began piano lessons at the age of five, later becoming a bassoonist in a youth orchestra. From 1980 to 1984 he studied at the Eastman School, Rochester, N.Y., where he was a pupil of Joseph Schwantner and Christopher Rouse. At Tanglewood he received composition lessons from Gunther Schuller. At Yale University (1984–85) he studied with Jacob Druckman. He was appointed the first associate composer with the Royal Scottish National Orchestra.

The Yellow Pages for chamber orchestra, composed in 1985, while he was a student at Yale, brought him instant recognition. Its cheerful repeated ostinati represent the user-friendly side of minimalist, with a hint of popular music and driving rhythms of jazz that characterize much of his later music.

As the titles of many of his pieces suggest, music and color have close associations for Torke. Among his orchestral works are *Ecstatic Orange*, performed by the Brooklyn Philharmonic Orchestra under Lukas Foss (1985); *Bright Blue Music* (1985); *Green* (1986); *Blue and White*, a ballet (1988); *Ash* (1989); *Red* (1991); *Javelin* (1994); *December* for strings (1995); *Brick Symphony*, a San Francisco Symphony Orchestra commission (1997); and *Lucent Variations* (2000).

For soloist(s) and orchestra Torke has written *Copper* for brass quintet and orchestra (1988); *Bronze*, a concerto in B-flat for piano and orchestra that the composer premiered as soloist (New York, 1990); a Piano Concerto, again premiered with the composer as soloist (1993); a Saxophone Concerto, for John Harle (1993), *Nylon* for guitar (1994); and a Percussion Concerto, subtitled *Rapture*, commissioned in 2000 by the Royal Scottish National Orchestra for Colin Currie. For the same orchestra he composed *An American Abroad* (2001).

Torke has composed three operas: *The Directions*, premiered in Iraklion, Crete in 1986; *King of Hearts*, produced on Channel 4 U.K. Television in 1993; and the one-act *Strawberry Fields* (1999), performed by Glimmerglass Opera. He is currently composing an

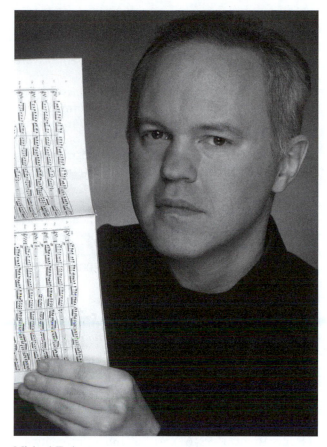

Michael Torke.
Photo: Robin Holland, courtesy the composer.

opera, *House of Mirth*, based on a story by Edith Wharton, for New York City Opera for the 2004–05 season.

In addition to the ballets *Purple* (1987) and *Slate* (1989), both staged by New York City Ballet, choreographers have been attracted to Torke's colorful scores for use in dance. In 1995 San Francisco Ballet staged *Terra Firma* (based on *Ash*, *Bright Blue Music*, and *Purple*). Other ballet compilations include *Time Torque*, produced by Ballet Chicago (*The Yellow Pages*, *Black and White*, and *Slate*) and *Three Bright Colors* (*Ecstatic Orange*, *Purple*, and *Green*). Grand Ballet Canadien has also choreographed *Bright Blue Music*. The ballet *The Contract*, with choreography by James Kuelka, was premiered in Toronto in May 2002 by the National Ballet of Canada.

Torke's many ensemble pieces include *Ceremony of Innocence*, performed at Tanglewood in 1983; *Vanada* for brass, keyboards, and percussion (1985); *Adjustable Wrench* (1987); *Rust* for piano and winds (1989); *Music on the Floor* (1992); *Chalk* for string quartet (1992); *Mondays and Tuesdays*, commissioned by the London Sinfonietta (1994); *Bone* for mixed ensemble (1994); *July* for saxophone quartet (1995); *Blue Pages, White Pages* (1995); *Flint* for chamber ensemble

(1995); *July 19* for string quartet (1996); *Overnight Mail* (1997); *Change of Address*, arranged from the television opera *King of Hearts* (1997); *Two Drinks* for saxophone and piano (2001); and *Two Harlequins are Looking at You* for piano trio.

His choral and vocal music includes a Mass for baritone, chorus, and chamber orchestra, performed at the Lincoln Center, New York in 1990; *Four Proverbs* for female voice and ensemble (1993); *Book of Proverbs* for soprano, baritone, chorus, and orchestra (1996); *Pentecost* for soprano, organ, and strings (1997); and a Disney Corporation commission, *Four Seasons* for children's chorus, chorus, and orchestra, premiered in October 1999 by the New York Philharmonic Orchestra conducted by Kurt Masur. Torke's most recent vocal composition is *Song of Isaiah* for soprano and orchestra, performed in Milwaukee in 2002.

TOWER, JOAN (PEABODY)
b. New Rochelle, New York, 6 September 1938

Joan Tower spent much of her childhood in South America, where her father was a mining engineer in Bolivia, Peru, and Chile. The family returned to the United States in 1955 after which she entered Bennington College, Vermont, where she was a pupil of Henry Brant (1958–61). At Columbia University she studied with Otto Luening, Chou Wen-chung, and Vladimir Ussachevsky (M.A. 1967; D.M.A., 1978).

In 1969 she was the pianist and founder of the Da Capo Players in New York, remaining with the group until 1984. Since 1972 she has taught at Bard College, Annandale-on-Hudson, New York, where she is currently Asher Edelman Professor of Music. She also was Composer-in-Residence with the St. Louis Symphony Orchestra (1985–87); *Silver Ladders* (1986), written during her residency for the orchestra, won the 1990 Grawemeyer Award for Music Composition; it has been made into a ballet in 1998 by choreographer Helgi Tomasson for the San Francisco Ballet. She was awarded a Guggenheim Fellowship in 1972, the Delaware Symphony's 1998 Alfred I. DuPont Award for Distinguished American Composers and Conductors, and induction into the American Academy of Arts and Letters. She serves as Composer-in-Residence with the Orchestra of St. Luke's (from 1999), the Yale/Norfolk Chamber Music Festival, and the Muir Quartet Festival at Park City, Utah. She was Composer-in-Residence at Tanglewood in 2000 and 2002.

Early influences on her music were Stravinsky and serial composers, before Tower's style after 1974 took on a freer, lyrical quality. She is best known for her orchestral music, which includes *Composition* (1967); *Amazon II* (1979), an orchestration of *Amazon I* for

Joan Tower.
Photo: Steve J. Sherman, courtesy the composer.

five instruments (1977); *Sequoia*, composed for the New York Philharmonic Orchestra in 1981; *Amazon III* for chamber orchestra (1982); *Music* for cello and chamber orchestra (1984); an overture, *Island Rhythms* (1985); a Piano Concerto, *Homage to Beethoven* (1985); a Clarinet Concerto (1988); *Island Prelude* for oboe and strings (1989); a Flute Concerto (1989); Concerto for Orchestra, a St. Louis Symphony Orchestra commission (1991); a Violin Concerto (1992); Concerto for chamber orchestra (1994); *Duets for Orchestra* (1994); *Tambor*, performed in New York by the National Symphony Orchestra of Washington in 1998; *Big Sky* for piano trio and orchestra (2000); and *Strike Zones*, a concerto for percussion written for Evelyn Glennie and the National Symphony Orchestra (2001).

Among her many instrumental pieces are *Pillars* for two pianos and percussion (1961); *Study* for two strings and two winds (1963); Percussion Quartet (1963, rev. 1969); *Brimset* for flute and percussion (1965); *Movements* for flute and piano (1968); *Opa Eboni* for oboe and piano (1968); *Prelude* for five players (1970); *Six Variations* for cello (1971); *Hexachords* for flute (1972); *Breakfast Rhythms I and II* for clarinet and five instruments (1974–75); *Black Topaz* for piano and six instruments (1976); *Platinum Spirals* for violin (1976);

Amazon I for flute, clarinet, viola, cello, and piano (1977); *Petrouchkates* for flute, clarinet, violin, cello, and piano (1980); *Wings* for flute (1981); *Red Garnet Waltz* for piano (1981); *Noon Dance* for flute (1982); *Fantasy . . . Those Harbor Lights* for clarinet and piano (1983); *Snow Dreams* for flute and guitar (1983); *Clocks* for guitar (1985); *Island Premiere* for wind quintet, also arranged for oboe and strings (1989); *Fanfares for the Uncommon Woman* for various brass ensembles (1986–93); *Elegy* for trombone and string quartet (1993); *Night Fields* for string quartet (1994); *Tres lent*, in memory of Olivier Messiaen for cello and piano (1994); *Turning Points* for clarinet and string quartet (1995); a Clarinet Quintet (1995); *Fascinating Ribbons* for wind ensemble (2001); and *In Memory* composed for the Tokyo Quartet in 2002.

Tower's ballet *Stepping Stones* for two pianos with choreography by Kathryn Posin was produced by Milwaukee Ballet in 1993.

TOWNSEND, DOUGLAS
b. New York, New York, 8 November 1921

Townsend graduated from the High School of Music and Art, New York in 1941. He later studied with Tibor Serly, Stefan Wolpe, Felix Greissle, and Otto Luening. At Tanglewood (1946) he was a pupil of Aaron Copland; he also received lessons from Louis Gruenberg (1948). Townsend taught at Brooklyn College (1958–69), Lehman College of the City University, New York (1970–71), the University of Bridgeport, Connecticut (1973–75), and the State University of New York, Purchase (1973–76). From 1977 to 1980 he was editor of the *Musical Heritage Review*, to which he contributed many articles. Townsend is active as a musicologist, discovering and editing works by F. X. Mozart, Leopold Mozart, Czerny, Donizetti, Rosetti, Alessandro Scarlatti, and others.

Townsend was active as a theater conductor and arranger and has composed three *Four-minute Operas* (1947); three *Folk Operettas* (1947); a chamber opera, *Lima Beans* (1954); an operetta for children, *The Floating Geezle* (1954); and a ballet, *The Infinite* (1951).

For orchestra he has written two chamber symphonies (1956, 1961); two symphonies for strings (1958, 1984); two suites for strings (1970, 1974); and three chamber concertos: no. 1 for violin and strings (1959), no. 2 for trombone and strings (1962), and no. 3 for flute, horn, piano, and strings (1971). Additional orchestral works include Divertimento for strings and wind (1950), *Fantasy* (1951), Sinfonietta (1954), *Adagio for Strings* (1956), *Fantasy on Motives of Burt Bacharach* (1979), and *Ode to Lincoln* for reciter and chamber ensemble. In addition he has composed a film

score, *8 x 8* (1957). Townsend has contributed several items to the band repertory: *The Gentlewoman's Polka* (1985); *The Ridgefield Rag* (1985); *Rag* for piano duet and band (1986); *Andante* (1989); *The 54th Street Rag* for piano and band (1989); two *Fantasias on Christmas Carols* (1988–90); *Rondino Scherzino* (2001); *Overture* (2002); and *Theme and Variations* (2002).

Among Townsend's instrumental works are two piano sonatinas (1945, 1951); a Brass Septet (1945); *Ballet Suite* for three clarinets (1953); *Canzona* for flute, viola, and bassoon (1954); *Four Fantasias on American Folk Songs* for piano duet (1956, orchestrated 1957); *Duo* for two violas (1957); *Tower Music* for brass (1959); *Dr. Jolly's Quickstep* for brass quintet (1974); Concertino for piano solo and four diverse instruments (1990); *Concerto in the Old Style* for three violins and strings (1994); and Concertino for four unaccompanied violins (2003).

Townsend's choral music includes a setting of *The Three Ravens* (1953), *Five Modern Madrigals* (1973), and a "cantatina" based on the tongue-twister *Betty Botter's Butter* for soloists, chorus, and piano.

TRAVIS, ROY (ELIHU)
b. New York, New York, 24 June 1922

Travis's college education at Columbia University was interrupted by his entrance into the U.S. Army in 1942. He became a combat engineer and saw active duty in the invasion of Germany. He studied briefly at the Guildhall School of Music, London, while a soldier awaiting return to the United States. He completed work for the A.B. degree at Columbia in 1947. At the Juilliard School (1947–50) he was a composition pupil of Bernard Wagenaar. At the same time, he studied Schenkerian analysis as a private pupil of Felix Salzer. He then studied with Otto Luening at Columbia (1950–51), receiving his M.A. in 1951; on a Fulbright Fellowship, he was a pupil of Darius Milhaud at the Paris Conservatory (1951–52). He taught at Columbia University (1952–53) and at the Mannes School of Music, New York (1952–57). He became a member of the music faculty of the University of California, Los Angeles (1957–91), where he was appointed professor in 1968. He is now retired.

Travis came to the attention of musicians with his *Symphonic Allegro*, composed in 1951, which won the Gershwin Prize and was performed and recorded by the New York Philharmonic Orchestra under Mitropoulos. Other early compositions include a String Quartet (1948), *Labyrinth* for orchestra (1950), Piano Sonata no. 1 (1954), and *Five Preludes* for piano (1956). Later orchestral works include *Collage* (1968) and *Songs and Epilogues*, settings of five Sappho poems in

English translation for voice and orchestra (1965, orchestrated 1975).

Since 1965, Travis has made increasing use of rhythms borrowed from authentic West African dances, mainly from Ghana. Works reflecting this interest in addition to the include *African Sonata* for piano (1966); *Duo Concertante* for violin and piano (1967); *Septet: Barma* (1968); Piano Concerto (1969); and *Switched-On Ashanti* for solo flute, pre-recorded African instruments and electronic synthesizers (1970–71). A Concerto for violin, tabla, and orchestra was premiered in a version with piano in London in 1996.

Travis's full-length opera in two acts, *The Passion of Oedipus*, was completed in 1965 and performed at the University of California, Los Angeles in 1968. In 1982 he completed a second opera in two acts to his own libretto, *The Black Bacchantes*, which combines elements of the ongoing black revolution and West African rhythms, within the dramatic framework of *The Bacchae* of Euripides. He is currently completing the orchestral score of an opera based on Shakespeare's *Hamlet*.

In addition to his primary activities as a composer, Travis has contributed articles to several scholarly journals. He is noted for his application of Heinrich Schenker's technique of linear-structural analysis to non-triadic works by such composers as Bartók and Stravinsky.

TREMBLAY, GEORGE (AMEDÉE)

b. Ottawa, Canada, 14 January 1911
d. Tijuana, Mexico, 14 July 1982

Tremblay was taken to the United States by his parents in 1919, settling eventually in Los Angeles, where he studied the organ with his father. His meeting with Arnold Schoenberg in 1936 had a profound effect upon his compositions, which thereafter adopted serial practices. He spent his life teaching privately in Los Angeles, and his students included many future film composers, notably John Beal, David Newman, and Jack Smalley.

For orchestra he composed three numbered symphonies: no. 1 in one movement (1949), no. 2 (1952), and no. 3 (1970); and two with titles only, *Chaparral Symphony* (1938) and *A Dance Symphony* (*The Phoenix*) (1982). His single work for concert band is *Prelude, Aria, Fugue and Postlude* (1967). Among his instrumental pieces are four string quartets (1936, 1946, 1962, 1963); *Modes of Transportation* for string quartet (1939); *In Memoriam* for string quartet (1942); three wind quintets (1940, 1950, 1962); Serenade for twelve instruments (1956); a Piano Quartet (1958); Trio for viola, cello, and piano (1959); *Epithalamium* for ten

instruments (1962); *Five Pieces* for oboe, clarinet, bassoon, and viola (1964); *String* Trio (1964); *Duo* for viola and piano (1966); Double Bass Sonata (1967); *Fantasy and Fugue* for bassoon and piano (1967); and Wind Sextet (1968). For piano Tremblay composed three sonatas (1939, 1939, 1957) and *Prelude and Dance* (1935).

Tremblay was the author of a book, *The Definitive Cycle of the 12-Tone Row and Its Application in All Fields of Composition, Including the Computer*, published in 1974.

TRIMBLE, LESTER (ALBERT)

b. Bangor, Wisconsin, 29 August 1923
d. New York, New York, 31 December 1986

At first Trimble trained as a violinist, but arthritis put an end to his career as a performer. He turned seriously to composition after receiving encouragement from Arnold Schoenberg, who heard an early string quartet. Trimble studied with Nicolai Lopatnikoff at the Carnegie-Mellon University in Pittsburgh (1945–48) and in Paris with Darius Milhaud, Arthur Honegger, and Nadia Boulanger (1950–52). At the Berkshire Music Center he had attended the classes of Milhaud and Aaron Copland.

On his return to the United States in 1952 Trimble became a music critic for the *New York Herald Tribune* and *The Nation* magazine until 1961; he was also managing editor of *Musical America* (1960–61). He abandoned full-time journalism when he was appointed general manager of the American Music Center. Two years later in 1963 he joined the faculty of the University of Maryland as professor of composition, resigning in 1968. Beginning in September 1967, he was for one year Composer-in-Residence with the New York Philharmonic Orchestra under Leonard Bernstein. From 1971 he taught at the Juilliard School. In 1964 Trimble was awarded a Guggenheim Fellowship. He also received the Award and Citation of the American Academy of Arts and Letters.

Symphony in Two Movements (1951) was his first large-scale work. Symphony no. 2, commissioned by the Koussevitzky Music Foundation and completed in 1968, was premiered in Lisbon in 1969. Also for orchestra Trimble wrote the Concerto for woodwinds and strings (1954); *Sonic Landscape* (1957, rev. 1968); *Five Episodes* (1961); *Notturno* for strings (1967); *Duo Concertante* (*To a Great American*) for two violins and orchestra (1968); a Violin Concerto (1977); *Panels* (1976, rev. 1983); a Flute Concerto (1980); and Symphony no. 3 (1984–85). For concert band he wrote *Closing Piece* (1957), *Concert Piece* (1965), and *Serious Song* (1965).

Among his instrumental work are an early *Duo* for viola and piano (1949); two string quartets (1949, 1955); Serenade for winds (1952); Double Concerto for instrumental ensemble (1964); *Solo for Virtuoso* (unaccompanied violin; 1971); *Music for Trumpet* (1974); and *Fantasy* for guitar (1978). He also composed a sequence of works for chamber ensemble entitled *Panels*: *I* for 11 players (1970), *II* for 13 players (1972), *III* for five players (1972–79), *IV* for 16 players (1973), *V*, String Quartet no. 3 (1974), *VI*, *Quadraphonics* for percussion quartet (1974), and *VII*, Serenade for nine players (1975).

Trimble's two-act opera *Boccaccio's Nightingale* (1969, rev.1983) remains unproduced. Three major items of vocal music are *Four Fragments from the Canterbury Tales* for soprano, flute, clarinet, and harpsichord (1958); *In Praise of Diplomacy and Common Sense* for baritone, male speaking chorus, two speaking voices, and percussion (1965); and *Petit Concert* for medium voice, violin, oboe, and harpsichord to texts of Blake and Shakespeare (1966). Trimble's solo songs include *Nantucket* (William Carlos Williams) for voice and piano (1949); *The Mistress of Bernal Francis* for medium voice and piano (1971); *To Mix With Time* for high voice and guitar (1980); and a song cycle, *Early Mornings* (1980). For men's chorus (with or without instrumental ensemble), he set Chaucer's words *Allas, Myn Hertes Queene* (1959). Other choral pieces include *A Cradle Song* for female voices (1967) and Psalm 93 (1973) and *Credo* (Herrick; 1973), both for mixed chorus.

Trimble provided scores for two documentary films produced by Gene Searchinger, *George Washington Bridge* and *A Portrait of Juan de Pareja* (*Valesquez*; 1974), and incidental music for *Little Clay Cart* (1953) and *The Tragical History of Dr Faustus* (1954).

He created two electronic music pieces, *Eden I* (1971) and *Hatteras* with percussion (1971).

TRYTHALL, (HARRY) GILBERT
b. Knoxville, Tennessee, 28 October 1930

Trythall is the older brother of Richard Trythall, also a composer. He studied at the University of Tennessee, Knoxville under David Van Vactor (1948–51), at Northwestern University, Evanston, Illinois with Wallingford Riegger (1952), and at Cornell University with Robert Palmer (1960). After serving as an assistant professor at Knox College, Galesburg, Illinois (1960–64), he was professor of theory and composition at George Peabody College for Teachers, Nashville, Tennessee (1964–75), where he was chairman of the music department (1973–75), From 1975 to 1981 he served as dean of the Creative Arts Center at West Virginia University,

Harry G. Trythall.
Courtesy the composer.

Morgantown. He was visiting professor of music at the Universidade Federal do Espírito Santo in Vitória, Brazil (2000–02).

Trythall first came to the notice of the musical public with Symphony no. 1, composed in 1958 and revised in 1961, a work planned on a large scale and showing the influence of Hindemith. Other orchestral pieces are *A Solemn Chant* for strings (1958); *Fanfare and Celebration* (1961); a Harp Concerto (1963); *Dionysia* for chamber orchestra (1964); *Cyndy the Synth* (*Minnie the Moog*) for synthesizer and string orchestra (1975); and *Sinfonia Concertante* (1989). His instrumental music includes a String Quartet (1961), a Flute Sonata (1964), *A Vacuum Soprano* for brass quintet and tape (1966), a *Prelude and Fugue* for organ, and a Brass Quintet.

In the 1960s Trythall began to use electronic tape, often in combination with instruments and other media. It is for these electronic and multimedia compositions that he is best known, including *Surfaces* for wind ensemble, tape, and lights (1962); *Entropy* for stereo brass, improvisation group, and stereo tape (1967); *Parallax*, an "environment" for between 4 and 40 brass instruments, electronic tape, slides, and audience (1968); *Chroma I* for an orchestra of winds and percussion, electronic tape, and slide projector (1970); and *Echospace* for brass, tape, and film, commissioned by the Atlanta Contemporary Dance Group (1971, rev. 1973). Other pieces include *Programmatic Sensation I* (electronic multimedia); *Push Tomato* for electronics and film; *The World, Mother, Apple Pie* for percussion, tape, film, and slides (1970); *Citizen Kane II* for electronics and film; *One Full Rotation of the Earth* for dancers, tape, and film; and *Luxikon I* for four synthesized percussion and laser patterns, premiered at the Georgia Unified Arts Conference in January 1980. For tape alone he has created *Music for Aluminum Rooms*, *The Play of Electrons*, *Breathing Bag no. 4* (with slides), *Two Pleasantries*, *The Electronic Womb* (1969), and *Luxikon II* (1981).

His solo vocal music includes *Love Songs* for soprano and piano; *Spanish Songs* for soprano and synthesizer (1986–87); *From the Egyptian Book of the Dead* for soprano, saxophone or wind controller and synthesizer (1990); *9.01: Hard Start Variations* for jazz soprano, wind controller, synthesizer, and sequencer (1991); *The Pastimes of Lord Chaitanya* for jazz soprano and synthesizer (1993); and *Intermission* for soprano and synthesizer (1994). Among his choral music are two pieces for chorus and tape, *In the Presence* (1968) and *A Time to Every Purpose* (1971), and a setting of the Mass in English and Spanish for congregation, organ, and descant (1988). Trythall has composed two operas, *The Music Lesson* (1960) and *The Terminal Opera* (1982, rev. 1987).

Trythall is the author of three books: *Electronic Music: Principles and Practice* (1973), *Eighteenth Century Counterpoint* (1993), and *Sixteenth-Century Counterpoint* (1994). He also is known for recording two albums of country music on synthesizer, *Country Moog* and *Switched-on Nashville*. He currently operates KBA Software, a company that makes music theory training material for computers.

TRYTHALL, RICHARD (AKRE)

b. Knoxville, Tennessee, 25 July 1939

Trythall, the younger brother of composer Gilbert Trythall, studied with David Van Vactor at the University of Tennessee, Knoxville (1958–61) and at Princeton University under Roger Sessions and Earl Kim (1961–63). In 1964 he won the Prix de Rome, which enabled him to study at the American Academy for three years. With the exception of his participation in the Center of the Creative and Performing Arts at the State University of New York, Buffalo (1972–73) and his tenure on the faculty of the University of California, Davis (1976), he has lived in Italy ever since 1964.

Trythall has been on the faculty of St. Stephen's School in Rome since 1966, and has been chairman of the arts department there for the past 25 years. Since 1970 he has been "music liaison" for the American Academy in Rome. In addition to his American citizenship, Trythall acquired Italian citizenship in 1996. Among his many awards, he was awarded a Guggenheim Fellowship in 1967, the Naumburg Recording Award, and a Fulbright Fellowship, as well as composition commissions from the Fromm Music Foundation, the Dorian Woodwind Quintet, and the Gruppo Percussione Ricerca (Venice, Italy).

For orchestra he has written an Overture (1959), a Symphony (1961), *Piece* for small orchestra (1963), *Construzione per Orchestra* (1966), and *Continuums*, first performed in 1968 at Tanglewood under the direction of Gunther Schuller.

Trythall, an accomplished pianist, was the soloist in the premieres of three works for piano and orchestra: *Theme and Variations* (1960), *Composition* (1965), and *Ballad* (1982–83). For keyboard he has composed many piano solos: *Three Pieces for Piano* (1962); *Coincidences* for piano solo (1970); *Recital One* (1979–81); *Arabesque* (1983); *Mirage* (1985–89); *Parts Unknown* (1990–91); *Two Haitian Ritual Dances* (for prepared piano; 1996); *Five Pieces in African American Styles* (1997); *Marisa* (2000); and *Out of Bounds* (2001), a "remix" of 11 of his earlier solo compositions. He has also composed a Suite for harpsichord and tape (1973), based on music by Domenico Scarlatti.

His instrumental music includes *Duets for treble instruments* (1958); String Quartet (1960); a Piano Trio (1964); *Variations on a Theme by F. J. Haydn* for wind quintet and tape (1976); *Salute to the 'Fifties* for solo percussionist and tape (1977); *Bolero* for four percussionists (1979); *Aria* for flute and piano (1989); *Memories Are Made of This* for string quintet, flute, clarinet, and piano (2003); and *Time and Time Again* for percussion quartet (2003).

For tape alone he has created *Study no. 1* (1967), *Verse* (1970–71), *Omaggio a Jerry Lee Lewis* (1975), and *Dance Music* (1978). *Verse* can be extended into a multimedia work with slides, film, and tape. The ballet *Capriccio*, for three percussion and tape, was completed in 1984.

Trythall has written two important vocal compositions, *Four Songs* to texts by Rilke for soprano and piano (1962) and *Penelope's Monologue* (1966), a concert aria for soprano and orchestra, setting excerpts of Joyce's *Ulysses*. For high school performance he has composed *A Christmas Cantata* (1974), *Three Fantasias of an Old Shoemaker* for baritone and chorus (1975), and *Mountain Songs* for chorus and guitars (1975).

David Tudor.
Courtesy Music Library, State University of New York, Buffalo, North American New Music Festival, Item 105.

TUDOR, DAVID (EUGENE)

b. Philadelphia, Pennsylvania, 20 January 1926
d. Tomkins Cove, New York, 13 August 1996

Tudor studied with Stefan Wolpe (composition), Irma Wolfe (piano), and William Hawke (organ). After acting as organist at St. Mark's Church, Philadelphia (1938–41) and at Swarthmore College, Pennsylvania (1944–48), he took on a career as a virtuoso pianist, especially in the field of avant-garde music. In much of his work he was associated with John Cage, Gordon Mumma, Christian Wolff, Morton Feldman, and Earle Brown.

Tudor's own compositions include *Fluorescent Sound*, premiered in Stockholm in 1964; *Bandoneon*, a mixed-media work (1966); *Four Pepsi Pieces* (1970); *Microphone* (1970, rev. 1973); *Monobird* (incorporating *Birdcage* by Cage; 1972); *Rainforest II* (incorporating *Murea* by Cage; 1972); *Untitled* (incorporating *62 Mesostics* by Cage; 1972, rev. 1994); *Rainforest IV* (1973); *Island Eye, Island Ear* (1974); *Pulsers* (1976); *Dialects* (1984); *Hedgehog* (1985); *Web I for John Cage* (1985); *Electronics With Talking Shop* (1986); *Web II for John Cage* (1987); *Five Stone* (1988); *Virtual Focus* (1990); *Coefficient I* (1991); *Coefficient: Frictional percussion and electronics* (1991); and *Neutral Network Plus* and *Neutral Syntheses 1 – 9* (1992–94).

Collective and group compositions include *Reunion* (with Cage, Mumma, and Marcel Duchamp; 1968);

Assemblages (with Cage and Mumma; 1968); *Rainforest III* (1973); *Video Pulsers* (1977); *Rotation* (1978); *Audio Laser* (1979); *Nine Lines Reflected* (1986); and *Toneburst: Maps and Fragments* (1996).

Tudor began collaboration with the Merce Cunningham Dance Company in 1953; he served as its musical director following Cage's death (1992). For Cunningham he provided the following scores: *Rainforest I* (1968); *Melodics for Amplified Bandoneon* (1972); *Toneburst (Sounddance*; 1974); *Forest Speech (Event*; 1976); *Weatherings (Exchange*; 1978); *Phonemes* (1981); *Likeness to Voices/Dialects* (1982); *Sextet for Seven* (1983); *Virtual Focus (Polarity*; 1990); and *Ocean Diary* (1994).

TURNER, CHARLES

b. Baltimore, Maryland, 25 November 1921

Turner studied violin at the Curtis Institute, Philadelphia (1939–41) and the Juilliard School (1945–47). He was also a composition pupil of Nadia Boulanger (1947) and Samuel Barber (1950–55). He taught at the Wykeham-Rise School, Washington, Connecticut (1968–70) and the United Nations School, New York (1970–78).

Turner's principal works are for orchestra: a Violin Concerto (1940); *Encounter*, a symphonic sketch premiered by George Szell (Cleveland, 1955); and *Marriage of Orpheus*, first performed by the New York Philharmonic Orchestra under Thomas Schippers (1966). A ballet, *Dark Pastorale*, was commissioned by the New York City Ballet and staged on 14 January 1957; other productions followed in Boston and Philadelphia.

Turner's instrumental music includes *Serenade for Icarus* for violin and piano (1959). He orchestrated Samuel Barber's final composition, *Canzonetta* for oboe and strings, the only complete movement of an intended Oboe Concerto.

TURNER, GODFREY

b. Manchester, England, 27 March 1913
d. New York, New York, 7 December 1948

Turner studied with Edward J. Dent at Cambridge University (1931–34) and Nadia Boulanger in Paris before going to the United States in 1936. He taught at the San Francisco Conservatory (1938–43) and was a music editor for Boosey and Hawkes in New York (1944–46). From 1946 until his suicide he was secretary of the American Music Center in New York.

Turner's best-known work is *Fanfare, Chorale and Finale* for brass, performed at the I.S.C.M. Festival in San Francisco in 1942. For orchestra he composed a *Sarabande and Tango*, *Sonata Concertante* for piano and strings, *Trinity Concerto* for chamber orchestra, and a Viola Concerto. The *Gregorian Overture*, performed in Columbus, Ohio, in 1947 won the BMI contest for an orchestral work. Among his instrumental pieces are a Wind Quintet and a *Little Suite* for four bassoons.

TUROK, PAUL (HARRIS)

b. New York, New York, 3 December 1929

Turok was educated at the High School of Music and Art, New York; Queens College, New York (B.A. 1950) with Karol Rathaus; the University of California, Berkeley (1950–51) with Roger Sessions; and at the Juilliard School (1951–53) with Bernard Wagenaar. From 1960 to 1963 he taught at City College, New York and at Williams College, Williamstown, Massachusetts (1963–64). In addition to his activities as a composer, for many years he has been an established critic, writing for the *New York Herald Tribune* (1964–65), *The Music Journal* (1964–80), *Ovation* (1980–89), and *Fanfare* (since 1980). A regular contributor of articles to the *New York Times* (1982–89), he is now the publisher and editor of *Turok's Choice*, a monthly newsletter reviewing classical recordings since 1990.

For orchestra he has written a Violin Concerto

(1953); a Symphony in two movements (1955); *Aspects of Lincoln and Liberty: Variations on an American Folk Song* (1958); *Four Studies* (1961); *Chartres West* (1968); *Homage to Bach* (1969); *Lyric Variations* for oboe and orchestra (1971); *A Scott Joplin Overture* (1973); *Great Scott!* (1973); *A Sousa Overture* (1975); *Ragtime Caprice* for piano and orchestra (1976); *Danza Viva* (1978); and *Threnody* for strings (1979).

Turok has composed a series of works for soloist(s) and orchestra entitled *Canzona Concertante*: no. 1 for English horn (1980), no. 2 for trombone (1982), no. 3 for flute, oboe, trumpet, and strings (1982), no. 4 for cello (1986), no. 5 for violin, piano, and winds (1988), no. 6 for bassoon (1995), no. 7 for viola, percussion, and strings (1999), and no. 8 for violin (2002). Other orchestral works include *Ultima Thule* (1981); *. . . from Sholem Aleichem* (1990); Concerto for two violins (1991); Piano Concerto (1998); and *Reeling in the New Year* (1999). His works for concert band include *March Militaire* (1955), *Joplination* (1975), and *Rhapsody* (1987).

Turok's stage works include three operas: *Scene Domestic*, a chamber opera in one act, composed in 1955 and premiered in Aspen, Colorado in 1973; *Richard III* in four acts (1975), produced by Philadelphia Lyric Opera in 1980; and *A Secular Masque* (1973); as well as two ballets, *Youngest Brother* (1953) and *Antoniana*, after Vivaldi (1977).

Instrumental pieces include four string quartets (1955, 1969, 1980, 1986); Suite for two violins (1948); *Variations on a Theme of Schoenberg* for string quartet (1952); *Concert Piece* for trombone and organ (1953); a String Trio (1954); a Wind Quintet (1956); *Elegy in Memory of Karol Rathaus* for brass ensemble (1963); *Duo Concertante* for winds (1969); *Picture* for wind quintet (1971); *Sarabande* for flute, horn, cello, and piano (1972); *Introduction and Gran' Scherzo* for five horns (1972); *Music for Nine Horns* (1973); *Prelude* for brass and organ (1973); a Clarinet Trio (1973); *Capriccio* for violin and percussion ensemble (1976); *Miniature Variations* for violin and piano (1977); Brass Quintet (1978); *Concert Variations* for trumpet and marimba (1978); *Parade* for solo clarinet (1978); *Three Virtuoso Caprices* (after Paganini) for two oboes and English horn (1978); Quintet for English horn and strings (1978); *Prelude and Fugue* for two oboes, oboe d'amore, and English horn (1980); *Sonata Jubilate* for brass and organ (1980); *Tourist Music* for oboe, clarinet, and bassoon (1985); *Gypsy Airs* for violin, clarinet, and piano (1989); *ABAC* for trumpet and organ (1990); Piano Trio (1992); *Fantasy on Rossini's 'Non piu mesta'* for four flutes and piano (1993); Sextet for piano and winds (2001); and *Elegy in Memory of Nathan Schwartz* for unaccompanied cello (2002).

Turok has composed sonatas for several instruments,

including unaccompanied cello (1952), organ (1961), harpsichord (1972), horn (1972), trumpet (1973), unaccompanied viola (1973), bassoon (1975), guitar (1977), two for cello (1977, 1996), two pianos (1984), alto saxophone (1988), violin (1989), and flute (2000). In addition there are *Partitas* for solo oboe (1954), English horn, clarinet, and bassoon (1991), and solo English horn (2001), and sonatinas for harp (1978) and solo flute (1979).

Among his piano compositions are *Passacaglia* (1955), *Little Suite* (1955), *Three Transcendental Etudes* (1970), *Piano Dance* (1987), and two pieces for two pianos, *Acres of Clams* (1994) and *Tourist Music II* (1997).

His vocal music includes *Evocations* for mezzo-soprano and piano (1955); *Chorus of the Frogs* (1956); *To Music* for soprano and piano (1957); *Sermon* for male voices and organ (1965); *True Thomas* for soprano, tenor, and piano (1969); *Three Popular Songs* for soprano and piano (1969); *The Calendar* for female voices and piano (1978); *Lanier Songs* for soprano and six instruments (1978); *Two Songs* for soprano, clarinet, and piano (1980); and *Behold, Thou art Fair, My Beloved* for chorus (2001).

TUTHILL, BURNET CORWEN

b. New York, New York, 16 November 1888
d. Knoxville, Tennessee, 18 January 1982

Tuthill was the son of William Burnet Tuthill, the architect of Carnegie Hall in New York. He studied at Columbia University (B.A., 1909; M.A., 1910) and conducted the Columbia University Orchestra (1909–13). He was general manager of the Cincinnati College of Music (1922–30) before being appointed director of the music department of Southwestern University, Memphis in 1935; he retired in 1959. In addition he was conductor of the Memphis Symphony Orchestra (1938–46) and was one of the founders of the National Association of Schools of Music. In 1945 he was granted leave of absence for a year to become director of Shrivenham American University in England.

For orchestra Tuthill composed a *Nocturne* for flute and strings (1933); *Bethlehem: a Pastorale* (1934); *Intrada* for small orchestra (1934); *Come 7*, a rhapsody (1935); a symphonic poem, *Laurentia* (1929–36); Symphony in C (1940); *Elegy* (1946); *Rowdy Dance* (1948); Clarinet Concerto (1948–49); *Flute Song* for flute, two horns, and strings (1954); *Rhapsody* for clarinet and chamber orchestra (1954–56); *Trombone Trouble* for three trombones and orchestra (1963); and concertos for saxophone (1965), trombone (1967), and tuba (1975). Tuthill also provided several works for wind band, including *Dr. Joe March* (1933); *Overture Brillante* (1937); a Suite, premiered at the Eastman School

Burnet Tuthill.
Courtesy Rhodes College.

(1946); *Processional* (1957); *Rondo Concertante* for two clarinets and band (1961); Concerto for double bass and band (1962); and *Fantasia* for tuba and band (1968).

Many of his instrumental pieces make use of wind instruments: *Intermezzo* for three clarinets (1927); *Fantasy Sonata* for clarinet and piano (1932); *Nocturne* for flute and string quartet (1933); Piano Trio (1933); *Variations on "When Johnny Comes Marching Home"* for wind quintet and piano (1934); *Sailor's Hornpipe* for wind quintet (1935); *Divertimento in Classic Style* for wind quintet (1936); Violin Sonata (1937); String Sextet (1937); Viola Sonata (1941); Trumpet Sonata (1950); *Family Music* for flute, two clarinets, viola, and cello (1952); String Quartet (1934); Quintet for four clarinets and piano (1957); *Six for Bass* for double bass and piano (1961); Saxophone Quartet (1966); Saxophone Sonata (1968); *Five Essays* for brass quintet (1969); *Slow Piece* for violin and harpsichord (1971); and *A Little English Suite* for English horn and piano (1971).

Tuthill's vocal music comprises four choral items: *Benedicite Omnia Opera* for double chorus (1933), *Big River* for soprano, female voices, and orchestra (1942), Requiem for soprano, baritone, chorus, and organ (1960), and *Thanksgiving Anthems* for mixed voices (1971).

In 1974 Tuthill published an autobiography, *Recollections of a Musical Life 1900–74.*

U-V

USSACHEVSKY, VLADIMIR (ALEXIS)
b. Harbin, Manchuria, 3 November 1911
d. New York, New York, 2 January 1990

Ussachevsky went to the United States in 1930, where he studied at Pomona College, California (1932–35). After graduating he attended the Eastman School of Music, Rochester, New York (1935–39), where his teachers included Howard Hanson and Bernard Rogers. During the Second World War he served in the U.S. Army. In 1947 he joined the music department of Columbia University. From 1970 to 1971 he was also Composer-in-Residence at the University of Utah, Salt Lake City. He was elected a member of the National Institute of Arts and Letters in 1975.

Ussachevsky's early works include *Theme and Variations* for orchestra (1935); *Jubilee Cantata* for chorus and orchestra (1938); *Piece* for flute and orchestra (1947); *Miniatures for a Curious Child* for orchestra (1950); *Intermezzo* for piano and orchestra (1952); and a Piano Sonata (1952).

After 1951 he took a special interest in electronic music, devising many new techniques for producing and recording sounds. In 1952 he began a collaboration with Otto Luening to create large-scale works using pre-recorded tape. With Luening, Sessions, and Babbitt he was a founder of the Columbia-Princeton Electronic Music Center in 1959.

In his own works, Ussachevsky sometimes combined instruments and tape. *Sonic Contours* (1952) uses taped sounds and instruments and mixes conversation with music. *A Piece for tape recorder* (1955) employs unusual percussion instruments. Later works in this category include *Colloquy* for solo instruments, orchestra,

Milton Babbitt, Peter Mauzey, and Vladimir Ussachevsky in front of the RCA Mark II Synthesizer the Columbia-Princeton Electronic Music Center, 1958.
Courtesy Columbia Electronic Music Center.

and tape (1976); *Pentagrams* for oboe and tape (1980); *Celebration 1980* for electronic valve instruments, strings, and tape (1980); *Celebration 1981* for six winds, strings, and tape (1981); and *Dialogues and Contrasts* for brass quintet and tape (1984). Other tape compositions include *Transposition, Reverberation, Experiment, Composition* (1951–52); *Underwater Valse* (1952); *Studies in Sounds* (1955); *Metamorphoses* (1956); *Improvisation on 4711* (1956); *Linear Contrasts* (1958); *Studies in Sounds Plus* (1959); *Wireless Fantasy* (1960); *Creation Prologue* (with choir) (1961); *Of Wood and Brass* (1965); *Two Images for a Computer Piece* (1968); *We* (1971), composed for CBS radio; *Two Sketches* (1971); and *Conflict* (1971).

Missa Brevis for soprano, chorus, and brass (without tape) was completed in 1972. A late work for orchestra alone is *Dances and Fanfares for a Festive Occasion* (1980). Ussachevsky composed incidental music for a play, *The Cannibals* (1969), a television score, *Mathematics* (1957), and five film scores: *Circle of Fire* (1940), *The Boy Who Saw Through* (1959), *No Exit* (1962), *Line of Apogee* (1967), and *Duck, Duck* (1970).

For his many works with Otto Luening, see Luening's separate entry.

VAN APPLEDORN, MARY JEANNE
b. Holland, Michigan, 2 October 1927

Van Appledorn studied at the Eastman School of Music, Rochester, New York (B. Mus., 1948; M. Mus., 1950; Ph.D., 1966), where she was a pupil of Cecile Straub Genhart for piano and Bernard Rogers and Alan Hovhaness for composition. She later attended the Massachusetts Institute of Technology. From 1950 to retirement in 2000, she was professor of composition at the Texas Technical University in Lubbock, becoming the Paul Whitfield Horn Professor in 1989.

For orchestra she has written *Concerto Brevis* for piano and orchestra (1954); *Passacaglia and Chorale* (1973); *Ayre* for viol da gamba ensemble and clarinet or saxophone choir (1989); *Terrestrial Music*, a double concerto for violin, piano, and strings (1992); *Rhapsody* for violin and orchestra (1997); and *Meliora Fanfare* (1999). To the concert band repertory she has contributed *A Choreographic Overture* (1957), Concerto for trumpet and band (1960), *Cacophony* (1980), *Lux Legend of Sankta Lucia* (1981), and *Cycles of Moons and Tides* (1995).

Van Appledorn has been a prolific writer of instrumental music: *Cellano Rhapsody* for cello and piano (1948); *Burlesca* for piano, brass, and percussion

Mary Jeanne Van Appledorn.
Courtesy Texas Tech University, Creative and Photographic Services.

(1951); *Sonnet* for organ (1959); *Matrices* for saxophone and piano (1979); *Liquid Gold* for saxophone and piano (1982); *Four Duets* for two saxophones (1985); *Sonic Mutation* for harp (1986); *Four Duos* for viola and cello (1986); *Sonatine* for clarinet and piano (1988); *Cornucopia* for trumpet (1988); *Windsongs* for brass quintet (1991); *Incantation* for trumpet and piano (1992); *Atmospheres* for trombone ensemble (1993); *Postcards to John* for guitar (1994); *Reeds Afire*, duos for clarinet and bassoon (1994); *Trio Italiano* for trumpet, horn, and bass trombone (1995); *Passages* for trombone and piano (1996); *A Native American Mosaic* for native American flute (1997); *Incantations* for oboe and piano (1998); *Galilean Galaxies* for flute, bassoon, and piano (1998); and *Gestures* for clarinet quartet (1999).

Her choral works include *Peter Quince at the Clavier* for women's chorus, narrator, flute, oboe, horn, and piano (1958); *Darest Thou Now, O Soul* for women's voices and organ (1975); *West Texas Suite* for chorus, symphonic band, and percussion (1976); a cantata, *Riding Night After Night* for three soloists, narrator, chorus, and orchestra (1978); and *Les Hommes Vides* for chorus (1994). Among her solo vocal pieces are *Danza Impresion de Espana* for vocal octet and ballet (1979); *Missa Brevis* for voice (or trumpet) and organ

(1987); *Freedom of Youth* for speaker and synthesizer (1986); *Five Psalms* for tenor, trumpet, and piano (1998); and *Songs Without Words* for two sopranos and piano (1999).

VAN DER STUCKEN, FRANK (VALENTIN)

b. Fredericksburg, Texas, 15 October 1858
d. Hamburg, Germany, 16 August 1929

Van der Stucken was born of mixed Belgian-German parentage. When he was eight, the family moved back to Europe and lived in Antwerp, where the boy first studied music. Later he became a pupil of Carl Reinecke at the Leipzig Conservatory (1877–79) and was a friend of both Grieg and Liszt. From 1881 to 1882 he was a conductor at the City Theater in Breslau (now Wroclaw, Poland). In 1883 he was invited by Liszt to give a concert of his own works in Weimar. He returned to the United States in 1884 to take up the post of music director of the Arion Choir in New York. In 1895 he was appointed the first conductor of the Cincinnati Symphony Orchestra, a post he held until 1907. He was also director of the Cincinnati College of Music (1896–1901) and the Cincinnati May Festival (1906–12, 1925–27). In 1908 he returned to Europe and spent most of his time there until his death.

Van der Stucken composed an opera, *Vlasa* (1883), incidental music for *The Tempest* (1882), and several orchestral works, including *Rigaudon* (1894), a symphonic poem, *Pax Triumphans* (1900), and a festival march, *Louisiana*. His orchestral prologue to Heine's tragedy *William Ratcliff* was performed in Weimar under the direction of Liszt.

VAN DE VATE, NANCY

b. Plainfield, New Jersey, 30 December 1930

Van de Vate studied piano at the Eastman School of Music (1948–49) before enrolling at Wellesley College (1949–52). She also attended the University of Mississippi (1955–58) and Florida State University, where she was awarded her doctorate in 1968. She taught at several institutions, including Memphis State University (1964–66), University of Tennessee (1967), Knoxville College (1968–69, 1971–72), Maryville College (1973–74), University of Hawaii (1975–77), and Hawaii Loa College, Hawaii (1977–80).

In 1975 she founded the International League of Women Composers. She has been much influenced by the music of places where she has lived or spent extended periods of time including Hawaii (1975–81), Indonesia (1982–85), and Eastern Europe. In 1985 she settled in Vienna where, with her husband, she established a recording company specializing in new music, Vienna Modern Masters, in 1990.

Van de Vate has composed five operas: *The Death of the Hired Man* (Robert Frost), completed in 1958 and revised in 1998; *In the Shadow of the Glen* (J. M. Synge; 1960, rev. 1994), performed in Cambridge,

Nancy Van de Vate, 2001.
Photo: Richard Howard, courtesy the composer.

Massachusetts in 1999; *Der Herrscher und das Mädchen*, an opera for children premiered in Vienna in 1995; *Nemo: Jenseits von Vulkania* (1995); and *All Quiet on the Western Front* (Remarque; 1999). She has also written three multimedia theater works: *A Night in the Royal Ontario Museum* for soprano and tape (1983); *Cocaine Lil*, produced in Bremen, Germany in 1988; and *Venal Vera: Ode to a Gezira Lovely* (2000).

Among her orchestral pieces are *Adagio* (1957); *Variations* for chamber orchestra (1958); a Piano Concerto (1968, rev. 1993), which she submitted for her doctorate; *Concertpiece* for cello and small orchestra (1978); *Dark Nebulae* (1981); *Gema Jawa* (*Echoes of Java*) for strings (1984); *Journeys* (1981–84); *Distant Worlds* (1985); two violin concertos (1985–86, 1996); *Pura Besakih* (*Besakih Temple, Bali*; 1987); *Chernobyl* (1987); *Krakow Concerto* for percussion and orchestra (1988); Viola Concerto (1990); *Adagio and Rondo* for strings (1994); *Suite From "Nemo"* (1996); Harp Concerto (1996); *A Peacock Southeast Flew*, a concerto for pipa and orchestra (1997); *Western Front* (1997); and *The Four Moods of Mechthild*, a suite for string orchestra (2000).

Van De Vate has composed much instrumental music, including *Short Suite* for brass (1960); Woodwind Quintet (1964); Viola Sonata (1964); String Quartet (1969); Oboe Sonata (1969); *Six Etudes* for solo viola (1969); *Three Sound Pieces* for brass and percussion (1973); Brass Quintet (1974, rev. 1979); String Trio (1974); Quintet for flute, clarinet, violin, viola, and piano (1975); Suite for solo violin (1975); *Music for viola, percussion, and piano* (1976); Trio for bassoon, percussion, and piano (1980); Piano Trio (1983); *Music for MW2* for flute, cello, piano (four hands), and percussion (1985); *Teufelstanz* for six percussionists (1988); *Seven Pieces* for violin and piano (1989); *Four Fantasy Pieces* for flute and piano (1993); Divertimento for harp and string quintet (1996); *Music in Five, Three and Seven* for saxophone quartet (2001); and Suite for marimba (2002).

For her own instrument, the piano, she has written two sonatas (1978, 1983); *Nine Preludes* (1974–78); *Contrasts* for two pianos, six hands (1984); *Twelve Pieces On One to Twelve Notes I and II* (1986, 2001); *Fantasy Pieces* (1995); and *Night Journey* (1996).

Choral music includes *The Pond* for chorus (1970); *An American Essay* (Whitman) for soprano, chorus, piano, and percussion (or orchestra; 1972); *Cantata* (*Voices of Women*) for female voices and seven performers (1979, orchestrated 1993); *Katyn* for chorus and orchestra (1989); *How Fares the Night?* for violin, women's chorus, and orchestra (1994); and *Choral Suite from "Nemo"* for chorus and orchestra (1997). Among her solo vocal compositions are *Four Somber Songs* for mezzo-soprano and piano (1970), orchestrated in 1992; *Letter to a Friend's Loneliness* (John Unterecker) for soprano and string quartet (1976); *Songs for the Four Parts of the Night* for soprano and piano (1984); and *Listening to the Night* for soprano and seven instruments (2001).

VAN HAGEN, PETER ALBRECHT, SR. (PETER ALBRECHT VON HAGEN, SR.)
b. Netherlands, 1755
d. Boston, Massachusetts, 20 August 1803

Van Hagen arrived in America in 1774, settling first in Charleston, South Carolina where he established a one-man conservatory, offering training in all woodwind and string instruments, in addition to singing and keyboard. He lived in New York from 1789 to 1796, appearing frequently in concerts with his wife (Elizabeth J. C. van Hagen, b. 1750, d. c.1809/10) and son (Peter A. van Hagen, Jr., b. 1779/81, d. 1837).

In 1796 he moved to Boston; changing his name to "von Hagen," he became established as a music publisher, theater music director, and organist. He composed a ballad opera, *The Adopted Child*, or *The Baron of Milford Castle*, and provided incidental music for a number of plays, including *Columbus, or The Discovery of America*; *The Battle of Hexham*; and *Zorinski, or Freedom to the Stones*. He is also credited with a *Funeral Dirge for George Washington*. The authorship of other works, such as songs, marches, and a *Federal Overture* (1797), is vague in terms of which family member should receive credit. However, Elizabeth van Hagen was definitely the composer of a piano sonata, two piano concertos, and *The Country Maid*, a set of keyboard variations.

VAN VACTOR, DAVID
b. Plymouth, Indiana, 8 May 1906
d. Los Angeles, California, 24 March 1994

Van Vactor studied medicine and music at Northwestern University, Evanston, Illinois (1924–28). There he learned the flute and received composition lessons from Felix Borowski. After a year at the Vienna Academy as a pupil of Franz Schmidt and Arnold Schoenberg, he returned in 1929 to the United States, where he played in the Chicago Symphony Orchestra from 1931 to 1943. In 1931 in Paris he was a pupil of Marcel Moyse for flute and Paul Dukas for composition. From 1936 to 1943 Van Vactor taught at Northwestern University. He was assistant conductor of the Kansas City Philharmonic Orchestra (1943–45) and head of the department of theory and composition at the Conservatory of Music (1943–47). In 1947 he founded the department of

David Van Vactor.
*Courtesy David L. Van Vactor and
Roger Rhodes Music.*

fine arts at the University of Tennessee and was appointed conductor of the Knoxville Symphony Orchestra, a position he retained until 1972. He retired from the university in 1976.

Several of Van Vactor's compositions are for his own instrument. These include a Quintet for flute and strings (1932); a Flute Concerto (1932); a Suite for two flutes (1934); *Concerto Grosso* for three flutes, harp, and orchestra (1935); *Pastorale and Dance* for flute and strings (1947); and *Concerto a Cinque* for three flutes and harp. He also composed a set of *Twenty-Four Etudes* for solo flute (1933) and a Sonatina for flute and piano (1945).

Van Vactor's most significant works are his eight symphonies. The First Symphony in D minor, dating from 1936, won a prize of $1,000 in a competition sponsored by the New York Philharmonic Orchestra, which performed it in January 1939 led by the composer. Symphony no. 2, subtitled *Music for the Marines: A Suite* (1943), was premiered by the Indianapolis Symphony Orchestra under Fabien Sevitzky. Symphony no. 3 in C (1938) received its premiere by the Pittsburgh Symphony Orchestra in April 1959. Symphony no. 4, *Walden* (1969) sets texts by Thoreau for chorus and orchestra; it was performed by the Knoxville Symphony Orchestra under the composer's direction in May 1971.

Symphony no. 5 (1975) was commissioned for the Bicentennial by the Tennessee Arts Center. Symphony no. 6 (1980) is scored for symphonic band or orchestra; Symphony no. 7 dates from 1983. A Symphony no. 8 remained incomplete at the time of his death.

Van Vactor's other orchestral compositions include *The Masque of the Red Death* (1929); *Five Little Pieces for Big Orchestra* (1929); *Passacaglia and Fugue in D minor* (1933); *Overture to a Comedy* no. 1 (1934); *Symphonic Suite* (1938); Divertimento for small orchestra (1939); Viola Concerto (1940); *Overture to a Comedy* no. 2 (*The Taming of the Shrew*; 1941); *Gothic Impressions* (*Variazioni Solenne*; 1941); *Fanfare* (1943); *Recitative and Salterello* (1946); *Prelude and March* (1950); Violin Concerto (1950); *The Trojan Women Suite* (1947–59); *Fantasia, Chaconne and Allegro* (1957); Suite for trumpet and strings (1962); *Sewanee Suite* (1963); *Sinfonia Breve* (1964); *Andante and Allegro* for saxophone and strings (1972); and *Chorale Prelude: Holy Manna* (1974). For string orchestra he composed six pieces: *Chaconne* (1928), *Five Little Bagatelles* (1938), *Adagio Mestoso* (1941), *Introduction and Presto* (1947), *Louise* (*Requiescat*; 1970), and *Prelude and Fugue* (1974).

Van Vactor wrote two ballets, *The Play of Words* (1931) and *Suite on Chilean Folk Tunes* (1963), with choreography by Irma Witt O'Fallon. He has a number of choral compositions to his credit: *Credo* for chorus and orchestra (1941), *Cantata* for female chorus and orchestra (1947), a *Christmas Cantata: The New Light* for narrator, soloists, chorus, and orchestra (1954), *Song of Mankind* (1971), and *Brethren We Have Met to Worship* (1975).

In addition to the pieces for flute, Van Vactor wrote much instrumental music, including a Quartet for four bassoons (1934); two string quartets (1940, 1949); Divertimento for string trio (1942); *Duettino* for violin and cello (1952); Suite for wind quintet (1959); Suite for piano (1962); Octet for Brass (1963); *Music for Woodwinds*, a collection of 36 pieces for various ensembles (1966–67); *Economy Band no. 1* for trumpet, trombone, and percussion (1966); *Economy Band no. 2* for horn, trombone, and percussion (1969); *Four Etudes* for winds and percussion (1968); *Episodes – Jesus Christ* for wind band (1970); a Tuba Quartet (1971); a Suite for trombone choir (1976); and *The Elements* for wind and percussion (1978).

In 1969 he composed the music for a film, *Jungle of the Soul*. He was also the author of a book, *Every Child May Hear* (1960).

VARÈSE, EDGAR (OR EDGARD)
b. Paris, France, 22 December 1883 (not 1885)
d. New York, New York, 6 November 1965

Varèse was born of an Italian father and Burgundian mother. His father intended that he should become an engineer, but against his parents' wishes he attended the Turin Conservatory and later returned to Paris to study with Vincent D'Indy and Albert Roussel at the Schola Contorum. He was also a pupil of Charles Widor at the Paris Conservatory. For a while Varèse conducted choirs in Paris and organized concerts of modern music. Here he mixed with the company of artists and writers, becoming a friend of Pablo Picasso, Max Jacob, Jean Cocteau, Amadeo Modigliani, Guillaume Apollinaire, and Erik Satie, and was acquainted with Lenin. In 1907 he moved to Berlin, where he came under the influence of Ferruccio Busoni. Richard Strauss encouraged him to compose and assisted in obtaining the first performances of several of his works.

His early works, all subsequently lost or withdrawn, include an opera, *Oedipus and the Sphinx* (1910–14), and a number of orchestral items: *Three Pieces for Orchestra* (1904), *Rapsodie Romane* (1905), and four symphonic poems: *Bourgogne* (1908), *Gargantua* (1912), *Mehr Licht* (1912), and *Les Cycles du Nord* (1914).

Varèse went to the United States in December 1915, where he presented concerts of new music. He became an American citizen in 1926. With the cooperation of Carlos Salzedo and Carl Ruggles, he founded the International Composers Guild for the promotion of concerts of advanced music. From 1928 to 1933 he lived again in Paris.

In the later works, Varèse developed a style of intricate rhythm and extreme dissonance that presented the audience with a new and incomprehensible language. The composer described his music as "organized sound" which possessed neither melody nor harmony in the accepted sense. The first composition he preserved, *Offrandes*, settings of two poems for soprano and small orchestra, was written in 1921. The influence of Debussy, whom he had known personally, can be detected in both the choice of surrealist poems and the treatment of the voice.

Amériques for large orchestra, completed in 1922 and revised in 1926, represents the composer's tribute to his new home. He explained the work: "When I wrote *Amériques* I was still under the spell of my first impressions of New York, not only New York seen, but more especially heard. For the first time with my physical ears I heard a sound that had kept recurring in my dreams as a boy, a high whistling C-sharp. It came to me as I worked in my West-side apartment where I could hear all the river sounds—the lonely foghorns, the shrill peremptory whistles—the whole wonderful river symphony which moved me more than anything ever had before. Besides as a boy, the mere word 'America' meant all discoveries, all adventures. It meant the unknown. And all this symbolical sense—new worlds on this planet—in outer space, and in the minds of man—I gave the title signifying 'Americas' to the first work I wrote in America." The melodic element is noticeably absent; instead, Varèse balances contrasting rhythms and colors of instrumental groupings, with the harmony arising from blocks of sound. *Amériques* was first performed in Philadelphia under Leopold Stokowski on 9 April 1926.

There followed *Hyperprism* for wind and percussion (1922–23) and *Octandre* for wind quintet, trumpet, trombone, and double bass (1924). Rhythm and color predominate in *Intégrales* for small orchestra and percussion (1925) and the remarkable *Ionisation* for 13 percussion instruments and two sirens (1931), performed in New York in March 1933 under Nicolas Slonimsky, to whom the work is dedicated.

Stokowski was the conductor of Varèse's second orchestral work, *Arcana*, performed in Philadelphia on 8 April 1927, almost a year to the day after the premiere of *Amériques*. It is scored for a large orchestra of 120 players (70 strings, quintuple wind, eight horns, five trumpets, three trombones, conrtrabass trombone, two tubas, two sarrusaphones, hecklephone, contrabass clarinet, and eight percussionists with 40 instruments).

The title is taken from *Hermetic Astronomy* by the sixteenth-century physician Bombastus Paracelsus, who is described as the "monarch of arcana." Although the inspiration came from the occult, the composer made it clear that the work is absolute, not program music: "I knew that someday I would realize a new kind of music, spatial music, and from then on I thought only of music as spatial."

During the next few years Varèse completed two further works. *Ecuatorial* (1934) was first scored for bass voice, brass, organ, percussion, and thereminovox; he later replaced the soloist with a chorus of men's voices and the obsolete thereminovox with two Ondes Martinot. The second piece, *Density 21.5* for solo flute, written in 1935, comprises a single page of music. It derives its title from the density of platinum and was written for George Barrère, who possessed a platinum flute.

After 1935 Varèse remained silent as a composer for almost 20 years. Lack of understanding by both musicians and audiences may account for his retirement. During this time he waited for the musical public to catch up with his visionary world. Only one work, *Ètude pour Espace*, for chorus, two pianos, and percussion, appeared in these years. Performed in New York under the composer's direction in 1947, it was part of a longer work begun in 1932 but later abandoned.

In 1953 Varèse produced *Déserts* for an orchestra of woodwinds, brass, piano,percussion, and two channels of magnetic tape transmitted stereophonically. His interest in electronic music dated back to the 1920's, and he had used an invention by Leon Theremin in the original *Ecuatorial*. Although there is no "program" to the music, Varèse stated that to him the title indicated "not only all physical deserts (of sand, sea, snow, outer space, of empty city streets) but also of the deserts of the mind of man; not only those stripped aspects of nature that suggests bareness, aloofness, timelessness, but also that remote inner space no telescope can reach, where man is alone, a world of mystery and essential loneliness." The music is divided into four sections for the instruments with three interpolations of the recorded sounds. *Déserts* was first performed in Paris by the Orchestre National, conducted by Hermann Scherchen (December 1954).

In 1955 Varèse composed *The Procession at Verges* for magnetic tape to accompany a film, *Around and About Joan Miró*. For the Philips Pavillion at the 1958 Brussels Exposition, Varèse composed *Poème électronique* for three-track tape. In the Pavillion, designed by Le Corbusier, it was played over four hundred loudspeakers spread throughout the building.

Varèse's last work, *Nocturnal*, for soprano, men's chorus, and orchestra, was premiered in an unfinished state (New York, 1961) and later completed by his pupil Chou Wen-Chung. It sets an excerpt from the novel *The House of Incest* by Anaïs Nin. At the time of his death he was also working on a symphonic poem, *Nuit*, to a text from the same book.

At the end of his life, Varèse was very much honored, and his music has had a profound effect upon young composers. His emphasis on "organized sound," spatial effects, and complex polyrhythmical textures, has exerted a lasting influence.

VERRALL, JOHN (WEEDON)
b. Britt, Iowa, 17 June 1908
d. Seattle, Washington, 15 April 2001

Verrall studied cello and composition at the Minneapolis College of Music (1928–31). In London at the Royal College of Music (1929–30) he was a pupil of R. O. Morris; he then studied composition with Zoltán Kodály in Budapest at the Liszt Conservatory (1931–32). After graduating in 1934 from the University of Minnesota, where he had been a composition pupil of Donald Ferguson, he taught at Hamline University, St. Paul, Minnesota (1934–42) and Mount Holyoke College,

John Verall.
Courtesy University of Washington Libraries, Neg. 1491-B, MSCUA.

South Hadley, Massachusetts (1942–46). During these years he continued composition lessons with Roy Harris (1938), Aaron Copland (1941), and Frederick Jacobi (1946–47).

Verrall was awarded a Guggenheim Fellowship in 1947 and a D. H Lawrence Fellowship in composition at the University of New Mexico in 1964. For a number of years he worked as a music editor with G. Schirmer and the Boston Music Company. In 1948 he joined the music faculty of the University of Washington, Seattle, retiring in 1973. One of his most famous composition students was William Bolcom, who enrolled at the university at the age of 11.

Verrall's orchestral music includes a Symphony (1939) and *Portrait of Man* (1940), both premiered by the Minneapolis Symphony Orchestra under Dimitri Mitropoulos; *Concert Piece* for strings and horn (1940); *Prelude and Allegro* for strings (1948); *Symphony for Young Orchestras* (1948); *Dark Night of St. John* (1949); *Variations on an Ancient Theme* (1955); *Portrait of St. Christopher* (1956), premiered by the Seattle Symphony Orchestra under Milton Katims; a Suite (1959); Symphony for chamber orchestra (1966); *Radiant Bridge* (1976), commissioned by the Port Angelus Symphony Orchestra; *Rhapsody* for horn and strings (1979); *Summerland Fantasy* (1985); *Olympic Sunset* (1984); and *Lyric Symphony* (1990). Verrall also composed concertos for violin (1947), piano (1959), and viola (1968). A few of his works for band are *Sinfonia Festiva* (1954), *Passacaglia* (1958), and *Chief Joseph Legend* for baritone, chorus, and band (1988).

For the stage, Verrall wrote three chamber operas: *The Cowherd and the Sky Maiden* (1951), *The Wedding Knell* (1952), based on a story by Hawthorne, and *Three Blind Mice* (1955), all produced at the University of Washington and directed by Stanley Chapple.

He is best known for his chamber music, especially the Viola Sonata no. 1 (1939) and the Fourth String Quartet. He composed seven string quartets in all (1941, 1943, 1948, 1949, 1952, 1956, 1961). Verrall's other instrumental works, which constitute the major part of his entire output, are two viola sonatas (1939, 1963); Divertimento for clarinet, horn, and bassoon (1941); Trio for two violins and viola (1941); two serenades for wind quintet (1944, 1950); a Piano Quintet (1953); sonatinas for violin, viola, cello, and oboe (all 1956); Wind Septet (1966); *Nonette* for wind and strings (1969); and sonatas for horn (1941), violin (1950), oboe (1956), and flute (1973), all with piano. For horn and piano, he composed *Eusebius Remembered* (1976) and *Invocation to Eos* (1983). His last instrumental pieces are *Fantasy Variations* for violin and piano (1989) and *Three Fantasy Legends* for horn and piano (1991).

Verrall's piano music includes *Four Pieces* (1949), his sonatas (1951, 1985), *Prelude en Suite* (1960), *Prelude, Intermezzo and Fugue* for two pianos (1965), and a Sonata for two pianos (1984). He also composed a score for a documentary film, *Minnesota Document* (1941).

Verrall was the author of three important books: *Form and Meaning in the Arts* (1958), *Fugue and Invention in Theory and Practice* (1966), and *Basic Theory of Scales, Modes and Intervals* (1969).

VINCENT, JOHN (CHARLES) JR.
b. Birmingham, Alabama, 17 May 1902
d. Santa Monica, California, 21 January 1977

Vincent was taught by Frederick Converse at the New England Conservatory of Music in Boston (1922–26), leaving to study privately for a year with George Chadwick. From 1927 to 1930 he taught in El Paso, Texas before accepting a position at George Peabody College in Nashville, Tennessee. From 1933 to 1935 he studied at Harvard University under Walter Piston.

In 1935 a John Knowles Paine Scholarship took him to Nadia Boulanger at the Ecole Normale du Musique in Paris, where he remained for two years. Upon his return to the United States in 1937 he was appointed head of the department of music at Western Kentucky State College, Bowling Green. A year's leave of absence (1941–42) enabled him to work with Roy Harris at Cornell University, where he obtained his doctorate. In 1946 he was appointed professor of music at the University of California in Los Angeles, following Arnold Schoenberg as teacher of composition. In 1952 he became director of the Huntington Hartford Foundation, and for seven years was conductor of the Los Angeles Chamber Orchestra. He retired from UCLA in 1969. He was president of the National Association of American Composers and Conductors (1975–76), helping to revive the organization after a period of dormancy.

Vincent's music is brightly tuneful with intricate rhythmical ingenuities. In many of his works he made use of a modern equivalent of medieval modes in the melodic invention. His most widely known work is the Symphony in D, subtitled *A Festival Piece in One Movement*. This exhilarating piece was first performed on 5 February 1955 by the Louisville Orchestra, which had commissioned it. Vincent revised the score in 1957.

For orchestra he also wrote a Suite (1929); a ballet *The Three Jacks* (1942); *Symphonic Poem After Descartes* (1958); *Overture to Lord Arling* (1959); *La Jolla Concerto* (1959); *Nude Descending a Staircase* (after Duchamp) for xylophone and strings (1950, rev. 1962); *Benjamin Franklin Suite* for strings (1962); *Rondo Rhapsody* (1966); a symphonic poem, *Phoenix, Fabulous Bird* (1966); and Symphony no. 2 (1966). The score of an early *Folk Song Symphony* (1931) has been lost.

His major chamber works are a String Quartet in G (1936) and *Consort* for piano and string quartet (1960), later revised as a Symphony for piano and string orchestra (1975). He also wrote *Prelude, Canon and Fugue* for flute, oboe, and bassoon (1936); a Second String Quartet (1967); *Nacre* (*Mother of Pearl*) for flute and piano (1925, rev. 1973); and a Suite for six percussionists (1973).

A one-act opera buffa, *Primeval Void*, to his own libretto, was completed in 1969. In 1954 Vincent provided incidental music for Richard Hubler's Christmas play *The Hallow'd Time*. He also wrote the score for a documentary film, *Red Cross* (1948). His vocal music includes *Three Grecian Songs* for double chorus (1935); *How Shall We Sing* (Psalm 137) for chorus and piano (1944, rev. 1951); *The Miracle of the Cherry Tree* for soprano and orchestra; *I Wonder as I Wander* for baritone, chorus, and orchestra; *Stabat Mater* for soprano solo and unaccompanied male chorus (1969); *Prayer for Peace* for soprano, alto, chorus, and organ (1971); and *Mary at Calvary* for chorus and organ (1972).

Vincent was the author of three books: *Music for Sight Reading* (1940), *More Music for Sight Reading* (1941), and *The Diatonic Modes in Modern Music* (1951, rev. 1974).

WAGENAAR, BERNARD

b. Arnhem, Netherlands, 18 July 1894
d. York, Maine, 19 May 1971

Wagenaar studied with his father, Johann, also a composer, and later at the Utrecht Conservatory. He began his musical career as a violinist, pianist, and conductor. When he came to the United States in 1921, he settled in New York and joined the New York Philharmonic Orchestra as a violinist and orchestral pianist. In 1925 he began teaching in the faculty of the Institute of Musical Art, New York. In the following year he became a naturalized American citizen. In 1927 he was appointed a teacher of composition at the Juilliard School, from which he retired in 1968. Among his pupils were Norman Dello Joio, Jacob Druckman, Bernard Herrmann, Ned Rorem, William Schuman, and Elie Siegmeister.

Wagenaar's music is usually immediately attractive, avoiding unnecessary complications. His single opera, *Pieces of Eight*, composed in 1944, is a light-hearted story of a pirate who attempts to find Captain Kidd's hidden treasure on Long Island.

The most important compositions of Wagenaar are his four symphonies. The First Symphony, composed in 1926, was given its premiere in 1928 by Willem Mengelberg and the New York Philharmonic. The Second Symphony (1930) received its first performance in 1932, also by the New York Philharmonic, under Toscanini. The composer himself conducted his Third Symphony with the Juilliard Orchestra in January 1937. The Fourth Symphony (1946) was given its first performance in 1949 by the Boston Symphony Orchestra, also under the baton of the composer. For orchestra Wagenaar also composed a Sinfonietta (1929), performed by Mengelberg and the New York Philharmonic. It was selected as the only American work to be per-

Bernard Wagenaar.
Photo: Shelburne Studios, Inc., courtesy The Juilliard School.

formed at the 1930 I.S.C.M. Festival in Liege. The Triple Concerto for flute, harp, and cello (1934) was first played by the Philadelphia Orchestra in 1938. This work also appeared at an I.S.C.M. concert in New York in 1941. A Violin Concerto dates from 1940.

Other pieces for orchestra are a Divertimento (1927), *Fantasietta on British-American Ballads* (1939), *Feuilleton* (1942), *Fanfare for Airmen* (1942), and *Song of Mourning* (1944). In 1953, to a commission from the Louisville Orchestra, Wagenaar composed his

Concert Overture. His last orchestral works were Divertimento no. 2 (1953), *Five Tableaux* for cello and orchestra (1955), and *Preamble* (1955).

Among his instrumental music are four string quartets (1926, 1931, 1936, 1960); a Violin Sonata (1925); a Piano Sonata (1928); a Cello Sonatina (1934); and Concertino for eight instruments (1942). His few vocal works include *Three Songs From the Chinese* for soprano, harp, and piano (1921); *From a Very Little Sphinx* for voice and piano (1925); *El trillo* for chorus, two guitars, and percussion (1942); and *No quiero tus avellanas* for alto, women's chorus, flute, English horn, two guitars, and percussion (1942).

WAGNER, JOSEPH F(REDERICK)

b. Springfield, Massachusetts, 9 January 1900
d. Los Angeles, California, 12 October 1974

Wagner studied at the New England Conservatory, Boston with Frederick Converse (1921–23) and at the College of Music, Boston University (1931–33). He also received private lessons from Alfredo Casella in Boston (1928) and Nadia Boulanger in Paris (1934–35). In addition, he studied conducting with Pierre Monteux in Paris and William Furtwängler in Berlin. He was music administrator of Boston schools (1929–40) during which time he also taught at Boston University. He was founder and first conductor of the Boston Civic Symphony Orchestra (1923–44). Later he was a member of the faculties of Hunter College, New York (1945–46); Brooklyn College (1945–47); Rutgers University; the University of Oklahoma; the Los Angeles Conservatory (1960–63); and Pepperdine College, Los Angeles (1961–73).

For orchestra Wagner wrote four symphonies (1934, 1945, rev. 1960, 1951, 1970); *Miniature Concerto* for piano (1919, rev. 1920); *Rhapsody* for clarinet, piano, and strings (1925, rev. 1937); *Two Movements Musical* (1927); a Piano Concerto in G minor (1929); two sinfoniettas, no. 1 (1930) and no. 2 for strings (1941); *Festival Processions* (1937); *From the North Shore: Four Miniatures* for strings (1939); *Variations on an Old Form* (1941, rev. 1958–59); *Dance Divertissement* (1942); *American Jubilee Overture* (1946); *Radio City Snapshots* (1946); Concertino for harp and orchestra (1947); *Northern Saga* (1948); *Music of the Sea* for strings (1954); a *Fugal Triptych* for piano, percussion, and strings (1936–37, rev. 1954); *Pastoral Costarricense* (1956); *Panorama* (1948–56); and *Litany* for strings (1959).

Wagner composed two violin concertos (1919–30, 1953–56); *Introduction and Scherzo* for bassoon and strings (1950–54); a Concerto for organ, brass, and percussion (1963); and a Harp Concerto (1964). He also

contributed several useful pieces to the band repertory: *Concerto Grosso* (1948); *Fantasy in Technicolor* for piano and band (1948); *Introduction and Rondo* for trumpet and band (1950); *Symphonic Transition* (1958); *Merlin and Sir Boss* (1963); and *Festive Fanfare* (1968).

Among his choral works are a Christmas cantata, *Gloria in Excelsis* (1925); *David Jazz* for baritone, men's chorus, and small orchestra (1933); *Psalm XXIX* for men's chorus and orchestra (1933); *Under Freedom's Flag* (1940); *The Pledge of Allegiance* (1940); *Song of All Seas, All Ships* (1946); *Ballad of Brotherhood* (1947); *Missa Brevis* (1949); *Missa Sacra* (1952); and *American Ballad* (1963).

Instrumental compositions include a string quartet (1940); sonatas for violin (1941), cello (1943), piano in B minor (1946), and two pianos (1965); Serenade for oboe, violin, and cello (1958); *Fantasy Sonata* for harp (1963); *Concert Piece* for cello and piano (1966); and *Twelve Concert Preludes* for organ (1974).

For the stage, Wagner wrote a one-act opera, *New England Sampler* (1964), and three ballets: *The Birthday of the Infanta* (1935), *Divertissement Dance* (1937), and *Hudson River Legend* (1941). He was the author of two textbooks, *Orchestration: A Practical Handbook* (1958) and *Band Scoring* (1960).

WALD, MAX

b. Litchfield, Illinois, 14 July 1889
d. Dowagiac, Michigan, 14 August 1954

Wald studied at the American Conservatory, Chicago, and with Vincent D'Indy in Paris (1922). He followed a career as a theater conductor before becoming chairman of the theory department of the Chicago Musical College.

For orchestra he wrote *Sentimental Promenades* (1922); *Retrospectives* (1924); a symphonic poem, *The Dancer Dead* (1931); a *Comedy Overture* (1937); *Three Serenades* for chamber orchestra (1937); and *In Praise of Pageantry* (1946). Chamber works include two piano sonatas, a violin sonata (1932), and a song cycle, *October Moonlight* for soprano and instrumental ensemble (1937). He also wrote a three-act opera, *Mirandolina* (1936), and a light opera, *Gay Little World* (1942).

WALKER, GEORGE THEOPHILUS

b. Washington, D.C., 27 June 1922

Walker's father was from the West Indies, and emigrated to the United States to study medicine, becoming a practicing physician in Washington, D.C. His mother gave him his first piano lessons, and Walker showed such

George Walker.
Courtesy the composer.

great talent that he gave his first recital at Howard University when he was fourteen. Walker was awarded a scholarship to Oberlin College, Ohio, to study piano, and graduated with highest honors (Mus.B., 1941). He later studied at the Curtis Institute, Philadelphia, where he was a pupil of Rosario Scalero, earning artist diplomas in piano and composition in 1945 and becoming the first African-American graduate of this renowned music school. In 1945 Walker made his concert debut as a pianist at New York's Town Hall and seemed destined for a career as a performer before turning to composition. He received his D.M.A. from the Eastman School of Music, Rochester, New York, in 1957. He also studied with Nadia Boulanger from 1957–59, and numbers Rudolf Serkin and Robert Casedesus among his teachers of piano. He taught at Dillard University, New Orleans (1953–54), The Dalcroze School of Music and the New School for Social Research, New York (1954–61), Smith College (1961–68), and the University of Colorado, Boulder (1968–69). In 1969 he joined the music faculty of Rutgers University, becoming chairman in 1976 and retiring in 1992.

Walker has been given numerous awards and prizes, including the Pulitzer Prize for *Lilacs* (1996), the first piece by an African-American composer to be so honored. Other awards include fellowships from the Fulbright and John Hay Whitney Foundations, both in 1957; two Guggenheim and two Rockefeller Fellowships; a Fromm Foundation commission; two Koussevitsky Awards; an American Academy of Arts and Letters Award; and a Mary Flagler Cary Charitable Trust Award. In 1997 Marion Barry, mayor of Washington, D.C. proclaimed George Walker Day in honor of the composer's 70th birthday. In 1999, he was elected to the American Academy of Arts and Letters. His early works show the influence of Stravinsky and Copland, but later he briefly adopted serialism in *Spatials* for piano (1961).

For orchestra he has written *Lyric for Strings* (1945, rev. 1990); a Trombone Concerto (1957); *Address* (1959, rev. 1991); a Symphony (1961); *Antiphonys* (1968); *Variations* (1971); a Piano Concerto (1975); a Violin Concerto (1975), revised as *Poème* (1991); *Dialogues* for cello and orchestra (1975); an overture, *In Praise of Folly* (1980), performed the following year by the New York Philharmonic Orchestra under Zubin Mehta; a Cello Concerto (1981); *An Eastman Overture* (1983); *Serenata* for chamber orchestra (1983); three sinfonias (1984, 1990, 2002); and three works for chamber orchestra: *Orpheus* (1994), *Pageant and Proclamation* (1997), and *Tangents* (1999).

A Mass for soloists, chorus, and orchestra (1976) was premiered by the Baltimore Symphony Orchestra, conducted by Sergiu Comissiona in April 1979. Other vocal music includes *Cantata* for soprano, tenor, boys' chorus, and orchestra (1982), *Lilacs* (1996), and *Canvas* for solo voices, chorus, and wind ensemble (1999).

Walker's important chamber works are two string quartets (1946, 1967); a cello sonata (1957); two violin sonatas (1958, 1979); *Perimeters* for clarinet and piano (1966); *Music for Three* for piano trio (1970); *Five Fancies* for clarinet and piano duet (1975); *Music for Brass* (1975); *Music for Diverse Instruments* (1980); a Viola Sonata (1989); *Modus* for chamber ensemble (1998); and *Windset* for wind quintet (1999). He has also composed many pieces for piano, including four sonatas (1953, 1960, 1975, 1984), *Spatials* (1961), and *Spektra* (1971).

WARD, ROBERT (EUGENE)
b. Cleveland, Ohio, 13 September 1917

Ward was educated at the Eastman School of Music, Rochester, New York (1935–39), where he studied composition with Howard Hanson and Bernard Rogers. At the Juilliard School (1939–42) he was a pupil of Frederick Jacobi (composition), Bernard Wagenaar (orchestration), and Albert Stoessel and Edgar Schenkman (conducting). At Tanglewood in 1941 he received lessons from Aaron Copland. During the Second World

War he served in the U.S. Army for four years in the Pacific, where as a bandmaster he added to his versatility in writing music in a variety of styles.

After returning to New York in 1946 Ward taught briefly at Columbia University before joining the faculty of the Juilliard School, where he remained for ten years (1946–56). Ward served as director of the Third Street Music School Settlement (1952–55) and was conductor of the Doctors' Orchestral Society of New York. From 1956 to 1967 he was managing director and executive vice-president of Galaxy Music Corporation and Highgate Press. In 1967 he became president of the North Carolina School of the Arts in Winston-Salem. In 1974 he resigned from this administrative position in order to devote more time to writing; he joined the faculty and taught composition there until 1979. In that year he was appointed the Mary Duke Biddle Professor of Music at Duke University, Durham, North Carolina, retiring in 1987.

Ward's first two successes were *Fatal Interview* for soprano and orchestra (1937) and *Ode for Orchestra* (1939), both given their first performances by Howard Hanson and the Rochester Symphony Orchestra. Ward has composed six symphonies (1941, 1947, 1950, 1958, 1975, 1988); the *Fifth*, subtitled *Canticles of America*, includes an important part for narrator, soloists, and chorus. *Adagio and Allegro* (1943) and *Jubilation: An Overture*, both written during the war in the Pacific while Ward was a bandmaster in the 7th Infantry Division, reveal the composer's interest in the rhythmical elements of jazz. Other notable orchestral works include *Slow Music* (1937), *Andante and Scherzo* for strings (1940), *Concert Music* (1948), *Night Music* (1949), *Euphony* (1954), and *Prairie Overture*. For narrator and orchestra he has written *Jonathan and the Gingery Snare* (1950).

Divertimento for Orchestra (1961) was composed for the Portland Junior Symphony Orchestra. *Music for a Celebration* (*Invocation and Toccata*) was commissioned in 1963 for the 20th anniversary of Broadcast Music Inc. (BMI). His Piano Concerto was completed in 1968. Later orchestral pieces include *Festive Ode* (1966), *Antiphony for Winds* (1967), *Sonic Structures* (1980), *Dialogues* for violin, cello, and orchestra (1983), a Concerto for tenor saxophone (1984), and *Byways of Memories* (1991).

Ward's first opera, *He Who Gets Slapped* (1956), originally entitled *Pantaloon*, a setting of the play by Andreyev, represents another side of Ward's technical skill. It was first staged by the Columbia University Opera Workshop in 1956 and later by the New York City Opera on 12 April 1959. His second opera, *The Crucible*, in four acts, is based on the play by Arthur Miller. Composed in 1961 under a commission from the Ford Foundation, it was produced that year by the New York City Opera. For this, his most important work, he was awarded the Pulitzer Prize. It was revived by the New York City Opera in 1968 and has received many performances by professional companies and university groups.

Ward's next opera, *The Lady From Colorado*, in two acts, was written for and produced by the Central City (Colorado) Opera in July 1964. In 1975 Ward completed another full-length opera, *Claudia Legare*, based on Ibsen's *Hedda Gabler*, which was premiered by the Minnesota Opera. Libretti for all four operas are by Bernard Stambler. A fifth opera, *Minutes to Midnight*, was performed at the New World Festival in Miami in July 1982 under the direction of Emerson Buckley. Ward has completed two further operas, *Abelard and Heloise* in three acts (1971) and *Roman Fever* (1993). His ballet *The Scarlet Letter* dates from 1990.

Ward's choral works include *Hushed Be the Camps Today* (1941); two cantatas, *Earth Shall Be Fair* for chorus, children's voices, organ, and orchestra (1960) and *Sweet Freedom's Songs* for baritone, narrator, chorus, and orchestra (1965); *Let the Word Go Forth* (John F. Kennedy) for chorus and ensemble (1965); and *Images of God* for chorus (1989). Among Ward's solo vocal music are *Three Songs* for soprano, tenor, and piano (1934); *Epithalamion* (Shelley) for high voice and piano (1937); *Fatal Interview* (Edna St. Vincent Millay) for soprano and orchestra (1937); three songs for high voice and piano, *As I Watched the Ploughman, Ploughing* (Whitman; 1938), *Sorrow of Mydath* (John Masefield; 1938); *Anna Miranda* (Stephen Vincent Benet; 1940); and *Sacred Songs for Pantheists* for soprano and orchestra (1951).

Ward's instrumental music includes an *Andante and Scherzo* for string quartet (1937); two violin sonatas (1950, 1990); *Fantasia* for brass and timpani (1953); *Ariosa and Tarantella* for cello (or viola) and piano (1954); a String Quartet (1965); *Celebration of God in Nature* for organ (1981); *Raleigh Divertimento* for wind quintet (1986); *Appalachian Ditties and Dances* for violin and piano (1989); and *Echoes of America* for clarinet, cello, and piano (1997).

WARD-STEINMAN, DAVID

b. Alexandria, Louisiana, 6 November 1936

Ward-Steinman studied at Florida State University from which he received his bachelor of music degree in 1957. From the University of Illinois he earned his master's and Ph.D. degrees in 1958 and 1961, respectively. His composition teachers included John Boda, Homer Keller, Wallingford Riegger, Darius Milhaud, Milton Babbitt, and Burrell Phillips. In 1958 he went to Paris for a year, where he was a pupil of Nadia Boulanger. In

David Ward-Steinman.
Photo: Patrice Madura, courtesy the composer.

1961 Ward-Steinman was appointed an assistant professor at San Diego State University, becoming associate professor in 1965 and full professor in 1968. From 1970 to 1972 he was Composer-in-Residence for the Tampa Bay, Florida area under a Ford Foundation grant.

Ward-Steinman's orchestral works include a *Concert Overture* (1957); a Symphony composed in Paris in 1959; *Concerto Grosso* for jazz combo and chamber orchestra (1960); two concertos for chamber orchestra (1961, 1962); *Prelude and Toccata* (1962); and a Cello Concerto (1964–66). Concert suites have been extracted from his two ballets, *Western Orpheus* (1964) and *These Three* (1966). Among his later orchestral pieces are *Season's Greetings* (1983); *Moire* for piano and chamber orchestra (1983); *Olympics Overture* (1984); *Chroma*, a concerto for multiple keyboards, percussion, and chamber orchestra (1985); *Elegy for Astronauts* (1986); *Winging It* for chamber orchestra (1986); *Cinnabar Concerto* for viola and chamber orchestra (1991–93); and Double Concerto for two violins and orchestra (1994–95).

For the stage Ward-Steinman has written incidental music for *The Oresteia* (Aeschylus; 1967), *A Day in the Death of Joe Egg* (Peter Nichols; 1971), and *The Puppet Prince* (Alan Cullen; 1971); two ballets, *Western Orpheus* (choreography by Richard Carter; 1964) and *These Three* (Eugene Loring; 1966); *Tamar* (1970–77), a multimedia music drama in three acts with li-

bretto by William Adams after the Robinson Jeffers poem; and *Rituals* for dancers and musicians (1971).

Ward-Steinman's major choral work, the oratorio *The Song of Moses* (1963–64), is scored for narrator, soloists, double chorus, and large orchestra. In 1968 he completed a Christmas cantata, *And in These Times*, with a libretto by the New England poet Douglas Worth. Other choral pieces include *Psalms of Rejoicing* for a cappella chorus (1961); *Antares* for gospel chorus, chamber orchestra, and synthesizer (or tape) (1963–65); *Of Wind and Water* (William Carlos Williams) for chorus, piano, and two percussionists (1982); and *Seasons Fantastic* (Robert Lee) for chorus and harp (1991–92).

Ward-Steinman's vocal music includes *Fragments from Sappho* for soprano, flute, clarinet, and piano (1962–65); *The Tale of Issoumbochi*, a Japanese fairy tale for narrator, soprano, and chamber ensemble (1968); *Grant Park* for baritone, oboe, clarinet, two trumpets, two trombones, percussion, and piano (1969); *And Waken Green* (Douglas Worth) for mezzo-soprano and piano (1983); and *Voices From the Gallery* for soprano, tenor, baritone, and piano (1990).

Ward-Steinman has also composed several instrumental works: *Three Songs* for clarinet and piano (1957); Brass Quintet (1958–59); *Duo* for cello and piano (1964–65); *Montage* for wind quintet (1968); *Child's Play* for bassoon, piano, and piano interior (1968); *Brancusi's Brass Beds* (Brass Quintet no. 2), commissioned in 1977 by the Bowling Green Brass Quintet; and *Night Winds* (Wind Quintet no. 2) (1993). For the piano he has composed a Sonata (1956–57), a *Sonata for Piano Fortified* (1972), and various shorter pieces, including *Elegy for Martin Luther King* (1968).

From 1970 in many of his works Ward-Steinman has made use of electronic tape: *Now-Music* for four tape recorders and dice (1957); *Putney Three* for wind quintet, piano interior, and synthesizer (1971); *Vega* for synthesized tape (1971); *Kaleidoscope*, a videotape for television for film, dancers, musicians, and synthesizer (1972); *Arcturus* for synthesizer and orchestra (1972), commissioned by the Chicago Symphony Orchestra; *Nova*, a collage for sound film, synthesizer, and tape (1972); *The Tracker* for clarinet, fortified piano, and tape (1976), based on a poem by Barney Childs; *Toccata* for synthesizer and slide projections (1978); and *Intersections I* for piano and tape (1981).

For wind ensemble or concert band Ward-Steinman has composed *Jazz Tangents* (1966–67), *Gasparilla Day* (1970), *Raga for Winds* (1972), *Scorpio* (1976), *Bishop's Gambit* (1979), and *Quintessence* (1985).

Ward-Steinman is the author of two books, *Comparative Anthology of Musical Forms* (with Susan Ward-Steinman; 1976) and *Toward a Comparative Structural Theory of the Arts* (1989).

WARREN, ELINOR REMICK

b. Los Angeles, California, 23 February 1900 (not 1906)

d. Los Angeles, California, 27 April 1991

Warren studied at Westlake School for Girls and at Mills College, Oakland, California. Later in New York she was a pupil of Paolo Gallico, Frank La Forge, and Clarence Dickinson. She also studied with Nadia Boulanger in Paris (1959) and Arnold Schoenberg in Los Angeles. She undertook a career as an accompanist to many leading singers, including Lawrence Tibbett and Richard Crooks.

For orchestra she composed *The Fountain* (1942); *Scherzo* (1950); *Along the Western Shore* (1954); Suite for Orchestra (1954, rev. 1958); *The Crystal Lake* (1958); *Sea Rhapsody* (1963); *Intermezzo* (1970); and a Symphony in one movement (1970).

Among Warren's numerous choral works are *White Horses at Sea* for male voices (1932); *The Harp Weaver* (Edna St. Vincent Millay) for baritone, female voices, chorus, and orchestra (1932); *The Passing of King Arthur* (Tennyson) for tenor, baritone, chorus, and orchestra (1940); *Christmas Candle* for chorus and piano (1940); *To My Native Land* (Longfellow) for chorus and orchestra (1942); *Winter Weather* (James Stephens)

Elinor Remick Warren in 1990.
Courtesy The Elinor Remick Warren Society.

for female voices and piano (1942); *Transcontinental* for baritone, chorus, and orchestra (1958); *Abram in Egypt* for baritone, chorus, and orchestra (1961); Requiem for soprano, baritone, chorus, and orchestra (1966); *From This Summer Garden* for female voices (1969); *Hymn of the City* for chorus (1969); *Night Rider* for chorus and piano (1974); *The Legend of King Arthur* (Tennyson) for tenor, baritone, chorus, and orchestra (1974); *Good Morning, America!* (Carl Sandburg) for narrator, chorus, and orchestra, commemorating the Bicentennial in 1976; *On the Echoing Green* for chorus and orchestra (1984); and *Now Welcome Summer* for chorus and orchestra (1984). Her vocal music includes *Four Sonnets* (Millay) for soprano and string quartet (1965, rev. 1970) and *Singing Earth* for soprano or tenor and orchestra (1978).

WASHBURN, ROBERT BROOKS

b. Bouckville, New York, 1 July 1928

Washburn was educated at the Crane School of Music, State University of New York College at Potsdam (B.S., 1949; M.S., 1955). After serving in the U.S. Air Force (1956–58), he studied with Bernard Rogers and Alan Hovhaness at the Eastman School of Music, Rochester, New York (Ph.D., 1960). He was also a pupil of Darius Milhaud at Aspen, Colorado (1963) and Nadia Boulanger in Paris (1964). From 1954 to 1985 he was professor of music at the Crane School of Music and is now dean emeritus and senior fellow in music.

For orchestra Washburn has written *Pastorale* for horn and strings (1949); a Symphony (1958); *Three Pieces* (1959); *Synthesis* (1959); Suite for strings (1959); *Festive Overture* (1960); *Prelude and Fugue* for strings (1961); *St. Lawrence Overture* (1962); Sinfonietta for strings (1963); *Serenade for Strings* (1966); *Song and Dance* for strings (1967); *North Country Sketches* (1969); *Blue Lake Overture* (1970); *Prologue and Dance* (1970); *Excursion* (1970); *Saturn V* (1973); *Elegy* (1974); and *Overture: Mid-America* (1976). More recent orchestral works include *Five Adirondack Sketches* for small orchestra (1989); *Saraswati Suite* for strings and tabla (1990); *New England Holiday* (1992); *Queen Noor Suite* for strings (1993); *Caravelle Overture* (1994); and *It's the Pizz!* for strings (1994).

Washburn has written extensively for the wind band repertory. Among his pieces are *March and Chorale* (1953); *Ode* (1955); *Burlesk* (1956); *Pageantry* (1962); Symphony (1963); *Partita* (1964); Suite (1967); *Ceremonial Music* (1968); *Impressions of Cairo* (1978); *Olympic March* (1979); *Kilimanjaro* (1981); *Equinox* (1983); *Pageant Royale* (1988); *Tower Bridge* (1992); *Temple on the Nile* (1992); *Hoosier Holiday* (1994);

Robert Brooks Washburn.
Courtesy the composer.

WAXMAN, DONALD
b. Steubenville, Ohio, 29 October 1925

Born in Ohio, Waxman's family relocated to Baltimore, Maryland, when he was very young. At the age of 15, Waxman won an RCA composition prize. He received his musical education at the Peabody Conservatory, Baltimore, where he studied with Elliott Carter, and at the Juilliard School, where he was a pupil of Bernard Wagenaar. A Guggenheim Fellowship allowed him to study in Paris in 1964–65. He was director of a private music school in Nyack, New York, and formed a successful piano duo with his wife, Jho. From 1970–90, Waxman was managing editor of Galaxy Music Corporation. In 1989, he was Composer-in-Residence at the Kang Nung (Korea) Music Festival. In 1998, he was awarded the Delius Society's Grand Prize for American chamber music compositions.

For orchestra Waxman has written *Paris Overture* (1965), *Overture to "Serenade Concertante"* (rev. 1987), *Songs and Supplications* for tenor, small chorus, and orchestra (rev. 1994), and *Announcement* (2003). His instrumental music includes *Fantasia* for flute and piano (1960); *Preludes, Canons and Inventions* for string trio (1960); a piano quartet (1962); Trio

Tidewater Festival Overture (1994); *Far East Fantasy* (1995); and *Song of Krishna* (1995).

Among his instrumental music are a Suite for wind quintet (1960); *Three Pieces* for flute, clarinet, and bassoon (or bass clarinet; 1961); a String Quartet (1963); Concertino for brass and wind quintet (1964); Wind Quintet (1967); Brass Quintet (1970); *Prayer and Alleluia* for organ, two trumpets, trombone, and timpani (1972); *Pent-agons* for percussion (1973); *Festive Fanfare* for brass and percussion (1975); *Five Miniatures* for brass (1979); *French Suite* for oboe, clarinet, and bassoon (1980); Piano Trio (1984); and *Hornography* for horn quartet (1990).

Washburn has written several choral works, including *Three Shakespearean Love Songs* for male voices, piano, and optional horn (1963); *Four Songs* for male voices and piano (1964); *Spring Cantata* for chorus (1973); *We Hold These Truths* (Thomas Jefferson) for narrator, chorus, and band (or orchestra; 1974); *Three Thoughts of Thoreau* for voices and piano (1976); *Sinfonia* for voices and instruments (1977); and *Insalatate Musicale* for chorus and piano.

He is the author of two textbooks, *Comprehensive Foundations in Musicianship* and *Crossroads in Music: Tradition and Conventions.*

Donald Wasman, 1996.
Photo: Arno Roslund, courtesy the composer.

for oboe, clarinet, and bassoon (1967); Trio for two flutes and piano (1985); *Arabesques* and Ostinato for two pianos (1995); and *Variations on a Waltz of Diabelli* for violin, clarinet, cello, and piano (1997).

Vocal music includes *Four Elegies* for tenor and string quartet and *Four Pastorals* (both 1960), *Lovesongs* for soprano, violin, and piano (1989), and *Tandaradei* for soprano and piano (rev. 2004). For chorus, Waxman has composed *Eight Thomas Hardy Songs* for mixed chorus a capella (1978), *Burgundian Noels* and *English Noels* (both 1985), and *Even During War Moments of Delicate Peace* for chorus, tenor solo, and piano (2003).

WAXMAN, FRANZ (FAMILY NAME: WACHSMANN)

b. Königschütte, Upper Silesia, Germany (now Chorzow, Poland), 24 December 1906
d. Los Angeles, California, 24 February 1967

Waxman entered the Dresden Music Academy in 1923 but soon transferred to the Berlin Conservatory. With the rise of the Nazis, he moved to Paris in 1933, where he composed his first film score for Fritz Lang's *Liliom*. In the following year he emigrated to the United States, settling in Los Angeles, where he later received lessons from Arnold Schoenberg. From 1935 to 1963 he composed the astonishing number of 147 film scores for Universal, M.G.M., and Warner Brothers. For these he maintained a high standard of craftsmanship and taste, never lapsing into mere routine. His work is still held in high esteem by experts.

Notable among the films he scored are *The Bride of Frankenstein* (1935); *Captains Courageous* (1940); *Rebecca* (1940); *The Philadelphia Story* (1940); *Dr. Jekyll and Mr. Hyde* (1941); *Suspicion* (1942); *Air Force* (1943); *Sorry, Wrong Number* (1948); *Sunset Boulevard* (1950; Academy Award); *A Place in the Sun* (1951); *My Cousin Rachel* (1952); *Rear Window* (1954); *Peyton Place* (1957); *Sayonara* (1957); *The Spirit of St. Louis* (1957); *The Nun's Story* (1959); *Taras Bulba* (1962); and *The Lost Command* (1966).

Waxman considered his concert music of primary importance; film music took second place in his estimation. His two major choral works are an oratorio, *Joshua* (1959), and a cantata, *The Song of Terezin* for mezzo-soprano, chorus, children's chorus, and orchestra, first performed in Cincinnati in 1965.

In addition to concert music derived from film music, he composed several orchestral pieces, including a symphonic fantasy on *A Mighty Fortress Is Our God* (1943); *Elegy for Strings* (1944); a comedy overture, *Athaneal the Trumpeter* (1945); a Trumpet Concerto (1946); *Paradine Case*: *Rhapsody* (1947); a popular

Fantasy on Carmen for violin and orchestra, written for Heifetz; *Three Sketches* (1955); Sinfonietta for strings and timpani (1955); *Theme, Variations and Fugato* (1956); *Goyana* for piano and strings (1960); and a Cello Concerto.

WEBER, BEN (WILLIAM JENNINGS BRYAN)

b. St. Louis, Missouri, 23 July 1916
d. New York, New York, 9 May 1979

After studying medicine for one year at the University of Illinois, Weber switched to music and attended De Paul University in Chicago. As a composer he was almost entirely self-taught, although he did receive some lessons in piano and singing and was encouraged by Arnold Schoenberg and Artur Schnabel. Weber was a Guggenheim Fellow in 1950 and 1951 and again in 1953. From 1959 to 1961 he was president of the American Composers' Alliance. For a while he was Composer-in-Residence at Yaddo, Saratoga Springs, New York; in 1966, he taught at the New York College of Music. In 1971 he was elected a life member of the National Institute of Arts and Letters.

Most of Weber's music is written serially in a musical language derived directly from Schoenberg. His most widely known work is the *Symphony on Poems of William Blake*, op. 33 for baritone and small orchestra, composed in 1950. His other orchestral music includes *Piece* for oboe and strings, op. 22 (1943–44); a *Sinfonia* for cello and orchestra (1945); *Two Pieces* for string orchestra, op. 34. (1950); a Violin Concerto, op. 41 (1954); *Prelude and Passacaglia*, op. 42, first performed in January 1955 by the Louisville Orchestra under Mitropoulos; *Serenade for Strings*, op. 46 (1957); *Rapsodia Concertante*, op. 47 for viola and small orchestra (1957); and a Piano Concerto, op. 52, commissioned by the Ford Foundation in 1960 and premiered by William Masselos and the New York Philharmonic Orchestra, conducted by Leonard Bernstein.

An important work, *Dolmen*, op. 58, an elegy for orchestra was composed in 1964 for the Louisville Orchestra. It was described by Virgil Thomson as "the saddest piece in the world." The title is a Breton word for a megalithic stone structure serving as a burial chamber. Later orchestral works are *The Enchanted Midnight*, op. 60 (1969); *Concert Poem*, op. 61, subtitled *Dramatic Piece* for violin and orchestra (1970); and *Sinfonia Clarion*, op. 62 for small orchestra (1972).

Weber's instrumental music includes two violin sonatas, no. 1, op. 5 (1941) and no. 2, op. 16 (1943); *Five Pieces* for cello and piano, op. 13 (1941); a Cello Sonata, op. 17 (1943); *Two Dances* for solo cello, op. 18 (1948) and op. 31 (1951); *Sonata da Camera*, op. 30

for violin and piano (1951); Concerto for piano, cello, and winds, op. 32 (1950); *Serenade*, op. 39 for flute, oboe, clarinet, and string quartet (1956); two string quartets: no. 1, op. 12 (1942) and no. 2 in one movement, op. 35 (1951); *Chamber Fantasie*, op. 51 (1961); *Prelude and Nocturne*, op. 55 (1963) for flute, celeste, and cello; *Consort of Winds*, op. 66 (1974); and *Three Capriccios* for cello and piano, op. 67 (1977).

In addition to the *Blake Symphony*, Weber wrote much vocal music, including *Concert Aria after Solomon* for soprano and orchestra, op. 29 (1949) and *Three Songs* for soprano and orchestra, op. 48 (1957); both for soprano and orchestra; and *Four Songs*, op. 40 for voice and cello (1953). For soprano and piano he composed *Five Songs*, op. 15 (1942); *Two Songs*, op. 53 (1962); a song cycle, *The Ways*, op. 54 (1962); and *A Bird Came Down the Walk*, op. 57 (1964).

Among Weber's keyboard works are *Five Bagatelles*, op. 2 (1938); Suite no. 1, op. 8 (1940–41); *Fantasia (Variations)*, op. 25 (1947); *Episodes*, op. 26a (1949); Suite no. 2, op. 27 (1949); *Humoreske*, op. 49 (1958); *Intermezzo*, op. 64 (1972); a Suite for piano, four hands, op. 56 (1964); and *Variazioni Quasi una Fantasia*, op. 65 for harpsichord (1974). A ballet, *The Pool of Darkness*, op. 26, was composed in 1949.

WEILL, KURT (JULIAN)

b. Dessau, Germany, 2 March 1900
d. New York, New York, 3 April 1950

Weill studied in Paul Dessau and briefly with Englebert Humperdinck at the Hochschule für Musik in Berlin.

From 1921 to 1924 he was a disciple of Ferruccio Busoni, although never his pupil in the conventional sense.

Weill's principal works composed in Germany are contemporary social satires in the form of singspiels and operas. The first two compositions for the stage were one-act operas. *Der Protagonist* with a libretto by Georg Kaiser was completed in 1925 and performed the following year in Dresden. *Royal Palace*, to a text by the surrealist poet Yvan Goll, received its premiere in Berlin in 1927 under Erich Kleiber.

Mahagonny, a singspiel, produced in Baden-Baden in July 1927, was withdrawn and reworked as a three-act opera, *Aufsteig und Fall der Stadt Mahagonny* (*The Rise and Fall of the City of Mahagonny*). With a libretto by Bertolt Brecht, it is a bitter satire on American capitalism. The opera was first produced in Leipzig in 1930. Another one-act opera, *Der Zar lässt sich photographieren* (*The Czar Has His Photograph Taken*), also to a libretto by Kaiser, was staged in Leipzig in November 1928.

Weill's greatest success, the ballad opera *Die Dreigioschenoper* (*The Threepenny Opera*) was performed in Berlin on 31 August 1928. With a libretto by Brecht, it is an updated version of John Gay's *The Beggar's Opera*. It was produced throughout Germany and in the Netherlands, France, Britain, Hungary, Russia, and Poland. It reached New York in 1933. Also in collaboration with Brecht, he wrote *Happy End* in 1929. Set in the underworld of Chicago, it reflects much of the atmosphere of *Die Dreigroschenoper*. After its initial production, it disappeared and, except for the song "Surabaya Johnny," the music was forgotten until it was

Kurt Weill.
Courtesy of the Weill-Lenya Research Center, Kurt Weill Foundation for Music, New York.

published in 1958. Weill's next works for the stage were *Der Jasager* (*He Who Says Yes*; Brecht), an opera for students based on a Noh play, performed in Berlin in 1930, and *Die Bürgschaft* (Caspar Neher; *The Bail*), a three-act opera staged in Berlin in 1932.

Following the Nazi banning of all his music, Weill left Germany. While living in Paris in 1933–34, he composed two musical plays: *Der Silbersee* (*The Silver Lake*) to a text by Kaiser, premiered in three German cities on 18 February 1933; and *Marie Galante* (Jacques Deval; Paris, 1934). Before going to the United States in 1935, he provided the music for a satirical play, *A Kingdom for a Cow*, staged at the Savoy Theatre, London in 1935.

American popular music and jazz were already an intrinsic part of Weill's style, so he felt at home in the world of Broadway. In addition, his European fame had preceded him to the United States. His first assignments were the music for a "war fable" by Paul Green, *Johnny Johnson* (1936) and the score for a biblical drama by Franz Werfel, *Eternal Road* (1937). His initial collaboration with Maxwell Anderson was the successful operetta *Knickerbocker Holiday* (1938), which includes "September Song." There followed *Lady in the Dark* (Moss Hart and Ira Gershwin; 1941), featuring Gertrude Lawrence and Danny Kaye; *One Touch of Venus* (S. J. Perelman and Ogden Nash; 1943); *Street Scene* (1947), a "Broadway opera," based on Elmer Rice's play with lyrics by Langston Hughes; and *The Firebrand of Florence*, an operetta (E. J. Meyer and Ira Gershwin; 1945).

Down in the Valley (1945–48) is a "college opera" for university and amateur performers. As with several of Weill's German stage works, the main figure, Brack, is a criminal. The score contains a number of American folk songs. It was first produced at Indiana University, Bloomington on 15 July 1948. *Love Life*, a "vaudeville" with lyrics by Alan Jay Lerner, was staged in New York in 7 October 1948 and enjoyed a run of 250 performances. Weill's final stage work was *Lost in the Stars* (1949), another collaboration with Anderson, based on Alan Paton's novel *Cry, the Beloved Country*. Described as a "musical tragedy," it marks a further move away from the conventional musical towards a more extended, serious operatic style. He left three other musicals incomplete: *Davy Crockett* (1938), *Ulysses Africanus* (1939), and *Huckleberry Finn* (1950). Marc Blitzstein's English version of *The Threepenny Opera* was first produced at Brandeis University, Waltham, Massachusetts on 14 June 1952 and led to the rediscovery of Weill's early works.

Weill's other music composed in Europe has been overshadowed by his stage successes. For orchestra he wrote Symphony no. 1 in one movement (1921), which Weill withdrew on the advice of Busoni. The score was lost in 1933 when the composer left Germany and was not rediscovered until 1958. Symphony no. 2 (1933–34) was first performed by Bruno Walter and the Concertgebouw Orchestra in Amsterdam in 1934, but the score was not published until 1966. Other orchestral works include *Fantasie, Passacaglia and Hymnus* (1923), Divertimento (1923), *Quodlibet* (1924), and Concerto for violin and wind instruments (1924), performed at the I.S.C.M. Festival in Zurich in 1926. He also composed two string quartets (1919, in B minor; 1923) and a Cello Sonata (1920).

Weill's choral and vocal music with orchestra include *Frauentanz* for soprano, viola, flute, clarinet, bassoon, and horn, performed at The I.S.C.M. Festival in Salzburg in 1924; *Rilke Lieder* for voice and orchestra (1925; lost in part); a cantata, *Der Neue Orpheus* for soprano, violin and orchestra (1925); *Vom Tod in Walde*, a ballad for bass voice and ten instruments (1927); and *Das Berliner Requiem* (1928).

Recordare (1923) is a Latin setting of the fifth chapter of the Lamentations of Jeremiah for four-part chorus and children's choir, but it was rejected by the conductor Hermann Scherchen as too difficult. The score was rediscovered by Oliver Neighbour in Paris in 1971, and its premiere given in June of that year at St. Pieterskirk, Utrecht. In honor of Lindbergh's flight across the Atlantic, Weill and Paul Hindemith collaborated on *Der Lindberghflug* (Der Ozeanlfug) (Brecht) (1927), a radio cantata for male soloists, chorus, and orchestra. Weill then set the text by himself; this version was performed in Berlin in December 1929.

Die Sieben Todsünden (*The Seven Deadly Sins of the Petite Bourgeoisie*; 1933) is a ballet with vocal soloists. The role of Anna is divided into singing and a dancing roles. One of Weill's most impressive scores, it was staged in Paris in 1933 (choreography by George Balanchine) with Lotte Lenya, the composer's wife, as the singing Anna.

The Ballad of Magna Carta with words by Maxwell Anderson was performed on CBS radio in February 1940. *Three Whitman Songs* for baritone and orchestra also date from 1940. In addition to screen versions of his musicals, Weill wrote four film scores: *You and Me* (1937–38), *The River is Blue* (1937–38), *Where Do We Go From Here?* (1943–44), and *A Salute to France* (1944).

WEISGALL, HUGO
b. Eibenschütz, Moravia (now Ivancice, Czech Republic), 13 October 1912
d. New York, New York, 11 March 1997

At the age of eight, Weisgall was taken to the United States, where he was brought up in Baltimore. He be-

Hugo Weisgall, conducting his opera, *Purgatory,* May 1966.
Photo: Milton Oleaga, courtesy The Juilliard School.

came a naturalized citizen in 1926. He attended the Peabody Conservatory in Baltimore (1928–31), and at Johns Hopkins University (1929–35, 1937–40) he obtained his doctorate with a thesis on seventeenth-century German lyric poetry. At the Curtis Institute, Philadelphia (1934–40) he studied composition with Rosario Scalero and conducting with Fritz Reiner. In New York (1933–40), he also received private composition lessons from Roger Sessions who exerted a strong influence upon him. He was awarded Guggenheim Fellowships in 1955, 1959, and 1966.

From 1937 to 1939 Weisgall conducted the Baltimore String Orchestra. After serving in the U.S. Army during the Second World War, he became cultural attaché in Prague in 1946. In 1949 he was appointed director of the Institute of Musical Arts in Baltimore. He founded the Baltimore Chamber Music Society in 1951. In 1959 he was visiting professor at Pennsylvania State University and the following year was appointed professor of music at Queens College of the City University of New York. From 1952 he had been chairman of the music faculty of the Cantors Institute of the Jewish Theological Seminary of America in New York. He also taught at the Juilliard School from 1956 to 1970.

It was through opera that Weisgall made his most significant contribution to music in America. His first two works in this medium are *Night* (1932) and *Lillith* (1934), both subsequently withdrawn. While he was musical director of the Hilltop Opera Company, Baltimore, he wrote the first of his important operas. In one act, *The Tenor,* completed in 1950 to a text taken from Wedekind, reveals a subtle treatment of character somewhat in the manner of Gian-Carlo Menotti. It was first performed in Baltimore in February 1952. In 1951

Weisgall based his next opera on the one-act Strindberg play *The Stronger.* The solo character is an actress who meets her former professional rival in a café on Christmas Eve. The development of her reactions shows the depth of her own neurotic jealousies and fears. The opera was first produced at Westport, Connecticut in August 1952.

These two works established a reputation for the composer that extended throughout the United States and to Europe, but their success tended to overshadow his other operas. Weisgall's remaining compositions for the stage have made use of full orchestral accompaniments. For the New York City Opera Company he wrote *Six Characters in Search of an Author* (1956), based on the play by Pirandello. It was not produced until 26 April 1959. It was followed by *Purgatory,* a setting of Yeats' one-act play, written in 1958 and presented at the Library of Congress, Washington, D.C., in February 1961.

Later operas were all produced in New York: *Athaliah,* based on Racine's biblical tragedy, in 1964; *Nine Rivers From Jordan,* to a libretto by Denis Johnston, on 9 October 1968; *Jennie,* or *The Hundred Nights,* derived from a Japanese Noh play, performed at the Juilliard American Opera Center in 1976; *The Garden of Adonis* (1959, rev. 1977–81); and *Esther* (1993). Also for the stage Weisgall wrote four ballets, all later withdrawn: *Quest* (1938), *Art Appreciation* (1938), *One Thing is Certain* (1939), and *Outposts* (1947).

Weisgall's early orchestral work. Overture in F (1942), was performed in London the following year. He wrote only three more pieces for orchestra, *Appearances, Entrances and Proclamation* (1960), *Prospect* (1983), and *Tekiator* (1985).

Choral music comprises settings of Jewish liturgical words and includes *Four Choral Etudes* (1935–60), *Five Motets* (1938–39), and *Hymn* for chorus and orchestra (1941). His last choral pieces was *Song of Celebration* for soprano, tenor, chorus, and orchestra (1975).

Weisgall composed several works for solo voice and orchestral or instrumental ensemble. These include *Soldier Songs* for baritone and orchestra (1946, rev. 1965); *A Garden Eastward*, a cantata for high voice and orchestra (1952); *Fancies and Inventions* (Robert Herrick) for baritone and five instruments (1970); and *End of Summer* for tenor, oboe, and string trio (1974).

Translations, seven songs for mezzo-soprano and piano, was commissioned in 1971 by Shirley Verrett. *The Golden Peacock* (*Seven Popular Songs from the Yiddish*) was completed in 1978. His last two sets of vocal music were *Liebeslieder: Four Songs with Interludes* for high voice and piano (1979) and *Lyrical Interval*, a cycle for low voice and piano (1985).

In 1966, under the collective title *Graven Images*, Weisgall wrote eight pieces separately scored for piano solo, wind instruments, and the last scored for solo voice, chorus, and piano. His instrumental music includes two works for piano, both later withdrawn: a Sonata in F-sharp minor (1931) and *Variations* (1939). A Second Piano Sonata, composed in 1982, survives, as do *Arioso and Burlesca* for cello and piano (1984) and *Tangents* for flute and marimba (1985).

WEISS, ADOLPH
b. Baltimore, Maryland, 12 September 1891
d. Van Nuys, California, 21 February 1971

Weiss was born of German parents into a musical family; his father had been a pupil of Ferruccio Busoni. After studying in New York and at Columbia University under Cornelius Rybner, he went to Vienna, where he attended Arnold Schoenberg's composition classes from 1924 to 1927. In 1932 he spent a further year in Europe on a Guggenheim Fellowship.

From 1907 to 1924 Weiss was a professional bassoonist in the Russian Symphony Orchestra of New York, New York Philharmonic Orchestra (under Mahler), and the Chicago Symphony Orchestra. From 1927 to 1932 he was secretary of the Pan-American Society of Composers in New York. In 1936 he moved to California, where he played in the San Francisco Symphony Orchestra, before settling in Los Angeles in 1938. He was a member of various film studio orchestras, becoming principal bassoon of the Los Angeles Philharmonic in 1951. He also conducted the San

Adolph Weiss.
Courtesy James P. Murphy Collection, Georgetown University Library.

Francisco Symphony and Opera Orchestras (1933) and the Los Angeles Philharmonic (1951).

The origin of Weiss's style can be traced to Schoenberg, but he developed his own particular use of the 12-note system. His method of composition involved a mathematical working with numbers that were later transcribed into notes. One of his most notable students was John Cage.

Weiss's important orchestral works are *I Segreti* (1922); *Chamber Symphony* for ten instruments (1927); *Ballad* (1928); a scherzo, *American Life* (1928); *Theme and Variations for Orchestra* (1931); a *Suite of Five Orchestral Pieces* (1938); *Ten Pieces* for low instruments and orchestra (1943); a Bassoon Concerto, which Weiss wrote for his own use (1949); and a Trumpet Concerto (1952).

Weiss wrote a large quantity of chamber music, including four string quartets (1925, 1926, 1932, 1942); *Sonata da Camera* for flute and viola (1929); a Wind Quintet (1932); *Petite Suite* for flute, clarinet, and bassoon (1937); a Violin Sonata (1941); *Passacaglia* for horn and viola (1942); Sextet for wind and piano (1947); Trio for clarinet, viola, and cello (1948); Trio for flute, violin, and piano (1955); *Rhapsody* for four horns (1957); *Tone Poem* for brass and percussion (1957);

and *Vade mecum* for wind instruments (1957). *Five Fantasias* for violin and piano (1956) are based on Japanese music he heard while on a tour of Asia with the Los Angeles Philharmonic Orchestra.

Weiss's vocal music includes the unpublished *Songs for Soprano* (1916–18), *Seven Songs* (E. Dickinson) for soprano and string quartet (1928), and *Ode to the West Wind* for baritone, viola, and piano (1945). For piano he wrote a *Fantasie* (1918), *Twelve Preludes* (1927), and a Sonata (1932). *Protest*, a dance score for two pianos, dates from 1945.

Weiss composed one full-length opera, *David*, and set *The Libation Bearers* (Aeschylus) for soloists, chorus, dancers, and orchestra (1930).

WERNICK, RICHARD

b. Boston, Massachusetts, 16 January 1934

At Brandeis University, Waltham, Massachesetts (1952–55), Wernick was a pupil of Irving Fine, Harold Shapero, and Arthur Berger. He also studied with Leon Kirchner at Mills College, Oakland, California, and at Tanglewood with Ernst Toch and Boris Blacher. Wernick was musical director and Composer-in-Residence with the Royal Winnipeg Ballet Company (1957–58). From 1958 to 1964 he worked in New York, providing scores for film, television, and the theater. After teaching at the State University of New York at Buffalo (1964–65) and the University of Chicago (1965–68), he joined the faculty of the University of Pennsylvania in 1968, becoming a professor in 1977; he retired in 1996.

For orchestra Wernick has written *Hexagrams* for chamber orchestra (1962); *Aevia* (1965); *Introits and Canon* for chamber ensemble (1978); a Cello Concerto (1980); *Fanfare for a Festive Occasion* (1981); a Violin Concerto (1984); a Viola Concerto, *"Do Not Go Gentle"* (1986); two symphonies (no. 1, 1988; no. 2, with soprano, 1993); a Piano Concerto (1989–90); Concerto for saxophone quartet (1991); and *Musica Camerata* for chamber orchestra (1999). For concert band he has composed two pieces, *Concert Overture* (1962) and *Snapshots* (1963).

Wernick's stage works comprise an opera, *Maggie*, based on a story by Hart Crane (1959), and five ballets: *The Twisted Heart* (1957), *Fête Brillante* (1958), *The Emperor's Nightingale* (1958), *The Queen of Ice* (1958), and *The Nativity* (1961). He has also provided incidental music for a number of plays, including *The Trojan Women* (1953), *Oedipus Rex* (1956), *Le Bourgeois Gentilhomme* (1957), and *The Geranium Hat* (1959).

Wernick's important compositions are for voice(s): *From Tulips and Chimneys* (e.e. cummings) for bari-

tone and orchestra (1956); *Lyrics I x I* (e.e. cummings) for soprano, vibraphone, marimba, and double bass (1966); *Haiku of Basho* for soprano, chamber ensemble, and tape (1970–71); *Moonsongs from the Japanese* for one to three sopranos and tape (1969); *Kaddish Requiem* for soprano ensemble and tape (1970–71); *A Prayer for Jerusalem* for voice and percussion (1970–71); *Songs of Remembrance* for mezzo-soprano and winds (1974); and *Visions of Terror and Wonder* for mezzo-soprano and orchestra (1976), which won a Pulitzer Prize.

Later vocal music includes *Contemplations of the 10th Muse* (Anne Bradstreet) for soprano and piano (1977); *And on the Seventh Day* for cantor and percussion (1979); *A Poison Tree* (William Blake) for soprano, four instruments, and piano (1980); *The Oracle of Shimon bar Yochai* for soprano, cello, and piano (1983); *I Too* for voice and piano (1984); *Oracle II* for soprano, oboe, and piano (1985); *Ball of Sun* for voice and piano (1989); *Two for Jan* (*Gaetani*) for soprano, mezzo-soprano, oboe, bass clarinet, and cello (1991); and *...and a time for peace* (*ve-yet shalom*) for mezzo-soprano and orchestra (1994).

Among Wernick's choral works are *Fantasia: Full Fadom Five* for chorus and chamber ensemble (1964); *what of a much of a which of a wind* for chorus and prepared piano/four hands (1964); *Beginnings* for chorus (1970); *Kee al Asher* for chorus (1972); *The 11th Commandment: No, Thou Shalt Not Xerox Music* for chorus, piano, and organ (1987) and *Fragment of Prophesy* for boys' chorus and mixed choir (1991).

Instrumental music includes seven string quartets (1953, withdrawn; 1963; 1973; 1988; 1990; 1995, with soprano; 1998); *Four Pieces* for string quartet (1955); Divertimento for clarinet, bassoon, viola, and cello (1956); *Duo Concertante* for cello and piano (1960); Trio for clarinet, violin, and cello (1961); *Music* for solo viola d'amore (1964); *Stretti* for clarinet, violin, viola, and guitar (1965); *Cadenzas and Variations I* for viola and piano (1967), *II* for violin (1970), and *III* for cello (1973); *Three Pieces* for string quartet (1967); and *Partita* for solo violin (1978). Later chamber music works are *In Praise of Zephyrus* for oboe and string trio (1980); *Formula P...M* for violin and cello (1981); Piano Sonata, *Reflections on a Dark Light* (1982); Cello Sonata, *Portraits of Antiquity* (1982); Brass Quintet, *Musica Ptolemica* (1987); *Cassation: Music Tom Jefferson Knew* for horn, oboe, and piano (1995); Piano Trio (1996); *Fagotten Memories* for solo bassoon (1997); Violin Sonata (1997); *Duettino* for oboe and violin (1998); *Techno's Acrobats* for bass clarinet (1999); *Trochaic Trot* for guitar (2000); Piano Sonata no. 2 (2000); *The Name of the Game* for guitar and 11 instruments (2001); and Cello Sonata no. 2 (2002).

WESTERGAARD, PETER (TALBOT)
b. Champaign, Illinois, 28 May 1931

At Harvard University (1951–53) Westergaard was a pupil of Walter Piston. On a Paine Traveling Fellowship he studied with Darius Milhaud at the Paris Conservatory (1953-54). On his return to the United States he attended Princeton University (1954–56) under Roger Sessions. A Fulbright Fellowship enabled him to study with Wolfgang Fortner in Detmold, Germany (1956–58).

He taught at the Staatliche Hochschule für Musik, Freiburg (1957) before joining the music faculty of Columbia University (1958–66). In 1967 he moved to Amherst College, Massachusetts, prior to taking up teaching at Princeton University in 1968, becoming professor in 1971. He was chairman of the department (1974–78, 1983–86) and named William Schubael Conant Professor in 1995.

For orchestra Westergaard has composed a *Symphonic Movement* (1954), *Five Movements* for small orchestra (1958), and a work for band, *Tuckets and Sennets* (1969). His instrumental music includes *Partita* for flute, violin, and harpsichord (1953, rev. 1956); *Inventions* for flute and piano (1955); a String Quartet (1957); Quartet for clarinet, violin, cello, and vibra-phone (1960); Trio for flute, cello, and piano (1962); *Variations* for six players (1963); *Divertimento on Discobbolic Fragments* for flute and piano (1967); *Noises, Sounds and Sweet Airs* for ensemble (1968); *Moto Perpetua* for flute, oboe, clarinet, bassoon, trumpet, and horn (1976); and *Two Fanfares* for brass sextet (1988).

Westergaard is best known for his operas: *Charivari* (1953), *Mr. and Mrs. Discobbolos*, based on Edward Lear (1966), and *The Tempest* (after Shakespeare) (1974).

Among Westergaard's vocal music are two cantatas: *I, The Plot Against the Giant* (Wallace Stevens) for female chorus, clarinet, cello, and harp (1958) and *II, A Refusal to Mourn the Death by Fire of a Child in London* (Dylan Thomas) for baritone and ten instruments (1958); *Spring and Fall to a Young Child* for voice and piano (1960); *Cantata III: Leda and the Swan* (W. B. Yeats) for mezzo-soprano, clarinet, vibraphone, marimba, and viola (1961); *There Was a Little Man* for soprano and violin (1982); *Ariel Music* for high soprano and chamber ensemble (1987); and *Ode* for soprano, flute, clarinet, violin, viola, and harp (1989).

WHITHORNE, EMERSON
b. Cleveland, Ohio, 6 September 1884
d. Lyme, Connecticut, 25 March 1958

Whithorne's family name was originally Wittern, and his parents were of Dutch origin. However, Thomas Whythorne, the sixteenth-century English composer, was one of his ancestors, so he took the name Whithorne. He grew up in a family of string players and, encouraged by his mother, he began piano lessons at the age of ten. In 1904 he studied in Vienna with Leschetizky (piano) and Robert Fuchs (composition), becoming a pupil of Artur Schnabel in 1905 and settling in London in 1907.

His reputation as a pianist, composer, and music critic for the *Pall Mall Gazette* led many to believe that he was an English musician. His *English Dances*, composed for the famous Shakespeare Ball organized by Lady Randolph Churchill, were so popular that they were even played throughout Germany by military bands. In 1915 he returned to America, where he became music editor for several publishers. From 1915 to 1920 he was editor for the Arts Publication Society of St. Louis. He retired in 1922 to devote himself entirely to composition; in addition, he was an active member of the League of Composers.

The following year his best-known work, *New York, Days and Nights*, a suite for piano, was heard at the Salzburg Chamber Music Festival. As with many of his large-scale piano pieces, it was later scored for orchestra, receiving its premiere in this form in New

Peter Westergaard, 1991.
Photo: John Simpson, courtesy the composer.

York in 1927. It established his fame as a truly American composer in spite of the years in Europe.

Poem for piano and orchestra was first heard in Chicago in 1927 under the direction of Frederick Stock. Even with the advocacy of Gieseking as soloist, the harsh dissonances, complex rhythms, and polytonal textures of the music alienated both critics and public.

Whithorne's other orchestral pieces are more conservative in character, often neo-romantic by nature. These include *The Rain* (1913); *La Nuit* (1917); a suite, *Adventures of a Samurai* (1919); a symphonic suite, *Ranga* (1920); *The Aeroplane* (1920); and two symphonic poems, *Fata Morgana*, performed by the New York Philharmonic Orchestra (1928), and *The Dream Pedlar* (1931). He composed three symphonies (1929, 1935, 1937) and a Violin Concerto (1928; Chicago, 1931). Other orchestral works include *Fandango* (1931); *Fandance* (1932); a tone poem, *Moon Trail*, first heard in Boston in 1933; *Sierra Morena*, performed by Pierre Monteux in 1938; *Stroller's Serenade* for strings (1943); and a symphonic poem, *The City of Ys*.

Outstanding among his chamber works are *Three Greek Impressions* for string quartet (1914), a Piano Quintet (1928), a String Quartet (1930), and a Violin Sonata (1932). For the stage he wrote *Sooner or Later*, a ballet in six scenes for chamber orchestra and chorus (1925). The scenario depicts in fantasy three different states of living: the primal tribal life, a modern city, and a scientific, futuristic mechanized existence. He also provided incidental music for Eugene O'Neill's play *Marco Millions* (1928), in which he used authentic Chinese music and instruments, and two oriental dramas, *The Yellow Jacket* and *The Typhoon*.

His large number of songs are unduly neglected. *Invocation*, a setting of Whitman's words "At the last, tenderly," is a particularly fine example of his expressive use of melodic line. In 1926 he set poems of the African-American writer Countee Cullen as *Saturday's Child*, for mezzo-soprano, tenor, and chamber orchestra. Although adopting an African-American idiom, the work avoids pastiche. The following year he set more poems by Cullen in a cycle for medium voice and string quartet, *The Grim Troubadour.*

WHITING, ARTHUR BATTELLE

b. Cambridge, Massachusetts, 20 June 1861
d. Beverly, Massachusetts, 20 July 1936

Whiting studied at the New England Conservatory of Music, Boston, with George Chadwick. In 1883 he went to Munich, where he became a pupil of Joseph Rheinberger. On his return to the United States in 1885, he taught in Boston before moving in 1895 to New York, where he made his permanent home and gained a

reputation as a teacher and concert pianist. He was one of the first American musicians to revive the harpsichord in the performance of Baroque music. One of his pupils was Edward Burlingame Hill.

As a composer, Whiting was very self-critical and therefore not prolific. He wrote a *Concert Overture* (1886), a Piano Concerto in D minor (1888), a Suite in G minor for horn quartet and strings (1891), and a *Fantasy* in B-flat minor for piano and orchestra (1897). He composed a Piano Quintet, a String Quartet, a Piano Trio, a Violin Sonata (1981), and a number of piano pieces.

The song cycle *Floriana* sets poems by Oliver Herford (1901). Other vocal music includes *Rubaiyat of Omar Khayyam* for baritone and piano (1901) and *Barrack Room Ballads* (Kipling) for baritone and piano. For the stage he provided music for a dance pageant, *The Golden Cage* (1926), inspired by the poems of William Blake.

WHITTENBERG, CHARLES

b. St. Louis, Missouri, 6 July 1927
d. Hartford, Connecticut, 22 August 1984

At the Eastman School of Music, Rochester, New York (1944–48), Whittenberg was a pupil of Bernard Rogers and Burrill Phillips. In 1962 he worked at the Columbia-Princeton Electronic Music Center, where he studied with Otto Luening. He received two Guggenheim Fellowships (1963–65) and spent a year at the American Academy in Rome (1965–66). He taught at Bennington College (1962–65), The Center for Liberal Arts, Washington, D.C. (1965–67), and the University of Connecticut (1967–77).

In his compositions, Whittenberg combined neo-classical elements with serialism. Most of his works are for chamber ensembles of various sizes. Principal among them are *Fantasy* for wind quintet (1961); *Triptych* for brass quintet (1962); *Chamber Concerto* for violin and seven instruments (1963); *Variations* for nine players (1964, rev. 1970); String Quartet no. 1 in one movement (1965); Sextet for flute, clarinet, bassoon, violin, cello, and double bass (1967); *Games for Five* for wind quintet (1968); Concerto for brass quintet (1969); *Composition* for winds (1969); *Correlatives* for chamber orchestra (1969); Serenade for strings (1971–73); String Quartet no. 2 (1974–75); and *Serenade on a Twelfth Night Carol* for flute, clarinet, and cello.

Other instrumental pieces include *Dialogue and Aria* for flute and piano (1959); *Concert Piece* for bassoon and piano (1961, rev. 1971); Cello Sonata (1963); *Set of Two* for viola and piano (1963); *Duo-Divertimento* for flute and double bass (1963); *Three Pieces* for solo clarinet (1963, rev. 1969); *Polyphony* for solo trumpet

(1965); *Conversations* for double bass (1967); *Iambs for two oboes* (1968, rev.1972); *Winter Music* for solo violin (1971); *Sonata-Fantasia* for solo cello (1973); *5 Feuilletons* for solo clarinet (1976); and *In Memoriam Benjamin Britten* for percussion (1977).

Among Whittenberg's keyboard pieces are *Piano Variations* (1963), *Four Forms and an Epilogue* for harpsichord (1965), *Three Compositions* for piano (1967, rev, 1969), and *Structures* for two pianos (1961).

Whittenberg's work at the Yale Electronic Studio produced several compositions for instruments and tape: *Study* for cello (1960); *Electronic Study* for double bass (1961); *Study* for clarinet with electronic extensions (1961); *Event* for chamber orchestra (1963); *Event II* for double bass, flute, and strings (1963); and *Electronic Collages: The Run Off*, incidental music for a play by R. Shure.

Whittenberg's vocal music includes *Three Songs on Texts of Rilke* for soprano and 9 instruments (1957, rev. 1962); *Concertante: Even Though the World* (Rilke) for baritone, flute, viola, and vibraphone (1961); *From the Sonnets to Orpheus* (Rilke) for narrator, soprano, baritone, and orchestra (1962); *Vocalise* for violin, viola, and percussion (1963); *From John Donne*, a sacred triptych for eight voices (1970–71); and *Two Dylan Thomas Songs*.

WIGGLESWORTH, FRANK

b. *Boston, Massachussets, 3 March 1918*
d. *New York, New York, 19 March 1996*

Wigglesworth studied at Bard College, Annandale-on-Hudson, New York (1937–40), Columbia University (1940–42), and Converse College, Spartanburg, South Carolina. He was a pupil of Otto Luening and Henry Cowell, and also worked with Edgar Varèse (1948–51). He taught at Converse College (1941–42), Greenwich House, New York (1946–47), Columbia University and Barnard College (1947–51); he began an association with the New School of Social Research, New York in 1954. He also taught at the City University of New York (1970–76). In 1981 he was appointed president of the America Composers' Alliance. Wigglesworth received a number of major awards, including one from the Alice M. Ditson Foundation in 1943 and one from the Institute of Arts and Letters in 1951.

For the stage he completed an opera, *The Willowdale Handcar* (1969), but left another incomplete at his death. He composed two ballets, *Young Goodman Brown* (1951) and *Ballet for Esther Brooks* (1961); a play with music, *Between the Atoms and the Stars* (1959); and incidental music for *Hamlet* (1960).

Wigglesworth's important works are three symphonies: no. 1 (1954), no. 2 for strings (1963), and no. 3, *Three Portraits* (1967–69). Other orchestral pieces are *New England Concerto* for violin and strings (1941); *Music for Strings* (1946); *Fantasia* for strings (1947); *Three Movements* for strings (1949); *Summer Scenes* (1951); Concertino for piano and strings (1953); *Concert Piece* (1954); *Telesis* for small orchestra (1955); Concertino for violin and orchestra (1965); *Overture for the American Composers Orchestra* (1977); Suite for Strings (1978–80); *Music for Strings II* (1981); *Aurora* (1983); and *Sea Winds* (1984).

Wigglesworth composed several choral works, including *Creation* for chorus and orchestra (1940); *Jeremiah* for baritone, chorus, and orchestra (1942); *Isaiah* for chorus and orchestra (1942); *Choral Study* for soprano and chorus (1947); *Sleep Becalmed* (Dylan Thomas) for chorus and orchestra (1948); *Alleluia* for female voices (1950); three short masses (1961, 1970, 1973); *Super Flumina* for chorus (1965); *Prayer* (1972); and Psalm 148 for chorus, three flutes, and three trombones (1973). He composed *Duets* (Robert Frost) for soprano and clarinet (1977–78).

Among his many instrumental compositions are a Trio for flute, banjo, and harp (1942); *Lake Music* for flute (1947); Serenade for flute, viola, and guitar (1952); a Viola Sonata (1959); a Brass Quintet (1958); *Sound Piece* for cello and piano (1959); Harpsichord Sonata (1960); Trio Sonata for two trumpets and trombone (1960); a Violin Sonata (1960); two wind quintets (1960, 1975); *Duo* for oboe and violin (or clarinet) (1961); Trio for three flutes (1963); Viola Sonata (1965); two string trios (1972, 1976); *Four Winds* for brass quartet (1978); a Sonata for solo viola (1978–79); Brass Quintet no. 2 (1980); and *After Summer Music* for flute, viola and guitar (1983).

WILDER, ALEC

b. *Rochester, New York, 16 February 1907*
d. *Gainesville, California, 24 December 1980*

Wilder received his musical education at the Eastman School of Music, Rochester, New York,, where he was a pupil of Edward Royce and Herbert Inch. During the 1930's and 1940's he was active as a songwriter and arranger for many bands and jazz orchestras.

Wilder's output of music is so prodigious that he himself could not recall much of what he had written. For orchestra he composed *Symphonic Piece* (1929); *Grandma Moses Suite* (1950); *Suite: Alice in Wonderland, A Child's Introduction to the Orchestra* (1954); *Carl Sandburg Suite* (1960); Suite for saxophone and orchestra (1965); Concerto for euphonium and wind ensemble (1971); *Rhapsody* for piano and orchestra; and two works for tuba and orchestra, *Effie Suite* and *Elegy for a Whale.*

Wilder composed several solo woodwind and brass concertos, often accompanied by wind ensemble. Among these are three for horn (1954, 1960, 1970), two for trumpet, and one each for flute, clarinet, oboe (1950), alto saxophone (1967), tenor saxophone, baritone saxophone, euphonium (1971), and tuba (1965). Other works for solo winds and orchestra include *Air* for horn and wind ensemble (1968); *Air* for bassoon and strings; Sonata for tuba and orchestra, and four suites with string accompaniment: clarinet (1947), brass quintet, horn, and tenor saxophone.

Besides his orchestral and stage works (see below), almost all of Wilder's other compositions are for wind instruments, including twelve wind quintets (1953–78); eight brass quintets (1970–77); a Wind Octet; a Nonet for brass (1969); seven *Entertainments* for wind ensemble (1961–71); and Serenade for winds (1977). Even his choral work, *Children's Plea for Peace* (1969), uses a wind ensemble to accompany the children's choir.

Like Paul Hindemith Wilder provided chamber music for the less popular instruments, with sonatas for alto saxophone (1960), bass trombone (1971), and English horn. There are also three sonatas for bassoon (1964, 1968, 1973); two horn sonatas (1954, 1957, 1965); two flute sonatas (1958, 1962); and one each for clarinet (1963) and oboe. There is also a multitude of suites for solo, duets, and trios of wind instruments with piano.

Wilder composed ten operas: the one-act *The Lowland Sea* (1951); *Sunday Excursion*, a one-act curtain raiser (1953); *Cumberland Fair* (1953); three two-act operas: *Kittewake Island* (1954), *Ellen* (or *The Long Way*) (1955), and *The Impossible Forest* (1958); *The Tattoed Countess* (1974); *The Truth About Windmills* (1975); and *The Opening* (1975). In addition there are three operas for children: *The Churkendoose, Racketty Packetty House*, and *Herman Ermine in Rabbit Town*; an operetta, *Miss Chicken Little* (1953); and a musical, *Jack in the Country*, based on Oscar Wilde's *The Importance of Being Ernest*. Also for the stage, Wilder wrote four ballets: *Juke Box* (1940), *False Dawn, Green Couch*, and *Life Goes On.*

Among his film scores are *The Grocer and the Dragon* (1955), *The Sand Castle* (1961), *Open the Door and See All the People* (1964), and two documentaries, *Albert Schweitzer* (1957) and *Since Life Began* (1961). In 1959 he also provided music for the 1928 silent film *The Fall of the House of Usher.*

Wilder was the author of two books, *The American Popular Song* (with James T. Maher) (1972) and *Letters I Never Mailed* (1975). His song "I'll Be Around" achieved wide success through performances by Frank Sinatra.

WILLIAMS, JOHN (TOWNER)
b. New York, New York, 8 February 1932

Williams studied orchestration at Los Angeles City College with the film composer Robert Van Epps and received composition lessons from Mario Castelnuovo-Tadesco. In New York in 1954 he became a piano student of Rosina Lhevinne. From 1980 to 1993 he was conductor of the Boston "Pops" Orchestra.

Although he is renowned as a composer of magisterial scores for Hollywood movies, Williams has composed many orchestral works for the concert hall. Most notable among these are *Essay* for strings (1966); a Symphony (1966); Sinfonietta for wind orchestra (1968); Concerto for flute, strings, and percussion (1969); a Violin Concerto (1974–76, rev. 1998); *Fanfare for a Festive Occasion* (1981); *Pops on the March* (1982); *Olympic Fanfare*, composed in 1982 for the Los Angeles Games; Tuba Concerto (1985) for Chester Schmitz and the Boston Symphony Orchestra; *Celebration Fanfare* (1986); a *Hymn to New England* (1987); *Liberty Fanfare* (1987); *Olympic Spirit* (1988); Clarinet Concerto (1991); Bassoon Concerto; *The Five Sacred Trees*, written in 1992 for the 150th anniversary of the New York Philharmonic Orchestra; a Cello Concerto for Yo-Yo Ma (1994); *Summons the Hero* (1995); and *Seiji* (1998), a tribute to Seiji Ozawa's 25 years with the Boston Symphony Orchestra.

Recent orchestral pieces include *TreeSong* for violin and orchestra, composed in 2000 for Gil Shahan; *Fanfare for the Winter Olympics* (2002); *American Journey* (2002); a Trumpet Concerto; *Song for World Peace*; *For New York*: Variations on a Theme of Leonard Bernstein (2002); *Soundings* (2003); and a Horn Concerto (2003). *America, the Dream Goes On* (1981) and *Summon the Heroes* (1996) are scored for chorus and orchestra.

Williams has composed more than 100 film scores, and has won five Academy Awards: *Fiddler on the Roof* (1971); *Jaws* (1975); *Star Wars* (1977); *E.T.* (1982); and *Schindler's List* (1993). Other films for which he has provided music are *Gidget* (1957); *Jane Eyre* (1970); *The Poseidon Adventure* (1972); *Towering Inferno* (1974); *Close Encounters of the Third Kind* (1977); *Superman* (1978); *The Empire Strikes Back* (1980); *Raiders of the Lost Ark* (1981); *The Return of the Jedi* (1983); *Indiana Jones and the Last Crusade* (1989); *Jurassic Park* (1993); *Saving Private Ryan* (1998); *Star Wars: The Phantom Menace* (1999); *Indiana Jones and the Lost Continent* (2001); *Star Wars:*

Episode II (2002); *The Minority Report* (2002); and *Catch Me If You Can* (2002).

WILLSON, (ROBERT) MEREDITH (REINIGER)

b. Mason City, Iowa, 18 May 1902
d. Santa Monica, California, 15 June 1984

Willson's versatilty is evident in the professional reputation he established as a flutist, conductor, musical director, songwriter, librettist, novelist, and composer for the concert hall, theater, films, radio, and television. As a child he studied piano with his mother and played the flute in the local band. He later attended the Institute of Musical Art in New York (now the Juilliard School) and received private tuition from Georges Barrère (flute; 1920–29), Henry Hadley (conducting; 1923–24), and Bernard Wagenaar and Mortimer Wilson (composition).

He was appointed principal flute in Sousa's band (1921–23), moving to a similar position in the New York Philharmonic Symphony Orchestra (1924–29), then conducted by Arturo Toscanini. In 1929 he became musical director of a radio company in San Francisco, joining NBC in 1932. From 1937 he provided songs for various Hollywood films while maintaining his radio work; he also created *The Meredith Willson Show*, which became a television program in the 1950s.

Willson acquired international fame relatively late in life with two highly successful musicals, *The Music Man* (1957) and *The Unsinkable Molly Brown* (1960). Two further works for the stage were a musical, *Here's Love* (1963), and an operetta, *1491* (1969). In addition to his many songs for films, he was musical director for Chaplin's *The Great Dictator* (1940) and provided music for the movie *The Little Foxes* (1941), both nominated for Academy Awards.

For orchestra Willson composed Symphony no. 1 in F minor, *A Symphony of San Francisco*, commissioned in 1936 to mark the 30th anniversary of the earthquake. Symphony, no. 2 in E minor, *The Missions of California*, was performed in 1940 by the Los Angeles Symphony Orchestra, conducted by Albert Coates. His other orchestral works include *O. O. McIntyre Suite* (1936), *The Jervis Bay* (1942), *Symphonic Variations on an American Theme*, *Song of Steel*, and *Anthem of the Atomic Age*.

Willson was the author of several books, including *What Every Young Musician Should Know* (1938), *And There I Stood With My Piccolo* (1948), *Who Did What to Fidalia?* (1952), *Eggs I Have Laid* (1955), and *But He Doesn't Know the Territory* (1959).

WILSON, MORTIMER

b. Charlton, Iowa, 6 August 1876
d. New York, New York, 27 January 1932

Wilson studied with Solomon Jadassohn, Harold Gleason, and Wilhelm Middelschultze in Chicago. From 1902 to 1907 he was director of the University of Nebraska School of Music, Lincoln. In 1907 he went to Germany, where he was a pupil of Max Reger and Hans Sitt. On his return to the United States he taught at the University of Nebraska, Lincoln. He was the conductor of the Atlanta Symphony Orchestra (1911–15) and taught at the Atlanta Conservatory. In 1915 he settled in New York, where he devoted himself to composition.

For orchestra he wrote five symphonies; an overture, *New Orleans* (*Mardi Gras*) (1920); a suite, *From My Youth*; a *Concerto Grosso* for strings; *Country Wedding Suite*; *Overture 1849*; and *Euterpean Lyrics* for strings. Instrumental works include three violin sonatas, two piano trios, two piano sonatas, and an Organ Sonata.

Wilson's music for the Douglas Fairbanks film *The Thief of Bagdad* (1924) was one of the first scores specially written to be played by a live orchestra in a movie theater. He also provided film scores for *The Black Pirate* (1926) and *Don Q, Son of Zorro* (1926).

He wrote three books: *The Rhetoric of Music* (1907), *Harmonic and Melodic Technical Studies* (1908), and *Orchestral Training* (1921).

WILSON, OLLY (WOODROW)

b. St. Louis, Missouri, 7 September 1937

As a youngster Wilson played the bass and piano in local jazz bands and was later a double bassist in the St. Louis Philharmonic and Cedar Rapids Symphony Orchestra. He studied at Washington University (B.Mus., 1959), the University of Illinois (M. Mus., 1960), where he was a pupil of Robert Wykes and Philip Bezanson, and at the University of Iowa (Ph.D., 1964). He returned to the University of Illinois in 1967 to work in the electronic music studios. He was awarded two Guggenheim Fellowships; the first (1971) enabled him to research the music of West Africa, the second (1977) took him to Rome. From 1960 to 1962 he taught at the Florida Agricultural and Mechanical University, moving to Oberlin (Ohio) College Conservatory of Music (1965–70). In 1970 he was appointed professor of music at the University of California at Berkeley. Wilson was elected to the American Academy of Arts and Sciences in 1995

For orchestra Wilson has written *Structure* (1960); *Three Movements* (1964); *Voices* (1970); *Akwan* for piano, electric piano, and orchestra (1972), influenced by his experiences in West Africa; *Reflections* (1978); *Trilogy* (1979–80); *Lumina* (1981); *Sinfonia* (1983–84); *Houston Fanfare* (1986); *Expansions II* (1990) and *III* (1993); and a Viola Concerto (1994). His chamber music includes *Prelude and Line Study* for flute, clarinet, bassoon, and bass clarinet (1959); Trio for flute, cello, and piano (1959); a String Quartet (1960); Violin Sonata (1961); *Dance Suite* for wind ensemble (1962); *Soliloquy* for double bass (1962); *Dance Music I* for wind ensemble (1963); Sextet for winds and brass (1963); *Dance Music II* for wind ensemble (1965); *Piece for Four* for flute, trumpet, double bass, and piano (1966); *Piano Piece* for piano and tape (1969); Piano Trio (1977); *Expansions* for organ (1979); *Echoes* for clarinet and electronic tape (1974–75); and *A City Called Heaven* for flute, clarinet, violin, cello, piano, and percussion (1989).

As a result of his time at the University of Illinois Electronic Music Studios Wilson produced four pieces for tape alone: *Cetus* (1967); a ballet, *The Eighteen Hands of Jerome Harris* (1970); incidental music for a play, *Black Mass* (1971); and *Black Martyrs* (1972).

Among Wilson's choral works are *Gloria* (1961); *Biography* with soprano solo (1966); *In Memoriam Martin Luther King, Jr.* with electronics (1968); and *Spirit Song*, a sequence of spirituals for soprano, double chorus and orchestra (1973).

His solo vocal music includes *Two Dutch Poems* for voice and piano (1960); two songs for tenor and percussion, *Wry Fragments* and *And Death Shall Have No Dominion* (Dylan Thomas; 1963); *Chanson Innocent* for alto and two bassoons (1965); *Sometimes* for tenor and electronics (1974–75); *No More* for tenor, flute, clarinet, violin, cello, harp, piano, and percussion (1985); and *I Shall Not Be Moved* for soprano and chamber ensemble (1992–93).

WILSON, RICHARD (EDWARD)
b. Cleveland, Ohio, 15 May 1941

After receiving piano, cello, and theory lessons at the Cleveland Music School Settlement (1954–59), Wilson entered Harvard University (B.A., 1963), where he was a pupil of Randall Thompson and Robert Moevs. He studied piano with Friedrich Wührer in Munich (1963) and composition with Moevs at the American Academy in Rome. He undertook post-graduate work at Rutgers University (M.A. 1966). Wilson began teaching at Vassar College, Poughkeepsie, New York in 1966, becoming professor in 1976 and serving as chairman of the music department (1979–82, 1985–88, 1995–98). He currently holds the Mary Conover Mellon Chair

Richard Wilson.
Photo © Barbara Trautwein, courtesy the composer.

in Music at Vassar. In addition he has been Composer-in-Residence with the American Symphony Orchestra (1992–93).

For orchestra Wilson has written *Fantasy and Variations* for chamber orchestra (1966); *Initiation* (1970); Concerto for violin and chamber orchestra (1979); Bassoon Concerto (1983); two symphonies (1984, 1987); *A Child's London* for narrator and orchestra (1987); *Silhouette* (1988); Suite for small orchestra (1988); *Articulations* (1989); a Piano Concerto (1991); *Agitations* (1994); Triple Concerto for horn, bass clarinet, and marimba (1999); *Intimations* for piano and orchestra (1999); *Peregrinations* for viola and orchestra (2002); and *Revelry* (2002). Two works for band are *Eleven Sumner Place* (1981) and *Jubilation* (1987).

Among Wilson's many instrumental pieces are a Suite for five players (1963); Trio for oboe, violin, and cello (1964); *Concert Piece* for violin and piano (1967); four string quartets (1968; 1977; 1982; 1997, rev. 2001); *Music* for violin and cello (1969); Quartet for two flutes, double bass, and harpsichord (1969); *Music* for cello (1971); *Music* for flute (1972); Wind Quintet (1974); *Serenade*: *Variations on a Simple March* for clarinet, viola, and double bass (1978); *Deux pas de trois*:

Pavane and Tango for flute, oboe, and harpsichord (1979); *Profound Utterances*, music for bassoon (1980); *Figuration* for clarinet, cello, and piano (1980); *Gnomics* for flute, oboe, and clarinet (1982); *Character Studies* for oboe and piano (1982); *Dithyramb* for oboe and clarinet (1982); and Suite for winds (1983).

Later chamber music includes *Line Drawings* for two clarinets (1984); *Flutations* for solo flute (1985); *Lord Chesterfield to His Son* for solo cello (1987); *Music* for viola (1988); *Contentions* for chamber ensemble (1988); Viola Sonata(1989); *Intonations*, five pieces for horn (1989); *Affirmations* for flute, oboe, violin, cello, and piano (1990); *Touchstones* for flute (1995); *Civilization and Its Discontents* for tuba (1992); *Three Interludes* for violin and piano (1996); *Motivations* for cello and piano (2000); *Canzona* for horn and string quartet (2001); and Piano Trio (2000). For piano solo he has written *Eclogue* (1974), *Sour Flowers* (1979), *A Child's London* (1984), *Fixations* (1985), and *Intercalations* (1986).

Wilson has written several important works for chorus: *August 22* (J. Unterecker) for chorus, piano, and percussion (1975–76); *A Dissolve* for female chorus (1968); *Can* (1968); *Light in Spring Poplars* for double chorus (1968); *Soaking* (1969); *Home From the Range* for double chorus (1970); *Elegy* (1971); *Hunter's Moon* (1972); *In Schrafft's* (W. H. Auden) for chorus, clarinet, marimba, and harpsichord (1979); and *Poor Warren* (John Ashbery) for chorus and piano (1995).

Wilson's only opera, *Aethelred the Unready*, was completed in 1994 and revised in 2001. Solo vocal music includes *The Ballad of Longwood Glen* for tenor and harp (1975); *A Theory* for soprano and vibraphone (1980); *Three Painters* for high voice and piano (1984); *Tribulations*, five songs for voice and piano (1988); *Persuasions* for soprano, flute, oboe, bassoon, and harpsichord (1990); *The Second Law* for baritone and piano (1991); *On the Street* for baritone and piano (or strings; 1992); *Pamietam* for mezzo-soprano and orchestra (1995); *Five Love Songs on Poems of John Skelton* for high voice and piano (1995); *Transfigured Goat* for soprano, baritone, clarinet, and piano (1996); and *Three Songs on Poems of John Ashbery* (2000).

WOLFF, CHRISTIAN

b. Nice, France, 8 March 1934

Wolff was taken to the United States in 1941, becoming an American citizen in 1946. Although he learned the flute and piano, he had no formal training in composition. At Harvard University he studied classics, receiving a doctorate in comparative literature in 1963. He taught classics at Harvard (1963–70) before being appointed professor of classics and music at Dartmouth College, New Hampshire in 1971 and professor of music in 1979, retiring in 2000. Wolff's early pieces from 1950 are notated with carefully judged silences. After 1957 he gave greater choice to performers with cues, later allowing for improvisation and less specific instruction.

Influenced by John Cage, even Wolff's earliest works are experimental in every way. He has adopted arithmetical progressions with regard to rhythm and makes considerable use of rests and long silences as a fundamental part of musical construction. In addition he imposes strict limitations on the number of different pitches. The *Duo* for two violins (1950) contains only three different pitches; Trio for flute, cello, and trumpet (1951) uses only four different pitches; and *For Piano I* (1952) is confined to nine pitches, as is *Nine for Nine Instruments* (1951), naturally.

Wolff has restricted himself almost entirely to instrumental compositions, and all those dating after 1957 contain indeterminate elements. As certain titles suggest, many works are for a flexible number of performers: *For Six or Seven Players* (1959); *For Five to Ten Players* (1962); *For One, Two or Three People* (1964); Septet for any instruments (1964); *Pairs* for two, four, six or eight players, any instruments (1968); and *Tilbury* for any instrument(s) (1969).

A basic feature of all his pieces is the element of choice presented to the players within a framework of instructions. A series of works entitled *Electric Spring* (1966–70) use two guitars with other instruments: no. 1 with horn and double bass, no. 2 with tenor and alto recorders and trombone, and no. 3 with violin and horn. *Edges* for any number of players and instruments dates from 1968. *Burdocks* was performed in London by the neo-Dada Scratch Orchestra in 1971. Another work written for performance in London, *Stones*, begins instructions to the performers with "Make sounds with stones." There is a companion work, *Sticks*.

Except for *Summer* (1961) and *Lines* (1972), both for string quartet, most of Wolff's compositions have explicitly objective titles, such as *In Between Piece* for three players (1963), and a series of *Duos*: for two violins (1950), two for two pianos (1957, 1958), for piano, four hands (1960) for horn and piano (1961), and for violin and piano (1961). His keyboard works include *For Prepared Piano* (1951); *For Piano I* (1952) and *II* (1953); Suite for prepared piano (1954); *For Pianist* (1959); *Snowdrop* (1970); and *Accompaniments* (1972); and Sonata for three pianos (1957).

Later compositions have included more specific and extended melodic material with radical political content. In *Accompaniments* (1972), the pianist declaims texts. *Changing the System* (1973) and *Wobbly Music*

(1974–75), both scored for chamber ensemble, require players to speak and sing extracts from political pamphlets. *Bread and Roses*, based on a political song, exists in four versions: for piano (1976), for violin (1976), *Bread and Roses For John 1982* for piano duet (1982), and *Exercise 23*: *Bread and Roses* for clarinet and small orchestra (1983).

In 1978 for Rohan de Saran, he composed *Cello Song Variations* (*Hallelujah I'm A Bum*) for solo cello. Other instrumental works include *Dark as a Dungeon*, versions for solo clarinet and for trombone and double bass (both 1977); *Braverman Music* for ensemble (1979); *Twenty Exercises*: 1 – 14 for chamber ensemble (1973–74), 15 – 18 for solo piano, trombone, and ensemble (1975), and 19 – 20 for two pianos (1980); *The Death of Mother Jones* for solo violin (1977); *Three Pieces*: *Rockabout, Instrumental*, and *About Starving to Death on a Government Claim* for violin and viola (1979–80); and *Peace March I* (*Stop Using Uranium*) for flute (1983–84), *II* for flute, clarinet, cello, percussion, and piano (1984), and *III* (*The Sun is Burning*) for flute, cello, and percussion (1984).

Recent ensemble works are *Isn't This a Time* (1982); Piano Trio (1985); *Bowery Preludes* for flute, trombone, percussion, and piano (1985–86); *Long Peace March* (1986–87); *For Si* for clarinet/bass clarinet, trumpet, two percussion, double bass, and piano (1990–91); *Merce* for 1 – 9 percussionists (1993); *Memory* for eight players (1994); *Bratislava* for eight players (1995); *Schoenen met Vetters* for seven players (1998–99); *Berlin Exercises 1–4* (2000); *Variations on Cage's "Fontana Mix"* for trumpet, double bass, and percussion (2001); and *Peace March 9* for brass and percussion (2003).

Among Wolff's latest instrumental pieces are *Malvina* for solo koto (1986); *Ruth* for trombone and piano (1991); *Look She Said* for solo double bass (1991); *Jasper* for double bass and violin (1991); *Ain't Gonna Study War No More* for timpani and marimba (1993); *Flutist and Guitarist* (1993); *Untitled* for electric bass guitar (1996); *Percussion Dances* for solo percussion (1997); *Pebbles* for violin and piano (1999); *Percussionist 1 – 6* (2000); *Pianist*: *Pieces* (2001); *She Had Some Horses* for viola and zither (2001); and *Touch* for piano (2002). In 2002 Wolff composed *Moving Spaces* for two to four players and optional 8-channel tape for Merce Cunningham's *Loose Times*.

In recent years he has turned to composing orchestral music: *Spring* for chamber orchestra (1995), *John, David* (1993, 1997–98), *Ordinary Matters* for three orchestras (2001), and *Peace March 8* (2002).

Wolff has published in Germany a collection of his writing under the title *Cues*: *Writings and Conversations*.

WOLPE, STEFAN
b. Berlin, Germany, 25 August 1902
d. New York, New York, 4 April 1972

Wolpe was born of Russian-Jewish and Austrian parents. From the age of fourteen he studied theory and composition at the Klindworth-Scharwenka Conservatory in Berlin, then spent one year at the Berlin Hochschule für Musik (1920–21) under Paul Juon. He regarded Ferruccio Busoni with his "aesthetic of new music" as his most important influence. Wolpe was also affected by the Dadaists. At the Bauhaus in Weimar he attended lectures and participated in studio classes of Johannes Itten and Paul Klee. He was active as composer and pianist in the left-wing Novembergruppe and in 1929 became more active politically, joining Hanns Eisler's workers' music movement. From 1931–33 he was music director of Die Truppe 1931. When Hitler seized power, he fled Germany and went to Vienna to study with Anton Webern during the fall of 1933. He emigrated to Palestine in 1934 and in 1935 attended Hermann Scherchen's course in conducting at Brussels. On returning to Jerusalem he taught theory and composition at the Palestine Conservatory.

In 1938 he emigrated to the United States, where he became a naturalized citizen in 1945. He taught at the Settlement Music School in Philadelphia (1939–1942), the Brooklyn Free Academy of Music (1945–48), the

Stefan Wolpe.
Courtesy Stefan Wolpe Society.

Contemporary Music School (1948–52), the Philadelphia Academy of Music (1949–52), Black Mountain College, North Carolina (1952–56), and Chatham Square Music School, New York (1957–63). From 1957 until he retired in 1967 Wolpe was head of the music department at C. W. Post College, Greenvale, New York.

Wolpe received many awards, including a Fulbright Fellowship, two Guggenheim Fellowships, and membership in the National Institute of Arts and Letters. His importance as a teacher was considerable. He numbered among his pupils composers who were influential in the fields of film, broadway, modern jazz, and concert music: Elmer Bernstein, Herbert Brün, John Carisi, Morton Feldman, Isaac Nemiroff, Raoul Pleskow, Ralph Shapey, and David Tudor.

Wolpe's compositions from the Berlin period show the influence of Schoenberg and Hauer, Bauhaus modernism, Dada, and jazz. In particular he explored the "music of stasis" as an alternative to the prevailing developing variation approach. Two music theater pieces, *Schöne Geschichten* (*Droll Stories*) (1927–29) and *Zeus und Elida* (1928), were performed as a pair at the Holland Festival in 1997. The Berlin years culminated in the *March and Variations* for two pianos (1932–33).

While studying with Webern he began working with the twelve-tone method. During the four years in Palestine he assimilated the concepts of Schoenberg, Hauer, Webern, and Busoni in *Four Studies on Basic Rows* for piano (1935–36). He found compensation for European modernism in classical Arabic music and the folklore of oriental Jewish communities. He incorporated elements from these traditions, such as the concept of *maqam*, in songs on Hebrew texts and instrumental pieces. Theodor Adorno in 1940 regarded Wolpe as "an outsider in the best sense of the word. It is impossible to subsume him." Wolpe's intensely dialectical music corresponds to Adorno's concept of negative dialectics.

In the music of the 1940's Wolpe assimilated diatonicism and dodecaphony in a continuous spectrum of resources, as demonstrated in the *Zemach Suite* (1939–41) and *Toccata* (1941), both for piano; the ballet *The Man from Midian* (1942); the cantata *Yigdal* (1945); *Battle Piece* for piano (1947); and the Violin Sonata (1949). In a series of compositional studies, *Music For Any Instruments*, he developed the concepts of spatial proportions and organic modes that formed the basis for the works he composed in the 1950s, while at Black Mountain College: *Quartet* for trumpet, tenor saxophone, percussion, and piano (1950, rev. 1954); *Enactments* for three pianos (1953); Symphony (1955–56); and *Piece* for oboe, cello, percussion, and piano (1955). These compositions provide a musical analog to the abstract expressionist canvases of the New York school of painters, many of whom were Wolpe's close friends.

Wolpe wrote lectures for the general listener and for specialists that he delivered with quasi-theatrical intensity. At Darmstadt in 1956 he presented a survey of contemporary music in America that emphasized the importance of jazz. While describing the music of Copland, Sessions, Carter, Babbitt, Feldman, Cage, and others, he emphasized the importance of the fantasy and the sense of intuitive form. He summed up his poetics in the lecture "Thinking Twice," which presents his ideas on organic modes and the conjunction of opposites as the basis for a music of "ever-restored and ever-advancing moments." His aesthetic of liberation and his vivid formulations were influential on younger composers.

Wolpe participated in the Webern revival and studied intensely the works of his former teacher. As a consequence his music of the 1960's is more spare and economical in means. *Form* for piano (1959) was succeeded by a series of masterful chamber works: *Piece in Two Parts* for flute and piano (1960); *Piece for Piano and 16 Instruments* (1961); *In Two Parts* for six players (1962); *Street Music*, a cantata (1962); *Piece for Two Instrumental Units* (1963); Trio for flute, cello, and piano (1964); two *Pieces* for *Violin Alone* (1964, 1966); *Chamber Piece* no. 1 (1964) and no. 2 (1967); and *Solo Piece for Trumpet* (1966). Many of these works are in two-part form that juxtaposes radically opposed aspects of the same material.

The onset of Parkinson's disease in 1963 made composing increasingly difficult, and Wolpe completed only a few works in his final years. These include *Cantata for Mezzo-Soprano, Three Women's Voices, and Instruments* (1963); String Quartet (1969), composed for the Juilliard Quartet; *From Here on Farther* for clarinet, bass clarinet, violin, and piano (1969); and *Piece for Trumpet and Seven Instruments* (1971).

During the 1960's Wolpe was rediscovered by a new generation in New York and thus influenced such younger composers as Mario Davidovsky, Harvey Sollberger, and Charles Wuorinen.

WOOD-HILL, MABEL
b. Brooklyn, New York, 12 March 1870
d. Stamford, Connecticut, 1 March 1954

Wood-Hill studied at Smith College, Northampton, Massachusetts, and with Cornelius Rybner at Columbia University. Although she was best known as a writer of songs and choral music, including a setting of Robert Burns's poem *The Jolly Beggars*, she composed several large-scale works, including a pantomime, *The Adventures of Pinocchio*, produced in New York in 1931; incidental music for Lady Gregory's play *Grania*; a tone poem, *The Land of Heart's Desire*; three orchestral suites, *The Wind in the Willows*, *Outdoor Suite*, and *Aesop's Fables*; *Courage*; *From Far Country*; and *Reactions to the Prose Rhythms of Fiona McLeod* for small orchestra. She also composed a suite for string quartet, *Out-of-Doors*.

WOOLF, BENJAMIN EDWARD
b. London, England, 16 February 1836
d. Boston, Massachusetts, 7 February 1901

Woolf was taken to the United States by his father in 1839. In New York he studied with W. R. Bristow and earned a living playing in the orchestra of New York theaters. He also led orchestras in Philadelphia and New Orleans. After settling in Boston he became a music critic for the *Boston Globe*, the *Boston Herald*, and *The Saturday Evening Gazette*.

For the stage Woolf composed six works, including three operettas, *The Doctor of Alcantara* (1862), *Lawn Tennis* (or *Djakh and Djill*; 1880), *Westward Ho!* (1894); and a two-act opera, *Pounce and Co* (1882), all performed in Boston. His other compositions include an overture, *The Comedy of Errors* (1887), two string quartets, and a Piano Trio.

WUORINEN, CHARLES (PETER)
b. New York, New York, 9 June 1938

Wuorinen studied at Columbia University (B.A., 1961; M.A., 1963), where he was a pupil of Jack Beeson, Otto Luening, and Vladimir Ussachevsky. He later joined the faculty and taught there from 1964 to 1971. He has been on the faculty of the Manhattan School of Music (1971–79) and Rutgers University (from 1984). In addition he has been a visiting lecturer at Princeton University (1969–71); a visiting professor at New England Conservatory, Boston (1968–71), University of Florida (1971–72), Yale University (1983, 1991), and the State University of New York, Buffalo (1989); and Composer-in-Residence with the San Francisco Symphony Orchestra (1985–89). In 2001 he was Composer-in-Residence at Tanglewood.

Wuorinen has been president of the Serious Music Society and was on the board of Composers' Recordings Inc., the American Composers' Alliance, and the American Music Center. His career as a conductor has been long established and he is co-founder and co-director of the Group for Contemporary Music and former chairman of the board of the American Composers' Orchestra. Wuorinen has received two Guggenheim Fellowship (1968, 1972), and his works have been awarded many prizes, including the New York Composers' Award (1958) and an award from the National

Charles Wuorinen, 2003.
Photo: Irene Haupt, courtesy Music Library, State University of New York, Buffalo.

Institute of Arts and Letters (1967). He has lectured widely throughout the United States and has appeared as a pianist and conductor with orchestras in Europe and America.

Remarkable among his early works is the Third Symphony, completed in 1959 when he was only 21. Although showing some influence of Aaron Copland and Roy Harris, it possesses strikingly original features. Other orchestral works of this period include Symphony no. 1 (1958); Symphony no. 2 (1959); *Concertone* for brass quintet and orchestra (1960); and *Evolutio Transcripta* for chamber orchestra (1961), which introduces new concepts of relating pitches and rhythmic structure.

Wuorinen's subsequent compositions use an extended 12-tone system imposing a discipline on pitch, intervals, register, and texture. He has at times employed certain electronic enhancement to his scores, as in *Orchestral and Electronic Exchanges* for orchestra and synthesized sound (1964), performed by the New York Philharmonic Orchestra in July 1965. Also for orchestra are *Music for Orchestra* (1956); *Contrafactum* (1969); *Grand Bamboula* for strings (1971); *Reliquary for Stravinsky* (1975); *Two-Part Symphony*, commissioned

503

in 1978 by the American Composers' Orchestra; *The Magic Art: An Instrumental Masque Drawn From the Works of Henry Purcell* (1979); *Short Suite* (1981); *Bamboula Squared* for orchestra and tape (1984); *Crossfire* (1984); *Movers and Shakers*, a Cleveland Orchestra commission (1984); *The Golden Dance* (1985–86); *Bamboula Beach Overture* (1987); *Machault Mon Chou* (1990); *Astra* (1990); *Delight of the Muses* (1991), staged as a ballet the following year; *Microsymphony* (1992); *The Mission of Virgil* (1993); *The Great Procession* (1995); *River of Light* for strings and percussion (1996); *Symphony Seven* (1997); and *Cyclops 2000*, commissioned by the London Sinfonietta.

Among Wuorinen's works for solo instrument and orchestra are five chamber concertos, for cello (1963), violin (1964), flute (1964), oboe (1965), and tuba (1970); three piano concertos (1966, 1973, 1983); Concerto for amplified violin and orchestra (1972); *Tashi* for clarinet, violin, cello, piano, and orchestra (1975–76); *Rhapsody* for violin and orchestra (1984); *Prelude to Kullervo* for tuba and orchestra (1985); *Five*, a concerto for amplified cello (1987); and Concerto for Saxophone Quartet (1992). He is currently composing Piano Concerto no. 4 for Peter Serkin and the Boston Symphony Orchestra.

Wuorinen's theater works include a masque in one act, *The Politics of Harmony* for three solo singers and ensemble, staged at Columbia University in 1968; a ballet, *Delight of the Muses* (1968); a two-act opera, *The W. of Babylon, or the Triumph of Love Over Moral Depravity* (libretto: Renaud Bruce; 1975), a Baroque burlesque with satirical allusions to operatic music by earlier composers, set in seventeenth-century France; and the recently completed opera, *Haroun and the Sea of Stories*, to a libretto by James Fenton based on the novel of Salmon Rushdie.

Wuorinen's major contribution to music has been in the realm of instrumental compositions. These include *Concert* for double bass (1961); *Duuiensela* for cello and piano (1962); *Flute Variations I* for solo flute (1963); *Composition* for oboe and piano (1965); *The Long and the Short* for solo violin (1965); *Duo* for violin and piano (1966); *Bicinium* for two oboes (1966); *Flute Variations II* (1968); *Adapting to the Times* for cello and piano (1969); *Nature's Concord* for trumpet and piano (1969); *Cello Variations I* for solo cello (1970); *Violin Variations* for solo violin (1972); *Grand Union* for cello and percussion (1973); *Fantasia* for violin and piano (1974); *Cello Variations II* (1975); *Fast Fantasy* for cello and piano (1977); *Six Pieces* for violin and piano (1977); Divertimento for alto saxophone and piano (1983); Piano Trio (1983); *Double Solo* for Horn Trio (1985); *Guitar Variations* (1994); Sonata for guitar and piano (1995); *Cello Variations III* (1997);

Epithalamion for two trumpets (1997); *Lepton* for celesta, harp, and piano (1998); *An Orbicle of Jasp* for cello and piano (1999); *Andante espressivo* for cello and piano (2001); and *Buttons and Bows* for cello and accordion (2001).

For ensembles Wuorinen has written four string quartets (1957, 1971, 1979, 2002); *Turetzky Pieces* for flute, clarinet, and double bass (1960); *Tiento sobre Cabezon* for flute, oboe, harpsichord, piano, and string trio (1961); Trio no. 1 for flute, cello, and piano (1961); *Bearbeitungen über Glogauer Liederbuch* for flute/piccolo, clarinet/bass clarinet, violin, and double bass (1962); Octet (1962); Trio no. 2 for flute, violin, and piano (1962); *Salva Regina: John Bull* for chamber ensemble (1966); and String Trio (1968). Later works include *Canzona (in memory of Igor Stravinsky)* for 12 instruments (1971); *Bassoon Variations* for bassoon, harp, and timpani (1972); *Harp Variations* for harp and string trio (1972); *On Alligators* for flute, oboe, bassoon, and string quartet (1972); *Speculum Speculi* for flute, oboe, bass clarinet, percussion, and double bass (1972); Trio no. 3 for flute, cello, and piano (1972); *Arabia Felix* for flute, bassoon, piano, electric guitar, vibraphone, and violin (1973); *Hyperion* for 12 instruments (1975); *Tashi I* for clarinet, violin, cello, and piano (1975); Wind Quintet (1977); *The Winds* for eight winds and piano (1977); *Archeopteryx* for bass trombone and ten instruments (1978); *Archangel* for bass trombone and string quartet (1978); *Fortune* for clarinet, violin, cello, and piano (1979); and *Joan's* for flute, clarinet, violin, cello, and piano (1979).

Recent works are Horn Trio for horn, violin, and piano (1981); Trombone Trio (1981); Trio for brass instruments (1981); *New York Notes* for flute, clarinet, violin, cello, and percussion (1982); Divertimento for string quartet (1983); Piano Trio (1983); Concertino for chamber ensemble (1984); *Spinoff* for violin, double bass, and conga drums (1984); *Horn Trio Continued* (1985); String Sextet (1988–89); Saxophone Quartet (1992); *The Great Procession* for flute, clarinet, violin, double bass, piano, and percussion (1995); Piano Quintet (1995); Brass Quintet (2001); and *Josquiniana* (2001) and *ALAP* (2002), both for string quartet.

Wuorinen has also provided several scores for percussion: *Prelude and Fugue* for four percussionists (1955); *Invention* for percussion quintet and piano (1962); *Janissary Music* for solo percussion player (1966); *Ringing Changes* for percussion ensemble (1969–70); the 45-minute *Percussion Symphony* for 24 players (1976), composed for and recorded by the New Jersey Percussion Ensemble; *Percussion Duo* for mallet instruments and piano (1979); and Percussion Quartet (1994).

His solo piano compositions include *Piano Variations* (1963), which contrasts quiet, long notes with rapid, violent outbursts of fast notes; three sonatas (1969, 1976, 1986); *12 Short Pieces* (1973); *The Blue Bamboula* (1980); *Capriccio* (1981); and *Bagatelle* (1987–88). For organ he has written *Evolutio* (1961) and *Natural Fantasy* (1985). *Time's Encomium* for synthesized and processed tape was created in 1968–69 to a commission from Nonesuch Records; in 1970 the work was awarded the Pulitzer Prize, making Wuorinen the youngest composer to win the this award.

Wuorinen has written several impressive choral works: a cantata, *Be Merry All That Be Present* (1957); *Sinfonia Sacra* for solo men's voices and chamber orchestra (1961); *Prayer for Jonah* for chorus and string orchestra (1962); *Super Salutem* for men's chorus, 9 brass players, percussion, and piano (1964); *Mannheim 87. 87. 87.* for chorus and organ (1973); *An Anthem for Epiphany* for chorus, trumpet, and organ (1974); an oratorio, *The Celestial Sphere* (1980); Mass for soprano, chorus, violin, and organ (1982); *O Solis Ortu* for chorus (1988–89); *Genesis* for chorus and orchestra (1989); *Missa Brevis* for chorus and organ (1991); *Missa Renovata* for chorus, flute, trombone, timpani, and strings (1992); and *The Haroun Songbook* for four solo voices and piano (2002).

Among his solo vocal music are *Dr. Faustus Lights the Lights* (Gertrude Stein) for narrator, clarinet, saxophone, bassoon, cello, piano, and percussion (1957); *Madrigale spirituale sopra salmo Secundo* for tenor, baritone, two oboes, two violins, cello, and double bass (1960); *A Message to Denmark Hill*, a cantata for baritone, flute, cello, and piano (1970); *A Song to the Lute in Musicke* for soprano and piano (1970); *Six Songs* (Coburn Britten) for countertenor and chamber ensemble (1977); Psalm 39 for baritone and guitar (1979); *Three Songs* (Coburn Britten) for tenor and piano (1979); *Twang* (Wallace Stevens) for mezzo-soprano and piano (1988–89); *A Winter's Tale* (Dylan Thomas) for soprano and piano (or chamber ensemble) (1992); *Fenton Songs I* (1997) and *II* (2002) for mezzo-soprano and piano trio; *Two Machine Portraits* (Les Murray) for tenor and piano (2001); *September 11* for tenor and piano (2001); *Stanzas Before Time* (John Ashbery) for tenor and harp (2001); and *Pentecost* (Derek Walcott) for tenor and harp (2002).

Wuorinen is the author of *Simple Composition*, a practical guide to composing music, published in 1979.

WYNER, YEHUDI

b. Calgary, Canada, 1 June 1929

Wyner is the son of the Russian-born composer, Lazar Weiner. At the Juilliard School (1944–46) he studied piano with Lonny Epstein. In 1946 he entered Yale University, where his teachers included Richard Donovan and Paul Hindemith. After graduating in 1951 he went to Harvard University, where he studied musicology and composition under Archibald Davison, Randall Thompson, and Walter Piston. Back at Yale in 1953 he continued his work with Hindemith for his M.Mus. degree. From 1953 to 1956 he was at the American Academy in Rome on Prix de Rome and University of California at Berkeley fellowships.

In New York (1956–60) he was a freelance pianist, conductor, and lecturer, and in 1958 he taught at the Hebrew Union College. From 1959 to 1960 he was on the faculty at Queens College, New York. In 1963 he was appointed associate professor at Yale, becoming chairman of the composition faculty at the School of Music there (1969–77). He was dean of music at the State University of New York College at Purchase (1978–82). In 1991 he was appointed Naumburg Professor at Brandeis University.

Wyner was music director of the Turnau Opera Association (1961–64) and the New Haven Opera Society (1969–73). Since 1967 he has established a career as accompanist to several professional singers, including his wife Susan Davenny Wyner, and as a pianist in chamber music groups.

Wyner has been associated with the Berkshire Music Center at Tanglewood since 1975. He has served as Composer-in-Residence at the Santa Fe Chamber Music Festival (1982) and the American Academy in Rome (1991), and has been a visiting professor at Cornell University (1987), Brandeis University (1987–89), and Harvard University (1991–93, 1996–98). He has been the recipient of many awards, including a Guggenheim Fellowship (1959), an American Institute of Arts and Letters grant (1961), a Brandeis Creative Arts Award (1963), and further grants from the National Endowment for the Arts and the Guggenheim Foundation in 1976. In addition he has received many commissions from musical organizations, including the Fromm Foundation (1960), the Koussevitzky Foundation (1960), and the Ford Foundation (1972).

Wyner's early piano works reflect the influence of his teacher Hindemith, as heard in the *Easy Suite* (1949), and Stravinsky, in the *Partita* (1952) and the Sonata (1954). Beginning with the *Concert Duo* for violin and piano (1955–57), the impact of the music of Berg, Schoenberg, Webern, and Elliott Carter exerted a profound change.

Wyner's important compositions are mostly for voice or instrumental ensembles. His chamber music includes *Dance Variations and Festival Wedding* for wind octet (1953, rev. 1959); *Concert Duo* for violin and piano (1955–57); Serenade for seven instruments (1958); *Passover Offering* for flute, clarinet, trombone, and cello (1959); *Three Informal Pieces* for violin and piano (1961); *Cadenza!* for clarinet and harpsichord (or piano;

1969); *De Novo* for cello and small ensemble (1971); *Dance of Atonement* for violin and piano (1976); *Intermezzi* for piano quartet (1980); *All the Rage* for flute and piano (1980); *Romances* for piano and string quartet (1980); *Tanz und Maissele* for clarinet, violin, cello, and piano (1981); and *Passage I* for seven instruments (1983).

Among his more recent chamber pieces are a Wind Quintet (1984); a String Quartet (1985); *Verzagen* for violin and piano (1986); *Composition* for viola and piano (1987); *Sweet Consort* for flute and piano (1988); *Sweet is the Work* for winds, brass, and piano (1990); *Trapunto Junction* for trumpet, horn, trombone, and percussion (1991); *Changing Time* for violin, clarinet, cello, and piano (1991); *Amadeus' Billiard* for violin, viola, double bass, bassoon, and two horns (1991); *Il Cane Minore* for two clarinets and bassoon (1992); *Brandeis Sunday* for string quartet (1996); Horn Trio (1997); *Madrigal* for string quartet (1999); Quartet for oboe and string trio (1999); and *Commedia* for clarinet and piano (2003).

Other works for piano include *Three Short Fantasies* (1963–71), *Wedding Dances from the Notebook of Suzanne de Venne* (1964–94), *Toward the Center* (1988), *New Fantasies* (1991), and *Post-Fantasies* (1993–94).

Compositions involving orchestra are relatively few in number: *Da Camera* for piano and orchestra (1967); *Intermedio* for soprano and string orchestra (1974); *Fragments from Antiquity* for soprano and orchestra (1978); *Tuscan Triptych*: *Echoes of Hannibal* for strings (1985, rev. 2002); *Prologue and Narrative* for cello and orchestra (1994); *Lyric Harmony* (1995); and *Epilogue* (1996).

The Jewish heritage is strongly reflected in Wyner's liturgical music, mostly written while he was musical director of the Westchester Reform Temple, Scarsdale, New York (1958–68). These include Psalm 143 (1952), *Dedication Anthem* (1957), and a number of worship services: *Friday Evening Service* for cantor, chorus, and organ (1963); *Torah Service* with instruments (1966); portions of a *Morning Service* (1966–74); a *Liturgy for the High Holidays* (1970); *Torah Service Responses* for chorus and instrumental ensemble (1994); and *Shir Hashirim* for chorus (1993, 1997). His music for the play *The Mirror* (1972–73), *Music for a Jewish Wedding* (1975), and *Dances of Atonement* for violin and piano (1976) also clearly draw upon traditional Jewish sources.

Other vocal music includes *Canto Cantabile* for soprano and concert band (1972); *Memorial Music* for soprano and three flutes (1971–73); *On This Most Voluptuous Night* (William Carlos Williams) for soprano and seven instruments (1982); *Leonardo Vincitore* for two sopranos, double bass, and piano (1988); *O To Be a Dragon* for women's voices and piano (1989); *Restaurants, Wines, Bistros, Shrines*, a cycle for soprano, baritone, and piano (1994); *A Mad Tea Party* for soprano, two baritones, flute, violin, cello, and piano (1996); *Praise Ye the Lord* for soprano and ensemble (1996); and *The Second Madrigal* for soprano and eleven players (1999).

Y-Z

YARDUMIAN, RICHARD
b. Philadelphia, Pennsylvania, 5 April 1917
d. Bryn Athyn, Pennsylvania, 15 August 1985

Yardumian was born of Armenian parents. Except for a few composition lessons from Virgil Thomson, he remained largely self-taught. His musical language combined Appalachian folk song with music from the Armenian tradition. Later he was influenced by Debussy and modal polyphony. For many years he was music director at the Lord's New Church, Bryn Athyn, a Swedenborgian church.

Yardumian's first success came with the premiere in 1945 of *Desolate City* by the Philadelphia Orchestra under Eugene Ormandy, who subsequently recorded the piece. Also for orchestra is the *Armenian Suite*, comprising seven short movements based on folk songs, written in 1937 when the composer was only 19. It was performed in March 1954, also by the Philadelphia Orchestra and Ormandy. Other early works include a *Symphonic Suite* (1939) and *Three Pictographs of an Ancient Kingdom* (1941).

Many of Yardumian's compositions were inspired by the Bible: the first of his two symphonies, dating from 1950, is a symbolic portrayal of Noah and the Flood. It received its premiere in 1961, again by the Philadelphia Orchestra. Symphony no. 2, a setting of psalms for medium voice and orchestra, was first performed in November 1964.

Cantus Animae et Cordis for string orchestra (or quartet; 1955) was performed in February 1956 by the Philadelphia Orchestra. They also presented *Chorale Prelude: Veni Sancte Spiritus* for chamber orchestra in March 1959. This work was commissioned by the Edward B. Benjamin Music Project. The same orchestra under Ormandy with Rudolf Firkusny as soloist gave the premiere of Yardumian's *Passacaglia, Recitative and Fugue,* subtitled Piano Concerto, in Philadelphia in January 1958. A second Piano Concerto was composed in 1973 and presented at the Festival de Royan in 1974 with John Ogdon as soloist. Yardumian wrote a Violin Concerto, originally comprising two movements composed in 1949, with a central movement added by the composer in 1960. *Epigram: William F. Kincaid*, completed in 1951, did not receive its premiere until 1973.

Among Yardumian's choral works is *Mass: Come Creator Spirit* for mezzo-soprano, chorus, and orchestra, commissioned by the Fordham University to celebrate its 125th anniversary. This setting of the Mass is in the vernacular with congregational participation. It was first performed at Carnegie Hall on 31 March 1967. *The Story of Abraham*, composed in 1971, is a cantata scored for soprano, mezzo-soprano, baritone, double chorus, and orchestra, with original color paintings by Andre Girard projected onto a screen. Yardumian also set Psalm 130 for tenor and orchestra, completed in 1947, and composed three shorter choral works: *Chorales* for a cappella chorus (1946–72); *Psalm 51: Create in Me a Clean Heart* for soprano and chorus (1962); and *Magnificat* for female voices (1965). *Poem to Mary in Heaven*, a setting of Robert Burns for mezzo-soprano and piano, was sketched in 1952 and orchestrated in 1979. His last vocal compositions were *Narek: Der Asdvadz* for mezzo-soprano, horn and harp (1983) and *Hrashapar* for chorus, organ, and orchestra (1984).

Yardumian's instrumental music includes *Monologues* for solo violin (1947), Flute Quintet (1951), and several works for piano, including *Three Preludes* (1938–44), *Danse* (1942), *Prelude and Chorale* (1944), and *Chromatic Sonata* (1946). He also wrote three chorale preludes for organ: *Ee Kerezman* (Resurrection) (1976), *Jesu Meine Freude* (1976), and *My God, My*

God, Why Hast Thou Forsaken Me? (1976), which he later orchestrated (1978–79).

YON, PIETRO ALESSANDRO
b. Settimo Vittone, near Turin, Italy, 8 August 1886
d. Huntington, Long Island, New York, 22 November 1943

Yon studied at the Milan Conservatory, the Turin Conservatory (1901–04), and the Academy of Saint Cecilia in Rome (1904–05). From 1905 to 1907 he was organist at the Vatican. He emigrated to the United States in 1907, where he became organist at St. Francis Xavier's, New York (1907–19, 1921–27). From 1927 to his death he was organist at St. Patrick's Cathedral, New York.

Except for an Oboe Concerto, most of Yon's compositions were choral or for the organ. His oratorio *The Triumph of St. Patrick* for choir and orchestra was performed in New York in 1934. He made 21 settings of the Mass for choir and orchestra or organ, including *Missa Solemnis*, *Missa Modica*, a Mass in G, *Mass of the Shepherd*, and *Missa Regina Pacis*. He is best remembered today for a Christmas carol, *Gesu bambino*, still seasonally popular.

In addition to *Concerto Gregoriano* for organ and orchestra (1920), Yon wrote many organ solo pieces, including three sonatas, two *Rhapsodies*, and 12 divertimenti. He was also the author of a book, *Organ Pedal Technic*, published posthumously in 1944.

YOUNG, LA MONTE (THORNTON)
b. Bern, Idaho, 14 October 1935

Young grew up in Los Angeles and Utah and studied at Los Angeles City College (1953–55), Los Angeles State College (1955–57), the University of California at Los Angeles (theory, composition, ethnomusicology; 1957–58), and the University of California at Berkeley (composition; 1958–60). He also studied with his father (saxophone) and privately in Los Angeles with William Green (saxophone and clarinet) and Leonard Stein (composition). For several years he performed on saxophone, clarinet, and guitar in various jazz groups.

At the Darmstadt Summer Course in 1959 Young was a pupil of Karlheinz Stockhausen. In New York he studied electronic music with Richard Maxfield at the New School of Social Research (1960–61). From 1970 he studied the Kirana style of Indian classical singing with Pandit Pran Nath until the latter's death in 1996.

Young was the first composer to investigate the long-term effects of continuous periodic sound waveforms and their effect on the human nervous system. His compositions include Trio *for Strings* (1959); *Two Sounds*

La Monte Young.
Courtesy Music Library, State University of New York, Buffalo, North American New Music Festival, Item 121.

(1960); *Composition 1960: Nos. 1–15*; *The Second Dream of the High-Tension Line Stepdown Transformer* from *The Four Dreams of China* (1962); *Studies in the Bowed Disk* (1963); *The Tortoise, His Dreams and Journeys* (1964–present); and *The Well-Tuned Piano* (1964–present). With his wife, the sculptor and light artist Marian Zazeela, he founded the Theater of Eternal Music in 1972.

During 1979–85 and 1989–90, he held a commission from the Dia Art Foundation to establish a permanent location for the research, design, and presentation of extended duration installations in New York City. Young and Zazeela formulated the concept of a "Dream House," a permanent space with sound and light environments in which a work is played continuously. They have presented sound environments in Espace Donguy, Paris (1990), Ruine der Künste, Berlin (1992), and the Musée Art Contemporain, Lyon (1999). The MELA Foundation Dream House: *Seven Years of |Sound and Light* opened in New York in 1993, extending into the new Millenium. In 2000 they created a four-month Dream House in Avignon, France with a continuous DVD projection of the six-and-a-half-hour collaboration on *The Well-Tuned Piano in Magenta Light* of 1987.

In 1990 Young founded the Forever Bad Blues Band, which has performed widely in the United States and Europe, presenting a continuous three-hour concert of Young's *Dorian Blues*.

ZADOR, EUGENE (ORIGINALLY JENÖ ZÁDOR)

b. Bátaszék, Hungary, 5 November 1894
d. Hollywood, California, 4 April 1977

At the age of six Zador began piano lessons. In 1911 he became a pupil of Richard Heuberger at the Vienna Conservatory; in 1912 he went to Leipzig to study with Max Reger. He was appointed to the faculty of the New Conservatory in Vienna, a position he held from 1921 to 1938. He also taught at the Budapest Academy of Music (1934–39).

To escape Nazi oppression Zador came to the United States in 1939, where he taught for a year at the New York College of Music. In 1940 he settled in Holly-wood, joining Metro-Goldwyn-Mayer as an orchestrator of film scores, including those by a fellow Hungarian émigré, Miklós Rózsa. He also devoted much time to composition and teaching. Richard Strauss and Reger were important influences upon his early works, but later much of his music acquired a powerfully rhythmic quality derived from Hungarian folk music.

Zador's major works were operas, 11 in all: *Diana* (Budapest, 1928); *The Island of the Dead* (Budapest, 1928); *Forever Rembrandt* (Gera, 1930); *Dornrischens Erwachen* (Saarbrucken, 1932); *Revisor* (*The Inspector General*), composed in 1928, revised 1952–57 (Los Angeles, 1971); *Azra* (Budapest, 1936); *Christopher Columbus* (New York, 1939); *The Virgin and the Fawn* (Los Angeles, 1963); *The Magic Chair* (Baton Rouge, 1966); *The Scarlet Mill* (Brooklyn College Opera, 1968); and *Yehu: a Christmas Legend* (1974). A ballet, *The Machine Man*, was composed in 1934.

Zador's output of orchestral works was considerable: a symphonic poem, *Bánk bán* (1918); *Romantic Symphony* (1922); *Variations on a Hungarian Folk Song* (1928); *Faschings Suite* (1928); *Chamber Concerto* for strings, two horns, and piano (1930); *Rhapsodie* (1930); *Sinfonia Technica* (1931); *Rondo* (1933); *Hungarian Caprice* (1935); *Dance Symphony* (1936); *Tarantella Scherzo* (1940); *Children's Symphony* (1941); *Pastorale and Tarantella* (1942); *Biblical Scenes* (1942); *Elegie and Dance* (1954); Divertimento for strings (1955); *Fugue Fantasia* (1958); *Christmas Overture* (1961); *Variations on a Merry Theme* (1963); *Festival Overture* (1964); *Five Contrasts* (1965); *Aria and Allegro* (1969); *Studies* (1970); Second Divertimento for strings (1974); *Hungarian Scherzo* (1975); *Dance Overture*; Serenade; and a symphonic poem, *Hannele*.

For solo instruments Zador composed a Trombone Concerto (1967); *Music* for clarinet, and strings (1968); *Rhapsody* for cimbalom and orchestra (1969); *Fantasia Hungarica* for double bass and orchestra (1970); *Duo Fantasy* for two cellos, strings, and harp (1973); and concertos for accordion (1972), harp (1975), and oboe and string orchestra (1975). His instrumental music includes a Piano Quintet, which was awarded a Hungarian State Prize in 1933; a Suite for brass (1961); a Suite for eight cellos (1966); a Wind Quintet (1972); and a Brass Quintet (1973).

For chorus and orchestra Zador wrote *Cantata Technica* (1961) and *Scherzo Domestico* (1961). *The Remarkable Adventures of Henry Bold* for narrator and orchestra was performed in Beverly Hills, California in October 1963. In 1974 Zador composed *The Judgement* (lyrics: Patrick Mahony) for chorus, brass, and percussion; and *Cain* (texts: Mahony and Rupert Hughes) for narrator and orchestra.

ZAIMONT, JUDITH LANG

b. Memphis, Tennessee, 8 November 1945

Zaimont was educated at the Juilliard School (1958–64) with Rosina Lhevinne; Queens College, New York (1958–64), and Columbia University (1966–68), where she was a pupil of Hugo Weisgall, Jack Beeson, and Otto Luening. In 1971 she went to Paris for a year to study with André Jolivet. From 1960 to 1967 she pursued a career as a duo-pianist with Doris L. Kosloff. In 1972 she joined the music faculty at Queens College, New York, moving to the Peabody Conservatory, Baltimore in 1980. From 1989 to 1991 she held the post of professor of music and chair of the music department at Adelphi University. Since 1992 she has been professor of composition at the University of Minnesota School of Music.

For orchestra Zaimont has written two symphonies, no. 1 (Philadelphia, 1996) and no. 2, *Remember Me* for strings (1999); a Piano Concerto (1972); a Concerto for two pianos (1976); *Elegy for Symphonic Strings* (1998); and *Movement for Orchestra*.

Most of Zaimont's music is for voices. Among her choral compositions are *Three Ayres* for chorus (1969); *Man's Image and His Cry* for baritone, alto, chorus, and orchestra (1970); a cantata, *The Chase* for chorus and piano (1972); *Sunny Airs and Sober*, five madrigals (1974); *Sacred Service for the Sabbath Evening* for baritone, chorus, and orchestra (1975); *Sir Patrick Spens* for 8 voices and piano (1980); *Devilry: Black Massing* for double chorus and percussion (1980–81); *Serenade to Music* (W. H. Auden) (1981); *Lamentation* for four soloists and double chorus (1982); and *Meditations at the Time of the New Year* for chorus and percussion (1999).

Her solo vocal music includes *Four Songs* (e.e.cummings) for mezzo-soprano and piano (1965); *The Ages of Love* for baritone and piano (1971); *Chansons nobles et sentimentales* for high voice and piano (1974); *Songs of Innocence* (William Blake) for

Judith Lang Zaimont.
Courtesy the composer.

soprano, tenor, flute, cello, and harp (1974); *Greyed Sonnets* for soprano and piano (1975); *The Magic World*: *Ritual Music for Three* for baritone, piano, and percussion (1979); *From the Great Land* (F. Buske) for mezzo-soprano, clarinet, piano, and drums (1982); *In the Theater of the Night*: *Dream Songs of Poems of Karl Shapiro* for high voice and piano (1983); *Deep Down* for medium voice and piano (1984); *New-fashioned Songs* for low voice and piano (1984); and *Nappens Monolog* (*Night Soliloquy*; 1985).

Among Zaimont's instrumental music are a Flute Sonata (1962); *Two Movements* for wind quartet (1967); *Grand Tarantella* for violin and piano (1967); *Capriccio* for solo flute (1971); *Music for Two* (1971); *Valse romantique* for flute (1972); *De Infinitate Celeste*: *Of the Celestial Infinite* for string quartet (1980); *Sky Curtains* for flute, clarinet, bassoon, viola, and cello (1984); *Dance/Inner Dance* for flute, oboe, and cello (1985); *Winter Music* for brass quintet (1985); *Folk Song Fantasy* for clarinet quartet (1998); *Parallel Play* for saxophone quartet (1999); and *Doubles* for oboe and piano.

For piano she has written *Portrait of a City* (1961); *Variations* (1965); *Toccata and Scherzo* (1968); *Snazzy Sonata* for four hands (1972); *A Calendar Set*: *12 Preludes* (1972–78); *Calendar Collection* (1979); *Stone*

(1981); *Blue Velvet Waltz* (1983); *Jupiter's Moons* (1999); and a Sonata (2000).

As an editor Zaimont has compiled *The Musical Woman*: *An International Perspective* (with Catherine Overhauer and Jane Gottlieb; 1983–93).

ZWILICH, ELLEN TAAFFE
b. Miami, Florida, 30 April 1939

As a child, Zwilich learned to play the piano, trumpet, and piano and in her early teens was composing piano pieces. She studied at the Florida State University, Tallahassee (B.M., 1956; M.M., 1962), where she was a pupil of John Boda. After graduating she taught in South Carolina before moving to New York, where she earned a living as a professional violinist in Leopold Stokowski's American Symphony Orchestra (1965–1972). In 1975 she obtained her D.M.A. in composition from the Juilliard School of Music, the first woman to do so. Among her teachers there were Elliott Carter and Roger Sessions for composition.

Zwilich's first orchestral work, *Symposium*, was written in 1973 for the New York Philharmonic Orchestra. Zwilich came to wide public recognition with her Symphony no. 1, originally entitled *Three Movements for Orchestra,* premiered in 1982 under the direction of Gunther Schuller. The work won the Pulitzer Prize, making her the first woman to win the music award. Other orchestral works that followed are *Prologue and Variations* for strings (1983); *Celebration,* performed by the Indianapolis Symphony Orchestra in 1984; Symphony no. 2, subtitled *Cello Symphony,* premiered in San Francisco in 1985; *Concerto Grosso* (1985), written to mark the 300th anniversary of Handel; and *Symbolon,* commissioned in 1988 for the tour of Russia by the New York Philharmonic under Kurt Masur. Symphony no. 3 was commissioned in 1992 to commemorate the 150th anniversary of the New York Philharmonic. Recent orchestral scores include *Fantasy* (1993), *Jubilation* (1996), *Upbeat!* (1998), and *Openings* (2001).

Compositions for solo instruments and orchestra occupy a significant part of Zwilich's catalog. The first of these, a Piano Concerto, was premiered in Detroit in 1984. It was followed by *Images* for two pianos and orchestra (1986); Concerto for tenor trombone (Chicago Symphony Orchestra: 1988); Flute Concerto, written for Doriot Anthony Dwyer and the Boston Symphony Orchestra (1989); Concerto for bass trombone (Chicago, 1989); Oboe Concerto (Cleveland, 1990); Double Concerto for violin and cello, commissioned in 1991 by the Louisville Orchestra; Bassoon Concerto (Pittsburgh,1992); *Romance* for violin and chamber orchestra (1993); Concerto for horn and strings

(Rochester, 1993); Trumpet Concerto, subtitled *American*, (1994); Triple Concerto for violin, cello, and piano (Minneapolis, 1996); *Peanuts Gallery* for piano and orchestra (1996); a Violin Concerto, written in 1997 for Pamela Frank; *Partita* for violin and strings (2000); *Millennium Fantasy* for piano and orchestra (2001); and a Clarinet Concerto (2002). She is currently composing *Rituals* for five percussionists and orchestra for performance by the Nexus Ensemble in 2004.

Zwilich's choral works include *Thanksgiving Songs* for chorus and piano (1986); *Immigrant Voices* for chorus, brass, timpani, and strings (1991); *A Simple Magnificat* for chorus and organ (1994); and Symphony no. 4, *The Gardens* for chorus, children's chorus, handbells, and orchestra, written in 1999 for Michigan State University. For solo voice she has written a song cycle, *Einsame Nacht* (Herman Hesse) for baritone and piano (1971); *Im Nebel* (Hesse) for contralto and piano (1972); *Trompeten* (Georg Trakl) for soprano and piano (1974); *Emlekezet* (Sandoe Petrofi) for soprano and piano (1978); and *Passages* (A. R. Ammons) for soprano and instrumental ensemble (1981) or orchestra (1982).

Zwilich's earliest extant instrumental piece, *Sonata in Three Movements* for violin and piano, was written in 1973–74 for her husband, the Hungarian-born violinist, Joseph Zwilich. It was followed by her String Quartet no. 1 (1974), performed at the I.S.C.M. Festival in Boston in 1976; *Clarino Quartet* for four trumpets (or clarinets; 1977); *Chamber Symphony* in one movement for flute, clarinet, violin, viola, cello, and piano (1979), dedicated to the memory of her husband; *De Celeste Infinitite* for string quartet (1980–82); String Trio (1982); Divertimento for flute, clarinet, violin, and cello (1983); *Intrada* for flute/piccolo, clarinet, violin, cello, and piano (1983); *Chamber Symphony* for flute/piccolo, clarinet/bass clarinet, double bass, piano, and percussion (1984); *Double Quartet* for strings (1984), Concerto for trumpet and five players (1984); Piano Trio (1987); *Praeludium* for organ (1988); Clarinet Quintet (1990); String Quartet no. 2, written in 1998 for the Emerson Quartet; *Lament* for piano (1999); and *Lament* for cello and piano (2000).

Zwilich has composed the music for a ballet, *Tanzspiel*, staged in New York in 1988.

Appendix

LEGACY: AMERICAN COMPOSERS AND THEIR STUDENTS

(a selective list)

MILTON BABBITT
(student of Roger Sessions)

Students: David EPSTEIN, Peter LIEBERSON, Donald MARTINO, Tobias PICKER, Frederic RZEWSKI, David WARD-STEINMAN

ERNEST BLOCH

Students: George ANTHEIL, Ernst BACON, Irvin BAZELON, Mark BRUNSWICK, Cecil BURLEIGH, Theodore CHANLER, Francesco DE LEONE, Herbert ELWELL, Isadore FREED, Ray GREEN, Ethel HIER, Frederick JACOBI, Leon KIRCHNER, Douglas MOORE, Roger NIXON, Quincy PORTER, Leroy ROBERTSON, Bernard ROGERS, Roger SESSIONS, Halsey STEVENS, Randall THOMPSON

NADIA BOULANGER

Students: Josef ALEXANDER, Leslie BASSETT, Marion BAUER, Robert Russell BENNETT, Arthur BERGER, Easley BLACKWOOD, Marc BLITZSTEIN, Will Gay BOTTJE, Paul BOWLES, Mark BRUNSWICK, Elliott CARTER, Theodore CHANLER, Paul CHIHARA, Israel CITKOWITZ, Henry Leland CLARKE, Ulric COLE, Paul COOPER, Aaron COPLAND, Arthur CUSTER, Ingolf DAHL, Robert DELANEY, Paul DES MARAIS, Robert Nathaniel DETT, David DIAMOND, Cecil EFFINGER, Herbert ELWELL, Donald ERB, Irving FINE, Ross Lee FINNEY, Arthur FRACKENPOHL, Peggy GLANVILLE-HICKS, Philip GLASS, Roger GOEB, Richard Franko GOLDMAN, Donald GRANTHAM, Alexei HAIEFF, Adolphus HAILSTORK, Donald HARRIS, Roy HARRIS, Frederic HART, Mary HOWE, Karel HUSA, Andrew IMBRIE, Harrison KERR, Leo KRAFT, Gail KUBIK,

Felix LABUNSKI, John LA MONTAINE, John LESSARD, Robert Hall LEWIS, Normand LOCKWOOD, Quinto MAGANINI, Robert MOEVS, Douglas MOORE, Anthony NEWMAN, Julia PERRY, Daniel PINKHAM, Walter PISTON, Bernard ROGERS, Harold SHAPERO, Elie SIEGMEISTER, David STOCK, Lamar STRINGFIELD, Howard SWANSON, Louise TALMA, Serge TCHEREPNIN, Virgil THOMSON, Lester TRIMBLE, Charles TURNER, Godfrey TURNER, John VINCENT, Joseph WAGNER, George WALKER, David WARD-STEINMAN, Elinor Remick WARREN, Robert WASHBURN

GEORGE CHADWICK

Students: John BEACH, Frederick CONVERSE, Mabel DANIELS, Elliot GRIFFIS, Henry HADLEY, Edward Burlingame HILL, Sidney HOMER, Lucius HOSMER, Werner JANSSEN, Daniel Gregory MASON, Horatio PARKER, Quincy PORTER, Florence PRICE, Leroy ROBERTSON, Arthur SHEPHERD, William Grant STILL, John VINCENT, Arthur WHITING

AARON COPLAND
(student of Nadia Boulanger, Rubin Goldmark)

Students: Samuel ADLER, David AMRAM, Josef ALEXANDER, Thomas BEVERSDORF, Paul BOWLES, Henry BRANT, Marc BUCCHI, Israel CITKOWITZ, Mario DAVIDOVSKY, Jacob DRUCKMAN, William FLANAGAN, Donald FULLER, Jack GOTTLIEB, Roger HANNAY, Charles JONES, Gerald KECHLEY, Karl KORTE, Dai-Keong LEE, William T. McKINLEY, Charles MILLS, Alex NORTH, Robert PALMER, Robert PARRIS, Daniel

PINKHAM, Gardner READ, Earl ROBINSON, Ned ROREM, Douglas TOWNSEND, John VERRALL, Robert WARD

HENRY COWELL
Students: Dominick ARGENTO, John CAGE, Lou HARRISON, Donald KEATS, William KRAFT, John LESSARD, Vernon MARTIN, Alan STOUT, Frank WIGGLESWORTH

LUIGI DALLAPICCOLA
Students: Dominick ARGENTO, Tod MACHOVER, Donald MARTINO, Frederic RZEWSKI

ROSS LEE FINNEY
(student of Nadia Boulanger, Edward Burlingame Hill, Roger Sessions)
Students: William ALBRIGHT, Leslie BASSETT, Donald HARRIS, Sydney HODKINSON

VITTORIO GIANNINI
(student of Rubin Goldmark)
Students: Will Gay BOTTJE, Marc BUCCHI, John CORIGLIANO, Nicholas FLAGELLO, Adolphus HAILSTORK, Anthony IANNACONNE, Ursula MAMLOK, Thomas PASATIERI

RUBIN GOLDMARK
Students: Nicolai BEREZOWSKY, Henry BRANT, Mark BRUNSWICK, Theodore CHANLER, Abram CHASINS, Arthur COHN, Ulric COLE, Aaron COPLAND, Lehman ENGEL, Amedeo di FILIPPI, George GERSHWIN, Vittorio GIANNINI, Alexei HAIEFF, Frederic Patton HART, Herbert HAUFRECHT, Frederick JACOBI, Philip JAMES, Carl McKINLEY, Charles NAGINSKI, Paul NORDOFF, Julia SMITH, Bernard WAGENAAR

HOWARD HANSON
Students: Domenick ARGENTO, Wayne BARLOW, Jack BEESON, William BERGSMA, Thomas BEVERSDORF, Will Gay BOTTJE, Emma Lou DIEMER, Anthony DONATO, Grant FLETCHER, William Parks GRANT, Weldon HART, Roger HANNAY, Herbert INCH, Dorothy JAMES, Ulysses KAY, John LA MONTAINE, William LATHAM, Robert Hall LEWIS, Martin MAILMAN, Peter MENNIN, Louis MENNINI, Ron NELSON, Robert PALMER,

Gardner READ, H. Owen REED, Paul SHAHAN, Vladimir USSACHEVSKY, Robert WARD

EDWARD BURLINGAME HILL
(student of George Chadwick, John Knowles Paine)
Students: Josef ALEXANDER, Leonard BERNSTEIN, Elliott CARTER, Irving FINE, Ross Lee FINNEY, Timothy SPELMAN, Randall THOMPSON, Virgil THOMSON

PAUL HINDEMITH
Students: Samuel ADLER, Easley BLACKWOOD, Howard BOATWRIGHT, Arthur CUSTER, Norman DELLO JOIO, Emma Lou DIEMER, Alvin ETLER, Paul FETLER, Lukas FOSS, Bernhard HEIDEN, Ulysses KAY, Donald KEATS, Mel POWELL, Charles SHACKFORD, Harold SHAPERO, Alan SHULMAN, Clifford TAYLOR, Francis THORNE, Yehudi WYNER

ARTHUR HONEGGER
Students: Leslie BASSETT, Thomas BEVERSDORF, Robert DELANEY, William FLANAGAN, Karel HUSA, Robert PARRIS, Daniel PINKHAM, John RILEY, Lester TRIMBLE

VINCENT D'INDY
Students: Seth BINGHAM, Isadore FREED, Daniel Gregory MASON, Quincy PORTER, Edgar VARÈSE, Max WALD

ERNST KRENEK
Students: Robert ERICKSON, George PERLE, Harold SHAPERO

OTTO LUENING
Students: CHOU Wen-Chung, Henry Leland CLARKE, Gloria COATES, John CORIGLIANO, Mario DAVIDOVSKY, Charles DODGE, John EDMUNDS, Roger GOEB, Ben JOHNSTON, Ulysses KAY, Donald KEATS, Karl KORTE, William KRAFT, Robert KURKA, Marvin David LEVY, William MAYER, Raoul PLESKOW, Eric SALZMAN, Elliott SCHWARTZ, Seymour SHIFRIN, Harvey SOLL-BERGER, Joan TOWER, Douglas TOWNSEND, Roy TRAVIS, Charles WHITTENBERG, Frank WIGGLESWORTH, Charles WUORINEN, Judith Lang ZAIMONT

OLIVIER MESSIAEN
Students: William ALBRIGHT, Easley BLACK-WOOD, William BOLCOM, Lalo SCHIFRIN, Leland SMITH

DARIUS MILHAUD
Students: Stephen ALBERT, Larry AUSTIN, Irwin BAZELON, Arthur BERGER, William BOLCOM, Michael COLGRASS, David DEL TREDICI, Charles DODGE, Jonathan ELKUS, David EPSTEIN, Robert FELCIANO, Arthur FRACKENPOHL, Donald FULLER, Philip GLASS, Ray GREEN, Everett HELM, Lee HOIBY, Stanley HOLLINGSWORTH, Ben JOHNSTON, Robert KURKA, Robert LINN, Ellsworth MILBURN, Frederic MYROW, Hall OVERTON, Thomas PASATIERI, Steve REICH, Jerome ROSEN, Peter SCHICKELE, Seymour SHIFRIN, Ezra SIMS, Leland SMITH, William Overton SMITH, Morton SUBOTNICK, Roy TRAVIS, David WARD-STEINMAN, Robert WASHBURN, Peter WESTERGAARD

JOHN KNOWLES PAINE
Students: John Alden CARPENTER, L. A. COERNE, Frederick CONVERSE, Blair FAIRCHILD, Arthur FOOTE, Edward Burlingame HILL, Daniel Gregory MASON, Walter SPALDING

HORATIO PARKER
(student of George Chadwick)
Students: Seth BINGHAM, Walter Ruel COWLES, Elliot GRIFFIS, Charles IVES, Quincy PORTER, Roger SESSIONS, David Stanley SMITH

VINCENT PERSICHETTI
Students: Hugh AITKEN, Seymour BARAB, Jacob DRUCKMAN, Robert EVETT, Philip GLASS, Karl KORTE, Lowell LIEBERMANN, Thomas PASATIERI, Claire POLIN, Steve REICH, Marga RICHTER, Peter SCHICKELE, Gitta STEINER, Conrad SUSA

BURRILL PHILLIPS
(student of Bernard Rogers)
Students: Jack BEESON, William FLANAGAN, Kenneth GABURO, Steven STUCKY, David WARD-STEINMAN, Charles WHITTENBERG

WALTER PISTON
(student of Nadia Boulanger)
Students: Samuel ADLER, Josef ALEXANDER, Leroy ANDERSON, Arthur BERGER, Leonard BERNSTEIN, Thomas BEVERSDORF, Gordon BINKERD, Elliott CARTER, Norman CAZDEN, Paul DES MARAIS, John EDMUNDS, Irving FINE, Everett HELM, Karl KOHN, Ellis B. KOHS, Gail KUBIK, Billy Jim LAYTON, Kirke MECHEM, Robert MOEVS, Conlon NANCARROW, Daniel PINKHAM, Charles SHACKFORD, Harold SHAPERO, Clifford TAYLOR, Serge TCHEREPNIN, Yehudi WYNER

OTTORINO RESPIGHI
Students: Samuel BARLOW, Walter HELFER, Normand LOCKWOOD, Jan MEYEROWITZ, Robert SANDERS

JOSEF RHEINBERGER
Students: L. A. COERNE, Frederick CONVERSE, Arne OLDBERG

WALLINGFORD RIEGGER
Students: Henry BRANT, Michael COLGRASS, Cecil Marion COWLES, Morton FELDMAN, Richard Franko GOLDMAN, Tom SCOTT, Elie SIEGMEISTER, Alan STOUT, Gilbert TRYTHALL, David WARD-STEINMAN

BERNARD ROGERS
(student of Ernest Bloch, Nadia Boulanger)
Students: Stephen ALBERT, Domenick ARGENTO, Jacob AVSHALOMOV, Wayne BARLOW, Jack BEESON, William BERGSMA, Gordon BINKERD, Will Gay BOTTJE, David DIAMOND, Emma Lou DIEMER, Anthony DONATO, William FLANAGAN, Grant FLETCHER, Arthur FRACKENPOHL, Charles FUSSELL, Kenneth GABURO, William Parks GRANT, Roger HANNAY, Weldon HART, Sydney HODKINSON, Hunter JOHNSON, Walter MOURANT, Ulysses KAY, Gail KUBIK, John LA MONTAINE, Robert Hall LEWIS, Martin MAILMAN, Salvatore MARTIRANO, Peter MENNIN, Louis MENNINI, Ron NELSON, Robert PALMER, Burrill PHILLIPS, Gardner READ, H. Owen REED, John RILEY, Paul SHAHAN, Donald SUR, Vladimir USSACHEVSKY, Mary VAN APPLEDORN, Robert WARD, Robert WASHBURN, Charles WHITTENBERG

ROSARIO SCALERO

Students: Samuel BARBER, Marc BLITZSTEIN, Carl BRICKEN, John EDMUNDS, Lukas FOSS, Charles HAUBIEL, Leonard KASTLE, Robert KELLEY, Gian-Carlo MENOTTI, George ROCHBERG, Virgil THOMSON, George WALKER, Hugo WEISGALL

ARNOLD SCHOENBERG

Students: Wayne BARLOW, Marc BLITZSTEIN, John CAGE, Lou HARRISON, Earl KIM, Leon KIRCHNER, Peter Jona KORN, Dika NEWLIN, Roger NIXON, Paul PISK, Gerald STRANG, David VAN VACTOR, Elinor Remick WARREN, Franz WAXMAN, Adolph WEISS

ROGER SESSIONS
(student of Ernest Bloch, Horatio Parker)

Students: Milton BABBITT, Marc BRUNSWICK, Israel CITKOWITZ, Edward T. CONE, Paul COOPER, David DEL TREDICI, David DIAMOND, Emma Lou DIEMER, John EATON, Lehman ENGEL, David EPSTEIN, Robert ERICKSON, Vivian FINE, Ross Lee FINNEY, Miriam GIDEON, Richard Franko GOLDMAN, Robert HANNAY, John HARBISON, Robert HELPS, Lejaren HILLER, Sydney HODKINSON, Andrew IMBRIE, Earl KIM, Leon KIRCHNER, Dai-Keong LEE, Robert LINN, Tod MACHOVER, Ursula MAMLOK, Donald MARTINO, William MAYER, Charles MILLS, Charles NAGINSKI, Conlon NANCARROW, Dika NEWLIN, Roger NIXON, Lionel NOWAK, Claire POLIN, Jerome ROSEN, Frederic RZEWSKI, Eric SALZMAN, Bruce SAYLOR, Leland SMITH, William Overton SMITH, Donald SUR, William SYDEMAN, Paul TUROK, Richard TRYTHALL, Hugo WEISGALL, Peter WESTERGAARD, Ellen Taaffe ZWILICH

RANDALL THOMPSON
(student of Ernest Bloch, Edward Burlingame Hill)

Students: Samuel ADLER, Leonard BERNSTEIN, Lukas FOSS, Karl KOHN, Leo KRAFT, Kirke MECHEM, Clifford TAYLOR, Ivan TCHEREPNIN

BERNARD WAGENAAR
(student of Rubin Goldmark)

Students: Hugh AITKEN, Norman CAZDEN, Norman DELLO JOIO, John DUKE, Cecil EFFINGER, Donald FULLER, Bernard HERRMANN, Ellis B. KOHS, Charles JONES, John LA MONTAINE, Alex NORTH, Mel POWELL, Ned ROREM, William SCHUMAN, Alan SHULMAN, Elie SIEGMEISTER, Julia SMITH, Roy TRAVIS, Paul TUROK, Robert WARD, Donald WAXMAN, Meredith WILLSON

CHARLES-MARIE WIDOR

Students: Seth BINGHAM, Eric DE LAMARTER, Richard DONOVAN, Blair FAIRCHILD, William HEILMAN, David Stanley SMITH, Edgar VARÈSE

STEFAN WOLPE

Students: Seymour BARAB, Morton FELDMAN, Romulus FRANCESCHINI, Ezra LADERMAN, Elliott SCHWARTZ, Ralph SHAPEY, Netty SIMONS, Douglas TOWNSEND, David TUDOR

Bibliography

Joseph ACHRON

Moddel, Philip. *Joseph Achron.* Tel Aviv: Israeli Music Publications, 1966.

John ADAMS

Christanssen, Rupert. "Filming Klinghoffer." *BBC Music Magazine,* June 2003.

Samuel ADLER

Lucas, J. D. "The Operas of Samuel Adler." PhD diss., Louisiana State University, 1978.

Stephen ALBERT

Humphrey, M. *Stephen Albert.* New York: Schirmer, 1993.

William ALBRIGHT

Reed, D. "The Organ Music of William Albright." PhD diss., University of Rochester, New York, 1976.
Salisbury, W. "Introduction to the Organ Music of William Albright." *Diapason* 63, no. 4 (1972).

John ANTES

McCockle, D. M. "John Antes: American Dilettante." *Musical Quarterly* 42 (1956).
Smith, W. J. "A Style Critical Study of John Antes' String Trios." Master's thesis, State University of New York, Binghampton, 1974.

George ANTHEIL

Pound, Ezra. *Antheil and the Treatise on Harmony with Supplementary Notes.* Chicago: P. Covici, 1927.
Whitesitt, Linda. *The Life and Music of George Antheil 1900–1959.* Ann Arbor: University of Michigan Research Press, 1983.

Theodore ANTONIOU

Hasagen, K. "Theodore Antoniou." *Musica* 22 (1968).

Dominick ARGENTO

Altman, P. "The Voyage of Dominick Argento." *Opera News* 40, no. 21 (1976).
"Dominick Argento." *ASCAP Today* 8, no. 1 (1976).
Steele, M. "Dominick Argento." *HiFi/Musical America* 25, no. 9 (1975).

Frederic AYRES

Upton, W. T. "Frederic Ayres." *Musical Quarterly* 18 (1932).

Milton BABBITT

Babbitt, Milton. *Milton Babbitt: Words about Music.* Edited by Stephen Dembski and Joseph N. Straus. Madison: University of Wisconsin Press, 1987.
Mead, Andrew. "Recent Developments in the Music of Milton Babbitt." *Musical Quarterly* 70 (1984).
———. *An Introduction to the Music of Milton Babbitt.* Princeton, NJ: Princeton University Press, 1993.

Ernst BACON

Fleming, W. "Ernst Bacon." *Musical America* 69, no. 36 (1949).
St. Edmunds, J. "The Songs of Ernst Bacon." *Shawnee Review,* October 1941.

Samuel BARBER

Broder, Nathan. *Samuel Barber.* Westport, CT: Greenwood, 1985. (Orig. pub. 1954.)
Hennessee, D. A. *Samuel Barber: A Bio-bibliography.* Westport, CT: Greenwood, 1985.
Heyman, Barbara B. *Samuel Barber: The Composer and His Music.* New York: Oxford University Press, 1992.
Saltzman, Eric. "Samuel Barber." *HiFi/Stereo Review* 17, no. 4 (1966).

Hans BARTH

"Barth at Miami Conservatory." *Musical Courier* 139 (January 1949).

Leslie BASSETT

Johnson, Ellen S. *Leslie Bassett: A Bio-bibliography.* Westport, CT: Greenwood, 1994.

Irwin BAZELON

Cox, David. "A World of Violent Silence: A Note on Irwin Bazelon." *Musical Times* 123 (1982).

H. H. A. BEACH

Block, Adrienne Freid. *Amy Beach: Passionate Victorian.* New York: Oxford University Press, 1998.
Brown, J. *Amy Beach and Her Chamber Music.* Metuchen, NJ: Scarecrow, 1994.

Jenkins, Walter S. *The Remarkable Mrs. Beach, American Composer: A Biographical Account Based on Her Diaries, Letters, Newspaper Clippings, and Personal Reminiscences.* Edited by John H. Baron. Warren, MI: Harmonie Park, 1994.

Merrill, E. L. "Mrs. H. H. A. Beach: Her Life and Music." PhD diss., University of Rochester, New York, 1963.

Supply BELCHER

Owen, E. "The Life and Music of Supply Belcher." PhD diss., Southern Baptist Theological Seminary, 1969.

Robert Russell BENNETT

Ferencz, George Joseph. *Robert Russell Bennett: A Bio-bibliography.* New York: Greenwood, 1990.

Nicolai BEREZOWSKY

Berezowsky, Alice. *Duet with Nicky.* Philadelphia, PA: J. B. Lippincott, 1943.

Arthur BERGER

Northcott, Bayan. "Arthur Berger: An Introduction at 70." *Musical Times* 123 (1982).

William BERGSMA

"The Music of William Bergsma." *Juilliard Review* 3, no. 2 (1956).

Leonard BERNSTEIN

Briggs, John. *Leonard Bernstein: The Man, His Works and His World.* Cleveland, OH: World Publishing, 1961.

Burton, Humphrey. *Leonard Bernstein.* New York: Doubleday, 1994.

Burton, William Westbrook. *Conversations about Leonard Bernstein.* New York: Oxford University Press, 1995.

Chapin, Saul. *Leonard Bernstein: Notes from a Friend.* New York: Walker, 1992.

Ewen, David. *Leonard Bernstein.* Rev. ed. London: W. H. Allen, 1967.

Gradenwitz, Peter. *Leonard Bernstein.* Leamington Spa, UK: Berg, 1987.

Laird, Paul. *Leonard Bernstein: A Guide to Research.* New York: Routledge, 2001.

Ledbetter, W. Steven. *Serenades and Tuckets.* Boston, MA: 1988.

Myers, Paul. *Leonard Bernstein.* London: Phaidon, 1998.

Peyser, Joan. *Leonard Bernstein.* New York: Beech Tree Books, 1987.

Secrest, Meryle. *Leonard Bernstein.* New York: Knopf, 1994.

William BILLINGS

Barbour, J. Murray. *The Church Music of William Billings.* East Lansing: Michigan State University Press, 1960.

McKay, David, and Richard Crawford. *William Billings of Boston.* Princeton, NJ: Princeton University Press, 1975.

Nathan, Hans. *William Billings: Data and Documents.* Detroit, MI: Information Coordinators, for the College Music Society, 1976.

Gordon BINKERD

Schackelford, R. "The Music of Gordon Binkerd." *Tempo No. 114,* September 1, 1975.

Arthur BIRD

Loring Jr., William C. "Arthur Bird, American." *Musical Quarterly* 29 (1945).

———. *The Music of Arthur Bird: An Explanation of American Composers of the Eighties and Nineties for Bicenten-* *nial Americana Programming.* Rev. print. 1977. Atlanta, GA: W. C. Loring, ca. 1974.

Marc BLITZSTEIN

Dietz, R. "The Operatic Style of Marc Blitzstein." PhD diss., University of Iowa, 1970.

Gordon, Eric A. *Mark the Music: The Life and Works of Marc Blitzstein.* New York: St. Martin's, 1989.

Ernest BLOCH

Bloch, Suzanne, and Irene Heskes. *Ernest Bloch: Creative Spirit.* New York: Jewish Music Council of the National Jewish Welfare Board, 1976.

Chapman, Ernest. "Ernest Bloch at 75." *Tempo No. 32,* 1955.

Jones, W. M. "The Music of Ernest Bloch." PhD diss., Indiana University, 1963.

Kushner, David Z. *Ernest Bloch: A Guide to Research.* New York: Garland, 1988.

———. *The Ernest Bloch Companion.* Westport, CT: Greenwood, 2002.

Minski, M. "Ernest Bloch and His Music." PhD diss., George Peabody College, 1945.

Newlin, Dika. "The Later Music of Ernest Bloch." *Musical Quarterly* 33 (1947).

Strassburg, Robert. *Ernest Bloch: Voice in the Wilderness.* Los Angeles: Robert Strassburg, 1977.

William BOLCOM

Hiemenz, J. "Musician of the Month: William Bolcom." *HiFi/Musical America* 26, no. 9 (1976).

Paul BOWLES

Bowles, Paul. *Paul Bowles on Music.* Edited by Timothy Mangan and Irene Herrmann. Berkeley and Los Angeles: University of California Press, 2003.

Dillon, Millicent. *You Are Not I: A Portrait of Paul Bowles.* Berkeley and Los Angeles: University of California Press, 1998.

Sawyer-Lauçanno, Christopher. *An Invisible Spectator: A Biography of Paul Bowles.* London: Bloomsbury, 1989.

Gena BRANSCOMBE

Marlow, L. A. E. "Gena Branscombe (1881–1977)." PhD diss., University of Texas, 1980.

Henry BRANT

Everett, T. "Interview with Henry Brant." *The Composer* 7 (1976–77).

Radie BRITAIN

Bailey, W., and N. Bailey. *Radie Britain: A Bio-bibliography.* Westport, CT: Greenwood, 1990.

Earle BROWN

Quist, P. L. "Indeterminate Form in the Works of Earle Brown." PhD diss., Peabody Conservatory of Music 1998.

Dudley BUCK

Gallo, W. K. "The Life and Church Music of Dudley Buck." PhD diss., Catholic University of America, 1968.

Cecil BURLEIGH

Fielder, N. C. *Complete Musical Works of Charles Wakefield Cadman.* Los Angeles: Cadman Estate, Security First National Bank of Los Angeles, Trustee, 1951.

Howard, John Tasker. *Cecil Burleigh.* New York: Carl Fischer, 1929.

Charles CADMAN

Perison, H. D. "Charles Wakefield Cadman: His Life and Works." PhD diss., Eastman School of Music, 1978.

Porte, J. F. "Charles Wakefield Cadman: An American Nationalist." *The Chesterian* no. 39 (1924).

Wakefield, C. W. *Complete Musical Works of Charles Wakefield Cadman*. Los Angeles: n.p., 1937.

John CAGE

Dunn, R., ed. *John Cage*. New York: Henmar, 1962.

Fetterman, William. *John Cages's Theater Pieces: Notation and Performance*. Amsterdam, Netherlands: Harwood Academic, 1996.

Fleming, Richard. *John Cage at 75*. Cranbury, NJ: Associated University Press, 1990.

Gena, P., and J. Brent, eds. *A John Cage Reader: In Celebration of His 70th Birthday*. New York: C. F. Peters, 1982.

Griffiths, Paul. *John Cage*. New York: Oxford University Press, 1981.

Johnson, Steven, ed. *The New York Schools of Music and the Visual Arts*. New York: Routledge, 2001.

Kostelanetz, Richard, ed. *John Cage: An Anthology*. Rev. ed. New York: Da Capo, 1991.

———, ed. *Writing about John Cage*. Ann Arbor: University of Michigan Press, 1993.

———. *John Cage (Ex)Plained*. New York: Schirmer, 1996.

———. *Conversing with John Cage*. 2nd ed. New York: Routledge, 2003.

Nicholls, David, ed. *The Cambridge Companion to John Cage*. Cambridge: Cambridge University Press, 2002.

Nyman, Michael. *Experimental Music: Cage and Beyond*. Cambridge: Cambridge University Press, 1993.

Paterson, David. "John Cage 1942-54: The Language of Changes." PhD diss., Columbia University, 1996.

———, ed. *John Cage: The Early Years*. New York: Routledge, 2001.

Perloff, M., and C. Junkerman, eds. *John Cage: Composed in America*. Chicago: University of Chicago Press, 1994.

Pritchett, James. *The Music of John Cage*. Cambridge: Cambridge University Press, 1993.

Revill, David. *The Roaring Silence: John Cage, A Life*. New York: Arcade, 1992.

Shultis, C. *Silencing the Sounded Self: John Cage and the American Experimental Tradition*. Boston, MA: Northeastern University Press, 1988.

John Alden CARPENTER

Downes, Olin. "John Alden Carpenter: American Craftsman." *Musical Quarterly* 16 (1930).

Gleason, H., and W. Becker. *John Alden Carpenter: 20th Century American Composer*. Music Literature Outlines IV. Bloomington: Indiana University Press, 1981.

O'Connor, J. *John Alden Carpenter: A Bio-bibliography*. Westport CT: Greenwood, 1994.

Pierson, T. C. "The Life and Music of John Alden Carpenter." PhD diss., University of Rochester, New York, 1952.

Pollack, Howard. *Skyscraper Lullaby: The Life and Works of John Alden Carpenter*. Washington, DC: Smithsonian Institution Press, 1995.

Benjamin CARR

Smith, R. L. "The Church Music of Benjamin Carr." PhD diss., Southwesten Baptist Theological Seminary, 1969.

Sprenkle, C. "The Life and Works of Benjamin Carr." PhD diss., Peabody Conservatory, 1970.

Elliott CARTER

Edwards, A. *Flawed Words and Stubborn Sounds: A Conversation with Elliott Carter*. New York: Norton, 1972.

Harvey, David H. *The Later Music of Elliott Carter: A Study in Music and Theory*. New York: Garland, 1989.

Knussen, Sue. "Elliott Carter in Interview." *Tempo No. 197,* July 1, 1996.

Link, John F. *Elliott Carter: A Guide to Research*. New York: Garland, 2000.

Restagno, Enzo. *Elliott Carter in Conversation with Enzo Restagno*. Brooklyn, NY: Institute for Studies in American Music, 1991.

Rosen, Charles. *The Musical Languages of Elliott Carter*. Washington, DC: Smithsonian Institution Press, 1980.

Schiff, David. *The Music of Elliott Carter*. 2nd ed. Ithaca, NY: Cornell University Press, 1998.

Whittall, Arnold. "The Writings of Elliott Carter." *Tempo No. 124,* 1978.

———. "Summer's Long Shadows." *Musical Times,* April 1997.

Mario CASTELNUOVO-TADESCO

Rossi, Nick. *Catalogue of Works by Mario Castelnuovo-Tedesco*. New York: International Castelnuovo-Tedesco Society, 1977.

Scalin, B. "The Operas of Mario Castelnuovo-Tadesco." PhD diss., Northwestern University, 1980.

Charles Whitefield CHADWICK

Faucett, Bill. *Charles Whitefield Chadwick: His Symphonic Works*. Lanham, MD: Scarecrow, 1996.

———. *George Wakefield Chadwick: A Bio-bibliography*. Westport, CT: Greenwood, 1998.

Yellin, Victor Fell. "The Life and Operatic Works of George Wakefield Chadwick." Master's thesis, Harvard University, 1957.

———. "Chadwick: American Realist." *Musical Quarterly* 61 (1975).

———. *Chadwick: Yankee Composer*. Washington, DC: Smithsonian Institution Press, 1990.

John Barnes CHANCE

Anthony, D. A. "The Published Band Compositions of John Barnes Chance." PhD diss., University of Southern Mississippi, 1981.

Theodore CHANLER

Nordgren, E. A. "An Analytical Study of the Songs of Theodore Chanler (1902–1961)." PhD diss., New York University, 1980.

Louis CHESLOCK

Sprenkle, E. R. "The Life and Works of Louis Cheslock." PhD diss., Peabody Conservatory, 1979.

Wen-chung CHOU

Frankenstein, Alfred. "The Sound World of Chou Wen-chung." *HiFi* 20, no. 7 (1970).

Philip Greeley CLAPP

Holcomb, D. R. "Philip Greeley Crapp: His Contribution to the Music of America." PhD diss., University of Iowa, 1972.

Michael COLGRASS

Horowitz, J. "Musician of the Month: Michael Colgrass." *HiFi/ Musical America* 27, no. 11 (1978).

BIBLIOGRAPHY

Frederick Shepherd CONVERSE

Garofalo, R. J. "The Life and Works of Frederick Shepherd Converse." PhD diss., Catholic University of America, Washington, D.C., 1969.

Severence, R. "The Life and Works of Frederick Shepherd Converse." PhD diss., Boston University, 1932.

Will Marion COOK

Carter, M. "Will Marion Cook: Afro-American Violinist, Composer and Conductor." PhD diss., University of Illinois, 1985.

Aaron COPLAND

Berger, Arthur. *Aaron Copland.* New York: Oxford University Press, 1953.

Butterworth, Neil. *The Music of Aaron Copland.* London: Toccata Press, 1986.

Copland, Aaron, and Vivian Perlis. *Copland 1900 thru 1942.* New York: St. Martin's, 1984.

———. *Copland since 1943.* New York: St. Martin's, 1989.

Dickinson, Peter. "Copland at 75." *Musical Times* 116 (1975).

———, ed. *Copland Connotations.* Woodbridge, UK: Boydell and Brewer, 2002.

———. "Aaron Copland in Interview." *Tempo No. 224,* April 2003.

Lewis, Gail, and Judith Tick. *Aaron Copland's America: A Cultural Perspective.* New York: Watson-Guptill, 2000.

Peare, C. *Aaron Copland: His Life.* New York: Holt, Rinehart and Winston, 1969.

Pollack, Howard. *Aaron Copland: The Life and Works of an Uncommon Man.* New York: Holt, 1999.

Robertson, Marta, and Robin Armstrong. *Aaron Copland a Guide to Research.* New York: Garland, 2000.

Skowronski, JoAnn. *Aaron Copland: A Bio-bibliography.* Westport, CT: Greenwood, 1985.

Smith, Julia. *Aaron Copland: His Work and Contribution to American Music.* New York: Dutton, 1955.

Henry COWELL

Cowell, Henry. *New Musical Resources.* With notes and an accompanying essay by David Nicholls. Cambridge and New York: Cambridge University Press, 1996. (Orig. pub. 1930.)

Daniel, Oliver. "American Composer: Henry Cowell." *Stereo Review* 33, no. 6 (1974).

Helm, Everett. "Henry Cowell: American Pioneer." *Musical America* 82, no. 4 (1962).

Hicks, Michael. *Henry Cowell, Bohemian.* Urbana: University of Illinois Press, 2002.

Higgins, Dick, ed. *Essential Cowell: Selected Writings in Music.* Kingston, NY: Documentext, 2000.

Lichtenwanger, W. *The Music of Henry Cowell: A Descriptive Catalog.* Brooklyn, NY: Institute for Studies in American Music, 1986.

Manion, Marion. *Writings about Henry Cowell: An Annotated Bibliography.* Brooklyn, NY: Institute for Studies in American Music, 1982.

Mead, Rita H. *Henry Cowell's New Music 1925-36.* Ann Arbor, MI: University Microfilms, 1981.

Nicolls, David. *The Whole World of Music: A Henry Cowell Symposium.* Amsterdam, Netherlands: Harwood Academic, 1997.

Saylor, Bruce. *The Writings of Henry Cowell: A Descriptive Bibliography.* Brooklyn, NY: Institute for Studies in American Music, 1977.

Weisgall, Hugo. "The Music of Henry Cowell." *Musical Quarterly* 14 (1959).

Ruth CRAWFORD

Gaume, Mary Matilda. "Ruth Crawford Seeger: Her Life and Works." PhD diss., Indiana University, 1973.

———. *Ruth Crawford Seeger: Memoirs, Memories, Music.* Metuchen, NJ: Scarecrow, 1986.

Seeger, Ruth Crawford. *The Music of American Folk Song.* Edited by Larry Polansky. Rochester, NY: University of Rochester Press, 2001.

Straus, Joseph N. *The Music of Ruth Crawford Seeger.* Cambridge: Cambridge University Press, 1995.

Tick, Judith. *Ruth Crawford Seeger: A Composer's Search for America's Music.* New York: Oxford University Press, 1997.

Paul CRESTON

Simmons, W. "Paul Creston: Maintaining a Middle Course." *Musical Journal* 34, no. 10 (1976).

Slomski, Monica J. *Paul Creston: A Bio-bibliography.* Westport, CT: Greenwood, 1994.

Bainbridge CRIST

Howard, John Tasker. *Bainbridge Crist.* New York: C. Fischer, 1929.

George CRUMB

Cohen, David. *George Crumb: A Bio-bibliography.* Westport, CT: Greenwood, 2002.

Gillespie, Don, ed. *George Crumb: Profile of a Composer.* New York: C. F. Peters, 1986.

Steinitz, Richard. "George Crumb." *Musical Times* 119 (1978).

Ingolf DAHL

Berdahl, J. N. "Ingolf Dahl: His Life and Works." PhD diss., University of Miami, 1975.

William DAWSON

Malone, M. H. "William Levi Dawson: American Music Educator." PhD diss., Florida State University.

Reginald DE KOVEN

De Koven, Anna Farwell. *A Musician and His Wife.* New York: Harper and Brothers, 1926.

Eric DE LAMARTER

Willis, T. C. "Music in Orchestra Hall." PhD diss., Northwestern University, 1966.

Norman DELLO JOIO

Baumgardner, Thomas A. "The Solo Vocal Music of Norman Dello Joio." PhD diss., University of Texas, Austin, 1973.

———. *Norman Dello Joio.* Boston, MA: Twayne, 1986.

Downes, Edward. "The Music of Norman Dello Joio." *Musical Quarterly* 48 (1962).

Sabin, Robert. "Norman Dello Joio." *Musical America* 70, no. 12 (1950).

Stuart DEMPSTER

Samson, V. "An Interview with Stuart Dempster." *The Composer* 9, no. 18 (1978).

Robert Nathaniel DETT

de Lerma, Dominique-René, and Vivian McBrier. "Introduction." In *The Collected Piano Works of Robert Nathaniel Dett.* Evanston, IL: Summy-Birchard, 1973.

McBrier, Vivian. *Robert Nathaniel Dett: His Life and Works (1882–1943).* Washington, DC: Associated Publishers, 1977.

Simpson, A. *Follow Me: The Life and Music of Robert Nathaniel Dett.* Metuchen, NJ: Scarecrow, 1993.

David DIAMOND

Friday, R. "Analysis and Interpretations of Selected Songs of David Diamond." PhD diss., New York University, 1984.

Kimberling, Victoria. *David Diamond: A Bio-bibliography.* Metuchen, NJ: Scarecrow, 1987.

Shore, C., ed. *David Diamond: A Celebration.* Stuyvesant, NY: Pendragon, 1995.

Lucia DLUGOSZEWSKI

Johnson, T. "Lucia Dlugoszewski." *HiFi/Musical America* 25, no. 6 (1975).

Jacob DRUCKMAN

Fleming, S. "Jacob Druckman." *HiFi/Musical America* 22, no. 8 (1972).

John DUKE

Compton, E. "The Singer's Guide to the Songs of John Duke." PhD diss., University of Rochester, New York, 1974.

John EATON

Frankenstein, Alfred. "Introducing John Eaton and His Pieces for Syn-ket." *HiFi* 18, no. 7 (1968).

Monson, Karen. "Eaton, Danton and Robespierre." *HiFi* 30, no. 7 (1980).

Cecil EFFINGER

Worster, L. *Cecil Effinger: A Colorado Composer.* Lanham, MD: Scarecrow, 1997.

Duke ELLINGTON

Collier, James Lincoln. *Duke Ellington.* New York: Oxford University Press, 1987.

Dance, Stanley. *The World of Duke Ellington.* Rev. ed. New York: Da Capo, 2001. (Orig. pub. 1970.)

Hasse, John E. *Beyond Category: The Life and Genius of Duke Ellington.* New York: Simon and Schuster, 1993.

Lambert, George E. *Duke Ellington.* London: Cassell, 1959.

Lawrence, A. H. *Duke Ellington and His World.* New York: Routledge, 2001.

Rattenby, Ken. *Duke Ellington: Jazz Composer.* New Haven, CT: Yale University Press, 1993.

Ulanov, Barry. *Duke Ellington.* New York: Creative Age, 1946.

Herbert ELWELL

Koch, F. *Herbert Elwell: Reflections on Composing.* Pittsburgh, PA: 1983.

Donald ERB

Felder, D. "Interview with Donald Erb." *The Composer* 10 (1980).

Arthur FARWELL

Culbertson, E. *He Heard America Sing: Arthur Farwell, Composer and Crusading Music Educator.* Metuchen, NJ: Scarecrow, 1992.

Farwell, Brice, ed. *A Guide to the Music of Arthur Farwell.* Briarcliff Manor, NY: B. Farwell, for the estate of Arthur Farwell, 1972.

Kirk, Edgar L. "Toward American Music: A Study of the Life and Music of Arthur George Farwell." PhD diss., University of Rochester, New York, 1958.

Richard FELCIANO

Christiansen, S. O. "The Sacred Music of Richard Felciano." PhD diss., University of Illinois, Urbana, 1977.

Morton FELDMAN

DeLio, Thomas, ed. *The Music of Morton Feldman.* Westport, CT: Greenwood, 1996.

Dickinson, Peter. "Feldman Explains Himself." *Music and Musician* 14, no. 11 (1966).

Feldman, Morton. *Morton Feldman Essays.* Edited by W. Zimmermann. Kerpen, Germany: Beginner Press, 1985.

———. *Give My Regards to Eighth Street: Collected Writings.* Edited and with an introduction by B. H. Friedman; afterword by Frank O'Hara. Cambridge, MA: Exact Change, 2001.

Griffiths, Paul. "Morton Feldman." *Musical Times* 113 (1972).

Hughes, Edward Dudley. "Softly, Softly." *Musical Times* 137 (November 1996).

Johnson, Steven, ed. *The New York Schools of Music and the Visual Arts.* New York: Routledge, 2001.

Potter, Keith. "An Introduction to the Music of Morton Feldman." PhD diss., University of Wales, Cardiff, 1973.

Vivian FINE

Von Gunden, H. *The Music of Vivian Fine.* Lanham, MD: Scarecrow, 1999.

Ross Lee FINNEY

Amman, D. "The Choral Music of Ross Lee Finney." PhD diss., University of Cincinnati, 1972.

Cooper, Paul. "The Music of Ross Lee Finney." *Music Quarterly* 53 (1967).

Gillespie, Don. *Ross Lee Finney: Profile of a Lifetime.* New York: C. F. Peters, 1992.

Hitchens, S. *Ross Lee Finney: A Bio-bibliography.* Westport, CT: Greenwood, 1996.

Manning, R. M. "The Published Songs of Ross Lee Finney." PhD diss., University of Miami, 1981.

Nicolas FLAGELLO

Cohn, Arthur, and P. L. Miller. "The Music of Nicolas Flagello." *American Record Guide* 31 (1965).

Simmond, W. "The Music of Nicolas Flagello." *Fanfare* 11, no. 1 (1978).

William FLANAGAN

Trimble, Lester. "William Flanagan (1923–1967): An Appreciation." *Stereo Review* 23, no. 5 (1969).

Carlisle FLOYD

McDevitt, F. J. "The Stage of Carlisle Floyd (1949–1972)." PhD diss., Juilliard School, 1975.

Senter, W. L. "The Monodrama 'Flower and Hawk' by Carlisle Floyd." PhD diss., University of Texas, Austin, 1980.

Arthur FOOTE

Alviani, D. "The Choral Church Music of Arthur Foote." PhD diss., Union Theological Seminary, 1966.

Cipolla, Wilma R. *A Catalog of the Works of Arthur Foote (1853–1937).* Detroit, MI: Information Coordinators, for the College Music Society, 1980.

Kopp, F. "Arthur Foote: American Composer and Theorist." PhD diss., University of Rochester, New York, 1957.

Moore, D. "The Cello Music of Arthur Foote (1853–1937)." PhD diss., Catholic University of America, 1977.

Tawa, Nicolas. *Arthur Foote: A Musician in the Frame of Time and Place.* Lanham, MD: Scarecrow, 1997.

Lukas FOSS

Perone, K. *Lukas Foss: A Bio-bibliography.* New York: Greenwood, 1991.

Sarz, A. "Lukas Foss: Musician of the Month." *HiFi/Musical America* 31, no. 1 (1981).

Yiu, Raymond. "Renaissance Man: A Portrait of Lukas Foss." *Tempo No. 221,* July 7, 2003.

Stephen Collins FOSTER

Elliker, Calvin. *Stephen Collins Foster: A Guide to Research.* New York: Garland, 1988.

Emerson, K. *Doo-Dah! Stephen Foster and the Rise of American Popular Culture.* New York: Simon and Schuster, 1997.

Howard, John Tasker. *Stephen Foster: America's Troubadour.* New York: T. Y. Crowell, 1962. (Orig. pub. 1934, 1940, 1953.)

Milligan, H. V. *Stephen Collins Foster: A Biography of America's Folk Song Composer.* New York: Schirmer, 1920.

Sonneck, Oscar G., and W. R. Whittlesay. *Catalogue of First Editions of Stephen Collins Foster.* Washington, DC: U.S. Government Printing Office, 1915.

Walters, R. *Stephen Foster: Youth's Golden Gleam; A Sketch of His Life and Background in Cincinnati, 1846–1850.* Princeton, NJ: Princeton University Press, 1936.

Isadore FREED

Steinharer, E. *A Jewish Composer by Choice: Isadore Freed.* New York: National Jewish Music Council, 1961.

Eleanor FREER

Foster, Agnes Greene. *Eleanor Everest Freer, Patriot, and Her Colleagues.* Chicago: Musical Art Publishing, 1927.

William FRY

Kauffman, B. F. "The Choral Works of William Henry Fry." PhD diss., University of Illinois, 1975.

Upton, William Treat. *The Musical Works of William Henry Fry in the Collections of the Library Company of Philadelphia.* Philadelphia, PA: Free Library of Philadelphia, 1946.

———. *William Henry Fry: American Journalist and Composer-Critic.* Rev. ed. New York: Crowell, 1974. (Orig. pub. 1954.)

Kenneth GABURO

Ferriera, D. "The Choral Music of Kenneth Gaburo." PhD diss., Cincinnati College Conservatory, 1977.

George GERSHWIN

Alpert, Hollis. *The Life and Times of Porgy and Bess: The Story of an American Classic.* New York: Knopf, 1990.

Armitage, Merle. *George Gershwin.* New York: Merle Armitage, 1938.

———. *George Gershwin: Man and Legend.* New York: Duell, Sloan and Pearce, 1958.

Carnovale, Norbert. *George Gershwin: A Bio-bibliography.* Westport, CT: Greenwood, 2000.

Ewen, David. *The Story of George Gershwin.* New York: Holt, 1943.

———. *George Gershwin: His Journey to Greatness.* Englewood Cliffs, NJ: Prentice Hall, 1970.

Gilbert, Steven E. *The Music of Gershwin.* New Haven, CT: Yale University Press, 1995.

Goldberg, Isaac. *George Gershwin: A Study in American Music.* New York: Simon and Schsuter, 1931.

Jablonski, Edward. *George Gershwin.* New York: Putnam, 1962.

———. *Gershwin Remembered.* Portland, OR: Amadeus, 1992.

Jablonski, Edward, and Lawrence D. Stewart. *The Gershwin Years.* Garden City, NY: Doubleday, 1958.

Kimball, Robert, and Alfred Simon. *The Gershwins.* New York: Atheneum, 1973.

Payne, Robert. *Gershwin.* New York: Pyramid, 1960.

Rosenberg, Deena. *Fascinating Rhythm: The Collaboration of George and Ira Gershwin.* New York: Dutton, 1991.

Schwartz, Charles M. *Gershwin: His Life and Music.* Indianapolis, IN: Bobbs-Merrill, 1973.

———. *George Gershwin: A Selective Bibliography and Discography.* Detroit, MI: Information Coordinators, for the College Music Society, 1974.

Vittorio GIANNINI

Mark, M. L. "The Life and Works of Vittorio Giannini (1906–1966)." PhD diss., Catholic University of America, 1970.

Parris, Robert. "Vittorio Giannini and the Romantic Tradition." *Juilliard Review* 1, no. 2 (1957).

Henry GILBERT

Downes, Olin. *Henry Gilbert, Nonconformist: A Birthday Offering to Carl Engel.* New York: n.p., 1943.

Longyear, K. E. "Henry F. Gilbert: His Life and Works." PhD diss., University of Rochester, New York, 1968.

William Walter GILCHRIST

Schleifer, M. F. *William Walter Gilchrist, 1846–1916: A Moving Force in the Musical Life of Philadelphia.* Metuchen, NJ: Scarecrow, 1985.

Philip GLASS

Jones, Robert T. "Philip Glass: Musician of the Month." *HiFi/Musical America* 29, no. 4 (1979).

———. "The Soul of Glass." *Opera News* 46, no. 1 (1981).

Kostelanetz, Richard, ed. *Writings on Glass.* New York: Schirmer, 1997.

Large, Nina. "Sound and Vision (Glass and Film Music)." *Classical Music,* December 21, 2002.

Maycock, Robert. *Glass: A Portrait.* London: Sanctuary, 2002.

———. "Glass on Film." *BBC Music Magazine,* June 2003.

Mertens, W. *American Minimal Music: La Monte Young, Terry Riley, Steve Reich, Philip Glass.* London: Kahn and Averill, 1983.

Nyman, Michael. "Steve Reich and Philip Glass." *Musical Times* 112 (1971).

Potter, Keith. *Four Musical Minimalists.* Cambridge: Cambridge University Press, 2000.

Schwarz, R. Robert. *Minimalists.* London: Phaidon, 1996.

Smith, D. "The Music of Philip Glass." *Contact* no. 11 (1975).

Richard Franko GOLDMAN

Lester, N. K. "Richard Franko Goldman: His Life and Works." PhD diss., Peabody Conservatory, 1984.

Stock, P. G. "Richard Franko Goldman and the Goldman Band." Master's thesis, University of Oregon, 1982.

Rubin GOLDMARK

Copland, Aaron, "Rubin Goldmark: A Tribute." *Julliard Review* 3, no. 3 (1956).

Rice, E. T. *Address Delivered in Memory of Rubin Goldmark, 6 April 1936.* New York: n.p., 1936.

Tomatz, D. J. "Rubin Goldmark: Postromantic Trial Balance in American Music." PhD diss., Catholic University of America, 1966.

Louis Moreau GOTTSCHALK

Doyle, J. G. "The Piano Music of Louis Moreau Gottschalk 1829–1869." PhD diss., New York University, 1960.

———. *Louis Moreau Gottschalk, 1829-1869: A Bibliographical Study and Catalog of Works.* Detroit, MI: Information Coordinators, for the College Music Society, 1982.

Gottschalk, Louis Moreau. *Notes of a Pianist.* Edited, with a prelude, a postlude, and explanatory notes, by Jeanne Behrend. New York: Knopf, 1964.

Korf, William. *The Orchestral Music of Louis Moreau Gottschalk.* Henryville, PA: Institute of Mediaeval Music, 1983.

Loggins, V. *When the World Ends: The Life of Louis Moreau Gottschalk.* Baton Rouge: Louisiana State University Press, 1958.

Perone, James E. *Louis Moreau Gottschalk: A Bio-bibliography.* Westport, CT: Greenwood, 2002.

Rubin, L. A. "Gottschalk in Cuba." PhD diss., Columbia University, 1974.

Snook, G. O. "The Gottschalk Legacy." Master's thesis, University of Nebraska, 1966.

Starr, S. Frederick. *Bamboula: The Life and Times of Louis Moreau Gottschalk.* Oxford: Oxford University Press, 1995.

Morton GOULD

Evans, Lee. "Morton Gould: His Life and Music." PhD diss., Columbia University Teachers' College, 1978.

Goodman, Peter W. *Morton Gould: American Salute.* Portland, OR: Amadeus, 2000.

Ray GREEN

Vise, Sidney R. "Ray Green: His Life and Stylistic Elements of His Music from 1938–1962." PhD diss., University of Missouri, 1976.

Charles Tomlinson GRIFFES

Anderson, Donna K. *Charles T. Griffes: An Annotated Bibliography-Discography.* Detroit, MI: Information Coordinators, for the College Music Society, 1977.

———. *The Works of Charles T. Griffes: A Descriptive Catalog.* Ann Arbor: University of Michigan Research Press, 1984.

———. *Charles Tomlinson Griffes: A Life in Music.* Washington, DC: Smithsonian Institution Press, 1993.

Boda, D. "The Music of Charles Tomlinson Griffes." PhD diss., Florida State University, 1962.

Henry, E. L. "Impressionism in the Arts and Its Influence on Selected Works of Charles Martin Loeffler and Charles Griffes." PhD diss., University of Cincinnati, 1976.

Howard, John Tasker. *Charles Tomlinson Griffes.* New York: Schirmer, 1923.

Maisel, Edward M. *Charles Tomlinson Griffes: The Life of an American Composer.* Rev. ed. New York: Knopf, 1984. (Orig. pub. 1943.)

Pratt, H. M. K. "The Complete Works of Charles T. Griffes." PhD diss., Boston University, 1975.

Louis GRUENBERG

Nisbett, R. F. "Louis Gruenberg: His Life and Works." PhD diss., Ohio State University, 1979.

Henry HADLEY

Berthoud, Paul, ed. *The Musical Works of Dr. Henry Hadley.* New York: National Association for American Composers and Conductors and the Henry Hadley Foundation, 1942.

Boardman, Herbert R. *Henry Hadley: Ambassador of Harmony.* Atlanta, GA: Emory University, Banner Press, 1932.

Canfield, J. "Henry Kimball Hadley 1871-1937: His Life and Works." PhD diss., Florida State University, 1960.

Howard HANSON

Carvine, A. J. "The Choral Music of Howard Hanson." PhD diss., University of Texas, 1977.

Monroe, R. "Howard Hanson: American Music Educator." PhD diss., Florida State University, 1970.

Perone, J. *Howard Hanson: A Bio-bibliography.* Westport, CT: Greenwood, 1993.

Plain, M. *Howard Hanson: A Comprehensive Catalog of the Manuscripts.* Rochester, NY: Howard Hanson Memorial Institute for American Music by Eastman School of Music Press, University of Rochester, 1997.

Tuthill, Burnet C. "Howard Hanson." *Musical Quarterly* 22 (1936).

Watanabe, Ruth T. *The Music of Howard Hanson.* Rochester, NY: University of Rochester Press, 1966.

John HARBISON

Seabrook, Mike. "John Harbison and His Music." *Tempo No. 197,* July 1, 1996.

Roy HARRIS

Slonimsky, Nicolas. "Roy Harris." *Musical Quarterly* 33 (1947).

Stehman, Dan. *Roy Harris: An American Musical Pioneer.* Boston, MA: Twayne, 1984.

———. *Roy Harris: A Bio-bibliography.* New York: Greenwood, 1991.

———. "The Symphonies of Roy Harris: An Analysis of the Linear Materials and of Related Works." PhD diss., University of Southern California.

Lou HARRISON

Garland, Peter, ed. *A Lou Harrison Reader.* Santa Fe, NM: Soundings Press, 1987.

Mellers, Wilfred. "The New Everlasting Feeling." *Musical Times,* May 1997.

Miller, Leta, and Frederic Lieberman. *Lou Harrison: Composing a World.* New York and London: Oxford University Press, 1998.

Rathbun, V. "Lou Harrison and His Music." Master's thesis, San Jose University, 1976.

Rutman, C. "The Solo Piano Works of Lou Harrison." PhD diss., Peabody Conservatory, 1983.

Von Gunden, Heidi, *The Music of Lou Harrison.* Metuchen, NJ: Scarecrow, 1995.

Thomas HASTINGS

Dooley, J. E. "Thomas Hastings: American Church Musician." PhD diss., Florida State University, 1963.

Scanlon, M. B. "Thomas Hastings." *Musical Quarterly* 32 (1946).

Bernard HEIDEN

Langosch, M. "The Instrumental and Chamber Music of Bernard Heiden." PhD diss., Indiana University, 1973.

Anthony HEINRICH

Barron, D. M. "The Early Vocal Music of Anthony Philip Heinrich." PhD diss., University of Illinois, Urbana, 1972 1973.

Bruce, F. N. "The Piano Pieces of Anthony Philip Heinrich." PhD diss., University of Illinois, 1971.

Maust, W. R. "The Symphonies of Anthony Philip Heinrich Based on American Themes." PhD diss., Indiana University, 1973.

Upton, William Treat. *Anthony Philip Heinrich: A Nineteenth Century Composer in America.* Rev. ed. New York: Columbia University Press, 1967. (Orig. pub. 1939.)

Victor HERBERT

Kaye, Joseph. *Victor Herbert: The Biography of America's Greatest Composer of Romantic Music.* New York: G. H. Watt, 1931.

Purdy, Claire Lee. *Victor Herbert: American Music Master.* New York: J. Messner, 1945.

Waters, Edward N. *Victor Herbert: A Life in Music.* Rev. ed. New York: Macmillan, 1978. (Orig. pub. 1955.)

Johannes HERBST

Falconer, J. O. "Bishop Johannes Herbst." PhD diss., Columbia University, 1969.

Gombosi, Marilyn P., ed. *Catalog of Johann Herbst Collection.* Chapel Hill: University of North Carolina Press, 1970.

Bernard HERRMANN

Bruce, G. D. "Bernard Herrmann: Film Music and Film Narrative." PhD diss., New York University, 1983.

Johnson, E. *Bernard Herrmann: Hollywood's Music Dramatist.* Rickmansworth, UK: Triad Press, 1977.

Smith, S. *A Heart at Fire's Center: The Life and Music of Bernard Herrmann.* Berkeley and Los Angeles: University of California Press, 1991.

James HEWITT

Howard, John Tasker. "The Hewitt Family in America." *Musical Quarterly* 17 (1931).

Wagner, John W. *James Hewitt: His Life and Works.* Bloomington: Indiana University Press, 1969.

John Hill HEWITT

Howard, John Tasker. "The Hewitt Family in America." *Musical Quarterly* 17 (1931).

Huggin, C. E. "John Hill Hewitt: Bard of the Confederacy." PhD diss., Florida State University, 1964.

Orr, N. Lee, and Lynn Wood Bertrand. *The Collected Works of John Hill Hewitt.* New York: Garland, 1994.

Winden, W. C. "The Life and Music Theatre: Works of John Hill Hewitt." PhD diss., University of Illinois, 1972.

Edward Burlingame HILL

Tyler, L. *Edward Burlingame Hill: A Bio-bibliography.* New York: Greenwood, 1989.

Oliver HOLDEN

Kroeger, K. D. "The Worcester Collection of Sacred Harmony and Sacred Music in America 1786–1809." PhD diss., Brown University, 1976.

McCormick, David W. "Oliver Holden: Composer and Anthologist." PhD diss., Union Theological Seminary, 1963.

Samuel HOLYOKE

Willhide, J. Laurence. "Samuel Holyoke: American Music Educator." PhD diss., University of Southern California, 1954.

HOMER, Sidney

McDonald, D. T. "Sidney Homer: Song Composer." Master's thesis, Women's College, University of North Carolina, Greensboro, 1963.

Thorpe, H. C. "The Songs of Sidney Homer." *Musical Quarterly* 17 (1931).

Francis HOPKINSON

Albrecht, Otto Edward. *Francis Hopkinson: Musician and Patriot, 1737–1937.* Philadelphia, PA: n.p., 1938.

Hastings, George Everett. *The Life and Works of Francis Hopkinson.* Chicago: University of Chicago Press, 1926.

Sonneck, Oscar G. T. *Francis Hopkinson, the First American Poet-Composer (1737–91) and James Lyon, Patriot, Preacher, Psalmodist (1735–94).* Washington, DC: H. L. McQueen, 1905. With new introduction by Richard A. Crawford. New York: Da Capo, 1967.

Charles HORN

Montague, R. A. "Charles Edward Horn—His Life and Works." PhD diss., Florida State University, 1959.

Alan HOVHANESS

Howard, Richard. *The Works of Alan Hovhaness: A Catalog, Opus 1-Opus 360.* White Plains, NY: Pro/Am Music Resources, ca. 1983.

Kunze, Eric. *Alan Hovhaness: A Discography.* Seattle, WA: E. Kunze, 1996.

Rosner, A. "An Analytical Survey of the Music of Alan Hovhaness." PhD diss., State University of New York, Buffalo, 1972.

Karel HUSA

Hartzell, L. W. "Karel Husa, the Man and His Music." *Musical Quarterly* 62 (1976).

Hitchens, S. *Karel Husa: A Bio-bibliography.* New York: Greenwood, 1991.

Henry Holden HUSS

Greene, G. *Henry Holden Huss: An American Composer's Life.* Metuchen, NJ: Scarecrow, 1995.

Jeremiah INGALLS

Klocko, David Grover. "Jeremiah Ingalls' 'The Christian Harmony or Songster's Companion' 1805." PhD diss., University of Michigan, 1978.

Charles IVES

Bernlef, J., and R. de Leeuw. *Charles Ives.* Amsterdam, Netherlands: De Bezige Bij, 1969.

Block, G. *Charles Ives: A Bio-bibliography.* Westport, CT: Greenwood, 1988.

Burkholder, J. Peter. *Charles Ives: The Ideas behind the Music.* New Haven, CT: Yale University Press, 1985.

———, ed. *Charles Ives and His World.* Princeton, NJ: Princeton University Press, 1996.

Cowell, Henry, and Sidney Cowell. *Charles Ives and His Music.* Rev. ed. New York: Oxford University Press, 1969. (Orig. pub. 1955.)

De Lenna, D. R. *Charles Ives (1874–1954): A Bibliography of His Music.* Kent, OH: Kent State University Press, 1970.

Dickinson, Peter. "Charles Ives 1874–1954." *Musical Times* 105 (1964).

Feder, Stuart. *Charles Ives: My Father's Song.* New Haven, CT: Yale University Press, 1992.

———. *The Life of Charles Ives.* Cambridge: Cambridge University Press, 1999.

Henderson, Clayton W. *The Charles Ives Tunebook.* Warren, MI: Harmonie Park Press, 1990.

Herrman, Bernard. "The Four Symphonies of Charles Ives." *Modern Music* 22 (1944–45).

Hitchcock, H. Wiley. *Ives: A Survey of the Music.* Brooklyn: Institute for Studies in American Music, Conservatory of Music, Brooklyn College of the City University of New York, 1977.

———. *Ives.* Rev. ed. London and New York: Oxford University Press, 1983. (Orig. pub. 1977.)

Hitchcock, H. Wiley, and Vivian Perlis, eds. *An Ives Celebration.* Urbana: University of Illinois Press, 1977.

Lambert, Philip. *Ives Studies.* Cambridge: Cambridge University Press, 1997.

———. *The Music of Charles Ives.* New Haven, CT: Yale University Press, 1997.

Oliver, Michael. "Ives on Record." *International Record Review,* August 2002.

Perlis, Vivian. *Charles Ives Remembered: An Oral History.* New Haven, CT: Yale University Press, 1974.

Perry, R. S. *Charles Ives and the American Mind.* Kent, OH: Kent State University Press, 1974.

Rossiter, Frank. *Charles Ives and His America.* New York: Liveright, 1975.

Sherwood, Gayle. *Charles Ives: A Guide to Research.* New York: Routledge, 2002.

Starr, Larry. *A Union of Diversities: Style in the Music of Charles Ives.* New York: Schirmer, 1992.

Swafford, J. *Charles Ives: A Life with Music.* New York: Norton, 1996.

Wallach, L. "The New England Education of Charles Ives." PhD diss., Columbia University.

Jean Eichelberger IVEY

Muemich, R. M. "The Vocal Works of Jean Eichelberger Ivey." PhD diss., Michigan State University, 1983.

Philip JAMES

James, Helga. *A Catalog of the Musical Works of Philip James (1890–1975).* New York: J. Finell Music Services, 1980. (Suppl. 1984.)

Hunter JOHNSON

Monaco, R. "The Music of Hunter Johnson." PhD diss., Cornell University, 1960.

Ben JOHNSTON

Von Gurden, Heidi. *The Music of Ben Johnston.* Metuchen, NJ: Scarecrow, 1985.

Werner JOSTEN

Werner Josten, 1885-1963: A Summary of His Compositions with Press Reviews. New York: Marchbanks, 1964.

Ulysses KAY

Hadley, R. "The Published Choral Music of Ulysses Kay." PhD diss., University of Iowa, 1972.

Hayes, L. "The Music of Ulysses Kay (1939–63)." PhD diss., University of Wisconsin, 1971.

Hobson, C., and D. Richardson. *Ulysses Kay: A Bio-bibliography.* Westport, CT: Greenwood, 1972.

Edgar Stillman KELLEY

King, M. R. "Edgar Stillman Kelley: American Composer, Teacher and Author." PhD diss., Florida State University, 1970.

Kent KENNAN

Wyss, J. A. "The Art Songs of Kent Kennan." PhD diss., University of Texas, Austin, 1981.

Harrison KERR

Kohlenberg, R. B. "Harrison Kerr: Portrait of a Twentieth-Century American Composer." PhD diss., University of Oklahoma, 1978.

Jacob KIMBALL

Wilcox, Glenn C. "Jacob Kimball (1761–1826): His Life and Works." PhD diss., University of South Carolina, 1957.

Leon KIRCHNER

Ringer, A. L. "Leon Kirchner." *Musical Quarterly* 43 (1957).

Peter Jona KORN

Duchtel, N., ed. *Peter Jona Korn.* Tutzing, Germany: H. Schneider, 1989.

Erich Wolfgang KORNGOLD

Carroll, B. G. "The Operas of Erich Wolfgang Korngold." PhD diss., Liverpool University, England, 1975.

———. *Erich Wolfgang Korngold: His Life and Works.* Paisley, Scotland: 1984.

———. *The Last Prodigy: A Biography of Erich Wolfgang Korngold.* Portland, OR: Amadeus, 1997.

Duchen, Jessica. *Erich Wolfgang Korngold.* London: Phaidon, 1996.

Hoffmann, R. S. *Erich Wolfgang Korngold.* Vienna: C. Stephenson, 1922.

Korngold, L. *Erich Wolfgang Korngold.* Vienna: Österreichischer Bundesverlag, 1967.

Tedeschi Turco, Mario. *Erich Wolfgang Korngold.* Verona, Italy: Cierre, 1997.

A. Walter KRAMER

Howard, John Tasker. *A. Walter Kramer.* New York: Schirmer, 1926.

Ernst KRENEK

Adorno, Theodor. *Theodor W. Adorno und Ernst Krenek Briefuechsel.* Frankfurt-am-Main, Germany: 1974.

Bowles, Garrett H. *Ernst Krenek: A Bio-bibliography.* New York: Greenwood, 1989.

Heurreman, A. G. "Ernst Krenek's Theories on the Sonata and Their Relations to His Six Piano Sonatas." PhD diss., University of Iowa, 1968.

Hughes, J. "Ernst Krenek: Festival Concerts." *Musical Quarterly* 61 (1975).

Krenek, Ernst. *Ernst Krenek: Die amerikanischen Tagebücher, 1937–1942; Dokumente aus dem Exil.* Edited by Claudia Maurer Zenck. Vienna: Böhlau, 1992.

Marckhl, E. *Rede fur Krenek.* Graz, Austria: 1969.

Maurer Zenck, Claudia. *Ernst Krenek ein Komponist im Exil.* Vienna: Lafite, 1980.

Saathen, F. *Erst Krenek: Langen-Mullers Kleine Geschenkbucher.* Munich, Germany: A. Langen, G. Müller, 1959.

Stewart, J. *Ernst Krenek: The Man and His Music.* Berkeley and Los Angeles: University of California Press, 1991.

Gail KUBIK

Lyall, M. D. "The Piano Music of Gail Kubik." PhD diss., Peabody Institute of Johns Hopkins University, 1980.

Wiktor LABUNSKI

Belanger, J. R. "Wiktor Labunski: Polish-American Musician in Kansas City 1937–1974." PhD diss., Columbia University, 1982.

BIBLIOGRAPHY

Ezra LADERMAN

Fleming, S. "Musician of the Month: Ezra Laderman." *HiFi/ Musical America* 30, no. 3 (1980).

Andrew LAW

Crawford, Richard. *Andrew Law: American Psalmodist.* Rev. ed. Evanston, IL: Northwestern University Press, 1981. (Orig. pub. 1968.)

Benjamin LEES

Cooke, Deryck. "The Music of Benjamin Lees." *Tempo No. 54,* 1959.

———. "The Recent Music of Benjamin Lees." *Tempo No. 64,* 1963.

———. "Benjamin Lees: 'Vision of Poets.' " *Tempo No. 68,* 1964.

O'Loughlin, Niall. "Benjamin Lees' String Quartet Concerto." *Tempo No. 93,* January 7, 1970.

Slonimsky, Nicolas. "Benjamin Lees in Excelsis." *Tempo No.113,* June 1, 1975.

Oscar LEVANT

Levant, Oscar. *The Memoirs of an Amnesiac.* New York: G. P. Putnam, 1965.

Kashner, S., and N. Schoenberger. *A Talent for Genius: The Life and Times of Oscar Levant.* New York: Villard, 1994.

Marvin David LEVY

Davis, P. G. "And We Quote . . . Marvin David Levy." *HiFi/ Musical America* 17, no. 3 (1967).

Robert Hall LEWIS

Gonzalez, L. "The Symphonies of Robert Hall Lewis." PhD diss., Peabody Conservatory, 1979.

Thirlow LIEURANCE

Kinsella, H. G. "Lieurance Traces American Indian Music to Oriental Origins." *Musical America* 37, no. 24 (1923).

Normand LOCKWOOD

Davis, T. M. "A Study of the Stylistic Characteristics in Selected Major Choral Works of Normand Lockwood." PhD diss., University of Missouri, 1980.

Norton, K. *Normand Lockwood: His Life and Music.* Metuchen, NJ: Scarecrow, 1993.

Charles Martin LOEFFLER

Colvin, H. "Charles Martin Loeffler: His Life and Works." PhD diss., University of Rochester, 1957.

Engel, Carl. "Charles Martin Loeffler." *Musical Quarterly* 11 (1925).

Henry, E. L. "Impressionism in the Arts and Its Influences on Selected Works of Charles Martin Loeffler and Charles T. Giffes." PhD diss., University of Cincinnati, 1976.

Knight, E. *Charles Martin Loeffler: A Life Apart in American Music.* Urbana: University of Illinois Press, 1993.

Meyer, A. H. "Loeffler at 70 Finds all Music Good." *Musical America* 51, no. 2 (1931).

Nicolai LOPATNIKOFF

Critser, W. *The Compositions of Nicolai Lopatnikoff: A Catalog.* Pittsburgh: University of Pittsburgh, 1979.

Otto LUENING

Hartsock, R. *Otto Luening: A Bio-bibliography.* Westport, CT: Greenwood, 1991.

Wentz, B. "Otto Luening at 85: An Interview." *HiFi/Musical America* 35, no. 11 (1985).

Edward MacDOWELL

Brancaleone, F. P. "The Short Piano Works of Edward MacDowell." PhD diss., City University of New York, 1982.

Currier, T. P. "Edward MacDowell as I Knew Him." *Musical Quarterly* 1 (1915).

Eagle, N. L. "The Piano Sonatas of Edward MacDowell." PhD diss., University of North Carolina, 1952.

Gilman, Lawrence. *Edward MacDowell.* New York: J. Lane, 1906.

Humiston, William Henry. *MacDowell.* New York: Breitkopf and Hartel, 1921.

Kefferstan, C. B. "The Piano Concertos of Edward MacDowell." PhD diss., University of Cincinnati, 1984.

Levy, A. *Edward MacDowell: An American Master.* Lanham, MD: Scarecrow, 1998.

Lien, B. "An Analytical Study of Selected Piano Works by Edward MacDowell." Master's thesis, Eastman School, 1940.

Lowens, Margaret Morgan. "The New York Years of Edward MacDowell." PhD diss., University of Michigan, 1971.

MacDowell, Marion. *Random Notes on Edward MacDowell and His Music.* Boston, MA: A. P. Schmidt, 1950.

Mumper, D. R. "The Four Piano Sonatas of Edward MacDowell." PhD diss., Indiana University, 1971.

Porte, John F. *Edward MacDowell, a Great American Tone Poet: His Life and Music.* Rev. ed. London: K. Paul, Trench, Trubner, 1978.

Sonneck, Oscar G. *Catalogue of First Editions of Edward MacDowell (1861-1908).* Rev. ed. Washington, DC: U.S. Government Printing Office, 1971. (Orig. pub. 1917.)

Daniel Gregory MASON

Burnet C. Tuthill. "Daniel Gregory Mason." *Musical Quarterly* 34 (1948).

Kapec, D. "The Three Symphonies of Daniel Gregory Mason Style—Critical and Theoretical Analyses." PhD diss., University of Florida, 1982.

Klein, M. J. "The Contribution of Daniel Gregory Mason to American Music." PhD diss., Catholic University of America, 1957.

Lewis, R. B. "The Life and Music of Daniel Gregory Mason." PhD diss., University of Rochester, New York, 1959.

Lowell MASON

Mason, H. L. *Lowell Mason: An Appreciation of His Life and Work.* New York: Hymn Society of America, 1941.

———. *Hymn Tunes of Lowell Mason: A Bibliography.* Rev. ed. Cambridge, MA: Harvard University Press, 1976. (Orig. pub. 1944.)

Pemberton, Carol A. "Lowell Mason: His Life and Work." PhD diss., University of Minnesota, 1971. Ann Arbor, 1985.

———. *Lowell Mason: A Bio-bibliography.* Westport, CT: Greenwood, 1988.

Rich, Arthur Lowndes. *Lowell Mason, "The Father of Singing among the Children."* Chapel Hill: University of North Carolina Press, 1946.

George Frederick McKAY

Coolen, W. T. "Creative Melodist the Life and Orchestral Works of George Frederick McKay (1899-1970)." Master's thesis, University of Washington, 1972.

William Thomas McKINLEY

Sposato, J. *William Thomas McKinley: A Bio-bibliography.* Westport, CT: Greenwood, 1995.

Colin McPHEE

McPhee, Colin. *Music in Bali.* New York: DaCapo, 1976. (Orig. pub. 1966.)

Mueller, R. "Imitation and Stylization in the Balinese Music of Colin McPhee." PhD diss., University of Chicago, 1983.

Oja, Carol J. *Colin McPhee: Composer in Two Worlds.* Washington, DC: Smithsonian Institution Press, 1990.

———. "Colin McPhee: A Composer Turned Explorer." *Tempo No. 148,* 1984.

Young, Douglas. "Colin McPhee's Music from West to East." *Tempo No. 150,* 1984.

Peter MENNIN

Hendl, Walter. "The Music of Peter Mennin." *Juilliard Review* 1, no. 2 (1954).

Gian Carlo MENOTTI

Ardoin, John. *The Stages of Menotti.* Garden City, NY: Doubleday, 1985.

Grieb, Lyndol. *The Operas of Gian Carlo Menotti (1937–72): A Selected Bibliography.* Metuchen, NJ: Scarecrow, 1974.

Gruen, John. *Menotti: A Biography.* New York: Schirmer, 1978.

Tricoire, R. *Gian Carlo Menotti: L'homme et son ouevre.* Paris: Seghers, 1966.

Spoleto Festival. "Official History." Spoleto, South Carolina, 1999.

David Moritz MICHAEL

Hahn, K. A. "The Wind Ensemble Music of David Moritz Michael." PhD diss., University of Missouri, 1979.

Roberts, D. A. "The Sacred Vocal Music of David Moritz Michael." PhD diss., University of Kentucky, 1978.

John Christopher MOLLER

Stetzel, R. D. "John Christopher Moller (1755–1803) and His Role in Early American Music." PhD diss., University of Iowa, 1965.

Meredith MONK

Jowitt, Deborah, ed. *Meredith Monk.* Baltimore, MD: Johns Hopkins University Press, 1997.

Sandon, Greg. *Invisible Theater: The Music of Meredith Monk.* Westport, CT: Wesleyan University Press, 1984.

Douglas MOORE

Glaeson, H., and W. Becker. *Douglas Moore.* Bloomington: Indiana University Press, 1981.

Reagan, D. J. "Douglas Moore and His Orchestral Works." PhD diss., Catholic University of America, 1972.

Weitzel, H. "A Melodic Analysis of Selected Vocal Solos in the Operas of Douglas Moore." PhD diss., New York University, 1971.

Justin MORGAN

Bandel, B. *Sing the Lord's Song in a Strange Land: The Life of Justin Morgan.* Rutherford, NJ: Fairleigh Dickinson University Press, 1981.

Robert MUCZYNSKI

Hawkins, J. A. "The Piano Music of Robert Muczynski." PhD diss., University of Maryland, 1980.

Nicolas NABOKOV

Wellens, Ian. *Music in the Frontline: Nicolas Nabokov's Struggle against Communism and Middlebrow Culture.* Aldershot, UK: Ashgate, 2002.

Conlon NANCARROW

Bruce, David. "The Manic Mechanic." *Musical Times,* April 1997.

Carlsen, P. *The Player-Piano Music of Conlon Nancarrow: An Analysis of Selected Studies.* Brooklyn, NY: Institute for Studies in American Music, 1988.

Gann, Kyle. *The Music of Conlon Nancarrow.* Cambridge: Cambridge University Press, 1995.

Reynolds, Roger. "Conlon Nancarrow: Interviews in Mexico City and San Francisco." *American Music* 2, no. 2 (1984).

Ethelbert NEVIN

Howard, John Tasker. *Ethelbert Nevin.* New York: Thomas Y. Crowell, 1935.

Thomson, Vance. *The Life of Ethelbert Nevin from His Letters and His Wife's Memories.* Boston, MA: Boston Music, 1913.

Dika NEWLIN

Albrecht, T. *Dika Caecilia: Essays for Dika Newlin, November 22, 1988.* Kansas City, MO: Park College, 1988.

Anthony NEWMAN

Satz, A. "Musician of the Month: Anthony Newman." *HiFi/Musical America* 22, no. 4 (1972).

Pauline OLIVEROS

Kefalas, E. "Pauline Oliveros." *HiFi/Musical America* 25, no. 6 (1975).

Taylor, Timothy D. "The Gendered Construction of the Musical Self: The Music of Pauline Oliveros." *Musical Quarterly* 77, no. 3 (1993).

Von Gunden, Heidi. *The Music of Pauline Oliveros.* Metuchen, NJ: Scarecrow, 1983.

Leo ORNSTEIN

Darter Jr., T. E. "The Futurist Piano Music of Leo Ornstein." PhD diss., Cornell University, 1979.

Martens, F. *Leo Ornstein: The Man, His Ideas, His Work.* Rev. ed. New York: Breitkopf and Hartel, 1975. (Orig. pub. 1918.)

John Knowles PAINE

Howe, M. A. De Wolfe. "John Knowles Paine." *Musical Quarterly* 25 (1939).

———. "John Knowles Paine." *Musical Quarterly* 25, no. 3 (1979).

Huxford, J. C. "John Knowles Paine: Life and Works." PhD diss., Florida State University, 1968.

Roberts, Kenneth C. "John Knowles Paine." Master's thesis, University of Michigan, 1962.

Schmidt, John C. *The Life and Works of John Knowles Paine.* Ann Arbor: University of Michigan Research Press, 1980.

Spalding, W. R. *Music at Harvard.* New York: Coward-McCann, 1935.

Robert PALMER

Austin, W. W. "The Music of Robert Palmer." *Musical Quarterly* 42 (1956).

Horatio PARKER

Chadwick, George W. *Horatio Parker.* Rev. ed. New Haven, CT: Yale University Press, 1972. (Orig. pub. 1921.)

"Horatio Parker." *Musical Times* 13 (1902).

Kearns, W. K. "Horatio Parker 1863-1919: A Study of His Life and Music." PhD diss., University of Illinois, 1965.

Parker, Horatio, ed. *Music and Drama.* Boston, MA: Hall and Locke, 1911.

————, ed. *Music and Public Entertainment.* Boston, MA: Hall and Locke, 1911.

Semler, I. Parker. *Horatio Parker: A Memoir for His Grandchildren.* Rev. ed. New York: G. P. Putnam, 1975. (Orig. pub. 1942.)

Stanley Smith, David. "A Study of Horatio Parker." *Musical Quarterly* 16 (1930).

Strunk, W. Oliver. "Works of Horatio W. Parker." *Musical Quarterly* 16 (1930).

Harry PARTCH

Bowen, Meirion. "Harry Partch." *Music and Musicians* 16, no. 5 (1968).

Dunn, David. *Harry Partch: An Anthology of Critical Perspectives.* Amsterdam, Netherlands: Harwood Academic, 2000.

Gilmore, Bob. *Harry Partch: A Biography.* New Haven, CT: Yale University Press, 1998.

Hackbarth, G. A. *An Analysis of Harry Partch's "Daphne of the Dunes."* Ann Arbor, MI: AMS Press, 1979.

Johnston, Ben. "The Corporealism of Harry Partch." *Perspectives of New Music* 13, no. 2 (1975).

McGeary, T. *The Music of Harry Partch: A Descriptive Catalog.* Brooklyn, NY: Institute for Studies in American Music, 1991.

Partch, Harry. *Bitter Music: Collected Journals, Essays, Introductions, and Librettos.* Edited, with an introduction, by Thomas McGeary. Urbana: University of Illinois Press, 1991.

————. *Barstow: Eight Hitchhiker Inscriptions from a Highway Railing at Barstow, California (1968 version).* Edited by Richard Kassel. Madison, WI: A-R Editions, for the American Musicological Society, 2000.

George PERLE

Knussen, Oliver. "George Perle, Composer." *Tempo No. 137,* 1981.

Kraft, Leo. "The Music of George Perle." *Musical Quarterly* 58 (1971).

Saylor, Bruce. "A New Work by George Perle." *Musical Quarterly* 61 (1975).

Swift, Richard. "A Tonal Analog the Tone-Centered Music of George Perle." *Perspectives of New Music* 21, nos. 1–2 (1982–83).

Vincent PERSICHETTI

Evett, Robert. "The Music of Vincent Persichetti." *Juilliard Review* 2, no. 2 (1958).

Paterson, Donald L., and Janet L. Paterson. *Vincent Persichetti: A Bio-bibliography.* Westport, CT: Greenwood, 1993.

Shackelford, R. "Conversations with Vincent Persichetti." *Perspectives of New Music* 20, nos. 1–2 (1981–82).

Simmons, W. "A Persichetti Perspective." *American Record Guide* 40, no. 6 (1977).

Webster, D. "Vincent Persichetti." *HiFi/Musical America* 35, no. 4 (1985).

Johann Friedrich PETER

Crews, C. *Johann Friedrich Peter and His Times.* Winston-Salem, NC: Moravian Music Foundation, 1990.

Rau, A. G. "John Frederick Peter." *Musical Quarterly* 23 (1937).

Schnell, W. E. "The Choral Music of Johann Friedrich Peter." PhD diss., Indiana University, 1973.

Daniel PINKHAM

Corzine, M. L. "The Organ Works of Daniel Pinkham." PhD diss., University of Rochester Eastman School, 1979.

Deboer, K., and J. Ahouse. *Daniel Pinkham: A Bio-bibliography.* Westport, CT: Greenwood, 1986.

Johnson, M. "The Choral Works of Daniel Pinkham." PhD diss., University of Iowa, 1966.

Raver, L. "The Organ Music of Daniel Pinkham." *American Organist* 17, no. (1983).

Stallings, M. E. "Representative Works for Mixed Chorus by Daniel Pinkham 1968–1983." PhD diss., University of Miami, 1984.

Paul A. PISK

Collins, T. W. "The Instrumental Music of Paul W. Pisk." PhD diss., University of Missouri, 1972.

Glowacki, J. *Paul A. Pisk: Essays in His Honor.* Austin: University of Texas, 1966.

Walter PISTON

Carter, Elliott. "Walter Piston." *Musical Quarterly* 32 (1946).

Lindenfield, H. N. "Three Symphonies of Walter Piston: An Analysis." PhD diss., Cornell University, 1975.

Pollack, Howard. *Walter Piston.* Ann Arbor: University of Michigan Research Press, 1981.

Roy, K. G. "Walter Piston." *Stereo Review* 24, no. 4 (1970).

Taylor, C. "Walter Piston for His 70th Birthday." *Perspectives of New Music* 3, no. 1 (1964).

Westergaard, Peter. "Conversation with Walter Piston." *Perspectives of New Music* 7, no. 1 (1968).

Quincy PORTER

Boatwright, Howard. "Quincy Porter 1897-1966." *Perspectives of New Music* 2 (1967).

John POWELL

Williams, P. L. "Music by John Powell in the John Powell Music Collection at the University of Virginia." Master's thesis, University of Virginia, 1968.

Mel POWELL

Thimmig, L. "The Music of Mel Powell." *Musical Quarterly* 55 (1969).

André PREVIN

Bookspan, Martin, and R. Yockey. *André Previn: A Biography.* Garden City, NY: Doubleday, 1981.

Greenfield, Edward. *André Previn.* London: Allan, 1973.

Previn, André. *No Minor Chords: My Days in Hollywood.* New York: Doubleday, 1991.

Ruttencutter, Helen D. *Previn.* New York: St. Martin's, 1985.

Florence PRICE

Brown, R. L. "The Orchestral Music of Florence Price (1888–1953): A Stylistic Analysis." PhD diss., Yale University, 1985.

Green, M. D. *Florence Price.* Boston, MA: Twayne, 1983.

Karol RATHAUS

Schwarz, Boris. "Karol Rathaus." *Musical Quarterly* 42 (1955).

Daniel READ

Bushnell, Vinson Clair. "Daniel Read of New Haven (1757–1836): The Man and His Musical Activities." PhD diss., Harvard University, 1978.

Gardner READ

Dodd, Mary Ann, and J. Engquist. *Gardner Read: A Bio-bibliography.* Westport, CT: Greenwood, 1996.

Steve REICH

Cowan, Robert Reich, and Wittgenstein. "Notes towards a Synthesis." *Tempo No. 157,* June 1986.

Hiller, Paul, ed. *Steve Reich: Writings on Music, 1965–2000.* New York: Oxford University Press, 2001.

Hoek, D. J. *Steve Reich: A Bio-bibliography.* Westport, CT: Greenwood, 2002.

La Barbara, Joan. "Three by Reich." *HiFi/Musical America* 30, no. 6 (1980).

Mertens, W. *American Minimal Music: La Monte Young, Terry Riley, Steve Reich, Philip Glass.* London: Kahn and Averill, 1983.

Nyman, Michael. "Steve Reich: Mysteries of the Phase." *Music and Musicians* 20, no. 6 (1972).

———. "Steve Reich." *Music and Musicians* 25, no. 5 (1977).

Potter, Keith. "Steve Reich: Thoughts on His 50th Birthday." *Musical Times* 127, no. 1715 (1986).

———. *Four Musical Minimalists.* Cambridge: Cambridge University Press, 2000.

Schwarz, K. Robert. "Steve Reich: Music as a Gradual Process." *Perspectives of New Music* 19 (1980-81).

———. *Minimalists.* London: Phaidon, 1996.

Alexander REINAGLE

Horton, C. "Serious Art and Concert Music for Piano in America from Alexander Reinagle to Edward MacDowell." PhD diss., University of North Carolina, 1965.

Roger REYNOLDS

Reynolds, Roger. *Mind Models: New Forms of Musical Experience.* New York: Praeger, 1975.

———. *Form and Method: Composing Music.* New York: Routledge, 2002.

Roger Reynolds: Profile of a Composer. New York: C. F. Peters, 1982.

Wallingford RIEGGER

Cowell, Henry. "Wallingford Riegger." *Musical America* 68, no. 14 (1948).

———. "A Note on Wallingford Riegger." *Juilliard Review* 2, no. 2 (1955).

Freeman, Paul D. "The Compositional Technique of Wallingford Riegger as Seen in Seven 12 Tone Works." PhD diss., Eastman School, 1963.

Gatwood, D. D. "Wallingford Riegger: A Biography and Analysis of Selected Works." PhD diss., George Peabody College for Teachers, 1970.

Golden, R. F. "Wallingford Riegger: Composer and Pedagogue." *Etude* 74, no. 8 (1956).

———. "Wallingford Riegger." *HiFi/Stereo Review* 20, no. 4 (1968).

Goldman, Richard Franko. "The Music of Wallingford Riegger." *Musical Quarterly* 36 (1950).

Orr, L. W. "An Analysis of the Later Orchestral Style of Wallingford Riegger." PhD diss., Michigan State University, 1970.

Savage, N. G. "Structure and Cadence in the Music of Wallingford Riegger." PhD diss., Stanford University, 1972.

Schmoll, J. B. "An Analytical Study of the Principal Instrumental Compositions of Wallingford Riegger." PhD diss., Northwestern University, 1954.

Spackman, Stephen. *Wallingford Riegger: Two Essays on Musical Biography.* Brooklyn, NY: Institute for Studies in American Music, 1982.

———. "Wallingford Riegger and the Modern Dance." *Musical Quarterly* 71, no. 4 (1985).

Terry RILEY

Mertens, W. *American Minimalist Music: La Monte Young, Terry Riley, Steve Reich, Philip Glass.* London: Kahn and Averill, 1983.

Potter, Keith. "Terry Riley Encountered" *Classical Music,* August 11, 1984.

———. *Four Minimalist Musicians.* Cambridge: Cambridge University Press, 2000.

Schwarz, K. Robert. *Minimalists.* London: Phaidon, 1996.

Leroy ROBERTSON

Wilson, Marian Robertson. *Leroy Robertson: Music Giant from the Rockies.* Salt Lake City, UT: Blue Ribbon, 1996.

George ROCHBERG

Bloch, Steven. "Progressive or Master Forger." *Perspectives on New Music* 21 (1982).

Dixon, J. *George Rochberg: A Bio-bibliography Guide to His Life and Works.* Stuyvesant, NY: Pendragon, 1991.

Kramer, Jonathan D. "Can Modernism Survive George Rochberg?" *Critical Inquiry* 11 (1984).

Reise, Jay. "Rochberg, the Progressive" *Perspectives on New Music* 19 (1980).

Ringer, A. "The Music of George Rochberg." *Musical Quarterly* 52 (1966).

Smith, J. T. "The String Quartets of George Rochberg." PhD diss., Eastman School, 1976.

Bernard ROGERS

Dershan, S. J. "Orchestration in the Orchestral Works of Bernard Rogers." PhD diss., University of Rochester, New York, 1975.

Diamond, David. "Bernard Rogers." *Musical Quarterly* 33 (1947).

Initili, D. J. "Text-Music Relationships in the Large Choral Works of Bernard Rogers." PhD diss., Case Western Reserve University, Ohio, 1977.

Ned ROREM

Atack, S. A. "Ned Rorem and His Songs." PhD diss., University of Nebraska, 1969.

Bloomquist, M. R. "Songs of Ned Rorem: Aspects of the Musical Settings of Songs in English for Solo Voice and Piano." PhD diss., University of Missouri, Kansas City, 1970.

Davis, D. "An Interview about Choral Music with Ned Rorem." *Musical Quarterly* 68 (1982).

Johnson, B. "Still Sings the Voice: A Portrait of Ned Rorem." *Tempo No. 153,* 1985.

Miller, P. L. "The Songs of Ned Rorem." *Tempo No. 127,* 1978.

McDonald, A. *Ned Rorem: A Bio-bibliography.* Westport, CT: Greenwood, 1989.

North, W. S. W. "Ned Rorem as a 20th Century Song Composer." PhD diss., University of Illinois, 1965.

Rorem, Ned. *Knowing Where to Stop: A Memoir.* New York: Simon and Schuster, 1994.

———. *A Ned Rorem Reader.* Edited by J. McClatchy. New Haven, CT: Yale University Press, 2001.

Christopher ROUSE

Shulman, Lawrence. "Christopher Rouse." *Tempo No. 199,* January 1997.

Miklós RÓZSA

Palmer, Christopher. *Miklós Rózsa: A Sketch of His Life and Work.* London: Breitkopf and Härtel, 1975.

BIBLIOGRAPHY

Dane RUDHYAR

Morang, A. *Dane Rudhyar: Pioneer in Creative Synthesis.* New York: 1939.

Rayner, Sheila Finch, ed. *Dane Rudhyar.* Long Beach: University Library, California State University, Long Beach, 1977.

Shere, J. *Dane Rudhyar: A Brief Biography with a List of Works.* San Jacinto, CA: 1972.

Carl RUGGLES

Archabal, N. M. "Carl Ruggles: Composer and Painter." PhD diss., University of Minnesota, 1975.

Babcock, D. "Carl Ruggles: Two Early Works and 'Suntreader.' " *Tempo No. 135,* 1980.

Faulkner, S. "Carl Ruggles and His 'Evocations' for Piano." Master's thesis, American University, Washington, D.C., 1973.

Gilbert, S. E. "Carl Ruggles (1876-1971): An Appreciation." *Perspectives on New Music* 11, no. 1 (1972).

Green, J. *Carl Ruggles: A Bio-bibliography.* Westport, CT: Greenwood, 1995.

Harrison, Lou. *About Carl Ruggles.* Yonkers, NY: O. Bradinsky, 1946.

Kirkpatrick, John. "The Evolution of Carl Ruggles." *Perspectives on New Music* 6, no. 2 (1968).

Peterson, T. E. "The Music of Carl Ruggles." PhD diss., University of Washington, 1967.

Saecker, J. "Carl Ruggles in Winona." PhD diss., Winona State College, 1967.

Seeger, Charles. "Carl Ruggles." *Musical Quarterly* 18 (1932).

―――. "In Memoriam: Carl Ruggles 1876-1971." *Perspectives on New Music* 10, no. 2 (1972).

Tenney, J. "The Chronological Development of Carl Ruggles' Melodic Style." *Perspectives on New Music* 16, no. 1 (1977).

Ziffrin, Marilyn. *Carl Ruggles: Composer, Painter and Storyteller.* Urbana: University of Illinois Press, 1994.

Frederic RZEWSKI

Wason, Robert W. "Tonality and Atonality in Frederic Rzewski's 'The People United Will Never Be Defeated.'" *Perspectives on New Music* 26 no. 1 (1988).

Carlos SALZEDO

Archambo, S. B. "Carlos Salzedo (1885-1961): The Harp in Transition." PhD diss., University of Kansas, 1984.

Lazare SAMINSKY

de Paoli, D., et al. *Lazare Saminsky: Composer and Civic Worker.* New York: Bloch, 1930.

Ernest SCHELLING

Hill, T. H. "Ernest Schelling (1876–1939): His Life and Contributions to Music Education through Educational Concerts." PhD diss., Catholic University of America, 1970.

Joseph SCHILLINGER

Burk, J. *Schillinger's Double Equal Temperament System.* Lawrence, Kansas: 1979.

Schillinger, Frances. *Joseph Schillinger: A Memoir by His Wife.* New York: Greenberg, 1949.

Schillinger, Joseph. *The Schillinger System of Musical Composition.* New York: C. Fischer, 1946.

Gunther SCHULLER

Carnovale, N. *Gunther Schuller: A Bio-bibliography.* Westport, CT: Greenwood, 1987.

Persea, B. "Two Works for Jazz Quartet and Ensemble by Gunther Schuller." Master's thesis, Eastman School, 1973.

Rich, Alan. "Gunther Schuller." *HiFi/Musical America* 26, no. 4 (1976).

William SCHUMAN

Adams, K. Gary. *William Schuman: A Bio-bibliography.* Westport, CT: Greenwood, 1998.

Broder, Nathan. "The Music of William Schuman." *Musical Quarterly* 31 (1945).

Dickinson, Peter. "William Schuman: An American Symphonist at 75." *Musical Times,* August 1985.

Keats, S. "William Schuman." *Stereo Review* 33, no. 6 (1974).

Robinson, H. "William Schuman." *HiFi/Musical America* 35, no. 8 (1985).

Rouse, Christopher. *William Schuman: Documentary Biography, Essay, Catalog of Works, Discography and Bibliography.* Philadelphia, PA: Theodore Presser, 1980.

Schreiber, Flora R., and Vincent Persichetti. *William Schuman.* New York: Schirmer, 1954.

Joseph SCHWANTNER

Stevens, D. P. "Joseph Schwantner." *HiFi/Musical America* 29, no. 12 (1979).

William SELBY

McKay, D. P. "William Selby, Musical Émigré in Colonial Boston." *Musical Quarterly* 57 (1971).

Roger SESSIONS

Campbell, M. I. "The Piano Sonatas of Roger Sessions: Sequel to a Tradition." PhD diss., Peabody Institute, 1982.

Cone, Edward T. "Sessions' Second String Quartet." *Musical Quarterly* 43 (1957).

―――. "Conversation with Roger Sessions." *Perspectives on New Music* 4, no. 2 (1966).

―――. "In Honor of Roger Sessions." *Perspectives on New Music* 10, no. 2 (1972).

Henderson, R. "Tonality in the Pre-Serial Instrumental Music of Roger Sessions." PhD diss., Eastman School, 1974.

Imbrie, Andrew. "Roger Sessions: In Honor of His 65th Birthday." *Perspectives on New Music* 1, no. 1 (1962).

―――. "The Symphonies of Roger Sessions." *Tempo No. 103,* 1972.

Kress, S. M. "Roger Sessions: Composer and Teacher." PhD diss., University of Florida, 1982.

Laufer, E. C. "Roger Sessions: Montezuma." *Perspectives on New Music* 4, no. 2 (1965).

Oja, Carol J. "The Copland-Sessions Concerts." *Musical Quarterly* 65 (1979).

Olmstead, Andrea. "Roger Sessions: A Personal Portrait." *Tempo No. 127,* 1978.

―――. "Roger Sessions' Ninth Symphony." *Tempo No. 133,* 1980.

―――. *Roger Sessions and His Music.* Ann Arbor: University of Michigan Research Press, 1985.

―――. *Conversations with Roger Sessions.* Boston, MA: Northeastern University Press, 1987.

Prausnitz, Frederik. *Roger Sessions: How a "Difficult" Composer Got That Way.* New York: Oxford University Press, 2002.

Rapaport, Paul. "Roger Sessions: A Discography." *Tempo No. 127,* 1978.

Schubart, M. A. "Roger Sessions: Portrait of an American Composer." *Musical Quarterly* 32 (1946).

Sessions, Roger. *The Correspondence of Roger Sessions.* Edited by Andrea Olmstead. Boston, MA: Northeastern University Press, 1992.

Ralph SHAPEY

Finley, P. *A Catalogue of the Works of Ralph Shapey.* Stuyversant, NY: Pendragon, 1997.

Oliver SHAW

Degan, B. "Oliver Shaw: His Music and Contribution to American Society." PhD diss., University of Rochester, New York, 1971.

Denison, F., A. Stanley, and E. Gleza, eds. *Memorial of Oliver Shaw.* Providence: Rhode Island Veteran Citizens' Historical Association, 1864.

Williams, T. *A Discourse on the Life and Death of Oliver Shaw.* Boston, MA: C. C. P. Moody, 1851.

Arthur SHEPHERD

Loucks, Richard. "Arthur Shepherd." PhD diss., University of Rochester, New York, 1962.

———. *Arthur Shepherd: American Composer.* Provo, UT: Brigham Young University Press, 1980.

Newman, W. S. "Arthur Shepherd." *Musical Quarterly* 36 (1950).

Seymour SHIFRIN

Boykan, M. "Seymour Shifrin: Satires of Circumstance." *Perspectives on New Music* 1 (1966).

Brody, M. "An Anatomy of Intentions: Observations on Seymour Shifrin's 'Responses' for Piano." *Perspectives on New Music* 19, nos. 1-2 (1980-81).

Morgan, R. P. "Remembering Seymour Shifrin (1926-1979)." *Perspectives on New Music* 19, nos. 1–2 (1980–81).

Elie SIEGMEISTER

Gallagher, J. "Structural Design and Motivic Unity in the 2nd, 3rd and 4th Symphonies of Elie Siegmeister." PhD diss., Cornell University, 1982.

Charles Sanford SKILTON

Howard, John Tasker. *Charles Sanford Skilton.* New York: C. Fischer, 1929.

Smith, J. A. "Charles Sanford Skilton (1868–1941): Kansas Composer." Master's thesis, University of Kansas, 1979.

David Stanley SMITH

Goode, E. A. "David Stanley Smith and His Music." PhD diss., University of Cincinnati, 1978.

Tuthill, Burnet C. "David Stanley Smith." *Musical Quarterly* 28 (1942).

Hale SMITH

Breda, M. "Hale Smith: Biographical and Analytical Study of the Man and His Music." PhD diss., University of Southern Mississippi, 1975.

John Philip SOUSA

Berger, Kenneth. *The March King and His Band.* New York: Exposition, 1957.

Bierley, Paul E. *John Philip Sousa: A Descriptive Catalog of His Works.* Rev. ed. Urbana: University of Illinois Press, 1984. (Orig. pub. 1973.)

———. *The Works of John Philip Sousa.* Columbus, OH: Integrity, 1984.

———. *John Philip Sousa: American Phenomenon.* New York: Appleton-Century-Crofts, 1986. (Orig. pub. 1975.)

Heslip, Malcolm. *Nostalgic Happening in the Three Bands of John Philip Sousa.* Laguna Hills, CA: M. Heslip, 1982.

Lingg, Ann M. *John Philip Sousa.* New York: Holt, 1955.

Newsom, Jon, ed. *Perspectives on John Philip Sousa.* Washington, DC: Library of Congress, 1983.

Simon, M. I. *John Philip Sousa, the March King.* New York: 1944.

Smart, James R. *The Sousa Band: A Discography.* Washington, DC: Library of Congress, 1970.

Sousa, John Philip. *Marching Along: Recollections of Men, Women, and Music.* Rev. ed. Edited by Paul E. Bierley. Westerville, OH: Integrity, 1994.

Stacy, W. "John Philip Sousa and His Band Suites: An Analytical and Cultural Study." PhD diss., University of Colorado, 1972.

Leo SOWERBY

Bading, D. C. "Leo Sowerby: Works for Organ and Orchestra or Ensemble." Master's thesis, University of Kansas, 1983.

Guiltinan, M. P. "The Absolute Music of Piano Solo by Leo Sowerby." PhD diss., University of Rochester, New York, 1977.

Huntington, J. M. "A Study of the Musical Contribution of Leo Sowerby." PhD diss., University of Rochester, New York, 1957.

Tuthill, Burnet C. "Leo Sowerby." *Musical Quarterly* 24 (1958).

Albert SPALDING

Sabin, Robert. "Albert Spalding: American Violinist." *Musical America* 70, no. 3 (1950).

Schwarz, Boris. *Great Masters of the Violin.* New York: Simon and Schuster, 1983.

Robert STARER

Dreier, D. "Robert Starer." *HiFi/Musical America* 33, no. 10 (1983).

Lewis, D. E. "The Major Piano Solo Works of Robert Starer: A Style Analysis." PhD diss., John Hopkins University, 1978.

Halsey STEVENS

Murphy, J. L. "The Choral Music of Halsey Stevens." PhD diss., Texas Technical University, 1980.

Vanderkoy, P. A. "A Survey of the Choral Music of Halsey Stevens." PhD diss., Ball State University, Indiana, 1981.

William Grant STILL

Ardoyno, D. "William Grant Still." *HiFi/Musical America* 35, no. 10 (1984).

Arvey, Verna. *William Grant Still.* New York: 1939.

———. *In One Lifetime.* Fayetteville: University of Arkansas Press, 1984.

Detels, Claire, ed. *William Grant Still: Studies at the University of Arkansas; A 1984 Congress Report.* Fayetteville: University of Arkansas, Fulbright College of Arts and Sciences, 1985.

Haas, Robert, ed. *William Grant Still and the Fusion of Cultures in American Music.* Rev. ed. Los Angeles: Black Sparrow, 1996. (Orig. pub. 1972.)

Simpson, R. "William Grant Still: The Man and His Music." PhD diss., Michigan State University, 1964.

Smith, Catherine Parsons, ed. *William Grant Still: A Study in Contradictions.* Berkeley and Los Angeles: University of California Press, 2000.

Still, Judith A., ed. *William Grant Still: An Oral History.* Flagstaff, AZ: Master-Player Library, 1998.

———. *William Grant Still: A Voice High-Sounding.* Flagstaff, AZ: Master-Player Library, 2003.

Still, Judith A., Michael J. Dabishus, and Carolyn L. Quinn. *William Grant Still: A Bio-bibliography.* Westport, CT: Greenwood, 1996.

Albert STOESSEL

McNaughton, C. D. "Albert Stoessel: American Musician." PhD diss., New York University, 1957.

Gerald STRANG

Berman, M. A. "Gerald Strang: Composer, Educator, American." Master's thesis, California State University, Long Beach, 1977.

Lamar STRINGFIELD

Nelson, D. R. "The Life and Works of Lamar Stringfield (1897–1959)." PhD diss., University of North Carolina, 1971.

George Templeton STRONG

Lawrence, Vera. *Strong on Music: The New York Music Scene in the Days of George Templeton Strong, 1836–1875.* New York: Oxford University Press, 1988.

Matthey, J. L. *Inventare du fonds musical George Templeton Strong.* Lausanne, Switzerland: 1973.

Gustav STRUBE

Klemm, G. "Gustav Strube: The Man and the Music." *Musical Quarterly* 28 (1942).

Morton SUBOTNICK

Johnson, Steven, ed. *The New York Schools of Music and the Visual Arts.* New York: Routledge, 2001.

Perkins, J. M. "Morton Subotnick: Serenade No. 1." *Perspectives on New Music* 11, no. 2 (1964).

Timothy SWAN

Murphy, S. E. "Timothy Swan and Yankee Psalmody." *Musical Quarterly* 61 (1975).

Webb, G. B. "Timothy Swan: Yankee Tunesmith." PhD diss., University of Illinois, 1972.

Richard SWIFT

Kohn, K. "Richard Swift: Concerto." *Perspectives on New Music* 11, no. 1 (1963).

Stauffer, T. "Richard Swift's Summer Notes." *Perspectives on New Music* 15, no. 2 (1977).

William SYDEMAN

Reich, N. B., ed. *A Catalog of the Works of William Sydeman.* New York: Division of Music Education, New York University, 1968.

Louise TALMA

Barkin, E. "Louise Talma: 'The Tolling Bell.'" *Perspectives on New Music* 10, no. 2 (1972).

J. Deems TAYLOR

Howard, John Tasker. *Deems Taylor.* Rev. ed. New York: C. Fischer, 1940. (Orig. pub. 1927.)

Pegolotti, James A. *Deems Taylor: A Biography.* Boston, MA: Northeastern University Press, 2003.

Raynor TAYLOR

Cuthbert, J. A. "Raynor Taylor and Anglo-American Musical Life." PhD diss., West Virginia University, 1980.

Alexander TCHEREPNIN

Arias, Enrique A. *Alexander Tcherepnin: A Bio-bibliography.* Westport, CT: Greenwood, 1988.

Chang, Chi-Jen. "Alexander Tcherepnin: His Influence on Modern Chinese Music." PhD diss., Columbia University Teachers College, 1983.

Reich, W. *Alexander Tcherepnin.* Rev. ed. Bonn, Germany: M. P. Belaieff, 1970. (Orig. pub. 1959.)

Tcherepnin, Alexander. "A Short Autobiography." *Tempo No. 130,* 1979.

Randall THOMPSON

Benser, Caroline C., and D. Urrows. *Randall Thompson: A Bio-bibliography.* Westport, CT: Greenwood, 1986.

Forbes, Elliott. "The Music of Randall Thompson." *Musical Quarterly* 35 (1949).

McGilvray, B. W. "The Church Music of Randall Thompson: An American Eclectic." PhD diss., University of Missouri, Kansas City, 1979.

Virgil THOMSON

Cook, E. "Virgil Thomson: The Composer in Person." *HiFi/Stereo Review* 19, no. 5 (1965).

Dulman, M. "Independent Spirit: Virgil Thomson Speaks Out." *Opera News* 41, no. 1 (1976).

Eyer, R. F. "Virgil Thomson." *Musical America* 64, no. 7 (1944).

Glanville-Hicks, Peggy. "Virgil Thomson." *Musical Quarterly* 35 (1949).

Hall, D. "Virgil Thomson: A Discography." *HiFi/Stereo Review* 14, no. 5 (1965).

Hoover, Kathleen, and John Cage. *Virgil Thomson: His Life and Music.* New York: Barnes, 1959.

Jackman, R. "The Operas of Gertrude Stein and Virgil Thomson." PhD diss., Tulane University, New Orleans, 1962.

Kostelanetz, Richard, ed. *Virgil Thomson: A Reader; Selected Writings, 1924-84.* New York: Routledge, 2003.

Meckna, Michael. *Virgil Thomson: A Bio-bibliography.* Westport, CT: Greenwood, 1986.

Mellers, Wilfred. "The Demotic Innocent." *Musical Times,* April 1997.

Page, T., and V. Page, ed. *Selected Letters of Virgil Thomson.* New York: Summit Books, 1988.

Schonberg, Harold C. "Virgil Thomson: Parisian from Missouri." *HiFi/Stereo Review* 14, no. 5 (1965).

Smith, C. "Thompson's 'Four Saints' Live on Broadway." *Musical Quarterly* 72, no. 7 (1952).

Smith, P. J. "Virgil Thomson: Musician of the Month." *HiFi/Musical America* 21, no. 11 (1971).

Soria, D. J. "Artist Life: Virgil Thomson." *HiFi/Musical America* 32, no. 2 (1982).

Tommasini, Anthony C. *The Musical Portraits of Virgil Thomson.* New York: Pendragon, 1985.

———. *Virgil Thomson: Composer on the Aisle.* New York: Norton, 1997.

Ernst TOCH

Jezic, Diane P. "Ernst Toch (1887-1964): Composer, Teacher, Philosopher, a Study of Selected Compositions and Writings." PhD diss., Peabody Conservatory, 1974.

———. *The Musical Migration and Ernst Toch.* Ames: Iowa State University Press, 1989.

Johnson, C. "The Unpublished Works of Ernst Toch." PhD diss., University of California, Los Angeles, 1973.

Pisk, Paul. "Ernst Toch." *Musical Quarterly* 24 (1938).

Weschler, Lawrence. *Ernst Toch 1887–1964: A Biographical Essay Ten Years after His Passing.* Los Angeles: n.p., 1974.

Joan TOWER

O'Brien, V. "Joan Tower: Musician of the Month." *HiFi/Musical America* 32, no. 9 (1982).

Douglas TOWNSEND

Edwards Jr., R., "A Brief History of the Trombone and a Survey of Douglas Townsend's Contribution to Contemporary Trombone Literature." Master's thesis, Southern Illinois University, 1979.

Lester TRIMBLE

Fleming, S. "And We Quote . . . Lester Trimble." *HiFi/Musical America* 17, no. 11 (1967).

Hodges, R. "Lester Trimble." *Stereo Review* 29, no. 5 (1970).

Burnet TUTHILL

Raines, J. I. "Burnet C. Tuthill: His Life and Music." PhD diss., Michigan State University, 1979.

David TUDOR

Holzaepfel, J. "David Tudor and the Performers of American Experimental Music 1950–59." PhD diss., City University of New York, 1993.

Johnson, Steven, ed. *The New York Schools of Music and the Visual Arts.* New York: Routledge, 2001.

Edgard VARÈSE

Barnard, Jonathan W. *The Music of Edgard Varèse.* New Haven, CT: Yale University Press, 1987.

Block, D. R. "The Music of Edgard Varèse." PhD diss., University of Washington, 1973.

Bredel, M. *Edgard Varèse.* Paris: Mazarine, 1984.

Chou Wen-chung. "Open Rather Than Bounded." *Perspectives on New Music* 1 (1966).

———. "Varèse: A Sketch of the Man and His Music." *Musical Quarterly* 3 (1966).

Clayson, Alan. *Edgard Varèse.* London: Sanctuary, 2002.

Jack, Adrian. "Edgard Varèse." *Music and Musicians* 24, no. 3 (1975).

Jolivet, Hilda. *Varèse.* Paris: Hachette, 1973.

Klaren, J. H. *Edgar Varèse: Pioneer of New Music in America.* Boston, MA: 1928.

MacDonald, Malcolm. *Varèse: Astronomer of Sound.* London: Kahn and Averill, 2002.

Morgan, R. P. "The Music of Edgard Varèse." *HiFi* 27, no. 2 (1977).

Ouellette, Fernand. *Edgard Varèse.* Rev. ed. Paris: Seghers, 1981. (Orig. pub. 1966; English version pub. 1968.)

Root, D. L. "The Performance Guilds of Edgard Varèse." PhD diss., University of Illinois, 1971.

Schuller, Gunther. "Conversation with Varèse." *Perspectives on New Music* 3, no. 2 (1965).

Varèse, Louise. *Varèse: A Looking-Glass Diary.* New York: Norton, 1972.

Vivier, Odile. *Varèse.* Paris: Éditions du Seuil, 1973.

John VINCENT

Parker, C. B. "John Vincent 1902–77: An Alabama Composer's Odyssey." PhD diss., University of California, Los Angeles, 1981.

Joseph WAGNER

Bowling, L., ed. *Joseph Wagner: A Retrospective of a Composer-Conductor.* Lomita, CA: Charade Record, 1976.

George WALKER

de Lerma, D. "The Choral Works of George Walker." *American Choral Review* 23, no. 1 (1981).

Delphin, W. *A Comparative Analysis of Two Sonatas by George Walker.* University of Southern Missouri, 1976.

Robert WARD

Fleming, S. "Robert Ward." *HiFi/Musical America* 32, no. 5 (1982).

Kreitner, K. *Robert Ward: A Bio-bibliography.* Westport, CT: Greenwood, 1988.

Elinor Remick WARREN

Bortin, V. *Elinor Remick Warren: Her Life and Music.* Metuchen, NJ: Scarecrow, 1987.

———. *Elinor Remick Warren: A Bio-bibliography.* Westport, CT: Greenwood, 1993.

Ben WEBER

Babbitt, Milton. "Ben Weber." *Perspectives on New Music* 17, no. 2 (1979).

Kurt WEILL

Farneth, D. *Kurt Weill: A Life in Pictures and Documents.* Woodstock, NY: Overlook Press, 2000.

Hinton, S., ed. *Kurt Weill: The Three-Penny Opera.* Cambridge: Cambridge University Press, 1990.

Hirsch, Foster. *Kurt Weill On Stage: From Berlin to Broadway.* New York: Knopf, 2002.

Jarman, D. *Kurt Weill: An Illustrated Biography.* Bloomington: Indiana University Press, 1980.

Kotschenreuther, H. *Kurt Weill.* Berlin-Halensee, Germany: M. Hesses, 1962.

Marx, Henry. *Weil—Lenya.* New York: Goethe House, 1976.

Mercado, Mario R., comp. *Kurt Weill: A Guide to His Works.* New York: Kurt Weill Foundation for Music; Valley Forge, PA: European American Music, 1989.

Rorem, Ned. "Notes on Weill." *Opera News* 10, no. 8 (1984).

Sanders, Ronald. *The Days Grow Short: The Life and Music of Kurt Weill.* New York: Holt, Rinehart and Winston, 1980.

Schebera, Jurgen. *Kurt Weill, 1900–1950: eine Biographie in Texten, Bildern und Dokumenten.* Mainz, Germany: Schott, 1990. (English version pub. 1995.)

Symonette, Lys, and Kim H. Kowalee, eds. *Speak Low When You Speak of Love: Letters of Weill and Lenya.* Berkeley and Los Angeles: University of California Press, 1996.

Taylor, Ronald. *Kurt Weill: Composer in a Divided World.* New York: Simon and Schuster, 1991.

Hugo WEISGALL

Balkin, A. "The Operas of Hugo Weisgall." PhD diss., Columbia University Teachers College, 1968.

Blumenfeld, M. "Hugo Weisgall's 66th Birthday and the New 'Garden of Adonis.' " *Perspectives on New Music* 16, no. 2 (1978).

Brooks Jr., J. A. "Technical Aspects of the Music in the Major Operas of Hugo Weisgall." PhD diss., University of Washington, St. Louis, 1971.

Leon-Cohen, L. "A Study Analysis and Performance of the Songs and Song Cycles for Voice and Piano by Hugo Weisgall." PhD diss., Columbia University Teachers College, 1982.

Rich, A. "Hugo Weisgall: Athalia." *Perspectives on New Music* 3, no. 1 (1964).

Saylor, Bruce. "The Music of Hugo Weisgall." *Musical Quarterly* 59 (1973).

Skulsky, A. "The Operas of Hugo Weisgall." *Etude* 74 (1956).

Adolph WEISS

George, W. B. "Adolph Weiss." PhD diss., University of Iowa, 1971.

Kopp, B. "The 12-Tone Techniques of Adolph Weiss." PhD diss., Northwestern University, 1981.

Peter WESTERGAARD

Crumb, George. "Peter Westergaard: Variations for 6 Players." *Perspectives on New Music* 3, no. 2 (1965).

Emerson WHITHORNE

Howard, John Tasker. *Emerson Whithorne.* New York: C. Fischer, 1929.

Alec WILDER

Alec Wilder: 1907–1980; An Introduction to the Man and His Music. Newton Center, MA: Margun Music, 1991.

Balliett, Whitney. *Alec Wilder and His Friends.* Boston, MA: Houghton Mifflin, 1974.

Demsey, D., and R. Pratter. *Alec Wilder: A Bio-bibliography.* Westport, CT: Greenwood, 1993.

Stone, David. *Alec Wilder in Spite of Himself: A Life of a Composer.* New York: Oxford University Press, 1996.

Wilder, Alec. *Letters I Never Mailed.* Boston, MA: Little, Brown, 1975.

Olly WILSON

Logan, W. "Olly Wilson: Piece for 4." *Perspectives on New Music* 9, no. 1 (1970).

Christian WOLFF

Barry, M. "Christian Wolff." *Music and Musicians* 26, no. 7 (1978).

Nyman, Michael. "Christian Wolff." *Music and Musicians* 20, no. 8 (1972).

Stefan WOLPE

Babbitt, Milton, Elliott Carter, L. Stempel, and Charles Wuorinen. "In Memoriam: Stefan Wolpe." *Perspectives on New Music* 11, no. 1 (1972).

Clarkson, Austin. *Stefan Wolpe: A Brief Catalogue of Published Works.* Islington, Ontario: 1981.

———, ed. *On the Music of Stefan Wolpe: Essays and Recollections.* Hillsdale, NY: Pendragon, 2003.

Hasty, C. "The Theory of Segmentation Developed from Late Works of Stefan Wolpe." PhD diss., Yale University, 1978.

Helin, J. "The Ever-Restored and Ever-Advancing Moment: Stefan Wolpe's Compositions, Philosophy and Aesthetic as Seen in 'Form' for Piano." Master's thesis, University of Texas, 1982.

Levy, E. "Stefan Wolpe for His 60th Birthday." *Perspectives on New Music* 2, no. 1 (1963).

Rosenfeld, Paul. "Stefan Wolpe's Music." *New Republic* 104 (1941).

Skulsky, A. "Stefan Wolpe: Liberation from Enslavement of the Twelve-Tone System." *Musical America* 71, no. 13 (1951).

Charles WUORINEN

Burbank, R. *Charles Wuorinen: A Bio-bibliography.* Westport, CT: Greenwood, 1994.

La Monte YOUNG

Cardew, Cornelius. "One Source: La Monte Young." *Musical Times* 9, no. 107/1485 (1966).

Gann, Kyle. "La Monte Young's Well-Tuned Piano." *Perspectives on New Music* 31, no. 3 (1993).

Mertens, W. *American Minimal Music: La Monte Young, Terry Riley, Steve Reich, Philip Glass.* London: Kahn and Averill, 1983.

Potter, Keith. *Four Minimalist Musicians.* Cambridge: Cambridge University Press, 2000.

Schwarz, K. Robert. *Minimalists.* London: Phaidon, 1996.

Eugene ZADOR

Zador, L. *Eugene Zador: A Catalog of His Works.* San Diego, CA: L. Zador, 1978.

Ellen Taaffe ZWILICH

Dreier, R. "Ellen Taaffe Zwilich." *HiFi/Musical America* 33, no. 9 (1983).

Index

Page numbers in italic refer to photo captions.

Names of people and individual works are only indexed when a substantial discussion appears in the text; brief mentions are not indexed.

Hovhaness (Chakmakjian), Alan (*continued*)
Fugue form, 215
Indian music, 215
St. Vartan Symphony, 217
study of Armenian religious music, 215
Symphony no. 2, *Mysterious Mountain,* 215–216, 217
Symphony no. 50 (*Mount St. Helens*), 216, 217
Howe, Mary (Carlisle), 217–218
Howland, William Legrand, 218
Hugo, John Adam, 218
Husa, Karel, 218–219
An American Te Deum, 219
Apotheosis of This Earth, 218–219
Monodrama, 219
Music for Prague, 1968, 218
Huss, Henry Holden, 219–220

I

Iannaccone, Anthony (Joseph), *221,* 221–222
Imbrie, Andrew Welsh, 222–223
String Quartet in B-flat, 222
Inch, Herbert Reynolds, 223
Ingalls, Jeremiah, 223
Ives, Charles Edward, *97,* 198, 223–228, *224,* 280
The Alcotts, 228
The Celestial Country, 224–225
Central Park in the Dark, 225
Emerson Piano Concerto, 228
experiments with musical material, 226
First Piano Sonata, 227
First String Quartet, 227
"General Booth Enters Into Heaven," 225
Hawthorne, 228
"Holidays Symphony," 226
The Housatonic at Stockbridge, 226
insurance career, 224
Largo, 227
major influences, 223–224
organist, 224
polytonality, 224
Psalm 67, 224–225
Putnam's Camp, 226
Second Piano Sonata, 227–228
Second Quartet, 227
Second Symphony, 225
A Set of Pieces for Theater Orchestra, 226
symphonies, 228
Symphony no. 4, 226–227
technical weakness, 225
Third Symphony, 225
Thoreau, 228
Three Harvest Home Chorales, 225
Three Places in New England, 228
The Unanswered Question, 225, 228
Universe Symphony, 18, 228
violin sonatas, 227
Ives, George, 223–224
Ivey, Jean Eichelberger, 228–229
Electronic Music Studio, 228

J

Jacobi, Frederick, *231,* 231–232
American Indian music, 231
Indian Dances, 231
String Quartet on Indian Themes, 231
James, Dorothy, 232, *232*
James, Philip (Frederick Wright), 232–233, *233*
Janssen, Werner, 233–234
conductor, 234
Johnson, Frederic Ayres, *see* **Ayres, Frederic**
Johnson, Hunter, 234
Letter to the World, 234
Johnson, Lockrem, 234
A Letter to Emily, 234
Johnston, Ben(jamin) Burwell, 234–236
just intonation, 235
microtonal tunings, 235
serialism, 235
Jones, Charles W., 236
Josten, Werner (Erich), 236–237, *237*
Jungle, 237

K

Kanitz, Ernst (Ernest), 239
Kastle, Leonard (Gregory), 239–240
Kay, Hershy, 240
Kay, Ulysses (Simpson), 240–241
Keats, Donald Howard, 241
Kechley, Gerald, 241–242, *242*
Keller, Homer T(odd), 242
Kelley, Edgar Stillman (Edgar Stillman-Kelley), 242–243
Kelly, Robert, 243–244
The White Gods, 243
Kennan, Kent Wheeler, 244
Night Soliloquy, 244
Kernis, Aaron Jay, 244–245
Kerr, Harrison, 245
Kessner, Daniel (Aaron), 245–246, *246*
Kim, Earl, *246,* 246–247
Kimball, Jacob Jr., 247
Kirchner, Leon, 247–248
pianist, 247
Kohn, Karl (George), 248–249
Kohs, Ellis Bonoff, 249
counterpoint, 249
Kolb, Barbara (Anne), 249–250
Korn, Peter Jona, 250
Korngold, Erich Wolfgang, *251,* 251–252
pioneer composer of film scores, 251
Korte, Karl (Richard), 252
Koutzen, Boris, 252–253, *253*
Kraft, Leo (Abraham), 253–254, *254*
Kraft, William, 254–255
percussionist, 254–255
Kramer, A(rthur) Walter, 255
Krenek, Ernst, *256,* 256–258
electronic tape, 258
Jonny Spielt Auf (Jonny Strikes Up), 256
Karl V, 256